Physiological
Psychology

THE DORSEY SERIES IN PSYCHOLOGY

EDITOR   HOWARD F. HUNT   *Columbia University*

BARNETTE (ed.)   *Readings in Psychological Tests and Measurements*   rev. ed.

BARON & LIEBERT (eds.)   *Human Social Behavior: A Contemporary View of Experimental Research*

BENNIS, BERLEW, SCHEIN, & STEELE (eds.)   *Interpersonal Dynamics: Essays and Readings on Human Interaction*   3d ed.

COURTS   *Psychological Statistics: An Introduction*

DENNY & RATNER   *Comparative Psychology: Research in Animal Behavior*   rev. ed.

DESLAURIERS & CARLSON   *Your Child Is Asleep: Early Infantile Autism*

DEUTSCH & DEUTSCH   *Physiological Psychology*   rev. ed.

FISKE & MADDI   *Functions of Varied Experience*

FITZGERALD & MCKINNEY   *Developmental Psychology: Studies in Human Development*

FLEISHMAN (ed.)   *Studies in Personnel and Industrial Psychology*   rev. ed.

FREEDMAN (ed.)   *The Neuropsychology of Spatially Oriented Behavior*

HAMMER & KAPLAN   *The Practice of Psychotherapy with Children*

HENDRY   *Conditioned Reinforcement*

KLEINMUNTZ   *Personality Measurement: An Introduction*

KOLSTOE   *Introduction to Statistics for the Behavioral Sciences*   rev. ed.

LIEBERT & SPIEGLER   *Personality: An Introduction to Theory and Research*

MADDI   *Personality Theories: A Comparative Analysis*   rev. ed.

MARKEL   *Psycholinguistics: An Introduction to the Study of Speech and Personality*

ROZEBOOM   *Foundations of the Theory of Prediction*

SALTZ   *The Cognitive Bases of Human Learning*

VON FIEANDT   *The World of Perception*

revised edition

Physiological Psychology

J. ANTHONY DEUTSCH

and

DIANA DEUTSCH

Both of the
University of California, San Diego
La Jolla, California

1973

THE DORSEY PRESS *Homewood, Illinois 60430*

IRWIN-DORSEY INTERNATIONAL *London, England* WC2H 9NJ
IRWIN-DORSEY LIMITED *Georgetown, Ontario* L7G 4B3

Revised Edition

First Printing, May, 1973
Second Printing, February, 1974

QP
360
D 48 | 15,539

ISBN 0-256-01081-1
Library of Congress Catalog Card No. 72–90772
Printed in the United States of America

Preface

The present textbook attempts to organize the subject matter of physiological psychology using two main principles. The first is that the experimental findings are organized around questions which arise from the study of behavior. We could have chosen to use neuroanatomical structures as a way of bringing order into the field. But it seems to us that the brain is an organ for the production of behavior and that it will be understood best by paying close attention to that product. The second is that we have used theories (frequently our own) to organize and sharpen the basic issues presented to the student. At the same time we give, as far as possible, the evidence for and against such theories. Our purpose in doing this is not to indoctrinate or even to persuade. We feel that whether a theory is accepted or not, it still serves to organize large amounts of data because it makes them meaningful. Experiments can better be remembered if they are thought of as either supporting some general hypothesis or tending to disprove such a hypothesis. Also, experiments become much more exciting and meaningful to the student if they are seen proving or disproving something beyond themselves. Furthermore, theories address themselves to issues. It is the awareness of general issues that serves to orient a student in the field and enables the student, when ready to perform research, to choose problems that have a general importance.

There are other points that can also be made. Physiological psychology is a subject where there are many unresolved issues and many unanswered questions. We have chosen to present the subject in this way where this is the actual case, giving the evidence for the various views but not coming to any conclusion ourselves where this seems at present to be unwarranted. We realize that this may produce a measure of mental discomfort in some students. However, we prefer to present a veridical picture of the subject. We also believe that it is salutary for the student to learn to suspend judgment, and that science is not omniscience.

ACKNOWLEDGMENTS

In the second edition, we each revised those chapters which we had written in the first edition with the exception that the two chapters written by Professors C. I. Howarth and I. P. Howard were revised by one of us (J.A.D.) We thank Professors Richard Kestenbaum, State University of New York, Stony Brook; Gabriel Frommer, Indiana University; Stanley Finger, Washington University, St. Louis; James D. Papsdorf, University of Michigan; Aryeh Routtenberg, Northwestern University; and Howard Hunt, Consulting Editor for The Dorsey Press, for their careful reading of portions of the manuscript and their valuable suggestions.

April 1973   J. A. DEUTSCH
                                                DIANA DEUTSCH

Contents

Introduction

It is the aim of psychology to understand the behavior of man and the animals. Some understanding of behavior may be obtained simply by noting what events in the environment correlate with certain types of behavior. For instance, we soon discover that food deprivation produces an enhancement of the tendency to eat. Or we may note what two behaviors correlate: we may observe that an increase of running speed to food correlates with a tendency to eat progressively more bitter food. We understand individual cases of behavior by realizing that they are only instances of widely and generally observed correlations.

However, our curiosity about behavior may go further. We may ask why the general correlations we observe actually occur. Why, for instance, does food deprivation lead to an increase of the tendency to eat? What goes on within the organism to produce such an effect? Some of the investigations of this question, of course, need not involve any physiological intervention and may consist simply of behavioral observation. Such investigations lie within the realm of experimental psychology as traditionally conceived. However, it has been found, and it is indeed obvious, that purely behavioral observation allows us to answer only a somewhat limited number of questions.

A convenient analogy is that of a man-made machine, such as a desk calculator, rather than a naturally occurring system such as a rat. If we use the analogy of the desk calculator, we can observe a large number of correlations by punching the keys and noting the output of the machine. We may test some of our explanations of why such correlations exist by performing more tests to produce predicted correlations between input and output. However, we would soon arrive at an impasse. There will be questions about how the desk calculator works which can be answered only by observing or directly manipulating the machinery inside the calculator.

Just as war has been called diplomacy by other means, physiological psychology is experimental psychology by other means. We still seek the explanation of behavior by experimental means. However, we do not restrict ourselves in our choice of experimental methods, as does

1

the experimental psychologist, and we take advantage of modern techno-logical advances to help us devise our experiments. Physiological psy-chology is therefore not different from experimental psychology in the questions it poses or the problems it attacks; it merely uses a wider, less restrictive range of methods.

When we explain the behavior of a machine, organism, or system, we describe the behavior as a result of a set of interactions of the components of such machines, organisms, or systems. Such descriptions may be of interactions of components which we have imagined or postu-lated, or they may be descriptions of the observed interactions of known components. Many theories are a mixture of the imagined and the real. If, therefore, we are interested in explaining behavior, we must know what has been observed about the underlying components of the living system and their interactions, so that we do not postulate imaginary mechanisms which are different from the actual, observed mechanisms. Knowing the characteristics of the components of the nervous system also helps us when we try to imagine how the whole system might work to produce behavior. For instance, each element in the nervous system is extremely slow compared with the components of a modern computer. This means that certain operations have to be carried out differently by the nervous system, and thus we cannot directly apply some computer models.

There is a second reason for knowing about the components of the nervous system. If we agree that an explanation of the behavior of an organism lies in the way that its components interact, then our experi-ments must try to find out how such components interact.

Such interactions may be discovered either by direct observation of the components, which is only rarely feasible, or by manipulating the components in some known way to observe the effects on behavior as a whole. In both instances it is obligatory to inform ourselves on what is already known about the components. Much of what is known will not tell us directly about the overall behavior of the organism. For example, knowing about transistors does not explain the behavior of a computer. However, if we wish to establish how a given computer works, it would be very useful to know how transistors operate to help us in our investigations.

How the components of the nervous system work is the subject of the first chapter. The second chapter is devoted to a description of how the large masses of such components are arranged. Again, such arrangement does not immediately lead to an understanding of behavior, no more than the position of the tubes inside the television set produces an explanation of the electronic production of pictures. However, if we wish to investigate the system, an understanding of the way it is connected and arranged will be useful.

chapter 1

The Neuron

In recent times we have learned that the functional unit of the nervous system is the individual nerve cell (for a summary of the arguments which lead to this conclusion, see Cajal, 1954). Nerve cells are called neurons and can be identified under the microscope by their structure. Figure 1–1 shows a selection of representative neurons from different parts of the nervous system. The histological investigation of the structure of the neuron preceded by a considerable period the development of techniques for investigating their activity.

The neuron is surrounded by a membrane 75 Å thick. Anatomically, the neuron may be divided into three parts: the cell body (or soma, perikaryon), the dendrites, and the axon. The cell body is very roughly spherical in shape and is composed of the nucleus and cytoplasm. Within the nucleus is the nucleolus. The nucleus contains the genetic material DNA, and thus mainly controls the protein composition of the whole neuron. In the cytoplasm around the nucleus are found small particles, called Nissl particles or Nissl bodies. These particles contain ribosomes, which in turn contain ribonucleic acid (RNA). This material is again concerned with protein synthesis. Also within the cytoplasm are the small rod-shaped particles known as the Golgi structures.

The dendrites arise from the cell body like fine roots (Fig. 1–1). They are shaped like branched trees, and hence their name (Greek *dendron*, tree). Another elongated process arises from the cell body; it is known as the axon, and it is through this that messages leave the neuron. At the end of the axon are end boutons, and these lie close to specialized portions of the membrane of the cell bodies or dendrites of other neurons. Where such contacts between neurons occur, messages pass from the axon to other neurons, and the structures subserving such transfer between neurons are called synapses.

When the nerve fiber (axon) is not conducting a message, the interior of the axon is about 70 millivolts negative to the exterior of the axon.

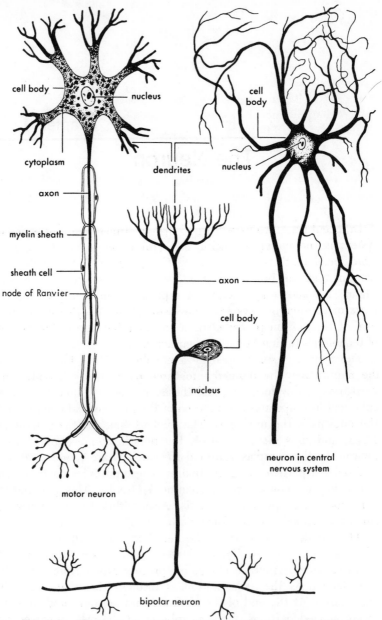

FIG. 1–1. Three neurons of common types. The one at the left shows the myelin sheath, formed from sheath cell membranes, rolled several layers thick around the axon proper. Many neurons are much longer, relative to the diameter of axon and cell body, and many have much thinner myelin sheaths or only a single cell membrane surrounding the axon. Within nerve trunks outside of the central nervous system, even the nonmyelinated axons lie inside sheath cells. (From Griffin, D. R., *Animal Structure and Function;* New York: Holt, Rinehart & Winston, 1962.)

This steady negative potential is called a resting potential. This resting potential is due to a different distribution of electrically charged atomic or molecular particles or ions inside and outside the axon. Inside the axon, the concentration of potassium is approximately twenty times as much as outside the axon. On the other hand, sodium and chloride ions are in much higher concentration outside the axon. The axon in the resting state may thus be regarded as polarized as there is a steady potential difference between the inside and outside of the axon.

This steady difference or polarization between the inside and the outside can be diminished by the application of some external stimulus, such as an electric current. This decrease in the potential across the axon membrane is called depolarization. Unless such depolarization reaches a certain threshold magnitude, the neuron returns to the resting potential after a fraction of a millisecond without any further activity after the depolarizing stimulus has been withdrawn. However, if the depolarizing stimulus goes beyond a certain point, it acts as a trigger. It triggers a nerve action potential or nerve impulse. Local depolarization of the axon membrane beyond the point forced by the initial stimulus takes place. Not only is the negative resting potential completely abolished but the inside of the axon becomes positive (for something like a tenth of a millisecond) with regard to the outside. The resting potential is therefore reversed during the action potential. This breakdown and reversal of the resting potential, which forms the first part of the action potential, is due to a sudden selective increase of local membrane permeability to sodium ions, which therefore flow into the axon. In about half a millisecond, the membrane begins to repolarize. Looked at electrically, there is a momentary change of polarization of one part of the membrane.

The ionic flows associated with this local change of polarization set up currents through neighboring parts of the axon, causing them to depolarize and produce nerve action potentials in their turn. Most axons beyond a minimum diameter are covered with a myelin shealth. This sheath prevents the flow of current through the axon membrane. However, the sheath is interrupted at regularly spaced points (at the nodes of Ranvier), and thus the excitation jumps from one node to another, with the effect that conduction along the fiber is speeded up. (Because excitation jumps from one node to another, such conduction is called saltatory.) After a nerve action potential has been initiated at a certain place on the fiber, the fiber is inexcitable for a small interval of time. This interval, called the refractory period, may last from 0.4 millisecond to 10 milliseconds. The thicker the fiber, the shorter the refractory period.

The nerve action potential is the message utilized by the nervous system to convey information over long distances along a particular neuron. As neurons are spatially discrete, another mode of propagation is utilized to carry the message from one neuron to another. When the nerve action potential reaches the end of the axon, it initiates a completely different series of events. At the end of the axon, where the axon comes very close to a part of the next neuron (the synapse), are stored packets (vesicles) of transmitter substances. When the nerve action potential arrives, the contents of such vesicles are forced into the space between the two neurons. The transmitter then diffuses across the synaptic cleft (the space between the two neurons) to depolarize the membrane on the other side of the cleft.

Such a membrane (the postjunctional membrane) has a set of specialized chemical receptors appropriate to the type of transmitter released by the previous neuron. The depolarization of the postjunctional membrane produces a new nerve action potential, and thus the neural message crosses the synapse. There are also postjunctional membranes which, instead of producing depolarization when a nerve action potential arrives, produce a heightened polarization. Such a heightened polarization counteracts any depolarization which may be produced at a neighboring synapse. Such an increase in polarization therefore tends to inhibit the transmission of an excitatory message.

There are also many different transmitter substances, the best documented of which are acetylcholine, norepinephrine, dopamine, and serotonin. Drugs which have psychological effects generally act by interfering with synaptic transmission in some way, either by boosting or diminishing it.

TRANSMISSION WITHIN NEURONS

The Nerve Spike

The modern era of neurophysiology began when sensitive thermionic tube amplifiers were developed in the 1920s. These enabled low-voltage activity of the neurons to be recorded. A still further advance came with the development of the cathode ray oscilloscope, which gives a recording system with as fast a response as the electronic tube amplifiers. Figure 1–2 shows a typical modern apparatus for recording the activity of single nerves.

The unit of neural activity is the nerve spike. This unit is a transient change in voltage of about 60 mv. and lasts about 0.4 to 1 msec. A continuously stimulated nerve will typically produce a train of these nerve spikes which travel at a constant rate away from the point of stimulation. Nervous conduction always involves spike activity, and the spike always has the same essential characteristics, whether recorded from simple nerve fibers or a nerve trunk, or from sensory or motor nerves. The amplitude of the spike potential is astonishingly constant for a given axon.

If a single, short stimulus produces a single spike, a second and similar stimulus will not produce a second spike unless there is a time interval of 0.4–2 msec. between the stimuli.

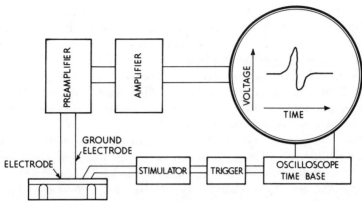

FIG. 1–2. Apparatus for recording the activity of single nerves.

The second stimulus at short intervals produces no second spike. At slightly longer intervals, a small second spike is produced, and at still longer intervals a full-size second spike develops. This experiment may seem to contradict what has just been said about the constant amplitude of the spike, but in this case the small second spike travels more slowly along the axon than the larger first spike. In this way the interval between the two increases, and at the same time the amplitude of the second spike increases until it equals the amplitude of the first spike. It then travels at the same speed as the first, so that the time interval between them now remains constant.

If the intensity of the second stimulus is increased, a second spike can be evoked at shorter intervals, but for intervals of the order of 1 msec., no second spike can be produced, no matter how intense the second stimulus. This interval, within which no second spike can develop, is called the absolute refractory period. The larger interval, within which a second spike can be produced, provided a strong enough stimulus is used, is called the relative refractory period. Preceding or following the relative refractory period, there may be a short interval when the second spike may be more easily evoked than the first. This is known as the supernormal phase; but it is not found in all nerves. These phases of changing excitability following the nerve spike show a very close correlation with the form of the electrical activity in the nerve just after the spike. Recent work with microelectrodes placed within the nerve cell has made it possible to understand these correlations.

Microelectrical Recordings

In the 1940s a number of techniques were developed for inserting electrodes into nerve cells (see Eccles, 1953). The first involved pushing electrodes down inside the cut end of a very large diameter axon. Later, workers made use of very fine electrodes which were pushed through the intact membrane of a nerve cell. In the latter case, the electrodes could be inserted into the cell body or into the axon. In all these studies it has been found that the nerve membrane has a charge across it of about 60 mv., being negative on the inside. (Such a decrease in voltage between the inside and the outside of the membrane is called depolarization; an increase is called hyperpolarization.)

When the membrane has been depolarized by a sufficient amount (usually to about 40 mv.), a spike potential develops. Following the spike, the original membrane potential is restored more or less rapidly. If the membrane stays relatively depolarized for a short time following the spike, then a smaller stimulus is needed to depolarize it to the threshold for a second spike. If it becomes relatively hyperpolarized, then a larger stimulus is needed to produce the threshold depolarization.

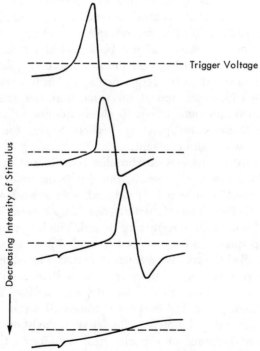

FIG. 1–3. Recording from interior of a cell subjected to increasing stimuli. (From Eccles, R. M., 1957; courtesy of The Johns Hopkins Press, Baltimore, Md.)

Variations in the degree of polarization following a nerve spike explain the variations in excitability of a neuron. When the membrane is relatively depolarized, the supernormal phase (enhanced excitability) is observed. When the membrane is hyperpolarized, this corresponds to the relative refractory period, when a stronger stimulus is necessary to produce a nerve spike. Figure 1–3 shows a typical microelectrode recording from the interior of a cell which was subject to successively stronger and stronger stimuli. The depolarization took place more rapidly to the stronger stimuli, and so the trigger voltage was reached more quickly.

The Resting Membrane Potential

The chemical composition of the axoplasm in the interior of the nerve cell is very different from the chemical composition of the tissue fluids which surround it. The membrane potential is developed because of the different concentrations of positive and negative ions on either side of the membrane. (An ion is an atom or molecule which has gained or lost electrons so as to acquire a net electrical charge. Such ions have complete electron shells and so are relatively inert chemically. However, their high electrical charge, combined with their small size, causes them to attract other ions strongly [as in a salt crystal] or molecules with a strong electrical dipole. In solution in water, the ions tend to be surrounded by a relatively permanently attached shell of water molecules attracted to the ions because of their strong electrical dipoles.)

The resting membrane is relatively permeable to the positive potassium ions which are found in their greatest concentration in the axoplasm. It may also be relatively permeable to the negative chloride ions which are found in the surrounding tissue fluid. The membrane is relatively impermeable to the positive sodium ions, which are in their greatest concentration in the tissue fluid, and also to the very large negative ions which are found in the axoplasm (Fig. 1–4). The net positive charge on the outside of the membrane is due to the distribution of these ions which will not pass through the membrane. The other ions will tend to pass through the membrane in such a way as to neutralize the charge developed across it by the ions to which it is impermeable. It seems likely that the presence of potassium ions in high concentration inside the membrane and of chloride in high concentration on the outside is a passive consequence of the distribution of the impermeable ions. Since potassium and chloride ions exist in such high concentrations on one side of the membrane to which they are freely permeable, they will tend to diffuse across the membrane toward the area of lower concentration. A state of equilibrium is achieved in which the diffusion gradient is opposed by the electrical gradient.

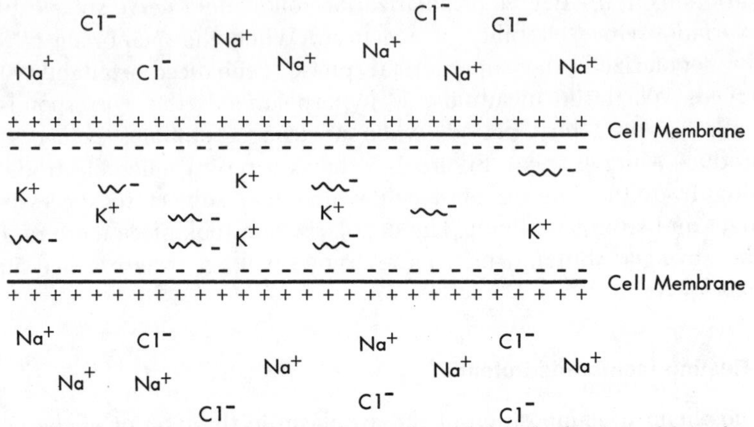

FIG. 1–4. Diagrammatic representation of the distribution of ions inside and outside a nerve cell. The cell membrane has a net positive charge in the outside largely because of an excess of positive sodium ions (Na^+) in the surrounding fluid and of negative organic ions ($\sim\!\!\sim\!-$) on the inside. Positive potassium ions (K^+) are in excess inside the cell and negative chloride ions (Cl^-) outside the cell, as a passive consequence of the distribution of the other two.

Such an equilibrium is known as a Donnan equilibrium. The relationship between the electrical gradient and the concentration gradient should, under these conditions, be given by the Nernst equation:

$$Er = \frac{RT}{-F} \log \frac{(Ki)}{(Ko)} = \frac{RT}{F} \log \frac{(Clo)}{(Cli)}$$

where Er is the membrane voltage, Ki and Ko are the potassium concentrations inside and outside, and Cli and Clo are the chloride concentrations inside and outside the membrane. T is the absolute temperature, $R = 8.2$ joules per mol.-degree abs., and $F = 96.500$ coulombs per mol.

The differences in concentration of most ions between the inside and outside of the membrane can be accounted for simply as a consequence these tend to be driven out of the electrically negative interior of the cell. For instance, in the case of the negatively charged chloride ions these tend to be driven out of the electrically negative interior of the cell (because negative charges repel each other). On the other hand, such a tendency to expulsion is countered by the opposite tendency to diffuse back into the cell. The negativity inside the cell of 70 mv. coming into balance with this tendency to diffuse is sufficient to produce the difference which is observed between the concentration of the chloride ions inside and outside the cell. On the other hand, some additional factor, besides such a balance, is needed to explain the difference in concentration between the interior and the exterior of the cell in the case of the sodium and potassium ions; thus an active process in which the cell expends energy to transfer ions has been postulated. It has been called the "sodium pump."

The membrane potential is largely maintained by such an uneven distribution of the impermeable sodium ions, and there is a great deal of evidence that the distribution of sodium across the membrane is largely determined by an active process (the sodium pump) which is clearly dependent upon metabolic energy for its operation. If a nerve is deprived of oxygen, then the concentration of sodium in the interior of the nerve cell slowly increases and the membrane potential decreases. The same result has been obtained by squeezing out the contents of a giant squid axon and replacing them by various electrolytes. When the axon is filled with isotonic potassium solution, the membrane has a normal potential and is normally excitable. If, on the other hand, it is filled with sodium solution, the membrane potential falls to zero and the membrane becomes inexcitable (Baker, Hodgkin, and Shaw, 1961).

Ionic Fluxes during the Nerve Spike

The nerve spike causes a sudden reversal of the membrane potential. The cause of this reversal is revealed by experiments which measure the resistance of the membrane. Coincident with the spike is a sudden decrease in the membrane impedance (resistance to alternating electrical current) (Cole and Curtis, 1939) which is primarily due to the membrane's becoming momentarily permeable to sodium ions (Hodgkin and Huxley, 1952). The detailed mechanism of the spike activity was investigated by Hodgkin and Huxley by the use of a voltage clamp. They inserted a core electrode 7 mm. into the cut end of a giant nerve fiber taken from a squid. Outside the axon was an external electrode. By means of an electronic feedback device, they were able to "clamp" the membrane voltage at any desired value. They then measured the strength and direction of the current which had to be applied to preserve the voltage at a particular value. The applied current is the exact inverse of the currents developing naturally in the membrane under these conditions.

Hyperpolarizing the membrane requires very little current to maintain the voltage. The resistance of the membrane remains high. A much smaller amount of depolarization produces a transient flow of current in such a direction as to cause a further depolarization. The voltage clamp has, therefore, to reverse the direction of its applied current for about 2 msec. in order to prevent the depolarization from increasing beyond the set value. After 2 msecs., the applied current again reverses, so that it is again in the direction one would expect in order to maintain the depolarization. The spontaneous initial flow of current is produced by a very great lowering of the membrane's resistance to sodium ions, which flow rapidly across the membrane under the influence of the electrical and concentration gradient.

It is this sudden inward flow of the positive sodium ions which produces the reversal of the membrane potential at the moment of the spike activity. When the sodium in the surrounding medium is replaced by chlorine, a large positive organic ion to which the membrane is impermeable, the transient inward flow fails to develop and the voltage clamp does not need to reverse the direction of the applied current. Instead, there is a slow decrease in the membrane resistance, which is due to an increased permeability to potassium ions which, in the absence of the clamp, would produce a net outward flow of current. The outward flow of potassium is almost certainly responsible for the fast recovery of the membrane potential to almost its initial value. The outward flow of potassium cancels, after a short delay, the effect of the inward flow of sodium. That sodium and potassium are largely responsible for the electrical activity of the nerve spike has been demonstrated by using radioactive traces, which show that spike activity produces a transfer of sodium and potassium across the membrane, but not of the other ions (Keynes, 1951; Eccles, 1957).

Saltatory Conduction

Mammalian nerves (except those of the smallest diameter) have an insulating covering (myelin) that is interrupted at small intervals of 0.5 to 1.5 mm. Such breaks in the insulation are called the nodes of Ranvier. The insulating covering of a nerve in the peripheral nervous system is produced by another cell, the Schwann cell, which wraps itself around the nerve fiber. In the central nervous system, the nerve fibers are covered in a somewhat similar way by glial cells (Bunje, Bunje, and Ris, 1961).

Because of the insulating properties of the myelin sheath, current which is generated by depolarization passes through an adjacent node of Ranvier rather than a neighboring portion of the neuron membrane. This causes depolarization to jump from one node to the next, accounting for the name saltatory (Latin for jumping). Such saltatory conduction speeds the rate at which an action potential moves along the nerve fiber. However, the advantage in terms of speed due to myelinization works only in the case of larger fibers. It has been calculated (Rushton, 1951) that in small diameter fibers a myelin covering would actually slow down conduction. This may account for the fact that small diameter fibers are nonmyelinated.

The distance between the nodes of Ranvier on the same fiber, according to Rushton's theoretical calculations, should be the main determinant of conduction velocity along the nerve fiber. It has been found that the larger the diameter of a fiber, the larger the distance between the nodes of Ranvier. It has also been shown that the speed of conduction in myelinated nerves correlates with fiber diameter. This supports Rushton's calculation. It also makes it possible to deduce the diameter of a nerve fiber if we know its conduction velocity (Fig. 1–5). Another

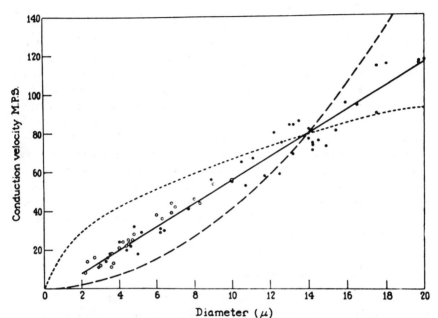

FIG. 1–5. The fastest conduction rate plotted against the diameter of the largest fiber for nerves of different velocities. The dots are data on adult cats; circles are data on kittens. The dotted and dashed lines represent the velocities calculated as the square root and square functions of the diameter. (From Hursh, J. B. (1939), "Conduction velocity and diameter of nerve fibers," *Am. J. Physiol.,* 127:131–39.)

correlation which enables us to deduce the diameter of a fiber is the length of its absolute refractory period. The thicker the fiber, the shorter the refractory period. As will be seen in the following chapters, such correlations can be put to good use in devising techniques to identify the anatomical characteristics of behaviorally functional neural circuits.

TRANSMISSION BETWEEN NEURONS

As has been stated above, the nerve spike travels along a nerve fiber from the point at which it has been initiated. When the nerve spike reaches the end of the nerve fiber along which it is traveling, the spike normally reaches a synapse, or a structure which enables the signal from one neuron to be transferred to another closely neighboring neuron. The nerve fiber which carries impulses to other neurons is generally the axon. This ends in a multitude of small structures called synaptic knobs. These knobs are in close contact with the cell body and dendrites of a neighboring neuron, separated only by a gap of about 20 millimicrons, called the synaptic cleft. Each knob contains a large number of small round sacs, called synaptic vesicles. Each of these synaptic vesicles contains minute quantities of transmitter substance, and when a nerve spike arrives, some of the sacs rupture, releasing the transmitter substance. This substance then diffuses across the synaptic cleft, altering the permeability of the membrane of the neighboring neuron to selected groups of ions. In this way, depolarization may occur at an excitatory synapse, and hyperpolarization at an inhibitory synapse, because of the different transmitter substances released.

While depolarization is frequently caused by the arrival of nerve impulses at the presynaptic terminals, transmitter release can occur through other kinds of depolarization. For instance, when the axon is very short, the graded potential generated at the post synaptic ending or the receptive surface spreads to the presynaptic terminals and causes transmitter release directly.

Excitatory and Inhibitory Potentials

It has already been mentioned that the nerve membrane merely has to be depolarized to a threshold value for the nerve spike activity to be triggered. By placing microelectrodes within the nerve cell body, it has been possible to record the activity of normal synapses (see summary by Eccles, 1957, 1965). Figure 1-6 shows the kind of record which is obtained from a spinal motoneuron when a small amount of excitation is produced by a weak stimulus to the appropriate sensory nerve. This activity is clearly very different from the nerve spike. It is of much smaller voltage. It is relatively slow, and its voltage varies with the intensity of the stimulus. It is the result of normal synaptic activity and has been labeled an excitatory postsynaptic potential (e.p.s.p.). It is due to synaptic activity producing a small amount of depolarization of the membrane, the amount of depolarization probably determined by the number of nerve spikes reaching the synaptic knob from the presynaptic fiber.

There is some evidence that the e.p.s.p.'s are quantized, in that there is a minimum size for the e.p.s.p. and that large e.p.s.p.'s are the sum of many quantal e.p.s.p.'s. Simple spatial summation of e.p.s.p.'s can

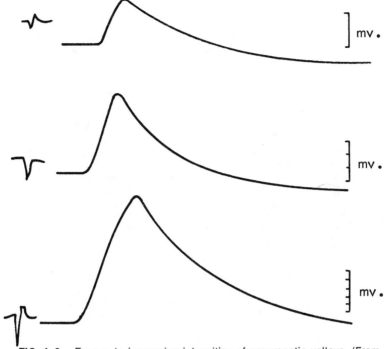

FIG. 1–6. E.p.s.p. to increasing intensities of presynaptic volleys. (From Eccles, R. M., 1957; courtesy of The Johns Hopkins Press, Baltimore, Md.)

also be demonstrated by stimulating two different sensory nerves which probably act on different synapses in the same motoneuron. Temporal summation can also be demonstrated very simply. These potentials are called excitatory potentials because they depolarize the nerve membrane. When they depolarize the membrane to a threshold degree, they produce spike activity in the same way as an applied electrical stimulus will elsewhere. In fact, Figure 1–3 was obtained from a motoneuron that was stimulated in this way. The slowly rising potentials are e.p.s.p.'s of progressively increasing amplitude.

Inhibitory Reactions. In some preparations, potentials resembling the e.p.s.p. but of opposite electrical sign have been observed (Fig. 1–7a). They produce a transient increase in the membrane potential and are clearly associated with inhibition. The simplest hypothesis about their activity is to assume that such i.p.s.p.'s (inhibitory postsynaptic potentials) subtract from the e.p.s.p.'s (excitatory postsynaptic potentials) the negative voltage of the i.p.s.p., cancelling the positive voltage of the e.p.s.p. It has been shown that such interactions in fact occur (Fig. 1–7b).

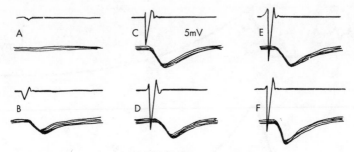

MILLISECONDS

FIG. 1–7a. Inhibitory postsynaptic potentials, recorded in a biceps semitendinosus motoneuron in the spinal cord of a cat, when a stimulus is applied to a sensory nerve from an antagonistic muscle, and quadriceps. The upper trace shows the afferent nerve activity recorded at the dorsal root. The lower curve shows the i.p.s.p. recorded simultaneously from a microelectrode in the motoneuron cell body. (From Coombs, Eccles, and Fatt, 1955; courtesy of *J. Physiol.*)

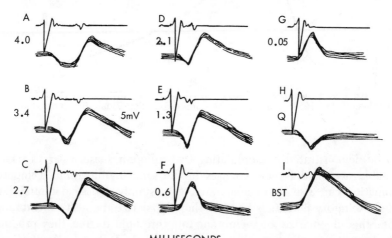

MILLISECONDS

FIG. 1–7b. The interaction of e.p.s.p. and i.p.s.p. in a biceps semitendinosus motoneuron. The upper trace shows afferent volleys recorded at the dorsal root for stimuli to quadriceps and biceps semitendinosus sensory nerves. The lower trace shows the interaction of i.p.s.p. and e.p.s.p. recorded with the microelectrode in the motoneuron cell body. The intervals in milliseconds between the volleys is marked on each trace. (From Coombs, Eccles, and Fatt, 1955; courtesy of *J. Physiol.*)

Nature of Synaptic Transmission. There has been some dispute about the physical nature of synaptic transmissions, whether it is due to a direct electrical influence of the presynaptic spike activity on the synaptic membrane or to the release of a chemical "transmitter" by the presynaptic membrane by the presynaptic spike activity, which then diffuses across to the subsynaptic membrane. The evidence now points solidly to the latter mechanism (see Eccles, 1953, 1957, and Nachmansohn, 1959). Perhaps the most direct evidence against the electrical theory of transmission was obtained by Bullock and Hagiwara (1956), who recorded from intracellular electrodes simultaneously in the presynaptic and postsynaptic regions of the giant synapse of the squid *Loligo.* They found that the depolarization of the postsynaptic membrane does not begin until the presynaptic spike potential is almost completely finished. The delay at the synapse is most easily explained in terms of the time taken for a transmitter substance to diffuse across the gap between the synaptic knob and the subsynaptic membrane.

A great deal more is now known about the chemistry of these transmitter substances, and notably acetylcholine, which has been shown to be involved in transmission across the neuromuscular junction, in sympathetic and in parasympathetic ganglia, and which are present at many other sites in the peripheral and central nervous system. These transmitter substances act on the subsynaptic membrane to produce the e.p.s.p.'s. and i.p.s.p.'s. They are probably synthesized within the presynaptic nerve fiber, are released when a nerve spike reaches the synapse, diffuse across the space between the pre- and postsynaptic membranes, and are then destroyed by the action of an enzyme, so that their activity lasts only a short time. Possibly the decomposition products then migrate back to the presynaptic fiber and are resynthesized into the transmitter substance.

A number of drugs interfere with this cycle. For example, curare is known to prevent transmission at the neuromuscular junction by blocking the sites on the synaptic membrane which receive acetylcholine. Strychnine and tetanus toxin appear to have a similar action at inhibitory synapses. Other drugs may have their effect by interfering with the breakdown or resynthesis of the transmitter or by preventing the release of the transmitter from the presynaptic membrane. Dale (1935) suggested that the transmitter substance released by a nerve is the same at all its synapses. This hypothesis has received some support; for example, the α motoneurons of the spinal chord, whose axons make synaptic connection with the muscle fibers of skeletal muscle, also make synaptic connection, via branching collateral fibers, with the small Renshaw cells within the spinal cord.

The evidence that acetylcholine is the transmitter at the neuromuscular junction is now overwhelming. It has also been found that anticholinesterases, which prevent the enzymatic breakdown of acetylcholine, greatly prolong the discharge of the Renshaw cells, so it appears likely that acetylcholine is the transmitter here also. Dale suggested that no nerve can have an excitatory and inhibitory action since, he supposed, the synaptic effect of a transmitter was characteristic of the chemical nature of the transmitter rather than the nature of the subsynaptic membrane. There seems to be no a priori reason to expect this to be the case, and in fact examples have been found recently in invertebrates where the same transmitter has both excitatory and inhibitory effects. Terzuolo and Bullock (1958) investigated the activity of the extrinsic inhibitory axon of the cardiac ganglion of the lobster and found that it could produce depolarization of some cells in the ganglion and hyperpolarization of others. Apparently, the same cell made direct synaptic connection with each neuron and so was having opposite effects on different cells. There is as yet no indication that this sort of thing occurs in vertebrates, but there is considerable evidence that inhibition is the function of specialized cells, probably small internuncial neurons (Araki, Eccles, and Ito, 1960).

Neurotransmitters

There is now considerable evidence that norepinephrine, dopamine, and serotonin act as transmitters in the central nervous system. These are called the biogenic amines, being formed from amino acids. Norepinephrine and dopamine are formed indirectly from the amino acid tyrosine whereas serotonin is derived from the amino acid tryptophan.

The number of nerve cells producing biogenic amines as transmitters is not large as a proportion of all nerve cells. Hillarp et al. (1960) have been able to render biogenic amines fluorescent and so have been able to identify neurons containing these transmitters. There are a few nuclei in the brain stem that send up fibers via the medial forebrain bundle, but even in the medial forebrain bundle such fibers account for a small proportion of fibers. The cells of origin of synapses using dopamine lie predominantly in the substantia nigra. The synapses themselves occur in the basal ganglia.

In Parkinson's disease, the production of dopamine by such cells seems drastically curtailed. Patients with this disorder suffer from tremor and the inability to initiate reflex or voluntary movement. While dopamine itself cannot pass from the bloodstream to the brain, treatment with dopamine is useless. However, treatment with L-dopa, the precursor of dopamine, which *does* pass the blood-brain barrier, has been successful in decreasing tremor and restoring mobility.

Most of the neurons that use serotonin have their origin in cell bodies within the raphe nuclei of the brain stem. Such cells send fibers to various areas of the forebrain. Various other substances have been suggested as transmitters on varying degrees of evidence, for instance, glutamic, glycine, and gamma-amino butyric acid (GABA).

Presynaptic Inhibition. Frank and Fuortes (1957) found a reduction in the effectiveness of stimuli to muscle sensory fibers in exciting α motoneurons in the spinal cord of the cat when sensory fibers from antagonistic fibers were also stimulated. The time course of this inhibition was considerably longer than the time normally observed, having its maximum effect about 10 msec. after the beginning of the inhibitory stimulus. Moreover, it did not correlate with any observable change in the excitability of the postsynaptic cell or with the production of any observable i.p.s.p.'s. Frank and Fuortes called this "remote inhibition" and suggested it could be due either to inhibitory synapses on the ends of the dendrites of the $\nu\alpha$ motoneurons which were so far from the recording electrode that their direct effect could not be recorded, or that it could be due to a reduction in the effectiveness of the afferent impulses at a presynaptic level.

Eccles (Eccles, Eccles, and Magni, 1961; Eccles, Magni, and Willis, 1962) has found impressive evidence for the latter mechanism. Under certain conditions, stimulation of muscle afferents will produce a dorsal root reflex, i.e., antidromic firing of other afferent fibers. The time course of this dorsal root reflex is the same as that of Fuortes' "remote inhibition," and conditions which favor the one also favor the other (cooling of the spinal cord and stimulation of flexor rather than extensor afferents). Moreover, they both correlate with the appearance of an oriented d.c. potential in the spinal cord, whose orientation is best explained in terms of depolarization of the terminal branches of the afferent fibers within the cord.

On the basis of this evidence, Eccles has suggested that there is a second mechanism of inhibition, which he has renamed presynaptic inhibition. If it is supposed that the afferent fibers make synaptic connections with the terminal branches of other afferent fibers, and that they produce depolarization of the subsynaptic membrane, then the correlation of the inhibition with the dorsal root reflex is explained. The depolarization may become enough to trigger spike activity, which will be conducted antidromically and appear as the dorsal root reflex. If the depolarization is not sufficient to trigger spike activity, its effect will be to reduce the amplitude of afferent spikes when they reach the depolarized terminal branch. It is a plausible hypothesis that these smaller spikes should release less transmitter substance than the normal-size spikes.

Hubbard and Willis (1962) have shown that direct artificial depolarization of the afferent nerve branches has an inhibitory effect, and Gray (1962) has observed structures in the spinal cord of the cat which could be small synapses overlaying the large synaptic knobs which are in contact with the ventral horn cells. Lundberg and Voorhoeve (1961) have observed what appears to be presynaptic inhibition in the spinal cord as a result of stimulation of the sensorimotor cortex, so that presynaptic inhibition may not be restricted to reciprocal inhibition of afferent fibers in the spinal cord but may be a widely used mechanism throughout the nervous system.

Receptor or Generator Potentials

"The characteristic feature of receptors is that they are normally activated by specific changes of their surrounding such as temperature, light, pressure etc. rather than by synaptic activity as in the case for other neurons" (Fuortes, 1971). Partly because of the different functions of the different receptors, such as light reception or sound reception, the shape of receptor cells varies widely. In general, receptor cells may be divided into two types. In the first, the membrane which is the analog of the postsynaptic ending is separated by a long fiber that reaches to the presynaptic part of the receptor cell. Examples of such cells are pressure receptors (Pacinian corpuscles), touch receptors (free nerve endings in the skin), and olfactory receptors, signaling odors. In these receptor cells, transmission of information requires the use of nerve impulses because of the distance a message has to travel. The second class of receptor cell is short—less than 1 mm. In this second class are light receptors (the rods and cones in the retina), sound receptors, vestibular receptors, and taste receptors. In these cells the part which is analogous to the postsynaptic ending generates an electrical potential which spreads directly to the presynaptic portion of the receptor cell. There this graded potential releases a chemical transmitter in the same way that the nerve impulse releases transmitter from the presynaptic ending of a neuron.

In the majority of receptor cells the receptor membrane becomes depolarized when the relevant stimulus (light, pressure, heat, etc.—depending on the receptor) is applied. The stimulus acts to produce a similar electrical change on the receptor membrane that transmitter causes when it is applied to the postsynaptic membrane. However, as in the case of some neurons, some receptors, such as the cones in the retina, hyperpolarize when the relevant stimulus is applied.

Integrative Activity of Neurons. It is clear that the nerve cell is capable of quite complex integrative activity. The mammalian motoneuron, whose cell body is only about 70 μ across, with dendrites up to 1 mm. (1,000 μ) long, may have as many as 100 synaptic connections on it coming from a very large number of afferent fibers and ascending and descending fibers in the spinal cord. Some neurons may act as simple summators of the excitatory and inhibitory influences acting upon them. But in other cells the interaction may be much more complex.

A great deal of new evidence concerning the integrative activity of single cells has come from work on invertebrates, where in a number of cases ganglia containing small numbers of comparatively large cells have proved particularly easy to work on. Vertebrate nerve cells may not have such complex activity as these invertebrate cells, but there is no good reason, except lack of evidence, to suppose that they have not. Bullock (1959) and Horridge (1963) have summarized a great deal of the vertebrate and invertebrate work on single neuron preparations, and Bullock has described the present situation as a "quiet revolution in our concepts of how nerve cells act alone and in concert."

Unfortunately, this quiet revolution has not resulted in a new ordering of the subject but has, instead, revealed new orders of complexity which still remain to be explored. The new complexity consists largely in the discovery of local differences within single cells. The classification of cellular potentials suggested by Bullock is shown in Figure 1–8. In any cell, many of these potentials may be simultaneously present. We have as yet very few quantitative data on their interaction. In addition, there may be changes in the state of the cell that are not revealed by the

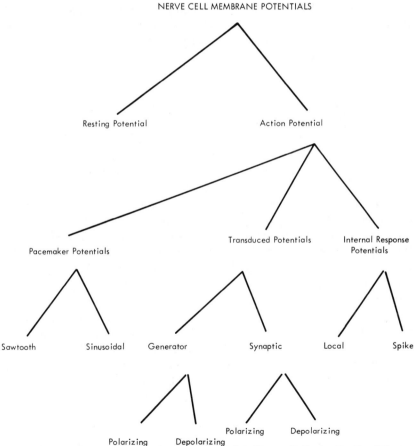

FIG. 1–8. Nerve cell membrane potentials. (From Bullock, T. H., "Neuron doctrine and electrophysiology," *Science*, 129, 1959.)

potentials. One example of this has already been dealt with in the account of inhibition produced by increased permeability of the cell membrane. Another example is facilitation, where successive impulses arriving at a synapse may produce successively larger e.p.s.p.'s, or diminution, where the reverse occurs. Neither effect correlates with a change in the membrane potential. If one adds to these effects the possibility of presynaptic inhibition, the theoretically possible but as yet unobserved presynaptic facilitation, and nonsynaptic interaction between nerve cells, it is clear that even in relation to the interaction of a small number of nerve cells the theoretical possibilities of interaction and integration are enormous.

Integrative Mechanisms

Input-output Relations in Simple Synaptic Systems.   The complexity of the interactive mechanisms revealed in the previous section may produce an extreme variety and complexity of possible modes of interaction between cells. We have some direct information concerning the input-output relations of single cells or groups of cells.

One piece of evidence comes from records from gross electrodes in the lateral geniculate (Bishop and McLeod, 1954). An electric shock applied to the optic nerve produces a synchronous volley of impulses which reach the lateral geniculate simultaneously and produce a sharp positive deflection recorded from the gross electrode on the optic tract or in the lateral geniculate. The electrode on the optic tract records only a single deflection, but the electrode in the lateral geniculate records two deflections with peaks separated by about 0.4 msec. The second deflection is probably the synchronized postsynaptic spikes appearing after the usual synaptic delay. Bishop and McLeod measured the relationship between the amplitude of the pre- and postsynaptic spikes, and an almost linear relationship was found (Fig. 1–9). Since only a single spike was evoked in each fiber, the data are relevant only to spatial interaction at the lateral geniculate. The very simple relationship may not be characteristic of other synaptic systems since the amount of spatial interaction in the lateral geniculate may be unusually small.

There seems to be no direct evidence concerning the relationship between the frequency of spike impulses reaching a synapse and the frequency of postsynaptic spikes. There is, however, some indirect evidence suggesting that the relationship may normally approach linearity. Hodgkin (1948) has shown that there is a linear relationship between the depolarization of the cell membrane and the frequency of nerve spikes generated. We also know that each spike will produce an e.p.s.p. of about the same amplitude and that these will summate. So, provided the spikes are not separated by too great a time, there should be a

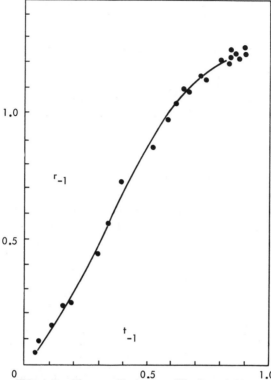

FIG. 1–9. The amplitude, in millivolts, of the post-synaptic r_1 spike plotted against that of the presynaptic t_1 spike, the strength of shock to the optic nerve being varied and all other conditions held constant. (From Bishop, P., and McLeod, *J. Neurophysiol.*, 17, 1954.)

linear relationship between the frequency of spikes and the amount of depolarization. An argument of this type is probably behind Rushton's assumption (1961) that excitatory interactions are linear.

There is a great deal of very elegant and quantitative work on inhibitory interactions in the eye of Limulus polyphemus, the horseshoe crab (Hartline and Ratliff, 1957, 1958; Hartline, Ratliff, and Miller, 1961) and on the inhibitory interactions of the Renshaw cells in the spinal cord with the α motoneurons of the ventral horn in the cat (Granit, 1961). In both cases the interaction appears to be almost linear. (Granit's experiment is conceptually simpler.) The Renshaw cells are stimulated by branching collaterals of the α motoneurons within the spinal cord. They have an inhibitory action of adjacent α motoneurons within the central horn. Their normal action is probably to reduce the total α motoneuron response to afferent or centripetal stimulation. They can be stimulated independently of an afferent stimulation by antidromic stimulation of the α motoneurons at the ventral root. Granit recorded the activity of a single fiber at one ventral root to varying degrees of afferent stimulation. He then recorded the activity produced by the same stimulation when the cell was inhibited by a standard stimulus to an adjacent ventral root and investigated the relationship between the normal frequency and the reduced frequency resulting from the standard amount of inhibition. The results could be fitted fairly well by the equation

$$fi = fu - c$$

where fi is the frequency when inhibited, fu the uninhibited frequency, and c a constant.

Hartline and his co-workers have obtained even better data from a more complex system (Fig. 1–10). Limulus has a faceted eye with

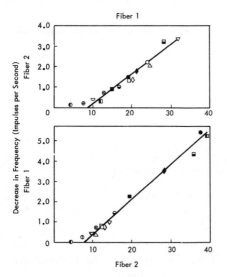

FIG. 1–10. Mutual inhibition of two receptor units in Limulus polyphemus. In each graph the magnitude of the inhibitory action (decrease in frequency of impulse discharge) exerted on one of the ommatidia is plotted on ordinate as a function of the degree of concurrent activity frequency of the other abscissa. The different points were obtained by using various intensities of illumination on ommatidia 1 and 2, in various combinations. The data for points designated by the same symbol were obtained simultaneously. (From Hartline and Ratliff, *J. gen. physiol.*, 1957; by permission of Rockefeller University Press.)

each ommatidium sending a fiber to the optic lobes in the crab brain. Hartline records from a single fiber and measures its frequency of firing as a function of light intensity when the appropriate ommatidium alone is stimulated (or a small number of ommatidia around the appropriate one). If a small group of adjacent ommatidia is simultaneously stimulated, the response of the first fiber is reduced by the inhibitory action of the adjacent ommatidia. The situation is complicated by the fact that the first group of ommatidia also inhibit the second, so that to describe the mutual interaction of single sensory cells in the Limulus eye Hartline has to set up sets of simultaneous equations, such as:

$$r_1 = e_1 - K_{1.2} \ \{ \ r_2 - r^{\circ}_{1.2}$$
$$r_2 = e_2 - K_{2.1} \ \{ \ r_1 - r^{\circ}_{2.1}$$

where r_1 and r_2 are the simultaneous frequencies of two fibers whose ommatidia are close enough to inhibit each other and are being separately stimulated, e_1 and e_2 are the frequencies with which each would fire if stimulated separately, $K_{1.2}$ and $K_{2.1}$ are constants expressing the degree of mutual interaction, while $r^{\circ}_{1.2}$ and $r^{\circ}_{2.1}$ are constants indicating that the inhibitory effect has a threshold so that when, for example, r_2 is less than $r^{\circ}_{1.2}$, the second fiber will have no inhibitory action on the first.

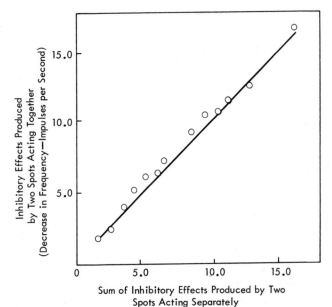

FIG. 1–11. The summation of inhibitory effects produced by steady illumination, at various intensities, of two widely separated groups of receptors. The sum of the inhibitory effects on a fast receptor (steadily illuminated at a fixed intensity) produced by each group acting separately is plotted as abscissa; the effect produced by the two groups of receptors acting simultaneously is plotted as ordinate. (From Hartline and Ratliff, *J. gen. physiol.,* 1958; by permission of Rockefeller University Press.)

Hartline has been able to show that these equations very accurately represent the behavior of this particular system, with the proviso that the expression in the brackets can take only positive values. Negative values are equivalent to zero since no inhibition occurs. Hartline has also shown that a number of the consequences which might be expected to result from the activity of such a system do in fact occur. Such a mechanism produces spatial contrast and the enlargement of activity at the edge of a patterned stimulus. And if a third ommatidium is stimulated, this may inhibit the second fiber to a greater degree than it inhibits the first fiber, so that stimulation of the third ommatidium may actually increase the rate at which the first fiber fires by releasing it from the inhibition exerted by the second. Hartline has compared this to the disinhibition which is observed in the interaction of spinal reflexes.

Hartline and Ratliff have also shown that when ommatidia are far enough apart to have no mutual inhibitory effect, their inhibitory effects on an intermediate ommatidium show simple summation (Fig. 1–11).

Inferences about the Nervous System

The physiological psychologist can only rarely directly observe how the nervous system produces behavior; most frequently, he must infer how the nervous system produces behavior from indirect evidence. It is interesting to note that the early neurophysiologists, hampered by inadequate technology, proceeded in the same way. Because they were extraordinarily successful, physiological psychologists have much to learn from their practical and logical methods.

Early ideas about the functioning of the nerve cell were developed from behavioral work on simple reflexes, notably by Sherrington and his school, who worked largely on the spinal reflexes of decerebrate preparations. Their method of investigation was to stimulate sensory nerves, either with a normal sensory stimulus or by electrical stimulation of the nerve itself, and then to measure the strength of the reflex twitch which developed, usually in one of the limbs. They investigated the relationship between the strength of the reflex response and the intensity and timing of the stimulus, and also investigated the effects of giving more than one stimulus at a time. Their main findings were as follows (Creed et al., 1932; Sherrington, 1906; Fulton, 1943).

1. As the intensity of the stimulus increased, the strength of the reflex response increased while its latency decreased.

2. If a simple stimulus was just below the threshold for evoking a response, a second stimulus immediately following it would sum with it to produce a reflex response. The size of the reflex response was usually greatest when the two subliminal stimuli were given simultaneously, and it deceased as the time interval between them was increased (Fig. 1–12).

3. A stimulus which produced contraction of one muscle would in general produce a relaxation of the antagonistic muscles (i.e., those

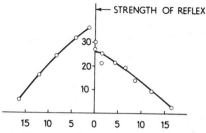

FIG. 1–12. Reflex responses of a muscle (*tibialis anticus*) to two stimuli (each of which is just threshold) at various intervals to two nerves (med. gastroc. n. and lat. gastroc. n.). Abscissae—stimulus interval in msec.; ordinates—tension in grams. To right of zero, lat. gastroc. n. is stimulated first; to left of zero, med. gastroc. n. first. Curve shows relation of stimulus intervals to resulting tension. (From Creed, R. S., et al., 1932, *Reflex Activity of the Spinal Cord;* courtesy of Clarendon Press, Oxford.)

muscles which tend to move the limb in an opposite direction). The first is attributed to the excitatory effect of the stimulus, and the second to its inhibitory effect.

4. If two stimuli each separately produced a response which affected the same muscles in the same way, the effect of both stimuli together was greater than the effect of either alone. In some cases, particularly when the stimuli were intense, the effect of the two together was less than the arithmetical sum of the two separate effects. In other cases, particularly when the stimuli were weak, the effect of the two together was greater than the arithmetical sum of the two separate effects.

5. If two stimuli produced effects in opposite directions, i.e., were antagonistic, then the two together produced an effect which was less than the effect of either alone. In general, the stimulus producing the greater response overcame the weaker, although there were many exceptions to this rule. Some reflexes which seem to have greater biological importance are, in Sherrington's term, prepotent and tend to overcome antagonistic reflexes even when the latter are of greater strength. Also, a reflex which has been in operation for some time can be overcome more easily than a reflex which is stimulated for the first time.

To explain these characteristics of reflex behavior, Sherrington developed some simple theories of nervous action which have since been largely confirmed by the more direct investigations made possible by improved physiological techniques. Sherrington made use of the concept of the neuron in developing his theory of nervous activity, although no records of the activity of neurons existed at that time. He argued that nervous activity was passed from one neuron to another through the "synapse" (Sherrington coined this word for the functional connection between one neuron and another). This activity must finally be transmitted to the muscles via the motor neurons, and since many kinds of activity are mediated by the same muscles and by the same motor neurons, there must be a great deal of "convergence" of sensory and other neurons onto this "final common path." The exact nature of this convergence must determine the effect of combined stimuli.

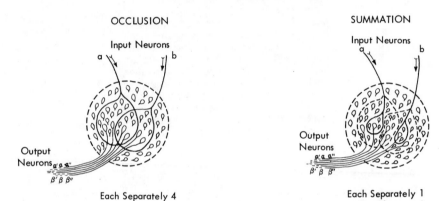

OCCLUSION

SUMMATION

Each Separately 4
Together   6

Each Separately 1
Together   6

FIG. 1–13. Sherrington's model of neural interaction. The dotted circles indicate the populations of neurons subliminally stimulated by each input neuron. The solid circles indicate the populations of neurons effectively stimulated by each input neuron. Neurons within the subliminal fringe of each input neuron are effectively stimulated by the summation of the two subthreshold effects.

Whether the effect for two simultaneous stimuli is more or less the sum of the effects of each separately is determined by the relative numbers of neurons subliminally or supraliminally excited by each stimulus, and the amount of overlap of the two populations. (Adapted from Creed, R. S., et al., 1932, *Reflex Activity of the Spinal Cord;* courtesy of Clarendon Press, Oxford.)

Sherrington's model of the interaction of neurons is shown in Figure 1–13. Each incoming neuron connects with several other neurons in a particular neuron pool. Some of these will be affected to a threshold level, and others only subliminally. The stronger the incoming signal, the greater the proportion stimulated above threshold. If the incoming signal is too weak, it may be inadequate, by itself, to produce any activity in the neurons in the pool. The subthreshold effects of two stimuli may, however, be enough to excite some neurons in the pool when they are combined. At a slightly higher intensity, each alone may excite a few neurons, which are likely not to be the same ones. Still more neurons will be excited by the combined effect of the two incoming signals, so that the combined effect of the two will be greater than the sum of the effects of each alone. At a higher intensity still, each incoming signal excites practically all the neurons in the pool, many of them being excited by both ("convergence"). In this case the combined effect of the two incoming signals will be less than the sum of each separately.

To account for the temporal characteristics of excitation and inhibition, Sherrington postulated a central excitatory state (c.e.s.) and a central inhibitory state (c.i.s.). Both were thought of as active persisting states in a pool of neurons which could combine algebraically—the c.e.s. having a positive sign and the c.i.s. having a negative sign. The output from a pool of neurons is determined by the positive result of the combined c.e.s. and c.i.s. Figure 1–13 shows the different modes of excitatory interaction. One can fairly easily extrapolate to the possible interactions of c.i.s. alone, or c.e.s. and c.i.s. combined. Figure 1–14 shows the temporal characteristics of the c.e.s. and c.i.s. for two spinal reflexes.

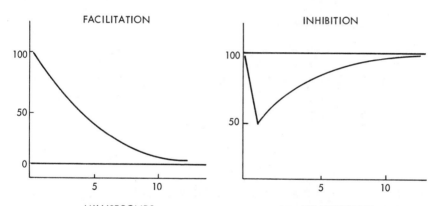

FIG. 1–14. The stimuli in these experiments were two short electrical stimuli to the sensory nerves, at different intervals (msec.) between them. Natural stimuli prolong the time relations because of the long latency of the sense organs. (From Lloyd, *J. Neurophys.,* 9, 1946.)

Modern methods of electrical recording reveal a great deal about the signals which are transmitted by the neurons and the nature of the c.e.s. and c.i.s. It seems clear, however, that Sherrington's c.e.s. (central excitatory state) can be identified with the e.p.s.p. (excitatory postsynaptic potential) and that experiments on the e.p.s.p. have dramatically confirmed many of the properties of the central excitatory state postulated by Sherrington. The effect of varying the interval between two stimuli is accounted for by the observed decay time of the e.p.s.p. If the second stimulus arrives soon after the first, the two sets of voltages sum together to produce a much higher voltage than if the second stimulus arrives after the first has partly decayed. An increased voltage produces a larger probability of spike initiation.

The shorter latency of a reflex with more intense stimulation is explicable in terms of the more rapid rise of the larger e.p.s.p.'s toward the threshold for spike activity. Temporal summation of e.p.s.p.'s evoked by successive spikes at a synapse can account for the longer latencies observed to prolonged low-intensity stimulation in the following way. If successive subthreshold stimuli arrive before the e.p.s.p. from the previous subthreshold stimulus has completely decayed, such e.p.s.p.'s gradually accumulate till the threshold for a reflex is reached.

Sherrington's c.i.s. (central inhibitory state) is the equivalent of the i.p.s.p. (inhibitory postsynaptic potential), and the algrebraic combination postulated by Sherrington between the c.e.s. and the c.i.s. is in fact the combination of positive and negative voltages across a neuronal membrane.

Basis of Drug Addiction

Despite the magnitude of the social problem caused by the ingestion of substances with some action on the nervous system, little of a definitive nature is known about the cause and persistence of such behavior. Almost 10 percent of those who drink ethanol are alcoholics. In Dublin, Ireland, 25 percent of all male first admissions to psychiatric facilities had a diagnosis of alcoholism and alcoholic psychosis. A similar problem is encountered through the use of cannabis (marijuana) in countries where it is legal. The mean incidence of patients who, following cannabis use, contracted schizophreniform or specific cannabis psychoses was 22.5 percent among psychiatric hospital admissions in Brazil, India, Morocco, and Nigeria (Wilson, 1968).

The actions of alcohol are physiologically almost all-pervasive. One well-established effect on the nervous system, that may well account for at least some of its addictive effects, is on cholinergic transmission. It has been shown that alcohol blocks or reduces the release of acetylcholine in slices of cerebral cortex. (Botulinus toxin also prevents the release of acetylcholine in cholinergic fibers.) The rate of synthesis of acetylcholine appears to be unaffected (Kalant et al., 1967). The decrease in acetylcholine release can be readily detected by pharmacological methods at doses which in the whole animal would cause moderate to heavy intoxication.

Perhaps the best-understood drug from the point of view of its action is nicotine, the most important pharmacological ingredient of tobacco. Nicotine is one of a class of drugs that stimulate autonomic ganglia at cholinoceptive sites. Its excitatory effect is blocked by hexamethonium.

At higher doses of nicotine, the stimulatory effect turns into a blockade of transmission through the production of persistent depolarization in the ganglia. (In contrast to this, muscarine and methacholine also stimulate autonomic ganglia, but the actions of these drugs are blocked not by hexamethonium but by atropine. At higher doses, methacholine produces blockade by hyperpolarization, not depolarization, as does nicotine). It is believed that autonomic cholinoceptive sites are of two types: one sensitive to nicotine and the other to muscarine. It is probable that these two types of site also exist in the central nervous system. While the initial stimulating and later blocking actions of nicotine are conceptually simple, the physiological actions of nicotine are complex and unpredictable because the drug has an effect on a large number of synapses simultaneously, as it can stimulate or block all autonomic ganglia. Nicotine also acts directly on the CNS, where cells sensitive to it have been directly identified. Nicotine can cause tremors, and in large doses convulsions. Nicotine can also cause vomiting, and it exerts an antidiuretic action. In larger doses (about 60 mg.), nicotine is one of the most rapidly acting poisons.

As a cigarette contains 20 to 30 mg. of nicotine and a cigar about 120 mg., it may be difficult to see why human beings develop such a powerful craving for tobacco. However, much of the nicotine is burned during smoking, while 90 percent is absorbed when the smoke is inhaled. Further, marked tolerance to the drug develops with continued use. Vomiting, one of the central effects of nicotine, often occurs in the novice, but soon fails to be triggered with continued use.

The same effect of tolerance occurs with all drugs of addiction. A drug exerts a steadily smaller effect with continuing use. This has the consequence that the user must secure a steadily greater dose to obtain the same effect. However, it is evident in the case of nicotine that the desired effect is not the vomiting but the tranquilizing effect.

How tolerance to a drug develops in physiological terms is a major problem for a basic understanding of addiction. A number of theories have been developed, all of which assume a homeostatic action on the part of the organism (Dole, 1970). If the drug has an action which drives the operation of some part of the organism in one direction, the organism develops some countermeasure to drive that part of the organism in the other direction. Some have suggested that the organism produces increased or decreased amounts of particular enzymes. Others, such as Jaffe and Sharpless (1968), have invoked alterations in the sensitivity of postsynaptic membranes to explain such homeostasis.

It has been observed that disuse at a synapse produces a greater sensitivity to a transmitter. If a synapse is pharmacologically blocked, its sensitivity can be expected to increase. As its sensitivity increases, more blocking agent will be necessary to keep it blocked. If the blocking agent is suddenly withdrawn, abnormally high activity in the system will occur. In fact, withdrawal symptoms are just what these theories would predict. They appear to be the opposite of the effects of the drug.

For instance, smokers attempting to stop smoking are nervous and on edge. Further, if the dose of drug is kept constant, tolerance develops, and the smoker who initially smoked to obtain a tranquilizing effect must maintain his smoking in order to feel the same as he felt before he began to smoke. Thus with tolerance a state of dependence is established. This is also true of the heroin addict. While a drug habit may initially be established to secure some pleasurable effect because it is positively reinforcing, it soon becomes maintained because cessation would be negatively reinforcing.

It has been possible to show alterations in synaptic sensitivity in a manner consistent with Jaffe and Sharpless's (1968) theory in the case of some drugs and in liver enzymes with other drugs. It would seem that addiction is a consequence of a long-term homeostatic property of the organism, perhaps at the postsynaptic ending or perhaps in some cases in the liver. However, the development of tolerance does not seem unescapable. Protein synthesis inhibitors block the development of tolerance to narcotics without blocking the actions of the narcotics in non-tolerant animals. Actinomycin D, administered with morphine, decreases the development of tolerance without impairing the analgetic effect of morphine. However, this inhibitor does not reduce morphine tolerance when it is given for short periods to animals that already are tolerant (Dole, 1970).

chapter 2

Anatomy of the
Nervous System

The first part of this chapter gives information to orient the beginning student to the mammalian nervous system. The balance of the chapter, which describes the nervous system in greater detail, is meant mainly for reference purposes should the student become interested in greater anatomical detail. It should be emphasized, however, that anatomical descriptions of specific systems are separately described throughout the text, wherever such descriptions help us understand the function of the systems. It also should be pointed out to the student that, in most instances, gross anatomy is useful mainly as a shorthand way of describing parts of the nervous system. The gross anatomy of a goose (Fig. 2–1) or octopus brain is markedly different from that of a mammal (Fig. 2–2). On the other hand, many forms of behavior of interest to

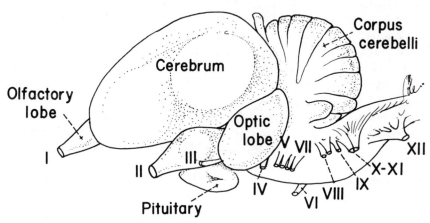

FIG. 2–1. Goose brain.

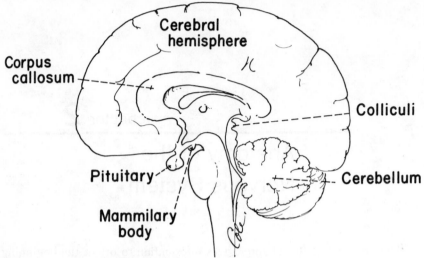

FIG. 2–2.   General schema of mammalian brain.

the psychologist are quite similar. This leads us to suspect that much of the neural circuitry at a finer level than that of gross anatomy will also turn out to be similar.

A simplified schema of a primate brain shows the cerebrum overlying such structures as the basal ganglia and the thalamus. Moving upward from the spinal cord, we arrive at the medulla oblongata, which changes into the pons (Fig. 2–3). The pons lies on the side close to the throat of the animal with the cerebellum attached at the back of the pons. Moving still further up, we have the midbrain or mesencephalon. Below the thalamus is the hypothalamus (Fig. 2–4, p. 36). It must be emphasized that these gross units, such as the medulla or the midbrain, are not functional wholes. Instead, they are heterogeneous collections of structures grouped into somewhat arbitrary units, often on the basis of gross visual resemblances. Each unit is made up of white matter and gray matter. Gray matter is made up of cell bodies and dendrites; the so-called nuclei and the cerebral cortex are made up of gray matter. Interconnections among nerve cells occur in the gray matter because synapses occur on the cell bodies or the dendrites. Axons connecting the nuclei are generally covered with a whitish myelin sheath; hence collections of such axons are called white matter. Such white matter therefore consists of connections between nuclei.

In the spinal cord, the cell bodies form the inner core of the cord and are surrounded by white matter on the outside of the cord (Fig. 2–5, p. 36). Sensory nerves enter the spinal cord through the dorsal roots (closer to the back of the animal). Motor nerves leave the spinal cord

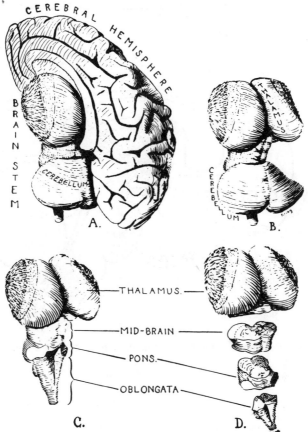

FIG. 2–3. Assembly diagram of the main parts into which the brain is divided for descriptive purposes: *A*, with only the left cerebral hemisphere removed; *B*, the brain stem and cerebellum; *C*, the brain stem alone; *D*, the segments of the brain stem. (From Krieg, W. J. S., *Functional Neuroanatomy*, 1966; Brain Books, Evanston, Ill.)

through the ventral roots (closer to the belly of the animal). Other nerves which directly leave the brain (not through the spinal cord) are called the cranial nerves. Some of the cranial nerves are sensory in function, others are motor, and some are mixed. The motor fibers thus far described do not have further synapses after they leave the central nervous system (brain and spinal cord). They control the musculature which causes limb movement, and are often called somatic nerves. However, there are other effector fibers that leave the brain and the spinal cord and *do* have synapses outside the central nervous system. These belong to the autonomic nervous system, which innervates muscle

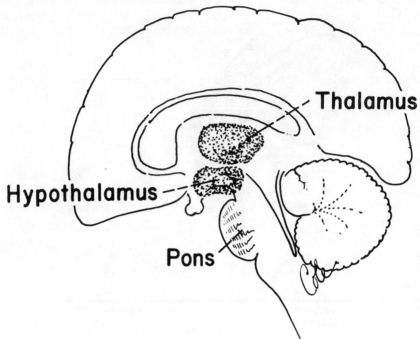

FIG. 2–4. Position of some major structures in the human brain.

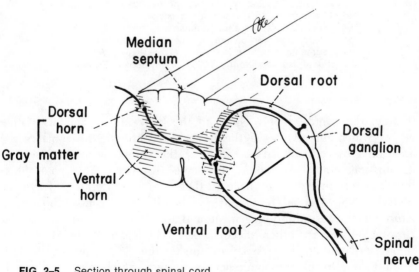

FIG. 2–5. Section through spinal cord.

in the gut, the heart, and various glands. The autonomic system is divided into two parts: the sympathetic and the parasympathetic. In general, the sympathetic system is active in states of stress and the parasympathetic in states of relaxation.

The medulla is in many ways a continuation of the spinal cord after it enters the skull. Most of the cranial nerves leave and enter the medulla. All the tracts connecting the brain with the spinal cord pass through it. In addition, the medulla contains nuclei that are important in breathing, heart beat, and control of the gastrointestinal tract. An upward continuation of the medulla is the pons (Fig. 2–3), containing some cranial nerve nuclei and fiber pathways leading to the cerebellum. The cerebellum lies on the dorsal surface and has some coordinating functions in movement. The midbrain or mesencephalon is an upward extension of the pons, and it merges at its other end into the hypothalamus and the thalamus. On the dorsal (toward the back) surface of the midbrain are the superior colliculi (connected with vision) and the inferior colliculi (connected with hearing). Further, the midbrain contains the red nucleus and the substantia nigra (both connected with movement). Together, the medulla, pons, and midbrain are grouped as the brain stem.

The thalamus can be subdivided into three groups of nuclei on functional grounds: sensory relay nuclei, association nuclei, and intrinsic nuclei. The sensory relay nuclei receive fibers from sense organs and send fibers signaling messages from the sense organs to the cortex. In this class are the lateral geniculate nucleus (vision), medial geniculate nucleus (hearing), and the ventrobasal nuclear complex (somesthesis). The association nuclei do not receive fibers directly from sensory pathways but send fibers to portions of the cortex. In contrast, the intrinsic nuclei do not send fibers to the neocortex. The functions of the association and intrinsic nuclei are obscure.

The hypothalamus lies forward of the midbrain and beneath the thalamus at the base of the brain. Composed of a large group of small nuclei, it is important in the regulation of drive and physiological regulatory functions. The main pathway, which takes up a large part of the hypothalamus, is the medial forebrain bundle. Stimulation of this bundle is rewarding.

The basal ganglia partially envelop the thalamus and are surrounded by the cerebral cortex and its underlying white matter. The basal ganglia are really a group of large nuclei comprising the caudate nucleus, the putamen, and the globus pallidus, together called the corpus striatum (Figs. 2–6, 2–8). These structures, part of the extrapyramidal motor system, send messages down into the spinal cord via the rubrospinal and reticulospinal tracts. In contrast, the pyramidal motor system originates in the cortex and sends messages into the spinal cord via the corticospinal

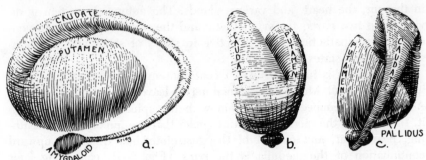

FIG. 2–6. Form of striatum of left side; (a) lateral aspect, (b) anterior aspect, (c) posterior aspect. (From Krieg, W. J. S., *Functional Neuroanatomy*, 1966; Brain Books, Evanston, Ill.)

tracts. The amygdaloid body, located in the middle of the. temporal lobe of the cortex, has connections with the olfactory system, and removal of the amygdaloid body removes some aversions.

Some idea of the position of the caudate and the amygdala is given by Figures 2–6 and 2–7. In Figure 2–7, these structures are shown in relation to the brain ventricles. The ventricles are a set of interconnected cavities inside the central nervous system and are filled with cerebrospinal fluid. In comparison, Figure 2–26 (p. 66) gives the position of the hippocampus in relation to the amygdala. Remember also that the hippocampus is situated on the floor of the inferior horn of the lateral ventricle and is therefore directly below the tail of the caudate nucleus in the same ventricle. The hippocampus, together with the olfactory bulb and

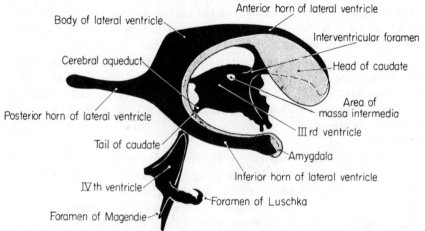

FIG. 2–7. The brain ventricles with caudate nucleus and amygdala. (Reprinted with permission of the Macmillan Company from *Correlative Anatomy of the Nervous System* by Crosby, Humphrey, and Lauer. Copyright 1962 by the Macmillan Company.)

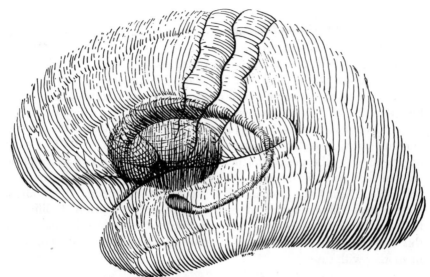

FIG. 2–8. Phantom of striatum within the cerebral hemisphere. (From Krieg, W. J. S., *Functional Neuroanatomy,* 1966; Brain Books, Evanston, Ill.)

some other structures, is part of the rhinencephalon. Some of these structures also are grouped together and are called the limbic system. They are thought to be involved in emotion.

Overlying the rest of the brain are the cerebral hemispheres. The exterior of these hemispheres is composed of a thin layer of gray matter called the cortex. Under this layer is white matter composed of axons, some connecting various areas of the cortex and others providing input to and output from the cortex. One of the largest structures in the white matter connecting the areas of the cortex is the corpus callosum, which connects symmetrical points in the left and right hemispheres. One of the largest tracts leading into and out of the cortex is the internal capsule (Fig. 2–23, p. 63).

ANATOMICAL METHODS

Most of the structures described in this chapter are plainly visible to the naked eye if a modicum of care is used in cutting up the brain. Most of them, in fact, were described before the advent of modern techniques of observation.

Modern techniques make extensive use of the light and electron microscopes. To facilitate microscopic examination, the brain is prevented from decaying by fixing the tissue in formalin or alcohol, and is then hardened by freezing or embedding it in paraffin or celloidin. Such hardening enables the anatomist to cut the neural tissue into thin sections suitable for mounting on a slide. A variety of stains has been developed which cause differential coloration of various kinds of neural tissue. Some strains attach only to myelin sheaths, others to cell bodies.

As the anatomist is frequently interested in connections between cells in the nervous system although the slices he can inspect are only 10 to 100 microns thick, tracing such connections would be all but impossible were it not for an interesting property of nerve cells. When an axon is cut, two types of degeneration take place. Within the central nervous system, usually the whole neuron, of which the axon is a part, degenerates. In the peripheral nervous system, degeneration takes place only in that part of the axon which is severed (by the cut) from the cell body. During the process of degeneration, the neural tissue alters its chemical characteristics so that it is possible to strain it differentially—so that it is plainly visible—in contrast with healthy tissue. In this way it is possible to trace a group of fibers from one thin slice to another with ease.

PERIPHERAL NERVOUS SYSTEM

The nervous system consists of a very large number of neurons. In the case of vertebrates the nervous system is generally subdivided into three main portions: (1) *the central nervous system,* comprising the brain and spinal cord; (2) *the peripheral nervous system,* comprising the cranial and spinal nerves; and (3) *the autonomic nervous system,* comprising the autonomic nerves and ganglia. (A nerve is a bundle of single nerve fibers.)

There are generally considered to be twelve pairs of cranial nerves which are attached to the brain at irregular intervals. These are highly specific in organization and function, and their anatomical arrangements are described where relevant in other portions of the book (Figs. 2–9, 2–10).

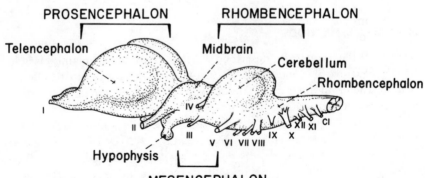

FIG. 2–9. The brain of a primitive vertebrate.

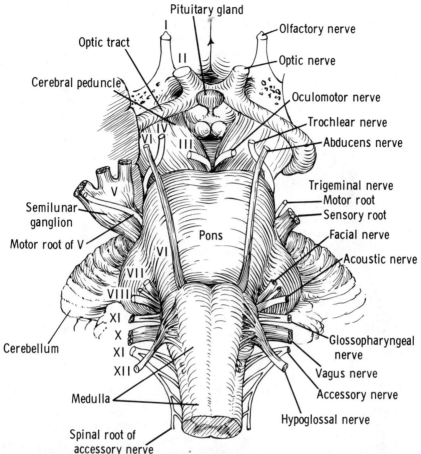

FIG. 2–10. Emergence of cranial nerves from the brain. View from base of brain. Note the position of the medulla, pons, and pituitary gland. (From Chusid, J. G., and McDonald, J. J., *Correlative Neuroanatomy,* 12th ed.; Lange Medical Publications, 1964.)

Thirty-one pairs of spinal nerves originate from the spinal cord. These consist of eight pairs of cervical spinal nerves, twelve pairs of thoracic nerves, five pairs of lumbar nerves, five pairs of sacral nerves, and one pair of coccygeal nerves.

Each spinal nerve is made of the union of two nerve roots passing out of the spinal cord. The first is the ventral root, which carries efferent fibers. The ventral root is a bundle of nerve fibers emerging from the spinal cord closest to the belly (Latin *ventralis,* belonging to the belly). Efferent fibers are fibers which carry information *from* the nervous system to the musculature and glands, causing them to function. The second is the dorsal root, which is composed of afferent fibers. (There are some exceptions to this functional division. The dorsal root is closer to the back (Latin *dorsalis,* belonging to the back). Afferent fibers are fibers which convey messages *into* the central nervous system. Thus they bring information from the sensory apparatus.

In the peripheral nervous system, both the afferent and efferent fibers are called axons. In the case of the afferent fibers, the fiber (axon) which conveys information into the cell body has to be very long as its cell of origin is in the central nervous system. In the central nervous

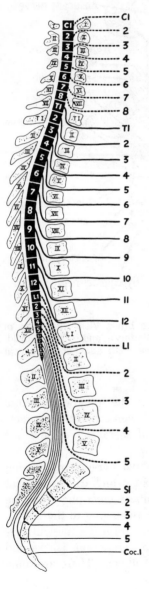

FIG. 2–11. Origin of the spinal nerves in the spinal cord. *C1-8* = cervical spinal nerves; *T1-12* = thoracic nerves; *L1-5* = lumbar nerves; *S1-5* = sacral nerves; *Coc. 1* = coccygeal nerve. The associated vertebrae are marked in Roman numerals. (From Haymaker, W., and Woodhall, *Peripheral Nerve Injuries; Philadelphia:* W. B. Saunders Company, 1953).

system, however, a fiber is called an axon only if it conveys information away from the cell body, as in the case of an axon belonging to an efferent fiber in the peripheral nervous system.

Just before the dorsal and ventral roots unite there is an enlargement or swelling on the dorsal root called the dorsal ganglion. This contains the cells of origin of the dorsal root fibers. The cells of origin of the ventral root fibers lie in the ventral horn of the gray matter of the spinal cord (Figs. 2–11, 2–12, 2–5). When we speak of cells of origin, we mean cell bodies whose fibers are an elongated part. The gray matter looks gray because it is composed of cell bodies which are unmyelinated. The white matter is composed of nerve fibers which are myelinated, and so look white because of their fatty covering of myelin.

Each spinal nerve makes its exit from the vertebral canal by means of an opening between the vertebrae (intervertebral foramen). It then branches into dorsal and ventral rami (Latin for branches). Many of the spinal nerves enter into complicated plexuses, where they intermingle

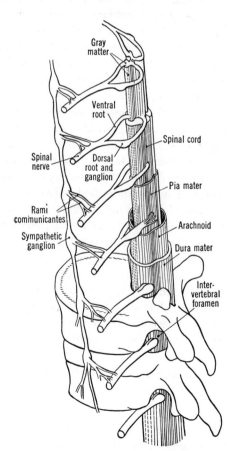

FIG. 2–12. Spinal cord and associated structures. (From Gardner, E. Q., *Fundamentals of Neurology,* 4th ed.; Philadelphia: W. B. Saunders Company, 1963.)

considerably. As a result, the regions supplied by the peripheral nerves arising from these plexuses do not correspond to the regions supplied by the spinal nerves entering the plexuses. That is, one spinal nerve may contribute to several peripheral nerves, and one peripheral nerve may distribute fibers derived from several spinal nerves. There is also considerable overlap between the areas supplied both by the spinal nerves and by the peripheral nerves.

AUTONOMIC NERVOUS SYSTEM

The outflows of the somatic and autonomic nervous systems may be distinguished on the basis of the types of effector organ which they innervate. Whereas the somatic ouflow is distributed to striated (striped) muscles, the autonomic outflow innervates the smooth muscle of the viscera and blood vessels, cardiac muscle, and glands.

Further distinctions between somatic and autonomic outflows are generally made on the basis of function. For instance, the somatic outflow is more under voluntary control than is the autonomic outflow. We find it easier to control the movements of our limbs than to control our heart rate, respirating, or body temperature, for example. Of course, this is only true as a general statement. A further distinction is that whereas the somatic nervous system is concerned with regulating external environment, the autonomic nervous system regulates our internal environment. Autonomic outflow regulates body temperature, blood pressure, heart rate, respiration, digestive function, and so on, thus maintaining constancy in our internal environment. However, exceptions could again be found to this general distinction.

The outflow of the autonomic nervous system has its own anatomical arrangement, as described below. One characteristic which distinguishes it from the somatic outflow concerns the location of the last neuron in the chain. Somatic motor neurons always have their cell bodies located inside the central nervous system. In the autonomic system (with the exception of the innervation of the adrenal medulla), the cell bodies of the ultimate neurons are located outside the central nervous system. Another interesting difference between the two outflows is that if autonomic effector organs are completely denervated, they usually will not degenerate but will continue to function autonomously. In contrast, striated muscle will atrophy after denervation.

Sympathetic and Parasympathetic Divisions of the Autonomic Nervous System

The autonomic nervous system has traditionally been classified into two divisions (Figs. 2–13, 2–14, 2–15). The first has been named the sympathetic or thoracicolumbar division, and the second the parasympathetic

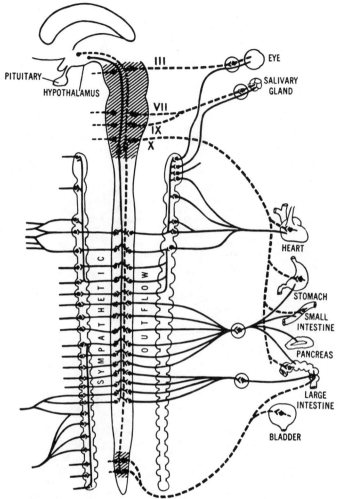

PITUITARY

HYPOTHALAMUS

III

VII

IX

X

EYE

SALIVARY
GLAND

HEART

STOMACH

SMALL
INTESTINE

PANCREAS

LARGE
INTESTINE

BLADDER

SYMPATHETIC OUTFLOW

FIG. 2–13. A simplified diagram of the general arrangement
of the autonomic nervous system. The projections from the
hypothalamus to the pituitary gland have been omitted, while
those to lower centers are shown in solid lines (sympathetic)
and broken lines (parasympathetic). The portions of the brain
stem and sacral cord from which the parasympathetic preganglionic fibers leave are indicated by oblique lines, and the
sympathetic outflow from the thoracic and upper lumbar cord
is labeled. Autonomic fibers to organs of the head and trunk
are shown on the right side, while those on the left side represent the sympathetic outflow to blood vessels, sweat glands,
and smooth muscle fibers attached to hairs. (From Gardner, E.,
Fundamentals of Neurology, 1969; W. B. Saunders Company.)

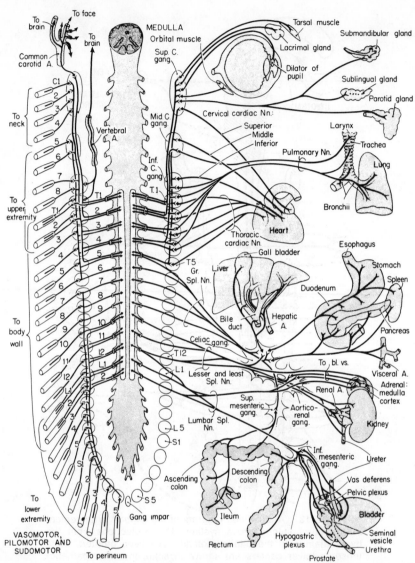

FIG. 2–14. Diagram to illustrate the sympathetic division of the autonomic nervous system. On the left side of the spinal cord is shown the innervation of the blood vessels, sweat glands, and pilomotor muscles. On the right is shown the innervation of the various viscera. (Reprinted with permission of the Macmillan Company from *Correlative Anatomy of the Nervous System* by Crosby, Humphrey, and Lauer. Copyright 1962 by the Macmillan Company.)

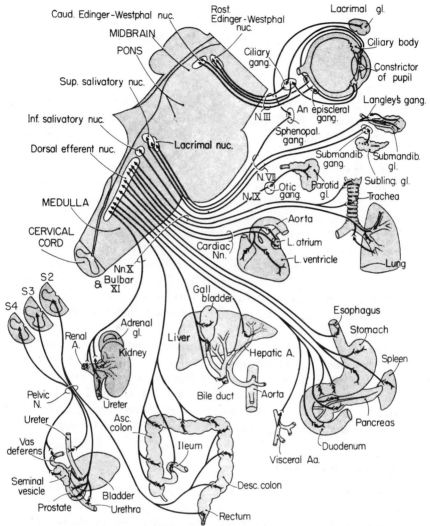

FIG. 2–15. The parasympathetic division of the autonomic system as it innervates the various viscera. (Reprinted with permission of the Macmillan Company from *Correlative Anatomy of the Nervous System* by Crosby, Humphrey, and Lauer. Copyright 1962 by the Macmillan Company.)

or craniosacral division. This classification has been made on several grounds. First, the two divisions originate in different portions of the central nervous system. Second, the sympathetic outflow is much more diffuse than the parasympathetic outflow. This is apparent, first, from the anatomical arrangements of the two systems (described below). Second, the sympathetic outflow innervates the adrenal medulla, which discharges epinephrine and norepinephrine into the blood stream. These substances are the sympathetic transmitter substances, and so such a release has the general effect of a diffuse sympathetic activation.

Figures 2–13, 2–14, and 2–15 provide a summary of the sympathetic and parasympathetic outflows and their functions. It will be noted that some of the autonomic effector organs are innervated only by sympathetic fibers. Others are acted on by both sympathetic and parasympathetic influences. In the latter case, the two influences often have antagonistic actions. For instance, sympathetic influences accelerate the heart and parasympathetic influences decelerate it. Again, in some cases sympathetic activation causes vasodilation and parasympathetic activation causes vasoconstriction. However, the two influences may act synergistically. For instance, both sympathetic and parasympathetic influences stimulate secretion of the salivary gland, but the secretions stimulated by the two pathways differ in viscosity.

Two points may be made concerning these contrasting effects. First, it appears that the sympathetic system is activated in states of emergency to mobilize body resources for such events as flight or fighting. Thus an animal under stress has dilated pupils, increased blood pressure, deepened respiration; it sweats, its hair stands on end—all of these are sympathetic effects. In contrast, parasympathetic functions, such as occur in the digestive tract, are inhibited. On this basis the general statement has been made that sympathetic activities predominate in states of stress, and parasympathetic activities in states of quiescence. But again this is a very general statement, to which exceptions may be found. Another function of this system of antagonistic innervation is that it can provide a very sensitive regulatory device, based on the two sets of tonic discharges impinging on the same effector organ.

Anatomical Organization

Autonomic outflow originates from *preganglionic neurons.* In the brain stem these are located in the nuclei of cranial nerves III, VII, IX, and X. Those in the spinal cord form a long column in the intermediolateral part of the gray matter. The small myelinated preganglionic fibers (axons of preganglionic neurons) leave the central nervous system by way of their corresponding cranial nerve or ventral root. They synapse with *postganglionic neurons,* located in ganglia outside the central nervous system. The unmyelinated postganglionic fibers (axons of postganglionic neurons) project to autonomic effectors. All such synapses use acetylcholine as transmitters.

Location of Autonomic Ganglia

Two long nerve trunks extend, one on each side, along the vertebral column. These are known as the *sympathetic chains* or *trunks,* and they consist of sympathetic ganglia and fibers joining them (Figs. 2–12, 2–13). There are 21 or 22 sympathetic ganglia in each chain. Sympathetic ganglia are also located elsewhere in the body. The parasympathetic ganglia are not arranged in trunks but are located in or near the effector organs which they innervate.

Sympathetic Outflow

Sympathetic preganglionic neurons are located in the thoracic and upper lumbar spinal segments. Their axons leave the spinal cord via the ventral roots and enter the corresponding spinal nerves. However, they leave these nerves via the *white rami communicantes* to enter the sympathetic trunks. Here a preganglionic fiber may pass up or down the trunk and then synapse with postganglionic neurons. In this case it would connect with postganglionic neurons located in several ganglia. It has been calculated that preganglionic fibers from a single white ramus may activate as many as eight ganglia. Alternatively, a preganglionic fiber may pass without synapse through the sympathetic trunk into a splanchnic nerve to reach other ganglia. Some preganglionic fibers in the splanchnic nerve directly innervate the adrenal medulla, without the intervention of postganglionic neurons.

Postganglionic fibers, originating in ganglia of the sympathetic trunk, pass through the *gray rami communicantes* to enter their corresponding spinal nerves. Running in these nerves, they reach the skin and subcutaneous tissue, and these innervate blood vessels, sweat glands, and smooth muscle of hair follicles. Some postganglionic fibers arising in the cervical and thoracic ganglia are distributed to structures in the thoracic cavity and the head.

Postganglionic neurons located in other sympathetic ganglia send fibers to various organs, as shown in Figures 2–13, 2–14, and 2–15.

Parasympathetic Outflow

The parasympathetic outflow may be divided into two portions: the cranial and the sacral. The preganglionic neurons of the cranial division are located in the nuclei of cranial nerves III, VII, IX, and X in the brain stem. Fibers arising therefrom proceed in these nerves and synapse with postganglionic neurons located close to or actually in visceral effectors in the thorax, abdomen, and head. The preganglionic neurons of the sacral division are located in the second, third, and fourth spinal segments. Their fibers leave the nervous system via the appropriate ventral roots and run in the pelvic nerves to synapse with postganglionic neurons located in ganglia close to or actually in the autonomic effector organs which they innervate. These include the bladder, colon, rectum, and blood supply to the genitalia. In contrast with the sympathetic system, interconnections between ganglia in the parasynpathetic system are very few, so that parasympathetic outflow is more discrete (Fig. 2–15). Parasympathetic postganglionic neurons also use acetylcholine as transmitters.

Directions in the Brain

Anatomists have developed a terminology to enable them to refer to directions in the brain. We shall first describe this terminology as it is applied to infrahuman forms. Structures toward the front of the head are called anterior; those toward the tail, posterior or caudal. Those toward the top of the head are called dorsal or superior; those toward the base, ventral or inferior. This is because in most animals dorsal (literally, belonging to the back) structures are in fact higher or superior to ventral (literally, belonging to the belly). In the human case, the nomenclature is often kept, as if man had not adopted upright posture and consequently bent the top of his nervous system 90 degrees. Structures at the base of the human brain are often called ventral (even though in terms of direction, with regard to the rest of the body, they should be called caudal).

Further, as the central nervous system is symmetrical about a midline or a plane, structures closer to the plane about which symmetry occurs are called medial, and those away from such a plane, lateral. The plane about which the nervous system is symmetrical is called the median plane. Any plane parallel to the median plane is a sagittal (Latin *sagitta,* arrow) plane. A coronal or frontal plane divides the brain in such a way that all points on one side of it are anterior to those on the other. A horizontal plane divides the brain so that all points on one side of it are superior to the points on the other side of such a plane. Such planes have to be specified, especially in the case of sections or cuts through the nervous system.

CENTRAL NERVOUS SYSTEM

At one stage of embryonic development a neural tube is formed, and it is from this that the mature nervous system is derived. The brain is formed from one part of the tube and the spinal cord from the rest. Together they form the central nervous system (Fig. 2–16).

Three enlargements develop in the portion of the tube which constitutes the brain. These are (*a*) the forebrain or prosencephalon, (*b*) the midbrain or mesencephalon, and (*c*) the hindbrain or rhombencephalon. Later the forebrain itself subdivides into two enlargements: (*i*) the endbrain or telencephalon and (*ii*) the interbrain or diencephalon. In Figure 2–9 (p. 40) these divisions are indicated on the brain of a primitive vertebrate.

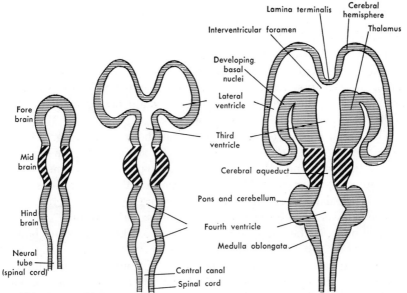

FIG. 2–16. Diagram of three- and five-vesicle stage in the development of the brain, with early development of the cerebral hemispheres. (From Gardner, E. Q., *Fundamentals of Neurology*, 4th ed.; Philadelphia: W. B. Saunders Company, 1963.)

With further development, the cerebral cortex, the corpora striata, and the rhinencephalon are derived from the telencephalon. From the diencephalon are derived the thalamus, epithalamus, and hypothalamus. The corpora quadrigemina and crura cerebri develop from the mesencephalon, and the cerebellum, pons, and medulla are finally derived from the rhombencephalon.

Brain Ventricles. The brain ventricles are derived from the cavity of the embryonic neural tube. They are filled with cerebrospinal fluid, which also circulates around the subarachnoid space surrounding the brain.

Running through the caudal portion of the medulla is a prolongation of the central canal of the spinal cord. This ultimately broadens into the diamond-shape *fourth ventricle,* and this is continuous with the relatively small *cerebral aqueduct,* which runs through the mesencephalon. The cerebral aqueduct opens into the *third ventricle,* a narrow cleft which runs through the diencephalon. This communicates through the interventricular foramina with the *lateral ventricles* of the cerebral hemispheres. The walls and roof of the fourth ventricle contain the lateral and median apertures, through which cerebrospinal fluid circulates to the subarachnoid space (Fig. 2–7, p. 38).

Spinal Cord

The spinal cord is most relevant to the subject matter on motor function and somesthetic mechanisms, for through it run pathways which produce movement in most of the body, and also pathways which convey sensory information from most of the body. Further, in the spinal cord itself, some of the information about the state of the body is applied to the pathways producing movement.

The spinal cord is deemed to begin at the foramen magnum (Latin *large opening*) at the base of the skull. It passes through a segmented hollow tube of bone called the vertebral column. The segments of this tube are called vertebrae. These vertebrae are divided into four groups: seven cervical (neck) vertebrae, twelve thoracic (chest) vertebrae, five lumbar (lower back) vertebrae, and the sacral vertebrae, fused into a single bone, at the end of the spinal column. The spinal cord, however, only extends just beyond the first lumbar vertebra (see Fig. 2–11), though separate nerve trunks and roots of spinal nerves continue to run through the vertebral column. This collection of nerves at the bottom of the spinal column is called cauda equina (Latin *horse's tail*) from its appearance. There are openings between the vertebrae from which pass the spinal nerves.

The spinal cord retains much the same arrangement throughout its

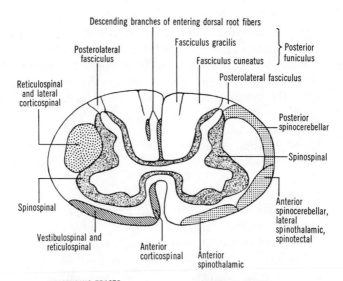

DESCENDING TRACTS   ASCENDING TRACTS

FIG. 2–17. Main tracts of the spinal cord. Only afferent ascending tracts are shown on the right; only efferent descending tracts are shown on the left. (From Gardner, E. Q., *Fundamentals of Neurology*, 4th ed.; Philadelphia: W. B. Saunders Company, 1963.)

length. It consists of two portions: the butterfly-shape gray matter, containing mostly cell bodies, surrounded by the second component, the white matter, made up of nerve fibers. Out of the gray matter emerge, on one side, the ventral roots and on the other side the dorsal roots. The tracts composing the white matter are illustrated in Figure 2–17. Their functional significance is dealt with in the chapters on somesthesis and motor function. There are local enlargements in the amount of gray and white matter in the spinal cord, where the nerve supply to the limbs leaves the cord, namely, in the cervical and lumbosacral regions. This leads to a local enlargement of the diameter of the whole cord.

The Brain

Hindbrain. The hindbrain consists of the medulla oblongata, pons, and cerebellum.

Medulla. As the cranial cavity is entered through the foramen magnum, we reach the region known as the medulla. Here there is a gradual rearrangement of the structures seen in the spinal cord, together with an addition of other structures, such as some of the nuclei of the cranial nerves (Fig. 2–18).

The cells of origin of the sensory components of cranial nerves lie outside the main neural column; this arrangement is similar to that found in the spinal dorsal roots and their ganglia. The ganglia found at the bulbar (adjectival form of the medulla) level belong to the trigeminal, facial, glossopharyngeal, vagus, cochlear, and vestibular nerves. On the sensory side, the fibers from the cells in these external ganglia of origin pass out to the periphery and also into the medulla, where they form synaptic connections with the cell bodies of sensory fibers of the second order. These aggregations of cell bodies and their afferent connections form various sensory nuclei within the medulla. From these second-order sensory neurons, connection is made to motor neurons (forming motor nuclei), which then pass out of the central nervous system to form the efferent components of the cranial nerves. Connections are also made by the second-order sensory neurons to centers higher in the nervous system. The spatial arrangement of these tracts and nuclei of these cranial nerves is illustrated in Figures 2–9 and 2–10.

An important change which takes place in the medulla, as mentioned above, lies in the gradual rearrangement of the components of the spinal cord as it passes upward. This is due mainly to two developments. First, the fibers in the ventral corticospinal tract and the lateral corticospinal tract come together to form one large corticospinal tract, called the pyramids (Fig. 2–18), which occupies the ventral and medial portion of the medulla. To do this, the lateral corticospinal tracts cross

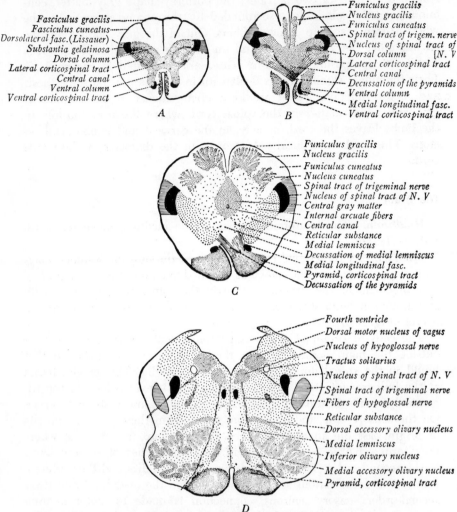

Fasciculus gracilis
Fasciculus cuneatus
Dorsolateral fasc.(Lissauer)
Substantia gelatinosa
Dorsal column
Lateral corticospinal tract
Central canal
Ventral column
Ventral corticospinal tract

A

Funiculus gracilis
Nucleus gracilis
Funiculus cuneatus
Spinal tract of trigem. nerve
Nucleus of spinal tract of
Dorsal column   [*N. V*
Lateral corticospinal tract
Central canal
Decussation of the pyramids
Ventral column
Medial longitudinal fasc.
Ventral corticospinal tract

B

Funiculus gracilis
Nucleus gracilis
Funiculus cuneatus
Nucleus cuneatus
Spinal tract of trigeminal nerve
Nucleus of spinal tract of N. V
Central gray matter
Internal arcuate fibers
Central canal
Reticular substance
Medial lemniscus
Decussation of medial lemniscus
Medial longitudinal fasc.
Pyramid, corticospinal tract
Decussation of the pyramids

C

Fourth ventricle
Dorsal motor nucleus of vagus
Nucleus of hypoglossal nerve
Tractus solitarius
Nucleus of spinal tract of N. V
Spinal tract of trigeminal nerve
Fibers of hypoglossal nerve
Reticular substance
Dorsal accessory olivary nucleus
Medial lemniscus
Inferior olivary nucleus
Medial accessory olivary nucleus
Pyramid, corticospinal tract

D

FIG. 2–18. Diagrammatic cross sections to show the relation of the structures in the medulla oblongata to those in the spinal cord: *A,* first cervical segment of spinal cord; *B,* medulla oblongata, level of decussation of pyramids; *C,* medulla oblongata, level for decussation of medial lemniscus; *D,* medulla oblongata, level of olive. (From Ranson, S. W., and Clark, S. L., *The Anatomy of the Nervous System;* Philadelphia: W. B. Saunders Company, 1959.)

from one side of the medulla, across the midline, to the other. This crossing is known as the decussation of the pyramids. In crossing over, the fibers also swing toward the ventral portion of the medulla (Fig. 2–19). The second change which modifies the appearance of the medulla as it passes upward is the termination of the fibers of the gracile and

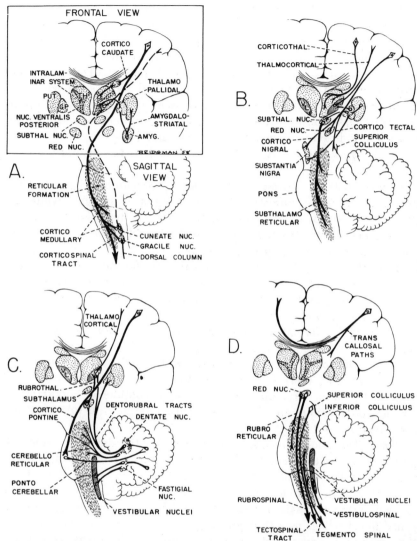

FIG. 2–19. A scheme of major corticosubcortical interrelations. In each figure the cerebral hemisphere has been drawn in coronal section and the brain stem in sagittal view. *A:* arrangement of the primary sensory pathway (dashed) and the corticospinal, corticomedullary, corticostriated, and amygdalostriated pathways. *B:* major corticothalamic, corticorubral, corticonigral, and rubroreticular connections. *C:* corticopontocerebellar, cerebelloreticular, cerebellovestibular, and cerebellorubrothalamic paths. *D:* origin of the main subcortical motor influences descending to spinal levels. (From Terzuolo and Adey, 1960, *Handbook of Physiology,* Vol. II; by permission of the American Physiological Society.)

cuneate fasciculi. The fibers of these fasciculi end in the nucleus gracilis and nucleus cuneatus, and synapse there with the cell bodies and dendrites of neurons whose axons pass upward and are known as internal arcuate fibers. These fibers cross the midline to the opposite side in what is known as the decussation of the lemniscus. They then pass upward to the thalamus in a fiber tract called the medial lemniscus. At about the level where the medial lemniscus appears is a set of prominent landmarks known as the olivary nuclei. The inferior olivary nucleus looks like a heavily crumpled gray band and encloses a tract known as the hilus of the olivary nucleus. Close to it is the medial accessory olivary nucleus.

A somewhat less conspicuous though very important occupant of this area is the reticular formation. This is a region of mingled white and gray matter occupying the spaces between the better-defined structures in the pons and the medulla. In it are the lateral reticular nucleus, the reticular nucleus of the pontine tegmentum, the paramedian reticular nucleus, the large-cell or gigantocellular reticular nucleus, the caudal reticular nucleus of the pons, and the oral reticular nucleus of the pons which extends up to the midbrain. Less conspicuous are the small-cell reticular nucleus and the ventral reticular nucleus.

The reticular formation sends fibers to the anterior portions of the spinal cord, and to many parts of the brain. There are also systems of fibers connecting the various parts of the reticular formation. On the afferent side, there is input from the main sensory pathways and from many brain structures. This region is considered important for a variety of functions, and there is particular interest in its role in arousal and attention.

Pons. The pons is composed of two parts: the dorsal or tegmental part and the ventral or basilar portion. The dorsal part is a direct continuation of the medulla. The ventral part is composed of three types of structure. The first consists of longitudinal fibers, that is, fibers passing parallel to the main axis of the nervous system. Some of these are corticospinal fibers which pass through the pons (and in the medulla become the pyramids), and yet others, called corticopontile fibers, end in the pons. The corticopontile fibers and collaterals from the corticospinal fibers make synaptic connections with the second set of structures in the pons, the nuclei pontis. These nuclei of gray matter, in turn, contain cell bodies whose fibers form the third structure in the ventral pons. These fibers run at right angles to the main axis of the nervous system, and the majority cross the midline to collect at the level of the pons in the large middle cerebellar peduncle which curves upward to enter the cerebellum, in company with the ventral spinocerebellar tract (Fig. 2–19).

Two other peduncles connect the cerebellum to the rest of the nervous system: the inferior cerebellar peduncle and the superior cerebellar peduncle. The first consists of ascending fibers of the dorsal spinocerebellar tract, the olivocerebellar tract from the inferior olivary nuclei, and dorsal and ventral external arcuate fibers arising from cuneate, arcuate, and lateral reticular nuclei. The second, or superior cerebellar peduncle, consists of efferent fibers to the red nucleus and the thalamus (Fig. 2–19).

The dorsal or tegmental part of the pons contains the dorsal and ventral cochlear nuclei. In these end the fibers of the cochlear nerve. Most of the fibers from the cochlear nuclei cross the reticular formation to and in the superior olivary complex, which may be divided into five main nuclear masses (see chapter on hearing). Some fibers arising in the cochlear nuclei end in the reticular formation, others travel to the ipsilateral superior olivary complex, and others join the tract of the lateral lemniscus. The tract of the lateral lemniscus arises mainly in the superior olivary complex. Also, efferent fibers from this complex run to back the ipsilateral and contralateral cochleae.

In this portion of the pons are also found the nuclei of the vestibular nerve, at the floor of the fourth ventricle. These nuclei contribute a large proportion of the fibers in the medial longitudinal fasciculus, which is especially concerned with the reflex control of the head and eyes. The pons also contains the motor nucleus of the facial nerve, the nucleus of the abducens nerve, and the nuclei of the trigeminal nerve. The medial lemniscus (carrying somatosensory fibers to the thalamus) also runs through the pons.

Cerebellum. The cerebellum, an entirely separate structure, will be described in the chapter on motor function. It is connected to the pons only by the structures described above.

Midbrain. The ventral portion of the midbrain is similar in certain features to the pons (Fig. 2–20). At the base are the cerebral peduncles. The outermost layers of these are occupied by a large plate of efferent fibers called the basis or pes pedunculi, which continue into the pons. Above this we observe a new feature, the substantia nigra, which divides the region of the efferent tracts from the rest of the mesencephalon. It consists largely of cells whose axons are sent into the structure just dorsal to it, the mesencephalic tegmentum. This is continuous with the reticular formation of the pons, being similar in structure. As in the case of the reticular formation of the pons and medulla, the midbrain has many nuclei and fiber tracts embedded in it. Among the nuclei are the ventral and dorsal tegmental nuclei. These receive fibers from the mammillary body (see below) via the mammillo-tegmental tract.

The most conspicuous fiber tract coursing through the tegmentum is the superior cerebellar peduncle. This decussates within the tegmentum, and soon after crossing the midline it reaches the red nucleus

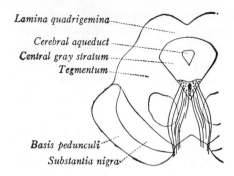

Lamina quadrigemina

Cerebral aqueduct

Central gray stratum

Tegmentum

Basis pedunculi

Substantia nigra

FIG. 2–20. Schematic cross section of the human mesencephalon. (From Ranson, S. W., and Clark, S. L., *The Anatomy of the Nervous System;* Philadelphia: W. B. Saunders Company, 1959.)

(nucleus ruber) and mostly ends within it. (However, some fibers from the superior cerebellar peduncle reach the ventral part of the thalamus.) Fibers from the red nucleus pass down to the medulla and to the spinal column to form the rubrospinal tract, and some pass back to the cerebellum and reticular formation. The fibers descending from the red nuclei to the bulbar and spinal levels cross the midline to form the ventral tegmental decussation, otherwise known as the decussation of Forel.

Moving upward and toward the midline, we come to the central gray stratum, surrounding the cerebral aqueduct. The central gray stratum contains the nuclei of the oculomotor and trochlear nerves and the mesencephalic root of the trigeminal nerve. Going still further up (dorsal), we come to the roof of the midbrain or the mesencephalic tectum. Here lie the corpora quadrigemina. These are two pairs of bodies: the superior colliculi and the inferior colliculi. Most of the fibers of the lateral lemniscus run to the inferior colliculus fibers, which form a part of the brachium of the inferior colliculus, running to the medial geniculate body. The majority of the afferent fibers to the superior colliculi come from the optic tract. Fibers arising from the superior colliculi sweep around the central gray stratum to form the dorsal tegmental decussation of Meynert, and then pass downward as the tectobulbar and tectospinal tracts.

Forebrain—the Diencephalon. The diencephalon connects the cerebral hemispheres with the mesencephalon. The thalamus, epithalamus, subthalamus, and hypothalamus are classified together as parts of the diencephalon. (The retinae and the optic nerves are embryologically part of this portion of the central nervous tissue.)

Subthalamus. The subthalamus forms a zone of connection between the dorsal thalamus and the mesencephalic tegmentum. Certain structures of the mesencephalon continue into it. These are the red nucleus, substantia nigra, and the reticular formation of the mesencephalon. (This last is called the zona incerta in the Mesencephalon.) Lateral to the subthalamus lies the internal capsule as it reforms into the basis pedunculi. The internal capsule consists partly of a sheet of fibers (enveloping much of the thalamus) which stream downward from the motor cortex on their way to the pons and the spinal cord and partly of fibers running from various portions of the thalamus to the cortex. Medial and rostral to the subthalamus is the hypothalamus. The subthalamus includes the subthalamic nucleus (or corpus luysii), whose connections are more elaborately described in the chapter on motor function. Some connecting bundles may be seen in the fields on Forel (divided into three parts H, H_1, and H_2). These are the fasciculus lenticularis, from the internal division of the globus pallidus, and the ansa lenticularis, also from the globus pallidus. These bundles are joined by others and collect together to form the thalamic fasciculus, which then runs to the anterior ventral nucleus of the thalamus.

Hypothalamus. The hypothalamus is one of the most essential structures in the brain. It plays a very important role in the regulation of many functions, including body temperature, water balance, hormone level, sleep and wakefulness, cardiovascular adjustments, eating and drinking, sexual activity, and emotion. Detailed descriptions of its role in several of these functions are given elsewhere in the book.

The hypothalamus lies on the ventral surface of the brain close to the third ventricle and ventral to the thalamus and subthalamus. Its anterior border is rostral to the optic chiasm, and its posterior border is caudal to the mammillary bodies, which appear on the surface of the brain as two rounded bodies (Latin *mammillaris*, breast). Anterior to this lies the tuber cinereum, which, as its Latin name betokens, is an ashen or gray excrescence, to which is attached the infundibulum (Latin *funnel*, so named for its shape). This forms the connection between the hypothalamus and the hypophysis (Fig. 2–21), whose functions are discussed in the section of the endocrine system.

Various cell groupings can be discerned in the hypothalamus. In the anterior (or supraoptic) region are the preoptic, supraoptic, and paraventricular nuclei. In the middle or tuberal region are the dorsomedial and ventromedial hypothalamic nuclei. In the posterior or mammillary region are the medial and lateral mammillary nuclei and the nucleus intercalatus.

The hypothalamus is also composed of large fiber tracts. Some of the most important afferent tracts are the medial forebrain bundle, which runs in a rostro-caudal direction; the fornix, connecting the hippocampus with the mammillary nuclei; the stria terminalis, connecting the amygdaloid nuclei with the anterior region of the hypothalamus; and the mammillary peduncle, through which fibers arising from spinal and tegmental structures reach the lateral mammillary nucleus.

On the efferent side, the supraopticohypophyseal tract arises from the supraoptic nucleus and courses through the infundibulum into the neural lobe of the hypophysis. Fibers from the tuber cinereum and

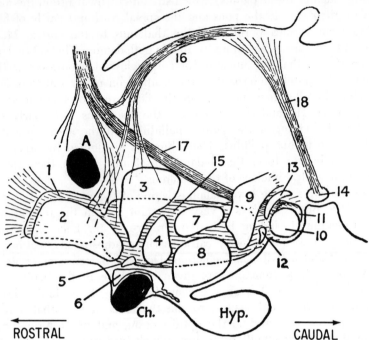

ROSTRAL   CAUDAL

FIG. 2–21. Diagram showing relative positions in sagittal plane of hypothalamic nuclei in typical mammalian brain, and their relation to fornix, stria habenularis, and fasciculus retroflexus. *A,* anterior commissure; *Ch,* optic chiasma; *Hyp,* hypophysis; *1,* lateral preoptic nucleus (permeated by the medial forebrain bundle); *2,* medial preoptic nucleus; *3,* paraventricular nucleus; *4,* anterior hypothalamic area; *5,* suprachiasmatic nucleus; *6,* supraoptic nucleus; *7,* dorsomedial hypothalamic nucleus; *8,* ventromedial hypothalamic nucleus; *9,* posterior hypothalamic nucleus; *10,* medial mammillary nucleus; *11,* lateral mammillary nucleus; *12,* premammillary nucleus; *13,* supramammilllary nucleus; *14,* interpeduncular nucleus (a mesencephalic element in which the fasciculus retroflexus terminates); *17,* fornix; *18,* fasciculus retroflexus of Meynert (habenulopeduncular tract). (From Le Gros Clark et al., *The Hypothalamus;* London: Oliver and Boyd, 1938.)

the paraventricular nucleus also end there. It is to be stressed that innervation from the hypothalamus reaches only one division of the hypophysis, namely, the neurohypophysis (sometimes referred to as the posterior hypophysis). This produces oxytocin and a vasopressor antidiuretic agent. The adenohypophysis (or anterior pituitary) is devoid of innervation by the hypothalamus, being instead controlled by secretions from the hypothalamus (as described in the section on the endocrines). There are three other major efferent tracts: the mammillothalamic tract of Vicq d'Azyr, which joins the medial mammillary nucleus to the anterior thalamic nuclei; the mammillotegmental tract, which connects the medial mammillary nucleus to the mesencephalon; and the dorsal longitudinal fasciculus, which interconnects a large number of structures in the thalamic and hypothalamic nuclei, mesencephalon, pons, and medulla.

Thalamus. The thalamus lies under the lateral ventricle and on the side of the third ventricle. It is divided by the internal medullary lamina (a vertical sheath of white matter) into lateral and medial masses. Anteriorly, this internal lamina divides to enclose the anterior nuclei (a third group) of the thalamus (Fig. 2–22).

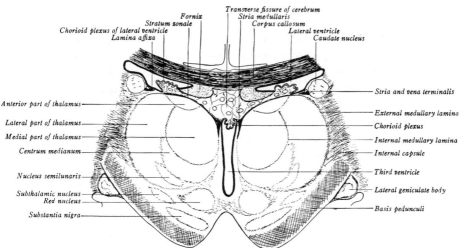

FIG. 2–22. Diagram of the frontal section through the thalamus and surrounding structures. (From Ranson, S. W., and Clark, S. L., *The Anatomy of the Nervous System;* Philadelphia: W. B. Saunders Company, 1959.)

The thalamic nuclei have been divided into five categories on morphological grounds. The anterior nuclei connect the mammillothalamic tract with the gyrus cinguli. The nuclei of the midline, lying along the edge of the third ventricle, are connected with the hypothalamus. The medial nuclei include the medialis dorsalis, which projects to the hypothalamus and prefrontal lobe, centrum medianum (center median of Luys), and the intralaminar nuclei. The center median and the intralaminar nuclei have no direct connections with the cortex.

The lateral nuclear mass contains the nucleus ventralis anterior, which is connected with the basal ganglia, the nucleus ventralis lateralis (which connects the superior cerebellar peduncle to the motor areas of the cortex), and the nuclei lateralis dorsalis and lateralis posterior, which receive fibers from other thalamic nuclei and are connected with the parietal lobe and the tip of the temporal lobe of the cortex. They are continuous with the pulvinar, which is part of the posterior thalamic nuclear complex. The nucleus ventralis posterior, also part of the lateral nuclear mass, is a relay station for the somesthetic pathways and taste. Its subdivisions and connections are described in the chapter on central somesthetic mechanisms.

The posterior nuclear group includes the pulvinar, the medial geniculate body, and the lateral geniculate body. The pulvinar is connected with other thalamic nuclei and has connections with the cortex in the posterior parietal and temporal lobes. The connections of the medial geniculate are described in the chapter on hearing and those of the lateral geniculate in the chapter on vision. It seems a common principle that connections between thalamic nuclei and the cortex run both ways.

There is evidence that several of the thalamic nuclei which do not have specific cortical connections are involved in the regulation of arousal and sleep. They have been termed the "thalamic reticular system," and a description of this system is given in the chapter on arousal and attention.

Another way to classify the various nuclei of the thalamus is in terms of their input and output connections. In these terms, they may be divided into sensory relay nuclei, association nuclei, and intrinsic nuclei. Sensory relay nuclei receive input from more peripheral sensory systems and send output to sensory regions of the cortex (lateral geniculate, medial geniculate, ventralis posterior nuclei). The association nuclei are also connected with the cerebral cortex but receive no direct input from sensory systems (medialis dorsalis, lateralis posterior nuclei, and pulvinar). The intrinsic nuclei do not project to the cerebral cortex, and they have connections with other thalamic nuclei (center median and intralaminar nuclei).

Epithalamus. The epithalamus is an area dorsal and rostral to the superior colliculi in the mesencephalon. It includes the pineal body (not composed of neural elements), the habenular nucleus, stria medullaris, and the posterior commissure. Some of the fibers of the posterior commissure connect the two superior colliculi. The stria medullaris ends in the habenular nucleus. It arises in the medial olfactory area, subcallosal gyrus, preoptic area, and amygdaloid nuclei. The habenular nucleus is connected with the interpeduncular ganglion in the mesencephalon via the fasciculus retroflexus of Meynert.

Forebrain—the Telencephalon. Basal Ganglia. The cerebral hemispheres consist mainly of a surface layer of gray matter together with a massive substructure of white matter or fibers. However, there are various masses of gray matter within the hemisphere. These are the caudate and putamen (collectively known as the striatum), globus pallidus, the amygdaloid nuclei, and the claustrum (Fig. 2–23).

The caudate nucleus (nucleus caudatus), as its name implies (Latin *caudatus,* tailed), has a long tail. The head of the caudate bulges into the anterior horn of the lateral ventricle. The tail is U-shaped and curves

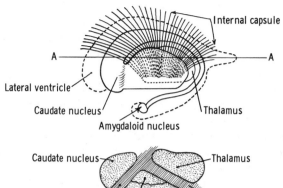

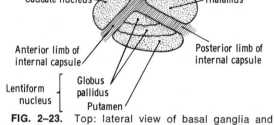

FIG. 2-23. Top: lateral view of basal ganglia and adjacent structures. Bottom: horizontal cross section at level *AA'* of top diagram. (From Chusid, J. G., and McDonald, J. J., *Correlative Neuroanatomy*, 12th ed.; Lange Medical Publications, 1964.)

caudal and ventral, and then rostral again, on the inferior ventricular horn to end as far rostral as the amygdaloid nucleus. The caudate is partly separated from the putamen by the internal capsule, though the two have the same histological structure. The putamen is separated from the globus pallidus (sometimes known as the pallidum) by the internal medullary lamina. (There is a terminological difficulty about these three structures. Together they are known as the corpus striatum. However, the caudate and putamen are together called the striatum. The globus pallidum and the putamen are together known as the lentiform or lenticular nucleus, because together they are shaped like a lentil [Latin *lens*, lentil].)

Fibers from the striatum pass to the pallidum and thence to the anterior part of the ventral thalamic nucleus, as described above.

The claustrum is a thin plate of cell bodies separated by the external capsule (a band of fibers) from the putamen, which lies medially and laterally by another band of fibers from the insula (a part of the cortex).

The amygdaloid body (Greek *amygdaloeides*, almond-like) is located in the roof of the inferior ventricular horn and is continuous with the cortex of the temporal lobe. It is divided into two main parts: the cortico-medial and the basolateral, which are further subdivided. The main efferent path of the amygdaloid body is the stria terminalis. This runs to the hypothalamus and preoptic regions. As is described in detail in the chapter on smell, the amygdaloid body also receives input from the olfactory system. This is why it is often classed as a part of the rhinencephalon, the name for those parts of the telencephalon credited at one time with olfactory function. These parts evolved earlier than the other parts of the telencephalon. The amygdaloid body is also considered to be important in a variety of functions, including emotion and the regulation of eating, drinking and sexual behavior.

Rhinencephalon. The literal meaning of rhinencephalon is "nosebrain," from the Greek *rhis, rhinos,* nose, and *enkephalos,* brain. The main structures comprising the rhinencephalon include the olfactory bulb and the olfactory tract, which divides into the lateral and medial olfactory striae. Further, there is the anterior perforated substance, composed of gray matter extending between the olfactory striae and the optic tract, and also the pyriform area, which includes the lateral olfactory gyrus, the uncus, and the anterior portion of the hippocampus (Figs. 2–24, 2–25). The hippocampus (Greek word meaning seahorse) is situated on the floor of the inferior horn of the lateral ventricle. The side which projects into the ventricle is covered by the alveus, a thin coating of fibers, which then continues into the fimbria of the hippocampus, which in turn is continuous with the fornix, the chief efferent

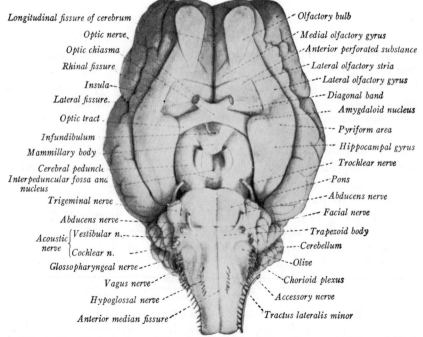

Longitudinal fissure of cerebrum
Optic nerve
Optic chiasma
Rhinal fissure
Insula
Lateral fissure
Optic tract
Infundibulum
Mammillary body
Cerebral peduncle
Interpeduncular fossa and nucleus
Trigeminal nerve
Abducens nerve
Acoustic nerve { Vestibular n.
Cochlear n.
Glossopharyngeal nerve
Vagus nerve
Hypoglossal nerve
Anterior median fissure

Olfactory bulb
Medial olfactory gyrus
Anterior perforated substance
Lateral olfactory stria
Lateral olfactory gyrus
Diagonal band
Amygdaloid nucleus
Pyriform area
Hippocampal gyrus
Trochlear nerve
Pons
Abducens nerve
Facial nerve
Trapezoid body
Cerebellum
Olive
Chorioid plexus
Accessory nerve
Tractus lateralis minor

FIG. 2–24. Ventral view of the sheep's brain. (From Ranson, S. W., and Clark, S. L., *The Anatomy of the Nervous System.* Philadelphia: W. B. Saunders Company, 1959.)

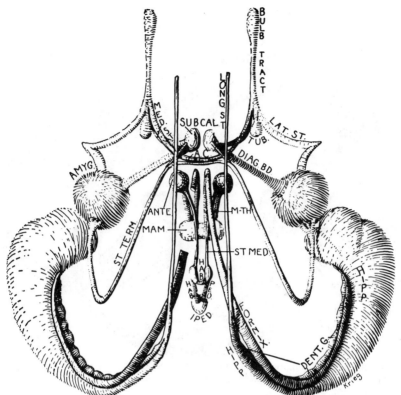

FIG. 2–25. Reconstruction of human rhinencephalon as seen from above. *Amyg.,* amygdala; *ante. comm., a.c.,* anterior commissure; *ante.,* anterior nucleus of thalamus; *bulb,* olfactory bulb; *comm. hipp.,* hippocampal commissure; *dent. g.,* dentate gyrus; *diag. bd.,* diagonal band; *hab.,* habenula; *hap-ped.,* habenulopeduncular tract; *hipp.,* hippocampus; *iped.,* interpeduncular nucleus; *lat. st.,* lateral olfactory stria; *long. st.,* longitudinal stria; *mam.,* mamillary body; *med. st.,* medial olfactory stria; *m.f.b.,* medial forebrain bundle; *m-th.,* mammillothalamic tract; *st. med.,* stria medullaris; *st. term.,* stria terminalis; *subcal.,* subcallosal gyrus; *tract.,* olfactory tract; *tub.,* olfactory tubercle. (From Krieg, W. J. S., *Functional Neuroanatomy,* 1966; Brain Books, Evanston, Ill.)

tract of the hippocampus (Figs. 2–24, 2–25, 2–26). The hippocampal commissure is a band of fibers connecting the two fornices close to the crus of the fornix (Latin *crus,* leg), a portion of the fornix. The anterior commissure joins the olfactory bulbs and the pyriform areas of the two cerebral hemispheres. A further structure, the analogue of which is proportionately much larger in rats than in man, in the septum. This is a thin-wall structure separating the lateral ventricles, placed between the fornix and the corpus callosum.

Some of the structures of the rhinencephalon form part of the central olfactory pathways (see chapter on taste and smell). Many rhinen-

COLUMNS
OF FORNIX

BODY OF
FORNIX

HIPPOCAMPAL
COMMISSURE

CRURA OF
FORNIX

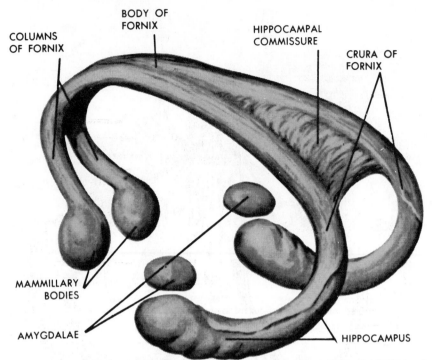

MAMMILLARY
BODIES

AMYGDALAE

HIPPOCAMPUS

FIG. 2–26. The hippocampus and associated structures (crura is the plural of crus). (From *The CIBA Collection of Medical Illustrations* by Frank H. Netter, M.D. Copyright CIBA.)

cephalic structures are considered to be important in the regulation of emotion. The hippocampus is thought to be intrinsically involved in memory functions.

Cerebral Hemispheres. The exterior of the cerebral hemispheres is covered by a thin mantle of gray matter called the cortex. This is composed of layers of cells between which may be seen layers of white matter. In most of the cortex, six layers may be seen. There have been various attempts at subdivision of the cortex on various classificatory schemes, such as Brodmann's (Fig. 2–27). His divisions of the cortex are the most commonly used and may be regarded as convenient. As the surface of the cortex has increased in area as one ascends the phylogenetic scale, it has become more and more folded or convoluted. In the rat, the surface of the hemispheres is smooth. In man, extensive folding has taken place, presumably to accommodate a larger cortical surface area without a corresponding increase in cranial size. The grooves which have arisen as a result of this folding are called fissures and sulci (Latin *sulcus*, furrow). The areas between the sulci are called

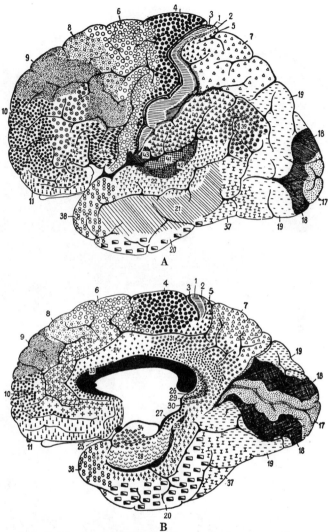

FIG. 2–27. Areas of the human cerebral cortex which possess a distinctive structure (according to Brodmann). *A,* lateral view; *B,* medial view. (From Ranson, S. W., and Clark, S. L., *The Anatomy of the Nervous System;* Philadelphia: W. B. Saunders Company, 1959.)

gyri or convolutions (Greek *guros,* round). These form landmarks on the surface of the brain, and have been labeled as indicated in Figures 2–28 and 2–29. However, there is some variation in folding from one individual to another. That is why functional localization prior to surgery is often necessary.

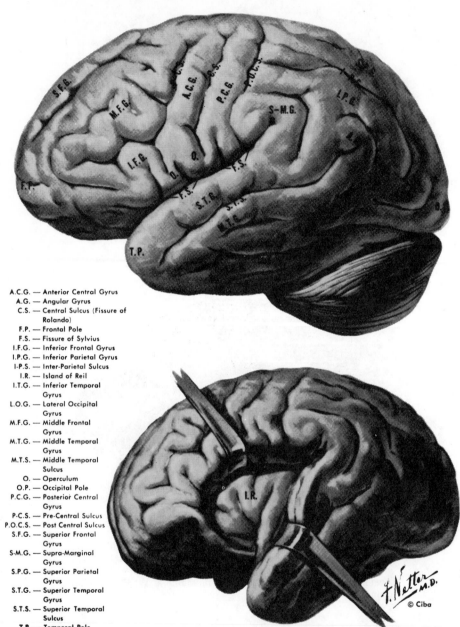

A.C.G. — Anterior Central Gyrus
A.G. — Angular Gyrus
C.S. — Central Sulcus (Fissure of
        Rolando)
F.P. — Frontal Pole
F.S. — Fissure of Sylvius
I.F.G. — Inferior Frontal Gyrus
I.P.G. — Inferior Parietal Gyrus
I-P.S. — Inter-Parietal Sulcus
I.R. — Island of Reil
I.T.G. — Inferior Temporal
        Gyrus
L.O.G. — Lateral Occipital
        Gyrus
M.F.G. — Middle Frontal
        Gyrus
M.T.G. — Middle Temporal
        Gyrus
M.T.S. — Middle Temporal
        Sulcus
O. — Operculum
O.P. — Occipital Pole
P.C.G. — Posterior Central
        Gyrus
P-C.S. — Pre-Central Sulcus
P.O.C.S. — Post Central Sulcus
S.F.G. — Superior Frontal
        Gyrus
S-M.G. — Supra-Marginal
        Gyrus
S.P.G. — Superior Parietal
        Gyrus
S.T.G. — Superior Temporal
        Gyrus
S.T.S. — Superior Temporal
        Sulcus
T.P. — Temporal Pole

FIG. 2–28. Lateral aspect of human cerebral hemispheres. The insula (or island of Reil) is shown by parting the lips of the lateral cerebral fissure. (From *The CIBA Collection of Medical Illustrations* by Frank H. Netter, M.D. Copyright CIBA.)

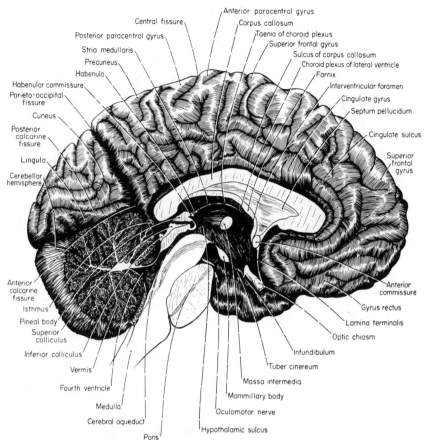

FIG. 2–29. The medial surface of the human brain. (Reprinted with permission of the Macmillan Company from *Correlative Anatomy of the Nervous System* by Crosby, Humphrey, and Lauer. Copyright 1962 by the Macmillan Company.)

The two hemispheres are separated by the longitudinal cerebral fissure. Each hemisphere may be divided into the frontal, parietal, occipital, and temporal lobes and the insula (Fig. 2–30). The insula lies within the lateral cerebral fissure and so cannot be seen from the surface except by parting the lips of this fissure (Fig. 2–28). The rhinencephalon has already been described (see Figs. 2–24, 2–25, 2–26).

Going hand in hand with an expansion of the area of the cortex or gray matter on the surface of the cerebral hemispheres, as we ascend the phylogenetic scale, is an increase in the mass of interconnecting fiber or white matter inside the cerebral hemispheres, streaming either up to or down from the cortex or interconnecting various portions of the cortex.

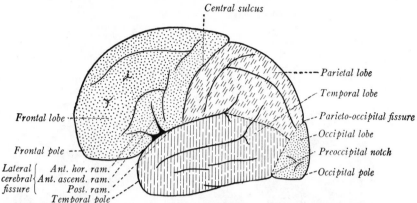

FIG. 2–30. Diagram of the lobes on the lateral aspect of the human cerebral hemisphere. (From Ranson, S. W., and Clark, S. L., *The Anatomy of the Nervous System;* Philadelphia: W. B. Saunders Company, 1959.)

One of the largest fiber tracts leading into and out of the cortex is the internal capsule (Fig. 2–23). The anterior limb of the internal capsule runs between the caudate and lentiform nuclei. In it runs fibers from the lateral nucleus of the thalamus to the frontal lobe. Fibers leaving the frontal lobe run through the anterior limb of the internal capsule to the pons. The posterior limb of the internal capsule, dividing the thalamus from the lentiform nucleus (globus pallidus and putamen), consists of fibers running from the thalamus to the cortex (the thalamic radiation) and various efferent tracts from the cortex (Fig. 2–19). Such efferent tracts comprise the corticobulbar tract (to the motor nuclei of the cranial nerves in the medulla), the corticospinal tract, the corticorubral tract (to the red nucleus), and the temporopontile tract (from the cortex of the temporal lobe to the pons). As the fibers diverge from the internal capsule to join their various connections in the cortex, the distinctive formation to which this gives rise is called the corona radiata.

The commissures joining the rhinencephalon together have already been described. However, the largest commissure in the nervous system is the corpus callosum, which joins together the two cerebral hemispheres. Most of the fibers composing this structure link symmetrical areas of the two hemispheres together.

Not only are there fibers leaving the cortex and arriving at the cortex from other structures, but many join different parts of the cortex together. These are known as association fibers.

chapter 3

Vision

In the study of vision we are concerned with the organism's response to light. Light is a form of electromagnetic radiation which may be viewed as consisting either of waves or of particles. As waves, light may be regarded as having a frequency, and since such waves travel at a certain speed, also a wavelength. When viewed as consisting of particles (quanta or photons), the energies of these particles depend on the wavelength of the light. Normally, light, when it travels, is treated as a continuous set of waves. However, when we deal with the emission or absorption of light, it is useful to consider light in terms of discrete particles.

The stimulation of the eye in vision is an instance of absorption of light. The eye in the dark is so sensitive that a retinal receptor, the rod, is excited by the absorption of one quantum of light, the smallest amount of light possible. However, a single quantum cannot be seen because vision depends on pooled information from a few rods.

The fact that light consists of separate packets of energy, the number of which becomes very small at low intensities, assumes considerable importance when we consider vision in low illumination. First of all, at a given low intensity of illumination the number of quanta reaching the eye fluctuates a great deal because of the random distribution in time of quanta. The absolute threshold of sensitivity of the eye must therefore fluctuate, if only because of the physical nature of the stimulus. Secondly, the spatial distribution of quanta on the receptor mosaic of the eye will also vary considerably during illumination at low intensities. This will lead to an indistinctness of vision, which again has physical as well as physiological or psychological origins.

Light may be regarded as the visible part of the spectrum of electro-magnetic waves which stretch from gamma rays to bands at frequencies used for broadcasting. The visible part of this spectrum ranges from about 380 mμ (millimicrons or millionths of a millimeter) to about 760 mμ. Normal white light, such as daylight, contains a mixture of all such wavelengths. When these wavelengths are seen unmixed (for instance, when they have been passed through a prism), the different wavelengths are seen as colors. The shortest wavelength is seen as violet. With increasing wavelengths, the appearance passes through blue to green, then yellow, orange, and finally to red. However, all wavelengths are not equally visible. Wavelengths taken from the extreme ranges of the spectrum require much higher energies to appear equally bright compared with wavelengths taken from the medium ranges. A similar function

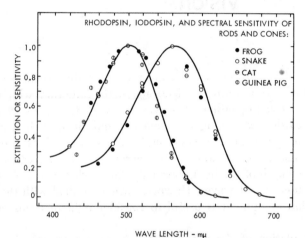

FIG. 3–1. The absorption spectra of chicken rhodopsin and iodopsin, measured by Wald, and photopic sensitivities of various animals as determined electrophysiological measurement, measured by Granit. (From Wald, G., *Handbook of Physiology,* 1960; by permission of the American Physiological Society.)

also holds for threshold intensities. Curves measuring such discrepancies in stimulating efficiency according to wavelength are called spectral sensitivity or luminosity curves (Fig. 3–1).

Besides varying in wavelength, light energy also varies in intensity, or in the amplitude of its wave form. Though this is a clear and unitary concept, a variety of measures and terminologies to define intensity has grown up for various reasons, some practical, others historical. We shall discuss the units most frequently used. The intensity of a source of light is measured by comparing it with the intensity of a standard candle (a standardized candle with a flame one inch high). When light from such a standard candle falls on a surface one foot away and one foot square, the level of illumination is defined as one footcandle. (An alternative system uses meters instead of feet, and according to this system one meter-candle is the level of illumination thrown by a candle on a surface of one square meter one meter away.) The amount of light reflected from an object, as distinct from that which is falling on it, is measured in millilamberts. One millilambert is the amount of light reflected from a perfectly diffusing and reflecting surface one foot square and illuminated by 0.93 footcandle.

THE EYE

The eye is roughly spherical in shape (Fig. 3–2). It admits light through its transparent anterior surface, the cornea. This light then passes to the posterior surface of the eye, having been brought into focus by the optical apparatus. The image-forming mechanism of the eye is not unlike that of a camera. Light rays are refracted or bent

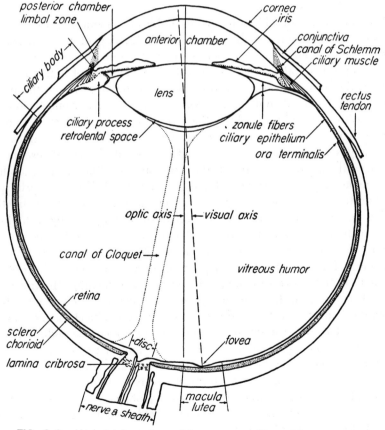

FIG. 3–2. Horizontal section of human eye. (From Walls, G. L., *The Vertebrate Eye;* Bloomfield Hills, Mich.: Cranbrook Institute of Science, 1942.)

upon passing into the eye. As refraction of light takes place when it passes from a medium of one density into that of another, refraction begins to take place as soon as light passes from air into the denser aqueous humor. (This is a fluid filling the anterior chamber of the eye in front of the lens.) More bending then takes place as the light passes into the denser substance of the lens, and again as it passes into the vitreous humor behind the lens. In a simple camera, only the lens is responsible for light refraction.

Differential amounts of focusing (or accommodation) are necessary, depending on the distance of the object being viewed. In the eye, as in the camera, such differential focusing is brought about by changes in the lens. In the camera, the lens is shifted in relation to the surface on which the image is formed. This is also the case in the eyes of some fish. However, in most vertebrate eyes, curvature of the lens is altered to produce the same results. Such alteration is accomplished by means of the ciliary muscles.

Another feature in which the eye resembles a camera is in the possession of an iris, which can be viewed as the analog of the diaphragm in the camera. The iris is a membrane resting on the outside of the lens. It controls pupillary diameter and thus the amount of light admitted through the lens. However, the range of diameter over which the pupil varies its size extends only from about 6.5 to 2.9 mm., while the range of intensities of light to which the eye is exposed is over a million to one. The iris therefore compensates only to a very limited extent for changes in illumination. This contribution of the pupil also helps improve the depth of focus of the lens, and so the focusing ability at extreme ranges of distance of the object viewed. This is a principle familiar to amateur photographers. A demonstration of its use by the ocular apparatus can easily be obtained by asking a subject to look at a small object, which is then brought slowly closer to his eye. It will be seen that as this is done the pupil begins to constrict.

Though for our purpose it is not necessary to review the optical mechanism of the eye in detail, it is important to mention the inversion which takes place in the eye during image formation. The eye resembles a pinhole camera in this respect. Points on the object being viewed are connected by straight lines (light rays) to corresponding points on the image being formed. All these lines must pass through a small aperture or pinhole between the object and the image. As a result, there must occur a left-right, up-down inversion of the image relative to the object being viewed. Consequently, objects which are seen in the upper right quadrant of the visual field actually impinge on the lower left quadrant of the retina.

A perception of light can be evoked in a particular part of the retina by applying pressure on a point close to it on the surface of the eye.

This is called a visual phosphene. The visual sensation is referred to a part of the visual field in accordance with the law of inversion stated above. For instance, deformation of the lower right part of the retina produces a visual sensation which appears to come from the upper left visual quadrant. That such a correlation between retinal locus and resulting appearance is unlearned is shown by the fact that when such phosphenes can be evoked in the congenitally blind they are perceived to proceed from the same place as in normal subjects.

Retina

In the normal human eye the image is formed on the retina. This is a complex structure consisting of receptors and neural layers lining about 180° of the eye on its posterior surface. In the center of the retina lies the macula lutea (yellow spot). Within this central region is a round depression, 1,500 μ in diameter, called the fovea centralis. This is the area which is used for vision of fine detail, and it is made up almost entirely of one class of visual receptor elements, the cones. The depression in the fovea centralis is due to the fact that blood vessels and nerve fibers run over the rest of the retina, whereas they bypass the fovea. Owing to a freak of development, the light-sensitive elements in the retina are actually obscured by blood vessels and the neural connections to the light-sensitive elements. These enter the eye through the optic disc, where consequently there is an interruption in the retina and the so-called blind spot.

The elements which translate energy in the form of light into neural events lie closest to the posterior surface of the eye. There are two main types of such elements: the *rods* and the *cones*. Their differences will be discussed below. These elements contain pigment, the state of which can be altered by light. The rods and cones make synaptic connections with *bipolar cells*. The next synaptic contact in the retina is between the bipolar and *ganglion cells*. Here, in the foveal region, it seems that three bipolar cells converge on two ganglion cells.

The axons of the ganglion cells form the fibers of the optic tract. The rather favorable ratio of receptors to fibers leaving the retina holds only in the fovea and in the case of the cones. Out toward the periphery, and in the case of the rods, convergence is extreme. Though there are about 125 million rods in the eye, only about one million myelinated fibers are to be found in the optic tract (Polyak, 1957). There is, however, a possibility that unmyelinated fibers also form the optic tract, and therefore the ratio of fibers to receptors may be much larger.

The connections described so far allow messages initiated by light to leave the retina. However, there are two other types of connection. The first type enables influences to be carried laterally within the retina itself at two levels. At the end feet of the receptors are *horizontal cells*, and between the bipolar and ganglion cell level are laterally spreading *amacrine cells*. It is thought (Granit, 1962) that these laterally spreading plexiform layers are inhibitory in function. Indeed, they would give an anatomical basis for the phenomena of contrast or lateral inhibition which is a pronounced feature in the visual system (see below).

Figure 3–3 is a detailed picture of the retinal network in primates

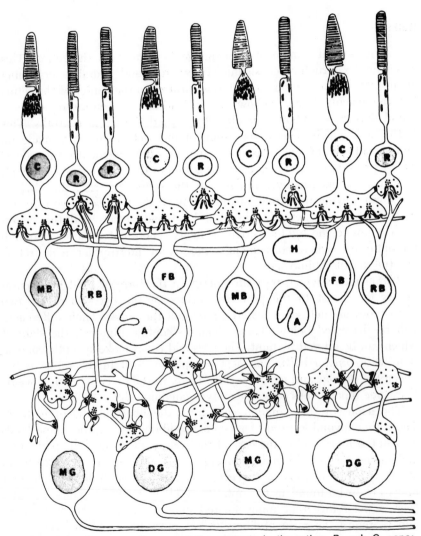

FIG. 3–3. Summary diagram of the contacts in the retina. *R*, rod; *C*, cone; *MB*, midget bipolar; *RB*, rod bipolar; *FB*, flat bipolar; *H*, horizontal cell; *A*, amacrine cell; *MG*, midget ganglion; *DG*, diffuse ganglion. (From Dowling, J. E., and Boycott, B. B., *Proceedings*, B. 166, 1966, by courtesy of the Royal Society.)

as described by Dowling and Boycott (1966). At the top of the figure are the two types of receptors, the rods (*R*) and the cones (*C*), which differ in shape. At the base of the cones, where these connect to other cells, is a flattened portion called a pedicle. In the case of the rod, the analogous part is smaller and rounded; it is called a spherule. The spherules and pedicles also differ in the number of synaptic invaginations (inlets in which synapses are found). In the rod spherules there is generally only one invagination. In the cone pedicle there are several invaginations. In the cone pedicle, only three dendrites run into each invagination. In the rod spherule, four to seven dendrites run into the single invagination it possesses.

It is also to be noted that the cone pedicles are connected with two kinds of bipolars, the midget bipolar (*MB*) and flat bipolar (*FB*), via separate synapses. The midget bipolars in the central retina connect with only one cone, but are connected with that cone through numerous synapses, as can be seen from the figure. The dendrite of the midget bipolar is always the middle of the three dendrites which run into each synaptic invagination. As you will recall, there are several such invaginations on each pedicle. The second type of bipolars, the flat bipolars, connect not to a single cone but to a group of cones, and not through an invagination of the pedicles (Fig. 3–4) and the spherules.

The rods make connections only with one kind of bipolar, the rod bipolar (*RB*). One axon of this type of bipolar makes both axodendritic and axosomatic contacts with the diffuse ganglion cells (*DG*) (An axodendritic contact is a synapse at which the presynaptic junction is on an axon and the postsynaptic junction is on a dendrite. An axosomatic contact is a synapse at which the presynaptic junction is on an axon and the postsynaptic junction is on the soma or cell body itself). Diffuse ganglion cells appear to make contacts with many bipolar cells of all varieties. In contrast, the midget ganglion cell (*MG*) synapses with only one midget bipolar (*MB*), but many times. (Such midget bipolars also are connected to only one cone.)

Yet to be described are the connections of the amacrine cells—cells without axons (Cajal, 1911). Their branches can be regarded both as dendrites and axons. Wherever bipolar cells make an axodendritic contact with a ganglion cell, an amacrine cell branch is brought into connection with the bipolar.

The bipolar transmits via a synapse with a synaptic ribbon to a ganglion cell dendrite and a branch of an amacrine cell (Fig. 3–5). The synaptic ribbon, drawn as a black bar in the figures, is found in the rod spherules, cone pedicles, and bipolar cells pointing directly between the two postsynaptic junctions. The ribbon is surrounded by synaptic vesicles. Its function may be to ensure a proper distribution of vesicles to each postsynaptic site. This arrangement is called a dyad synaptic

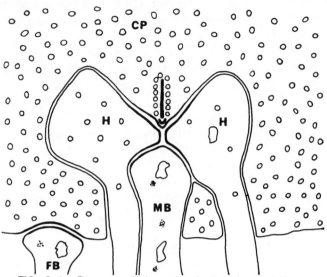

FIG. 3–4. Diagram of the synaptic junctions of the cone pedicles. Under each ribbon in the cone terminal are three processes. The more deeply inserted, usually containing some synaptic vesicles, are the horizontal cell processes (*H*); the central element is a midget bipolar dendrite (*MB*). The bipolar dendrite is separated from the membrane underlying the synaptic ribbon by a space of about 800 to 1,000 Å, which is bounded by the horizontal cell processes. The ribbon synaptic junctions in the rod spherules are similar to this arrangement except that there are usually 2 or more central (bipolar) elements. On the basal surface of the cone pedicles, dendrites from the flat bipolars (*FB*) make superficial contacts. These junctions show little morphological specialization. (From Dowling, J. E., and Boycott, B. B., *Proceedings,* B. 166, 1966, by courtesy of the Royal Society.)

contact. The amacrine cells also make synaptic contacts of the normal, less complex variety with other amacrine cells, ganglion cell dendrites, and cell bodies. Close to the postsynaptic ending on the amacrine cell branch is a presynaptic junction complete with synaptic vesicles, opposite which is a postsynaptic junction on the bipolar cell.

It should be noted that this description of neural connections within the retina is found in primates. This, along with that of cats, is the simplest organization of retinal neural connections so far found. The retinae of frogs and pigeons are the most complex; those of rabbits and pigeons are intermediate. This correlates with the complexity of information processing which occurs at the retinal level in these various forms (Dowling, 1968).

It has been possible to record intracellularly from the various types of cells in the retina of Necturus maculosus (mudpuppy) because of

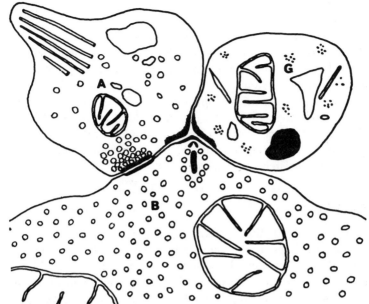

FIG. 3–5. Diagram of the dyad synaptic contacts of the bipolar terminals (*B*) with ganglion cell dendrites (*G*) and amacrine cell processes (*A*). Frequently the amacrine cell process makes a synaptic contact back onto the bipolar terminal, forming a reciprocal contact between bipolar terminal and amacrine process. Membrane thickenings are drawn as seen in glutaraldehyde-preserved material. Cytoplasmic organelles characteristic of each of the three types of processes are diagrammatically represented. (From Dowling, J. E., and Boycott, B. B., *Proceedings, B.* 166, 1966, by courtesy of the Royal Society.)

the large size of these cells in this animal's eye (Werblin and Dowling, 1969). Spikes (action potentials) are generated only by the ganglion cells which transmit visual information from the eye to the brain, a relatively large distance, and amacrine cells. Signals for transmission inside the retina (except for amacrine cells) consist entirely of graded potentials, either of the depolarizing or hyperpolarizing type, and chemical messengers. The electrical potential produced by the breakdown of photopigments by photons is linear with the number of photons absorbed by the photopigments in that part of the visual receptor cell where the photopigment is located. However, by the time this electrical potential reaches the synaptic region of the receptor, it is related to the light input by a function resembling a logarithmic function. Both this electrical potential and that observed in the horizontal cells is a graded hyperpolarization. The bipolar cells is Necturus show hyperpolarization to stimuli in the center of their receptive field and depolarization when stimuli are applied to the outer portions of the receptive field.

In some bipolar cells this relation of hyperpolarization to depolarization is reversed.

The second type of connection which has been postulated, and about which there is some doubt (Granit, 1962), is represented by centrifugal fibers or fibers sending messages into the retina from other parts of the central nervous system.

Light and electron microscopy has revealed evidence for centrifugal fibers in vertebrates only in the eye of birds (Cowan and Powell, 1963; Dowling and Cowan, 1966). However, similar evidence is lacking for centrifugal fibers in the primate. There is therefore intense skepticism regarding their existence (Dowling and Boycott, 1966).

Rods and Cones

Though the distinction between rods and cones was originally made on the basis of shape, there seems to be a considerable amount of overlap morphologically between the two types of receptor. Probably the best preliminary distinction between them can be made on functional grounds. The cones are used mainly when light is plentiful. They have developed in cases where high selectivity of information is at a premium. Rods, however, have developed to detect low levels of illumination. For instance, in the human eye cones predominate in the fovea centralis, which has a high capacity for color discrimination. However, rods predominate at the periphery, which is much more sensitive to light after dark adaptation but where color discrimination is absent. Similarly, diurnal animals have retinae composed mostly of cones whereas nocturnal animals possess only rods.

It has been shown by direct measurement of pigments in individual cones (MacNichol, 1964) that three kinds of cones are distinguished from each other by their possession of a different pigment. Each type of cone contains a pigment which breaks down most readily in light from a particular portion of the spectrum. The first type has its peak sensitivity at a wavelength of 447 mμ (blue-violet), the second type is maximally sensitive at 540 mμ (green), and the third at 577 mμ (yellow). This has been shown to be true of the macaque and also of man. This finding is important in understanding the basis of color vision (see below). The rods, on the other hand, contain a pigment, rhodopsin, with a peak of sensitivity close to 500 mμ. The properties of the pigments in the receptors determine many psychophysical results in vision, as will be seen later. The pigment in the rods and cones is contained in the outer segments of these cells. The outer segments are those parts of the rods and cones closest to the chorioid (Fig. 3–2). It has been estimated that 15 to 30 percent of the dry weight of a whole rod consists of rhodopsin (Hubbard 1953; Wald, 1954).

These light-sensitive molecules seem to be an integral part of membranes inside the outer segments. The membranes of which the light-sensitive molecules are a part enclose discs, which are stacked like a pile of coins inside the outer segments. It seems that the inside space of these discs is connected with the extracellular space in the case of cones but not in the case of rods (Laties and Liebman, 1970). So far this has been shown to be true in amphibians, and remains to be demonstrated in other vertebrates. However, if the bleaching of a molecule of visual pigment causes a leak in the membrane of which such a molecule is a part, it is easy to see why depolarization of the membrane should take part.

A correlation appears to exist between color sensitivity in different parts of the human visual field and the presence of different cone pigments. The center of the fovea is more sensitive to red light than the rest of the fovea, and is less sensitive to blue. By measuring what wavelengths of light are best absorbed in the foveal region, Weale (1968) was able to show that the center of the fovea absorbed more red light and less blue light than the rest of the fovea. This makes it plausible that there are differences in photosensitive pigments in different parts of the fovea, which correlates with the differential color sensitivity of these regions.

Visual Pigments

Light must be absorbed in order to have any physical effect. For this to happen, light-absorbing substances or pigments must be present which are changed in some way when they absorb light. In the case of vision, this change must be such as to produce nervous excitation.

Visual pigments break down when they absorb light. Therefore, in order for visual functioning to be continuous, the change caused by light on the pigment must be reversible. Furthermore, the change in the pigment which gives rise to neural excitation must be short lasting or be quickly removed. Otherwise the eye could not detect rapid decreases of light.

Four visual pigments are known at present: rhodopsin and porphyropsin in rods and iodopsin and cyanopsin in cones. Of these, probably rhodopsin, and perhaps iodopsin, occur in the human visual apparatus. These four pigments have been shown to be combinations of two forms of retinene and two forms of opsin. Opsin is a protein and retinene is a carotenoid closely related to vitamin A. Rhodopsin, when it absorbs light, passes into $retinene_1$ via some intermediates and rod opsin. $Retinene_1$ may then be modified into vitamin A_1, or it may recombine with opsin to form rhodopsin again. If $retinene_1$ is modified into vitamin A_1, $retinene_1$ can be resynthesized from this vitamin. $Retinene_1$ and opsin will then form rhodopsin again. There are therefore two processes whereby rhodopsin is regenerated: a fast one from retinene$_1$ and opsin and a slow one, ultimately from vitamin A$_1$ and opsin.

A similar process occurs in the case of the other visual pigments. Rhodopsin and iodopsin (a cone pigment extracted from the retinae of chickens) are both composed of retinene$_1$, and differ only in the protein to which this retinene is attached. Rhodopsin contains a protein called rod opsin, whereas iodopsin contains a protein called cone opsin. There is a similar relation in the case of porphyropsin and cyanopsin. Instead of containing retinene, these two pigments contain a closely similar carotenoid, retinene$_2$. Porphyropsin is formed by retinene$_2$ and rod opsin, whereas cyanopsin is composed of retinene$_2$ and cone opsin. Though the chemistry of these four naturally occurring photopigments is well understood, it is not yet clear how the dissociation of such pigments into their components by light produces neural excitation.

Measurements have been made of the rates at which monochromatic lights decompose the visual pigments and how much they are absorbed by such pigments. In the case of rhodopsin there is a striking parallel between the sensitivity of the human dark-adapted eye to various portions of the visible spectrum and the amount of light in these same portions absorbed by this pigment. Of the other pigments, iodopsin, the cone pigment extracted from the chicken retina, comes fairly close to the sensitivity of the human light-adapted eye, though its peak of sensitivity is displaced toward the longer wavelengths. The slight chemical differences present in these various pigments produce differences in their absorption spectra (Fig. 3–1).

On the basis of electron microscopic studies, Sjöstrand (1961) believes that rhodopsin forms part of a continuous membrane. This membrane, made up of lipid and protein molecules, is highly folded in the end of the receptor cells, as is illustrated in Figure 3–3. Most of the rhodopsin molecules are so oriented as to absorb light which strikes parallel to the long axis of the receptor cell (Wald et al., 1963).

One consequence of the properties of photosensitive pigments on vision relates to dark adaptation. One of the most striking properties of the visual system is the range of intensities over which it can function. The ratio of intensities from threshold to the upper limit of visual tolerance is approximately ten billion to one. This is a range of approximately 100 decibels. However, if an eye has been functioning at higher light intensities, it takes time for it to become efficient and to see at lower light intensities. We have all had the experience of entering a dim room from a sunlit scene, and initially we can see very little, as everything seems dark. Soon, however, the dim room appears brighter and vision becomes clear. It takes about 30 minutes for the dimmest light to become visible after the eye has been exposed to bright light, as is shown in

Figure 3–6. It seems that this slow change in visual sensitivity is mediated by the resynthesis of visual pigment.

DARK ADAPTATION

It was suggested by Hecht (1937) that the amount of unbleached rhodopsin present in rods was regulated by the rate at which it was being bleached by light and also by the rate at which it was being resynthesized by the eye. Therefore if the amount of light falling on the retina was sharply cut down, there would be an increase in the amount of unbleached rhodopsin in the rods because the average length of time that a resynthesized rhodopsin molecule would stay unbleached would be longer. Further, the larger the number of unbleached rhodopsin molecules, the greater the chance that a quantum of light, on entering the eye, would strike an unbleached molecule. When a quantum of light is absorbed by an unbleached molecule, energy is released, which will in turn contribute to the stimulation of the neural receptor, and so to a visual sensation. Thus the less light there is, the more sensitive to light the eye becomes.

We should expect, from the above, that the increase in light sensitivity of the eye when it is placed in the dark should parallel the resynthesis of visual pigments by the eye. That such is the case can be seen from Figure 3–6. The way this evidence was obtained is most ingenious. Rushton (1962) has determined the rate of resynthesis of rhodopsin in the intact eye by measuring how much light, shone into the eye, is reflected from it. Since less light is reflected when rhodopsin is unbleached, one can determine the rate at which rhodopsin is resynthesized, while at the same time taking reports of sensation from the subject. The subject whose curve of increasing sensitivity and rhodopsin resynthesis is illustrated in Figure 3–6 was chosen by Rushton because he was a "rod monochromat." In a "rod monochromat" the cones do not function; consequently, foveal vision is almost absent, acuity is poor, and there is total color blindness. On the other hand, the properties of such an eye are not complicated by the presence of cones, so there should be a direct match between the properties of rhodopsin and behavioral response. It can be seen from Figure 3–7 that this is the case.

In the normal eye, cones are also present, so we should expect dark adaptation to be a function of the resynthesis of the cone pigments as well as of rhodopsin. It appears that the cone pigments do not ever become as light sensitive as does rhodopsin, however long we stay in the dark. On the other hand, using the above method, Rushton has measured the rate at which cone pigments are resynthesized in the eye and he found that this rate is very much faster than that of resynthesis of rhodopsin. This is in agreement with Wald's (1959) measurement

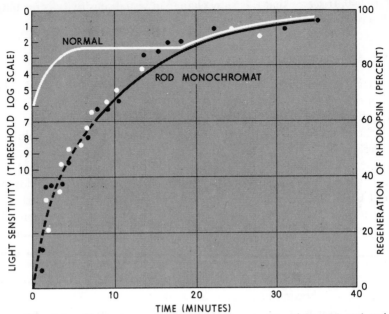

FIG. 3–6. Comparison of dark adaptation curves of normal and rod monochromat subject. The dots indicate rate of regeneration of rhodopsin of both subjects. This rate of regeneration is the same for both subjects as the dots do not divide into two populations. (From Rushton, W. A. H., "Visual Pigments in Man," *Scientific American,* 207, 12, November 1962. Copyright 1962 by Scientific American, Inc. All rights reserved.)

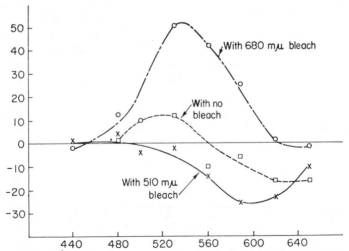

FIG. 3–7. Plot of the responses of a cell excited by green and inhibited by red to various monochromatic lights. Conditions indicated on curves. (From De Valois, R. L., *Contributions to Sensory Physiology,* W. D. Neff (ed.); New York: Academic Press, 1965.)

of the rate of synthesis of cone and rod pigments in solution. We should therefore expect, if we compare the rod monochromat with the normal subject, that the normal man will initially adapt more quickly as his cone pigments resynthesis but will soon hit a temporary ceiling of sensitivity as the concentration of cone pigment quickly reaches its maximum. After a while the slower but eventually more sensitive rhodopsin will resynthesize to the point where the rods, or rhodopsin-containing elements, become as sensitive as the cones, while still not reaching their own point of maximum sensitivity. As the rods become even more sensitive, the sensitivity of the normal eye begins to increase again to a final plateau. That this is the case can be seen from curves of dark adaptation (Fig. 3–6) in the normal subject. As was mentioned above, rods predominate in the visual periphery, and as a result we should expect the same type of curve from the periphery of the normal eye as that to be found in the monochromat. This is also the case.

As we explained above, the various visual pigments are each maximally sensitive in a different part of the spectrum. When they are all taken together, the cone pigments are most sensitive toward the red end of the spectrum, whereas rhodopsin is most efficient in the blue part of the spectrum. This accounts for the common observation that blue and green objects appear to be much brighter in relation to yellow and red objects in dusk than in daylight. This phenomenon is known as the Purkinje shift. Furthermore, because of the insensitivity of rhodopsin to the red end of the spectrum, dark adaptation (resynthesis of rhodopsin) also can take place unhindered if we are placed in deep red light, though we are not actually in the dark.

This insensitivity of rhodopsin to deep red light is put to interesting use by the Bronx Zoo. At this zoo, small nocturnal mammals with all-rod retinae are placed in deep red light, which they cannot see during the day, and in white light at night. In this way their activity cycle is reversed. Since they are active during the day, they can be viewed as such by their human observers, whose cone pigments are sensitive to the longer wavelengths. In zoos where this is not done, such animals are almost invariably asleep when visitors are admitted.

It appears from various measurements (Rushton, 1962; Wald, 1959) that the bleaching of very small amounts of rhodopsin leads to a very large decrease in sensitivity in the dark-adapted human subject. According to Wald (1959), visual sensitivity is reduced 8.5 times by the bleaching of only 0.006 percent of rhodopsin, whereas sensitivity is reduced 3,300 times by the bleaching of 0.06 percent of rhodopsin. It appears that it is the logarithm of sensitivity which varies with the concentration of rhodopsin. To explain this, Wald has suggested the theory that rhodopsin resides in a large number of compartments within the rod. Each compartment contains a large number of rhodopsin molecules, but only the bleaching of the first molecule within each compartment produces excitation, even though the other molecules in the compartment continue to absorb light. In this way a high state of light adaptation can be produced by the bleaching of a very small quantity of rhodopsin. The observed logarithmic relation would be generated by such a system.

INCREMENTAL THRESHOLDS AND NOISE

The smallest perceptible increase of illumination at any level of illumination is always the same proportion of that level. This is known as Weber's law and is expressed as $\dfrac{\Delta I}{I} = K$, where ΔI is the smallest perceptible increment of light at a particular level of illumination, I is that particular level of illumination, and K is some constant number. For K to remain the same, as it does, as I increases ΔI also has to increase. This means that at a high background level of illumination the increment of illumination has to be relatively high in order to be seen. It has to be much higher than when the background illumination is weak. Thus the physical magnitude of the smallest detectable difference is light intensity (ΔI) proportional to the intensity of the background illumination (I).

While the proportion between the background and the difference that can be detected is constant over most of the range of light intensities, it does not hold at very low intensities. At very low intensities the proportionate difference between background illumination and a just detectable change from it becomes larger and larger. Thus, for the sake of an arbitrary example, we can no longer detect an increment of one tenth of the background illumination, but we may need an increment of one half of the background illumination. In fact it has been repeatedly found in human experiments that below a certain point in background illumination (I)—the least increment of illumination which is required to be seen—is a constant amount of light, rather than a constant proportion of the background amount of light. One way to explain this would be to assume that as we decrease the amount of background light arriving in the eye, this amount becomes smaller than some quantity of "light" generated in the eye itself. In other words, we are saying that it is impossible to turn down the background light (against which a difference is judged) below a certain point. While we can control the external light source, we cannot normally control the "light" generated inside the eye.

Barlow (1957) suggested that this "light" could be due to the breakdown of visual pigment molecules due to body heat. This random breakdown of visual pigment molecules sets up signals in the visual system against which any increment of signal coming from the outside must be judged. As this level of internally generated "noise" normally stays constant, we would expect that, below a certain point of external background illumination level, such an external background will become a negligible proportion of the total signal ascending the visual pathway, most of the signal being contributed by a breakdown of visual pigment molecules, by body heat. Any increment of illumination will have to be judged against this total signal, which will remain effectively the same as the external background illumination is turned down. Consequently, the value of the least perceptible difference (ΔI) will remain the same in absolute terms as we plot it against the external background illumination. Such a theory assures that the formula $\frac{\Delta I}{I} = K$ remains true even at very low levels of illumination as far as the nervous system is concerned. Its apparent failure at very low levels is due to our failure to control the input to the nervous system. If we assume that $\frac{\Delta I}{I} = K$ remains true, we can work out how much "noise" or "light" is being generated by the eye by the apparent deviation from such a formula.

In an ingenious experiment, Muntz and Northmore (1957) tested Barlow's explanation of the breakdown of Weber's law at low intensities. The basic notion was that if breakdown of visual pigment molecules due to body heat could be diminished, Weber's law should hold for lower background intensities of illumination. To achieve this, Muntz and Northmore trained fresh-water turtles to discriminate a plain, illuminated background from a background with a brighter spot on it. Background illumination was varied, as was the brightness of the superimposed spot. The turtles were tested at 30 degrees C. and at 20 degrees C., and the results are shown in Figure 3–8. While the threshold is unaffected by temperature at high values of background illumination, the value of ΔI is clearly lower at 20 degrees C. than at 30 degrees C. at low values of background. Barlow's theory is the most plausible explanation of such a relationship.

COLOR AND BRIGHTNESS

As was described above, various types of receptors in the eye are differentiated on the basis of the pigment they contain. These receptors feed into a second stage, the bipolar cells, which in turn feed into ganglion cells. There are also two layers corresponding to the junction zones between these cells which provide means of horizontal interaction. Such an anatomical picture suggests that there may be an interesting recombination of the information from the receptor layer. More direct evidence from electrophysiological recording confirms such a notion. Two main types of combination of the basic information supplied by the receptor cells have been discovered. The first type consists of combinations of

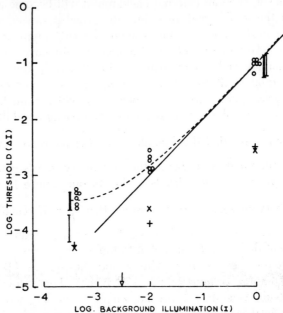

FIG. 3–8. Increment thresholds for the six individual turtles at the different values of *I* (open circles). Where more than one point falls on the same position, they have been displaced to the right for clarity. Solid line shows the expected relationship if Weber's law holds. The dashed line is given by $\Delta I = K(I + X)$; the value of *X* is shown by the arrow on the abscissa. Thresholds for two human subjects are shown by crosses. Ninety five percent confidence limits for the mean threshold values obtained at 30° C. (thick vertical bars) and 20° C. (thin vertical bars) in the second experiment are also shown. The results at a background of $5 \cdot 1 \times 10^{-4}$ ft. lamberts are shown in their correct position on the abscissa; results at $1 \cdot 6$ ft. lamberts have been shifted to the right. A value of zero on the abscissa equals $1 \cdot 6$ ft. lamberts; on the ordinate, zero equals approximately $0 \cdot 376$ μW/ster. cm². (From Muntz, W. R. A. and Northmore, D. P. M., "Background Light, Temperature and Visual Noise in the Turtle," *Vision Research,* Vol. 8, 1968.)

like sign, and the second type of combinations of opposite sign. In the first category, signals from receptor cells converge onto a ganglion cell, and in some cases each signal excites the cell and in other cases each signal inhibits it. In the second category, the ganglion cell is excited by input from one class of receptor and inhibited by input from another. It will be seen that the like-sign channel conveys information about overall brightness regardless of color and the unlike-sign channel carries information about color almost regardless of intensity.

Evidence concerning these two types of channel was first discovered in the retinae of certain fishes by Svaetichin (Svaetichin and MacNichol, 1958). Recording with micropipettes, Svaetichin found a negative resting potential in the retina which increased with the intensity of light, regardless of wavelength. However, some wavelengths were more effective in producing a change than others. Another type of potential, however, changed from negative to positive as the illuminating wavelength shifted from the blue end to the red end of the spectrum. Both these potentials Svaetichin called S-potentials. They are not spike potentials but steady potentials, and it is unclear from which structures they originate. Some of the potentials which reverse sign have their highest sensitivity in the red and green regions (one corresponding to the peak of negativity and the other corresponding to the peak of positivity). Another type has its two peaks in the blue and yellow regions of the spectrum. Perhaps at the ganglion cell level these graded or steady potentials are translated into the usual type of spike potential, or the inhibition of spike activity, as the case may be. In higher forms, such information is then carried, probably without much change, to the cells in the lateral geniculate, in which the axons of the ganglion cells (the optic nerve) mainly terminate. It is most profitable to consider the activity as it appears at the level of the lateral geniculate because this has been excellently investigated by De Valois (1965) in the macaque monkey. DeValois and his collaborators have shown, by careful psychophysical procedures, that the visual systems of the macaque and man are virtually identical. That is why their neural recording from the macaque has most relevance for color vision as we understand it. Let us first consider the evidence from cells combining signals of like sign.

Like-Sign Summators

These cells have also been called broad-band cells. They are functionally similar to the retinal ganglion cells described by Granit (1962), which he calls dominators.

Using microelectrodes, DeValois was able to demonstrate the existence of cells in the lateral geniculate of the macaque which reacted in the same way, qualitatively, to all wavelengths in the visible spectrum. Some cells would react by inhibition, others by excitation. The cells showed the same sensitivity to different parts of the visible spectrum as did the whole monkey in behavioral tests. It seems, therefore, that these cells carry brightness (luminosity) information.

From the overall sensitivity of these cells it is often possible to see to what receptors they are linked at the periphery. Some have a sensitivity curve which corresponds to that of rods. Others show a rod curve at low intensities, and yet at higher intensities the luminosity curve characteristic of daylight vision. Thus the Purkinje shift can be seen in a single cell. This indicates that these cells are indirectly connected both to rods and cones. Other cells in this class show curves which are like some of the curves for two cone pigments added together.

Opposite-Sign Summators

These are cells on which inputs converge, some of which excite and some of which inhibit ongoing activity. These inputs come from receptor cells with different sensitivities, that is, the blue, green, and yellow cones. Good examples of these have been demonstrated among ganglion cells in the retina of goldfish (Wagner et al., 1960). When an excitatory input from a receptor arrives, such a cell fires at the onset of the light stimulus. If, on the other hand, the stimulating light excites a receptor which sends inhibitory messages to the ganglion cell, inhibition of spontaneous activity occurs and the ganglion cell fires when the stimulating light is switched off. (This is known as postinhibitory rebound and commonly occurs in units of the nervous system.) When the stimulating light is of an intermediate wavelength, such as to affect both those receptors which excite the cell and those which inhibit it, the ganglion cell fires both on the "on" and the "off" of the stimulating light. To test the correctness of this interpretation of the linkage of receptors with these ganglion cells, experiments were done to selectively bleach out the pigment belonging to one of the receptors thought to be linked to a given ganglion cell. When this was done and the receptor inhibiting the cell had been thus desensitized, an "on" response could be obtained by almost any wavelength in the spectrum. Clearly, the inhibitory process had been inactivated, and it could not cancel out the excitatory process anywhere in the spectrum. The ganglion cells were connected to receptor processes most sensitive in the red and the green regions of the spectrum.

Similar results have been obtained by DeValois (1965) in the lateral geniculate of the macaque (Fig. 3–7). Most of the cells found here were excited by green and inhibited by red, or vice versa. Other cells responded in a similar way to blue and yellow. Further combinations were also identified; some cells, for instance, being inhibited by colors at both ends of the spectrum but excited by colors in the middle ranges. It was found that the relative excitation or inhibition of a particular cell is determined by the proportions in which the receptor cells indirectly connected to it are excited by the incident light. The pigments producing the excitation in each receptor cell (such as the green and yellow cones) have greatly overlapping sensitivities, which in fact differ only slightly over most of the spectrum. The visual mechanism adopts a good stratagem by processing the information in such a way that the excitation which is common to both types of receptor cancels out and that which is not common is registered. (A similar principle is used in the differential amplifier which is employed in neurophysiological recording.) Consequently, there is a great sharpening of the signal concerning color, which now corresponds to the difference between the two curves. However (as in the case of the differential amplifier), such a scheme of cancellation produces a difficulty. The cancellation tends to differ, depending on the absolute as well as the relative magnitudes of the signals which are summed. This is because it is difficult to adjust such a device so that both channels respond to an increase in the signal (in this case light) according to precisely the same function. One channel may register the same increase of light intensity with a slightly smaller increase in firing rate than the other. In this case a wavelength which produces perfect cancellation at one intensity (since here the two channels are equally excited) may fail to do so at another intensity, and cancellation at the second intensity will occur at a different wavelength. Because of this, a shift should be expected in the peak of excitation in a lateral geniculate cell as the intensity of a stimulating light is raised. DeValois (1965) has noted that such a shift of peak sensitivity in the cells of the lateral geniculate does indeed occur and that it is highly similar to the change in color which is perceived with increasing intensity by the human observer. This is known as the Bezold-Brücke effect, and the neurophysiological data presented above explain it in a very satisfying manner.

It should also be noted that in an arrangement where two curves cancel with regard to their common sensitivity, the peaks of sensitivity of the two initial curves are shifted away from each other. Thus the peak of sensitivity of the deep yellow pigment at the cones is effectively shifted at the lateral geniculate into the red. Similarly, the green pigment is shifted toward the blue when it is linked with the deep yellow. For the same reason, a linkage of the green and blue cones in an opposite-sign summator would lead to a shift of the green curve into a maximum in the yellow region and some shift of the blue toward even shorter wavelengths. In this way three primary pigments would give rise to four basic colors.

Figure 3–9 shows the main combinations arriving at ganglion cells in the retina. It is to be noted that there are two main systems in the four opposite-sign summators. The $+Y-B$ system, giving rise to a sensation of yellow, is excited by cones with a maximum sensitivity in the 570-mμ region. The $+B-Y$ system, giving rise to a sensation of blue, is the reverse. In these two systems the output of cones with sensitivity in the two extreme regions of the visible spectrum are subtracted from each other. The other main systems (RG) subtract from each other the cones whose maximum sensitivity is in the 570-mμ region of the

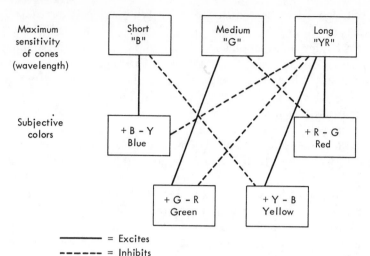

FIG. 3–9. The combination of three types of cones to produce
color sensation.

spectrum (also used in the *YB* system) and the cones whose maximum
sensitivity is in the middle of the spectrum 540 mμ. The +*G*—*R* system
produces a sensation of green whereas the +*R*—*G* system produces
a sensation of red. Whereas the *YB* system is somewhat responsive
to brightness differences (though more sensitive to color differences),
the *RG* system is almost entirely responsive only to color differences.

There are some other phenomena of color vision which the physiological data presented so far also explain. It has been known for a long
time that any three colors (such that no one of them could be matched
by a mixture of the other two) could be mixed by a separate adjustment
of their intensities to match any single color. Three colors conforming
to the above properties are called primaries, and one set of such primaries is red, green, and blue. The fact that no less than three different
primaries are needed to produce a match implies that there are at least
three channels which convey information about a single color, and also
that probably there are only three. This is the basis of the Young-Helm-
holtz three-color theory. Now that it has been possible to show that
there are three types of cones each with a maximal sensitivity to a
different wavelength, we see that the three-channel hypothesis is right.

On the other hand, we can also see that a regrouping of the three
channels takes place as the nervous system takes the information from
the three types of receptor and recombines it. This recombination, in
which the basic three channels are made to oppose or cancel each other
in various ways, generates another set of phenomena which could not
be explained in a very straightforward way by a simple three-channel

theory. Many phenomena suggest the existence of two specially related pairs of colors, red and green on one hand and blue and yellow on the other. These are called complementaries. Together, such complementaries cancel out, that is, they make white or gray. Secondly, a color leaves its complementary as an afterimage. Also, yellow and blue are seen much further into the periphery of vision than red and green, and the fields within which the two pairs of colors can be seen are almost coextensive for the two colors of each pair. Such observations led Hering (1874) to formulate his opponent-process theory, which has been developed by Hurvich and Jameson (1957).

It can readily be seen that the phenomena described above fit readily into the neurophysiological picture of two main types of opposite-sign summators, the red-green and blue-yellow.

Color Blindness

Color blindness is a generic term for a large number of different conditions in which color discrimination is abnormal. Such abnormalities are observed in 8.2 percent of the male population and 0.4 percent of the female (Marriott, 1962). Before more direct information was obtained, these conditions were intensively studied in the hope that they might shed some light on the mechanism of color vision. In a way, color blindness may be regarded as a lesion made by nature, and lesions are studied to obtain evidence on the working of the intact organisms. However, it has been impossible to make any unique interpretation of the color-blindness symptoms prior to knowledge of how the mechanism works, based on more direct types of evidence.

Color blindness may be divided into three main groups: dichromatism, monochromatism, and anomalous trichromatism. Monochromats can match any color simply by adjusting the intensity of any other color. Their condition is normally due to a complete absence of cone function. There are also rare cases where cone function is present, and these could be due to an absence of opposite-sign summators. Dichromats can match any colored light with two colors, one from the red and the other from the blue end of the spectrum. One type of dichromat, the protanope, is completely unable to see light at the deep red end of the spectrum. According to Rushton (1962), who made measurements of the light reflected from the retina of protanopes, the cone pigment most sensitive in the red region is missing in this condition. On the other hand, deuteranopes, another class of dichromat, have, according to Rushton (1962), a different cone pigment missing, which is most sensitive in the green region. However, other data suggest that deuteranopes stems from a fusion of the red and green systems (Weale, 1968). Both deuteranopes and protanopes confuse reds, yellows, and greens. The third class of dichromat, the tritanope, confuses shades of blue with green and also pink with orange. From reports of subjects who are color blind in one eye and normal in the other (Graham and Hsia, 1958; Judd, 1948), reds, yellows, and greens appear as yellow and the rest of the spectrum as blue in the case of both a protanope and a deuteranope. The anomalous trichromats, classified into protans, deutans, or tritans, are seemingly intermediate between, respectively, the protanopes, deuteranopes, and tritanopes on one hand and the normal on the other. They are perhaps to be regarded as having a weakly developed aspect of their color mechanism rather than a complete absence of such an aspect.

SPATIAL INTERACTIONS

So far, some account has been given of how the eye processes information from light falling on it without much regard for the spatial arrangement of such light. However, the eye functions not only to detect light and its differences in wavelength but also to interpret information about the relative spatial distribution of patches of light on the retina.

The general picture which emerges from recording studies from ganglion cells or their axons (composing the optic nerve) is as follows. First, each ganglion cell receives excitation upon stimulation of a small area in the retina. Second, it is inhibited by stimulation of the region surrounding the small area from which it receives excitation. In some cases, the situation is reversed, and the ganglion cell is inhibited by stimulation of a small retinal area and excited by stimulation of a field surrounding this small area. This has been shown by Kuffler (1953) in the cat's light-adapted eye. He placed a microelectrode in a ganglion cell and recorded activity in this cell as he moved a small exploring light spot on the retina. When the light was shone within about ½ mm. of the ganglion cell, the cell gave a burst of spikes. When the light was placed about 1 mm. away and switched on, there was no response; instead, the ganglion cell gave a burst of spikes when the light was switched off. In an intermediate zone, the cell discharged both when the light was switched off and when it was switched on. It is probable that when a cell fires at the offset of a stimulus it is being inhibited, or partly inhibited, by such a stimulus. So it seems that the recorded cell was being excited by impulses from receptor cells within a central area and inhibited by impulses from those outside the area.

However, this organization of the retina occurs only in the light-adapted eye. Barlow, Fitzhugh, and Kuffler (1957) found that in the dark-adapted eye of the cat the outer zone of opposite sign was lost. In the case of the cells whose "surround" produced an off response when it was illuminated, this no longer happened in the dark-adapted state. Only the response to a light being switched on in the center of the field remained. This would indicate that during dark adaptation there is not only a change due to the visual pigments' being in an altered state but also a neural reorganization, whose mechanism is at present obscure.

LATERAL INHIBITION

The results quoted in the preceding section on the light-adapted eye suggest that not only does excitation over small areas of the retina summate but that inhibition of one excited area by another also takes place when larger distances are involved. This sideway spread of inhibition is called lateral inhibition, and has been studied in a quantitative manner by Hartline (1949) in the eye of *Limulus,* the horseshoe crab. This animal has a compound eye and the different elements can be separately illuminated. It can be shown that if two such elements are stimulated by two lights of different intensity, one inhibits the other in proportion to their relative rates of discharge. The more active an element, the greater the inhibition it exerts. The amount of inhibition decreases and the threshold which inhibition must reach to be effective increases with distance from the element exerting such inhibition. Elements exert such inhibition upon each other. It follows from this that if there are two neighboring regions (consisting of a large number of elements), one of which is excited and the other is not, the elements in the excited region will inhibit each other. However, those elements in the excited region which are closest to the unexcited region will be least inhibited because of the absence of excited neighbors at least on one side. Therefore most excitation will be at the border of the two regions. Such a mechanism has been postulated as the basis of contrast phenomena (Hartline, 1949) and also of figural aftereffects (Deutsch, 1963). Similar interactions have been shown to occur in the eye of the cat (Kuffler, 1953).

More complex interactions underlying the responses of retinal ganglion cells have also been found. Hartline (1940) observed that movement of a light spot was particularly effective in eliciting responses in single optic fibers in the frog. Even more remarkable are the observations of Barlow and Hill (1963) in the rabbit and Maturana and Frank (1963) in the pigeon. There are ganglion cells in the retina that respond not only to moving stimuli but also only to stimuli moving in a particular direction.

An investigation of ganglion cells in the movement-sensitive retina has been carried out by Michael (1968) on the eye of the ground squirrel (*Citellus mexicanus*). This mammal has an all-cone retina. It is diurnal in its habits as its night vision and dark adaptation are very limited.

Indeed it is said to be unable to find its way back to its burrow at night, being effectively blind at low levels of illumination. In the optic nerve of the ground squirrel Michael found fibers (axons of ganglion cells in the retina) which gave relatively small responses when a light was first shone on a small area and when such a light was removed. This area, defined as the field center, subtended 0.5 to 1.0 degree of visual angle. (1 degree of visual angle covers about 115 μm on the retina in the ground squirrel.) This field center was surrounded by an area which, if simultaneously illuminated with the field center, inhibited the response of the field center to such illumination. It is therefore called an inhibitory surround. No activity in the monitored nerve fiber was evoked by shining a light on the inhibitory surround. The investigated fibers were therefore unresponsive to diffuse light.

While the field center was somewhat excited by the onset of a stationary light spot, a much larger response occurred when the spot was moved in a particular direction, called the preferred direction. When the light spot was moved in the opposite direction, no response was recorded. This response to a light spot was also shown to a black spot, and to a black-white or white-black edge moving in the preferred direction. It therefore seems that the property of movement in a particular direction, independent of other properties, is already abstracted at the ganglion cell level in the retina of the ground squirrel. Similar cells have been observed in the rabbit by Barlow and Hill (1963), Barlow and Levick (1965), and Levick (1967).

Twenty-three percent of the optic fibers studied by Michael in the ground squirrel were directionally sensitive. It seems that such fibers do not travel to the lateral geniculate nucleus of the thalamus but project to the superior colliculus. It seems that in the ground squirrel about half the fibers and in the optic nerve project to the superior colliculus while the other half project to the lateral geniculate nucleus of the thalamus.

TECTAL LOBES OR COLLICULI OF THE FROG

That the retina possesses a remarkable capacity for perceptual analysis has been shown in the frog by Maturana et al. (1968). Instead of using spots of light, they used the kinds of stimuli that the frog has to distinguish in its natural environment in order to catch its food, flies, and escape predators. Microelectrode recordings were taken from the terminations of optic nerve fibers in the tectum, which receives most of the output from the retinae in the frog. The first kind of fiber Maturana described produces a burst of activity when an edge, lighter or darker than the background, is moved across a small area of the retina. If the edge stops moving within this area, the neural response persists, though at a lower frequency. When the illumination is switched off, the response disappears. When the light is switched on again, the response reappears. Further, if an edge is introduced during darkness, a neural response also appears when the light is switched on again. Wide variations in illumination do not affect the characteristic responses described above. The second kind of fiber signals the occurrence of a curved edge in a small area of the retina, reacting best to small dark spots. Though these fibers will continue to signal the presence of such spots if they had been moved into a particular area and then made stationary, such a signal will cease if the general illumination is turned off and then on again. Nor will a signal be given if such spots are introduced into the area during a period of darkness which is then followed by general illumination. However, wide variations in general illumination do not change its responsiveness to the effective stimuli, dark spots. A third class of cells responds only to a moving edge, and never when such an edge is stationary. In the fourth class of cells, activity is evoked by a general dimming of the illumination, whereas in the fifth a steady activity signals the general level of the illumination, increasing as illumination decreases. These results emphasize the value of teleological thinking in the experimental analysis of biological systems. The experiments were undertaken, as is explained by Maturana et al., by considering the function of the frog's eye and its biological purpose.

Superior Colliculi

The retina in all vertebrates is mapped into the superior colliculi, which, with the inferior colliculi, comprise the corpora quadrigemina. Axons from the ganglion cells of the retina project to the superior colliculi, where neighboring points on the retina are connected to neighboring points of the colliculi. In the lower vertebrates, such as the goldfish and the frog (Fig. 3–10 [Trevarthen, 1968, p. 308]), the collicular map is the only one subserving vision. In mammals such as the rat and the cat, there is a second visual map in the cortex. In the cat, however, not only are retinal fibers mapped into the superior colliculi but there is also a projection of fibers from the visual cortex (Altman, 1962; Barris et al., 1935). The center of the visual field in the goldfish, frog, rat, and cat is connected to a different point on the surface of the superior colliculi. However, Trevarthen (1968) points out that if we view the map in terms of the body of the animals concerned, a considerable similarity emerges. The eyes of the various species concerned, and so the center of the visual field, point in different directions in relation to the main rostro-caudal axis of the body. It seems that the center of the visual field has been connected differently to the colliculus, depending on the direction of the eyes. For instance, in the cat the eyes

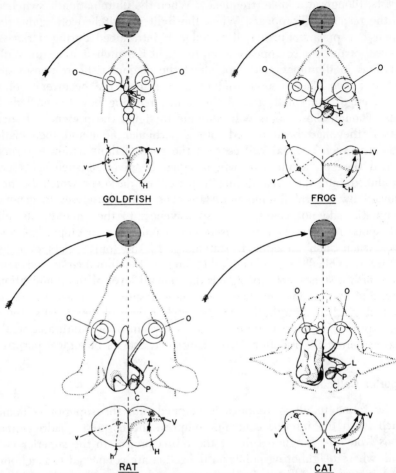

GOLDFISH

FROG

RAT

CAT

FIG. 3–10. Colliculus maps in several vertebrates. *O*, optical axis; *L*, lateral geniculate (and other visual nuclei of dorsal thalamus); *P*, pretectum; *C*, optic tectum = superior colliculus; *h* and *v*, horizontal and vertical meridia of the optical visual field; *H* and *V*, horizontal and vertical meridia of the body-centered behavioral visual field. The shaded line on the right tectum indicates the border of the binocular field. The striate areas of the cortex are shown for the rat and cat with the central or foveal areas in black. The dotted areas of cortex are also implicated in visual functions. (From Trevarthen, C. B., "Two Mechanisms of Vision in Primates," *Psychologische Forschung*, Vol. 31, 1968; courtesy of Springer Verlag, N.Y. Inc.)

point almost directly forward. Hence the center of the visual field is connected to the anterior tip (somewhat laterally displaced) of the superior colliculus. In the rat, however, the eyes point sideway. That part of the rat retina which relays informatian about space almost directly forward is connected to a similar place in the colliculi as the center of the cat's visual field. However, the center of the rat's visual field which looks sideway is connected to part of the colliculus similar to that part of the cat's visual field which picks up information from the same part of space as the rat's center of the visual field (relative to the animal's head) rather than a map of the visual field.

Functions of the Superior Colliculi

G. E. Schneider (1967) has shown that after ablation of the visual cortex, hamsters fail to discriminate visual patterns but are able to localize visual objects in space. On the other hand, when the superior colliculus was ablated the animals were unable to orient to the position of a visual stimulus, though their ability to discriminate patterns was intact. Without the superior colliculus, animals were unable to localize sunflower seeds visually, while visual cortical ablation did little to impair this ability. In a task where the hamsters had to discriminate between two patterns fastened on two doors, behind one of which was the reward, those with cortical lesions were unable to do so. However, the hamsters with lesions of the superior colliculus discriminated such patterns but could not guide themselves correctly toward them. Thus they would run to the incorrect pattern but would not attempt to push through it to obtain a water reward. Instead, they would run until they reached the correct pattern and then push.

Barnes, Smith, and Latto (1970) investigated the functions of the superior colliculus in the rat. Animals were trained to jump toward the dark door and avoid the light doors in a six-choice jumping stand. Rats with bilateral lesions of the superior colliculi were severely impaired in such a task, jumping indiscriminately toward the correct and the incorrect stimuli. However, the apparatus was then modified so that the rats could run round to the various choices, and they would attempt to enter only the correct box. In another experiment, the animals would learn to approach a box if it was dark. The goal box contained two sugar pellets when it was dark and nothing when it was lit.

The rats ran much more slowly when the box was lit, thus showing they could discriminate. It could be concluded, therefore, that rats with bilateral lesions of the superior colliculi could discriminate visual stimuli but could not orient toward them, thus supporting Schneider's (1967) conclusion. However, Barnes et al. (1970) noted that while jumping mainly to the incorrect door in the jumping apparatus, the rats never missed the aperture to the boxes or hit the partition between the boxes. They state: "It appears that the animals can jump accurately towards the outline of the aperture of the box without being able to orient to the correct brightness one." This poses an interesting problem. Sprague and Meikle (1965) conclude that the function of the superior colliculi in cats includes not only control of head and eye movements but also what could be termed aspects of visual attention and perception.

Interactions between the Superior Colliculus and Visual Cortex

When the visual areas of the cat cortex are ablated unilaterally, the cat becomes permanently and completely blind in that half of the visual field opposite the lesion (total contralateral hemianopia). Sprague (1966) made the surprising discovery that if after the visual cortical removal the contralateral superior colliculus is removed as well, vision returns to that half of the field which was rendered blind by the initial cortical lesion. The return of vision to that half of the visual field blinded by the cortical ablation was immediate on the removal of the contralateral superior colliculus. If instead of ablating the contralateral colliculus, fibers connecting the two colliculi (commissure of the superior colliculus) were split, blindness also was reversed, but in this case it took three weeks for vision to return. While the reason for such results is not entirely clear, the latter show a complex interaction between the superior colliculi and the visual cortex. The results also show that evidence from lesions to the CNS must be interpreted with caution.

Single-Unit Studies of the Superior Colliculi

Sterling and Wickelgren (1969) have studied the receptive fields of single units in the superior colliculus of the cat. In the cat, inputs from the retina and the visual cortex converge in superficial layers of the superior colliculus. Most collicular units can be stimulated through input to either eye. The units respond well to moving stimuli and weakly or not at all to stationary stimuli. About 75 percent of the units are sensitive to stimuli moving in a particular direction. While the cortex seems to have approximately equal numbers of cells sensitive to movement in any direction, most of the cells in the colliculus are sensitive to movement in a similar direction. They are sensitive to movement with a strong horizontal component away from the center of the visual field. Such a property is useful in tracking objects visually to keep them within the visual field.

There are other differences between collicular and cortical movement detectors in the cat. In the cortex, the least amount of activity is elicited in a unit by movement 90 degrees to the direction of the movement which elicits the maximum activity. More activity is elicited by movement 180 degrees to the direction of movement eliciting the maximum activity than by movement 90 degrees away from it. In some sense, such cortical units are orientation detectors almost as much as direction detectors. In collicular units, however, movement at 90 degrees to the direction eliciting maximum response is often quite effective in producing a discharge, whereas movement 180 degrees away from the direction eliciting maximum discharge is quite ineffective as a stimulus. Whereas cortical units are very sensitive to small movements of ¼ degree or less, collicular cells are unaffected by such small movements. Further, collicular cells are much less sensitive to differences in size or shape of the stimulus. The receptive fields of the collicular units consist of an activating region in the center from which responses can be elicited. This is surrounded by an area from which no responses can be elicited. In fact this surround seems to be antagonistic to the activating center because stimuli become less efficient in stimulating the activating center if they extended into the surround.

In a further study, Wickelgren and Sterling (1969) investigated the influence of the visual cortex on receptive fields in the superior colliculus. As has been mentioned above, fibers from the cat's visual cortex project to the superior colliculus. The area of origin of such fibers which reach the superficial gray and the optic layer is areas 17, 18, and 19 of the cortex (Fig. 1, Wickelgren and Sterling). The projections from the cortex are almost all ipsilateral (i.e., the cortex projects to the colliculus on the same side) and the projection from the retina is almost all from the contralateral eye.

Whereas collicular units are initially unresponsive after the removal of the visual cortex, they begin to respond one to four weeks after the operation. However, their characteristics change completely. Collicular units now respond to stationary stimuli and are not directionally selective. Further, units can be driven only by the contralateral eye. This contrasts with the properties described by Sterling and Wickelgren (1969) and summarized above, where it was shown that most collicular units, when there is input from both the retina and the cortex, respond only to moving stimuli and are directionally selective.

In this connection it is interesting to consider research on the function of the colliculi in the behavioral testing of animals in which the visual cortex is ablated. Humphrey (in press) has trained monkeys without the visual cortex to reach for quite small objects for a reward. They could not, however, make learned discriminations of such objects. In interpreting his results, Humphrey explicitly assumes (about the superior colliculi) "that their role in the intact animal is just that which they play in an animal with the visual cortex removed." However, it has been shown above that the colliculi alter their properties as a result of the ablation of the visual cortex. Of course, unless Humphrey's type of assumption is made in interpreting the results of ablation studies, it is difficult to see how they can be interpreted at all.

VISUAL DEPRIVATION AND THE CORTEX

It seems that the organization of the visual system is based on a very high specificity of anatomical connection to achieve the recognition of basic perceptual elements like lines, tilt, color, and so on. How far such capacities are innate and how far they are acquired has long been a matter of dispute among psychologists. If the connections which exist in the adult could be shown to exist in a neonatal organism, the basis for at least some forms of perception could be shown to be innate. Recording from four kittens less than 20 days old with essentially no visual experience, as in one the eyes had not opened, Hubel and Wiesel (1963) found that responses from cortical cells, though sluggish, were essentially like those obtained from adult cats. Most of the cells responded maximally to lines with a particular orientation.

Further experiments (Wiesel and Hubel, 1963a, 1963b, 1965) suggest that prolonged absence of stimulation of the visual system leads to various patterns of atrophy. If one eye is occluded for two to three months after birth, the kittens behave as if they are blind if they are allowed to look only through that eye. Microelectrode recording revealed that almost no cortical cells were affected by stimulation of the previously occluded eye. Further, it appeared on histological examinations that the cells receiving input from that eye in the lateral geniculate had atrophied. In contrast, when both eyes had been occluded while the animals behaved as if blind, 41 percent of the sampled cells in the visual cortex were normal, as shown by microelectrode recording. It would seem that if one eye suppresses the other, atrophy is more complete.

Early visual experience can influence the receptive field organization in other ways. Hirsch and Spinelli (1970) gave differential exposure to the eyes of a kitten. One eye was permitted to see only horizontal bars and the other eye only vertical bars. As a result of this treatment, it was found that all cortical units responsive to bars responded only to input from only one of the two eyes and that the neurons responsive to horizontal bars were stimulable only through the eye that had been exposed to them and the neurons responsive to vertical bars were stimulable only through the eye that had been exposed to vertical bars. Blakemore and Cooper (1970), in a somewhat different experiment, reared some kittens in a visual environment consisting only of vertical stripes and other kittens in an environment consisting only of horizontal stripes. When stripes at right angles to those previously exposed were shown, no units responding to them were found. However, normal neural responsiveness was found to stripes shown in the previously experienced orientation. Concurrent with this neural pattern of responsiveness, evidence of behavioral blindness was found to contours in the orientations which had not previously been exposed. Freeman, Mitchell, and Millodot (1972) found an analog of this condition in human subjects suffering from astigmatism. In this condition, contours running in one orientation cannot be brought into focus. It seems that even when proper optical compensation for such a condition is made, so that no optical blurring is present, many persons suffering from astigmatism still exhibit a blurring of vision along orientation consistent with their previous inability to focus in that orientation.

VISUAL DEPRIVATION AND THE SUPERIOR COLLICULUS

The responses of retinal ganglion cells or lateral geniculate cells are little affected when kittens are deprived of vision in one eye. However, most cortical cells, generally driven by either eye, respond exclusively to the eye which was not deprived of vision. Most collicular cells respond to visual deprivation in one eye in the same way as cortical cells do. They cease to respond to messages coming from the deprived eye. Wickelgren and Sterling (1969b) showed that this altered responsiveness of the colliculi, following monocular deprivation, is due to the influence of the cortex. The deprived eye becomes much more effective in driving collicular cells after removal of the cortex. It appears that the cortical input prevents collicular cells from responding to their retinal input if the cortex itself is unresponsive to retinal input consequent upon visual deprivation.

SPATIAL RESPONSES IN THE HIGHER VISUAL CENTERS

Each retina may be pictured as being divided by a vertical line drawn through the fovea. The half of the retina thus established which is closer to the nose is called the nasal hemiretina; the other half is the temporal hemiretina. The fibers from the nasal hemiretina cross the midline at the optic chiasm whereas those from the temporal hemiretina continue without crossing. In consequence, the fibers from the nasal hemiretina in one eye and those from the temporal hemiretina in the other eye proceed to the same hemisphere (Fig. 3–11). The left nasal hemiretina and the right temporal hemiretina both receive light from the left half of the visual field. It follows that objects in the left half of the visual field are represented by messages going to the right hemisphere whereas those in the right visual field find their destination in the left hemisphere. This is true in man. As we descend the phylogenetic scale, there is an increasing tendency for the fibers in each optic nerve to cross to the opposite hemisphere.

The most important visual pathway in man passes to the lateral geniculate nucleus (LGN). The LGN is made up of six layers of cells

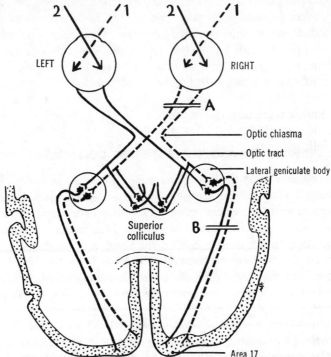

FIG. 3–11. The visual pathways. Arrows *1* indicate the light from objects in the right visual fields (when looking straight ahead) reaches the left halves of the retinae. The reverse is true for the opposite visual fields. The collaterals from the visual path (to the superior colliculi for reflexes) are really separate fibers and not branches of true visual fibers. Cutting the optic nerve at *A* causes complete blindness in that eye. A lesion at *B*, however, causes blindness in the left half of each field of vision (arrows 2). (From Gardner, E., *Fundamentals of Neurology*, 4th ed.; Philadelphia: W. B. Saunders Company, 1963.)

separated by layers of fibers. The fibers from the nasal hemiretina of the opposite side terminate in cell layers 1, 4, and 6. The fibers from the ipsilateral temporal hemiretina end in the other layers. No significant interaction at the LGN between the inputs from the two eyes has been demonstrated, either from anatomical or electrophysiological evidence.

Axons of the ganglion cells of the retina terminate in boutons on cell bodies in the LGN. These cell bodies send axons to the fourth layer of the striate cortex. In the monkey LGN (Glees and Le Gros Clark, 1941), there are no terminations on the same cell from more than one axon coming from the retina. Instead, each axon sprays out into five or six branches which terminate on a single geniculate cell. In such a way there is divergence, but no convergence or overlap. In the cat, however, in line with its lower visual acuity (Glees, 1941), there is definite overlap, which could lead to the pooling of information from several fibers coming from the retina. There are also so-called association cells in the LGN, with short axons which terminate in dense arborizations. Such cells could be the basis of lateral interaction, perhaps of an inhibitory kind, between the various channels passing through the LGN.

Hubel and Wiesel (1961), working on the cat, were able to show that a geniculate cell behaves in much the same way as the retinal ganglion cells which feed into it. LGN cells tend to have roughly circular peripheral receptive fields. These consist first of a central region, circular in shape, a discrete stimulus to which excites the cell (the "on" response). This is surrounded by a larger field, again roughly circular, a stimulus to which tends to inhibit the "on" response, and which excites the cell when the stimulus is switched off (the "off" response). The one difference between the behavior of the LGN cells and the ganglion cells of the retina is that diffuse illumination of both the "on" and the "off" region simultaneously produces no response in the LGN cells, whereas some "on" activity may be seen in the retinal ganglion cells. This implies that there is a more precise balancing out of the excitatory and inhibitory influences on a cell at the level of the LGN. As was seen with the ganglion cells of the retina, not only are there cells, the centers of whose receptive fields produce excitation and the peripheries of which produce inhibition, but there are also cells with receptive fields, the centers of which exercise an inhibitory influence, whereas the peripheries produce excitation. It should also be mentioned that adjacent points in the LGN are stimulated by neighboring points on the retina. Such an orderly projection is preserved when we reach the destination of the axons of the LGN cells in the cortex. A disproportionately large part of the LGN projection is occupied by the central part of the retina.

The axons from the LGN reach the posterior portion of the cortex by the geniculocalcarine tract. The area of cortex receiving these projections is also known as the striate (striped) area. In the gray matter of the cerebral cortex are two white laminations of myelinated nerve fibers which lie parallel to the surface of the cortex. These two laminations appear as white bands where the cortex is sectioned and are called the inner and outer lines of Baillarger. In the striate cortex, only the outer line or band is visible, but it is more conspicuous than elsewhere. It is here called the line of Gennari, and gives this portion of the cortex its striped appearance. In man, most of the visual area as defined by the projection of fibers from the LGN is buried in the depths of the calcarine fissure, the deep cleft separating the two hemispheres in their occipital portion. Fibers representing the center of the retina or the macula are mapped at the more posterior end of the fissure, close to

the exterior. This macular region of the retina occupies a disproportionately large part of such a map.

Electrophysiological studies have shown, however, that there are three
maps of the retina in the cortex which lie adjacent to each other. These
are known as areas I, II, and III. The existence of the first two has
been shown in the cat, rabbit, and monkey (Thompson, Woolsey, and
Talbot, 1950; Hubel, 1963). The third has been described by Hubel
and Wiesel (1963) in the cat. The second and third representations
are not in the striate area but adjacent to it (Fig. 3–12).

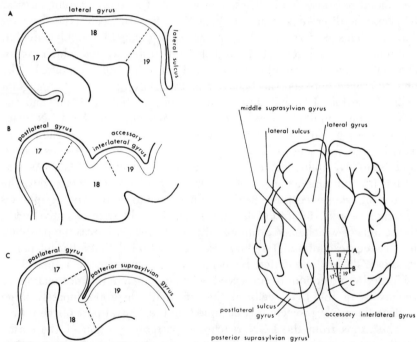

FIG. 3–12. Composite diagram showing coronal sections at three antero-
posterior levels through visual areas I, II, and III (or 17, 18, and 19). Boundaries
are based on several criteria, including histology as studied in Nissl- and myelin-
stained sections, distribution of projections from area 17 to nonstriate visual cortex
by the silver-degeneration technique, and physiological recordings. (From Hubel.
D. H., and Wiesel, T. N., *J. Neurophysiol.*, 28, 1965.)

Microelectrode studies (Hubel and Wiesel, 1962) have revealed a
most remarkable organization among cortical cells subserving vision.
Instead of finding the type of cell whose receptive field is circular and
composed of two concentric regions, one of which tends to inhibit and
the other exite, they have found fields divided by straight lines. Cells
here also are excited by stimuli falling on one small region of the retina

and inhibited by stimuli impinging on a neighboring region. However, the shape of the boundaries between any two such regions is in the form of a straight line, and one of the two fields is not necessarily within the other (as it is at the level of the retinal ganglion cells and the LGN).

There are in fact two main types of receptive field at the cortex. The first is composed of a narrow central strip (which may be excitatory or inhibitory), divided by two straight lines from two flanking fields. These flanking fields are inhibitory if the central strip is excitatory and excitatory if the central strip is inhibitory. Such fields, when they have an "on" center, produce their highest discharge to a visual stimulus consisting of a narrow strip and coinciding exactly with the position of the "on" center. If the stimulus encroaches on the "off" portion of the field, reduction in firing takes place as might be expected. The second type of field is composed of an "on" area divided on only one side by a straight line from an "off" area. Exact superimposition of an edge along the boundary of the receptive field produces the largest effect. The balancing between the excitatory and inhibitory parts of the field is such that these cells do not respond to changes in diffuse illumination.

As the width of the central strip in many of the receptive fields of these cells resembles in size the width of the central regions of the receptive fields of LGN cells, Hubel and Wiesel believe that each cortical cell receives projections from a set of LGN cells and that these LGN cells have receptive fields which, taken together, form a straight line.

A further complication is introduced by the fact that at least 12 directions of such strip or boundary-detecting cells have been found. This means that different cells are most sensitive to different slants or directions of lines, if these are directly superimposed on a specific retinal locus. The cells just described have been called "simple" cells by Hubel and Wiesel because they respond only to stimulation at a specific locus. Another class of cells they termed "complex." In spite of displaying complete specificity with regard to the orientation of lines or edges by which they will be activated, they will respond to such lines located anywhere within a certain small portion of the visual field. It appears that they are linked to the output of a large number of simple cells, all responding to lines of the same orientation.

In this way complex cells respond to the orientation of a line, independent of specific loci. Complex and simple cells have also been found in the cortex which respond only to lines or edges which move. Some are sensitive not only to a particular direction of movement but also to its speed.

Whereas little or no binocular interaction occurs at the level of the LGN, Hubel and Wiesel (1962) reported that 84 percent of the units in the cortex responded to stimulation from corresponding points on the two retinae, and this could very well be an underestimate. If the two stimuli on the two corresponding points were the same, their effects summed. If the excitatory part of the field was stimulated in one eye and the inhibitory portion in the other, the effects tended to cancel. The responses obtained from the cell to stimulation of the two eyes were not always equal; one eye would produce a stronger response than the other.

An interesting aspect of the functional organization of the orientation-sensitive cells, both simple and complex, is that they are arranged in columns with each column at right angles to the surface of the cortex. Each column has in its cells, both simple and complex, sensitive only to one orientation. The various cells in the column, however, are not from only one point on the retina; they are simply from the same neighborhood.

Hubel and Wiesel (1965) reported the discovery of further kinds of cells in the visual cortex. So far the cells we have described come from visual area I. There are, as we have seen, at least two other areas in the cat in which there is a topographical map of the retina—visual II and visual III (Fig. 3–12). Recording from these areas. Hubel and Wiesel found what they term hypercomplex cells and hypercomplex cells of higher order. Hypercomplex cells are of various kinds. Some give a maximal response to a line in one particular orientation, but only if the end of the line does not extend past a particular point. If the line is progressively extended past this point, the response diminishes and then ceases altogether. In another kind of cell, extending a line in either or both directions abolishes the response. It is as if two or more simple cells described above were all connected to another cell, one connection being excitatory and the others inhibitory. Still other hypercomplex cells give their maximal response to two precisely positioned boundaries at right angles to each other, the response varying as a function of the angles between the two boundaries. The amount of firing from this last class of cells could serve as the basis of recognition of angle, irrespective of rotation. This ability is probably basic to shape recognition (Fig. 3–13).

Hypercomplex cells of higher order are found mainly in visual area III. These mostly stand in a similar relation to hypercomplex cells as simple cells stand to complex cells. They may signal the ends of lines of a certain orientation anywhere within a given region of the retina. There are also other cells, classified by Hubel and Wiesel, in this category. These are sensitive to lines in a particular orientation and ending at a particular point, and also to lines at right angles to them. McCollough (1965) has shown some interesting perceptual consequences of the existence of orientation-specific edge detectors which presumably occur also in the human visual system. Observers were shown alternating

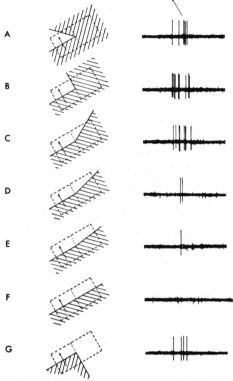

FIG. 3–13. Stimulation of a cell with two intersecting edges across its retinal receptive field, as shown on left of the figure. The response, as seen on the right, varies as a function of the angle between the two intersecting edges. (From Hubel, D. H., and Wiesel, T. N., *J. Neurophysiol.*, 28, 1965.)

fields of orange-vertical and blue-horizontal stripes. After such an exposure, a test pattern consisting of black-vertical stripes appeared blue, green and black-horizontal stripes appeared orange. If the field was tilted 45 degrees, the colored afterimage disappeared. If the inspection of the colored stripes was made with one eye, no colored afterimage was seen with the other. This experiment then demonstrates the presence of edge detectors in the human visual system, and further that some or all of these edge receptors are specific to color. Because the afterimage shows no "interocular" transfer, the experiment also shows that such edge detectors function at a stage in the visual pathway before the inputs from the two eyes have converged.

McCollough's finding (1965) on color-contingent aftereffects has now been confirmed and extended by others (Helper, 1968; Stromeyer and

Mansfield, 1970; Held and Shattuck 1971). Observers were shown red stripes alternating with green stripes. The red stripes were tilted clockwise off vertical and the green stripes counterclockwise off vertical. In the test condition, vertical red stripes appeared to the observers to be tilted counterclockwise and vertical green stripes to be tilted clockwise.

Favreau, Emerson, and Corballis (1972) report a further example of a color-contingent aftereffect. Plateau (1851) found that when a spiral is rotated, it appears to expand when rotated in one direction and to contract when rotated in the other direction. If the spiral appears to expand when moving, a stationary spiral viewed after the rotating spiral appears to contract. If the spiral appeared to contract when moving, stationary spiral viewed just after appears to expand. Favreau et al. (1972) rotated a spiral in one direction in green light, alternating this with rotation in the other direction in red light. There were two test conditions. In the first, the observer was shown the spiral rotating in white light in one direction and then the other. The color afterimage was found to be appropriate to the direction of movement. For instance, if the spiral was shown in green light rotating clockwise, clockwise rotation in white light produced a red afterimage. In the second condition, the spiral was shown stationary in either green or red light. Here the direction of the illusory movement was appropriate to the color in which the stationary spiral was exposed. The reported direction of illusory motion (expansion or contraction) for a color in which the stationary spiral was exposed was opposite to that direction associated with that color during training. Such results create a strong presumption that there are motion detectors in the human system, some of which at least are color specific.

However, in this experiment, as in the ones that follow in this section, it is difficult to rule out alternative explanations of the results besides the operation of various types of cellular detectors. Sekuler (1965) found that gratings of various orientations when exposed after a briefly exposed test bar would mask such a bar. The amount of masking decreased as the tilt of the test bar diverged from that of the grating up to about 45 degrees. Similar results were obtained by Moulihan and Sekuler. However, in their experiment the grating preceded the test bar. The author attributes the results to directionally sensitive contour analysers of the type discovered by Hubel and Wiesel (1962). Other behavioral experiments which seek to establish the existence of similar analysers by psychophysical means have been performed by Pantle and Sekuler (1968). Enroth-Cugell and Robson (1966) have identified cells in the visual system which tend to be maximally responsive to certain sizes of stimulus Pantle and Sekuler (1968) showed an elevation of threshold for bars of a particular width after the inspection of bars of a similar width. More recently, Weisstein (1970) has attempted to measure neural symbolic activity by using psychophysical measures of the type outlined in this section. If a smaller object is placed in front of a larger object, we see the smaller object in front of a continuous larger object. That is, just because we do not see that position of the larger object with the smaller object in front of it, we still perceive the larger object as continuous or without a hole in it.

Weisstein attempted to demonstrate that a neural model exists corresponding to that part of the object which, while unseen, was still in a way perceived. To do this, she placed a cube in front of a larger plane that was marked with horizontal black and white bars. She found a decrease in contrast between the black and white bars, not only where the bars had been visible but also in that part of the visual field where they had been hidden from view. Her conclusion is that such a change "may indicate the existence of a neural mechanism which conveys the information 'in back of.'" Whether this is the real explanation, further experimental work must determine.

COLUMNAR ORGANIZATION OF THE CORTEX

As was mentioned above, orientation-sensitive cells are arranged in columns with each column at right angles to the surface of the cortex. Each column has cells sensitive to a certain orientation. It has been noted by anatomists (Lorente de No', 1943) that most intracortical connecting axons run at right angles to the surface of the cortex rather than parallel to the surface. Further, the efferent fibers of cells in every cortical layer run downward into the white matter underlying the cortical gray matter. The functional significance of this anatomical arrangement was first made apparent by the studies of Mountcastle (1957). Experimenting on the primary somatosensory cortex of the cat, he found narrow columns of tissue running perpendicular to the surface of the brain which were exclusively concerned with a specific submodality of somethesis. Some columns were exclusively devoted to light touch, others to deep pressure, and so on. Similar results have been obtained in the auditory modality by Hind (1960), Oonishi and Katsuki (1965), and Abeles and Goldstein (1970). It seems that neurons sensitive to a particular frequency are grouped together in the same column.

BINOCULAR INTERACTION

The significance of such a columnar arrangement in the processing of sensory information begins to be understood when we consider binocular interaction. In the visual cortex of the monkey, Hubel and Wiesel (1968) have found that 80 percent of the cells can be driven from either of the two eyes. They are therefore binocularly activated.

It has been found that the two regions (one in each eye) that activate a given binocularly driven unit are related in a highly specific manner. The two retinae may be regarded as two sheets of graph paper with the squares on the two sheets numbered in the same way. When an image of a line is placed on the two sheets so that the squares that are numbered the same are covered in both cases, only one image is seen. The distance at which it is seen depends on how much the eyes converge. If the eyes converge a great deal, the image is seen as close. If the eyes hardly converge at all, the image is seen as far away. In a second case, when an image of a line is placed on the two sheets so that the line falls on squares far from each other on the two sheets, two separate lines are seen. However, the intermediate case yields a somewhat surprising result. When the image of a line is placed on the two sheets so that the squares covered are slightly displaced from each other, then only one line is seen, but it is seen at a different distance from the case where the line falls on the squares numbered the same on each sheet. (This principle is employed to produce a sensation of apparent depth from two completely flat images in stereoscopes.)

The physiological basis of this transformation of information is that not only the squares with the same number on each sheet are connected to the same neuron in the CNS, the same applies to squares which are close neighbors on the two sheets. These are also connected to a common neuron in the CNS. The stimulation of such common neurons then signals relative distance in depth. Different neurons have retinal points attached to them which differ in the degree that they are displaced from each other on the two retinal sheets. It seems, therefore, that different neurons signal different distances in depth (Barlow, Blakemore, and Pettigrew, 1967; Nikara, Bishop, and Pettigrew, 1968; Blakemore, 1969). Blakemore and Pettigrew (1970) have found that the neurons in a given cortical column signal the same depth. A given column appears to have neurons representing a patch of a thin sheet of space. All the cells in a column, though they represent the same distance in depth (the third dimension), also represent neighboring points in the other two dimensions. This is the first type of column found by Blakemore and Pettigrew (1970). A second type of column also exists in which all the cells also are binocularly driven. However, they are all identical when we consider the first two dimensions, but differ along the third dimension, that of depth. Instead of representing a sheet at a certain depth, they represent a thin cylinder of space projecting outward away from the eye. It seems that each point in visual space is represented once in a column, specifying a particular distance away from the two eyes, and again in another column, specifying a particular direction away from the eye. However, it should be noted that the two types of column found by Blakemore and Pettigrew (1970) are not sensitive to points in a literal way. Each column is sensitive only to line segments in a specific orientation, so that each line segment is connected to a particular column on the basis of its orientation, its distance in depth, and its direction away from the eye.

TEMPORAL FACTORS IN VISION

The eye cannot follow changes in illumination which occur above a certain rate. For instance, if the interval between light flashes is too short, these flashes are not seen as separate. Practical interest attaches to this property of eye because it is the basis of cinema and television.

The properties of the eye in reacting to the temporal characteristics of stimulation are probably best considered by starting with the initiation of neural impulses at the retina. Any limitation in the ability to follow rapid changes there is bound to be a limitation imposed on the whole visual system. If no signal reporting a change arises peripherally, the visual system has no information that such a visual change has occurred, whatever the changes in the physical stimulus. Therefore, if we find that the limitations of our visual capacities, determined behaviorally, coincide with the limitations in the speed of the photochemical responses on the retina, the behavioral data are adequately explained.

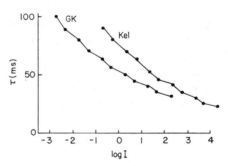

FIG. 3–14. Variation of the critical time τ as a function of the logarithm of luminance. *GK* represents the results of Graham and Kemp (in milli-lamberts). *Kel* indicates the results of Keller (in trolands). (From Pieron, II., *Contributions to Sensory Physiology*, W. D. Neff (ed.); New York: Academic Press, 1965.)

When light reaches the retina, no neural activity leaves the retina for 20 to 70 msec. This is known as retinal lag, and it is shorter for bright lights and longer for dim lights. Related to this is a certain period known as the critical time, or τ, over which the light stimulus is averaged by the eye. The same number of photons, however, distributed in time within a certain brief period, produces the same visual sensation. This is known as Bloch's law, and is a special case of the Bunsen-Roscoe law. (This states that the product of intensity of stimulus and its total time is constant $[i \times t = k]$.) The length of the critical time decreases with increasing intensity of the stimulating light (Fig. 3–14). Though most of the evidence relating to the critical time, τ, has been obtained through psychophysical methods, Grusser and Kapp (1958) obtained an τ value of 25 msec. recording action potentials from ganglion cells in the cat's retina. Whatever the spacing of the same two flashes within this critical time of 25 msec., the same number of action potentials was recorded. As this time is close to what would be expected from results from psychophysical data (Piéron, 1965), it seems that the averaging over a certain small interval of time (which has been described above) is a characteristic of the visual process before, or at, the ganglion cell level.

The eye's ability to distinguish steady from intermittent stimulation (flicker) has been extensively studied by behavioral methods. Various general relationships have emerged at the psychophysical level. It is approximately true that flicker fusion frequency (the frequency at which flicker becomes indistinguishable from a steady light) rises as the logarithm of the intensity of stimulating light. This is called the Ferry-Porter law. More accurate measurement shows that the curve relating stimulus intensity to fusion frequency is divided into two parts with a kink in the middle. The steeper rise at higher intensities is attributable to the cones.

On the neural side, a suggested limitation on the rate at which flicker can be perceived lies in the frequency at which the optic tract discharges at a given level of steady illumination. One might argue that flicker can only be detected by successively more frequent and less frequent groupings of action potentials. This cannot occur unless the rate of neural discharge at a given level of intensity is much higher than the rate of flicker imposed on the eye. However, as we saw above, there are ganglion cells which respond with a discharge only at the "on" and others only at the "off" position of illumination. Such elements might therefore signal intermittency without the limitation which has just been described.

But the limitation on the perception of rate of flicker occurs before we reach the optic nerve. Studies on ganglion cells in the retina of the cat have been undertaken by Enroth (1952, 1953), Grusser and Rabelo (1958), and Reidemeister and Grusser (1959). From such studies it seems that the fusion point of flicker is determined chiefly by the averaging of stimulation over the critical time, τ, which occurs before the message from the retina is translated into action potentials at the ganglion cell level. Discharges, indistinguishable from those in response to steady illumination, occur in ganglion cells at rates close to those expected from the critical time, τ, as measured by Grusser and Kapp (1958). Ganglion cells of the "on-off" variety (discharging when illumination comes on and goes off) produce a response indistinguishable from their discharge under steady illumination at a frequency of about 35 flashes per second. Slightly lower rates are necessary for "on" and "off" types of ganglion cells to produce a discharge such as that which is given to steady illumination. Measurements were taken at a similar intensity as that used in the experiment of Grusser and Kapp, who used double flashes. Given a critical time, τ, of 25 msec., over which perfect averaging takes place, we would expect a rate of 40 flashes per second to be indistinguishable from a steady light.

Another interesting phenomenon is associated with intermittent stimulation: the Brücke phenomenon, discovered in 1864. When flicker occurs at about 10 per second, and while it is clearly perceived as flicker, the flickering light appears brighter than a steady light and brighter than other flickers. Such a brightness enhancement seems to have its origin before, or at, the level of the ganglion cells in the retina. Grusser and Creutzfeldt (1957) have shown a similar enhancement of activity in the ganglion cells of the retina in the cat.

Eye Movements and the Visual Image

Because visual adaptation is rapid, frequent changes in illumination are necessary for the continuous functioning of elements of the visual system. Ditchburn and Ginsborg (1952) and Ratliff (1952), by the use of ingenious optical systems, were able to compensate for the movements of the eye and so to stabilize the image thrown on the retina. Under such conditions, the image fades out within a few seconds. Normal vision can be maintained only by making the image move across the retina or by introducing flicker (Cornsweet, 1956). Such fading is normally counteracted by small, rapid eye movements. However, considerable fading can occur in spite of small eye movements even under conditions of voluntary fixation. A black bar on a white ground will tend to fade if it is steadily fixated for about a minute, as the reader can readily observe, and the whole visual field will even become obscured, as observed by Aubert (1865). In the periphery, disappearance is even more rapid. This is called the Troxler (1804) phenomenon.

Though it was stated above the visual adaptation is rapid and that movement of the image is therefore necessary to maintain continued visual functioning, it is not clear at what level such adaptation takes place, or indeed whether it can be considered adaptation in the usual sense. It has been shown that neural activity at the retina (Hartline, 1938; Barlow and Sparrock, 1964) and at the cortex (Burns et al., 1962; Hubel and Wiesel, 1962) declines substantially during stimulation by a stationary pattern and that movements of such a pattern which mimic those induced by eye movements induce strong neural activity. However, Riggs and Whittle (1967) measured evoked neural activity at the retina and at the occipital part of the scalp (overlying the visual areas) and found no corresponding loss of electrical activity during subjective fading of the image due to stabilization (Fig. 3–15). They used a flickering pattern

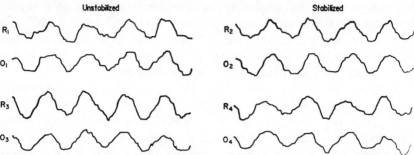

FIG. 3–15. Sample records of potential waves evoked by alternation of black and white stripes viewed under unstabilized (left) and stabilized (right) viewing conditions. R_1 and O_1 are simultaneously cumulated potential waves from retinal and occipital leads respectively during normal (unstabilized) viewing. R_2 and O_2 are simultaneous records during stabilized viewing. R_3 and O_3, and R_4 and O_4 are further examples of the same kind. Each record is a 0.1 sec. segment representing 2,048 cumulations of potential waves produced by stripe alternation at the rate of 47.4 alternations per second in subject R. Median amplitudes of retinal potentials are 1.3 and 1.1 microvolts respectively during unstabilized and stabilized viewing; median occipital potentials are 1.0 and 1.0 μV respectively for unstabilized and stabilized viewing. Subject reported almost complete disappearance during stabilized viewing. (From Lorrin A. Riggs and Paul Whittle, "Human Occipital and Retinal Potentials Evoked by Subjectively Faded Visual Stimuli," *Vis. Res.*, 7:441–51, 1967.)

in order to produce an electrical signal that could be readily detected. The image faded in spite of the intermittent nature of the stimulus. The fact that such fading occurred during flicker also tends to rule out an explanation in terms of simple adaptation. It is possible that images which do not move with respect to the retina are actively suppressed and that this may be a mechanism for getting rid of troublesome afterimages.

Such suppression of unwanted images takes place in the case of binocular rivalry. If two quite different images are placed in the two retinae, in most cases there is not a perception of an average of what the two eyes see separately. Instead, we see only one of the two different images. The other one is suppressed. Riggs and Whittle (1967) found from occipital scalp recordings that evoked potentials were undiminished. Van Balen (1964) and Lansing (1964), investigating the same phenomenon under slightly different conditions, found a small decrement in the evoked occipital potentials.

VISUAL ACUITY

Visual acuity, or the capacity to resolve or discriminate fine detail, depends on (a) the configuration and illumination of the stimulus, (b) where such detail falls on the retina, and (c) whether the retina is stationary with regard to the object being viewed or is in motion. Because of the difference the configuration of the stimulus makes, that is, what kind of detail we are interested in resolving, three main tests of acuity have been adopted, though other tests would give yet different results. In the first type of test, acuity is measured by the minimum separable. Here we determine how small a white gap between two black lines or blocks can be made before such lines or blocks are seen as one. Under good conditions of illumination, the gap that can be seen corresponds well with the diameter of a single cone, as estimated by Polyak (1941). This subtends about 24 seconds of visual angle at the center of the fovea. As illumination decreases, so does acuity. One obvious reason for low acuity at low intensities is that the total number of light quanta striking the retina from the region of the gap may be below the threshold for vision. Increasing the size of the gap increases the number of quanta reflected from the gap, and so a larger gap becomes visible (Pirenne, 1962). Further, at low intensities, rods will detect light when it is below the cone threshold. Consequently, the observer is forced to use regions of the retina outside the fovea centralis, where rods occur. Not only does each of these receptors subtend a larger visual angle, but it is probable that excitation from many rods converges on a single fiber. Hence illumination is averaged over a larger area and detail is thereby lost.

Even under optimum conditions of illumination, acuity may be considerably worse than the diameter of a single cone. This can be due to defects of the image-forming mechanism. It has often been pointed out that even the best the eye is capable of in bringing a line half a minute of arc into focus still leaves a considerable blurring of the image on the retina. The illumination from such a narrow strip will to a large extent be distributed over a few cones. However, the important thing to consider is the gradient of illumination formed by the image. If the disparity in the amount of light falling on one or more receptors (compared with neighboring receptors) is greater than the differential threshold for brightness, a change of illumination, and so a gap, should be seen. It is true that the gap may be seen as wider than it actually is, but the test of acuity is whether it can be seen, not whether it can be seen as the correct size.

A similar argument can be applied to the second measure of acuity, the minimum visible. In this test a fine black line is superimposed on a white ground. Acuity here is measured by the minimum width of such a line which can be seen. Using such a measurement, one can detect a line whose width subtends an angle of 1 second, which is much smaller than the diameter of a single cone. This may be explained on the same lines as above. Provided the image of the line decreases the illumination on a row of cones, however large or numerous they may be, by more than the differential threshold for brightness, the line will be reported as seen.

It is of interest to note that acuity is better when the eye is not moving, as might be expected. This has been shown by Riggs et al. (1953) and Ratliff (1952), who concluded: "It has also been demonstrated that the relatively large changes in the position of the eye as a result of the rapid tremor are a hindrance to monocular acuity." This finding is in contradistinction to the fact that if the image remains fixed on the retina, fading occurs, with a consequent loss of acuity (Riggs et al., 1953).

A third test of acuity determines the smallest misalinement of two lines. Starting with a single long vertical line, one of the two halves is shifted parallel to itself. The smallest deviation from the continuation of the line which can be detected is called a measure of vernier acuity. Optimal values are of the order of 5 to 10 seconds of arc, deteriorating if the two lines are shortened. This judgment probably depends on our ability to extrapolate the course of a line.

CEREBRAL LESIONS AND VISION

Total destruction of the visual cortex in man appears to produce total blindness (Teuber, 1961). In the monkey after such a loss, differences in the total amount of light reaching the eye may still be reacted to, but pattern vision is absent (Kluver, 1942). Similarly, pattern vision is destroyed in the cat and rat (Teuber, 1961). An exception to this has been reported by Doty (1961). Apparently, if the striate cortex is destroyed in kittens, they will perform normally as adults in tests of shape discrimination.

In animals, destruction of the striate cortex leads to a loss of retention of habits based on the discrimination of visual intensity. However, such habits may be relearned. The explanation of such an apparent memory loss is obscure. There are many possibilities. One is that the animal relearns by using another part of its neural apparatus which is still intact, perhaps by reacting on the basis of different cues. This possibility is supported by the observations of Kluver (1942) and Bauer and Cooper (1964). Kluver found that monkeys with lesions of the striate area can no longer make discriminations on the basis of brightness (luminous flux per unit area) but are still capable of distinguishing on the basis of total luminous flux. That is, the monkey can still perceive the total amount of light reaching the eye but can no longer discriminate between its arrival on different parts of the retina. It is therefore possible for the lesioned monkey to relearn a task (originally learned on the basis, say, of pattern) on the basis of differences in total luminous flux between the discriminanda. Bauer and Cooper have shown that rats with translucent plastic cups over their eyes show good retention of a light-dark discrimination after striate area removal. This contrasts with the poor retention of such a habit after striate removal by a group which learned the habit with unobstructed vision. The wearing of plastic cups over the eyes would force learning on the basis of luminous flux before striate area removal.

It is interesting to note that rats with removal of the striate area can still learn logically complex visual tasks, provided the original visual discrimination remains within their capacity. Bauer and Cooper (1964) were able to train rats with striate lesions to go left when the lights were off and right when they were on. The same task with black and white cards, instead of lights, proved insuperable to the lesioned rats.

A second possibility is that a so-called generalization decrement has occurred. It is possible to produce a "memory loss" in a perfectly normal rat simply by altering an aspect of the total training situation which is seemingly irrelevant to such a discrimination. A third explanation could be that the stimuli to be discriminated still impinge on the animal but that they have altered in appearance to the animal as a result of the lesion. This notion is supported by an experiment of Thompson (1960), who ablated the striate cortex in two stages, which would be expected to make the transition from one kind of appearance to another more gradual. Under these conditions, he found good postoperative retention of the habit.

The fact that animals can relearn (or retain) a visual intensity discrimination after destruction of the striate cortex and subsequent degeneration of the LGN means that other parts of the central nervous system besides the LGN and striate cortex receive fibers from the optic tract. Two such areas are known. The first is the superior colliculus; the second is the pretectal area.

In the cat, at least, there is a good point-to-point projection of the retina to the colliculi (Apter, 1945). Blake (1959) has found that pattern discrimination in this animal is grossly impaired after lesions of this area. In man, these structures are credited with a role in the control of eye movement. The pretectal area, on the other hand, seems concerned with the light reflex of the pupil. It therefore seems that other portions of the nervous system besides the pathway to the LGN and striate cortex can subserve visual function. However, though discrimination of the total amount of light is possible, the differential threshold for such a discrimination is sharply raised.

Partial lesions of the striate area in man produce scotomata or regions of the visual field in which normal object vision is absent. However, it seems that when figures are exposed to that there is a continuity of contour between the part of the figure exposed outside and inside the scotoma, such figures can be "completed" (Teuber, 1961). Parts of the figure which would not be seen within the scotoma if they were presented alone seem to be in some sense visible when they are connected to parts of the figure falling on an area outside the scotoma where vision is normally possible. However, impairment of vision as a result of brain lesion does not manifest itself only as a scotoma. There may be areas of the visual field where objects can be seen, but only as long as other objects are not present in less impaired parts of the visual field. They may either become less distinct ("obscuration") or disappear altogether ("extinction") (Bender, 1952). When the object in the less impaired part of the field is removed, the object in the more impaired part of the field reappears. Similar phenomena occur in the somatosensory system (see Chapter 6).

Two other types of visual sensory deficit appear after brain lesions. The first are associated with injuries causing scotomata; the second with any brain injury at all. The first kind of change may be exhibited by parts of the visual field where object vision appears normal. Contours fade more rapidly, flicker fusion thresholds are reduced, dark adaptation is impaired, as is perception of real and apparent movement. The second type of visual change is linked with lesions anywhere, whether in the striate cortex or not. The patient finds it hard to detect figures which are embedded in other shapes. In animals such as the rat and the monkey, it seems that only small islands of striate cortex need be spaced, when lesions are made, to preserve the ability to discriminate patterns (Lashley, 1939; Harlow, 1939; Settlage, 1939). However, it is not known whether there are more subtle deficits, as are found in human patients, in the remaining parts of the visual field.

We may ask if the striate area of the cortex is the only one needed for the processing of visual information. In the rat, Lashley found that any lesion, provided it spared the visual cortex, did not interefre with visual discriminative capacity. In the cat, however, Myers (1956) and Sperry (1958) found that increasing ablation of areas other than the visual cortex produces increasing visual deficit. Evidence from human head injuries also strongly suggests that other areas of the cortex are involved in visual perception. Injuries to the posterior parts of the parietal lobe and adjoining occipital cortex cause a syndrome known as visual disorientation (Holmes, 1918). Many aspects of the perception of space are disturbed. The patient finds it difficult to estimate the distance of objects and is unable to estimate length and size. Objects, though seen, are not reacted to (visual inattention). It may be that such symptoms are not due to a destruction of the parietal cortex but, instead, to interruption of tracts which connect the striate area with a part of the cortex of the temporal lobe, an area of which appears to subserve visual functions.

The role of the temporal lobe in visual function can be discerned

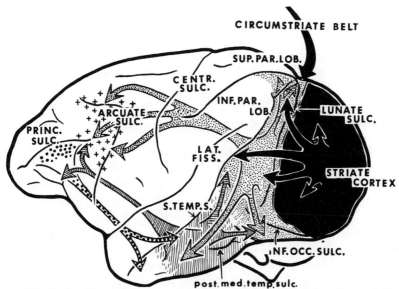

FIG. 3–16. Diagrammatic representation of some of the corticocortical fiber connections observed by Kuypers et al. (From Kuypers, H. G. T. M., et al., *Experimental Neurology;* New York: Academic Press, 1965.)

in some of the symptoms of the Kluver-Bucy syndrome (see Chapter 10). Following the bilateral removal of the temporal lobes in the monkey, there is found, among other symptoms, a visual agnosia. That is, the animal does not seem to recognize objects even though it can see them.

It is mainly the lesion of the inferotemporal or ventral temporal cortex which produces the visual deficit which has been noted (Mishkin, 1954). The connections between the striate area and this area are transcortical. Monkeys with lesions of the inferotemporal area seem to show a disproportionate difficulty with visual discriminations, requiring a considerable degree of abstraction.

Further information about the role of the inferotemporal cortex comes from microelectrode studies. Gross et al. (1969), working on the monkey, have shown that single units in this area respond to complex visual properties. For instance, one unit responded most strongly to a cut out of a monkey's hand.

Through an ingenious combination of behavioral and surgical techniques, Mishkin (in press) showed that the inferotemporal region in the monkey is connected to the striate area on both sides via a belt of cortex, surrounding the striate area, termed by Kuypers et al. (1965) "a circumstriate cortical belt." This belt comprises the parastriate and preoccipital areas, analogous to visual areas II and III in the cat (Figs. 3–12, 3–16) and corresponds to areas 18 and 19 in Brodmann's classification. This circumstriate belt sends fibers to the inferior part of the temporal lobe and to the frontal lobe around the arcuate sulcus. The inferior part of the temporal lobe sends fibers back to parts of the circumstriate belt and to the lateral and ventrolateral surface of the frontal lobe. Finally, the frontal lobes send fibers to the inferior part of the temporal lobe.

CENTRIFUGAL EFFECTS IN THE VISUAL SYSTEM

It has been suggested that there are pathways leading to the retina in such a way as to influence its activity. The anatomical evidence for such pathways is difficult to assess. Walter (1958), in one of the more recent studies, confirms the existence of fibers running into the retina (because not all fibers in the optic tract degenerate when the retina is removed). However, whether such fibers are directly connected to the visual system is in doubt because at least some of these centrifugal fibers run to blood vessels in the retina. Granit (1955) has studied the problem by using electrophysiological techniques. He stimulated the brain stem while placing microelectrodes close to ganglion cells in the retina. He was able to show that brain stem stimulation could inhibit and excite single ganglion cells, and he attempted to argue (1962) that the observed effects could not have been due to vascular changes.

Evidence for centrifugal effects at higher levels of the visual system is less equivocal. There is evidence, for instance, that the striate area of the cortex sends impulses back to the lateral geniculate (Niemer and Jimenez-Castellanos, 1950). Further, in mammals there is an increase in development of the projection from the visual cortex to the tectum (Crosby and Henderson, 1948) as we ascend the phylogenetic scale. This development goes hand in hand with a decrease in importance of the superior colliculi. This suggests that the cortex assumes increased control over eye movements.

Visual Afferents to the Brain Stem

Activity due to strong visual stimulation is not only relayed to areas with a specific visual function, such as the lateral geniculate, but also to large areas of the brain stem. Though the anatomical basis for this is obscure, evoked potentials with long latencies (45–25 msec.) have been recorded in the brain stem in response to a strong light flash by Ingvar and Hunter (1955). The long latencies recorded imply that such effects are carried either by very thin fibers or across a large number of synapses.

chapter 4

Hearing

Before embarking upon a description of the organ which enables us to detect sound, it may be well to say a few words about some elementary physical properties of the stimuli which excite the ear. In the present context, it is not necessary to consider how sound is generated or propagated but simply what kind of changes are sensed by the ear when they arrive at its receptor surfaces. Such changes can be brought about by straightforward mechanical stimulation, as was done by Wilska (1935). He placed a thin rod against the membrane of the eardrum and was in this way able to move this membrane rapidly in and out, producing a sensation of sound. When we hear sounds in the normal manner, the eardrum is moved in and out in a similar way, but the movements are imparted by rapid in and out motions of the air molecules impinging on the eardrum, instead of a solid rod. In order to produce such a sensation of sound, the number of in-out movements has to be between about 30 per second to about 20,000 per second. The displacement of the drum membrane which will produce a just detectable sensation of sound when the number of in-out motions is 1,000 per second is about 10^{-8} cm., a surprisingly small distance.

In describing sound vibrations or waves, it is customary to specify the number of times per second the in-out cycle occurs, for example, 1,000 cps. (cycles per second). Further, the physically most simple and important case of in-out movement is depicted by a sine wave. This is a curve which traces the up-down movement of a point traveling on the periphery of a circle rotating at a constant speed around its center and displays this up-down movement of the point as a function of time. For instance, such a curve would show how the height of the crank handle on a wheel rotating at a constant speed varies with time (Fig. 4–1). The usefulness of such a specification of sound will be apparent when it is stated that any wave motion can be represented as a sum of sine components of differing frequencies and extents of movement, according to Fourier's theorem.

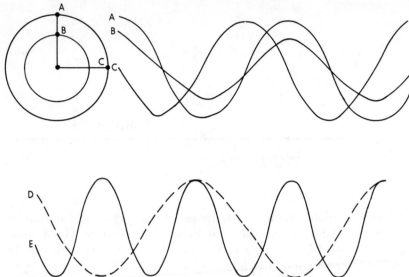

FIG. 4–1. The curves A, B, and C are sine waves traced by the height of the points *A*, *B*, and *C* as the disc on which these points are drawn rotates at a constant speed. Curves *A* and *B* do not vary in phase, because points *A* and *B* lie on the same straight line passing through the center of the disc. The curves *A* and *B* are, however, of different amplitude, as point *A* lies on a circle of larger radius than point *B*. Curves *A* and *C* are 90 degrees out of phase because the lines connecting them to the center of the circle form an angle of 90 degrees. They are, however, of the same amplitude because the points *A* and *C*, whose motions they trace, art on the same circle.

Curves *D* and *E* depict two sine waves traced out by the same point on the periphery of a circle. In the case of curve *E*, the circle was rotating at twice the speed than when it was tracing out curve *D*. Consequently, the frequency depicted by curve *E* is double the frequency depicted by curve *A*.

If we take vibrations which can be described by a simple sine wave, the frequency per second of these vibrations moving the eardrum corresponds closely to a perceived attribute of sound—its pitch. Another property of the sound wave that it is useful to consider is its phase. For instance, if we take the example we used above, we can imagine a wheel with two crank handles rotating at a constant speed. We can plot the height of the two handles separately as a function of time. If the two handles are set 90 degrees apart on the wheel (the angle having its apex at the center of the wheel), then the two sine waves traced by the two handles are said to be 90 degrees out of phase. If this is the case, it can easily be seen that as one wave attains its peak the other is always halfway between them, and vice versa. If the two waves are generated by points 180 degrees out of phase, the lowermost portion of one curve occurs at the same time as the uppermost portion of the other. The excursions above the center of the imaginary wheel may be regarded as positive (pushing the eardrum inward) and those below as negative (pushing the eardrum outward). This is important, as the eardrum in responding to such movements adds them, so that two sound waves of the same frequency and in-out movement will cancel out completely if they are 180 degrees out of phase.

When considering vibrations, it is useful to specify not only their frequency and phase but also the distance of the displacement of the vibrating body. For instance, two sounds can be identical in frequency, but one may produce larger vibrations. To specify their difference, it would be possible to refer to the distances of displacement caused by the two sounds. However, owing to the extremely small size of such distances they are difficult to measure. Consequently, measurements are made in terms of pressure generated by sounds on a surface on which they impinge. Such pressure is directly proportional to the displacements during vibration, provided that the frequency of vibration is kept constant, and also the physical properties of the vibrating medium. Given the same amount of displacement of a medium (to-and-fro extent of movement), pressure increases in direct ratio as the frequency of vibration goes up. Thus a measurement of pressure is another way of specifying the displacement during a vibration, except that the frequency of the vibration and the physical properties of the vibrating medium are also taken into account.

However, measurements of the amplitude of sounds are not made directly in terms of pressure (dynes per square centimeter). Instead, a logarithmic measure of comparison is used, and this for two main reasons. In making discriminations of loudness, the ear works according to Weber's law; thus a threshold difference is always approximately the same logarithmic increment. Second, the range of pressures that the ear can respond to before sound becomes painful is of the order of $10^{6.5}$ to 10 (630 dynes per sq. cm. to 0.0002 dynes per sq. cm.). Direct numerical comparisons of sound pressures would therefore be unwieldy. Consequently, sound pressures are compared by using the decibel (db.) notation. The difference in the pressure of two sounds in decibels is the 20th multiple of the logarithm (to base 10) of the ratio of the two sound pressures being compared. For instance, a tenfold increase in pressure is an increase of 20 db.

The organs of hearing make it possible for animals to respond to the minute rapid vibrations described above. Most of the features of the outer and middle ear are such as to minimize the loss of energy when such vibrations are transferred from air to the rather denser media of which the apparatus of the inner ear is composed. This apparatus in the inner ear translates the vibrations imposed upon it into neural activity, extracting their temporal characteristics, such as frequency, time of arrival, and amplitude.

The outer ear consists of the pinna or auricle, the familiar ear flap, which apparently is of little functional significance in hearing in man, and a short tube, about one inch in length, called the auditory meatus, which leads to the eardrum, or tympanic membrane. The characteristics of this tube are of functional significance since it acts as a resonator by virtue of its length and shape. Because of its resonant characteristics, the meatus produces a pressure amplification of between 5 and 10 db.

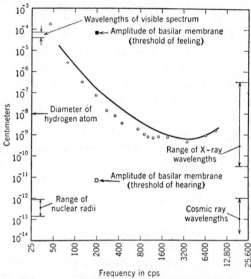

FIG. 4–2. Amplitude of vibration of the eardrum at threshold of hearing. Circles: data of Wilska. Solid line: amplitude of vibration of air molecules at threshold intensity as calculated by Stevens and Davis. (From Bekesy and Rosenblith, Chapter 27 in *Handbook of Experimental Psychology*, S. S. Stevens (ed.); New York: John Wiley, 1951.)

over the range from 2,000 to 5,500 cycles per second, dropping off outside these limits. This range corresponds to the region of greatest sensitivity of the ear (see Fig. 4–2). Further, the meatus protects the eardrum mechanically against damage, which it would sustain were the eardrum mounted on the body surface, and against variations in humidity and temperature, which would greatly affect its elastic characteristics.

The eardrum is a thin membrane at the base of the meatus; it has the form of a flattened cone, with its apex pointing inward relative to the exterior of the head. Most of the cone is relatively rigid, a flaccid fold on the lower rim permits the cone to move in response to imposed vibrations. Such movements in response to sounds encountered at the threshold of hearing are exceedingly minute, being the same order as the diameter of a hydrogen molecule (10^{-8} cm.). The eardrum has an area of 69 sq. mm.

The motions of the eardrum are then transmitted to the apparatus of the middle ear. This consists of a chain of little bones or ossicles. The first, the malleus (hammer), is connected to the eardrum and also to the second ossicle, the incus (or anvil), which in turn is attached to the stapes (or stirrup). The footplate of the stapes is implanted in the oval window by the annular ligament. The three ossicles are connected by the articulate ligaments. The whole system of ossicles is suspended in the cavity of the middle ear by eight ligaments, two of which lead to small muscles: the tensor tympani and the stapedius. These two muscles contract reflexly, with a latency of about 10 msec., in response to strong sounds in such a way as to decrease transmission of sound down the ossicular chain. This tends to protect the mechanism of the inner ear against potential damage by loud sounds. The middle ear has a second mode of defense against loud sounds. The ossicles are so suspended on their ligaments that they can vibrate in two different modes. Normally the stapes rotates on an axis at one end of the footplate and perpendicular to it. When, however, vibrations of large amplitude occur, the stapes rotates about an axis at right angles to the first mode, on an axis lying through and parallel to the footplate, thus reducing the efficiency of transmission to the oval window.

Though the detailed motions of the ossicular chain in transmitting sound are not completely agreed upon, there seems no doubt that the complex ossicular chain performs two functions. First, it performs the function of a lever in reducing the amplitude of excursion at the eardrum to a much smaller displacement at the oval window. The second function is to apply the energy acting on the larger surface of the eardrum to the much smaller surface of the oval window under the footplate of the stapes, which is about 3.2 sq. mm. This means, therefore, that the pressure (force per unit area) to the oval window is much greater than pressure applied to the eardrum. The effect of these two functions of the middle ear is to increase the efficiency of energy transfer from the air to the denser media of the inner ear, acting like a transformer to match the two impedances. It can be calculated from the mechanical properties of the inner ear and air that 99.9 percent of the intensity of sound (30 db.) falling on the ear would be lost by being reflected back if it were not for the mechanism of the middle ear. Such a figure is in agreement with the degree of hearing loss (again upward of about 30 db.) in patients who have lost their middle ear apparatus. The middle ear has a resonant frequency of about 1,700 cps. This, in combination with the resonant frequency of the auditory meatus, gives the ear its overall sensitivity curve (Fig. 4-2).

The vibrations of the stapedial footplate are transmitted to the cochlea via the oval window (Fig. 4–3). The cochlea is shaped like a snail shell—a spiral bony duct. This duct is further divided into three divisions: the scala vestibuli, the scala tympani, and the cochlear duct or scala media (Fig. 4–4). The scala vestibuli and the scala tympani contain perilymph and are joined at the apex of the cochlea through a small opening called the helicotrema. At the basal end of the scala tympani lies the round window, closed by a thin membrane. Thus the stapedial footplate can move into the oval window as it can displace the incompressible fluid in the inelastic bony duct out through the round window. The scala vestibuli is divided from the cochlear duct by the thin Reissner's membrane (which does not seem to contribute significantly to

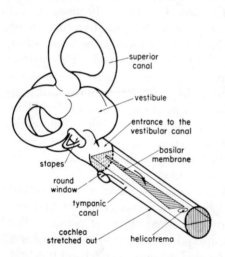

FIG. 4–3. Schematic drawing of the cochlea and labyrinth. The cochlea, normally wound, has been stretched out to form a straight tube. Note that the basilar membrane widens toward the helicotrema. (From Rasmussen, G. L., and Windle, W. F., *Neural Mechanisms of the Auditory and Vestibular Systems;* courtesy of Charles C Thomas, Publisher, Springfield, Ill.)

the mechanical properties of the inner ear). On the other side, the cochlear duct is divided from the scala tympani by the basilar membrane. The length of the basilar membrane in man is about 35 mm. It is about 0.04 mm. wide at the stapes and increases in width toward the helicotrema (as the cochlea itself narrows) to 0.5 mm. The membrane is not under tension but exhibits a decrease in stiffness of at least 100 to 1, and increases in mass as we ascend from the end near the stapes to that near the helicotrema. Because of this gradation in its mechanical properties, the basilar membrane serves to analyze the incoming sound waves.

When the stapes vibrates, pressure is transmitted to the fluid in the cochlea which travels virtually instantaneously to the round window. Hence a driving force is applied to the whole of the basilar membrane almost simultaneously. As Békésy (1960) was the first to observe (in 1928), when this occurs a wave appears to travel up the basilar mem-

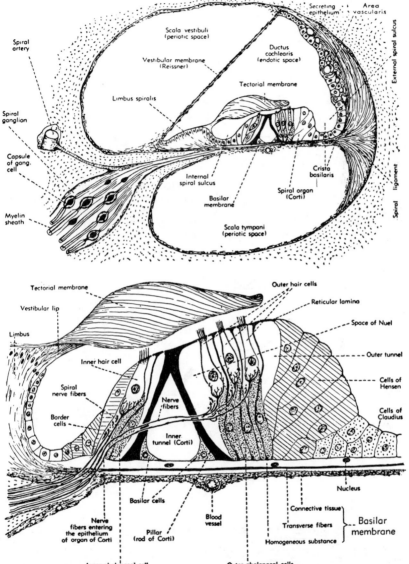

FIG. 4-4. Upper: Vertical section of human cochlea. Lower: Organ of Corti, basilar membrane, and tectorial membrane in greater magnification.

brane from the stapes. The amplitude of such traveling waves increases as they go from the oval window up the basilar membrane, reaching a maximum at a point on the membrane, the location of which depends on the frequency of the imposed oscillation (Figs. 4–5, 4–6). High frequencies give rise to waves which end very close to the stapes. Lower

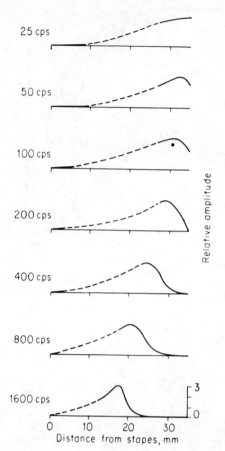

25 cps

50 cps

100 cps

200 cps

400 cps

800 cps

1600 cps

Relative amplitude

3

0

0   10   20   30
Distance from stapes, mm

FIG. 4–5. Maximum displacement of the basilar membrane at various imposed frequencies of sound. (From Békésy, *Akust Zeits,* 1943. 8. 66. Courtesy of S. Hirzel Verlag.)

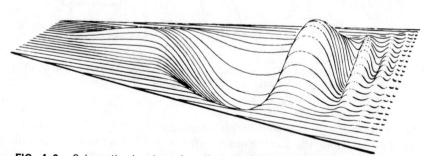

FIG. 4–6. Schematic drawing of a displacement pattern on the basilar membrane when a sound is transmitted to the cochlea. (From Rasmussen, G. L., and Windle, W. F., (eds.), *Neural Mechanisms of the Auditory and Vestibular Systems,* 1960; courtesy of Charles C Thomas, Publisher, Springfield, Ill.)

frequencies produce waves which travel further toward the helicotrema before tapering off. The direction of travel from the stapedial end toward the helicotrema is the same whether or not the initiating vibrations are applied from the stapedial end, for instance, where sound is transmitted through the bone of the skull. According to Békésy (1960), such a system is closely analogous to a set of reeds, each with increasing resonant frequency. If a driving signal of a certain frequency is applied simultaneously to all the reeds, that reed whose resonant frequency is closest to the driving signal will vibrate maximally. This is essentially the model of the basilar membrane's action put forward by Helmholtz (1863) just over a century ago. However, in Helmholtz's model there is no traveling wave. The appearance of traveling waves in such a model, to conform to observations of the basilar membrane, is easily provided by elastic coupling between the reeds. This is done by weaving a narrow rubber band to connect the reeds to each other. In this way a mechanical interconnection between the resonators is obtained as it presumably exists in the basilar membrane, which is, after all, a continuous strip (Fig. 4–7). In the model of interconnected reeds, traveling waves originate at one end independently of where the driving frequency is applied.

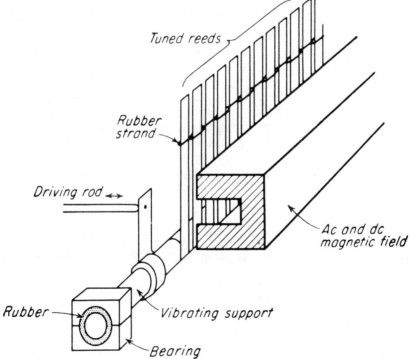

FIG. 4–7. Arrangement of resonant reeds to demonstrate traveling wave. (From Bekesy, *J. Acoust. Soc. Amer.*, 27; courtesy of Acoustical Society of America.)

As in the cochlea, the largest amplitude of movement of the waves occurs close to the point where the resonant frequency of the reeds corresponds to the frequency of the driving waves. As can be seen from Figure 4–8, there is a fairly sharp falling off beyond this point. In such a way, the frequency of a sound wave is translated into a place of maximum movement along the basilar membrane. However, it should not be assumed from the foregoing that the traveling wave generated on the basilar membrane adds nothing to the resonance analysis of sound impinging on the cochlea. Tonndorf (1962) suggested that the traveling waves generated especially by brief sounds (e.g., clicks, thumps) prob-

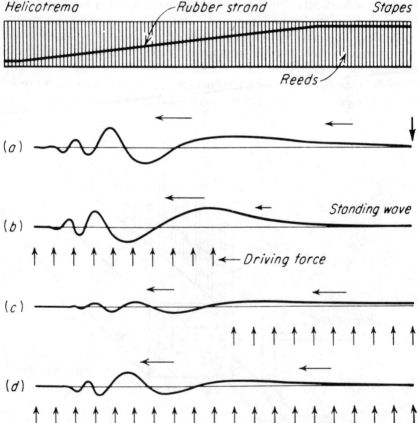

FIG. 4–8. The upper drawing shows how the rubber band was interlaced among the reeds to give coupling that produced traveling waves like those of the cochlea. The waves shown below represent different ways of actuating the system. In *a*, vibrations were applied to one reed on the right, in *b*, to the more flexible half of the reeds on the left, in *c*, to the stiffer half of the reeds on the right, and in *d*, to the support. (From B́ekésy, *J. Acoust. Soc. Amer.,* 27; courtesy of Acoustical Society of America.)

ably provide an important method of analysis and identification of such sounds.

So far we have seen how the minute vibrations of the sound waves are transmitted to the basilar membrane and how they are translated into motions of this organ. We now have to consider how the motions of the basilar membrane produce nervous activity giving information about the pitch and loudness of sounds. The translation from movement to neural activity in the cochlea is accomplished by the expedient of placing sensory cells all along the length of the cochlear duct.

These sensory cells lie in the organ of Corti, which in turn lies on the basilar membrane, on the side of the basilar membrane, which bounds the cochlear duct. The sensory cells are known as hair cells because hairs protrude from them. These hairs protrude into the tectorial membrane (and so are embedded on their other end in it [Fig. 4–4]). The tectorial membrane overlaps the organ of Corti in the cochlear duct and is hinged on one side of cochlea only, a little way above the basilar membrane. When the basilar membrane is displaced, the tectorial membrane also moves. However, being hinged at a different point, a shearing action occurs between it and the basilar membrane, carrying the organ of Corti. That is, as the basilar membrane takes the tectorial membrane up with it, a sideways displacement of the two membranes occurs because they are hinged at different points. As the hairs of the hair cells are effectively embedded in the membranes simultaneously, the hairs are bent sideways as the membranes vibrate up and down. This lever-like arrangement is thought to increase the efficiency of energy transfer from fluid to the cells themselves.

The hair cells are divided into two groups: the internal and external hair cells. The internal hair cells lie in one row close to the bony shaft around which the cochlea is wound. They are flask shaped, about 12 μ in diameter, and there are about 3,500 of them in the cochlea. The external hair cells lie in three or four rows. They are about 8 μ in diameter and 20,000 in number. Each external hair cell has a large number of hairs protruding out of it (more than 100 in man), set in the form of a W. In the internal hair cells, the hairs are set in two almost straight rows. Such morphological differences may be correlated with differences in function (Keidel, 1962).

The bending of the hairs by the displacement of the basilar and tectorial membrane somehow initiates activity in the auditory nerve. Such activity in the nerve is of the usual all-or-none type. The triggering of the auditory nerve by the bending of the hairs, however, seems to be mediated through an intervening electrical process called the cochlear microphonic. The movement of the hairs in some way causes changes in electrical potential which can be recorded from the round window of the cochlea. This change in electrical potential follows with considerable fidelity the sound transmitted by the stapes, in the manner of a microphone. If electrodes are placed in the scala tympani or scala vestibuli, the potential variations recorded from them give a good index of the movement of the basilar membrane closest to the electrode. A second type of potential which arises on stimulation is called the summating potential. This seems to be produced by loud sounds, is slowly changing in comparison to the cochlear microphonic, and may be either negative or positive in sign. It is possible that the source of the electrical energy of these varying potentials may be the endolymphatic potential. The cochlear duct is filled with endolymph, a fluid unusually rich in potassium. The cochlear duct has a steady positive potential of about 80 millivolts, which appears to originate in the stria vascularis (which lines one of the sides of the cochlear duct). It may be that this steady energy is released by the bending of the hairs on the organ of Corti to produce the cochlear microphonic, which in turn stimulates the auditory nerve.

The nerve endings of the auditory nerve reach the hair cells through the bony spindle around which the cochlear is wound. In the hollow of this spindle is a long spiral ganglion (the spiral ganglion of Corti), containing some 28,000 cells. The axon-like dendrites of the cells then pass through fine openings in the bone of the cochlea to reach the inner and outer hair cells. Whereas the fibers running to the internal hair cells innervate from one to three such cells, most of these crossing to the external hair cells may be connected to a large number of cells and each cell in turn to a large number of fibers.

This is a good point at which to consider the contribution of the mechanical part of the hearing apparatus to our overall hearing ability. It was seen that different parts of the basilar membrane show a maximum vibration depending on the frequency of vibration imposed upon them. It was also noted that different parts of the organ of Corti (lying upon the basilar membrane) stimulate different nerve fibers. It looks, therefore, as if information concerning the frequency of sound impinging on the ear could be read off simply by seeing what nerve fibers are made active. However, if we look at the diagrams of the traveling wave as it has been observed by Békésy (Fig. 4–5) a relatively large portion of the membrane seems to be vibrating at roughly the same amplitude. That is, the crest of the disturbance on the basilar membrane is rather flat. On the other hand, our ability to discriminate pitch is much finer than would be expected from these properties of the basilar membrane. For tones up to 2,000 cps., we are able to discriminate differences of 2 to 4 cps. at 40 db. above threshold.

To overcome such a lack of selectivity at the mechanical level, Gray (1900) suggested that neural impulses rising on each side of the peak of excitation were somehow suppressed. He called this the principle of maximum stimulation. Békésy (1960) has proposed a "funneling" action on the part of the nervous system. This is a combination of the principles of lateral inhibition and summation. There are instances in which a stronger stimulus adjacent to a weaker one suppresses it. There are also instances where neighboring stimuli simply sum. Békésy proposes that in the cochlea they sum to produce a sensation of loudness but inhibit each other to produce a sharply localized sensation of pitch. He has shown such ideas to be plausible by ingenious experiments in-

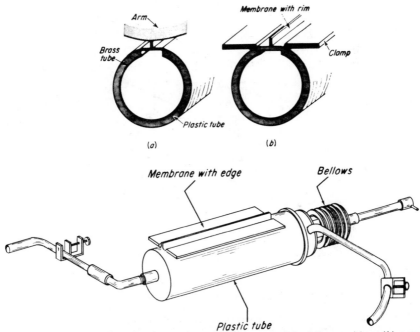

FIG. 4–9. Two cross sections of a dimensional model of the cochlea: (b) near the driving end and (a) near the other end. Detailed view of the model. (From Békésy, *J. Acoust. Soc. Amer.*, 29; courtesy of Acoustical Society of America.)

volving the sensation of vibration along the skin. In one experiment to show inhibition, he applied traveling waves such as he had observed in the cochlea to the skin of the forearm by means of a large mechanical model of the cochlea (Fig. 4–9). He was able to show that the sensation of vibration was sharply localized to the peak of the traveling wave and was not felt at other neighboring points, though the physical extent of vibration was almost identical. In another experiment, he set off vibrators at different frequencies at equally spaced points on the forearm (Fig. 4–10). These were individually adjusted in amplitude so as to produce a sensation of equal magnitude. When they were set to vibrate together, the vibration was felt only at a peak in the center of the whole row of vibrators. The frequency of vibration felt was that of the vibrator in the center. However, the amplitude of vibration felt was much larger than when the center vibrator was the only one vibrating. Such an experiment confirms the notion of funneling. Only one frequency is felt since other frequencies are inhibited. However, the other frequencies, though not perceived, contribute to the felt amplitude of the frequency which inhibits them. Of course, experiments on the properties

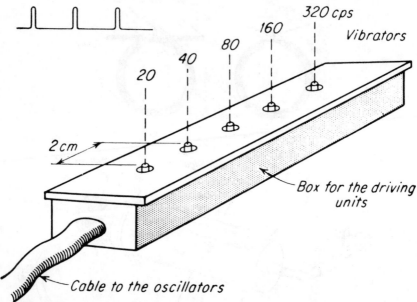

FIG. 4–10. Arrangement of a series of vibrators to show funneling (inhibition and summation). (From Békésy, *J. Acoust. Soc. Amer., 29;* courtesy of Acoustical Society of America.)

of skin sensitivity can serve only as analogies. But if the sensory innervation of the skin produces a sharpening effect, it is plausible to believe that a similar sharpening effect can take place on the basilar membrane.

Other Mechanisms of Frequency Discrimination

A mechanism reading off the place of the biggest bulge on the basilar membrane, as outlined above, could determine what sound frequency was impinging on the ear. However, such a mechanism would lose certain information about the incoming sound wave. It would not indicate, for instance, the precise point in time, during each cycle of pressure change, when a certain portion of the cycle occurred. In other words, such a mechanism would indicate frequency while losing information about phase. To obtain information about phase, messages must be sent indicating when, in time, an increase or decrease in pressure is occurring during each sound cycle. That such accessory information about the phase of a cycle is available can be seen from the performance of the observer in sound localization. It is possible for an observer to localize the source of a continuous sine wave by differences in phase at the two ears. The two ears are some distance apart and sound takes time to travel. Therefore, if the source of sound is nearer one ear, an increase of pressure at the nearer ear will be followed by a similar increase at the other ear some while later. This suggests that information about the precise time of a particular portion of the sound wave is picked up by the ear. There is also evidence from simultaneous unit recordings of firing in the auditory nerve and pressure changes that neural elements fire on the same position on the sound wave. Such information is useful in localizing tones up to frequencies of 1,500 cps. (Cherry, 1961). It therefore seems that information about the temporal spacing of pressure changes is useful up to this frequency even when comparison has to be made between the two ears about the precise timing of a portion of a pressure wave. The usefulness of such timing in identifying pitch might extend to even higher frequencies if successive events occurring in the same ear were being measured by the nervous system, and so might serve as an accessory mechanism of pitch recognition.

One of the apparent limitations of such a system of identifying pitch is the refractory period of the nerve fiber. Having initiated a spike discharge, an auditory nerve fiber cannot fire again for about 1 msec. after, being only 3 to 5 μ in diameter. This would place an upper limit of about 1,000 cps. on the frequency at which any single neuron could follow. However, due to differences between neurons, some neurons could fire on one cycle and others on the next, so that information about frequency could be preserved in a whole bundle of fibers taken together. This is known as the volley principle, and direct recordings of the auditory pathway shows that such a principle could operate up to a frequency of 4,000 cps. Whether information about pitch is actually extracted from the incoming signal simply by an analysis of the frequency of neural impulses is difficult to know. A phenomenon, known as the residue phenomenon of Schouten, is often quoted in support of the idea that the true temporal relations between events in the auditory nerve can produce sensations of pitch. Schouten (1938) has been able to demonstrate that if a high-frequency tone (e.g., 3,000 cps.) is turned on and off 100 times per second, we can hear a 100 cps. tone. It is generally argued that such a sensation cannot be due to a place of resonance at the cochlea, but simply to the periodicity of interruption of the high-frequency tone. However, whether such an argument is entirely correct is open to question. Voots (1962) has shown that the tone corresponding to the frequency of interruption can be heard by patients who cannot hear the high tone being interrupted. These patients must therefore have been obtaining their information from the portion of the cochlea that normally signals low tone information. It could therefore have come either by volleying or by place coding. The behavioral evidence is therefore still equivocal on this point.

Some interesting consequences emerge from the analysis of frequency by the mechanical properties of the cochlea. Because of the rather broad, somewhat flat response of the basilar membrane to a single frequency, a neural mechanism is superimposed to inhibit neurons which are excited on each side of the peak. In this way the information about the movements of the surrounding basilar membrane, which does not mirror the incoming frequency pattern, is disregarded and only the incoming frequency is heard, instead of a whole band of frequencies around it. In order to achieve such a suppression efficiently, the inhibitory function of the peak of oscillation of the basilar membrane should not be symmetrical. It will be remembered that the basilar membrane oscillates only at one end (the basal end) when high frequencies are applied to the cochlea and that the cutoff of the vibration is sharp toward the other (apical), and where the lower frequencies have their maximum effects. We would, therefore, expect that the neural inhibition generated by maximum vibration will be smaller toward the apical portion of the basilar membrane than toward the basal because the basal portion of the membrane always tends to move if any portion more apical is also moving, especially at the higher intensities of imposed vibration. This means that if no neural inhibition was superimposed on the mechanism of the basilar membrane, real lower tones would always introduce a wide band of higher tones, but real higher tones would not in turn lead to an illusion of a wide band of accompanying lower tones.

That a mechanism of suppression or inhibition operates in this way seems to be demonstrated by the phenomena of auditory masking. Two tones fairly close in frequency sometimes actually sound together in the environment, and unfortunately the nervous system still acts according to its usual rule for suppressing illusory tones and tends to inhibit the activity produced by one of the real tones. The tones affected in this way are what we would expect from the considerations about the efficient suppression of illusory tones. That is, lower tones mask higher tones to a much greater degree than higher tones mask lower tones. In this way the auditory system, by excluding signals which it itself introduced, also on occasion excludes information about the environment. The inhibition of unit responses in central structures to one tone by the presentation of another tone is described later.

In the following sections we shall discuss the neural substrate of hearing. We shall discuss what is known of unit activity in central auditory structures, examine the results of ablation studies, and, finally, report on the efferent control of messages arising in the cochlea.

CENTRAL AUDITORY MECHANISMS

The Classical Auditory Pathway

The axons forming the cochlear branch of the eighth cranial nerve arise in the spiral ganglion of Corti and are arranged in an orderly fashion, preserving their original positions relative to each other. As they reach the cochlear nuclei, those fibers arising in the apex bifurcate lateroventrally, those arising in the base, dorsomedially, with each fiber sending branches to the dorsal and ventral cochlear nuclei respectively. Each fiber branch terminates on many cells in the cochlear nuclei, and it is inferred that each cell in the cochlear nuclei receives many fibers.

The cochlear nuclei are composed of a number of different cell groups, and these are usually divided into two major groupings: the dorsal and the ventral cochlear nuclei. However, for various reasons, especially because of recent evidence concerning the organization of frequency-sensitive neurons in this complex, it has been argued that the ventral group should be further divided into the posteroventral nucleus and the anteroventral nucleus. No significant differences have been shown regarding the functioning of single units in these different subgroupings.

Most of the fibers leaving the cochlear nuclei cross the reticular formation and terminate in the contralateral superior olivary complex. Some, however, terminate in the reticular formation, others travel to the ipsilateral superior olivary complex and yet others join the tract of the lateral lemniscus. The superior olivary complex may be divided into five main nuclear masses: the S-shaped segment, the accessory nucleus, the nucleus of the trapezoid body, the medial preolivary and the lateral preolivary (Galambos et al., 1959).

The tract of the lateral lemniscus arises mainly in the superior olivary complex and terminates mainly in the inferior colliculus, though some of its fibers immediately join the brachium of the inferior colliculus to pass to the medial geniculate body of the thalamus. Scattered groups of cells lying amongst the fibers of this tract constitute the nucleus of the lateral lemniscus.

The brachium of the inferior colliculus, though containing some lemniscal fibers, consists mainly of fibers arising in the ipsilateral and contralateral inferior colliculi. The tract terminates in the medial geniculate body of the thalamus.

The medial geniculate body may be divided into two main portions: the small-celled, densely populated pars principalis, and the larger-celled, loosely packed pars magnocellularis. Of these, only the pars principalis should be considered a major auditory area (Rose and Galambos, 1952).

The main outflow of the pars principalis of the medial geniculate is to the auditory areas of the cortex, which are described in detail below. Connections to these areas are made by way of the posterior limb of the internal capsule.

Other Auditory Pathways

In addition to the classical afferent pathways described above, various other auditory pathways should be mentioned. Galambos et al. (1961) have demonstrated that a more medial pathway of considerable importance must also exist, since transection of the classical pathway at the level of the brachium of the inferior colliculus does not significantly alter the pattern of evoked activity at the cortex following click stimulation to the ear. Behavioral studies involving lesions of the classical pathway confirm this supposition (see below). Responses to auditory stimulation have been found to occur in the brain stem reticular formation and also in the more medially placed thalamic nuclei. A fairly direct pathway to the cerebellum must also exist, though its exact course is unknown. Further, there are a complex set of descending connections, which are described at the end of the chapter.

Responses of Neurons in the Auditory Pathways to Acoustic Stimuli

Before embarking on a description of the activity found in the auditory pathways, it would be of value to consider the types of analysis which must be performed by these structures. Let us assume that a complex sound is presented to the organism. Initially, a specific analysis must be made of the component stimulus frequencies and their intensities. Once this is achieved, the information thus obtained must be recoded in various ways. The component frequencies of the complex sound must be abstracted in a way analogous to the recoding of visual stimuli necessary for shape recognition (see Chapter 3). Similar recoding must be done for the intensity components of the stimulus. The durations of the different stimulus components must be analyzed. Another important type of analysis provides information as to the localization of the sound source. It is demonstrated from psychological experiments that such information is derived from binaural differences in time of arrival, phase, and intensity of the sound stimulus.

Once the types of recoding are established, higher-order encoding must take place. Take, for instance, the example of auditory localization. Based on a successive series of determinations as to the localization of a sound source, information would then be obtained as to the direction in which this source is moving. Rhythm is another example. Once the durations of a series of stimuli have been established, their relationships would be encoded as a rhythmic pattern.

One might expect, therefore, to find that at the earliest stages in the auditory pathway only the simplest stimulus characteristics are represented. Then, as the auditory pathway is ascended, one would expect to find units which respond in an increasingly complex fashion to acoustic signals. This is indeed the case. Upon comparing the lowest with the highest level in the auditory pathway, one finds in the auditory nerve a remarkably regular response to the frequency and intensity of a sound stimulus. Yet at the level of the auditory cortex, one third of the neurons can be stimulated only by complex sounds or by tones of changing frequency; that is, they are unresponsive to single tones of a steady frequency (Evans, 1968). Many auditory cortical neurons are remarkably sensitive to such complex auditory stimuli as clicks and voice sounds (Katsuki et al., 1960; Bogdanski and Galambos, 1960; Evans and Whitfield, 1964).

In this section we shall describe the different types of auditory analysis and how integration is carried out.

FREQUENCY

Frequency Discrimination

Response Areas. One method which experimenters have employed to determine the response of neurons in the auditory pathway to tonal frequency is the plotting of response areas. The response area of a unit is obtained by determining the threshold intensities necessary to activate the unit at various stimulus frequencies. The frequency at which the unit is activated at lowest intensity is known as its characteristic frequency. This method has provided valuable information on the frequency specificity of central neurons.

However, two reservations should be made concerning this method. First, certain experimenters have found that a neuron may have the lowest threshold for stimuli of one tonal frequency and yet have the greatest responsiveness to suprathreshold stimuli of another frequency. This has been shown, for instance, by Rose et al. (1963) and Hind et al. (1963) in the inferior colliculus and by Greenwood and Mayurama (1965) in the cochlear nucleus. Second, it should not be assumed that a unit which responds to a certain range of frequencies with the use of steady tones as stimuli would under no circumstances be responsive to tones of other frequencies. When the stimuli are tones of constantly changing frequency, some units respond vigorously to those tones at frequencies quite outside their response area as determined by the conventional method. Such units have been described by Nelson et al. (1966) in the inferior colliculus of the cat and by Whitfield and Evans (1965) in the auditory cortex of the cat.

With these reservations established, let us turn to a description of response areas at various levels of the auditory pathway. In discussing peripheral auditory mechanisms we saw that different parts of the basilar membrane vibrate maximally at different frequencies, and therefore that different auditory receptors are maximally stimulated at different frequencies, depending on their location on the organ of Corti. We saw further that the crest of the traveling wave on the basilar membrane was rather flat, and therefore that some additional mechanism would have to be postulated to explain the fineness of our ability to discriminate pitch. One such possible mechanism is lateral inhibition, that is, an inhibitory interaction between neighboring fibers such that the fiber firing more strongly would suppress the fiber firing more weakly. It might be hoped that the response areas in the auditory nerve would correspond with what would be expected from the mechanical characteristics of the cochlea, but that farther along the auditory pathway the response areas of some units would show much more specificity with regard to sound frequency.

Response Areas of Single Auditory Nerve Fibers. Recording from the auditory nerve of the guinea pig, Tasaki (1954) reports that response areas were characterized by a steep rise in threshold intensity when the stimulus frequency exceeded a certain optimum, and by a gradual rise as the stimulus frequency declined. The frequency at which the intensity threshold was lowest was found to be a function of the position of origin of the fiber at the cochlea. Those fibers arising in the basal turn of the cochlea had high cut-off frequencies, and those arising in the apical turn had low cut-off frequencies and therefore responded only to low tones. Similar findings have been reported for the cat (Tasaki and Galambos, reported by Tasaki, 1957; Katsuki et al.; 1958; Katsuki, 1961). The general shape of this threshold frequency curve corresponds well with what might be expected on Békésy's model of traveling waves in the cochlea, yet the high-frequency cut-off in auditory nerve fibers is much sharper than that of the mechanical movement of the cochlear partition or of the amplitude of the microphonic response recorded in the upper turns of the cochlea. Tasaki suggests that this sharp cut-off might be due to a complex mechanical motion of the cochlear partition near the point of maximum vibration.

In cats, Katsuki (1961) reports a second type of response area in addition to the type described above. The second type was obtained mainly from units with low characteristic frequencies, and in it the threshold rose gradually on the high-frequency side of the optimum frequency as well as on the low-frequency side. He suggests that neurons with such response areas may innervate the outer hair cells, and that neurons with response areas of the former type may innervate the inner hair cells. Katsuki et al. (1962) also demonstrated the existence of two types of unit with different shapes of response area in the monkey. They describe two partially overlapping populations of neurons: those with low-intensity thresholds and those with high-intensity thresholds. Their rates of firing were the same, however, for sounds of very high intensity. This is because the low-threshold units increased their frequency of firing at a more gradual rate than those with high thresholds. The units with high thresholds were unresponsive to sounds of low intensity. However, as soon as their threshold was exceeded, any further increment of intensity brought about a much larger increase in rate of firing than did the same increment in the low-threshold neurons. Such a division into high- and low-threshold elements was apparent only in the low- and middle-frequency range.

Kiang (1968) contends, however, that the apparent separation of auditory nerve fibers into two separate populations with different types of response areas may be artefactual and based on inadequate stimulus control. He argues that the sound system used in these experiments did not give sufficient energy at the high frequencies to enable the characteristic frequencies of these fibers to be determined. Further, dips in the tuning curve may have been produced by middle ear distortion, and these may in turn have been mistaken for the characteristic frequencies of the units. This would account for the apparently high thresholds of some units.

Inhibitory areas.   Although it had earlier been thought that inhibition of one neuron by another did not take place below the first relay station, a recent study of Sachs and Kiang (1968) is a beautiful demonstration of two-tone inhibition in the auditory nerve of the cat. This inhibition was found in all the fibers they studied. As shown in Figure 4–11, the inhibitory areas arise systematically on both sides of the characteristic frequency of the unit. The inhibitory areas overlap the response areas slightly. It has been shown that such inhibition is not conveyed by an efferent pathway since it also occurs in animals in which the olivocochlear efferents have been transected (Kiang, 1968). This study demonstrates lateral inhibition in the auditory pathway analogous to that found by earlier investigators in the visual and somatosensory pathways (see pp. 95 and 226). One might assume that this would produce a sharpening of frequency discrimination.

Response areas of neurons in the cochlear nucleus.   Several investigators have studied the response areas of units in the cochlear nuclei. Some found areas very similar to those obtained in the auditory nerve (Tasaki and Davis, 1955) with perhaps a less gradual decline on the

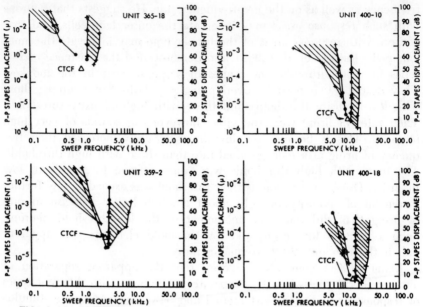

FIG. 4–11. Response and inhibitory areas for four fibers. The inhibitory areas are hatched; the dots represent the boundary of the response area. The relevant data for the four units are:

Unit	CF in kHz	Rate of Spontaneous Activity	Rate of Response to CTCF Alone
365–18	1.13	10/sec	40/sec
359–2	3.17	8/sec	12/sec
400–10	12.2	1/sec	30/sec
400–18	13.7	1/sec	10/sec

(From Sachs, M. B., and N. Y-S. Kiang, *Journal of the Acoustical Society of America*, Vol. 43:1120–28, 1968.)

low-frequency side (Tasaki, 1954; Katsuki et al., 1958; Katsuki, 1961). Recently, however, much more complex response areas have also been found at the level of the ventral cochlear nucleus. It appears that these areas have a large variety of shapes. In some cases, ineffective bands exist within the limiting frequencies of the response area, and such a tonal band may be inhibitory as well as ineffective (Moushegian et al., 1962). Further, a unit may be responsive to scattered frequency bands outside its response area (Fig. 4–12).

Mikaelian (1966) has described two types of unit in the cochlear nucleus of the mouse. One type had lower thresholds, narrower response areas, and a small dynamic intensity range. This type of unit showed two-tone inhibition, and there the inhibitory frequences usually lay on both sides of the characteristic frequency of the unit. The other type

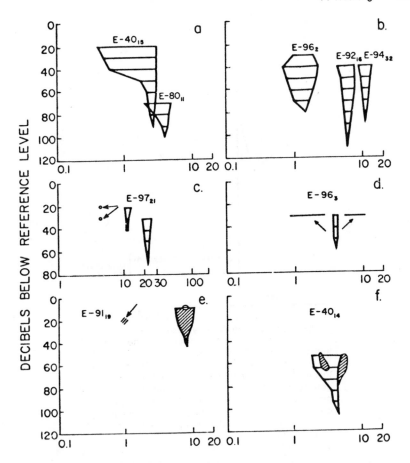

FREQUENCY IN KILOCYCLES

FIG. 4–12. Frequency response areas of ventral cochlear nucleus units. All units in this figure, except *E 40–15* and *E 80–11* are from unanesthetized cats. *A* and *b:* classical response areas. Solid lines indicate tone band over which units respond. *C:* unit showing two response areas as well as additional response bands at −20 and −30 db. (arrows). *D:* unit responding to frequency bands higher and lower than those found in its response area. Unit lost after measurements at 30 db. were made. *E:* an inhibitory response area for unit of Figure 4–11 driven at 7.8 kc. only. Hatched area encloses tones inhibiting spontaneous discharge. Note (arrow) the additional sharp inhibition outside the inhibitory response area. *F:* asymmetrical response area showing inhibition (hatched regions) within and bordering it. (From Moushegian et al., *J. Neurophysiol.*, 25, 1962).

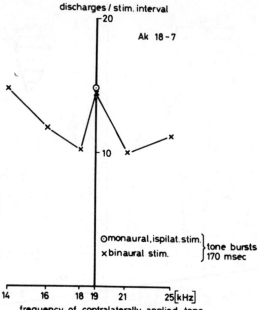

discharges / stim. interval

FIG. 4–13.   Number of discharges per stimulus interval as a function of the contralaterally applied tone. Each point an average of 100 responses. Ipsilateral cat stimulated with 19 kHz., the characteristic frequency of neuron; approximately 40 dB SPL, constant throughout experimental procedure. Tone on contralateral side, when present, the same. (From Klinke R. et al., *Pflügers Arch.,* 306:165–75, 1969.)

of unit had higher thresholds, broader response areas, and a larger dynamic intensity range. This type of unit almost never demonstrated two-tone inhibition.

Klinke et al. (1969a, 1969b), studying single-unit responses in the cochlear nucleus of the cat, found that contralateral stimulation would reduce the response of a unit to ipsilateral stimulation. The strongest inhibition was produced by frequencies adjacent to the test frequency, as shown in Figure 4–13. This is another example of lateral inhibition, in this case produced by a contralaterally applied tone. Klinke et al. conclude that this effect is mediated by efferent fibers of the crossed olivocochlear bundle (see p. 167).

Higher Auditory Centers

Various studies have been made of response areas at levels higher in the auditory pathway: in the superior olivary complex, the inferior colliculus, the medial geniculate, and the cortex (see, for instance,

Galambos, 1952; Galambos et al., 1959; Hilali and Whitfield, 1953; Katsuki et al., 1958, 1959, 1962; Hind et al., 1960; Rose et al., 1963; Evans and Whitfield, 1964; Oonishi and Katsuki, 1965; Tsuchitani and Boudreau, 1966; Goldstein et al., 1968). They have employed varying techniques, and it is difficult to draw any firm conclusions from them. The impression, however, is that as the auditory pathway is ascended, response areas become progressively narrower, up to the level of the medial

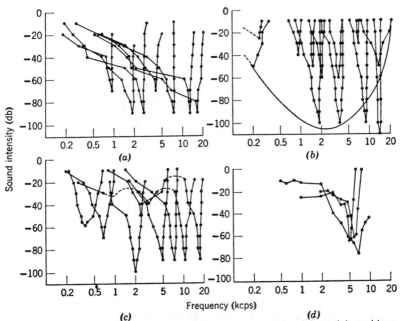

FIG. 4-14. Response areas of single neurons obtained from (a) cochlear nerve, (b) inferior colliculus, (c) trapezoid body, and (d) medial geniculate body. (Reprinted from *Sensory Communication,* Walter Rosenblith, (ed.), by permission of the M.I.T. Press, Cambridge, Mass. Copyright 1961, the M.I.T. Press.)

geniculate. At the cortical level, however, the picture becomes complex. Although some cortical units have narrow response areas, others have response areas with more than one peak, and yet others have very broad response areas (Katsuki et al., 1959; Hind et al., 1960; Oonishi and Katsuki, 1965; Goldstein et al., 1968). Some examples of response areas at various levels of the auditory pathway are shown in Figures 4–14 and 4–15. It seems that the analysis of simple frequency characteristics is accomplished at the subcortical level, and that the auditory cortex is concerned with the integration and recoding of such information. This conclusion is substantiated by studies of the effect of cortical lesions

UNIT DEPTH LATENCY   RESPONSE AREA

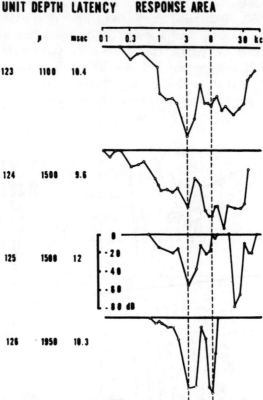

FIG. 4–15. Response areas and latencies of the auditory neurons obtained in a single penetration. The number of unit, depth, and latency are shown on the left and the response areas on the right. The abscissa and the ordinate indicate the frequency and intensity of sound respectively. Responses of U-124 and U-125 were simultaneously recorded. Two deep units had two peaks in each of their response areas, and were classified as the multipeak type. (From Oonishi, S., and Y. Katsuki, 1965, *Japanese Journal of Physiology.*)

on the ability to make simple frequency discriminations. As described on page 165, cats can still make such discriminations after extensive bilateral lesions of the auditory cortical areas (Goldberg et al., 1958; Goldberg and Neff, 1961a).

Periodicity Information

As discussed in the section on peripheral auditory mechanisms, one possible mode of transmission of frequency information is by reproduction of the periodicity of the sound wave. As described above, the auditory nerve as a whole is capable of following such periodicity up to 4,000 to 5,000 cps.

Studies on single units in the auditory nerve of the guinea pig, cat, and monkey have shown that the firing of such units is phase-locked to the stimulus waveform; that is, the fiber fires on the same position on the sound wave. Tasaki (1959) found such phase-locking to stimuli up to at least 2,000 cps. in the guinea pig; and similar findings have been obtained by Rupert et al. (1963) in the cat. Kiang et al. (1965) obtained phase-locking up to 4,000 to 5,000 cps. in auditory nerve fibers of the cat. Rose et al. (1967) also found such phase-locking up to 4,500 to 5,000 cps. in the squirrel monkey (though this became progressively more blurred as stimulus frequencies increased above 2,000 cps.). Interspike intervals recorded from these fibers were shown to be grouped around integral multiples of the stimulus period. The stimulus frequency alone determined this periodicity of firing, and it was unaffected by

UNIT 65-107-1

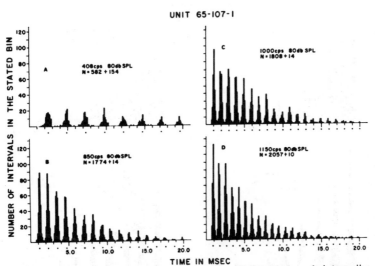

FIG. 4–16. Neuron 65-107-1. Periodic distributions of interspike intervals when pure tones of different frequencies activated the neuron. Stimulus frequency in cycles per second (cps.) is indicated in each graph. Intensity of all stimuli: 86 db. SPL. In all figures the sound pressure level (SPL) is given in decibels (db.) re 0.0002 dyne/cm². Tone duration: second. Responses to 10 stimuli constitute the sample upon which each histogram is based. *Abscissa:* time in milliseconds; each bin = 100 μsec. Dots below abscissa indicate integral values of the period for each frequency employed. *Ordinate:* number of interspike intervals in the bin. N = number of interspike intervals in the sample. N is given as two numbers: the first indicates the number of plotted intervals; the second is the number of intervals whose values exceeded the maximal value of the abscissa. (From Rose, S. E., et al., 1968, *Hearing Mechanisms in Vertebrates*, CIBA.)

such factors as the characteristic frequency of the unit, or its threshold, or the duration or strength of the stimulus. An example of the following of periodicity of stimulus of different frequencies by a single neuron is shown in Figure 4–16.

Further research by this group has been concerned with the response of auditory nerve fibers to two tones presented simultaneously. Under such conditions, the response of a neuron may be in any one of three modes: (*a*) its periodicity may mirror that of the first tone only; (*b*) it may mirror that of the second tone only, or (*c*) its periodicity may be determined by those of both tones. The factors determining the mode of response appear to be the intensity of the component stimuli and their position within the response area of the unit. However, whatever the mode of response, the total number of spikes remains essentially the same. Figure 4–17 shows the response of a neuron when it is presented with two tones separately, and together at different relative intensities.

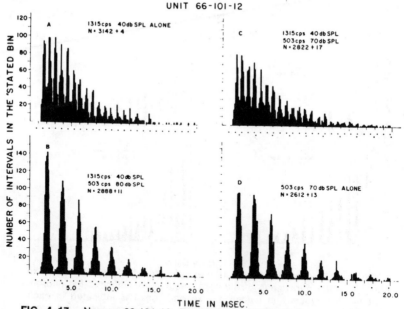

FIG. 4–17. Neuron 66-101-12. Distributions of interspike intervals when a tone of 1,315 cyc./sec. at 40 db. SPL was sounded together with a 503 cyc./sec. tone at indicated intensities.

Duration of all tones: 8 sec. *A:* response pattern to 1,315 cyc./sec. tone alone; *B* and *C:* response patterns when both tones were sounded together; *D:* response pattern to 503 cyc./sec. tone alone at 70 db. SPL. *Abscissa:* time in milliseconds: each bin = 100 μsec. Dots below abscissa indicate integral multiples of the period of the component tones. *Ordinate:* number of intervals in each bin. All graphs are scaled to correspond to two tonal presentations of 8 sec. duration. (From Rose, S. E., et al., 1968, *Hearing Mechanisms in Vertebrates,* CIBA.)

It can be seen that under this latter, when the response of the fiber is determined jointly by the periodicity of both tones, interspike intervals must necessarily occur which would not occur to either tone independently. Rose et al. (1969) hypothesized that such interspike intervals might be correlated with what is known behaviorally of difference tones. It was found that interspike interval distributions occurred which corresponded to certain difference tones.

The above studies are powerful evidence that periodicity pitch information is conveyed along the auditory nerve. However, such following is much more difficult to find beyond this level. Phase-locking has been shown to exist at higher auditory centers (Mayurama et al., 1966; David et al., 1969; Moushegian et al., 1967), but this is far less prominent than that found in the auditory nerve. It is likely that periodicity pitch information is translated into a place code as the acoustic pathway is ascended.

TONOTOPIC ORGANIZATION OF FREQUENCY

It is generally the case in the nervous system that when there is place coding of stimuli which can be ordered along one dimension, units responding to these stimuli are arranged so that those responding to adjacent values along the dimension lie adjacent to each other (see, for instance, the chapter on vision and somesthesis). For this reason, it is of interest to investigate the presence of tonotopic organization for frequency in the central auditory structures. Many auditory nuclei show a tendency to tonotopic localization. However, as seen in the preceding discussion of response areas, we should not think of a unit which is characterized as having a "best frequency" as being specifically sensitive to that frequency. We have seen that response areas are a very complex affair, and except at threshold intensities, units generally respond over quite a wide range of frequencies.

Cochlear Nucleus

Rose et al. (1959) present convincing evidence that units in the cochlear nuclei are arranged in an orderly manner with respect to their characteristic frequencies (i.e., frequencies which activate the unit at lowest intensities). The authors divide the cochlear nuclei into three major groupings: the dorsal cochlear nucleus, the posteroventral nucleus, and the anteroventral nucleus. (Although the ventral cochlear nucleus is not usually divided into two, anatomists had previously suggested this idea.) They demonstrated that in all three of these divisions the neurons are arranged in a dorsoventral sequence in general, from high to low with respect to their characteristic frequencies. This finding is in accord with anatomical studies which showed that the cochlear fibers are arranged in an orderly manner and that fibers from different cochlear coils bifurcate in an orderly dorsoventral sequence.

Superior Olivary Nuclei

Medial Superior Olivary Nucleus. Goldberg and Brown (1968) found evidence for tonotopic organization in the medial superior olivary nucleus of the dog. This nucleus in the dog is folded into a U shape, with the hilus of the U opening laterally. Units with high characteristic frequencies were found to be located in the ventral limb of the U, and units with low characteristic frequencies in the dorsal region. The characteristic frequency of a unit was found to be the same whether the stimulation was to the ipsilateral or the contralateral ear.

S-Segment. Tsuchitani and Boudreau (1966) describe a tonotopic arrangement of neurons in the S-segment of the cat. Units in the ventral limb were found to be selectively responsive to high tones, and those in the dorsolateral limb to low tones. The intermediate frequencies were represented in an orderly arrangement between these extremes, following the curvature of the nucleus (see Fig. 4–18).

Inferior Colliculus

Rose et al. present evidence for tonotopic organization in the inferior colliculus of the cat. They found that there is probably a sequence of best frequencies as the rim of the external nucleus of the inferior colliculus is transversed in a ventral, oral, and medial direction. They further demonstrated a consistent sequence of best frequencies arranged from low to high as the central nucleus is traversed (Fig. 4–19).

Medial Geniculate

Galambos (1952) failed to discover an orderly tonotopic organization in the pars principalis of the medial geniculate. Further, in a study by Rose and Woolsey (1958) it was concluded that each cross section of the pars principalis is probably connected with all cochlear turns.

Auditory Cortex of the Cat

The auditory regions in the cortex of the cat may be divided on its cytoarchitectural characteristics into four main areas, according to

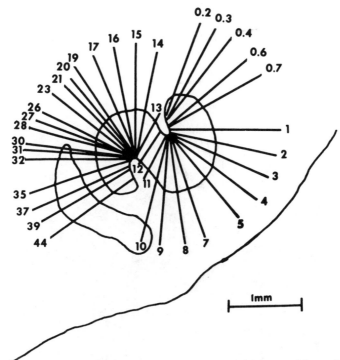

FIG. 4–18. Tonotopic organization of the S-segment of the cat. Units with the characteristic frequencies indicated are located in a spoke-like arrangement within the confines of the S-segment cell layer. A tracing of a histological section through the right SOC was used as a standard to construct this map from 87 unit recordings in 22 cats. (From Tsuchitani, C., and J. C. Boudreau, *Journal of Neurophysiology*, 1966.)

Rose (1949): AI, AII, EP, and a dorsal fringe sector which he named SF or the suprasylvian fringe sector (Fig. 4–20). Woolsey and Walzl (1942) showed that the basal turn of the cochlea projected to the anterior portion of AI and the apical turn to its posterior portion. However, in AII (Fig. 4–21), which lies just ventral to AI, the basal end of the cochlea projects to the posterior portion and the apical end to its anterior portion. As regards EP, it has been shown that there is an area responsive to stimulation of the basal cochlea (Downman, Woolsey, and Lende, 1960) and that ventral to this area there is another, responsive to stimulation of the apex of the cochlea. There is also a frequency representation in the suprasylvian fringe sector. Woolsey (1961) reports that when the lateral bank of the suprasylvian sulcus and the adjoining lateral surface of the hemisphere were explored, a regular increase in represented frequency along the suprasylvian sulcus from the anterior to the caudal end was exhibited. This confirms the earlier, less complete evidence from Hind (1953, 1960). Figure 4–21 illustrates these findings.

The question remains whether these cortical areas receive independent input, or whether some areas are "secondary" or dependent on others. Kiang (1955) demonstrated not only that there was some de-

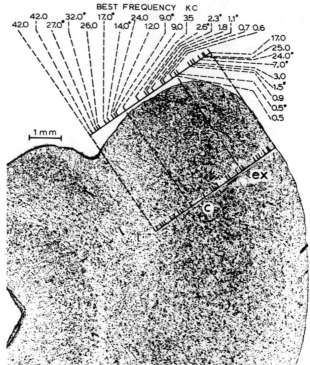

FIG. 4–19. Photomicrograph of a frontal section at the level of the inferior colliculus in cat 61–215. Nissl stain. A cell-sparse external nucleus (*ex*) and a cell-dense central nucleus (*c*) can be distinguished within the complex of the inferior colliculus at this level. A part of the electrode tract is visible to the left of the designation *ex*. The solid black line is a projection of the electrode track on the photograph. The track is assumed to be 0.5 mm. longer than is apparent from examination of histological sections. Bars indicate the depth of the successive points at which a single unit or a cluster of units was isolated by the electrode and a determination of best frequency made. Values marked by a dot indicate best frequencies of single neurons; other values show the upper limit of the effective frequency range which, for small clusters of units, is taken as an approximation of best frequency. Note that, neglecting a few irregularities, there is a sequence of best frequencies from high to low in the external nucleus and a sequence from low to high in the central nucleus. (From Rose et al., *J. Neurophysiol.*, 26, 1963).

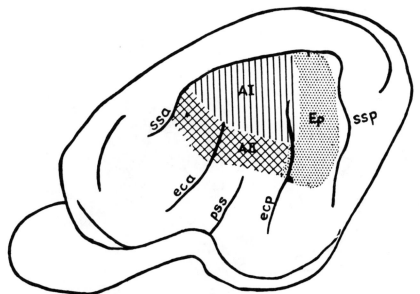

ssa—anterior branch of suprasylvian sulcus
ssp—posterior branch of suprasylvian sulcus
eca—anterior ectosylvian sulcus
ecp—posterior ectosylvian sulcus
pss—pseudosylvian sulcus

FIG. 4–20. Sulci on cortex of cat, important in discussion of hearing. Superimposed are cytoarchitectonic fields of auditory region according to Rose
(1949). (From Rasmussen, G. L., and Windle, W. F., Neural Mechanisms of the
Auditory and Vestibular Systems, 1960; courtesy of Charles C Thomas, Publisher,
Springfield, Ill.)

pendence of EP on AI but also that AII and EP may be activated
independently of AI. He found that when strychnine was applied to
a point in AI, the frequency response curve for any point in ventral
EP was similar to that for the point of strychnine application in AI.
When strychnine was applied to a different point in AI, the frequency
response curve from EP changed accordingly. He found this characteristic to be peculiar to EP, and concluded that ventral EP receives projections from AI.

However, Kiang established that both AII and EP may be activated
independently of AI by the following method. He isolated small patches
of cortex by ablating all other auditory areas and found that normal
surface positive responses persisted after a small area was isolated and
disappeared when this area was undercut. This he found to be true
for AI and AII and ventral EP, and he concluded that they all received
primary afferent projections. Corroborative evidence comes from Downman et al. (1960), who report that after bilateral removal of AI,

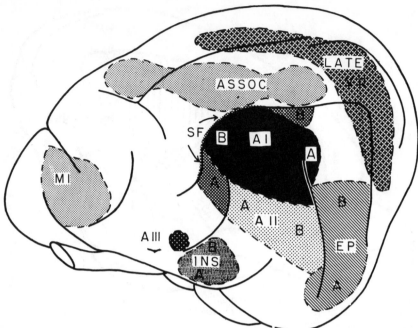

FIG. 4–21. Summary diagram showing four central areas with cochlea represented anteroposteriorly from apex *A* to *B* in the suprasylvian fringe sector (*SF*), from base to apex in *AI*; from apex to base in *AII*. In *Ep*, representation is base above, apex below. In insula (*INS*), evidence suggests base represented above, apex below. *AIII* is Tunturi's third auditory area. "Association" cortex (*ASSOC*) and precentral motor cortex gave responses to click with 15-msec. latencies under chloralose. Visual area II *(LATE)* gave responses with 100-msec. latency, also under chloralose. (From Rasmussen, G. L., and Windle, W. F., *Neural Mechanisms of the Auditory and Vestibular Systems*, 1960; courtesy of Charles C Thomas, Publisher, Springfield, Ill.)

middle AII and EP could be activated by clicks and by cochlear nerve stimulation.

Auditory Responses in the Second Somatic Area

Following a report by Tunturi (1945) on the dog that responses to auditory stimulation may be elicited in an area separate from those previously described, which lies partly in the second somatic area, a series of reports indicating that auditory stimuli also elicit responses in SII in the cat has appeared. Mickle and Ades (1952) found these responses to auditory as well as vestibular and somaesthetic stimuli were of such brief latency that they conclude that this is an example of polysensory primary receiving area, in which correlation of messages from various modalities may be performed immediately without the messages' having to be relayed farther to a secondary area.

Insular Area

Pfaffmann and Woolsey (reported by Woolsey, 1961) obtained evidence that part of the insular cortex responded to auditory stimulation. Loeffler (1958) showed that the base and apex of the cochlea were differentially represented in this region (Fig. 10–16). Desmedt and Mechelse (1959) found that responses may be elicited in this area to visual as well as auditory stimuli and that an interaction occurs between such responses. They further present evidence that this area initiates an efferent control of incoming auditory stimuli (see below).

Longer-Latency Responses

Longer-latency responses (about 15 msec.) to auditory stimulation are forthcoming from the suprasylvian and anterior lateral gyri and the precentral motor area. These areas are also responsive to visual and somatic stimuli (Buser and Borenstein, 1959). Late responses of 100 msec. latency to auditory stimuli may be obtained in the second visual area. No evidence of frequency representation has been found in these areas, which are also shown in Figure 4–21.

Thalamo-Cortical Projections to the Main Auditory Areas

Some light is shed upon the organization of the auditory cortex by considering its connections. AI is connected to the pars principalis of the medial geniculate. Rose and Woolsey (1949) also conclude that it is connected to the pars magnocellularis. AII and EP are also separately connected to the pars principalis. There is also a projection from the posterior region of the pars principalis to the temporal and insular cortex. It also seems that AII, EP, the insular and temporal cortex are separately connected to the pars magnocellularis (Rose and Woolsey, 1949). However, Rose and Galambos (1952), who studied single-unit responses to clicks in the medial geniculate, were unable to find sufficient responsiveness in the pars magnocellularis to justify the conclusion that this was indeed a major auditory area.

Auditory Cortex of the Monkey

Studies on this problem using the monkey as experimental animal have been far fewer than those on the cat, partly because of the technical difficulties involved in reaching the cortical areas concerned without injuring other parts of the cortex unduly. After studying degeneration in the monkey cortex following lesions in the medial geniculate, Poliak (1932) concluded that the cortical projection area for audition comprised most of the superior surface of the superior temporal gyrus. Le Gros

Clark (1936) and Walker (1937), studying retrograde degeneration in the medial geniculate following cortical lesions, also delineated as auditory an area on the superior surface of the superior temporal gyrus. However, the area they mapped was smaller than that of Poliak and was confined to the posterior section of this location. Ades and Felder (1942), studying click responses in the cortex, found a responsive area similarly located to those of Le Gros Clark and Walker but somewhat larger, though not so large as that mapped by Poliak.

Later, Pribram et al. (1954) employed a different operative technique, and so managed to avoid much of the damage which had been incurred in the course of previous experiments. They report responsiveness to clicks over a much wider area than had previously been considered auditory: the posterior supratemporal plane, the superior temporal gyrus, insula, and inferior parietal lobe.

Walzl and Woolsey (Walzl, 1947) explored, in the macaque, cortical responses to stimulation of nerve fibers in the osseous spiral lamina. They found that stimulation of fibers in the basal coil of the cochlea caused responses in the posterior medial part of the auditory cortex. Stimulation of fibers at the apical turn caused responses in the anterior lateral part of the area. Licklider and Kryter (1942) studied responses in the auditory cortex of the macaque evoked by stimulation with tones of differing frequencies. Using the definition of the auditory area that was delineated by Ades and Felder, they report that the higher frequencies produced maximal responses in the posterior medial part of the region. The lower frequencies activated the anterolateral part of the area. Since the basal turn of the cochlea is concerned with high-tone reception and the apical turn with low, this accords well with the findings of Walzl and Woolsey.

It should be pointed out, however, that tonotopic localization in the cortex is not strictly point to point. Evans (1968) has recently contended that although an ordering of best frequencies in the auditory cortex certainly exists, it is so blurred that it would be more appropriate to regard such an arrangement as a substratum for the performance of higher-order integrative functions rather than to assume that it is used for the purpose of frequency discrimination. This is consistent with the results of ablation studies showing that extensive bilateral ablation of auditory cortical areas does not produce a deficit in the performance of frequency discriminations.

Higher-Order Analysis of Frequency Information

Response to Changing Frequency.   The organism must be able to detect not only the absolute frequencies inherent in an acoustic stimulus but also if they vary, and in what way. Recently, interest has developed in the response of central auditory neurons to tones of constantly changing frequency. Units responsive to this type of stimulus occur at all levels of the auditory pathway above and including the superior olivary nuclei. However, such units are encountered only very rarely in the cochlear nucleus (Evans, 1968).

Watanabe et al. (1968) describe neurons in the superior olivary complex of the cat which respond to frequency-modulated sound. Some units responded only to sounds of ascending frequency; others only to sounds of descending frequency; and yet others responded irrespective of the direction of change of frequency of the sound. Similar results were obtained by Nelson et al. (1966) from units in the inferior colliculus of the cat. These authors also found that for some units the critical factor determining the degree of activation of a neuron was the rate of change of stimulus frequency. The higher the rate of change, the greater the response. Yet other units showed a greater response to a slower rather than a faster rate of modulation. Sometimes the response areas for steady and for modulated tones coincided; in other units the range of frequencies evoking response to frequency-modulated tones lay entirely outside the response area of the unit as established by steady tones.

Suga (1964) investigated responses to frequency-modulated tones in the posterior colliculus of the bat. Neurons were found which were specifically sensitive to changes in sound frequency in either the upward or the downward direction.

Whitfield and Evans (1965) found that about 10 percent of the neurons in the auditory cortex of the cat would respond to a tone only if its frequency was changing. Further, frequency-modulated tones produced vigorous and consistent responses in neurons which responded only inconsistently to steady tones. Many of these units were directionally sensitive in their response. Other units responded to one direction of frequency change at certain frequencies and to the opposite direction at other frequencies. As was found by Nelson et al. (1966) in the inferior colliculus, response areas to frequency-modulated tones were sometimes separate from those to steady tones, though in other units they coincided. Only a small degree of modulation was necessary to evoke a response in these neurons, that is, about a semitone. The average range of effective modulation rate varied between about 1 cps. to 20 cps.

INTENSITY

Responses of Single Units to Stimuli of Different Intensities

The most frequent effects of increasing the intensity of a stimulus on the discharge of a unit are (a) a decrease in the latency of response, (*b*) an increase in the probability of response, (*c*) an increase in the number of spikes per response. However, those effects do not always occur (Galambos et al., 1952; Galambos et al., 1959; Erulkar et al., 1956; Galambos and Davis, 1943; Rose et al., 1963). Sometimes increasing stimulus intensity leads to an increase in the latency of response, sometimes to a decrease in the probability of response. Some units respond best at certain intensities and less well at both higher and lower intensities than the optima (see, for instance, Goldberg and Greenwood, 1966). It is apparent that inhibitory influences must in these cases play a role in determining the degree of response of a unit to a given stimulus. Some units show an increase in the number of spikes per response with increasing stimulus intensity until a plateau is reached, which may be at a relatively low intensity (for example, Mihaelian, 1966; Tsuchitani and Boudreau, 1967). Some units have been reported in which there is a lack of correlation between stimulus intensity and number of spikes per response, or between stimulus intensity and response latency (Katsuki et al., 1959; Galambos et al., 1959).

When there is clearly an increase in the number of spikes per response correlated with stimulus intensity, such a relation is often found to be sigmoid. Katsuki et al. (1958, 1959, 1961) observed such a relation at all levels of the auditory pathway, but reported that the curve relating stimulus intensity with discharge frequency was steep at the more peripheral levels and became flatter the more central the regions studied.

Responses of Single Units to Amplitude-Modulated Stimuli

It is obviously important for the organism to know not only the absolute intensity of an acoustic signal at any given time but also if it is changing, and if so, in which direction and at what rate. Neurons which appear to transmit such information have been studied by Nelson et al. (1966) in the inferior colliculus of the cat. These neurons respond in different ways to changes in stimulus amplitude. Some units respond with increased firing to increasing amplitude; others respond selectively to decreasing stimulus amplitude. One unit was studied which changed its response pattern from one which was proportional to the amplitude of the stimulus when this was constant to one which reflected the rate of change of the stimulus amplitude.

Responses to binaural Differences in Stimulus Intensity

Responses of single units to dichotic stimuli of which the intensity at each ear differed have been studied at various levels of the auditory pathway. A discussion of these findings is deferred to the section on auditory localization (p. 161).

Single-Unit Responses at Threshold Intensity

Psychological studies have demonstrated that a reciprocal relationship exists at threshold between the intensity and duration of an acoustic stimulus (Garner and Miller, 1944; Garner, 1947; Miller, 1948). An interesting neurophysiological correlate for this phenomenon has recently been described by Radionova (1966), who recorded responses from neurons in the cochlear nucleus of the cat to bursts of noise. It was found that as the duration of the signal decreased from 100 msec. to about 10 msec., threshold intensity rose by about 10 db.

LOCALIZATION OF SOUND IN SPACE

Psychophysical experiments on human subjects clearly indicate that the localization of sound in space is determined by an interaction of messages from the two ears. If two clicks of equal intensity are delivered simultaneously one to each ear, the observer hears only one sound located in the median plane. Increasing the intensity of one of these clicks causes the sound to be heard nearer the side of the louder click, and the more the intensity is increased, the farther to that side the click is heard. Also, if one of the clicks is delivered slightly before the oth⸺ the sound is heard nearer the side of the first click. Phase differences between two sounds also contribute to apparent localization. Recently, considerable attention has been devoted to the neurophysiological substrates of these analyses.

Single-Unit Studies in the Superior Olivary Complex

Medial Superior Olivary Nucleus. Rupert et al. (1966) studied the responses of neurons in this complex of dichotic clicks. Three types of neuron were described. The first type responded with one spike to a click delivered to the ipsilateral ear. Dichotic stimulation affected the spike latency and probability; the contralateral click was inhibitory in its effect. The second type of neuron fired twice to each ipsilateral click, and this firing was also inhibited by contralateral stimulation. The degree of inhibitory interaction in both these types of neuron was sensitive to small changes in time differences between presentation of the stimulus to the two ears. The third type of neuron always fired to a click at either ear, firing occurring predominantly to the click at the first ear. Binaural interactions occurred in this type of neuron when there were large differences between presentation of the stimulus to the two ears (about 10 msec.). Watanabe et al. (1968) have also found that neurons which respond only to clicks delivered to one ear showed inhibitory interactions with brief time courses, and that neurons which respond to clicks presented to either ear show long-lasting inhibition.

Moushegian et al. (1967) have found that when clicks are delivered to both ears simultaneously, the spike response can be totally inhibited. Such inhibition is shown in Figure 4–22. These authors also found that with low frequency tones, at the characteristic frequency of the unit,

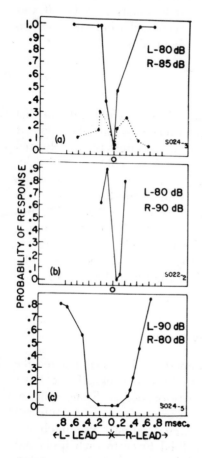

FIG. 4–22. Binaural inhibitory interactions of three neurons in response to dichotic clicks. The abscissa represents the time differences between the N_1 peaks, which are recorded near the round windows of the left and right cochleae. Most of the data points were determined from at least 50 stimulus presentations. Neuron in *a:* driven by a left ear click, occasionally produced two spikes to one monaural click presentation. Latency to first spike is 3.73 msec. from N_1. The dashed curve is the probability of firing for the second spike. Neuron in *b:* driven by right ear click; latency from N_1 is 3.23 msec. Neuron in *c:* driven by left ear; latency from N_r is 2.8 msec. (From Moushegian et al., *J. Neurophysiol.,* 1966.)

the degree of inhibitory interaction was a function of interaural phase. Similar findings are reported by Goldberg and Brown (1969).

The effect of a dichotic stimulation in units of this nucleus is not always inhibitory. Goldberg and Brown (1969) report the presence of some cells in this region, the firing of which is augmented by dichotic stimulation.

S-Segment. Cells in this nucleus are excited only by ipsilateral sounds, but they can be inhibited by contralateral stimulation (Galambos et al., 1959; Boudreau and Tsuchitani, 1968). Inhibitory and excitatory response areas in these neurons generally coincided. The main factor determining spike output from this nucleus is the relative difference in intensity of stimulation between the two ears, rather than the absolute levels of stimulus intensity employed. However, no inhibitory interactions were found for neurons with a characteristic frequency below 1,000 cps.

Inferior Colliculus. Rose et al. (1966) studied neurons in the inferior colliculus of the cat where firing depended on interaural phase. Different cells exhibited maximal firing at different specific values of phase angle when the frequency was kept constant. However, when frequency was varied, a given neuron would show an essentially consistent value of "characteristic delay" in terms of absolute time, and not in terms of phase angle, for all frequencies to which it responded. For instance, as frequency rose, phase angle would also increase because the absolute delay between the two sine waves causing maximal firing stays constant. These authors also describe neurons which usually respond to contralateral stimulation; but this response can be greatly reduced, or even abolished, when stimuli of the same frequency are presented binaurally. The degree of such inhibition was generally a function of interaural intensity differences. Geisler et al. (1969) also describe neurons which are sensitive to binaural intensity differences. With tones as stimuli, this effect of interaural intensity difference is independent of overall intensity levels. However, with noise bursts there is also a dependence on overall level. Geisler et al. (1969) also describe neurons which are sensitive to interaural time delay; and these appear to have a maximal or minimal discharge rate for a fixed value of delay regardless of the frequency or intensity of the sound stimulus.

Altman (1968) describes neurons in the inferior colliculus of the cat which appear to detect the direction of sound source motion. This investigator presented trains of clicks binaurally, gradually diminishing and raising the time interval within each pair of clicks. This was equivalent to the movement of a sound source from one ear to the midline and back again. Some cells were found which responded to apparent motion in one direction and others which responded to apparent motion in the other direction. An analogy may be made with units described in the visual system which respond only when a light source is moving in a certain direction.

Medial Geniculate. Adrian et al. (1966), studying single-unit activity in the medial geniculate of the cat and the rabbit, found that some units respond only to ipsilateral stimulation, others only to contralateral stimulation, and a third category responded to stimulation of either ear, or to both. Some units of the third category showed binaural interaction, which would be excitatory or inhibitory. Spike output was influenced by variations in time of arrival between the two ears or differences in relative stimulus intensities at the two ears. As was found in other nuclei, the best inhibitory frequency generally coincided with the best excitatory frequency.

Auditory Cortex. Rosenzweig (1951) studied the representation of the two ears in the auditory cortex by means of gross electrodes. He found that for most localizations the contralateral gross response was larger than the ipsilateral response. However, both ears were represented in both hemispheres. This is very consistent with the findings of Neff et al. (see p. 167) that unilateral cortical ablation produces only a slight deficit in auditory localization; however, bilateral ablation gives rise to a very severe deficit.

Single-unit studies in the auditory cortex have produced findings consistent with those described above. Hall and Goldstein (1968) studied the response of neurons in the left auditory cortex of cats to tone bursts, noise bursts, and clicks. More cells were found to respond to monaural stimulation of the right (i.e., contralateral) than to the left ear. However, there was extensive overlap of populations representing the two ears. Most units showed some form of binaural interaction. Generally, this took the form of summation; but in some units the interaction was inhibitory and in others there was a combination of summation and inhibition.

Brugge et al. (1969) describe cells in the auditory cortex which were excited by contralateral stimulation and inhibited by ipsilateral stimulation. The responses of these neurons were very sensitive to interaural phase when frequency was constant. These cells exhibited "characteristic delays" similar to those described by Rose et al. (1966) in the inferior colliculus.

Evans and Whitfield (1965) found that 56 percent of the neurons they studied in the auditory cortex of the cat showed a preferential response for a particular stimulus location. Preferences for contralateral locations were predominant. A few units responded either preferentially or only when the sound source was placed in the median sagittal plane anterior to the head of the animal. Changing the stimulus location of only a few degrees abolished the response of these units.

TEMPORAL CHARACTERISTICS OF RESPONSE

The temporal course of responding found in the lowest levels of the auditory pathway generally lasts for the duration of the stimulus and ceases when the stimulus ceases. An example of such a response is shown in Figure 4–23 (though in this case the unit recorded was from the auditory cortex). As the auditory pathway is ascended, more complex patterns of response emerge. Many units are spontaneously active in the absence of stimulation, and respond with inhibition while the acoustic stimulus

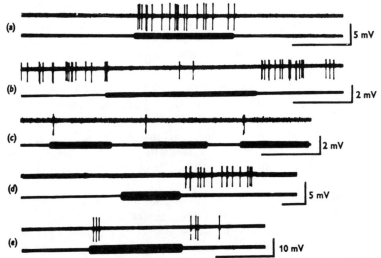

FIG. 4–23. Examples of unit responses. Tones are represented by thickening of the lower trace. Time bars are 0.5 sec. Negativity in the spike records is indicated by upward deflexion. (a) sustained excitation: 28 kc/s at +52 db. (b) sustained inhibition: 24 kc/s at +54 db. (c) 'on' response: 27 kc/s at +47 db. (d) 'off' response: 30 kc/s at +70 db. (e) 'on-off' response: 2.8 kc/s at +84 db. (From Evans, E. F., and I. C. Whitfield, 1964, J. Physiol., Cambridge, England.)

is present. Other units respond only at stimulus onset. Yet others respond only at the termination of a stimulus. Another category of units responds phasically both when the stimulus is turned on and when it is turned off (Fig. 4–23). Further units show a phasic "on" response, but with an initial delay. Evans (1968) describes units in the auditory cortex which display a more vigorous "off" response after a long stimulus presentation; others exhibit a more vigorous "off" response after a short stimulus presentation. The response of many auditory cortical units was found to be dependent on particular stimulus durations.

It is clear that this variety and complexity in the temporal characteristics of response to acoustic stimuli found in the higher auditory centers must play a role in higher integrative functions of acoustic stimulation, especially those involved in relative duration or rhythm.

EFFECT OF BRAIN LESIONS ON AUDITORY FUNCTIONS

Frequency Discrimination

After extensive bilateral lesions of the cortical auditory areas, cats can be shown still to be able to make frequency discriminations (Goldberg et al., 1958; Goldberg and Neff, 1961a) provided adequate testing procedures are used. However, it is not known whether the difference threshold for frequency discrimination is altered by this procedure.

After bilateral section of the brachium of the inferior colliculus, cats are also able to perform frequency discriminations (Goldberg and Neff, 1961b). Under such conditions potentials are still evoked in the cortex by auditory stimuli (Galambos et al., 1961). However, animals with bilateral sections of the brachium of the inferior colliculus, which also extend medially (with the result that potentials are no longer evoked at the cortex by auditory stimuli), are unable to perform frequency discriminations. It appears that a medially placed pathway, running parallel to the classical afferent pathway, is of importance for frequency discrimination.

Such medially placed structures may also be important in the human case. Landau et al. (1960) report the case of a boy who died at age ten and at autopsy was found to have severe bilateral degeneration of the medial geniculate and auditory cortex. He had been studied intensively before death, and it was found that he could understand speech and carry out simple conversations, uttering the speech sounds correctly. It was therefore apparent that he could discriminate frequency as well as intensity of sound.

Tonal Pattern Discrimination

Diamond and Neff (1957) found that when AI, AII, and EP were completely ablated, the ability to discriminate tonal patterns (i.e., the same tones arranged in a different order) was lost. Later, Goldberg, Diamond, and Neff (1957) extirpated the temporal and insular cortex, sparing SI, AII, and EP, and found a profound loss in ability to perform such tasks. Thus it seems that the ability to store the sequence of tonal events is lost by lesions in the auditory cortex.

Absolute Intensity Threshold

A series of early experiments, including a study by Kryter and Ades (1943), on the cat led to the conclusion that ablation of auditory cortical areas did not significantly affect absolute intensity threshold if a postoperative recovery time was allowed before testing. These authors found that if, in addition to the auditory cortices, the medial geniculate bodies were destroyed, a loss of 40 db. to 50 db. resulted, which would only be termed a mild deafness.

Discrimination of Intensity Differences

Another early series of experiments, including studies by Raab and Ades (1946) and Rosenzweig (1946), both on the cat, demonstrated

that the ability to discriminate differences in intensity was not significantly affected by auditory cortical ablations. Raab and Ades showed
that when the inferior colliculi were bilaterally ablated in addition, DLs
were increased. Oesterreich and Neff (reported by Neff, 1961) report
little change to DLs after bilateral extirpation of all known auditory
cortex. When, in addition, the inferior colliculi were ablated, a DL increase of 5 to 7 db. was noted. When the brachium of the inferior
colliculus was sectioned bilaterally, DL changes of up to 10 db. were
noted. Discriminations of large differences in intensity can still be performed after sections of the brachium of the inferior colliculus which
extend medially so that potentials are no longer evoked in the cortex
by acoustic stimuli.

Localization of Sound in Space

Neff, Fisher, Diamond, and Yela (1956) and Neff and Diamond
(1958) showed that bilateral, though not unilateral, ablations of AI,
AII, and EP in the cat lead to a severe deficit in the ability to localize
sound in space. More recent studies (Neff, 1961) indicate that bilateral
transection of the brachium of the inferior colliculus produces a complete
loss in the ability to localize sound in space. Also, a slight deficit may
result from unilateral cortical lesions which include AI, AII, EP, SII,
IT, and SS (suprasylvian gyrus). A small deficit has also been shown
to result from unilateral transaction of the brachium of the inferior colliculus. Small deficits were also noted to result from bilateral ablations
of portions of the auditory cortex.

AUDITORY EFFERENT PATHWAYS

Auditory centrifugal pathways arising at all levels from the cortex
to the periphery have been demonstrated in the auditory system. (Rasmussen, 1955, 1958; Desmedt and Mechelse, 1958, 1959) (see Fig. 4–24).
The first complete description of such a centrifugal pathway was that
of the olivocochlear bundle provided by Rasmussen (1942, 1946).
Galambos (1956) showed that stimulation of this bundle caused suppression of auditory nerve activity. Desmedt (1962) confirmed this inhibitory
effect. Further, Desmedt (1960) showed that lemniscal stimulation produced an inhibitory effect on responses in the contralateral cochlear
nucleus.

Comis and Whitfield (1966) have shown that stimulation in the S-segment of the superior olives produces facilitation in many units of the
ipsilateral ventral cochlear nucleus. In some units, a lowering of threshold
to sound stimuli was obtained. Stimulation of nuclei of the lateral lemniscus produced either facilitation or inhibition in the contralateral dorsal
or ventral cochlear nuclei.

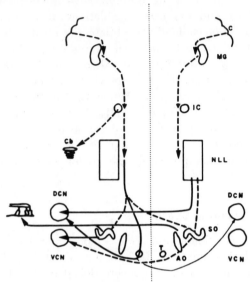

FIG. 4–24. Centrifugal connections of the auditory pathway. Connections not firmly established anatomically are shown by dashed lines. *DCN,* dorsal cochlera nucleus; *VCN,* ventral cochlear nucleus; *Cb,* cerebellum; *AO,* accessory olive; *SO,* lateral olipary nucleus; *T,* nucleus of the trapezoid body; *NLL,* nuclei of the lateral lemniscus; *IC,* inferior colliculus; *MG,* medical geniculate body; *C,* cortex. (From Whitfield, I. C., "The Auditory Pathway." Monographs of the Physiological Society No. 17, 1967.)

Starr and Wernicke (1968) stimulated the olivocochlear bundle at its point of decussation in cats. This decreased response rate to tonal stimuli in some units of the cochlear nucleus, increased it in others, had no effect in yet others, and produced mixed effects in a fourth category of unit. Similarly varied effects on spontaneous firing in cochlear nuclear units were found. These effects persisted after destruction of the cochlea ipsilateral to the recording site.

Pfalz (1966) showed that spontaneous firing in the left cochlear nucleus was inhibited in some neurons and facilitated in others when trains of clicks were delivered to the right ear after destruction of the left cochlea. These effects were almost certainly produced by a loop running to the superior olivary nuclei and back toward the periphery via the olivocochlear bundle. This same loop probably mediated the effects of Klinke et al. (1969a,b), described on page 146, where it was found that stimulation of the contralateral cochlear nucleus reduced the response of neurons in the ipsilateral cochlear nucleus to tonal stimuli.

The effect described by these investigators was frequency dependent and took the form of lateral inhibition (Fig. 4–12). This would almost certainly have a sharpening effect on frequency discrimination. Support for this assertion is given by the finding of Capps and Ades (1968) that sectioning of the olivocochlear bundle produced a significant decrease in pitch discrimination in the squirrel monkey. Another possible function of this efferent pathway was investigated by Dewson (1968), who found that masking was reduced under the influence of the olivo-cochlear bundle.

chapter 5

Peripheral
Somesthetic
Mechanisms

In this chapter we shall be concerned with the physiological processes underlying the various types of sensation which are elicited by stimulation of the skin surface. These include, for instance, warmth, heat, cold, touch, pressure, vibration, pain, tickle, itch, and sexual feelings. Of course a much larger list could be made up of such sensations, and an even greater variety is introspectively apparent. The study of these processes is made complex by the fact that many distinct sensations cannot be identified with particular physical stimuli in any simple way. Apart from differences in the type of stimulus energy employed (such as heat, mechanical stimulation, acid), differences in spatial and temporal patterning of stimulation alone may give rise to qualitatively distinct sensations. For instance, the sensations produced by stroking, itch, and vibration are qualitatively distinct, yet they are all brought about by light mechanical stimulation.

For this reason, experiments correlating activity in the nervous system with sensory quality are best classified into two groups. The first group correlates neural activity with physically defined stimuli and the second group correlates neural activity with experienced sensation (or, in the case of animals, with behavior). Both groups of experiments are of importance. Much knowledge may be gained by the study of nervous activity in response to physical stimulation, yet this does not tell us how such activity is interpreted by central structures. For instance, if a nerve fiber is found to respond to two distinct types of physical stimulus, this may mean one of two very different things. Either the fiber is treating the stimuli as the same, that is, it is confusing them, or it is relaying information concerning both types of stimulation. In the latter case, the fiber would be relaying more information than one which responds specifically only to one type of stimulus. In some cases, experiments correlating neural activity with sensation can decide to which of the two categories such a fiber might belong.

The way in which the different sensory qualities are transmitted in the nervous system has been one of the major interests of workers studying the skin senses. The classical theory maintains that there are four "primary sensory modalities," namely, touch, warmth, cold, and pain, and that other sensations are just derivations of these. Each primary sensory modality has its own morphologically distinct receptor type. Another view is that different physical stimuli activate the same pathways, but cause a different temporal and spatial patterning of activity in these pathways. The different sensations result from these different temporal and spatial patterns. A third view was suggested by Head (1920), who proposed that apart from the system subserving deep sensibility there are broadly two peripheral sensory systems: the phylogenetically older *protopathic system,* which subserves rather poorly defined sensations, and the phylogenetically younger *epicritic system,* which is capable of relaying the finer grades of sensation. It has further been suggested (Bishop, 1961) that not two but several sensory systems may exist in the same organism, each representing a different level of phylogenetic development. The newer the system phylogenetically, the more discrete the sensory information it carries.

A further view is that some pathways may become less specific as they progress from periphery to center. Wall (1960) presents evidence that there are cells at the level of the first relay which behave as though several fibers, conveying different sensory modalities, terminate on them. Or a system of temporal patterning at the periphery may lead to a spatial separation according to modality at more central structures (in some cases), as suggested by Hunt and McIntyre (1960d). We shall return to this question of modality transmission several times during the course of this chapter.

SPATIAL DISTRIBUTION OF THE SKIN SENSES

The ease with which different sensory qualities may be elicited varies for different regions of the skin surface. This is true, firstly, when large regions of the body surface are compared. Weber (1835), on the basis of experiments on himself and others, was the first to demonstrate that tactile sensitivity varied depending on the part of the body investigated. Weinstein (1968), on the basis of a series of experiments, showed that the more distal regions of the body are more sensitive than the more proximal regions for both point localization and two-point discrimination.

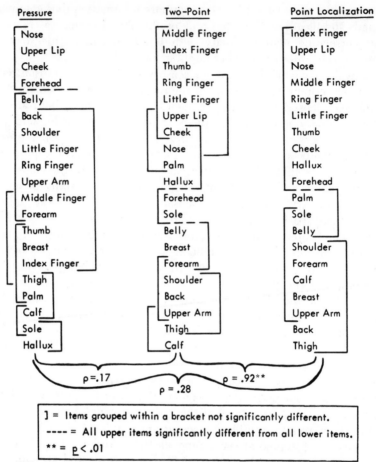

Pressure	Two-Point	Point Localization
Nose	Middle Finger	Index Finger
Upper Lip	Index Finger	Upper Lip
Cheek	Thumb	Nose
Forehead	Ring Finger	Middle Finger
Belly	Little Finger	Ring Finger
Back	Upper Lip	Little Finger
Shoulder	Cheek	Thumb
Little Finger	Nose	Cheek
Ring Finger	Palm	Hallux
Upper Arm	Hallux	Forehead
Middle Finger	Forehead	Palm
Forearm	Sole	Sole
Thumb	Belly	Belly
Breast	Breast	Shoulder
Index Finger	Forearm	Forearm
Thigh	Shoulder	Calf
Palm	Back	Breast
Calf	Upper Arm	Upper Arm
Sole	Thigh	Back
Hallux	Calf	Thigh

$\rho = .17$ $\rho = .92**$

$\rho = .28$

] = Items grouped within a bracket not significantly different.
---- = All upper items significantly different from all lower items.
** = $\underline{p} < .01$

FIG. 5–1. Rank order of body parts for three measures of tactual sensitivity. (From Weinstein, S. *The Skin Senses,* D. R. Kenshalo, ed., 1968. Courtesy of Charles C Thomas Publisher, Springfield, Ill.)

This did not, however, hold for pressure sensitivity (see Fig. 5–1). Different degrees of sensitivity were found for the left, compared with the right, side of the body (the subjects were righthanded). The left side of the body tended to be more sensitive than the right for pressure sensitivity and two-point discrimination but not for point localization. It was also found that women are more sensitive to pressure than men.

Sensitivity to pain also varies considerably, but in a different fashion. The cornea and conjunctiva of the eyes are very sensitive to pain, and the fingertips are insensitive. The mucous lining of the cheeks is particularly insensitive to pain, one region, known as Kiesow's area, being totally analgesic. The thresholds for thermal sensation also vary depending on body region. The threshold for warmth is low on the forehead and high on the foot (Maréchaux and Schäfer, 1949).

Secondly, if a small area of the skin is systematically tested spot by spot, it is found that some spots are particularly sensitive to touch, some to pain, some to warmth, and some to cold. Figure 5-2 shows typical maps of cold and warm spots. The number of spots per unit area sensitive to a certain type of stimulus varies for different regions of the body. Further, those body regions which contain a very large number of spots for one type of stimulus often do not contain such a proportionately large number of another type of stimulus.

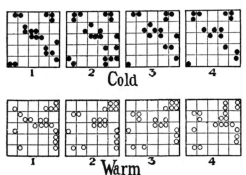

FIG. 5–2. Maps of cold and warm spots on the skin of the upper arm. The same square centimeter of skin was mapped repeatedly to locate sensory spots. The results are presented in the upper four squares for cold spots and in the lower four squares for warm spots. (From Dallenbach, K. M., 1927; permission of *Amer. J. Psychol.,* p. 39.)

When physiological techniques were not so well developed, so that it was difficult to analyze directly the activity of neural structures, much of the discussion concerning specificity within the skin senses centered around whether or not the sensory spots for the different modalities were stable when tested on different occasions. It was argued that if spots sensitive to a particular modality appeared consistently in the same locations, then receptors sensitive to this stimulus modality must be located beneath these spots. This would not, of course, prove the point. Variations in skin sensitivity, even consistent variations, could occur for many different reasons. Yet it was disputed by others that such sensory spots were not stable, but varied from day to day, mirroring only temporary differences in local skin sensitivity. Many experiments were therefore conducted to determine how stable such sensory spots were, and many varied results were obtained. However, modern electrophysiological methods have enabled us to provide much more direct and convincing answers to questions concerning specificity of skin receptors; so the controversy over the stability of sensory spots now assumes less importance.

An interesting group of mapping experiments concerns the application of nonadequate stimuli to previously mapped sensory spots. A nonadequate stimulus is one to which a spot is relatively insensitive. Von Frey (1894) found that a painful stimulus (sharp needle) applied to a pressure spot often gave only a sensation of pressure. Kiesow (1895) reported that applying pressure or electrical stimuli to a previously mapped cold or warm spot often gave reports of cold or warmth. These experiments indicate the existence of receptors which may be activated by more than one type of stimulus, yet their excitation is always interpreted as signaling one particular sensory mode.

Another example is the phenomenon of paradoxical cold. Von Frey (1895) found that previously mapped cold spots will respond to hot stimuli with a sensation of cold. The stimulus temperature needed to obtain this effect had to be high—around 45 degrees C. or abve. This fits in very well with the neurophysiological finding that single cold receptors maintain a steady discharge at temperatures below 41 degrees C., and also at 45 degrees C. and above (see below).

It is still not really known whether sensory spots are regions innervated by modality-specific receptors or whether they are simply due to favorable conditions for transfer of the appropriate form of stimulus

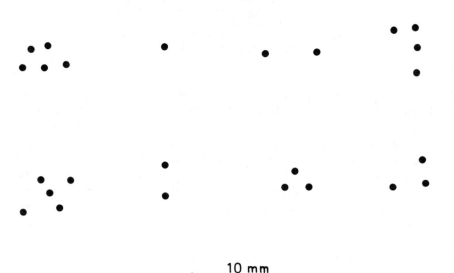

10 mm

FIG. 5–3. Examples of the distribution of receptive spots taken from eight touch units in the sural nerve of the cat. (From Hunt, C. C., and McIntyre, A. K., 1960; by courtesy of *J. Physiol.*, 15.)

energy. However, neurophysiological studies are providing evidence that sensory spots are regions innervated by modalityspecific receptors.

Hunt and McIntyre (1960a) describe a group of fibers in the sural nerve of the cat which respond to tactile stimulation, which receptive fields limited to a few distinct spots arranged about 1–5 mm. apart (Fig. 5–3). These spots might correspond to touch spots in human skin. Other experimenters have also described peripheral fibers with punctate receptive fields (Marushashi et al., 1952; Iggo, 1963). Indeed, Iggo (1968) has found, upon examination of such spots, that each spot forms a dome, roughly hemispherical in shape, which contains between 30 to 50 receptors, which he identifies as Merkel's discs (see Fig. 5–4).

Receptive fields comprising several spots have also been found in a class of nociceptors responding to damaging mechanical skin stimulation in the cat (Burgess and Perl, 1967) and squirrel monkey (Perl,

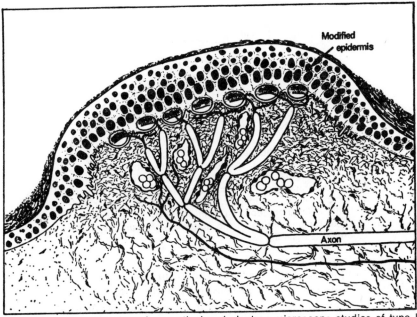

FIG. 5–4. Diagram based on optical and electron microscope studies of type I slowly adapting cutaneous mechanoreceptors ("touch corpuscle," Iggo, 1963). The diagram shows the basic structure of the cutaneous receptor with the afferent myelinated axon penetrating up through the dermis to end in Merkel's cells at the lower border of the epidermis. At this region the epidermis is thickened and the subjacent dermis is also much denser than in the adjacent region. Within the Merkel's corpuscle (M) the nerve ending forms an expanded disc of tissue about 10μ in diameter, 1μ to 2μ thick. The nerve ending is totally encased by the enclosing cell, which is probably the Merkel's cell shown in an electron micrograph. C: capillaries in the dermal core; M: myelinated axon; NM: nonmyelinated accessory axons; D.C.: dense collagen. (From Iggo, A., in O. E. Lowenstein (ed.), CIBA Foundation Symposium: Touch, Heat and Pain; London: Churchill, 1966).

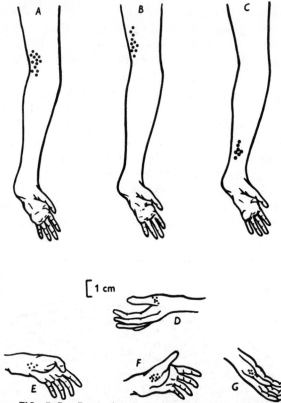

FIG. 5–5. Receptive fields of high threshold mechanoreceptors. *A* to *C,* posterior femoral cutaneous nerve. *D* to *G,* radial nerve. *A,* nociceptor. *B,* low sensitivity mechanorecepter. *C,* moderate pressure receptor. *D,* nociceptor. *E,* nociceptor. *F,* nociceptor. *G,* low sensitivity mechanoreceptor. (From Perl, E. R., *J. Physiol.,* 1968. By permission of the *Journal of Physiology,* Cambridge, England.)

1968). Examples of such spots in the squirrel monkey are shown in Figure 5–5. This unevenness of sensitivity within the receptive field just described is not limited to peripheral fibers. For instance, Perl et al. (1962) describe single neurons in the nucleus gracilis in which there is a spotlike distribution of sensitivity over the receptive field.

MORPHOLOGY OF THE SKIN RECEPTORS

In man, most of the body surface is composed of hairy skin. There are *free nerve endings,* which are formed by repeated division of fibers as they near their terminations. After several divisions, the fiber branches lose their myelin sheaths and then the neurilemma, leaving only the naked axis cylinders. These free nerve endings are arranged in plexiform fashion, and the nerve nets formed by different fibers overlap freely. Other fibers end in basket-like networks around hair follicles. A specialized type of ending, known as Merkel's discs, is also found (Weddell and Miller, 1962).

Nonhairy skin (palms of the hand, soles of the feet, etc.) also contains free nerve endings, and in addition Merkel's discs, and *Meissner's corpuscles,* an encapsulated ending. In various specialized body areas, such as the lips, nipples, and genital organs, there occur in addition a large variety of encapsulated endings. These include *Krause end bulbs* and *Ruffini cylinders,* among others, which are so varied and numerous that it is difficult to classify them. Present in many body regions, especially

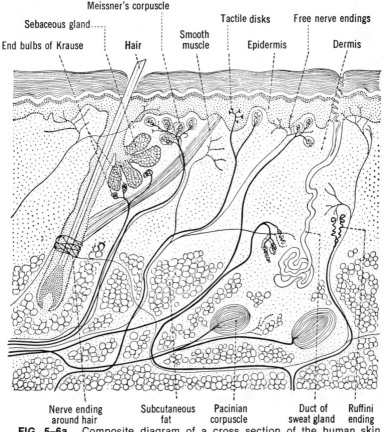

FIG. 5–6a. Composite diagram of a cross section of the human skin (From Gardner, E., 1947, *Fundamentals of Neurology;* by courtesy of W. B. Saunders Co., after Woollard, Weddel, and Marpman, *J. Anat.,* 1940.)

in deep locations, are *Pacinian corpuscles*. This corpuscle is very large (often large enough to be seen with the naked eye) and is composed of a large number of thin layers of tissue surrounding the end of a large fiber, rather like onion layers (Figs. 5–6a and b).

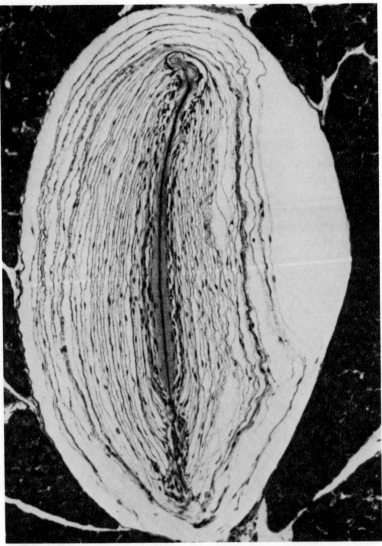

FIG. 5–6b. Longitudinal section through a Pacinian corpuscle. (From Quillian, T. A., *Touch, Heat, and Pain,* Little, Brown & Company, 1966. By permission from CIBA Foundation Symposium *Touch, Heat, and Pain;* London: Churchill.)

Functions of the Different Types of End Organs

It was once thought that the different sensations could be attributed to the activation of end organs of the appropriate morphological type. Von Frey concluded that the Krause end bulb was the organ responsible for the sense of cold, the Ruffini cylinder for warmth, Meissner's corpuscle for touch, and the free nerve ending for pain. This proposal has been attacked on the grounds that most of the skin surface, which is composed of hairy skin, contains only free nerve endings and terminations around hair follicles, and yet all the sensory qualities are perceived from such skin. Sinclair, Weddell, and Zander (1952) found that all sensory modalities were adequately represented in the human auricle (hairy skin). Hagen et al. (1953) compared thresholds for warmth and cold for the mucous membrane of the lip (which contains many encapsulated endings) with those for an adjacent piece of hairy skin (no encapsulated endings) and found no significant differences between them. Further, cornea has been found to contain only free nerve endings, yet Lele and Weddell (1956) were able to evoke, in addition to reports of pain (which was classically supposed to be the only sensation obtainable from the cornea), consistent reports of touch at contact with a fine nylon thread, and of warmth and cold at contact with copper cylinders and jets of air at the appropriate temperature. Indeed, no differences in sensation were found when the skin and the exposed mucous membranes of the lip were similarly stimulated. It is clear from this that the various skin sensations may be perceived without the presence of encapsulated end organs.

Weddell and his colleagues have argued that since a variety of sensations may be aroused through the activation of free nerve endings, these endings are not modality specific. They propose instead that the various sensory modalities are conveyed by means of different patterns of activation of the end organs. However, this conclusion does not of necessity follow from the findings. These have shown only that different sensory modalities may be conveyed by receptors which do not, with our present techniques, exhibit any morphological differences. As will be described later, recordings from single fibers in the peripheral nerve have disclosed many examples of receptor specificity. It is to be expected that advances in microscopic techniques will lead to the discovery of morphological differences among free nerve endings.

The question still remains whether the various types of encapsulated end organ are modality specific, as suggested by the classical hypothesis of Von Frey. Strughold and Karbe (1925) mapped the cold spots on the conjunctiva of the eye and found good agreement between this map and that of Krause end bulbs as seen under the microscope. In a later experiment, Bazett et al. (1932) attempted to correlate the number of cold and warm spots found in the prepuce with that of Krause end bulbs and Ruffini cylinders respectively. Making various allowances, they found that the two counts agreed fairly well.

Further, as referred to earlier and described in detail on p. 189, there is good evidence that Merkel's discs are receptors for certain slowly adapting units responding to pressure, and which exhibit highly specific characteristics (Iggo, 1968). The Pacinian corpuscle is another example of a highly specific mechanoreceptor; it has a very low threshold, adapts very rapidly, and is very sensitive to vibration (Skoglund, 1960; Hunt, 1961; Lindblom, 1966). This receptor is also insensitive to temperature changes (Loewenstein, 1961).

RESPONSES IN THE PERIPHERAL NERVE

Classification of Fiber Type

Fibers in the peripheral nerve are found to vary with regard to diameter size, height and characteristics of action potential, and degree or presence of myelination—these characteristics all correlating with each other. Various classifications of fiber type on the basis of these attributes have been made, but the one most commonly used is that proposed by Gasser and his collaborators (Gasser, 1943). Gasser denoted as A fibers all the myelinated fibers in the somatic nerves (though some in the visceral nerves were also included). He subdivided the A fibers into five groups of diminishing diameter and conduction velocity: α, β, γ, δ, and ϵ. Their diameters varied from 16 to 20 μ for α fibers, to 2 to 4 μ for ϵ fibers; and their velocity varied from 90 to 115 m/sec for α fibers, to about 10 m/sec for ϵ fibers. He denoted as C fibers the unmyelinated fibers in the sensory nerves, and these have diameters of 2 μ or less and conduct at from 0.6 to 2 m/sec. Also, each component of the action potential of a C fiber lasts much longer than the corresponding component of an A fiber's action potential. B fibers are myelinated, and have a very different type of action potential from those of A and C fibers, but since they occur only in visceral nerves we shall not be concerned with them.

It was originally hoped that different fiber sizes might be correlated with the various sensory modalities; that is, that fibers of one size might be concerned with touch, fibers of another size with pain, and so on. As it turns out, however, the sizes of fibers responding to different sensory modalities overlap considerably.

A number of experiments have shown that mechanical stimuli may evoke responses in fiber throughout the spectrum of sizes. This was shown in the early work of Adrian (1930) and Zotterman (1939), among others. More recently, Wall (1960) demonstrated that fibers sensitive to pressure occur throughout the A fiber range. Hunt and McIntyre (1960b) divided A fibers responding to mechanical stimulation into several groups: hair, touch, pressure, and probably nociceptive. They plotted the number of fibers in each group against conduction velocities and calculated diameters as shown on Figure 5–7. Each class of units has a characteristic distribution, but it is obvious that considerable overlap occurs, even among these subgroups.

Brown and Iggo (1967) and Iggo (1966) have also subclassified various mechanoreceptors and drawn up similar histograms (see Fig. 5–8). Furthermore, recent studies (Douglas et al., 1960; Iggo, 1960; Iruichijima and Zotterman, 1960) have confirmed that many C fibers respond to mild mechanical stimulation.

Fibers responding to thermal stimuli belong to the Aδ and C group. Aδ fibers sensitive to temperature have been studied in the tongue of the cat and the dog (Zotterman, 1936; Hensel and Zotterman, 1951a; Dodt and Zotterman, 1952), in the trigeminal area of the cat and hamster (Hensel, 1952b; Raths et al., 1964), and in the skin of the monkey (Iggo, 1963) and man (Hensel and Bowman, 1960). Unmyelinated C fibers responsive to thermal stimulation have been studied in the skin of the cat, dog, and hamster (Hensel et al., 1960; Iruichijima and Zotterman, 1960; Raths et al., 1964).

Regarding nociceptive stimulation, Zotterman (1939) found that burning, without inducing mechanical deformation of the skin, gave rise to Aδ and C potentials in the saphenous nerve. Etching the skin with acids produced similar results. Needle prick gave rise to initially large potentials (accounted for by mechanical deformation of the skin), followed by Aδ and C potentials. Maruhashi et al. (1952) also found small myelinated and C fibers responsive to noxious mechanical stimuli and to acid. Iggo (1959a) and Iruichijima and Zotterman (1960) describe some C fibers which responded to temperature changes only when they were extreme enough to be considered painful.

MODALITY SPECIFICITY IN THE SENSORY PATHWAYS

Information from the environment reaches our skin surface in temporal and spatial patterns and is relayed by the nervous system in temporal and spatial patterns. It is obvious that some of our sensations can only be obtained by the preservation of such patterning; among these are the sensations of tickle, vibration, roughness, and smoothness. However, there are basically two competing views regarding the importance of such patterning in the overall analysis of skin sensation. In one view, the somatosensory system is regarded as divisible into several subsenses, each with a separate transmission system; the total sensory picture is thought of as more or less a sum of the different types of information arriving at the various central analyzing mechanisms. This

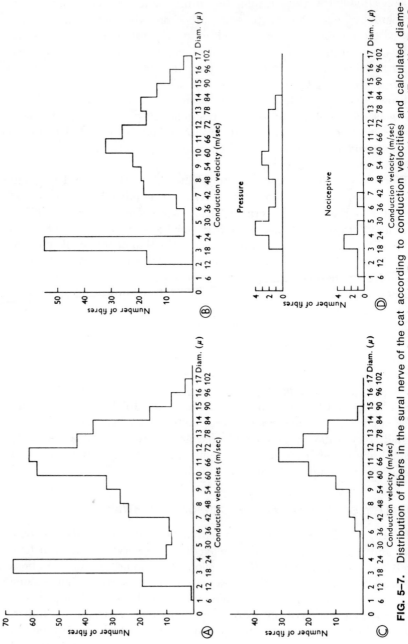

FIG. 5-7. Distribution of fibers in the sural nerve of the cat according to conduction velocities and calculated diameters. A, total sample of 421 sural fibers. B, hair units. C, touch units. D, pressure and nociceptive units. (From Hunt, C. C., and McIntyre, A. K., 1960; courtesy of *J. Physiol.*, 153.)

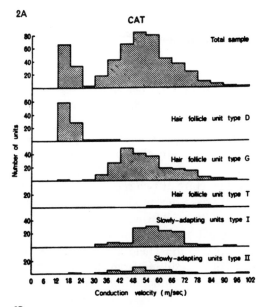

2A

CAT

Total sample

Hair follicle unit type D

Number of units

Hair follicle unit type G

Hair follicle unit type T

Slowly-adapting units type I

Slowly-adapting units type II

0 6 12 18 24 30 36 42 48 54 60 66 72 78 84 90 96 102

Conduction velocity (m/sec)

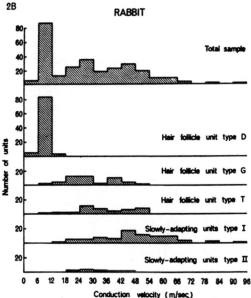

2B

RABBIT

Total sample

Number of units

Hair follicle unit type D

Hair follicle unit type G

Hair follicle unit type T

Slowly-adapting units type I

Slowly-adapting units type II

0 6 12 18 24 30 36 42 48 54 60 66 72 78 84 90 96

Conduction velocity (m/sec)

FIG. 5–8. Histograms to show the relation between the conduction velocity of the axons and the afferent unit types in the saphenous nerve of (a) the cat and (b) the rabbit. In both animals, almost without exception, the most slowly conducting myelinated fibres (Aδ) innervate type D follicle units. The remaining four classes of unit are all innervated by faster axons, and no clear-cut distribution of units according to conduction velocity is evident, except that in the rabbit the slowly adapting type I units are supplied by the fastest axons and in the cat the type T follicle units are not innervated by axons with conduction velocities of less than 54 m/sec. (From Iggo, A., *Touch, Heat, and Pain*, 1966, Little, Brown & Company. By permission from CIBA Foundation Symposium *Touch, Heat, and Pain*; London: Churchill.)

view does not deny that interactions take place between the different senses. A pain in one part of the body will cause someone to ignore a tactile stimulus to another part. At the physiological level, there are many examples of interaction between units subserving different sensory modalities, both inhibitory and excitatory. However, the basic picture is one of relatively independent transmission systems which interact with each other. After all, such interactions at both the experiential and the physiological levels are also known to take place between entirely different senses—such as vision and audition—but this does not detract from the basic picture of two separate senses in these instances.

Another view emphasizes the importance of spatial and temporal patterning of neural activity, and would rather regard the whole of the skin senses as one great transmission system, with different types of output. In the first place, it is held that a perceived sensory quality should be regarded not as resulting from the activation of one particular type of fiber but rather as a function of the working together of fibers of many different types. In this view, if one type of fiber were to be rendered inactive, there should not result a sensory loss limited to only one modality, but the total sensory experience should change since the overall pattern of impulses arriving at the central analyzing mechanism would be changed. With relevance to this expectation, clinical studies on partial sensory loss are particularly important. For if the skin senses were divided into several subsenses with separate transmission systems, then a loss of one modality should leave other modalities on the whole undisturbed. But in the other view there should be a total disturbance of the sensory apparatus.

Secondly, proponents of the "pattern theory" hold that information concerning different sensory modalities may be conveyed in the same fiber by different temporal patterns of activity. For instance, one stimulus modality may be conveyed in a particular fiber by firing in the high-frequency range, and another modality by firing in the low-frequency range. In such a system, confusion would be expected to arise between the different sensory modalities. This, however, is not in itself an argument against the pattern theory, since such confusions do indeed arise. The study of such confusions and the attempt to correlate them with what is known of unit activity is one of the most fascinating aspects of this problem.

Of course, if the reasonable assumption is made that, at the final level of integration, spatially separate structures underlie the different sensory modalities, then the proposed system of temporal patterning would require some analyzing mechanism at the highest level to decode the transmitted information. If information concerning the different modalities were transmitted independently, this would not be necessary. This makes a system of separate mechanisms preferable on the principle of parsimony.

To confirm or disconfirm the hypothesis of temporal patterning, investigators have studied the response of single fibers to different modalities of stimulation. For those fibers which respond to only one modality, the temporal pattern theory cannot hold. For those which respond to more than one modality, this theory provides a possible interpretation of the findings: such a fiber may be relaying information concerning both modalities. Alternatively, however, the fiber, though responding to both types of physical stimulus, may instead be treating them as one. For instance, touch and cold stimuli may activate the same fiber, the activity of which is always interpreted by the central structures as conveying touch. The only type of evidence which will convincingly decide between these interpretations is evidence involving subjective experience, both clinical and experimental.

In some cases, such "nonspecific" fibers may not be concerned with sensation at all but with some reflex activity. Certain types of reflex activity, such as the flexor reflex and startle response, are to a large extent independent of stimulus modality. Nonspecific fibers may mediate such responses.

Neurophysiological Evidence

Fibers responding specifically to one modality of stimulation and fibers responding to more than one have been described. In an early report, Zotterman (1936) described an experiment demonstrating not only that some mechanoreceptors are unresponsive to thermal stimuli but also that some thermoreceptors are unresponsive to mechanical stimuli, and some pain receptors are unresponsive to mild mechanical and thermal stimuli. Recording from a fine branch of the lingual nerve in the cat, Zotterman found that when the tongue was laid free in the air there was evoked a volley of small spikes which increased in number when the tongue was exposed to draft or to a fine stream of air from a syringe. However, if the air in the syringe was warmed, these small spikes disappeared; so Zotterman concluded they came from cold fibers. If the air from the syringe was forceful enough to produce a deformation on the tongue, large spikes also appeared, and remained whether the air was cool or warm. Thus they must have come from specific pressure fibers. Similar large spikes appeared at the impact of a drop of water falling onto the tongue. When a drop of hot water was applied to the tongue, besides the large pressure spikes two different types of spike appeared, one of which Zotterman concluded came from warm fibers and the other from pain fibers.

A large number of later experiments have demonstrated the existence of fibers specifically responsive to thermal or mechanical stimuli and of others which responded to more than one stimulus modality. Many of these are summarized in Table 5-1.

TABLE 5-1
Electrophysiological Studies of Cutaneous Receptors

References	Type of Lead	Fiber Size	Specific Fibers — Cool and Cold	Specific Fibers — Warm and Hot	Specific Fibers — Mech.	Nonspecific Fibers — Cold and Mech.	Nonspecific Fibers — Hot and Mech.	Nonspecific Fibers — Hot, Cold, and Mech.	Nonspecific Fibers — Temp. Mods. Mech.
CAT									
Tongue									
Hensel & Witt, 1959 (55)	Single	A	+						
Infraorbital nerve									
Boman, 1958 (8)	Single	A	+			+			
Iriuchijima & Zotterman, 1960 (63)	Single	C	+	+	+	+	+	+	
Saphenous and sural nerves									
Iggo, 1959 (60)	Single	A	+	+	+				
Witt & Hensel, 1959 (153)	Single	A	+		+				
Hunt & McIntyre, 1960 (56)	Single	A		+++	+++	+++	++	+++	
Hunt & McIntyre, 1960 (57)	Single	A		+	++++	++	++	+++	++
Wall, 1960 (127)	Single	A		+	+	+	+	+	+
Douglas & Ritchie, 1957 (23)	A-dromic	A							
Iggo, 1959 (59)	Single	C	+++	+	+	+	+	+	
Iggo, 1959 (60)	Single	C	+	+		+			
Iggo, 1960 (61)	Single	C	+						+
Hensel, Iggo & Witt, 1960 (54)	Single	C			+	+	+	+	
Iriuchijima & Zotterman, 1960 (63)	Single	C			+	+	+	+	
Douglas & Ritchie, 1957 (23)	A-dromic	C	++		+			+	
Douglas & Ritchie, 1959 (24)	A-dromic	C₁ / C₁	+		+	+			
Douglas, Ritchie & Straub, 1959 (25)	A-dromic	C / C			+	+		+	
Witt, 1961 (152)	Single	C / C							

	Type of lead	Nerves tested							
Ishiko & Loewenstein, 1960 (64)	Single	A					++		
Loewenstein, 1961 (89)	Single	A					++		
Cornea									
Lele & Weddell, 1959 (81)	Bundle	A				++		++	
Weddell, 1960 (122a)	Bundle	A				++		++	++
				DOG					
Infraorbital nerve									
Boman, 1958 (8)	Single	A	+	+	+		+		
Iriuchijima & Zotterman, 1960 (63)	Single	C	+	+	+		+	+	
Saphenous nerve									
Iriuchijima & Zotterman, 1960 (63)	Single	C	+	+	+		+	+	
				RAT					
Infraorbital nerve									
Boman, 1958 (8)	Single	A	+	+	+		+	+	
Saphenous nerve									
Iriuchijima & Zotterman, 1960 (63)	Single	C	+	+	+		+	+	
				RABBIT					
Ear									
Weddell, Taylor & Williams, 1955 (142)	Bundle	A		+	+				
				MAN					
Radial nerve, superficial branch									
Hensel & Boman, 1960 (53)	Single	A	+	+	++		++		
Hensel, 1961 (52)	Single	A	+		++		++	+	

Crosses indicate fibers activated by the cutaneous stimuli indicated. On account of wide variations in experimental approach, it is impossible to make any quantitative comparisons. See papers cited against each author for more detailed information.

Type of lead.—Single: single fiber preparation, either teased or isolated by collision technique, or microelectrode intracellular recording. Bundle: lead from a bundle. A-dromic: antidromic recording technique.

Nerves tested.—A: fibers described by the authors as Group A or myelinated. C (C₁ or C₂): Group C fibers.

Specific fibers.—Cool and cold: warm and hot: fibers activated by stimuli below or above skin temperature respectively. Mech.: fibers activated by any kind of mechanical stimulus.

Nonspecific fibers.—Cold and mech.: cold or cool fibers responding also to mechanical stimuli. Hot and mech.: warm or hot fibers responding also to mechanical stimuli. Hot, cold, and mech.: fibers activated by positive and negative heat transfer and to mechanical stimuli. Temp. mods. mech.: mechanoreceptors, the afferent discharge of which is modulated by a change of temperature.

(From Weddell G., and Miller S., *Annu. Rev. Physiol.*, 1962.)

Fibers responding to Mechanical Stimuli. It is apparent from the table that many fibers respond specifically to warming, to cooling, or to mechanical stimulation. But the degree of specificity shown by many of these fibers is much greater than is suggested by these three classifications. Within the class of mechanoreceptors, for instance, various types of specificity have been demonstrated. In a study of individual A fibers in the sural nerve of the cat, Hunt and McIntyre (1960a and b) found several patterns of response to mechanical stimulation. One group of fibers, which they termed "hair receptors," were activated by hair movement, which did not necessarily involve skin deformation. These fibers adapted rapidly, even if the hair was maintained in a bent position. Their receptive fields varied widely in size (in general between 3 mm.^{2} and 185 mm.^{2}) and showed a large amount of overlap. These fibers would not respond to temperature changes. A second group, termed "touch receptors," would usually discharge only upon actual touching of the skin. They were slow in adapting, and would usually maintain their discharge for the duration of the tactile stimulus. Their receptive fields were discrete, and limited to a few distinct spots, clustered about 1 to 5 mm. apart. These fibers also responded to temperature changes. A third group, designated "pressure receptors," discharged only to pressure stimuli of considerably greater intensity than that necessary to activate touch receptors, though such stimuli were not noxious. These fibers were slow adapting, but did not exhibit discrete receptive spots, and did not respond to temperature changes. A fourth group, called "probably nociceptive receptors," discharged only to heavy pinching of the skin or pinprick.

Iggo and his colleagues (Iggo, 1966, 1968; Brown and Iggo, 1967) have classified mammalian cutaneous afferent units with myelinated fibres into two main categories; the first being rapidly adapting and the second slowly adapting.

The rapidly adapting units respond to displacement of a hair or of the skin around hair follicles. The initial frequency of discharge upon stimulation is related to the rate of displacement (Brown and Iggo, 1966a, b). These rapidly adapting units are subclassified into three subcategories, according to the following criteria: (*a*) type of hair follicle innervated, (*b*) type of receptive field, (*c*) how sensitive the receptor is to displacement, and (*d*) the afferent fiber diameter. Those in the most sensitive category were termed type D units. These innervate down hairs and have Aδ fibers. The units innervating large hairs have large myelinated fibers and are less sensitive to hair movement. These were classified as type G and type T units. The number of hairs innervated by a single axon was always larger for the Aδ fibers than for the faster-conducting fibers; yet their receptive fields were similar in area.

The slowly adapting units responded to pressure on the skin with a persistent or slowly adapting discharge. This response is evoked from spotlike areas of the skin (Frankenhauser, 1949; Hunt and McIntyre, 1960; Iggo, 1963). Each individual fiber innervates one to five spots which are closely grouped together. This type of unit is very sensitive both to the amount and the rate of skin displacement. Brown and Iggo (1966a and b) have further subclassified this type of unit into two subcategories. The first (type I) almost never discharges spontaneously at normal skin temperature (Iggo, 1963). Generally, these units are excited only by displacement of the spot itself, and not by movement of the surrounding skin or by movement of hair. These units adapt slowly with continued stimulation, but the discharge ceases abruptly when the displacement is terminated. These units exist in clusters of one to five spots per fiber, and any spot is innervated by only one fiber. The second type of slowly adapting unit (type II) often emits a low-frequency spontaneous discharge in the absence of external stimulation. This discharge can be increased by stretching the skin or by injection of pain-producing substances (Fjallbrant and Iggo, 1961). These units generally have a single highly sensitive spot, though they are less sensitive to mechanical displacement than Type I units.

Upon examination of the spots in type I units of the cat, it was found that each spot formed a roughly hemispherical dome, which was clearly visible under the microscope. Iggo (1968) concludes that each spot contains 30 to 50 receptors which may be identified as Merkel's discs (see Fig. 5–4).

All the units described by Iggo and his colleagues are to a greater or lesser extent sensitive to changes in skin temperature. This is described on page 194.

A further type of specific mechanoreceptor was described by Fitzgerald (1940), who investigated fibers innervating the vibrissae around the mouth of the cat. These fibers were highly sensitive and responded within a virtually nonadapting discharge to a change in the position of the vibrissae, which decreased the angle at which they emerged from the skin. The discharge frequency in the fiber depended on the amount of change of position of the vibrissae. Releasing the hairs to their original position immediately terminated the discharge.

Another example of specificity within the group of mechanoreceptors lies in their ability to follow the frequency of repetitive stimulation. A large number of mechanoreceptors discharge with each cycle of low-frequency vibration (around 40 c/s) but cannot follow higher frequencies. Yet the Pacinian corpuscle will follow vibration at frequencies in the range of about 50 to 800 c/s (Fig. 5–9).

The thermal receptors studied by Zotterman and his colleagues in the chorda tympani and lingual nerve of the cat (e.g., Hensel and Zotterman, 1951a; Dodt and Zotterman, 1952a) demonstrated an exquisite

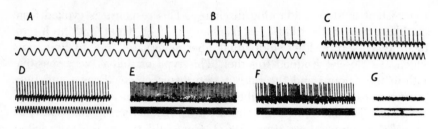

FIG. 5–9. Response of an isolated Pacinian corpuscle to vibration. Afferent impulses were found to follow each cycle of vibration in a 1:1 ratio over a frequency range from 90 to 600 cps. The upper trace displays nerve impulses; the lower trace displays the frequency of vibration applied to the corpuscle. Final frequencies (cps): *A*, 90; *B*, 102; *C*, 180; *D*, 550; *E*, 650; *F*, 700; *G*, 1,000. Time marker, 10 msec. (From Hunt, C. C., 1961; courtesy of *J. Physiol.*, 155.)

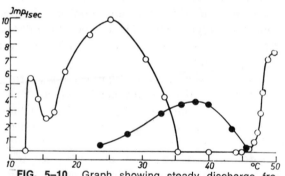

FIG. 5–10. Graph showing steady discharge frequency of a single cold fiber (open circles) and a single warm fiber (filled circles) as a function of static temperature level within the range of 10 to 50° C. (From Zotterman, Y., 1953; courtesy of *Ann. Rev. Physiol.*, 15.)

degree of specificity. The different fibers were found to have optimal discharge frequencies at different temperatures, and each fiber exhibited a finely gradated response, which varied with the different conditions of thermal stimulation.

If the surface of the tongue is maintained at a constant temperature, cold fibers will maintain a steady discharge, the frequency of which depends on the temperature, over long periods, sometimes hours. The maximum frequency of this discharge lies at around 10 imp/sec.; and the temperature at which it is elicited varies from fiber to fiber, but lies within the range of 20 to 34 degrees C. The frequency of the steady discharge as a function of temperature falls on both sides of this maximum (Fig. 5–10), the highest temperature at which the steady discharge may be elicited being around 41 degrees C. and the lowest temperature being around 10 degrees C. At temperatures above 45 degrees C., however, the steady discharge gradually returns, the frequency of discharge increasing with increasing temperature to a maximum of 7 to 7.5 imp/sec. at around 50 degrees C. Above this temperature the discharge disappears. (This discharge at high temperatures is known as the paradoxical discharge of cold fibers, and is held to be the explanation of the "paradoxical cold sensation" described by Von Frey, who discovered that stimulating single cold spots with temperatures above 45 degrees C. produced a sensation of cold.)

One might hypothesize that in hibernators the range of temperatures producing a steady discharge in cold receptors would be different, since it is known that thermoregulation in hibernators functions at body temperatures as low as 5 degrees C. Raths et al. (1964) and Raths and Hensel (quoted in Hensel, 1968) recorded from fibers in the trigeminal nerve and the infraorbital nerve of the hamster and found that the maximum discharge rate plotted in both Aδ and C fibers at constant temperature was frequently as low as 4 or 5 degrees C. These cold receptors did not behave differently depending on the season of the year; so it was concluded that these findings represent a species difference in the type of unit present in these animals.

Zottermann (1959) stresses that the frequency of discharge of these cold fibers at constant temperatures is determined solely by the prevalent temperature and not at all by how it was reached.

When the temperature of the tongue is made to drop suddenly, a cold fiber will produce a short burst of high-frequency discharges, though it will quickly adopt the steady discharge frequency appropriate to the new temperature (Fig. 5–11). The frequency of this rapid discharge depends mainly on the rate of temperature change, though the temperature range in which the drop occurs also affects it. The maximum discharge frequency observed to sudden cooling was 140 imp/sec., which occurred to rapid cooling from 40 to 2 degrees C. Rapid cooling may produce this discharge from cold fibers even when the temperature range concerned is above the upper limit for steady discharge.

When the temperature is made to rise rapidly, a cold fiber will briefly cease to discharge before adopting the frequency appropriate to the new temperature. The rate of warming and the temperature range in which it occurs determine the length of this inhibition of discharge. If the rate of warming is slow, or the degree of warming small, the discharge may not disappear entirely.

It was found that warm fibers, as well as cold fibers, maintain a steady discharge at constant temperatures, the frequency of the discharge depending on the temperature (Fig. 5–10). The maximum frequency of steady discharge occurred in the temperature range of 37.5 to 40 degrees C. and was around 1.5 to 3.7 imp/sec. The upper tempera-

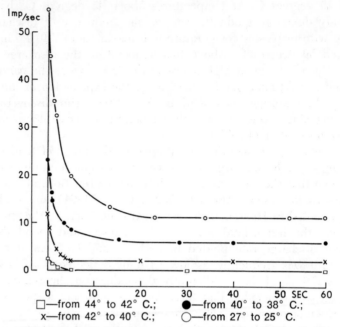

□—from 44° to 42° C.;   ●—from 40° to 38° C.;
x—from 42° to 40° C.;   ○—from 27° to 25° C.

FIG. 5–11. Discharge frequency of a single cold fiber in the lingual nerve of the cat during sudden lowering of the temperature of the tongue. Cooling starts at time 0. (From Hensel, H., and Zotterman, Y., 1951; courtesy of *Acta Physiol. Scand.,* 23.)

ture limit necessary to evoke a steady discharge was in the region of 47 degrees C. and the lower limit around 20 degrees C. In contrast to the discharge recorded in cold fibers, the discharge exhibited by warm fibers tended to be rather irregular.

A rapid rise in temperature in warm fibers produces a brief high-frequency discharge, before they adopt the frequency appropriate to the new temperature. A fall in temperature of 8 to 15 degrees also gives rise to a brief increase in discharge frequency of very short latency, the effect being greater for more rapid temperature drops (Dodt and Zotterman, 1952; Dodt, 1953).

Cutaneous thermoreceptors in rats, cats, and dogs (Iruichijima and Zotterman, 1960; Hensel, Iggo, and Witt, 1960) of C fiber diameter have been described whose behavior is very similar to that of the A thermoreceptors in the tongue described above. However, the warm fibers show no paradoxical discharge during cooling (Hensel, Iggo, and Witt, 1960).

Fibers Responding Specifically to Painful Stimuli. Pain sensations may be aroused by a variety of means. Extreme mechanical stimuli of various types, such as pinching, needle prick, extreme heat, extreme cold, and the application of various chemicals to the skin, may all cause pain in man. Yet these stimuli all differ from each other physically. The problem of specificity in pain pathways is therefore particularly interesting, for we must ask not only whether fibers exist which respond only to pain-producing stimuli but also whether these fibers respond to *all* pain-producing stimuli, or whether, instead, a modality separation amongst pain fibers themselves exists.

It has been found that an adequate stimulus for pain in the skin is either potentially or actually productive of tissue damage. Hardy et al. (1952) found that the thermal radiation threshold for pain is at a skin temperature of around 45 degrees C. This temperature is at the threshold range for tissue damage (Moritz and Henriques, 1947). Lewis (1942) showed that needle prick at pain threshold will produce skin damage, as manifested by redness later. A chemical change accompanying a slight degree of tissue damage may therefore be the common basis for the perception of pain. This will be discussed in greater detail below.

Fibers have been found which are activated only by painful stimuli. In this category fall fibers responding only to those mechanical stimuli judged painful by man, such as pinprick and pinching of the skin. These have been found in the Aδ range (Dodt, 1954; Hunt and McIntyre, 1960b) and the C range (Iggo, 1959a, 1960).

Some fibers have also been reported to respond only to those temperature changes judged painful by man. Pain thresholds in man are variable, but such reactions occur roughly at skin temperatures above 45 degrees C. (Hardy et al., 1952) and below 17 degrees C. (Wolfe and Hardy, 1941). Fibers activated by warming the skin only to high temperatures exist in the Aδ range (Dodt, 1954) and the C range (Hensel, Iggo, and Witt, 1960; Iggo, 1959b; Iruichijima and Zotterman, 1960), and those activated by cooling the skin only to very low temperatures (Boman, 1959) in the C fiber range (Iggo, 1959a; Iruichijima and Zotterman, 1960).

However, it is not possible to make the generalization that all individual pain fibers respond to all painful stimuli. Instead, it appears that some fibers respond only to one kind of painful stimulus, others to two kinds, and yet others to more. For instance, Dodt (1954, 1959) found that Aδ fibers in the lingual nerve of the cat responded to extreme heat and to painful mechanical stimuli but not to cold. Iggo (1959a), recording impulses from C fibers in the saphenous nerve of the cat, found some fibers sensitive only to intense mechanical stimuli and heat from stimulators 48 degrees C. or hotter; others responded to intense mechanical stimuli and cold from stimulators 10 degrees C. or cooler; only one fiber was found which responded to both heat and cold. He further describes C fibers sensitive to noxious mechanical stimuli but not to temperature change.

Further, Burgess and Perl (1967) describe fibers in the hindlimb of the cat which responded only to damaging mechanical stimulation of the skin (that is, pinching or cutting). No effect was obtained from application of noxious heat, noxious cold, acid, or injection of bradykinin. The receptive fields of these fibers were in the form of spots separated by unresponsive areas (see p. 174). Perl (1968) also found fibers which were specifically responsive to noxious mechanical stimulation (but not noxious temperature change) in the squirrel monkey. These also had receptive fields consisting of clusters of spots.

Some fibers appear to respond to heat, cold, and mechanical stimulation not necessarily noxious. Iruichijima and Zotterman (1960) describe C fibers which responded to strong thermal changes in the skin in both directions, and also to mechanical stimulation such as touch and pressure as well as pinching and pinprick. One might wonder whether such fibers are really nociceptive in function since they respond to touch. Yet Iggo (1959b) describes C fibers sensitive to extremes of temperature which were initially responsive to mechanical stimuli only if they were severe. Repeated heating and cooling of the skin sometimes led to a lowering of the mechanical threshold. Such behavior parallels the development of hyperalgesia as a result of trauma (see below) and may form part of its basis.

Fibers Responding to Both Mechanical and Thermal Stimuli. A number of fibers have been described which responded both to mechanical stimulation and to cold. Hensel and Zotterman (1951b) describe a group of mechanoceptive fibers in the lingual nerve which may be activated by cooling. However, their response to cooling was different from that of the "true" cold fibers which they had studied, for they could only be activated by severe cooling and ceased to respond as soon as the low temperature was made constant. A different pattern has been described by Hensel and Boman (1960) in fibers from a superficial branch of the radial nerve in human subjects. Here fibers responded sensitively to mechanical stimulation, and in addition exhibited a steady discharge at indifferent skin temperature without mechanical stimulation. Cooling led to an increase in discharge frequency, but this increase was small compared with that due to mechanical stimulation. Witt and Hensel (1959) describe similar receptors in the cat (see Fig. 5–12).

It is probable that the receptors described above mediate a mechanical sensation. First, their thermal sensitivity is very low compared with their mechanical sensitivity. Second, this assumption would explain the illusion of pressure which is produced by cooling, known as Weber's illusion. On the other hand, mechanical stimuli may produce a cold sensation (Kiesow, 1895).

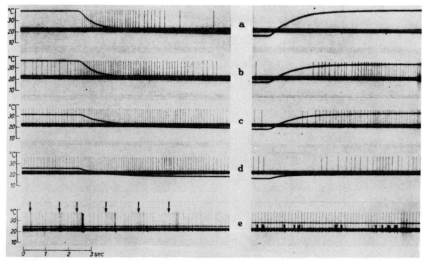

FIG. 5–12. Response of a nonspecific A fiber in the saphenous nerve of cat during thermal (a-d) and mechanical (e) stimulation. (From Witt, I., Hensel, H., *Pflugers Arch. Ges. Physiol.*, 1959, 268, 582.)

Lippold et al. (1960) report that a proportion of the muscle spindles which they studied in the cat responded to cold in a fashion similar to that found in specific cold fibers, while still having a normal response to stretch. The function of such a response is as yet unknown.

Hunt and McIntyre (1960a) describe a group of fibers which they call "touch units." These fibers were highly sensitive to mechanical stimulation, and yet displayed a background discharge in the absence of mechanical stimulation. The average frequency of this discharge depended on skin temperature. One group of such units showed a maximum discharge frequency in the 28 to 38 degrees C. range, the frequency gradually falling on either side of the optimum temperature, which varied for different units (Fig. 5–13). Other units discharged only at high skin temperatures. Others responded with an increased discharge to cooling, and an inhibition of discharge to heating, in a manner similar to that of specific cold receptors. It was also found that responses to constant tactile stimuli varied depending on temperature. Below 22 degrees C. and above 42 degrees C. touch units often failed to respond to mechanical stimulation. In the temperature range between these extremes, warming or cooling led to rapid adaptation of the receptor, and to the evocation of fewer discharges by the mechanical stimulus.

Hunt and McIntyre suggest that in this group of units, sensory information relating to both touch and temperature may be conveyed by the same fibers—possibly that low discharge frequencies convey temperature and high frequencies touch. Such a system would not provide

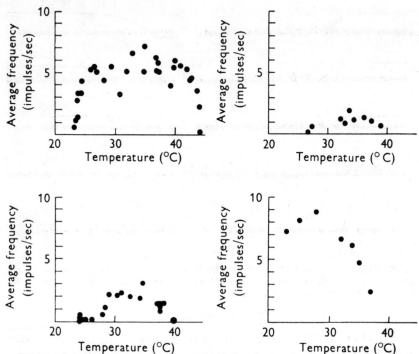

FIG. 5–13. Relation between baseline discharge frequency and static temperature level in four touch units in sural nerve of the cat. (From Hunt, C. C., and McIntyre, A. K., 1960, by courtesy of *J. Physiol.*, 153.)

very good differentiation of the two types of information. The finding that sufficient raising or lowering of the skin temperature causes faster adaptation and fewer discharges in response to a tactile stimulus may be related to what is known of variations in tactile threshold with temperature changes. Allers and Halpern (1921) found that pressure thresholds are related to skin temperature by a concave function, with maximal sensitivity between 36 and 38 degrees C.

Iggo (1968) has also described various types of mechanoreceptor which respond to temperature changes. The most sensitive are type II units. A fall in temperature produces an increase in the discharge frequency of these units. Further, their spontaneous discharge is affected by temperature, being maximal at some value between 20 and 40 degrees C. Type I units show a similar pattern, though this is less marked. Further, some type D, T, and G units may be excited by a steep fall in temperature.

Wall (1960) also describes pressure-sensitive fibers which responded to temperature changes. Some were spontaneously active and responded to an increased temperature with an increased discharge frequency;

some became constantly active when skin temperature was increased; in others the rate of adapation was decreased by heating the skin.

Explanation of Double Specificity. When a fiber responds both to mechanical and to thermal stimulation, this may have several causes. One possibility is that the double response is due to a physical artefact. For instance, changes in skin temperature might cause movement of blood vessels and so excite mechanoreceptors. However, in well-controlled experiments such artefacts may be ruled out (Wall, 1960). Secondly, one receptor responding to mechanical stimuli and another responding to temperature changes may originate impulses converging onto the same fiber. Thirdly, a single receptor might itself respond to the two different types of stimulation. But even here one cannot conclude, without very careful controls, that the receptor in question can be excited independently by both forms of energy. It has been found that the amplitude and rate of rise of a mechanically elicited generator potential in the Pacinian corpuscle increases greatly with temperature. Yet it has been demonstrated (Ishiko and Loewenstein, 1960) that here the receptor membrane is excited by mechanical stimulation, yet not by temperature change per se. However, changes in temperature alter the rate and amount of charge transferred through the mechanically excited receptor membrane. Loewenstein (1960) has also shown that in the Lorenzinian ampulla of selachians temperature changes will alter activity, but only when physiological levels of pressure in the ampulla are maintained. When pressure is reduced to subphysiological levels, the receptor will not respond to thermal changes. In each receptor type under investigation, therefore, very careful studies have to be performed before the nature of the double response can be determined.

Experiential and Behavioral Evidence regarding Modality Specificity

In the spinal cord, fibers are to some extent segregated according to modality, and so studies on patients with limited lesions of the cord have been very fruitful in the investigation of modality specificity from the sensory point of view. Unfortunately, fibers in the peripheral nerve are not grouped according to modality; so such studies cannot be performed here. However, some evidence for sensory modality specificity does exist for the peripheral nerve.

That only tactile sensations may be aroused when only certain tactile fibers are conducting is indicated by the correlation of the results of certain psychophysical and neurophysiological experiments in which conduction in the peripheral nerve is blocked by cocaine. In man, cocaine block leads to a disappearance of the various modalities of sensation in sequential order, touch being the last to remain. Gasser and Erlanger (1929) showed that injection of cocaine blocked conduction first in the smallest fibers, then the middle ones, and finally the largest. It can thus be inferred that the largest fibers in the cutaneous nerves convey only tactile sensations. More direct evidence on this point derives from an experiment by Heinbecker, Bishop, and O'Leary (1933). They were able to stimulate directly exposed peripheral nerves in conscious man and found that activating the largest fibers in these nerves gave rise to tactile sensations, and no other, though they evoked painful sensations when smaller nerve fibers were activated.

In a study on the frog, Adrian, Cattell, and Hoagland (1931) also present evidence that large tactile fibers are not concerned with nociception. They found that stimulating the skin by an intermittent air blast gave rise to discharges of frequency as high as 200 to 300/sec., which is almost the maximum frequency the nerve fiber can carry. However, intact frogs, when stimulated in this fashion, showed no pain reactions. A similar conclusion was drawn by Gernandt and Zotterman (1946) in a study on the cat. They report activation of large medullated fibers in the splanchnic nerve in response to the most gentle pressure to the exposed mesentery. However, stimulation of such fibers would not elicit any meso-enteric reflex or any other noticeable response. The authors thus conclude that these fibers are not concerned with nociception.

Though these experiments do not absolutely prove the point, they present convincing evidence that at least some tactile fibers (in the large group) convey only messages concerned with touch, even though they might be activated in response to noxious stimulation.

Heinbecker et al. (1933) correlated δ fiber activity with the sensation of pain. They stimulated exposed nerves in the leg of a conscious man and report that he gave a response of pain at that stimulus which produced a δ elevation in the electroneurogram.

Further, Collins, Nulsen, and Randt (1960) stimulated the exposed sural nerves of eleven human subjects and simultaneously recorded the action potentials. They found consistently that A-β and A-β-γ stimulation was not painful; however, when the Aδ group was also stimulated, this produced definite pain.

In another study, Clark, Hughes, and Gasser (1935) found that in the saphenous nerve of the cat, when C as well as A fibers were activated, this produced greater effects on blood pressure and respiration than when only A fibers were activated. When all fibers other than those in the C group were blocked by compression or asphyxia, stimulating the C fibers alone was sufficient to produce reflexes. Further, under those experimental conditions where it can be shown in animals that all fibers other than C fibers were blocked by asphyxia, human subjects report only pain and warmth when stimulated.

Kenshalo and his collaborators (1968) have conducted a series of behavioral experiments on the temperature sensitivity of the cat in an attempt to correlate their findings with the neurophysiological evidence. An avoidance response to electric shock was established, with warmth as the conditioned stimulus. When the stimulus was applied to the shaved skin of the thigh, it was found that the stimulator temperature had to be raised to 51 degrees C. to produce a response, irrespective of the initial level of adaptation. It has been shown that such a temperature is in itself noxious to the cat (Kenshalo, 1964; Rice and Kenshalo, 1962). It can be concluded that the cat is not sensitive to mild warming of the inner thigh. However, further avoidance experiments have shown that the cat can detect a temperature increase of about 1 degree C. applied to a 4-cm.^{2} area around the nose. Kenshalo (1968) concludes that warm fibers in the saphenous nerve (innervating the inner thigh) do not mediate a temperature sensation but that warm fibers in the infraorbital nerve (innervating the area around the nose) do.

MECHANISMS OF IMPULSE INITIATION

Mechanoreceptors. Little is as yet known about the mechanisms involved in impulse initiation by mechanical stimuli. Recently various possibilities have been suggested for the Pacinian corpuscle. Loewenstein (1961) recorded the generator potential in the Pacinian corpuscle resulting from mechanical stimulation of the nerve terminal after he removed the outer lamina. He found that potentials evoked by stimuli applied to different places along the receptor axons summated. Also, the generator potential decreased with distance from the site of stimulation. From this, among other evidence, he concluded that the size of the generator potential was determined by the area of the receptor membrane excited.

Thermal Receptors. Various theories have been put forward to explain the initiation of impulses by thermal stimuli. It has been suggested (Ebbecke, 1917; Bazett, 1941) that this is based on a thermal gradient between the different skin layers, that is, a difference in the temperature of the skin at various depths. It was thought that the receptors were activated by an alteration in such thermal gradients. However, Hensel and Zotterman (1951c) demonstrated that thermoreceptors were excited by thermal stimuli independently of intracutaneous gradients. They used nerve preparations containing cold fibers innervating only the upper surface of the tip of the tongue. Cooling the upper or lower surfaces of the tongue, or injecting cold solutions in the lingual artery, produced cold receptor discharges, and at latencies expected from the time the cold would take to penetrate to the regions supplied by the cold fibers. Yet the spatial temperature gradients would differ in each case. Arrest of blood flow for a short while did not materially affect the results.

Another suggestion was that a temporal thermal gradient is necessary for excitation of thermal receptors; that is, the receptor must be subjected to a changing temperature. However, we have seen that although a change in temperature briefly produces a rapid discharge in the appropriate fiber, warm and cold fibers have been found to discharge at a steady rate for several hours to a constant thermal stimulus. A temporal thermal gradient is therefore not necessary for the excitation of thermal receptors either. Zotterman (1959) concludes that thermal receptors are probably excited by some chemical process, since they do not depend for their activation on any exchange of thermal energy. The nature of such a chemical change is at present unknown.

PAIN

It is believed that the excitation of pain fibers is chemically mediated. It is very likely that various chemicals are involved and that different substances predominate, depending on the situation (Keele, 1970). Pain can be produced by intra-arterial injections of such chemical substances as hypertonic solutions, potassium salts, acids, alkalis, and some amines and peptides in amounts which are not necessarily injurious (Keele and Armstrong, 1964; Kimura, 1955; Moore, 1938; Boissones et al., 1963; Elliott et al., 1960, 1961). There is also evidence that bradykin-like peptides are formed in injured tissues as they become inflamed (Cerletti et al., 1961; Cohn and Hirsch, 1960; Elliott et al., 1960, 1961). Rosenthal (1968) has also produced evidence for the mediation of pain by histamine. First, it was found that the amount of histamine liberated from the skin (Fig. 5–14) was directly related to the intensity of the pain-pro-

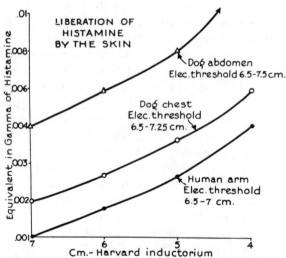

FIG. 5–14. Liberation of histamine from the skin. (From Rosenthal, S. R., in *The Skin Senses*, D. R. Kenshalo, ed., 1968. By courtesy of Charles C Thomas, Springfield, Ill.)

ducing stimulus in the cat, guinea pig, rabbit, and man (Rosenthal, 1964; Rosenthal and Minard, 1939). Further, the introduction of histamine into the skin of human subjects elicited pain in direct relation to the concentration of histamine (Rosenthal, 1950; Rosenthal and Sonnenschein, 1949). Further, the antihistamine substance thymoxyethyldiethylamine produced cutaneous anaesthesia without having a central action (Rosenthal, 1964, 1965, 1968; Rosenthal and Minard, 1939) in dogs, monkeys, guinea pigs, and human subjects.

It should be remembered, however (p. 193), that there is evidence for afferent units subserving certain types of pain but not others. It may be that there are both generalized pain receptors which respond to chemicals as described above and, in addition, nociceptors which transmit only specific types of painful information.

PAIN STATES

Cutaneous Hyperalgesia

When an area of skin is traumatized, for instance by scratching, heating, freezing, or electrical irritation, there results a lowering of the pain threshold in this region. In addition, the pain sensation now felt has an intense burning, diffused quality. This hyperalgesia may last for hours or even days.

Echlin and Propper (1937) found that scraping the skin of the frog produced an increase in the number of impulses traveling at speeds appropriate to pain fibers and a lowering of threshold for their evocation. Recently, Iggo (1959b) found C fibers sensitive to temperature extremes which at first responded to mechanical stimuli only if they were severe. Repeated heating and cooling of the skin sometimes led to a lowering of the mechanical threshold. This provides a possible basis at the nerve fiber level for hyperalgesia.

The hyperalgesic region gradually spreads, and may finally extend over a much larger area than the original region of trauma. Lewis (1942) suggests that a special system of fibers with large receptive field must be involved in this effect, but this view has come under criticism, mainly because such a system of fibers has not been found. A second line of explanation rests on two phenomena. The first is that a peripheral nerve fiber is divided into fine branches in the area it innervates. When one of these branches is stimulated, the evoked activity not only travels up the main fiber but also propagates antidromically down the other branches. The second phenomenon, demonstrated by Habgood (1950) in the frog, is that antidromic stimulation of pain fibers releases some substance in the skin which then evokes activity in neighboring pain fibers. Accordingly, it is supposed that a noxious stimulus in the normal case provokes activity in a branch or branches of a nociceptive fiber.

Some of this activity spreads antidromically to neighboring skin areas via the other branches of this same fiber. There is a release in these further areas innervated by these fibers of a substance which in turn is capable of stimulating branches of fibers not originally involved. In such a way, the pain spreads from the point to which the noxious stimulus was applied.

Another suggestion is that this spread of hyperalgesia is centrally produced. A constant barrage of impulses up one pain pathway may cause irritation of adjacent pain pathways from neighboring regions of skin. Stimulation of a nerve proximal to a procaine block can cause hyperalgesia (Hardy et al., 1950), and this would suggest the hypothesis of a central origin.

It may well be that both the peripheral and the central explanations are correct. Hyperalgesia after trauma has a very important function in that it tends to prevent an injured region from being further traumatized, so that healing processes will be unimpeded. It is very possible that in this case more than one mechanism exists to produce the same end result.

Hyperpathia Resulting from Peripheral Nerve Lesions

When one or more cutaneous nerves is cut, there appears in the corresponding peripheral field a region which is totally anaesthetic, surrounded by a region which is partially anaesthetic. Sensation in the region of partial anaesthesia soon develops an altered quality. The threshold for touch is still raised, but once a stimulus is above this elevated threshold, it may appear painful. Pinprick now gives rise to a diffused, poorly localized pain which is very unpleasant. Sometimes a spontaneous burning pain appears. As regeneration proceeds, stimulation of the previously anaesthetic zone may also produce such sensations.

Such effects have also been produced when a peripheral nerve trunk is blocked with a local anesthetic, or when a limb is compressed with a pressure cuff (Weddell et al., 1948).

Various explanations for this have been suggested. Prominent among these is the explanation of Head (1920), who suggests that, apart from the system subserving deep sensibility, the peripheral sensory apparatus consists of two systems. The phylogenetically older "protopathic system" is capable of responding to painful cutaneous stimuli and to extremes of heat and cold. The response of this system is diffuse, and is not accompanied by any real appreciation of the location of the stimulus. The phylogenetically younger "epicritic system" responds to light touch with a well-localized sensation. It is responsible for our capacity to discriminate two points: to localize stimuli effectively and appreciate the finer grades of temperature.

Head proposes that normally the epicritic system exercises an inhibitory influence on the protopathic system. After a nerve has been damaged, the protopathic fibers regenerate more quickly than the epicritic fibers, so for a while the protopathic system is released from inhibitory control. The hyperpathia is due to the uncontrolled activity of the protopathic system.

Foerster (1927) also suggests that hyperpathia is produced by the activation of pain pathways without the concomitant activation of pathways for touch and pressure, which have an inhibitory action.

Against this explanation, it has been pointed out that the regions in which pain has this abnormal quality are not directly correlated with the regions of anesthesia to touch. Trotter and Davis (1909) found in one case that there were more spots hypersensitive to pinprick actually outside the region of anaesthesia. Lanier et al. (1935) describe a region in which pain sensibility was diminished and the peculiarly unpleasant pain was felt, although there was no loss of touch sensibility.

Another version of the explanation in terms of a loss of inhibition which would meet the above objection is that this abnormal pain is usually inhibited by the normally felt pain. Landau and Bishop (1953) conclude from their experiments on differential nerve block that the block of Aδ pain fibers releases the perception of C fiber pain.

Others, such as Trotter (1926), have suggested that the phenomenon is due to abnormal activity in the regenerating fibers. Granit et al. (1944) have demonstrated the appearance of "artificial synapses" at the point of injury, and through such a mechanism abnormal activation could appear.

Another finding which may have bearing on the phenomenon is the ingrowth of fibers from adjoining nerves. Pollock (1919) postulated such an ingrowth, since recovery was not lost after a second section of the regenerating nerve. Weddell (1941) actually demonstrated that unmyelinated fibers grow into the anaesthetic area. How such an ingrowth could explain the findings on hyperpathia is, however, still obscure.

SENSATION OF PAIN

Pain may be aroused by a variety of means. It may be aroused from the skin surface by severe mechanical thermal, chemical, or electrical stimulation. It is possible that there is a common basis underlying pain produced on the skin surface—perhaps the release of some chemical which occurs at intensities of stimulation strong enough to produce tissue damage, though this has not been demonstrated (see pp. 200–202). Distention of various visceral organs also causes pain. Severe arterial dilation and arterial constriction producing ischaemia have also been shown to produce pain. Inflammation has the effect of lowering the pain threshold both for the skin and for deeper structures.

In a well-controlled situation, it can be demonstrated that differences in intensity, of pain can be detected. Hardy et al. (1952) have shown that 21 j.n.d.'s of pain may be distinguished by trained observers. With a constant pain stimulus, it has also been shown (Dallenbach, 1939) that pain sensations adapt to eventual disappearance.

Are There Two Types of Pain?

From the neurophysiological studies described in a previous section, it appears that fibers mediating pain may be found both in the group of small myelinated fibers and in the C group. It has been held, further, that these two groups of fibers subserve two distinct types of pain, which have been called fast pain and slow pain.

There have been three main lines of argument for the existence of two separate types of pain. The first is that two temporally discrete sensations are often felt to noxious stimulation, such as pinprick. The second is that during experimental nerve block the type of pain felt when only A fibers are conducting is qualitatively quite different from that felt when only C fibers are conducting. And the third is an attempted correlation of the delay in pain perception and reaction time to pain when the peripheral nerve is blocked by ischaemia with the extra time taken by C fibers in conduction.

Many early experimenters (e.g., Gad and Goldschneider, 1892; Thunberg, 1902) have reported two painful sensations to a noxious stimulus separated by a time interval, and many have confirmed this experience. Yet others have asserted that two such distinct sensations were not clearly apparent. Jones (1956) points out that it is very easy in this type of experiment to stimulate two receptors sequentially and thus produce a double sensation of pain by an artefact. For instance, heat stimuli, which are considered very effective in producing double pain, will penetrate the tissues with time and stimulate more remote receptors even after the stimulator is removed. Pinprick, too, may stimulate more than one receptor sequentially, especially if the needle is not rigidly mounted. Also, pulling the needle out restimulates the receptor. When Jones employed as stimulus a square-wave pulse from a Grass stimulator, this type of stimulation ensuring that if more than one receptor were stimulated they would be stimulated simultaneously, no reports of double pain were given. She also noted that no case was cited in the literature of double pain provoked by a single electrical stimulus.

The second argument for the existence of two types of pain, this time identifying the different types with transmission by different fiber groups, is that different qualities of pain are produced when the two groups of fibers are blocked differentially. Following perineural injection of cocaine, the C fibers in the peripheral nerve are blocked first and the A fibers last. And if a cuff is placed around the limb so as to block circulation, conduction in A fibers disappears first and that in C fibers last. It has been asserted by many that when only A fibers are conducting, the pain felt is a brief, pricking pain; when only C fibers are conducting, the experience is of a slow, long-drawn-out burning pain. Some assert, further, that "C-fiber pain" is much more unpleasant than A fiber pain. However, others have criticzed such experiments on the grounds that such introspective data have not been reproduced consistently (Sinclair and Hinshaw, 1950a and b). Thirdly, there have been attempts to correlate changes in reaction time to a painful stimulus when only C fibers are conducting with the difference in conduction rate between A and C fibers. Zotterman (1933) reports that when A fiber conduction is blocked, the pain that persists is a delayed pain, the reaction time to which agrees with that reported by Thunberg (1902) for second pain. Attempting to calculate conduction rate in fibers mediating this delayed pain, from this reaction-time data he concluded that it agreed with the known conduction velocity of C fibers. Various other workers have obtained similar correlations. This work has, however, come under heavy criticism (see, for instance, Sinclair and Hinshaw, 1951). Delays in reaction time to a stimulus under abnormal conditions may occur for a large number of reasons, of which difference in peripheral conduction time is only one. Also, *all* cutaneous sensory systems show a delay in perception under ischemic conditions. A delay also occurs with procaine blocks, during which A fibers alone are conducting, and therefore there should be no delay.

SENSATION OF PRESSURE

The absolute threshold for pressure sensation has been found to be constant, for any one locus of stimulation, at a given degree of tension or force per linear extent of skin surface contacted (Von Frey and Kiesow, 1899). The application of pressure alone does not arouse a pressure sensation, as can be demonstrated by dipping a finger into a jar of mercury. Under these conditions, a pressure sensation is felt only at the surface of the mercury, where there is a difference between the pressure exerted by the mercury and by the air above it.

Von Skramlick (1937) showed that the incremental threshold for pressure varied for different regions of the body, on the whole correlating with the absolute threshold. It also varies depending on the state of adaptation to the initial stimulus. Thus it is smaller when the increment is applied rapidly, and if both stimuli are brief, it is larger with short interstimulus intervals (Kolbe, 1936; Grindley, 1936).

The pressure sense adapts very rapidly. Von Frey and Goldman (1915) found that after three seconds of application of a pressure stimulus it appeared weaker than a momentary pressure of only 25 percent of its value. We have seen that there are many types of rapidly adapting receptors responsive to mechanical stimulation. The time orders of adaptation to pressure may be a result of the sequential stimulation of various fast-adapting receptors as the skin adjusts to the pressure stimulus. Nafe and Wagoner (1941) showed that pressure sensations due to the application of a weight on the skin occurred only while the skin was moving. When the skin stopped moving, the subject reported no pressure; yet when the weight was removed so that the skin started returning to its normal position, the subject again reported a pressure sensation.

Nafe and Kenshalo (1958) obtained parallel findings in the discharge of peripheral nerves underlying the pressure sensation. They recorded neural discharges from the dorsal cutaneous nerve of the frog and the femoral nerve of the rat. Depression of the skin evoked a discharge in these nerves, which adapted rapidly. Further depression evoked another rapidly adapting discharge. Release of the tissue, which had the effect of producing movement in the opposite direction, again produced a transient discharge.

TEMPERATURE SENSATIONS

The absolute threshold for temperature sensation varies with different bodily regions. Further, the threshold is lower when the number of thermally sensitive spots is increased (Hardy and Oppel, 1938). Such summation can take place over small and large areas. As for summation over small areas, the experiment of Kenshalo and Gallegos (1967) provides an elegant neurophysiological substrate. These experimenters showed that a single thermal fiber in the monkey innervates several spots over areas up to 1.7 cm.^{2}, and that an increase in afferent activity was produced with an increase in the number of spots stimulated.

The rate of change of the stimulus temperature is an important factor governing the size of the threshold. The slower the rate of change, the higher the threshold. This is also consistent with the neurophysiological findings (p. 190). Another factor is the temperature to which the skin is adapted before application of the stimulus. At room temperature, thermal stimuli of around skin temperature (32 degrees C.) do not arouse sensations of warmth or cold. When the fingers are dipped in warm or cool water, a change of 0.15 degrees C. in either direction is needed to produce a thermal sensation. When the skin has previously been adapted to a higher or lower temperature, a greater temperature change is needed to produce a thermal sensation.

The course of temperature adaptation is in the form of a negatively accelerated curve (Hahn, 1930). The time taken to adapt depends upon the temperature applied. At temperatures close to normal, this time is very short, and as temperatures deviate from normal skin temperatures adaptation time becomes increasingly lengthened. At temperature extremes (below 20 degrees C. and above 40 degrees C.), the thermal sensation does not disappear (Hensel, 1950). However, when only single spots are stimulated, adaptation is rapid even at temperature extremes.

Adaptation to a certain temperature brings with it not only a lack of senasion at this temperature but also a change in the perception of other thermal stimuli. Thus when the skin is at normal temperature (around 32 degrees C.), temperatures above this will appear warm and those below cold. After the skin has adapted to 38 degrees C., stimuli below 38 degrees C. will appear cold and those above 38 degrees C. will appear warm. Similarly, with an adaptation temperature of 26 degrees C., temperatures above 26 degrees C. will appear warm and those below it cold. In other words, physiological zero corresponds to the temperature to which the skin is adapted, and stimuli are felt as warm or cold depending on whether they are higher or lower in temperature than physiological zero at the time.

The increase in time to adaptation as temperature extremes are approached would be easily explicable if warm and cold peripheral fibers each showed a monotonic increase in rate of steady discharge with increased constant warm and cold temperatures respectively. One would simply have to assume that the peripheral warm and cold fibers projected onto central neurons of the same sign which adapted to their discharges. The time to complete adaptation would be longer the higher the frequency of incoming impulses, and therefore as temperature extremes were approached.

The shift in physiological zero could also be easily explained on this model. For at a given state of adaptation a central neuron would fire only to a new temperature which produces an increased steady discharge rate in peripheral fibers. Thus at an adaptation temperature of 38 degrees C. and a new temperature of 39 degrees C., the peripheral warm fibers would increase their steady discharge rate, and the peripheral cold fibers would decrease theirs. Therefore only the central warm neurons would fire. With the same adaptation temperature of 38 degrees C. and a new temperature of 37 degrees C., the peripheral warm fibers would decrease their steady discharge rate and the peripheral cold fibers would increase theirs. Therefore only the central cold neurons would fire.

However, it is not clear from the neurophysiological data that peripheral warm and cold fibers do indeed show a monotonic increase in steady discharge frequency depending on temperature, or that this function is derivable from averaging the activity of several neurons. Some figures

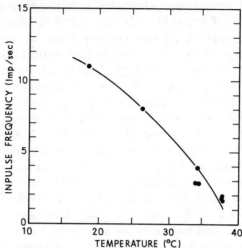

FIG. 5–15. Graph plotting the frequency of steady discharge against constant skin temperature in a single "cold" fiber from a superficial branch of the radial nerve in a conscious human subject. (From Hensel, H., and Boman, K., 1960; courtesy *J. Neurophysiol.*, 23.)

support this model (see, for instance, Fig. 5–15), but others show fibers with a peak firing frequency at a certain temperature, with a gradual decline in steady discharge frequency with temperatures on either side of this optimum (Fig. 5–10). On such a model, the sensory data could not be explained in the same way. One explanation of the adaptation findings applicable to the second model (and the first, too) is that peripheral warm and cold fibers, in addition to exciting central neurons of the same sign, have inhibitory connections to central neurons of opposite sign. On this hypothesis it is the reciprocal inhibition which causes adaptation. Making the simple quantitative assumption that peripheral warm and cold fibers progressively inhibit central cells of opposite sign at a rate proportional to the degree to which they excite central neurons of their own sign, one would predict the curve relating time to adaptation with stimulus temperature that has been obtained. This would follow since the proportional difference in steady discharge of cold and warm fibers is lowest in the medium temperature range and increases toward the temperature extremes. One would also expect that at those temperatures where only either the warm or the cold peripheral fibers show a steady discharge, but not both, there should be no adaptation. Such a correlation is indeed obtained. According to Hensel (1950), who used very carefully controlled thermal devices, constant sensations appear at above 40 degrees C. and below 20 degrees C., and the upper limit for steady discharge of the cold fibers is 41 degrees C. and the lower limit for warm fibers is 20 degrees C. (Zotterman, 1959).

It has been found that when single warm or cold spots are tested, adaptation is very rapid, even at temperature extremes, in contrast to the findings when relatively large areas of skin are tested. This would follow if reciprocal inhibition were the cause of thermal adaptation. Suppose a large skin area were stimulated at 41 degrees C. This stimulus would cause the cold fibers to stop discharging. Therefore they would not inhibit the central warm neurons and so no adaptation would take place. However, if only one warm spot were stimulated, this will not cause neighboring cold fibers to stop firing. They would continue to fire at a steady rate, approximately appropriate to room temperature, and would therefore still exert an inhibitory influence on the central warm neurons to which the stimulated warm fiber projected, and so adaptation would occur.

ITCH

Itching is a unique sensory experience with a unique and well-defined behavioral response—that of scratching. Yet the stimuli which evoke it are not unique. Mechanical, thermal, and electrical stimuli may produce itching, as can the application of various chemicals to the skin.

The aversive nature of itching, as well as its arousal by a variety of stimuli, gives rise to the possibility that it is related to pain. This is made more probable by the finding that itching cannot be aroused from skin made analgesic by severing the spinothalamic tract, or in cases of congenital analgesia, yet it is unaffected in cases of touch anaesthesia (Foerster and Gagel, 1932; Arthur and Shelly, 1959). Yet whether or in what way it is related to pain is not clearly known. Certainly itching is not simply diminutive pain, as some have suggested, for a gradual reduction in the intensity of a pain stimulus produces simply a gradual lessening and final elimination of the pain, without producing itching (Keele, 1958; Moulton, Spector, and Willoughby, 1957).

With punctate stimulation it can be shown that some spots on the skin are sensitive to itch and others insensitive (Von Frey, 1922), as with other types of sensation. Hyperalgesia greatly increases the number of itch points on an area of skin. It is generally held that itching is conveyed by C fibers. In the frog, topical application of itch-producing substances produces impulses characteristic of C fiber activity. Also, only C fibers display an after-discharge to stimulation and may be activated by extremely mild mechanical stimulation (Zotterman, 1939); and such an after-discharge may partly underlie the prolonged itch sensation which occurs even after withdrawal of the stimulus.

The release of various chemical substances in the skin has been suggested as the cause of itching. Histamine may produce itching when introduced into the skin, and it has been suggested that histamine liberation is the cause of itching. However, whenever histamine produces itching it also invariably produces whealing, and if diluted may produce whealing without itching. Yet itching can occur in skin with normal appearance. Itch has also been produced upon application to the skin of weak solutions of acetic formic acid (Lebermann, 1922). The fat soluble methyl bromide may also cause itch (Watrous, 1942). However, intradermal injection of histamine liberators produces itch (Lecomte, 1956). The tropical plant cowhage or itch powder (*Mucana pruriens*) causes itch, but its mechanism is uncertain (Shelly and Arthur, 1955). Arthur and Shelly (1955, 1959) report that protinease produces itching very effectively without producing gross changes in the appearance of the skin. Protinease is a naturally occurring substance which may be released or activated to produce itching, and Arthur and Shelly (1959) suggest that this happens in various states leading to pruritus.

VIBRATION

The sensation produced by vibration of a tuning fork or other device against the skin is quite distinct from that of pressure. The lower limit of frequency needed to produce the feeling of vibration is difficult to define, but it would not be under 10 cps or as high as 100 cps. The upper limit is also ill defined but may be as high as 10,000 cps or higher (Geldard, 1953).

Studies on patients with neurological lesions have demonstrated that the sense of vibration may be impaired by specific lesions. Damage to the posterior columns often results in impairment whereas damage to the anterolateral columns does not. Superficial cortical lesions usually do not impair vibratory sensibility, though deep lesions, which may involve the thalamus, more often do.

As for the peripheral receptor, there has been considerable controversy over whether the same receptors are used to convey both pressure and vibration or whether separate receptors are responsible for the two.

At the sensory level, Geldard (1940) conducted a convincing experiment indicating that touch and vibration are conveyed by the same receptors. He mapped out pressure-sensitive spots on an area of skin and found that these had low and consistent vibratory thresholds. Those spots which were pressure insensitive had much higher vibratory thresholds (Fig. 5–16). Geldard (1953) also points out that vibratory sensitivity varies as a function of skin temperature, in a similar fashion to pressure sensitivity. Weitz (1941) showed that vibratory thresholds were lowest around 4 degrees C. above normal skin temperature, and

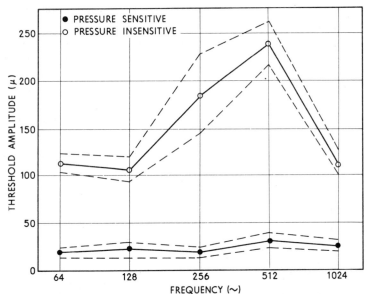

FIG. 5–16. Vibratory thresholds for two populations of sensory spots, one very sensitive to pressure and the other very insensitive. The dotted lines indicate the variability of measurement. (From Geldard, F. A., 1940; courtesy of *J. Gen. Psychol.,* 22. By permission of the Journal Press.)

rose rather steeply on either side of this optimum. Allers and Halpern (1921) also found pressure thresholds to be lowest at around 36 to 38 degrees C. and to rise on either side of these temperatures.

However, neurophysiologists have recently taken another view. They point out that Pacinian corpuscles are exquisitely sensitive to applied vibration but they are less suited to convey pressure. These corpuscles have been found in the periosteum, near tendons, joints, and muscles, where they are very well located for sensing vibration transmitted through the skeletal system. Hunt (1961) reports that various hair and touch receptors can follow low-frequency sinusoidal vibration (around 40 cps); that is, they can discharge with each cycle of movement. Muscle receptors can follow vibration frequencies up to about 150 cps. But the only known receptor capable of following frequencies about 200 cps is the Pacinian corpuscle. This responds to sinusoidal vibration in the range of about 50 to 800 cps (Fig. 5–9).

It might be concluded from this that a correspondence between pressure and vibration spots should be found with low vibration frequencies but not with high. But this has not been the finding. Geldard (1940) obtained a correspondence between pressure and vibration-sensitive spots for frequencies including 64 cps to 1,024 cps.

It may then be concluded that vibration sensitivity does not rest on the ability of a fiber to follow the vibration frequency of the stimulus. The function of vibration frequency discrimination is much more likely to depend on the ability of a fiber to follow different stimulus frequencies. This is a difficult function to test since subjective intensity also varies with frequency. Goff (1959) controlled for this variable by using equal-loudness stimuli varying in frequency. Under these conditions, she found that a very low frequencies frequency discrimination was good, but starting from below 100 cps. it very rapidly deteriorates (Fig. 5–17). It is obvious, therefore, that vibration frequency discrimination

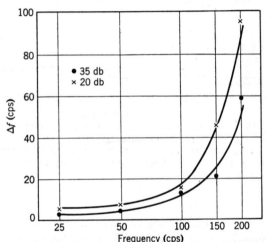

FIG. 5–17. Differential frequency discrimination of mechanical vibration applied to the fingertip, in a single subject. (Reprinted from *Sensory Communication,* edited by Walter Rosenblith (figure from F. A. Geldard after G. D. Goff); by permission of the M.I.T. Press, Cambridge, Mass. © 1961, the M.I.T. Press.)

at high frequencies must be very poor indeed. There is therefore no need to exclude as possible vibration receptors those which cannot follow high frequencies accurately. In addition, the Pacinian corpuscle will not follow frequencies above 1,000 cps., and we can perceive stimuli vibrating at frequencies higher than this.

This does not mean that Pacinian corpuscles are not involved in vibration perception but only that there is no reason to exclude other mechanoreceptors from this function. Geldard (1940) has shown that with areal stimulation the skin is most sensitive to vibration of around 250 cps, thresholds rising on either side of this. Plumb and Meigs (1961) recently confirmed that sensitivity was greatest in the region between

200 and 400 cps. This correlates with the behavior of the Pacinian corpuscle, which has its lowest threshold at around 300 cps (Sato, 1961).

Taking all this evidence together, it seems that vibration may be subserved both by pressure receptors and by specialized receptors which do not respond to maintained pressure.

In a recent set of experiments by Mountcastle and his associates (Mountcastle et al., Talbot et al.), thresholds for vibration perception were measured for the human hand, and these were correlated with afferent activity produced by identical stimuli to the monkey hand. Measurements were taken for stimuli up to 300 cps.

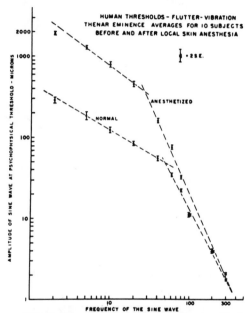

FIG. 5–18. Relation between the amplitude of a sine-wave oscillatory movement of the skin and the human threshold for the perception of movement, at a series of different frequencies. Stimuli delivered to the glabrous skin of the thenar eminence of the hand. Points on the graphs are the means for ten observers. Cutaneous anesthesia by cocaine iontophoresis elevated the thresholds for perception of low-frequency stimuli (2–40 cycles/sec) by factors of 5 to 10; sensitivity to high-frequency oscillation was little affected by skin anesthesia. Dissociation by cutaneous anesthesia of the double limbed threshold function suggests that the sense of flutter-vibration on the hand is served by two sets of primary afferents, one terminating in the glabrous skin, the other in deeper tissues. (From Talbot, W. H., et al., *J. Neurophysiol.*, 1968.)

In the human case it was found that the average threshold values, when plotted against stimulus frequency, were best fitted by two straight lines in log-log coordinates, intersecting at from 40 to 50 cps (Fig. 5–18). When the skin was anaesthetized by cocaine iontophoresis, thresholds rose considerably in the 5 to 40 cps. range but remained virtually unchanged for the upper values. This led to the conclusion that vibration sensitivity was subserved by two types of afferent: the first innervating the skin and responsive to low vibration frequencies (or "flutter") and the second innervating the deep tissues and subserving higher vibration frequencies.

In the case of the monkey, two corresponding sets of afferents were found. One, which innervated the skin, was sensitive to low-frequency vibration (Fig. 5–19) and the second, which terminated in deep tissue

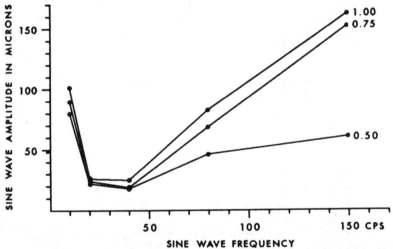

FIG. 5–19. Tuning curves for a quickly adapting afferent innervating the glabrous skin of the monkey hand, isolated by microdissection of the median nerve. The three curves plot the amplitude of the sine wave, at a series of frequencies, required to raise the probability to the levels indicated that an impulse will be evoked by each cycle of the stimulus. (From Talbot, W. H., et al., *J. Neurophysiol.*, 1968.)

and probably ended in Pacinian corpuscles, was highly sensitive to vibrations at higher frequencies (Fig. 5–20).

Mountcastle (1961) reports that with very light anaesthesia, cortical neurons follow repetitive cutaneous stimuli beat for beat at frequencies up to about 75 to 100 per second. At higher frequencies, the response equilibrates. It may be that vibration frequency discrimination depends on the ability of central neurons to follow the stimulus frequency.

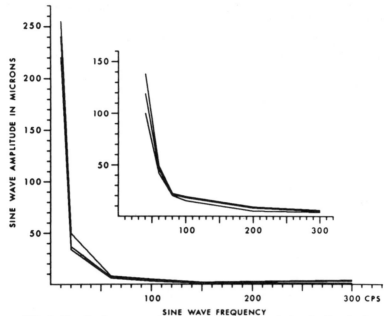

FIG. 5–20. Tuning curves for two Pacinian afferents terminating in deep tissues of the monkey hand, each isolated separately by microdissection of the median nerve. Stimuli were delivered to palmar skin. The three curves in each plot, from upper to lower, the amplitude required to raise the probability to 1.0, 0.75, and 0.50 respectively that an impulse will be evoked by each cycle of the stimulus. Inset curves are typical of Pacinian afferents; the other curves are those for the Pacinian with the widest frequency sensitivity observed. It was unique in this respect. (From Talbot, W. H., et al., *J. Neurophysiol.*, 1968.)

HEAT

At temperatures roughly above 45 degrees C. a sensation of heat, which is quite distinct from that of warmth, emerges. It has long been thought that this sensation is linked to the paradoxical discharge of cold receptors. As described above, Von Frey (1895) found that at temperatures above 45 degrees C. previously mapped cold spots will respond with a sensation of cold. Dodt and Zotterman (1952b) placed this on a neurophysiological basis by showing that at temperatures above 45 degrees C. a steady discharge of cold fibers occurs, with a maximum frequency at 50 degrees C. (Fig. 5–11).

Alrutz (1900) proposed that the sensation of heat was due to a fusion of warmth and paradoxical cold. That mixed warm and cold sensations can cause the impression of heat is demonstrated by the "heat grill." This consists of a grill made of parallel tubes which are alternately warm and cold (but none hot). Touching this grill will often give an impression of heat. Also, the simultaneous stimulation of a single cold spot with a cold stimulus and a single warm spot with a warm stimulus may produce the impression of heat (Alston, 1920). However, under normal conditions, stimuli described as "hot" are also above the pain threshold. Therefore a discharge from pain receptors also usually underlies the sensation of heat.

chapter 6

Central Pathways
for the Skin Senses

PROJECTION PATHWAYS

Spinal Cord to Thalamus

Fibers conveying sensory information through the spinal nerves enter the spinal cord by way of the dorsal roots. The cell bodies for these fibers lie in the spinal ganglion, which is an enlargement or swelling of the dorsal root. A dermatome is that skin area which is supplied with afferent fibers by one dorsal root. There is considerable overlap between dermatomes of neighboring roots. As each dorsal root enters the cord, it branches into many filaments. Each filament separates into a large medial division which contains large fibers and a small lateral division containing small fibers.

Fibers of the medial division enter the ipsilateral dorsal columns without synapse and there ascend the cord. Some terminate at various levels in the gray matter of the cord. The remaining fibers terminate in the dorsal column nuclei of the medulla (the nuclei gracilis and cuneatus) and there synapse with second-order neurons.

Fibers arising in the dorsal column nuclei cross the midline and ascend in the tract of the medial lemniscus to end mainly in the lateral part of the ventrobasal complex of the thalamus. Some fibers terminate in portions of the posterior nuclear group of the thalamus, especially the magnocellular and suprageniculate nuclei of the medial geniculate complex (Bowsher, 1961; Perl and Whitlock, 1961).

Fibers ascending the dorsal columns give off collaterals at various levels, which synapse in the dorsal horns. Second-order neurons arising therefrom cross to the opposite side and ascend as part of the spinothalamic tract in the anterolateral region of the cord.

Fibers of the lateral division of the dorsal root enter the tract of Lissauer (dorsolateral fasciculus) located at the tip of the dorsal horn, ascend there a segment or two, and terminate in the substantia gelatinosa Rolandi. From here arise second-order neurons which cross to the opposite side and ascend there as part of the spinothalamic tract.

It is generally believed that the collaterals of the dorsal column fibers contribute to the ventral spinothalamic tract and that fibers from the lateral division of the dorsal root contribute to the lateral spinothalamic tract. However, this dissociation has been questioned.

The spinothalamic pathway projects bilaterally onto the thalamus, which it enters as lateral and medial bundles (Bowsher, 1961). The main lateral distribution is to the lateral part of the ventrobasal complex of the thalamus. Some fibers end in portions of the posterior nuclear group (Poggio and Mountcastle, 1960), especially the magnocellular and suprageniculate nuclei of the medial geniculate body. The medial part of the tract is distributed to several intralaminar nuclei, and also to the centrum medianum, according to some definitions but not others (Bowsher, 1961; Whitlock and Perl, 1961).

Instead of ascending to the thalamus, many spinothalamic fibers terminate in various portions of the brain stem reticular formation (Mehler et al., 1960; Mehler, 1961). In return there is a strong input from the reticular formation to the diffuse thalamic nuclei.

In the cat, a further afferent pathway has been demonstrated which ascends in the dorsomedial part of the lateral funiculus (Morin, 1955; Lundberg and Oscarsson, 1961). The first neuron relays in the dorsal horn on the same side as its entrance to the cord (Eccles, Eccles, and Lundberg, 1960). The second neuron relays in the lateral cervical nucleus of the same side, and the third in the ventrobasal complex of the contralateral thalamus (Busch, 1961).

Trigeminal Pathways to the Thalamus

Fibers transmitting sensory information from the face and head enter the pons through the sensory root of the trigeminal nerve. Most of these fibers bifurcate, a fine branch ending in the main sensory nucleus of the pons and a larger branch following the spinal tract of the trigeminal nerve to end in the spinal nucleus of the medulla (Cajal, 1955). Other fibers connect only with the main nucleus, and yet others only with the spinal nucleus.

Fibers arising in the main sensory nucleus cross the midline and, lying adjacent to the medial lemniscus, ascend to the medial component of the ventrobasal complex of the thalamus. Other fibers, originating in the main sensory nucleus, form a dorsal pathway, which some believe to be both crossed and uncrossed, others only uncrossed. This pathway is believed to terminate in the medial component of the ventrobasal complex, or in the centrum medianum, or both.

Fibers arising in the spinal nucleus ascend as the bulbothalamic tract, the exact course of which is unclear, though it runs for a while in the reticular substance of the brain stem tegmentum. This tract is believed to terminate in the medial component of the ventrobasal complex and the centrum medianum. Some fibers of the spinal nucleus appear to contribute to the medial lemniscal projection (Gordon, Landgren, and Seed, 1961).

Pathways from the glossopharyngeal and vagus nerves also exist, but these have been less well worked out.

Thalamus to Cortex

The primary cortical sensory receiving area (SI) is located in the postcentral gyrus and receives projections from the ventrobasal complex of the thalamus, and possibly also from the posterior nuclear group. The second somatic area (SII) is located in the anterior ectosylvian gyrus in the cat (and the corresponding region in primates) and probably receives projections both from the posterior nuclear group of the thalamus and also from the ventrobasal complex (Andersson, 1962). The precentral gyrus also receives sensory projections (Gardner and Morin, 1953; Kruger, 1956), and the lateral and suprasylvian gyri should probably be included as part of the cortical sensory projection area (Albe-Fessard and Rougeul, 1955).

SOMATOTOPIC ORGANIZATION

First- and Second-Order Neurons

Centrally projecting fibers in the dorsal columns are arranged in an orderly lamination, such that fibers from each progressively higher body segment are arranged just lateral to those from the segment immediately below (Fig. 6–1). There is very little overlap between fibers from different segments, though overlap between fibers from the same segment occurs. In the dorsal column nuclei the lamellar arrangement is preserved, fibers from the caudal segments terminating medially and those from the higher segments laterally (Kuhn, 1949). At all rostro-caudal levels of the dorsal column nuclear complex, a somatotopic organization is apparent both along the medio-lateral axes and the dorso-ventral axes, with the caudal regions of the body represented medially and the limb apices dorsally (Kruger et al., 1961).

A somatotopic representation of the face, with the mandibular division

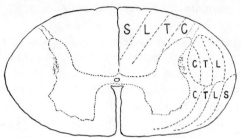

FIG. 6–1. Diagram of the cervical spinal cord showing lamination in various tracts. Since there is considerable overlapping and intermingling of fibers, the dividing lines shown here are arbitrary. *C,* cervical. *T,* thoracic. *L,* lumbar. *S,* sacral. (From Ranson, S. W., and Clark, S. L., 1959, *The Anatomy of the Nervous System,* after Walker, A.; courtesy of W. B. Saunders Co., Philadelphia.)

lying dorsally, the opthalmic division ventrally, and the interior of the buccal cavity medially, occurs at all rostro-caudal levels of the sensory trigeminal nuclear complex. That is, each point on the face is projected onto a column of cells extending from the rostral portion of the main sensory nucleus to the caudal portion of the spinal nucleus (Kruger and Michel, 1962a; Wall and Taub, 1962; Eisenman et al., 1963). In fact, if a cross section were taken through the dorsal column nuclei and the caudal part of the descending trigeminal nucleus together, the "distribution can best be visualized as a cat lying on its back which forms the floor of the DCN complex, with its tail extending to the midline; the hindlimb, forelimb and face successively more lateral, and the paws of each foot pointed up and located at the dorsal edge of the DCN complex" (Kruger et al., 1961). This representation is shown in Figure 6–2. The projection is entirely ipsilateral, except that the perioral region has some bilateral representation.

Fiber tracts in the anterolateral columns are also laminated. Here fibers from the more caudal body segments lie lateral to those from higher segments (Fig. 6–1). However, much intermingling of fibers from different skin segments takes place. This considerable overlap is confirmed in the spinothalamic tract in midbrain regions by stimulation studies in man during mesencephalectomy for the relief of intractable pain (Spiegel and Wycis, 1961).

Thalamus

Neurons of the trigeminal nuclear complex project onto the medial division of the ventrobasal complex of the thalamus, and those from the dorsal column nuclei onto its lateral division, in an orderly fashion.

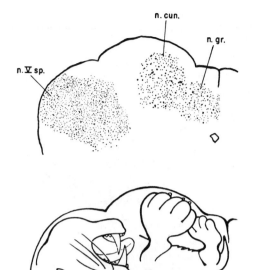

FIG. 6–2. Sensory representation in a cross section through the dorsal column nuclei and the caudal part of the descending trigeminal nucleus of the cat. (From Kruger, L., et al., *J. Neurophysiol.*, 1961, 24.)

Spinothalamic neurons projecting onto the ventrobasal complex intermingle in the same somatotopic organization (Whitlock and Perl, 1959). A similar organization is apparent at the thalamic level, as at the level of first relay, though reversed mediolaterally (Kruger et al., 1961).

In detailed studies on the rabbit, cat, and monkey, Mountcastle and his collaborators (1949, 1952, 1959) have shown that the body surface is projected contralaterally onto the ventrobasal complex, with the head posteromedial, the tail anterolateral, the back superior, and the feet inferior. The perioral and intraoral regions project ipsilaterally as well as contralaterally. Stimulation studies on patients during the course of thalamotomy for the relief of intractable pain have yielded a map of the body surface similar to that found in the monkey with the use of recording techniques (Monnier, 1955).

No clear somatotopic organization is apparent in the posterior nuclear region of the thalamus (Whitlock and Perl, 1961; Poggio and Mountcastle, 1960). Nor does such an organization exist at the centrum medianum or the intralaminar nuclei.

Cortex

The projection of fibers from the ventrobasal complex to the postcentral gyrus of the cortex is orderly, so that the topographic relationships in the former region are preserved in the latter, though in reverse position. The medial region of the ventrobasal complex (face area) projects near the Sylvian fissure. The lateral region of the lateral portion of the ventrobasal complex (leg area) projects dorsomedially. Fibers from intermediate regions of the ventrobasal complex also project into intermediate regions of the cortical area (Fig. 6–3). Penfield and his col-

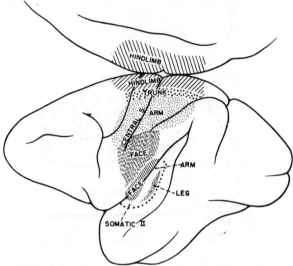

FIG. 6–3. Sensory representation in the cortex of the monkey. In this diagram the medial aspect of the hemisphere is shown as adjoining the dorsolateral aspect. Somatic area II extends into the superior bank of the Sylvian fissure. The area enclosed by open circles is normally in the depths of the fissure and so not visible in this view. (From Terzuolo, P., and Adey, W. R., in *Handbook of Physiology*, Vol. II; by permission of the American Physiological Society.)

laborators have shown by studies on patients that a somatotopic organization also exists in the postcentral gyrus in the human case (Fig. 6–4).

A detailed somatotopic projection of the body surface is also apparent at the second somatic area, though in a different order. The face areas of SI and SII are adjacent to each other (Fig. 6–3). The projection to SII, however, is bilateral.

The somatosensory cortex is organized in a series of vertical columns oriented perpendicular to the cortical surface. All neurons forming part of a vertical column appear to have roughly similar receptive fields and to respond to the same type of stimulus modality. This is true both of SI (Mountcastle, 1961) and SII (Carreras and Levitt, 1959).

The proportional amount of tissue accorded centrally to a given body

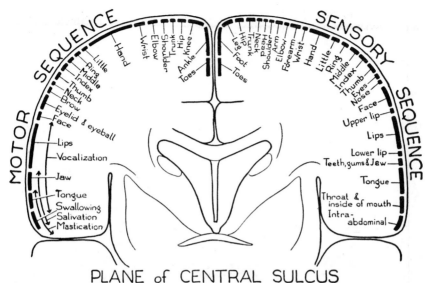

PLANE of CENTRAL SULCUS

FIG. 6–4.   Diagram of sensory and motor sequences in the cortex of man. The bars indicate roughly the extent of cortical area devoted to each body region. (From Rasmussen, G., and Penfield, W., *Fed. Proc. 1947*, 455.)

region does not mirror its actual proportional size. Regions which possess greater peripheral innervation density are accorded a correspondingly larger portion of central tissue. Receptive fields in these areas are also smaller. For instance, receptive fields located on progressively more distal portions of a limb are found to be progressively smaller. Table 6–1

TABLE 6–1

Region	A: Hair		B: Touch	
	Avg. Area, Sq. Mm. (Range)	No. of Units	Av. Area, Sq. Mm. (Range)	No. of Units
Digit.................	48 (6–200)	46	444 (228–765)	3
Foot	280 (28–900)	30	1,818 (500–4,500)	19
Leg..................	733 (50–1,140)	5	4,121 (950–7,100)	13
Thigh	1,620 (100–2,550)	4	6,416 (3,150–12,000)	16
Hip and flank........	2,010 (600–6,600)	7	10,742 (4,050–28,900	13
Tail.................	1,466 (900–2,300)	5	6,800	1

Average receptive field sizes for two types of neuron in the nucleus gracilis of the cat: hair units (A) and touch units (B). The neurons are here classified by their location on the limb. For both of neurons, the receptive fields located on progressively more distal regions of the limb are shown to be progressively smaller. (From Perl, E. R., *et al., J. Neurophysiol.*, 1962, 25).

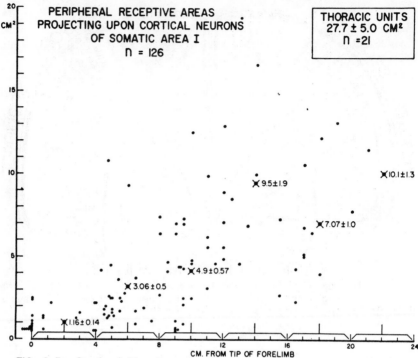

FIG. 6–5. Graph plotting the areas (in sq. cm.) of excitatory peripheral receptive fields of cortical neurons against the distances of the centers of these receptive fields from the tip of the contralateral foreleg of the cat. The crossed dots represent the means of these peripheral receptive field sizes when these are grouped into classes by 4 cm. distances from the limb tip. Standard errors are also given. (From Mountcastle, V. B., *J. Neurophysiol.*, 1957, 20, 408.)

shows such a relation at the level of the dorsal column nuclei and Figure 6–5 at the somatosensory cortex. The same variation in receptive field size may exist at the level of the peripheral nerve (Yamamoto et al., 1956). These factors are further correlated with the degree to which the animal employs the body region in question. Thus the face is always accorded a disproportionately large amount of central tissue, as are the distal as opposed to the proximal portions of the limbs. Also, when different species of animal are compared, the amount of central tissue devoted to a body region varies with the degree to which that species of animal employs this particular organ. Thus the rabbit has a very large trigeminal representation. And in the monkey, much more than in the rabbit, the paws are extensively represented.

These correlations are of course to be expected since the more complex or sensitive the functions carried out by a body region, the more information has to be conveyed from the periphery and processed by central structures.

Weinstein (1968) attempted to correlate the amount of cortical area subserving each body part in the human tactile sensitivity as determined by various measures. He found that such a correlation exists for point localization and two-point discrimination, but not for pressure sensitivity. Receptive field sizes have been determined mainly in subhuman species, and a meaningful comparison cannot be made in absolute terms between these and the two-point threshold in man. However, the relative size of receptive field in animals taken from different regions of the body correlate very well with relative differences in two-point threshold determined in man for the different bodily regions.

RECEPTIVE FIELD CHARACTERISTICS

It has found at the level of the peripheral fiber that a receptive field may show a gradient of sensitivity. Stimulation at the center of the field may evoke discharge at shortest latency, highest frequency, and slowest adaptation. Sensitivity diminishes with distance from the center of the field (Iggo, 1960). In some cases this would be expected on physical grounds. For instance, if the head of a pin is pressed into the skin, the resultant skin deformation would be maximal at the center. A discrete thermal stimulus would also transfer most heat at the center of the field of stimulation. This explanation would hold only under some conditions, for instance, if the receptive field were not larger than the zone of deformation produced may be mechanical stimulus.

At the level of the first relay, several peripheral fibers converge onto the same central cells, and the same peripheral fiber sends branches to several central cells. Receptive fields at this level are therefore considerably larger and also overlap more than those of peripheral fibers. This pattern of convergence-divergence would be expected in itself to give rise to a gradient of sensitivity, sensitivity being again greater in the middle of the receptive field since here the synaptic linkages are strongest. Such is in fact the case. The studies of Mountcastle and Powell (1959) on single units in the cortex have shown that cells in the middle of the cortical discharge zone discharge the largest number of impulses with the greatest probability and at shortest latencies. The farther from the center a cell is located, the fewer the number of discharges and the longer the discharge latencies. Reciprocally, a given cortical cell will be excited maximally by one point on the receptive field, and less so by points located nearer the periphery of the field. This gradient of sensitivity could provide a means whereby information as to the locus of a peripheral stimulus is preserved in spite of enlarged and overlapping receptive fields.

Some neurons with extremely large receptive fields have been found at each stage in the sensory pathway. Several units in the thalamus and cortex were found to cover one half of the entire animal; some cover the entire body surface (see below). The functions of these units 'remain unknown. Many are activated only by noxious stimuli. It may be that these mediate gross withdrawal responses. In other cases, where the units also respond to light mechanical stimuli, it may be that they are integrating information arriving simultaneously from various body areas. Greater sensitivity can also be obtained by summing information over large regions of the body.

LATERAL INHIBITION

Evoked responses in many central neurons may be inhibited by stimulation of a different region of skin. The inhibitory receptive field may surround the excitatory field, or may lie adjacent to it, or even be removed from it. In those cases where the zone of inhibition surrounds the zone of excitation, this has the effect of sharpening the receptive field and therefore providing better spatial acuity. Lateral inhibition has been found as early in the somatosensory pathway as the nucleus gracilis (Perl et al., 1962) and as far up as the cortex (Mountcastle, 1961; Andersson, 1962). Temporal and spatial summation of such inhibitory effects occur (Mountcastle, 1961). Figure 6–6 shows some inhibitory and excitatory fields in the second somatic area of the cortex. Lateral inhibition also occurs in other sensory systems and is especially prominent in the visual system (see Chapter 3).

MODALITY SPECIFICITY IN THE CENTRAL PATHWAYS

Dorsal Columns

In the spinal nerve, fibers sensitive to different kinds of sensory stimulation are intermingled. In the cord, however, some separation according to modality occurs. The clinical evidence shows that the dorsal columns contain fibers subserving touch, pressure, and kinesthesis, and complex discriminatory functions related to these. Destruction of the dorsal columns in man leads to an inability to determine the position and movement of limbs as well as to recognize vibratory stimuli. There is also an impairment of localization of sensory stimuli and of appreciation of spatial and temporal stimulus sequences. These symptoms are also found in tabes dorsalis, a disease in which there is degeneration of the dorsal columns.

In man, pain is generally held not to be mediated by the dorsal columns. Very good evidence for this view lies in the high success rate of anterolateral cordotomy for the relief of intractable pain. This opera-

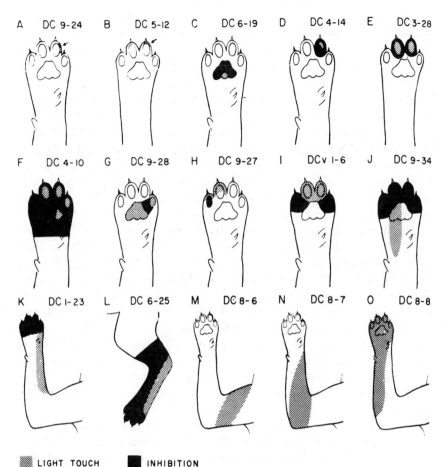

A   DC 9-24   B   DC 5-12   C   DC 6-19   D   DC 4-14   E   DC 3-28

F   DC 4-10   G   DC 9-28   H   DC 9-27   I   DCv 1-6   J   DC 9-34

K   DC 1-23   L   DC 6-25   M   DC 8-6   N   DC 8-7   O   DC 8-8

░ LIGHT TOUCH   ■ INHIBITION

FIG. 6–6. Typical excitatory and inhibitory receptive fields for units in the second somatic area of the cortex in cats with intact dorsal columns. These units were activated by light stimulation of the skin of contralateral limbs. B, E and L represent hindlimbs; all the drawings represent forelimbs. (From Andersson, S. A., Acta Physiol. Scand., 56, suppl. 194, 1967, 16.)

tion spares the dorsal columns. However, the evidence in this regard is not completely clear cut. Severe tingling has on occasion been obtained upon stimulation of the dorsal columns (Foerster and Gagel, 1932; Sweet, 1959). Also, Browder and Gallagher (1948) found that relief of pain in a phantom limb was obtained in three out of four patients by division of the dorsal column.

In animals, it may be that the dorsal columns also play a role in pain perception. Lesions in the anterior region of the cord do not abolish pain responses in dogs or monkeys (Cadwalder and Sweet, 1912; Mott, 1892), in contrast to the human case.

Single-unit studies in the nucleus gracilis have also yielded information concerning modality transmission in the lemniscal pathway (Wall, 1961; Perl et al., 1962). Perl et al. (1962) found that most of the units here could be classified into three groups. The first group of units discharged to hair bending and adapted rapidly. The second group responded to light touch and adapted slowly to a maintained tactile stimulus. They also demonstrated a background discharge in the absence of mechanical stimulation, the frequency of which varied with changing temperature. The relation between discharge frequency and skin temperature depended on the rate and duration of the temperature change, rather than on the absolute temperature level. The third group responded well to jarring or vibratory stimuli, and were able to follow the frequency of applied vibration in the range from 70 to 350 cps. A few units responding to joint movement were also found. The response characteristics of the first three types of unit were considered very similar to these of certain peripheral units studied by Hunt and McIntyre (1960a and b) and Hunt (1961) (see Chapter 5). The authors conclude that these receptors had separate and specific projections to gracilis neurons. However, many of the receptive fields of these second-order neurons were much larger than those of the peripheral fibers. Many second-order touch units, for instance, had fields which extended almost throughout the lateral or medial half of the hind limb (though quite small receptive fields were also found). It was therefore concluded that several peripheral fibers of the same modality converged onto a single second-order neuron.

In the case of hair units, it was further found that evoked responses could be inhibited by stimulation of the skin surrounding the excitatory receptive field. The other types of unit did not show this inhibitory interaction.

This study therefore demonstrates both the preservation of response characteristic and also some further organization of the incoming information at the level of the second-order neuron.

Anterolateral Columns

Clinical evidence shows the spinothalamic tract to contain fibers subserving pain (including visceral) and temperature as well as touch. In syringomyelia, a disease in which fibers crossing in the anterior commissure are disrupted, there occurs a loss of pain and temperature sensibility in the corresponding body segments, though tactile sensitivity appears unimpaired. Also, anterolateral cordotomy, that is, surgical interruption of the anterolateral columns (generally undertaken for the relief of intractable pain), produces little change in tactile sensibility, though there is an increase in tactile threshold. However, pain and temperature sensations are lost. (Visceral pain is lost if the operation is bilateral.) Sometimes the sense of tickle may also be lost, and disturbances in sexual sensations occur.

Classically, it is thought that the ventral spinothalamic tract is concerned with touch and the lateral with pain and temperature. However, there is no concrete evidence that this is the case (Rose and Mountcastle, 1959). The difficulty in establishing the exact locus of tactile fibers is partly due to the fact that since the dorsal columns also mediate tactile sensations, there is little demonstrable loss in tactile sensibility when the anterolateral columns are sectioned.

It is also classically believed that fibers concerned with temperature lie separate to those concerned with pain in the lateral spinothalamic tract (Foerster, 1936; Foerster and Gagel, 1932). However, when anterolateral cordotomies are performed, analgesia and thermanesthesia usually occur together. Yet a few cases have been reported of the loss of thermal sensibility without loss of pain sensibility, and vice versa. There also occur, sometimes, cases of dissociated loss of sensibility to heat or to cold (Head, 1920). The existence and yet rarity of such dissociations leads one to conclude that there probably are separate pain and temperature fibers in the spinothalamic tract but that they are on the whole intermingled. Sweet (1950) found that stimulation of the spinothalamic tract in conscious patients yielded reports of either pain or temperature (mainly heat), though no touch. The fibers mediating the different sensations appeared intermingled.

Single-unit studies on dorsal horn cells have added some further potential information concerning modality transmission in the spinothalamic pathways. However, the projections of the axons of the neurons studied are in most cases unknown; so it is difficult to draw specific conclusions from these studies. Some neurons responded only to one modality, such as touch or noxious stimulation; others responded to more than one (Kolmodin and Skoglund, 1960; Wall, 1960). Receptive fields varied from small to very wide, some being scattered (Hunt and Kuno, 1959). In some cases, stimulating one skin area produced an increased discharge frequency while the same stimulus to another area produced inhibition of discharge in the same neuron. Here it is apparent, as in the dorsal column nuclei, that many peripheral fibers must converge onto a single second-order neuron. But it seems that here the convergence is not restricted to fibers of the same modality.

Wall (1960, 1961) describes a group of neurons in the dorsal horn which responded in a different manner to several types of peripheral stimulus. They responded as though afferent fibers sensitive to different degrees of pressure converged onto them. Also, single cells responded both to pressure and to warming of the skin—to the latter with an increased average frequency of spontaneous discharge. Effects of high pressure and high temperature stimulation (which both produce pain in man) were similar; and application of vibration and an itch-producing substance to the skin also produced characteristic patterns of response.

Unfortunately, it is not known whether these neurons (studied by Wall) form part of a true sensory pathway or whether they are involved merely in the formation of reflexes for which discrimination among the different modalities of stimulation would be unnecessary. However, Wall and Cronley-Dillon (1960) present some evidence that these cells may actually be transmitting information concerning different sensory modalities by means of different patterns of discharge.

Wall argues that if information concerning stimulus modality were transmitted via the discharge pattern of a cell, factors altering the discharge pattern should also alter the experienced sensation. Further, where the discharge pattern to two types of stimuli was identical, one should expect these stimuli to be confused at the sensory level. Wall points to two such examples. The first concerns the effect of a vibratory stimulus applied to a given region of skin on the simultaneous application of another stimulus to the same region. Such vibratory stimuli cause the cells under discussion to produce a characteristic pattern of alternating activition and inhibition, and considerably raise their threshold for the emission of the high-frequency discharge which is characteristic on the presentation of other types of stimulus to the skin. Wall argues that if these cells really did convey information concerning stimulus modality, vibrating an area of skin in man should cause sensitivity to other modalities of sensation in that region to decrease. It was indeed found that light vibration raises the threshold in this region in man for touch, pain, and temperature. Another example is the similar response of such cells to extreme heat and high distorting pressures to the skin, which cause similarly painful sensations in man.

The lateral tract located in the dorsomedial part of the lateral funiculus appears to transmit specific tactile information. Lundberg and Oscarsson (1961) report that single units in this tract responded effectively to light touch over a restricted receptive field and did not respond with increased activation to stronger mechanical stimuli. Further, Norsell (quoted by Andersson, 1962) reports that in dogs, unilateral interruption of the lateral tract in the dorsomedial part of the lateral funiculus abolished unilaterally a conditioned response established to puffs of air applied to the hindlimbs.

Sensory Trigeminal Nuclear Complex

The clinical evidence indicates that the main sensory nucleus is primarily concerned with tactile information and the spinal nucleus with pain and temperature. Sjöqvist (1938) found that sectioning afferent fibers to the caudal part of the spinal nucleus (trigeminal tractotomy) produced a severe loss of pain and temperature sensibility in the face, yet very little impairment in tactile sensibility. However, single-unit studies in the cat have produced results at variance with these findings. Many authors have reported the presence of neurons in the spinal nucleus as well as in the main sensory nucleus sensitive to light tactile stimuli (Gordon et al., 1960; Kruger et al., 1961; Kruger and Michel, 1962b; Eisenman et al., 1963). Also, differences could not be found between these two nuclei concerning responsiveness to noxious stimuli. Kruger and Michel (1962b) and Wall and Taub (1962) were unable to find units in either of the trigeminal nuclei which responded specifically to noxious stimulation. In contrast, Eisenman et al. (1963) found many cells which discharged only to noxious stimuli. Some responded to noxious mechanical stimuli but not to noxious thermal stimuli; others to both. However, these units were found in the main sensory nucleus as well as in the spinal nucleus, and the authors conclude that the two nuclei could not be separated on this basis.

Specific temperature fibers in the trigeminal nuclear complex have not been found. However, Wall and Taub (1962) describe certain pressure-sensitive cells that also responded to changes in temperature.

Single-unit studies performed on the cat have failed to explain the clinical evidence on separation of function within the sensory trigeminal nuclear complex in man. It may be, however, that this is due to the difference in species investigated. Perhaps similar studies on the monkey will produce results more in line with the clinical evidence.

Brain Stem between Spinal Cord and Thalamus

Lesions in the brain stem between the spinal cord and the thalamus may give rise to analgesia and thermanesthesia. However, appreciation of pain, warmth, or cold may be impaired independently (Von Monakow, 1908; Mann, 1892; Head, 1920). There may result a raising of the tactile threshold, and sometimes an impairment of more complex functions, such as tactile localization, two-point discrimination, or appreciation of passive movement. In some cases, a pain syndrome may result. The affected regions lie in the contralateral side of the body. Stimulation of the spinothalamic tract in patients during mesencephalotomy for the relief of intractable pain may produce pain of a tingling, burning, or pricking quality. "Electrical" sensations have also been reported (Spiegel and Wycis, 1961). These sensations are usually projected to the side opposite that of stimulation, though bilateral sensations can occur. In some cases the pain is diffusely localized; in others it occurs in relatively specific regions of the body, such as the face, arm, chest, or leg.

Central Midbrain Structures

It will be recalled that many spinothalamic fibers feed into various regions of the brain stem reticular formation. There is good reason to suppose that at least some of these fibers are concerned with pain, for if the spinothalamic tract is interrupted at the midbrain level, a pain syndrome may develop. Various writers (Walker, 1943; Bowsher, 1957; Spiegel and Wycis, 1961) attribute this pain sensibility following mesencephalic tractotomy to the functioning of the more medially placed structures.

Also, stimulation of various centrally placed midbrain regions has been found to give rise to reactions of fear and rage, and though some of these have been interpreted as demonstrating the existence of fear and rage "centers," the possibility that this stimulation causes pain or some unpleasant sensation is very strong in some cases. Spiegel et al. (1954) interpreted the reactions of cats upon stimulation of the mesencephalic tectum as being pain suggestive, and Delgado (1955) came to a similar conclusion upon observing the reactions of monkeys upon stimulation of the inferomedial part of the mesencephalic central gray matter. Further, Spiegel and Wycis (1961) report that, in patients, stimulation in the midbrain tegmentum, probably of neurons of the reticular system, elicited pain sensations which were projected mainly contralateral to the point of stimulation; and Reyes et al. (1951) found that stimulation of the midbrain tectum produces pain in patients, projected to the contralateral side.

Thalamus

Ventrobasal Complex. Studying single-unit responses to various forms of mechanoreception, Poggio and Mountcastle (1960) concluded that neurons in this region showed a high degree of modality specificity, with small contralateral receptive fields. Perl and Whitlock (1961) also found, in animals with spinal lesions sparing only the anterolateral tracts, that single units in the ventrobasal complex demonstrated a high degree of specificity, responding either to light touch, joint rotation, hair displacement, deep pressure, or heat of tissue-damaging intensity with very restricted contralateral receptive fields. The effect of thermal stimuli in the medium ranges was not investigated in either of these studies.

Landgren (1961), studying responses of single ventrobasal units to stimulation of the tongue of the cat, also found that most of the neurons were responsive to only one stimulus modality. Of these, touch cells comprised a large proportion. Cold cells also were numerous. One thalamic cell was activated by warming. He found some cells which responded both to touch and cooling.

Some ventrobasal neurons were found to be exquisitely sensitive to the stimulus parameters employed. The cold cells investigated by Landgren behaved in a fashion similar to those found in peripheral nerve fibers (see Chapter 5). Sudden drops in temperature caused an immediate increase in discharge frequency, and warming the tongue caused a decrease in firing frequency. With a constant temperature, the fiber adapted to a steady discharge. These cold cells also discharged to very high peripheral temperatures (paradoxical cold discharge). The frequency of steady discharge in these thalamic neurons was both higher and less regular than that of peripheral cold cells. Other ventrobasal neurons responded only phasically to drops in temperature.

Similarly, Poulos and Benjamin (1968) have found two types of neuron in the ventrobasal complex of squirrel monkeys which responded to thermal stimulation of the tongue. One type of neuron responded to cooling and mechanical stimuli, and the other type responded only to cooling. The response of the latter type of unit was very similar to that found in the analogous peripheral fibers. Intermingled with these thermal units were others which responded only to mechanical stimulation.

A similar exquisite sensitivity to stimulus parameters has been found in units activated by joint rotation (see below).

Posterior Nuclear Region. Units in the posterior nuclear region were found regularly to have very large receptive fields, which were often stocking-like in shape and frequently bilateral (Poggio and Mountcastle, 1960; Perl and Whitlock, 1961). Some receptive fields were so large as to include all four limbs; some were scattered. Perl and Whitlock (1961) found that most of these units responded to light mechanical stimuli. In contrast, Poggio and Mountcastle (1960) found that nearly 60 percent of these neurons could be activated only by noxious stimulation, the remaining cells responding to light mechanical stimuli. Some units were activated by light mechanical stimuli over one part of their receptive field and by noxious stimuli over another (Fig. 6–7). This discrepancy between the two sets of findings may be due to a difference in the anaesthetic levels employed, or to a difference in anatomical location of the units studied. Complex patterns of excitation and inhibition exist in this region. Some cells were activated from one side of the body and inhibited from the other side. Others were excited from small fields, and yet could be inhibited from almost the entire remaining body area.

Some cells in this region were found to be activated by acoustic and vibratory as well as simple somatic stimuli; occlusion between somatic and auditory inputs occurred commonly. Other cells in this

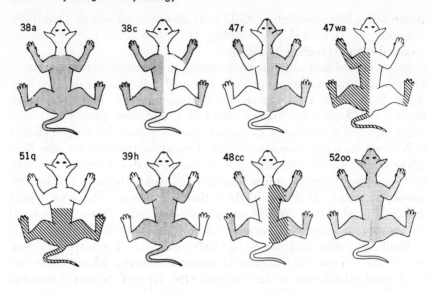

Receptive fields of units driven by mechanical stimuli

Receptive fields of units driven by noxious stimuli

FIG. 6–7. Typical receptive fields for neurons in the posterior nuclear group of the thalamus. The righthand side of each figurine drawing represents the ipsilateral side of the body, relative to the recording electrode. (From Poggio, G. F., and Mountcastle, V. B., *Bull. Johns Hopkins Hosp.*, 1960, 106.)

region were sensitive only to acoustic stimuli. Also, although discrete thermal stimuli were not employed, changes in general skin temperature produced profound changes in the activity of these cells.

Intralaminar Nuclei and Centrum Medianum. Units located in the intralaminar nuclei and centrum medianum responded only to noxious stimuli, receptive fields being very large, and bilateral (Perl and Whitlock, 1961). Albe-Fessard and Kruger (1962) report that cells in the centrum medianum-parafascicular complex responded only to noxious stimuli localized anywhere on the body. Some neurons fired at short latency and others only after a delay. A few units emitted both short and long latency responses. The long latency response of such units may be related to the phenomenon of second pain (see Chapter 5).

Lesion studies in patients have further implicated this area in pain sensitivity. Ervin and Mark (1961) report that lesions in the ventroposterior nuclei did not alleviate pain of terminal cancer in patients. However, lesions in the centromedian and intralaminar nuclei provided relief of pain. Hécaen et al. (1949) found that a marked reduction in the perception of painful stimuli resulted from lesions located mainly in the centrum medianum. Interestingly enough, however, they did not produce pain upon stimulation of this structure. Another finding which is against the supposition that these units underlie pain sensitivity is that they will not respond to a slowly applied pinprick, or to light touch on the cornea, both of which are painful (Kruger, 1959).

Thalamic Lesions and Deficits in Sensibility. Thalamic lesions often result in a raising of tactile thresholds in the affected regions, which lie on the side of the body contralateral to the lesion. Vibration sense is often disturbed. Appreciation of posture and passive movement are often affected, as are stimulus localization, two-point discrimination, and other tests of discriminative function. The appreciation of heat and cold may be defective. Pain sensibility is often disturbed, and a pain syndrome may develop (Head, 1920).

Cortex

First Somatic Area. Mountcastle (1961), studying the response of SI neurons only to various forms of mechanoreception, concluded that most neurons were specific as to mode and place. However, other cells in this region displayed very large receptive fields and showed complex patterns of excitation and inhibition (Mountcastle and Powell, 1959). For instance, some could be excited by ipsilateral stimuli and then inhibited by stimuli located in the equivalent region on the opposite side. Others could be activated only by noxious stimuli and then inhibited by light tactile stimuli applied to the same body region.

Landgren (1957, 1961) studied cortical neurons responding to stimulation of the tongue. He found the majority of these cells responded only to one modality, these being mainly touch and cold cells, though one warmth cell was isolated. Some cells responded to two modalities, and some to even more. All cortical cells which responded to more than one stimulus modality fired at short latency to touch or "stretch" stimuli. Yet thermal and taste stimuli activated these same cells more effectively, though at longer latencies.

As at the thalamic level, cold cells were found to have different discharge patterns in response to cooling. Some manifested only phasic responses, but others behaved very like the peripheral cold fibers described by Hensel and Zotterman (1951).

Another example of exquisite sensitivity to the parameters of stimulation employed is given by neurons activated by joint rotation. Some only respond phasically to joint rotation. However, most of these neurons both respond rapidly to transient rotation of the appropriate joint and discharge steadily when the joint is maintained at a certain angle, adapting to this only very slowly. The angle of joint displacement which causes excitation varies for different neurons. The degree and rate of joint movement determine the onset transient, whereas the joint angle alone determines the steady discharge. Some pairs of neurons were described which are reciprocally related to a given joint. The first neuron, but not the second, is activated when the joint moves in one direction, and when the direction of movement is reversed the second cell is activated, but not the first. The behavior of two such neurons is shown in Figure 6–8. It can be seen that the discharge frequency for each

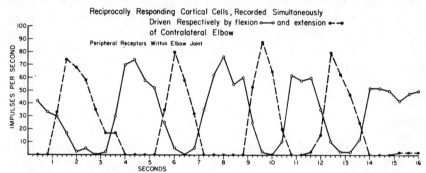

FIG. 6–8. Graph showing the impulse frequency of two neurons which responded reciprocally to alternating flexions and extensions of the contralateral elbow. The neurons, located in the postcentral gyrus of the cat, were observed simultaneously. The graph plots continuously the average frequencies for each consecutive 400 msec. period. During the fourteenth and fifteenth seconds the joint was held steady. (From Mountcastle, V. B., *J. Neurophysiol.*, 1957, 20.)

neuron reaches zero when the joint is in the position which maximally excites the other neuron. As yet, it is not known whether this reciprocity is central or peripheral in origin.

Second Somatic Area. Many units in SII respond specifically to one modality of stimulation over small contralateral receptive fields (Andersson, 1962). However, receptive fields in this area vary greatly from small to very large (Carreras and Levitt, 1959). In animals with spinal lesions, it was shown (Andersson, 1962) that some units had very large receptive fields, often stocking-like, sometimes bilateral and symmetrical, sometimes discontinuous, and sometimes including the whole animal. Some units were only responsive to strong stimuli; others were activated by light stimuli over one area but only by strong stimuli over another. These units were very slow adapting. Some showed no adaptation and continued to fire with a gradual decrease in frequency after the stimulus was withdrawn. Some units were also activated by auditory stimuli, and interaction between responses to somatic and auditory stimuli was observed. A few units were driven by vibratory stimuli.

These units are similar to those found in the posterior nuclear complex of the thalamus (Poggio and Mountcastle, 1960; Perl and Whitlock, 1961). Andersson (1962) suggests that this type of response is mediated via the posterior nuclear complex whereas the specific type of response is mediated via the ventrobasal complex. He further suggests that in the intact animal the less specific pathways are inhibited both by descending tracts exerting a tonic inhibitory influence at the first relay and by inhibitory effects from ascending specific projection pathways interacting at higher levels.

Andersson found that the responses evoked from large body regions were obtained mainly in the posterior portion of SII. The more anterior portion of the area contained units which were much more specific in their response patterns; that is, similar to those typical in SI (Fig. 6–9).

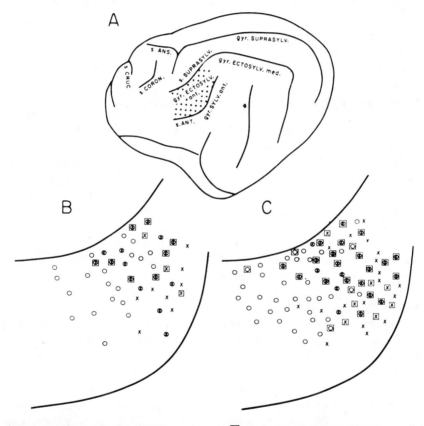

O CONTRALATERAL FORELIMB FIELDS   ⊡ BILATERAL FORELIMB FIELDS
X CONTRALATERAL HINDLIMB FIELDS   ⊠ BILATERAL HINDLIMB FIELDS
● CONTRALATERAL FORE- AND HINDLIMB FIELDS   ⊞ BILATERAL FORE- AND HINDLIMB FIELDS

FIG. 6–9. Distribution of penetrations in the second somatic area of the cat. *A,* schematic drawing of the cortex of the cat with the area investigated stippled. *B,* distribution of 47 penetrations with intact dorsal columns. *C,* distribution of 87 penetrations with intact lateral tract. In both *B* and *C,* each point was classified according to the maximum peripheral field, estimated both by single units and by evoked potential waves at all levels in the penetration. (From Andersson, S. A., *Acta Physiol. Scand.,* 56, suppl. 194, 1962, 60.)

Sensations Evoked in Patients by Cortical Stimulation

Stimulation of various cortical structures in patients has been found to evoke sensory responses. Most of these responses are obtained from the postcentral gyrus, though some are obtained from the precentral gyrus and a small number from neighboring points. Sensations evoked from the postcentral gyrus are somatotopically organized with respect to the body surface (Fig. 6–4). The sensations evoked are generally contralateral but may be bilateral. Foerster (1927) reports that sensations obtained upon postcentral stimulation were discretely localized, but those obtained from the superior parietal lobule were localized much more diffusely.

The most commonly occurring sensations are tingling, a feeling of "electricity," and numbness (Penfield and Jasper, 1954). Pain has occasionally been reported (Foerster, 1927), including visceral pain.

CORTICAL LESIONS AND DEFICITS IN SENSIBILITY

In man, parietal lesions may produce a variety of symptoms, notably in the somatosensory field. With superficial lesions, sensory thresholds are often little affected, but marked deficits in discrimination and synthesis of sensory information may appear. There may be impairment of postural sensibility, the recognition of passive movement of a joint, or of the position in space held by a limb. The affected limb may appear too heavy or too light. Deficits may occur in stimulus localization, two-point discrimination, or stereognosis (the recognition of objects by tactile means). Also, the patient, though able to perceive a stimulus to the affected limb when presented alone, may yet be unable to perceive it when presented together with a stimulus to the normal side of his body (Critchley, 1953).

Sometimes parietal lesions may give rise to anaesthesia instead of or in addition to the above symptoms. In this case, the anaesthesia is not usually distributed evenly over one half of the body; instead, scattered islands of sensory loss with blurred boundaries appear. Sometimes a dissociated loss for some but not other sensory modalities occurs. Kleist (1934) reports deficits in pain and temperature sensation, or pain alone, in some patients. Foerster (1936) and Kroll (1930) report pain deficits. Marshall (1951) showed by careful investigation that pain sensation could be severely impaired as a result of such lesions, yet in other cases temperature sense could be severely impaired with no loss of pain.

Sometimes a pain syndrome may develop, as discussed in the next section. Occasionally, asymbolia for pain is found; the patient may feel pain but does not react aversively to it, and may even seek it.

More severe symptoms may also result from parietal lesions, such as an inability to copy simple drawings or simple models (constructional apraxia), or to write (agraphia), or perform calculations (acalculia). The patient may manifest considerable right-left disorientation in his movements.

The body image may become severely impaired or distorted. Sometimes there develops what is known as "unilateral neglect." Here there is considerable poverty of movement on the affected side, but if specifically commanded to do so, the patient will use the affected limbs. In extreme cases the patient will not tend to one half of his anatomy: he will comb his hair only on one side of his head, shave only one side of his face, leave one half of his body unclothed. Yet reflex movements on the affected side remain normal. An interesting test of this syndrome demonstrates that it is the sensory needs of the affected side which suffer rather than the desire to move it. If the left side is deficient and the patient is told to put on a pair of gloves, he will use his left hand to put a glove on his *right* hand (but not vice versa).

A strikingly concomitant of such disorders is that the patient often evinces complete unconcern for the affected limbs. Even in cases of paralysis, the patient is not troubled by the deficit. In fact, he often goes to great lengths to deny this very loss. He will assert that he can indeed move his paralyzed limb, and invent many excuses to explain his not using it. In worse cases, the patient will disown his affected part, complain of it, ask that it be removed, claim that it belongs to someone else. Sometimes bizarre delusions are formed concerning the identity of the affected limbs. At other times the patient may feel as though nothing exists in the affected regions. Interestingly, Critchley concluded that it is injury to the *non*dominant parietal lobe which is best correlated with disorders of the body image.

It is difficult to know to what extent the extreme symptoms related to disorders of the body image are somatosensory in origin and how much is due to a general loss of spatial sense, or even to personality disorder. Sensory loss alone cannot explain the refusal to admit paralysis, or denial of ownership of a limb, since this does not happen in cases of sensory loss and paralysis due to peripheral lesions. One consideration still involving the sensory system, but which may explain a part of these bizarre symptoms, is that in the case of normal sensory loss the central representation for the affected area is intact, and the patient decides that a limb is paralyzed or numb on the basis of certain types of information, or lack of it, which is registered in the central representation. However, if the central representation itself is lost, this cannot happen. The information that there is a lack of sensation, or lack of movement, cannot be registered in the usual way. This might explain the feeling of nothingness in place of a limb, and the feeling that the limb is not really a part of one's body. Some such factor may be the basis of denial of a defect such as paralysis, if the registration of movement or lack of it does not occur.

However, it is unlikely that such considerations can explain the bizarre confabulations that some patients adopt to account for their deficit. A patient may believe that his limb has embarked on a long journey, or that he is attached to a limb belonging to some person of his acquaintance, or he might hold long conversations with his affected part. Other evidence of extreme personality disorder is also often apparent in such patients, and it may be necessary to postulate an additional general personality disturbance to account for these extraordinary symptoms. However, it is not very surprising that a consistent and extreme distortion of an individual's sensory world should alone cause a collapse of the sense of reality.

Correlation of Different Subdivisions of the Sensorimotor Region with Different Types of Sensory Function in Man

Various clinicians have attempted to assign special functions to the different subdivisions of the sensorimotor region. According to the traditional view, the postcentral gyrus (or primary receiving area) is concerned with basic sensations and the posterior parietal lobule (the association area for somaesthesis) is concerned with analysis and integration of these experiences. One might therefore expect lesions confined to the postcentral gyrus to give rise mainly to deficits in tests of simple sensation, such as sensory threshold. Lesions of the posterior parietal lobule might be expected to give rise to deficits in tasks testing integrative functions, such as stimulus localization, two-point discrimination, sense of movement, and so on.

On the other hand, Head (1920) proposed that, in general, lesions of the precentral gyrus lead to a deficit in the appreciation of spatial relationships, lesions in the postcentral gyrus lead to a deficit in the recognition of similarities and differences between objects, and lesions of the posterior parietal area result in defect in response to graduated intensities (such as pressure sensitivity).

A completely different view is taken by Goldstein (1927, 1942), who denies that separate functions are localized in different areas. He suggests that lesions, wherever placed, result in the same basic disorder of function, which manifests itself differently on the various tests employed but varies according to the individual patient. According to his hypothesis, one should not be able to point to any consistent variation in type of performance deficit resulting from lesions differently localized.

Semmes et al. (1960) carried out an extensive study on war veterans with discrete long-standing lesions of the sensorimotor cortex. They classified lesions as involving various subsectors of the sensorimotor area (precentral, postcentral, and posterior parietal regions), contralateral to the hand tested, or other cortical regions. For each hand, they then studied pressure sensitivity, resolution of two points, point localization, and discrimination of the direction of passive movement of a joint. They concluded that it was not possible to correlate lesions involving a particular subsector of the sensorimotor region with specific deficits, as measured by these tests. Their study therefore failed to support either the classical hypothesis or Head's hypothesis of gross anatomical localization of function. However, though they found that scores for the right hand on all tests were highly related, this was not the case for the left, forcing the postulation of more than one basic disturbance of function. Therefore Goldstein's hypothesis of a unitary impairment of function also was not corroborated.

Semmes et al. made a further interesting observation when they compared performance of the right with the left hand. Although they found that the presence of defects in the right hand was maximal after left sensorimotor injuries, compared with lesions in other regions of the left hemisphere, right sensorimotor lesions did not have a significantly greater effect on the left hand than did other lesions in the right hemisphere. It therefore appears that sensory mechanisms, at least for the hand, are more concentrated in the left hemisphere than in the right.

Animal Studies

In rats, Zubek (1951a, 1952) found that lesions in SI and SII did not lead to a complete abolition of the capacity to perform roughness and tactile form discriminations, though there was some loss. In one cat, Zubek (1951b) found that ablation of SI and SII led to a permanent loss of the ability to make roughness discriminations. However, one cannot conclude much on the basis of one animal. In dogs, Allen (1947) found that bilateral lesions of SI and SII did not abolish a positive CR to tactile stimulation, although a differential foreleg response was abolished.

Ruch and Fulton (1935) and Ruch, Fulton, and German (1938) report that in the monkey, chimpanzee, and man, lesions in the postcentral gyrus or posterior parietal region did not abolish the ability to discriminate differences in weight, roughness, or tactile form. However, retraining was needed to reestablish the ability. Blum et al. (1950) found in one monkey with ablation of the entire parietal cortex that, with prolonged retraining, somesthetic discrimination was possible.

Kruger and Porter (1958) found that ablation of SI and SII led to a severe tactile deficit in the contralateral limbs, though with unilateral and bilateral ablations a single somesthetic form discrimination could be relearned. Ablation of the precentral-cortex led to a temporary tactile

deficit but no deficit in somaesthetic form discrimination. Unilateral ablation of the precentral and postcentral arm area combined led to a severe
sensory loss in the arm contralateral to the lesions. The two subjects
tested were unable to carry out the somaesthetic task with the affected
limb, though they were able to perform a visual discrimination task
utilizing that limb.

Further, Diamond et al. (1964) trained cats to avoid shock when
a touch to a hindlimb was changed to alternately touching the hindlimb
and the forelimb. They then ablated SI and SII, and this necessitated
the relearning of the avoidance response. Later they transected the
dorsal columns and the habit was again relearned. It would appear
from the ability demonstrated in these animals to relearn somaesthetic
habits impaired by ablation of central structures that considerable re-
dundancy exists in the regions subserving certain somaesthetic functions.

CENTRIFUGAL CONTROL OF SENSORY INFLOW

As in other sensory systems, there is evidence that centrifugal fibers
modulate sensory information arriving at the somatosensory relay sta-
tions. Kuypers (1960a, 1960b) demonstrated that fibers originating in
the precentral, postcentral, and posterior parietal cortices descended
in the pyramidal tract to end in the dorsal column nuclei. Occlusive
interaction has been found in units of the dorsal column nuclei between
pyramidal and sensory inflows (Magni et al., 1959). Some units here
can be driven by sensorimotor cortex stimulation; others inhibited
(Chambers et al., 1960; Guzman et al., 1961). Some reticular fibers
also end in the dorsal column nuclei (Kuypers et al., 1960). Stimulation
of the midbrain reticular formation produces inhibition in this area;
however, when the sensorimotor cortex is ablated, this changes to facilitation (Guzman et al., 1961).

There also appear to be descending fibers originating in the cortex
and ending in the ventrobasal complex of the thalamus. Iwama and
Yamamoto (1961) found that stimulation of the somatosensory cortex
altered activity in the ventrobasal complex evoked from the dorsal
columns.

SENSORY PATHWAYS FROM THE VISCERA

Sensory information from the viscera is carried peripherally by sympathetic and parasympathetic fibers, as well as by some somatic afferents
which innervate the visceral cavities. Some types of stimulus which cause
pain when applied to the skin do not produce sensation when applied
to the viscera. Procedures as drastic as cutting or burning a visceral
organ need not cause sensation. However, visceral afferents will discharge effectively, for instance, to certain chemical irritants, spasms,

or sudden distention. Inflammation renders visceral pain fibers more sensitive. Visceral pain is subjectively different from cutaneous pain, being in general more severe and long lasting and having a diffuse irradiating quality.

Many visceral afferents are concerned only with the initiation of reflexes and do not have a sensory function. Such reflexes are mediated mostly by the parasympathetic system, though reflexes secondary to pain may be mediated by sympathetic fibers.

Most visceral pain impulses are carried by sympathetic nerves. However, there are exceptions to this. The parasympathetic pelvic and vagus nerves convey pain impulses from organs which they innervate (White, 1943).

Fiber Size and Modality Specificity in Visceral Afferents

Gernandt (1946) and Gernandt and Zotterman (1946) found that noxious stimulation to the diaphragm and the intestine set up impulses in the Aδ and C range in the phrenic and splanchnic nerves respectively. Light stimulation of the mesentery gave rise to Aβ fiber activity in the splanchnic nerve. The diameters of the fibers responding to the two different types of stimulation were therefore similar in these instances to those found in afferents from the skin.

Central Pathways

Not very much is known about the central visceral pathways. According to Aidar et al. (1952), splanchnic afferent pathways in the cat appear to traverse two routes. A fast route was found to travel by way of the ipsilateral posterior columns, and nucleus gracilis and, from there to the contralateral medial lemniscus and lateral portion of the ventrobasal complex. Splanchnic impulses occurred in regions between those for the fore- and hindlimbs. Much slower impulses were also traced bilaterally in the region of the lateral spinothalamic tract in the cord, and also bilaterally in the posterior hypothalamus and caudal thalamus. Amassian (1951a) also recorded impulses evoked by splanchnic stimulation bilaterally in the anterolateral region of the cord, using rabbits, cats, and dogs. Patton and Amassian (1951) demonstrated a splanchnic projection to the lateral part of the ventrobasal complex of the thalamus, intermingled with the topographic projection of the somatic afferents. It has been hypothesized that the sensation of visceral distention is mediated by the posterior columns and that of visceral pain by the anterolateral columns.

Cortical responses to visceral afferent stimulation have also been found. Amassian (1951b) showed that stimulation of the splanchnic nerve evokes activity in the contralateral postcentral gyrus, in a region between the arm and leg areas. Stimulation of the cortex in conscious patients has yielded visceral sensations (Penfield and Jasper, 1954). Foerster (1936) also reports visceral pain (cardiac and abdominal) upon stimulation of the postcentral gyrus in the appropriate regions of the topographic projection field.

Convergence has been observed between the somatic and visceral systems at the thalamic and cortical levels (MacLeod, 1956; Amassian, 1952). Central responses to visceral afferent stimulation may be blocked by preceding somatic stimulation.

HYPERPATHIA

Various lesions of the central nervous system may give rise to an alteration in the quality of pain sensation felt in the corresponding region of the body. Although the threshold for the experience of pain may not be lowered, and may even be raised, the pain, once felt, is more intense and much more disagreeable. The term hyperpathia is employed to describe such abnormalities of sensation.

Hyperpathia Due to Midbrain Lesions

Pain syndromes have been noted to occur after midbrain lesions. Dogliotti (1938) reports that patients in whom pain pathways in the midbrain had been cut on one side experienced diffuse unpleasant sensations in the contralateral half of the body. Drake and McKenzie (1953) and Walker (1943) report similar findings. It was suggested that such pain could be mediated by fibers in the midbrain reticular formation or tectum, probably together with activity in the hypothalamus. Bowsher (1957) also proposes that while the spinothalamic system might mediate short latency, sharply localized pain, the spinoreticulothalamic system might mediate the diffuse long-lasting pain found in these syndromes. One might assume, therefore, that the spinothalamic system, or some other pathway traversing the same area, normally inhibits the more diffuse system, and that the lesions had the effect of releasing the latter from inhibition. Or, alternatively, one could suppose that the lesion had the effect of irritating the diffuse sensory pathways, so as to cause an abnormal increase in their activity, thus producing the abnormal sensations.

Hyperpathia Produced by Thalamic Lesions

The thalamic syndrome of Déjérine and Roussy (1906) occurs when a large portion of the thalamus, including much of the ventrobasal complex, is destroyed as a result of thrombosis of the thalamogeniculate artery. After an initial period of sensory loss, sensory stimuli come to evoke pain of long latency, which is persisting, diffuse, poorly localized, and intensely unpleasant. Though the threshold for their perception may be high, it often happens that painful sensations come to be provoked by normally innocuous stimuli, such as touch, vibration, or even sound. This condition may become steadily worse, until the patient is in a state of spontaneous agonizing pain.

Whether it is due to irritation or loss of inhibition (see below), one may speculate about the possible thalamic regions involved in this syndrome. In the posterior nuclear region, receptive fields are commonly very large, and activity in such units might explain the diffuseness and poor localizability of the sensations experienced. Also, several of these units have been found to be activated by vibratory and auditory stimuli (Perl and Whitlock, 1961; Poggio and Mountcastle, 1960), which also produce these unpleasant sensations in such patients. Another region which may be involved is the centrum medianum and adjoining structures. Here units respond only to noxious stimuli over very large receptive fields (Perl and Whitlock, 1961; Albe-Fessard and Kruger, 1962). Some of these neurons respond only at long latency (Albe-Fessard and Kruger, 1962). Against implicating this region is the finding that receptive fields here are bilateral. However, Walker (1943) reports a case of pain syndrome in which autopsy revealed destruction of almost the entire ventrobasal complex and the equivalent of the posterior nuclear group, but in which centrum medianum and intralaminar nuclei were spared. Also, Hécaen et al. (1949) found that centrum medianum lesions produce an improvement in thalamic pain.

Hyperpathia and the Cortex

Pain syndromes have also been described following lesions of the cerebral cortex. Kleist (1934) reports cases of hyperpathia resulting from localized parietal lesions. Michelson (1943) also reports several cases of pain states resulting from cortical lesions, and Hamby (1961) corroborates this. Further, central pain may sometimes be abolished by excision of the appropriate parietal regions (Hamby, 1961; Eriksen et al., 1952). Biemond (1956) suggests that the second sensory area may be involved in the experiencing of such abnormal sensations. He reports a case of hyperpathia and spontaneous pain over the entire half of the body, contralateral to an area of softening involving SII, with retrograde degeneration in the posteroventral nucleus of the thalamus. Davison and Schick (1935) also describe a case of hyperpathia and spontaneous pain where there was a lesion largely in SII and no thalamic lesion.

In SII, as in the posterior nuclear group, many units have been found with wide receptive fields, and many were activated only by noxious stimulation. And, as in the posterior nuclear group, many units were also activated by vibratory and acoustic stimuli. These findings increase the likelihood of the involvement of this region in pain states.

Explanation of Hyperpathia Caused by Lesions of the Central Nervous System

Head (1920) suggests that the thalamic syndrome is due to a release of the thalamus from the inhibitory control of the cortex. He proposes that the cortex and the thalamus are two separate "centres of consciousness." The thalamic center is concerned with the emotional aspects of sensation and the cortex with discriminative aspects. Also, the threshold of the thalamic center is high, but once this is reached its response is "of excessive amount and duration, and this it is the business of the cortical mechanism to control. The low intensity of the stimuli that can arouse the sensory cortex and its quick reaction period, enable it to control the activity of the cumbersome mechanism of the thalamic centre." Head suggests that corticofugal inhibitory fibers end in the lateral nucleus of the thalamus, so that destruction of this thalamic nucleus destroys the termination of most of these pathways. On this hypothesis, those cortical and subcortical lesions, which are so situated that they destroy such corticofugal inhibitory pathways, should also produce hyperpathia.

The suggestion that as one ascends the phylogenetic scale new and more discriminative integrating centers for sensory experience are produced, which exert an inhibitory influence on the older, cruder centers, has been proposed by others with reference to the problem of pain states. Walker (1943) proposes that there are three such integrating centers which may be related in this way: the oldest in the tectum mesencephali, the next in the thalamus, and the third in the cortex. Bishop (1961) has reaffirmed this conception of a hierarchy of brains on the basis of embryological studies.

An example of direct observation at the unit level of tactile pathways inhibiting pain pathways is provided by Mountcastle (1961). He reports the existence of units in the postcentral gyrus which respond only to noxious stimuli, but are then inhibited by the presentation of tactile stimuli to the same peripheral locus. Another related neurophysiological study is that of Andersson (1962). He found that lesions in the spinal cord produce a considerable increase in the proportion of cortical units with wide receptive fields, including those which respond only to noxious stimulation. He attributes this change to the severing of a centrifugal inhibitory pathway, as well as to the loss of inhibitory effects from ascending specific projection pathways interacting at higher levels.

There are also neurophysiological grounds for supposing that the sensory cortex modulates activity in the sensory region of the thalamus. It has been shown (Iwama and Yamamoto, 1961) that stimulation of the somatosensory cortex may affect activity in the ventrobasal complex of the thalamus which is evoked from the dorsal columns.

One argument against Head's hypothesis concerns the lack of complete correlation between pain syndromes and loss of discriminative sensibility. It very often occurs that there is a loss of discriminative ability without a pain syndrome being produced. Destruction of the dorsal columns, both as a result of disease and through operation, results in a loss of discriminative sensibility (Browder and Gallagher, 1948; Pool, 1946; White and Sweet, 1955). However, in the vast majority of instances pain syndromes are not produced. Such findings are also common with lesions elsewhere in the central nervous system. The reverse dissociation also has been noted. Pain syndromes have been shown to occur as a result of lesions in the CNS without a concomitant loss of discriminative sensibility. Biemond (1956) reports a case of hyperpathia due to cortical lesions in which the discriminative senses of the patient were all intact. Michelson (1943) also remarks on the occasional absence of disturbances in discrimination in patients with centrally produced pain states.

These are not watertight arguments against Head's hypothesis. One could argue that, provided some impulses reached the cortex, it could still control the thalamus effectively, even if its discriminative capacity was impaired. Also, it might be possible to sever a corticofugal inhibitory pathway discretely without disturbing the discriminative capacities of the cortex. But they cast doubt on this view.

An alternative explanation is that such syndromes are caused by irritation of structures adjacent to the lesion. Several factors may be pointed out in favor of this latter hypothesis. First, it is more parsimonious to postulate an irritative factor affecting certain structures than to propose a loss of a postulated inhibitory pathway which has not been shown to have the necessary characteristics. A second, and very strong, factor is the variability and unpredictability of the pain states produced. For example, mesencephalic tractotomy has in various cases given rise to pain states, as has been described. But this is by no means always the case; similar operations have not produced pain. Also, although surgical operation of the posterolateral thalamus may produce pain states, many such operations have produced no pain syndrome (Ervin and Mark, 1959). Further, a patient's symptoms may vary considerably during the course of his illness. Discussing patients with pain due to cortical lesions, Michelson (1943) stresses the variability and reversibility of their symptoms and concludes that irritative factors are probably the cause of the pain states.

REFERRED PAIN

Although pain from a visceral organ may be correctly localized, at times it appears to arise instead from some area on the skin surface. Such pain is referred to those regions of the skin, or dermatomes, which are supplied by the same posterior roots as those through which the visceral afferents enter the spinal cord. Pain arising from other deeply placed structures may also at times be referred to the skin surface.

Various hypotheses have been put forward to account for referred pain. McKensie (1893) suggested that sensory impulses from the viscera produce an irritable focus in the spinal cord, which in turn facilitates transmission along pain pathways arising from the skin, with the resultant excitation of the spinothalamic tract. This theory is known as the convergence-facilitation theory (Hinsey and Phillips, 1940).

Another suggestion is that visceral and cutaneous afferents converge into the same neurons at some level in the central nervous system, so that in these instances the information as to whether the impulses are visceral or cutaneous in origin is lost. The fact that the opposite confusion does not arise (i.e., pain arising from the skin is not referred to a viscus) may be explained by assuming that the central mechanism always interprets pain coming from these common pathways as arising from the skin. Another explanation is that since the skin is a much more frequent source of afferent impulses than the visceral organs, a message which may have arisen from either is interpreted as coming from the skin, as this is the most likely place of origin.

Direct evidence of convergence of impulses from visceral and cutaneous sources onto the same neuron has been obtained in the posterolateral ventral nucleus of the thalamus. McLeod (1956) found that most of these cells which responded to splanchnic delta afferents were also activated by stimulation of the skin, usually in the trunk region. He found occlusion to occur between impulses derived from the different sources. At the cortical level, Amassian (1952) also found convergence of visceral and cutaneous afferents onto single neurons.

Various writers have suggested that a factor in referred pain is the existence of a constant barrage of impulses from the skin which are usually not numerous enough to cause the perception of pain, and which may be facilitated by visceral discharges so that the pain threshold is exceeded. To test this hypothesis, experimenters have injected procaine into the cutaneous area of reference to see whether this would abolish the pain. Some have found no effect of procaine injection (e.g., Woollard et al. [1932], who investigated pain caused by stimulation of the phrenic nerve). However, others have found that the pain was ended or made to migrate by these means (for example, Weiss and Davis, 1928). Another demonstration of facilitation was reported by Cohen (1944) on two patients with cardiac anginal pain, both of whom referred their pain to the elbow region after trauma to the elbow but not before. These findings, though variable, are not inconsistent with each other. In some cases, pain impulses arising from the viscera alone may be numerous enough to give rise to pain; in other cases pain may not be experienced unless facilitated from other sources, because the visceral barrage is not quite powerful enough to produce the sensation of pain. It is also likely that suggestion is an important factor in pain reference.

It has also been suggested as an explanation of referred pain that viceral afferents produce reflexes in the corresponding superficial regions, that is, viscerocutaneous or visceromotor reflexes (Wernoe, 1925; Verger, 1927). Spameni and Lunedei (1927) suggest that visceral impulses, having reached the spinal cord, activate efferent pathways to the skin. This would result in physiochemical changes which would in turn give rise to afferent activity. Pollack and Davis (1935) found some evidence to support this hypothesis. Rosenthal (1968) has produced evidence suggesting that pain referred from the viscera is produced by impulses traveling to the skin, where histamine is liberated, which in turn activates pain receptors.

DEPRESSED REACTIONS TO PAIN

Insensitivity to Pain. Very occasionally, individuals are found who do not appreciate painful stimuli as such. This appears to be not a psychologic or emotional but a sensory loss. It may be accompanied by other sensory changes. Kunkle and Chapman (1943) report the case of a young man with almost complete insensitivity to pain, and also a moderate impairment of heat and cold sensation. He also showed an absence of itching. However, the reflexes shown to be associated with activation of pain pathways were not all lost. For instance, the cold pressor effect was retained. (Immersing the hand in ice-cold water produces a rise in arterial blood pressure, together with slight tachycardia, and this has been shown to be mediated by pain fibers [Wolff and Hardy, 1941].) Thus in this case it appeared that pain impulses traveled enough to elicit a reflex blood pressure rise but yet did not go far enough to reach consciousness.

Pain Asymbolia. Cases of pain asymbolia may arise as a result of parietal lesions. In these cases pain is felt, but the aversive reaction to it is lost. The patient may even seek out painful stimuli. There is often a concomitant lack of concern over threatening gestures and other potential dangers. Such patients often show other extreme symptoms associated with parietal disease (see above), and this pain asymbolia may therefore be related to the other symptoms.

Indifference to Pain after Frontal Lobotomy. Frontal lobotomy typically produces a state of indifference to pain, and therefore has been performed in cases of intolerable and intractable pain. Here the indifference does not appear to be to the pain immediately felt but to lie, rather, in a considerable diminution of the prolonged psychologic disturbance which constant pain induces. Thus lobotomized patients are still distressed by painful events such as childbirth (Freeman and Watts, 1950), and their actual pain threshold appears, if anything, lower than normal (Chapman et al., 1948). However, the pain does not make them so miserable, and they appear less engrossed in their feelings and sensations and make fewer spontaneous complaints. It is suggested that lobotomy produces a loss of perserveration, which extends also to disturbing thoughts, whether connected with pain or with other anxiety-producing situations.

COMPLEX NATURE OF PAIN PERCEPTION

Pain as a sensory modality is particularly complex in that motivational and cognitive determinants play an unusually prominent role in its perception. One example of the importance of extrasensory factors in pain perception comes from studies of soldiers wounded in battle. Beecher (1959) has described how soldiers wounded in battle often perceived such little pain that they did not wish for medication to relieve it. As a further example, patients who have undergone frontal lobotomy for the relief of pain rarely complain about the pain, or ask for medication, though their actual pain threshold may even be lowered. Lack of the aversive component in the response to pain has also been described above (in the section on pain asymbolia).

Further, Hill et al. (1952a) have shown that anticipation of pain can have a profound effect on pain response. Similar conclusions have been drawn concerning anxiety and attention (Hill et al., 1952b), suggestion and placebos (Beecher, 1959; Melzack et al., 1963), cultural background (Chapman and Jones, 1944), hypnosis (Barber, 1959), and early experience (Melzack and Scott, 1957). A remarkable example of the effect of prior conditioning is provided by Pavlov (1927, 1928), who found that dogs which are repeatedly fed after skin damage to one site of the body soon respond to stimuli by salivating without showing signs of pain. However, if the same stimuli are applied to a different part of the body, they exhibit normal pain responses.

It is apparent from these examples that both cognitive and motivational factors are important determinants of pain perception. Melzack and Casey (1968) emphasize the complex and intricate nature of pain pathways and suggest that structures in the reticular formation and limbic system (see Chapters 9 and 11) are responsible for the aversive nature of pain, and that cortical efferents (particularly those from the frontal cortex) modify both the sensory and motivational systems after cognitive evaluation of the pain-producing situation.

Site of Action of Analgesics

Various experiments have shown that certain analgesics affect pain receptors whereas others are central in their action.

A set of elegant experiments (Lim et al., 1964a, b; Hashimoto et al., 1964; Lim, 1970), using intra-arterial injections of bradykinin to evoke pain in dogs, has shown that the NA analgesics (e.g., aspirin, sodium salicylate, N-acetyl-p-aminophenol, aminopyrine, and phenylbutazone) block the action of bradykinin at the peripheral receptor whereas morphine and other narcotic analgesics block pain at a central locus.

In one experiment, cross-perfusion was performed of the vasoisolated but innervated spleen of a recipient dog R by a donor dog D. Pain was then produced in dog R by bradykinin injections into the splenic artery of dog R. Then aspirin, or another NA analgesic, was injected into the blood of dog D, which perfused the spleen of dog R. This blocked the pain response. However, when these same analgesics were injected intravenously into the circulation of dog R, pain in this dog was not blocked. However, morphine and other narcotic analgesics blocked such bradykinin-evoked pain in dog R only when they were injected intravenously into dog R, and not when they were injected into the blood of dog D perfusing the spleen of dog R.

It has further been shown, in man as well as in dogs, that intraperitoneal injection of Na-aspirin blocked the intraperitoneal pain induced by bradykinin. However, the same dosage of aspirin when injected intravenously had no effect on the intraperitoneal bradykinin-evoked pain response.

In another experiment, intravenous injection of aspirin blocked splanchnic nerve potentials evoked by intra-arterial injection of bradykinin into the splenic artery of dogs. However, injection of morphine by the same route produced no blocking effect.

Further, it was found that after intra-arterial injection of bradykinin the pain response was blocked by aspirin with less than 10 percent of the dosage necessary for blocking by intravenous injection when aspirin was given directly into the spleen. However, eight times the intravenous dose injected into the brain failed to block the pain response.

A further experiment has demonstrated that the peripheral blocking of pain by Na-aspirin is not due to peripheral nerve block. The application of aspirin to the splanchnic nerve in dogs did not block impulses produced by electrical stimulation. Since the peripheral action of aspirin is not due to nerve block, the evidence is very strong that it acts on the receptor terminals.

chapter 7

Taste and Smell

TASTE

The sense of taste plays an important part in the selection of sub-stances to eat or drink. It is important to the organism not only in feed selection but also in the regulation of the amount eaten or drunk. These roles are discussed in detail in the chapter on hunger and thirst. The way that taste enters into the determination of behavior is chiefly discussed in those chapters. Here we shall be concerned mainly with the physiological modus operandi of this sensory avenue.

Taste is concerned with the detection of chemical substances in solu-tion. As a result, most experiments on taste are concerned with the qualitative and quantitative variation of solutions. The quantitative as-pect of solutions is measured in terms of the weight of a substance as a proportion of the solvent, which is usually distilled water. One method where the solution is described in percentage terms is to describe as a 2 percent saline solution a mixture of two grams of salt and enough water to make up 100 cc. of solution. Similarly, a 15 percent concentra-tion of glucose consists of 15 grams of glucose in distilled water to make up 100 cc. of solution. Another method of specifying the strength of solution is in terms of molarity, that is, the number of molecules that are added to a fixed amount of solvent, but of course only indirectly. A solution of 1 mole is prepared by placing the molecular weight of a substance in grams in distilled water to make up 100 cc. of solution. The molecular weight times grams of a substance is the mass of 6.023×10^{23} molecules. Therefore two solutions of different substances (both of the strength of one mole) contain the same number of mole-cules. To obtain a solution of 0.1 mole, one tenth of the molecular weight in grams is placed in water to make up 100 cc. of solution.

In the case of taste, four basic qualities have been postulated more by convention than rigorous experimental evidence. These four are salt, sweet, sour, and bitter. It is believed that any taste can be matched by a mixture of these four qualities. However, this would seem intuitively unlikely because of the great variety of tastes in everyday life which seem to have other ingredients. The answer to this would be that one must be careful to exclude "tastes" which are really odors, or which arise though the stimulation of free nerve endings of the trigeminal nerve in the oral cavity to produce "hot" tastes (as those of some spices) or through the direct stimulation of cold receptors to produce "cool" tastes (as that of menthol). That such "tastes" are numerous can be surmised from the fact that people without a sense of taste are frequently unaware of their handicap as long as their sense of smell is intact (Moncrieff, 1951).

A reason for belief in the four basic taste qualities is that it is possible to affect the perception of these four qualities separately, or to differing degrees, the order depending, say, on the kind of drug painted on the tongue. For instance, gymnemic acid produces a temporary inability to taste sweet-tasting substances. After chewing the berry of the West African shrub *Synsepalum dulcificum,* sour foods taste sweet. Our confidence in the inference that salt, sweet, sour, and bitter are the basic taste qualities is further increased by the results of electrophysiological investigation, to be described below.

Organs of Taste

The organs of taste are called taste buds. In fish these buds may be distributed over large parts of the body surface. However, in man, as in mammals generally, they lie mainly on the tongue. These organs each consist of 10 to 15 taste cells, together with other cells. These other cells have been thought by some to be sustaining cells. However, it has been suggested that these sustaining cells are in reality old or aged taste cells, which are no longer innervated (Fig. 7–1).

Each taste cell has a set of fine hairlike structures projecting through pores onto the surface of the tongue. These structures are about 4 microns in length and about 0.2 microns in diameter. Most of the taste buds are placed in the circumvallate, foliate, and fungiform papillae. In man, the taste buds at the tip of the tongue are more sensitive to sweet substances and those at the back of the tongue are more responsive to bitter substances. There are also taste buds in the larynx and pharynx.

Bekesy (1964) stimulated single fungiform papillae with trains of brief (0.5 msec.) pulses through small electrodes. Only one taste sensation could be elicited from each papilla and this was always either sweet, bitter, sour, or salty. However, there were some large papillae near the edge of the tongue where one taste, salty, was elicited by stimulation of one side of the papilla and another taste, sour, was evoked by stimulation of the other side. In another experiment, Bekesy (1966) stimulated

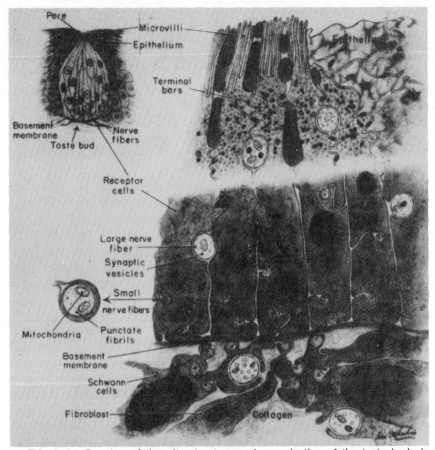

FIG. 7–1. Drawing of the ultrastructure and organization of the taste buds in the foliate papilla of the rabbit. (From Lorenzo, A. J. D., *Olfaction and Taste,* Zotterman, Y. [ed.], 1963; courtesy of the Pergamon Press.)

single papillae with taste solutions that were bitter, sweet, salty, and sour. Most papillae were again sensitive only to one quality. However, Harper, Jay, and Erickson (1966), in an experiment differing in some details, found only four papillae out of the ten tested were specific to only one taste. However, the papillae they used were large papillae near the edge of the tongue, and Békésy observed dual or even multiple sensitivities from such papillae.

Mode of Stimulation of the Taste Receptors

It seems likely that it is the tiny hairs or microvilli which project through the taste pores to the surface of the tongue that are the structures actually stimulated by taste solutions. Each microvillus is surrounded by a single thickness of membrane of about 80 Å. This membrane is probably made up of oriented protein and phospholipid. It seems that such a membrane has a number of receptor sites which combine with the taste solution in a highly specific way. Beidler (1954) has argued that such a combination involves a physical rather than a chemical reaction. Van de Waals forces, hydrogen bonding, dipole-dipole interactions, and ionic forces have been suggested as producing the interaction between receptor site and the adsorbed substance. Evidence that the reaction involved in stimulating a taste receptor is not chemical but physical is provided by Dethier and Arab (1958). These workers stimulated the tip of the chemosensory hair of the blowfly with sugar and showed that a change of temperature of 0–35 degrees C. did not affect the efficiency of stimulation, as it would in the case of most chemical reactions. If the whole cell or animal were altered in temperature, then, of course, it might be expected on the grounds that the response of the whole system would be affected. By using the tip of the chemosensory hair alone, such an alteration was avoided.

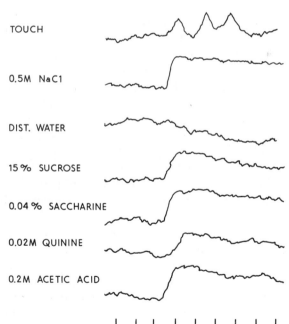

FIG. 7–2. Integrated electrical responses of the whole chords tympani of man to sapid solutions poured on the tongue. Note that water depressed the spontaneous afferent activity. Time in seconds. (From Diamant et al., *Olfaction and Taste,* Zotterman, Y. (ed.), 1963; courtesy of Pergamon Press.)

It is probable that the basis taste stimuli all have specialized receptor sites associated with them. Sourness is clearly associated with acids, the hydrogen ion being an important determinant of sour taste. The positive and negative ions of salts in solution produce a salty taste. (Though common salt [NaCl] is the only salt which has a pure salty taste, it is somewhat paradoxical that weak solutions of it taste sweet.)

Dastoli et al. (1968) isolated a protein from bovine tongues which combines with saccharine and various sugars according to their degree of sweetness. This makes it probable that the isolated protein is identical with the protein which acts as a sugar receptor. Hansen (1969) puts forward evidence that the receptor protein (at least in some insects) is the sugar splitting enzyme α-glucosidase and that sugar is detected at the receptor membrane by the formation of a sugar-glucosidase complex.

The physical bases of bitterness are obscure. It has also been shown that, in certain species, water leads to an increase of activity in certain fibers. However, in the rat, and probably man (Diamant et al., 1963), water leads only to a decrement in firing in the salt fibers (Fig. 7–2).

INITIATION OF THE ELECTRICAL CHANGE

The stimulating particle probably produces a change in the configuration of a macromolecule at the receptor site when it is bound to it. Such a change may form a hole which allows potassium to leak out of the cell (Beidler, 1963). In this way, a part of the receptor cell becomes depolarized, and the depolarization spreads electrotonically to the site on the cell at which the spike impulse is generated. Browne and Hodgson (1962) have shown that in the blowfly chemoreceptor an impulse can be initiated less than 4 msec. after the application of the stimulus. This is similar to the latency of response to an electrical stimulus with an anodal pulse in mammalian receptors of 5 to 7 msec. found by Pfaffmann (1941). But the latency to chemical stimulation in mammalian preparations is about 35 to 40 msec.

In the case of the mammalian receptor cell, the work of Kimura and Beidler (1961) suggested that the site of spike initiation is not on the taste cell itself. It seems as if the depolarization of the taste cell is transmitted either chemically or electrically to the nerve fiber with which the taste cell is in intimate contact. A spike impulse is first initiated on the nerve fiber which innervates the taste cell. An increase in the amount of depolarization produced by chemical stimulation of the taste cell produces a linear increase in steady-state single fiber firing (Fig. 7–3). Equal increases in depolarization also produce the same number of j.n.d. differences in taste (Fig. 7–4), showing that, in this

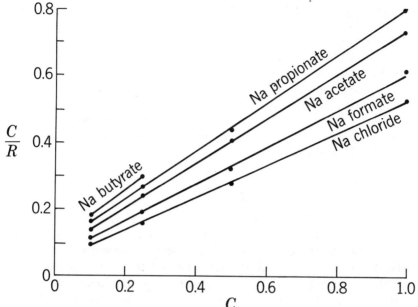

FIG. 7–3. Ratio of the molar concentration of the stimulus and the magnitude of the integrated response of the taste receptors is plotted against the molar concentration of the stimulus. The ratio of the molar concentration of the stimulus and the magnitude of the receptor potential plotted against molar concentration also produces a straight line. (Reprinted from Beidler, L. M., in *Sensory Communication,* Walter Rosenblith (ed.); by permission of the M.I.T. Press, Cambridge, Mass. Copyright 1961, the M.I.T. Press.)

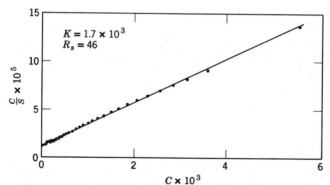

FIG. 7–4. Ratio of the molar concentration of the stimulus and the number of consecutive taste j.n.d.'s (ΔS) for man is plotted against the molar concentration of the stimulus. (Data from Lemberger, 1908).

instance, the psychophysical relations are due to a property of the transducer at the cell membrane.

Beidler (1954) has proposed a theory of stimulation of taste receptors. He assumed that each receptor is a cell with a number of receptor sites to which the molecules to which the cell is sensitive are adsorbed. If a substance at a certain concentration is applied to a cell with unfilled receptor sites, only a certain number of receptor sites will be filled at that concentration. He further assumed that the highest response of a cell occcurs when all the receptor sites are filled. He thus arrived at the fundamental taste equation:

$$\frac{C}{R} = \frac{C}{R_s} + \frac{1}{KR_s}$$

where C is the concentration of the stimulus, R the magnitude of response, R_s the magnitude of maximum response, and K the equilibrium constant. All these parameters can be directly measured except K. However, if the theory is correct, when the ratio of the concentration stimulus and the magnitude of receptoral response is plotted against the concentration of the stimulus, a straight line should be obtained. That this is so can be seen from Figure 7–3.

The equilibrium constants which Beidler has calculated from these and similar results are low. From these and other experiments, he concluded that the process of taste stimulation is not an enzymatic reaction but a physical process of adsorption to proteins. Though this theory was originally proposed by Beidler to account for the taste of salts, he has found it applicable, with certain complications, to the case of acids, sugars, and bitter substances.

Of interest is the fact that the taste equation proposed by Beidler has been applied by him to psychophysical data. Assuming that a j.n.d. of taste represents an equal increment of response of the taste receptor to the stimulating substance, the concentration divided by the cumulative number of j.n.d.'s plotted against the concentration should yield a straight line (Fig. 7–4).

Specificity of Taste Cells

There are various kinds of receptor sites, each adsorbing different substances. A specific type of receptor site can adsorb different kinds of ions or molecules with different binding energies and different stimulating efficiencies. Further, it seems that different types of sites coexist on the same cell. It is possible to measure the amount of depolarization of a taste cell when taste solutions are applied by penetrating the cell membrane with a microelectrode. Kimura and Beidler (1961) have been able to show by this means that a taste cell is normally sensitive to

TABLE 7-1
Response in Millivolts of the Hamster Taste Receptor
to Basic Stimuli of Four Taste Qualities

Taste Receptor	0.1 M NaCl	0.1 M Sucrose	0.02 M Quinine	0.01 M HCl
1..........	10.5	2	4.5	—
2..........	8.5	2	7.5	0
3..........	9	1	4.5	—
4..........	11.5	5	8	22.5
5..........	10	6.5	9	12.5
6..........	6.5	1.5	5	—
7..........	9.5	2.5	7	9
8..........	14	0	5	14

K. Kimura and L. M. Beidler, *J. Cell, and Comp. Physiol.*, 58:137, Table 3.

salt, sucrose, hydrochloric acid, quinine, and so on in varying combinations. Table 7-1 shows some of the sensitivities of two single taste cells.

INNERVATION OF TASTE CELLS

A single fiber in the chorda tympani nerve branches extensively before making contact with taste cells. One fiber therefore makes contact with at least 25 different taste cells (Beidler, 1969).

De Lorenzo's (1963) electron microscope studies show the way taste cells are innervated (Fig. 7-1). Under each taste bud are seen myelinated fibers from 1 to 6 μ in diameter. On their way toward the taste bud, they lose their myelin sheath. The unmyelinated fibers, upon entering the taste bud, establish synaptic contiguity with the taste cells. Two types of nerve fibers appear to terminate on the taste cell. The larger type (0.5 to 1.0 μ in diameter) appears always to terminate on one receptor cell only. However, De Lorenzo is not sure whether the smaller fibers are not branches of the larger fibers. Further, one cell may be doubly innervated. Recordings of single fibers also show that specific responding to a basic quality such as "sweet" is rare. This of course might be expected, as receptor cells themselves are rarely specific, and because a single nerve fiber appears to be joined to more than one receptor cell. Work on single fibers has been reported by Pfaffmann (1955), Fishman (1957), and Cohen et al. (1955).

Fishman (1957) pointed out certain difficulties in interpreting the sensitivity profiles of taste fibers which have a lower threshold to quinine than to salt. However, the maximum rate of responding obtainable with quinine will be very low whereas the maximum rate attainable with salt will be much higher. Presumably, such properties can be explained if we assume that there are receptor sites of two types on the same receptor cell. If there are only a few "bitter" sites with a high sensitivity and a large number of "salt" sites with a lower sensitivity, we would obtain the relationship Fishman found. He argued that such relations make it difficult to classify any one fiber. If it is grouped according to threshold, it might be classified as bitter, but salty if suprathreshold levels of rate of discharge are considered. Fishman's observations suggest a possible explanation for alterations in certain tastes such as that of salt, at low intensities, when salt tastes sweet. Sweet receptor cells may have salt sites of low threshold which saturate at low intensities. Consequently, at low concentrations of salt most of the discharge comes from units whose firing is normally interpreted as signaling the presence of sugars. The same rate of discharge would occur from these receptors if sugar were applied to them.

The problem of innervation of receptor cells is complicated in the case of taste because taste receptors are constantly dying and being replaced by new cells. Cells from the epithelium migrate into the taste buds at the rate of one cell every ten hours. Each such cell has a life span of about 11 days, after which it degenerates (Beidler and Smallman, 1965). Mature taste cells do not appear to undergo division. Instead, taste cells are replaced by epithelial cells which move into the taste buds where they become innervated and are transformed into taste cells. As they age, they move inward into the taste bud and are replaced by fresh epithelial cells migrating inward into the taste bud. However, it seems that the innervation of the taste cell does not remain with it as the cell migrates, so that each cell on its journey inward into the taste bud will send signals down a succession of fibers. In order that a fiber innervating the receptors should send the same information irrespective of the receptor cell connected to it, we must assume that each innervating taste fiber determines the quality of the receptor sites located on the cell to which it becomes attached. When innervation from the taste nerves to the tongue is removed, all taste buds quickly disappear. As the nerve regenerates, differentiation of the cells again occurs, and the taste buds re-form from the epithelial cells. This shows that the nerve is capable of modifying the characteristics of the cells with which it comes in contact. (It has, however, also been reported that some branches of the fibers innervating the taste buds end in the epithelium surrounding the taste buds [Kolmer, 1927]; such fibers may be responsible for the mechanical and temperature sensitivity seen in many single-taste fibers.)

Gustatory Pathways

The taste buds in the fungiform papillae of the anterior two thirds of the tongue send messages to the central nervous system via the lingual and chorda tympani nerves. These are branches of the seventh cranial nerve (facial nerve and nervus intermedius) (Fig. 7–5). The cells of

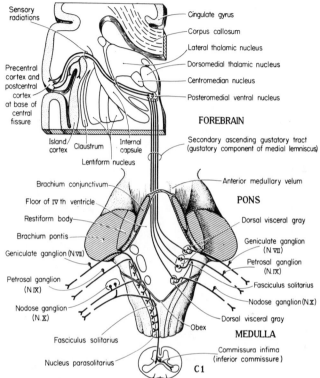

FIG. 7–5. Diagram to illustrate the gustatory pathways and their regions of termination in the dorsal thalamus and the cerebral cortex. The general visceral afferent fibers and their central relationships are also shown. (From Ranson, S. W., and Clark, S. L., *The Anatomy of the Nervous System*; Philadelphia: W. B. Saunders Company, 1959.)

origin of this nerve lie in the geniculate ganglion. The taste buds in the circumvallate and foliate papillae of the posterior third of the tongue are connected to the central nervous system via the ninth cranial or glossopharyngeal nerve. The cells of origin of this nerve are in the petrosal ganglion. The taste buds in the larynx and pharynx are supplied by the vagus or tenth cranial nerve, probably by way of the internal laryngeal nerve. The cells of origin of this nerve lie in the nodose ganglion. All the diverse peripheral connections turn into the tractus solitarius and the nucleus of the tractus solitarius (called nucleus parasolitarius where well developed) in the medulla. Electrophysiological studies of the tractus and nucleus of the tractus solitarius have been carried out by Pfaffmann et al. (1961), Makous et al. (1963), and Doetsch et al. (1969). Similar characteristics of response to those obtained more peripherally were seen. There was a wide range of responsiveness to chemical stimuli, and the threshold to stimulation was also similar. Some of the results obtained are illustrated by Figure 7–6. There

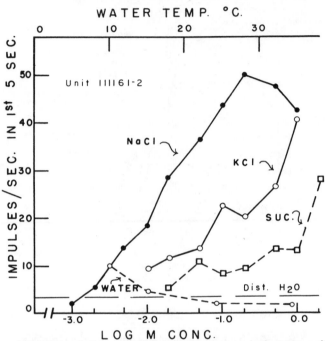

FIG. 7–6. Action potential frequency of a single taste unit to chemical and thermal stimulation of the tongue. The axis, "Water Temp. °C," refers only to the curve labeled "Water." The average level of activity to distilled water is plotted as a horizontal dashed line parallel to the x axis. (From Makous, W., et al., *Olfaction and Taste,* Zotterman, Y. [ed.], 1963; courtesy of Pergamon Press.)

are also wide variations in the reactivity of units, similar to those found in the periphery. Further, Makous et al. (1963) reported that out of 21 taste units tested, 13 responded to mechanical stimulation of the tongue. Also, out of 24 taste units tested, 21 responded to tap water if it was cold (9–12°C.). However, the firing frequency of such nongustatory responding appears small compared with the responses to taste stimuli. Similar results are reported by Pfaffmann et al. (1961). Responses to mechanical and temperature stimuli occur even in the chorda tympani taste fibers (Pfaffmann, 1941; Fishman, 1957; Sato, Yamashita, and Ogawa, 1969). Doetsch et al. (1969) report that there is almost a fivefold increase in firing rate in the nucleus of the tractus solitarius (second-order neurons) over that found in the fibers of the chorda tympani nerve (first-order neurons) to the same stimulus. Therefore there seems to be a rate of response amplification by the second-order neurons. Furthermore, the initial burst of activity found in the chorda tympani fibers when a stimulus was applied was attenuated by the second-order neurons.

Not only do taste units show mechanical sensitivity, there is a great deal of intermingling of gustatory and somesthetic units at all levels of the nervous system, as if the gustatory sensitivity of the tongue were treated more or less as another modality of the somesthetic system, much like cold or mechanoreception. This picture is only partially correct, however, as some segregation of the taste modality has taken place. However, even where such segregation occurs, as on the cortex of the rat, it occurs inside the somatic sensory face area. Cohen et al. (1957) and Landgren (1957) reported that gustatory, tactile, and thermal units were all intermingled in the somatic sensory tongue area of the cat.

In the thalamus, the relay intermediate between the nucleus of the tractus solitarius and the cortex, Frommer (1961), Frommer and Pfaffmann (1961), Pfaffman, Erickson et al. (1961) showed that the area for taste was not coextensive with other modalities in the rat. This area is the ventral part of the nucleus ventralis of the thalamus at its medial tip. The responses to taste stimuli found in this area resemble those found in the chorda tympani nerve and the medullary relay. A somewhat similar separation has been shown to exist at the thalamic level in the monkey (for example, Benjamin, 1963).

It has been shown (Ables and Benjamin, 1960; Oakley and Pfaffmann, 1962) that removal of this thalamic area produces a marked reduction in "preference" of various solutions such as salt and sugar. Besides establishing an anatomical point, such results also show that the overdrinking of such solutions is due to their taste.

In the rat, the taste area in the thalamus projects to the somatic sensory face area. Bilateral removal of this area produces impairment of taste discrimination (Benjamin and Pfaffmann, 1955; Benjamin and Akert, 1959). Further, removal of all the rest of the neocortex, while the taste area was spared, left discrimination normal. However, it is to be remembered that removal of the cortical area also causes degeneration of the thalamic taste relay. Benjamin (1955a, 1955b) found that removal of the cortical taste area alone did not alter the aversion threshold to quinine when the animal was under high drive and drinking was restricted to an hour. The threshold was the same as that of normal animals under high or low drive. However, if more extensive lesions of the cortex were made, an elevation of threshold manifested itself. If, on the other hand, the animals with a lesion only of the taste area were tested under low drive, when drinking was ad libitum, an increased threshold to quinine was shown. This interesting result is at present difficult to interpret.

In the rabbit, Bremer (1923) has shown that taste deficit is caused by the ablation of cortical areas concerned with mastication. Ruch and Patton (1946) have shown that discrete lesions of the parainsular cortex deep in the sylvian fissure in chimpanzees and monkeys produce gustatory impairment. Penfield and Rasmussen (1950) reported that stimulation of this region in patients elicits reports of taste sensations. A diagram of the gustatory pathways appears in Figure 7–5.

Temporal Characteristics of Stimulation

When a taste stimulus is applied to a taste receptor, a steady change in receptor potential occurs. No rapid initial increment followed by a decrement is observed. This rapid increment followed by a decrement is found when recording is done from single-taste fibers, which suggests that the initial overshoot and its subsidence originate at the site where the action potentials are generated.

It seems, from the experiments of Krakauer and Dallenbach (1937), that complete adaptation, measured by behavioral methods, is rather fast, ranging from 1.5 to 3 minutes. However, electrophysiological data, at least in the case of salt (Beidler, 1963), do not show such a process of adaptation to occur peripherally, though it does so subjectively. Beidler (1957) stated that neural activity consequent to salt stimulation drops somewhat during the two seconds after the stimulus has been applied and then remains at a steady level when monovalent salts such as NaCl are used. However, such a lack of peripheral adaptation, as contrasted wth subjective adaptation, occurs in monovalent salts only. When divalent salts such as $CaCl_2$ are used, complete adaptation occurs slowly. It is to be noted that the same receptor cells respond both to NaCl and $CaCl_2$.

The discrepancy between electrophysiological recordings and psychophysical observations of adaptation to NaCl turn out not to implicate central processes of adaptation but are due, surprisingly enough, to a species difference. Beidler (1963) recorded from rats. Diamant and Zotterman (1969) recorded from the chorda tympani nerve in rats and in human patients undergoing surgery for deafness caused by bony growth around the ossicles of the middle ear (otosclerosis). It is clear that in man adaptation to NaCl is quite rapid whereas in the rat such adaptation is very slow, if not absent (Diamant and Zotterman [Fig. 7–7]).

A further fact of great interest in this regard is that there is very little cross-adaptation between NaCl and $CaCl_2$ at the peripheral neural

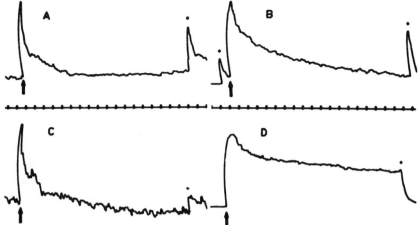

FIG. 7-7. Summated chorda tympani response to a continuous 3-min. flow of 0.2 M NaCl. A, B, C are human responses for patients no. 1, 2, 3, respectively, and D is a rat response. Dots indicate response during application of distilled water; arrows onset of salt. Tape-recorded data processed under identical conditions with rise and fall time constants of 1.5 sec. The tape recorder was off at beginning of B. Time base in 10-sec. intervals (Diamant, H. B., et al., *Acta Physiol. Scand.*, 1967.)

level. Adaptation to calcium chloride can be complete and yet the response to sodium chloride be almost undiminished. In line with this is the finding of Hahn (1949), on the subjective level, that no cross-adaptation occurs between a sample of 24 inorganic salts. However, in the case of sour, adaptation by one acid transfers to the sour taste of other acids, while for bitter and sweet cross-adaptation occurs only between some stimuli.

Generally, cross-adaptation between different stimuli is taken to imply that they both stimulate a common receptive pathway. On the other hand, where there is no cross-adaptation the argument must be made that the receptive mechanisms for the two stimuli must be separate and different. We would therefore have to conclude from Hahn's results that there must be separate channels for each of the 24 inorganic salts between which he found no cross-adaptation. However, McBurney (1969) reports that while there is very little cross-adaptation when detection threshold is used as a measure, there is cross-adaptation when subjects are asked to rate the salts in terms of their saltiness. It seems that it is the other taste qualities of the salts which enabled threshold detection to take place in Hahn's experiment. We do not, therefore, need to postulate a large number of different receptor mechanisms for salts. However, the story is not yet complete. If the salty taste component adapted out as a result of exposure to salt, the threshold for the detection of other salts should increase because one of the components is missing.

The reason why the threshold does not increase seems to be, as McBurney (1969) reports, that the adaptation to salt potentiates the sour taste of some salts and the bitter taste of others. While it is difficult to see how the threshold to sour and bitter could be reduced after adaptation to salt (NaCl), the most probable explanation in the view of the writer is that the various taste components, such as salt and bitter, normally mask each other, thus increasing the threshold for each other. When one taste quality is removed through adaptation, such masking is removed and the threshold for the other quality therefore decreases.

Hahn's results on adaptation show that the threshold for salt after adaptation finally reaches a value just above the concentration of the adapting stimulus. McBurney and Pfaffmann (quoted as Pfaffmann, 1963) measured such an effect at saline concentrations close to threshold (Fig. 7–8). They were able to establish clearly that saliva normally acts

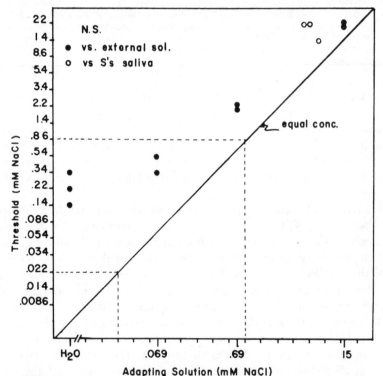

FIG. 7–8. Relation between adapting solution on the tongue and threshold. Each point shows the threshold obtained on one experimental determination; solid dots for adaptation to water or salt, open circles where the tongue is adapted to saliva with a Na+ composition shown on the abscissa as determined by flame photometry. (From Pfaffmann, C., *Olfaction and Taste,* Zotterman, Y. [ed.], 1963; courtesy of Pergamon Press.)

as an important adapting stimulus, greatly elevating the absolute threshold.

Pfaffmann reported that when adaptation to the salt solutions occurred, there was no salt sensation even for the strongest concentrations used. Pfaffmann concluded a process of central adaptation must occur.

McBurney and Pfaffmann's result is interesting because it enables us to reconcile results obtained by electrophysiological means with data obtained by psychophysical methods on man. Changes in taste threshold when salt deprivation or changes in fluid intake occur have been reported from psychophysical studies by de Wardener and Herxheimer (1957) and Yensen (1959). However, electrophysiological studies of neural responses in sodium-deprived rats have consistently failed to show any differences in sensitivity to NaCl. Pfaffmann (1963) explained this discrepancy by pointing out that during electrophysiological studies the rat's tongue is constantly rinsed with distilled water. If we assume no change in the sensitivity of the receptor but merely changes in the constitution of the saliva in the psychophysical tests, then changes in the saliva causing differential levels of adaptation will bring about variations in threshold. It is to be expected that the constitution of saliva would change sufficiently in human subjects, depending on their physiological state, to produce the observed discrepancy.

Though the NaCl threshold rises above the saline solution to which the tongue is adapted, this does not mean that solutions below such a threshold are tasteless. They are tasteless in the immediate vicinity of the adapting stimulus. Distilled water after the tongue is adapted to a saline solution tastes bitter or sour (Bartoshuk, McBurney, and Pfaffmann).

Other tastes also show complementarity, which however, is inconsistent. Adaptation to a sweet-tasting substance makes water subsequently taste sour, while adaptation to sour substances makes water taste sweet. On the other hand, adaptation to quinine hydrochloride, a bitter-tasting substance, also makes water sweet. It is difficult to find a compound besides urea which will make water taste salty. It is possible that some of these inconsistencies would disappear if taste masking could be shown to occur for some taste components of the adapting compounds. The masked tastes, while not perceptible in conjunction with the other tastes of the adapting compound, would nevertheless produce their own adaptation at the receptor. This adaptation by the masked taste could subsequently alter the perceived taste of a subsequent stimulus.

Another interesting effect emerges from these findings on adaptation. McBurney (1963) asked his subjects to rate the magnitude of sensation irrespective of quality after adaptation to various NaCl solutions. He found that the magnitude of taste sensation was lowest around the solution to which adaptation had taken place (Fig. 7–9). Solutions above

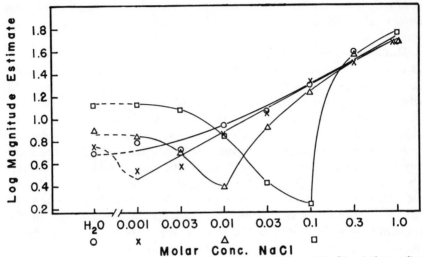

FIG. 7–9. Plot of estimate of magnitude of sensation of NaCl solutions after preadaptation to various salt solutions. Curve obtained after preadaptation with H_2O marked *o*; with 0.001 molar conc. NaCl marked *x*; with 0.01 molar conc. NaCl marked △; with 0.1 molar conc. marked □. (Courtesy of McBurney.)

the adapting solution were rated as increasing in saltiness; those below as increasing in sourness or bitterness. Further, adaptation to higher concentrations of NaCl did not simply make the tongue less sensitive to NaCl by a constant amount or fraction. It can be seen from the curves (Fig. 7–9) that when there is adaptation to the 0.1 concentration, the 0.3 concentration is judged as intense as when there is adaptation to distilled water. As a result, there is a marked deviation from a simple power function when a 0.1 adapting solution is used. (It can be seen that when a 0.001 molar concentration of NaCl is used, a straight line is obtained when the logarithm of the concentration is plotted against the logarithm of the magnitude estimate. This indicates that the two magnitudes are related according to a simple power law.) If there was some kind of overall decrement in sensitivity due to adaptation, then a solution of 0.3 molar after an adapting stimulus of 0.1 molar should taste equally strong as a solution of 0.003 molar after an adapting stimulus of 0.001 molar. But this, or anything like it, is not the case. Instead, 0.3 molar tastes as strong whether the adapting stimulus was 0.1 or 0.001 molar in concentration. In other modalities it has been shown that the difference threshold is smallest around the adapting value. For instance, after adaptation to distilled water the j.n.d. at 0.1 M

NaCl is 0.018 M NaCl. On the other hand, when the tongue was adapted to 0.1 M NaCl, the j.n.d. was 0.009 M NaCl (McBurney et al., 1967). On the other hand, there is a much smaller reduction of sensitivity at 0.3 M NaCl than at 0.1 M NaCl, when an adapting stimulus of almost 0.1 M NaCl is used. The j.n.d. at 0.3 molar is almost unaffected by this adapting stimulus. The results correspond closely to the data obtained by McBurney by the method of magnitude estimation (Fig. 7–9).

SMELL

The sense of smell is probably one of the most important sensory avenues for many mammals. For instance, most mammals possess scent glands which are used for trail and territorial demarcation and to modify endocrinological responses (e.g., Whitten, 1969; Schultze-Westrum, 1969). Such scent signals are called pheromones. One such pheromone is secreted by male mice in their urine, and the smell of this pheromone stimulates the release of gonadotrophin from the anterior pituitary of females not in estrus, so that the next period of estrus will occur earlier.

Though it appears to have declined in importance in the primates, olfaction still plays a large part in food selection and in the maintenance of a clean environment. The effective stimuli to the sense of smell are molecules of volatile substances. To be smelled, substances must be airborne and in a finely divided state. Such substances are brought in proximity with the sensory surface by breathing or sniffing. To this end, the olfactory receptor surface, or olfactory mucosa, lies in the upper portion of the nasal cavity.

In higher vertebrates the surface of the receptor surface, or olfactory mucosa, is covered by a thin layer of mucus secreted by Bowman's glands located under the epithelium. In man, the sensitive surface occupies about 2.5 cm² in each nostril. This sensitive surface is not in the direct flow of the inspired air. Consequently, the air carrying odorous particles reaches the sensitive surface by eddying. The magnitude of such eddying is increased by sniffing. Adrian (1956) reported that different compounds tend selectively to stimulate different parts of the sensory surface. Etheral smells in weak concentration usually stimulate the anterior parts of the receptor surface whereas heavy oils have their maximum effect on the posterior parts.

In the case of smell, the functions of sensory cell and nerve cell are not separate, as is the case in taste. The sensory element in olfaction is the specialized dendrite of a bipolar neuron. The cell body of this neuron is about 5 to 10 μ in diameter (Fig. 7–10). Below the nucleus, the cell narrows to form the olfactory nerve fiber, about 0.2 μ in diameter, which runs directly to the olfactory bulb, which is a part of the central

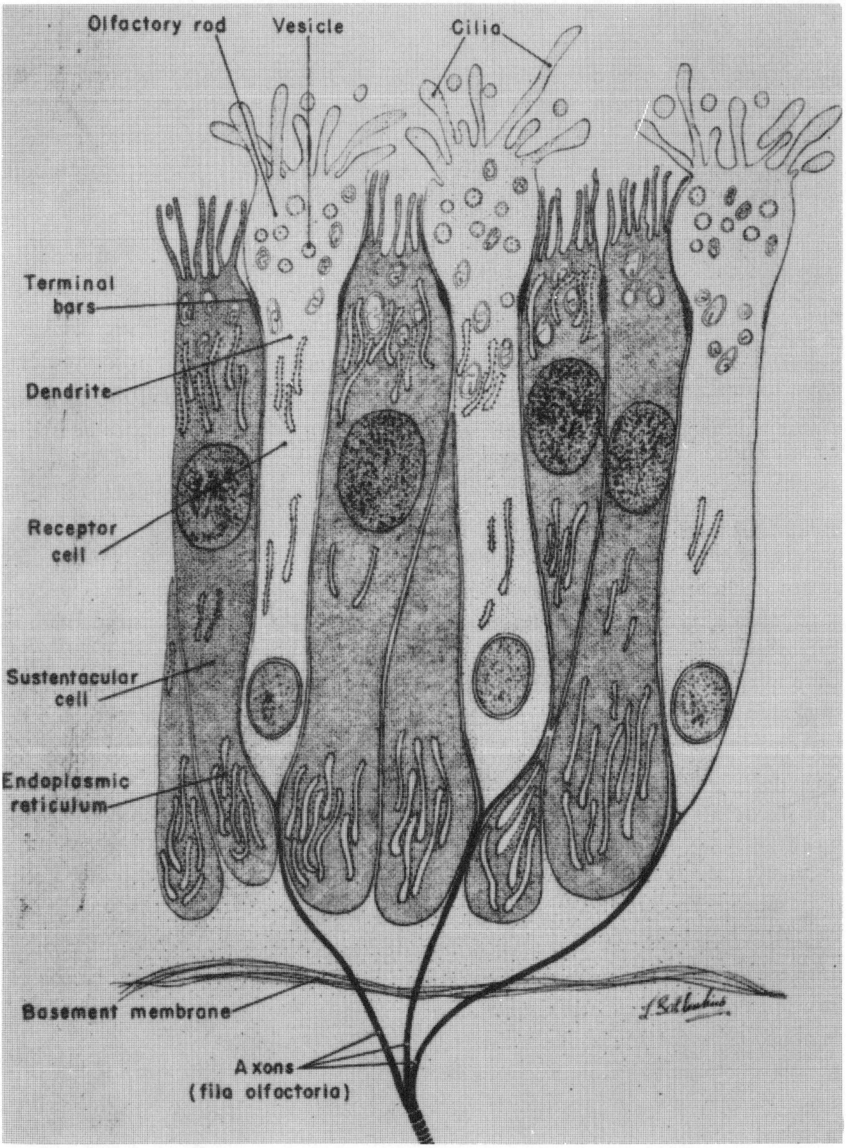

FIG. 7-10. Schematic drawing of the olfactory mucosa showing the relationships of the various cell types, based upon DeLorenzo's observations with the electron microscope. (From DeLorenzo, A. J. D., *Olfaction and Taste*, Zotterman, Y. [ed.], 1963; courtesy of Pergamon Press.)

nervous system. The receptor cells are cylindrical in shape and are wedged between sustaining or sustentacular cells of a similar shape. Most of the receptor cell is entirely surrounded by the sustentacular cells. However, the dendrite of the receptor cells juts out at the surface above the surrounding sustentacular cells. This bare end, called the olfactory rod, has on its end 6 to 12 fine hairlike structures or cilia, probably about 100 μ in length and about 0.1 to 0.2 μ in diameter. However, both the length and the number of cilia are subject to much variation between species (Steinbrecht, 1969). It would seem that it is this exposed part of the neuron which comes in contact with and reacts to the molecules of odorous substances. The function of the cilia is presumably to increase the surface area of the receptive cell. In the rabbit there are 100 million cells in the olfactory area with a density

TABLE 7–2

Stimulus	Cells Sampled	Cells Responding
n-Amyl Alcohol	25	14
Musk Xylene	38	20
Benzaldehyde	36	19
Benzyl Acetate	12	6
Geraniol	18	9
Benzonitrite	22	11
Pyridine	32	15
Indole	19	9
Camphor	32	14
Methyl Salicylate	18	8
Butyric Acid	30	13
Linalool	14	6
Pinene	7	3
n-Butanol	47	19
c-Hexanol	20	8
Nitrobenzene	42	16
Triethylamine	14	5
Ethyl Butyrate	31	10
Mercaptoacetic Acid	19	6
Valeric Acid	13	4
Limonene	17	5
Coumarin	22	6
Carbon Disulfide	28	7
Cinnamaldehyde	25	6
Methyl Anthranilate	6	1
Salicylaldehyde	21	3

The stimuli used in various experiments by Gesteland et al. (1963), the number of cells on which each was tried, and the number of those which responded with an increase in discharge rate are tabulated here. Weak and strong responses are lumped together. (From Gesteland, R. C., et al., *Olfaction and Taste,* Zotterman, Y. [ed.] 1963; courtesy of Pergamon Press.)

of about 125,000 receptor cells per square millimeter. Each receptor cell is separately connected via its own axon directly to the olfactory bulb.

Single-Receptor Cell Recordings

Recently, Gesteland et al. (1963) reported that they were able to record from single receptor units in the olfactory mucosa of the frog. They found that the action potential is long in duration (3 to 5 msec.) from extracellular recording sites near the axon hillock. The maximum repetition rate of neural discharge is 20 per second and is seen only rarely. A common rate of response to a stimulus is 1 to 5 per second. The resting rate of discharge is extremely low.

Each receptor shows selectivity to groups of odors. Each responds strongly to some odors, weakly to others, and to some not at all. Table 7–2 shows the proportions of cells sensitive to the various stimuli used. From an analysis of the sensitivities of the receptor cells sampled, it was possible to suggest a grouping of the receptors:

		Sensitive to—	Less Sensitive to—
Group	1	Limonene (lemon)	Carbon disulphide (rotten egg)
		Camphor (moth repellent)	
		Pinene (carrot seed turpentine)	
	2	Coumarin (new-mown hay)	
		Musk (heavy putrid)	
	3	Butyric acid (rancid butter)	
		Valeric acid (rancid butter)	
		Mercaptoacetic acid (offensive)	
		Cyclohexanol (peppermint-like)	
	4	Benzaldehyde (bitter almond)	
		Nitrobenzene (crude bitter almond)	
		Benzonitrite (bitter almond)	
		Musk (heavy putrid)	
		Amyl alcohol (flowery fragrant)	
	5	Pyridine (burnt)	
		Musk (heavy putrid)	
		Cinnamaldehyde (cinnamon)	
		N-butanol (glue solvent)	
	6	Musk (heavy putrid)	Benzaldehyde (bitter almond)
	7	Pyridine (burnt)	Nitrobenzene (bitter almond)
	8	Butanol (glue solvent)	
		Ethyl butyrate (pineapple)	
		Amyl alcohol (flowery fragrant)	
		Geraniol (geranium)	

Gesteland and co-workers are of the opinion that there are other, rarer groups also. From their results on single neuron stimulation, they believe that there are different types of receptor sites, distributed over each receptor cell. Different groups of cells could differ by having different ratios of receptor types on them. In this way, the receptoral scheme in smell seems to be like that seen in taste, except that there seems to be a larger number of special receptor sites.

Slow potential changes are also recorded from units in the olfactory epithelium when an olfactory stimulus is applied. Such potential changes may be in polarization in the receptor membrane which triggers action potentials. Chemoreceptors respond with a slow positive potential to

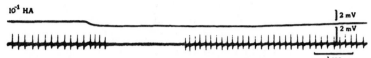

FIG. 7–11a. Inhibition of the "background" activity of an olfactory unit in the nose of the turkey vulture *(Cathartes aurea)* during hexylacetate stimulation. (From Shibuya and Tucker, *Olfaction and Taste III,* Pfaffmann [ed.], Rockefeller University Press, 1969.)

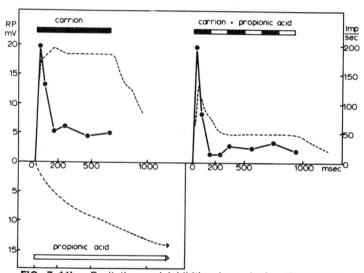

FIG. 7–11b. Excitation and inhibition in a single olfactory unit of an antennal sensillum basiconicum of the carrion beetle *Thanatophilus rugosus.* Upper left diagram shows the excitation under stimulation with carrion odor (black bar). Dotted line indicates the slow potential (left ordinate, *RP*); solid line represents the impulse frequency (right ordinate). Lower diagram, inhibitory slow potential going in positive direction under stimulation with propionic acid (white bar). Diagram at top right shows the excitation under a combined stimulation with carrion odor and propionic acid (black and white bar). Note the undiminished peak frequency and the lowered plateau. (From Dzendolet, E., in *Olfaction and Taste,* Pfaffmann (ed.), Rockefeller University Press, 1969. By permission from Boeckh, Jurgen, "Electrical Activity in Olfactory Receptor Cells.")

a substance which inhibits firing by the receptor. A negative potential develops to a substance which produces firing at the receptor. If an inhibitory and an excitatory substance are presented simultaneously, the potentials sum algebraically (Boekh, 1969). However, the presence of even a strong inhibitory stimulus does little to reduce the frequency of the initial burst of firing to an excitatory stimulus (Figs. 7–11a and 7–11b). A good review of further studies on the electrical activity of olfactory receptor cells is given by Boekh (1969).

Kaissling (1969) has shown the connection between odor concentration and the amplitude of the potential in the receptor by means of the mass action law in a way that Beidler (1954) developed for taste. The assumption is that, at a certain concentration, only a certain proportion of receptor sites are occupied by molecules. Such molecules are absorbed to the receptor sites. The maximal response occurs when all the receptor sites are occupied. It seems, therefore, that taste and smell receptors have a very similar physical mode of operation.

Mode of Stimulation of Olfactory Receptors

In the previous section we saw how olfactory stimuli are placed in different qualitative classes by the stimulation of different types of specific receptors. Before this experimental work was done it had been suggested that qualitative differences in smell were due to spatial or temporal patterns of a homogeneous population of receptor cells. The question to be asked now is related to the previous problem: What general kind of interaction occurs between the stimulating molecule and the receptor cell? Though many different theories have been suggested, based on radiation or chemical interaction, they have not received much support. An interesting approach to this problem of the physical process producing receptor excitation has been made by Jones (1955). He measured the absolute threshold for a large number of substances, calculating the relative number of molecules necessary to produce a sensation for each substance. He then attempted to correlate the stimulating efficiency of the various substances with various physical properties, such as their water solubility, vapor pressure, dipole moment, and standard free energy of formation. He discovered that vapor pressure had a very high correlation with stimulating efficiency in terms of the number of molecules necessary to reach absolute threshold. The results are plotted in Figure 7–12. As, in general, substances of lower vapor pressure are more readily adsorbed, he concluded that the most likely physical process involved in excitation of the receptors is the adsorption of molecules on the receptor surface. In this way, the mechanism of receptor excitation in smell would be similar to that in taste.

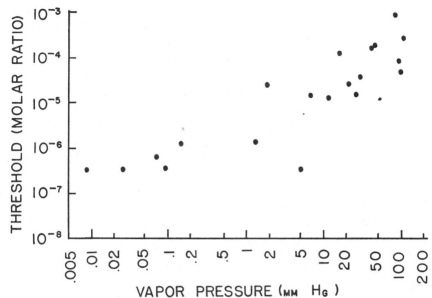

FIG. 7–12. Log_{10} of the undiluted vapor pressures plotted against median thresholds. (From Nowell Jones, 1955, *J. Psych.*, 40; by permission of the Journal Press.)

Laffort (1963) was able to obtain a linear relationship between the olfactory threshold for various substances in the aqueous phase and their molecular volume, taking the air-water partition coefficient into account. The important role of the aqueous mucus, in which the olfactory cilia are bathed, is indicated by the necessity of considering the aqueous phase of the molecules and the air-water partition coefficient. The odorant molecules must dissolve in the mucus before they can stimulate the cilia.

While different chemical series were related linearly to molecular volume, the slopes of this relationship are different for the different series (such as the acids, esters, and alcohols). Laffort (1969) was able to eliminate these differences in slope by plotting olfactory threshold against an index combining molecular volume with two other physical parameters of molecules, the hydrogen bonding index and atomic volumic polarizability.

If the mechanism of stimulation of olfactory receptors is analogous to that proposed for taste, we should expect various loci on the membrane of the receptor cell selectively to adsorb molecules as a result of certain highly specific properties, such as a particular shape. Depending on further properties of the adsorbed molecule, a change in the permeability to ions of the membrane at the receptor site results when the molecule has been absorbed. This results in a lowering of the electrical potential across the cell membrane. In the case of the smell receptor, if the lowering of the potential is sufficiently drastic, then as this change spreads electronically across the membrane of the cell, it reaches a region on the membrane at which an action potential is generated. This action potential is then propagated along the cell and its axon. Ottoson (1963) argued that the part of the membrane producing the initial alteration in potential does not produce the action potential. He has measured this initial depolarization of the cell membrane from the surface of the epithelium (Ottoson, 1956) and has found that it is not affected by antidromic stimulation of the olfactory nerve, which shows that the action potential is not conducted to this region. He quoted examples on impulse initiation in the lobster's stretch receptors (Edwards and Ottoson, 1958), in spinal motorneurons (Coombs, etc., 1957), and the giant cells of Aplysia (Tauc, 1962), where the cell body does not participate in the production of impulses, and suggested that olfactory receptor neurons are similar.

The characteristics of the change in potential when odors strike the olfactory mucosa are of considerable interest. Ottoson (1956) was the first to detect such changes by recording with large electrodes from the surface of a very large number of receptors simultaneously. When a prolonged odorous puff is passed over the frog's mucosa, after an initial decline of electrical activity little adaptation takes place. This is in agreement with the observations of Adrian (1950) on the secondary neurons in the olfactory bulb of the rabbit. This lack of adaptation shown by electrophysiological methods at more or less peripheral loci is at variance with the rapid adaptation to smells as it occurs in our perception. We very soon fail to be able to smell an odor when we are continuously exposed to it. To explain this discrepancy, Adrian (1950) suggested that the signals from the receptors are suppressed by the intrinsic activity in the olfactory bulb. Work on efferent control of the olfactory bulb (see section below) suggested that such signals may be inhibited by efferent fibers reaching the olfactory bulb from other points in the central nervous system.

Ottoson has been able to measure the relation between the increase of the potential at the mucosa and stimulus strength. By plotting the amplitude of potential against the logarithm of stimulus strength, a curve of increasing slope is obtained. This means that a larger proportionate increase of stimulus is needed at lower intensities to produce the same absolute change in amplitude of potential than at higher intensities. At higher intensities, a smaller proportionate change will produce the same absolute change. Let us assume that when we discriminate different intensities of the same odor, a discriminable difference is always the same absolute difference between potentials. For instance, we could assume that we can detect a difference between any two levels of an odor whenever the difference between the potentials to which they give rise is more than a tenth of a millivolt. If this reasonable assumption is made, there is good qualitative agreement between Ottoson's result and the results of psychophysical experiments. According to Zigler and Holway (1935), a much larger proportionate increase at low intensities of odor is necessary to produce a noticeable difference than at high. That is, $\Delta I / I$ decreases as I increases. It would therefore seem that the psychophysical law as applied to smell reflects some property of the membrane covering the end of the olfactory receptor cell.

One of the noteworthy features of the olfactory receptor is its extreme sensitivity. De Vries and Stuiver (1961) have calculated that the largest estimate of mercaptan molecules necessary to stimulate a receptor cell is 6 and that, at the most, 40 receptor cells have to be stimulated to produce a sensation. Neuhaus (1955) showed that olfactory receptors in dogs could react to a single molecule of fatty acids.

Many cases of odor "blindness" have been discovered. Amoore (1969) reports specific anosmias for 62 different chemical compounds. This would indicate a considerable individual variability in human olfactory receptor sites.

Theories of Olfactory Quality

There have been many suggestions about the physical properties to which the receptor is sensitive. Most of the theories proposed so far are not capable of encompassing more than a small proportion of the evidence, and many have conclusive evidence against them. These have been well reviewed by Jones and Jones (1953).

There have also been a number of attempted classifications of odors (Zwaardemaker, 1925; Henning, 1924; Crocker and Henderson, 1927). However, it is not even clear how many of the smells thus classified actually represent stimulation of olfactory receptors, rather than taste receptors giving rise to sweet or sour "smells," or of free nerve endings belonging to the trigeminal nerve, capable of reacting to chemical stimuli giving rise to pungent "smells," or of cold fibers stimulated by certain substances, such as menthol, giving rise to fresh "smells." Such classifications may be descriptively useful, but it is dubious whether they shed any great insight on the mechanism of olfaction.

Factor analysis has been applied in a preliminary but promising manner to the problem of basic olfactory qualities by Jones (1957). He obtained recognition thresholds for 20 substances on a large number of subjects. From the intercorrelations of these thresholds, he was able to conclude that individual differences in thresholds are systematic, that there are many varieties of receptor, and that his results corresponded to no existing scheme of odor classification.

The theory which has so far received the strongest measure of experimental support is, in its outline, due to the Roman poet, the Epicurean Lucretius. He believed that different substances give off molecules of different shapes and sizes. These then entered pores of differnt shapes and sizes in the palate and accordingly were perceived as different odors. This stereochemical theory of odor was restated in modern times by Moncrieff (1951). Molecules of various odorants, by virtue of their shape and size, were thought of as fitting into different-shape receptor sites on the surface of the receptor membrane. Amoore (1964) has made this theory more specific by working out the shapes and sizes of such receptor sites. He postulates seven varieties of receptor site (Amoore et al., 1964). These, according to him, correspond to seven primary odors: camphoraceous (like moth repellent), musky (like angelica root oil or heavy putrid odor), floral (like roses), pepperminty, ethereal (like drycleaning fluid), pungent (like vinegar), and putrid (like bad eggs). The pungent molecules stimulate not because of their shape but because they are positively charged. Similarly, putrid molecules stimulate because they are positively charged. It is claimed that from these seven primary odors it is possible to match any other known odor. Because of their shape, some molecules will fit into more than one type of receptor site, and this is held to account for mixed odors. It is further proved possible to predict the odor of a new compound from its shape and to modify it in a predicted direction by changing the shape. Molecules of the same shape but belonging to different chemical substances were found to have the same odor; quite different chemicals of the same overall molecular shape were quite often indistinguishable.

Supporting evidence for the stereochemical theory of odor has been reported by Amoore and Venstrom (1966, 1967) and Higashino et al. (1969).

Central Connections

The receptor cells send their axons directly to the central nervous system and there is no interconnection between the receptor cells at the peripheral level. The axons penetrate the cribriform plate of the ethmoid bone to end in the olfactory bulb (Fig. 7–13). The axons from the anterior and dorsal parts of the olfactory mucosa connect to the anterior part of the olfactory bulb, and those from the ventral and posterior parts project to the posterior part of the bulb. Each of these axons belonging to the receptor cells then passes into a glomerulus and ends there. It does not branch until it passes into the glomerulus. The glomerulus is a spherical bush of dendrites belonging to the tufted, mitral

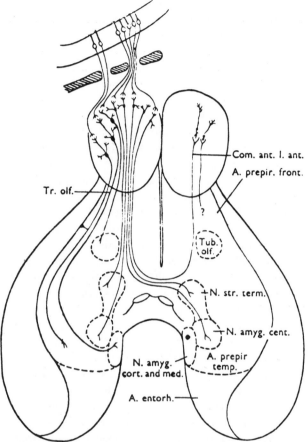

FIG. 7–13. Diagrammatic representation of the secondary olfactory pathways in the mammalian brain: *a. prepir. front,* frontal part of the prepiriform area; *a. prepir. temp.,* temporal part of the prepiriform area; *a. entorh,* entorhinal area; *n. amyg. cent.,* central amygdaloid nucleus; *n. amyg. cort.,* cortical amygdaloid nucleus; *n. amyg. med.,* medial amygdaloid nucleus; *tr. olf.,* olfactory tract; *tub. olf.,* olfactory tubercle; *com. ant. l. ant.,* commissure anterior lateralis anterior; *n. str. term.,* nucleus of the stria terminalis. (From Allison, A. C., 1953; courtesy of *Biological Reviews,* 28.)

and external granular cells lying more deeply in the olfactory bulb (Allison, 1953). It is interesting to note that the connection between the receptor cells and the mitral and tufted cells is of an unusual type. The axon of the receptor cell connects to the dendrites of the mitral and tufted cells (axo-dendritic connection) instead of connecting directly with the cell body (axosomatic connection), which is the usual arrangement found in the higher vertebrates. The axodendritic mode of connection is typical of the nervous system of invertebrates and lower vertebrates, and is considered to be less rapid and efficient in the transmission of impulses. It is also to be noted that the sense of smell possesses another primitive feature inasmuch as the functions of receptor cell and conductive neurons are combined. This is different from the case of taste, and again resembles the sensory arrangement to be found in invertebrates (for instance the blowfly, Dethier and Arab, 1958).

The axons of the mitral cells (the dendrites of which the receptor cells connect in the glomeruli) form the lateral olfactory tract, which flows into the primary olfactory cortex. It should also be noted that as well as possessing dendrites which meet the incoming fibers in the glomerulus, each mitral cell has accessory dendrites which lie close to the dendrites of other mitral cells in the external plexiform layer. This is also true of the tufted cells. Further, both the mitral and tufted cells divide their axons into two as these axons pass out of the olfactory bulb. One branch runs out. The other branch of the axon doubles back (and is therefore called recurrent collateral) to end on the accessory dendrites of its own class in the olfactory bulb. The axons of the tufted cells pass into the anterior commissure and run into the contralateral olfactory bulb. There they form synaptic connections with granule cells. The axons of the granule cells extend toward the surface to end on the accessory dendrites of mutual and tufted cells. Each glomerulus in the rabbit has 26,000 axons from receptor cells ending in it. From each glomerulus, information runs through 24 mitral cells to higher olfactory centers, and through 68 tufted cells to the contralateral olfactory bulb. There are about 60,000 mitral cells in each olfactory bulb of the rabbit. It seems likely that axons from receptors cells of similar sensitivity to specific odors collect on the same glomerulus and that mitral cells in different regions of the olfactory bulb tend to respond selectively to different odors (Adrian, 1953; Mozell and Pfaffmann, 1953). Using small electrodes to record from the layer of mitral cells in the rabbit's olfactory bulb, Adrian (1953, 1956) reported that such cells are differentially sensitive to odorous stimuli. He stated that mitral cells can be divided into at least four or five groups, depending on their peak sensitivity:

Group 1. Aromatic compounds (benzol, toluol) (lighter fluid, dry-cleaning fluid)
      2. Esters of fatty acids (amyl and ethyl acetate) (fruity)
      3. Paraffin hydrocarbons (pentane and homologues) (gasoline)
      4. Terpenes (limonene, cedar oil, eucalyptus) (lemon, etc.)
      5. Sulphur compounds (mercaptan, H_2S) (foul, rotten eggs)

A slow potential change, paralleling that recorded from the olfactory mucosa, can be recorded from the olfactory bulb. This is thought to arise from the glomeruli and to represent a summed dendritic potential. Superimposed on this slowly rising bulb potential are a series of faster rhythmic waves. Some interesting observations on this phenomenon have been made by Moulton (1963) on unanaesthetised rabbits with chronically implanted electrodes. He reported that occasionally low-amplitude asynchronous waves in the range of 75 to 90 cps. could be recorded from the bulb even when the rabbit was breathing filtered air. When an odor was introduced, high-amplitude sinusoidal waves appeared in the record, varying from 50 to 85 cps. Spike discharges recorded from the bulb did not always coincide with the rhythmic activity.

The spike discharges recorded by Moulton did not show any regular relation to the strength of the presented odor, as repeated presentation of the odor brought about habituation. When he paired shock with a previously habituated odor, enhancement of the response appeared, though quantitative relations still remained inconsistent. This suggests some relation to states of arousal or attention of the amplitude of response. The effect of various attentional states on activity in peripheral sensory structures is discussed further in Chapter 11.

Békésy (1964) has shown that if an odor arrives in one nostril a few tenths of a millisecond before it arrives in the other nostril, it will completely suppress the sensation in the second nostril. A similar effect is obtained when the concentration in one nostril is only 10 percent higher than in the other. Recently, Leventeau and MacLeod (1969) investigated the physiological substrate of this reciprocal inhibition, which presumably functions in odor localization. By recording from the glomeruli, they were able to show some interesting interactions.

The response to an odor in one nostril was roughly halved in the glomerular layer connected to that nostril when an equal-intensity stimulus was applied about 3 msec. before to the opposite nostril (Leventeau and MacLeod, 1969). The interactions between different concentrations to the two nostrils show unexplained discrepancies.

Efferent Influences on the Olfactory Bulb

Cajal (1911) and Cragg (1962) have shown that a very large number of centrifugal connections end in the olfactory bulb. These end on the granule cells of the bulb, some arising in the prepyriform cortex. It has been shown by Kerr and Hagbarth (1955) and Hagbarth and Kerr (1954) that both the resting and induced activity of the olfactory bulb may be modified by stimulation of the prepyriform cortex, amygdaloid nucleus, olfactory tubercle, and anterior commissure. Kerr (1960) demonstrated the inhibition of induced waves in one bulb by strong olfactory stimulation of the contralateral bulb. Efferent effects have also been described by Yamamoto and Iwama (1961) and Walsh (1959).

Moulton (1963) described the effect of severing the efferent fibers to on bulb and its connections with the opposite bulb. This was done by a lesion to the anterior olfactory areas through which run efferent fibers to the bulb (Cragg, 1962) and to the anterior commissure, through which run the fibers from the opposite bulb. A better correlation between input to the bulb and recorded output was obtained on the side with no efferent input. There also appeared a larger and more regular response. Whereas diminution of response with repeated presentation of the same stimulus occurred in the side whose efferent input was intact, no such diminution was observed on the contralateral side. Kerr and Hagbarth (1955) obtained similar phenomena in cats and could not decide whether the depression of activity represents some form of desynchronization, such as occurs on activation in the cortex, or a true inhibition of activity in the olfactory bulb.

Connections of the Olfactory Bulb with Other Areas

Direct connections of the mitral cells in the olfactory bulb with the rest of the nervous system are made via the lateral olfactory tract (see Fig. 7-13). This terminates ipsilaterally in the olfactory tubercle parts of the prepyriform cortex and the cortical and medial groups of the amygdaloid nuclei. The tufted cells are connected via the anterior limb of the anterior commissure in the nucleus of the stria terminalis and the central amygdaloid nucleus. They are also connected to the granule cells in the contralateral olfactory bulb. The olfactory tubercle, the cortical, medial, and central amygdaloid nuclei, and the nucleus of the stria terminalis receive connections from nonolfactory areas also. It is therefore difficult to know whether their efferent connections have a specifically olfactory function or whether they themselves have such a function. The only area which is specifically olfactory is the prepyriform cortex, according to Allison (1953). When the prepyriform cortex is electrically stimulated in the dog, spikes can be recorded 3 msec. later in the ventrolateral portion of the prefrontal area and from no other area (Allen, 1943b). The agranular insular cortex is considered by Allison (1953) to be equivalent to the area described by Allen. Allison (1953) found that in the rabbit, degeneration of fibers passing into the agranular insular cortex occurs after destruction of the prepyriform area. Ablation of this prefrontal area has been shown by Allen (1940, 1941) to yield a behavioral deficit. He found that this area is necessary for conditioned differential response to olfactory stimuli and impairs other olfactory learning to some extent. The differential conditioned response which was so severely affected meant, in effect, that the dog had to learn to decide in seven seconds whether to jerk its foreleg when it smelled cloves and not to jerk it when it smelled asafetida. In a control experiment, Allen (1943a) found that the same lesion had no effect on the learning of the same habit to auditory, cutaneous, and visual stimuli, thus ruling out an interpretation of the result in terms of general intellectual impairment. Other lesions designed to test the extent of the brain areas necessary for olfactory discrimination have yielded negative results. Swann (1934, 1935) designed a test in which a rat had to dig through wood shavings scented either with oil of anise or creosote to obtain food. That is, the rat had to discriminate between two paths leading to food on the basis of odor. However, lesions of the septum, amygdaloid complex, pyriform lobes, hippocampus, fimbria, fornix, and habenula had no effect on the discrimination. Brown and Ghiselli (1938) also failed to observe any effect on olfactory discrimination after a variety of subcortical lesions, as did Lashley and Sperry (1943), who severed the cortical radiations coming up from the anterior group of thalamic nuclei.

Traditionally, the rhinencephalon as a whole used to be credited with olfactory function. This view has not been substantiated by recent evidence. Though it is possible to record from a large number of structures events initiated by stimulating the olfactory bulb, it is not clear at present how many of these are concerned with smell in any direct manner.

Behavioral Phenomena

Perhaps the most important and difficult problem in research on olfaction concerns the method of stimulation. Various instruments and procedures have been designed to ensure the delivery of a known and uniform amount of odorous substance to the sensory surface. The difficulties inherent in this have been ably reviewed by Wenzel (1948). Zwaardemaker (1925) designed an instrument called an olfactometer. This consists of an outer tube, the inner surface of which is impregnated with the substance to be tested, and an inner tube of glass. This inner tube fits into the outer tube, and is slid into it to varying extents. The farther it is slipped in, the less surface is exposed when the subject sniffs the free end of the inner tube. In this way, some gradation of odorous intensity is achieved. Instead of relying on the sniffing power of the nose, it is possible to attach a pump to the tubes in such a way that air is blown into the nostril for a fixed amount of time. A further refinement of technique has been introduced by Elsberg and Levy (1935), called the blast injection method. In this technique, varying amounts of air are forced into a bottle with an odorous substance in it. As a consequence, varying amounts of pressure build up and are then suddenly released into the nostrils of the subject. However, this technique has been brought into question by Jerome (1942), Wenzel (1949), and

Jones (1953). The differences in threshold found cannot be related to the concentration of odorous substance but rather to pressure. To overcome these difficulties, Wenzel (1955) introduced a technique with satisfactory reliability in which threshold measurements are taken during normal breathing. The whole head is placed in a plastic box with the face and hair covered, leaving access only to the nostrils. Then a stream of air, to which various amounts of odor can be added, is blown into the box.

An olfactometer which gives close control over the duration, volume, pressure, and temperature of the stimulus and permits specification of dilution of odorant, has been designed by Jones (1954). It is illustrated in Figure 7–14 (Jones, 1954). Basically, it consists of a syringe (*B*) which

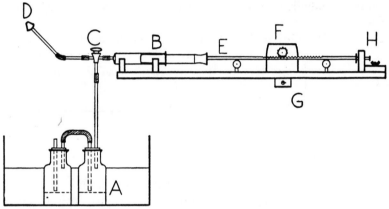

FIG. 7–14. Diagram of the essential portions of the olfactometer designed by Nowell Jones. (From Nowell Jones, 1954; courtesy of *Amer. J. Psych.,* 67.)

may be filled with differing proportions of pure air and a certain dilution of the odor to be tested. What proportions of the odorant and air are sucked into the syringe by withdrawing the plunger is controlled by turning the three-way stopcock at *C*. Air is taken in from a purified source (not shown in the diagram) which connects separately to the stopcock and to the bottles of odorant at *A*. When the syringe is full, the odorant mixture is delivered into the subject's nose through the nosepiece (*D*) by switching on the electric motor at *F*. This engages the toothed rack (*E*) to drive the plunger of the syringe (*B*). A stop is mounted at *H* to ensure that the plunger travels through the same distance every time the subject is stimulated. A blast of 40 cc. is delivered to the subject in 0.8 sec.

It has already been mentioned that complete adaptation to an odor, as shown by subjective reports, occurs. Zwaardemaker (1925) has shown that the rate of elevation of absolute threshold is higher with stronger stimuli. Not only do odors diminish with perceived intensity, but there are some which also change qualitatively as adaptation proceeds. Presumably, rates of adaptation to various components differ. Adaptation is to a certain extent specific. Threshold for oil of clove and eucalyptus and for ether are elevated by previous exposure to camphor. However, adaptation to benzaldehyde leaves the threshold for these odors relatively unaltered. Such relationships presumably reflect differences in the receptor sites occupied by different odorous molecules. However, as can be seen from the case of taste, this is not necessarily so. It is also possible to produce a new odor by mixing odors. Also, an odor may be rendered imperceptible by the presence of another, a phenomenon analogous to that of auditory masking. The physiological bases of these observations are at present obscure.

chapter 8

Motor System

Ian P. Howard*

In any logical account of the motor system, each step assumes a knowledge of what is to follow. This is because the various parts of the system are interdependent and are involved in closed control loops. For purposes of exposition (and experimental analysis), these control loops must be broken into, but for a final understanding their integrity must be restored. The student is thus asked to read through this account more than once. Things which are not understood at the first reading, because they anticipate facts explained later, should become clear on subsequent readings.

MUSCULAR CONTRACTION

Muscle, together with its associated skeletal structures, is a machine that converts chemical energy into mechanical energy. There are two main types of muscle; striated muscle and smooth muscle. All skeletal muscles, that is, muscles attached to tendons and bones, are striated, but a few striated muscles are not skeletal, for instance, muscles in the iris and heart. Most striated muscles are under voluntary control and are often called voluntary muscles on this account. Smooth or unstriated muscle is never skeletal and is normally not under voluntary control.

There are about 400 skeletal muscles in the human body, comprising almost one half of its total weight. There are about 250 million muscle fibers or cellular units, supplied by about half a million myelinated nerve fibers. Thus many muscle fibers are supplied by one efferent nerve fiber, and any such group of muscle fibers is known as a *motor unit*.

---

* Revised by J. A. Deutsch.

Motor units vary in size in different parts of the body. Those muscles involved in fine, precise movements have smaller motor units than those involved in cruder movements. The muscle fibers belonging to any one unit are scattered at random in a particular muscle. Contiguous muscle fibers are bound together by connective tissue into bundles. Many bundles make up a skeletal muscle. Each end of a skeletal muscle is attached by a tendon to a bone in such a way that contraction of the muscle causes movement at a joint.

Each striated muscle fiber consists of a mass of parallel *myofibrils,* each 1 to 2 μ thick. Each fibril shows cross striations when viewed under a microscope, and the fibrils are so arranged that their patterns of striation are in step. The pattern of striations is repeated down the length of the fibrils, and each unit or segment of the pattern is bounded by highly refractive bands, between which stretch parallel molecular *filaments.* These filaments are therefore parallel to the direction of the muscle fibrils and fibers. Thicker filaments, composed largely of *myosin,* are interleaved with thinner and longer filaments, composed largely of another muscle protein, *actin.*

The contraction of the muscle involves a contraction of the myofibrils. The contraction of the fibrils is caused by the myosin and actin molecular filaments sliding past each other, presumably because of obliquely acting forces between them. Neither the myosin filaments nor the actin filaments are contractile—it may be seen under the electron microscope that the length of the filaments does not alter. Contraction consists of an increased overlapping of the two sets of filaments. For further details of this theory of muscular contraction, see H. E. Huxley (1956).

An older view (Fulton, 1955) was that contraction involves an alteration in the length of the actin and myosin chain molecules by a process of "molecular folding." This is now known to be wrong, but perhaps the obliquely acting forces between the actin and myosin filaments involve "molecular folding."

Something is known about the biochemical processes by which energy is made available for the contractile process. However, a discussion of these processes is beyond the scope of this book. The student is referred to Fulton (1955) and *British Medical Bulletin* (1956).

Smooth Muscle

Smooth, unstriated muscle is innervated by the unmyelinated nerves of the autonomic nervous system, and is not, in any obvious way, organized into motor units. It typically lines body cavities, such as the bladder, uterus, intestine, and blood vessels. Many smooth muscles contract rhythmically even in the absence of nerve impulses. Smooth muscle, like striated muscle, contains myofibrils and the same muscle proteins, actin and myosin; however, the myofibril segments of smooth muscle are not aligned with each other, which accounts for its smooth, unstriated appearance. This lack of alignment is probably due to the fact that smooth muscle fibrils do not have to pull in concert against a skeletal member but, rather, in all directions over a sheet of contractile tissue so as to control the volume of the body cavity of which they form the lining.

Neuromuscular Junction

Figure 8–1 is a diagramatic representation of a neuromuscular junction on a striated muscle fiber. It shows one dendritic terminal bouton

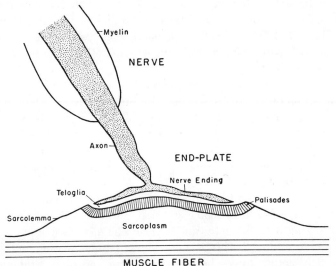

FIG. 8–1. Diagram of endplate region. (Adapted by Couteaux from Acheson, G., *Fed. Proc.,* 1948, 7:447.)

in close proximity to the motor endplate of a muscle fiber. The motor endplate is a very specialized part of the muscle membrane. The nerve impulse stimulates the release of acetylcholine in the synaptic junction. Acetylcholine is known as a transmitter, and acts by increasing the permeability of the muscle membrane to sodium and potassium ions. This leads to a transient "puncture" of the endplate membrane, which causes its resting potential to drop and a wave of depolarization to spread over the muscle membrane. The mechanism by which this membrane potential is conducted is similar to that by which the action potential in a nerve axon is conducted (see p. 6). It quickly spreads to all parts of the fiber, to each fibril, and finally to each actin and myosin filament.

When the nerve impulse has ceased, the acetylcholine must be removed rapidly, or the muscle would continue to contract. An enzyme, acetylcholinesterase, is responsible for the breakdown of the transmitter. Poisons—for instance, physostigmine—combine with the acetylcholinesterase and prevent it from working. Small amounts of such poisons are sufficient to cause rapid death upon the permanent contracture of all the muscles of the body. Other poisons, for instance, curare, interfere with the action of acetylcholine and produce muscle paralysis. These drugs are useful in the experimental analysis of muscular function, as well as clinically. There are several diseases, some of which are inherited—for instance, family periodic paralysis and myasthenia gravis—which affect the processes of neuromuscular transmission (see Brain, 1952).

Mechanical Aspects of Muscular Contraction

Contracting muscle is subject to certain internal physical restraints which impede its free movement, quite apart from any external load which may be imposed. These restraints are the inertia due to the muscle's mass, internal friction, the muscle's elasticity, and the extent of any damping. Each of these restraints affects contraction in a different way.

Inertia is a function of mass and is a measure of the extent to which the moving part resists any change in velocity. According to classical mechanics, the force required to move a body is equal to the product of its mass and acceleration. Thus the mass or inertia of a limb affects its movement only when it is required to change its speed of movement.

Friction resists change of position, and is especially high when a limb moves from rest, but may be regarded as a constant when movement has started.

Elasticity is a measure of the force which is required to extend the muscle at any particular length. It increases as a function of length and tends to restore the muscle to its original length. Resting muscles are always under some elastic tension, so that elasticity would facilitate muscular contraction except that every striated muscle is balanced by its antagonist, which resists its contraction. The elastic forces which arise when a muscle is stretched have two components: the first is due to the elasticity of the tendons and other elastic elements in series with the muscle fibers; the other is due to the active contraction of fully innervated muscle in response to the stimulus of stretching (the stretch or myotatic reflex). The physical elasticity is practically independent of the rate at which the muscle is stretched and is dependent only on the amount of stretch, at least up to the point of injury. The active elastic component is a complex function of many factors and depends on the integrity of a complete reflex arc.

Damping is a measure of the forces which resist movement in proportion to the velocity of movement. One form of damping is a consequence of the viscosity of the tissues. A second form of damping is provided by the adaptation of the reflex arcs which control the muscle's contraction. This topic will be mentioned again.

These are the basic properties of muscle which determine the way a muscle will contract to a given stimulus, assuming there is no external load. Figure 8–2 may help to clarify these matters. The relative spatial

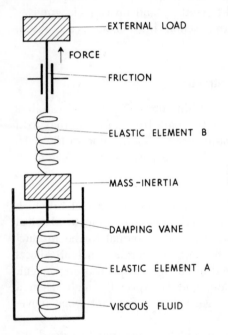

EXTERNAL LOAD

↑ FORCE

FRICTION

ELASTIC ELEMENT B

MASS – INERTIA

DAMPING VANE

ELASTIC ELEMENT A

VISCOUS FLUID

FIG. 8–2. Diagrammatic representation of the mechanical elements of muscle.

arrangement of the inertial, frictional, elastic, and damping elements is important. For instance, the elastic element *A* in Figure 8–2 is "outside" the inertial mass and damping; on release of tension, this part of the system will contract rapidly, as it will not have to move a mass or overcome damping. The elastic element *B* is "inside" the inertial and damping elements, and will therefore contract only slowly. Both types of elasticity are present in muscle. The relative positions of other elements are equally important. In practice, they are distributed, though not evenly, throughout each muscle. Such mechanical models are a useful aid to understanding, but give only an approximation of the actual state of affairs. In reality, the elements we have discussed do not function independently; a change in one brings about a change in another. In other words, living systems are *nonlinear*.

The behavior of muscle under different conditions of external load will now be considered. If a muscle is stimulated by a brief electric shock, it responds with a *"twitch."* If the stimulus is repeated, even before the first response has died away, the muscle will again contract. With high-frequency stimulation, the individual twitches fuse into a smooth, continuous contraction, or *tetanus*. If a muscle is anchored to a rigid tension-measuring device, it will be unable to shorten when stimulated, but the tension developed will increase with the strength of the stimulus. The muscle is said to be contracting *isometrically*. On the other hand, if it is attached to a light lever which records movement rather than tension, the muscle will shorten at constant tension, and is said to be contracting *isotonically*. The tension developed in isometric contraction is a function of the extent to which the muscle is initially stretched, and is maximum when the muscle is as long as it is in the resting limb. In the body, the maximum tension is also a function of the number of muscle fibers arranged in parallel, but a balance is struck between the need for strong "in parallel" muscles and the need for "in series" muscles which have a greater range of shortening. When muscle under isometric tension is suddenly released, there is a rapid shortening due to the endogenous elasticity of the tissues, followed by a slower shortening due to active contraction.

Under isotonic contraction, the muscle takes time to shorten to its full extent. This *latent* period is a function of the tension against which the muscle has to pull; when there is no external load, the speed of contraction is maximal and is determined by the muscle's internal mass, friction, elasticity, and damping constants. At the other extreme, when the muscle contracts isometrically, its speed of shortening is zero. The velocity varies enormously between different muscles in the body and between different species. Striated (voluntary) muscle is, on the whole, faster than unstriated (involuntary) muscle. The wing muscles of insects contract in less than 1 msec.; they are the most rapidly contracting of all muscles. At the other extreme, the unstriated circular muscle of the column of the sea anemone, *Metridium senile*, requires five or six minutes for a single "twitch." For further details on this subject see Wilkie (1956).

Gradation of Muscular Contraction

In the intact animal, the gradation of the strength of muscular contraction in a particular muscle is controlled by the number of motor units which are stimulated and by the frequency of the efferent neural discharge. Records of the changes in electrical potential which accompany muscular contraction (electromyography) have revealed that more units are recruited with increased muscular tension, and that the neural discharge rate to a single motor unit varies from 5 to 50 per second, as the strength of contraction increases, although contraction rarely involves complete tetanus. It used to be thought that the individual muscle fibers obey the all-or-none law; that is, that they contract fully or not at all. It is now known that fatigue, drugs, and disease may modify the strength of contraction of a fiber, even though the nerve impulses remain constant (Merton, 1956). The γ-fiber system is also an important mechanism for controlling the strength of muscular contraction (see p. 295).

Muscular contraction must not only be graded in strength but also be smooth and balanced in operation. At the cellular level, all the fibrils in a particular muscle fiber and all fibril segments receive impulses practically simultaneously, for each fiber receives many terminal boutons from any single neuron, and the action potential spreads quickly over the fiber membranes. The muscle fibers comprising a motor unit are scattered throughout the whole muscle, and they also contract simultaneously because they are supplied by the same neuron. However, the different motor units do not fire in synchrony, but those units that are firing at any time are evenly and randomly spread throughout the muscle. It is rare for all the units to fire together; they fire in rotation like the cylinders of a car engine. The final effect is that the contraction is smoothed, just as the running of the car engine is smoothed by the out-of-step firing of the cylinders. If the firings were not well distributed at any one time, one end of the muscle would contract before or more than the other end, or one side would contract before the other side; the movement would be off balance. It is the random distribution of the fibers comprising each motor unit that ensures this balance of the contractile process. Muscle is indeed a well-designed machine.

Other Properties of Striated Muscle

Most muscles contain a mixture of three different types of muscle fiber in different proportions (although each motor unit contains only one type of muscle fiber). These three different types of muscle fiber have been designated A-, B-, and C-type fibers. A fiber contains only a few mitochondria and has very few (if any) capillaries to furnish a blood supply. They are also larger in size than the B and C muscle fibers. C fibers are the smallest fibers, with a high mitochondrial content and the largest density of capillaries surrounding them. B fibers are intermediate in size between the A and C fibers, in the number of mitochondria they contain, and in their vascular supply. The A fibers look pale whereas the C fibers look dark. The C fibers are brought into use by the nervous system most frequently because of their innervation, as will be seen later, and the A fibers least frequently. The distinction between A, B, and C fibers is not absolute, and they may also be regarded as a continuum.

It seems that the innervation of the muscle fiber determines what characteristics it will develop. When nerves are transposed from muscles which normally contain mainly A fibers to muscles which normally contain C fibers, and vice versa, the character of the muscles changes. A fibers appear where C fibers would predominate with normal innervation, and vice versa.

The contraction speeds of the three classes of fiber vary greatly. At one extreme, C fibers are slow in contracting and do not fatigue rapidly, whereas at the other extreme A fibers are fast in contracting and fatigue rapidly. As was stated above, each motor unit contains muscle fibers of only one class. Each motor unit contains widely varying numbers of muscle fibers. Some of the smaller motor units consist of only 39 fibers, according to Henneman's (1968) estimate. Others may contain as many as 2,000 motor fibers. The smallest units contain C fibers and large units contain A fibers.

Innervation of Motor Units

A motor neuron pool is that group of motor neurons which innervates a particular muscle. In the case of large muscles, such pools may be spread over two or three segments of the cord. The axons of such motor neurons pass out to the muscles through two or three ventral roots.

Each motor unit is controlled by a single α motor neuron. This means that in some cases one nerve axon can branch into as many as 2,000 terminals because there is approximately that number of muscle fibers in a motor unit, each with its own nerve terminal. The larger the α motor neuron, the larger the number of muscle fibers in the motor unit it controls. As a result, there is a linear relation between the conduction velocity of the axon of a motor neuron and the maximum tension of the motor unit the axon innervates. (The larger the neuron, the thicker its axon, and so the faster its velocity.) Thus it may be concluded that the larger the α motor neuron, the larger the motor unit it controls.

This gradation of size among motor units, together with the fact that smaller α motor neurons control smaller motor units, has great functional importance because of a gradation of excitability. The smallest neurons have the lowest threshold of excitability, and the threshold increases with the size of the neuron. Consequently, when the excitation reaching the motor neuron pool is weak, only the smaller motor neurons fire. As these cause the contraction of small motor units, the whole muscle develops only a small tension. As the excitation reaching the motor neuron pool increases, a larger number of motor neurons fires, as those of a larger size are now recruited. From this it follows that the larger units are never active without the participation of smaller units. It also follows that as tension increases it must increase by progressively larger quanta because progressively larger motor units begin to contract. Hence there is an analogue of Weber's law in sensation: each successive increment of tension is a constant proportion of the tension already developed (rather than a constant amount). Henneman (1968), to whom much of this understanding is due, points out that "the usage of any motor unit, in fact, is probably in inverse ratio to its size." Small units must therefore not be prone to fatigue, and many of the largest and most powerful motor units must hardly ever be used.

The largest α motor neurons have a surface area of 50,000 to 60,000 μ^2 and may have as many as 10,000 synaptic knobs on their soma and dendrites. These cells may also have axons of up to 20 μ in diameter connecting them with their muscle. The smallest α motor neurons have surface areas of 10,000 to 15,000 μ^2 and a correspondingly smaller number of synaptic knobs and axons, of about 9 μ in diameter.

Every motor neuron algebraically sums the excitatory and inhibitory effects impinging on it. Not only are larger neurons less excitable, they are more susceptible to inhibition. Henneman's discoveries require some revision of Sherrington's theories about the organization of a motor neuron pool. Sherrington had assumed that effects like summation were due to the overlap of two subliminal zones and their consequent addition to surmount the threshold of firing. The phenomenon of summation can be demonstrated when two subliminal stimuli are evoked in two spatially different nerves, both impinging on the same motor neurons. The two stimuli, while ineffectual alone, sum to produce a response. Sherrington had assumed that lack of the two entering stimuli would excite two spatially separate but partly overlapping populations of neurons. Where the zones of excitation overlapped, the two subliminal stimuli would add or sum to produce a response. According to Henneman, input to the pool is distributed to all the member cells in it. Larger cells need more input to fire them. Consequently, two subliminal stimuli will both impinge on the same cells and will fire them if they jointly surmount the excitability threshold. This will not depend on a spatial distribution of the excitation. Occlusion occurs when the combined output of the two suprathreshold stimuli is less than the sum of their outputs where they occur separately. In Sherrington's theory, such occlusion was held to occur when the zones of excitation overlapped, and so the neurons in the zone of overlap were fired simultaneously to produce one response, rather than firing twice and so producing twice the output if the stimuli were applied separately. In Henneman's hypothesis, there would again be overlap but of a different kind. A simultaneous excitation of motor neurons, up to a certain size, would not produce twice the output of such neurons stimulated by half the input.

Muscular Fatigue

Muscular fatigue has been attributed at different times to the central nervous system, the neuromuscular junction, the action potential which triggers the fibrils, and the contractile process itself. Merton (1956) convincingly demonstrated that muscular fatigue (as distinct from boredom) is due to a failure of the contractile process itself. He showed that there is no falling off of the muscle action potential in a fully fatigued muscle, so that muscle fatigue is not due to blockage at the central nervous system or the neuromuscular junction. He also showed, contrary to an earlier belief, that it is not possible to contract a muscle by stimulating the fibrils directly, after the muscle has been fully fatigued by voluntary effort. This rules out the action-potential-to-fibril trigger mechanism as the cause of fatigue, and the only possibility left is that fatigue occurs in the final contractile process, perhaps because of the exhaustion of a biochemical process. In support of this conclusion, it was found that cutting off the blood supply to a fatigued limb prevented recovery and induced rapid fatigue in an unfatigued muscle.

Muscle Spindles

In contrast with the muscle fibers innervated by the axons of α motor neurons (also called extrafusal muscle fibers), there is a class of muscle fibers that are innervated by smaller fibers, the axons of γ motor neurons. The number of these smaller fibers is about one third the total number of motor neuron axons leaving the spinal cord. Whereas the axons of the α motor neurons range from 9 to 20 μ in diameter, the axons of the γ motor neuron vary between 1 to 8 μ in diameter. In keeping with the diameter of the axons of the γ motor neuron, the γ motor neurons are small and, it seems, very excitable. This is shown by their high rate of "spontaneous" discharge and high rates of discharge upon stimulation.

As stated above, γ motor neurons innervate intrafusal muscle fibers. From 2 to 12 of these thin muscle fibers form a component of an organ called a muscle spindle (from its shape). These thin muscle fibers are enclosed by connective tissue and surrounded by a fluid-filled bag halfway along their length. The portion of the muscle fibers enclosed by the fluid-filled bag probably does not contract but is more like a tendon. Each end of the spindle (and so the intrafusal muscles which are components of it) is attached to an extrafusal muscle fiber, so that if the extrafusal fiber contracts, tension on the intrafusal fibers relaxes. Muscle spindles are interspersed among the ordinary muscle fibers in most if not all muscles of the body.

The intrafusal muscle fibers are further divided into two types. The first is called "nuclear bag" fibers. While these fibers are less than half the diameter of the extrafusal fibers, they are longer and thicker than the second class of intrafusal fibers, called "nuclear chain" fibers. These nuclear chain fibers are about half the length and diameter of the nuclear bag fibers. The ends of the nuclear chain fibers are attached to the longer nuclear bag fibers. There are usually two nuclear bag fibers within each muscle spindle, and four nuclear chain fibers. According to one view, the termination of the γ motor neuron axons on the two types of intrafusal fibers is different. The ending of the nuclear bag fibers are connected to the γ motor neuron axons through discrete motor end-plates which are found mainly on the ends of the motor fibers. The ending on the nuclear chain fibers is a fine mesh, network, or "tract" which may envelop the motor fiber from the center right down to the attached ends of the motor fiber. (However, some opinions have it that both the nuclear bag and nuclear chain fibers receive both types of ending).

So far we have described two constituents of the motor spindle, the intrafusal motor fibers and their innervation, which cause them to contract. We shall now describe the sensory endings, which also are a component of the motor spindles. There are two types of sensory endings in most spindles. The first are primary (annulospiral) endings from nerve fibers 12 to 21 μ in diameter (group Ia). These group Ia afferents divide into two branches: One branch winds around a nuclear bag fiber and the other around a nuclear chain fiber. (Lloyd [1943] divided A fibers [myelinated somatic afferent and efferent fibers] into three groups based on diameter: group I, 12 to 21 μ; group II, 6 to 12 μ; and group III, 1 to 6 μ.) Each spindle has one group A primary sensory fiber, which divides into two branches. In contrast, each muscle spindle has a somewhat more variable number (0 to 5) of secondary sensory (flower-spray) endings. These are spread predominantly around the nuclear chain muscle fibers. These secondary endings each come from nerve fibers 6 to 12 μ in diameter (group II).

Tendon organs comprise another class of receptors whose task is to monitor the state of muscles. These tendon organs of Golgi are near the junction between the muscle fibers and tendons. Instead of being placed "in parallel" to the muscle fibers, they are placed "in series." The sensory fibers (type IB) divide into myelinated branches inside a capsule and then form sprays of unmyelinated fibers with clasplike swellings adhering to the surface of the tendon fascicles. Slight elongation of these fascicles probably stimulates the nerve endings.

The afferent fibers in the muscle spindle are excited whenever they are subjected to stretch, and they may be stretched in two different ways. First, the extrafusal fibers to which the spindle is attached may lengthen. This may happen because the extrafusal fibers relax or because there is an increase of load on the muscle. Under these conditions, the excitation in the afferent fibers feeds back onto the α motor neurons, innervating the extrafusal fibers and causing contraction. In this way a particular limb position can be set, and any deviation due to external load or relaxation is automatically corrected by a feedback system of which the muscle spindle is the adjustable sensing element. The adjustment or setting of the sensing element is accomplished by adjustment in the length of the intrafusal muscle fibers in the muscle spindle.

The second way that the muscle spindle afferents can be excited is by the firing of γ motor neurons, which cause contraction in the intrafusal muscle fibers. When this occurs, the sensing elements in the muscle spindle will fire and excite α motor neurons, which will shorten the more powerful extrafusal muscle fibers to which the muscle spindles are attached. This has been called the "γ leading" process because the γ motor neuron system leads induces the appropriate activity in the α motor neuron system.

The muscle spindle system therefore has an important part to play in the initiation of some reflexes and perhaps some types of voluntary movement (Granit, 1970). However, in most cases of contraction, recording has shown that both α and γ activity occurs synchronously to produce the contraction (Hunt, 1952; Vallbo, 1970). Phillips (1969) has presented evidence that both α and γ motor neurons are activated together by electrical stimulation of the baboon motor cortex.

The primary and secondary endings have a low-frequency, resting discharge, which ceases during muscular contraction. This so-called pause demonstrates that the muscle spindles are in parallel (in line abreast) with the muscle fibers; when the muscle contracts, tension is taken off the spindles by the muscle fibers and the end organs cease firing until the slack in the spindles is taken up by the active contraction of the muscle fibers within the spindles.

The discharge from primary spindle endings is approximately proportional to the amount of stretch applied to the passive muscle, but adaptation is rapid, and therefore the maximum discharge will depend as much on the rate at which the muscle is stretched as on the absolute tension. The discharge from the secondary endings depends on the rate of change of stretch only to a minor extent, and mainly by the stretch itself, independent of the rate at which it is applied. The secondary endings, unlike the primary, do not show significant adaptation.

Spindle afferents feed into the spinal cord by way of the sensory dorsal roots. They initiate the local, monosynaptic stretch reflex (see page 309) and feed into tracts which ascend to the cerebellum.

The tendon organs have a higher threshold to external stretch and do not show any resting discharge. Therefore spindles produce a greater discharge than tendon organs at lower tensions, but as the tension increases, more and more tendon organs start to discharge. Tendon organs discharge during muscular contraction when the spindles show their pause; that is, they behave as if they are in series (in tandem) with the contracting muscle fibers, and anatomical evidence supports this conclusion. They respond to the total tension in the muscle, whether this be produced by active contraction or by passive stretch.

The tendon organ afferents go by way of the sensory dorsal roots into the spinal cord. They initiate the clasp-knife reflex (as described on p. 309) and, like the large afferents from muscle spindles, ascend in the dorsal cerebellar tracts to the cerebellum. Group I afferents also project to the motor cortex.

Independent Bias of Primary and Secondary Spindle Afferents

The sensitivity of spindle primary (group Ia) and secondary (group II) afferents can be controlled by the activity of γ motoneurons through the contraction of intrafusal muscle fibers. Γ motoneurons can be divided into two classes. The first class, called static, alters the sensitivity of the primary and secondary afferents. Increased activity of static γ motoneurons increases the discharge rate of primary afferents to maintained stretch and reduces their sensitivity to the rate of change of stretch. It is as if the primary afferents were caused to show less adaptation. At the same time, increased activity in these static motoneurons increases the rate of discharge of secondary afferents at a given muscle length (Matthews, 1964; Appelberg et al., 1966). The second class of γ motoneurons is called dynamic. Increased activity of the dynamic group alters only the responsiveness of the primary spindle afferents, making them more sensitive to rates of change of stretch. The vestibulospinal tract connects directly with static γ motoneurons of extensor muscles whereas fibers in the reticulospinal tract project directly to flexor static γ motoneurons (Grillner, et al., 1969).

While the control of dynamic γ motoneurons is different from that of the static ones, its precise connection is at present uncertain.

POSSIBLE FUNCTIONS OF THE GAMMA FIBER SYSTEM

Evidence (which is the subject of much controversy [Granit, 1970]) suggests that in normal muscular contraction the spindle muscle fibers may contract before the main extrafusal muscles. This spindle contraction produces very little tension in the muscle, but it induces afferent discharges from the spindle receptor end organs, which reflexly facilitate contraction of the main muscles, a process known as *proprioceptive recruitment*. When the extrafusal muscle fibers have "caught up" with the contracted spindles, the tension in the spindle is relieved and facilitation of muscular contraction cases. This process also is called γ leading because the voluntary contraction of the muscle precedes a reflex firing of the α motorneurons, which then produce a contraction of the extrafusal fibers.

The spindle receptors, in effect, signal the difference in length between muscle and spindle fibers (Eldred, Granit, and Merton, 1953). Hyde and Gellhorn (1949) were still able to elicit muscular contractions from the gastrocnemius muscle of a cat after sectioning the afferent fibers from the muscle spindles, although the response was weaker than with intact afferents. Variations in the strength of the electrical stimulus applied to the motor cortex still affected the strength of the muscular contraction, showing that gradations in muscle responses can be independent of proprioceptive recruitment. Conditioned motor responses have been found to survive limb deafferentation (Knapp, Taub, and Berman, 1959), although not without some change in the pattern of the response (Gorska and Jankowska, 1963).

Cerebellar and Brain Stem Control of Muscle Spindles and the Control of Servo-oscillation

Granit and his co-workers, in an extensive series of experiments, found that the γ system could be either activated or inhibited by stimulating either the anterior cerebellum or the diencephalic reticular formation, and that only in the presence of the anterior lobe of the cerebellum does γ firing facilitate muscle contraction. Reflex activity, however, survives removal of the cerebellum, and the conclusion is that in this case the direct α system is used to initiate muscle contraction without facilitation by γ outflow. In the intact animal, either system is available; the direct α system is probably used for ballistic and well-practiced movements, and the indirect γ leading system for exploratory movements. The cerebellum apparently controls whether the γ leading system or the direct system is used.

Any control system which, like the spindle control system, depends upon negative feedback is potentially unstable. This is because the error signal takes time to generate a corrective response, which therefore has its effect after the limb has moved beyond the target position. A second correction has to be applied in the opposite direction, which also results in overshooting, and soon the limb oscillates about the target position. In order to compensate for this oscillation, the reflex control system must have an output determined by both position error (length misalignment) and the rate of change of muscle length. This latter information enables the system to anticipate the future position of the limb and adjust the corrective signal accordingly. We have already mentioned that damping is a rate-dependent function, and therefore damping in any of its forms should be able to provide the necessary rate-of-movement information. Purely mechanical damping is provided by the viscosity of the muscle tissues and joints. Damping is also provided by sensory adaptation in spindle receptors, which attenuates the muscle to a spindle-length misalignment signal. Damping is also provided by inhibitory control from the tendon organs. The cerebellum also probably helps to control this rate-dependent adjustment by timing γ outflow in relation to the α outflow. After the cerebellar ablation, cats are ataxic (see p. 318), and although they recover to some extent, they are never again normal (Higgins and Glaser, 1964). Tremor due to cerebellar disease in man (see p. 317) may represent a disturbance of the same system.

To summarize, the prime function of the γ system (i.e., fibers and intrafusal fibers) is to prevent the muscle spindles from becoming flaccid during muscular contraction; the spindles are kept in trim and their threshold is maintained at a usable level. The γ system also serves to initiate, or at least facilitate, voluntary contraction by the process of γ leading, and contributes to the stability of muscular control. See Granit (1955, 1970) for further details.

Recurrent Collaterals of Motor Neurons

We have already discussed how muscular contraction is inhibited by increased discharge from Golgi tendon organs; but muscular contraction is also reflexively inhibited by activity in the Renshaw loop, so called after its discoverer (Renshaw, 1941). Alpha motor neurons send signals to the muscles via their axons. However, these axons also have a branch which loops back; hence these branches are called recurrent collaterals. These recurrent collatrals run back via the ventral horns into the spinal cord. Where they form synapses with small interneurons called Renshaw cells. These cells are excited by input from the recurrent collaterals of the motor neurons. The axons of the Renshaw cells terminate on motor neurons in neighboring sections of the spinal cord, usually causing their inhibition. Renshaw cells can also be excited or inhibited by input from the skin, muscles, and higher portions of the CNS. The function of this sytem is obscure.

Receptors in the Joint Capsule and Skin

The articular surfaces of free-moving or diarthrodial joints are lined with cartilaginous material and a limiting synovial membrane. The synovial fluid is secreted into the joint and lubricates it. Ligaments bind the joint to form the joint capsule (for further details of joint physiology, see Gardner, 1950). The ligaments of mammalian joints are well provided with sensory endings. The receptors in the skin surrounding the joint may be considered to be joint receptors also.

The afferents from joint receptors (and skin receptors) are known to project via the dorsal root into the spinal cord and up to the thalamus and sensory cortex. They are therefore truly sensory. The discharge patterns of the various neurons, both in the nerve and at the cortex, show a range of types. Most neurons show an initially high, transient discharge, followed by a slowly adapting discharge when the joint is held at a particular angle. Some units are active at any joint position: others are maximally active at small joint angles; and others are maximally active at large joint angles. Some pairs of spatially related cortical cells are reciprocally related, one cell being active as the joint moves in one direction and the other being active when the joint moves in the other direction. For references and details, see Rose and Mountcastle (1959).

KINESTHESIS

Kinesthesis is best understood as a behavioral term. It includes the discrimination of the positions of body parts, the discrimination of movement, and the amplitude of movement of body parts, both passively and actively produced. Visual and auditory information is assumed to be absent. Afferents from muscles and tendons do not reach the cortex and therefore are probably not directly involved in kinesthesis. Afferents from joints and skin, and the pattern of motor innervation, are almost certainly involved in kinesthetic judgments. We define kinesthesis, therefore, as the discrimination of the positions and movements of body parts based on information other than visual, auditory, or verbal.

There are many types of kinesthetic judgment. The main ones are set out in Table 8–1, and they will be discussed in that order.

Kinesthesis in Passive Movement

The basic measure of kinesthetic sensitivity is the threshold of passive movement. Like all other thresholds, it varies with the conditions; the speed of movement, the position of the limb, and the type of joint are important variables. A value as low as 0.2 degrees has been found for the arm moving at 0.3 degress per second (Goldscheider, 1889; Cleghorn and Darcus, 1952). Movement through larger angles is necessary before the direction as well as the presence of movement is detected. Proximal joints are more sensitive than distal ones. No reliable figures

TABLE 8–1
Types of Kinesthetic Judgment

Passive Movement	Threshold of movement Judgment of position (indication when previous position is regained) Threshold of direction of movement Accuracy of direction judgments Judgment of amplitude of movement Judgment of speed of movement
Active Movement	Steadiness and fineness of movement Judgment of position Accuracy of direction of movement Accuracy of amplitude of movement Accuracy of pressure production Accuracy of speed of movement

exist to indicate the accuracy with which people can judge the position, direction, amplitude, or speed of passively moved limbs.

Kinesthesis in Active Movement

Active movements can be produced which are finer than the passive threshold, but the steadiness and fineness of control of active movements depend upon the limb use, fatigue, and the health of the system. There are various ways of studying the active position sense of a limb: (1) the blindfolded subject may be asked to place a limb in a given position and then to regain the same position after the limb has been displaced; (2) the blindfolded subject may be asked to bring the two index fingers together, or to duplicate the position of one limb by its partner. Cohen (1958) used the first method and found that his subjects could reduplicate a position of their extended arm to a mean accuracy of 3.3 cm. This error is the sum of the inaccuracy in the registration of the initial position and the inaccuracy of the reproductive movement. If it is assumed that the accuracy of a single movement is half this, it follows that over 1,000 positions of the extended arm are discriminable in this way. The second method, in which the index fingers are brought together, constitutes a well-known clinical test of kinesthetic-motor sensitivity.

There seem to be no data on the accuracy with which directions of movement may be discriminated.

The ability to estimate an amplitude or extent of movement may be studied by two methods: (1) the subject may be asked to move a limb through a given distance and then to duplicate the movement; (2) the subject may be asked to run his finger between two stops and then to estimate whether subsequently executed movements between stops are the same. Kramer and Moskiewicz (1901) used the first method and found a tendency for the arm to move a shorter distance in the reproduction than in the initial movement. This is a time-order error which contaminates the method insofar as measurements of kinesthetic sensitivity are concerned. Breternitz (1934) used the second method and found that accuracy varied with the joint used and the distance moved.

For a discussion of the judgment of pressure, the student is referred to Provins (1957). A related topic is weight judgment.

Having discussed the various types of kinesthetic judgment, we shall now inquire into the sensory and motor mechanisms involved.

Sensory and Motor Conditions for Kinesthesis

On the sensory side, kinesthesis in any or all of its forms may depend on the muscle-spindle and tendon receptors and/or the joint receptors. Tactile receptors may also be involved. On the motor side, active-movement kinesthesis may depend upon the motor-outflow information reaching whatever centers are involved in kinesthetic judgments. In order to study each of these factors, the others must be removed. The techniques for each component are shown in Table 8–2, together with a statement of the types of judgment possible in each case.

The muscle spindles and tendon organs are considered together, as

TABLE 8–2
Procedures for Isolating Sensory and Motor Components of Kinesthesis and the Known Judgments Possible in Each Case

Receptors Left Active	Procedures	Known Types of Judgment Possible
Spindle-tendon receptors	Passive movement of tongue, eye, or joint with anesthetized capsule	No passive kinesthesis
	Direct stimulation of motor neurons	No information available
Joint receptors	Passive movement with severed tendons	No information available
Motor outflow	Active movements with anesthesia of all afferents	No passive kinesthesis Active appreciation of amplitude of movement as long as the limb is not loaded

there is no known technique for separating them. The eye and the tongue contain no joint receptors, and when the conjunctiva or skin is anesthetized, these organs provide a means of studying muscle-tendon receptors. Irvin and Ludvigh (1936) showed that a surface-anesthetized eye has no kinesthetic sense of any kind when passively moved, although they found that the position and extent of movement of the surface-anesthetized eyes may be judged when they are moved actively. It would seem, therefore, that spindle-tendon receptors are not sufficient to indicate the position or movement of the passively moved eye. However, the pattern of discharge from spindle-tendon receptors is not the same for passive movement as it is for active movement, and it is possible that these organs play a role in the appreciation of active eye movements. Whatever the role of spindle-tendon organs in eye muscles, they may be involved, along with other receptors, in the appreciation of passive and active movement in jointed limbs. There are no reliable data for the tongue.

The second procedure for isolating the effects of spindle-tendon receptors is to anesthetize the joint capsule of a limb joint. Anesthesia may be induced by electric currents, drugs, or cutting off the blood supply to the joint capsule, leaving the muscles intact. This procedure has a long history, and the results are controversial, but it may fairly be concluded that the appreciation of passive movement in all its forms is either absent or severely impaired by joint anesthesia, which suggests that the joints contain the receptors necessary for passive kinesthesis (see Provins [1958] for details).

Active movements of specified extent are still accurately executed when the joint capsule is anesthetized, although the position of the limb when at rest cannot be judged. Either the motor outflow or the active spindle-tendon discharge, or both, are responsible for this active kinesthesis.

An experiment which Lashley carried out in 1917 suggests that the motor outflow is involved in normal active kinesthesis. He observed a patient with loss of afference from the leg joints and muscles due to a bullet wound in the spinal cord and found that, although the patient had no passive kinesthesis, he could move his legs through specified distances as accurately as a normal subject. This latter ability in the patient, but not in the normal subject, was lost when the leg had to pull against a spring. This suggests that either the spindle-tendon organs or the joint receptors compensate for load changes when judgments of the extent of active movements are made with varying resistances to the movement. Theoretically, either or both types of receptor could serve this function, but the experiments to decide which have not been done. One possible experiment would be to test whether the ability to move through a given distance with varying load is possible in a limb in which the joint has been anesthetized. If this ability were intact under these circumstances, it would demonstrate that the spindle-tendon organs serve to compensate for load changes; it would not, of course, prove that the joint receptors cannot do the same thing. Nobody has been able to study the role of spindle-tendon organs when both the joint receptors and motor outflow are absent. One way of doing this would be to anesthetize a joint, stimulate the motor nerve directly, and ask the blindfolded subject to estimate the extent of the resulting movement and position of the limb.

Very rapid movements, such as those involved in piano playing, may be complete before there has been time for muscle spindle or capsule receptor activity to have any effect. It has been shown that the reaction time for kinesthetic feedback is 160 msec. (Vince, 1948). Ballistic movements must therefore be wholly under the control of the motor outflow. Such a dead-reckoning system works well for well-practiced movements when the resistance is normal. Part of the business of learning a motor skill is the building up of central motor programs which may, when required, produce accurate, rapid sequences of movements without the need for feedback from peripheral receptors.

In conclusion, it may be said that joint receptors are necessary and spindle-tendon organs are not sufficient for passive kinesthesis. Whether spindle-tendon receptors are involved in active kinesthesis is not known. Active movements of given extent are possible in the absence of all afferents, as long as the limb is not loaded. But whether load compensation is a function of the joint receptors or the spindle-tendon receptors is not known.

SPINAL CORD AND REFLEX ACTIVITY

Structure of the Cord

The spinal cord of man is an extension of the central nervous system, extending from the brain to about halfway down the back. It is about as thick as a fountain pen and has the consistency of jelly. Such a delicate structure needs protection. This is afforded by two enveloping membranes, the dura mater and the pia mater, and the spongy, shock-absorbing arachnoid, which is contained between them. The protecting structures are known as the *meninges* and cover the whole central nervous system. The spinal cord and meninges lie inside the bony vertebrae of the spine. A central canal, continuous with the cerebral ventricles, runs the length of the cord carrying spinocerebral fluid, which also surrounds the cord. Deep folds, or sulci, penetrate the cord, one from the dorsal surface and one from the ventral surface.

Between each pair of vertebrae, on each side, a pair of spinal nerves emerges to innervate the muscles and sense organs of the body segment. The dorsal (posterior) root of each pair is the sensory nerve, and the ventral (anterior) root of each pair is the motor nerve. This separation of sensory (afferent) and motor (efferent) nerves was first described by Charles Bell and François Magendie in the first half of the eighteenth century. It became known as the *Bell-Magendie law,* and was one of the first scientifically based observations on the functions of the nervous system. It is now known that there are some afferent fibers in the ventral root, but the Bell-Magendie law is still regarded as an important generalization.

The central gray core of the cord contains synapses and neuron cell bodies; the outer white regions contain parallel, longitudinal bundles of myelinated axons interspersed with a feltwork of neuroglia cells which probably serve to maintain the metabolic functions of the nerve cells proper. The gray matter extends in the directions of the four roots to form the four horns. Incoming and outgoing fibers run in the horns from or toward their appropriate root. The six bundles of white matter are known as funiculi: two dorsal (posterior), two ventral (anterior), and two lateral. Each funiculus contains smaller regions known as *fasciculi* and *tracts* which carry axons up and down the cord. Axons running across the cord traverse the *commissure* of the gray matter. The axons in the white matter nearest the gray matter (fasciculi proprii) run a short distance before reentering the gray matter; the axons farther out run longer distances to or from the brain stem.

General Properties of Reflex Activity

On entering the dorsal root, the neurons from the various somesthetic sensory end organs split into many branches, some of which ascend without synapse in the spinal cord (see Chapter 6). Others ascend or descend for some little distance before each of them synapses either in the dorsal or the ventral horn. The postsynaptic fibers have one of several destinations. (1) Some run out to ipsilateral (same side) or contralateral (opposite side) motor roots without synapsing further, and mediate so-called *monosynaptic reflexes.* (2) Others synapse again with ipsilateral or contralateral motor neurons in the same segment of the cord. The latter are known as *internuncial neurons,* mediating *segmental reflexes.* Some internuncial neurons send off collateral branches which synapse with other internuncial neurons to form closed chains or loops round which discharges may reverberate. (3) Others run in the fasciculi proprii and reenter the ventral horns of other segments to synapse with ipsilateral or contralateral motor neurons. These internuncial neurons mediate *intersegmental reflexes.* (4) Others enter one or another *spinal somesthetic pathways* in the funiculi and ascend to the brain stem, thalamus, cerebellum, or cerebral cortex. Stimulation of any one afferent somesthetic neuron may initiate activity in all these separate routes.

On the motor side, each motor axon which leaves by the ventral root originates in the ventral horn from a large cell body upon which may converge as many as 1,400 dentrites from many different sensory neurons, from internuncial neurons, and from neurons which have descended in the motor tracts from higher centers (see Fig. 8–3). A group

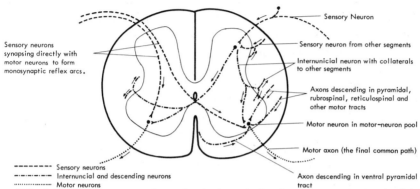

Sensory Neuron

Sensory neurons synapsing directly with motor neurons to form monosynaptic reflex arcs.

Sensory neuron from other segments

Internunicial neuron with collaterals to other segments

Axons descending in pyramidal, rubrospinal, reticulospinal and other motor tracts

Motor neuron in motor-neuron pool

Motor axon (the final common path)

-------- Sensory neurons
-·-·-·-·- Internuncial and descending neurons
·················· Motor neurons

Axon descending in ventral pyramidal tract

FIG. 8–3. Transverse section of spinal cord showing fiber tracts involved in spinal reflexes.

of motor neurons belonging to a particular muscle is known as a *moto-neuron pool.*

It should be obvious from the above description of the ramifications of afferent discharges in the dorsal horn and of the convergence in the ventral horn that reflex arcs, as individual and separate circuits, do not exist. They are convenient abstractions for the purpose of analysis. Each afferent neuron is in structural synaptic contact, directly or indirectly, with all the neurons of the central nervous system (spinal cord and brain). Inhibitory barriers prevent an impulse in a neuron firing off the entire system. These barriers may be broken down locally with drugs such as strychnine, and when this is done, any disturbance fires off a large part of the system. Reflexes are functional routes in this inhibitory matrix of synapses. Discharges along these routes are not separate from each other, but interact, sometimes facilitating each other and summating their effects, and at other times inhibiting each other.

Once a motor axon has been fired, nothing can normally prevent the muscle from contracting, and there is no normal way in which the muscle can be made to contract except by discharges arriving along those motoneurons which supply it. Any given muscle may take part at different times in many reflexes, yet all these reflexes must finally funnel their impulses through the same motor axons. This common part of the system is therefore called the *final common path*.

If two reflexes which share a final common path are stimulated at the same time, they may be allied and summate, or they may be antagonistic, when one will be inhibited by the other. The stretch reflex and the extensor thrust reflex are allied and summate to support the animal against gravity. If two antagonistic reflexes occur at the same time, they must compete for the final common path. Generally, one of them gains a *total victory* over the other. Which one does so, depends upon the relative strength and the relative importance of each of the two reflexes. For instance, nociceptive reflexes—that is, those which involve withdrawal from painful stimuli—would normally have precedence over the scratch reflex. If antagonistic reflexes take command over the final common path in rhythmic succession, the resulting pattern is known as *successive induction*. Walking is an example of such a mechanism.

Other reflexes may be antagonistic—not because they share a final common path but because they are functionally incompatible. For instance, the hindlimb scratch reflex is incompatible with the forelimb withdrawal reflex because the animal would lose its balance if both responses occurred together.

Reflexes do not occur in vacuo but against an ever present pattern of postural reflexes and voluntary movements. Nor do reflex responses necessarily remain constant over time; they show fatigue and are influenced by higher centers and hence by learning.

If several stimuli occur in succession, the activity they engender may summate to give a larger response than any of the stimuli would have evoked separately. Stimuli which individually are at a subthreshold (subliminal) level may converge at one time or in quick succession upon a single motor neuron to produce a discharge. This *summation* is thought to occur at the spinal synapse of the motoneuron; any activity there sets up a *central excitatory state*, which, if sufficiently intense, discharges the motor axon. If the central excitatory state is subliminal, it diminishes to zero in a period of about 10 to 20 msec.

Each reflex has a characteristic *latency*, which is the time delay between the application of the stimulus and the arrival of action potentials at the muscle. The latency of the receptor end organ, the afferent and efferent conduction times, and the central synaptic delays and conduction time all contribute to the overall latency of the reflex. The weaker the applied stimulus, the longer the latent period.

Reflex muscular contractions are often rhythmical, for instance, the scratch reflex. They often outlive the stimulus, when they are said to show an *afterdischarge* or rebound which may be due to continuing activity in internuncial closed chains.

Antagonistic muscles work as a pair; when one contracts, the other is reflexly inhibited so as to allow the limb to move. This is known as *reciprocal innervation*. In some reflex patterns, such as the startle pattern, which occurs in response to a loud noise, agonists and antagonists contract together, but the functional significance of this response is obscure.

Segmental Reflexes

The segmental reflexes are known as *myotatic, autogenetic,* or *myogenic reflexes.* They are a response of a muscle to stimuli arising in that same muscle or its antagonist. The *stretch reflex* is a myotatic reflex invoked by pulling on the tendon of a muscle or, in the intact animal, by pushing against a limb. It serves to compensate for changes in external load which limbs may encounter, particularly those limbs which support the animal against gravity. The afferent signals which trigger the reflex arise in the muscle-spindle receptors and travel to the dorsal horn of the cord in large myelinated fibers. These fibers synapse directly with motor neurons, both ipsilaterally and contralaterally. Internuncial neurons are not involved; the reflex is *monosynaptic.* The response is limited to the stimulated muscle and to its antagonist: the neural response to the ipsilateral muscle facilitates contraction, and that to the contralateral muscle inhibits contraction.

The "tendon jerk," an example of which is the knee jerk (produced by a tap on the patellar tendon), is related to the stretch reflex.

If an increasing pressure is applied to the limb of an animal, a pressure will be reached when the resistance to movement of the limb suddenly collapses. This is the *lengthening* or *"clasp knife" reflex.* It too is a monosynaptic, myotatic reflex. The sudden onset of the reflex occurs when the tension in the tendon reaches the threshold of the tendon receptors. As soon as this happens, the discharge from these receptors inhibits the opposing stretch reflex arising from the lower-threshold spindle receptors, and the extensor muscles relax. Tension on the tendon is thus relieved, and the stretch reflex again takes command until the external pressure on the limb builds up once again to produce a second clasp-knife reflex. A succession of shortening reactions thus occurs as pressure is applied to a limb. The shortening reaction is presumably a safety device protecting the limb from the effects of too much tension.

Cutaneous reflexes are segmental reflexes triggered off by stimuli applied to the skin. One example is the *extensor thrust* of the leg elicited by pressure on the feet. It serves to maintain the animal in a standing posture. It is a two-synapse reflex involving internuncial cells in the spinal cord. Most stimuli applied to the skin induce ipsilateral reflex flexion and contralateral extension. The extensor thrust is an exception to this rule.

The Babinski reflex is another example of a cutaneous reflex. This occurs in young children, and often in sleeping or diseased adults, and is a useful clinical sign. It consists of the turning up of the great toe in response to a scratch on the sole of the foot, and probably serves a withdrawal function. A further interesting segmental cutaneous reflex is the *grasp reflex,* which is an automatic grasping induced by an object touching the palm of the hand. Infants and brain-damaged patients may show this reflex; the patient may be unable to let go of whatever he is holding. It enables the young mammal to cling to its mother.

Intersegmental and Suprasegmental Reflexes

Intersegmental reflexes are those in which the stimulus is applied to receptors in one segment of the body and the response occurs in another. Internuncial neurons running in the fasciculi proprii form the link between the segments. The *scratch reflex* in the dog is a well-known intersegmental reflex. The receptors lie in the skin on the back and sides of the animal; the response is a rhythmic scratching movement by the hindlimb.

Suprasegmental reflexes depend on centers in the brain stem or higher centers. Breathing involves a complex of suprasegmental reflexes coordinated in the medulla. Eye reflexes, swallowing, and other reflexes in the head are suprasegmental. Postural reflexes are suprasegmental, and in view of their behavioral importance will be discussed in a separate section.

For further reading on reflex activity, see Sherrington's *Integrative Action of the Nervous System* (1947) and Denny-Brown et al. (1938).

THE PYRAMIDAL SYSTEM

The pyramidal tracts are thought to be the main pathways involved in the voluntary control of movement. In man, about 40 percent of the fibers in these tracts originate in the so-called *precentral motor areas* in the cerebral cortex (see p. 335). The rest originate largely in the prefrontal and parietal lobes of the cerebral cortex. The large pyramid-shaped *Betz cells* of the precentral motor areas together contribute about 30,000 large axons to the pyramidal tracts but account for only about 3 percent of the total number of fibers in the tracts. About 40 percent of all the fibers in the tracts are unmyelinated, and most of those that are myelinated are very small.

The tracts descend on each side in the white matter of the cortex, making up part of the internal capsule (see Fig. 8–4). The two halves descend and form the peduncle in the ventral midline region of the upper brain stem. Most of the fibers decussate or cross to the opposite side at this level to form the lateral pyramids or lateral corticospinal

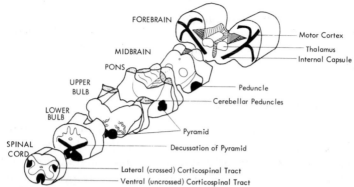

FOREBRAIN

MIDBRAIN

PONS

UPPER BULB

LOWER BULB

SPINAL CORD

Motor Cortex

Thalamus

Internal Capsule

Peduncle

Cerebellar Peduncles

Pyramid

Decussation of Pyramid

Lateral (crossed) Corticospinal Tract

Ventral (uncrossed) Corticospinal Tract

FIG. 8–4. Diagrammatic representation of the pyramidal pathways. (Adapted from Elliot, H. C., *Textbook of Neuroanatomy,* 1963; courtesy of Pitman Medical Publishing Co., London.)

tracts; the undecussated fibers continue as the ventral pyramids or ventral corticospinal tracts. The bundles of decussating fibers form a pyramid-shaped structure, from which the pyramidal system derives its name. The fibers which supply the motor nuclei of the head muscles depart from the main tract at the level of the pons. Collateral branches in the brain stem feed into the extrapyramidal system (see next section).

The axons of the spinal pyramidal tracts are the longest in the body. In primates, some of these axons terminate directly in motoneurons in the ventral horns, but most of them terminate in internuncial neurons. Their influence on motoneurons is studied by recording the effect which pyramidal stimulation has upon monosynaptic reflex pathways. This influence is invariably facilitatory. A small percentage of the fibers in the pyramidal tracts are afferent fibers ascending to the cortex, but their function is not known.

Electrical stimulation of the motor cortex excites extrapyramidal as well as pyramidal pathways, and for this reason cortical stimulation elicits muscular contractions even after pyramidectomy. The contribution of the pyramids may be studied by electrical stimulation at lower levels, where the pyramids are uncontaminated by extrapyramidal fibers. The movements elicited show great variability, apparently because of the internuncial neurons which are interposed between the pyramidal axons and the motoneurons, and perhaps because of varying spread of the electric stimulus to neighboring structures.

In primates, unilateral pyramidectomy leads to contralateral paresis or plegia involving the musculature from the neck down. The paretic muscles are hypotonic, weak, and incapable of executing fine, skilled movements. Skin reflexes are weak or absent. No clear cases of pyramidectomy are known in man; any damage involves extrapyramidal tracts as well, and the symptoms are those of spasticity (see next section). Evarts (1967) has trained monkeys to release a telegraph key in response to a flash of light, rewarding them for moving as fast as possible. The reaction time of pyramidal tract cells is 120 msec. Thus a great deal of processing probably occurs before the signals reach the pyramidal tract cells.

THE EXTRAPYRAMIDAL SYSTEM

Central motor control mechanisms other than the pyramidal system and the cerebellum are known as the extrapyramidal system. Lower vertebrates have no pyramidal system and their only motor centers are those structures which are homologous with the extrapyramidal subcortical nuclei. The extrapyramidal nuclei receive connections from the precentral motor cortex (Brodmann's area 4) as well as from other cortical areas, and the distinction between the two systems at the cortical level is obscure.

The main subcortical nuclei comprising the extrapyramidal system are the following:

Basal ganglia
{
  Diencephalic nuclei
  {
    Corpus striatum
    {
      Caudate nucleus
      Putamen
      Pallidum
    } Lenticular nuclei
    Subthalamic nucleus and other thalamic nuclei
  }
  Mesencephalic nuclei
  {
    Red nucleus
    Niger nucleus or substantia nigra
    Reticular formation
  }
}

The nuclei comprising the corpus striatum surround the halves of the internal capsule—the massive V-shape bundles which contain the fibers going to and from the cortex. The putamen and pallidum (globus pallidus) are tucked into the V of the capsule and are therefore lens shaped—hence their name, lenticular nuclei. The subthalamic nucleus is situated under the thalamus in the diencephalon or subcortical forebrain. The red and niger nuclei are bilateral structures near the midline in the midbrain or mesencephalon. The reticular formation extends in the midline down the medulla.

Each of these nuclei has connections, directly or indirectly, with each other and with the cerebellum, thalamus, and cortex. The spinal outflow from the system takes its origin from the red nucleus and the reticular formation as the rubrospinal and reticulospinal tracts respectively.

Clinical Extrapyramidal Syndromes

Damage to the extrapyramidal system in man leads to one of two syndromes: hyperkinetic-dystonia or *spasticity* on the one hand and hypokinetic Parkinson's disease on the other.

Spasticity is characterized by hyperactive stretch reflexes, that is, by reflexes released from central inhibitory influences which normally arise in the extrapyramidal system (Magoun and Rhines, 1947). The commonest cause of the disease is injury to the central nervous system at birth. The manifestations vary, depending on which part of the system is damaged.

Damage to the putamen and caudate nucleus leads to the *choreic syndrome,* involving irregular, rapid, involuntary jerky movements and impairment of voluntary movement. The same syndrome may also arise from damage to the cerebral cortex and subthalamus. Damage to the striatum, but particularly the pallidum, leads to the *athetoid syndrome,* involving involuntary, spasmodic, wormlike movements, especially of the peripheral limb segments. These movements are slower than the choreic movements; the joints become fixed in abnormal postures and voluntary movements are again impaired. Damage to the subthalamic nucleus of one side leads to contralateral *hemiballismus,* involving violent tossing movements of the limbs, sometimes so violent that the patient falls down; the limbs can hardly be moved voluntarily. Damage to the reticular formation leads to *myoclonus,* involving arrhythmic contractions of single muscles or muscle groups. The consequences of damage to the red nucleus are very variable and may be any or all of the syndromes so far mentioned.

The *hypokinetic Parkinsonian syndrome* arises from damage to the substantia nigra; it does not involve spontaneous, large involuntary movements but, rather, stiffness of the limbs and fine tremor when the limbs are at rest, the so-called *tremor at rest.* For more details of these clinical conditions, see Benda (1952).

Functional Significance of the Extrapyramidal System

Only recently have experimental physiological procedures confirmed information derived from clinical observation. Some of the experiments on the effects of stimulating extrapyramidal structures in the diencephalon are discussed in the section on righting reflexes.

The extrapyramidal system functions along with the cerebellum in controlling movements. The red nucleus receives fibers from the cerebellum and relays them to the motor cortex, which in turn connects to the cerebellum via the pons, thus completing a feedback loop. Fibers also descend to the motoneurons of the cord from the red nucleus, influencing movements of the limbs, which in turn induce activity in muscle afferents and perhaps vestibular afferents which feed back to the cerebellum and cortex, completing another control circuit. These two examples, among many, serve to demonstrate the functional integrity of the whole motor and motor afferent system, including the vestibular system. The γ efferent system must not be forgotten either, because of its role in initiating and controlling movements.

Voluntary movement involves the setting up of a central spatial-temporal template of the required action, presumably in the cortex initially. Corresponding instructions are fed into cerebellar, extrapyramidal, and spinal centers, where they are translated into effective discharge patterns to the motoneurons after being integrated by these centers into the ongoing reflex and postural-background activity in the body's musculature. Feedback from proprioceptors, exteroceptors, and the vestibular apparatus informs the cerebellum and motor cortex whether the movements have been executed as planned. If this *reafferent* copy does not correspond to the central pattern, corrective impulses are discharged after due allowance has been made for the time delays in the system. Many subroutines are stored in the system at various levels: as reflex patterns in the spinal cord and brain stem, as postural stereotypes in the vestibular, cerebellar, and extrapyramidal systems, and as complex movement "templates" in the neocerebellum. The cortex is thus relieved of the necessity of controlling the innate routines and well-learned skills, and is free to devote itself to the mastery of new patterns of movement, which in practice means the adaptation of subroutines into new movement sequences. For a fuller discussion of the extrapyramidal system, see Jung and Hassler (1960).

THE CEREBELLUM

Structure and Connections

The cerebellum is a large, convoluted part of the central nervous system, consisting of many nuclei and fiber masses. It sits above the fourth ventricle and is connected to the rest of the nervous system by six large peduncles or stalks, three on each side. The cerebellum has two principal subdivisions.

1. The flocculo-nodular lobe is the most primitive part. It is situated at the base of the cerebellum immediately above the fourth ventricle. Its position makes it difficult to approach, and for this reason experimental studies have been hampered. The component structures have remained relatively undeveloped in higher mammals. It is the only part which has direct two-way connections with the vestibular nerve and nuclei.

2. The corpus cerebelli, or cerebellar cortex, is particularly well developed in higher mammals, and its development has paralleled that of the cerebral cortex. It is divided into an anterior or paleocerebellar

lobe and a posterior or neocerebellar lobe (Larsell, 1960). The cortex is highly convoluted into folia, and consists mainly of white matter covered with three layers of gray matter; a superficial molecular layer, a Purkinje cell layer, and a deep granular layer. Incoming impulses arrive in the so-called mossy fibers which synapse profusely with the complex dendritic endings of the granular cells of the granular layers. Outgoing fibers originate entirely in the massive Purkinje cells. The granular cells send ascending and intricately bifurcating axons into the outer molecular layer, where they envelop dendritic expansions from the Purkinje cells. The Purkinje cell dendrites are also enveloped by dendrites from "star cells" and "basket cells" in the molecular layer (see Fig. 8–5).

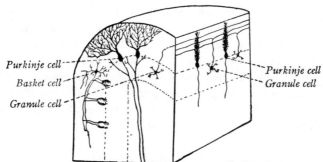

FIG. 8–5. Schematic representation of neuronal arrangement in a transverse and longitudinal section of a cerebellar folium. (From *Handbuch der Mikroskopischen Anatomie des Menschen,* ed. by W. v. Mollendorf, Vol. IV, part 8, 1958; courtesy of Springer-Verlag.)

The incoming mossy fibers deliver impulses from many sources: from the spinal cord via dorsal and ventral spinocerebellar tracts, from the cerebral cortex via pontine nuclei, from the reticular formation and basal ganglia, and from the vestibular system.

The Purkinje cell axons run into the cerebellar white matter and terminate largely in gray nuclear masses in the white matter (fatigii, globosus, emboliformis, and dentate nucleus). From the nuclei arise the main outflow from the cerebellum (Jansen and Brodal, 1954).

Changes in electrical potential at the cerebellar surface may be evoked by stimulation of the vestibular apparatus, muscle spindles, and tendon, joint, cutaneous, visual, and auditory receptors, as well as by artificial stimulation of the sensory and motor areas of the cerebral cortex (Adrian, 1943; Brookhart, 1960). Each sensory end organ evokes potentials in a particular part of the cerebral cortex according to its location in the body. In other words, the cerebellum is *topographically organized.*

This topographical organization has an approximate point-to-point correspondence with the topographical organization of the sensory-motor cerebral cortex. Cerebellar cortical tracts run via the red nucleus and thalamus, and a corticocerebellar tract runs via nuclei in the pons.

Even in the absence of external stimulation, the cerebellar cortex maintains a rhythmic, asynchronous discharge with a frequency of 150 to 250 oscillations per second. This rhythmic activity originates in the Purkinje cells, and is particularly vulnerable to anesthesia and the effects of drugs (Dow, 1938). One may conclude that incoming influences exert their effects by altering the rate of discharge of the Purkinje cells, increasing it or decreasing the basic frequency, rather than initiating activity in otherwise quiescent cells. The basic rhythmic activity is continually modified by impulses from very diverse sources. This continual flow of information into the cerebellum from all sensory and motor systems which are concerned with reflex and voluntary sensory-motor coordination clearly means that the cerebellum has a central role in sensory-motor coordination. The cerebellum has no direct access to the spinal cord, and therefore cannot influence motor neurons directly. Its influence is funneled through brain stem nuclei, including the red nuclei, the vestibular nuclei, the reticular formation, and basal ganglia, and through the motor areas of the cerebral cortex.

Functions of the Cerebellum

Stimulation of the anterior or the posterior lobe with high-frequency (over 40 cps.) impulses leads to a depression of muscular tonus (hypotonus) through the body. If decerebrate rigidity is present (see p. 328), stimulation of the anterior lobe promptly inhibits it. At least part of this hypotonus must be a consequence of the inhibition of the gamma system which follows from cerebellar stimulation (see p. 299). Stimulation of the anterior lobe with lower frequency impulses leads to facilitation of muscular tonus or hypertonus (Terzuolo and Terzian, 1953). This hypertonus is coupled with, and will to some extent be caused by, augmented gamma fiber activity, although Granit (1955) considered that both gamma and alpha motor neurons are directly influenced by cerebellar activity.

Stimulation of the posterior lobe produces conjugate deviation of the eyes. But the main effects of stimulating the posterior lobe are the inhibition and facilitation of voluntary motor activity. This control is mediated by impulses from the cerebellum acting on the cerebral motor cortex and extrapyramidal system (basal ganglia and reticular formation).

One may conclude from present-day physiological evidence that the anterior lobe of the cerebellum is concerned with the control of the distribution of tonus in reflex activity, both spatially in the various muscles, and temporally in the sequence of movements. This control is over both postural reflexes and other reflexes, and is funneled via the rubrospinal and reticulospinal tracts.

The posterior lobe or neocerebellum also controls reflex activity, but is mainly concerned with the spatial and temporal organization of voluntary motor activity or skills. Its influences are funneled through the motor cortex and pyramidal system, as well as through brain stem nuclei of the extrapyramidal system. Voluntary activity can take place only against a background of reflex and particularly postural reflex activity. It is the integration of voluntary activity into the pattern of reflex and postural adjustments which is the function of the neocerebellum. The physiological evidence upon which the above conclusions are based was obtained for the most part from decerebrate animals (see Brookhart [1960] for further details). Caution must be exercised in applying the results to man. However, the conclusions from anatomical and electrophysiological evidence are confirmed by evidence from extirpation experiments in animals and by clinical evidence in man.

Holmes (1922) classified the disorders of motility due to cerebellar disease in man. The following are the principal effects:

1. *Muscular Hypotonia.* In cerebellar hypotonia, the muscles are flaccid and show a diminished resistance to passive movement. If a hypotonic limb is shaken passively, the terminal segments of the limb flop about loosely on their joints. If the lesion is confined to one cerebellar hemisphere, the hypotonia is confined to the same side of the body. Cerebellar hypotonia probably depends upon (a) depression of vestibular centers which normally facilitate tonus, (b) decreased gamma fiber activity, and (c) direct depression of alpha motor activity.

2. *Disturbances of Posture.* With a unilateral lesion, the affected side often sags; the weight of the body is put on the unaffected leg, and the head is turned to that side. The patient may be unable to stand, and tends to fall toward the affected side. If he is able to walk, he veers to the affected side.

3. *Cerebellar Ataxia.* Voluntary movements are disturbed or ataxic. They are weak, easily fatigued, and show a long reaction time. They are *dysmetric;* that is, their range is poorly controlled; and the harmonious synthesis of movements at different joints and of different limbs is lost. This last disorder is also called *asynergia.* Reaching movements oscillate about their target. This "*intention tremor*" is especially evident in skills involving finely controlled movements of the fingers. If a patient is asked to hold his forearm against an applied pressure, his arm jerks in an uncontrolled ballistic movement when the applied pressure is released. Normally such uncontrolled *rebound* would be controlled by the reflex contraction of antagonistic muscles. In the early phases after cerebellar damage, the eyes may show a skew deviation. Spontaneous

nystagmus is common, especially when the eyes are deviated toward the side of a unilateral lesion.

In lower mammals, cerebellar ablation commonly leads to overactivity of extensor muscles; if the animal attempts to stand, the forceful extension of the forelimbs often throws the animal onto its back. There is some recovery from these symptoms after a time. Primates show little of this overactivity, which is due primarily to a release of vestibular impulses from cerebellar inhibitory control (Bach and Magoun, 1947; De Vito, Brusa, and Arduini, 1956), but probably also to enhanced gamma fiber outflow and direct facilitation of alpha motor outflow.

VESTIBULAR APPARATUS

In mammals, the vestibular apparatus is a set of sense organs in the bony labyrinths of the inner ear. These sense organs, like the auditory cochlea, with which they are associated, contain a sensory epithelium covered with sensitive hair cells which cause neural discharges when displaced. The cochlea is "tuned in" to high-frequency vibrations, whereas the organs of the vestibular apparatus are "tuned in" to very low-frequency mechanical disturbances produced by accelerations of the head. This selectivity of response is largely due to the mechanical resonant properties of the structural components of the sense organs rather than to the end organs (sensory receptor cells) themselves.

There are three main components of the vestibular system: the three canals, the utricle, and the sacculus. The function of the sacculus is unknown and will not be discussed further.

The anatomical arrangement of the vestibular organs and cochlea are shown in Figure 8–6. All these organs are suspended in perilymph fluid. The internal cavities of the organs are linked together and filled with endolymph fluid.

The utricles are often called static receptors because one of their functions is to indicate the position of the head in relation to gravity, and the canals are often called dynamic receptors because they indicate rotary acceleration. This is a false distinction. The canals, as a triplet, are sensitive to both the direction of rotary acceleration and its amount; and, similarly, the utricles are sensitive to both the direction of linear acceleration and its amount. The distinction between them is that the canals respond to rotary acceleration and the utricles respond to linear acceleration. Gravity is one form of linear acceleration; in relativity theory, we may be regarded as accelerating away from the center of the earth at 32 feet per second per second. Our dynamically neutral state is the state of free fall achieved only by cosmonauts for any length of time. In this state we are weightless and our utricles are not stimulated.

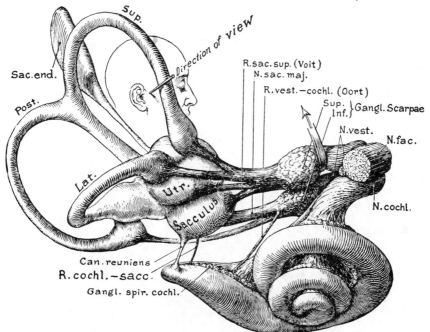

FIG. 8–6. Diagram of the inner ear, showing the semicircular canals, utricle, sacculus, and cochlea, together with the nerves innervating them. (After Hardy, M., 1934, *Anat. Rec.,* 59, 412.)

Vestibular Canals

In man, the canals lie in planes approximately at right angles to each other. Each canal has a contralateral parallel partner with which it forms a synergic pair. In spite of the fact that the three canals share a common cavity in the utricle, each one functions independently of the others, as if each were a complete and independent fluid circuit. Their usual name, semicircular canals, is therefore misleading.

At one point in each canal, near its junction with the utricle, is a swelling or *ampulla* which contains the sensory epithelium or *crista ampullaris*. The structure of a crista is shown in Figure 8–7. It is a ridge of epithelium protruding into the cavity or lumen of the ampulla and carrying many multiciliated sensory cells interspersed with structural cells. The cilia of all the cells project into a common gelatinous mass or cupula reaching to the far side of the ampulla, which is arched at this point so that the cupula may swing from side to side like a swinging door (see Fig. 8–8). In each sensory cell, the cilia membranes are continuous with the cell membrane. A resting potential of about 160 millivolts exists across the membrane; the cell interior is negative with respect to the outside. The whole structure is thus a charged "condenser."

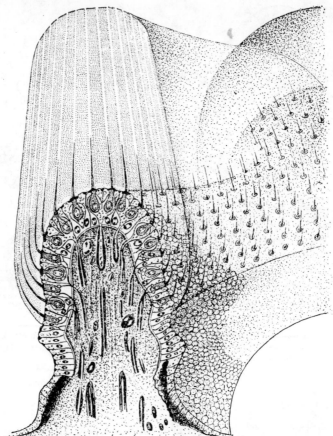

FIG. 8–7. Schematic drawing of one half of a crista ampullaris, showing innervation of its epithelium. Thick nerve
fibers forming nerve calyces round type I hair cells at the
summit of the crista; medium-caliber fibers innervating type I
hair cells on the slope of the crista; medium-caliber and fine
nerve fibers forming a nerve plexus innervating hair cells of
type II. The sensory hairs pass from the hair cells into fine
canals in the cupula, which is separated from the epithelium
by a narrow subcuplar space. (From Wersäll, 1956, *Acta oto-
laryngol*, suppl. 126.)

Each sensory cell synapses with a sensory neuron. The neurons gather
together to form the vestibular branch of the eighth or acoustic cranial
nerve.

Mach and other early theorists did not realize that the cupula seals
the lumen of the ampulla, and consequently thought that the endolymph
flowed over the cristae. In 1931, Steinhausen observed the true functioning of the cupula in a living fish by injecting india ink into the endolymph. Modern electrophysiological methods enable microelectrodes to

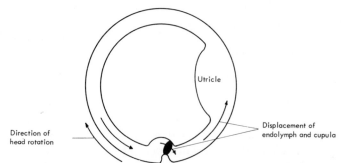

FIG. 8–8. Schematic diagram of a vestibular canal showing the complete fluid circuit. The arrows depict the consequences of a clockwise rotation of the head in the plane of the canal.

explore both the resting membrane potential and the discharge patterns consequent upon stimulation. The results of these investigations have given rise to the following account of the functioning of the canals.

Consider the right horizontal canal. When the head is rotated to the right in the plane of the canal, the inertia of the endolymph causes it to lag behind and flow to the left relative to the walls of the canal. The cupula is consequently deflected toward the utricle. The cilia are deflected, which results in a decrease in the resting membrane potential (depolarization). The mechanism of this depolarization is not understood, but it causes an increase in the frequency of firing in the sensory neurons. In the same way, a rotation of the head to the left is accompanied by an outward deflection of the cupula, an increase in the resting potential (hyperpolarization), and a decrease in the frequency of the afferent discharge. The end organ is thus bidirectional, although the sensory membrane as a whole is more sensitive a depolarization than to hyperpolarization at least in lower animals. This asymmetry of function is known as Ewald's law of vestibular directional preponderance (see Lowenstein [1956] and Gernandt [1959] for further physiological details).

Steinhausen described the behavior of the cupula by the well-known differential equation for the torsion pendulum. Experimental findings have confirmed that, within limits, this equation adequately describes the behavior of the end organ. However, as we shall see, the formula only partially accounts for the behavioral consequences of rotations of the body.

During a period of rotation at *constant angular velocity*, the endolymph catches up with the canal walls, the cupula returns to its resting position, and the discharge ceases. If the body is now brought to rest, the deceleration displaces the cupula in the opposite direction. It takes about 30 seconds before it regains its central position, and during this recovery period the subject will behave as if he is still decelerating. He will fall to one side, his eyes will move nystagmically, and he will experience turning sensations and nausea.

If an acceleration is followed immediately by a deceleration, the two opposed deflections of the cupula cancel out, leaving no residual deflection and no aftereffects. If a *steady rate of acceleration* is continued for several minutes, the subject will report that the rotation is stopping, even though the cupula remains deflected. It is not known whether this adaptation effect depends on a peripheral or central process (Ek, Jongkees, and Klijn, 1960).

Determinations of the threshold of angular acceleration have been made with a variety of methods—a recent determination gave $0.5°/sec^2$ (Groen and Jongkees, 1948). For short time intervals, the product of the acceleration and the time required to reach threshold is constant; for instance, shorter times of application require greater accelerations to reach threshold. This relationship is analogous to Bloch's law in vision (see page 113).

Utricles

The utricle or statolith organ is a sac at the junction of the three vestibular canals. It contains a sensory organ, *the macula*, which responds to the extent and direction of linear acceleration, including the linear acceleration due to gravity. Organs sensitive to position with respect to gravity are very old in the evolutionary scale. They are represented in every animal phylum, and are known as statocysts in invertebrates. One of the neatest ways of studying their function is provided by the crayfish's habit of using its pincers to replace grains of sand in its statocyst after every moult. These grains serve to stimulate the statocyst as the crayfish moves about. If iron filings are the only small particles available, the crayfish will place these in its statocyst cavity, and will then alter its orientation in response to the movements of a magnet. See Lowenstein (1950, 1956) for details of the comparative aspects of otolith functioning.

The mammalian utricle is filled with endolymph which has nearly the same specific gravity as water. The macula consists of an epithelium of ciliated sensory cells covered by a gelatinous substance containing calcium carbonate particles or *otoconia*. The specific gravity of the otoconia is greater than that of the surrounding endolymph, so that the heavy otoconia are displaced by changes in the extent or direction of linear acceleration. When the head is erect, the macula is in an approximately horizontal position, and the sensory hairs are vertical with the otoconia lying on top of them.

Trincker (1962) recorded the potential changes inside the macula of the guinea pig and found that only shearing forces produced by tangential displacements of the hair cells are effective in producing neural responses. Pressure or tension applied at right angles to the macula epithelium has no effect. A shearing-force mechanism produces a utricular response that is a sine function of the angle of tilt, whereas a tension mechanism would produce a response that is a cosine function of tilt (see Fig. 8–9). Trincker was able to demonstrate the sine function in

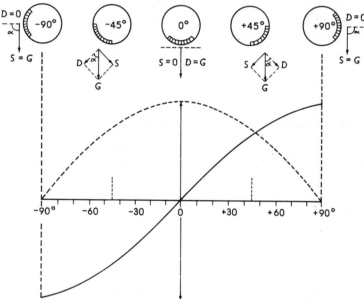

FIG. 8–9. Stimulation of the macular sensory epithelium by shearing force and the characteristic curve representing information input. Above: schematic drawings of the utricle, with its macula and statolithic membrane, undergoing tilting in both directions around the horizontal rostro-occipital axis of the head. Forces on the sensory epithelium represented as vector parallelograms. G, gravity; S, shearing force (the component of gravity, acting tangentially on the epithelium); D, pressure (or tension), the component, acting vertically on the macula. In a normal position, $S = 0$; at 90°, $D = 0$. Below: the relationship of shearing force (continuous line) and pressure (broken line) to degree of inclination (abscissa); shearing gives a sine relationship, while pressure gives the cosine. (From Trincker, 1962, *S.E.B. Symposium*, 294.)

actual recordings from the tilting macula of the guinea pig. Wing (1963) has not been able to record any consistent potential changes in the mammalian vestibular ganglion in response to head tilt, and suggested that the utricle is largely vestigial in higher mammals, where vision and kinesthesis are dominant in maintaining balance.

Labyrinthine Pathways

The vestibular part of the eighth nerve on each side passes to four *vestibular nuclei,* which sit astride the cerebellar peduncle. The vestibular nuclei on each side of the head are connected together directly, as well as by fibers running through the reticular formation. Other fibers from the vestibular nuclei form the *medial longitudinal fasciculus,* which ascends to the oculomotor centers of the brain stem to mediate the vestibular nystagmus reflex. Other fibers descend into the spinal cord as the vestibulospinal tract, which terminates in motoneuron pools in the cord and mediates vestibulospinal reflexes. Some fibers pass directly to the cerebellum and reticular system. Although doubted for a long time, it is now established that the vestibular apparatus projects via the thalamus to the cerebral cortex, principally to the contralateral superior ectosylvian fissure.

Behavioral Consequences of Labyrinthine Stimulation

The foregoing account of the complex ramifications of the vestibular afferents throughout the central nervous system suggests that the behavioral consequences of vestibular stimulation are equally complex. At the same time, the paucity of cortical projections suggests that these behavioral consequences are largely at the unconscious, reflex level. When a person rotates about his body axis, the eyes execute a series of slow movements in the opposite direction to the rotation, alternating with quick return sweeps. This pattern of eye movements is known as *vestibular nystagmus* and may be elicited in a horizontal, vertical, or frontal plane (torsional nystagmus), depending upon which of the three canals is in the plane of rotation of the body.

The speed of the slow phase is roughly proportional to the speed of rotation for moderate speeds and clearly serves to retain, as far as possible, a stationary image of the visible world on the retina. The quick phase is mediated by brain stem centers, and is not controlled by proprioceptive impulses from the eyes. The whole reflex occurs in the dark and is therefore not dependent on vision, although when the eyes are open the nystagmus is more nicely geared to the speed at which the retinal image moves. It is thought that, although the vestibular apparatus initiates the nystagmus, optokinetic or visually induced nystagmus takes command when the eyes are open (Dodge, 1923). An illusion of visual movement accompanies postrotational nystagmus, especially when only a single point of light is visible. This illusory movement has been called the *oculogyral illusion* (Graybiel and Hupp, 1946), and it may outlast the nystagmus, so that the movement of the eyes is not the only cause of the illusion (Guedry, Collins, and Sheffey, 1961).

An absence of postrotational nystagmus has often been taken to signify defective labyrinths, although it often is not present in normal subjects. A rotating chair in which people may be tested in this way is known as a Bárány chair. A vast clinical literature has grown up on the basis of this and similar tests. If the duration of postrotational nystagmus is plotted as a function of the logarithm of the rate of deceleration (cupula deflection), a straight-line function known as a *cupulogram* is obtained (Ek, Jongkees, and Klijn, 1960). The duration of postrotational nystagmus would logically seem to represent the time which the cupula takes to return to equilibrium and the slope of the cupulogram would seem to represent the rate of this recovery. However, the cupulogram slope changes with practice, and there is no evidence that a change in the rate of cupula recovery is responsible for this change. As an example of the effects of practice on the cupulogram, look at Figure 8–10

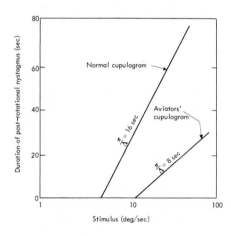

FIG. 8–10. A normal cupulogram compared with that of the average cupulogram of 18 experienced aviators. (Adapted from Groen, 1960, *Acta oto-laryngol.*, p. 60).

and compare the averaged cupulograms from ordinary people with the averaged cupulogram from practiced aviators. The slope of the cupulogram from the experienced aviators is less than normal, reflecting a high degree of cortical suppression of vestibular aftereffects, an obviously desirable accomplishment in aviators. For further details of cupulometry, see Cawthorne, Dix and Hallpike (1956).

The decline, with practice, of postrotational nystagmus and other postrotational effects is known as *vestibular habituation*. The mechanism of vestibular habituation is not understood, although it presumably depends on central factors. It is well established that drowsiness and lack of attention speed up vestibular habituation (Collins, 1962) and that arousal restores postrotational nystagmus, although not to its prehabituation level. It may be concluded that habituation depends upon a reduction of arousal, but not entirely on this factor. Habituation is especially marked when the eyes are open, and probably the most important factor in habituation under these conditions is an increased stabilization of the eye by visual fixation. It may be supposed that postrotational phenomena are normally habituated to some extent because of the rotations to which people are continually subjected. If this is so, newborn infants should manifest an unusually low threshold for, and an extralong duration of, postrotational nystagmus. This seems to be the case (Groen, 1963), although the child's poorly developed mechanism of visual fixation is also a probable contributory factor, and the infant, like the adult, must be kept alert in order that the nystagmus may be elicited.

The central adaptive control of the effects of angular and linear accelerations is further illustrated by the well-known acclimatization to the movements of a ship. It is as if the person learns to anticipate each movement by producing a central "copy" of the particular sequence and by partialing this out from the afferent signals as they come in. When one returns to land, the firm ground seems to pitch and roll because the partialing-out process persists for hours or even days.

Effects of Loss of Labyrinthine Function

Unilateral loss of vestibular function is followed by a period of acute discomfort. The patient is unable to move his head without feeling distressed, nauseated, and disoriented; the skin is pallid, pulse rate is high, and vomiting is frequent. He has nystagmus and falls to the undamaged side. These symptoms subside after some days or weeks, presumably because of a change in the way in which the central nervous system makes use of an asymmetrical vestibular input.

A patient with bilateral vestibular loss shows none of the nausea, distress, or nystagmus symptoms. He is unable to stand steadily upright with eyes closed, and he is likely to swim downward instead of upward when submerged in water. Some recovery of stability takes place, especially in man, who is able to rely on proprioceptive and visual signals.

Motion Sickness

Motion sickness is a state that develops in animals and humans when they are subjected to accelerations over which they have no control. It manifests itself in nausea, vomiting, and distress.

The literature on this subject was reviewed recently by Chinn and Smith (1955) and Loftus (1963). There is abundant evidence that the vestibular apparatus is implicated in the etiology of motion sickness. Bilateral labyrinthectomy or sectioning of the vestibular-cerebellar tracts in animals and man renders the subject immune to motion sickness. Caloric or electrical stimulation of the vestibular apparatus induces motion sickness. Modern evidence suggests that both canal and utricular stimulation may be involved. Low-frequency, high-amplitude oscillations seem to be more effective than high-frequency, low-amplitude oscillations. However, the most potent stimulus seems to arise when there is a complex series of changes in the amplitude and direction of both linear and rotary acceleration. Even if the person is subjected to a simple sinusoidal rotation or swing, complex forces will act on his head every time he moves it. These forces arise through interaction between the forces produced by the movements of the swing and those produced by the movement of the head. If the head is strapped in one position, motion sickness symptoms are much reduced (Johnson and Taylor, 1961). Most people adapt to sickness-inducing conditions after a time. For instance, Graybiel, Clark, and Zarriello (1960) observed volunteers living in a slowly rotating room for many days. The initial distress and incapacity gradually diminished.

Thus complex stimulation of the vestibular apparatus is the main etiological factor in motion sickness. However, the fact that adaptation takes place demonstrates that central factors are also important.

Summarizing our knowledge about the vestibular apparatus, it may be concluded that the differential equation for the torsion pendulum adequately describes the behavior of the peripheral organ. However, central factors modify the effects which the afferent discharge has on behavior, and probably the afferent discharge itself. This is a typical situation: behavioral mechanisms are "layered," and the top control layers must be stripped away to reveal the simpler mechanisms, which are ultimately describable in terms of differential equations. An experimental psychologist must understand the basic physiology and physics of peripheral mechanisms, and no physiologist should ignore the complex nonlinear central mechanisms. The study of vestibular mechanisms is a field where important contributions have been made both by physiologists and physicists working on peripheral mechanisms (Mach, Ewald, Groen, Jongkees, etc.) and by psychologists working on the central mechanisms (Dodge, Dunlap, Mowrer, Graybiel, etc.).

POSTURAL REFLEXES

There are two main types of postural reflexes. The first type—the tonic reflexes—are concerned with the control of the attitude of parts of the body in relation to each other but not in relation to gravity. The second type—the righting reflexes—maintain the body in a constant orientation to gravity. Many of the segmental reflexes discussed in the last section, such as the stretch reflex and crossed extensor reflex, are tonic postural reflexes. The suprasegmental reflexes will be discussed in this section.

Magnus, while working in Sherrington's laboratory in Liverpool, noticed that the distribution of tonus in the body of a decerebrate cat is affected when its head is passively moved about. He went on to study postural reflexes over the next fourteen years with his co-workers, Rademaker, de Klejn, and others, in the University of Utrecht. His classic work, *Körperstellung*, appeared in 1924; an English summary is contained in the Cameron Prize Lectures of 1926. In man, postural reflexes are overlaid by complex learned motor response patterns. The young child, however, does not possess a functional cerebral cortex, and may therefore exhibit postural reflexes in their primitive form. This work has been thoroughly reviewed by Peiper (1963).

Tonic Reflexes of the Decerebrate Animal

When the brain stem is sectioned just above the vestibular nuclei, the extensor muscles throughout the body go into continuous spasm, resulting in a rigid extension of the limbs. This postural pattern is known as *decerebrate rigidity* and is due to the release of vestibular tonic centers from control by extrapyramidal centers.

When the head of such a decerebrate preparation is placed in different positions, the distribution of tonus in the whole body musculature is changed. Two reflexes are involved in this response: (1) a *tonic neck reflex*, resulting from stimulation of neck-muscle receptors, and (2) a *tonic labyrinthine reflex*, resulting from stimulation of the utricles.

In order to study the tonic neck reflex in isolation from the tonic labyrinthine reflex, the labyrinths must be removed. Under these circumstances, rotation of the head causes extension of the fore- and hindlimbs on the side toward which the jaw is rotated ("jaw limbs") and relaxation of the limbs on the side toward which the back of the head is rotated ("skull limbs"). Inclination of the head toward one shoulder causes extension of the jaw limbs and relaxation of the skull limbs. Lowering or dorsiflexion of the head causes an extension of the forelimbs and relaxation of the hindlimbs. Elevation or ventroflexion of the head causes flexion of the forelimbs and extension of the hindlimbs.

Tonic neck reflexes occur in many human infants during the first six months of life, before the cerebral cortex has gained control over the lower reflex centers. Figure 8–11 shows the typical reflex pattern induced by a sideway head position in a newborn infant; it is known as the "fencing position" for obvious reasons.

In order to study tonic labyrinthine reflexes in isolation from the tonic neck reflexes, the head is immobilized in relation to the body by a plaster jacket, or the tonic neck reflex outflow is interrupted by cutting the first three cervical roots of the spinal cord.

When such a preparation is moved into different positions in relation

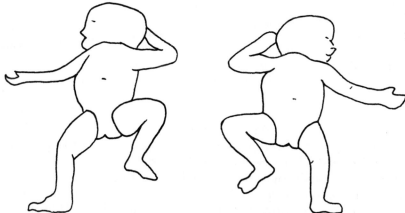

FIG. 8–11. Asymmetrical neck tonic reflex (fencing position) in an infant girl age 2 months 9 days. (Drawn from a photograph in Peiper, 1963, p. 157.)

to gravity, the extensor tonus changes in the same way in all four limbs. The tonus is maximal when the animal is in the supine position and the otoliths are pulling down on the macular epithelium; tonus is minimal when the animal is in the prone position and the otoliths are pressing on the macular epithelium. In other positions, extensor tonus is intermediate.

In the presence of both neck and labyrinthine reflexes, the pattern of tonus in the body represents the algebraic sum of their effects. For example, if the head of a prone, decerebrate cat is flexed ventrally, the forelimbs will relax under the influence of both reflexes, but the hindlimbs may not change, as they are influenced in opposite directions by the two reflexes.

These attitudinal reflexes last as long as the head is held in a certain position, and it is for this reason that they are called "tonic." They may be seen in the active behavior of intact animals. For example, a cat when reaching for food on the ground lowers the head, which causes the forelimbs to relax. When a cat reaches up, the head elevates and the forelimbs extend, but the hindlimbs do not change markedly in their position. These reflex tonic attitudes are not easy to detect in intact primates, but may be seen in decerebrate preparations and in clinical conditions in humans.

Righting Reflexes

The reflexes discussed so far may be elicited in a decerebrate animal where the section is made just rostral (toward the head) to the vestibular nuclei. If the section is more rostral and leaves the midbrain and thalamus intact, the preparation is known as a thalamic preparation. The animal no longer manifests the extensor contracture of decerebrate rigidity and is able to restore itself to an upright posture when disturbed.

Five groups of reflexes which cooperate in righting responses were identified by Magnus. In order to demonstrate any one of these components, the animal must first be placed in such a state that none of them is active. This so-called zero condition is fulfilled if a thalamic animal, after bilateral labyrinthectomy, is suspended freely out of contact with any surface. In lower animals, which do not have optic-righting reflexes, it is not necessary to cover the eyes; in higher mammals, this is necessary.

Labyrinthine-Righting Reflexes.   All blindfolded, thalamic mammals with intact labyrinths show the labyrinthine-righting reflexes. If the animal is held by the pelvis, its head remains in the upright position as far as possible, no matter how the pelvis is moved (see Fig. 8–12). These reflex head movements depend upon the utricle and perhaps also the sacculus, and are therefore absent in labyrinthectomized animals (see Fig. 8–13). They are only faintly demonstrable in the neonate

FIG. 8–12. Head-down suspension of a thalamus preparation of a rabbit. The head does not follow gravity, but is brought into normal position in space by the labyrinthine righting reflex. (Sketch by Peiper after Magnus, 1924.)

FIG. 8–13. (*a*) rabbit without labyrinths; (*b*) intact rabbit in suspended lateral position. In the animal without labyrinths, the head responds to gravity; in the intact animal, the labyrinthine-righting reflex raises the head to normal position. (Sketch by Peiper after Rademaker, 1926.)

human, but develop during the first year of life. They enable the growing infant to lift his head, and later to sit up and stand.

Neck-Righting Reflexes. The neck-righting reflexes orient the body in relation to the head. If the body is tilted, the head regains the upright position by the action of the vestibular-righting reflexes; consequently the neck becomes twisted, which evokes the neck-righting reflexes, which in turn cause the thorax and then the lower parts of the body to be brought back into line with the upright head.

Body-Righting Reflexes. If a labyrinthectomized animal is held freely in the lateral position and lowered onto a surface, it immediately brings its head into a normal position with regard to the surface. The asymmetric stimulation of the touch receptors in the skin evokes this reflex. If the tactile stimulation on each side of the body is made symmetrical by pushing a board against the animal, the head will return under the influence of the neck-righting reflex to the lateral position. If the head of the animal is held firmly in the lateral position as the animal is lowered onto a surface, its body will right itself. This reflex is also induced by the asymmetrical stimulation of the skin, and it occurs in spite of the opposing neck-tonic reflex, which tends to keep the body in line with the laterally placed head.

Optic-Righting Reflexes. In intact higher mammals, such as cats, dogs, and primates, the orientation of the head is controlled largely by vision. If an animal with labyrinths removed but otherwise intact is freely suspended in the air, its head remains disoriented until the eyes are opened and the animal fixates on something in the environment.

All these reflexes normally work together to maintain the upright posture of the unconstrained intact animal. The head always leads; if the animal is disoriented, the head is first restored to the vertical position through the mediation of visual-, vestibular-, and tactile-righting reflexes. The thorax is then brought into line with the head through the mediation of neck-righting reflexes and tactile body-righting reflexes. Finally, the hindquarters and legs are brought into line by spinal and tactile-righting reflexes. This sequence of events is called a chain reflex and may be seen in the way a cat rights its body when falling. This chain reflex may also be demonstrated in infant humans.

Central Control of Postural Reflexes

The way in which postural motor patterns are organized by the central nervous system has been studied by Hess (1957) and his co-workers in Zurich. They found that electrical stimulation delivered by fine electrodes embedded in the diencephalic region of an otherwise intact cat induces reproducible attitudinal responses of the head, or head and body. A head-lowering–legs-flexing response is induced by stimulation of the posterior commissure. An opposed response is induced by stimulation in a zone over the posterior hypothalamus, or in the rubrospinal tract. The head rotates in response to stimulation of the thalamus or subthalamus, the direction of turning depending on the exact site of stimulation. Head turning is induced by stimulation of the lateral thalamus. All but this last response show rhythmic activity synchronous with low-frequency stimulation.

The various head responses produced by diencephalic stimulation are similar to the postrotational vestibular reflex head movements induced by the various vestibular canals. Hess concluded that the normal mode of stimulation of these diencephalic centers was from the vestibular canals, via the cerebellum and brachium conjunctivum. He also traced routes from the sensory tracts of the body and head, namely, the spinothalamic and trigeminal tracts, which presumably carry information regarding the relative position of body parts to these diencephalic centers.

A further set of responses from the diencephalon were observed which involved lifting the forelimbs and perhaps the whole side of the body. That these were not related to nociceptive (pain) reflexes was evident from the calm demeanor of the animal. Hess concluded that these responses correspond to postural reflexes under the control of proprioception, such as the crossed extensor reflex.

These results do not prove that basic motor patterns are controlled solely by central processes irrespective of proprioceptive inputs. There has been a long dispute about the relative importance of central and proprioceptive factors in the control of basic motor response patterns. On the one hand, the chain reflex theory holds that rhythmical motor patterns, such as walking, result from the successive interaction of proprioceptive and tactile reflexes. On the other hand, claims have been made that walking movements may occur in limbs in which all sensory nerves have been cut. However, Gray (1950) suggests that walking movements in a deafferented limb depend on the integrity of sensory nerves in other limbs. The most recent evidence is that walking and other movements are possible even with complete deafferentiation of the body (Taub, 1965).

Maintenance of the Postural Vertical

In order to study the ability of a person to judge when his body is in an upright position, it is usual to seat the blindfolded subject in a chair which can be tilted. In the absence of visual information, a person is able to set his body to the vertical to within one degree. However, many factors upset his judgment, such as the degree to which he was initially tilted before being allowed to restore himself to the vertical, the direction of the initial tilt, the speed of return to the vertical, and the duration of delay in the tilted position. For details of experimental work on these factors, see Howard and Templeton (1966).

Other work has been concerned with the sensory modalities involved in setting the seated body to the vertical. These modalities could include vision, touch, kinesthesis, and the labyrinths. Garten (1920) tested subjects with defective inner ears and found that they could accurately set their bodies to the vertical in a tilting chair. He concluded that the labyrinths are not important for this ability. He also found that the performance of normal subjects was affected by complete immersion in water, although anaesthetizing the skin areas which were in contact with the chair (by cooling the buttocks) had no effect on performance. He concluded that kinesthesis must therefore be the crucial modality for this ability. This conclusion, however, is not valid. If a person is able to use any one modality to set his body to the vertical, removing one, as Garten did, would not affect accuracy even though each modality could be important when it alone is present. However, it seems that tactile stimulation of the skin is not an essential factor in the ability to set the body to the vertical, at least for the seated person.

Some recent evidence has been put forward in support of Garten's suggestion that the labyrinths are not essential for body orientation. Thetford and Guedry (1952) studied five subjects with unilateral labyrinth loss, under a variety of conditions on the tilting chair. They performed just as well as normal subjects. This was probably because the subjects had become adapted to the asymmetrical vestibular input. One cannot conclude from these experiments that vestibular stimulation is unimportant for setting the body to the vertical in normal people. Errors have been found to be greater when the head of a normal subject is held upright than when it is fixed in the median plane of the body (Fleishman, 1953; Solley, 1960). Only in the latter condition is the utricle brought into action, which suggests that normal subjects use their utricles in judging the orientation of their bodies.

The influence of the visual frame on the setting of the body to the vertical has been studied by Passy (1950). The subjects adjusted themselves to the vertical in the tilting chair from an initial tilt of 45 degrees with the frame tilted to various angles up to 20 degrees to either side. The constant error in the direction of the frame tilt was found to increase as the tilt of the frame was increased, particularly when the frame was tilted to the same side as the body. The maximum effect of the tilted frame on the constant error was, however, only 2 degrees. The subjects at all times set their bodies much nearer to the true vertical than to the position of the visual frame.

The method of using a passive, seated subject for studying the ability to set the body to the vertical has little relevance to man's capacity to maintain a vertical posture in conditions where he is free to move actively. In a real-life situation, the usual task is that of maintaining body balance while standing or moving about.

It has already been pointed out that people with defective labyrinths are largely able to compensate for their disability, even when their eyes are closed. The most important modality for the maintenance of upright posture is undoubtedly proprioception. The joint-capsule receptors in proximal joints, particularly the hip joints, are very sensitive to body sway. It is apparent from studies of the electromyographic activity of the antigravity muscles that control of posture is not by steady contraction of these muscles but by intermittent correction of balance. If one stands on one leg with eyes closed, the intermittent nature of posture adjustment is apparent (see Eldred [1960] for further details).

The extent of the body sway when the eyes are closed is affected by many factors: age, the height and weight of the body, drugs, and suggestion. The sway amplitude is easily measured; such a measure is known as the *sway test*. It is used in the diagnosis of disorders of the proprioceptive system, as a test of drunkeness, and as a test of suggestibility or hypnotizability (see Edwards [1942]).

MOTOR AREAS OF THE CEREBRAL CORTEX

Fritsch and Hitzig reported in 1870 that electrical stimulation of certain areas of the dog's cerebral cortex produced movements of parts of the body. This was the first demonstration that motor functions are localized in the cerebral cortex. Similar motor areas were reported in primates by Leyton and Sherrington in 1917, and in humans by Penfield and Rasmussen in 1950. The so-called classical motor area from which these responses were elicited is situated in Brodmann's area 4, just in front of the central sulcus in the precentral gyrus. It forms a strip extending from deep in the longitudinal fissure down into the lateral fissure. Figure 8–14 shows the distribution of the body parts which are maximally aroused by stimulation of given loci in the motor strip.

Although motor responses are most readily elicited from the classical motor area, this is not the only part of the cortex to produce motor responses when stimulated artificially; motor responses may be elicited from the neighboring postcentral gyrus, which is normally considered to be the somesthetic area (see page 221), and from so-called secondary motor areas in the frontal and parietal lobes.

In addition, cortical centers for eye movements exist in the occipital and frontal lobes; and centers producing autonomic motor responses, such as hair erection, changes in heart beat, etc., exist in the frontal and temporal lobes.

Stimulation of other widespread areas of the cortex may cause any ongoing motor activity to be suppressed. These so-called suppressor

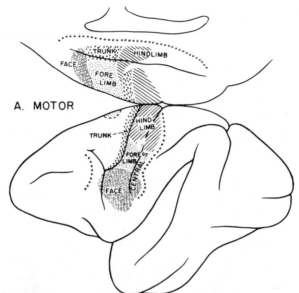

FIG. 8–14. Diagrammatic representation of the precentral motor areas in the brain of the monkey, showing the topographical localization of body areas.

areas are not localized, as was once thought; whether a particular area excites or suppresses depends to some extent upon the nature of the electrical stimulation.

The precise muscle group responding to stimulation of any particular locus of the precentral motor cortex depends upon the strength and frequency of the stimulus and the nature of the preceding stimulation (Murphy and Gellhorn, 1945; Liddell and Phillips, 1950). Furthermore, Ward (1938, 1952) showed that stimulation of a particular locus of the motor cortex of an unanaesthetized cat brought a limb to a particular final position whatever the initial position of the limb, although the final position was affected by the position of the head. Any one locus of the motor cortex must therefore send impulses to many spinal motor neurons, and the particular response elicited at any time must depend upon the postural state of the body, that is, on kinesthetic feedback and the background activity in spinal, vestibular, cerebellar, extrapyramidal, and cortical motor centers.

However, the coordination that Ward's experiment implies does not seem to be brought about by the activity of the motor cortex itself but by mechanisms farther downstream. When the motor cortex is removed and the underlying white matter (consisting of axons leaving the motor cortex) is stimulated, the same results are obtained as when the cortex itself was stimulated. However, interruption of the afferent pathway at the spinal level by a section of the dorsal roots abolished this coordination. It seems as if the motor cortex sends out a message setting a target for the mechanisms lower down. This target is then aimed at, and reached, by the operation of feedback loops, unless these are surgically interrupted. On the other hand, it is not certain that the feedback loop controlling position does not involve the motor cortex itself. Group I muscle afferents have been shown to project to the motor cortex of both the monkey and the cat (Albe-Fessard et al., 1965; Oscarsson, 1966). Ward's experiment would seem to show that the motor cortex sent commands to the periphery, which signaled the final position of a limb.

On the other hand, other studies stimulating the motor cortex have shown that threshold punctate stimuli of this region cause contraction of a single muscle (Chang et al., 1947). This suggests that the commands sent out from the motor cortex signal the pull to be exerted by a muscle, rather than a position to be attained. Strong support for this comes from an experiment recording the activity of pyramidal tract neurons during movement. Evarts (1968) trained monkeys to flex their wrists quickly while grasping a rod, which was weighted so that the monkey had to exert differing degrees of force either during flexion or extension. During steady applications of force, the greater the force, the more rapid was the firing in pyramidal tract neurons. During changes of rate of application of force, there was an extra burst of neuronal firing just before an increase of force and a decrease in firing before a reduction in force.

At present, the contradictory evidence about the type of command sent out by the motor cortex is unresolved. It is possible that there are two types of neuron and that the neurons that signal force are already lower in the chain of command to the neurons that set the position of the limb as a target.

It is an interesting fact that patients undergoing brain surgery report that the movements induced by stimulation of the motor cortex occur as if "someone were pulling the strings." That is, the patients do not feel they are making the movements themselves.

Removal of area 4 results in a general flaccid paralysis, from which considerable recovery takes place. Presumably, other motor areas take over the functions of area 4 to some extent. However, if the spinal cord is damaged, the loss of motor function is more severe and permanent, although more localized. Destruction of motor neurons of the final common path produces irreversible and complete paralysis of particular muscles, which subsequently atrophy.

Relative paralyses of motor function which result from lesions in the pyramidal system are known as *plegias*. A plegia occurs on the side contralateral to the lesion when the lesion is rostral to the decussation.

When affecting the whole of one side of the body, the plegia is known as a *hemiplegia;* when affecting the upper or lower part of the body, it is known as a *paraplegia.*

Damage to any part of the motor system, including the pyramidal and extrapyramidal systems and cerebellum, produces incoordination of movement in certain muscles. Any such loss of muscular control is known as *ataxia.*

Damage to cortical motor areas outside area 4, particularly damage to area 6, is usually accompanied by what is known as *apraxia.* An apraxic patient is able to move his limbs normally in simple tasks, but is unable to plan and execute complex learned skills. The motor system itself is intact, but cannot be marshaled adequately into spatial-temporal patterns. Apraxias may be more or less specific to one type of skill. *Agraphia* is an inability to write. Dressing apraxia is an inability to carry out the manipulations involved in getting dressed.

Such disturbances of higher motor functions cannot be considered in isolation from defects in related abilities. For instance, motor incoordination will result from disorders to the *body scheme,* that is, the frame of reference in terms of which the positions and movements of body parts are judged and acted upon. Body scheme disorders are associated with damage to the parietal lobes (see Critchley, 1953). A defect in the ability to comprehend the spatial relationships of objects, which may also arise through parietal lobe damage, could affect motor coordination when an attempt is made to manipulate objects. It is impossible to specify any one center that is solely concerned in the control of a complex skill; a motor skill is the end product of the complex interaction of many subsystems, and may suffer through damage to any one subsystem. At the same time, the nervous system, especially that of higher mammals, is adept at compensating for localized damage, either by recovery or by substituting alternative means of control.

One of the main tasks of voluntary movements is the control of the movement of limbs in relation to visible objects. There are several experimental approaches to this problem of visual-motor coordination:

1. The surgical rearrangement of nerve-to-muscle connections, sensory inputs, or tendon-to-bone insertions.

2. The displacement of the optical array entering the eyes and the study of the subsequent adaptation of visual-motor coordination.

3. The rearing of animals under restricted conditions of growth.

Surgical Rearrangement

The nerves of amphibians, especially young ones, may be readily transplanted so that they innervate atypical muscles (Sperry, 1945). For instance, the nerves to an agonist and antagonist in the forelimb of the frog may be transposed. When this is done, and the animal has regained the use of the limb, it is found that this limb walks backward relative to the other limbs; the same muscles contract in the same sequence as before, even though the resulting movements are maladjustive. The frog never learns to walk normally. In ther words, it is the muscle itself which decides how it is to contract, and not the nerves innervating the muscle. Each muscle of the body must somehow instruct the central nervous system to make central patterns of synaptic connections so that that muscle will contract in a way determined by the type of muscle it is. Weiss (1941, 1950) summarized this state of affairs by saying that "muscles have names," and this theory has become known as the myotypic theory of muscular control. It is not known how the muscles instruct the nervous system to make appropriate central connections.

Not only muscles determine central neural connections, sense organs apparently do the same. For instance, if an extra cornea is grafted onto the cheek of a frog and allowed to become innervated by a branch of the trigeminal nerve, it will cause a blink of the normal eyes when touched. The grafted cornea has somehow instructed the trigeminal branch to make those central motor connections appropriate to that other branch of the trigeminal nerve which normally innervates the cornea. This type of rearrangement of central connections works only within the field of any one peripheral nerve. For instance, it is not possible to make the auditory nerve act like an optic nerve by grafting the retina into the place of the cochlea.

Tendons may be easily regrafted onto atypical bones. Lower animals never learn to adapt their behavior to such a rearrangement. Tendons are sometimes regrafted in human patients, and a considerable degree of relearning takes place. This modifiability is presumably related to the development of the motor cortex in man.

Displacement of the Optical Array

If wedge prisms are worn which displace the optical array to one side, reaching movements toward visible objects are disturbed. The human subject readily adapts his movements to a visual displacement if he is informed of his errors. On moving the prisms, accuracy is again disturbed for a while. This type of visual-motor adaptation is normally specific to the particular arm used in training but is not specific to the particular eye which is open during training. However, if training consists of moving the eyes until they are fixated on an immobile finger which remains unseen until the end of the movement, the training is not specific to the hand that is used. The rule seems to be that the training is specific to whichever part of the body is required to change its normal movement during training.

Von Holst and Mittelstedt (1950) concluded from their observations on insects and fish that the important thing in visual-motor coordination is the relationship between self-produced movements of the body or parts of the body and changes in the pattern of stimulation of the sense organs which these movements produce. Such changes in sensory stimulation consequent upon self-produced movement were called *re-afference*. Changes in sensory stimulation produced solely by changes in the external world were called *ex-afference*. An animal capable of orientating itself must be capable of distinguishing between re-afferent and ex-afferent stimulation. It does this by disregarding the changes in sensory stimulation which a given pattern of muscular innervation normally produces. This theory has something in common with Helmholtz's theory of unconscious inference.

Held (1962) has recently applied this theory to the case of visual-motor adaptation to prisms. His basic procedure was to compare the effectiveness of self-produced movement with that of passive movement in the adaptation of visual-motor coordination to a displaced visual input in adult human subjects. Only the self-produced movement led to any adaptation, and Held concluded that re-afference is necessary for adaptation. However, it has been demonstrated by others that, under appropriate conditions, visual-motor adaptation may occur without self-produced movement during training (see Howard and Templeton, 1966), though not as effectively as with self-produced movement.

Restricted Rearing

Held and Hein (1963) have recently claimed that, for kittens at least, reafferent experience is essential for the development of visual-motor skills such as the blink response, paw placing, and avoidance of the visual cliff. This conclusion, however, may be questioned because the control group of kittens which were denied reafferent experience were also denied many types of exafferent stimulation, which may have been sufficient for the development of the skills mentioned.

There is a general difficulty with all experiments involving early deprivation. The procedures may not merely prevent the development of the relevant motor abilities but may cause the degeneration of control mechanisms which were originally present.

chapter 9

Emotion I

WHAT IS EMOTION?

The word emotion is not amenable to precise definition. As pointed out by Mandler (1962), it is rather to be regarded as a "chapter-heading term" which, in common with other such terms, does "no more than collect under one rubric what are believed to be related phenomena, experiments and observations. . . . The collection of these instances has no clearly definable boundaries; it arises historically and empirically, with the structure of the boundaries rarely spelled out, and, most frequently, appreciated intuitively." The study of emotion, therefore, consists in the investigation of various classes of events, such as emotional experiences, the environmental events which arouse emotion, behavior during emotional states, and so on. In this chapter we shall investigate the physiological changes which occur during emotional states. There is a large variety of conditions which are generally classified as emotions. These include, for example, love, joy, euphoria, hate, pity, disgust, sadness, fear, and rage. However, physiological psychologists studying emotion have been concerned mainly with fear and rage, since these are most readily produced in animals.

Manifestations of Fear and Rage

The somatic manifestations of fear and rage, as is well known from common observation, include running, immobility, fighting, tremor, crying, and screaming, to mention a few. A large number of autonomic changes accompany these states, including, for instance, changes in blood pressure, size of pupil, heart rate, skin temperature, respiration, salivary secretion, sweating, and gastrointestinal activity. Both the sympathetic and parasympathetic divisions of the autonomic nervous system are involved in these effects, though the sympathetic nervous system plays a predominant role on the whole (Gellhorn and Loofbourrow, 1963).

Various endocrine changes also occur, notably the increased secretion of epinephrine by the adrenal medulla and the release of ACH by the adrenal cortex. The electroencephalogram in emotion displays a pattern indicating a high degree of arousal, and Lindsley (1951) has emphasized the role of the reticular activating system in emotion.

THE JAMES-LANGE THEORY AND THE ROLE OF AUTONOMIC AROUSAL IN EMOTION

It is apparent that in emotional states a high level of autonomic activity accompanies the emotional feeling. One of the major questions which has exercised psychologists of emotion is how these two conditions, that is, the autonomic arousal and the feeling state, are related. Sherrington (1906) put the question thus:

Does (1) the psychical part of the emotion arise and its correlate nervous action then excite the viscera? Or (2) does the same stimulus which excites the mind excite concurrently and *per se* the nervous centres ruling the viscera? Or (3) does the stimulus which is the exciting cause of the emotion act first on the nervous centres ruling the viscera, and *their* reaction then generate visceral sensations; and do these latter, laden with affective quality as we know they will be, induce the emotion of the mind? On the first of the three hypotheses the visceral reaction will be secondary to the psychical, on the second the two will be collateral and concurrent, on the third the psychical process will be secondary to the visceral.

Basically, the James-Lange theory of emotion is hypothesis 3. It proposes that emotional feeling is produced by and is secondary to the autonomic discharge generated by the stimulus. James also included motor responses along with autonomic discharge as determiners of emotional feeling. Thus, for instance, our feeling of fear is our awareness of the bodily changes such as dryness of the mouth, muscular tremor, and so on, which are part of the state of fear.

If this hypothesis were correct, then depriving an organism of information as to the state of its peripheral autonomic and somatic apparatus should result in a lack of emotional feeling. However, there are cases where injury to nervous pathways prevents the patient from feeling his body reactions, yet the patient nevertheless reports emotional states. Related experiments have been performed on animals. Sherrington (1906) demonstrated that dogs deprived of a considerable proportion of their sensory input would still manifest emotional behavior (anger, joy, disgust, fear). It could be argued against such animal studies that the hypothesis under discussion is one correlating feeling or introspectible states with autonomic and motor responses, and that this is possible only with human subjects. This objection is well taken if one is concerned only with James' original formulation. However, others have adapted his hypothesis to propose an effect of autonomic discharge on emotional behavior as well as on introspectible states, and the animal studies argue against this amended hypothesis.

Some have argued against the objection based on interference with the nervous system, that before these lesions were made, central events had been conditioned together through the mediation of peripheral autonomic responses, and that once such conditioning had taken place the peripheral autonomic changes were no longer necessary. To test this hypothesis, it would be necessary to deprive animals of autonomic information very early in life, so that such conditioning would not have a chance to take place. It should be pointed out in this regard that a dog described by Sherrington was very young when tested, and had never before had a chance to display one emotion that it was tested for: disgust for dog's flesh, which is a highly specific emotion.

A further criticism of the James-Lange theory, put forward by Cannon (1929), is that the visceral changes apparent in various emotional states do not differ sharply, as might be expected in this hypothesis. In fact, Cannon argued, the visceral discharge accompanying emotion is diffuse, and could not form the basis of our clearly differentiated emotions. Following such objections, attempts were made to correlate different patterns of visceral discharge with different emotional states. Ax (1953) and Schachter (1957) found that fear and anger were correlated with a similarly high level of autonomic arousal, but that they differed on some indices. Wolf and Wolff (1947) were able to observe physiological responses of the stomach wall in a patient with a gastric fistula. They found that fear and anger were correlated with different visceral patterns. However, not enough work has been done on this problem to state with confidence that fear and anger can be reliably differentiated on this basis. In addition, these studies do not elucidate whether the visceral changes were caused by, or themselves caused, the emotions.

Another line of criticism stems from work by Mandler (1962) and his co-workers, who concluded on the basis of various experiments that although people may be aware of a rather diffuse and global condition of emotional arousal, they are unable to discriminate discrete changes in autonomic discharge. If we are unable to detect such differences, they argue, it is difficult to see how they could form the basis of clearly differentiated emotions.

Further studies point to the conclusion that autonomic arousal influences emotional states in a rather global and diffuse fashion. Marañon (1924) injected patients with epinephrine, which mimics the action of the sympathetic nervous system. He found that some patients reported that they felt "as if" they were experiencing some emotion such as fear or happiness. A few experienced genuine emotion as a result, when reminded of emotion-arousing subjects. In a well-controlled study,

Schachter and Singer (1962) report that injection of epinephrine was found to invoke states of enhanced emotion, which were either anger or euphoria, depending on the social situation the subject was in. This effect depended on the subjects' not being correctly informed of the autonomic effects of the drug. It appears, therefore, that the subjects, unless informed otherwise, interpreted the autonomic effects of the drug as part of their feelings of emotion.

Schachter and Wheeler (1962) injected subjects with epinephrine, a placebo, or chlorpromazine (a sympatholytic agent). The degree of amusement which these subjects then displayed to a slapstick movie was found to be correlated with the degree of sympathetic activation produced by the injections.

Singer (1963) reports that rats given epinephrine showed more fear than controls in fear-producing situations, but that there was no difference in situations which were not fear producing. An analogous effect of depression of fear by chlorpromazine was also found.

These experiments indicate that the level of autonomic arousal generally affects the degree of emotion manifest, though generalized autonomic arousal alone does not appear to produce specific emotions. It might be pointed out that epinephrine, besides mimicking the action of the sympathetic nervous system, also has various effects on the central nervous system. The effect of epinephrine on emotion may therefore be due to any of several factors. Of course, this does not invalidate the hypothesis that its effect on emotion is due to its sympatheticomimetic action.

THE SYMPATHETIC NERVOUS SYSTEM AND AVOIDANCE LEARNING

The adrenal medulla secretes epinephrine and norepinephrine, and this activity is controlled entirely by pathways from the sympathetic nervous system. Conditions of stress, such as cold, pain, anxiety, exercise, or anoxia, will greatly increase this activity. Epinephrine and norepinephrine themselves mimic the action of the sympathetic nervous system.

Several learning theorists believe that the activity of the autonomic nervous system is a vital link in the process underlying avoidance learning. Mowrer (1950) suggests that autonomic responses produced by a noxious UCS become conditioned to a neutral CS by a process of classical conditioning. These autonomic responses themselves produce stimuli (SD), the termination of which is reinforcing to the animal. The animal therefore learns by instrumental conditioning to terminate those unpleasant SD which occur in the presence of the CS, by performing whichever act removes the CS. In this way the animal avoids the

UCS. Mowrer considered the SD produced by noxious stimuli and conditioned to the CS to be exclusively autonomic. Since the secretions of the adrenal medulla have an effect mimicking the action of the sympathetic nervous system, removal of the medulla should remove a large number of these SD and so should retard avoidance learning (since the degree of SD reduction should determine the degree of learning).

However, experiments investigating the effects of adrenal demedullation on avoidance conditioning have yielded conflicting results. Moyer and Bunnell (1959) performed a bilateral adrenal demedullation on a group of rats and found that this group did not differ significantly from operated or nonoperated controls with respect to the number of trials to criterion or number of shocks during avoidance training in a shock alley. Nevertheless, Levine and Soliday (1962), using a shuttle box, found that with efficient training procedures adrenal demedullated rats performed fewer avoidance responses than controls. Also, Caldwell (1962) reports that demedullated mice, trained in a shuttle box before operation and then tested for retention, took longer to reach criterion and showed longer latencies at first than did operated or nonoperated controls when they were first tested.

Other workers have studied the effects of injection of epinephrine on fear-motivated behavior. Kosman and Gerard (1955) injected rats with epinephrine and then tested them for escape and avoidance responding in a shuttle box. A decrease in the frequency of escape and avoidance responses was noted, but the authors considered the effect due to general debilitation caused by the drug. Moyer and Bunnell (1958) report that injections of epinephrine did not alter the acquisition of a CAR. However, Latané and Schachter (1962) conclude that if the correct dosage is given, a facilitation of avoidance learning can result from epinephrine injection. Rats injected with a weak dose learned an avoidance response more quickly and effectively than placebo-injected rats, but rats given a heavy dose did not differ significantly from placebo-injected rats.

In another experiment to test the importance of the autonomic nervous system in avoidance conditioning, Wynne and Solomon (1955) blocked the peripheral autonomic reactions of dogs by various procedures, and trained them in a shuttle box. These animals were retarded both in their escape and avoidance of shock, though they could in fact learn. The authors conclude that autonomic responses play an important role in avoidance conditioning, but that aversive SD must also be produced in other ways.

The suggestion that avoidance learning is critically dependent on the degree of antonomic arousal related to a fear state is not without difficulties. Some have found that when measures of fear are taken at various stages of learning and extinction, they do not correlate with what should be expected on such a hypothesis. Kamin *et al.* (1963), for instance, observed the suppressive effect of the CS in a Skinner box at various stages of acquisition and extinction of a shuttle box avoidance response. They found that subjects which had been trained to a moderate extinction criterion were still very fearful of the CS. The decline in fear seemed to be an effect rather than a cause of the extinction procedure. They write: "The data on the whole reveal a considerable lack of parallelism between fear and instrumental behavior." Using heart rate as an index of autonomic behavior during avoidance acquisition and extinction, Black (1959) also describes a lack of parallel between autonomic and behavioral responses during extinction.

THE ADRENAL CORTEX AND AVOIDANCE LEARNING

The adrenal cortex secretes various steroids which are important for the maintenance of health and combating the effects of stresses of various kinds, including cold, heat, pain, and infection. Bilateral removal of the adrenal cortex results in a very much greater susceptibility to all kinds of trauma. Adrenal cortical function is controlled almost completely by ACTH released from the pituitary. Almost any environmental change will increase the secretion of ACTH, including cold, heat, pain, fright, and infections.

Since fear is a potent stimulus to ACTH secretion, psychologists have been interested in the consequences of increasing or reducing the degree of adrenal cortical activity on fear-motivated behavior. For instance, Solomon and Wynne (1954) propose two ways in which neuroendocrine discharge might enter into the process of avoidance learning. First, they propose that such a discharge is part of the pain-fear reaction to aversive stimuli, which also includes autonomic discharge, skeletal motor discharge, and higher nervous activity. This neuroendocrine discharge, they suggest, results in chemical feedback, the termination of which is reinforcing to the animal. They in effect espouse a two-factor theory such as that of Mowrer, except that they also assign a role to feedback stimuli other than autonomic. Second, in order to explain the extreme resistance to extinction displayed by animals after avoidance conditioning, they propose that avoidance training results in a permanent increase in the probability of occurrence of an anxiety reaction in the presence of the conditioned stimulus ("the principle of partial irreversibility"). They suggest that the action of the adrenal cortex may play an important role in this permanent change, which they propose takes place in the central nervous system. Selye (1950) also proposes a "general adaptation syndrome," characterized by a permanent partial reorganization of hormonal functioning under conditions of stress.

The body of experimental evidence, however, has not led to any definite conclusions concerning this hypothesis. Mirsky et al. (1953) found that monkeys injected with ACTH showed less fear-motivated inhibition of a bar-press response for food than controls. Also, monkeys injected with ACTH during extinction of a habit acquired to avoid shock showed more rapid extinction than controls. However, Murphy and Miller (1955) found, using a shuttle box procedure, that rats given ACTH during conditioning took significantly longer to extinguish than did controls. No significant effect was found on the number of trials to criterion, however, and the administration of ACTH during extinction was found ineffective. Miller and Ogawa (1962) tested adrenalectomized rats and found that ACTH administration during learning delayed extinction of the avoidance response in this group too. And, as with Murphy and Miller's experiment, there was no effect on conditioning. Since these rats were adrenalectomized, the authors conclude that ACTH must have exerted its effect through some extra-adrenal mechanism.

Moyer (1958) showed that animals subjected to bilateral total adrenalectomy were not retarded in the performance of an escape response, as compared with operated and nonoperated controls. Furthermore, Levine and Soliday (1960) made lesions in the median eminence of the tuber cinereum in the hypothalamus, which has the effect of blocking ACTH release to trauma (McCann, 1953), though constant amounts of ACTH continue to be secreted. They found that lesioned subjects paradoxically showed *superior* avoidance learning in a shuttle box, and suggest that a high degree of anxiety may make learning less efficient and that secretion of ACTH during stress may actually be a disadvantage in such situations. An alternative interpretation of these results is that the lesions made the animals hyperactive; but even if this were correct, the experiment still shows that releasing ACTH during stress does not appear to be of vital importance in learning situations.

ADRENAL FACTORS AND FEAR INCUBATION

Kamin (1957) showed that aversively conditioned responses are better retained initially and after 24 hours than at times intermediate between these. There is an initial decrement in avoidance responding, which is then followed by an improvement. (The large number of studies of this phenomenon have been reviewed by Brush, 1970.) It has been suggested by Levine and Brush (Levine and Brush, 1967; Brush and Levine, 1966) that the ability to perform the avoidance response is related to the hormonal state of the animal after stress. After shock, a corticotropin-releasing factor produced by the hypothalamus causes the release of ACTH (adrenocorticoptropic hormone) from the anterior pituitary. After an aversive stimulus is applied, the plasma concentration of ACTH rises to a maximum in approximately 2.5 to 5 minutes and subsides to near normal levels in 5 to 10 minutes (Hodges and Veruikos, 1959; Sydnor and Sayers, 1954). The adrenal cortex responds to the circulatory ACTH by a release of corticosteroid hormones. Such corticosteroid hormones reach their maximum concentration in the plasma after one to two hours and subside to low levels after four to eight hours (Fortier, 1959; Jones and Stockliam, 1966). This longtime course occurs after such stress as is produced by surgery. The time course of corticosteroid response after footshock can be much shorter (Fortier et al., 1959; Friedman, 1967). Brush and Levine (1966) and Levine and Brush (1967) have shown a correlation in time course between the decrease in corticosteroids and a decrement in performance which occurs after avoidance training in the shuttle box. Further, they showed that injections of ACTH or hydrocortisone one hour after training, when performance was normally depressed, abolished such a depression. It seems, therefore, that low levels of corticosteroids lead to poorer levels of performance in the shuttle box and that increase in such levels improves performance.

However, neither active avoidance learning nor shuttle box learning is affected by adrenalectomy (Applezweig and Moeller, 1959; Bohus and Endroczi, 1965; Moyer, 1958). More directly, the Kamia effect was found in rats below the age at which the corticosteroid response to stress develops (Klein and Spear, 1969) in hypophysectomized rats (Marquis and Suboski, 1969) and in adrenalectomized rats (Suboski et al., 1970). Recent studies have suggested that the decrease in performance, followed by an increase, is more likely to be a memory phenomenon. Klein and Spear (1970a) and Bintz (1971) trained rats on an avoidance task, the acquisition of which was retarded by the previous learning of another avoidance task. Interference between the two tasks was least at times when there was the greatest degree of depression in the performance of the first task. Interference was greatest when the second task was learned immediately after training on the first task and 24 hours later. If the decrement in performance on the first task at intermediate times was due to lessened fear or lowered hormones, it is difficult to see how these factors could lead to an increased efficiency of performance of a similar but conflicting task. However, if the memory of a conflicting task is poorer, it is easier to acquire another task.

Klein and Spear (1970b), in another experiment, retested rats at various times after avoidance training, each test being preceded by footshock. The footshock was meant to reestablish cues present during original learning. Such treatment led to an abolition of impairment of performance at intermediate times. Performance at intermediate times was as good as immediately after learning and 24 hours later. While it is claimed that the footshock reactivated the memory of original learning and so improved performance, this explanation is difficult to reconcile with the results of the experiments (Klein and Spear, 1970a; Bintz, 1971), where training on a conflicting habit was actually superior at intermediate times. It is difficult to see why the footshocks applied during training of the conflicting habit did not also reinstate the memory of the first habit at intermediate times.

A further contradiction in these findings is found in an experiment by Spear, Klein, and Riley (1971). In this experiment, simple footshock has no apparent effect in producing memory decrement 24 hours later, when administered 2.5 hours before passive avoidance learning. On the other hand, active avoidance learning, instead of simple footshock, did have an effect. So in one experiment footshock had an effect in producing cues similar to those in avoidance learning (Klein and Spear, 1970a) whereas in another experiment simple footshock had no such effect (Spear, Klein, and Riley, 1971). Spear, Klein, and Riley (1971), when they gave rats active avoidance training 2.5 hours before passive avoidance training, found poor retention of the passive avoidance training 24 hours later, compared with groups where the active avoidance had preceded passive avoidance training either by 5 minutes or 24 hours. Footshock 2.5 hours before the passive avoidance training had no such effect. The authors interpret their finding in terms of state dependency. The difference in the state of the rat 2.5 hours after stress (corticosteroids, etc.) and 26.5 hours after is greater than 24 hours and 48 hours after. Unfortunately for this interpretation, the number of trials required to learn the passive avoidance task 2.5 hours after the active avoidance was much smaller than when such training took place 5 minutes or 24 hours later. If such a reduction is due to a general tendency to freeze at the 2.5-hour interval, the real learning of the task may actually be very poor. When the general tendency to freeze has worn off, it will manifest itself as poor "retention."

THE LIMBIC SYSTEM

"Limbic system" refers loosely to a group of structures and their interconnections that are thought to be concerned with the development and elaboration of various emotions. Though different writers vary in their definition of the exact scope of the system, the structures involved generally include the cingulate and hippocampal gyri, hippocampus, orbitoinsulatemporal polar region, amygdala, septum, hypothalamus, epithalamus, and the dorsomedial and anterior thalamic nuclei. Other terms, such as "rhinencephalon," "olfactory brain," and "visceral brain," have also been employed to refer generally to the same group of structures. Historically, the term "limbic system" derives from Broca's term "limbic lobe," which he employed to refer to the cingulate and hippocampal gyri. These regions have recently been held to be important components of the anatomical substrate of emotion.

Papez (1937) first emphasized the possibility that some anatomical "circuit" involving limbic structures may underlie emotional thought and expression. He wrote:

The central emotive process of cortical origin may then be conceived as being built up in the hippocampal formation and as being transferred to the mammillary body and thence through the anterior thalamic nuclei to the cortex of the gyrus cinguli.

He thus hypothesized a circuit underlying emotion that runs as follows: hippocampus—fornix—mammillary bodies—mammillothalamic tract—anterior thalamic nuclei—thalamocortical radiations—gyrus cinguli.

The basis for Papez's choice of these structures rested mainly on a few clinical observations. For instance, in rabies, a disease characterized among many other things by emotional outbursts, brain lesions occur in the hippocampus (as well as in other areas). He also cites a case report of the association of degeneration in the gyrus cinguli with emotional outbursts. But in spite of this paucity of evidence, his hypothesis gave rise to a vast amount of animal experimentation, involving stimulation and ablation of these and related structures. As other regions of the brain were also found by these experiments to be implicated in emotional processes, various attempts were made to elaborate and subclassify this ever growing group of related structures and interconnections.

Maclean (1949) was one of the first to elaborate the Papez circuit. Later, different investigators tended to include different structures and classify them along different principles. Brady (1958, 1960) divided limbic structures into three main groups. The first group, the paleocortical or allocortical portions of the system, comprised those surface structures meeting the criteria for "cortex" suggested by Rose and Woolsey (1948), and included the hippocampus, pyriform lobe, and the olfactory bulb and tubercle. The second group, the juxta-allocortical portions of the system, intermediate between the phylogenetically old and phylogenetically young cortex, included the cingulate gyrus, presubiculum and, frontotemporal cortex. The third group was made up of subcortical structures and included the amygdaloid complex, septal region, certain portions of the thalamus and hypothalamus, and also—perhaps—the caudate nucleus and the midbrain reticular formation.

Pribram and Kruger (1954) subdivided the limbic system according to a different principle, olfactory connections. The first group, termed rhinal, consisted of structures with direct connections with the olfactory bulb. These included the olfactory tubercle, area of diagonal band, prepyriform cortex, and corticomedial nuclei of the amygdaloid complex. The second group, termed paleol, consisted of structures with direct connections with the first system but none with the bulb, and included subcallosal and frontotemporal juxta-allocortex, septal nuclei of the amygdaloid complex, and "olfactory" portions of the corpus striatum. The third group, termed hippocampal-cingulate, consisted of structures with direct connections with the second system but none with the bulb or with the first system, and included Ammon's formation and the entorhinal, retrosplenal, and cingulate juxta-allocortex (Fig. 9-1).

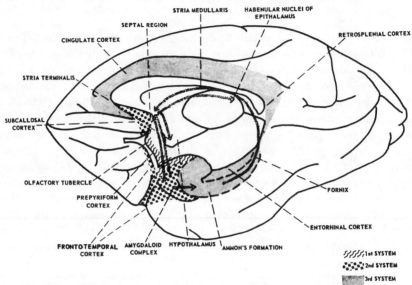

FIG. 9-1. Mediobasal surface of the monkey brain, showing limbic structures classified into three systems according to olfactory connections. (From Pribram, K. H., and Kruger, L., 1954, *Annals of The New York Academy of Sciences,* 58:116.)

It should be pointed out, however, that though there is some usefulness to be derived from classifying these limbic structures in an orderly fashion, a "true" classification of the system as it is involved in emotion can be arrived at only after the exact nature of the involvement of each of these structures and their interrelations in emotional processes has been thoroughly understood. At present we are far from this goal. Therefore we shall investigate what is known from stimulation studies of the involvement of central nervous structures in fear and rage.

STIMULATION STUDIES

Midbrain and Diencephalon

Stimulation of various regions in the midbrain and diencephalon has been found to give rise to reactions of fear and rage. Using lightly

anaesthetized cats, Ranson and Magoun (1933) obtained splitting movements upon stimulation of the subfornical component of the medial
forebrain bundle. Magoun et al. (1937) obtained in the lightly anaesthetized cat and monkey coordinated facial and vocal activity closely resembling that occurring during the expression of unpleasant emotion in
the normal animal when they stimulated the central gray matter and
tegmentum of the midbrain, and also certain hypothalamic areas. In
the unanesthetized cat, Hess (1928) obtained various manifestations
of rage from brain stem areas. Masserman (1941) produced rather
stereotyped and undirected rage manifestations from the hypothalamus.
Later Hess and Brugger (1943) and Hess, Brugger, and Bucher (1945)
obtained from the perifornical nucleus and preoptic area of the hypothalamus and the ventral septal region complex manifestations of rage
during which the animal would effectively direct its attack. Ingram
(1952) found that stimulation of the dorsomedial nucleus of the hypothalamus gave rise to expressions of rage. Spiegel, Kletzkin, and Szekely
(1954) produced defensive behavior when they stimulated in the peri-
aqueductal gray matter and neighboring areas. Delgado, Roberts, and
Miller (1954) obtained a fear-like reaction in cats upon stimulation
of the superior part of the tectal area and the lateral nuclear mass
of the thalamus. Maclean (1957) found that chemical stimulation in the
region of the central gray matter would produce a furious animal.

Some have observed a distinction between brain stem placements
yielding flight and those yielding aggression. Hess (1954) reports that
stimulation of the posterior hypothalamus yielded flight and more anterior
placements yielded rage. In the cat, Hunsperger (1956) obtained an
aggressive reaction from the perifornical region of the hypothalamus
and also from the central gray matter of the midbrain. These two regions
he found to be surrounded by a larger common field, from which flight
responses were obtained (Fig. 9–2). Nakao (1958) reports that aggressive responses were generally elicited in the cat from sites in the middle
hypothalamus and flight reactions from rostral hypothalamic or preoptic
sites.

Roberts (1958a) also divides aversive responses elicited from the
brain stem into two main groups. The first, which he termed "flight,"
was obtained upon stimulation of a small area in the posterior hypothalamus. The second, which he termed "alarm," and which included a much
more heterogeneous group of responses, could be obtained from placements scattered widely through the midbrain and diencephalon (Fig.
9–3). Roberts (1962) obtained fear-like behavior upon stimulation of
the cat thalamus. He classified these responses into three groups: a
visual searching response, a pain-like response (elicited mainly from
the posteroventral nucleus), and a crouching response (elicited mainly
from a region around the dorsomedial nucleus).

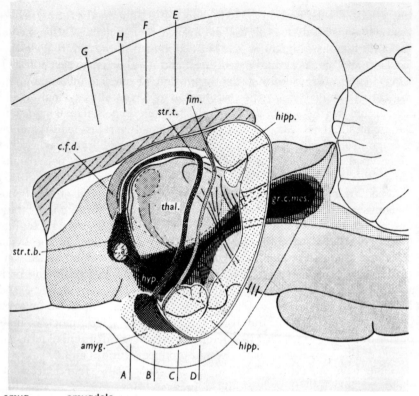

amyg.	amygdala
c. a.	commissura anterior, anterior commissure
c. f. d.	columna fornicis descendens, descending column of the fornix
fim.	fimbria
gr. c. mes	griseum centrale mesencephali, central gray matter of the mesencephalon
hipp.	hippocampus
hyp.	hypothalamus
str. t.	stria terminalis
str. t. b.	stria terminalis bed
thal.	thalamus

FIG. 9–2. Regions in the forebrain and brain stem of the cat from which affective responses were obtained by Hunsperger (1956) and de Molina and Hunsperger (1959). Two saggital levels are plotted in this figure. (From de Molina, A. F., and Hunsperger, R. W., 1959, courtesy of *J. Physiol.*, 145.)

Cholinomimetic agents produce aggressive behavior and killing in rats. Cholinergic blocking agents reverse the effect. The experimental areas were the lateral hypothalamus (Smith et al., 1970) and the amygdala (Igic et al., 1970).

The dissociation between the two different types of effect obtained by these various authors is not complete. Hess (1957) reports that,

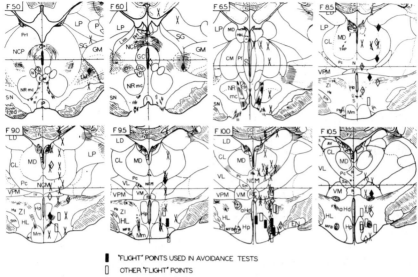

I   "FLIGHT" POINTS USED IN AVOIDANCE TESTS
[] OTHER "FLIGHT" POINTS
♦ "ALARM" POINTS USED IN AVOIDANCE TESTS
◊ OTHER "ALARM" POINTS
X POINTS ELICITING LITTLE OR NO EMOTIONAL BEHAVIOR
? POINTS RESEMBLING BOTH "FLIGHT" AND "ALARM"

FIG. 9–3. Series of frontal sections through the diencephalon and midbrain of the cat, showing sites yielding flight and alarm responses. (From Roberts, W. W., *J. Comp. Physiol. Psychol.*, 51; courtesy of the American Psychological Association.)

with the same stimulation, one type of reaction may be transformed into another. Also, Hunsperger (1959) found that increasing the intensity of the stimulation in the same placement may sometimes change an aggressive reaction to one of flight, or the other way round. Nakao (1958) writes that in some animals the reaction appeared mixed, including both attack and escape elements. Also, the fear and rage areas suggested by the various authors differ considerably, and there is considerable overlap in the pooled results. Further, caution should be observed in view of the report (de Molina and Hunsperger, 1959) that the individual character of the animal may affect the type of response obtained: a timid cat would tend to show flight for instance. Since reported findings represent the pooled effects obtained from many animals, it is difficult to say how much this factor of individual difference may have influenced results. Nakao, who used 50 cats, reports that only in three animals could he elicit either flight or aggression, depending upon which placement was used—a very small number.

However, separate regions for defensive and aggressive behavior have been reported in the opossum (Roberts, Steinberg, and Means, 1967).

Stimulation of a ventral zone in the midhypothalamus (including the ventromedial nucleus) produced defensive threats. On the other hand, stimulation of the dorsolateral midhypothalamus and the dorsolateral preoptic area produced biting attacks in other animals. Such responses are not completely stereotyped and depend in part on an appropriate object for their evocation. For intance, more attacks were made on live animals than on dead animals or inanimate objects.

MacDonnell and Flynn (1964) have found points in the thalamus which produced hunting-like behavior. Stimulation of sites in the midline thalamus and the medial portion of the dorsomedial nucleus of the thalamus produced stalking and hunting behavior in the cat. The behavior was a somewhat specialized form of aggressive behavior because hissing, vocalization, arching of the back, and striking movements were never elicited. Instead, the attack was often preceded by a slight crouch. If the rat was at some distance, "the typical movement was a sudden, low to the ground, direct-line approach followed by a hard-biting attack." Such a description makes it unlikely that the cat was attacking because it was being hurt. Some of the thalamic points elicited attacks when stimulated as above, and these were divided into two classes: stimulation of the first *facilitated* attack behavior elicited from hypothalamic sites, and stimulation of the second *suppressed* attack elicited from hypothalamic sites. Other thalamic sites, while not eliciting attack in themselves, facilitated attack from hypothalamic sites.

Interpretation of the Effects

Are True Rage and Fear Produced by This Stimulation? Masserman (1941, 1943) claimed, on the basis of his observations on hypothalamically elicited "fear" and "rage" responses, that stimulation merely evoked the motor manifestations of fear and rage and that the reactions did not indicate true emotionality. He gave various reasons for this:

1. An animal made "aggressive" by hypothalamic stimulation would not appropriately direct its attack; neither would an animal thus made "fearful" appropriately direct its escape.

2. The induced reaction ceased abruptly and completely upon cessation of the electrical stimulus.

3. The stimulus, while inducing the reaction, would not inhibit any other behavior in which the animal was indulging. A cat would continue to lap milk, clean itself, and purr in response to petting, while at the same time exhibiting the motor and autonomic manifestations of rage and fear.

4. No conditioned reaction to a light or sound stimulus could be obtained after it had been paired a very large number of times with the hypothalamic stimulation.

He therefore concluded (1941) that "the activity induced by hypothalamic stimulation is mechanical, diffuse, stereotyped, stimulus-bound, and seems to carry no greater emotional connotation than would the contraction of a skeletal muscle induced by the stimulation of an efferent nerve."

However, the findings of later investigators are on the whole at variance with those of Masserman. An animal stimulated in this way would be provoked to a well-directed attack on the experimenter (Hess and Akert, 1955; Akert, 1961; Nakao, 1958) or would make well-directed attempts to escape (Nakao, 1958; de Molina and Hunsperger, 1959). After cessation of the stimulus, the threshold for angry behavior remained at a low level for a longer period (Hess and Akert, 1955), and mewing and snarling often persisted after discontinuation of the stimulation (Nakao, 1958). Eglin (1953) (reported by MacLean, 1955) found (corroborating Masserman's findings) that animals receiving injections of physostigmine and acetylcholine in the lateral and posterior groups of nuclei in the hypothalamus also showed hissing, growling, and other manifestations of aggressive behavior, while at the same time licking the examiner's face between growls. However, Nakao (1958) reports that a hypothalamic stimulus, too weak even to cause overt responses, repeatedly caused a cessation of other behavior; for example, the animal would stop lapping milk.

Furthermore, a number of recent studies have shown that such hypothalamic stimulation may indeed serve as an unconditioned stimulus in conditioning experiments. Cohen et al. (1957) point out that in the usual avoidance conditioning situation the unconditioned stimulus, such as pain, produces an innate response on which the conditioned reaction may be based (e.g., electric shock applied to the feet induces running or jumping). They therefore selected for their experiment only those animals which included locomotor behavior of the running and jumping kind as part of their response to the hypothalamic stimulation. They then demonstrated that animals would learn to shuttle from one compartment to another in response to a tone in order to avoid the hypothalamic shock. They noted, further, that presentation of the CS would evoke generalized agitation in these animals.

Nakao (1958) found that after many presentations of a buzzer followed by hypothalamic stimulation the buzzer alone induced various signs of agitation. Animals learned to escape from a compartment in which the hypothalamic stimulation had been given and to avoid a dish of milk in the observation cage when this had been associated with stimulation. Further, animals which had learned to push a paddle to escape and avoid shock to the feet pushed the paddle on the first trial that hypothalamic stimulation was administered. Earlier, Delgado et al. (1954) reported that stimulation of brain stem areas which elicited a fear-like reaction in cats could motivate the performance of a response previously established to avoid shock. Such animals would also learn to escape from a compartment in which they had been stimulated and to avoid food which had been associated with the stimulation. Delgado et al. (1956) also found that stimulation of various subcortical structures in the monkey, including the amygdala and central gray matter, elicited a previously learned avoidance response.

It has been suggested (Akert, 1961) that the reason why Masserman failed to obtain conditioning to hypothalamic stimulation may have been that this stimulation set up afterdischarges antidromically in the hippocampus. Such hippocampal seizures have been shown to disrupt learning.

Another possibility as to why Masserman's animals would not react to a conditioned stimulus is that the hypothalamic stimulation may have been rewarding as well as aversive. Roberts (1958a) reports that animals with "flight" placements would not show an emotional reaction to a CS, nor would they learn a response to avoid the stimulation. They would, however, learn to escape it. In contrast, "alarm" placements elicited avoidance learning. Roberts (1958b) then showed that stimulation of "flight" placements was also rewarding to the animals, and concluded that this was probably the cause of the lack of avoidance. Bower and Miller (1958) also produced rewarding, along with aversive, effects when they stimulated placements in the middle to anterior portions of the medial forebrain bundle.

Finally, various investigators (e.g., Hunsperger) have reported that in addition to placements yielding integrated defense reactions, other placements have yielded various components of aversive responses, such as growling, without eliciting the whole pattern. It is possible that Masserman was studying these borderline placements. In sum, it appears that stimulation of some placements yields reactions which appear to have the properties of a true emotion, and with other placements there is some doubt about this.

Causes of such Rage and Fear Reactions.   Assuming that true fear and rage can be produced by stimulation of at least some brain stem loci, there are two main possibilities to account for this. The first is that some central mechanisms specifically concerned with fear and rage are being stimulated, and the second is that these effects are due to pain or some other unpleasant sensation. If the latter were the case, then these findings would be more relevant to the study of central somesthetic mechanisms than to the study of emotion. On the other hand, as though we were tapping regions which are normally excited in the presence of certain stimuli (such as the sight of a predator or prey) to produce behavior connected with fear and aggression. Of course nothing definite can be concluded about an animal's sensations. This is where stimulation studies on human patients provide us with valuable information.

The hypothesis that these emotional responses are due to pain has been examined by several investigators. With stimulation of these areas, it is always possible that current spread to structures such as the dura, blood vessels, or classical pain pathways might cause pain, or that pain pathways as yet uninvestigated are being stimulated. Miller (1961) describes an animal in which a rage reaction was evoked upon stimulation, and in which the tip of the electrode was later found to be below the base of the brain. Further, the exact course of the nervous pathways mediating sensation, including pain, is still unclear (see Sweet, 1959; Perl, 1963), but it appears diffuse and may well include several regions from which emotional responses have been elicited. And some workers have actually concluded that their effects probably were due to pain. An animal, when hurt, displays a characteristic set of reactions which an experimenter may come to recognize. Such reactions have been reported from hypothalamic stimulation in cats and monkeys by Karplus and Kreidl (1928), by Spiegel et al. (1954) in cats upon stimulation of the mesencephalic tectum, and by Delgado (1955) in the monkey upon stimulation of the lateral part of the tegmentum, central gray, posteroventral nucleus of the thalamus, crus of fornix, and posterior hippocampus.

Further evidence that stimulation of the midbrain tegmentum may produce pain arises from human studies. Spiegel and Wycis (1961) report that after lesions involving a large area of the spinothalamic system (the classical pain pathway), stimulation a few millimeters ventrally, apparently in the midbrain tegmentum, elicited conscious pain sensations. Also, Reyes et al. (1951) found that stimulation of the mesencephalic tectum produces pain in patients.

However, others have concluded that the reactions they obtained from animals upon stimulation in these areas were definitely not pain-suggestive. For instance, a description which is often chosen of a cat so stimulated is that it behaves as if confronted with a dog (Hess, 1957; Hunsperger, 1959). But this does not exclude the possibility of a sensory artifact of some sort. Different unpleasant sensations may give rise to different behavioral reactions. Consider, for instance, the development of an intense itch, or a feeling of suddenly being too hot. One sensation might make an animal feel that another animal is responsible, and so make it attack the nearest object in sight, and another might make it want to run away. This possibility should be considered especially if we bear in mind that some brain stem areas yielding defense and flight responses overlap with areas yielding other types of response. For instance, with stimulation of the preoptic area of the hypothalamus, "the animal then behaves as if exposed to a rather high ambient temperature" (Akert, 1961). Sneezing, retching, and vomiting also occur from regions overlapping with some of the areas evoking affective responses.

Roberts (1958a) reports that animals with "alarm" placements showed very variable behavior, with a number of interfering effects, and suggests a possible sensory explanation for effects obtained from these regions. Behavior elicited from "flight" placements, however, did not give this impression.

In human patients, although White (1940) reports no sensory changes resulting from hypothalamic stimulation, Heath and Mickle (1960) write that the patients report "marked discomfort" in the form of tachycardia, flushing, etc., resulting from stimulation.

Perhaps the answer is that with some placements the effect is due to sensory phenomena, but that with other placements this is not so. Placements in the anterior hypothalamus, investigated by Roberts and Kiess (1964), appear to be related directly to aggression. Stimulation of these regions caused normally placid cats to attack rats ferociously, and during such stimulation cats would learn a Y maze to obtain a rat which they could attack; that is, the performance of the attack was positively reinforcing. With regard to fear, an experiment by Deutsch and Howarth (1962) indicates that stimulation of certain placements is related to fear motivation, and here it is very difficult to see how a sensory artifact could account for the results. Deutsch and Howarth first trained rats to press a lever to obtain brain stimulation, and then held them away from the lever until they lost interest. They then found that fear-producing stimuli (buzzer and shock) recalled the rat to the lever (though its pressing on these occasions never produced further brain stimulation), and also increased rates of lever pressing for long periods. This occurred often in animals with tegmental placements but infrequently in animals with hypothalamic placements. The authors conclude that "electrical self-stimulation in some sites may be caused by an activation of mechanism underlying normal fear and escape."

Amygdala

Manifestations of fear and rage have also been obtained upon stimulation of the amygdala. Kaada, Anderson, and Jansen (1954) obtained these manifestations when they stimulated the lateral part of the basal nucleus and the lateral nucleus. Ursin and Kaada (1960) obtained an attention response, and fear and rage effects, from the basal and lateral nuclei and also from an area extending medially through the area of the central nucleus and into the internal capsule. Magnus and Lammers (1956) implicated the central, medial, basal, and mediobasal nuclei in emotional responses. Shealy and Peele (1957) implicated basal, lateral, central, and medial components. Wood (1958) obtained emotional responses from basal and central nuclei. De Molina and Hunsperger (1959) produced affective responses from the dorsal portion of the basal nucleus and adjacent parts of the central nucleus and medial nucleus, that is, in a field from which several components of the stria terminalis arise. They also traced affective reactions along the pathway of the stria terminalis into the bed nucleus of this tract at the level of the anterior commissure. At this level, they report, the field spreads out and joins the region producing emotional effects in the hypothalamus and midbrain (Fig. 9–2).

Opposite effects have, however, also been reported. Anand and Dua (1956) found that amygdaloid stimulation in some cases had a quieting effect on animals. In one case sleep was produced. Fonberg and Delgado (1961) report that in some cases amygdaloid stimulation appeared to make cats friendlier and less hostile. Egger and Flynn (1963) write that in some cats normal mousing was blocked by amygdaloid stimulation. Also, hypothalamically elicited attack of rats was blocked by amygdaloid stimulation. Amygdaloid placements producing these effects were found in the medial portion of the lateral nucleus and the magnocellular portion of the basal nucleus. However, in other regions, noticeably in the area of the dorsolateral portions of the lateral nucleus, electrical stimulation facilitated the attack response.

Various investigators have claimed that regions yielding fear and rage are to some extent topographically separate. Ursin and Kaada (1960) conclude that the two areas yielding fear and rage run approximately parallel in a medio-dorso-caudal direction. Fear results from stimulation in an area extending from the rostral part of the lateral nucleus and the preamygdaloid area through the region of the central nucleus. Anger is induced from more ventro-medial and caudal regions. Both zones extend into the internal capsule (Fig. 9–4). They write: "In our experience fear and rage have been obtained from the same electrode on two occasions only." Magnus and Lammers (1956) report that fear occurred from the periamygdaloid area and the central, medial, and mediobasal nuclei. Anger was elicited from the medial nucleus and the ventral part of the basal nucleus. Shealy and Peele (1957) obtained an escape reaction from basal and lateral components and a few central placements, and a rage reaction from medial and central areas.

Others have concluded that no such topographical division exists. De Molina and Hunsperger maintain that points yielding flight lay scattered between those yielding rage, the former being much less common than the latter. Some have gone even further and asserted that fear or rage may be elicited from the same placements. Gastaut et al. (1952) report that attention occurs with low stimulation, fear and flight with higher intensities, and rage with intensities which are higher still.

Interpretation of These Effects

As was discussed for brain stem stimulation, the question arises whether the induced fear and rage may be secondary to some unpleasant

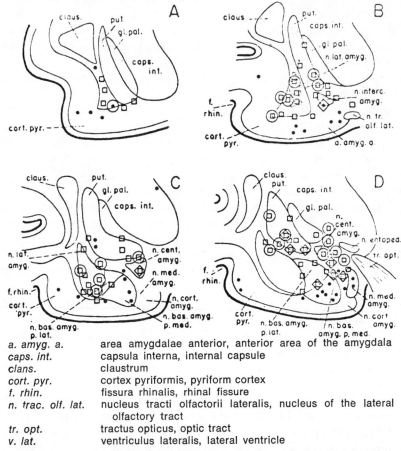

a. amyg. a.	area amygdalae anterior, anterior area of the amygdala
caps. int.	capsula interna, internal capsule
clans.	claustrum
cort. pyr.	cortex pyriformis, pyriform cortex
f. rhin.	fissura rhinalis, rhinal fissure
n. trac. olf. lat.	nucleus tracti olfactorii lateralis, nucleus of the lateral olfactory tract
tr. opt.	tractus opticus, optic tract
v. lat.	ventriculus lateralis, lateral ventricle

FIG. 9–4. Series of frontal sections through the amygdala in the rostro-caudal direction showing points yielding attention, anger, fear, and combined effects. (From Ursin, H., and Kaada, B., 1960; by permission of *EEG Clin. Neurophysiol.*, 12.)

sensation caused by the stimulation. In a large proportion of cases, stimulation of the amygdala produces fear or rage and is accompanied by other effects, such as micturition, defecation, spitting, salivation, motor effects, behavior resembling an attempt to eject a foreign body from the mouth or throat, and so on. Magnus and Lammers point out that licking movements obtained upon weak stimulation may change into gagging and vomiting with higher intensities, and finally to flight and attack with the highest intensities.

One argument against the sensory explanation is that these supplementary effects are also elicited from regions outside those producing

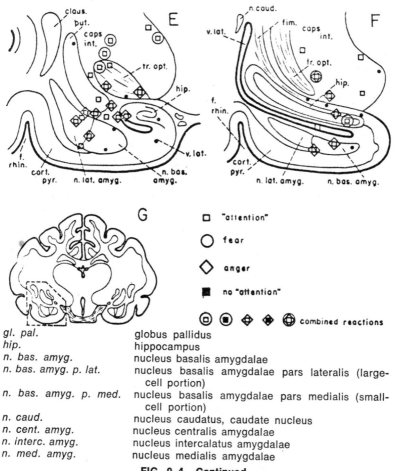

gl. pal.   globus pallidus
hip.   hippocampus
n. bas. amyg.   nucleus basalis amygdalae
n. bas. amyg. p. lat.   nucleus basalis amygdalae pars lateralis (large-cell portion)
n. bas. amyg. p. med.   nucleus basalis amygdalae pars medialis (small-cell portion)
n. caud.   nucleus caudatus, caudate nucleus
n. cent. amyg.   nucleus centralis amygdalae
n. interc. amyg.   nucleus intercalatus amygdalae
n. med. amyg.   nucleus medialis amygdalae

FIG. 9–4—Continued

affective reactions (de Molina and Hunsperger, 1959; Ursin and Kaada, 1960). This argument is not entirely conclusive, however, since the degree of resultant distress might be the factor determining whether or not the animal will react emotionally.

In some cases the effects may be caused by unpleasant hallucinations. Ursin and Kaada (1960) write that anger elicited from rage placements "seemed to be directed towards something imaginary." Extracts quoted by Magnus and Lammers from their protocols include: "Looks as if she were seeing something." "Shrinks back to the Lt. and tends to turn over to the Lt. as if she had a disagreeable hallucination."

Possibility of Seizures. Naquet (1954) has pointed out that stimulation of the amygdala may give rise to an electrical afterdischarge projected to the septum, hypothalamus, and parts of the cortex. Such a discharge may produce various autonomic and motor phenomena, and also, sometimes, growling and fear manifestations. Injection of alumina cream into the amygdala will produce spontaneous seizures which mimic the effects of stimulation, including the fear manifestations. Amygdaloid stimulation will also sometimes trigger hippocampal seizures which may give rise to fear and rage manifestations.

One should be able to decide on behavioral grounds whether fear symptoms produced by stimulation are actually the result of a seizure process. With seizures, the behavioral symptoms occur after a delay and may considerably outlast the stimulation. The animal underreacts to external stimuli and its fear does not appear to be related to any object in the environment. This fits some descriptions of stimulated animals, but other experimenters report symptoms which arise and cease concomitantly with the stimulation, during which time the animal is prone to attack any object in its environment. It therefore appears that only some fear and rage symptoms resulting from amygdaloid stimulation are due to a seizure process.

Hippocampus

Fear and rage reactions have been produced by some upon stimulation of the hippocampus (Kaada, Jansen, and Anderson, 1953; Gastaut et al., 1952; MacLean and Delgado, 1953), though negative results have also been reported (Liberson and Akert, 1955). De Molina and Hunsperger (1959) write that the hippocampus is on the fringe of the area which produces affective reactions, and only marginally yields emotional responses.

Delgado (1955) obtained pain-suggestive responses in monkeys upon stimulation of the posterior hippocampus and crus of fornix. Kaada et al. (1953) favor an interpretation in terms of hallucinations for the affective reactions which they evoked upon hippocampal stimulation in cats. The animals would direct their attention toward something imaginary, and there was a diminished reactivity to actual stimuli in most cases. The possibility that these effects are due to seizure discharge is very strong.

Neocortex

Fangel and Kaada (1960) obtained definite manifestations of fear and flight in cats upon stimulation of a few points in the lower ends of the posterior sylvian, ectosylvian, and suprasylvian gyri, and from some placements in the cingulate cortex. Rage was never obtained from cortical placements by these experimenters. Sano (1958) also reports anxiety and fear in cats upon stimulation of the posterior suprasylvian gyrus, but not rage. A much lower proportion of "affective" placements was found in this area as compared with the amygdala. Kaada, Jansen, and Anderson (1953) obtained behavioral effects upon stimulation of the cingulate and hippocampal gyri similar to those found for the hippocampus and fimbria. Finally, Anand and Dua (1955) found that stimulation of the temporal tip in cats and monkeys produced "irritability." Stimulation of the posterior orbital surface of the frontal lobe produced viciousness in cats only for placements very near the tip of the temporal lobe. Stimulation of other placements in this area, both in cats and monkeys, made the animals very quiet. Stimulation of the anterior cingulate gyrus produced irritability in monkeys and intense rage in cats.

However, since high intensities are necessary to produce "affective" responses from the cortex, as opposed to the amygdala and the brain stem, one cannot be certain that these cortical structures are really responsible for the effects (Hunsperger, 1959).

Temporal Lobe Stimulation in Patients

The responses of patients to brain stimulation are particularly enlightening since they provide introspective reports as well as behavior to study. Such reports may help us to decide whether the fear and rage manifestations observed in animals are due to direct activation of fear and rage mechanisms or whether they are secondary to some unpleasant sensation or hallucination.

During operation, epileptics have frequently been found to report feelings of fear upon stimulation of parts of the temporal lobe. Such feelings appear to be a genuine result of the stimulation, and not due to a general fear of the operative procedure, since they occur only with stimulation of some regions and not others. Such effects have been obtained from the anterior and inferior surfaces of the temporal lobe (Penfield and Jasper, 1954; Penfield, 1958; Roberts, 1961). In contrast, anger and other types of emotion were not evoked.

Jasper and Rasmussen (1958) found practically no emotional responses upon stimulation of the amygdala and hippocampus. However, sensory responses, sometimes unpleasant, were often produced. They concluded from these findings that the amygdala and hippocampus are not important integrating centers for emotional experience. Pampiglione and Falconer (1960) further report that out of 17 patients suffering temporal seizures, stimulation of the hippocampus evoked fear or rage in none. Sensory effects occurred sometimes.

In contrast, Chapman et al. (1954) and Chapman (1958) describe feelings of fear and anxiety upon amygdaloid stimulation in four out of five epileptic patients. Assaultiveness was never obtained, even though the patients were spontaneously assaultive. Heath and Mickle (1960) report reactions of both fear and rage resulting from stimulation of the amygdala and rostral hippocampus in schizophrenics. Heath et al. (1955) found that in one schizophrenic woman the evoked response, using the same placement and the same parameters of stimulation, was variable, sometimes eliciting fear and sometimes rage.

Interaction with the Patient's Illness. The advantages of being able to obtain introspective reports from patients undergoing electrical brain stimulation are qualified by the fact that all such patients are seriously ill. The responses of schizophrenics should be viewed with suspicion since their spontaneous speech and behavior are very abnormal. Further, many have affirmed that temporal lobe stimulation produces only psychical responses in patients who had previously had epileptic discharges in the temporal lobe (Baldwin, 1960; Penfield and Jasper, 1954; Jasper and Rasmussen, 1958). Stimulation of the temporal cortex even in patients with epileptic foci in the parietal or frontal lobe does not result in such responses. It has also been observed that the responses emitted by these patients may closely resemble those forming part of the patient's seizure pattern, though this is only sometimes true. This does not necessarily mean that such data obtained from epileptics do not shed light on normal function. It may simply be that epilepsy renders the cortex more susceptible to stimulation, and the results obtained may genuinely reflect the function of these regions under normal conditions. This is especially so when a good topographical agreement between different types of response can be shown upon comparing results from different individuals.

CLINICAL STUDIES OF BRAIN PATHOLOGY

Emotional changes have been shown to occur in patients with brain lesions caused by various factors, including physical trauma, infections, disease, and hereditary and other disorders.

Encephalitis lethargica is an example of an infectious disease which produces acute emotional changes. This disease affects the whole of the central nervous system in small disseminated foci, but particularly affects the brain stem (Von Economo, 1931). In its acute form, great apathy is often manifest, and lack of emotion often occurs in its chronic form. Outbursts of extreme emotion can also appear. In rabies, which also produces lesions located mainly in the brain stem, extreme emotional outbursts occur too.

Patients with tumors involving the hypothalamus and surrounding structures may show emotional changes. Alpers (1937) describes a patient with extensive destruction of the hypothalamus who became very aggressive and defensive. Cushing (1932) reports cases of tumors in the pituitary region which were accompanied by emotional changes such as periods of fright or emotional negativism. A case of a tumor involving the chiasm and spreading into the ventricle was associated with extreme symptoms of rage, such as shrieking, clawing, and scratching, alternating with periods of somnolence. From another point of view, Gibbs (1956) correlated abnormalities of electrical activity in the brain with various abnormalities of behavior and concluded that the presence of rage was correlated with abnormal activity assumed to emanate from the thalamus and hypothalamus. However, it should be stressed that emotional changes are not listed among the most common symptoms produced by hypothalamic lesions (Le Gros Clark et al., 1938).

Zeman and King (1958) note that a clinical syndrome of hyperemotionality, including outbursts of violence and constant crying, may be associated with tumors of the anterior midline structures, especially the septum pellucidum and the fornix.

Patients with brain disease involving frontal tissue often show outbursts of emotionality. In addition, a pathological appearance of frontal tissue was found by Slocum et al. (1959) to be associated with symptoms of extreme anxiety and depression. Ackerly and Benton (1948) describe a case of bilateral frontal lobe defect in which the patient was unable to form any but superficial and transient emotions.

In psychomotor epilepsy, which results from seizure discharges originating in the mesial temporal region, feelings of fear may occur at the start of an attack (Macrae, 1954; Weil, 1956; Williams, 1956). Such ictal symptoms of fear have been shown not to be due to fear of the oncoming fit or to any other such circumstance but to occur simply in isolation as auras, analogous to the somatic, gustatory, or other sensations which may occur at the onset of an attack. Rage has only rarely been reported to occur as an aura (Gastaut et al., 1955). However, aggressive behavior often appears once the attack is in full swing. This may be related to the finding that stimulation of the amygdala only very rarely causes aggression in patients, even those about to be operated on for intractable assaultativeness (Chapman, 1958, 1960). Perhaps, for aggression to occur, the discharge must spread from the amygdala to other structures.

Patients suffering from psychomotor epilepsy often exhibit personality disturbances which may be described as in some ways the reverse of the Kluver-Bucy syndrome (see Chapter 10): a tendency to explode into violent anger, loss of sexual urge, and appetite disturbances (Gloor, 1960). This may result from a continuous irritative process due to the lesion.

Finally, in view of the many though divergent findings on limbic system structures, a report of normal mentality associated with gross anatomical defects in rhinencephalic areas is of special interest. Nathan and Smith (1950) report the case of a man who died of cancer and who, before death, was intensively studied as part of a program concerned with operation for the relief of pain. He was intelligent, social, and popular, and appeared perfectly normal both intellectually and emotionally. When he died and his brain was examined, it was found, however, that in place of a corpus callosum and gyrus cinguli there was an irregular mass of white matter covered by overlying gray matter. The fimbria and fornix were absent, as was the septum pellucidum. The amygdala was grossly abnormal. The hippocampus was very small and abnormal, and its only efferent pathway was to its fellow on the opposite side. This well-documented study demonstrated that at least in one individual a number of limbic structures are not indispensable for emotion.

chapter 10

Emotion II: Ablation Studies

EARLY ABLATION AND TRANSECTION STUDIES AND THE PROBLEM OF SHAM RAGE

Early experimenters investigated emotional changes resulting from extensive ablation or transection procedures. The early preparations were classified into two main groups. *Decorticate preparations* typically (Dusser de Barenne, 1920; Rothman, 1923; Cannon and Britton, 1925; Bard, 1928) exhibited fully fledged rage responses, which were, however, poorly directed. These responses would often occur not only to noxious stimuli but also to normally innocuous stimuli, such as those produced by light stroking. *Decerebrate preparations* (Woodworth and Sherrington, 1904; Bazett and Penfield, 1922) exhibited signs of rage, sometimes even to normally innocuous stimuli (Keller, 1932), but their repertoire of response was limited compared with that of decorticate preparations.

Later, full-scale experiments utilizing large numbers of animals were carried out in order to define more precisely the nature of the emotional changes resulting from various lesions. From such studies Bard and his collaborators arrived at the following generalizations:

1. Bilateral removal of neocortex alone induces a state of extreme placidity.

2. Further destruction of certain forebrain structures, even ablations large enough to include most of the diencephalon, produces a ferocious animal, with much lower rage threshold than normal, but with poorly directed attack.

3. This integrated rage response may be elicited in preparations with extensive forebrain damage, provided the caudal half of the hypothalamus remains intact. When this is removed, as in the decerebrate preparation, the rage response becomes more circumscribed, less well integrated, and of higher threshold.

4. The lower the level of decerebration, the more fragmentary the rage response becomes (Bard and Macht, 1958).

Bard and Mountcastle (1948) concluded that destruction of the amygdaloid complex and the transitional cortex of the midline was crucial to whether or not decortication rendered an animal placid or ferocious. They therefore concluded that the cortex normally exerts an inhibitory (as well as facilitatory) influence on rage-provoking mechanisms in the brain stem, this inhibitory influence being mediated via the amygdaloid complex and transitional midline cortex. When this inhibitory influence is removed, the rage threshold is lowered.

Bard adopted the term "sham rage" (introduced by Cannon and Britton, 1925) to describe animals with a lowered rage threshold resulting from decortication. He explained (1934) that the term "sham" was chosen not as a behavioral description but because the conscious aspects of emotion are assumed to be missing in animals without neocortex. However, the term is generally employed to refer to a characteristic group of symptoms. Bard and Mountcastle (1948) present a vivid description of such an animal, whose lesions are shown in Figure 10–1.

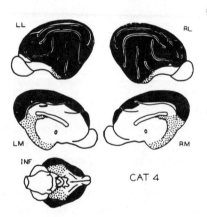

CAT 4

FIG. 10–1. Diagrams showing the extent of lesions produced in cat 4. Solid black: regions removed in the first and second operations, which resulted in a state of placidity. Stippled areas; regions left intact in the first and second operations but ablated in the third operation, which produced a state of ferocity. (From Bard, P., and Mountcastle, V. B., 1948; courtesy *Res. Publ. Assn. Nerv. Ment. Dis.*, 27.)

When the cat was lifted from her cage she growled, spat and bit. Light pinching of the skin of her tail, flnak or back produced growling, spitting, biting and striking, acceleration and deepening of respiration, marked dilatation of pupils, and piloerection. In her poorly directed attack she bit herself viciously.

From the second day after the third operation until she was sacrificed 160 days later, *Cat 4* invariably responded to the most trifling disturbance by a savage exhibition of rage. Tactile, pressure and vibratory stimuli were equally effective in eliciting all the motor phenomena which make up the full expression of feline anger. Merely placing a hand lightly on her flank or back produced hissing with lips retracted and tongue curled, growling, flattening of the ears, tail-lashing, acceleration of respiration, dilatation of pupils, erection of hair over tail or back, and profuse sweating from the toepads. Any stimulus of the body extremities or tail greater than a gentle stroke evoked in addition savage biting and striking with unsheathed claws. If the stimulus was applied to the tail or near the midline of the body the attack was directed forward or downward and sometimes she bit her forepaws. When it was applied well to one side of the midline she turned a little to the stimulated side but never sufficiently to reach the source of the stimulation. The threshold for effective tactile stimulation was higher around the neck, occiput and top or sides of the head than over the trunk, tail and extremities. A light puff of air directed at her face sufficed to provoke spitting, growling, retraction of ears, widening of pupils, piloerection, and the assumption of a belligerently defensive stance, but this reaction was not produced by tapping her on the nose. The cat occasionally hissed in the absence of any apparent external stimulus but we never observed any spontaneous development of an integrated rage reaction. . . .

Provided she was in her cage, tapping it always elicited several definite signs of anger. The same response could be obtained by knocking on a table when she was sitting or crouching on it. We were never able to induce any sign of pleasure. Stroking her back or lightly rubbing her head or cheeks invariably caused growling and spitting.

One explanation of decorticate sham rage, alternative to that of a release of rage mechanisms from cortical inhibition, is that the changes observed are really sensory in origin, and that these animals are hyperalgesic. Human cases of hyperpathia resulting from subcortical lesions present a picture with various relevant features (see Chapter 6). Often the response to noxious stimulation is greatly exaggerated, and a discrete stimulus such as a pinprick may give rise to a very disagreeable diffuse sensation localized over a large area of the body. Later, stimuli not usually considered painful at all, such as light touch and vibration, may produce this same intense disagreeable sensation. In some cases a state of perpetual intense pain may develop. In comparison, sham rage preparations exhibit rage to normally innocuous stimuli; the rage reaction is typically poorly localized (which may indicate a diffuse sensation), and different parts of the body have different "rage thresholds." The animals' reactions appear at times more appropriate to pain than to rage: they were described on occasion as licking themselves, and as biting themselves rather than their environment. Such animals would also constantly rub themselves. The stimulus threshold for rage often became progressively lower, until sometimes the animal would bit itself constantly. Finally, although most of these preparations were bilateral, Bard and Rioch (1937) report several animals with unilateral ablations which exhibited a lower rage threshold only to stimuli on the ipsilateral side. Cat 244, for instance, which sustained ablation of the right cortex, exhibited violent rage upon light mechanical stimulation of the right side. The threshold, though low over the entire right half of the body, was especially low at the ear and the feet. Stimuli adequate to evoke the reaction on the right side failed to do so on the left.

If decorticate sham rage phenomena are really due to sensory changes, then the notion of a cortical inhibitory influence on brain stem rage mechanisms should be reexamined. Perhaps future experimentation will elucidate this further.

LESIONS IN VARIOUS BRAIN STRUCTURES AND THEIR EFFECTS ON EMOTIONALITY

Midbrain

Kelly, Beaton, and Magoun (1946) found in cats that lesions in the central gray matter of the midbrain and adjacent parts of the tegmentum produced a specific loss in certain kinds of emotional response. Facio-vocal expression of negative emotions was greatly impaired, whereas other ways of expressing these emotions, such as clawing and flight reactions, were preserved, as were other facio-vocal activities such as purring. Recent experiments of Hunsperger (1956) and de Molina and Hunsperger (1962) on the cat indicate that midbrain structures are indeed critically involved in fear and rage. They found that after bilateral lesions in the midbrain region, from which hissing was obtained upon stimulation, hissing could no longer be elicited from the hypothalamus. Further, a unilateral lesion in this midbrain area suppressed ipsilaterally, but not contralaterally, the aggressive response obtained upon stimulation of the amygdala. Finally, bilateral lesions in this region produced a permanent impairment of naturally elicited aggressive reactions. Since this placidity did not occur with similar lesions in the hypothalamus or amygdala, de Molina and Hunsperger conclude that the central gray of the midbrain is of supreme importance in the elicitation of defensive behavior.

Hypothalamus

Lesions involving various parts of the hypothalamus have been found to produce either a loss in emotional responsiveness, or an increase in fear and rage reactions, or no emotional changes. Such differences can to some extent be correlated with the locus of the hypothalamic lesion.

Bard considered the presence of the caudal half of the hypothalamus to be of critical importance for the elicitation of a well-integrated rage response. This conclusion was arrived at as a result of observations on large numbers of animals in which varying amounts of forebrain had been removed (Bard, 1928, 1934; Bard and Rioch, 1937). Bilateral lesions in the caudal hypothalamus have been found by others (Ranson, 1939; Ingram et al., 1936) to produce a loss in emotional responsiveness, in addition to somnolence and depression of general activity. Masserman (1938, 1943) reports similar findings. He cautions, however, that animals in this condition suffer gross impairment of bodily functions, so that this loss in emotional responsiveness is difficult to evaluate. This is especially so since those animals which survive long enough to reestablish their bodily functions to nearly normal levels also recover emotionally.

Others have described animals with large circumscribed hypothalamic lesions which can exhibit well-integrated rage reactions. Kelly, Beaton, and Magoun (1946) report that two cats in which the hypothalamus was completely destroyed at the mammillary level exhibited growling, crying, and spitting to nociceptive stimulation, and pupillodilatation, retraction of the nictating membranes, piloerection, spitting, and striking movements in the presence of barking dogs. Magoun and Bard (quoted by Bard and Mountcastle, 1948) observed three cats with very extensive hypothalamic lesions which displayed "vigorous well-integrated rage reactions."

In an earlier experiment Keller (1932) produced a "typical rage response" in what was essentially a pontile animal, this differing from the normal only in that the "somatic effectors are not coordinated into an escape or defensive pattern." This, he remarks, is only to be expected in an animal which "lacks sight, hearing, smell, and the ability to localize disturbances at the periphery." The threshold for rage in such an animal was found to be very low since it was evocable by gentle handling and even the animal's own sneezing. From such experiments it appears that hypothalamic mechanisms are not indispensible for the elicitation of rage.

De Molina and Hunsperger (1962) also conclude that hypothalamic mechanisms are less critical than midbrain mechanisms in the elicitation of rage. They observed that bilateral lesions of the hypothalamic zone which yielded hissing upon stimulation abolished the electrically induced affective response obtained from the amygdala, but did not abolish the response obtained from the midbrain (Hunsperger, 1956). In contrast, midbrain lesions abolished the response from the hypothalamus. A unilateral hypothalamic lesion produced an ipsilateral suppression of the pattern evoked from the amygdala. However, naturally evoked aggressive behavior was unaffected by such lesions, in contrast with midbrain lesions.

Wheatley (1944) describes a dramatic increase in ferocity in cats with lesions in the ventromedial nucleus of the hypothalamus. Similar results were obtained by Anand and Brobeck (1951) on rats. Wheatley suggests that the ventromedial nucleus usually exerts an inhibitory influence on rage-producing mechanisms. Hunsperger (1959), however, favors the possibility that the effect is due to a chronic irritative effect of the lesion on structures from which fear and rage may be elicited. Wheatley himself doubts the irritative hypothesis since the effect is long lasting, but this is not conclusive since permanent irritative scars can be formed.

Thalamus

The dorsomedial and anterior nuclei of the thalamus project to the granular cortex of the frontal lobe and the cingulate gyrus respectively. These areas are of special interest to neurosurgeons concerned with providing relief from various neurotic and psychotic symptoms (see below).

Anterior Thalamic Nuclei. Schreiner et al. (1953) report that destruction of the anterior thalamic nuclei in the cat produced an elevated rage threshold and overly solicitous responses to pleasurable stimuli. However, Brierley and Beck (1958) found no such changes in either the cat or the monkey.

Dorsomedial Nuclei. Although Spiegel et al. (1949, 1951) observe that a reduction in aggressiveness and anxiety results from lesions in the dorsomedial nuclei in animals as well as in patients, Schreiner et al. (1953) found increased irritability and rage to result in cats. Chow (1954) obtained no behavioral changes as a result of bilateral lesions in the dorsomedial nuclei (but his lesions were small). Pechtel et al. (1955) stress that the preoperative and postoperative treatment of the subjects are crucial in determining the ultimate effects of such a lesion. On the whole, increased aggressiveness seemed to occur if the cats had been made experimentally neurotic before operation. Also, regular contact with other cats and human beings after the operation led to increased friendliness, which was not shown by animals kept in isolation. Brierley and Beck (1958) write that bilateral dorsomedial lesions in cats produce no changes in emotionality. However, the same lesions in the monkey produce hyperactivity, loss of fear reactions, and distractibility, together with a vacant facial expression. They conclude that the symptoms appear to be those characteristic of the frontal lobe syndrome, therefore justifying the attention of those interested in therapeutic effects of lobotomy and similar procedures.

Temporal Lobe

Kluver and Bucy (1937) found that bilateral anterior temporal lobectomy in monkeys results in a variety of extraordinary behavioral changes. (These were first noted by Brown and Shäfer in 1888, but were later forgotten.) These changes include (1) a loss of fear and rage reactions; (2) changed dietary behavior, often described as "indiscriminate"; for instance, the monkeys, usually frugivorous, would eat all kinds of meat; (3) an increase in sexual activity and also "perverted" sexual behavior; (4) hypermetamorphosis, or a tendency to attend to and, if possible, touch all things seen; (5) a tendency to examine all objects by mouth; and (6) visual agnosia, or an inability to recognize the meaning of objects presented visually.

Faced with this wide variety of symptoms resulting from one extensive ablation, other investigators have attempted both to separate the different symptoms anatomically by making more discrete lesions and to explain the various symptoms by postulating a change in a single underlying factor. A dissociation of the symptoms by anatomical means has not been very successful. There is, however, some evidence that visual agnosia may be separated from the loss of fear and rage reactions. Lesions in the ventrolateral portion of the temporal lobe produce considerable impairment in visual discrimination, seemingly alone (Mishkin, 1954; Mishkin and Pribram, 1954). Orbito-insulatemporal lesions or more restricted anteromedial lesions appear to produce the other components of the Kluver-Bucy syndrome without impairment of visual discrimination (Pribram and Bagshaw, 1953; Walker et al., 1953). However, Akert et al. (1961) found that, in monkeys, ablations restricted to the neocortical gyri of the temporal lobe, in which encroachment on rhinencephalic structures was functionally insignificant, produced a partial Kluver-Bucy syndrome, including psychic blindness, oral tendencies, and a taming effect. However, in this case the symptoms (other than psychic blindness) diminished considerably after three months.

The Amygdala

It is now generally believed that the structure most critically involved in the emotional (along with some other) changes in the Kluver-Bucy syndrome in the amygdala. Lesions in the amygdala (which also usually damaged the pyriform area in the cat and the uncus in the monkey) have been observed by many to result in increased tameness. This has been found true for rats (Anand and Brobeck, 1952; Woods, 1956), cats (Shreiner and Kling, 1953, 1956), lynxes and agoutis (Schreiner and Kling, 1956), and monkeys (Rosvold et al., 1954; Weiskrantz, 1956; Schreiner and Kling, 1956).

However, ablation of the amygdala has also been found to result in entirely opposite changes. Spiegel et al. (1940) and Bard and Mountcastle (1948) report a drastic increase in aggressiveness resulting from bilateral amygdalectomy. Wood (1958) observed the same effect with discrete bilateral lesions in the basal and central nuclei of the amygdala.

(Interestingly, these were the structures found by the same author to produce fear and rage when stimulated.)

Extensive amygdaloid ablations have been reported by others to produce no change in overt emotionality. King (1958) makes this observation in the rat, though he suggests that his animals may not have been emotional enough initially for a taming effect to become manifest. Hunsperger (1959) also found that extensive lesions in the amygdala produced no change in emotionality.

A complex result has recently been obtained by Ursin (1965a). He found that flight behavior in wild cats was significantly reduced by small bilateral lesions in the flight zone of the amygdala, previously mapped by stimulation experiments (Chapter 9, Fig. 9–4). However, no significant correlation was obtained between lesions of the previously mapped defense zone and a reduction of defensive behavior, though such a reduction was also obtained. However, in tame cats neither type of behavioral change was noted.

Various explanations for these discrepancies have been put forward. For instance, it has been suggested that the symptoms resulting from amygdalectomy are really due to inadvertent damage to other structures. Hunsperger (1959) suggests that concomitant damage to the pyriform area may be a critical factor. In support of this is the finding of Adey et al. (1956), who observed that damage to this area that leaves the amygdala intact produces tameness. However, Wood (1958) reports that discrete lesions in the pyriform cortex result in no behavioral changes.

Green, Clemente, and de Groot (1957a) emphasize that amygdalectomy may interfere with the blood supply to the hippocampus, producing damage which may render the animal prone to hippocampal seizures. Such seizures may include manifestations suggestive of fear and rage (see Chapter 9). Indeed, Green et al. (1957b) observed that bilateral lesions in the amygdala and surrounding tissue produced increased aggressiveness only in those animals which developed seizures, and in all of these there was extensive hippocampal involvement. In addition, these animals appeared hyperesthetic to peripheral stimulation.

Schreiner and Kling (1954) observed that animals made initially placid by amygdalectomy became hostile at the onset of hypersexuality, and suggest that this may be the basis for the reported discrepancies. However, as Gloor (1960) points out, Bard and Mountcastle's cats were not hypersexual; so this cannot wholly explain the differences.

Other writers have stressed that the emotional changes produced cannot simply be described in terms of "increased" or "decreased" aggressiveness or fear. In a study on dogs in which there were extensive lesions in the pyriform area and hippocampus in addition to the amygdala, Fuller et al. (1957) found that different tests yielded very different results. For instance, though these operates would not take the initiative and start a fight with other animals, they were capable of fighting as fiercely as the controls when aroused. Again, though they tended to keep away from people, they did not display various submissive forms of behavior usually associated with such timidity. Similarly Rosvold et al. (1954) report that amygdalectomy in monkeys results in all the subjects' appearing more aggressive in the individual cage situation. However, in the group cage situation, two out of three animals fell from the top to the bottom of the hierarchy.

The preoperative and postoperative treatment of the animals have also been considered crucial (Masserman and Pechtel, 1956). In the experiment of Rosvold et al., though two operates fell from the top to the bottom of the hierarchy, the third appeared more aggressive. This animal had been dominant for the longest time, and was after operation confronted with only submissive animals. Weiskrantz (1956) has also emphasized the importance of the way animals are treated in the postoperative recovery period. If the animals are constantly "tested" for reactivity to noxious stimulation, for instance, the constant unpleasant stimulation could make them become very wild. He suggests also that the effect of amygdalectomy may be mainly cognitive. The animals may find it difficult to recognize reinforcing stimuli as such, whether they be positive or negative. Sometimes this difficulty may be apparent in overgeneralization, as when an animal attempts to ingest anything or copulate with anything. On the other hand, it may also be manifest in an absence of response to normally fear- or rage-producing stimuli.

This cognitive hypothesis is attractive since it purports to explain other effects of amygdaloid lesions simultaneously with the resultant loss of fear and rage. Schwartzbaum (1960) carried out an experiment demonstrating that amygdalectomized monkeys did not react to a change in the degree of reinforcing value of stimuli as did normals. The amygdalectomized monkeys did not show the usual change in rate of lever pressing when the amount of reward was changed. However, a lack of emotionality could also have accounted for Schwartzbaum's results, as he points out. One difficulty with the cognitive hyothesis is that it does not explain why the amygdalectomized animal tends to eat more but be afraid less, rather than eat less and be afraid more; that is, the *direction* of the changes is not explained. Perhaps this could be related to the difference between autonomous drives and drives depending on peripheral stimulation for their arousal. Eating is not dependent on peripheral stimulation but fear and rage are. Sex is to some extent, but considerably less so than fear or rage.

Combined Lesions Involving the Amygdala and Other Structures

Amygdala and Ventromedial Nucleus of the Hypothalamus. In an experiment by Schreiner and Kling (1953), one male cat, rendered docile by amygdalectomy, later sustained lesions of the ventromedial nucleus of the hypothalamus. The effect of this second lesion was to make the animal very ferocious. However, Anand and Brobeck (1952) report that a rat, made ferocious as a result of lesions in the ventromedial nucleus, and which then sustained lesions in the lateral group of amygdaloid nuclei, was rendered quite tame by the second operation.

The above studies obviously did not employ enough animals for any definite conclusions to be drawn from them. In a larger study by Kling and Hutt (1958), four cats rendered ferocious by bilateral lesions in the hypothalamus, three of them in the ventromedial nuclei, sustained bilateral amygdalectomies. The second lesion in no way reduced the ferocity of these animals. Also, cats which had been rendered tame by lesions of the amygdala were rendered ferocious by the superimposition of bilateral hypothalamic lesions.

These findings set a limit to the number of possible hypotheses concerning the functions and interactions of these two structures with regard to fear and rage. One hypothesis consistent with the findings is that the amygdala exerts an inhibitory influence on structures in the ventromedial nucleus and that this nucleus in turn inhibits other structures responsible for the elicitation of fear and rage. The results of single-unit studies also indicate that the amygdala may exert an inhibitory influence on the ventromedial nucleus. Sawa et al. (1959) write that stimulation of the lateral, medial, and intermediate nuclei of the amygdala in cats caused either an inhibition of single-unit firing in the ventromedial nucleus or a transition of the responses from inhibition to facilitation, usually depending upon the characteristics of the stimulus. However, with repetitive stimulation of the amygdala, the effect on single-unit discharge in the ventromedial nucleus became much more strongly inhibitory. Evidence of other interactions between the amygdala and various other hypothalamic areas is discussed in the section on stimulation studies.

Amygdala and Septum.   King and Meyer (1958) studied the effects of superimposed septal and amygdaloid lesions in the rat. They found that rats showed a striking increase in emotionality with septal damage, and the effect of superimposing an amygdaloid lesion (mainly the lateral and basal nuclei were damaged) was to suddenly reduce this hyperemotionality to approximately preoperative levels. When the first produced lesion was in the amygdala, this had the effect of preventing the appearance of a full-blown septal syndrome.

Amygdala, Hypothalamus, and Midbrain.   On the basis of certain stimulation and lesion studies in the cat, de Molina and Hunsperger (1962) propose a different system of interaction between the regions yielding emotional responses in the amygdala and brain stem (Chapter 9, Fig. 9-2). They found that unilateral coagulation of the affective region in the midbrain suppressed ipsilaterally the affective pattern evoked from the amygdala. Bilateral coagulation of the midbrain field suppressed the pattern evoked from the hypothalamus. Unilateral coagulation of the affective field in the hypothalamus also suppressed ipsilaterally the pattern evoked from the amygdala. However, unilateral and bilateral coagulation of the amygdala did not affect the response obtained from the hypothalamus. Furthermore, unilateral coagulation of the stria terminalis suppressed ipsilaterally the pattern obtained from the amygdala, but did not affect the pattern obtained from the hypothalamus. In addition, coagulation of the amygdala or the hypothalamic affective region did not affect spontaneous affective behavior, whereas coagulation of the midbrain region produced placidity. (Hilton and Zbrozyna [1963] have produced evidence that the path carrying signals from the amygdala to the hypothalamus is the ventral amygdalofugal path of Nauta, a flat band of fibers lying above the optic tract.)

On the basis of these findings, de Molina and Hunsperger suggest that the system governing defensive behavior is organized at three levels of progressively increasing importance, the amygdala ranking lowest in the hierarchy and the affective region of the midbrain highest.

Hippocampal Fornix System and Septum

Ablation experiments involving the hippocampal fornix system and the septum have also produced equivocal results. Spiegel et al. (1940) report that lesions in the hippocampal fornix system, particularly those in which the lesions of the fornices encroached on the septum pellucidum, produced marked aggressiveness. Brady and Nauta (1953) observed that rats with septal lesions showed a significant increase in emotional reactivity and startle response. They demonstrated later, however (Brady and Nauta, 1955), that these symptoms disappeared within 60 days after operation. Study of the lesions led the authors to the conclusion that the fornix and hippocampus were probably involved in these effects. King (1958) also reports that rats with septal lesions show a dramatic increase in overt emotionality. However, Rothfield and Harmon (1954) found that bilateral interruption of the fornix resulted in a definite lowering of the rage threshold only in cats in which the neocortex had been removed.

However, many negative results have also been obtained. Hippocampal ablation in rats (Brady, 1958) and cats (Bard and Mountcastle, 1948) did not lower the rage threshold. Allen (1948) observed no emotional changes in dogs following removal of Ammon's horn or transection of the fornix on both sides. Destruction of the fornices produced no behavioral changes in cats (Wheatley, 1944) or monkeys (Garcia-Bengochea et al., 1951). Bond et al. (1957) found that bilateral lesions of the septum and fornix in cats resulted in no increase in rage reactions;

and Kling et al. (1960) report that lesions of the posterior septum, fornix, and anterior commissure did not produce even transient irritability.

One possible explanation for these discrepancies is that the regions investigated here are on the fringe of those for producing definite affective responses upon stimulation (de Molina and Hunsperger, 1959). The lesions may therefore sometimes produce chronic irritation of these areas.

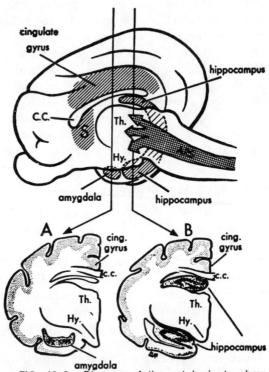

FIG. 10–2. Diagram of the cat brain to show limbic-system structures: the septum (*S*), the cingulate gyrus, the hippocampus, and the amygdala. At the top is a medial view of the brain after it has been sagitally sectioned. Diagrams *A* and *B* are cross sections through the halfbrain at the levels indicated by the vertical lines in the top diagram. While the cingulate gyrus and the septum are midline structures, the hippocampus and amygdala are located deeper in the cerebral hemisphere, as shown in *A* and *B*. All of these limbic structures are present bilaterally (*c.c* = corpus callosum, *cing. gyrus* = cingulate gyrus, *Hy.* = hypothalamus, *S* = septal area, *Th.* = thalamus). (From McCleary, R. A., and R. Y. Moore, 1965, *Subcortical Mechanisms of Behavior.* Courtesy of Basic Books, New York.)

The sometimes reported transient nature of the emotional effects, together with the variability of the findings, would tend to indicate an irritative factor. The exact placement of the lesion may be an important factor in determining whether such an irritative effect occurs.

Green (1960) points out that the hippocampus has an extremely low threshold for seizure discharge. In addition to other symptoms, behavior suggestive of fear and rage often occurs during such seizures, and the animal may appear hyperesthetic. Such lesions may produce an irritative scar which results in a chronic tendency to seizure discharge. Of course, if the behavioral effects under discussion occur during seizures, we cannot be sure that the hippocampus is involved in this particular behavior, since it may be initiated in some other part of the brain to which the seizure is propagated. It must also be stressed that different experiments have employed different species of animal, and some of the discrepant results may be due to anatomical differences between the species investigated (see Fig. 10–2).

Temporal Ablations in Human Patients

Many unilateral ablations of the anterior temporal lobe in man have been carried out for the relief of seizures, and no significant emotional effects have resulted. Bilateral lesions in the anterior temporal area have been produced in patients with severe psychomotor epilepsy and in patients with assaultive psychosis. A decrease in aggressiveness has been obtained in several instances (Green, Duisberg, and McGrath, 1951; Pool, 1954; Terzain and Ore, 1955), though the results have been very variable. Increased rage immediately after the operation, which later subsided, was observed in some cases (Sawa et al., 1954). Other symptoms analogous to those found in animals upon similar operations have also been reported by several investigators (Terzian and Ore, 1955; Pool, 1954; Sawa et al., 1954). On the whole, however, the findings in this area have been very variable, and it is difficult to conclude much from the studies since the patients involved were all very deteriorated before operation.

Anterior Cingulate Region

A temporary alteration in behavior, best generally described as a decrease in fear, has been reported by several investigators after anterior cingulate ablation in monkeys. Smith (1944) found this, as did Ward (1948), who also observed a lack of aggression and affection, and a general social indifference toward other animals. Glees et al. (1950) made similar observations, stressing the general abnormality of response to animate objects, which resulted both in decreased fear and aggression, and yet also an increased tendency to act in a provocative fashion. However, Mirsky et al. (1957) report that though such monkeys appeared less fearful of man, no gross abnormalities were apparent in the group cage situation, and the animals did not appear socially indifferent. Pribram and Fulton (1954) found that the sole effect of bilateral anterior cingulate lesions was a decrease in the duration of an avoidance reaction caused by a sudden frustration.

However, increased aggressiveness and a general overreactivity have also been observed with such lesions. Kennard (1955a) made this observation on cats, though she found the equivalent lesion in monkeys produced a nonaggressive attitude (1955b). It has been pointed out that the lesions sustained by Kennard's animals were not really in the anterior cingulate area; however, Brutkowski et al. (1961) found a similar increase in rage in dogs resulting from lesions in the genual portion of the anterior cingulate area, and so well within the region ablated by the above experimenters. Pechtel et al. (1958) also found an increase in aggression and a lowered threshold for startle responses as a result of ablation of the anterior cingulate area in cats and monkeys. Brutkowski et al. favor the hypothesis that increased rage is here due to hyperalgesia and is therefore sensory and not emotional in origin. Their animals appeared afraid of being touched. Such an intepretation is also very consistent with the other descriptions of such animals. Smith (1944) also observed an apparent increased cutaneous sensibility and vigorous reaction to very slight cutaneous stimulation.

Clinical Studies of Frontal Lobotomy

Following a report by Fulton and Jacobsen (in 1935) that bilateral prefrontal lesions in chimpanzees may reduce reactions to frustrating situations, Moniz (1936) carried out frontal lobotomies on several mental patients, with encouraging results. Relief from anxiety was found to follow this procedure, along with a certain "flattening" of the emotions; that is, such patients may be prone to emotional outbursts, but they are said to feel emotions less deeply and more briefly. Patients after this operation also display a general lack of perseveration.

More recently, attention has been focused on the more limited ablations of the anterior cingulate area and the posterior orbital cortex. Following reports from animal studies that anterior cingulate ablation appears to reduce fear, this operation was performed by various neurosurgeons in place of the more extensive lobotomy procedures to provide relief for patients suffering from chronic anxiety and obsessions (Tow and Whitty, 1953; Tow and Armstrong, 1954; Le Beau, 1954; Whitty, 1955). Success has been claimed especially for the treatment of chronic anxiety. Pathological worrying was greatly reduced, and, at least according to some investigators, this was accompanied by a reduction of other associated traits, such as self-consciousness, timidity, and excessive perseveration (Tow and Whitty, 1953). No intellectual deficit resulted from these lesions, and less "blunting of personality" than occurred following standard lobotomy.

A limited ablation of the posterior orbital cortex has been attempted especially for patients who are depressed and suffer from low psychomotor activity, mainly on the basis of the finding that posterior orbital ablations cause hyperactivity in monkeys (Dax and Radley-Smith, 1943). Some success has been claimed for this procedure (Fulton, 1951).

Recently, Slocum, Bennett, and Pool (1959) carried out a very thorough long-term study on 18 patients they had selected for frontal lobe surgery. All were suffering from very severe long-term anxiety which had proved unamenable to other treatment. They claim that excellent results were obtained. Interestingly, the operation revealed a pathological appearance of frontal tissue in a high proportion of patients. The authors therefore suggest that some organic brain disease may sometimes underlie such extreme anxiety symptoms.

LEARNING EXPERIMENTS INVOLVING LESIONS

Recently, investigators have become dissatisfied with the use of simple observation or rating scales for the detection of changes in fear-motivated behavior and have increasingly been testing animals in learning situations. They have hoped by this method to obtain a clearer picture of the nature of the resultant changes, for instance, in the case of decreased fear, whether fear responses were simply lost or whether they extinguished more rapidly, or whether perhaps the deficit was one of retention of previously learned fear responses.

However, once the animal is tested in a learning situation, many more factors must be taken into consideration in accounting for the observed changes than is necessary with simple observation. One reason why an animal may not learn an avoidance habit is that his fear and therefore his motivation to avoid has been reduced; an alternative explanation is that his general learning capacity has been rendered defective.

Another factor concerns the direction of the motivational change. When fear is extremely low, avoidance performance will obviously be inefficient. However, it appears that in some situations performance may also be less efficient when fear is very high. In a study of children, Penny and Croshery (1962) found that anxious subjects performed an avoidance response less well than nonanxious subjects. Levine and Soliday (1960) report that animals deprived of the ability to release ACTH under stress learned a shuttle box avoidance problem faster than controls, and this study also suggests that highly anxious animals may perform less well than animals which are less anxious. More specifically, in the shuttle box situation, one important factor in the acquisition of an avoidance response is that of overcoming a tendency to perform competing responses, such as freezing or leaping straight up into the air. From observation of animals in this situation, it appears that those which have been made very anxious tend to perform more of these competing responses. Therefore if a lesioned animal is shown to perform less well in a shuttle box, then, in the absence of further behavioral criteria, one may hypothesize that the animal is either much less frightened or much more frightened.

Another methodological point is made by Harvey et al. (1965). They found that septal-lesioned rats showed a deficit in shock-produced suppression of a lever-pressing response for water. However, the manifestation of this deficit depended critically on the strength of shock employed. They state: "Had the study employed only strong shocks the lesion would have appeared to be without effect; had it employed only weak shock the lesion would have appeared to block the aversive conditioning completely. The quantitative character of the effect only appeared with intermediate shock intensities." The parameters of the aversive stimulation used are therefore of critical importance in avoidance experiments.

A further possible source of error has been emphasized in a very interesting paper by McCleary (1961). Following the findings of Kaada (1951) that stimulation of the subcallosal cortex produced motor inhibitory effects whereas stimulation in the medial and anterior cingulate gyrus resulted in facilitation (Fig. 10–3), McCleary hypothesized that subcallosal lesions should disrupt avoidance behavior under circum-

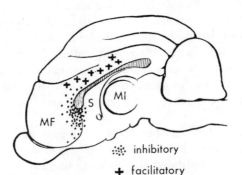

:::: inhibitory

+ facilitatory

FIG. 10–3. Midsaggital drawing of cat brain, indicating the regions on the mesial cortex yielding inhibitory and facilitatory motor effects. (From McCleary, R. A. 1961, data from Kaada, B.; courtesy of *J. comp. physiol. Psychol.*, 54, and American Physiological Association.)

stances requiring inhibition of responding (passive avoidance) and that lesions in the cingulate gyrus should disrupt avoidance behavior under circumstances requiring the making of an active response (active avoidance). He found that when avoidance was tested by measuring the degree to which a cat was inhibited in returning to a food trough after it had been shocked while eating, animals with subcallosal lesions appeared totally incapable of inhibiting their approach response, whereas both normal and cingulate lesioned animals very quickly inhibited their response. It was shown later (Lubar, 1964) that cingulate-lesioned animals actually avoided a source of punishment longer than normals. Yet when avoidance was tested in a shuttle box situation, cats with bilateral cingulate lesions were grossly deficient in avoidance, though they exhibited clear fear responses to the CS, whereas cats with bilateral subcallosal lesions were at least as efficient as normals, and the data suggest that their performance was in fact superior.

As for the question whether subcallosal and septal lesion should be treated separately, McCleary (1966) states that subcallosal lesions invade the septal area to one degree or another. Further, lesions limited to the septum are equally effective in producing the behavioral abnormalities produced by subcallosal lesions. The reason for this may be that the pathway leading from the subcallosal area courses through the septum to hypothalamic areas. There is electrophysiological evidence for such a pathway.

It has yet to be clarified to what the dichotomous results found by McCleary are due. One possibility is that they are due to changes in general activity. It has been found that animals with posterior orbital ablations suffer from motor restlessness. McCleary also reports that his subcallosal subjects were hyperactive in their home cages. Such hyperactivity might prevent them from avoiding a source of shock but might, if anything, facilitate shuttle box conditioning. McCleary did not observe any activity changes in his cingulate-lesioned animals, though he did not test specifically for this.

Another possibility is that such lesions interfere with the animals' ability to *initiate* a voluntary movement, or else to keep still purposely to attain some end—that is, that the deficits are in the "start" and "stop" systems (Vanderwolf, 1962). Thus an animal might be "reflexly" hyperactive but still be unable to initiate a movement to attain an end.

Thirdly, the effects may be specific to fear-producing situations. In such a situation an animal has two innate responses: it can run or it can freeze. A lesion may increase a tendency to freeze in an avoidance situation and so interfere with the animal's ability to escape effectively, but not with its ability to passively avoid a source of food. Or the lesion may increase the animal's tendency to run rather than freeze, so that it becomes unable to inhibit a movement to avoid shock. In a related study, Hearst and Whalen (1963) report that administration of d-amphetamine facilitated discriminated avoidance performance in a lever-pressing situation. However, rates of lever pressing in non-CS periods were unaffected. They interpret these results as due to the effect of amphetamine in breaking up freezing patterns.

Further, Vanderwolf (1963) found that rats which had been subjected to a series of electroconvulsive shocks learned a shuttle box task more readily than controls. The convulsed subjects were not hyperactive, however, and the author attributes their improved performance to the breaking up of freezing patterns by the ECS.

A further complication in the interpretation of these experiments arises from the findings that when cingulate-lesioned cats were trained in a one-way active-avoidance apparatus (instead of the shuttle box), they did not perform significantly worse than controls (Lubar, 1964). Two possible reasons for these contrasting results may be considered. Firstly, since the shuttle box task is a harder one to learn than either the passive-avoidance or the one-way active-avoidance tasks, the cingulate-lesioned animals may really be suffering an intellectual impairment. Secondly, it may be that freezing tendencies become particularly strong in the shuttle box situation. This is not unexpected, since in the shuttle box the animal is required to return to the compartment which it had just been required to avoid, and thus a "position conflict" is set up.

An experiment by Thomas and Slotnick (1963) makes it very likely that the explanation in terms of increased freezing in the shuttle box is correct. They conditioned sham-operated control and cingulate-lesioned rats in a double-grill box under high and low hunger drives. They found that although cingulate-lesioned rats under a low drive showed a significant deterioration in avoidance performance, cingulate-lesioned rats under a high hunger drive showed no performance deficit. It therefore appears that the hyperactivity caused by hunger counteracts the increased freezing tendency of the cingulate-lesioned animals. If their original deficit had been due to intellectual impairment, hunger should not result in improved performance.

Lubar (1964) also found that animals with cingulectomies in addition to limbic cortex-septal lesions showed normal passive avoidance. Thus the reduction in activity produced by the cingulate lesions counteracted the increase in activity produced by the limbic cortex lesions.

Other studies also point to the conclusion that cingulate lesions result in an increased tendency to freeze. Peretz (1960) reports that rats with anterior cingulate lesions required a greater number of trials to learn a shuttle box avoidance response than did sham operates. However, they performed better than normals on bar-pressing and discrimination tasks with food as the motivation. But in both the control tasks used, decreased motility may be associated with improved performance (see

Maher and McIntire, 1960). Also, active-avoidance deficits may be due to a tendency to freeze. Thus this experiment does not argue against McCleary's hypothesis.

Thomas and Slotnick (1962) observe that in rats bilateral damage to the cingulum produced significant retardation in the acquisition of an avoidance response in a double-grill box. However, maze learning was not significantly affected by the lesion. They hypothesize that this impaired acquisition of the CAR derives from an increased tendency to freeze. The worse performers in the experiment did indeed freeze more. (It seems, however, that the behavioral deficits thought to be characteristic of cingulate lesions are the consequence of damage to an adjacent structure, the lateral gyrus [Lubar et al., 1966, 1967]. Lesions of the cingulate gyrus alone produce little deficit in avoidance learning.)

Another interesting approach has recently been adopted by Hunt and his colleagues (Harvey et al., 1965; Harvey and Hunt, 1965). They point out that passive avoidance tasks rely heavily on appetitive drives. In one passive avoidance measure, the CER (conditioned emotional response), a lever-pressing habit is established for a reward (e.g., water). The animal is then presented several times with a CS followed by shock. The CS soon comes to elicit a suppression of the lever-pressing rate, together with crouching and defecation. The degree to which lever pressing is inhibited is then taken as a measure of avoidance. In other passive avoidance tasks the animal is required to inhibit its response to obtain food and water in order to avoid shock. One would therefore expect an animal's desire for food or water to affect its performance in these situations.

However, active avoidance tasks (such as shuttle box conditioning) do not also rely on appetitive drives. Supposing, therefore, that a lesion had the effect of making the animal more hungry or thirsty, this would reduce the effectiveness of shock in suppressing a food or water-obtaining response. However, this would not also impair shuttle box performance. It might be suggested further that the facilitation observed in shuttle box conditioning in such animals is also due to increased appetitive drive. Thomas and Slotnick (1963) found that cingulate-lesioned rats improved their shuttle box performance when they were hungry.

The hypothesis that passive-avoidance deficit is secondary to increased hunger or thirst has been intensively investigated for the septum. Animals with septal lesions exhibit a diminished strength of CER and also a deficit in the suppression of lever pressing by punishment (Brady and Nauta, 1953; Harvey et al., 1961). Further, the lesions with which McCleary (1961) obtained deficits in passive but not active avoidance (his "subcallosal" group) also invaded the anterior septal region. Also, Kaada et al. (1962) produced deficits in passive avoidance (avoidance of an electrified water dish) in rats with septal lesions. However, such animals will learn a shuttle box avoidance problem more rapidly than normals (King, 1958). This improvement of performance of rats with septal lesions in a two-way shuttle box has been confirmed (Krieckhaus et al., 1964; Kenyon and Krieckhaus, 1965a). On the other hand, septal lesions impair performance in a one-way shuttle box (Kenyon and Krieckhaus, 1965b).

Harvey et al. (1965) found that septal lesions produced deficits in discriminated shock-produced suppression of lever pressing for water reward. However, they also found that lesions in the septal region caused a consistent increase in water intake after deprivation. Furthermore, increasing the amount of water deprivation in sham-operated controls offset the differences in suppression between them and the septal animals. Harvey and Hunt (1965) showed that the effect of increased thirst on lever-pressing is manifested to a greater or lesser extent depending on the type of lever-pressing schedule used. Very careful controls are therefore necessary to establish whether or not a change in hunger or thirst occurs as a result of a lesion.

Septal lesions also increase food intake in the rat and the cat (Harvey and Hunt, 1961). A similar interpretation of the effect of septal lesions in impairing a shock-produced inhibition of responding for food therefore also appears reasonable.

Another factor to be considered in evaluating the effect of a lesion which alters avoidance responding is that of sensory changes. Harvey et al. (1965) measured the latency to tail flick in response to radiant heat in septal lesioned and sham-operated control rats. No differences were obtained. However, it appears that septal rats are slightly more sensitive to painful electrical shock as measured by the flinch-jump technique. Unfortunately, very few studies of this nature have been performed.

FURTHER STUDIES OF THE SEPTAL SYNDROME

McCleary (1961) suggested that the effect of subcallosal-septal lesions was to prevent an inhibition of responding, as stated above. Rats with septal lesions emit more responses than normal controls when working for reinforcement on fixed interval schedules, where an increase in response rate does not produce additional reward (Ellen and Powell, 1962). Even on schedules where frequency of reinforcement is lowered if responses are too frequent, septal rats respond more than normal controls (Ellen, Wilson, and Powell, 1964). Septal rats are also inferior to controls at staying away from a situation which produces punishment (passive avoidance) (Kaada, Rasmussen, and Kveim, 1962). Sodetz (1970) tested McCleary's theory by using a Sidman avoidance schedule.

On this schedule brief electric shocks are delivered to the animal at regular intervals in the absence of responding. When the animal responds, the shock is prevented from occurring for a fixed time after the response. If the animal responds again before shock has occurred, the shock is again postponed for an equal time. This means that if the animal responds at intervals which are less than the time for which a shock is postponed as a result of a response, then the animal can avoid all shocks. The optimal performance for the animal is to respond just before shock is due to occur. If the animal responds prematurely, he will have to respond more frequently in a given session in order to avoid all shocks. In McCleary's hypothesis, a septal rat would be expected to respond more frequently than a normal, and the results were quite striking. To quote Sodetz: "The septals acquired avoidance more rapidly than the control animals. The septals maintained the same terminal shock rate as the controls while consistently emitting fewer responses. The septal animals were found to have a higher probability of emitting responses with relatively long interresponse times." The results are clearly at variance with McCleary's hypothesis, which would predict the opposite result.

Because of the discrepancy between previous work on the septal syndrome and the findings of Sodetz (1970) (supported by those of Morgan and Mitchell, 1969), Kelsey and Grossman (1971) attempted to reconcile the differences by the use of the following hypothesis. They noted that in the experimental paradigms which have shown disinhibitory effects of septal lesions, the rats had been pretrained on habits requiring different types of responding. For instance, in many studies the rats were reinforced for every response (a CRF or continuous reinforcement schedule). The poorer performance of septal rats when another schedule was imposed in the experiment proper may have been due to interference. Instead of having to argue that the septal rats were less able to perform on various schedules, we can simply assume that septal rats are more susceptible to the effects of interference from previous training. In the experiments of Morgan and Mitchell (1969) and Sodetz (1970), no interfering pretaining had been used. In this way Kelsey and Grossman's hypothesis would explain the discrepancy between previous work and that of Sodetz and Mitchell and Morgan.

Such a hypothesis is rendered plausible by the analogy of hippocampectomized rats. Once a hippocampectomized rat has been trained on a schedule that reinforces every response (CRF), it cannot be trained to respond on a schedule which differentially reinforces low rates of responding (DRL). On the other hand, such a rat can be trained on a DRL schedule if this schedule is used from the start and no CRF pretraining is used (Clark and Isaacson, 1965; Schmaltz and Isaacson, 1966).

However, when Kelsey and Grossman tested septal rats in a task in which premature responding delays reinforcement for food (DRL schedule) without any other previous training, septal rats were still inferior to controls. They made more premature responses, and also often waited much longer than necessary to make a response after they had completed the delay necessary to obtain another reward. However, when an external one, signaling the end of the delay interval, was provided, the performance of the septal rats was similar to that of the controls. Ellen and Butter (1969) have also reported an improvement in the behavior of septal rats when a stimulus is provided which signals the end of the required pause in responding. It is as if the septal rat is no longer able to discriminate lapses of time. (This, of course, is unlikely to be the only impairment.)

While there is a great deal of evidence (summarized above) that septal lesions result in a lessened ability to inhibit responding or a lessened tendency to freeze, it is not clear whether this is the sole explanation of the behavioral change following septal lesions. As has been pointed out by Duncan (1971), there could also be a lessened ability to learn in aversive situations. In order to dissociate initial learning from subsequent performance, Duncan adopted the interesting technique of reversible lesion. He implanted cannulae into the septum and produced a temporary dysfunction by injecting procaine into the cannulae. The state produced by the injection of this local anaesthetic closely resembled the signs commonly observed after irreversible lesioning of the septum. He then proceeded to test the rats' ability to acquire a CER in a state of temporary septal dysfunction. (This consisted of pairing a shock with a tone, while the animal was lever pressing for food, in order to determine the degree of lever pressing suppression caused by the tone.) Duncan found that there was impairment in the learning displayed by the rats. While this could have been due to the rat's lessened tendency to freeze, Duncan's method enabled him to separate this performance variable from the learning variable. He tested his animals in the same situation after the anaesthetic had long worn off. He found that while there was no loss of a general tendency to freeze, there was less suppression of lever pressing than in controls. This could indicate that septal dysfunction had impaired initial conditioning. However, the results might also be the consequence of a generalization decrement as the afferent input could change considerably from the learning to the testing situation because of the difference in drug state.

Thalamus

Studies on animals with medial thalamic lesions point to the conclusion that such lesions produce an exaggeration of the freezing component of the reaction to fear-producing stimuli.

Thompson (1963) observed in the rat that bilateral lesions in either the diffuse thalamic nuclei or the dorsomedial nucleus impaired the performance of a jumping and gripping response to avoid shock which was acquired prior to operation. However, such rats also clearly showed fear reactions to the CS in spite of not responding. It appears unlikely that this deficit was motor in origin since the majority of the subjects that failed to relearn the habit (with the exception of those with dorsomedial lesions) made many spontaneous responses.

Vanderwolf (1962) investigated the effects of lesions in the medial thalamic nuclei (including habenulae, medial nuclei of the thalamus, intralaminar nuclei, and nuclei of the midline). Animals were required to run from a black compartment into a white one within five seconds, in order to avoid shock. The lesioned animals were found quite unable to avoid shock, although they showed all signs of fear to the black box (squealing, defecating, etc.). However, they were able to *escape* shock as well as normals. They also performed better if allowed fifteen seconds to run instead of five. Such animals typically sat motionless in this situation, and if they ran, they did so with explosive suddenness. They were also shown capable of sitting still on a platform surrounded by a charged grid in order to avoid shock, so they showed no passive-avoidance deficit. Yet in spite of this inability to run quickly to avoid shock, animals with such lesions tend generally to be hyperactive, and will run faster than normals to obtain food (Replogh, quoted by Vanderwolf, 1962).

Roberts and Carey (1963) studied cats with dorsomedial lesions (which also encroached on other medial thalamic nuclei). These animals displayed a considerable increase in crouching and decrease in flight attempts in classical fear conditioning. Their tendency to crouch excessively also interfered with the learning of a locomotor flight response. However, these cats did not differ significantly from controls in speed of approach to a food box.

It therefore appears from these studies that medial thalamic lesions result in an increased tendency to freeze in avoidance situations, thus producing an inefficiency in avoidance performance. This reduction in motility appears to be specific to fear-producing situations since it does not occur in food-getting tasks. A further study by Vanderwolf (1964) also demonstrates that this reduced capacity to avoid is not due to learning impairment. He found that rats with medial thalamic damage which fail on an active avoidance test will improve their avoidance performance as a result of a second lesion in the septal area. Septal lesions have the effect of making normal animals hyperactive (see above) and so would break up the freezing patterns. If the original deficit were due to learning impairment, a further lesion would not lead to an improvement in performance.

Amygdala

The nature of the effect of amygdaloid lesions on avoidance learning is unclear. Brady et al. (1954) observe that amygdalectomy in cats produced an increase in the number of trials needed to learn an avoidance response in a double-grill box, though it did not impair retention of such a habit. However, King (1958) in a study on ra*s found that amygdaloid lesions lengthened response latencies but did not alter rates of acquisition of an avoidance response. He points out, however, that the task he used was simpler than that set by Brady et al., and so perhaps his test was less sensitive. Weiskrantz (1956) reports that amygdalectomized monkeys also tended to take longer in acquiring a conditioned avoidance response. They also extinguished more rapidly a habit acquired preoperatively, though no difference in the degree of retention of such a habit was found.

Horvath (1963) obtained different results in a study on cats depending on task difficulty. He found that cats with lesions restricted to the basolateral division of the amygdala showed a severe deficit in acquisition of a complex active-avoidance response, and significant but smaller deficits in the performance of a passive-avoidance response and in the acquisition of a simple active-avoidance response and in the acquisition of a simple active-avoidance response. For the complex active-avoidance response there was a very good correlation between retention deficit and damage to the basolateral nuclei. No such correlation was shown for the other tests. He therefore suggests that the basolateral nuclei are essential for the performance of an avoidance response of a high order of complexity.

However, Ursin (1965b), using different experimental procedures, arrived at a different conclusion. He found that lesions in the rostral part of the lateral nucleus and in the region containing fibers projecting from it (his "flight" zone) (Fig. 9–4) impaired the acquisition of an active-avoidance response. Lesions encroaching on the medial nucleus or the stria terminalis impaired passive avoidance.

Hippocampus

The results of studies on the effect of hippocampal lesions on avoidance responding on the whole support the notion that increased activity is an important factor. This increased activity may be due to increased hunger or thirst, but this has not been investigated yet. On the whole, deficits have been demonstrated in passive-avoidance but not in active-avoidance situations.

Brady (1958) reports that lesions in the hippocampus can virtually eliminate the CER in the rat. Teitelbaum and Milner (1963) found that hippocampal rats were hyperactive compared with normal and brain-damaged controls. Others (e.g., Kim, 1960; Kaada et al., 1961) observed little if any increase in activity, but their measures of activity were different. Teitelbaum and Milner also found that these animals were unable to inhibit movement to avoid shock. The animals were unable to sit still on a "safe" platform, as did normals, but instead kept jumping on and off.

Other deficits following hippocampectomy (summarized by Douglas, 1967, and Kimble, 1968) include prolongation of extinction, increased distractibility to novel stimuli, and impairment of spontaneous and learned alternation. Douglas and Kimble conclude that this type of lesion impairs an inhibitory mechanism. It has become increasingly clear that the hippocampus is in many ways not a unitary structure in rats or cats. Anatomically, its projections have been shown to be quite heterogeneous (Elul, 1964; Raisman, Cowan, and Powell, 1966).

On the behavioral level, Kimura (1958) reports that whether or not hippocampal animals show a deficit in a passive-avoidance task depends on the exact placement of the lesion. He tested latency of running to food after the rat was shocked while eating and found that rats with lesions in the posterior part of the dorsal hippocampus were deficient in this avoidance compared with normal controls. However, those with anterior lesions showed no such difference.

That the consequences of lesions in the hippocampus vary with the exact placement of the lesion within that structure has been stressed by other investigators besides Kimura (1958)—for instance, Grant and Jarrard (1968), Jackson (1968), and Nadel (1968). Fried (1971) has reported a behavioral difference between dorsal hippocampal and ventral hippocampal lesions. In a task requiring rats to change approach responding to avoidance responding (and vice versa), whereas ventral hippocampal lesions produced a small impairment of avoidance performance, dorsal hippocampal lesions caused a faster change from avoidance behavior to approach behavior, compared with controls.

Some negative results have also been obtained. Kaada et al. (1962) presented water-deprived rats with an electrified water dish and recorded the total number of shocks accepted by the animals. He found that though lesions in various other brain structures greatly increased the number of shocks accepted, the number received by hippocampal operates did not increase significantly. No significant difference was found between animals with anterior and those with posterior hippocampal lesions. Kimble (1963) also found that although hippocampal rats showed less passive avoidance following shock than did normals, they did not show significantly less than did cortical lesioned controls.

It might be expected from the above findings that, in active-avoidance tests, hippocampals should perform, if anything, better than normals.

This has been observed in several instances. Brady et al. (1954) report that cats with hippocampal lesions do not show poorer learning than normals in a double-grill box situation. Isaacson et al. (1961) found that when rats with extensive hippocampal lesions were tested in a shuttle box avoidance problem, they actually reached learning criteria sooner and exhibited lower response latencies than did normals. Similar improvements have been observed by Green, Beatty, and Schwartzbaum (1967).

It has also been shown that hippocampectomized animals find it difficult to change a learned mode of responding. For instance, once a hippocampectomized rat has been trained on a schedule which reinforces every response (CRF), it cannot be trained on a schedule which differentially reinforces low rates of responding (DRL). On the other hand, such a rat can be trained on a DRL schedule if this schedule is used from the start and no CRF pretraining is used (Clark and Isaacson, 1965; Schmaltz and Isaacson, 1966). Whether the hippocampectomized rat can switch from a previously learned mode of responding is a function of the degree to which the previous learning had been ingrained. Hippocampectomized rats have no difficulty in inhibiting an approach to food—when this is subsequently punished—if the approach response to food is rewarded only a few times before punishment is instituted (Stern and Kirkby, 1967).

Frontal Lobotomy and Fear-Motivated Behavior

Various studies involving passive avoidance have been carried out in order to investigate the effect of lobotomy on anxiety. Lichtenstein (1950) reports that lobotomized dogs showed a partial or complete loss of a preoperatively acquired feeding inhibition. This may be due to a reduction in anxiety, but there are two other factors which may also account for this finding. First, prefrontal lobotomy increases feeding (Brutkowski, 1959); so the results may simply be due to increased feeding activity. Second, prefrontal lobotomy increases motility, as has been studied by several authors, including French and Harlow (1955), and this should be expected to produce a passive avoidance deficit.

Streb and Smith (1955), using the rat, measured the amount of crouching displayed after several trials to the sound of a buzzer which terminated with shock. They found that frontal lobotomy resulted in fewer crouching responses and also a greatly increased motility score. It would therefore be difficult to conclude anything about anxiety here since this effect also may simply be due to increased motility.

Maher and McIntire (1960) carried out an experiment to test the increased motility explanation of CER reduction following frontal ablation. Rats in which a CER (immobility and defecation) had been established were subjected to bilateral frontal ablation. Postoperatively, the subjects showed a loss of immobility but no loss of the defecation component. They conclude that the effect of the operation is to increase motility rather than reduce anxiety. These findings were confirmed by Maher et al. (1962), using a different apparatus.

In a different type of experiment, Waterhouse (1957) trained monkeys to overturn one cup to obtain food and another to avoid shock, using discriminant CSs. Prefrontal lobotomy led to a marked loss in performance accuracy for both tasks, though retraining was possible. A slightly greater effect on fear than on food responses was noted. However, since lobotomy produces an increase in food-related responses (Brutkowski, 1959), an effect on anxiety is not conclusively shown here.

Indeed, Auleytner and Brutkowski (1960) claim that bilateral prefrontal lobotomy in dogs produces an increase rather than a decrease in responsiveness to noxious stimuli and defensive behavior when the classical conditioning procedure is used. However, Brutkowski (1959) also demonstrated an increased responsiveness with other types of behavior; so we cannot be sure that his effect is specifically related to fear.

In general, it appears that deficits in passive-avoidance situations resulting from lesions are secondary to some effect other than on emotion. It may well be that with lesions producing an increase in passive avoidance and a deficit in active avoidance, these effects are due to an increased freezing tendency, although the exact causes of this change have yet to be elucidated.

chapter 11

Arousal, Sleep, and Attention

As we all know, the events which we notice form only a small proportion of those which impinge on our sense organs. We fail to notice events when we are unconscious or asleep, and also when we are attending to some other aspect of our environment. In this chapter we shall deal first with factors underlying general arousal and then with those underlying selective attention.

ELECTROENCEPHALOGRAM (EEG) AND STATES OF ALERTNESS

An important difference betwen the conditions of the awake and the sleeping organism is demonstrated by means of the electroencephalogram (EEG). This is a record of the gross electrical activity of the brain, and is obtained by attaching two electrodes to the scalp without physiological interference with the organism. The electrical activity of the cortex, when the subject is awake and relaxed, is characteristically a 10/sec. synchronized wave form known as the alpha rhythm (Fig. 11–1). With increasing drowsiness, the frequency of the rhythm is reduced and low-amplitude slow waves occur occasionally. Light sleep is characterized by slow waves and occasional high-voltage "sleep spindles." In deep sleep, large, very slow waves appear in a random irregular pattern. When the subject is alert and attentive, low-amplitude fast waves appear which are only partially synchronized. In states of emotion, brain rhythms become totally desynchronized (Lindsley, 1952).

Although the correlation between states of alertness and type of EEG pattern is generally good, especially at the extremes, it is possible to separate the two. Gastaut (1954) quotes a number of clinical cases where certain states of alertness are accompanied by cortical rhythms

EXCITED

RELAXED

DROWSY

ASLEEP

DEEP SLEEP

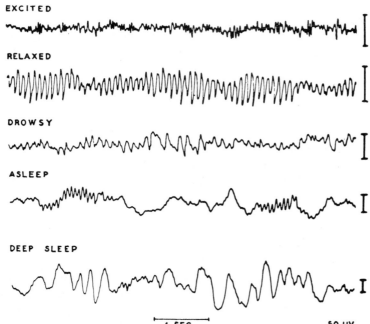

1 SEC   50 μv.

FIG. 11-1. Characteristic EEG records from different stages of sleep and wakefulness. (From Jasper, H. H., Penfield, N., and Erickson, J. C., *Epilepsy and Cerebral Localization*, 1941; by permission of Charles C Thomas, Publisher, Springfield, Ill.)

characteristic of other states. For instance, in comas brought about by hypoglycemia, very frequently the most superficial comas are concomitant with the slowest rhythms. When extreme coma is brought about in patients through some complication in the administration of anaesthesia, the patient's EEG shows very rapid desynchronized rhythms. Also, during artificial hibernation (a procedure in which coma is produced in a patient by means of the administration of drugs and the concomitant lowering of temperature), rapid, desynchronized rhythms may often accompany loss of consciousness. Similarly, normal alpha waves may be shown to occur during comas, as in cases reported by Gastaut in which the coma was produced by lesions in the lower brain stem. Feldman and Waller (1962) found that lesions in the posterior hypothalamus produced a permanent sleeplike state during which it was possible to produce electrical activation (desynchronized low-voltage rhythms in the cortex) either by stimulation of the midbrain reticular formation or by peripheral stimulation, without behavioral arousal or alerting. Desynchronized rhythms also occur periodically in normal sleep, and this has been described as "paradoxical sleep."

But even more compelling are the cases cited of the concomitance of perfectly normal states of alertness with chronically slow cortical rhythms. Gastaut describes the case of a girl who had rhythms of a frequency of 3 cps. for some years following recovery from a coma and yet was, in fact, the brightest pupil in her class. Hess further observes (1954) in cats in which natural sleep was induced by stimulation of a "sleep center" that, while in most cases there appeared in an EEG pattern characteristic of sleep, on some occasions the electrical activity of the brain was found to have a waking pattern while the cat was lying in a sleeping position, and vice versa. Feldman and Waller (1962) report that limited lesions of the midbrain reticular formation can lead to attentive behavior, though the EEG rhythm is of high voltage and low frequency—that is, characteristic of sleep. It has also been observed that overtired people, whose EEGs manifest a definite sleep pattern, may still perform calculations.

Certain drugs have also been shown to produce a dissociation between states of alertness and their characteristic EEG patterns. Funderbunk and Case (1951) demonstrated that atropine induces a synchronized EEG in animals which nevertheless seem quite alert. Bradley and Elkes (1953) and Wikler (1952) confirmed this finding. On the other hand, Killam et al. (1957) demonstrated that reserpine induces drowsiness in animals, which nevertheless maintain a desynchronized EEG. And chlorpromazine causes a slight increase in stimulus threshold for EEG desynchronization upon brain stimulation, but greatly raises the threshold for behavioral arousal (alertness) upon stimulation of the same region. It seems, therefore, that it may be wiser to consider EEG patterns as by-products of the mechanism underlying arousal and sleep rather than as an integral part of this mechanism.

Many attempts have been made by neurophysiologists to correlate EEG rhythms with certain neural "states" of the cortex. However, little success has so far been obtained. Kogan (1960) reports that, during conditioning, the presentation of an auditory CS results in generalized desynchronization in all cortical areas; yet some regions demonstrate increased excitability and other regions decreased excitability, though they both show the same EEG patterns. Jasper, Ricci, and Doane (1960) found that desynchronization of EEG rhythms in the cortex may be accompanied by an increase, decrease, or no change in the discharge frequency of a cortical unit. And they conclude: "States of excitation or inhibition in the cortex are not related in a simple manner to the presence or absence of slow waves in the surface ECG as judged by rates of firing of cortical cells." Schlag (personal communication) feels, however, that though there may be a lack of correlation when we look at the activity of individual units with microelectrodes, a better estimate may be formed if simultaneous recording from a number of units is used. Using somewhat larger electrodes, Schlag found a good correlation between unit activity and EEG rhythms. Desynchronization is accompanied by an increase in the activity of the majority of units.

A related problem is that of gross evoked responses. These are electrical changes recorded with large electrodes from the central nervous system in response to some stimulus. Fox (1970) has put forward evidence that the shape of the gross evoked response indicates the probability of single-unit discharge in a large population of neurons. The higher the recorded voltage of the gross evoked response, the larger the number of single units discharges on the average in response to light flashes. However, most other studies indicate that postsynaptic depolarization potentials are generating gross evoked potentials as they sum together (e.g., Creutzfeld, 1966).

AROUSAL AND THE RETICULAR SYSTEM

The term "reticular system" refers to a number of subcortical structures thought to be concerned, among other things, with the regulation of wakefulness and the electrical activity of the brain. These structures have been divided into two main groups which to some extent subserve separate functions. The first group has been called the "brain stem reticular formation" and the second group the "thalamic reticular system."

Brain Stem Reticular Formation

Anatomically, the brain stem reticular formation is found to extend upward from the medulla through the central core of the brain stem, traversing the pons, midbrain, hypothalamus, subthalamus, and thalamus (Fig. 11–2). It probably projects to the cortex by two routes, one via various nonspecific thalamic nuclei and the other bypassing the thalamus and reaching the cortex directly by way of the internal capsule.

Reticular regions of the brain are of vital importance for a number of functions (Magoun, 1963). Here we are concerned only with their relevance to arousal and attention. One of the first studies demonstrating the importance of brain stem structures in the maintenance of arousal was that of Bremer (1937), who placed an animal in a permanent state of sleep, indicated both behaviorally and by its electrocorticogram, by a midbrain transection (the "cerveau isolé" preparation). Bremer assumed at the time that his results were due to deafferentation of the cerebrum. However, in 1950 Lindsley et al. showed in the cat that if the classical afferent pathways are severed at the level of the midbrain, the animal is able to move around and demonstrates a waking EEG. Nevertheless, if lesions are made in the reticular formation and the specific sensory pathways are left intact, the animal is permanently asleep and shows a sleeping EEG (Fig. 11–3).

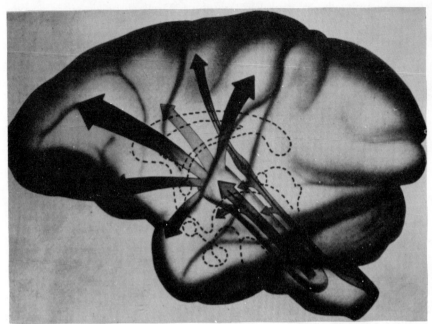

FIG. 11–2. Lateral view of the monkey brain, on which is projected a representation of the ascending reticular system. (From Magoun, H. W., (ed.), *Brain Mechanisms and Consciousness*, 1954; by permission of Blackwell Scientific Publications.)

AWAKE : MIDBRAIN LESION AFFERENT PATHS

A′

CC-17 21ST PO. DAY

ASLEEP : LESION MIDBRAIN TEGMENTUM   *100 μV*

B′

CC-18 12TH PO DAY   *1 SEC.*

FIG. 11–3. *A′:* waking EEG in a cat with bilateral section of the classical sensory pathways in the midbrain, sparing the central tegmentum. *B′:* sleeping EEG in a cat with interruption of the mesencephalic tegmentum, sparing the sensory pathways. (From Lindsley, D. B., et al., 1950; by permission of *EEG Clin. Neurophysiol.,* 2.)

French and Magoun (1952) demonstrated that in the monkey, too, injury to the cephalic brain stem produces a permanently comatose animal with a chronically synchronized EEG. Similar findings have been reported in man by various workers, including Penfield (1938), French

(1952), and Jefferson (1952). It was also found that increasing the size of chronic lesions in the brain stem reticular formation induces a progressively deepening stupor. However, it now seems that the state of sleep in the cerveau isolé preparation may be somewhat less than permanent. It seems that after a few days the cerveau isolé preparation recovers its sleep-waking cycle after a few days (Villablanca, 1965).

Corroborating evidence that the brain stem reticular formation is involved in arousal derives from experiments involving stimulation of various portions of this structure. Moruzzi and Magoun (1949) found that stimulation in the region of the brain stem led to a cessation of synchronized cortical rhythms and their replacement by low-voltage desynchronized activity. Further, using animals with chronically implanted electrodes, Segundo, Arana, and French (1955) found that stimulation of the reticular formation produced behavioral arousal from sleep, in addition to a desynchronization of EEG rhythms; and they argue that this effect did not seem to be secondary to pain or movement. However, this cannot be excluded.

Pathways into the Reticular Formation. Important sensory connections to the reticular formation have been demonstrated. Collaterals to the reticular formation from afferent pathways subserving all the sensory modes have been established at many levels. Starzl et al. (1951) recorded potentials evoked in the brain stem of cats by sciatic stimulation and auditory clicks. They concluded that collaterals from the ascending somatic paths feed into the brain stem reticular formation through almost its entire length from the medulla to the posterior thalamus, and that the distribution of collaterals from the auditory system is almost identical. Similar findings have been reported with reference to other modalities. Anatomical studies (Mehler et al., 1960; Bowsher, 1957, 1961) emphasize the connection with pain pathways. There does not seem to be any topographical subdivision of the reticular formation with respect to reception of impulses via the different modalities. Even single units have been shown to respond to stimulation via various sensory modes. However, the various modalities of stimulation are not equally powerful in exciting the reticular formation. Simulation of the visual system seems to be least powerful, and stimulation of the somatic pathways most powerful. Magoun (1963) points out that the potent arousing quality of painful stimuli would lead one to expect pain pathways have a particularly intimate relation with the reticular formation.

Important connections from the cortex to the reticular formation have also been shown to exist. Segundo, Naquet, and Buser (1955) found in the monkey that single-shock stimulation of various cortical loci caused generalized EEG arousal. French, Hernandez-Peon, and Livingston (1955) found, also in the monkey, that stimulation of certain discrete cortical regions gave rise to evoked potentials throughout the extent of the brain stem reticular formation. These regions were located in the frontal oculomotor fields, sensorimotor cortex, cingulate gyrus, orbito-frontal surface, temporal tip, first temporal gyrus, and the paraoccipital region (Fig. 11–4). It has also been demonstrated (Bremer and Terzuolo, 1953) that brief faradization of various cortical areas produces behavioral awakening in a sleeping animal as well as inducing desynchronized EEG rhythms.

 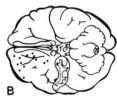 

A   B   C

FIG. 11–4. Lateral (A), basilar (B), and medial (C) surfaces of the monkey cortex, showing loci, stimulation of which induced evoked potentials in the central cephalic brain stem. (From French, J. D., et al., 1955; by permission of *J. Neurophysiol.*, 18.)

The importance of these pathways from the cortex is indicated by the finding of Hernandez-Peon and Hagbarth (1955) in cats, that potentials evoked in the reticular formation by cortical stimulation are larger and more widespread than those evoked by afferent stimulation. Further, "meaningful" stimuli, which presumably must be analyzed as such by the cortex, seem to be especially efficient in inducing arousal. Gangloff and Monnier (1956) report that a rabbit will be aroused much more effectively by the appearance of a human being than by strong stimuli such as bright lights or loud noises. In the human case, a person will awake at the sound of his own name, a mother at the sound of her baby's cry, and yet be undisturbed by quite loud noises. Fischgold and Lairy-Bounes (1952) report that in the case of a comatose patient, calling his name would evoke EEG arousal, whereas intense stimuli were without effect.

One might explain spontaneous waking from sleep, for instance when a nightmare is out of hand, by means of such corticofugal messages. Stimulation of the superior temporal gyrus and the hippocampal gyrus are extremely effective in evoking potentials in the reticular formation, and there is evidence that these areas play an important part in processes connected with memory and dreaming (Penfield, 1958).

Pathways to the reticular formation have also been found to arise from the cerebellum (Snider, 1952), basal ganglia (Sprague, 1953), and rhinencephalic structures (Adey, Sunderland, and Dunlop, 1957; Green and Adey, 1956).

Convergence of Input to the Reticular Formation. It is characteristic of the reticular formation that it responds in a much more generalized fashion to incoming stimulation than do relay nuclei on the primary sensory pathways. Potentials may be evoked throughout this structure by excitation of various sensory systems (French et al., 1952; Starzl et al., 1951) and various cortical structures (Bremer and Terzuolo, 1954; French et al., 1955). Occlusive and facilitatory interactions between responses evoked in the reticular formation from very different sources have further been observed (Bremer and Terzuolo, 1952, 1954; French et al., 1955). Single-unit studies have demonstrated a convergence of input from several sources (Amassian and DeVito, 1954; Scheibel et al., 1955; Palestini et al., 1957; Bradley and Mollica, 1958). Figure 11–5

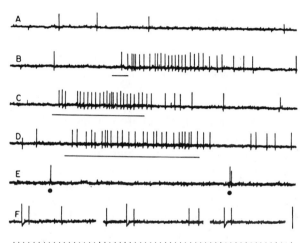

FIG. 11–5. Convergence onto the same pontile reticular unit of tactile, acoustic, and cortical stimuli. *A,* spontaneous discharge. *B,* tapping the ipsilateral forelimb. *C,* rubbing the back. *D,* touching whiskers. *E,* hand claps. *F,* single shocks to the ipsilateral sensori-motor cortex) indicated by the stimulus artefact). (From Palestini, M., et al., 1957, *Archives Italiennes de Biologie,* 95.)

shows the response of a single neuron in the reticular formation to several different stimuli. Neuroanatomical evidence further indicates that the reticular formation may function in a diffuse manner (Scheibel and Scheibel, 1958, 1967).

However, it has also been observed that the convergence of input onto individual reticular neurons is not absolute; that is, units could not be made to respond to all types of stimulation (Amassian and DeVito, 1954; Hernandez-Peon and Hagbarth, 1955; Scheibel et al., 1955). Furthermore, some reticular units have been found to be more responsive than others. Also, due to artefacts introduced by experimental techniques, it is difficult to asses just how generalized the reticular response to stimulation is under normal conditions. It has been found, for instance, that individual units exhibit larger receptive fields under chloralose anesthesia than under syncurarine. We cannot say with certainty, therefore, how large the receptive fields would be in animals under no drug at all. Again, the type of stimulation employed is important. Hernandez-Peon and Hagbarth (1955) report that units which were unresponsive to stimuli applied as single shocks responded quite well when stimuli were applied repetitively.

Another finding which retains the possibility that information as to the source of an incoming stimulus may be preserved in the reticular formation is that individual units will respond with different patterns and latencies of firing depending on their source of input. Theoretically, it is possible to encode information by means of such differences, though such a system would be cumbersome and would require a very complex decoding apparatus.

Lack of Topographical Projection to the Cortex. French, Amerongen, and Magoun (1952) stimulated various regions in the brain stem of monkeys and concluded that there was no correlation between the site of stimulation of the activating system and the area of cortical response. What they did find, however, was that some areas of the brain stem were more excitable than others, and stimulation of these areas gave rise to activation throughout the cortex. Stimulation of less excitable brain stem areas gave rise to a response which tended to be frontally oriented. The frontal and parietal areas of the cortex were found to be most easily excited, the temporal region less easily, and the occipital region least. Magoun (1954) also found that stimulation of any part of the brain stem region gave rise to a desynchronization of the EEG which was generalized all over the cortex, though it was most pronounced and persisted longer in the anterior part of the hemisphere.

A Synchronizing Influence in the Lower Brain Stem. It has been demonstrated by numerous experiments (described earlier) that lesions in the brain stem reticular formation produce coma and a permanently synchronous EEG. However, a series of experiments initiated recently under Moruzzi have complicated this picture. It was found that cats with transections at the midpontine level show desynchronized EEG rhythms for most of the time, with only a few brief periods of synchrony. According to Batini et al. (1958), this preparation (the midpontine pretrigeminal preparation) displayed a waking EEG for at least 70 percent and frequently 90 percent of the total time it was recorded, as contrasted with a normal animal, which displayed a waking EEG from 20 percent to 50 percent of the time. Such an animal could follow with its eyes an object passing across its visual field, and display pupillary dilation when an emotionally significant stimulus was presented. These ocular signs appeared only when the EEG was desynchronized.

Various experiments indicate that this effect may not be accounted for by irritative or humoral factors. It was postulated, therefore, that the midpontine transection excludes the influence of a synchronizing structure in the lower brain stem. If the transection is made a few millimeters rostrally (the rostropontine preparation), EEG synchronization is induced; so it was also inferred that structures immediately rostral to the midpontine transection were essential for producing a desynchronized EEG (see Fig. 11–6).

Effects of Anesthetics on the Reticular Formation. Activity in the brain stem reticular formation is easily depressed by anesthetic agents (Arduini and Arduini, 1954; French, Verzeano, and Magoun, 1953), in contrast with activity in the cortex and primary sensory pathways (through activity in the latter regions is also modified). It has been suggested (Brazier, 1954) that this particular susceptibility is due to that fact that anesthetic agents block synaptic transmission much more than they do nerve fiber conduction, and the reticular formation is a multisynaptic system. Generally, anesthetics, as well as blocking activity in the reticular formation, also produce EEG changes in the direction of synchrony.

Thalamic Reticular System

The thalamic reticular system consits of a closely interconnected network of neurons involving those thalamic nuclei which do not have specific projections to the cortex (Fig. 11–7). These include the midline and intralaminar nuclei, the anteroventral nucleus, and the lateral reticular nucleus. Just as was found with the brain stem reticular formation, this system receives collaterals from the classical sensory pathways subserving various sensory modalities, and input from these pathways is distributed here in a nonspecific fashion. Important projections from the cortex have also been demonstrated, as from other areas, such as the cerebellum and rhinencephalon (Lindsley, 1960).

Although its name implies that is is a single system, the thalamic reticular system does not in fact function in a unitary fashion. On the one hand, it appears to have an activating function similar to that found in the brain stem reticular formation. On the other hand, it also has effects which antagonize the arousal system. We shall describe these latter effects first.

The Recruiting Response. Morison and Dempsey (1942) discovered that during stimulation of the intralaminar nuclei of the thalamus at frequencies of 6 to 12 per second there is an increment of response at the cortex with successive shocks. The cortical wave reaches a maxi-

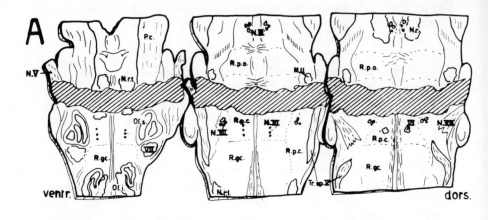

FIG. 11–6. EEG patterns following midpontine and rostropontine transections. Horizontal sections of the brain stem of the cat with cross-hatched areas indicating the level and extent of the brain stem lesion in the midpontine (*A*) and rostropontine (*B*) pretrigeminal preparations. Below each set of drawings are shown the EEG patterns typical for each preparation, recorded from the right (*F.d.*) and left (*F.s.*) frontal areas. (From Batini, C., et al., 1959, *Archives Italiennes de Biologie, 97.*)

mum after two to five successive stimuli. As repetitive stimulation continues, the response at the cortex may decrease again, exhibiting spontaneous waxing and waning (Fig. 11–8). This phenomenon is known as the recruiting response, and resembles the spindle bursts which occur spontaneously during sleep.

The exact pathways involved in this effect on the cortex are uncertain. It had been thought that connections were made with the cortex by way of the specific thalamic nuclei. However, Hanbery and Jasper (1953) demonstrated that recruiting responses could be obtained in a given cortical area after destruction of the specific thalamic nucleus known to be connected with this region. For instance, the recruiting response obtained from the visual area of the cortex was unimpaired after destruction of the lateral geniculate body of the thalamus. Similar findings were obtained for the auditory and somatosensory areas. Indeed, even better recruiting was obtained in a cortical region for which the appropriate specific thalamic nucleus was destroyed. Generally, recruiting responses are easier to elicit and of higher voltage in the frontal and motor cortex and the anterior cingulate region than in the cortical sensory areas and posterior parietal areas.

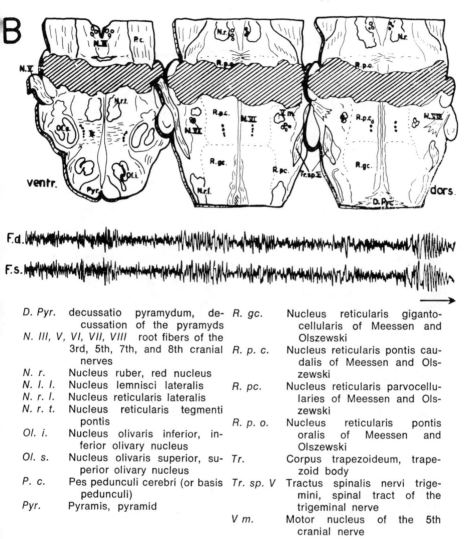

D. Pyr. decussatio pyramydum, de-
cussation of the pyramyds
N. III, V, VI, VII, VIII root fibers of the
3rd, 5th, 7th, and 8th cranial
nerves
N. r.   Nucleus ruber, red nucleus
N. l. l. Nucleus lemnisci lateralis
N. r. l. Nucleus reticularis lateralis
N. r. t. Nucleus reticularis tegmenti
pontis
Ol. i.   Nucleus olivaris inferior, in-
ferior olivary nucleus
Ol. s.   Nucleus olivaris superior, su-
perior olivary nucleus
P. c.   Pes pedunculi cerebri (or basis
pedunculi)
Pyr.   Pyramis, pyramid

R. gc.   Nucleus reticularis giganto-
cellularis of Meessen and
Olszewski
R. p. c. Nucleus reticularis pontis cau-
dalis of Meessen and Ols-
zewski
R. pc.   Nucleus reticularis parvocellu-
laries of Meessen and Ols-
zewski
R. p. o. Nucleus reticularis pontis
oralis of Meessen and
Olszewski
Tr.   Corpus trapezoideum, trapezoid body
Tr. sp. V Tractus spinalis nervi trige-
mini, spinal tract of the
trigeminal nerve
V m.   Motor nucleus of the 5th
cranial nerve

FIG. 11–6—Continued

Sterman and Clemente (1962a) have reported that low-frequency
stimulation of a circumscribed region is the basal forebrain of the cat,
just rostral to the optic chiasma, gave rise to an immediate and sustained
cortical synchronization. This response was similar in many respects
to the thalamic recruiting response. However, differences in the responses
obtained from the two loci did exist. For instance, the synchronization
evoked from basal forebrain stimulation was also prominent in the primary sensory areas. Further, this response was blocked by nembutal;

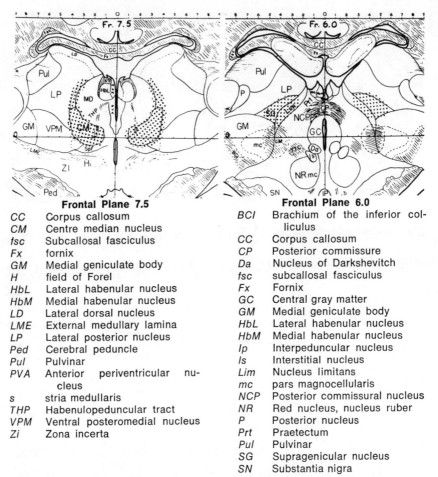

Frontal Plane 7.5

CC	Corpus callosum
CM	Centre median nucleus
fsc	Subcallosal fasciculus
Fx	fornix
GM	Medial geniculate body
H	field of Forel
HbL	Lateral habenular nucleus
HbM	Medial habenular nucleus
LD	Lateral dorsal nucleus
LME	External medullary lamina
LP	Lateral posterior nucleus
Ped	Cerebral peduncle
Pul	Pulvinar
PVA	Anterior periventricular nucleus
s	stria medullaris
THP	Habenulopeduncular tract
VPM	Ventral posteromedial nucleus
Zi	Zona incerta

Frontal Plane 6.0

BCI	Brachium of the inferior colliculus
CC	Corpus callosum
CP	Posterior commissure
Da	Nucleus of Darkshevitch
fsc	subcallosal fasciculus
Fx	Fornix
GC	Central gray matter
GM	Medial geniculate body
HbL	Lateral habenular nucleus
HbM	Medial habenular nucleus
Ip	Interpeduncular nucleus
Is	Interstitial nucleus
Lim	Nucleus limitans
mc	pars magnocellularis
NCP	Posterior commissural nucleus
NR	Red nucleus, nucleus ruber
P	Posterior nucleus
Prt	Praetectum
Pul	Pulvinar
SG	Supragenicular nucleus
SN	Substantia nigra

FIG. 11–7. Diagram of the thalamic reticular system in the cat. Areas giving rise to recruiting responses are shown by the stippling. Successive frontal planes are shown. (From Jasper, H. H., 1960, in *Handbook of Physiology,* Vol. 2.)

in contrast, the recruiting response from the thalamus may even be potentiated by this drug.

Behavioral Sleep Produced by Stimulation of Areas from Which the Recruiting Response Is Obtained. As Sterman and Clemente (1962a) observe, the relevance of the recruiting phenomenon consists in its similarity to the rhythms recorded from the cortex during sleep and allied states. It lies also in the fact that stimulation of areas from which the electrical phenomenon of recruiting can be induced often produces behavioral sleep in freely moving animals.

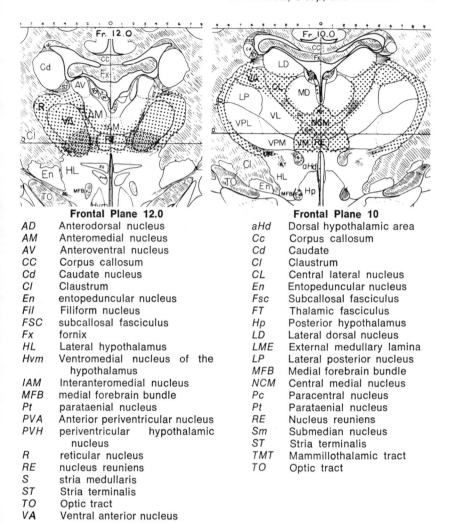

	Frontal Plane 12.0		**Frontal Plane 10**	
AD	Anterodorsal nucleus	ahd	Dorsal hypothalamic area
AM	Anteromedial nucleus	Cc	Corpus callosum
AV	Anteroventral nucleus	Cd	Caudate
CC	Corpus callosum	Cl	Claustrum
Cd	Caudate nucleus	CL	Central lateral nucleus
Cl	Claustrum	En	Entopeduncular nucleus
En	entopeduncular nucleus	Fsc	Subcallosal fasciculus
Fil	Filiform nucleus	FT	Thalamic fasciculus
FSC	subcallosal fasciculus	Hp	Posterior hypothalamus
Fx	fornix	LD	Lateral dorsal nucleus
HL	Lateral hypothalamus	LME	External medullary lamina
Hvm	Ventromedial nucleus of the hypothalamus	LP	Lateral posterior nucleus
		MFB	Medial forebrain bundle
IAM	Interanteromedial nucleus	NCM	Central medial nucleus
MFB	medial forebrain bundle	Pc	Paracentral nucleus
Pt	parataenial nucleus	Pt	Parataenial nucleus
PVA	Anterior periventricular nucleus	RE	Nucleus reuniens
PVH	periventricular hypothalamic nucleus	Sm	Submedian nucleus
		ST	Stria terminalis
R	reticular nucleus	TMT	Mammillothalamic tract
RE	nucleus reuniens	TO	Optic tract
S	stria medullaris		
ST	Stria terminalis		
TO	Optic tract		
VA	Ventral anterior nucleus		

FIG. 11–7—Continued

FIG. 11–8. Recruiting response, showing waxing and waning, produced by repetitive stimulation of the intralaminar nuclei of the thalamus at the frequency indicated by the signal. This record was taken from the middle suprasylvian gyrus. (From Dempsey, E. W., and Morison, R. S., 1942, *Am. J. Physiol.*, 135.)

For instance, Hess (1944, 1954) observed that repetitive stimulation in an area overlapping with that from which recruiting is obtained at low voltage and a frequency of eight per second produces sleep in cats. Hess stresses the resemblance of this phenomenon to that of natural sleep. The animal does not fall asleep suddenly but first chooses a convenient place and settles down in it. The EEG pattern in indistinguishable from that recorded in natural sleep (Hess, Koella, and Akert, 1953), and the animal may be aroused by peripheral stimulation. Employing dogs as subjects. Akimoto et al. (1956) also demonstrated that repetitive stimulation at low voltage and low frequency (five to ten per second) in the intralaminar nuclei induces sleep in unanesthetized animals. Here also the EEG pattern produced was very similar to that found in natural sleep. Further, Sterman and Clemente (1962b), using cats, found that stimulation of the basal forebrain synchronized area, described above, induces the rapid onset of behavioral sleep. In this case the effect could be obtained by high- as well as low-frequency stimulation (5 to 250 cps.).

Interaction between the Recruiting System and the Arousal System. Various kinds of evidence indicate that the activating effect of the brain stem reticular formation acts as an antagonist to the recruiting system. Best recruiting is obtained in animals with the mesial portion of the reticular formation destroyed. Furthermore, it is difficult to obtain recruiting in unanaesthetized animals which are aroused by sensory stimulation. Rapid stimulation of the brain stem reticular formation concomitantly with stimulation of the intralaminar nuclei to obtain recruiting will block the recruiting response. The interaction between the basal forebrain synchronizing area and the brain stem reticular formation is more complex. Here the order of application of the two types of stimulation is important. Cortical arousal produced by high-frequency stimulation of the brain stem reticular formation will be blocked if the basal forebrain zone is then stimulated simultaneously at low frequency; that is, cortical syncronization will result. However, if the basal forebrain zone is stimulated first, the opposite will be the case (Sterman and Clemente, 1962a).

Activating Function of the Thalamic Reticular System. Large bilateral lesions of the anterior portion of the thalamic reticular system may produce coma analogous to that produced by lesions of the midbrain (French and Magoun, 1952; Lindsley et al., 1950), though the depth of coma invoked by the thalamic lesions is less profound. It seems, therefore, that the thalamic reticular system also has an activating function.

Further evidence arises from stimulation studies in this region. It is possible to produce EEG desynchronization upon high-frequency stimulation of the thalamic reticular system, though activation so produced is shorter lasting than is that mediated by the brain stem reticular formation. In the two studies cited above, demonstrating the induction of sleep by low-frequency thalamic stimulation (Hess, 1954; Akimoto et al., 1956), raising the stimulus frequency in the same locus produced the opposite effect: it would arouse a sleeping animal.

Such findings have led to speculation as to whether these two opposite effects, obtained from the same locus, are due to stimulation of the same system in different ways or to stimulation of two separate systems by the use of different stimulus parameters. Recent work has made it very likely that the latter interpretation is correct, and that the contrasting effects are due to the stimulation of two separate systems which partially overlap anatomically. Schlag and Chaillet (1963) were able to show that different points within the thalamic reticular system tended to give rise either to recruiting or to desynchronization in the cortex. Further, cortical desynchronization could not be elicited in a third of their cats when the connection of the thalamic reticular formation with the mesencephalic reticular formation was severed, whereas the recruiting response could still be elicited. Enomoto (1959) had shown that a sagittal section of the massa intermedia and corpus callosum abolishes the recruit response on the contralateral cortex. Schlag and Chaillet were able to confirm this finding and to show, in addition, that stimulation at a high frequency at the same thalamic site in Enomoto's preparation was able to produce a desynchronization of the contralateral hemisphere. It may therefore be that the desynchronizing effect of stimuli to one component of the thalamic reticular system is actually transmitted to the cortex by first traveling back to the midbrain reticular formation. The path which transmits the synchronizing influence to the cortex appears to be more direct.

Paradoxical Results Following Lesions of the Reticular System

Adametz (1959) and Chow and Randell (1960) report that if lesions are made in the midbrain reticular formation in several stages, allowing for recovery between each stage, animals with large lesions may yet remain alert and capable of learning. The explanation of why inflicting such lesions in stages should prevent coma is as yet unclear. Doty et al. (1959) also report that cats with massive midbrain lesions might recover and demonstrate EEG desynchronization if given intensive nursing care. Similar results have also been obtained by Sprague, Chambers, and Stellar (1961) and Batsel (1960). It is possible, therefore, that the brain stem reticular formation might prove to be less vital for the maintenance of arousal than it has been considered to be. Chow et al. (1959) found also that massive lesions in the thalamic reticular system need not produce comas.

THEORIES ON THE PROCESS OF FALLING ASLEEP

There have been two main approaches to the study of sleep. The first approach regards sleep as a "passive" process; that is, it is assumed that sleep is brought about by some impairment or depression of nervous system function. A modern version of this view stresses the finding that wakefulness depends on the integrity of ascending pathways from the brain stem reticular formation, and that coma results from lesions in these pathways. It is therefore proposed that sleep is brought about by reduction in the activating influence of the reticular formation. This may be produced by several factors, such as synaptic fatigue and reduction in sensory influx. This view was stated by Bremer (1954), when he wrote:

The physiological process of falling asleep may be explained, without necessary recourse to the hypothesis of a hypnogenic centre, by the cumulative de-activation (de-facilitation) of the encephalic neuronal networks resulting from synaptic fatigue and favored by a reduction in the exteroceptive and proprioceptive sensory afflux. In this process of neuronal de-activation which culminates in sleep the functional slackening of the brain stem reticular formation, by reason of the latter's central situation in the nervous apparatus of arousal, plays without doubt an essential role.

Another view suggests that sleep is brought about by the influence of an active sleep-producing mechanism. This view is supported by various lines of evidence. Firstly, lesions in the anterior part of the hypothalamus have given rise to states of sleeplessness both in encephalic patients (Von Economo, 1918) and in rats (Nauta, 1946). It may be suggested that sleep-inducing structures are damaged in these cases. Secondly, stimulation in various diencephalic regions (including structures in the anterior hypothalamus) can produce sleep, as shown by the experiments of Hess and his collaborators (1944, 1953, 1954), Akimoto et al. (1956), and Sterman and Clemente (1962) quoted above.

Moruzzi (1960) presents the hypothesis that sleep may be induced by an ascending flow of impulses arising from synchronizing structures in the lower brain stem which inhibit or antagonize the reticular activating system. He suggests that while the reticular activating system is excited by sudden environmental changes, "the synchronizing structures of the brain stem are endowed with the opposite property of responding with an avalanching increase of their activity whenever a prolonged sequence of monotonous sensory stimulations is applied to a large group of receptors." In support of this notion, he cites experiments of Pavlov and his followers which indicate that sleep may be brought about more quickly and consistently in the presence of repeated identical stimuli than if such stimuli were omitted. Moruzzi's hypothesis was not intended to account for the whole process of induction and maintenance of sleep, but he argues that it may be an important factor at least in the case of sleep initiation.

Moruzzi's hypothesis is supported by two main lines of evidence. Firstly, cortical EEG synchronization can be produced by stimulation in the region of the nucleus of the solitary tract in the medulla. The second line of evidence comes from experiments which surgically separate parts of the nervous system from each other. When a section is made between the medulla and the spinal cord (encéphale isolé preparation), EEG synchronization and ocular signs of sleep occur from time to time. However, if the section is made in the middle of the pons (the midpontine pretrigeminal preparation), desynchronization is present for most of the time (Fig. 11-6). It is therefore argued that some structure which lies between the middle of the pons and the junction between the spine and medulla is responsible for exerting a synchronizing influence.

Further evidence that there are separate mechanisms for sleep and for arousal comes from experiments involving the injection of cholinergic and adrenergic agents into the relevant brain sites. Hernandez-Peon et al. (1963) report that injection of noradrenaline into sites in the preoptic area elicited alertness, whereas injection of cholinergic substances into the same sites produced sleep. This makes it very likely that separate arousing and sleep-inducing pathways exist and employ different chemical mediators, though they overlap anatomically. It is at present unclear how the active sleep-inducing process exerts its effect. It could, for instance, inhibit the arousal system directly, or it could antagonize its effects at various structures.

This does not mean that the reticular deactivation view of sleep is incorrect. It is apparent from common experience that the onset of sleep is facilitated by a quiet environment. Even when sleep was induced by brain stimulation, it was found that this could be affected by such conditions as external stimulation and the animal's emotional state. It seems, therefore, that a low level of activity in the arousal system is prerequisite for the induction of sleep. Both processes, the active and the passive, are important.

However, here as elsewhere in this particular area, contradictory findings have arisen. Myers (1964) implanted crystals of carbachol (a cholinergic drug, a synthetic form of acetylcholine) in areas where Hernandez-Peon et al. reported obtaining sleep. Instead of somnolence, the drug produced nervousness, and in larger doses aggressive behavior. MacPhail and Miller (1968) were similarly unable to evoke sleep by injections of carbachol solutions into the sites used by Hernandez-Peon et al., and, like Myers, observed only fearful and aggressive behavior.

PARADOXICAL SLEEP

Paradoxical sleep is so named because it is deep behavioral sleep accompanied by a fast desynchronized EEG record, normally characteristic of behavioral alertness (Dement, 1958; Hubel, 1960; Moruzzi, 1964). In spite of this resemblance to the waking state, paradoxical sleep seems to be a deeper stage of sleep than that characterized by slow synchronized rhythms. For instance, on going to sleep the organism passes from the synchronized stage of sleep to the desynchronized stage. Further, on being disturbed in the desynchronized stage by some externally applied stimulus, the organism passes into synchronized sleep and then perhaps wakes up. Also, during paradoxical sleep antigravity reflexes are diminished, as shown, for instance, by loss of muscle tone in the neck muscles. However, this stage of sleep is accompanied by fast eye movements, and it seems that it is during this stage that dreaming occurs (Jouvet, 1962). Further, subjects are often more difficult to awaken from paradoxical sleep than from normal sleep.

Paradoxical sleep generally occurs every 90 minutes, and lasts 20 minutes in adults. However, during an infant's first few weeks of life about 80 percent of the time spent in sleep is occupied by paradoxical sleep.

It is possible to deprive both animals and humans of paradoxical sleep selectively (Dement, 1960; Jouvet et al., 1964). They are awakened whenever rapid eye movements occur or the tonus of the neck muscles disappears. When this occurs, the tendency for paradoxical sleep increases. In contrast to animals deprived of similar amounts of normal sleep, cats deprived of paradoxical sleep were restless, hyperphagic, and hypersexual (Dement, Henry, Cohen, and Ferguson, 1967).

It has been shown that the desynchronized stage of sleep is induced by activity in the pontile tegmentum (Jouvet, 1962). It appears that the pathways carrying this effect from this nucleus run to the higher parts of the nervous system through the ventral and medial part of the upper brain stem, and are separate from the pathways responsible for desynchronization during behavioral wakefulness.

HUMORAL FACTORS INVOLVED IN CORTICAL ELECTROGRAPHIC CHANGES

Although most studies investigating the effect of reticular changes on the electrical activity of the cortex have concentrated on the neuronal pathways and mechanisms involved, it has also been demonstrated that such an influence can occur in the absence of a neural pathway. Ingvar (1955) observed that electrical stimulation of the reticular activating system caused electrographic changes in neuronally isolated cortex, and concluded that neurohumoral factors must also play a role in regulating cortical electrical activity. Purpura (1956), using the cross-perfusion technique in cats, found that stimulation of the bulbar reticular formation in the donor produced cortical EEG arousal in the recipient. He concluded that this effect was due to the release of a neurohumor from the donor's brain. In a similar situation, Kornmuller et al. (1961) found that stimulating the central lateral nucleus, the ventral medial nucleus of the thalamus, and the caudate nucleus in the donor produced electrographic sleep effects in the recipient as well as in the donor.

Monnier et al. (1963) performed cross-circulation experiments an rabbits. They found that stimulation of the mediocentral intralaminary thalamus in the donor produced a statistically significant increase in high-voltage slow activity in the recipient as well as in the donor. Stimulation of the midbrain reticular system in the donor produced a statistically significant decrease in high-voltage slow activity in the recipient as well as in the donor. This substantiates the hypothesis of an extraneuronal humoral agent influencing cortical electrical activity following reticular changes. However, injections derived from the blood of a naturally sleeping rabbit did not make the recipient rabbit sleep (Monnier and Hösli, 1964).

There are profound physiological changes in brain metabolism during both normal and paradoxical sleep. While there is a small increase in cerebral blood flow during normal sleep with no increase of oxygen consumption, during paradoxical sleep blood flow doubled while metabolism increased (Kety, 1967). This corresponds to the observation of Evarts (1964) that there is a large increase of neural activity during paradoxical sleep. About three times the amount of gamma aminobutyric acid (GABA) is released during sleep as during waking (Jasper et al., 1965). (It is believed that GABA may be an inhibitory synaptic transmitter).

Matzusaki et al. (1964) have produced paradoxical sleep lasting as long as 70 hours with continuous infusions of short-chain, fatty acid compounds such as sodium butyrate. Lower doses produce unconscious states resembling sleep. On the other hand, Jouvet (1967) has found that normal sleep is produced by drugs which increase the effective level of serotonin in the brain (for instance, monoamine oxidase [MAO] inhibitors). Paradoxical sleep seemed to be inhibited by this treatment.

More recently it has been shown that the administration of physostigmine and reserpine jointly produce all the signs of paradoxical sleep (Karczmar et al., 1970). Rats, rabbits, and cats were used. In all these species, EEG desynchronization occurred after the administration of the two drugs—hippocampal theta waves, eye movements, and complete muscular relaxation, especially in the neck. Physostigmine reduces the rate of destruction of acetylcholine by binding with acetylcholinesterase.

There is thus less acetylcholinesterase to destroy acetylcholine. In line with this action of physostigmine, atropine completely abolished the action of physostigmine in producing paradoxical sleep jointly with reserpine. Atropine occupies the receptor sites otherwise available to acetylcholine at muscarinic cholinergic synapses. It occupies such receptor sites, however, without depolarizing the postsynaptic membrane. In this way atropine antagonizes the action of physostigmine. Atropine prevents access to receptor sites to the increased quantities of acetylcholine, increased through the action of physostigmine. At the doses of reserpine employed in this study (10 to 20 mg/kg.), there is an almost complete depletion of serotonin and catecholamines, norepinephrine and dopamine. However, besides affecting serotonin and the catecholamines, reserpine also affects acetylcholine and gamma aminobutyric acid (GABA), which has been implicated as an inhibitory transmitter.

HABITUATION OF THE AROUSAL RESPONSE

When a stimulus is repeatedly presented, it gradually ceases to elicit EEG arousal. This habituation of the arousal response may develop even when many minutes intervene between successive presentations of the same stimulus, and may persist for hours or even days. The presentation of a novel stimulus may abolish habituation established to an old stimulus (disinhibition), and pairing a stimulus with a motivationally relevant stimulus such as shock (conditioning) will greatly retard the habituation process. These findings show that habituation is a type of learning and not just the result of receptor fatigue or nerve accommodation.

Even when extinction of the generalized arousal response is complete, the localized activation pattern in the cortical region receiving the afferent stimulus may persist much longer. Voronin and Sokolov (1960) report that visual stimuli continue to produce blocking of the posterior alpha rhythm even after hundreds of presentations.

This type of habituation has been shown to be very specific to the stimulus parameters presented. Sharpless and Jasper (1956) recorded responses to auditory stimuli in naturally sleeping cats. They found that habituation was specific to the frequency of the tone used, and even to the pattern in which various tones were presented. For instance, an animal habituated to a tone falling in pitch from 5,000 to 200 cps. would be aroused by the same combination of tones rising in pitch. A comparison of the effect of Sharpless and Jasper's lesions on specificity of habituation, with the effect of similar lesions on the ability to discriminate between stimuli, suggests that habituation may be as specific as the animal's ability to discriminate between stimuli. Bilateral lesions of the auditory cortex destroyed specificity of habituation to tonal patterns but did not destroy frequency-specific habituation. In comparison, tonal pattern discrimination is abolished by ablation of auditory cortical areas; yet animals with auditory cortex ablated can still make frequency discriminations (see Chapter 10).

Evidence from studies on human subjects also indicates that habituation of the arousal reaction is very sensitive to changes in stimulus parameters. Voronin and Sokolov (1960) found that a diminution in intensity of a light or sound stimulus, or even the omission of a stimulus which has been regularly repeated, will produce dehabituation. If habituation is established to a complex of three stimuli, then the presentation of one of these without the others will induce arousal. In experiments employing verbal stimuli, they found that when habituation is established to a group of words similar in meaning but different in sound, arousal occurred to a word with a different meaning. However, some generalization of habituation has also been demonstrated. The more similar a stimulus is to the habituatory stimulus, the less likely it is to produce alpha blocking.

Speed of habituation depends on the type of stimulus employed. Sharpless and Jasper (1956) report that habituation to a click stimulus needed only six trials, whereas habituation to a modulated tone changing continuously in pitch required 60 trials. Voronin and Sokolov found that against a background of habituation to words indifferent to the subject, words with particular significance were not habituated to.

Habituation of the arousal response seems to be independent of changes in the primary sensory pathways. Sharpless and Jasper (1956) showed that after such habituation in sleeping cats, cortical potentials evoked by the habituatory stimulus were undiminished. Furthermore, it does not seem to depend on changes occurring in the nonspecific ascending pathways, since high amplitude potentials may also be recorded from the reticular formation in response to the habituatory stimulus (Jouvet, 1961). Parts of the cortex seem vital to this function, however. Jouvet (1961) reports that it is not possible to obtain habituation of the arousal response in chronic mesencephalic or neodecorticated cats. In animals with partial cortical ablations, the smaller the area of cortical surface left intact, the longer it takes for an animal to habituate. Sharpless and Jasper (1956) showed that habituation to auditory stimuli occurred in animals with total ablations of the auditory cortex; so the primary cortical receiving areas do not seem to be essential to this process. The frontal cortex, however, appears to be of critical importance. Jouvet found that almost complete ablation of the frontal cortex led to a considerable slowing down of the habituation process. Konorski (1956) reports that ablation of the frontal lobes in the dog led to a substantial retardation of the process of inhibition. On the basis of such evidence, Jouvet (1961) postulates that habituation depends on the action of a rostral inhibitory system, of which the neocortex is an essential part, which acts downward on the reticular system. However, Horn and Hill (1966a) have found single units that show habituation in the mesencephalon of a decorticate animal, and Spencer and Thompson (1966a, b, c) have found habituating units in a spinal cord severed from the rest of the central nervous system.

SELECTIVE ATTENTION

Human Behavioral Studies

It is apparent from everyday experience that we are aware of only a limited sample of the happenings around us. Such a limitation is not due only to the relatively restricted range of our sense organs. Many things which excite our sense organs do not appear to be registered by us. Instead, we seem to select small samples of the input from our receptors and to deal with these samples one at a time. We can also switch from one sample to another when we wish, but we cannot attend to everything at once even if we would like to do so. Why this is the case is one of the main problems of selective attention.

An experiment by Cherry (1953) illustrates how very little we may be aware of from one information source when we are attending to another. Subjects were required to repeat a continuous stream of speech delivered to one ear, while at the same time another stream of speech was being fed into the other ear. In the middle of the experiment the nature of the stimulus to the "irrelevant" ear was changed: some subjects were presented with a pure tone; others with a woman's voice instead of a man's; others with German instead of English words; and still others with "reversed" speech with the same spectrum as normal speech, though devoid of meaning. It was found that though the changes to a female voice and a pure tone were readily noticed, the subjects could say nothing about the content of the irrelevant message—not even what language it was in! And only some of the subjects presented with the reversed speech noticed "something queer" about it.

One question which arises here is where in the nervous system the messages to which we do not attend are lost. One of the ways of deciding where the nervous system discards information with which it is not at the moment dealing is to consider the complexity of selection between messages. If, for instance, the nervous system will exclude a message only on the basis of which ear is receiving it (as in the experiment of Cherry), it would be plausible to assume that the selection is performed at a low level, simply by blocking the path leading from one ear. If, on the other hand, the meaning of messages is utilized in enabling us to attend to one message and to discard another, it is evident that both messages must have been examined as to their content prior to the rejection of one. It is most unlikely that such an examination could be carried out at the purely peripheral level, and a central or cortical theory of selection therefore becomes plausible.

In the attempt to determine which cues we utilize in making such a selection, the experimental situation preferred by most workers has been the simultaneous presentation of two auditory sequences. Localization cues have been shown to be important in this situation. Broadbent (1954) presented, simultaneously, sequences of messages in pairs, and required subjects to answer only one sequence. He found that the presentation of the messages through spatially segregated loudspeakers increased efficiency, as did stereophonic separation (which, as Broadbent remarks, controlled other possible factors, such as changes in the quality of the sound produced by moving the speaker, or the subject's moving his head nearer to one speaker). Furthermore, he found that if the speech was reproduced through headphones stereophonically, better results were obtained than if the voices were presented through the headphones conventionally mixed. Further evidence for the importance of localization cues is presented by Poulton (1953), Spieth, Curtis, and Webster (1954), and Webster and Thomson (1954), who investigated the monitoring of more than two channels at a time.

Experiments on listening to messages against a background of noise are also of relevance here, since "noise" may be considered a second channel competing for the subject's attention. Hirsh (1950) investigated this phenomenon in a well-controlled situation, using a room free of echoes. When the speech was delivered through one loudspeaker and the noise through another, he found that better results were obtained if the speakers were separated than if they were adjacent. Furthermore, if one loudspeaker was placed in front of the head and the other behind, efficiency was lower than if the speakers were separated but differently placed, and it is interesting that the latter condition provides more localization cues than the former, in which the only available cue is provided by the shadow of the external ear.

Another cue shown to be important in this respect is the frequency of the sound occurring in the messages. Increasing the difference between the mean frequency (pitch) of the relevant and the irrelevant messages increases efficiency in attending to the former and ignoring the latter (Spieth, Curtis, and Webster, 1954; Egan, Carterette, and Thwing, 1954).

So far the evidence quoted is consistent with the notion that the separation of one message from another in selective attention may be done on the basis of relatively few simple characteristics, such as localization and frequency. If messages were discarded on some simple criterion such as frequency, then the selected message could proceed alone for more complex analysis. The mechanisms for more complex analysis could then handle the single message more efficiently than if they were being flooded by a large number of messages. Such a view has been put forward in a detailed form by Broadbent (1958). He supposes that messages are selected by a "filter" which is capable of simple and few discriminations. This filter allows only one message out of many to proceed to the central analyzing mechanisms, thus reducing the load of discrimination which they have to perform. At the time, such a notion of a filter agreed with neurophysiological observations on diminution of evoked potentials at relatively peripheral levels during attention (see below). However, further research has produced a more complicated picture of these phenomena, so that the neurophysiological findings, on the whole, do not really support the notion of a peripheral filter.

Further, behavioral research makes such a notion of a filter implausible because of the complexity of discrimination required in many tasks involving selective attention. Various findings demonstrate that the selection of wanted from unwanted speech is a central phenomenon, and not due simply to the blocking of the unwanted information at a peripheral level. Peters (1954) found that if two messages similar in content are played simultaneously to the subject, it is more difficult for him to select one of them than if the contents of the messages àre different. This tends to show that the contents of two messages are taken into consideration before one of them is selected.

The operations performed on incoming information before the selection of a message have been shown to be very complex. Gray and Wedderburn (1960) performed an experiment in which two meaningful sequences of syllables or words were used. Instead of playing one of these sequences consistently to one ear or the other, they took the two sequences and switched them between ears. Sequence A would start on the left ear and sequence B on the right; thus a syllable or word would be fed into each ear. However, the second word or syllable in sequence A would be fed into the right ear and the second word or syllable in sequence B would go into the left ear. It was found that though the sequences were continually switched from one ear to the other, the subjects would select the speech in such a way that a meaningful sequence was reported back to the experimenter. The subjects were, therefore, analyzing the meaning of the speech sounds in the process of selecting some and rejecting others, and this analysis could not possibly have been carried out at the periphery. Gray and Wedderburn's (1960) experiment shows that the nervous system, prior to making its selection, can make use of its memory of the transition probabilities of the items presented. Some word or sound sequences are more probable than others, and it looks as if in this experiment the more likely combinations were chosen as belonging together, in spite of their occurring in different ears.

Further evidence of the use of such transition probabilities is presented by Treisman (1960). She played two messages, one to each of a pair of earphones. Subjects were asked to repeat what they heard in one of their ears. In the middle of the experiment the messages were switched from one ear to the other. There was a tendency to stay with a message for a few words in spite of the switch, this tendency being proportional to the transition probability of the words in the message.

It has also been shown that there is a surprising specificity about the items which will redirect attention. Moray (1959) has shown that if a subject is attending to a message in one ear, it is possible to have him switch to the other ear in a certain proportion of instances by calling his name in the ear and the message to which he was otherwise unaware. No other stimulus was found to be effective. The special status of one's own name in the attention process has been confirmed in other instances. In a well-controlled experiment, Oswald, Taylor, and Treisman (1960) found that a subject shows EEG changes during sleep in response to his own name much more so than to any other name. Howarth and Ellis (1961) used another type of situation to investigate this problem. Subjects were required to identify various names when they were fully awake and listening with both ears, but when there was masking by noise. The investigators found that the probability of the subject's recognizing his own name was significantly higher than that of his recognizing other names. Comparing the probabilities of recognition in their experiment with those derived by Moray (1959) and Oswald, Taylor, and Treisman (1960), they conclude: "It seems an obvious conclusion to suppose that the same pattern analysing mechanism is required to account for behavior during dichotic listening or during sleep."

If the same structure is responsible for recognition in the case of normal listening and during selective attention, it is most likely that selection is performed at the highest neural level. The above evidence therefore leads us to conclude against the hypothesis that selection in attention is achieved by a two-stage process, including a preliminary discriminating mechanism or filter which allows only certain items to proceed to the highest level. It is more consistent with the behavioral evidence to suppose that messages proceed to the same destination whether they are selected in attention or not. Then, as a result of activity in the regions to which the messages proceed, further changes will take place in these and associated regions if such messages are selected for attention.

Localized EEG Arousal

Since general behavioral arousal is correlated with widespread EEG desynchronization, it might be expected that selective attention to a specific stimulus would be associated with EEG arousal localized to the appropriate cortical region. Such an association has indeed been found under certain conditions. Adrian (1947) showed in human subjects that the presentation of visual stimuli led to the blocking of the occipital alpha rhythm. Shifting attention from the visual to an auditory stimulus caused the occipital alpha to return. He also found that visual stimuli, if confined to a part of the visual field, selectively block only the alpha-rhythm in the contralateral parieto-occipital region. Penfield (1954) describes localized activation in a patient during operation. When the patient was told to make a fist of his hand, the resting rhythms in the hand area of the contralateral precentral and postcentral gyri disappeared, but they continued in the face area and in the cortex lying anterior and posterior to the Rolandic hand area. The resting rhythms returned as the patient maintained his hand in that position. While the patient, upon instruction, touched his thumb with one finger after the other of the same hand, resting rhythms in the Rolandic hand area disappeared again, not to return until the maneuver was completed.

However, this localized activation can be demonstrated only under certain conditions. The presentation of a relatively novel stimulus gives rise to a number of behavioral reactions, involving the activation of widespread areas of the cortex. With repeated presentations of the same stimulus, however, most of these general reactions tend to disappear, and concomitantly the EEG arousal response becomes localized to the appropriate cortical region. For instance, the initial presentation of a light stimulus induces blocking of the alpha rhythm in the occipital and motor areas of the cortex, along with other effects such as changes in respiration, GSR changes, and eye movements. After a few presentations these behavioral effects tend to disappear, along with the alpha blocking of the motor area. However, alpha blocking in the occipital region may continue for even hundreds of presentations. With the presentation of a tactile stimulus, the blocking of occipital alpha disappears after the first few presentations while the GSR changes and blocking of the Rolandic rhythm continues. With proprioceptive stimuli, blocking of the Rolandic rhythm and the GSR changes continue even longer. Thus the appearance of localized activation coincides with the disappearance of the generalized behavioral response to a novel stimulus (Voronin and Sokolov, 1960).

We may ask further what functional change such EEG activation reflects. When we attend to an object, various processes can be seen to occur by common observation. We may make receptor adjustments to see the object more clearly and to approach it, and we are in a state of readiness to respond to it. We are also able to report the various features of the object afterward if called upon to do so. So it seems that when we are paying attention to certain stimuli, various circuits in the areas concerned with the reception of these stimuli are activated. These circuits are concerned with motor output, memory storage, and so on. The generalized EEG arousal accompanying the presentation of a novel stimulus is thus associated with a considerable degree of activity in motor and autonomic pathways. However, with repeated stimulus presentations, fewer of these circuits are activated, and this is reflected in a more localized EEG desynchronization. Certain pathways, concerned with the reception and analysis of the signal, of course continue to be activated.

The discovery by Hubel, Henson, Rupert, and Galambos (1959) of units in the auditory cortex of the cat, which responded only when the animal was paying attention to a sound source, might be interpreted in this light. One unit they describe almost never responded to clicks, tones, or noise, but responded readily to squeaks emitted by a toy mouse, to a human voice, and to hissing when the animal was paying attention to these stimuli. Another unit responded to the sound of keys being jingled outside the room, but only when the cat looked toward the door. It also responded to the rustling of a paper, but only when the cat looked toward the paper. The authors conclude that about 10 percent of the units in the auditory cortex of the cat are of this type. Other units, in contrast, responded reliably to stimuli presented by loudspeaker, regardless of whether the animal was awake or asleep. We might suppose that these "attention" units formed part of circuits responsible for such things as the appropriate motor response to the stimulus, or memory storage, or that they lay on the pathway to these systems. Thus we should expect these units to be inactive even if impulses evoked by auditory stimuli were reaching the cortex, provided the animal was not paying attention to these stimuli.

The Selection Process in Selective Attention

So far we have concluded that the discarding of information to which we are not attending does not occur at a peripheral level, since the discriminations required to separate the ascending messages before one of these is selected are often extremely complex. The problem of how the nervous system discriminates or separates the vast mixture of ascending impulses so that they are appropriately grouped to correspond with the many concurrent events stimulating the organism is not basically one of selective attention. It is, rather, a problem in perception. However, there is another question which is more limited to the sphere of selective attention. This is how one of the messages, once they have been separated, is efficiently selected by the nervous system. There is an extremely large number of possible messages, from which one is to be selected at any one time. If we wish to select one item out of a set according to some criterion, this involves us in a process of comparison among the items of such a set. If the set is large, it seems at first sight that the number of comparisons to be made among its various items will be enormous. For such a task to be performed by the nervous system, one would have to postulate a neural connection for every comparison that might have to be made.

However, we can envisage a much simpler system which would choose the largest item of a group (Deutsch and Deutsch, 1963). If there is a group of boys and we wish to select the tallest, we can proceed by placing a horizontal board over their heads to see which boy's head it touches. The boy whose head it touches will know he is the tallest boy in the group. If he leaves the group, the board will descend until it touches the head of the tallest boy who is left. The principle of operation of this system is that the tallest will raise a general level to his own height and so will be the only one to be at that level.

Deutsch and Deutsch (1963) describe in detail how signals might be selected for attention on this analogy. Then propose that the reticular system may, as part of its function, act as a diffuse system capable of taking a level appropriate to the greatest amount of excitation being fed into it. Such excitation would occur as a result of cortical analysis of a signal. For those signals whose resultant excitation is lower than that appropriate to the level in the diffuse system, the relevant motor and memory storage pathways, etc., would be blocked. Thus only one signal would be attended to (Fig. 11–9).

Such a system could be independent of the mechanism underlying general arousal (though it need not be). Beh and Barrett (1965) present evidence for such an independence of general and specific alerting systems. This question needs to be investigated further.

Changes in the Evoked Potential Related to Shifts of Attention and Habituation

Attention Shifts. Hernandez-Peon, Sherrer, and Jouvet (1956), recording responses evoked in the dorsal cochlear nucleus to clicks in unanaesthetized animals, found that the presentation of a visual stimulus (in this case mice in a jar) or an olfactory stimulus (fish odors) greatly diminished the amplitude of the evoked response to clicks. When the "distracting" stimuli were removed, responses in the cochlear nucleus returned to their original amplitude. A similar effect has been reported in visual and somatosensory pathways (Hernandez-Peon, Guzman-Flores, Alcarez, and Fernandez-Guardiola, 1957; Brust-Carmona and Hernandez-Peon, 1959). In man, Jouvet (1957) studied the effect of various attentional states on responses in the optic radiations to light flash. When the subject was asked to attend to and count the flashes, there resulted an enhancement of responses in the optic radiations. The

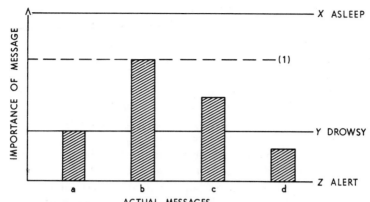

ACTUAL MESSAGES
FIG. 11–9. Diagram to illustrate the operation of a hypothesized specific alerting system and its interaction with the mechanism underlying general arousal. This system involves a shifting reference standard which takes up the level of the most important arriving signal. The interrupted horizontal line (*1*) represents the "level" of importance in the specific alerting system which is raised and lowered according to the incoming messages. The solid horizontal lines represent levels of general arousal. At *X* the organism is asleep and none of the incoming messages produce alerting. At *Y* the organism is drowsy and only some of the incoming messages could produce alerting. At *Z* the organism is awake and all incoming messages could produce alerting; however, only *b* is heeded because of the operation of the specific alerting system. (Adapted from Deutsch, J. A., and Deutsch, D., 1963, *Psych. Rev.*, 70.)

responses diminished when distracting stimuli were introduced, or when the subject was asked to perform calculations.

Habituation. It has been claimed that when a stimulus is repeatedly presented, evoked potentials recorded from the cortex and relay nuclei along the primary sensory pathways, as well as from the reticular formation and other subcortical structures, show a decrement in amplitude which follows a waxing and waning course. Various factors, such as a period of rest and the presentation of extraneous stimuli (disinhibition, will bring about a return to high amplitude potentials. Such habituation has been alleged to occur at such peripheral levels as the dorsal cochlear nucleus (Hernandez-Peon and Scherrer, 1955; Galambos et al., 1956; Hernandez-Peon, Jouvet, and Scherrer, 1957), the retina (Palestini, Davidovich, and Hernandez-Peon, 1959), the olfactory bulb (Hernandez-Peon, Alcocer-Cuaron, Lavin, and Santibanez, 1957), and the lateral column of the spinal cord (Burst-Carmona and Hernandez-Peon, 1959). Habituation at higher levels on the primary sensory pathways, including the cortex, has been found in various structures (Hernandez-Peon, Guzman-Flores, Alcarez, and Fernandez-Guardiola, 1958; Moushegian et al., 1961). In the cortex, habituation of the evoked potential often occurs considerably faster in regions other than the primary projection area for the appropriate stimulus. It has also been reported that cortical-evoked potentials may disappear at a faster rate than evoked potentials at lower levels (Hernandez-Peon, 1960).

Involvement of the Brain Stem Reticular Formation in These Effects. It has been inferred from a variety of evidence that the changes in evoked potential (described above) are brought about by some mechanism involving the brain stem reticular formation. One such type of evidence is that stimulation of the reticular formation may cause a reduction in amplitude of the evoked response similar to that produced by distraction and habituation, or a facilitation of the evoked response similar to that obtained in conditioning (see Chapter 12).

Granit (1955) demonstrated both facilitation and inhibition of the firing of individual ganglion cells of the retina as a result of stimulating the midbrain tegmentum. A similar control of activity in the spinal and brain stem relays has been demonstrated: stimulation of the reticular formation inhibited responses in the posterior columns (Hagbarth and Kerr, 1954) and inhibited conduction in the nucleus gracilis (Hernandez-Peon, Scherrer, and Velasco, 1956). Activity in the sensory nucleus of the fifth nerve could be similarly affected (Hernandez-Peon and Hagbarth, 1955).

Hernandez-Peon, Scherrer, and Velasco (1956) report that stimulation of the reticular formation resulted in a depression of the evoked response to photic stimulation in the lateral geniculate. Under some conditions a facilitatory effect can also be demonstrated (Bremer and Stoupel, 1959). At the cortical level also, both inhibitory and facilitatory effects of reticular stimulation of the evoked potential have been shown (Bremer and Stoupel, 1959; Dumont and Dell, 1958). Lindsley (1958) found improved resolution of cortical response to two light flashes closely separated in time as a result of reticular stimulation.

Nevertheless, stimulation of other central structures may also influence the size of evoked responses. This has been shown, for instance, for the cortex, cerebellum, and various structures in the rhinencephalon. (Such effects are mentioned in other chapters in this book dealing with specific sensory afferents.)

Further evidence that the brain stem reticular formation is involved in the habituation of the evoked response is based on the finding that lesions in this structure may eliminate such habituation (Hernandez-Peon, 1960). The reticular formation does not appear to act nonspecifically in this respect, however. Pontine lesions were shown to eliminate habituation of postrotatory nystagmus but not to affect olfactory habituation. Yet mesencephalic lesions eliminated acoustic and olfactory habituation but did not prevent habituation to vestibular stimulation. Barbiturate anaesthesia, especially, is known to depress activity in the reticular formation. Animals under this anesthetic will not demonstrate habituation, and if this anaesthesia is administered after habituation has taken place, evoked potentials will, as a result, return to their original high amplitude. On the other hand, such a return to high-amplitude responses does not occur under light physiological sleep (Hernandez-Peon, 1960). However, despite the seeming necessity for the intactness of reticular structures in some instances, it has also been shown that habituation of the evoked potential is possible in preparations lacking a reticular formation. Hernandez-Peon and Brust-Carmona (1961) report that habituation may occur in isolated spinal cord in cats, as do Spencer and Thompson (1966a, b, c).

Interpretation of the Changes in Size of the Evoked Potential at the Peripheral Sensory Synapses

Hernandez-Peon (1960) suggests that the reduction in amplitude of response which occurs at the peripheral sensory synapses with attention shifts, habituation, and reticular stimulation is due to "centrifugal plastic inhibition acting at those peripheral sensory synapses" originating from the brain stem reticular formation. There are indications from recent experiments, however, that these effects may at least (in some cases) be due to peripheral factors. Hugelin, Dumont, and Paillas (1960) report that when the middle ear muscles were cut, stimulation of the reticular formation failed to produce an attenuation of the evoked response to clicks at the cochlear nucleus. They suggest that the reticular control of auditory input may be due to motor effects. They further point out that the mean diminution of microphonic potentials resulting from reticular stimulation was less than five decibels, which is very small from the point of view of auditory sensation.

Naquet et al. (1960) report that changes in the evoked potential at lower levels of the visual pathway, resulting from reticular stimulation, may be due to accompanying changes in pupillary diameter. The pupil dilates during desynchronization of the EEG (whether or not this desynchronization is due to reticular stimulation) and contracts during EEG synchrony. It has been found that during desynchronization flash-evoked responses at the optic chiasma and lateral geniculate were increased, and that they were reduced at the visual receiving area of the cortex. The reverse occurred during synchrony. When the size of the pupil was fixed by topical application of atropine, the size of the evoked potentials remained constant at the optic chiasma and lateral geniculate, though they continued to vary at the cortex.

Another line of criticism is put forward by Worden and Marsh (1963) in a study on cats with intact middle ear muscles. They found that fluctuations in the amplitude of evoked response occurring in the cochlear nucleus with repeated stimulus presentations were quite inconsistent. Increases in amplitude of evoked response occurred as well as decreases. Amplitude changes in opposite directions could be recorded between placements in the right and left cochlear nuclei, and also between two adjacent placements within one cochlear nucleus. No correlation was found between placement of electrode tip and direction of amplitude shift in the evoked response. Opposite results were even obtained from the same placement on different occasions. It may therefore be that earlier results showing a decrease in evoked potential at peripheral levels during repeated stimulus presentations were due to sampling bias.

In a well-controlled experiment, Wickelgren (1968a, b) recorded click-evoked responses at various levels in the auditory pathway. He could detect no changes in amplitude to a repetitious click in the cochlear nucleus, superior olive, and inferior colliculus. However, changes were observed as the click stimulus was repeated in the medial geniculate of the thalamus and the auditory cortex. At the cortex, the only change observed was a decrement in the late surface negative component of the gross evoked potential.

Habituation has also been studied at the single-unit level. Many of the units in the brain stem reticular formation show that habituation often ceases to respond after five or six stimuli. It is the units that show a lack of specificity in responsiveness that are most prone to habituate. In unanaesthetized preparations, dishabituation of the response has been shown (Bell, Sierra, Buendia, and Segundo, 1964; Horn and Hill, 1966b; Scheibel and Scheibel, 1965). Whereas most units in the primary sensory projection areas show no habituation (Horn, 1963), hippocampal units show habituation within 10 to 20 trials. The responses of hippocampal units are somewhat unspecific (Vinogradova, 1965, 1968). Intracellular recordings from units in the mesencephalon show an attenuation of postsynaptic potentials as the only observable change during habituation (Segundo, Takenaka, and Encabo, 1967).

Interpretation of the Changes in Evoked Potential at the Cortical Level

Changes in the evoked response at the cortex have not been shown to be due to peripheral factors. We saw above that when the size of the pupil was fixed by atropine, flash-evoked responses in the visual receiving area of the cortex continued to show lability (Naquet et al., 1960). Further, Moushegian et al. (1961), using animals in which the middle ear muscles had been cut, found that evoked responses at the auditory cortex still demonstrated diminution with habituation and attention shifts, as well as enhancement with conditioning (Fig. 11–10).

However, some disagreement exists concerning the functional inter-

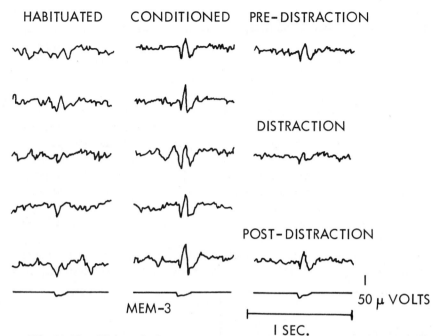

HABITUATED   CONDITIONED   PRE-DISTRACTION

DISTRACTION

POST-DISTRACTION

MEM-3

50 μ VOLTS

I SEC.

FIG. 11–10. Click-evoked potentials recorded from the auditory cortex of cats deprived of middle ear muscles. The first column shows potentials taken from a cat in the "habituated" state. The middle column shows enhancement of evoked potentials produced by the reinforcing of selected clicks with a puff of air directed at the cat's face. The last column shows evoked potentials recorded immediately before, during, and after visual distraction. (From "Evoked Cortical Potentials in Absence of Middle Ear Muscles," Moushegian, G., et al., *Science,* 133: 282, 24 Feb. 1961. Copyright 1961 by the American Association for the Advancement of Science.)

pretation of these changes at the cortex. Using human subjects, Jouvet (1957) and Garcia-Austt et al. (1964) found that the visual evoked responses to flash stimuli were enhanced in amplitude when the subjects were required to attend to and count the flashes. On the other hand, Horn (1960) recorded flash-evoked responses in the visual cortex of cats, both when the cat was watching a mouse and when it was resting. He found that when the cat was watching the mouse, responses were attenuated, and when it ignored the mouse, the amplitude of the responses remained high. Horn proposed, therefore, that diminution in evoked responses might indicate increased rather than reduced sensitivity in the appropriate region. Callaway et al. (1965) obtained results from human patients pointing to the same conclusion. They found that when the subjects were attending to auditory stimuli, they manifested a decrease rather than an increase in the auditory evoked response. A further conflicting result was obtained by Van Hof et al. (1962), who report that attending to and counting flash stimuli did not affect the amplitude of the evoked response to the flashes.

Lindsley and his co-workers suggest that these conflicting results (in the human case) may have been due to differences in the methods by which an attentive set was established in the subjects. Some tasks also involve a degree of distraction of attention from the test stimuli (such as may occur if numerical calculation is required). In a situation which they felt minimized this factor, Spong, Haider, and Lindsley (1965) required subjects to make perceptual discriminations. They recorded cortical evoked responses to flashes and to clicks, and found that when attention was directed toward the visual stimuli the responses to flashes evoked from the occipital area were larger, and when attention was directed to the auditory stimuli the responses to clicks evoked from the temporal area were larger. Earlier, Haider, Spong, and Lindsley (1964) found that poorer signal-detection performance in a vigilance task was associated with a reduced amplitude of visual evoked responses at the cortex (Fig. 11–11). It is evident from these careful studies that

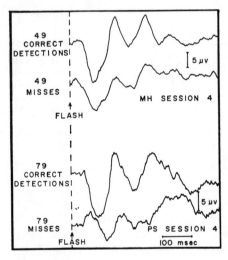

FIG. 11–11. Computer-averaged cortical-evoked potentials for equal numbers of detected and missed signals in two human subjects. (From "Attention, Vigilance and Cortical Evoked Potentials in Humans," Haider, M. A., *Science,* 145: 180–82, 10 July 1964. Copyright 1964 by the American Association for the Advancement of Science.)

close attention must be paid to behavioral variables in order to reach agreement on this question.

Another variable which influences the results of attention experiments has been pointed out by Satterfield (1965). Satterfield separately measured the early evoked potential from the scalp over the sensory areas, and a later and larger potential occurring at a latency of more than 100 msec.—most readily recorded from the vertex of the head, and therefore called the vertex potential. While the short-latency sensory evoked potentials were unaffected by changes in attention, fluctuations in the vertex potential were induced by changes in attention.

chapter 12

Neural Bases of
Learning

NATURE OF THE PHYSICAL CHANGE IN LEARNING AND MEMORY

Though it is at present impossible to say what change occurs in the brain when a sensory event is registered in memory, there is both clinical and experimental evidence to indicate some properties of the change we are looking for. The passing of time makes interesting alterations in the stability of memory, which presumably reflect the characteristics of the underlying physical change. Some of the more remarkable evidence comes from clinical cases of amnesia.

AMNESIC PHENOMENA

Two main types of amnesia due to organic processes (such as head injury or poisoning) can be distinguished. The first is posttraumatic amnesia, or an inability to remember events which occurred after an accident. The second is retrograde amnesia, or an inability to recall happenings before an accident.

In the majority of accidents leading to amnesia, there is concussion. In this state there is a paralysis of cerebral function including motor, sensory, mental, and reflex manifestations. During the period of concussion there can be no registration of events in the environment, and as a result there a complete amnesia for events which occurred at this time. With the return of consciousness, mental functions gradually recover. The more complex functions are the last to return. The period of recovery may vary from a few minutes to weeks.

During the period of recovery, memory is usually uniformly hazy. However, in a few cases there are reappearances of memory which will again disappear. Sometimes posttraumatic amnesia is delayed; that is, everything at the time of the injury and some time after is clearly remembered, but later there follows a period of confusion and amnesia. Such cases of posttraumatic amnesia are probably due to the delayed effects of injury, such as hemorrhage. There are also cases in which paralysis of mental function does not occur during posttraumatic amnesia. There are cases of football players and boxers who continue to play or fight after a head injury and who later remember nothing of the game or fight that occurred after the injury. Such a state is similar to that of postepileptic automatism, where whole sequences of action may not be amenable to recall following a seizure. There are also cases when the patient on recovery will describe a "vision" which refers to something seen before the accident. However, the circumstances surrounding this isolated memory cannot be recalled.

The second type of amnesia of traumatic origin is found in cases of head injury, acute cerebral anoxia, after administration of electroconvulsive shock, and such accidents as carbon monoxide poisoning. This is retrograde amnesia. The memories which are lost in this type of amnesia cover the time period preceding the accident. It appears that it is always the period closest to the accident which is not remembered. That is, the gap in memory covers a continuous stretch of time, with one end anchored to the accident. There is, then, a memory gap extending backward, and this gap may shrink, with the memories most distant always returning first.

The period covered by such a gap is often very long, sometimes extending over years. For instance, during gradual recovery of consciousness a patient, on being asked, may give the current date as several years earlier and his age as correspondingly younger. In most cases the posttraumatic gap in memory shrinks ultimately to a few minutes or seconds before the accident occurred. Russell and Nathan (1946), in their extensive review, stress that recovery of memories in retrograde amnesia occurs not in order of importance but in order of time. The long past memories, however trivial they are, are the first to return.

Another type of retrograde amnesia occurs in the Korsakoff psychosis. Such a psychosis is often the consequence of alcoholism and is marked by a progressive loss of memory. Memory for progressively more remote events disappears until the patient may remember only childhood events. Memory of the events of the last few moments is preserved (Talland, 1965). Victor (1964) finds that the loss of memory in this syndrome is correlated with damage to the medial dorsal nuclei of the thalamus.

RELATIONSHIP OF RETROGRADE AMNESIA TO THE PHYSICAL CHANGE IN MEMORY

The symptoms of retrograde amnesia are so striking and paradoxical that we would expect them to tell us something important about the physical change responsible for memory. It is not older memories or less important memories, which introspectively seem fainter, that are selectively knocked out. On the contrary, the more recent memories are the most likely to disappear. This suggests that the physical change on which our capacity to remember rests becomes progressively more resistant to injury. It also suggests that a physical change is not laid down once and for all, but that it continues to consolidate so that it becomes more difficult to obliterate. The simplest way of accounting for this would be to assume that the physical change which was initiated during the act of registration continues to grow in magnitude. This would then explain the loss of more recent memories by assuming that the physical change initiated by the act of registration had not built up to a sufficient level to overcome obliterative effects imposed by injury or disease. Given a certain level of disruptive physical effects, we would expect all the memories laid down before a certain date to remain and all those registered after such a date to disappear.

However, it does not seem that the process can be quite so simple. The scheme suggested above ignores the fact that memories in retrograde amnesia do recover. If memories do return, then it seems that the changes underlying them must have remained in the interim but that they had somehow been inaccessible. It could be argued that the physical change on which memory rested had really diminished below a certain threshold of magnitude, this magnitude being necessary for the memory change to be accessible. During recovery such subliminal changes which were preserved could grow again until they exceeded the threshold of accessibility. This idea does not seem plausible because it implies an enormous range of subthreshold magnitudes of the memory change. Since less recent memories return first, we would have to assume that even though memories stretching say over five years were all inaccessible or below threshold, the relative amounts of past threshold of accessibility. This idea does not seem plausible because it implies an enormous range of subthreshold magnitudes of the memory change. Since less recent memories return first, we would have to assume that even though memories stretching say over five years were all inaccessible or below threshold, the relative amounts of past strengthening would still have to be preserved because otherwise an orderly return of the memories would not be possible. If a large number of discrete steps of consolidation can be preserved below threshold, it would imply that the normal mechanism of recall is very inefficient in utilizing a memory change. The preservation of a large number of informationally discrete steps below threshold implies that threshold could be much lower than it is.

Another way of accounting for the phenomena of retrograde amnesia which does not run into the above difficulties is as follows. We could assume that the change that subserves memory increases in some way with time but that it does not diminish during retrograde amnesia. Instead, as a result of injury or disease, another change occurs which makes it impossible to utilize a certain fixed amount of the memory change. If the accumulated memory change is large, a greater change due to injury or disease is necessary to counteract its normal function. Such a view would account both for the retrograde character of some amnesias—that is, the fact that the gap in memory extends back from the time of the injury—and also for the fact that recovery of memory is also possible. At present it is impossible to be sure whether such a view is the correct view. On the other hand, it seems highly plausible that some process of progressive strengthening or consolidation does in fact occur.

Temporal Lobes and Memory

Both damage to and stimulation of structures within the temporal lobes lead to various types of interference with memory. Penfield (1958), by electrically stimulating parts of the temporal lobe during operation on patients, was able to evoke memories of previous experiences. Such memories were experienced almost with the strength of hallucinations. The same point on the cortex would evoke the same memory repeatedly. However, excision of the tissue at operation, the stimulation of which had given rise to the memory, did not lead to its loss. That is, the electrical stimulation of the tissue led to an evocation of a complex memory. However, loss of the tissue did not abolish the memory or the capacity for its retrieval (Penfield, 1965).

Hippocampal stimulation in patients (Bickford et al., 1958; Chapman et al., 1967) produces quite different effects on memory. Retrograde amnesia is produced (for events up to two weeks past with bilateral stimulation). The length of the gap in retrograde amnesia increases with the length of the period of hippocampal stimulation. The retrograde amnesia was temporary, lasting only a few hours, and suggesting that the electrical stimulus produced some selective inability to retrieve recent memories. However, the inability to retrieve did not affect very recent memories, which would be called short-term memory by human experimental psychologists. For instance, the ability to repeat strings of digits (digit span) was unaffected by the hippocampal stimulation.

Lesions of the hippocampus in the human (accompanied by at least a unilateral lesion to the temporal lobe) produce a disturbance of memory that is different in some ways to that produced by electrical stimulation of the hippocampus. The patient is, as a rule, unimpaired in his ability to repeat strings of digits (short-term memory). Similarly, he can recall events which occurred before the operation. However, he seems unable (with certain exceptions noted below) to form new memories after the operation.

The patient is grossly impaired in learning a visual (Milner, 1965) or tactile (Corkin, 1965), recurring visual (Kimura, 1963) and auditory (Milner, 1968) material, and delayed matching from sample of visual stimuli (Sidman et al., 1968). This impairment of memory, measured in the laboratory, faithfully mirrors the everyday disability of such patients. Such patients cannot remember meeting people they conversed with a few minutes ago. On the other hand, not all mnemonic functions are equally impaired. A patient is able to learn to draw an object while watching his hand only through a mirror and sustain his improvement 24 hours later, even though he does not remember having performed the task before. Furthermore, a patient can learn to recognize an incomplete figure with greater ease, performing as well as normals (Gollin, 1960; Warrington and Weiskrantz, 1971; Milner and Teuber, 1968). In this task drawings of objects are presented to the subject with large portions of the outline missing. On successive exposures, more of the outline is left in the picture until the complete picture is presented. Once the subject has learned what the picture is, he will recognize the picture from a much more fragmented and incomplete outline than was necessary for him to recognize the picture when it was initially presented. When the task is performed with incomplete words, material which cannot be recalled or recognized by the amnesic patients using the conventional methods of memory testing is nevertheless remembered well within normal limits when parts of the stimulus are presented.

Temporal Lobe Lesions in Animals

As we saw above, damage to the temporal lobes, including the hippocampus, produces striking memory deficits in man in everyday life and deficits in recent memory in most laboratory tests. Brown and Schafer (1888), who observed the effects of large bilateral lobe lesions on monkeys, described one of the symptoms as follows:

His memory and intelligence seem deficient. . . . Every object with which he comes in contact, even those with which he was previously most familiar, appears strange and is investigated with curiosity . . . and he will on coming across the same object accidentally a few minutes afterwards go through exactly the same process as if he had entirely forgotten his previous experience.

Until recently, further experimental work has failed to support Brown and Schafer's observations. For instance, Orbach, Milner, and Rasmussen (1960) designed an elaborate set of tests for monkeys with lesions designed to be equivalent to those producing amnesia in patients. Delayed responding was unimpaired even though the monkeys were distracted with a free peanut during the waiting period. Also, there was no impairment on an object-discrimination task whose trials were widely interspersed among trials of other discriminations. However, there was a decreased ability to perform delayed alteration and a smaller decrement in the learning of visual and tactile discrimination. Thus Orbach, Milner, and Rasmussen's study failed to disclose any specific memory deficit as a result of medial temporal lesions. These results are supported by certain learning situations, such as concurrent learning (Correll and Scoville, 1967), on cats (Flynn and Wasman, 1960), and rats (Isaacson and Wickelgren, 1962; Kimble, 1968).

On the other hand, lesions in this area have effects on behavior and certain learning situations, such as concurrent learning (Correll and Scoville, 1965a), visual matching from sample (Correll and Scoville, 1965b), sequential tasks (Kimble and Pribram, 1963), reversal tasks (Mahut and Cordeau, 1963; Webster and Voneida, 1964), and maze learning (Kaada, Rasmussen, and Kvein, 1961). Other deficits, summarized by Douglas (1967) and Kimble (1968), include prolongation of extinction, increased distractibility to novel stimuli, impairment of passive avoidance, and spontaneous and learned alteration. Instead of supposing that there is a memory deficit, Douglas and Kimble suppose that hippocampal damage (with accompanying damage to the temporal lobe) is due to an impairment of an inhibitory mechanism. An inability to inhibit a response could give rise to a seeming inability to learn in many situations. More recently, however, Iversen and Weiskrantz (1970) and Iversen (1970, 1971) have shown what seems best interpreted as a memory deficit as a result of fairly discrete lesions in the anterior temporal lobe. Visual discriminations were learned to criterion, followed by another discrimination learned to a similar criterion, and some time later (typically 24 hours), after other discriminations had been interpolated, a monkey was tested on a discrimination that it had learned previously. Iversen (1970, 1971) was able to show that, despite an insignificant impairment in initial acquisition, memory for the previous learning was reduced.

OVERLEARNING AND RETROGRADE AMNESIA

Chow and Survis (1958) and Orbach and Fantz (1958) have shown that the retention of visual habits is less severely affected by temporal neocortical ablations when these habits have been overlearned. While there probably is no strict comparability between the practice of a habit and the age of a memory, these experiments suggest that the greater resistance of a memory to destructive influences might be caused by dissemination of the memory throughout the central nervous system as practice or time proceeds. Such an explanation is put forward by Chow and Survis (1958): "As the habit becomes well ingrained, the neural changes must involve or spread to more and more additional regions." However, an alternative explanation need not postulate such a spread, or an unequal destruction of the physical counterpart of the visual memory. One need only assume that irrelevant tendencies which obscure learning are ironed out during prolonged training, so that if an equal amount of destruction of the memory trace for the visual memory is assumed, the overtrained habit would be less affected because there would be fewer irrelevant tendencies to compete with it than with the undertrained habit. This alternative interpretation is supported by the finding of Chow and Survis (1958) that six out of the eight monkeys in their study retained a color discrimination which was taught as a pretraining problem and was not overlearned but was followed by overtraining on a different visual problem. However, this pretraining color discrimination was lost following ablation of the same cortical regions under identical conditions in monkeys to whom no subsequent visual overtraining was given before operation (Chow, 1952). Since the color problems were not overlearned in this study, a spread due to practice cannot be postulated. On the other hand, irrelevant tendencies, which would interfere with the habit, could have been diminished by training on other discriminations. This was shown by Harlow (1959) in his studies on the acquisition of learning set.

EXPERIMENTS ON THE CONSOLIDATION OF THE MEMORY TRACE: ELECTROCONVULSIVE SHOCK

Muller and Pilzecker (1900) and Hebb (1949) have suggested that a temporary preseveration of neural activity occurs after the reception of a sensory message and that during the time of this preseveration a permanent change gradually takes place. Thus the permanent change should be observed to consolidate during the temporary perseveration of neural activity. If this suggestion is correct, it should be possible to impair or even improve the process of learning by various types of treatment which might influence the temporary perseveration of neural activity after a learning trial. Such effects have indeed been found. It has been shown that learning can be impaired by the administration of electroconvulsive shock after a learning trial (Duncan, 1949; Thompson and Dean, 1955; Thomson et al., 1961). In this procedure a brief current is passed between the ears of the rat so that a convulsive seizure, followed by unconsciousness, occurs. By showing that the loss of memory also occurred when the current was applied to an animal under ether anaesthesia and no seizure followed, McGaugh (1966) demonstrated that the loss-of-memory effect obtained was not due to the seizure caused by the electroconvulsive shock (ECS). Effects similar to that of ECS have been shown in the case of hypoxia (oxygen lack) (Thompson and Pryer, 1956) and when depressant drugs were administered (Leukel,

1957; Pearlman et al., 1961). Cerf and Otis (1957) found that narcosis, produced by heating goldfish at various intervals after a learning trial, produced decrements in learning that were larger the closer the narcosis had been to the preceding trial. Such a temporal relation has also been demonstrated in the case of ECS. The closer the ECS to the end of a preceding learning trial, the severer the learning loss.

It has also been shown that the loss-of-memory effect cannot be attributed to possibly punishing effects of electroconvulsive shock because the same shock applied across the hindlegs of rats under the same conditions produces no such decrement of learning (Duncan, 1949) except at the shortest interval (20 seconds) (see also p. 437). Thomson et al. (1961) have demonstrated different effects of ECS on learning in rats that were descendants of the Tryon maze-bright strain and of the Tryon maze-dull strain. In the maze-dull strain, ECS produced a learning decrement after a much longer interval than that observed in the maze-bright strain. This evidence indicated to Thomson et al that the process of consolidation takes a longer time in the Tryon maze-dull strain. Such results are of particular interest because it has been shown in McGaugh's laboratory (1961) that the maze-dull strain is only inferior to the maze-bright strain in learning mazes if the trials are massed. If the trials are spaced, the difference in learning rate between the two strains disappears. It is, of course, possible that such results are only coincidental. It could be argued that the maze-dull strain is in some way more sensitive to a given level of electric shock. Against this argument is the finding of Woolley et al. (1960) that the maze-bright animals have lower thresholds in terms of current for seizures than the maze-dull rats, but such a finding is not conclusive because the threshold being measured is for seizure and not for effects on memory processes.

The hope behind the many investigations employing ECS seemed to be that "consolidation" of the memory trace could be studied. The notion was that the memory trace, shortly after being laid down, was labile and susceptible to destruction, but that it soon changed state and became impervious to disruption. If the time it took the memory trace to consolidate could be measured, some clue to its physical identity might be found. However, no constant time over which ECS disrupts memory after training has been found. For instance, Quartermain, Paolino, and Miller (1965) and Chorover and Schiller (1965) have found an interval in the order of seconds. On the other hand, Kopp, Bohdanecky, and Jarvik (1967) have found effects six hours after training, and McGaugh (1966) reports effects on memory three hours after training. Some of these discrepancies are due to the amount of current passed through the animal.

It has been shown in many studies that increased current intensity and increased duration of ECS produce increasing amnesia (McGaugh,

1966; Jarvik and Kopp, 1967; Dorfman and Jarvik, 1968; Pagano et al., 1968; Alpern and McGaugh, 1968; Zornetzer and McGaugh, 1970). There is another factor which might alter the gradient of retrograde amnesia in ECS. Lewis et al. (1968, 1969) have reported that if animals are familiar with the environment in which they are subsequently shocked, memory of the shock either is not eliminated by ECS or ECS is effective only in producing amnesia when ECS is administered very close to the shock. However, this effect of environmental familiarity is not always found, for reasons which are not well understood—for instance, in two experiments by Dawson and McGaugh (1969).

Whether ECS effects are seen at all may be influenced by competing responses. Gerbrandt et al. (1968) report failure to find an effect of ECS on memory of a discrimination training using hooded rats. In a subsequent experiment, Bures and co-workers (1968) found such an effect only in albino rats. Also, they found an adverse effect of ECS on the memory of a reversal habit when overtraining was given on the original habit. This effect was observed both in hooded and albino rats.

Further evidence on the process of consolidation comes from the injection of anaesthetic drugs in rats at various times after a learning trial. Working with a water maze, Leukel (1957) found some impairment in learning when thiopental was injected intraperitoneally one minute after each daily trial. However, if the injection was made 30 minutes after the end of each trial, no such effect was noted. Pearlman et al. (1961) have studied the effects of phentobarbital and ether administered at different intervals after the end of the learning trial. They trained rats to press a lever for a reward of water. After each animal had reached a certain criterion, it received an electric shock through the lever. Administration of the drugs occurred after this single learning experience. An attempt was made to produce equal amounts of anaesthesia in all groups. Retention tests were made 24 hours after learning. There was little or no effect if ether was administered at an interval of 10 minutes after the learning trial; if administered 10 seconds after the learning trial, the animals would press the lever at 30 percent of their initial rate; if administered 5 minutes after the learning trial, the rate would fall to 17 percent. Phentobarbital had a more profound and long-lasting effect. When phentobarbital was administered after a 10-second interval, the rate of lever pressing was 76 percent of the previous rate, which means that memory of the shock was almost obliterated; when administered after a 10-minute interval, the rate of lever pressing was only 23 percent of the previous level; and when administered after a 20-minute interval, memory of the shock was intact, as the rate of bar pressing was only 1 percent of the previous level.

The picture of two qualitatively different processes—one susceptible to ECS and the other an invulnerable consolidated memory trace—seems no longer so plausible. That some change is occurring during the foot-shock-ECS interval has been made clear. However, ECS seems to be capable of interfering with memory up to an ill-defined point on a merely quantitatively changing continuum. The notion of a quantitatively changing continuum is supported by the amnesic effects of other agents. For instance, flurothyl (hexafluorodiethyl ether), when compared in efficacy to ECS by Bohdanecky, Kopp, and Jarvik (1968), showed an effect longer after training than did ECS. The curves of amnesic effect of these two agents presented by Bohdanecky, Kopp, and Jarvik (1968) run parallel and, except for the degree of amnesic effect, seem qualitatively similar.

OTHER EXPLANATIONS OF ECS EFFECTS

On the basis of their experimental findings, Coons and Miller (1960) have recently put forward an ingenious argument about the effects of ECS on the retention of a habit. They point out that the work demonstrating "loss of memory" for a given habit after ECS is vitiated by the fact that if the shock were felt, it would produce avoidance of a response which could be mistaken for amnesia. Accordingly, these workers used a somewhat complex design in which ECS, if felt, would facilitate learning. The results of their study support their contention. However, more recent results (Abt et al., 1961, using ether; McGaugh, 1961, using ECS; and Pearlman et al., 1961, using anaesthetic drugs to produce amnesia) do not support Coons' and Miller's findings. Abt et al. (1961) and McGaugh (1961) created a simpler situation by placing a rat on a small, restrictive platform raised slightly above a much larger platform. Very shortly the rat stepped off the small platform and onto the larger platform, where it obtained an electric shock. When these same animals were placed on the small platform a second time, they stayed there when no amnesic agent had been applied. If an amnesic agent was applied immediately after the animal stepped off the small platform and the animal was then placed on the platform a second time, he would step off again. As in the studies already quoted, the effect of the amnesic agent diminished when application was postponed in relation to the crucial response. In this situation, the effects of ECS and shock to the feet should summate if the animal is avoiding the electroshock. The same argument could be applied to the more complex situation devised by Pearlman et al. (1961), when an animal "forgot" that it had been punished after pressing a lever. In each of these cases the amnesic agent, instead of increasing fear or avoidance, produced what is most plausibly interpreted as an amnesia. This conclusion is strengthened by the result of an experiment conducted by McGaugh and Madsen (1964). These investigators showed that rats eventually learned to avoid a place when they were given ECS on successive occasions. However, such learning was slow compared with the learning of rats when the shock was of a lower intensity but was not strong enough to produce a convulsion. They further showed that when ECS was administered five seconds after the shock in amounts insufficient to produce a convulsion, it slowed down acquisition of avoidance learning of the place where such shocks were given. Supporting evidence has been reported by Quartermain, Paolino, and Miller (1965).

Perhaps the most damaging criticism of ECS as a tool is that it does not produce a retrograde memory deficit at all. Routtenberg and Kay (1965) and Kopp et al. (1967) have provided evidence that ECS causes decreased latencies, and thus could produce an appearance of amnesia in tests where an increase in latency is taken as evidence of retention. However, such findings by themselves could not explain why small differences in time of ECS after learning (the retrograde effect) should produce differences in amount of amnesia. However, Schneider and Sherman (1968) have now shown why this explanation, in terms of reduced latency, could fit the retrograde effect. Schneider and Sherman found that the critical variable to produce an appearance of amnesia was the interval between footshock and ECS. When rats were shocked upon stepping off a platform, ECS 0.5 seconds later produced amnesia 24 hours later. ECS administered 30 seconds or 6 hours later produced no amnesia. However, if a second footshock was given 0.5 seconds before the ECS (given either 30 seconds or 6 hours later), "amnesia" was produced.

Schneider (personal communication) states that the combination of footshock and ECS can be given outside the test situation, either before or after the step-off task, and apparent amnesia for the step-off task will still result. It seems that some interaction between footshock and ECS is responsible for the quasi-retrograde amnesia normally observed. It is difficult to see how this explanation could be extended to situations where there is an apparent amnesic effect of ECS even where shock is not used before ECS, as in the study of Peeke and Herz (1967). However, the "amnesia" in their experiment may have been a simple performance decrement due to ECS, as no retrograde action of the ECS was demonstrated. There does seem to be an interaction between ECS and footshock. Coons and Miller (1960) showed that ECS side-effects were greater if ECS was administered sooner after footshock.

Another experiment casting doubt on the retrograde amnesic nature of ECS was performed by Misanin, Miller, and Lewis (1968), who propose a hypothesis which would cover ECS results found in appetitive situations. They trained rats to lick when thirsty. The rats were then exposed to a burst of intense white noise. The offset of this noise coincided with footshock. A control group showed that 24 hours later such noise depressed the rate of licking. The rate of licking was equally unaffected in the group given ECS immediately after the noise-footshock training and in the group where ECS was administered 24 hours later, immediately after a second exposure to the noise. When the white noise was omitted just prior to ECS treatment 24 hours later, memory was not significantly affected, as judged by depression in the rate of licking. The authors explain the result by assuming that ECS has an effect on memory when the memory trace is activated and "that the memory system must be in a state of change at the time of ECS."

However, Dawson and McGaugh (1969) repeated the experiment and were not able to find the same effect as Misanin et al. (1968). Reactivation of the memory trace before ECS did not produce amnesia. Dawson and McGaugh state: "We have been unable to discover any procedural details that could explain our failure to replicate the findings of Misanin et al. (1968)."

PERMANENCE OF ECS EFFECTS

Turning back to the original hypothesis which appeared to motivate research with ECS, it was hoped to show that there was a phase during which memory was labile and so subject to destruction by ECS. If this were the case, the application of ECS at some interval after learning should lead to a permanent amnesia for the habit learned (Duncan, 1949). Chevalier (1965) found no diminution of ECS amnesia after a month. Zinkin and Miller (1967) found an apparent recovery of memory after ECS under conditions of repeated testing of a single group. Luttges and McGaugh (1967) found no such effect if separate groups were tested at different time intervals, so that each mouse was retested only once. No apparent recovery of memory occurred after one month, even though control animals had not forgotten the task. Kohlenberg and Trabasso (1968), on the other hand, found that mice given ECS performed at the same level as controls 48 hours after treatment, but were markedly inferior after only 24 hours. It is to be noted here that there was a considerable degree of forgetting in the controls after 48 hours. Such a trend can also be seen in the data of McGaugh and Alpern (quoted by McGaugh, 1966). There are, therefore, discrepancies both in the time course of memory after ECS and without ECS.

Some of the differences with respect to recovery of memory after ECS are resolved by Peeke and Herz (1967), who showed an apparent recovery in mice 72 hours after learning when such mice had been tested 24 and 48 hours after learning, but no such recovery when mice were tested only 72 hours later. Schneider and Sherman (1968) present data which suggest that recovery of memory after ECS occurs when there is stronger initial learning, as produced by increasing the number of footshocks, but not when such learning is weaker. Another possible reason for this discrepancy in the ECS data has been given by Pagano et al. (1968). They have shown that whether memory returns after ECS treatment depends upon the intensity of ECS. Relatively low ECS intensity permitted a return of memory of a step-down task within 24 to 48 hours. There was amnesia at one hour after ECS, in contrast with the results of Geller and Jarvik (1968). Such amnesia was only observed when ECS was administered 0.5 seconds after footshock. No amnesia was observed when the footshock-ECS interval was 30 seconds. On the other hand, high ECS intensity led to an amnesia which lasted 48 hours, the longest time after ECS that the rats were tested.

IS ECS AMNESIA IMMEDIATE?

An interesting sidelight on the initial hypothesis of consolidation which motivated work with ECS is cast by a study of Geller and Jarvik (1968). These workers found that memory remains for a few hours after ECS but disappears by 24 hours, the interval after which animals treated with ECS have been traditionally tested.

The persistence of a memory a short while after ECS and its disappearance only later has been confirmed by McGaugh and Landfield (1970). These results create something of a paradox for the simple consolidation model. It is difficult to see how memory could persist after the labile stage of memory has been destroyed by ECS. There are alternate possibilities to explain Geller and Jarvik's result. The first would be to suppose that two processes were involved, both beginning with the learning experience. The first would be transient and immune to ECS. The second process would normally be long lasting but ECS could prevent its initiation. This type of explanation has been suggested in connection with the protein synthesis data. A second explanation would be to assume that there was a single process and that ECS accelerates forgetting. The data do not compel us to accept a two-stage model.

EFFECTS OF ECS ON OLDER HABITS

Effects of ECS given after a longer time span have been reported by Hunt and Brady (1951), and a whole series of investigations designed to elucidate these effects has been reported by Hunt (1965). When a sound is used to signal impending unavoidable shock, the sound will suppress ongoing operant behavior, such as pressing a lever for water. This suppression of behavior caused by the sound can be eliminated by giving a rat a whole series of ECS treatments. Such treatments were applied four days after the end of training a rat to press a lever for a reward of water. The suppression of responding caused by the sound disappears for one or two weeks after the ECS treatments. The rat can be trained again during this period to reacquire the behavior. However, the loss of suppression of lever pressing when the sound occurs is only temporary, and suppression reappears again spontaneously. Though this effect of the electroconvulsive shock looks like an amnesia in some respects, only the warning function of the sound seems forgotten. There is no amnesia for the lever-pressing habit for obtaining water. Other possible interpretations are discussed by Hunt (1965).

Another interesting phenomenon connected with ECS and older habits has recently been reported by Robbins and Meyer (1970) and Howard and Meyer (1971). The phenomenon could be related to that reported by Schneider and Sherman (1968). Rats were taught three two-choice visual discrimination problems one after another. Two different motivations were used: some discriminations were motivated by shock avoidance and others by food approach. As soon as the rat had completed learning the third discrimination problem, ECS was administered. Twenty-four hours later, the rats were retested to establish their retention of the first or second discrimination. Either the first or second discrimination would have been motivated in the same way (shock or food) as the third discrimination, immediately after the acquisition of which the rat was convulsed. Whether the first or second discrimination was similar in motivation to that of the third depended on the group assignation of the particular rat. It was found that the retention of a problem was impaired only if the problem had been learned under the same motivation as the problem that had been followed by ECS. Whether the problem had been learned first or second in the series made no difference in retention.

ECS AMNESIA AS ACCELERATED FORGETTING

Because ECS experiments had been designed to show that a memory was initially in a labile state and that it needed some time to become fixed, it seemed quite adequate to test animals 24 hours later. If animals could not remember at that time, it was assumed that the short-term labile memory had been knocked out before it had become fixed. Geller and Jarvik's (1968) experiment showed that ECS did not knock the memory out; instead, it seems that there is a time just after the experience during which ECS simply accelerates forgetting. Secondly, if animals could remember 24 hours after ECS, it was assumed that fixation had taken place. However, this assumption has now been shown to be false by Hughes, Barrett, and Ray (1970a, b). They showed that while lower intensities of ECS or longer intervals between learning and ECS had no significant amnesic effect at 24 hours, these factors produced premature forgetting at a later test time. These results lead to a radically different model of memory consolidation, so that it looks as if there is a gradual change in the memory trace with time.

Agents such as ECS, protein synthesis inhibitors, KCl, etc., alter the rate at which consolidation takes place; that is, they alter the slope of growth by some constant factor. The alteration may be so large that the slope of growth may actually become negative if the agent is strong enough. From this it follows that if an agent of a given strength is applied early during the process of growth, then, if the slope of growth becomes negative, the memory trace will shrink to zero after some time. If the same agent at the same strength is applied after the process of consolidation has reached twice the level later in the process of growth, then it will take twice as long for the memory trace to shrink to zero (Hughes, Barrett, and Ray, 1970b). If two agents of unequal strength are applied at the same point in the process of consolidation, it will take longer for the memory trace to shrink to zero after the weaker agent (Hughes, Barrett, and Ray, 1970a).

CHOLINERGIC SYSTEMS AND ECS

How does ECS operate to produce its effects on memory? While ECS undoubtedly has many behavioral effects, many of which can be mistaken for effects on memory, on balance it seems reasonable that ECS *does* have some effect on memory. Recent research strongly suggests that ECS has its amnesic effect via a change in the cholinergic system. The release of bound acetylcholine as a result of ECS increases the activity of cholinergic neurons (Richter and Crossland, 1969). As a result of the release of such acetylcholine, there may be induction of the enzyme acetylcholinesterase (Adams, Hobbit, and Sutker, 1969). Adams et al. found elevations in acetylcholinesterase levels after a series of four ECS treatments. In a behavioral assay for memory, they trained rats to avoid footshock when a light appeared. After training, three ECS treatments were administered and the rats were retested four hours later. Half an hour before retest, the rats were injected with either physostigmine or scopolamine or saline (physostigmine increases acetylcholine levels while scopolamine reduces the effect of a given level of acetylcholine on the postsynaptic ending). While ECS amnesia was not affected by saline, physostigmine enhanced and scopolamine reduced such amnesia. Physostigmine alone, without ECS, also produced some retention loss. These results suggest that ECS raises acetylcholine concentrations, which then lead to synaptic block and consequent amnesia (see section on cholinergic synapse and memory).

That ECS has an effect on memory analogous to cholinergic drugs has been shown in a very interesting experiment by Wiener (1970).

Wiener trained animals in a single session in a Y maze to escape shock by running to the lit alley to 10 consecutive correct trials. Then, at various times after training (5 minutes to 31 days), rats were given ECS and retested 24 hours later. The results of the retest were very similar to those obtained with anticholinesterases (Fig. 12–1). There

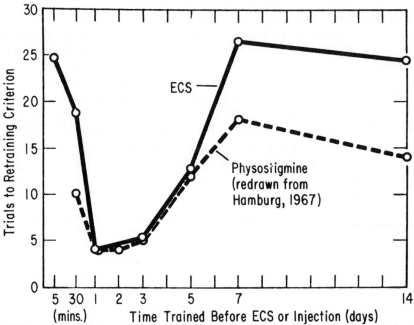

FIG. 12–1. Mean number of trials required for retraining of animals given four ECS treatments compared with those injected with physostigmine. (From Wiener, N. I., "Electroconvulsive Shock-Induced Impairment and Enhancement of Learned Escape Response," *Physiology and Behavior,* 1970, 5:971–74. Courtesy of Brain Research Publications, Inc.)

was an initial amnesic effect (5 minutes to 1 day), followed by no effect at 1 to 3 days. At 7 to 14 days, there was again amnesia. At 31 days, where controls show considerable forgetting, the ECS-treated animals actually show facilitation much as they do as when they are treated with anticholinesterase. Wiener also found that scopolamine acted as a complete antidote against the amnesic effects of ECS while physostigmine augmented the effect of EFC.

Davis et al. (1971) also studied the effects of cholinergic agents on ECS-induced amnesia, but in a one-trial passive-avoidance habit. Physostigmine was administered before the learning trial and ECS protected memory four hours later from disruption. Scopolamine, injected prior to the retention trial, served as an antidote to the memory disruption produced by ECS (alone) in the control group.

State-Dependent Learning

When an animal is trained to perform a habit during one drug state, it may be unable to perform such a habit on a subsequent occasion if the drug is absent or changed. The original learning is then called state dependent and the failure to transfer is called dissociation. Such state-dependent learning has been reviewed by Kumar et al. (1970). It is difficult to predict what drug or what learning will produce state-dependent learning. As noted by Kumar et al., state-dependent learning has not been observed with drugs that have only peripheral effects.

The explanation of state dependency is not clear. One possible explanation is in terms of generalization decrement. There are many cases where a change in the stimuli—often apparently irrelevant—produces severe impairments of performance (Bindra, 1959). It is possible that drugs can produce a change in the stimuli similar to those that can be produced in the environment. While Overton (1964) has shown that manipulating environmental stimuli is not as effective as altering the drug state, some of his manipulations were almost as effective. It is consequently possible that drug administration and environmental stimulus change give rise to the same underlying process, differing only in degree.

On the other hand, no experiment rules out the interpretation that stimulus change and drugs give rise to different processes which result in qualitatively similar effects that differ in degree. Interesting human evidence comes from an experiment of Osborn et al. (1967): while thiopental produces state-dependent learning in rats, no such dependency occurs in human subjects. The subjects showed impairment for material presented while under sedation by thiopental, after the drug had worn off, 24 hours later. However, the subjects could remember materials learned before sedation while they were sedated, and their memory of material presented under thiopental was no better then recall occurred under sedation 24 hours later than when no drug was administered. If learning under thiopental had been state dependent, then recall in the drugged condition should have been superior to the undrugged condition.

In the absence of experimental evidence for state-dependent learning in man, it is more parsimonious to assume that generalization decrement accounts for the apparent state dependency in animals. Animals show much more pronounced effects of generalization decrement than man.

INTEROCULAR TRANSFER AND STORAGE
OF THE MEMORY TRACE

The bilateral symmetry of the nervous system offers interesting opportunities for its investigation. We may ask whether information which the animal has obtained through learning is stored in both hemispheres, whether it can be made available to a hemisphere even if at the time of learning this hemisphere received no direct sensory input, and so on. Most of the experiments on this subject involve the sectioning of the corpus callosum, a massive structure of nerve fibers which join the two halves of the cortex. Studies of learning employing this technique were initiated by Bykoff (1924). This investigator taught a dog to expect food after a mechanical stimulus to the skin on one side of the animal. This causes the animal to salivate when the mechanical stimulus is applied. In the intact animal, salivation is produced without further training when the contralateral point on the skin is stimulated. However, in the animal with callosal section no such transfer was observed.

Beritoff and Chichinadze (1936, 1937) studied the problem of interhemispheric transfer in pigeons. There is complete crossover of visual fibers from one eye to the opposite hemisphere in the pigeon; therefore information from one eye only travels to one hemisphere. These authors found that habits learned with one eye were not transferred when testing was done with the other eye. However, later studies by Levine (1945, 1952) and Siegel (1953) have shown that such transfer can occur. Since there is complete crossover of visual fibers, it seems that such transfer must be mediated at a fairly high neural level. The contradiction with the earlier Russian work has been explained as being caused by the use of different retinal loci. In the pigeon, transfer depends on the part of the visual field stimulated during training.

For the cat, monkey, and man, each hemisphere receives input from both retinae in such a way that each hemisphere has projected on it about half the visual field; therefore training on only one eye means that both hemispheres are receiving messages from this eye. However, if the optic chiasma is cut in the sagittal plane, the animal becomes hemianopsic when either eye is shut, but has a complete visual field with both eyes open, except for nasal interference. The two hemispheres can then be trained separately by restricting vision to one eye only. Myers (1955) found that cats with such a section of the optic chiasma could transfer from one eye what they had learned with the other eye. Also, Myers (1956) and Sperry et al. (1956) found that if the corpus callosum was sectioned in addition to the optic chiasma, no transfer of learning from one eye to the other occurred. However, Merkle and Sechzer (1960) found that this was not true for the simple task of brightness discrimination. Such a discrimination still transfers after a section of both the optic chiasm and the corpus callosum. Further, Sechzer (1964) has shown that after optic chiasm–corpus callosum section, interocular transfer of a horizontal-vertical discrimination resulted when shock avoidance was the motivation used and not food approach. Food approach had been used in all the studies of this problem.

It seems that the transfer found in the first study of Myers was carried from one hemisphere to the other by fibers in the corpus callosum. It has further been found that such interhemispheric transfer is contingent upon the intactness of a posterior portion of the corpus callosum. It appears from Myers' (1959) data that there is a considerable degree of functional equivalence between the various parts of the posterior portion of the corpus callosum. The intactness of any posterior part of the structure leads to interocular transfer after section of the chiasma. It seems that in different cats entirely different parts of the posterior corpus callosum sufficed for transfer of the same visual discrimination problem. However, around 2 to 3 million callosal fibers were needed for successful transfer (though not all of these were visual fibers).

Such findings lead logically to other experiments. The lack of communication between the left and right hemispheres that is caused by callosal section apparently prevents the left hemisphere from utilizing information laid down in the right. On this theory, we may ask whether this is because information is laid down in both hemispheres during normal learning at the time of training or whether one hemisphere draws on information stored in the other during the time of testing. Work by Myers (1957), Sperry, Stamm, and Miner (1956), and Sperry (1958) would indicate that, for some types of visual discrimination, storage appears to be bilateral, whereas it is unilateral for more difficult visual discriminations. In tests with the contralateral eye, sectioning of the corpus callosum or removal of the cortex to which visual information passed during learning (prior to testing with the contralateral hemisphere) results in almost perfect retention. However, this has been found true only where the patterns to be discriminated are vertical and horizontal striations. For instance, where the patterns are small, filled circles against larger unfilled wide ones, such transfer does not occur. The obvious conclusion is that there is carryover of information from one hemisphere to the other during learning when the discrimination is simple, but no such carryover when the discrimination is more complex. Whether this conclusion is correct will be decided by further investigation.

It has also been found that the animal with sectioned chiasma and callosum can learn diametrically opposed habits with no interference between the two habits (Myers, 1956; Sperry, 1958). Such results have been obtained with the monkey and the cat (Sperry, 1958; Trevarthen, 1960).

Work has also been undertaken on the transfer of somesthetic habits in animals with a section of the corpus callosum. As has been mentioned above, Bykoff (1924) found an absence of the usual transfer of a touch stimulus to the contralateral side. Stamm and Sperry (1957) found no transfer when cats with sectioned callosum had been trained to discriminate between two levers on the basis of touch. When the front paw on one side had been trained, there was no transfer to the other paw. Similar results have been obtained by Glickstein and Sperry (1960) and Ebner and Myers (1960) in the case of tactile object discrimination in monkeys, and by Myers and Henson (1960), who worked with chimpanzees.

Sperry (1959) has found a remarkable autonomy of function of the somesthetic cortex in cats, that is, independence from the part of the cortex of the same hemisphere. The removal of most of the cortex on the same side, together with callosal section, did not affect the retention of learned somesthetic discriminations by the somesthetic cortical remnant, nor the speed of new learning. A similar autonomy has not been found for the visual cortex (Sperry et al., 1960).

It has been suggested that the transfer of learning of a pattern discrimination from one eye to the other depends on previous experience with some patterned light in the second eye. However, this has been shown in a conclusive experiment not to be necessary (Meyers and McCleary, 1964).

Studies of interocular transfer in relation to memory have also been made with fish (Sperry and Clark, 1949; Schulte, 1957; McCleary, 1960). The study of this animal is of some interest because there is a complete crossover from a retina to the contralateral portion of the nervous system. This means that each eye is represented separately and unilaterally. Further, since there is no neocortex, there is also no corpus callosum; there are, however, commisural fibers. Sperry and Clark (1949) and Schulte (1957) covered one eye of the fish, which were then required to swin toward the correct one of two stimuli to obtain food. When the original eye used in the training was covered and the "naive" eye uncovered, transfer was evident, and the fish chose the correct stimuli for food. McCleary (1960) found interocular transfer in fish with a simple type of avoidance situation which used conditioned heart rate as an index. When a skeletal motor response of a simple nature was learned with one eye while the other eye was covered, no transfer occurred. However, when the naive eye was left uncovered during training (though it could not see the training stimuli), transfer did occur. Covering an eye, however, did not prevent transfer if conditioned heart rate was used as an index. When a simple swimming escape response was required, failure of transfer occurred even if both eyes were covered with translucent binders during training, and also in the transfer tests. The stimulus was a thin beam of white light which was focused on one blinder during training and on the other blinder during transfer tests. The explanation of these findings is obscure.

A variant of the technique of callosal sectioning in the study of memory has been introduced by Bures and Buresová (1960), using Leão's spreading depression. If a high concentration of a chemical agent such as potassium chloride is placed on the dura, a series of waves of depression is generated in the cortex with no recovery between them. In such a case, electroencephalographic activity may remain depressed for several hours. The production of such a depression in both hemispheres does not anaesthetize an animal; the animal moves around much as usual. However, during the depression it does not manifest signs of previous learning.

A depression produced in one hemisphere does not spread to the other hemisphere, and this is what makes it a convenient tool in the study of interhemispheric transfer. Using this technique, Bures and Buresová trained rats in a simple avoidance habit. When the same hemisphere was depressed on the two successive days of learning, there was considerable saving in the retention of the habit on the second day. However, if one hemisphere was depressed on the first day and another hemisphere on the second day, there was no saving of learning on the second day. These authors suggest that the memory trace had remained localized in the hemisphere which had been involved in learning on the first day. On the second day this first hemisphere was inactivated so that the trace of the learning on the first day was unavailable to the animal. It follows from this reasoning that there was no transfer of a memory trace between the two hemispheres during the 24 hours or so during which they both functioned normally. Russell and Ochs (1961) reported that such inferred transfer occurs very quickly if the unilaterally learned habit is practised while both hemispheres are functioning.

It has been shown earlier in work on callosal sectioning that it is possible to train the two hemispheres separately in conflicting habits without any signs of interference. Bures and Buresová (1960) were also able to show the coexistence of traces of conflicting habits in the two hemispheres, even when the callosum was intact. Animals were trained to escape by going to the left when one hemisphere was inactivated and to the right when the other was inactivated. On the second day they would choose to go either left or right, depending on which hemisphere was not activated. It was also observed that on recovery from spreading depression, memory traces of habits learned before the depression were left intact.

However, as in the work on callosal sectioning, complexities have appeared. Thompson (1964) reported that rats under bilateral spreading depression can learn a simple avoidance habit. Travis and Sparks (1963) obtained similar results using an escape habit. Further, Tapp (1962) found that the emotional components of a habit learned with the cortex normal transferred to the training situation when bilateral spreading depression was instituted. Also, Bures, Buresová, and Fifková (1964) reported partial transfer of a passive-avoidance reaction from one hemisphere to the one inactivated by cortical spreading depression during training. The rat was given electric shock in one compartment of an apparatus while cortical spreading depression was applied to one hemisphere. The originally unaffected hemisphere was then placed under spreading depression while the affected one recovered, and the amount of time spent by the rat in the compartment where it had been shocked was measured. Rats showed some retention of the avoidance habit when the hemisphere which was inactivated during training was active and the other hemisphere active during learning was depressed. This transfer occurred even in animals with a transected corpus callosum, showing that the memory trace could not have traveled from one hemisphere to the other via the corpus callosum. Further to exclude the possibility that the memory trace had somehow traveled from one hemisphere to the ather, retention of the habit was demonstrated in rats where cortical spreading depression in the hemisphere used during training was evoked before the other hemisphere used in the retention test was allowed to recover. It looks, therefore, as if subcortical structures are somehow involved.

However, subcortical structures are not left unaltered by the application of spreading depression to the cortex. The activity of 90 percent of thalamic and hypothalamic units is severely depressed during cortical spreading depression, whereas the activity of over 60 percent of reticular units is increased. Even more perplexing is the finding that rats trained to go, say, to the left when one hemisphere is depressed, go right when the other hemisphere is depressed (1964, 1965). While it is true that the rats did not perform the original habit of going left when spreading depression was shifted to the other hemisphere, it is somewhat surprising that their behavior deviated from random performance to the same extent as before the hemispheres were switched. While this was claimed as a loss of the learned habit, it could equally well be interpreted as an acquisition of the mirror-image habit by some mysterious means. However, a simpler explanation is that the rats during initial training had learned by orienting themselves with respect to the lateralized symptoms to which unilateral spreading depression gives rise. Then when the side of the cortex which is depressed is switched, the rats will perform the mirror-image habit. No forgetting has taken place.

Recent work suggests a completely different explanation of the experiments on interhemispheric transfer. This explanation is based on the old principle of generalization decrement. An instance of this was described by the seventeenth-century philosopher, Locke: "It is of a young gentleman, who having learnt to dance, and that to a great perfection, there happen'd to stand an old trunk in the room where he learnt. The idea of this remarkable piece of household stuff had so mix'd itself with the turns and steps of all his dances, that though in that chamber he could dance excellently well, yet it was only while that trunk was there." Changes in apparently irrelevant aspects of the environment can lead to partial or complete disruption of a learned habit. It is probable that such changes can be brought about by physiological as well as by environmental manipulations. It may also be the case that in spreading depression an inability to switch hemispheres is not due to the fact that the memory resides in one hemisphere alone, but rather to the stimulus change brought about by a change of hemispheres.

Such considerations prompted Schneider (1967) to reinterpret the results obtained with the use of spreading depression. As was stated above, the basic assumption of this work was that if an animal has been trained with one hemisphere depressed, it cannot perform when the state of the two hemispheres is reversed. This shows that the memory of the habit must have been confined to the hemisphere which was nondepressed during original learning. Though this is an appealing argument, it is by no means a compelling one, and Schneider has set about showing why it is often wrong. Schneider's alternative hypothesis is that the rat's inability to transfer is due to generalization decrement. It is probable that there is a change in the stimulus complex concomitant with changes of cortical depression. It is also known that changes in stimulus conditions between training and test conditions can lead to apparent forgetting on the part of the animal.

To support his thesis, Schneider has to show that certain propositions are true. The first is that spreading depression can act as a stimulus to the rat. Schneider and Kay (1958) trained rats in an operant situation, reinforcing responses emitted under unilateral spreading depression but not reinforcing those with cortex normal. It was found that during extinction more responses were emitted under unilateral spreading depression than without depression. The second proposition which then has to be demonstrated is that stimulus change due to spreading depression does act to interfere with performance. To test this, Schneider (1966) trained rats to perform an avoidance task. Two groups of animals were trained in a shuttle box to avoid shock. One group (*ND*) was trained on two successive days with no spreading depression and then on the third day with both hemispheres depressed. The second group (*CD* and *AD*) was trained on the first day with one hemisphere depressed, on the second with the other hemisphere depressed, and on the third with both hemispheres depressed. According to the notion that memory is stored in a nondepressed hemisphere, we should expect no savings or equal savings on the third day of training in both groups when both hemispheres were depressed. On the other hand, if transfer depends on the degree of stimulus change brought about by spreading depression, then the group trained under unilateral spreading depression would be expected to transfer much better to the condition of bilateral spreading depression than the group with no experience of spreading depression. This is shown in Figure 12–2.

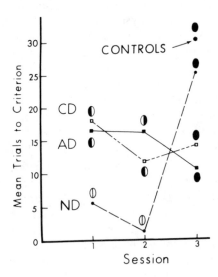

FIG. 12–2. Retention under spreading depression. Mean trials to reach criterion in each avoidance session. The control point represents the mean trials taken by each control group to reach criterion during the final session. The shading of the circles near each data point represents the depressed hemisphere or hemispheres. (Courtesy of Dr. Schneider.)

However, this experiment may be criticized on two grounds. First, no controls were run for the effects of repeated spreading depression. There may be physiological effects due simply to repeated treatment. Second, Schneider (1967) purports to show that unilateral spreading depression produces subcortical memory storage. Such subcortical storage, according to him, does not occur when the cortex is undepressed. It seems that this, rather than degrees of stimulus change, could explain his experiment, as he himself states (1967).

To counter this objection, Schneider (1967) ran another experiment in which he trained rats in a passive-avoidance task of the step-down variety. Two groups were trained under unilateral spreading depression. One was subsequently tested under the same unilateral depression, whereas the other was tested with cortex normal. During this test the performance of the rats tested with cortex normal was greatly inferior to those tested under unilateral depression.

In another experiment, Schneider and Hamburg (1966) again used a shuttle box to train animals in an avoidance task. They investigated the notion that there is fast transfer from one hemisphere to the other when training occurred with both hemispheres undepressed, interposed between training with one and then the other hemisphere depressed as had apparently been shown (e.g., Russell and Ochs). With no training between the depression of one hemisphere and then the other, no transfer occurred, as has been shown by other investigators (see Fig. 12–3).

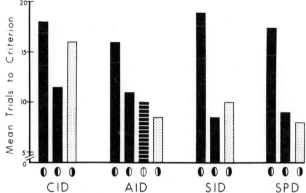

FIG. 12–3. Interhemispheric transfer and the mean number of trials to criterion (excluding the criterion trials) during each session. The first two sessions consisted of conditioning with the same hemisphere depressed (unilateral conditioning); the final session consisted of conditioning with the initially trained hemisphere depressed (contralateral retention). The third session in the *AID* group represents the number of trials required for 5 avoidance responses during the interdepression period. The shading represents the relationship between the depressed and the nondepressed hemispheres. Group *CID* received only unilateral training and contralateral test sessions. (Courtesy of Dr. Schneider.)

With avoidance training under no depression interposed between training with one hemisphere depressed and then the other, transfer occurred between the situation where one hemisphere was depressed (group *AID*). However, the same transfer occurred in two other situations as in this last situation, where avoidance training occurred between the two training sessions with unilateral depression on one cortical hemisphere in the first session and on the other hemisphere in the second session.

These two situations are as follows. The rat is placed in the apparatus with both hemispheres undepressed between the two training sessions with unilateral depression and simply given nonavoidable shock in the shuttle box (group *SID*). This procedure produced transfer of avoidance responding between the condition where one hemisphere was depressed to the condition where the other was depressed. The results in the second situation are even more surprising on the memory trace transfer hypothesis. In the second situation, animals were given experience of the unavoidable shock with both hemispheres undepressed before any training with unilateral spreading depression (group *SPD*). Training with unilateral spreading depression was then begun, and the bilateral experience with shock led to no better learning rate than was obtained in initial learning with the other groups. Evidently the effect of the unavoidable shock had not been simply to facilitate learning under unilateral depression. When, however, the other hemisphere was depressed with no training or treatment given between the session with one hemisphere depressed and then the other, perfect transfer occurred. This is quite inconsistent with the notion that memory traces move from one hemisphere to the other to produce behavioral transfer of a habit learned under spreading depression. It is, on the other hand, again completely consistent with an explanation based on generalization decrement. The experience the animal had of the situation first with both hemispheres undepressed and then with unilateral depression enabled it to generalize better from this wider sample.

An even more damaging experiment to the interpretation of interhemispheric memory transfer was carried out by Schneider and Ebbesen (1964). Their experiment was very similar to that of Russell and Ochs except that they added a control group. Besides the group which was given a rewarded trial with both hemispheres undepressed, another group was given the rewarded trial under identical circumstances except that the rewarded trial was given with the trained hemisphere depressed. Both groups were then tested for responding during extinction with the trained hemisphere depressed. Transfer from the trained to the untrained hemisphere was observed for both groups. However, the group given the single intervening trial with the trained hemisphere depressed showed very much more transfer than the group given the intervening rewarded trial with both hemispheres undepressed. Here it is difficult to see how a memory trace could have been induced to transfer from a depressed hemisphere to the undepressed hemisphere by the rewarded trial. On the other hand, the result is much more comprehensible in terms of the stimulus generalization hypothesis of Schneider (1968).

So it appears that the memory engram remains as elusive as ever. It seems that we were not tracking the memory trace after all but indulging in a procedure analogous to moving Locke's "remarkable piece of household stuff." Squire and Liss (1968) have pointed out that it is difficult for Schneider to account for all the data on the generalization decrement hypothesis. It may very well be that there is some effect on memory when spreading depression is used. On the other hand, there is also some effect on generalization decrement. As the relative contributions of these two factors (memory and generalization decrement) are difficult to assess, the use of spreading depression to provide information about memory localization must be viewed with skepticism.

Spreading Depression and Retrograde Amnesia

Rabedeau (1966) and Paolino and Levy (1971) have shown that the amnesia produced by cortical spreading depression does not occur if cortical spreading depression is applied immediately after a training trial, or over three hours later, but is substantial when depression is applied 16 minutes after training. From this it is argued that the memory trace is initially subcortical and so invulnerable to cortical spreading depression until the memory becomes cortical after a lapse of time. However, as aversive training was used, we may instead be dealing with an interaction between shock recency and susceptibility to the amnesic effects of spreading depression. A recent shock may have a protective value against the amnesic effect of cortical spreading depression.

HABITUATION AT THE NEURAL LEVEL

Habituation is said to occur when there is a decrement in response to a stimulus without a negative or positive consequence to the organism when such a stimulus is repeated. Such a decrement of response upon stimulus repetition also has other characteristcs; namely, the response recovers in the absence of stimulation. There is also generalization from one stimulus to another. When habituation occurs to one stimulus, it is found that response decrement occurs to other stimuli. Further, there is also the reappearance of the habituated response after the administration of some other suitably arousing stimulus. A habituation is a simple form of learning and as it is manifested by organisms with very simple nervous systems (as well as by organisms with no specialized nervous systems), attempts have been made to establish the neurophysiological substrate of habituation in simple organisms as well as in vertebrate nervous systems.

It is possible to demonstrate phenomena akin to habituation at the purely neurophysiological level. For instance, Horn and Wright (1970) have stimulated the presynaptic portion of the giant synapse of the squid stellate ganglion, recording postsynaptically. Twenty electrical pulses for half a second were delivered every ten seconds. As stimulation progressed, the rate at which the excitatory postsynaptic potential e.p.s.p. developed as a result of each pulse became progressively slower. As the trigger point at which the action potential occurred remained at the same voltage, there was a progressive increase in latency as pulses were applied. Eventually the later pulses in each group of 20 fail to elicit action potentials altogether, and such failure of transmission takes many seconds to dissipate. Horn and Wright (1970) believe that the presynaptic action potential eventually fails to release transmitter sufficient to produce depolarization at the postsynaptic membrane.

Bruner and Kennedy (1970) have described a more complex system in a giant motor neuron which partially innervates the crayfish's fast abdominal flexor reflex. Here stimulation at a low frequency results in a decrease of responsiveness. Three stimuli one minute apart cause a decrease in responsiveness from which it takes five minutes to recover. However, at higher stimulus frequencies (with a maximum at two per second) there is a facilitation of the response. It seems that, here again, the decrements in responsiveness are probably due to presynaptic changes, which are not, however, due to a simple depletion of presynaptic transmitter stores. The habituation of withdrawal responses in the earthworm and other annelids has also been investigated neurophysiologically (Roberts, 1962a, b; Roberts, 1966; Horridge, 1959, 1969). Sensory nerves make synaptic connections to giant fibers, which then make synaptic connections with motor neurons innervating the longitudinal muscle. The first few stimuli to the organism produce a facilitation of the withdrawal response. This is due to an increase in transmission between the giant and motor neurons. Subsequent decrease in responsiveness is due to a decrease in transmission between the sensory neurons and the giant fiber neuron and also between the giant fiber neuron and the motor neuron. Neither the sensory neuron nor the motor neuron nor muscle shows much decrement of responsiveness with repetitive stimulation. In insects, also, Huber (1965) has shown the cockroach that it is not the receptor which shows fatigue. The afferent (cercal) nerve can follow frequencies of at least one per second. On the other hand, both behavioral startle responses and the responses of the giant fiber which synapses with the afferent (cercal) nerve show habituation when the interstimulus interval is 30 seconds. It seems, then, that the change responsible for overall behavioral habituation is due to some change at the synapse connecting the afferent nerve and the giant fiber. Again, fatigue of the peripheral receptor does not produce habituation.

Neural bases of habituation and dishabituation have been studied in *Aplysia*. In this marine gastropod, a large number of nerve cells are extremely large. They can be identified visually and it is easy to record intracellularly for prolonged periods. Bruner and Tauc (1966) studied the habituation of a tentacle contraction. The neural correlate of this tentacle habituation is the waning of an e.p.s.p. (excitatory postsynaptic potential) in a giant cell in the left pleural ganglion. Shocks delivered to other cells produce potentials which are as large or greater than the potentials before habituation occurred. This suggests that dishabituation is the result of an excitatory system which can even outbalance the effects of habituation.

Further studies in *Aplysia* have made use of the gill withdrawal reflex (Pinsker, Kupferman, Castellucci, and Kandel, 1970; Castellucci, Kupferman, Pinsker, and Kandel, 1970). Here the reflex seems to be monosynaptic; that is, the sensory neuron from the skin is connected directly to the motor neuron which produces gill withdrawal.

The responsiveness of the motor neuron to direct electrical stimulation by intracellular depolarization does not change during habituation. It seems that the change during habituation occurs somewhere in the synaptic connection between the sensory and motor neuron, and it is attributed to some attenuation of transmission in the presynaptic terminals of the sensory neuron. The motor neuron not only has monosynaptic sensory input which triggers the withdrawal response and is subject to habituation, it also has polysynaptic sensory input which, when active, potentiates the postsynaptic potential. In this way the parallel polysynaptic input to the motor neuron facilitates the monosynaptic reflex and overrides habituation. This, then, appears to be the substrate of dishabituation.

A similar dual system appears to operate in the vertebrate, as we shall see later. However, monosynaptic reflexes in the vertebrate spinal cord do not display habituation—but habituation in the polysynaptic spinal reflex in the vertebrate spinal cord was described by Sherrington (1906), who called it "fatigue." This phenomenon has been studied with the use of microelectrodes (Spencer, Thompson, and Neilson, 1966a, b, c; Wickelgren, 1967a, b; Groves and Thompson, 1970). Intracellular recordings of motor neurons during habituation show a decrease in both depolarizing and hyperpolarizing synaptic potentials. This is probably due to some reduction in transmission in the interneuron population. (Interneurons are those neurons in the chain from sensory to motor neurons which are not themselves sensory or motor but are interposed between the sensory and motor neurons.)

The pattern of interneuron firing in response to afferent input during habituation has been determined by Groves and Thompson (1970). There are three types of interneurons. The first shows no change with repeated afferent stimulation. The second type shows progressive attenuation of firing. Characteristically, this type also emits short-latency, high-frequency discharges. The third type shows an increase in firing during early trials and subsequent reduction in firing. The flexion reflex which is produced by the activity in these units also shows initial sensitization or increase before the reduction of responsiveness called habituation.

Impinging on the neurons in the polysynaptic pathway is a diffuse excitatory system which is apparently responsible for dishabituation. A large number of studies (reviewed by Leiman and Christian, 1973) has shown habituation in neurons in the central nervous system. However, such studies do not shed much light on the mechanism of habituation. As Leiman and Christian point out, it is difficult to know whether the habituation takes place in such units or whether "they are not themselves controlled by other habituating systems." Even greater difficulties arise with studies made on the central nervous system with gross potentials. (These are discussed in the chapter on arousal and attention.)

ELECTROPHYSIOLOGICAL STUDIES OF ASSOCIATIVE LEARNING

The large neurons in *Aplysia*, the large marine gastropod, have made it a favorite subject of study. The right giant cell which can be individually identified in the aplysian abdominal ganglion has been most extensively studied in connection with a phenomenon known as heterosynaptic facilitation. This means that if the neuron is fired by the activity of one synapse, it will be more readily fired by the activity of another synapse. If the heterosynaptic facilitation is nonspecific, the second synapse will be made more efficient even though the firing through the first synapse occurred independently in time. If the heterosynaptic facilitation is specific, the second synapse is made more efficient only if the excitations of the first and second synapses occur close to each other in time. In the right giant cell, heterosynaptic facilitation is nonspecific because the repetitive excitation of the cell through one synapse alone produces a subsequent increase in the amplitude of an e.p.s.p. through another synapse by as much as 100 to 700 percent (Kandel and Tauc, 1965a, b). Heterosynaptic facilitation lasts from 10 to 30 minutes, but whether heterosynaptic facilitation can be specific is at present a matter of controversy (Leiman and Christian, 1972). The physiological basis of such facilitation is at present unknown, though it is argued that the change in transmission is due to some presynaptic change (Epstein and Tauc, 1970).

There are in the abdominal ganglion of *Aplysia* some large cells which produce bursts of spikes, followed by quiescence at regular intervals. With weak stimulation of a neuron with efferent input into such a rhythmic neuron, different effects were obtained, depending on the timing of the applied stimulus with respect to the phase of the endogenous rhythm. If the stimulus was applied close to the beginning of the endogenous burst, the subsequent quiescent period was shortened. However, if the stimulus was applied later during the burst, or during the period of quiescence, the cycle was lengthened. The effect was progressively augmented by a repetition and lasted over a number of minutes (Frazier, Waziri, and Kandel, 1965; Pinsker and Kandel, 1967). Input to the spontaneously rhythmic cell can be produced directly by depolarizing the cell via an intracellular electrode. Such depolarization can be applied at some other rhythm (von Baumgarten, 1970). Some neurons will alter their spontaneous rhythm to match a rhythm imposed by the external depolarization. This acquired rhythm is maintained briefly even when the rhythmic external depolarization is withdrawn.

NEUROPHYSIOLOGICAL RECORDING AND LEARNING
IN THE VERTEBRATE NERVOUS SYSTEM

In addition to the above studies, a multitude of experiments shows changes in rates of firing of neurons in the mammalian nervous system. While these studies show that the nervous system has changed during learning and not by behavior alone, they give little clue to how such change has come about (an excellent review is contained in Leiman and Christian, 1973). Attempts have been made to modify the rate of firing of single units by administering a reinforcer (such as a brain reward) after an increase in frequency of firing of the neuron (Olds and Olds, 1960). However, it soon became obvious that it was actually movements or receptor adjustments that were being rewarded. A neuron would fire if the rat sniffed or moved its leg, and reward would be administered; consequently the rat would again sniff or move its leg. It could be doubted if the experiment showed more than that movements could be conditioned and that such movements were brought about by some neural activity. Fetz (1969) also showed that the rate of single-unit discharge can be altered by food reinforcement, but such changes were again often correlated with the learning of gross movements. In an attempt to obviate the problem of movement, rats were reinforced only if they remained motionless for a short while (Olds, 1965, 1968; Olds and Hirano, 1969). However, in many of these cases there were still slight twitches of the head, nose, or whiskers. But even if no such movements could be shown, there is another much more pervasive objection: the monitored cell may be one which, by an increase of its firing, produces inhibition of movement.

Phillips and Olds (1969) have concluded that "there are single cells in the midbrain which can make discriminatory responses to the significance of different sensory signals." The units only increase or sustain their rate of firing if the sensory stimulus signals the occurrence of a reward relevant to the motivational state of the rat at the time. Otherwise, firing is reduced.

Rats were trained to hold down a lever motionlessly for two seconds. At the end of one second (after the beginning of the lever press), one of three tones would announce whether the reward was to be food, water, or nothing. Units were found that would increase or sustain their rate of firing if the tone announced food while they were hungry or water when they were thirsty. Otherwise, if the rat was disappointed, rates were lowered. It was shown that the significance of the tones could be reversed and that therefore the units were not sensory units simply responding maximally to some frequency. While the authors' conclusion about the discriminatory function of the units is consistent with the results, other interpretations are also possible. For instance, the penalty for movement after a tone has announced the forthcoming reward depends on the motivation of the animal. If the animal is hungry and water or nothing is announced by the signal, the animal can afford to relax. However, if food is announced, the rat might very well redouble its efforts to stay motionless because it has learned that if it moves no reward will be presented, in spite of the signal. Thus we can still argue that recordings were made from inhibitory motor units.

An interesting method to ensure that the changes in neuron firing occur in the neuron being observed and not as a result of some distant event has been used by Bures and his associates (Bures and Buresová, 1967, 1970; Gerbrandt, Skrebitsky, Buresová, and Bures, 1968). The first stimulus (the conditioned stimulus) can be a tactile or acoustic stimulus or current delivered to neighboring neural tissue by a second electrode. The second stimulus (the unconditioned stimulus) is a weak DC anodal polarizing current delivered through the recording microelectrode to a neuron. The procedure produced an alteration of responsiveness of the monitored neuron to the conditioned stimulus in about 10 percent of the neurons monitored in various areas (with the exception of the cortex). These changes often outlasted the pairing of the stimulus by some minutes. Whether such changes reflect specific changes in excitability to the conditioned stimulus or some more general sensitization is not completely clear yet. Continuous polarization can produce a general increase in excitability.

The above studies have attempted to modify the activity of single neurons as a result of some learning or quasi-learning paradigm. In addition, a number of studies have observed changes in single units concomitant with learning. For instance, Woody, Vassilevsky, and Engel (1970) studied changes occurring in the responsiveness of units to the conditioned stimulus before, during, and after the acquisition of a classical conditioned eye blink response in cats. Measurements of the sensitivity of units to the CS (a click) were taken in the coronal-precruciate area, one of the cortical regions mediating eye blink. After conditioning, many of the units in the area had much shorter latencies to the CS. There was also an increase in the frequency and length of activity of units to the CS.

OTHER STUDIES OF SIMPLER NEURONAL SYSTEMS

One of the problems of investigating the physiological basis of learning has been our inability to pinpoint the locus of learning change. However, Horridge (1965) discovered that leg posture could be learned by the ventral cord ganglia when the brain was absent in cockroaches, locusts, and similar large insects. Careful controls were undertaken to exclude possible factors other than associative learning. The relevant ganglion which did the learning contained only about 3,000 cells.

Further work on this type of learning in the headless insect (the Horridge preparation) has been done by Hoyle (1965). By recording directly off the efferent nerve, he was able to train the headless insect to maintain a certain rate of firing in that nerve by administering shocks to the afferent nerve if the rate of firing in that nerve deviated from the arbitrarily chosen level the experimenter had selected.

The Horridge preparation has also been examined in pharmacological and biochemical studies by Kerkut et al. (1970) and Oliver et al. (1971). The rate at which the isolated metathoracic ganglion can be trained to keep its leg out of solution to avoid shock can be altered by the administration of various drugs. Various RNA and protein synthesis inhibitors (such as actinomycin D, acridine orange, congo red, chloramphenicol, and cycloheximide) retard learning. On the other hand, facilitation of learning occurs after administration of various anticholinesterases, and amphetamine facilitates learning—as does an increase in temperature. (However, the experiments do not allow us to distinguish between an effect on performance and learning.) During learning (or perhaps performance) there is a rapid decrease in the cholinesterase activity in the metathoracic ganglion. Gradual forgetting over 72 hours is paralleled by a return of cholinesterase activity to normal. Whether this striking correlation between cholinesterase activity and memory is the result of a cause-and-effect relation remains a challenge to further research.

Electrophysiological Phenomena: Epileptiform Phenomena and Learning

We saw above that electrically and chemically induced convulsions produced memory disorders. Memory defects have also been observed in epileptic patients. These defects may be caused either by the seizures themselves, as in the case of the electrically induced seizure, or by the activity of the epileptogenic focus of abnormal activity alone. Such a focus can be demonstrated in the electroencephalogram as a steady discharging focus of abnormal activity. This is sharply localized, and it spreads to the surrounding tissue to produce a seizure only on occasions that may be months apart. In a series of interesting studies, Morrell (1956, 1957) has been able to shed light on the relation of these foci of abnormal activity to learning by using the technique of the alpha-block conditioning. When a visual stimulus is presented to a subject (for instance, a bright flash of light to a subject with his eyes shut), the 8 to 13 c.p.s. alpha rhythm is not affected when a sound or touch of sufficiently low intensity impinges on the subject. However, if such a sound or touch is paired with the light stimulus, a normal subject will later show blocking of his alpha rhythm in response to the sound or touch alone. The number of paired presentations of sound or touch with light required in a normal subject varies from 1 to 20 trials. Morrell (1956) investigated the ability to form such alpha-block conditioned responses in patients with sharply localized temporal lobe spike foci. In such cases it is expected that the auditory system would be especially involved.

To obtain a measure of the selective impairment of auditory function, Morrell (1956) used not only auditory but also tactile stimuli. It was found that in these patients the capacity to form an alpha-block conditioned response to a tone was extremely impaired whereas learning to a tactile stimulus remained essentially normal. However, Morrell found no difference in these patients in the motor reaction time to touch and to tone stimuli. This finding may be related to that by Chow and Obrist (1954) in which production of an epileptogenic focus does not interfere with habits previously acquired.

In a similar study with monkeys, Morrell (1957) was again able to show that epileptic foci selectively impair the formation of an alpha-block conditioned response. Epileptic foci were experimentally created by the placement of aluminum hydroxide cream in selected locations in the central nervous system. This substance gives rise to chronically discharging seizure foci, resembling those of epileptic foci when electrographically recorded. Morrell was able to show that extreme impairment of learning occurred under these conditions. Animals with foci in the auditory cortex showed a deficit in conditioning to tone but not to touch. Those with foci in the postcentral leg area showed a deficit to touch but not to tone. Morrell (1957) was also able to show that if the paired stimuli were presented when a small and well-circumscribed focus was quiescent, alpha block which was conditioned to touch would appear. However, though such learning was well established, blocking to the conditioned stimulus (touch) would suddenly and completely disappear when a pairing of the stimuli occurred during a spike discharge. The unconditioned alpha block to light was, on the other hand, unaffected. Less than a minute later, when the spike discharge subsided, the next trial with the touch stimulus produced an alpha block, showing that learning had remained intact. When the excisions of the discharging focus were unilateral, a marked improvement in the formation of an alpha-block conditioned response was evident. It seems, therefore, that if excision is unilateral, the abnormal discharge of a focus causes a greater deficit than the simple absence of the discharging tissue. The contralateral tissue can then presumably function without interference.

Other investigators (Kraft et al., 1960; Stamm and Pribram, 1960) have confirmed Morrell's observation that learning of a particular type is affected, depending on the site of the discharging focus. Kraft et al., for instance, found that monkeys with occipital implants of aluminum hydroxide cream showed impairment in learning visual discrimination tasks. However, no deficit was evident in their learning of an alternation task. Stamm and Pribram (1960) demonstrated a learning deficit for an alternation task when aluminum hydroxide cream was placed bilaterally on the frontal cortex. Though this learning deficit was very large, no detectable deficit was found in the retention of the same habit acquired preoperatively. These data should be contrasted with the findings of Chow (1961), who found that when a bilateral electrographic discharge was induced in their temporal cortices, monkeys had an inability to learn and retain visual habits. However, retention was not disturbed with bilateral hippocampal or occipital discharge.

STEADY POTENTIAL SHIFTS AND LEARNING-LIKE PHENOMENA

Following the work of Rusinov (1953), Morrell (1961) demonstrated that after the application of low (2 to 10 μa) anodal constant current to a part of the motor cortex, phenomena resembling learning occurred. This constant current does not produce limb movement by itself. However, the limb movement that one would expect as a result of adequate stimulation of the motor area with other kinds of current was triggered as a result of a flash, sound, or touch. Even after the current has been switched off, such a movement can be produced by various stimuli for a period up to half an hour. The experiment was also conducted another way. A group of stimuli was selected, and all members of this group were repeated individually until habituation (as judged by the EEG record) to them occurred. Then one of these stimuli was chosen to be presented repeatedly while the constant anodal current was applied to the motor area of the cortex; this stimulus then elicited a limb movement and continued to do so even when the current was switched off. The other members of the group to which habituation had occurred and which had not been paired with the constant current did not elicit such a movement. However, other stimuli (to which habituation had not taken place and which were outside the previously selected group) elicited the limb movement for some time after the constant current had been switched off.

It seems that the steady current applied to the motor area renders it hyperexcitable and liable to be triggered by any disturbances. However, the process of habituation of a stimulus appears to attenuate the functional connection between the receiving area for this stimulus and the motor regions. The pairing of a habituated stimulus with the constant current application, however, results in a loss of this habituation, so that this stimulus becomes effective in eliciting the appropriate limb movement.

Another interesting phenomenon obtained in the same study concerns the application of the constant anodal current to the visual receiving area. Recordings were obtained from single neural units which responded to a single flash by a high-frequency burst of spikes. These units responded by a similar burst after each flash when such flashes were delivered at the rate of three per second. The effect of the constant current seemed to be that it would induce such a single unit to respond to a single flash delivered up to 20 minutes after the end of the three per second flicker by a series of bursts of spikes spaced at three per second (Fig. 12–4). Morrell reported that no trace of such rhythmic

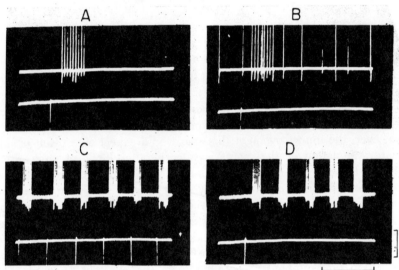

FIG. 12–4. Conditioning of a rhythmic burst response to a single flash in a single neuron in the visual cortex. Anodal polarization was applied to the visual receiving area. Single flash elicited a single burst in a quiescent (*A*) and in a randomly firing cell (*B*). Three per second stroboscopic stimulation (*C*) produced driving of unit discharge at frequency. A single flash (*D*), delivered 30 seconds after termination of the rhythmic stimulus, resulted in repetitive unit discharge at about 3 per second. Unit potentials are seen in the upper channel of the oscilloscope; stimulus artifacts in the lower channel. Amplitude calibration: 2 millivolts. Time calibration: 500 milliseconds (*A* and *B*) and one second (*C* and *D*). (From Morrell, F., in Fields, W. S., and Abbot, W., *Information Storage and Neural Control*, 1963; courtesy of Charles C Thomas, Publisher, Springfield, Ill.)

activity was apparent in the record during this interval. These findings are evidence against the notion that reverberating circuits are necessary as short-term storage of information in the central nervous system.

Such grouping of single cell discharge has been observed by Jasper et al. (1960) with the monkey during low-frequency flicker and by Strumwasser and Rosenthal (1960) with the frog during intermittent direct-current stimulation of single neurons. However, these authors did not report storage of the pattern of stimulation during the time stimulation was absent. It may well be that the steady potential shifts induce, mimic, or produce some physiological changes to be found in the normal functioning of the central nervous system. Goldring and O'Leary (1957) have reported negative DC shifts of cortex when the midline thalamic reticular system is stimulated. Findings of a similar nature are also reported by Arduini (1958). Morrell (1961), coupling an auditory signal with stimulation of the midline thalamic reticular nuclei (which produce a negative DC shift), found that this shift would occur after 30 paired trials to a tone alone. Working with the rabbit, Morrell used low-frequency (four to five per second) unilateral stimulation of the centromedian nucleus. Such stimulation produced a negative DC shift in the central cortex on the same side as the stimulated area.

ELECTRICAL ACTIVITY OF THE BRAIN AND ITS RELATION TO THE MEMORY TRACE

We shall now turn to a brief review of EEG phenomena in an effort to assess the possibility that the electrical events recorded by the electroencephalogram are used by the central nervous system as a signal in transmission or storage.

When a novel stimulus is presented to an animal, a desynchronization of its EEG rhythm occurs. The resting brain rhythms are replaced by low-voltage, fast electrical activity.

What does this measure of brain activity tell us about other behavior of the nervous system? Kogan (1960) measured thresholds of neural excitability during desynchronization. He found that the threshold for such excitability decreased in the primary sensory area to which the alerting sensory stimulus was relayed, but that it increased in other areas, though all showed EEG desynchronization. It has been shown by Ricci et al. (1957) that activity of individual units can be increased, decreased, or unaffected by desynchronization. Schlag (personal communication) has evidence that some of the above results are due to poor sampling inherent in the methods of microelectrode recording. Using larger electrodes, he shows a good correlation between desynchronization and enhanced unit activity.

When a novel stimulus is repeatedly presented alone, a gradual decrease in the period of desynchronization occurs until it fails to develop altogether. Such a process is termed "habituation" and is selective and specific. A stimulus differing only slightly from that previously presented repeatedly will cause desynchronization (Sokolov, 1960; Sharpless and Jasper, 1956).

When habituation to a signal is complete, training is begun. The stimulus to which habituation has occurred is paired with some other stimulus which has either rewarding or punishing properties; arousal to the previously habituated stimulus tends to occur under such circumstances. Many papers (e.g., John and Killam, 1960; Morrell, 1960) describe the distribution of responses to a flickering light during conditioning. With avoidance conditioning there develops an enhancement of the response to the flicker in the reticular formation and the hippocampus. Later in training, such an enhancement occurs in the nucleus ventralis anterior and structures of the visual system. However, it seems that when reward rather than punishment is introduced, the sequence of changes during learning is altered. These experiments raise the question whether we are observing in the EEG some signal which is identifiable with a short-term or long-term memory trace or its transmission or whether, instead, we are observing other side-effects of the learning situation. One example of such localized changes in EEG rhythms may be taken. High-frequency (40 cps.) activity in the amygdala arises during certain phases of learning. Gault and Leaton (1963) have shown that such discharges occur only when the animal sniffs. The EEG record is therefore a somewhat circuitous way of measuring olfactory exploration on the part of the animal.

The unlikelihood of identifying EEG rhythms as signals used by the central nervous system either in transmission or storage is increased by an excellent experiment by Chow (1960). He implanted electrodes in the inferior temporal cortex of the monkey and then required the animal to learn a discrimination which it is less able to perform without this part of the cortex. The animal was presented with visual patterns, the significance of which changed according to the frequency of the flicker in which they were displayed. No signs of this discontinuous stimulation appeared on the EEG record in the temporal area, even though it was an ingredient which had to be distinguished by the animal. The EEG changed in the temporal area only during the middle trials, being the same at the beginning and the end of learning. This is most plausibly interpreted by Chow as being caused by attentional factors. One might conclude, as did Morrell (1961), that "the experiment of Chow serves to demonstrate that the material basis of the engram or durable memory trace is not likely to be revealed by the techniques of electrophysiology."

Various other EEG phenomena have been noted during conditioning. Slow waves appear when an animal is required to wait or to suppress a response. John, Leiman, and Sachs (1961) claimed that "inhibition of conditioned response is consistently accompanied by slow waves." However, they also reported that such slow waves also occur in relation to excitation as well as to inhibition, and there appeared to be no differences between the waves under these two circumstances.

It has also been noted by numerous workers (e.g., Morrell, 1957) that slow waves can be elicited by a steady tone, if this tone has been coupled with a flickering light. The experimental procedure used to show this was as follows. A pure tone of low intensity was presented to an animal repeatedly until it produced no alteration in the electro-encephalographic record. At this point a low-frequency visual flicker was introduced at a fixed time after the beginning of the tone. The frequency of flicker was 3 to 12 per second, and it produced "photic driving" of the EEG rhythm. By this we mean that an EEG rhythm of the same frequency as the light flicker could be observed from the visual cortex. After the few trials in which the tone and flicker were presented together, the tone alone began to produce a desynchronized EEG record in the same way that it did before habituation to the tone had taken place. This has been called stage I, and it may last from 15 to 60 trials, depending on the animal. In stage II, when the tone was sounded and before presentation of the visual flicker, an EEG rhythm appeared, similar in frequency to that evoked by the flicker itself. This stage was brief (two to ten trials) and was soon replaced by stage III, which was a desynchronization localized to the visual cortex and which persisted, so that it may be regarded as the final stage. However, it is the frequency of the discharge in stage II after the tone is sounded and before the light appears that is of main interest here. It has been regarded by some workers as a neural memory trace of the flicker which the nervous system produces in order to compare an incoming frequency of flicker with those flicker frequencies which have already been presented. However, Morrell, Barlow, and Brazier (1960) reported two points of interest in relation to such a hypothesis. They found, contrary to general impression, that the shift in EEG frequency was not directly or linearly related to the shift in flash rate. For example, when one animal was first conditioned with a three per second flash, it developed a conditioned response at six per second. A second experiment, using a four per second flash, resulted in a conditioned response at three per second. A third experiment, using a six per second flash rate, resulted in a response that was at or very close to six per second. These authors also examined the records from stage III with the help of a computer in order to see whether anything resembling the frequency of the flash appeared in the desynchronized record. When a large number of successive records were superimposed and the fluctuations for each moment of the record were averaged, random components tended to be ironed out, which may have accidentally biased the single record in a positive or negative direction. The average record then emerged, and this should reveal any regularly repeating changes which are masked by random fluctuations on the individual records. Using this technique to see whether the fluctuations of stage II persisted in stage III, Morrell et al. found evidence, which they considered unequivocal, that the rhythm of stage II disappears.

In view of these results, these investigators raised the possibility that the slow rhythms described in stage II represented the hippocampal arousal pattern which consists of slow waves and which occurs at a certain stage in the conditioning procedure described. It has been suggested by some that the occurrence of slow rhythms during stage II is a part of a memory storage mechanism. For instance, John et al. (1961) write: "A mechanism of this sort would appear to provide means for storage of a representation of a temporal sequence of events, lasting beyond the duration of the events themselves. Such a mechanism for internal representation of a past event seems, on logical basis, to be essential to enable an animal to perform two differentiated responses to two similar stimuli, either of which may be presented in a given experimental situation." This view is reminiscent of ancient theories of hearing in which it was considered that in order to recognize a sound it had to be compared with a similar sound stored in the ear. It is clear that such a mechanism is not essential on logical bases. It is merely a possible, though somewhat clumsy, mechanism. We can equally well suppose that there are arrangements of cells which are differentially set into activity by different incoming frequencies in a manner analogous to resonators. We do not, then, need to suppose that the occurrence of a frequency is stored by having a copy of it played by the nervous system. We only need to suppose that a record is kept of which "resonator" system has been activated by an incoming set of signals.

Whatever the theoretical possibilities are, the notion that the rhythms detected by the electroencephalogram carry information which is used by the nervous system has received experimental attention. Chow, Dement, and John (1957) used an avoidance task in which a cat had to jump from one compartment to another in order to avoid shock. The imminence of the shock was signaled by a flickering light. The light also produced an EEG wave at the frequency of the flicker, or photic driving, as it is called, which is usual in such a situation. In time the cat would jump from one compartment to another simply when the flicker occurred. After this phase of the experiment, a tone was sounded before the flickering stimulus, outside the avoidance situation. When animals had reached stage II in this procedure—that is, when the tone alone produced a low-frequency EEG rhythm similar to the photic driving—they were placed once again in the avoidance situation. The tone was sounded, and it produced the same EEG as the flicker. However, it did not produce any behavioral response. It does not, therefore, seem that the signal generated by flicker and picked up by the EEG electrodes is used by the nervous system itself as a signal.

chapter 13

Chemical Bases of Memory

DRUG FACILITATION OF LEARNING

Not only is it possible to impair learning by various procedures after a training trial, but apparently it is also possible to improve learning, as we might expect if the consolidation hypothesis is correct. In an impressive series of studies, McGaugh and co-workers have demonstrated that administration of various stimulant drugs, such as strychnine and picrotoxin, both before and after a training trial, increases the rate at which learning proceeds.

The evidence that learning can be improved with injections of stimulants after a training trial is of greater interest to us. Any effect of improved learning that is associated with injections which are given before the trial could be attributed to an increase of motivation, alertness, or some other such factor not necessarily connected with the process of storage per se. On the other hand, injection of a stimulant after the completion of a trial makes it much more likely that any observed improvement of learning is caused by the drug acting on some process set up by experience during the last preceding trial. Of course, it is possible that the drug's action persisted until the next batch of trials. However, McGaugh (1961) has shown that the closer the injection to the previous trial, the greater the improvement in performance on the succeeding trial. If the drug affected some process occurring during a learning trial and not one occurring immediately thereafter, then we should expect the opposite result; that is, the further the injection from the previous day's trial, the greater the likely influence of the drugs on the succeeding day's test. So if we obtain less effect with an injection closer to the succeeding day's test than with one which is closer to the previous day's trials, we may conclude that the effect of the drug was on some process occurring and diminishing after a day's trial.

In their two strains of rats, McGaugh and co-workers (1961) have also found striking differences in the facilitative effects of drugs on learning. These differences can be compared with those they had previously found in reactions to ECS (see p. 436). They used a newly synthesized compound (1757 I.S.), similar in effect but not in structure to strychnine. This was injected ten minutes before daily massed trials in a complex alley maze. They found that the descendants of the Tryon maze-dull animals which were injected with the drug showed a significant improvement over controls of the same strain which were not injected with this drug. On the other hand, no facilitation of learning was found in the descendants of the maze-bright animals. The number of errors made by the injected maze-bright animals was not lower than that of controls of the same strain which had not been injected with 1757 I.S. It is interesting that without the drug there was a large difference between maze-dull and maze-bright strains in the mean number of errors: the mean number of errors was 12.86 (S.D., 4.64) for the maze-bright strain as compared to 33.15 (S.D., 18.12) for the maze-dull strain. When we compare the two strains under the influence of the drug, we find that the mean number of errors for the maze-bright animals was 15.71 (S.D., 8.94) while that of the maze-dull was 17.33 (S.D., 10.30). In other words, when the drug is used, the difference between the strains under massed conditions of learning tends to disappear. As noted above, the learning ability of the maze-dull strain is inferior to the maze-bright strain only when the trials are massed.

If injections of a stimulant will abolish the difference between the maze-bright and maze-dull rats under massed conditions by leading to an improvement of the maze-dull rats, then we naturally might expect that the stimulant would cause the maze-dull rats to actually surpass the maze-bright rats under spaced conditions of learning. Breen and McGaugh (1963) found this to be true. In their study, the rats were given an injection of the stimulant picrotoxin after each day's trial (only one trial was given each day). Three different levels of dosage were used. As can be seen from Table 13–1, when under the drug's influence, the maze-dull rats were superior to the maze-bright animals.

It is tempting to assume, as McGaugh assumed, that the observed differences in the effects of ECS, stimulants, and distribution of practice of the maze-dull and maze-bright animals are caused by a difference in the consolidation rate of the neural trace. However, this view presents difficulties which further research may resolve. For instance, it is difficult to understand why the assumption that the stimulant increased the consolidation speed of a neural trace after each trial can be considered as an explanation for the fact that the maze-dull animals became as efficient as the maze-bright animals under massed conditions when a stimulant was administered. We would further have to assume that if

TABLE 13–1
Effect of Picrotoxin on Maze Learning

	Control Group 0.9% Saline			Low-Dose 0.75 Mg./Kg.			Medium-Dose 1.0 Mg./Kg.			High-Dose 1.25 Mg./Kg.		
Strain	N	M	S.D.	N	M	S.D.	N	M	S.D.	N	M	S.D.
Maze-bright......	10	26.5	4.48	10	25.6	8.67	10	25.9	5.94	12	20.2	5.35
Maze-dull........	10	22.2	2.99	10	16.6	9.41	11	14.5	7.28	11	13.8	4.57

Note: M, Mean Number of Errors Made on Trials 2 to 7; $S.D.$, Standard Deviation of Mean; N, Number of Animals.

a new process of consolidation was started before the previous process had finished, less of a neural trace would be laid down than if both processes of consolidation had gone on to completion. However, this would not explain why the drug-treated maze-dull animals made fewer errors than the treated or untreated maze-bright animals when the trials were spaced a day apart. In this case it seems that the postulated process of consolidation would reach an asymptote within 24 hours, even when the animals are untreated. (At least this is used as an argument concerning the consolidation hypothesis and to account for the lack of a difference between the maze-bright and maze-dull animals when the trials are widely spaced. It is argued that under these conditions the processes of consolidation do not overlap.) A speeding up of the processes of consolidation should therefore have no effect if the trials are widely spaced. If the overlap factor of consolidation is already minimal, a further speeding up of the consolidation process by drugs can hardly have an effect.

There may be no single explanation for the above experiments. Many factors unconnected with learning per se, such as a tendency to alternation or other biases, enter into the performance of a task, especially in a complex T maze. These factors obscure the expression of learning as it is manifested in performance. The tendency toward spontaneous alternation decreases with time between trials; therefore, a greater tendency to alternate on the part of the maze-dull rats could make their performance worse when trials are closely spaced. Wide spacing of the trials greatly reduces this tendency, and consequently we should find, as is the case, that the difference in errors between the maze-bright and the maze-dull rats should diminish greatly. The maze-dull and maze-bright rats differ in many ways, many of them apparently unconnected with the qualities for which they were originally selected. For instance, it has been found in the writer's laboratory that there exist not only large differences in the amounts of saline and water drunk but also divergencies in the very manner of drinking. Thus it is entirely possible that accidental correlations of drug sensitivity are confounding the results of the experiments in which different genetic strains are used.

However, such criticisms cannot be leveled at studies illustrating drug facilitation of learning in general. Westbrook and McGaugh (1964) have shown that such drug facilitation occurs during latent learning. It seems that learning is increased when rats in a complex maze are administered 1757 I.S. (a drug with a strychnine-like action) during a period of non-reward after each daily trial. When a food reward was introduced, injections were discontinued. However, the rats that had received the injections while unrewarded made significantly fewer errors than uninjected controls when reward was introduced (Fig. 13–1). While interactions between hunger drive induced by previous injections and per-

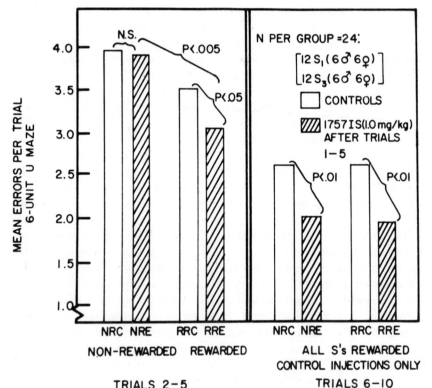

FIG. 13–1. Facilitation of latent learning when drug is injected only during period of unrewarded runs. *NCR,* nonrewarding controls, injected with saline only. *NRE,* nonrewarded experimental animals, injected with 1757 IS after trials up to trial 5. *RRE,* rewarded experimental animals, injected with 1757 IS after trials 1–5. *RRC,* rewarded control animals, injected with saline after each trial. In trials 6–10 all animals were treated in identical fashion—rewarded and injected with saline after each trial. (From McGaugh, J. L., in Kimble, D. P. [ed.], *The Anatomy of Memory,* Palo Alto, Calif.: Science and Behavior Books, 1965.)

formance were not evaluated in this study, the design is potentially powerful.

Facilitative effects on the learning of a wide variety of tasks by the posttrial injection of stimulants have been reported. Posttrial injections of strychnine facilitate visual and oddity learning (Hudspeth, 1964), delayed alternation (Petrinovich et al., 1965), passive- and active-avoidance learning (Franchina and Moore, 1968; Bovet et al., 1966), and conditional stimulus transfer in a two-way avoidance task in mice (Oliverio, 1968). Other stimulants have also been shown to have facilitatory effects—among them, picrotoxin, pentylenetetrazol (metrazol), amphetamine, caffeine, nicotine, and bemigride (Dawson and McGaugh, 1971).

However, strychnine facilitation of learning has not always been obtained (Prien et al., 1963; Louttit, 1965; Stein and Kimble, 1966; Schaeffer, 1968). The reason for these discrepancies may lie in an interaction between the drug and environmental factors. Facilitation of maze learning with the use of strychnine is found in rats reared in an enriched environment but not in an impoverished environment (Shandio and Schaeffer, 1969; Le Boeuf and Peeke, 1969). Further, strychnine facilitates discrimination learning if rats are placed in a quiet environment after learning but not a noisy one (Calhoun, 1966).

Further complications concerning drug facilitation of learning have been described by Krivanek and McGaugh (1968, 1969). Mice were trained in a visual discrimination habit to obtain food. Different groups were injected with various drugs in varying quantity at differing times after the last trail each day. They ran three trials per day. With strychnine, the dose-response curve is biphasic. The largest effect of facilitation was obtained with the smallest doses (0.25 to 0.1 mg./kg. of body weight IP [injected intraperitoneally]) and the largest doses (1.0 to 1.25 mg./kg. IP). Smaller facilitation of learning was found with intermediate doses (0.2 to 0.8 mg./kg. IP). With pentylenetetrazol, facilitation increased with increasing dose up to 10 mg./kg., where increasing the dose led to no further facilitation. With D-amphetamine there is again an increase of facilitation with increasing dose, except that at the highest dose used (2.5 mg./kg.) the effect is smaller than at lower doses.

When the drugs were injected at different times after learning, strychnine continued to be effective if injected within an hour of the last trial. Pentylenetetrazol was ineffective if administered after a time delay longer than 15 minutes. D-amphetamine has to be injected immediately after the last trial of the day to have facilitatory effect.

Complicating this subject even further is the finding that different doses of the same drug produce their maximal effects at different times of injection after learning (Hunt and Bauer, 1969). Rats were injected with pentylenetetrazol either immediately or 15 minutes after discrimination training. A dose of 7.5 mg/kg. produced a larger facilitation of learning if injected immediately after training than if injected 15 minutes later. However, a 10 mg/kg. injection was more effective in producing facilitation when administered 15 minutes after training than if injected immediately. It is obvious that we cannot infer the length of some postulated stage of memory by observing how long after it has been recorded it is susceptible to enhancement.

Facilitation of Learning by Drugs Affecting RNA and Protein Synthesis

Experiments have been carried out to see if drugs which stimulate RNA or protein synthesis also facilitate learning. Schmidt and Davenport (1967) report that tricyanoaminopropene (TCAP) facilitates maze learning in rats. TCAP has been shown to increase nucleoprotein production in the rabbit brain and ribosomal RNA synthesis in the lateral vestibular (Deiter's nucleus in the rabbit) (Hyden and Harteluis, 1948; Hyden and Egyhazi, 1962). However, other investigators have not been able to show a facilitating effect of TCAP on learning (Brush et al., 1966; Otis and Pryor, 1968). Claims have also been made that magnesium pemoline increases RNA synthesis and facilitates learning (Plotnickoff, 1966a, b, 1967). However, not only have the chemical effects of magnesium pemoline been questioned (Stein and Yellin, 1967) but it is doubtful whether the changes it produces are concerned with learning (Beach and Kimble, 1967; Bowman, 1966; Stein et al., 1968). Changes in overall activity or the tendency to freeze in a shuttle box situation (as was used in the original study) could produce an appearance of enhanced learning.

Another attempt to increase levels of RNA has been made by feeding rats large quantities of an alkaline hydrolystate of yeast. Cook and Davidson (1968) report that this procedure speeds up the learning of a pole-climbing task, and prolongs its retention, but has no effect on Sidman avoidance learning. The effect on the pole-climbing task could have been due to an enhancement of activity and responsiveness to shock. Yeast RNA has been shown by Brown (1966a, b) to enhance activity and responsiveness to shock.

EXPERIMENTS ON PLANARIANS (FLATWORMS)

Corning and John (1961) reported that tails of planaria regenerating in ribonuclease do not retain a conditioned response which is retained by tails regenerating in pond water. Since ribonuclease destroys RNA, it might be argued on the basis of this experiment that the RNA which supposedly stores the planarian memory had been dissolved by the ribonuclease. However, it is difficult to know how much of the so-called conditioned response to a paired light and shock represents simply a general sensitization (Jensen, 1965). Further, morphological anomalies were produced by the treatment with ribonuclease and these might interact with the rather complex factors governing the response of planaria to light recently discovered by Van Deventer and Ratner (1964).

Some other experiments support the notion of sensitization as an explanation of apparent conditioning in planaria (Halas et al., 1962; Bennett and Calvin, 1964). However, attempts to condition European species seem to have been more successful. In two of the species tested, one was refractory to conditioning. However, the other species showed an effect resembling classical conditioning (Chapouthier, Legrain, and Spitz, 1969).

There seems to be some evidence that planarians are capable of discrimination learning (Best and Rubinstein, 1962; Chapouthier, Pall and Ungerer, 1968; Corning, 1964; Humphries, 1961; Griffard and Pierce, 1964; Block and McConnell, 1967). However, following a run of correct responses there seems to be a rejection phase in which the animal chooses the "wrong" stimulus (Best and Rubinstein, 1962; Chapouthier et al., 1968; Corning, 1964). This type of behavior may represent learning or simply a tendency to respond to runs.

MEMORY TRANSFER IN PLANARIANS

Hungry planarians will eat other planarians when the latter are cut up into pieces. By feeding trained planarians to their naive fellows, McConnell (1962) claims to have observed transfer of classical conditioning. Jacobson et al. (1966) claim to have produced transfer of training by injecting RNA from trained animals into the digestive cavity of untrained planarians. However, other experiments (Hartry et al., 1964; Chapouthier et al., 1969a) suggest that what may have been "transferred" is some general tendency to respond rather than a specific habit.

McConnell (1966) reports the transfer of discrimination learning through cannibalism. However, negative results are reported by other laboratories (Picket et al., 1964; Chapouthier, 1971).

MEMORY TRANSFER IN VERTEBRATES

The problem of what is transferred occurs again when we consider similar work with vertebrates, where extracts of trained animals were injected into untrained animals. It has been claimed (Babich et al., 1965) that intraperitoneal injections into untrained rats of RNA extracted from the brains of trained rats transferred the training. However, in spite of many efforts by excellent investigators (e.g., Luttges et al., 1966; Gross and Carey, 1965) it has been impossible to substantiate such claims. Further, it has been shown (Luttges et al., 1966; Eist and Seal, 1965) that such RNA injected intraperitoneally reaches the brain in negligible quantity, if at all. However, even intracerebral injections of such RNA fail to produce transfer.

It seems that the substance that produced transfer was an impurity in the RNA. There is now a sufficient number of positive studies to make it appear that there is something in the extract to alter behavior—probably not RNA, but some other substance (for a review, see Chapouthier, 1973). Studies which claim the transfer of a specific learned habit are not solidly supported. Perhaps the most indicative study so far has been reported by Frank, Stein, and Rosen (1970). Some donor mice were either shocked in a part of a shuttle box that recipient mice would be required to avoid or rolled about in a glass jar. Other donor mice were simply placed in the same part of the shuttle box without being shocked. Recipient mice were then injected with brain or liver homogenates of mice from one of the three groups of donors. Those recipients injected with brain or liver homogenates from donors shocked in the maze or rolled in the jar performed better in the avoidance task in the shuttle box. Further, recipients of homogenate from mice rolled in the jar performed even better than the recipients of homogenate from mice shocked in the place to be avoided. The results of this experiment show that something was transferred which improved performance during learning. Frank et al. (1970) conclude that some substance produced because of general stress was transferred and modified the behavior of the recipient mice. While the study does not rule out the existence of some substance which transfers specific information, it makes such a postulation unparsimonious given the experimental evidence so far.

CHEMICAL CHANGES DURING LEARNING

A more direct attempt to measure learning changes in the biochemical constitution of selected parts of the nervous system has been made by Hyden and Egyhazy (1962, 1963) and Hyden and Pigon (1960). Rats learned to obtain food by traversing a kind of tightrope. An analysis was then made of the composition of RNA in the nuclei of Deiter's cells (in the first vestibular relay) and of the surrounding glial cells. Changes in the base composition of the RNA were found. However, it is not clear that such changes were brought about by learning rather than by stimulation of the vestibular apparatus during climbing. It is true that there were "control" groups subjected to rotation, but it does not seem that these animals experienced equivalent vestibular stimulation. A priori, it seems unlikely that any skill of motor coordination the animal might have to learn in balancing would be represented by modifications in the almost peripheral vestibular apparatus.

A large number of studies report various chemical changes which occur in the brain during learning (see Chapouthier, 1973). However, it has been calculated (Deutsch, 1971) that, at best, only one two-thousandth of the substrate of learning in the brain can be altered by a particular learning experience. It is most unlikely that such a small percentage of change could be measured by existing biochemical methods even if we knew the substrate of memory. As a consequence, it may be said that if a change during learning is detectable by biochemical methods, it cannot be the change which forms the substrate of memory. To be detectable, it must be too large.

Protein and RNA Synthesis Inhibition and Memory

A considerable amount of research has been devoted to an attempt to show that RNA is involved in the process of memory storage. These attempts have been inspired by the belief that RNA molecules are capable of carrying coded information in very large quantities, and because this large information carrying capacity of DNA and RNA is used in the biological system in the mechanism of heredity transmission. The identification of RNA is made plausible by the further argument that a change in the excitability of a cell could not be permanent unless there was some change in the genetic information in the cell. All other cell constituents have a high rate of turnover, and there must be something which causes these constituents to remain different after learning. However, it seems that there are other possibilities which should not be forgotten. There are phenomena, such as the influx of melanin into the neurons of the nucleus niger in horses (Jung and Hassler, 1960), which suggest that the contents of a cell may be stably modified without any presumptive change in its genetic apparatus. It is also within the bounds of possibility to suppose that such a change of intracellular content might modify the excitability characteristics of the cell. If such suppositions are accepted, we need only postulate a sudden increase of permeability to a specific substance on the reception of a given signal to provide for an equally plausible learning substrate. It is easy to conceive that such a process would have the characteristics of high vulnerability at the outset, before permeation was complete, and that permeation could continue slowly over a long period of time to give the characteristics of long-term consolidation.

RNA is involved in protein synthesis, and, as a result, differences in rate of stimulation on neurons are reflected in the RNA content of neurons as activity leads to increased protein turnover in cells transmitting impulses. For instance, decreased activity leads to a decrease in RNA in relatively inactive cells. It has been reported that there is a lowering of cytoplasmic RNA concentrations in the cells of the receptor and bipolar layers of the retina in animals which have been reared in the dark (Riesen, 1960; Rasch et al., 1959). Such a relation makes it very difficult to prove experimentally that RNA actually stores information in learning, rather than that it is, like water, simply necessary in any neural change or activity. Other research has attempted to discover if proteins are involved in memory storage.

Dingman and Sporn (1961) reported that when 8-azaguanine—a purine analog which can cause formation of nonfunctional RNA—is given to rats, it depresses to a small extent the learning of a new maze, though it does not affect the performance in an obviously well-learned maze. Unfortunately, when compared with a well-established habit, new learning is very sensitive to all kinds of influence, so that the result obtained is at best inconclusive (Singh, 1964).

A more convincing approach to the problem has been adopted by Gerard and co-workers (1963). When a unilateral brain lesion such as a cerebellar lesion is made, a postural asymmetry results. If the spinal cord is transected immediately after the brain lesion has been made, such an asymmetry disappears. However, such asymmetry persists if the transection of the spinal cord is delayed. Taking such a fixation of function as an analog of fixation in memory, it was possible to study the effect of pharmacological agents on the time before a postural asymmetry due to a lesion of the central nervous system would become irreversible in spite of the interruption of the spinal pathway. When 8-azaguanine is administered, it takes longer for the postural asymmetry caused by a cerebellar lesion to become irreversible, whereas another agent, believed to increase RNA content of neurons, decreased the interval necessary for a postural asymmetry to become fixated. It remains for future research to determine the relation of this phenomenon to learning as it is normally conceived.

Puromycin, a powerful protein synthesis inhibitor, has been used by Flexner and his collaborators (1963) to test if protein synthesis is involved in memory storage. Mice are taught an escape task in a Y maze, and puromycin is injected intracerebrally 1 to 60 days after training. The mice are then retested 3 to 4 days after the injection. Mice injected one day after training with 90 micrograms of puromycin in the temporal region of the brain lose their memory of the habit.

Unfortunately, it is impossible to tell just how large such a memory loss is because of the way the savings score is calculated by Flexner and his collaborators— memory loss is expressed in terms of a percentage savings score. "These percentages are calculated by subtracting the number of trials or errors to criterion in the retention tests from the number to criterion in training, dividing by the number in training and multiplying by 100." (1967).

Such a score could produce a serious overestimate of the amount of amnesia if the rate of learning is slowed down by the drug. Unless there is an independent estimate through the use of preinjected controls of the effect of the drug on the rate of learning, the number of trials to criterion during retest does not specify the relative contributions to the total relearning score made by amnesia and by altered rate of learning. Flexner et al. (1967) say of puromycin-treated mice: "Some reach criterion on second learning in practically the same number of trials with the same number of errors as on first learning; in others, second learning is substantially more difficult than first learning." There is, therefore, reason to believe that rate of relearning was affected in this set of experiments. Given this measure, then, it is possible that in these experiments a trivial degree of forgetting would look like a complete amnesia if on retest the mouse learned very slowly.

Flexner et al. (1967) infer that the memory trace spreads as it becomes older. Mice injected one day after training with 90 μg of puromycin, using injection into the temporal region of the brain, lose their memory of the habit. On the other hand, with an interval of 11 days between training and injection, injection into the temporal region appears no longer sufficient to cause amnesia. The dose has to be distributed into at least three sites (temporal, ventricular, and frontal) bilaterally symmetrical. This is taken to be evidence of the spread of the memory trace with time after learning.

However, alternative conclusions can be drawn. No preinjected controls are ever run; consequently, we do not know whether the widely injected mice are more impaired in their capacity to learn than their counterparts injected only in the temporal region. Further, the difference obtained may be attributed to effective dose rather than spread of the memory trace. We could suppose that the memory trace is scattered over a large number of ties and that soon after learning the memory substrate is sensitive to a lower level of drug. It has been shown that an injection of puromycin into the temporal cortex produces only low protein synthesis inhibition in all other sample areas of the brain (1967). This low effect might therefore be sufficient to block memory initially. However, a combined set of injections (temporal, ventricular, and frontal) causes a very much higher puromycin inhibition of protein synthesis in other areas besides the temporal. Thus while a temporal injection may no longer cause amnesia because the traces in other sites require a larger depression to be blocked, this can be achieved by a different spatial distribution of the injection.

Subsequent to these results with puromycin, which support the idea that protein synthesis is necessary for the formation and maintenance of memory, Flexner and Flexner (1967) have reported that intracerebral injections of small quantities of saline at various times after puromycin treatment abolished the puromycin-induced amnesia. It therefore seems that puromycin simply blocked retrieval in some way and that the memory trace itself was in fact unimpaired by puromycin. In this experiment, puromycin injections were made one day after training, with the exception of subsidiary groups where injection was made after a longer interval. Saline was then injected at intervals varying between 4 hours and 60 days.

Why, then do Flexner and Flexner conclude that puromycin appears to interfere with consolidation of memory? After all, mice treated with puromycin just after training showed a significantly smaller amnesia when injected with saline than when they were not injected with saline. Their conclusion that there is an effect on consolidation is based on a further comparison. Flexner and Flexner compare the effect of saline injection on restoring memory in mice injected with puromycin immediately after training with mice injected with puromycin one day after training. Flexner and Flexner claim there is a difference. Our earlier results on the efficacy of saline in restoring memory after treatment with puromycin referred to 47 mice in which puromycin was given one or more days after training and was followed 30 hours to 60 days later by intracerebral injections of saline. These savings are marginally significantly greater ($p < .05$) than those obtained when puromycin, given immediately after training, was followed 5 days later by saline. It is doubtful if the group of 47 animals is in fact a proper control group, because it differs in other ways besides the time after training when puromycin was injected.

One of these differences which seems important concerns the time between the puromycin and saline injections. Inspection of . . . the previous experiment (1967) describing this group shows that there seems to be an interaction between time between puromycin injection and saline injection and subsequent recovery from amnesia. For instance, when the interval is 30 hours, no mice lose their memory, one has impaired memory, and 7 retain their memory. On the other hand, when the intervals between puromycin and saline injections are from 2 to 12 days, one animal loses its memory, 9 have impaired memory, and 13 retain their memory. Both the 30-hour group and the 2-to-12-day 6 intracerebral injections of puromycin 13 to 15 days after training. and were used as a part of the same baseline comparison group of 47 mice. Yet the probability that the 30-hour and 2-to-12-day groups are different is greater than the probability that the 2-to-12-day group and the group injected with puromycin immediately after training are different.

The marginal difference between the mice injected with puromycin immediately after training and those injected one day later could therefore be due to the fact that they were also injected with saline at different times after puromycin. Furthermore, the group of 47 mice injected at least one day after training, used as a baseline of comparison of the mice injected immediately after training and with saline 5 days later, is also heterogeneous in another way. One subgroup was given 6 intracerebral injections of puromycin 13 to 15 days after training. The Ns in each subgroup are quite unequal, so that the total baseline becomes almost completely arbitrary. Therefore, it cannot be safely concluded that saline is relatively less effective in restoring memory when puromycin has been administered immediately after learning.

Flexner et al. (1967) also report that acetoxycycloheximide, an extremely potent protein synthesis inhibitor, does not have an amnesic effect when injected one day or more after training. However, when acetoxycycloheximide is injected in mixture with puromycin, it protects against the amnesic effects of puromycin. Flexner et al. (1967) attempt to explain this in terms of the ways in which the two drugs inhibit protein synthesis. On the other hand, it has never been demonstrated that puromycin or any other protein synthesis inhibitor has its action on memory through a direct effect on protein synthesis rather than through some indirect or side effect. Koenig (1965), for instance, has shown that puromycin depresses cholinesterase synthesis and that actinomycin-D has the opposite effect (1967).

Flexner and Flexner (1967) found that other chlorides besides Na Cl, ultrafiltrates of blood serum, and even water would restore memory when they were injected, and thus reverse puromycin amnesia. They interpret this effect as being due to the washing off of the abnormal peptides produced by the puromycin injection. Their hypothesis for explaining the fact that acetoxycycloheximide suppresses the action of pyromycin on memory is that acetoxycycloheximide suppresses the synthesis of abnormal peptides which are otherwise formed by puromycin. While Reinis (1969) claims to have found such peptides by their effect on behavior, Ungerer, Spitz, and Chapouthier (1969) were unable to find them.

PUROMYCIN AND IMMEDIATE MEMORY

Barondes and Cohen (1966) trained mice in a situation similar to Flexner's, either in the presence of puromycin or with puromycin injected immediately after learning. They found in both cases that memory was present for 45 minutes after training but was almost lost after 3 hours. Therefore puromycin also seems to have an effect on the formation of memory. Flexner and Flexner (1968) attempted to discover whether this effect of puromycin on presumed memory formation was also reversible by saline injection. Flexner and Flexner (1968) summarize the results of their studies with puromycin followed by saline as follows.

It was shown that puromycin administered to mice one or more days after maze-learning blocks expression of memory; the blockage can be removed by intracerebral injections of saline. We present evidence that intracerebral injections of saline are relatively ineffective in restoring memory when puromycin is administered either before or immediately after training; in these two situations puromycin appears to interfere with consolidation of memory.

Such an important conclusion should be examined further. We shall consider only the group injected after training, as it is the only one which is comparable to other groups which have been run. This group was trained, injected with puromycin immediately upon being trained, injected with saline 5 days later, and then retested 10 days after original training. The difference in retention between the mice treated with puromycin and other saline and those treated only with puromycin was clearly significant. Injection of saline therefore seems to reverse the amnesia produced by puromycin injected immediately after training.

Ungerer (1969a) was unable to obtain an effect of puromycin on mice trained for positive reinforcement in an operant situation. The dose and place of injection of the drug were the same as was effective in producing amnesia for a maze habit. It is possible that the operant habit was better trained. Flexner et al. (1967) have claimed that puromycin is ineffective in producing amnesia for an overtrained habit.

Cohen, Erwin, and Barondes (1966) have shown that puromycin produces abnormal electrical activity in the central nervous system, and they believe that the effect of this drug is due to such side-effects rather than to its properties as a protein synthesis inhibitor. Acetoxycyclohexamide, another protein synthesis inhibitor, has also been used.

Barondes and Cohen (1968) have reported that subcutaneous injection of 240 μg of acetoxycycloheximide in mice 5 minutes to 5 hours before training in a T maze produces amnesia for the habit. The mice were trained to a criterion of 5 out of 6 correct. This result is in marked contrast with previously reported results by these workers (1967), where intracerebral injections of the same substance which produced at least as high protein synthesis inhibition at the time of training were without effect on a well-trained habit. (However, an amnesic effect on a habit learned to a criterion of 3 out of 4 correct was observed.) Barondes and Cohen (1968) also found that memory was unimpaired at 3 hours, although amnesia set in 6 hours after training. From this it is argued that "a different process is utilized for memory storage during this period and that the absence of a long-term process, which is apparently dependent on cerebral protein synthesis, does not become manifest until the short-term process has decayed sufficiently." (1968).

The argument seems to be based on two premises. (1) If a process persists after the injection of a drug, it must therefore be invulnerable to that drug. (2) If a process persists for a time after the injection of a drug and then ceases, another process similar to the first but vulnerable to the drug did not start. But when stated this way, the premises are obviously not necessarily true. If we put hot water into an ice bucket, it takes some time for the ice to melt, but we do not argue that there is a short-term ice invulnerable to the hot water and a long-term ice which is vulnerable to the hot water. That the hot water–ice analogy is probably correct can be shown by quoting from Flexner et al. (1967): "In mice trained to criterion both recent and longer-term memory are maintained for 10 to 20 hours after injection of puromycin; then they disappear permanently."

Applying the argument used to erect the short- and long-term stages of memory, we would have to suppose that there was a large, possibly infinite number of stages of memory in long-term memory to account for the persistence of a stage of memory after injection for 10 to 20 hours followed by an amnesia. It would be much more parsimonious to assume that there is a single process which is reversed gradually by the application of a treatment.

Actinomycin-D inhibits the transcription of DNA into RNA. Injections of this drug into mice which cause almost complete inhibition of RNA synthesis are without any effects on learning either a passive-avoidance task (Barondes and Jarvik, 1964) or a maze-learning task (Cohen and Barondes, 1966). There was no effect on retention up to four hours later, after which the high toxicity of the drug made further testing impossible.

Another group of studies on amnesia and protein synthesis inhibition has been performed by Agranoff and his associates. Goldfish are taught to avoid shock in a shuttle box apparatus. They are given a fixed number of trials, at the end of which only a little learning has occurred. Treatment is given either before or soon after training, and retesting is done at different times after training. Agranoff and Klinger (1964) have found that injection with puromycin immediately after training causes goldfish to forget after 3 days. Potts and Bitterman (1967) added an element of discrimination to the shuttle box situation used by Agranoff. Instead of using a white light as a warning stimulus, the goldfish could discriminate what color light was followed by shock. They trained the goldfish, giving 20 trials a day on 6 training days one week apart. Each set of trials was followed by an injection of 170 μg of puromycin intracranially. The results showed that the puromycin-injected goldfish learned to avoid, though at a slower rate than the controls. However, it seems that the relative efficiency of discrimination (given different baselines of responding) was about the same for the experimental as for the control fish. Potts and Bitterman (1967) suggest that puromycin does not interfere with the consolidation of memory in general but with the consolidation of conditioned fear.

An alternative explanation may be suggested. As the ECS experiment of Schneider and Sherman (1968) indicates, the effect may be due to an obliteration of diminution of fear by an interaction between fear arousal and treatment when these are temporally continuous. Memory consolidation may not be involved in the puromycin effect at all.

That the effect of puromycin resembles that of ECS in the parameters of retrograde amnesia it produces in goldfish has been shown by Davis, Bright, and Agranoff (1965). Agranoff et al. (1967) report that actinomycin-D, injected intracranially immediately after learning, produces partial amnesia. An injection of the drug three hours after training does not produce amnesia. A similar effect is reported with injections of acetoxycycloheximide (it is not reported how long memory persists after the injection). The authors state: "Since protein synthesis is not significantly inhibited for several hours after the injection of actinomycin-D, we suggest that this drug impairs memory not by blocking protein synthesis but by some other means, presumably by its well-known role in blocking DNA-mediated RNA synthesis."

Agranoff has reported (1967) that intracranial injections of 6 percent KCl into the goldfish produce retrograde amnesia for 12 to 18 hours, a much longer time span than is effected by protein synthesis inhibitors. Memory, apparently, also takes 12 to 18 hours to disappear after treatment.

Davis (1968) has reported evidence for an environmental trigger to memory fixation in the goldfish. It has been shown that puromycin gradually has less effect the longer after the learning experience it is injected. Davis reports that if the goldfish is left in the training environment after training, the time is extended during which the memory is vulnerable to puromycin. Davis interprets this to mean that memory fixation is suppressed by conditions in the training environment. This conclusion must be accepted with caution. It can be seen from Davis's data that uninjected controls show a memory deficit which rapidly increases with the time they are left in the training environment. Such a deficit does not occur if such controls are returned to their home tanks. It can be argued, then, that puromycin injections, given to fish that have been left in the training environment for increasing times, are acting on a rapidly decreasing memory substrate, as indicated by a behavioral impairment of memory. For instance, a puromycin injection made immediately after training affects a memory where the normal retention index 72 hours later would be −0.38. The same injection made 3.5 hours after training affects a memory where the normal retention index would be −1.22—significantly different from the case where the goldfish is removed immediately from the training environment. After 24 hours in the training environment, retention deficits of controls are very large and not significantly different from deficits shown by the groups which received puromycin after 24 hours in the same environment. It is possible that a weaker memory remains susceptible to puromycin for a longer time than a stronger one, and Davis has not excluded this possibility. Until the nature of the decrement observed in untreated fish kept in the training environment is clarified, the fact that puromycin remains an effective agent for longer after training when fish are kept in the training environment can hardly be taken as evidence for an environmental trigger of memory fixation.

CHOLINERGICS AND MEMORY

There has long been clinical evidence that scopolamine produces amnesia—for instance, when it has been administered during childbirth (Gauss, 1906). The memory of the patient of the time spent under scopolamine is hazy or absent. In animals, anticholinergic drugs (atropine and scopolamine), when injected before training, impair learning of discrimination (Whitehouse, 1964) and passive avoidance (Buresová et al., 1964).

Also, Bohdanecky and Jarvik (1967) have reported the impairment of one-trial passive-avoidance memory in mice by injection of scopolamine or physostigmine before the learning trial. Memory was impaired 24 hours later, and the effect was not peripheral because control injections of scopolamine methylbromide or neostigmine did not have the same effect. Scopolamine methylbromide and neostigmine are quaternary nitrogen analogs of scopolamine and physostigmine and cross the blood-brain barrier with difficulty. On the other hand, physostigmine and scopolamine are tertiary nitrogen compounds and cross the blood-brain barrier with ease. On the other hand, it is probable that the exclusion of scopolamine methylbromide by the blood-brain barrier is not absolute. There are indicators in Bohdanecky and Jarvik's (1967) experiment that at least some of the scopolamine methylbromide may have reached the CNS. Further, Paul-David et al. (1960) have shown EEG effects similar to atropine with atropine methylnitrate, a quaternary nitrogen analog, after moderately heavy doses of this drug.

Davis, Thomas, and Adams (1971) have also observed an impairment of retention of a one-trial passive-avoidance habit by administration of scopolamine or physostigmine before the learning trial.

Herz (1959) found that these anticholinergic effects depressed performance only in the earlier stages of training. Anticholinesterases facilitate learning when injected just before (Bures et al., 1962) or just after (Stratton and Petrinovich, 1963) learning.

When rats are repeatedly exposed to a stimulus and this stimulus is subsequently used as a conditioned stimulus, learning is not as efficient, presumably because the rats have habituated to the stimulus. Better learning occurs without extensive pre-exposure. Carlton and Vogel (1965) showed that if the pre-exposure took place while the rat was under scopolamine, it did not show a subsequent decrement in learning. They suggested that this was because scopolamine prevented habituation and that, since habituation is a part of behavioral inhibition, scopolamine blocked behavioral inhibition which was assumed to be mediated by the cholinergic system. Warburton and Groves (1969) have shown, however, that habituation is not completely blocked but only slowed down by scopolamine. They also suggest that reduced habituation is produced by an amnesia due to scopolamine. The rat cannot habituate to some thing it cannot remember. Scopolamine is used clinically to produce a blurring of memory, and overdosage with anticholinergics can produce disturbances of memory in patients.

ADRENERGIC EFFECTS ON MEMORY

Some recent evidence opens the possibility that norephinephrine may also play a role in memory storage (Randt et al., 1971). Diethydithiocarbanate (DDC) decreases the synthesis and brain concentration of norepinephrine by inhibiting the enzyme dopamine (B-hydroxylase). DDC was injected into mice 30 minutes before passive-avoidance training and the mice were placed in an apparatus consisting of two compartments. They were put in the smaller of the two compartments, and, after passing into the larger compartment, were given a 2-second shock 18 seconds after entry. Latencies to enter the large compartment were longer in the DDC-injected mice as compared with saline controls on retest 1 and 5 minutes after training, suggesting an enhancement of memory. On the other hand, on retest 1, 6 and 24 hours later, latencies of entry into the larger compartment were very much shorter than those of the saline controls, indicating that there might be an amnesia. We must remember, however, that tests of passive avoidance measure not only memory but also activity levels and fear. An experimental design based on discrimination tends to minimize the role of activity. Further, escape training is superior to avoidance training because performance is based on the motivating properties of pain rather than fear. However, no situation is ideal, and a whole battery of memory tests should be used before we can be confident that memory function has been altered.

In the experiment noted above, DDC injected 2 hours after training produced no change in performance 24 hours later. If this control proves repeatable, the case for an effect on memory will be good.

CHOLINERGIC SYNAPSE AND THE SITE OF MEMORY

The idea that learning and memory are due to some form of change of synaptic conductance is very old, having been suggested by Tanzi in 1893. It is a simple idea, and in many ways an obvious one. However, the evidence that learning is due to changes at the synapse has hitherto been meager. Though changes occur at a spinal synapse as a result of stimulation, there is no evidence that these changes are utilized in the nervous system for information storage. To use an analogy, if we pass large amounts of current across resistors in a computer, temporary increases in temperature and perhaps even permanent increases in resistance occur. However, such an experiment shows only that the computer could store information by using "poststimulation" alterations in its resistors—not that this is the *actual* way in which the computer stores information. Further, Sharpless (1964) has pointed out that learning is not due to simple stimulation of a pathway, and he therefore questions whether the phenomena studied by Eccles (1961, 1964) have anything to do with learning as observed in the intact organism. Nevertheless, this does not mean that learning is not due to synaptic changes of some sort; it means only that a different experimental test of the possibility must be devised.

After blows to the head sustained in accidents, events which occurred closest in time prior to the accident cannot be recalled (retrograde amnesia). Such patches of amnesia may cover days or even weeks. The lost memories tend to return with those most distant in time from the accident becoming available first (Russell and Nathan, 1946). In the Korsakoff syndrome (1965), retrograde amnesia may gradually increase until it covers a span of many years. An elderly patient may end up remembering only his youth, having no useful memory of the more recent intervening years. From such evidence concerning human retrograde amnesia we may conclude that the changes that occur in the substrate of memory take a relatively long time and are measurable in hours, days, and even months. If we suppose from this that the substrate of memory is synaptic and that it is slowly changing, it may be possible to follow such synaptic changes by using pharmacological methods. If the same dose of a synaptically acting drug has different effects on remembering, depending on the age of the memory (and this can be shown for a number of synaptically acting drugs), we may assume that there has been a synaptic alteration as a function of time since learning, and we may infer that such a synaptic change underlies memory.

Pharmacological agents are available which can either increase or decrease the effectiveness of neural transmitters (Goodman and Gilman,

1965). For instance, anticholinesterase and anticholinergic drugs affect transmission at synapses utilizing the transmitter acetylcholine. Such cholinergic pathways exist in the brain (McGeer et al., 1969: Olivier et al., 1970).

During normal transmission, acetylcholine is rapidly destroyed by the enzyme cholinesterase. Anticholinesterase drugs, such as physostigmine and diisopropyl fluorophosphate (DFP), inactivate cholinesterase and thus indirectly prevent the destruction of acetylcholine. In submaximal dosage, these drugs inactivate only a part of the cholinesterase and hence only slow down—but do not stop—the destruction of acetylcholine. The overall effect at such submaximal levels of anticholinesterase is to increase (by some constant) the lifetime of any acetylcholine emitted into the synapse and thereby to increase to acetycholine synaptic concentrations resulting from a given rate of emission. Up to a certain level, the greater this concentration, the greater the efficiency of transmission—that is, the conduction across the synapse. Above that level, which is set by the sensitivity of the postsynaptic membrane, any further increase in acetylcholine concentration produces a synaptic block (Goodman and Gilman, 1965, 1934; Feldberg and Vartiainen, 1934). Thus the application of a given dosage of anticholinesterase, by protecting acetylcholine from destruction, will have different effects on the efficiency of synaptic conduction, depending on the rate of acetylcholine emission during transmission and on the sensitivity of the postsynaptic membrane. At low levels of emission of acetylcholine or low sensitivity of the postsynaptic membrane, an application of anticholinesterase will render transmission more efficient. Such a property is used to good effect in the treatment of myasthenia gravis. In the treatment of this disorder anticholinesterase is used to raise the effective concentration of acetylcholine at the neuromuscular junction so as to reduce apparent muscular weakness. On the other hand, the same dose of anticholinesterase that caused muscular contraction in the myasthenic patient produces paralysis at the neuromuscular junction in a man with normal levels of function.

If there are changes with time after learning in the level of acetylcholine emitted at the modified synapse, such a synapse should show either facilitation or block, depending on when (after learning) we inject the same dose of anticholinesterase. A similar argument with regard to the action of anticholinesterase can be applied if we assume that, instead of a presynaptic increment in transmitter, it is the postsynaptic membrane which becomes more sensitve to transmitter as a function of time after learning. But the use of an anticholinesterase does not allow us to decide which of these alternative versions of the hypothesis of the increment of synaptic conductance actually holds for the learning situation. Later, however, we shall indicate how the use of other types of drugs, such as the cholinomimetics, allows us to surmise that postsynaptic sensitization is the more likely mechanism.

The first two experiments (Deutsch et al., 1966; Deutsch and Leibowitz, 1966) show that facilitation or block of a memory can be obtained with the same dose of anticholinesterase simply as a function of the time of injection since original learning, as might be expected if synaptic change formed with the substrate of memory.

Experiments with Cholinergic Agents on Long-Term Memory

In the first experiment, rats were trained on a simple Y maze; then an intracerebral injection of anticholinesterase was made at different times after initial training, the time being varied from one group of subjects to another. Twenty-four hours after injection, all rats, irrespective of the group to which they were assigned, were retested. Thus the time between training and injection was varied; the time between injection and retest was kept constant. Any difference in remembering between groups was therefore due to the time between initial training and injection.

Rats were placed on an electrified grid in a Y maze. The lighted arm of the Y was not electrified, and its position was changed randomly from trial to trial. The rats therefore learned to run into the lighted arm. The learning criterion was met when they had chosen the lighted arm ten trials in succession, whereupon training was concluded.

Then, at various times after training, the rats were injected intracerebrally with DFP dissolved in peanut oil. This dose did not increase the number of trials to criterion in a naive group of rats, thus showing that learning capacity during training was not affected by the drug in the amounts used. At 24 hours after injection, the rats were retrained to the same criterion of 10 successively correct trials. The number of trials to criterion in this retraining session represented the measure of retention.

The first group was injected 30 minutes after training. Its retention was significantly worse than that of a control group injected only with peanut oil. By contrast, a group injected with DFP 3 days after training showed the same amount of retention as the control group. Thus up to this point it seems that memory is less susceptible to DFP the older it is. In fact, a subsidiary experiment has established that injections of DFP on habits 1 and 2 days old have no effect, showing that the initial stage of vulnerability lasts less than 1 day. Beyond 3 days, however, the situation seems to reverse itself: the memory is *more* susceptible to DFP the older it is—because a DFP group injected 5 days after training showed only slight recollection at retest, and a further group, injected 14 days after training, showed complete amnesia.

The score of the group trained 14 days before injection was the same as the score of the naive group which had not been trained before but had simply been injected with DFP 24 hours prior to testing. The amnesia of the DFP group trained 14 days before injection was not due to normal forgetting, since other controls showed almost perfect retention over a 15-day span. Similar results have been obtained by Hamburg (1967) with intraperitoneal injections of the anticholinesterase physostigmine, using the same escape habit. Biederman confirmed the shape of the amnesic function with physostigmine in an operant situation. He used a latency measure of forgetting and a bar press response. Further evidence that the sensitivity of memory to cholinergic drugs alters with the age of the memory is presented by Squire et al. (1971). However, the results show that, at least in their situation, some of the effect was due to an interaction between central and peripheral factors.

To make sure that we were not observing some periodicity in fear or emotionality interacting with the drug, another experiment, employing an appetitive rather than an escape task, was conducted. The rats were taught to run a reward of sugar water, the position of which always coincided with the lit arm of a Y maze (Wiener and Deutsch, 1968). The results (Fig. 13-2), when compared to the maze results from the preceding experiments, show a very similar pattern of amnesia as a function of time of learning before injection. It is therefore most likely that we are in fact studying memory. The divergences in the curves after seven days are probably due to differences in rates of forgetting among the three groups.

In the first set of experiments, which dealt with the effects of the anticholinesterases DFP and physostigmine on habits which are normally well retained, the effects of these drugs were to decrease the retention of a habit depending on its age. Thus one of the predicted effects of anticholinesterase was verified. However, the other predicted effect, facilitation, was not shown. The reason for this is that the acquired habit was so well retained without treatment over 14 days that one could not, on methodological grounds, show any improvement of retention subsequent to injection of the drug. It may be that 1-, 2-, and 3-day-old habits were facilitated instead of merely being unaffected, but the design of the experiment would not allow us to detect this because there is an effective ceiling on performance. Therefore an attempt was made to obtain facilitation where it was methodologically possible to detect it; namely, where retention of the habit by a control group was imperfect. For example, it was found that 29 days after learning the escape habit described above was almost forgotten by a group of animals injected with peanut oil only 24 hours before. On the basis of this observation, a second kind of experiment was devised.

Rats were divided into four groups. Two groups were trained 14 days

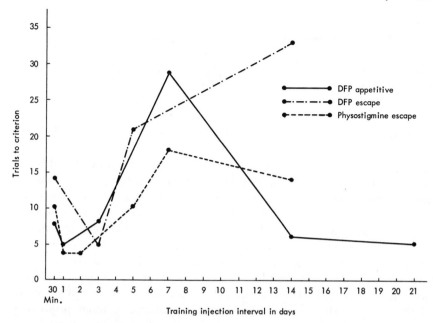

FIG. 13–2. Effect of anticholinesterase injection on memories of different age, shown in three separate experiments. Trials to criterion during retest are plotted against the time which elapsed between retest and original learning. A larger number of trials to criterion during retest signifies greater amnesia. The time between injection and retest was constant. The differences past the 7-day point probably represent differing rates of forgetting in the three situations. (The three experiments are by Deutsch et al. [1966], Hamberg [1967], and Wiener and Deutsch [1968].) (From Deutsch, J. A., 1971, by permission of *Science*, vol. 174, pp. 788 ff. Copyright 1971 by the American Association for the Advancement of Science.)

before injection and the other two groups 28 days before injection. One of the 28-day and one of the 14-day groups were injected with the same dose of DFP; the remaining 28- and 14-day groups were injected with the same volume of pure peanut oil. The experimental procedure and dosage were exactly the same as previously described.

On retest, poor retention was exhibited by the 14-day DFP group and 28-day peanut oil group. By contrast, the 28-day DFP group and the 14-day peanut oil group exhibited good retention. The anticholinesterase injections show a large and clear facilitation of the otherwise almost forgotten 28-day-old habit and confirm the obliteration of the otherwise well-remembered 14-day-old habit demonstrated in the previous experiments (Fig. 13–3a). The same facilitation of a forgotten habit was shown by Wiener and Deutsch (1968) using an appetitive habit and by Squire (1970) using physostigmine-injected mice. Biederman (in press) showed an improvement in memory in pigeons when physostigmine is injected 28 days after a line-tilt discrimination is partly learned. A well-learned color discrimination, acquired by the same subjects, showed no such improvement under the same conditions. Thus these results also lend strong support to the notion that forgetting is due to a reversal of the change in synpatic conductance which underlies learning (Fig. 13–3b). It must be emphasized, however, that both the block and the facilitation of a memory are temporary, wearing off as the injected drug wears off.

So far it has been shown the the anticholinesterase drugs DFP and physostigmine have different effects on memories of different age. Though their actions on memory are consistent with, and plausibly interpreted by, their anticholinesterase action, some other property besides their indirect action on acetylcholine could in some unknown manner produce the same results. It was therefore desirable to conduct an independent check on the hypothesis that the observed effects are due to an effect of acetylcholine. This check can be provided by using an anticholinergic drug (like atropine or scopolamine), which reduces the effective action of a given level of acetylcholine at the synapse without actually changing the level. It does this, apparently, by occupying some of the receptor sites on the postsynaptic membrane without producing depolarization. It thus prevents acetylcholine from reaching such receptor sites and so attenuates the effectiveness of this transmitter. We would therefore expect an anticholinergic to block conduction at a synapse where the postsynaptic membrane is relatively insensitive, while simply diminishing conduction at synapses where the postsynaptic membrane is highly sensitive. If the interpretation of the effects of DFP is correct, we would then expect the reverse effect with the administration of an anticholinergic drug. That is, we would expect the greatest amnesia with anticholinergics precisely where the effect of anticholinesterase was the least, and we would predict the least effect where the effect of anticholinesterase on memory was the largest. It will be recalled that the last effect of anticholinesterase was on habits one to three days old.

In a third set of experiments (Wiener and Deutsch, 1968; Deutsch and Rocklin, 1967), the anticholinergic agent was scopolamine, and it was injected in exactly the same amount of oil and location as in the previous experiments with DFP. The same experimental procedure also was used. A group that was injected 30 minutes after training showed little if any effect of scopolamine. However, a group injected 1 and 3 days after training showed a considerable degree of block. Groups injected 7 and 14 days after training showed little if any effect. The results in the appetitive and escape situations were very similar.

As far as the experimental methodology will allow us to discern, the effect of an anticholinergic is the mirror image of the anticholinesterase effect (Fig. 13–4). There is an increase of sensitivity between 30 minutes

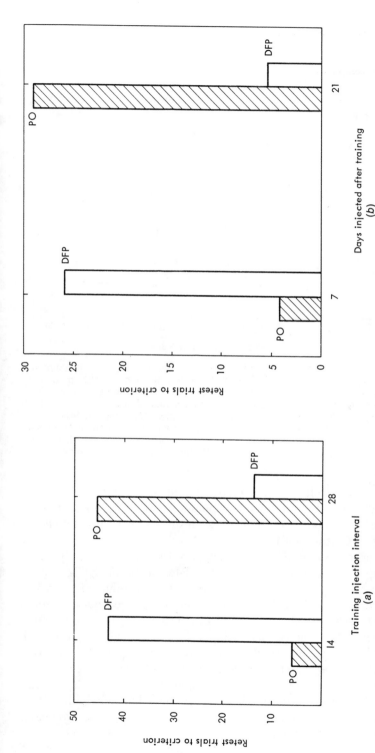

FIG. 13-3. Effect of injection of the anticholinesterase DFP (diisopropyl fluorophosphate) and PO (peanut oil), the drug vehicle, on well-retained or almost forgotten habits. Trials to criterion are plotted against time between retest and original training. When controls remember well, DFP-injected animals forget. When controls forget, DFP-injected animals remember well. (After Deutsch and Leibowitz, 1966, and Wiener and Deutsch, 1968). (From Deutsch, J. A., 1971, by permission of *Science*, vol. 174, pp. 788 ff. Copyright 1971 by the American Association for the Advancement of Science.)

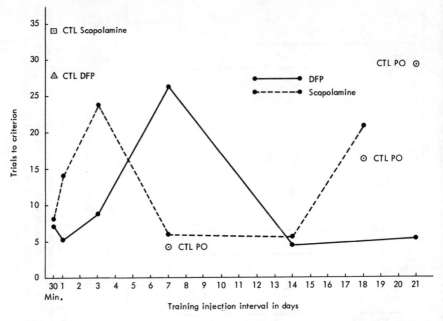

FIG. 13–4. Effects of injection of the anticholinergic scopolamine compared with that of the anticholinesterase DFP and control injections of PO (peanut oil) on the retention of an appetitive task at various times after original learning. Time between injection and retest was constant. Also indicated are the number of trials to criterion when rats were injected with scopolamine (CTL scopolamine) or DFP (CTL DFP) before original learning to give an estimate of actual amount of amnesia produced. (From Deutsch, J. A., 1971, by permission of *Science,* vol. 174, p. 788 ff. Copyright 1971 by the American Association for the Advancement of Science.)

and 1 to 3 days, followed by a decrease of sensitivity. This further confirms the notion that there are two phases in memory storage. Finally, it is of interest to note that amnesia can result in man from anticholinergic therapy (Cutting, 1964).

The experiments outlined above support the idea that at the time of learning some unknown event stimulates a particular group of synapses to alter their state and to increase their conductivity. At this point we may ask why such an increase in synaptic conductivity does not manifest itself with the passage of time when no drugs are injected. Why has it not been noted that habits are better remembered a week after initial learning than, say, three days after learning? Various answers are possible. One is that the phenomena we have described are some artifact of drug injection. Another is that animal training has, in general, stretched over days in other studies, so that time blurred the initiation of a memory. In addition, and partly as a consequence of the foregoing, it is difficult to find studies where the age of the habit, measured in days, has been used as an independent variable in studies of retention.

However, should we not have seen such an improvement in recall in our control groups? This would have been unlikely for the methodological reason that our animals were trained to the very high criterion of ten out of ten trials. Given a score which was initially almost perfect, it was thus well nigh impossible to observe any subsequent improvement in retention that might actually exist.

To rid ourselves of this methodological limitation, we devised a study using escape from shock in which rats were initially undertrained. The rats were given 15 trials. We then waited to see how many trials it would take these rats on some subsequent day to reach our strict criterion (Huppert and Deutsch, 1969). No drugs were used. We found that the rats took only about half the number of trials to reach criterion when they waited seven to ten days as when they waited one or three days (Fig. 13–5). Huppert (personal communication) has shown an

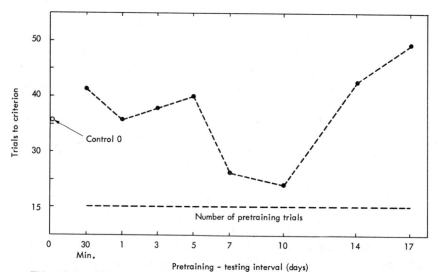

FIG. 13–5. Effects of delay between original partial training (15 trials) and subsequent training to criterion. Trials to criterion in subsequent training are plotted against time since original partial training. Control 0 indicates the number of trials to criterion taken by a group which received its training all in one session. (From Deutsch, J. A., 1971, by permission of *Science*, vol. 174, pp. 788 ff. Copyright 1971 by the American Association for the Advancement of Science.)

analogous improvement using an appetitive task. Finally, Dr. J. L. McGaugh pointed out to me that there are animal studies which purport to find similar effects (Anderson, 1940; Bunch, 1933, 1939; Huppert, 1915). This shows that our conclusions about the varying substrate of memory were not due to some pharmacological artifact.

We may now ask ourselves whether the inferred modification of a synapse represents an all-or-none or a graded process. In other words, can a synapse be modified only once during learning or does a repetition of the same learning task after some learning has occurred further increase conductance at a single synapse? If we postulate an all-or-none process, how, according to such a model, can we explain empirical increases in "habit strength" with increased training? Possibly they are due to a progressive involvement of fresh synapses and a spread involving more parallel connections in the nervous system. In support of a graded process, we may hypothesize that successive learning trials modify the same synapses in a cumulative way by producing an increase either in the rate at which conductance increases or in the upper limit of such conductance, or both.

There are tests of these two alternatives. If, with increased training, a synapse becomes more conductive, then a habit should become increasingly more vulnerable to anticholinesterase with increased training. Furthermore, the memory of the same habit should be facilitated when its level of training is very low. In other words, we should be able to perform the same manipulations of memory by varying the level of training as we were able to perform when we varied time since training.

If, on the other hand, increases in training simply involve a larger number of synapses but no increase in the level of transmitter at any one synapse, increases in training should not lead to an increased vulnerability of a habit to anticholinesterase. Rather, the opposite should be the case. As the number of synapses recruited is increased, some of the additional synapses will, by chance variation, be less sensitive to a given level of anticholinesterase. Thus a larger number of synapses should be left functional after anticholinesterase injection when we test an overtrained habit. Three experiments (Deutsch and Leibowitz, 1966; 1967, S. F. Leibowitz, Deutsch, Coons, in preparation) show a large and unequivocal effect. Poorly learned habits are enormously facilitated and well-learned habits are blocked (Fig. 13–6). This supports the hypothesis that a set of synapses underlying a single habit remains restricted and each synapse within such a set simply increases in conductance as learning proceeds.

So far the results have been interpreted in terms of the action of drugs on synapses which alter their conductance as a function of time since training and amount of training. We can use the model we have developed to generate a somewhat different kind of prediction. An anticholinesterase in submaximal concentrations simply slows the rate of destruction of acetylcholine. Since we have hypothesized that amnesia is due to a block resulting from an acetylcholine excess, we should predict no amnesia if we spaced our trials so that all or most of the acetylcholine emitted on the previous trial is destroyed by the time

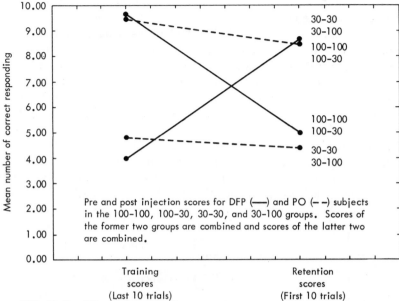

FIG. 13–6.   Effects of anticholinesterase injection (DFP) on the retention of
well-learned and poorly learned habits. The mean number of correct responses of the last 10 of 30 trials or two groups is shown on the left. One
group had to learn to run to alley illuminated by 30v. bulb; the other had to
learn the same task, except that the bulb had 100v. across it. As can be seen
from the last 10 trials, the dim light of the 30v. group posed a difficult task
which produced little learning by the end of the 30 trials. The group learning
the brighter cue (100v.) displayed excellent acquisition. Because of the different rates of acquisition of the 100v. and 30v. habits, half of each group
was shifted to retest on the other brightness and half was retained on the
same brightness (30-30, 100-100 retested on the same brightness, 30-100
trained on 30, retested on 100, 100-30 trained on 100, retested on 30.) The
scores of animals trained on the same brightness are combined. Half the
animals were injected with DFP, the other half with peanut oil (PO). There
is little change in the scores of the PO animals. However, there is a complete crossover of the drug-injected animals, showing block of the well-
learned habit and facilitation of the poorly learned habit. (From Deutsch, J. A.,
1971, by permission of Science, vol. 174, pp. 788 ff. Copyright 1971 by the
American Association for the Advancement of Science.)

of the next trial. It has been shown by Bacq and Brown (1937) that
(with an intermediate dose of anticholinesterase) block at a synapse
occurred only when the intervals between successive stimuli were
shortened. Accordingly, an experiment was performed where we varied
the interval during retest between 25 and 50 seconds (Rocklin and
Deutsch, unpublished). Using a counterbalanced design, we found that
rats tested under physostigmine at 25-second intervals showed amnesia
for the original habit. Those tested at a 50-second intertrial interval
under physostigmine showed no amnesia.

In a second experiment, the rats during retest had to learn an escape habit the reverse of the one they had learned during training. Therefore to escape shock during retest they had to learn not only to run to the dark alley but also to inhibit the original learning of running to the lighted alley. Thus, provided that the original habit was remembered at the time the reversal was being learned, the time to learn the reversal should take longer than the time to learn the original habit. But if the original habit was not remembered, there should be no difference in trials to criterion between original learning and retest. The results showed that at 50 seconds between trials, animals in both the physostigmine and the saline control groups took almost twice as long to reverse as it took them to learn the original habit, indicating that they remembered the original habit (Fig. 13–7). At 25 seconds between trials,

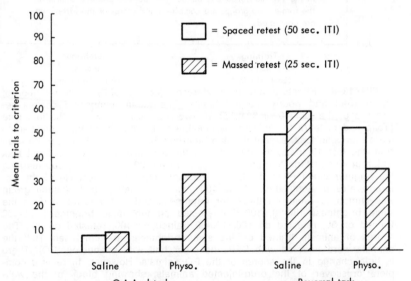

FIG. 13–7. Effect of massing and spacing trials during retest on anticholinesterase-induced amnesia. Left: retest consisted of relearning original habit (run to light, avoid dark). Right: retest consisted of unlearning original habit. On retest the animal had to learn to run to dark and avoid light (reversal). *ITI* = intertrial interval; *PHYSO* = physostigmine. (From Deutsch, J. A., 1971, by permission of *Science,* vol. 174, pp. 788 ff. Copyright 1971 by the American Association for the Advancement of Science.)

the physostigmine animals learned the reversal as quickly as the original habit, whereas the saline animals again took much longer. This second experiment shows that the amnesia of the 25-second physostigmine group in the first experiment was not due to disorientation or an incapacity to perform or learn but to an amnesia. We might explain the high relearning scores for the same habit of the rats run at 25-second intervals under physostigmine by saying that the rats were somehow incapacitated by the physostigmine if they had to run at 25-second intervals. However, it is difficult to see how such incapacitation could produce abnormally low learning scores for the reversal habit. This dependence of the amnesia on the precise interval of trials during retest should not, of course, be seen with anticholinergics or cholinomimetics but only with anticholinesterases. This further prediction from the hypothesis should be tested.

So far, then, it seems that the drugs we are using to block or facilitate memory have their effect on synaptic conductance. However, what is it that changes when synaptic conductance alters? As was mentioned previously, the two main hypotheses are that (a) the amount of transmitter emitted at the presynaptic ending increases or (b) the postsynaptic ending increases in its sensitivity to transmitter. To test this idea, carbachol (carbamolycholine) was injected before retest. This drug, a cholinomimetic, acts on the postsynaptic membrane much like acetylcholine; however, it is not susceptible to destruction by the enzyme acetylcholinesterase. Therefore, by injecting this drug we can test the sensitivity of the postsynaptic membrane. It seems that seven-day-old habits are blocked by a dose of this cholinomimetic which leaves a three-day-old habit unaffected (Table 13–2). This would indicate that

TABLE 13–2
The Effect of Carbachol Injection on Recall of Habits That Were Three and Seven Days Old. (Criterion was seven correct trials in succession. Numbers in parentheses indicate number of rats tested.)

Treatment	Median number of trials to criterion	
	3 days	7 days
Carbachol.........	6.0 (15)	20 (15)*
Saline............	4.0 (8)	0 (7)

* $P < .01$ compared with saline, Mann-Whitney U test.
From Deutsch, J. A., 1971, by permission of *Science*, vol. 174, pp. 788 ff. Copyright 1971 by the American Association for the Advancement of Science.

it is probably the postsynaptic membrane that has increased its sensitivity and so increased synaptic conductance.

One of the questions that often arises is why the drugs we use do not block all cholinergic synaptic activity. As was seen above, rats learn appetitive tasks at a normal rate under drug doses which, under some circumstances, produce complete amnesia. There is very little in the overt behavior of the rat to indicate that it has been drugged. The drug doses produce no apparent malaise or incoordination. Clearly, the doses we use seem to affect only what one might call the memory synapses. It would therefore seem that these are more sensitive to our drugs, but such an abnormal sensitivity may be more apparent than real. We know that there are levels of training and times after training when a habit is unaffected by the dosage of drug, and this shows that "memory" synapses are not always affected. It therefore seems more plausible to think of the "memory" synapses as traveling through a much larger range of postsynaptic sensitivity, while normal synapses remain fixed somewhere in the middle of the range of sensitivity variation of the memory synapse. In other words, the "memory" synapse has to swing from extreme insensitivity to transmitter to extreme sensitivity in order to manifest those changes in conductance which we have demonstrated. It will therefore be much more susceptible to anticholinergic agents when conductance is low and to anticholinesterases and cholinomimetics when conductance is high. In the middle of the range, sensitivity to all agents will resemble that of a normal synapse, and only grossly toxic doses will affect memory. This speculation, of course, will have to be further tested. The experiments so far reported implicate the cholinergic system in memory. It is of course possible that other systems, such as the adrenergic, will also turn out to have a similar function, and this, too, we hope to test.

When an animal is rewarded for performing a habit, such a habit will be learned or acquired. However, when the habit is no longer rewarded, the animal will cease to perform it. Another kind of learning takes place, and this is called extinction. If initial learning consists of the formation of some synaptic (or other) connection, does extinction consist of the weakening or uncoupling of this connection? Or is it the formation of some other connection which then works to oppose the effects of the first ("learning") connection? If extinction consists of weakening the connection set up in original learning, then an extinguished habit should be similar to a forgotten habit pharmacologically. Because we have already shown that an almost forgotten habit is facilitated by anticholinesterase, we would, on the "weakening hypothesis" of extinction, expect an injection of an anticholinesterase to produce less amnesia of an extinguished habit than of the same unextinguished habit. If, on the other hand, another habit is acquired during extinction which inhibits the expression of the original habit, another pattern of results should be discernible after injection with an anticholinesterase. If original learning occurs seven days before anticholinesterase injection and retest, there should be amnesia for the original habit. If extinction of the habit is given close in time to its acquisition, there should be amnesia for both the original learning and for extinction. If, on the other hand, original learning is seven days before injection and retest, and the extinction is three days before injection and retest, the original habit should be lost but the extinction habit retained. (As we noted above, three-day-old habits are unaffected by our dose of anticholinesterase.) When extinction was given to rats close in time to the original training, both the original training and extinction were blocked by physostigmine (Deutsch and Wiener, 1969). These rats took the same number of trials to relearn as control animals, which were trained, not extinguished, and then drugged. However, when extinction was three days before injection and retest, it took the rats—during retest after drug injection—approximately twice as many trials to learn as control animals (unextinguished and drugged), showing that extinction had been retained while the original habit was blocked (Fig. 13–8). This supports the idea that extinction is the learning of a separate habit, opposing the performance of the initially rewarded habit.

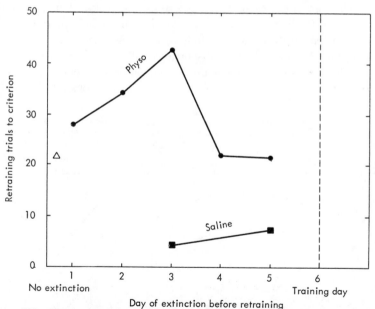

FIG. 13–8. Effect of physostigmine on retraining after extinction. The time between original learning and retraining is the same for all groups. When time of extinction is close to original learning, there is amnesia, but no difference from a group receiving no extinction. At extinction 3 days before learning, the number of trials to relearn is almost double. *SALINE* = scores of controls injected with saline; *PHYSO* = scores of animals injected with physostigmine. (From Deutsch, J. A., 1971, by permission of *Science*, vol. 174, pp. 788 ff. Copyright 1971 by the American Association for the Advancement of Science.)

It has also been suggested (Carlton, 1969) that different systems, such as excitatory or inhibitory systems, are subserved by different transmitters. Habits acquired during extinction have been viewed as inhibitory. However, the last experiment we have outlined also shows that extinction placed close to original learning is equally vulnerable to anticholinesterase as original learning. Habits probably cannot be classified into synaptically inhibitory and excitatory on the basis of behavioral excitation or inhibition. However, as all habits compete for behavioral expression, excitation and reciprocal inhibition must be connected with all habits.

Conclusions

A simple hypothesis can explain the results obtained to date if we disregard those results when we wait 30 minutes after original learning to inject. The hypothesis is that, as a result of learning, the postsynaptic endings at a specific set of synapses become more sensitive to transmitter. This sensitivity increases with time after initial learning and then declines. The rate at which such sensitivity increases depends on the amount of initial learning. If the curve of transmission plotted against time is displaced upward with anticholinesterases, the very low portions will show facilitation and the high portions will cause block (Fig. 13–9). The middle portions will appear unaffected (unless special experimental tests are made). If the curve of transmission is displaced down with

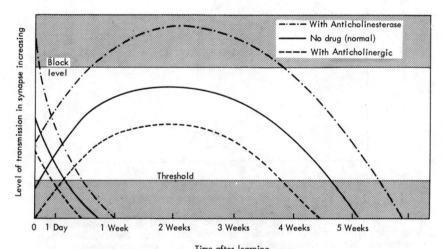

FIG. 13–9. Hypothesized changes in "memory" synapses with time after training and with pharmacological intervention. (From Deutsch, J. A., 1971, by permission of *Science,* vol. 174, pp. 788 ff. Copyright 1971 by the American Association for the Advancement of Science.)

anticholinergics, the middle portion will appear unaffected and only the very early or late components will show block.

Taken together, then, the results which have been obtained are evidence that synaptic conductance alters as a result of learning. It seems that (1) Cholinergic synapses are modified as a result of learning and it is probably the postsynaptic membrane which, up to a certain point, becomes increasingly more sensitive to acetylcholine with time after learning. (2) After this point, sensitivity declines, leading to the phenomena of forgetting. (3) There is also good evidence that there is an initial phase of declining sensitivity to cholinesterase or increasing sensitivity to anticholinergics. This could reflect the existence of a parallel set of synapses with fast decay serving as a short-term store. (4) Increasing the amount of learning leads to an increase in conductance in sets of synapses without an increase in their number. (5) Both original learning and extinction are subserved by cholinergic synapses.

chapter **14**

Learning and
Intracranial
Self-Stimulation

NATURE OF THE PROBLEM

In this chapter we shall be concerned with what is known about learning from the physiological point of view. A great deal is known from the descriptive or behavioral point of view about the adaptive changes which occur when an animal is repeatedly placed in the same situation. Such changes, or the capacity for such changes, are the property of some mechanism, or a set of mechanisms, to be found within the animal. It will be our task to consider what these mechanisms are.

Ideally, the discovery and description of such mechanisms appear simple. In order to discover the mechanism of learning, we should observe the nervous system while learning is proceeding, much as we look at the works of a clock in order to discover how it keeps time, and this should tell us what the mechanism is which produces learning. Unfortunately, such a simple approach is not possible. The functional units of the nervous system are too small and numerous for us to be able to view their interactions simultaneously. We are, therefore, driven to less direct methods of discovering the mechanisms of learning. Since only certain kinds of observation are open to us, we must construct guesses about the kind of mechanism at work and then see what observations of the type available to us we should expect if such hypotheses were correct. Such observations might either be on the behavior of the intact organism, which are placed in the domain of experimental psychology, or on organisms where some interference, pharmacological or surgical, has occurred. These latter are collocated under the name of physiological psychology. The distinction that is here drawn between experimental and physiological psychology does not refer to a different theo-

504

retical purpose but simply to the method or technique employed. The facts we use as we attempt to frame hypotheses about the mechanisms which enable an animal to learn will be drawn both from studies on intact animals and from physiological methods. Both sets of data reflect the workings of the mechanism which in our hypotheses we attempt to discern. Both kinds of evidence can function as evidence for or against hypotheses about the mechanism.

PROBLEMS IN THE MECHANISM OF LEARNING

What is it about the nervous system that we are attempting to discover when we study learning? There are many questions which may be asked and which it will be useful to keep separate. We may wish to help engineers who are interested in constructing computers that display some of the advantageous features of biological learning systems. For instance, biological learning systems are capable of storing an enormous amount of information. Though this could be explained by the large number of components in biological systems, the speed with which stored information can be drawn upon by such systems (for instance, the speed with which we recognize) cannot be explained in such a way. On the contrary, the elements of which the nervous system is composed act very slowly in comparison to the vacuum tubes or transistors available to the engineer. The problem of storage and retrieval may be illustrated by the following example. Storage of signals on magnetic tape in very large quantities presents little problem. Long sequences of music, for instance, can be faithfully recorded. They can also be accurately reproduced, so that if we wish to know all that has been recorded in the machine we can ascertain this simply by playing back what has been recorded. However, we may not simply wish to know all that has been recorded. We may wish to know whether a given piece of music has already been recorded on the tape. In order to find this out, we have to arrange for a comparison of all that has been recorded with the piece of music which may or may not have been recorded. The problem is how to find this out quickly. In order to decide that the piece of music has not occurred before, it would be necessary to play the whole tape on which recording had been made. If the process of recognition was carried out in this way, the time would rise with the amount already recorded. Such a process of "recognition" is clearly lengthy and inefficient. When we hear a melody, recognition is prompt. We do not have to search in series through all the tunes we have heard. An explanation of this property of fast access or retrieval will not lie in the speed of each component of the nervous system. Rather, the explanation of the speed with which stored information can be tapped will be found in the way in which the rather slow-acting components are arranged.

That is, in animals and man the system of storage and retrieval is probably different from that in man-made devices. If this is the case, the engineer will be able to build a system with properties similar to the nervous system out of components such as tubes or transistors and so be able to construct more efficient machines. It is common to have the interconnections of the components, rather than their individual properties, determine the performance of the overall system. It is for this reason that it is possible to build a computer having the same repertoire out of physically quite different components, such as vacuum tubes or transistors. While the physical principles on which the basic units function are different, the interactions of these elements or basic units are kept the same.

On the other hand, we may be interested in determining the precise physical change which occurs in the nervous system when an animal learns. There is presumably some long-term alteration of a physical nature in the nervous system on which an animal's learning depends. Such a question is not directed at the explanation of learning in the same way as that concerning the learning system, which could be asked without an attempt to know the physical specification of the parts composing the system. It is a question about the physical embodiment of an operation within the system. Even if we knew the precise physical change which occurred during learning, we could not, without a knowledge of the system within which it functions, predict the behavior of the organism when it learns. In the same way, we cannot predict the storage performance of a computer merely by knowing that magnetization is the long-term change which occurs in the computer when it stores information. However, the answer to this question is important from another point of view. It would perhaps tell us why, for instance, cooling a biological system does not destroy learned habits or why more recent memories are affected after concussion while those of more distant events are left intact.

There is a third class of questions that we may wish to ask about learning and its relation to the nervous system. We may be interested to know what parts of the nervous system are necessary for learning. This may be thought of as a question about the problems we discussed above; that is, where in the nervous system the structures or neural organization subserving learning are to be found and where the physiological change necessary in learning is located. The answer to these questions would not, of course, enable us to understand behavior better than if we did not know where in the nervous system certain neural organizations are placed. Knowing the precise lesion which will produce aphasia still leaves us in ignorance of the mechanism of speech. However, though the answer to the question of places does not have direct implications for the understanding or explanation of behavior, it might in many instances be a prerequisite to the study of a system by direct neurophysiological means. A Martian invader might note that most cars in the United States are made in Detroit, but this tells him virtually nothing about how cars are made. However, it would direct his attention to Detroit if he wished to find out.

THE LEARNING SYSTEM

There are in nature many instances of systems which alter their behavior on successive exposures to a situation. These may all, to some extent, be regarded as instances of learning systems. At one end are examples which only tenuously fit our notion of what we could consider to be learning. For instance, a pane of glass displays different behavior the second time a stone is thrown through it. At the other end, and much nearer to what we would wish to call learning, is the mechanism acquired immunity. Here one exposure to a pathogenic organism can alter the reactions of the body in such a way that resistance specific to this pathogenic organism is built up when subsequent exposures take place.

Though there are many natural systems which display what we might wish to call learning, as psychologists we are interested in explaining changes in behavior. It is therefore necessary to consider whether suggested systems (or theories, as they can be called) tally in their properties with those exhibited by living organisms.

Stimulus-Response Linkage as a Learning System

One of the most widely held views about learning is that it occurs as a result of the linkage of an afferent pathway in the nervous system (which conveys the stimulus) to an efferent pathway (activity which results in a response). There are differences in opinion among those who hold this general view about the precise conditions under which such a linkage occurs. What is common is the notion that the occurrence in close temporal contiguity of a stimulus and a response under certain conditions lead to a state of affairs in the nervous system such that on the next occasion the stimulus occurs the afferent pathway down which it travels will be joined to the efferent pathway, so that the same response will occur again. On this view we should make at least two predictions about learning. The first is that learning a habit should not occur without the execution of the responses involved in this habit. Stimuli must be followed by responses. Otherwise, no linkage between them can occur. The second prediction is that once a habit has been learned, interference with the execution of the responses which occurred during the learning of the habit should lead to a disappearance of the habit. If a habit consists of a series of stimuli, each evoking a particular response, an abolition of the responses should lead to a disappearance of the habit.

There is a great deal of evidence against the first prediction that learning should not occur without the execution of responses involved in a habit. First, there is a group of experiments in which animals are conveyed through an environment by the experimenter and subsequently allowed to move through it themselves to see if they have learned anything. Such an experiment was first suggested by Thorndike (1946), but it fell to Gleitman (1955) to be the first to perform it. In Gleitman's experiment, the rats were drawn through an environment in a Plexiglas car and given an electric shock in a particular place. This shock was then terminated in another place. The rats were subsequently released and their avoidance of the place where they had been shocked was observed. The rats gave evidence of learning. They preferred the place where the shock was terminated to that where it was started.

McNamara, Long, and Wike (1956) adopted a similar procedure in a T maze, rewarding their rats with food after a ride to one of the sides. They used two experimental groups of rats. One was carried through an elevated maze rich in external cues, the other through a maze where visual cues were considerably reduced. Two control groups were run through these same mazes, and their performance compared to that of the rats which were carried alone. In the test trial when the experimental groups were allowed to run the maze, it was found that the group which had been carried in the environment rich in external cues had been equal or better in learning the maze. As was to be expected, however, the carried group in the maze where external cues were deficient was inferior to the control group. Dodwell and Bessant (1960) performed an experiment designed to ascertain whether learning without performance could occur in more complex tasks. These experimenters used a water maze with eight successive choice points. They used two groups of rats. The first group learned to swim the maze for a reward of food. The second group was placed on a wooden trolley whose upper surface projected above the water. The rats in this group were then propelled through the maze on the trolley for ten trials and at the end of each trial rewarded with food in the goal box. After such treatment, this group was then made to swim the maze to see if there was any saving in the number of trials to criterion as compared with the group which had not been given the experience of being pushed through the alley. There was considerable saving due presumably to learning without performance. The mean number to criterion of trials for the trolley group was 5.6; for the swimmers only, it was 9.6.

These experiments suggest that what is learned is not what response to make to what stimulus, but rather what stimulus follows what. Such a conclusion is supported by the type of experiment initially performed by Brogden (1939). Two stimuli, such as an auditory and a visual one, are repeatedly paired. One of these stimuli is conditioned to a response. It is then found that there is a tendency for the other member of the pair of stimuli to evoke that response without any further training.

A more direct way of observing the linkage of one stimulus to another is made possible by the technique of EEG measurement. It is possible to demonstrate by use of the EEG that a stimulus, say an auditory one, when it is paired with a visual stimulus will produce in time the same EEG response as the visual stimulus. A light shone into a subject's eyes in the dark will cause the alpha rhythm to disappear while it is on. It was noted by Durup and Fessard (1935) and Loomis et al. (1936) that alpha waves could be blocked not only by light stimuli but also by sounds when these sounds had been paired with the light. This type of learning is quite fast. For instance, Morrell and Jasper (1956) demonstrated such learning in eight monkeys in an average of about 11 trials. However, this phenomenon is somewhat irregular in its appearance. For instance, in a large study Gastaut et al. (1957) were able to obtain this "alpha block conditioned reflex" in only 60 percent of human subjects.

The second prediction concerns the disruption of a learned habit if the responses made during the learning of the habit are disrupted or made impossible. Here also the stimulus-response linkage theory of learning fails to be substantiated. Once a habit has been learned, the animal can execute it using a wide variety of alternative means of responding. As Lashley (1930) states: "If we train an animal in a maze and observe carefully his subsequent errorless running, we find little identity of movement in successive trials. He gallops through in one trial, in another shuffles along, sniffing at the cover of the box. If we injure his cerebellum, he may roll through the maze. He follows the correct path with every variety of twist and posture, so that we cannot identify a single movement as characteristic of the habit" (Lashley and McCarthy, 1926). Lashley (1924) also reports a case of a cebus monkey trained on puzzle box problems. This animal had a lesion in the motor area of the right hemisphere. Consequently, the left arm was not used by the animal during training on the problem. Subsequently a similar lesion was placed in the left hemisphere. Now weakness and spasticity of the right arm led the animal to use its left arm, which by now had considerably recovered. This arm had not been used at all during training on the problem boxes.

This plasticity on the part of the nervous system does not accord with the stimulus-response linkage theory of learning. However, as any other theories advanced by psychologists to explain these phenomena were imprecise and smacked of mysticism, these phenomena of plasticity tended to be ignored or dismissed. As is often the case, the evidence became identified with the dubious theories which quoted it in support.

There is a set of experiments which at first sight appear to be relevant to the hypothesis under discussion. Many experiments have been performed which show that learning to respond to a conditioned stimulus can occur without the performance of such a response when the unconditioned stimulus is presented. For instance, Kellogg et al. (1940) and Light and Gantt (1936) crushed the motor nerves leading to one of the legs of a dog. An avoidance conditioning procedure was then carried out. Though the appropriate response was impossible at the time of conditioning, the dog gave the appropriate response once the nerves had regenerated. Finch (1938) and Crisler (1930) carried out salivary conditioning while blocking salivation with atropine. However, when tests were made without atropine, it became clear that learning had taken place. In another study, Harlow and Bromer (1942) produced motor paralysis in monkeys by applying a drug to the motor cortex. There was evidence that avoidance learning had occurred in spite of this paralysis.

Though these experiments are of interest in other context, they cannot be used as evidence to show that stimulus-response linkage is not the basis of learning. They are evidence against the view that a response as viewed by the observer is paired with a stimulus, but not against the notion that events within the nervous system which normally evoke behavioral responses are linked to incoming messages. In the experiments quoted above it is not unreasonable to suppose that events within the nervous system were occurring to evoke the particular responses which appeared later, but that they were simply prevented from evoking their normal consequences.

Cortical Stimulation and Learning

Connected with the techniques which show learning even when the response is prevented from occurring are experiments which circumvent the normal sensory channels and yet demonstrate learning. Loucks (1935, 1938) showed that direct electrical stimulation of the motor cortex could serve as a conditioned stimulus for forelimb flexion. Such conditioning occurred even when sensory messages resulting from the movement of the hindleg evoked by the cortical stimulation could be ruled out. This investigator also showed that direct electrical stimulation of the visual cortex could also serve as a conditioned stimulus. Doty et al. (1956) have extended these findings, being especially careful to exclude any possible sources of artifact, such as the direct stimulation of the membranes surrounding the brain, the blood vessels, or similar effects. They trained cats to lift their paw to escape a shock. The signal for the shock was electrical stimulation applied to the cortex. Areas of the cortex where such stimulation was effective included a point on the frontal cortex and the marginal, postlateral, middle suprasylvian, middle and posterior ectosylvian gyri.

Other workers have produced drive by the use of electrical stimulation applied directly to the nervous system, not only in cortical but also in subcortical structures. Delgado et al. (1954) have found that electrical stimulation of thalamic, mesencephalic, and limbic structures in cats can produce learning to escape this stimulation. Stimulation in these loci produces similar behavior as occurs after peripherally applied electric shocks. In the procedure used, these workers sounded a tone or shone a flickering light as a warning. The cat could prevent electrical brain stimulation if it turned a wheel within five seconds of the warning. The cats learned to do this after 16 to 92 trials. It is difficult to evaluate the significance of these findings. Even though we might agree that afferent pain pathways can be excluded, the experiments simply demonstrate that there are central areas which when directly stimulated produce similar effects to those produced by afferent pathways.

Electrical stimulation of subcortical structures cannot only have punishing effects, but can also lead to the repetition of the behavior which occurred just prior to the administration of the shock (Olds and Milner, 1954; Seward et al. 1960). A rat can in this way be trained to press a lever or perform in a runway. The loci were such stimulation is effective are in the midline structures of the hypothalamus and rostral midbrain or in the limbic system. These experiments will be discussed more fully below (pp. 515–45). Behavior produced in this way shows interesting discrepancies, with behavior rewarded under more normal conditions. Such discrepancies will best be understood when we consider the system which probably produces learning.

What Information Is Stored in Learning?

According to the stimulus-response hypothesis, the information that is stored in learning is what response should be evoked by a particular stimulus when this stimulus occurs. Such storage can be readily imagined to consist of a connection which is made between a receptor and a motor area. However, the likelihood is very small that it is information about the relation of a stimulus to a specific response which is stored in learning. Learning, as was shown above, can occur without the performance of a response. The response is not necessary during learning. (It is only necessary to enable us to verify that learning has taken place; without appropriate responses on some later occasion we could not observe that an organism had learned.) Similarly, disruption of response mechanisms does not cause learning to disappear.

The following is the simplest assumption which emerges from the evidence we have considered. What is stored is information about the sequence of stimuli which the organism encounters. However, though this hypothesis appears in some ways to be obvious, there are difficulties if we attempt to use it to account for the organism's performance once it has learned. In the stimulus-response view, it is easy to see how learning, once it has occurred, leads to performance. The occurrence of a stimulus will evoke that specific response to which the stimulus was linked during learning. In the stimulus linkage view, it is difficult to see how the occurrence of a stimulus produces any action at all. This is a real difficulty, but we must remember that the question we are attempting to answer is not how the information stored during learning is utilized but what information is stored during learning. We shall now turn to the question of the utilization of the information.

How Is the Information Laid Down during Learning Utilized in Subsequent Performance?

If we agree that what is stored is the sequence of stimuli the animal encounters in the environment, then the question concerning the utilization of this information resolves itself into two parts. The first is: How can the occurrence of stimuli (whose sequential order has been stored) be translated into some useful or appropriate motor act? The second question is: How is the stimulus which is associated with motor activity selected? That is, why are some stimuli effective and not others?

We will consider the first question about the relation of the stored stimulus sequence and activity. It will be recalled that when we were examining the stimulus-response view of behavior we saw that an animal's overall performance was remarkably unaffected by interference with motor components. The animal can, it seems, run a maze correctly even when it is forced to make quite different component movements, for instance, by cerebellar ablation. Similarly, the correct performance of an animal is extremely variable. It looks as if the animal can employ different means to achieve the same end. These observations lead us to suspect that the type of mechanism is a feedback type. Such mechanisms possess the flexibility of performance we observe. Take a very simple example of this type of mechanism built into a learning machine (Deutsch, 1954). A part of it is a trolley with a conical beam of light thrown forward from it. The trolley has two wheels, each separately driven by a reversible motor. Near the trolley is a set of light-sensitive photocells which pass a signal when the light beam from the trolley impinges upon them. One of these light-sensitive photocells is selected (by a separate mechanism) to pass a signal back to the trolley. When there is no signal relayed back to the trolley, one of the motors reverses.

This has the result that the trolley turns round on its axis. As soon as the beam of light strikes the photocell, the motor which has been reversing goes forward. As a consequence, the whole trolley moves forward, and so approaches the photocell. If the trolley starts in a wrong direction or does not run a straight course, as soon as its beam leaves the photocell the trolley will begin to rotate again. As soon as its beam strikes the cell again, the trolley goes forward and so gradually approaches the cell. The ability of the trolley to approximate to the cell persists even if the wheels do not drive forward at the same speed, making the trolley as a whole move forward in a curve. Similarly, placing obstacles in the way of the trolley may alter the particular pattern of movements ("rotate," "go forward") but does not prevent final approximation of the trolley to the cell, provided success is possible in the face of the obstacles.

There are of course more complex and efficient steering or guidance systems than that outlined above. It is, nevertheless, an example of systems where the external stimulus does not simply trigger a movement, which then runs its course independently (as in the stimulus-response paradigm). The external stimulus in such systems modifies the response as it is made. For instance, the external stimulus can act as a target, and any deviation from the course toward the target is taken and translated into a compensatory movement. Without entering into a prolonged discussion of the precise mechanisms by which this might be achieved in the animal, we shall assume that an external stimulus is "steered toward" through the action of a feedback system. The appropriate motor act into which the occurrence of a particular stimulus is translated is that of steering toward this stimulus.

Motivation and Selection of Behavior Sequences

We now know that there are regions in the hypothalamus which contain cells monitoring various bodily states. Artificial stimulation of such cells produces activity of the same type as that which occurs in the animal when it is naturally motivated. Minute injections of hypertonic saline in the hypothalamus make the animal drink or perform tasks which it had learned to obtain water, and analogous experiments have shown that the same is true for eating or mating. Nevertheless, the question still remains how such cells within the hypothalamus communicate with the rest of the nervous system so that lines of action are evoked which are appropriate to a particular motivated state or drive. For instance, Kendler (1946) has shown the following. A rat which is both hungry and thirsty is taught a maze shaped like a T. In the goal box at one end of the arm of the T there is water and in the other end food. On the critical trial the rat is made only hungry (or alternately only thirsty). It is found that the rat can choose the arm of the T which is appropriate to its motivational or drive state. A hungry rat chooses the food arm and a thirsty one will turn into the arm containing water, even though the water or the food cannot be detected at the choice point.

The most likely supposition to explain how one set of cells in the hypothalamus produces running toward one goal box when the animal is hungry is that such a set of cells sends messages to another set of cells within the brain, which in turn direct the action of running toward a particular set of signals, such as those which emanate from one of the alleys in the T maze. We would naturally expect such messages to travel down a particular set of fibers from one set of cells to the other. Such simple assumptions might help us to understand how, when a particular motivational state such as hunger is present, the rat will perform one set of actions rather than another.

However, we still have the problem in our simple model of how the two sets of cells become connected. During the course of learning the animal seems to be able to connect the cells in the hypothalamus which signal when it is thirsty to at least two different sets of cells. The activity of these two sets produces different actions in the T maze. (The same argument, of course, applies to the cells which signal when the animal is hungry.) There is, during learning the maze, a connection of one set of cells, rather than another, to the cells in the hypothalamus which signal thirst. Further, this connection is also an appropriate one to produce a particular outcome, such as the finding of water. That is, the thirst-signaling cells are connected to that set of cells which when active bring the animal toward cues at the end of that alley previously found to contain water and not the alley containing food.

How could such a selection take place? It looks as if the fibers leading from one set of cells to both other sets must already be there. Adult rats do not seem to be able to grow fibers in their central nervous system, and even if they could, the process of growth would have to be extraordinarily rapid. Some habits can be learned practically instantaneously. The problem, if we keep to our model, is to open a set of connections which are already there—to open one set of sluice gates rather than another in channels which have already been dug.

One way in which this might be done is as follows. We can imagine that as the animal runs toward a set of cues in the T maze, signals impinge on one set of cells (those concerned with locomoting toward that set of cues), and not on the set of cells which is concerned with locomoting to another set of cues. Shortly after such signals impinge, the rat finds water. Other signals are then generated which in turn impinge on the set of cells signaling thirst. In other words, the relevant set of cells receives a signal from the sense organs just before the thirst-signaling cells receive their own signal from the sense organs. We simply have to assume that two sets of cells receiving signals from the sense organs in close succession are connected. As we speculated above, such a connection probably consists of making a preexisting connection functional. There must be some connection, and one that is already functional, between the two groups of cells in order for this change to take place. When these two groups of cells have received a message from the sense organs, a message down this connection between the two groups will open the other connection between them. This, as we have decided, carries signals when the animal becomes thirsty.

We now have a model in which groups of cells are joined by two kinds of connection. The first conveys messages from cells signaling bodily states of various kinds. Such connections may for convenience be called motivational connections. The second conveys messages which lead to the opening of motivational connections between groups of cells which have received messages from the parts of the sense organs connected to them in close succession. These we may call reinforcement pathways. Given such a model, we are now in a position to imagine in rather a general way what could be happening to the rats in Kendler's experiment. A host of other phenomena uncovered by rat psychologists on motivation and reward and learning can also be understood by a development of the notions described above. A learning machine devised on the above principles shows considerable simplicity (Deutsch, 1953, 1954, 1960). Such a hypothesis also enables us to analyze physiological manipulations of the central nervous system to produce learning. The hypothesis has been introduced to organize the facts concerning intracranial self-stimulation introduced in the next section.

Analogy between Reward and Electrical Stimulation in Certain Areas of the Central Nervous System. A discovery of Olds and Milner (1954) disclosed that electrical stimulation of certain subcortical centers can produce a repetition of the activity which just preceded the electrical stimulus. The characteristics of the behavior elicited by such stimulation, as will be seen below, correspond in some respects with behavior rewarded in a normal manner. However, there are also some striking differences between these two types of behavior. Such effects are produced chiefly by the stimulation of the medial forebrain bundle and connected pathways.

The electrical stimulation of these structures can be carried out through chronically implanted monopolar electrodes. The electrode, consisting of a stainless steel thin insect pin, is insulated almost to the tip, which is placed in the brain structure to be stimulated. The other end is embedded in a block of dental cement and is further connected to a thicker wire or a plug. The dental cement is poured around tiny screws inserted in the skull. In this way the electrode is firmly anchored in place. The ground electrode is an uninsulated piece of stainless steel wire spread flat against the skull under the dental cement. While many types of electrical stimuli have been used, the best on many grounds (Gallistel, 1971) is a 0.1-msec. negative-going monophasic pulse. (A simple and convenient circuit for producing this type of stimulus has been described by Deutsch [1966].) The interval between the brief pulses is typically 10 msec., and a train of pulses is set to last 0.5 seconds. These parameters are sufficient to produce a nearly maximal brain reward when the current which flows during each pulse is from 250 to 700 micro-amperes in intensity (Gallistel, 1971).

The ends of the wires which protrude from the skull are connected to the source of stimulating current through some type of switch, which is usually placed under the animal's control. The switch allows current to pass when a rat presses a lever, and thus the rat delivers an electrical stimulus to its own brain. Most of the switches have a device which limits the temporal duration of the current, typically to half a second. In this way an animal is forced to repeat a bar press in order to maintain the electrical stimulation. It would be difficult to evaluate or compare the performance of rats which simply hold the bar down. By interrupting the current after a certain time, we can obtain an estimate of the rate of responding as a function of various factors.

Most of the studies on electrical brain stimulation have employed the technique of placing the rat in a box with a lever in it. The lever, when touched, delivers a current of short duration through implanted electrodes. The rate of bar pressing is then recorded on a cumulative recorder. Such a technique is therefore superficially analogous to that employed in Skinnerian instrumental conditioning. In the basic situation of this kind, an animal presses a lever and is rewarded for this lever press by a pellet of food dropping into a container through a chute. The animal then has to move to the container to collect the reward and back from the container to the reward in order to press the bar again. Animals find it difficult at the beginning of training to learn to move away from the food container once they have found food there. They have to learn that food is to be found in the container if, and only if, they have pressed the lever.

In the case where electrical brain stimulation serves as "reward," the "reward" is delivered as the animal presses the lever. It does not have to learn a conditional relation between two situations, as in the case of instrumental responding for food. The situation is less like an instrumental response and more like a consummatory response, say, of drinking, where each tongue movement "delivers" the reward. This point may sound like a quibble but is nevertheless very important. Unless we know what type of normal behavior learning for brain stimulation most resembles, it is difficult to make any straightforward comparison or interpretation.

Anatomical Loci of Brain Reward. While there is agreement that stimulation of the medical forebrain bundle produces brain reward, it has been difficult to map the sites yielding this phenomenon. Wetzel (1968) has pointed out that the main obstacles have been the variety of behavioral techniques used to establish the phenomenon and the inadequate reporting of the locus of stimulation. Intracranial self-stimulation has been obtained from the amygdala (Hodos, 1965; Valenstein and Valenstein, 1964; Wurtz and Olds, 1963), olfactory bulbs (Phillips and Mogenson, 1969), hippocampus (Ursin, Ursin, and Olds, 1966), caudate (Olds, 1960), and thalamic reticular system and central gray (Cooper and Taylor, 1967). As will be shown later, the intracranial self-stimulation phenomenon in the rat has some strange and striking properties when evoked from the medial forebrain bundle. Whether we are dealing with a phenomenon with the same properties when instrumental learning occurs as a result of the stimulation of these other structures is unknown. The same ambiguity arises when we examine reports of intracranial self-stimulation in other species, especially man.

Claims of a similar phenomenon have been made for other species: man (Bishop et al., 1963; SemJacobsen and Torkeldsen, 1960), dolphins (Lilly, 1962), dogs (Stark and Boyd, 1963), cats (Justesen et al., 1963; Roberts, 1958), and monkeys (Brady, 1960; Lilly, 1960).

Further Anatomical Studies. It has often been claimed that the sites of intracranial self-stimulation fall within the so-called limbic system (see chapter on emotion), for instance, by Brady and Conrad (1968) and Albino and Lucas (1962). However, Gallistel (1971) has argued that self-stimulation sites show little correlation with the limbic system. No pronounced effects on intracranial self-stimulation have been found after extensive lesions of structures said to make up the limbic system, such as the hippocampus, amygdala, fornix, dorsal thalamus, septum, and the mesencephalic gray (Ward, 1960, 1961; Valenstein, 1966; Asdourian, Stutz, and Rocklin, 1966).

However, many investigators have found that lesions in the medial forebrain bundle do not cause large decrements in intracranial stimulation if the rat is allowed a long postoperative recovery. Extensive lesions in the medial forebrain bundle rostral or caudal to the stimulating electrode have little effect on self-stimulation (Valenstein, 1966). Lesions placed simultaneously both caudal and rostral to the stimulating electrode reduce self-stimulation performance only slightly (Lorens, 1966). However, Olds and Olds (1969) have shown substantial decrements in self-stimulation with lesions in the medical forebrain bundle even after an eight-week recovery period. Such a decrement occurred only in electrodes rostral but not caudal to the lesion. That is, intracranial stimulation is reduced when there is an interruption of pathways leading posteriorly but not anteriorly. This could mean that the signals generated by the electrode (which are of course propagated both anteriorly and posteriorly) exert their effect posteriorly. However, this conclusion is not necessary. It should be remembered that, after eight weeks, degeneration of an axon interrupted by the lesion should have taken place both anteriorly and posteriorly to the lesion. The medial forebrain bundle is mainly composed of axons with very few cell bodies.

Other Effects of Intracranial Self-Stimulation. Rats with electrodes in the septal nuclei show transient decelerations of heart rate during self-stimulation (Malmo, 1961). On the other hand, rats with lateral hypothalamic placement show an acceleration of heart rate (Perez-Cruet et al., 1963). However, it seems that the contradictory results obtained with septal and lateral hypothalamic electrodes are more apparent than real. Apparently, stimulation in both placements produces an initial, brief acceleration followed by a longer depression of heart rate (Meyers et al., 1963). Lateral hypothalamic stimulation produces much higher rates of spontaneous responding, evoking the early cardiac acceleration and preventing deceleration by the first self-administration of the next stimulus. However, such cardiac deceleration could be observed with lateral hypothalamic placements when rats were placed on a partial reinforcement schedule where the intervals between successive brain stimuli were longer.

Increases in heart rate and blood pressure during intracranial self-stimulation through lateral hypothalamic electrodes have been observed in dogs (Perez-Cruet et al., 1965). Are such autonomic phenomena mere side-effects? The injection of dibenzyline (an adrenergic blocking agent) abolished the effects on blood pressure and heart rate without affecting intracranial self-stimulation. Similar conclusions follow from an experiment where there was bilateral removal of the sympathetic chain and sectioning of the vagus and the pelvic splanchnic nerves in cats. No impairment of intracranial self-stimulation was evident as a result of this surgical intervention (Ward and Hester, 1969).

Seizure-like activity has been observed in the EEG records of animals while they were self-stimulating (Porter et al., 1959; Newman and Feldman, 1964), leading to suggestions that animals self-stimulated in order to produce epileptiform seizures. However, such seizure activity does not accompany intracranial stimulation in many cases (Bogacz et al., 1965), and in cases where it does, anticonvulsant drugs increase the amount of intracranial self-stimulation (Reid et al., 1964).

Pharmacology of Brain Reward

It has been suggested (e.g., Wise and Stein, 1969) that the transmitter in the pathways producing brain reward is norepinephrine. As evidence for this, Wise and Stein showed that the rate of bar pressing for brain reward was greatly reduced in rats injected with disulfiram, a potent inhibitor of norepinephrine synthesis. If the presynaptic endings in the neurons mediating brain reward are depleted, such neurons cannot function efficiently and we must expect a reduction in brain reward. However, Roll (1970) showed that rats given disulfiram while working for brain reward were drowsy or asleep, which would naturally reduce the total number of lever presses they could execute. When aroused from their slumber, the rats pressed at a normal rate, which suggests that the pathways for brain reward were functionally unimpaired.

Characteristics of Learning Produced by Electrical Brain Stimulation

When electrical stimulation is used as a "reward," the course of acquisition of a response is as gradual as it is in learning for a water or food reward (see, for instance, Seward, Uyeda, and Olds, 1959). When learning is complete, very high rates of lever pressing occur. Rates of 7,000 per hour have been reported. In order to learn and perform, animals do not have to be in any drive state. They can be satiated for all their conceivable needs and yet will keep on pressing the lever.

Rats will self-stimulate for hours at high rates (Olds, 1958; Hine and Bivens, 1968). The higher the rate of intracranial self-stimulation, the longer (in general) it will persist (Raye et al., 1968). The only natural reward which produces similar persistence and lack of satiation is a mixture of saccharine and extremely dilute sucrose (Valenstein, Cox, and Kakolewski, 1967).

It has further been noted that bar pressing under conditions of brain stimulation tends to continue until the animal is physically exhausted. In contrast, under ordinary conditions of reward, satiation occurs and so a rat's rate of responding slows down. If the intracranial stimulus is made sufficiently intense, rats will cross a more highly charged grid for an intracranial stimulus than for food when they are 24 hours hungry (Olds, 1958).

In spite of extreme persistence of responding while the shock supervenes on each response, a very rapid decrement of responding occurs when the current is switched off. This is very unlike the type of performance to be found in the instrumental conditioning situation for food, where there is often an initial increase in rate of responding with nonreward, gradually tapering off to a chance level. In the case of animals that learn through electrical stimulation, there is a sharp immediate decline (e.g., Seward, Uyeda, and Olds, 1959).

This tendency to quickly lose interest in the level once no more stimulation occurs appears to manifest itself in other situations. It has been found by Sidman et al. (1955) that animals will not learn to press the bar in situations where a brain stimulus is infrequent. For instance, the experimenter may arrange the apparatus in such a way that the animal obtains only one electrical stimulus for a great number of lever presses (the so-called fixed ratio schedule). Animals learn well under such a schedule when food or water is used as reinforcement, but not when an intracranial stimulus is the reinforcing agent. It seems likely that this difficulty is due to the very rapid "loss of interest" in bar pressing once it is not followed by a brain stimulus. The animal may press for a short while after the brain stimulus has been turned off, but not a sufficient number of times to bridge the gap between one "rewarded" response and the next, when the fixed ratio between "rewarded" and "nonrewarded" is high. However, Sidman et al. found that the fixed ratio performance of rats with certain electrode placements improved when they were hungry.

Keesey and Goldstein (1968) ran an experiment with brain reward to parallel an experiment by Hodos and Kalman (1963) with sugared milk to investigate partial reinforcement schedules. While rats performed well to obtain a small amount of the sugared milk (0.025 ml.) even when only 2 in every 200 responses was rewarded, Keesey and Goldstein could not maintain responding even with high-amplitude intracranial reward if the number of unrewarded responses before a reward was more than 30. It seems that rats working for a brain reward could not tolerate between-reward intervals of more than 15 seconds whereas those responding for a normal reward would maintain response even with between-reward intervals of more than 60 seconds.

So far we have discussed the properties of brain stimulation as reward in an adapted Skinner box. There have also been efforts to have rats learn complex mazes with brain stimulation as a "reward," and this has been found difficult or impossible, with certain exceptions. Olds (1956) found that it was possible to train animals with electrode tips in the basomedial forebrain when the animals are running under 18 to 24 hours of food deprivation. (This is reminiscent of the results of Sidman et al., quoted above, who found that hunger improved the fixed ratio performance of their animals.) As compared with rats running for a food reward in the same experiment, the electrically stimulated animals improved their performance in the maze very markedly during the 15 massed trials each day. However, there was a sharp decrement on the first trial of the next day. The rats seemed to have lost interest in running until stimulation was applied next day. There was, however, a day-to-day improvement.

Seward, Uyeda, and Olds (1960) were also successful in teaching animals to perform in runway and grid-crossing situations under conditions of both spaced and massed practice. Of the 17 animals, 10 had electrode tips implanted in the ventromedial hypothalamus, 6 in the dorsolateral, and one in the medial thalamic nucleus. In contrast to the previous maze experiment by Olds (1956), these animals were deprived of neither food nor water. Animals received 10 trials a day for 12 sessions. The interval between trials for the group receiving spaced training was 15 minutes. Again, a sharp improvement occurred within one day's session for the massed group, together with an overnight decrement in performance. These features are absent in the group for which the trials are spaced. In spite of the difference in rates of improvement within a day's trials and the sharp overnight decrement for the massed group, the rate of acquisition—taking the first trials of each day only—is comparable for both groups (Seward, personal communication).

There is another feature of learning for electrical brain stimulation which is different from learning for a food or water reward. Responding after extinction reappears quite suddenly at full strength when the current is again connected to the switch. There is no gradual warm-up period (Olds, 1955; Lilly, 1958).

Often rats which have learned a habit for brain reward do not perform it because the time elapsed since the last brain reward has been too long. Under these circumstances, performance can be revived by giving the rat a free brain reward, even outside the apparatus (Deutsch, Adams, and Metzner, 1964; Gallistel, 1969a, b; Wetzel, 1963). The administration of such a free brain reward to induce further performance of a habit is called "priming." Priming does not produce a general effect. Wetzel (1963) has found that priming does not induce performance for a food reward, and Deutsch et al. (1964) that priming produces temporary preference for brain reward as opposed to water. Such a preference decays as a function of time since priming.

In contrast with brain reward, normal rewards given before the performance of a habit learned for such rewards in general reduce overall speed (Bruce, 1938; Morgan and Fields, 1938). Gallistel (1973) makes the point that while Bruce (1937, 1938) claimed to show that small prewaterings augmented the speed of rats running for a water reward, his data do not bear this out.

Poor performance on various schedules, the day-to-day decrements, and the improvement within a day's session if trials are massed may all be viewed as effects of intertrial interval (ITI). Many studies have shown decrements in performance as a function of a small increase in ITI (Gallistel, 1966, 1967; Johnson, 1968; Newman, 1961; Panksepp et al., 1968; Spear, 1962; Wetzel, 1963). Below ITIs of five seconds or less, performance is brisk. But with ITIs over 15 seconds, performance becomes somewhat sluggish. When the ITI exceeds several minutes, some rats will not run at all (e.g., Gallistel, 1967). However, where control groups have been running for normal rewards under the same circumstances as for intracranial reward, the results show a trend in the opposite direction (Newman, 1961; Wetzel, 1963; Deutsch and

Howarth, 1963; Gallistel, 1967). It has of course been shown that spaced trials (longer ITIs) produce better learning and faster performance with normal rewards (Ulrich, 1915; Lashley, 1958; Mayer and Stone, 1931).

It might be argued that increasing the ITI in intracranial reward is due to a lessened reward value of the brain stimulus. However, Gallistel (1967) and Panksepp et al. (1968) showed deterioration in performance on the very first trial that ITI was lengthened and improvement on the first trial that the ITI was shortened—before the rat can have experienced any change in reward magnitude. However, the decrement of performance seen with increasing ITI has not been uniform. For instance, Scott (1967) found no overnight decrement when he compared running speed on the first trial of the day with succeeding trials of the same day. As he used a 15-minute ITI within a day's trials, running speed had probably declined as far as it was going to. A similar difficulty exists with the results of Wasden et al. (1965), who used a one-minute ITI interval and found no overnight decrement in half their animals.

Kornblith and Olds (1968) induced their rats to run a maze with a 24-hour ITI by using a large open-field start box and a small goal box. How far the performance was due to agoraphobia (fear of open spaces) or to a real motivation for brain reward is undetermined, although they had difficulty inducing many rats to perform before they began to use the large start box. Kent and Grossman (1969) have observed some rats in which temporal decay phenomena are prominent but other rats in which they are not observed (probably due to inappropriate testing). This agrees with the writer's observations and those of other workers (Wetzel, 1963; Wasden et al., Valenstein, 1966). Deutsch et al. (1964) found that prolonged suprathreshold stimulation of the reward electrode produced animals with a greatly enhanced persistence and less sensitivity to increased ITIs.

A HYPOTHESIS ABOUT INTRACRANIAL SELF-STIMULATION

As we reasoned above, groups of cells, sensitive to bodily deficits and hormones, are connected to other groups of cells, which underlie various actions, by two separate pathways. The first pathway, called a motivational pathway, conveys excitation from the cells sensitive to bodily deficits to the groups of cells underlying various actions. In this way, when a certain deficit arises and excites the cells sensitive to it, this deficit also indirectly excites other cells which then produce certain actions.

This hypothesis assumes that motivational pathways convey excitation to other cells only under certain circumstances. The cells sensitive only to physiological deficits convey messages to the "action" cells as a result of learning. It is assumed that a connection exists before learning takes place but that messages cannot pass down this connection. During learning, the connection is made functional (so that messages can pass down it) by the activity of another pathway, called a reinforcement pathway, which also connects the two groups of cells. However, this pathway does not carry information about physiological deficit, but only signals information about the arrival of afferent sensory messages to the two groups of cells. When the two sets of cells receive their different afferent sensory messages in close temporal succession, the motivational pathway between the two groups of cells becomes functional, so that excitation can pass between the two groups of cells.

We may assume that the electrode in intracranial self-stimulation stimulates both the reinforcement and motivational pathways between groups of cells. In this way a stimulus will not only render a motivational pathway functional by a stimulation of the reinforcement path but also send excitation down the same motivational pathway, thus causing a certain action to be executed. In this way an intracranial stimulus will provide not only the "reward" for the last action but also motivation for the next. Such induced motivation decays rapidly down to the level which was present in the motivational pathway before the electrical stimulus was applied. If we are stimulating a pathway which is normally excited when the animal is hungry, the level to which the induced drive will decay may be high if the animal is hungry, but low if it is satiated.

The facts we have summarized agree with the assumption that each brain stimulus excites a drive pathway, and that in the removal of such a stimulus such excitation decays. Such an assumption would explain why during massed training there is a very great improvement within a day's trials and a very large overnight decrement, whereas if trials are spaced there is no such improvement within a day's trials. It is easy to imagine that closely spaced brain shocks will summate, whereas if they are more widely spaced no such summation will take place. We can also see why rats did not perform in a situation such as Sidman's, when he spaced his shocks too far apart. The "drive" generated by one bar press would dissipate before the animal obtained the next "injection" of drive, with the consequence that it will stop bar pressing. We can also see why "relearning" after extinction should be so abrupt compared with normal relearning in such a situation. There has been no "unlearning" as in ordinary extinction but only a cessation of "drive." As a consequence, when we "inject" drive again, the learned habit will reappear at full strength.

The assumptions about drive induction and decay which follow from this theory can be more rigorously tested. For instance, it should be demonstrable that cessation of responding during extinction of habits learned for intracranial stimulation is a function simply of time since the last intracranial stimulus. In the case of habits learned for a normal reward, cessation of responding is almost entirely a function of the number of unreinforced trials, and not time since the last reward.

Accordingly, a series of experiments was performed in the Skinner box (Howarth and Deutsch, 1962) to test this prediction. After the rats had been well trained to press the lever to obtain an intracranial stimulus, they were tested under two conditions. In the first condition the current was switched off and the number of responses to cessation of responding was counted. Then the total number was counted, excluding those responses made during the first 2.5 seconds; then the total number, excluding those responses made during the first 5, 7.5, and 10 seconds. In the second condition, responding was prevented by withdrawing the lever at the beginning of extinction for 2.5, 5, 7.5, and 10 seconds, and the number of responses to extinction was counted after the lever was reinserted. If, as in normal habits, the number of responses to extinction was a function mainly of the number of unreinforced responses, the number of responses without lever withdrawal and after each interval of lever withdrawal should have been the same. On the other hand, cessation of responding could be a function of time since the last brain stimulus.

According to such a hypothesis, the number of responses made to extinction after the lever was reinserted after, say, 5 seconds, should be the same as the number of responses made to extinction in the first condition, when we exclude the presses made during the first 5 seconds. The data are presented in Figure 14–1, and it is clear that the prediction from the hypothesis is strongly supported.

That "extinction" in intracranial self-stimulation in the Skinner box occurs as a function of time has been replicated by Pliskoff and Hawkins (1963) and Quartermain and Webster (1968). Quartermain and Webster also showed that such time dependency did not occur in thirsty rats trained for a reward of water.

To test the generality of the result in the Skinner box, another experiment was designed in a grid-crossing situation. If drive decayed after an intracranial stimulus, speed of grid crossings in a well-learned habit should be slower after a delay of 30 seconds than after no delay between successive trials. On the other hand, with thirsty animals running to cross the grid, no slowing down after 30 seconds should be observed. The results of the experiment are in agreement with this prediction.

Because it could have been argued that all that had been shown in the previous experiments was some decrease in the level of general activity after an intracranial stimulus, with a consequent slowing down of activity, another kind of test was devised. In this test it was shown that it was the specific motivation to obtain an intracranial stimulus which decayed, and not some factor of general activity. Animals were trained to obtain water in one side of a T maze and intracranial stimula-

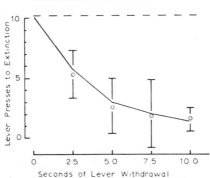

FIG. 14–1. Effect of seconds of lever withdrawal on lever presses to extinction. (The circles show the average effect of withdrawing the lever from the box for a given time, before replacing it, on the number of lever presses to extinction which immediately follow the replacement of the lever. The dashed line shows the expected result if extinction were a function of the number of unreinforced lever presses. The solid line shows the expectation from the hypothesis that extinction in this case is a simple function of time since the last brain stimulus. The way this curve is derived is shown on the top line in the figure which represents a typical extinction record obtained on an event recorder. Ten presses altogether are made. Four of these occur before 2.5 seconds, so that one would predict that 6 lever presses should be made if the lever were removed for 2.5 seconds before starting the extinction trials.) (From Deutsch, J. A., and Howarth, C. I., 1963, *Psych. Rev.*, 70; courtesy of American Psychological Association.)

tion on the other. They were then run under varying degrees of thirst and were given a choice after varying delays after the previous intracranial stimulus. If run close to the last intracranial stimulus, they would choose it again. However, as the interval after the previous intracranial stimulus increased, the probability of the choice of such a stimulus decreased. The results are presented in Figure 14–2. The motivation for intracranial stimulation falls off with the time after the previous intracranial stimulus.

The drive decay hypothesis of extinction in intracranial self-stimulation has been questioned by Pliskoff and Hawkins (1963), who trained rats in the Skinner box under two conditions. In the first, rats were

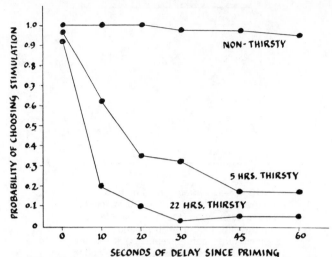

SECONDS OF DELAY SINCE PRIMING

FIG. 14–2. Probability of choice of brain stimulation as a function of delay and competing drive. (Effect of delay since last brain stimulus on the probability of choice of brain stimulation, as against water, when the rat is 0, 5, and 22 hours thirsty.) (From Deutsch, J. A., and Howarth, C. I., 1963, *Psych. Rev.*, 70; courtesy of American Psychological Association.)

rewarded by an intracranial stimulus for returning to the lever after the current had been switched off for some time. In the second condition, other animals were not rewarded for returning to the lever after the current had been switched off.

Pliskoff and Hawkins found that the first group emitted a larger number of responses after the current was switched off. Pliskoff and Hawkins argued that the drive decay hypothesis of extinction must be modified because differential training was shown to affect the number of responses to extinction. However, their results are perfectly compatible with the hypothesis. Given different amounts of training, a habit will need different degrees of drive to be evoked. The first group of rats had been given training to return to the lever, the second had not. The first group would therefore be expected to perform at a lower level of drive than the second, and so continue to press longer as drive subsided.

Another objection to the drive delay theory has been that there is no real difference between brain reward and other types of learning. Gibson et al. (1965) have suggested that the rapid extinction for brain reward, as opposed to the longer extinction for normal reward, is due to the fact that in brain reward the operant response (the lever press in the Skinner box) is also the consummatory response. The rat obtains the primary reward at the same time it presses the lever. In the normal reward, the consummatory reward is eating, which occurs after the lever press. In their experiment, hungry rats were trained to obtain either brain reward or sugar water under two conditions. The first was a condition under which the primary reinforcement was delivered as soon as the operant response was made (the normal brain-reward situation), and in the second the operant response was followed by the consummatory response (the usual or normal reward situation). During extinction, it was shown that the rate of extinction depended upon the relation of the instrumental response to the reward rather than upon the nature of the reward. That is, extinction was somewhat swifter for the two groups which obtained the reward immediately upon executing the instrumental response or for which the instrumental and consummatory responses were identical.

However, it should be noted that the rats working for brain reward in this experiment were severely hungry and that their electrodes were in loci known to produce normal extinction performance (e.g., Deutsch and DiCara, 1967). Hence they were comparing animals working for brain reward, whose extinction should have been the same as for animals working for normal reward, according to the drive decay theory. While, therefore, there is relatively small effect on extinction exerted by the type of habit extinguished, the experiment of Gibson et al. does not show that this is the reason for the large difference between normal extinction and extinction after brain reward. It is in fact most unlikely to be the reason, because Gallistel (1967) found no performance decrement after longer ITIs when he arranged the presentation of a water reward to resemble the presentation of a brain reward.

Further, Quartermain and Webster (1968) performed an experiment in which they equated responding for water and brain reward along the dimensions thought to be crucial by Gibson et al. (1965) in producing the difference between brain reward and normal extinction. In spite of this equation, rats working for a brain reward still showed "extinction" as a function of time since the last reward, whereas the rats working for water did not.

Relationship between Drive Induced by Intracranial Self-Stimulation and Normal Motivation

It has been noted that many placements from which intracranial self-stimulation can be obtained are close to sites in the hypothalamic region, which, upon stimulation, produce such motivated behaviors as thirst, hunger, or sex. On the hypothesis used to view the data, one would expect that pathways which are held to be stimulated by intracranial self-stimulation are close to such areas. As the hypothesis assumes separate pathways for the various drives, such as hunger and thirst, we would expect an interaction between specific drive states and electrical stimulation. The internally generated messages down the motivational pathways would be expected to sum with the externally introduced message.

If animals are hungry, for instance, they (*a*) bar press more rapidly for a given level of electrical stimulus (Hoebel and Teitelbaum, 1962; Brady et al., 1957; Olds, 1958); (*b*) perform better on a task where brain stimuli are widely spaced (fixed ratio schedule) (Sidman et al., 1955); and (*c*) learn to run complex mazes, as in the experiment of Olds (1956), where the "rewards" are widely spaced.

The intimate relationship between lateral hypothalamic brain stimulation and hunger has been amply demonstrated in an impressive series of studies by Hoebel and co-workers (Hoebel, 1968; Balagura and Hoebel, 1957; Hoebel, 1965; Mount and Hoebel, 1967). They have shown that whatever factors tend to increase hunger also increase brain reward, and whatever factors decrease hunger also decrease brain reward in lateral hypothalamic placements. This has been shown to be true of manipulations such as lesions, stomach loads, deprivation, and glucagon and insulin injections. However, brain reward usually is not affected by hunger or satiety when the stimulating electrode is in the septum.

Other examples point strongly to the conclusion that the electrodes which produce brain reward do this by stimulating drive-reward mechanisms (hunger, thirst, sex) within the central nervous system. Rats with septal placements continue to press for brain reward, ignoring water almost to the point of death. Rats with electrodes in the lateral hypothalamus continue to prefer brain reward over food in a T maze even when extremely hungry, whereas those wih electrodes in other structures switched their preference to food as deprivation increased (Spies, 1965). A somewhat extreme case of this was reported by Routtenberg and Lindy (1965), where the rats with electrodes in the lateral hypothalamus starved themselves to death, preferring brain reward to food. Rats with electrodes in other areas chose food as they became more hungry.

It seems that in these cases the excitation proceeding from the physiologically excited groups of cells sums with the artificially "injected" excitation to increase the amount of "drive" excitation. The same summation would prolong the effect of the electrical stimulus at a level suprathreshold for action.

This idea was more directly tested by Deutsch and Metzner (quoted by Deutsch, 1963). They measured running speed in a T maze as a function of delay between an intracranial stimulus and succeeding trial. They found that running speed decreased as a function of time since the last brain stimulus and the rate at which it decreased was significantly altered by thirst in some electrode placements.

As we have argued that normal "drive" excitation can sum with "injected drive" excitation, it is entirely possible that in the cases where performance has been obtained in a learning situation, even where brain stimulation is widely spaced (such as Seward et al., 1959), normal "drive" was present.

However, all the cases quoted above could be accounted for in other ways than by assuming a summation of internally generated and artificially produced drive excitation. It could be said that, owing to biochemical changes during drive states, tissues were electrically more sensitive, or the stimulus became more rewarding. These arguments could not be used if it could be demonstrated that a habit previously learned for an intracranial reward could be evoked by a natural drive in the absence of further intracranial stimulation. Accordingly, two groups of rats were used by Deutsch and Howard (1962), one with electrode implants in the lateral hypothalamus and the other with implants in the ventral tegmentum. Both groups were then trained to lever press in a Skinner box. When any of the rats were held away from the lever for a short while, they failed to return. When the rats were subsequently frightened by a buzzer or shock, only those animals with ventral tegmental implants returned to press the lever, which was now disconnected from the current. A further experiment showed that time to extinction was extremely prolonged when animals with tegmental implants were frightened, whereas those with hypothalamic electrodes tended to show such a prolongation when they were hungry. This supports the idea that the same pathways as produce normal motivated behavior when they are active are also stimulated during intracranial self-stimulation.

Herberg (1963) has claimed that the number of presses to extinction is uninfluenced by the drive state of the rat in placements which produce higher rates of responding during such a drive state. Unfortunately, it seems that his animals had been repeatedly extinguished during training so that the average number of responses to extinction was around three. Rats learn to stop pressing, irrespective of drive level, as soon as reward is withdrawn if the process of extinction is often enough repeated. In support of this interpretation of Herberg's failure to obtain the effect, there is the fact that he also failed to find (in the same experiment) a correlation between strength of current obtained by the rat for a lever press and number of trials to extinction. A high correlation exists, as is shown by Deutsch and Howarth (1963) (Fig. 14–3).

In fact, it has been found by Deutsch and DiCara (unpublished) that there is a very large effect of drive on the number of presses during extinction. Furthermore, there is a high correlation between the number of presses during extinction and elevation of response rates when the animals are pressing for an intracranial reward when they are hungry in both conditions. To obviate the objection that a higher rate of responding (due to hunger) would lead to a larger number of responses

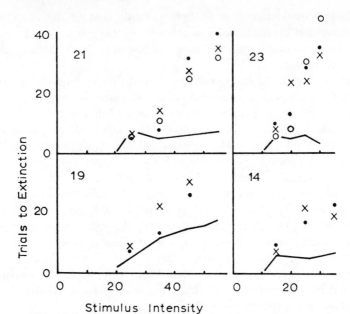

FIG. 14–3. Effect of intensity on rate of responding and time and presses to extinction. (Effect of intensity of brain stimulation on lever pressing rates: solid line. Number of presses to extinction: circles. Time to normal extinction: crosses. Time to extinction without lever pressing: dots.) (From Deutsch, J. A., and Howarth, C. I., *Psychol. Rev.,* 70; courtesy of American Psychological Association.)

before the extinction period and so, indirectly perhaps, to a larger number of responses during extinction (so leading to a spurious confirmation of the theoretical prediction), the rats were run on a current level which produced maximal rates of responding whether the rats were hungry or satiated. Elevation of rate due to hunger was measured after extinction trials had been concluded. Current was lowered during the elevation of rate determination to bring about a 25 percent reduction in rate of lever pressing. In this way the ceiling effect, which had been purposely used in the first part of the experiment, was avoided.

It has been suggested above that Herberg obtained a different result (i.e., no effect of drive on number of lever presses in extinction in animals showing elevation of rate while under that drive) because repeated extinction had already taken place during training, before the experiment proper was conducted. Accordingly, Deutsch and DiCara continued to test their animals, giving them repeated experience of rewarded bouts of responding followed by extinction. The extinction scores both during hunger and satiation conditions declined rapidly, until both reached the same low asymptote. A test conducted after six extinction sessions would have showed no difference in the number of trials to extinction between the hungry and satiated condition. It therefore seems that Herberg's discrepant finding can be accounted for (Fig. 14–4).

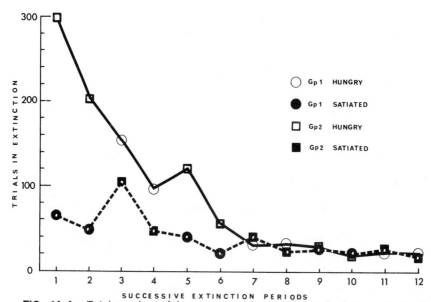

FIG. 14–4. Total number of lever presses in successive 3-minute periods of extinction made by rats, displaying elevation of rate of lever pressing when they were hungry. The rats were divided into 2 groups for 2 extinction periods. One group was run satiated during extinction while the other was run hungry. Such an alternation was maintained until the end of the experiment. As can be seen, there is a large discrepancy between extinction scores in the initial extinction periods. This difference disappears rapidly as the rats learn that once current is switched off, no more intracranial reward will be available.

A prediction analogous to that on extinction can be made concerning secondary reinforcement. Rats should continue to press to obtain a stimulus previously paired with intracranial reward only if some drive was present at the time of testing. For instance, rats which show an elevation of lever pressing for an intracranial reward should press only if they are hungry for a tone previously paired with the intracranial reward (Gallistel, 1964). DiCara and Deutsch (unpublished) have found that there is a high correlation ($r = 0.89$, $N = 12$) between the rate of responding for brain stimulation measured during hunger and the degree of secondary reinforcement obtained under the same drive condition. Using group data, Stein (1958) has shown that a significant overall secondary reinforcement effect can be obtained when an intracranial reward is used as primary reinforcer. However, reporting individual scores, Seward et al. (1959) found that a secondary reinforcement effect appears in only a small proportion of their rats. This discrepancy can readily be explained if we take variability in placement into account and assume that the appearance of the secondary reinforcement effect depends on the presence of a relevant drive during testing.

Two Pathways in Intracranial Self-Stimulation

The suggested hypothesis of intracranial self-stimulation assumes that two sets of pathways, each with a different function, have to be stimulated to produce the phenomenon. To test this feature of the theory, various electrical parameters were used to see if the presumed pathways showed differential sensitivity to them. It is known mainly from studies on peripheral nerves that nerve fibers differ among themselves in various aspects of electrical excitability. For instance, they show differences in rates of adaptation to a gradually rising electrical stimulus, in absolute threshold to an applied stimulus, and also in the time during which they are unexcitable following a suprathreshold stimulus (refractory period).

If the drive pathways had a lower threshold of excitability than the reinforcement pathways, then it should be possible to elicit drive without reinforcement simply by using a lower stimulating current. In such a way a learned response could be maintained even when the intracranial stimulus occurred randomly in relation to the previously rewarded action. Thus it should be possible to maintain the animal's response during extinction. If, on the other hand, the reinforcement system were also excited with each random stimulus, it should not only maintain motivation, but reward new actions and so lead to a diminution of performance of the already learned habit. In the experiment done to test this relation (Deutsch et al., 1962), it was found that stimulation at approximately half the intensity necessary for training would increase the number of emitted responses during extinction when such stimulation was applied randomly with respect to the previously rewarded act.

Gallistel (1969a) performed an ingenious experiment which also separates reward from drive effects. If a rat is given some normal reward for performing a habit, increasing the amount of the reward increases the reward value only up to a certain point, at which reward value becomes asymptotic. For instance, Crespi (1942), using a runway, was able to show that running speed increased as the size of the food reward was increased from 0.20 gram to 1 gram. Past this amount, the rate of increase in running speed decreases. The points at which increments in the physical size of the reward fail to produce a significant increase in running speed are the same, independently of the drive of the animal (Reynolds and Pavlik, 1960). Even though the absolute running speeds vary with level of drive, the points at which increases in speed due to increased reward level off are the same for various levels of drive. An increase in the physical amount of a reward, such as food, does not lead to an increase in the psychological amount of reward past a certain point. This point does not vary with the amount of drive present during the test.

Gallistel (1969a) measured the point at which brain reward ceased to increase with increasing brain stimulation. Using 0.1-msec. negative going pulses at 200 pulses per second, he found in all cases that increasing the number above 64 resulted in no further increase in reward value. Though such a stimulus appears to be maximal in terms of reward or incentive, it produces very little drive as measured by persistence of responding. The rats given this maximal amount of reward would hardly run if the time between the reward and the next trial exceeded 5 to 10 seconds. However, if the amount of stimulation before the next trial was increased, an increase in the persistence of running was obtained. Again, an increase in the amount of stimulation past a certain point produced no further increase in persistence.

However, this psychological maximum point was not reached until the amount of stimulation was 10 to 20 times as great as the point at which the reward maximum had been reached. At the maximum drive point, brisk responding persisted for 10 to 15 minutes. In the case of the drive system, the long time over which stimuli sum is probably due to the long time each quantum of excitation takes to decay. In the case of the reward system, the small number of rewarding pulses after which no further pulses have an effect is probably due to rapid accommodation or adaptation in these pathways. Further experimental work is necessary to determine the reason for the two different maxima found for the reward and drive effect of the intracranial stimulus.

The next set of experiments (Deutsch, 1964) tried to find if the refractory period of the reinforcement and motivation pathways was different. If two brief pulses are applied to a nerve, there is an interval during which the second will be ineffective in triggering a second spike. However, if the two pulses are shifted apart, there is a point at which the second pulse will also initiate a spike. If we stimulate, say, a motor pathway with double pulses, we should see a sudden increase in the effect of the stimulation as we apply the two pulses progressively further apart in time from each other. In a similar way, if we stimulate a pathway which produces reward (or drive) with double pulses, we should see a sudden increment in the rewarding (or drive producing) efficacy of the physical stimulus as the second pulse falls outside the refractory period of the nerve.

To test whether such a difference in refractory periods exists, animals were given stimuli consisting of two brief (0.1 msec.) pulses, separated from each other by intervals varying from one test session to the next.

These pulses were negative going because this is the more effective direction of stimulation, and were repetitiously applied for 0.5 seconds, 10 msec. elapsing between the first pulses in each pair. The intrapair distance was varied between 0.2 and 2 msec., this being the range in which to expect the appearance of the neural absolute refractory period. This varies from 0.4 to 2 msec., depending on the diameter and type of fiber in peripheral nerves (Grundfest, 1940). A series of situations to measure reward and drive was then devised. These were designed to show at what interval between the two pulses reward or drive would suddenly increase. The rate of lever pressing in a Skinner box was used as one measure of drive. The lowest level of voltage compatible with consistent lever pressing with an intrapair pulse interval of 2 msec. was first determined, and then rates of lever pressing as this voltage were determined in random order for other intrapair pulse intervals. Five-minute rest intervals were given between tests to allow the drive induced by one test to decay before the next test. As can be seen (Fig. 14–5), there is a sudden increase of the effectiveness of the second pulse when it is more than 0.8 msec. after the first. A second test of drive was also used. A rat was taught to traverse a straight alley for a reward of an intracranial stimulus which was always kept the same. Trials were spaced so that running did not occur spontaneously unless an intracranial stimulus was used as a "primer" in the start box. The drive-inducing effectiveness of double pulses at various spacings was measured by running speed. As in the lever pressing test, an enhancement of effectiveness occurs after the pulses are spaced more than 0.8 msec. apart.

Tests to measure the reward effect of the intracranial stimulus were also devised. For instance, rats were given a choice between two rewards in a T maze, each consisting of an intracranial stimulus with a certain intrapair pulse interval. It can be seen that 0.7 msec. is consistently preferred over smaller intervals, but treated as equal to longer intervals (Fig. 14–6). This suggests that the second pulse is already having a full effect at 0.7 msec., unlike the result which emerged in the drive tests. A further reward test confirms this difference. Rats were trained to press in a Skinner box for a high 60 cps. stimulus. Repeated extinction trials were then run, until the rat stopped responding within five seconds. (During the first few extinction trials the rat would respond for over one minute.) In this way the animal was trained to stop when no further reward occurred. At this stage the irregular periods of extinction (in which the animal was abruptly shifted from receiving a high 60 cps. stimulus for a bar press to receiving nothing) were removed from the training schedule. Instead, the animal was abruptly shifted from receiving the high 60 cps. stimulation for a lever press, to receive some level of double pulse stimulation. Since the animals were in a high state

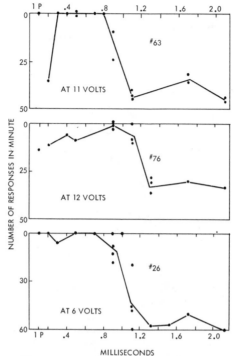

FIG. 14–5. Rate of lever pressing at different pulse-pair intervals with voltage kept constant. Each point represents a single score (lever presses during 1 minute). The curves of 3 rats are shown. *1P* = 1 pulse per 10 msec. Instead of 2 as in rest of tests. (From Deutsch, J. A., 1964, *J.C.P.P.*, 58; courtesy of the American Psychological Association.)

of drive following the 60 cps. stimulation and had been taught not to press when reward was discontinued, it was expected that they would continue to press for voltage-pulse couple combinations which were above the threshold for reward when they were switched to these after the 60 cps. standard. However, it was thought they would cease pressing abruptly when the effective strength of the voltage-pulse couple combination was below the threshold of the reward effect. The criterion for the continuation of lever pressing was that the animal should press for more than 30 seconds of the minute after the stimulus obtained by lever pressing had been changed from the high-intensity 60 cps. standard to the pulse-pair stimulation at varying voltages. The duration of a minute after the standard was taken because lever pressing initially persisted for at least a minute after the standard was switched off, thus

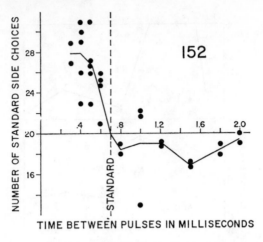

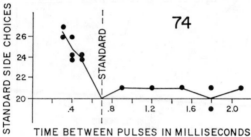

TIME BETWEEN PULSES IN MILLISECONDS

FIG. 14–6. Number of choices of goal containing stimulus at 0.7 msec. intrapulse-pair interval against other intrapulse-pair intervals at the same voltage in a T maze. (Each point represents the results of a session of 40 trials.) (From Deutsch, J. A., 1964, *J.C.P.P.*, 58; courtesy of American Psychological Association.)

showing that induced drive sufficient to motivate lever pressing continued for at least this length of time. In this way the double pulse stimulus would only need to supply reward, the drive component having already been induced by the standard 60 cps. stimulation.

It was hoped by this method to measure the threshold of the reward component of intracranial self-stimulation. We would expect a higher voltage to be necessary to sustain responding after the standard has been switched off if only one pulse in each pulse pair is effective and a lower voltage to be sufficient if both pulses were effective. The curve plotting the lowest voltage necessary to sustain reponding at each interval between the two pulses in each pair should then show a sharp inflection at the end of the refractory period. The obtained curves are illustrated in Figure 14–7. As can be seen, the inflection in the curve occurs at the

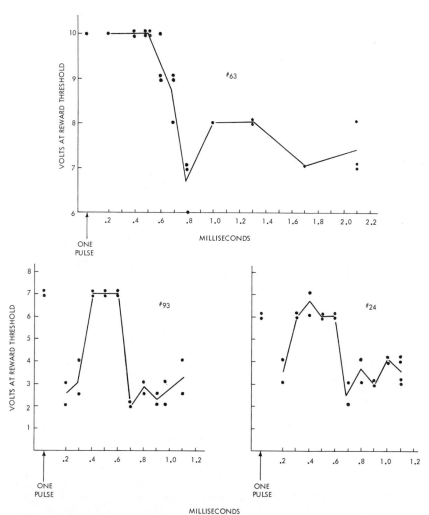

FIG. 14–7. Minimum voltage required to keep rat pressing for intracranial stimulation in reward test. Results for three rats. Each point represents a single determination. (After Deutsch, J. A., 1964, *J.C.P.P.*, 58; courtesy of American Psychological Association.)

same point as in the curve (Fig. 14–6) plotting the data from the preference test of reward.

Some of the advantages of the Skinner box single-lever method of measurement of reward threshold are that the same animal can easily be used both in the rate of lever-pressing experiment and in the reward threshold experiment, and that the voltages used in both experiments are comparable. Results from both experiments performed on the same animals are shown in Figure 14–8.

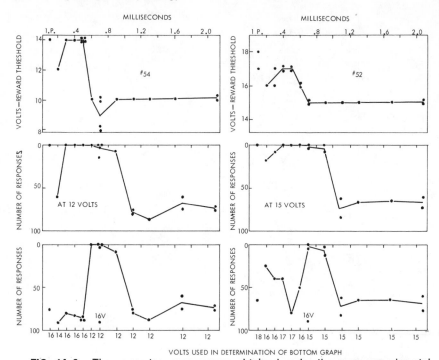

VOLTS USED IN DETERMINATION OF BOTTOM GRAPH

FIG. 14–8. The upper two curves were obtained under the same experimental conditions as the curves in Figure 14–7. The middle two curves were obtained under the same conditions as the curves in Figure 14–5. The bottom two curves show the number of responses in the second minute of a session (sessions 5 min. apart) with a voltage at reward threshold in rat no. 52. In the case of no. 52 rat, the reward threshold was determined again in the critical beginning part of the curve, after the test plotted in the bottom curve, to check for possible order effects. The points thus repeated are also indicated in the top curve to give an indication of consistency. In the case of rat no. 54, the fixed voltage was two volts above threshold, as lever pressing could not consistently be induced at reward threshold. Where the voltages at which the test was conducted are the same for the two "number of responses" tests, they are plotted on both graphs. Again, each point represents the result of one determination. The inset point on the bottom curve shows the effect of raised voltage on responding at a pulse-pair interval. (After Deutsch, J. A., 1964, *J.C.P.P.*, 58; courtesy of American Psychological Association.)

Another way of showing that there are two components or two refractory periods involved in the phenomenon of intracranial self-stimulation is to measure the rate of lever pressing for various pulse intervals at a higher voltage. In the original experiment, reported above, rats were run at a voltage sufficient to produce a steady level of responding when pulses were 2 msec. apart. Little lever pressing occurs when the voltage is determined in this way when pulses are closer than 0.9 msec. apart. At a higher voltage, however, an increase in the rate of lever pressing occurs as soon as the shorter refractory period is exceeded. It seems that at the lower voltage both refractory periods have to be exceeded to give rise to instrumental behavior. When the voltage is increased, only one refractory period has to be exceeded. (At higher voltages still, ceiling rates of responding occur whether the pulse interval is within both refractory periods or not.) We can in this instance, then, obtain a "reward" curve using the same response as the one yielding the "drive" curve (Fig. 14–9).

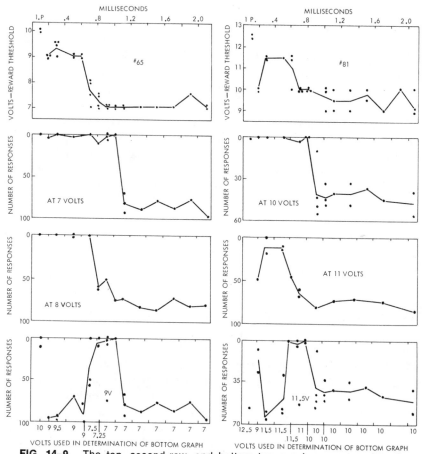

FIG. 14–9. The top, second-row, and bottom two graphs correspond to those described in Figure 14–8, in that order. They represent results for another two animals. The two graphs next to the bottom represent the rates of lever pressing at varying pulse intervals at a voltage higher than in the second two graphs. (After Deutsch, J. A., 1964, *J.C.P.P.,* 58; courtesy of American Psychological Association.)

Another interesting finding emerges from the experiments with double pulses. It will be noticed that on many of the curves presented above there is a short period of about 0.2 msec. during which the second of the two pulses seems to have an effect on the animal's behavior. This is probably due to a neural phenomenon known as latent addition. For a nerve spike to be triggered, a certain threshold has to be exceeded. As a pulse of current is applied to the nerve, a charge builds up, and if the applied current is withdrawn before such a charge has built up sufficiently to trigger a spike, the charge will persist for a short while and finally decay. If, during this period of decay, another normally subthreshold pulse is applied, the process of charging will resume, adding itself to the charge still left. In this way the two together may exceed the critical threshold where either one alone would not. The period during which two normally subthreshold pulses sum to produce a spike is called the period of latent addition. When we stimulate a large number of pathways simultaneously through an implanted electrode, the fibers close to the tip of the electrode, charging at a higher rate, will produce nerve spikes. However, fibers at a longer distance will charge more slowly and will therefore not have reached the critical threshold when the electrical stimulus is withdrawn. However, if the identical subthreshold pulse is repeated within the period of latent addition (about 0.2 msec. for A and B fibers in the peripheral nerve), the critical threshold will be exceeded. In this way fibers which are not normally excited by the electrode are recruited.

It can therefore be surmised that the enhancement of effect at very short intervals (0.2 msec.) before the end of the refractory period is due to the recruitment of a different population of fibers in the subliminal fringe, whereas the enhancement of effect at the end of the refractory period is due to a doubling of activity within the same population of fibers. The effect might be useful in investigating fine differences in localization. However, whether such an effect is found is dependent, among other things, on the spatial arrangement of the stimulated fibers. For instance, if the electrode is stimulating all the fibers to an adequate extent with the first pulse, there will be no subliminal fringe.

Another way of separating the refractory periods of the drive and reward component in brain reward was devised by Gallistel, Rolls, and Greene (1969). A straight runway was used with priming before each trail and with a brain reward in the goal box. Running speed was measured as a function of intrapair pulse interval. There were two main conditions. In the first, the intrapair pulse interval of the priming stimulus was varied while the brain reward in the goal box was kept constant. In the second, the intrapair pulse interval of the brain reward in the goal box was varied while the priming stimulus was kept constant. The results obtained by an independent laboratory are indistinguishable from those published by Deutsch (1966), and confirm his findings by using a different behavioral method.

The results of this last series of experiments support the view that "reward" and "drive" have a separate anatomical substrate in terms of separate pathways, and that both these pathways are stimulated to produce intracranial self-stimulation.

As a check on the validity of the neurophysiological interpretation given above, direct recordings from animals exhibiting intracranial self-stimulation were undertaken. The rats were placed in a stereotaxic instrument under nembutal anaesthesia and a recording macroelectrode was inserted in the medial forebrain bundle 5 mm. anterior of the previously implanted and behaviorally tested stimulating electrode. Stimuli were then applied through the stimulating electrode and evoked potentials recorded from the anteriorly placed recording electrode. The experiment was performed in two parts. In the first a single pulse was used as a stimulus. If two pathways with different refractory periods were being stimulated, they should also differ in conduction speed. The thicker the fiber, the lower the refractory period, and the faster the conduction speed. It should therefore be possible to see two evoked potentials arriving at different times at the recording electrode. This provides an independent check on the previous interpretation. It can be seen from Figure 14–10 that two evoked potentials appear, the first being smaller than the second. However, the distances available in the rat's brain are very small, so that the electrical stimulus used to trigger the neuronal discharge tends also to be picked up (to an undesirable extent) by the recording electrode, and it does not lie down sufficiently by the time some fast-traveling potentials have arrived at the recording site. This interference (or stimulus artefact) can act as a confounding factor when we interpret records. It could be that the first evoked potential which arrives is actually bigger than it appears. On the other hand, in some cases at least, it could simply be a stimulus artefact.

In the second part of the experiment, pulse pairs separated by varying intervals were used as stimuli. It is difficult to see anything of the faster arriving evoked potential as it tends to get obliterated by the second pulse. It can, however, be seen from various records that the second evoked potential only repeats when the time interval between the two pulses is on the order of 1 msec., showing a clear refractory period of the magnitude expected from the behavioral measure (Fig. 14–11).

Gallistel et al. (1969) have used microelectrodes to measure the refractory periods and other characteristics of single neurons or units excited by pulses at loci previously found to produce brain reward. They found two sets of units, each with a refractory period close to those revealed by the behavioral work. The units with a refractory period characteristic of the drive component were found in the medial thalamus. The units with the shorter refractory period characteristic of the reward component were found in a different area in the lateral thalamus. Within each set of units excited by the brain reward electrode were two subsets

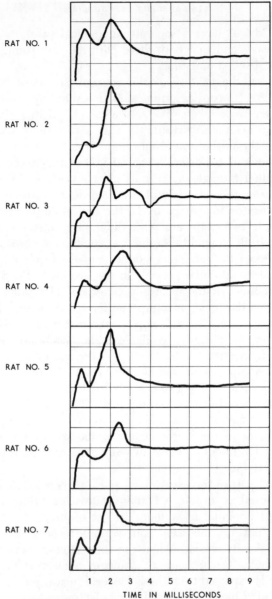

RAT NO. 1

RAT NO. 2

RAT NO. 3

RAT NO. 4

RAT NO. 5

RAT NO. 6

RAT NO. 7

1 2 3 4 5 6 7 8 9
TIME IN MILLISECONDS

FIG. 14–10. Evoked potentials recorded in the medial forebrain bundle by stimulating with one brief pulse through an electrode, known to produce responding for intracranial stimulation. The distance between recording and stimulating electrodes was about 0.5 cm. For rats 1 to 3 the stimulating electrode was in the posterior hypothalamus; for rats 4 to 7 it was in the lateral hypothalamus. Two evoked potentials, arriving at different times, can be seen. Each record is composed of at least 10 superimposed traces. (Deutsch, J. A., unpublished.)

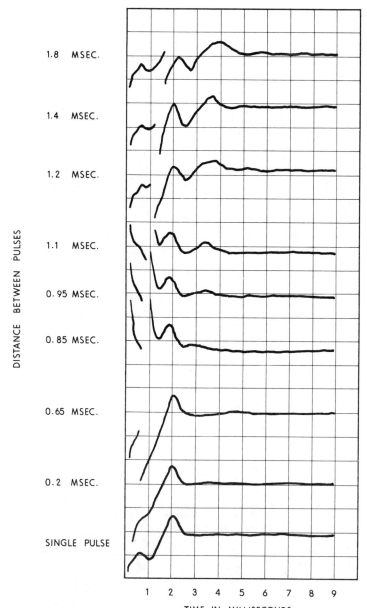

DISTANCE BETWEEN PULSES

1.8 MSEC.

1.4 MSEC.

1.2 MSEC.

1.1 MSEC.

0.95 MSEC.

0.85 MSEC.

0.65 MSEC.

0.2 MSEC.

SINGLE PULSE

TIME IN MILLISECONDS

FIG. 14–11. Evoked potentials recorded in the medial forebrain bundle by stimulating with two brief pulses at various time intervals from each other. These pulses were applied through an electrode known to produce responding for intracranial stimulation. The distance between recording and stimulating electrodes was about 0.5 cm. Each record is composed of at least 10 superimposed traces. The second pulse has no effect until it occurs after about 0.85 msec., thus showing that there is a refractory period. (Deutsch, J. A., unpublished.)

of units, as shown by the speed of arrival of the signal at the recording electrode. The first set of units from which microelectrode recordings were made was from the same axon as was being stimulated by the brain reward electrode. There, each negative going stimulating pulse produced an action potential or nerve spike as recorded by the microelectrode, except when the stimulating pulses were below the refractory period of the axon. The second set of units from which microelectrode recordings were made was connected to the stimulated axon via a synapse (or perhaps synapses). In these units the time between stimulus and neural activity was relatively longer and there was no longer a direct one-to-one relation between stimulating pulse and recorded action potential. However, refractory periods could still be inferred from an average diminution of the frequency of recorded action potentials as a function of the pulse-pair intervals in trains of stimulating pulses.

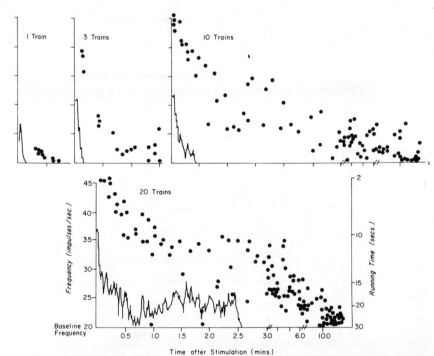

Time after Stimulation (mins.)

FIG. 14–12. Persistence of firing as a function of length of initial stimulation in a synaptically driven unit classified, on the basis of the refractory period effect, as belonging to the priming or "drive" class. The jagged lines are the post-stimulation firing frequency, as indicated by an RC averaging circuit with a time constant of less than ½ sec. To facilitate comparison with behavioral data, the point plots of post-priming running speed are superimposed. The behavioral data are from a massed trial runway performance (for a 16 pulse reward) as a function of time since priming and number of priming trains (64 pulses/train). Priming occurred at the outset of a series of massed trials. (Courtesy of C. R. Gallistel.)

Again, the refractory periods were divided into the same two groups as shown when recording was from the same neurons being stimulated. As must be inferred from the phenomena of drive decay, we would expect the activity in the drive pathway to outlast imposed stimulation and for such activity to persist longer the longer the preceding stimulation. No such persistence of activity is suggested by the behavioral observations concerning the reward pathway. Interestingly enough, once one or more synapses are crossed, the units driven by the long refractory period neurons display a discharge which persists in time beyond the original stimulating pulses. Also, the longer the initial stimulating train, the longer the persistence of the activity of these units, as is shown in Figure 14–12. In contrast, the units driven by neurons with the shorter refractory period do not show any tendency to fire for a longer time after stimulation stopped as the preceding stimulation train was lengthened.

FURTHER THEORIES OF BRAIN REWARD

Stein (1964) and Olds and Olds (1965) have suggested similar theories of brain reward. They assume that the implanted electrode excites reinforcement or pleasure. It is further assumed that stimuli associated with reinforcement acquire properties which arouse previously rewarded behavior. Trowill et al. (1969) postulate a further interaction in the Olds-Stein type of theory: that activating the reinforcement system arouses behavior most strongly when the organism is satiated and the reinforcement is of high quality. On the whole, these theories have difficulties when brain reward has different properties from natural reward, for instance, where drive decay can be demonstrated. However, such theories have the advantage where no ITI decrement is demonstrated.

REWARD

If an animal is deprived of food or water and then finds some food to eat or water to drink, it will tend to repeat the sequence of actions which led up to its finding the needed substance. Various notions of what makes eating or drinking rewarding have been advanced. For instance, Hull (1951) believed that it was the reduction of a physiological need which originally led to a connection in the nervous system such that the behavior leading to this need reduction would occur again. Sheffield and his associates have attempted to test this belief that physiological need reduction must occur for an activity to become rewarding. Sheffield and Roby (1950) have shown that saccharin, a sweet-tasting nonnutritive substance, will function as a reward in runway performance and that it will continue to do so without losing its effectiveness as a reward. This finding demonstrates that reinforcement can occur without need reduction.

This interpretation of the experiment has been questioned by Smith and Capretta. They point out that in the conditions of Sheffield and Roby's experiment the digestion of previously eaten food would have been taking place when saccharin was being drunk. They therefore argue that the reward value of saccharin to the animal is derived from the physiological need reduction due to the digestion of other substances at the time that the rat drinks saccharin.

In order to test this possibility, Smith and Capretta used two groups of rats. One group of rats was given saccharin only when the processes of digestion were complete. For this group, saccharin diminished in value as a rewarding agent during the course of the experiment. However, saccharin kept its effectiveness as reward for a second group to which saccharin was given not long after ordinary food. Such an experiment, on the face of it, would confirm this argument. Unfortunately, the effect of saccharin is not simple. Saccharin at high concentrations tastes bitter. It also produces a bitter taste when injected intravenously. The build-up of concentration of saccharin in the bloodstream when it has been drunk by an animal on an empty stomach may be very much swifter and rise further than when it is mixed with food in the intestine. In other words, saccharin drunk on an empty stomach may have unpleasant side-effects. It would be interesting to repeat the experiment of Smith and Capretta on animals with esophageal fistulae or with nonnutritious sweet-tasting substances other than saccharin where some of the complicating properties of saccharin are absent.

De Snoo (1937) found that fetuses in utero would respond to an introduction of saccharin into the amniotic fluid by drinking. It is difficult to see how the presence of saccharin could be correlated with the reduction of physiological need in this instance.

Some theorists have adopted an amended view that drive reduction, not necessarily accompanied by need reduction, is reinforcing. A reduction in physiological need or deficit can, for instance in hunger, take a long time. Further, there are cases where an activity is rewarding, for instance mating, where there is no obvious physiological deficit which is corrected. Nor is it easy to argue that the rewarding nature of such an activity arises through association with a reduction of a physiological deficit of another kind. The shift of emphasis from need reduction to drive reduction is easy for a Hull-type theory. On this theory, a physiological need or deficit is held to give rise to afferent stimuli (called drive stimuli). A rewarding state of affairs is said to arise when there is a rapid diminution of the physiological deficit, which in turn would cause drive stimuli to decrease. It is a simple modification of the theory to leave out physiological deficit and simply to talk in terms of reduction in drive stimuli.

Sheffield et al. (1951) set out to test the view that drive reduction is reinforcing. They used copulation as a reward for male rats. However, they allowed them to intromit without permitting them to intromit a sufficient number of times for ejaculation to take place. As we will see in the chapter on mating, a rat intromits and withdraws a number of times before the final ejaculatory mount. Sheffield et al. found that this procedure would function as reward for males with no previous sexual experience. In this situation it is difficult to argue that any reduction in drive stimulation had taken place, since the animals were not allowed to ejaculate. In fact, a commonsense view of the matter would be that there had been a drive increase. Of course, we can always say that if such a procedure was rewarding it must have been drive reducing, but this would make the concept of drive reduction circular and untestable.

Kagan (1955) has further investigated the reward value of incomplete coition in rats. He found that naive male rats, not allowed to proceed to ejaculation, would find copulation rewarding to begin with, though they develop some kind of conflict. They run up to the female but show reluctance to mount her. It may be that the observed conflict is due to some kind of discomfort produced by incomplete coition. However, Whalen (1961) found no decrement in reward with incomplete copulation, and criticizes Kagan's design.

Sheffield, on the basis of his findings, proposes that it is the evocation of a consummatory response which is rewarding. However, it is unlikely that this is the case. Miller and Kessen (1952) found that a rat will learn to choose the arm of a T maze where a nutrient solution is directly inserted into the stomach, showing that reward can occur even when the usual consummatory activities are absent. So it seems that both an explanation of reward solely in terms of consummatory activity or in terms of drive reduction are rendered implausible by the above evidence.

It is, however, possible to look at the evidence another way. We can assume that it is some specific stimulation which is correlated with reward. For instance, we may adopt the view that it is the taste of water which is rewarding to the animal. Putting this in more physiological terms, we can say that it is a signal ascending certain pathways which is correlated with reward when the animal is thirsty.

This can be illustrated by considering the physiological correlates of taste preference. In rat and man (Zotterman and Diamant, 1959), when water is placed on the tongue, there is a reduction in the spontaneous firing of a certain type of fiber. If a salt solution above a certain concentration is placed on the tongue, there is an increase in the amount of firing from the same type of fiber. If samples of water with an increasing admixture of salt are placed on the tongue, there is progressively less reduction of spontaneous firing. A reduction of spontaneous firing in this fiber signals water, and it seems to be the cumulated reduction of firing in this fiber while the animal drinks that determines how much the animal will drink. If the animal is presented with a solution of saline which reduces the spontaneous firing in this water-salt fiber by only a small amount, the animal will drink this solution for a much longer time than if it drinks water. Further, if the animal is given such a solution of saline in its cage together with water, the amount being unlimited, it will drink much more of the saline. However, when rats are presented with equal volumes of the same saline solution and water in the maze and they have to choose between them, they find the water more rewarding and learn to run to the water side. This can be explained by saying that the same volume of water will produce a larger cumulative reduction in the firing of the water-salt fiber (Deutsch and Jones, 1960). These findings indicate that it is a particular afferent message which leads to the neural changes which underlies the phenomena of reward. In terms of the system we discussed above, the function of the afferent message would be to make a connection between two sets of cells more permeable to the passage of excitation.

It seems that such an account of reward in terms of a specific afferent message can be applied to other types of activity. Hagstrom and Pfaffmann (1959) have pointed out that there is a correlation between the amount of activity in the chorda tympani nerve (a part of the afferent taste pathways) generated by various sweet-tasting solution and the reward value of these solutions. This observation extends the previous work of Hutt (1954) and Gutman (1954). Hutt found that the rate of responding of rats in a Skinner box for a given solution was a function of the taste of the solution as well as of its amount. Guttman reported that those solutions of glucose and sucrose which are judged equally sweet by human observations are equally reinforcing to rats.

Is the Association between Reward and Need Reduction Learned?

It might be suggested that the association between reward and need reduction is learned. For instance, it could be said that the animal learns that a particular sensory message brings in its wake a certain amount of physiological need reduction. In this way the role of afferent impulses would be a secondary and not a primary relation. However, Sheffield's work on the rewarding effects of coition would be difficult to reconcile with this viewpoint, since he used naive rats. However, there is other work bearing on this question. For instance, Coppock and Chambers (1954) attempted to pair an arbitrarily chosen event with physiological need reduction. They tried to reward hungry rats with an injection of glucose into the bloodstream when they turned their heads in a certain direction. Their rats were 72 hours hungry, apparently without having been placed on a feeding schedule previously. This would have produced extremes of depletion. (It is usual to accustom animals to a regular feeding schedule before an experiment.) In spite of such extreme treatment, the results of this experiment are highly equivocal. Though 32 animals were used in this study, significant differences were not obtained for absolute frequency of head turns or their absolute duration, or for the relative number of moves toward the rewarded position, but only for the relative duration of preference for the rewarded position. Further, the controls used in this study consisted of animals which had physiological saline injected. This would not have the same reviving effect as an injection of glucose in the experimental group. Any difference could therefore have been due to some factor of revival rather than of learning. At best, the experiment shows that such learning, if it occurs at all, is very inefficient. Chambers (1956a, b) extended the experiment to dogs and rabbits. His animals were given an injection of glucose when they were in one area in a box and xylose (a nonnutritive sugar) or saline in other areas. Chambers found that dogs (which were satiated, or starved one to three days) did not learn. The rabbits (starved six, four, or three days) found the glucose injections rewarding. It was found that a relatively short time after glucose injection there followed a significant rise in body temperature. It seems likely that a sudden removal of noxious symptoms could serve as a reward in this situation. It is known (as we have seen in the chapter on hunger and thirst) that this can constitute a way in which animals learn to select certain dietary components. However, as we also saw, such a way of learning to ingest the appropriate substance in the quantity appropriate to a deficit is inefficient and breaks down when the choice given the animal is large.

The inefficiency of learning by need reduction alone is illustrated in an experiment by Thomson and Porter (1953), where the need was produced by sodium deficiency. In this experiment, six rats were rendered ageusic (unable to taste) and anosmic (unable to smell). These six rats, and eight normal rats, were fed on a sodium-deficient diet. Saline, below taste threshold for the ageusic group but not for the normal group, was placed in one arm of a T maze and water in the other. The normal group learned within ten days, in which four trials a day 15 minutes apart were given. The ageusic group received the same treatment but did not learn. They were then placed on a complex and lengthy training procedure, as a result of which four out of the six ageusic animals appear to have learned. The two animals which did not learn learned promptly as soon as the strength of the saline solution in the maze was increased above their taste threshold.

That the reward value of the taste of salt is unlearned is further supported by an experiment of Epstein and Stellar (1955). They showed that rats would drink an amount of saline proportional to their deficit as soon as it became available, without previous experience.

In summary, then, the most plausible way of interpreting experimental evidence on reward agrees well with common sense and introspection. It is the taste of water, the feeling of satiety, the sensations from the genitalia that an animal finds rewarding. The connection of these sensations with need reduction is not one which is made by each individual animal. Such a connection between reward and physiological deficit has been made by the process of natural selection. Only those animals which have found certain sensations rewarding have survived. Learning with physiological need reduction as reward has already occurred in the species; the individual need not recapitulate it.

CONCLUSION

In this chapter we have reviewed some of the evidence both from physiological and behavioral experiments which shows us something about the mechanism which produces the adaptive change known as learning. In the first part of the chapter we saw that it is unlikely that learning consists in the linkage of stimulus with response. In the section dealing with learning to obtain the reward of an intracranial stimulus, we showed how more specific models of brain function could be tested and verified by a combination of stimulation of the central nervous system in animals under simultaneous behavioral test. In the section on reward, it was shown that primary reinforcement is in all probability due to the excitation of certain receptor systems. It is in this area of learning that the distinction between experimental and physiological studies is becoming obliterated, as physiological studies have shown themselves capable of testing theoretical issues generated by behavioral work.

chapter 15

Reproductive Behavior

Behavioral Considerations

Courtship and copulation take many forms among the vertebrates. Since most of the physiological evidence quoted in this chapter is restricted to mammals—especially the rat and the cat—some account of the behavior of these two species will be given.

After the male rat has found an estrous female, he attempts to approach her. However, she darts forward, fluttering her ears, and stops, repeating this behavior until the male mounts her. In response to this tactile stimulus she arches her back and raises and exposes the genitalia (lordosis). Having intromitted, the male dismounts and licks his own genitalia and then mounts again. The male intromits about 12 times before ejaculation occurs. Each intromission lasts about one third of a second and is separated from the previous one by an interval of 45 to 60 seconds.

An intromission consists of a number of shallow thrusts around the vaginal orifice, followed by a deep thrust. During the ejaculatory intromission, the male makes several deep thrusts into the vagina, making an insertion which is about three times longer than during a normal intromission. He also grasps the flanks of the female much more tightly during the ejaculatory mount (Bermant, 1965). The ejaculate congeals rapidly upon contact with air to form a vaginal plug, a viscous mass which lodges within the vaginal orifice.

The female cat shows pronounced and well-defined sexual responses which make it a convenient subject for study. Activities which precede mating include low vocalization, rubbing, rolling, and crouching accompanied by treading. This last kind of behavior consists of a lowering of the front part of the body, a raising of the pelvis, turning the tail

551

to one side, and a treading movement of the hind legs. In many cats this action occurs quite spontaneously without any apparent external stimulus. In other cats this behavior is induced either by a grasping of the neck by the male or simply by his presence or by stimulation of the genitalia. When genital stimulation or intromission of the male occurs, the female utters a loud cry, shriek, or growl. After coitus, the so-called afterreaction occurs, and this is somewhat variable. It usually consists of a "frantic rubbing, squirming, licking and rolling" (Ranson, 1940). This is accompanied, as is described below (p. 562), by electrical changes in parts of the hypothalamus. It is tempting to compare this reaction to orgasm in the human female.

It has been observed that the disposition of female cats to allow copulation varies. Some will permit only a very determined male to mate. It has also been claimed (Green et al., 1957) that the female is affected by the location where she meets the male. She is much more receptive in strange territory than in her own cage. In the male cat, situational factors are similarly important. In contrast to the female, the male will copulate only in a place where he regards as his own territory and not in a strange place. In order to regard a place as his territory, he must explore it to become familiar with it. When a female is introduced into his territory, he first behaves with great caution, and only after a prolonged period does he seize the female by the neck and mount her. However, if on a subsequent occasion another cat is introduced into his territory, he will mount it at once, regardless of its sex. On the other hand, he becomes quite wary if another cat is already in his territory when he appears, and he cautiously observes the other cat. It seems that the cat resembles the rabbit in this respect. The writer has observed that male rabbits in their own territory will attempt to mate with newly introduced males, until these bite and a fight develops. Homosexual mating is avoided only through the noncompliance of the sex object and not through a discriminatory object choice of the initiating male.

Hormonal Influence and Mating Behavior

As opposed to hunger, the biochemical changes which initiate sexual activity are well understood. In general, the occurrence of mating behavior is correlated with the presence of certain hormones. The androgens, secreted mainly by the male testes, are associated with masculine mating patterns. The estrogens, secreted by the female ovaries, are connected with female sexual behavior. This has been shown by observing behavior when these hormones are absent and also when they are present. For instance, fully developed mating behavior tends to occur after puberty, that is, after the gonads have become functional. Absence of the gonads, and therefore the gonadal hormones, tends to be correlated with an absence of mating activity, especially in females.

Birds

Castration. In birds, castration reduces the frequency of elements of mating behavior, especially if the operation is performed prepuberally (Collias, 1950). The amount of such reduction varies greatly. In some male pigeons, copulatory behavior continues for as long as eight months after postpuberal castration (Carpenter, 1933). Observations of secondary sexual activities revealed increases in billing after castration (Carpenter, 1933a). In avian females, as contrasted with males, removal of the gonads leads to a complete cessation of all sexual activity.

Hormone Administration in Immature Birds. Noble and Zitrin (1942) have found that when male chicks were injected with testosterone propionate, they exhibited all the sexual behavior of the adult cock, such as crowing and a complete copulatory pattern. These authors also reported that when female chicks were given daily injections of estrogen since they were 15 days old, they squatted for treading males after about three weeks, thus prematurely showing the pattern typical of an adult hen. Boss (1943) induced sexual behavior in immature herring gulls by injecting testosterone.

These experiments can be considered evidence for two things: first, that sexual behavior occurs as a result of the presence of hormones; and second, that immature animals have a neural organization which is capable of producing sexual behavior, although this is not usually observed because of the absence of the relevant hormone.

Mammals

Castration before Puberty. There is a very large diminution of sexual activity in mammalian males which have been castrated before puberty and in females whose ovaries have been removed prepuberally. Studies on this have been carried out on rats (Beach, 1942; Beach and Holtz, 1946), hamsters (Rosenblatt and Aronson, 1958, 1958a; Warren and Aronson, 1957), guinea pigs (Sollenberger and Hamilton, 1939), and cats (Aronson, 1958). The example of a prepuberally castrated male chimpanzee (Clark, 1945) is often quoted to show that male sexual activity of primates is independent of the gonadal hormone. This chimpanzee was allegedly capable of vigorous sexual activity in adulthood. However, in reviewing this case Rosenblatt and Aronson (1958a) drew attention to the fact that this animal was under hormone therapy and that there is no published record showing that it copulated before administration of testosterone.

Castration in Adulthood. Many experimental observations have also been made on mammalian males castrated in adulthood. For instance, Stone (1927) reported that male rats castrated in adulthood lost their capacity to ejaculate before they failed to copulate. Forty-five percent of the castrates failed to copulate after two months. This percentage gradually increased with time. Thorek (1924) found that when male rhesus monkeys were castrated in adulthood they made no mating attempts at the end of the sixth month after the operation. Other investigators have found a much greater length of persistence. Rosenblatt and Aronson (1958) reported that one of their castrated male cats intromitted four years after the operation. Many of their cats continued to make mating attempts, such as mounting, for years. However, considerable variability is found from one animal to another with regard to the persistence of mating activity after castration. Experience of mating prior to castration is an important factor here, as has been shown by Rosenblatt and Aronson (1958). They found that male cats with sexual experience before castration were more likely to exhibit the full mating pattern after castration than cats that have not had such experience.

Hormone Administration. Another line of evidence relating to the importance of hormones as initiating factors in sexual behavior comes from the effects of their administration. As in birds, sexual behavior can also be evoked in mammals through appropriate dosage with sex hormones. Beach (1948) reported cases of precocious sexual activity after giving mammals sex hormone treatment. Such results have been obtained in young male and female rats, mice, and dogs, but only weak results were obtained in guinea pigs (Gerall, 1958).

Injection of testosterone brings about sexual behavior in previously castrated males even when castration was performed before puberty. Such effects occur in all mammals. Stone reported that the return of sexual behavior in the rat after the injection of testosterone was the reverse order of its loss of sexual behavior following castration (Stone, 1939). For example, treatment with androgens results first in a return of copulatory behavior and later a return of ejaculation. Similar effects have been noted with estrogen injection in spayed females. Sexual receptivity occurs after estrogen injection in the female dog, cat, and rabbit. When an injection of progesterone in addition to a priming injection of estrogen is given to the rat, mouse, guinea pig, or hamster, sexual receptivity is increased. Similar effects are produced from various classes of normal animals that are not sexually active, such as senile animals and animals which have a seasonal quiescence of mating behavior. Minnick, Warden, and Arieti (1946), for example, restored copulatory activity in 28-month-old male rats. Beach (1948) reported a number of cases where various methods of manipulating the hormone level elicited mating behavior in animals which were out of season.

Dependence of Mating on Sex Hormones

All the evidence available from animal studies suggests that females are completely dependent on gonadal hormones in their mating behavior (Beach, 1948). Evidence of any type of independence from gonadal hormones of mating activity is found only in prepuberally or post-puberally castrated males. It may be that the neural centers responsible for sexual behavior in the male are capable of residual activity without the biochemical stimulus normally supplied by sex hormones. On the other hand, it is also possible that in the male the neural centers which respond to hormonal influence are less specific in their sensitivity and consequently will continue to respond to a large range of biochemical factors after the gonads have been removed.

P-chlorophenylalanine, which has been described as an aphrodisiac (Tagliamonte, 1969; Ferguson et al., 1970), produces long-lasting sexual excitement which is reversed by 6-hydroxytryptophan. The effect may only be homosexual (Whalen and Luttge, 1970) and may not enhance normal activity with a receptive female (Zitrin and Beach et al., 1970). Dopa also has aphrodisiac effects.

Dependence of Hormones on Mating

In mating, as in hunger and thirst, there is a close interaction between the physiological substrate and behavior. Not only do physiological factors such as hormonal changes evoke mating behavior, but mating behavior influences physiology in a direct manner. Two interesting instances of this are the effect of mating in the male on the size of the reproductive organs and the effect of genital stimulation on the probability of conception in the female.

Male rats living and copulating with females have larger sexual organs and kidneys than males living without females (Drori and Folman, 1964). It seems that it is heterosexual mating in the rat which prevents the relative atrophy of the reproductive system (as social conditions and exposure to female odors have only minor effects) (Folman and Drori, 1966). Further, it has been shown (Folman and Drori, 1969) that the weight of the penis, perineal muscle, seminal vesicle tissue, and the hypophysis significantly increased with the amount of copulation allowed male rats. The total amount of body fat decreased with increasing amount of sexual intercourse. In another study, Herz, Folman, and Drori (1969) have shown that the testosterone content of rat testes increases with mating. Similar effects have been shown in the rabbit by Endroczi and Lissak (1962) and Saginor and Horton (1968), where copulation increases the testosterone content of blood for several hours. As the hypophysis enlarges through copulation, it is probable that the increase in testosterone output is due to an action of hypophyseal trophic hormones on the testes.

The second instance where the behavioral pattern of mating closely affects physiology is genital stimulation and the probability of pregnancy in the female. The female rat has a short estrous cycle of four to five days, and during this cycle the corpora lutea do not secrete enough progesterone during their brief existence to enable implantation of the fertilized egg to occur. It appears, however, that sufficient progesterone is secreted as a result of stimulation by the male during mating. Wilson et al. (1965) found that when female rats received six or more intromissions before the male ejaculated, 90 percent became pregnant. When females received three or less intromissions before the male ejaculated, only 22 percent became pregnant.

This supports the hypothesis that stimulation from repeated intromissions initiates a neuro-endocrine reflex which leads to the secretion of sufficient progesterone to permit implantation of the ovum. Adler (1969) has been able to show that this increase in fertility is due to the stimulus of penile insertion into the female genitalia. At ejaculation in the rat, part of the ejaculate coagulates or hardens in the vagina, forming what is called a vaginal plug. Such stimulation could have been partly responsible for pregnancy—in conjunction with penile insertion.

However, Adler was able to rule out the vaginal plug as a necessary stimulus to increased fertility by preventing its formation by pharmacological means. Mounting without penile insertion had no effect on indices of receptivity four or five days later, thus showing no enhancement of release of progesterone due to mounting alone. However, it seems that progesterone release consequent on multiple penile insertion is not the only factor which enhances fertility. Adler was able to show that more sperm penetrated into the uterus when ejaculation followed a large number of intromissions. It seems, therefore, that multiple intromission in the rat enhances fertility in two ways: by a release of progesterone to permit implantation and an increase in sperm transport into the uterus by a mechanism as yet undefined.

LOCUS OF ACTION OF HORMONES: PERIPHERAL THEORIES

It has been believed that hormones produce mating behavior by their effect on peripheral bodily structures—in many ways a plausible idea. The presence of hormones causes changes in peripheral structures. For example, during estrus female monkeys develop conspicuous reddening and swelling of the skin around the genitalia. It was assumed that the stimulus which produced sexual behavior arose from the altered afferent messages arising from peripheral bodily structures. Such views are discussed and criticized by Lashley (1938). There is now considerable evidence against such peripheral theories since sex drive remains unimpaired by the removal or denervation of structures affected by sex hormones.

Ball (1934) demonstrated that female rats show normal patterns of mating behavior after the uterus and vagina have been removed. Bard (1935) obtained similar results in the female cat. Denervation of the sex organs of a cat (both the sensory fibers and the efferent sympathetic fibers) does not alter its mating behavior. In the male cat, desensitization of the genitalia by sectioning a part of the lower spinal cord still does not alter copulatory attempts (Root and Bard, 1947). Pauker (1948) found that ablation of the prostate and seminal vesicles in the hamster was without effect on mating behavior or on the rate of mating behavior disappearance after removal of the testes. Beach and Wilson (1963) have shown that ablation of the seminal vesicles does not change the mating behavior of the rat.

CENTRAL LOCUS OF SENSITIVITY TO HORMONES

In the study of hunger and thirst, we have seen that there are structures in the hypothalamus which appear to translate biochemical factors into neural activity. The same is true in mating activity. Stimulation of restricted regions in the hypothalamus with minute quantities of hormone produces sexual activity (Fisher, 1956; Davidson and Sawyer, 1961). Restricted lesions in the hypothalamus abolish integrated mating behavior, even in the presence of adequate supplies of the appropriate hormone and the intactness of the development of genital structures and secondary sexual characteristics (Soulairac and Soulairac, 1956; Sawyer and Robinson, 1956). Such results will be more fully described in the next section when we consider central nervous structures which are critically involved in mating behavior.

Evidence from Ablation Studies

In general, it may be said that two different effects may arise from lesions in the central nervous system, both serving to abolish mating behavior; however, these effects have not always been distinguished. The effect of the first kind of lesions is to produce abolition of mating through gonadal atrophy in the following way.

Hypothalamic loci which are concerned with the regulation of the gonadotropic secretions of the anterior pituitary are destroyed with the result that the gonads (testes or ovaries) become nonfunctional. Therefore the outcome of lesions of the first type is in effect the same as that of castration or ovariectomy because the supply of gonadal hormones is removed. This effect on mating behavior must be regarded as secondary, especially since mating behavior may be restored by the administration of the appropriate hormone. The effect of the second type of lesion is the complete abolition of spontaneous or integrated mating behavior even though no gonadal or genital atrophy results, and even in spite of the presence of adequate supplies of the appropriate hormone. Such lesions probably destroy the central nervous tissue which translates certain biochemical states into neural activity or the pathways leading from biochemically sensitive tissue. Consequently, the presence of hormones cannot be translated into the neural activity which produces mating behavior.

With this in mind, let us consider various ablation studies in detail. Soulairac and Soulairac (1956) found that two types of lesions served to abolish mating behavior in the male rat. The first type of lesions involves the medial and lateral mammillary nuclei. Reduction of copulatory behavior is sudden in animals with such lesions. In the presence of receptive females, male animals with such lesions show an undirected hyperactivity which often turns into aggressive behavior. Atrophy of the gonads and genitalia also results from these lesions. The second type of lesion consists of bilateral lesions of the preoptic area and of the suprachiasmatic nucleus. Mating behavior progressively decreases, until it is completey abolished within 15 days after the operation. There is no atrophy of the testes or genitalia as a result of this type of lesion.

In male and female guinea pigs, lesions of the ventral portion of the anterior hypothalamus (between the optic chiasma and the stalk of the pituitary) eliminate mating behavior (Brookhart and Dey, 1941; Dey et al., 1940). Injection of gonadal hormones does not evoke mating behavior in these guinea pigs (Brookhart et al., 1940). Sawyer and Robinson (1956) produced lesions in the anterior hypothalamus of female cats. These lesions were produced rostral to the ventromedial nuclei and either medial to or within the area of the medial forebrain bundle. In most cases, such lesions result in a disappearance of estrous behavior in spite of estrogen administration. There is no ovarian regression, and ovulation can be induced by direct electrical stimulation of the ventromedial nucleus. Lesions of the ventromedial nucleus and destruction of the mammillary body or the premammillary region also result in anestrus. But such disappearance of estrus is due to ovarian regression, probably through a decline in the secretion of gonadotropic hormone by the anterior pituitary. Here mating behavior can be restored by administration of estrogen (Fig. 15-1).

However, Sawyer (1957) found that in the female rabbit the site of lesion which produces anestrus without ovarian atrophy is in the mammillary region. Small bilateral lesions in this region led to an absence of estrous behavior, and this behavior could not be induced by administration of estrogen. The ovaries did not atrophy, and ovulation

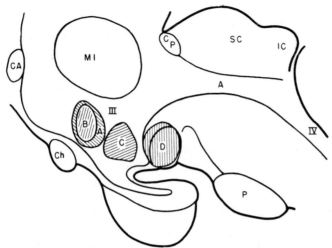

FIG. 15–1. Site of lesions in the female cat which interfere with reproductive behavior. *A* and *B* are anterior hypothalamic lesions which produce permanent anestrus, which is not reversible by administration of estrogen. *C* is a lesion of the ventromedial hypothalamus, which induced ovarian atrophy. However, mating behavior could be evoked by administration of estrogen. *D*-mammillary lesions with the same effect as in lesion illustrated in *C*. In *E* the reconstructions of the lesions are all projected on a midsagittal map: *CA,* anterior commissure; *ch,* optic chiasm; *CP,* posterior commissure; *MI,* massa intermedia; *P,* pons; *IC,* inferior colliculi; *SC,* superior colliculli; *III,* third ventricle. (From Sawyer, C. H., *Handbook of Physiology,* 1960, p. 1232.)

could be produced by stimulation of the hypophysis. However, ventral tuberal lesions involving the arcuate and the base of the ventromedial nuclei led to a failure of ovulation, and in some animals such lesions led to ovarian atrophy. If a supply of estrogen was present, these animals would mate.

From this evidence it seems that the release of ovulatory hormones by the pituitary is controlled by the basal tuberal area. On the other hand, the system involved in the initiation of mating activity appears to be in a different location in the cat than in the rabbit. In the cat, this system is rostral to the basal tuberal area; in the rabbit, it is caudal to the basal tuberal area. Nevertheless, there is a possibility that there are also effects on mating behavior in female rabbits when the anterior part of the hypothalamus is damaged. Sawyer reports that animals with damage in this area did not survive long enough to be tested. Experiments involving electrical recording from the anterior part of the hypothalamus (Green, 1954) suggest that this area is indeed involved (see below).

Different types of lesion effects have recently been obtained. Law and Meagher (1958) found in the rat that lesions of the midventral hypothalamus resulted in behavioral estrus without vaginal estrus. They found, further, that spayed female rats with such lesions also displayed behavioral estrus. Goy and Phoenix (1963) reported the latter condition in the guinea pig also after anterior ventral lesions of the hypothalamus. It remains to be determined whether such results are due to the destruction of some sexual inhibitory mechanism or represent simply the irritative consequences of a lesion.

Evidence that mechanisms for both male and female behavior are present in females has been found by Hillarp et al. (1954). They made small bilateral lesions in the basal preoptic area of female rats and found that within 20 to 30 minutes after awakening postoperatively from anaesthesia 18 animals (a small minority of their subjects) began to show male patterns of copulation directed indiscriminately at male or female animals. This behavior was continuously repeated for a few hours and then disappeared. It seems plausible to interpret this behavior as due to an irritative effect of the lesion.

Evidence for the separate neural representation of male and female patterns in the rat female has been obtained by Singer (1968). Lordosis was abolished completely by lesions, mainly of the anterior hypothalamic nucleus. Such lesions did little to impair masculine mounting responses in the same females. On the other hand, lordosis was unaffected by lesions in the medial and lateral preoptic nuclei of the hypothalamus, which greatly reduced mounting responses.

Evidence from Local Hormonal Stimulation

Fisher (1956) has obtained further interesting evidence on hormone-sensitive loci within the hypothalamus. He used a technique similar to that which Andersson and co-workers used when studying thirst (see Chapter 16). This method involves the use of microinjections of substances thought to evoke certain behavior in order to determine the locus of their action on the nervous system. The substances are used in such minute quantities that their general effect after they have diffused would produce no noticeable reaction. Therefore if thirst or mating activity is produced by this method, it is likely that the excitatory substance has been injected very near the site of the cells which translate a particular biochemical state into specific behavior patterns. Fisher found that injections of 0.003 to 0.05 mg. of sodium testosterone sulfate (suspended in saline) in the region of the lateral preoptic area produced exaggerated sexual behavior. The elicited behavior often continued for more than 90 minutes following the injection. Though Fisher emphasized the possibility that causes other than hormonal may have produced this behavior, control injections of physiological saline, neural excitants, and electrical stimulation did not have the same effect in this experiment (but see p. 596).

However, male mating responses are not the only responses which have occurred after such treatment. Fisher describes responses such as nest building, retrieving, grooming litters of young, respiratory changes, diffuse hyperactivation, long-lasting exploratory-like behavior, repetitive localized muscular response, digging, leaping, and seizures. The effects of the hormone on the lateral preoptic region are therefore not clear cut. It is possible that a high concentration of one hormone may excite centers which are maximally sensitive to other hormones.

Harris (1958) and Harris et al. (1958) reported that behavioral signs of estrus appeared when estrogen was placed into the hypothalamus of ovariectomized cats in quantities too small to be active if normally injected. Also, Kent and Liberman (1959) injected into the lateral ventricles of the brain doses of hormone which were too small to have any effects systemically. By this means they were able to provide further evidence of the central action of hormones on behavior. Having primed a castrated hamster with estrogen, they were able to produce behavioral estrus by an injection of progesterone into the ventricles.

Davidson and Sawyer (1961) used the technique of implanting estrogen-filled hypodermic needles into brain sites of rabbits, while Lisk (1962) used the same technique with rats. Again we see that it is possible to produce a state of behavioral receptivity by implants of estrogen in quantities too small to have an effect if normally injected. Using C^{14}-labeled estrogen for his implants in cats, Michael (1962) has shown that the spread of estrogen from the implant is very small (400–600 microns around the tip of the implant tube). Further, uptake of the hormone is restricted to a few cells, and there also seems to be a relation between the number of cells showing uptake of the estrogen around the implant and the behavioral effect of estrogen in promoting mating. This suggests that cells sensitive to the hormone are intermingled with cells having other functions.

Evidence from Electrical Stimulation

In the rat, Vaughn and Fisher (1962) have induced mounting, erection, and seminal emission as a part of coordinated sexual behavior by electrical stimulation in the anterior lateral hypothalamic area. MacLean and Ploog (1962) were able to produce erection in the squirrel monkey by stimulation in the septopreoptic area, septum, anterior and midline thalamic nuclei, hypothalamus, and cingulate gyrus. MacLean et al. (1962) obtained seminal discharge in the squirrel monkey by stimulating parts of the thalamus, especially from the parafascicular centromedian complex.

Evidence from Recordings of Electrical Activity

Porter et al. (1957) have used electroencephalographic (EEG) recording from the hypothalamus during or after vaginal stimulation in the cat. Following copulation, the female cat exhibits a marked afterreaction that lasts for several minutes. During this afterreaction, bursts of high-amplitude EEG activity were observed in the medial forebrain bundle but never in the posterior hypothalamus. Such changes were seen only in the records of cats which were in estrus or to which estrogen had been administered.

Green (1954) obtained records of heightened electrical activity from the anterior hypothalamus of the female rabbit during sexual activity. He used the technique of chronic implantation of electrodes, which enabled him to record when the animals were unanesthetized and unrestrained. As a result he was able to observe hypothalamic response during courtship and mating. Sawyer (1960) reported that he and Kawakami, using the same animal and a similar technique, have observed an afterreaction following copulation or vaginal stimulation. High-amplitude slow waves appear in the limbic cortical and hippocampal regions while the rabbit remains quiescent. The females in which this was observed had been treated with estrogen or a combination of progesterone and estrogen. In relation to studies using ablation techniques, a point of interest is that this EEG afterreaction can be evoked by low-frequency electrical stimulation of the ventromedial region of the hypothalamus. Sawyer reports that neither vaginal nor hypothalamic stimulation evokes the EEG afterreaction when the female rabbit is anestrous.

Transection Studies

Spinal Copulatory Organization. Many components of sexual activity can be demonstrated at the level of the spinal cord. It is possible in male animals to obtain erection of the penis and ejaculation through tactile stimulation following a supralumber transection to the spinal cord. These responses may be obtained in spinal dog and spinal man. Sherrington (1900) noted that in the male dog tactile stimulation following genital stimulation gives rise to movements which closely resemble those found during copulation, such as bilateral extension of the knees and ankles, depression of the tail, and ventral curvature of the back. "These

reflex movements suggest themselves as belonging to the act of copulation, and this suggestion is strengthened by failure to obtain similar
movements on touching the analogous parts of the spinal bitch." This
may be due to differences in peripheral morphological development
which distinguishes the sexes.

More recently, Hart and Kitchell (1966) have found that the pattern
of penile erection and contraction of penile muscles involved in ejaculation of the semen are similar in dogs with spinal transection and intact
dogs. When such dogs have recovered from spinal shock (a depression
of reflex activity consequent upon spinal transection), the intensity of
ejaculation seemed much greater than in an intact male dog. Ejaculation
was produced in both cases by genital stimulation in the absence of
a receptive female. This suggests that the ejaculatory reflex occurs by
means of disinhibition from higher centers rather than by excitation
by them. In a further comparison between spinal and normal male dogs,
Hart (1967) showed that some aspects of mating behavior (especially
the copulatory lock and the intense ejaculatory reaction) are probably
completely mediated at the spinal level. Further, the sexual refractory
period (a postcoital depression of mating activity) seems to be caused
by a refractoriness of neural mechanisms within the spine.

Hormones at the Spinal Level. Do such neural mechanisms at the
spinal level need sex hormones to render them functional? A study by
Bromiley and Bard (1940) tends to rule out the notion that hormonal
effects are necessary for copulatory reflexes at the spinal level. These
workers examined decapitated cats, both males and females in and out
of estrus. They found that treading movements of the hindlegs and dorsal
flexion of the pelvis occurred when the vulva or perineum of the female
cat was gently rubbed. Also, if one or the other side of the midline
was touched, the tail moved to the opposite side and the pelvis turned
toward the stimulated side. Such reactions occurred whether the females
were fully in heat or fully anestrous; therefore it appears that these
lower neural systems are not themselves sensitive to hormonal influences
in a way similar to certain portions of the hypothalamus, and that the
lower neural systems operate well without such hormones. Bard (1940)
states: "In fact one of the best examples of this spinal 'treading' was
found in an animal which had been spayed thirty-nine months before
and had never been treated with estrin; its genital tract was markedly
atrophic." Dempsey and Rioch (1939) also found no change in spinal
reflexes of the female guinea pig which could be ascribed to administration of estrogen and progesterone.

Bromiley and Bard stated that all the parts of the female copulatory
reaction which they described in the female, they obtained in decapitate
males. However, tail deflection was apparently less marked in males,
and sometimes was absent. Thus in the tail deflection part of the female

copulatory pattern of the cat, the spinal nervous mechanisms subserving tail deflection are insensitive to hormonal influence and are, to a large extent, common to both sexes.

Results on cats which are decerebrate (where only the medulla, pons, and lower mesencephalon are left intact) have also been reported by Bard and Bromiley (1940). In spite of the decerebrate rigidity found in such animals, an attitude suggestive of the feline estrual crouch can be elicited by stimulation of the vagina. Whether or not this response can be elicited does not depend on the hormonal condition of the animal. It can be in estrus or out of estrus.

Components of Copulation. The component reactions observed in copulation are produced by neural mechanisms other than those found in the hypothalamus, but these spinal mechanisms in the intact animal are a functional part of the system which is brought into activity when its hypothalamic component is hormonally stimulated. The responses which we have been considering are parts of the copulatory or end stage of sexual activity. However, mating behavior as elicited by hormones consists also of a large number of activities leading up to copulation. Many of these involve the detection and correct orientation toward a member of the opposite sex. Such activities presuppose a high degree of elaboration of afferent messages, especially those concerned with distance reception. In mammals, most of these activities are necessary for proper execution of the mating patterns of the male, while the female tends rather to provide a source of stimulation. It is therefore not surprising (as can be seen from Beach [1940, 1948] and Bard [1940]) that mating depends on cortical intactness to a greater degree in the male than in the female. Cortical ablation in the male cat may lead to the execution of copulatory movements before the animal has moved into the normal position for mating and therefore actual mating fails.

BEHAVIORAL STUDIES AND THE NEURAL EXCITATORY POOL IN COPULATION

A set of studies on latencies to ejaculation in the rat suggest an interesting set of quantitative interactions to be explored at the neural level. As has been stated above (p. 551), the male rat intromits about 12 times before ejaculation occurs. Each intromission lasts about one third of a second and is separated from the previous one by an interval of 45 to 60 seconds. It has been found by Larsson (1956) and Rasmussen (quoted by Beach and Whalen, 1959b) that if this interval between intromissions is artificially lengthened by removing the female after the male has dismounted, the number of intromissions prior to ejaculation is decreased. This occurs only if the period between intromissions is increased to 3 to 5 minutes. If the delay is increased to 10 minutes, some males may not achieve ejaculation while other males will increase the number of intromissions before ejaculation.

Beach and Whalen interpreted these findings by saying that the stimulus of each intromission begins a process of excitation which rises for at least three minutes. Since this level of excitement must reach a certain threshold before ejaculation can occur, an enforced waiting period after each intromission will increase the excitatory store beyond the normal level. As a result, the excitatory level will reach an ejaculatory threshold after fewer intromissions. It could be suggested, as an alternative, that each intromission causes a swiftly occurring sensory change, such as adaptation, to occur to the receptors in the penis; this adaptation would cause withdrawal, and could gradually wear off after each withdrawal. Thus we can assume that only incoming stimulation is stored and added to the excitatory pool; and we can assume that a longer spacing of the intromissions will bring in more stimulation (or more of the correct kind of stimulation) with each intromission since there is more time for adaptation to wear off between intromissions. It would not, according to this alternative hypothesis, be necessary to assume that the level of the excitatory pool increased spontaneously while the rat was inactive. If we assume, as in the previous explanation, that there is also a spontaneous decay of excitation in the excitatory pool, we can account for the data that relate the interval between intromissions with the speed of ejaculation, together with the fact of withdrawal.

The alternative hypothesis (Deutsch and Deutsch, 1966) that adaptation causes withdrawal and that such adaptation wears off with time receives strong support from an experiment by Bermant et al. (1969). When there is an enforced delay between intromissions of 5 minutes, the average duration of genital contact is 331 msec., as compared to 265 msec. during self-paced copulation.

However, penile stimulation through intromission is not the only way that the pool of excitation can increase. While mounting a female with a surgically sutured vagina does not lead to sufficient excitation to lead to ejaculation, it shortens the latency of ejaculation in an immediately subsequent copulatory situation with a normal female (Hard and Larsson, 1968).

In a further study of this problem, Beach and Whalen (1959) allowed male rats to intromit one, four, or seven times and then, after an imposed interval ranging from 75 to 120 minutes, they observed how many more times the rats would have to intromit before ejaculating. It appears from their results that the greater the number of initial intromissions, the smaller number of additional intromissions needed to produce ejaculation when there are delays of at least 30 minutes following initial intromissions. In general, this study confirms the notion that in some way each intromission added to a pool of excitation that decays at a slow rate but increases with each successive intromission until the threshold for ejaculation is reached (providing delays between intromissions are not too long).

It has been observed that after the first ejaculation the male rat will rest for about five minutes before he will begin to mate again. The second set of intromissions leading to ejaculation differs from the first set as follows: (1) the time between intromissions is less, and (2) fewer intromissions occur before ejaculation (e.g., Larsson, 1956; Beach and Jorden, 1956). This change continues in subsequent bouts of copulation in the series until mating ceases. Beach and Whalen (1959) found that the effect of the first ejaculation, that is, a reduction in time between intromissions, upon the subsequent copulatory bouts in the series lasted up to five hours. Similarly, the effect of the first ejaculation on the number of times intromission is necessary for a subsequent ejaculation was shown to persist for 90 minutes. During this time the number of intromissions necessary to produce an ejaculation was smaller than during the first set of intromissions leading to an ejaculation. The length of time between an ejaculation and a subsequent bout of intromissions also increases as a function of immediately preceding ejaculations. Such behavioral results are likely to be due to an interplay of ejaculatory mechanisms (which can function autonomously at the spinal level, at least in dog and man) and other mechanisms higher in the nervous system.

While there is evidence of mounting excitation with increasing genital stimulation in the male, as measured by readiness to ejaculate, the evidence for the female seems to point in the opposite direction. (This may be because of the different indices used.) A female rat in estrus can be trained to perform a response to obtain sexual stimulation (Bermant, 1961; Pierce and Nuttall, 1961). Using this method, it has been shown that the smaller the amount of preceding sexual stimulation, the faster the response to obtain the next sexual stimulation. A female, for instance, responds much more quickly to obtain more stimulation after a nonpenetrating mount than after nonejaculatory nonpenetrating contacts. Bermant and Westbrook (1966) extended these observations by showing (for instance) that a vaginal plug decreased female motivation for further stimulation whereas anesthetic agents, applied topically to the vaginal opening, increased it, as measured by the reduced latency of the next response. However, it is not certain whether an increase of latency of response after stimulation, such as ejaculation, is due only to a waning of positive motivation or an increase in an aversive component of the stimulation. Female rats in estrus will perform an escape response from a group of sexually active males. Such a response was longest in duration and highest in probability after ejaculatory penetrations by a male and least frequent and shortest in duration after simple mounts.

HORMONES VERSUS SEX OF ANIMAL AS DETERMINANTS OF BEHAVIOR

We have seen that the absence of hormones, male or female, tends to abolish sexual behavior. We may ask whether the type of behavior evoked depends on the specific hormone present or on the sex of the recipient. To state it more concretely, will estrogen injected in a castrated male produce female mating behavior or male mating behavior? The safest generalization is that the behavior produced on administration of a hormone, whether it is androgen or an estrogen, is the behavior appropriate to the sex of the recipient. Castrated males will respond by exhibiting male behavior after the administration of estrogens. This has been shown in rats (Ball, 1939, and Beach, 1942), in capons (Goodale, 1918), and in cats (Green et al., 1957). However, it seems that the effectiveness of estrogens in producing this behavior is not strong. On the other hand, there is only slight evidence that estrogens injected into castrated males may produce female behavior. The evidence on the injection of androgens into spayed females is complicated by the fact that a great deal of masculine behavior is manifested by normal females or by spayed females injected with estrogens. The evocation of female behavior by spayed females treated with androgens has been reported in rats by Beach (1942) and in cats by Green et al. (1957).

Pharmacological Effects on Mating

Drugs that activate adrenergic pathways (low doses of LSD-25, d-amphetamine, methamphetamine, and cocaine) appear to facilitate sexual behavior in males (Bignami, 1966; Leavitt, 1969) whereas anticholinergic agents (scopolamine, atropine) produce disruption of mating. Atropine also almost abolishes lordosis and mounting in female rats (Singer, 1968). Spectacular effects on male sexual behavior have been obtained by reducing brain serotonin levels. Tagiamonte et al. (1969), by administering p-chlorophenylalamine, lowered the brain content of serotonin to about 10 percent of normal, whereas the concentration of norepinephrine fell to 71 percent of that in normal animals. A state of great sexual excitation was produced. Pargyline is a monoamine oxidase inhibitor which increases brain levels of norepinephrine. When pargyline was injected along with p-chlorophenylalamine, sexual excitement became intense. Serotonin concentrations rose to 20 percent of normal, whereas norepinephrine concentration was equal to that of normal animals. This finding suggests that sexual excitation is controlled by a balance between adrenergic and serotoninergic mechanisms in the brain.

Sensory Effects on Mating

Among the lower mammals, the sense of smell is perhaps the most important in mating. For instance, Murphy and Schneider (1970) have found that removal of the olfactory bulbs in the male golden hamster (*Mesocricetus auratus*) led to a complete cessation of mating activity, as well as to a loss of territorial and social behavior. In the rat, the effect of anosmia seems less profound. Black (1942) and Heimer and Larsson (1967) found a considerable decrease in responsiveness among inexperienced males. Bermant and Taylor (1969) investigated these findings further. It could be thought that the anosmic males' decrement was due to the fact that they could not detect the female or that she was in estrus. However, the anosmic males were not slower than normals in achieving initial intromission or to recover from the effects of an ejaculation. The deficit consisted in a large prolongation of the time required to achieve ejaculation once intromission had occurred. These observations held for the first hour of the three-hour test. During the last two hours the differences between normal and anosmic rats tended to disappear, especially when a second female was introduced. A second experiment was made with inexperienced males, and it was found that both initial mounting and ability to achieve ejaculation in the normal time were affected. While olfactory bulb removal has a definite effect on mating, the effect may be through a decrease of testicular function, which has also been noted (Whitten, 1956; Magnotti, 1936).

SEXUAL DIFFERENTIATION

From the above evidence it seems that the effect of a hormone depends on the sex of the recipient, or, more specifically, on the characteristics of the neural tissue which have been established by a process of differentiation at the fetal or neonatal stage. While it seems that in the adult the action of the hormone is merely to activate, it appears that it has a differentiating function while the organism is developing. In the mammal, the presence of testosterone during fetal development (usually supplied by the immature fetal testes) leads to the development of male morphological characters. For instance, if testosterone is administered in utero to female fetuses, such as female rhesus monkeys (Young et al., 1964), a penis and scrotum develop. In the castrated fetal male, on the other hand, there is a development of female sexual apparatus, presumably because testosterone is absent. Of profound importance to the student of behavior is the observation that a similar type of differentiation occurs in the central nervous system as well as in the peripheral sexual apparatus under the same hormonal fetal conditions. The presence of androgens during early stages of development produces an adult that will react to the presence of sex hormones by exhibiting male behavior. Such a behavioral effect has now been demonstrated in rats, guinea pigs, and rhesus monkeys (Young et al., 1964). It has also been possible to show that if males are castrated before the period of differentiation by testosterone, they will develop into adults that display feminine behavior when injected with estrogen and progesterone. In the rat, such a demonstration is feasible. In this species the period in which differentiation occurs appears to be postnatal rather than prenatal, and it ends about the tenth day after birth. It has been reported (Young et al., 1964) that, when primed with female sex hormones, males castrated before they were five days old displayed a very large increase in feminine behavior compared to males castrated at or after the tenth day after birth. "On the one hand, females treated with androgen during the appropriate period show a regression or inhibition of feminine behavior and an accentuation of masculine behavioral traits. Males deprived of the principal source of endogenous androgen during a comparable period show accentuated feminine behavior and the absence of, or greatly diminished capacity for, masculine behavior" (Young et al., 1964).

Of great interest also is the finding in the rhesus monkey that not only is sexual behavior altered but that social patterns characteristic of a particular sex are also reversed in a similar manner. Female monkeys treated with androgens during the stage of differentiation closely resemble males on such indices as facial threats or play patterns.

Cases have been described (Goldfoot et al., 1969; Stern, 1969) where treatment has produced individuals in whom both male and female substrates of behavior have been preserved. For instance, Goldfoot et al. injected neonatally castrated rats with androstenedrone for 20 days after birth. (Androstenedione is an androgen, a male sex hormone secreted along with testosterone by the fetal testes.) When injected with testosterone as adults, they displayed male intromission responses and ejaculation whereas under estrogen and progesterone they showed lordosis, which is a part of the female pattern in rats. It is therefore possible that the function of testosterone in early development is a trophic effect on the substrates of male behavior, together with a suppressor effect on the neural substrates of female behavior.

Genesis of Mating Behavior in Man

The conditions which can be brought about experimentally in rats, guinea pigs, and rhesus monkeys also occur as a result of disease or mishap in man. Individuals may be born with gonads (testes, ovaries) belonging to one sex but a genital morphology resembling the other sex in varying degrees. These are called pseudohermaphrodites. One class of pseudohermaphrodite possesses ovaries but a masculine external genital morphology. This is due to the presence of androgens during fetal development, which may come about in various ways. For example, the mother may be given androgens or the orally active progestational compounds during her pregnancy for therapeutic reasons; or, in a condition known as congenital adrenal hyperplasia, the adrenal cortex of the fetus secretes excessive amounts of androgens. In a second class, the pseudohermaphrodite possesses testes, but a female external genital morphology. This may be caused by subnormal testicular function in the male fetus.

Such pseudohermaphrodites are generally reared as male or female depending on their external genital morphology. In later life they behave in the manner expected of the sex of their upbringing and not of their biological sex as determined by their possession of one or other type of gonad. Because of this conflict between biological sex and cultural or social sex, such cases have been quoted to support the argument that learning and not biologic sex determines sexual behavior (e.g., Hardy, 1964). Such an argument is, however, invalid. From the evidence in animals, we have seen that if hormones during fetal life produce a male type of genital morphology, they also result in male sexual behavior in later life, irrespective of the type of gonad present. Since a pseudohermaphrodite tends to be brought up according to the morphology of the genitalia, we would expect the same result on both the cultural and physiological view of the genesis of sexual behavior.

EFFECTS OF EXPERIENCE ON MATING

In view of the fact that mating behavior tends to be dependent on the presence of certain hormones, we may ask whether the hormones evoke entire integrated sequences of behavior when they first stimulate the relevant parts of the nervous system or whether mating behavior is gradually perfected through experience. Species differences appear to be a factor governing the role of experience in mating.

Rats, both male and female, mate in the same way on the first occasion as on subsequent occasions; and so do some dogs and cats (Beach, 1958). However, Nissen (1953) reported that sexually naive chimpanzees need many periods of contact before they will mate. It is difficult to assess the importance of experience in the development of mating activity and other instinctive activity. Many assume that sexual activity is partially learnt. But it has not been made entirely clear what is meant by learning sexual activity. Is it learning in the sense of maze learning where the animal begins to manifest correct responses rather than incorrect responses? Or is it learning in the sense that a rat learns to eat in an originally unfamiliar place, where fear of strange surroundings had interfered with the feeding response?

There have been many studies on this problem. Hayward (1957) has shown that when immature male rats were trained to avoid females in heat, they would show inhibition of mating behavior when they became mature. Similarly, Rasmussen (1955) found that when male rats were given an electric shock whenever they attempted to mount females, they would later attempt to copulate with other males more frequently than with females. Also, Beach et al., (1956) were able to inhibit sexual responsiveness in male rats by subjecting them to electric shock every time they attempted to mate. These studies show that sexual behavior is similar to other types of behavior in that it is susceptible to interference effects. Particularly interesting are studies which have shown enhancement of sexual activity when as a result of learning one would expect the opposite to occur. Kagan and Beach (1953) reared immature male rats under two conditions: (1) one group of rats was periodically exposed to females, and (2) another group of rats was completely isolated from females. It was found that during testing the isolated group copulated more frequently than the group which had been given prepuberal contact. Kagan and Beach attributed this result to the interfering effects of previously learned playful activity. These results show the importance of interfering behavior tendencies which may mask behavior patterns which are not learned. However, in similar studies, Zimbardo (1958), who worked with the rat, obtained the opposite result of Valenstein et al. (1955), who worked with the guinea pig. Supporting the notion that some deficit occurs during isolated rearing are the studies of Gerall et al. (1967) and Folman and Drori (1965), who found the deficit to consist of inappropriate of clumsy responses toward the female and not of a lack of interest or motivation.

Another experiment, with results at first sight paradoxical, has been reported by Beach and Fowler (1959). These authors subjected male rats in a particular environment to a series of painful electrical shocks. They found that these rats later mated in this environment but that the number of intromissions to ejaculation was actually lower than in rats in a normal environment. As explanation for this behavior, these workers suggested that autonomic arousal due to fear of shock has a facilitatory effect on orgasm.

Barfield and Sachs (1968), continuing this line of inquiry, selected males for sexual vigor and gave them electric shock every 30 seconds during mating tests. Almost three quarters of the intromissions occurred within five seconds of the electric shock. The continuing shock also had the effect of shortening by about a third the interval between ejaculation and the next copulatory bouts. A similar facilitation of sexual responding was demonstrated by Caggiula and Erberger (1969) with inexperienced males. While electric shock was effective in enhancing the amount of copulation with receptive females, loud noise was ineffective. It is therefore difficult to reconcile this observation to the notion that autonomic arousal is responsible for this enhancement effect. It is possible that copulation in the natural state is accompanied by rivalry and fighting between males. A copulatory situation without such agonistic behavior may therefore lack an important natural ingredient.

A series of experiments performed by Rabedeau and Whalen (1959) is especially pertinent to the idea that experience in mating leads to increased speed toward copulation mainly through elimination of competing responses. In their first experiment, they were able to show that male rats selected on the basis of their slowness to initiate coitus showed a very large decrement in latency to copulate as a result of copulatory experience. The results of this experiment could be explained in terms of an increase in arousability or learning to initiate copulation. However, in their second experiment of the series Rabedeau and Whalen selected males that initated coitus quickly. These rats were then divided into two groups. The first group was allowed to have sexual experience while the second group was not. To see if learning in terms of a higher "arousability" through experience had taken place, these workers castrated both groups of animals. This had the effect of lengthening latencies to coitus, presumably by lowering sex drive. Without such a procedure, latencies would have been so short for both groups that any effect of experience could not have been detected. However, in this second experiment no significant difference due to prior experience could be found, although latencies to coitus were increased to a range where differences due to experience should have been detected.

It may be that a competing tendency has to wear off in rats which are slow to initiate coitus, whereas such a tendency is absent in animals which initiate coitus without delay, so that experience does not differentially remove a competing tendency.

In such species as the dog, cat, and rat, a sexually inexperienced female will mate and no learning is apparent in subsequent matings. However, Whalen (1963) has shown that sexually inexperienced female cats permit coitus more quickly after experience of intromission, thus showing a learning effect. From Whalen's description it seems that such learning was due to a lessening importance of conflicting aggressive tendencies. Whalen describes this as follows: "Naive female cats would not readily mate in the laboratory even though they had been treated extensively with endogenous estrogen, and would assume the mating posture either spontaneously in the home cage or in response to perineal tapping by the investigator. When placed with a male, the naive queen would hiss and strike at the male when he approached. Usually this resistance by the female was rapidly overcome when the investigator held the female permitting the male to mount and achieve the initial intromission. Thereafter, mounting and intromission occurred without intervention."

ABNORMALITIES OF SEXUAL BEHAVIOR AND BRAIN LESIONS

Kluver and Bucy (1939) noted that animals with their temporal lobes removed manifested, among other symptoms, "hypersexuality" (see Chapter 10). Schreiner and Kling (1956) demonstrated similar effects in the agouti, monkey, cat, and lynx, with more restricted lesions confined mainly to the amygdala and the overlying pyriform cortex. These effects appear mostly in the male and do not occur in the absence of sex hormones. Green et al. (1957) reported that the so-called hypersexual symptoms could be produced by lesions of the pyriform cortex alone, without damage to the neighboring amygdala. They found that male cats with such lesions differed from normal cats by copulating with other species, anaesthetized animals, and kittens; by masturbating; and by indulging in sexual activities outside their own territory (Fig. 15–2).

It might be argued that the effect of this lesion is irritative and that it acts simply to increase male copulatory tendencies in a similar way as the lesions inflicted on females by Hillarp et al. (1954). This argument is strengthened by the results of an experiment conducted by Green and co-workers where they inflicted similar lesions on female cats. After the operation a few of these cats began to show male sexual patterns, such as pouncing, mounting, neck grips, and genital sniffing. This behavior persisted in spite of vicious rebuffs by the animal being molested. That some abnormality of stimulation of the hypothalamus may have been occurring is indicated by the finding that one of these female cats ovulated spontaneously. In normal cats, ovulation only occurs as a consequence of mounting by a male through the intermediacy of the hypothalamic control of the anterior pituitary. However, Gastaut (1952) has reported that cats with rhinencephalic lesions show estrous behavior without accompanying changes in the reproductive organs. This finding is against the hypothesis of Schreiner and Kling that the "hypersexuality" observed in their male animals is due to an increase in sex hormones produced by the lesion. If this were true, then physiological signs of estrus should have been produced by such lesions in females. On the other hand, it is possible that differences in lesions were such that no direct comparison could be made. However, such findings do not exclude a direct irritative effect on mechanisms subserving sexual arousal in the hypothalamus.

On the other hand, it would be equally plausible to assign this disorder

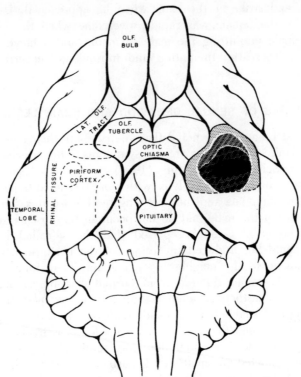

FIG. 15–2. Site of lesion which produces "hypersexuality" in cats. (Fig. 2, Green, J. D., Clemente, C. D., and DeGroot, J., *J. Comp. Neur., 108,* 522)

to causes similar to those responsible for indiscriminate eating due to lesions of the amygdala. In this case it was argued that an animal must avoid various properties possessed by certain substances which would be deleterious if ingested. The disruption of this mechanism was postulated as an explanation of the effects of amygdalectomy on feeding habits. Here it might similarly be argued that the occasions for copulation must also be delimited by attractions toward certain properties and repulsions from other properties. Copulation with "unsuitable" sexual partners could be interpreted as due to an absence of repulsion from them, rather than as an increase in their attractive properties. In support of this view is the finding that these animals also tend to show increased tameness. Fear and rage often seem to be absent. If these factors were absent, it would be natural to expect copulatory attempts in an environment where these attempts would normally be inhibited by fear and on animals which would ordinarily evoke fear or aggression.

There have also been reports of human cases where similar areas of the brain have been excised (as in the animal studies quoted above) in attempted to ameliorate the condition of patients suffering from epilepsy or schizophrenia. Terzian and Dalle Ore (1955) reported the case of a young male epileptic with a bilateral removal of the anterior portion of the temporal lobes and the amygdaloid nucleus (similar to the lesions inflicted by Kluver and Bucy). This unfortunate man was reduced to a state bordering on imbecility, and he became docile and manageable in contrast to his previous dangerously violent tendencies. Besides other symptoms unrelated to sex, there appeared frequent masturbation and exhibitionistic, and some homosexual, tendencies. However, with the exception of masturbation, these tendencies were only verbal in their expression. Sawa et al. (1954) reported the case of five male schizophrenics and one male epileptic with bilateral amygdalectomy. (This lesion appears to correspond to the area removed by Schreiner and Kling.) Though the patients were observed up to four months after the operations, little accentuation of sexual behavior was found. "There was no such sexual response as a frequent erection of the penis as was reported in Kluver and Bucy's monkeys; the patients simply enjoyed talks on sexual topics to the nursing women, going no further than taking hands" (Sawa et al., p. 326). Taken in the context of the patients' other symptoms, such behavior can hardly be taken to represent hypersexuality. However, in these cases it is difficult to be sure of the precise extent and location of the lesion.

MATERNAL BEHAVIOR

Maternal behavior is a name for a set of behavior tendencies involved in care of the young. This may include such heterogeneous activities as nest building, retrieving of young, and feeding the young. In the cage-bred rat, maternal behavior consists of building a nest, cleaning the pups, nursing them, and retrieving them when they leave the nest. With the probable exception of retrieving, such behavior is similar also for the caged domestic rabbit. However, when the same rabbit is released and permitted to live under seminatural conditions, a much larger repertoire of maternal activity is discovered. The pregnant female digs a tunnel that terminates in a spherical chamber; the tunnel is then sealed from the outside. Some time later the female gathers wisps of dry grass, opens up the nest again, and lines the base of the spherical chamber with the grass. She also plucks fur from her belly to lay on top of the grass. The entrance to the tunnel is again sealed. The female again enters the tunnel when the young are born. She nurses them once a day and seals up the entrance of the tunnel after every visit. When the female stops nursing, she makes a hole in the sealed entrance just large enough for the young to emerge through. During the period of nursing the female keeps well away from the entrance of the tunnel. The sealing of the entrance is so well executed that it is almost impossible for the human eye to distinguish it from the surrounding earth. If one of the young is taken out of the nest and placed near the nursing female, there is no reaction besides sniffing. It is clear that retrieving has no place in the natural repertoire of this species of animal.

Thus maternal behavior is a complex of activities which differs from one species to another. Such behavior is evoked by an administration or withdrawal of hormones. A combination of hormones found in a pregnant female just before parturition is effective in producing maternal behavior. However, prolactin or lactogenic hormone secreted by the anterior pituitary is the most important of these hormones. Prolactin causes the development of the mammary glands and milk secretion. Estrogen, on the other hand, has been shown by Hain (1935) to inhibit maternal responses, even when the dose is too small to interrupt lactation. Injections of prolactin into virgin females and males also cause retrieving of the young. However, Leblond (1940) found that such activities will appear when these animals are simply exposed to young. Such cases could be analogous to the observation of Witschi (1935), who found that when a female pigeon saw another incubating female this was sufficient to evoke secretion of lactogenic hormone by the pituitary, thus inducing the changes necessary for crop milk secretion.

The stimuli which evoke maternal behavior vary greatly even within one species. The writer has observed a rat which would repeatedly retrieve its own tail. It would leave the nest, see its tail, pick it up carefully between its teeth, and deposit it in the nest. Models of young rats possessing varying levels of crudity can also produce retrieving behavior. In general, however, it seems that the younger the pups, the greater the tendency for maternal behavior to be evoked (e.g., Wiesner and Sheard, 1933). This does not mean that occasionally even adult animals will not evoke maternal behavior. The writer has observed female ferrets (*Putorius vulgaris*) retrieving other adult female ferrets with great persistence and vigor.

The execution of maternal activities such as nest building and retrieving young depends to a large extent on exteroceptive cues. For instance, the young must normally be seen or heard squealing after they have left the nest before the mother will retrieve them. However, it seems that various sensory avenues are to some extent interchangeable in the rat. Wiesner and Sheard (1933) found that rats rendered anosmic and deaf still built nests and retrieved young. Somewhat similar findings have been reported by Beach and Jaynes (1956). These authors, however, found that blinding, rendering rats anosmic, and severing the sensory nerves to the snout at the same time completely destroyed maternal behavior. A combination of two of these handicaps produced serious impairment in the care of the young.

That sensory avenues are not always interchangeable for maternal behavior is shown by the behavior of the hen. If the hen can only *see* a distressed chick that manifests its distress clearly to a human observer, then the hen takes no notice. However, the hen need only *hear* the distress call of the chick, and *not* see it, for appropriate maternal action to take place.

A decrease in parental efficiency has also been reported by Beach (1937), Stone (1939), and Davis (1939) after extensive cortical lesions, the size of the lesion being reported as more important than its placement. However, Stamm (1955) observed that removal of portions of the cingulate and retrosplenial cortex, comprising only about 16 percent of the cortex, impairs maternal behavior very seriously, whereas control lesions of a similar size elsewhere were without noticeable effect. Rosvold (1949) reported that, in a rat, extended electroconvulsive shock during the last half of pregnancy abolishes nest building and care of the young. Though such a finding is not unexpected, its explanation is obscure.

Nest Building

In a majority of instances, domestic rabbits that are permitted to live under seminatural conditions will work at nest building or burrowing only during pregnancy. In many other species, however, we find that some nest building or shelter construction takes place with no particular relation to the care of the young. However, there may be an enhancement of nest building during pregnancy, as in the case of the laboratory rat (Kinder, 1927) and mouse (Koller, 1952, 1956). Koller (1952) also observed that administration of prolactin did not induce nest building in the mouse. It has been observed that hypophysectomy or thyroidectomy in rats leads to increased nest building (Richter, 1941). Such effects are probably due to the efforts of the animal to conserve heat, since there is a drop in the animal's temperature. Koller (1956) has induced increased nest building in mice by shaving their hair, and Kinder (1927) has increased nest building in rats by lowering room temperature. It seems that progesterone levels are important in regulating nest building. Koller (1952, 1956) has observed that administration of progesterone to male and female mice leads to an increase in nest building. However, administration of estrogens leads to a decrease in nest building in females but an increase in males. A relationship in the contrary direction exists in rabbits, where it has been shown that removal of the corpus luteum during pregnancy leads to immediate nest-building behavior, including plucking of fur (Klein, 1952, 1956).

THE ENDOCRINE SYSTEM

Because of the importance of glandular factors in instinctive activities, it is necessary to summarize the relevant information about the functioning of the endocrine glands. These glands secrete into the blood stream minute amounts of substances called hormones. They enter into and modify various biochemical processes in the body and thus exert their influence on various aspects of physiological functioning.

Many of the endocrine secretions directly affect the functioning of the nervous system. The secretions of the thyroid influence metabolism and the utilization of carbohydrates. In adulthood, an absence of thyroid hormone can cause mental dulling and even psychotic symptoms (myxedematous madness). A congenital malfunction of this gland causes cretinism, which manifests itself by extreme mental retardation and lack of growth.

Another organ secreting a hormone important in nervous function is the adrenal medulla. Epinephrine, which is secreted by the gland, has widespread effects that chiefly reinforce the sympathetic nervous system. It increases heart rate, induces more rapid blood clotting, increases sugar output by the liver, and in addition influences the central nervous system. It has been claimed that epinephrine acts directly on the reticular formation (Bonvallet et al., 1954; Dell, 1958). EEG activation can be induced by the administration of epinephrine. Porter (1952) also reports EEG activation of the posterior hypothalamus in response to epinephrine. In this way, secretion of epinephrine by the adrenal medulla might prolong and intensify arousal of the organism.

Other glands are important as regulators of the balance of various substances in the body. The beta cells of the pancreas secrete insulin, which maintains the level of sugar in the blood by promoting metabolism of glucose. A deficiency of insulin secretion, as in diabetes mellitus, leads to an excess of glucose, causing hyperglycemia. The alpha cells of the pancreas, on the other hand, produce glucagon which may promote glucose uptake.

Another gland that is useful in regulating levels of various substances in the blood in the parathyroid. This gland maintains calcium and phosphorus balance in the blood. Its removal causes loss of calcium and enhanced levels of phosphorus with consequent tetany. The potassium-sodium balance is maintained by hormones of the adrenal cortex. Among other symptoms, such as general muscular weakness, removal of the adrenal gland leads to rapid loss of sodium.

Of great importance from the behavioral point of view are the gonads. The male gonads secrete testosterone, which causes development of the male physical characteristics. These physical characteristics vary from species to species; in man, these are the changes seen at puberty. There is growth of pubic hair, growth of facial hair, increased hirsutism (though this varies from one genetic group to another), changes in the voice, development of the penis, and an increase in muscular development. On the other hand, decrease in testosterone level, as in castration, causes changes on the surface and structure of the penis (Beach and Levinson, 1950). Ovarian hormones in the female influence physical development by causing changes in the genitalia and the appearance of secondary sexual characteristics. Ovarian secretions are for the greater part cyclic. These cycles are intimately connected with the activity of the anterior pituitary, which in turn is under the control of the hypothalamus.

Anterior Pituitary and Sex Hormones

The endocrine glands are controlled partly by the nervous system but mainly by chemical factors in the blood. Of these chemical factors, the most important comes from the anterior pituitary gland. This organ secretes a set of hormones that in turn stimulate many other endocrine glands to secrete their particular hormones. For instance, the anterior pituitary secretes a luteinizing hormone that causes the development and maintenance of the interstitial cells of the testis and also affects the ovaries. The anterior pituitary also liberates follicle-stimulating hormone which causes the development of spermatozoa-producing tissue in the testis. The same hormone also causes the development of the ovary follicles. Under the influence of the luteinizing hormone from the pituitary, the testes produce their own hormones, called the androgens (testosterone, androstenodione). These in turn produce secondary sex characteristics and the behavioral tendencies of the male. Similarly, the female gonads (the ovaries) secrete hormones which produce female secondary sex characteristics in a complex cycle called the estrous cycle.

At the beginning of the estrous cycle, the follicles of the ovaries begin developing when the anterior pituitary secretes a follicle-stimulating hormone. As the immature follicle develops, it secretes estrogen. Estrogen then stimulates the anterior pituitary to produce the luteinizing hormone. The combination of the follicle-stimulating hormone and luteinizing hormone causes further development of the follicle, which thus secretes more estrogen. These large amounts of estrogen have two main effects: they alter the uterus and vagina (including their epithelium) and they change the ratio in which the pituitary secretes luteinizing and follicle-stimulating hormone. As a result, more luteinizing and less follicle-stimulating hormone is secreted. As this occurs, the ovum is released by the rupture of the follicle (ovulation). After the ovum has left it, the ruptured follicle develops into the corpus luteum, continuing to secrete estrogen and also progesterone, a hormone which occurs in large quantities in pregnancy. These two hormones prepare the epithelium of the uterus for implantation of the ovum should fertilization of the ovum occur. If it does not, the corpus luteum regresses, and also the level of estrogen and progesterone. This drop in the level of these hormones causes the pituitary to secrete follicle-stimulating hormone again. This begins the next estrous cycle.

Parallel to these physiological changes is a behavioral cycle of female receptivity, called heat, which occurs at the time of ovulation. In mammals with short estrous cycles, like rats and mice, progesterone is not secreted during the estrous cycle. It is, however, produced through the development of the corpus luteum if fertilization of the ovum, and then pregnancy, occurs.

The outline of events occurring during the estrous cycle is basically similar for all spontaneously ovulating mammals. In the human, however, the lining of the uterus is sloughed off with resultant menstrual bleeding, which should not be identified with heat or estrus in lower mammals. In most spontaneously ovulating mammals, copulation occurs only during the estrus or heat. However, as we ascend the phylogenetic scale from monkey to man, a progressive independence of intercourse with time of ovulation is observed. In some mammals, such as the rabbit, ovulation does not occur in spontaneous cycles but only after sexual excitement is produced in the female by a mounted male or by genital stimulation.

Neural Influence on the Anterior Pituitary

It has been shown that the secretions of the anterior pituitary are of the greatest importance in regulating sexual functions. However, this structure is itself under the influence of neural factors. For instance, the estrous cycle has been described as if it were merely due to an interplay between the anterior pituitary and the ovary. However, it is known that in at least a part of this cycle the hypothalamus plays an indispensable role. Similar evidence for the importance of neural factors will be described as suggested by behavioral evidence and then by physiological methods.

Birds. Most birds are seasonal breeders. Gonadal development, which is under the control of the pituitary, and plumage changes, which may be under direct pituitary control or under indirect influence of the pituitary through the gonads, occur only at certain times in the year. Some birds adapt themselves immediately to a change of seasons when transported across the equator (Marshall, 1942). It has been shown that seasonal changes in light intensity stimulate pituitary gonadotropic activity in many species (Rowan, 1938). It seems that ovulation, which is under the control of the pituitary, occurs only during daylight in the domestic fowl (Warren and Scott, 1936). Artificial exclusion of light during the day and night lighting can lead to a reversal in the time of ovulation.

However, the dependence of endocrine changes on ambient illumination varies from one species to another. In the sparrow (*Passer domesticus, Linnaeus*), ovarian development is relatively unaffected by manipulation of the length of light to which this bird is exposed. Neural factors which emanate from nesting and mating activities seem to be important in bringing about the sparrow's ovarian development (Riley and Witschi, 1938). Darling (1938) has brought forward evidence that stimulation from other members of a flock may be a strong factor in bringing about the requisite endocrine development in the individual member of a flock. A good example of the importance of this type of stimulation occurs in the pigeon. A female pigeon in isolation does not ovulate. However, homosexual activity between two female pigeons causes both of them to lay eggs. Further, ovulation occurs if a female is simply placed within sight of a male pigeon, or another female, or even if she is supplied with a mirror so that the reflection of herself acts as the stimulus. Further, when the male pigeon sees an incubating female, a lactogenic hormone is secreted by the pituitary of the male pigeon, thus inducing the changes necessary for crop milk secretion (Witschi, 1935).

For any species of bird, the female generally lays a constant number of eggs in a clutch. It seems that the control of the number of eggs laid is through an inhibition of the ovulatory process (initiated by the pituitary), caused by stimulation produced by the eggs themselves after laying has occurred. If eggs are withdrawn as they are laid, laying continues (Witschi, 1935).

Mammals. In mammals, neural factors also play an important role in regulating pituitary secretion. As in the case of birds, transporting mammals across the equator to the opposite hemisphere leads to a change in their breeding rhythm that corresponds with an alteration of the seasons. Such changes have been observed in sheep, deer, and many other species (Marshall, 1937). The reproductive rhythm of many common mammals is affected by variations in environmental lighting. Harris (1960) quotes as examples the mouse, rat, ferret, hedgehog, cottontail rabbit, cat, raccoon, and goat. The influence of environmental lighting has been most extensively studied in the ferret (*Putorius vulgaris*). In the northern hemisphere, the female of this species does not exhibit estrous activity between September and February. However, estrus can be induced by placing the animal in 16 hours of light per day during this period. It has been demonstrated (Harris, 1960) that this dependence of estrus on light exists because of a connection between the hypothalamus and the anterior pituitary gland.

In some mammals, ovulation is dependent not on a cycle but on some form of external stimulation (as was seen in some birds). Such is the case in the rabbit, ferret, cat, ground squirrel, and mink (Harris, 1960). Here ovulation depends on stimulation from a male or stimulation of parts of the genitalia, which results in a gonadotropic discharge from the pars distalis of the anterior pituitary.

There is also a neural influence on other endocrines through the anterior pituitary. Selye (1950) has drawn attention to and summarized much of the work showing the effect of emotional stress on the adrenal cortex. Discharge of adrenal cortical hormone follows stress in many species, such as the mouse, rat, rabbit, and human.

There is also evidence that the action of the thyroid is to some extent dependent on the nervous system. Emotional and physical stress lead to a lowered secretion of thyroid hormone (e.g., Brown-Grant et al., 1954). It also seems that overactivity of the thyroid in Graves' disease follows upon emotional disturbance (e.g., Thompson and Blount, 1954). Therefore it is thought that the endocrine system is to a large extent controlled by the nervous system acting through the anterior pituitary.

Mechanism of Anterior Pituitary Control by the Hypothalamus

The behavioral evidence discussed above showing how sensory signals may modify the working of the endocrine system naturally leads us to ask how this control is exercised. Anatomically speaking, the anterior pituitary is close to the hypothalamus, joined to it by the hypophyseal stalk. The anterior lobe of the pituitary (also called the adenohypophysis) is subdivided into the pars distalis, pars tuberalis, and pars intermedia. The main secretory center is in the pars distalis.

It seems clear that messages from the hypothalamus excite the anterior pituitary to secrete gonadotrophic, adrenocorticotrophic, and thyrotrophic hormones. First, electrical stimulation of the hypothalamus releases these hormones from the pituitary. However, direct electrical stimulation of the anterior pituitary does not produce this effect (Harris, 1948). Second, transplantation of the anterior pituitary to other parts of the brain, away from the hypothalamus, causes absence of normal function by the transplant even though an adequate blood supply redevelops. Harris and Jacobsohn (1952) found that in such transplant cases there were no estrous cycles and that organs of reproduction suffered complete atrophy. Animals with a transplanted pituitary also showed marked atrophy of the adrenal cortex, though not to quite such a degree as when the pituitary was completely removed. Similar findings have been made concerning thyroid activity following a pituitary transplant.

However, the mode of control of the hypothalamus over the anterior pituitary is not by means of nervous pathways. It appears that the pars distalis is devoid of innervation by the hypothalamus. It seems, instead, that the anterior pituitary is stimulated to secretion by blood-borne chemical messages originating in the hypothalamus. The normal functioning of the anterior pituitary correlates well with the intactness of the blood supply passing from the hypothalamus and its state of regeneration after section of the hypophyseal stalk. Transplants of anterior pituitary tissue begin to function normally when their blood supply from the hypothalamus develops. It seems that there are cells in the hypothalamus (which have been called neurosecretory cells) that secrete substances capable of causing the anterior pituitary, in turn, to secrete hormones. These neurosecretory cells send out fibers that come into close proximity with blood vessels running into the anterior pituitary. It is thought that the secretion passes from these fibers of the neurosecretory cells into the circulatory system supplying the anterior pituitary, thus stimulating it to secrete, or inhibiting it from secreting.

Role of the Hypothalamus in Anterior Pituitary Control. As was stated above, the anterior pituitary secretes luteinizing hormone and follicle-stimulating hormone, besides other hormones. These secretions have a gonadotrophic effect in both sexes. In the female, the release of these hormones is cyclic; in the male, such a cycle as the estrous cycle is absent. It has been demonstrated that the pituitary itself is not sexually differentiated but that the cyclic character of its secretion in the female is imposed by the hypothalamus. A pituitary taken from a male rat and transplanted into the appropriate position in a female maintains a normal estrous cycle and pregnancy (Harris and Jacobsohn, 1952). If ovarian tissue is transplanted into a castrated male rat, follicular ripening occurs, but the cycle of phenomena described above is absent. This shows that it is not the presence of the ovary and its influence on the pituitary which causes the cycle.

It has also been shown by Harris and Jacobsohn (1952) that when pituitaries are taken from neonate rats and transplanted under the tuber cinereum of adult females that had been hypophysectomized, they produced an estrous cycle long before this cycle would have appeared in the original animal from which the pituitary had been taken. It therefore seems that the onset of puberty is also in some way produced by neural mechanisms. It has also been found that precocious puberty in young rats can be induced by hypothalamic lesions (Donovan and van der Werff ten Bosch, 1956). Such findings should be compared with clinical observations where precocious puberty occurs in cases of small hypothalamic tumors (Bauer, 1954). In these cases the location of the tumors is different; they are found in the region of the mammillary bodies. Further evidence that hypothalamic lesions affect pituitary function is provided by Sawyer and Robinson (1956), who reported genital atrophy and anestrus in female cats following lesions of the ventromedial nucleus, premammillary region, and the mammillary body. Similar findings have been reported on rabbits with tuberal lesions involving the arcuate and the base of the ventromedial nuclei (Sawyer, 1957).

The fact that this hypothalamic area is involved as a detector in the homeostatic regulation of hormone level is shown by the work of Lisk (1962) on the rat and by Davidson and Sawyer (1961) on the rabbit. Implants of estrogen in the basal tuberal-medial eminence region produce ovarian atrophy.

In guinea pigs and rats, lesions of the paraventricular nuclei behind the optic chiasma result in a state of permanent vaginal estrus. This effect seems to be due to the abolition of the rhythmic release of luteinizing hormone and the constant secretion of follicle-stimulating hormone. Such estrus, however, is correlated not with behavioral receptivity but with lack of receptivity. However, Greer (1953) found that if daily injections of small amounts of progesterone were given to these animals, the return of cyclical changes in the vagina followed. Caging with a male can also lead to an interruption of estrus in these animals. It should be noted in this regard that ovulation can be blocked in rats by exposing them to continuous illumination (Bunn and Everett, 1957).

Donovan and van der Werff ten Bosch (1956a) reported that estrus was brought on early in ferrets by the placement of lesions bilaterally behind the optic chiasma. A similar result has been obtained by these workers (1956) in bringing about precocious puberty in the rat.

Experiments involving direct electrical stimulation also confirm the view that signals from the hypothalamus control the activity of the anterior pituitary. Harris (1948) found that stimulation of the tuber cinereum for three minutes was sufficient to produce ovulation. On the other hand, if such stimulation was applied as long as 7.5 hours directly to the anterior pituitary, ovulation did not occur.

With regard to the thyrotropic and adrenocorticotrophic function of the pituitary, a certain amount of spontaneous secretion occurs even when the anterior pituitary is independent of the hypothalamus. This may be contrasted with the case of the gonadotrophic function of the anterior pituitary, which depends overwhelmingly on hypothalamic influence.

Feedback Mechanism Controlling Hormone Level. Injection of adrenal cortical hormone in an intact animal leads to atrophy of the adrenal cortex. Administration of thiouracil, which lowers the effective level of thyroid hormone in the body, leads to an enlargement of the thyroid gland. Such phenomena, coupled with the fact that the level of testicular, thyroid, and adrenal cortical hormone stays constant, suggest the action of a feedback mechanism. Indeed it seems that the anterior pituitary increases its secretion of thyrotrophic hormone when the thyroid level falls. This has the effect of stimulating the growth of the thyroid and its secretion of the thyroid hormone. However, when the thyroid level rises, this has the effect of decreasing secretion of thyrotrophic hormone by the pituitary. When the thyroid level decreases below a certain point as a result of a decrease in the secretion of thyrotrophic hormone by the pituitary, the production of thyrotrophic hormone increases. Such an arrangement will evidently serve to keep the level of thyroid hormone stable around a certain point.

Nature of the Hormone-Stabilizing Mechanism

As has been stated above, an excess of a certain hormone leads to a lessened output of this hormone by the appropriate gland as the trophic hormone output of the anterior pituitary, provoking this secretion, is cut down as a result. We may ask whether the excessive hormone acts directly on the pituitary, causing a decrease by this organ of the relevant trophic hormone, or whether it acts on the hypothalamus, which then cuts down its activation of the relevant part of the anterior pituitary. It seems that both mechanisms may be partly involved. It appears that the anterior pituitary can react directly to an excess of hormone by cutting down its output. For instance, in the case of the thyroid, von Euler and Holmgren (1956) reported that when extremely small doses of thyroxine were injected into the pituitary, the action of the thyroid gland was inhibited. On the other hand, an excess of hormone does not lead the hypothalamus to cut its activation of the thyrotrophic secretion of the pituitary. It was found by von Euler and Holmgren that injections of similar doses of thyroxine into the hypothalamus were without effect. However, a hormonal deficiency does not stimulate the pituitary to increase its output of the relevant hormone, or (to be entirely safe) does not do so in the absence of certain hypothalamic tissue. In a normal animal a partial excision of the thyroid gland or a unilateral adrenalectomy leads to a hypertrophy of the remaining glandular tissue. Similarly, administration of thiouracil, which diminishes the effective concentration of thyroid, leads to hypertrophy of the whole thyroid in an intact animal. However, in the rat, large anterior lesions of the hypothalamus prevent these compensatory responses of the thyroid (Greer, 1952).

Lesions in the region of the anterior median eminence have a similar effect in the case of the adrenal cortex. This has been demonstrated by Ganong and Hume (1954) on dogs and Fulford and McCann (1955) on rats. However, it was found in the dog that such lesions still led to adrenal atrophy following administration of exogenous sources of cortisone. This agrees with the view, stated above, that the pituitary itself responds to an increase in the relevant hormone by diminishing output of the matching trophic hormone, but that hypothalamic centers have to be intact if an increase of trophic hormone is to occur in response to a deficit of the matching hormone. The areas that on removal impair the ability of the pituitary to increase trophic hormone secretion in response to a deficit of hormone have been found upon electrical stimulation to provoke discharge of trophic hormones. Lesions of these regions also result in slow atrophy of the glands responsive to the trophic hormones. It seems from the above findings that the stabilizing mechanism operating in hormonal control is of some complexity. It is not completely understood.

chapter 16

Hunger and Thirst

People and animals usually become hungry or thirsty when they have not had anything to eat or drink for some time. When food or water is then made available, they usually will not only consume the appropriate substances but also ingest them in the right amount. In this way they are able to maintain themselves in good health and regulate their body weight within close limits. What is known of the mechanism which accomplishes the quantitative regulation of eating and drinking will be the subject of the first section of this chapter. In the second section we shall discuss the way in which qualitative regulation is carried out; that is, how in response to its bodily needs an animal selects its diet from among the many substances in its environment.

We shall begin by considering how a shortage of food or water is translated by the body and the nervous system into the actions of eating or drinking.

Nature of the Initiating Physiological Change in Thirst

Osmotic Thirst. Though we usually drink when we are short of water, water loss in itself is not the immediate cause of drinking. Thirst may occur when there is no decrease in total body volume of water. For instance, an injection of hypertonic saline will produce a strong thirst. Further, depletion of water may occur under some circumstances without producing thirst. Darrow and Yannet (1935) report that dogs lacking in water and also salt depleted showed no thirst. One interpretation of this finding is that salt depletion had lowered the effective concentration and consequently the osmotic pressure of the extracellular fluids. Therefore there was no withdrawal of intracellular water, even though there had been a total water loss which, under normal conditions, would have been sufficient to withdraw water from inside the cells.

An alternative hypothesis is that there has to be an increase in salt concentration in the whole body before thirst can occur. However, Gilman (1937) made it clear that thirst is not merely a reflexion of the hypertonicity of the whole body system but that thirst is caused by the withdrawal of water from inside the body cells. He produced equal increments of osmotic pressure in dogs by injecting urea or sodium chloride. He found that drinking was greater after saline injections than after urea injections. It is known that urea passes easily through cell membranes whereas sodium chloride does not. As a result, there would be very little alteration in the relative osmotic pressure gradient between the intra- and extracellular fluid after injecting urea but a great deal of change in this gradient after injecting sodium chloride. Hence the sodium chloride would act to withdraw water from inside the body cells into the extracellular fluid until the osmotic pressures inside and outside the cell were more nearly equal.

This mechanism of the initiation of thirst has an interesting though paradoxical practical consequence. Dill (1938) reported that the loss of equal amounts of water through perspiration produced unequal amounts of thirst, depending on whether this loss occurred in men who are acclimatized or unacclimatized to heat. Men that were unacclimatized felt less thirst after they had lost a given amount of water through perspiration than men who were acclimatized. The reason for this is that men who were not acclimatized lost more salt in an equal volume of sweat than men who were acclimatized. As a result, there was more increase in extracellular osmotic pressure where more salt was retained per unit of water excreted as sweat (that is, in the acclimatized man, whose sweat is less salty).

Further evidence for the osmometric theory of the genesis of thirst is provided by another experiment of Darrow and Yannet (1935). If thirst is the consequence of the effective osmotic pressure of extracellular fluids on the body cells, but not of total water loss, then relative dehydration of the extracellular fluids should not produce thirst, provided that water is not withdrawn from inside cells. This was achieved by the intraperitoneal injection in dogs of 5 percent glucose. After this solution had made its way into the cells, the investigators withdrew an equivalent volume of fluid from each animal. As a result, though the tongue and mucous membranes of the mouth became dry, the animals did not display any signs of thirst. Sufficient water from the glucose solution had entered the body cells.

Extracellular osmotic pressure also promotes release of antidiuretic hormone which reduces water excretion (Gilman and Goodman, 1937).

Volemic Thirst. There is now some doubt whether a simple increase in extracellular osmotic pressure is the only cause of drinking. Fitzsimons (1961) found that simple decrease in fluid volume, such as that caused by bleeding, can also induce drinking. Experimenting with rats, Fitzsimons (1961) compared drinking induced by bleeding with that induced by an injection of sodium chloride. Onset of drinking was immediate in the chloride-treated group; in the other group there was no drinking in the first half hour. However, the total amount of drinking during six hours was much smaller in the rats treated with sodium chloride. This would suggest that some further mediating change occurs when there is isotonic volume depletion. (However, blood loss does not always result in increased drinking [Oatley, 1964; Fitzsimons, 1961; Schnieden, 1962].)

In contrast to osmotic thirst, where the increased osmotic pressure of the extracellular fluid acts directly on the central nervous system, volemic thirst has to be translated into biochemical changes at the peripheral level. It is these biochemical changes which, in turn, act on the central nervous system to produce volemic thirst (Fitzsimons, 1969). When intravascular fluid volume is decreased, a reduction in the local blood flow of the kidney occurs. The kidney releases renin in response to this reduction, and renin acts on a substrate in the blood to release angiotensin. Injections of angiotensin into the central nervous system evoke drinking (Epstein, Fitzsimons, and Simons, 1969). Furthermore, rats, given a choice between an isotonic salt solution and water, choose water when suffering from osmotic thirst. However, during volemic thirst they choose isotonic saline (Smith and Sticker, 1969).

Almli (1970) has recently reported that hypovolemic thirst, produced by reduction in blood volume through bleeding, results in significant increases of tonicity of extracellular body fluids at the same that a rat begins to drink. These changes are large enough to produce the drinking that is observed, and they occur at the time that the rat begins to drink. Whether other methods of reducing extracellular fluid volume produce such an elevation of extracellular osmotic pressure remains to be determined. This finding sheds some doubt on the concept of volemic thirst.

To clarify the results showing that fluid volume loss can lead to thirst, the following distinction has been proposed (Stricker, 1966; Stricker and Wolf, 1969): intravascular fluid (plasma), extracellular fluid, and intracellular fluid. (Extracellular fluid is also extravascular, that is, outside the circulatory system. Intravascular fluid is fluid within the circulatory system and is also extracellular.) Stricker (1966) shifted fluid between these three compartments: intravascular, extracellular, and intracellular.

The first manipulation was the insertion of water (5 percent of the animal's body weight) by tube into the animal's stomach. This has the effect of diluting all the body fluids, and it caused a simultaneous increase in volume of both the intracellular and the intravascular fluid. This procedure did not produce drinking.

The second manipulation consisted of the injection of 2.5 cc. of 1.5 percent formalin. This diminished intravascular fluid volume while it increased extracellular and intracellular fluid volume. The increase in intracellular fluid volume was of the same order (1 to 2 percent) as in the case where water was placed in the stomach. Here the animals drank large amounts, showing that thirst was elicited when intracellular and extracellular fluid increased at the expense of intravascular fluid.

The third manipulation was a subcutaneous injection of 5 cc. of 10 percent polyethylene glycol. This has the effect of withdrawing fluid from the intravascular compartment into the extracellular compartment without causing a measurable alteration in the volume of intracellular fluid. This manipulation again produced drinking.

These experiments show that either increase in extracellular fluid or decrease in intravascular fluid produces thirst. The reasonable conclusion from these experiments is that a decrease in intravascular fluid produces thirst (called volemic thirst, in contrast to osmotic thirst, produced by hypertonicity of extracellular fluid).

In a further study (Stricker and Wolf, 1969), increasing concentrations of propylene glycol produced increasing amounts of drinking by increasing the amount of fluid withdrawn from the intravascular compartment. When thirst is induced by a decrease in the volume of intravascular fluid, such thirst can be reduced or eliminated by giving the animal isotonic saline through a stomach tube (Stricker and Wolf, 1967). However, no such relief of thirst caused by a decrease in the volume of intravascular fluid (volemic thirst) took place if water was given instead of the saline. On the other hand, it was found that thirst induced by increasing the tonicity of the extracellular and intravascular fluid (osmotic thirst) was not inhibited by isotonic saline but was inhibited by water.

Nature of the Initiating Change in Hunger

The precise change, or changes, which act to initiate and maintain hunger have not been discovered. However, a number of theories have been proposed, each with some evidence to support it. One of the reasons why changes occasioning hunger have been difficult to pinpoint is that most theories have assumed that hunger is due to a physiological state and satiation is due to its absence. However, as we shall see, satiation seems to occur before the removal of a state of bodily depletion. Therefore it seems that there are two factors involved in hunger: the first to initiate it and the second to switch it off, independently of the continuance of the first. A further difficulty in deciding what changes produce hunger is that there are many different types of hunger, each mirroring deficiencies in various components of the diet. Each type of hunger will probably have its own special factors which act to start it and other factors which will signal that enough of a particular substance has been ingested.

Various theories of the physical changes producing hunger have been advanced. The three most prominent are the thermostatic theory of Brobeck, the glucostatic theory of Mayer, and the lipostatic theory of Kennedy.

Thermostatic Theory. Brobeck (1948) proposed that "animals eat to keep warm, and stop eating to prevent hyperthermia." It can be shown that body temperature rises after the ingestion of food, the amount of rise differing with various dietary constituents. This propensity to cause an increase in temperature is called the "specific dynamic action" of a food. In support of the hypothesis that eating is regulated by body temperature is the fact that eating is depressed by high temperatures and enhanced by low temperatures. Secondly, foods with a high specific dynamic action, such as proteins, have a high value in producing satiety but foods with a low specific dynamic action are not as effective in producing satiation.

Kennedy (1953) has objected to the thermostatic hypothesis since animals which are fed on a fat diet should become obese, which is not the case. Animals should also be food satiated by exercise, which raises body temperature by a far greater amount than does the ingestion of food.

An experiment which supports the thermostatic theory is reported by Andersson and Larsson (1961). They found that local cooling in the preoptic area and rostra hypothalamus induces eating in the satiated goat. On the other hand, warming of the same area produces drinking and inhibits eating. Cooling also inhibits drinking. However, the shifts in temperature used to obtain these effects seem very large. Further, ablation of the area which causes alterations of intake with changes in temperature did not seem to cause abnormalities of food intake. The only result of the lesion was that the goat would eat at body temperatures at which normal goats will not eat and that the lesioned goat would not drink more at temperatures which elevate drinking in normal goats. Excessive eating would be expected in the thermostatic hypothesis. It is reasonable to conclude that temperature can affect eating and drinking in the normal animal, but that it is not the main or exclusive regulator of hunger.

Glucostatic Theory. Mayer (1953) has suggested that hunger occurs when glucose is unavailable for metabolic purposes and satiation supervenes when glucose is made available. One measure of the availability of glucose which has been suggested is the absolute level of glucose (Carlson, 1916), but this suggestion has been rejected (Mayer, 1955). Another purposed measure is the arteriovenous glucose difference. If there is no difference between the arterial and venous content of glucose, no glucose is being taken up by the tissues en route between the arteries and the veins. The available glucose is therefore zero. If, on the other hand, there is a large difference, this must be due to the fact that glucose is being taken out by the tissues. Correlations between arteriovenous glucose differences and hunger have been demonstrated by Stunkard et al. (1955). Furthermore, Herberg (1960) has shown that minute injections of glucose into the ventricles of a rat depress food intake.

That some aspect of glucose metabolism is important in the initiation of hunger is implied by experiments with 2-deoxy-D-glucose (2-DG). 2-DG is a specific inhibitor of glucose utilization inside the cell. Injections of 2-DG increase food intake in a number of different species (Likuski, Debons, and Clouttier, 1967; Smith and Epstein, 1970; Houpt and Hance, 1971).

That restoration of glucose level is not the factor producing satiation has been shown by Koopmans (1972) in an ingenious procedure. Koopmans used parabiotic rats whose intestines had been partially crossed. (Parabiotic rats are a pair of highly inbred rats joined together along their flank, somewhat like artificial siamese twins.) The rats are highly inbred so that no tissue rejection phenomena occur. Koopmans crossed a portion of the small intestines of one rat over to the small intestines of the other. In this way, whichever rat fed (called the donor), the food from its stomach would end in the small intestines of its partner (the recipient) and be partially absorbed there. Koopmans was able to show that glucose levels in the blood did not correlate with the amount eaten. In spite of large amounts of glucose absorbed by the rat into whose small intestines food had been passively placed by the other rat's eating, there was no diminution of the amount of food ingested when the recipient rat was allowed to eat at various times after the donor rat had eaten.

Further discussion of this theory will be given when we consider factors producing satiation.

Lipostatic Theory. Kennedy (1953) has suggested that an animal is in some way sensitive to the overall fat stored in its body, perhaps through biochemical alterations which occur in the contents of its circulation as its fat depots enlarge. It is evident that some explanation must be given of the fact that an animal is capable of long-term regulation of its weight, which would be difficult to account for on the thermostatic or glucostatic theories. For instance, rats which have been artificially fattened lose weight rapidly and soon reach their previous size when allowed to regulate their own weight unhindered (Teitelbaum, 1962) (Fig. 16–1).

Locus of Action of Initiating Changes in Hunger and Thirst

Peripheral View. In the preceding sections we have considered some of the facts and theories about the changes which produce hunger and

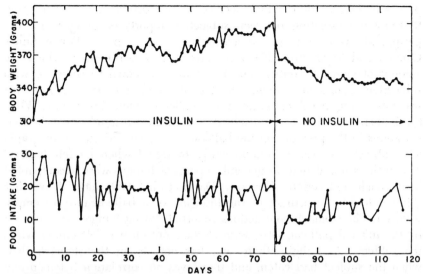

FIG. 16–1. A normal rat, made obese by insulin injections, allows its weight to return to a normal level when injections are discontinued. The top graph gives changes in weight, the lower graph changes in food intake. (From Teitelbaum, P., *Excerpta Medica,* No. 47, 1962, p. 700.)

thirst. We shall now inquire as to where these changes act, or are translated into neural activity. This, again, has been the subject of various theories. Historically, the most important theories can be classified into two general hypotheses: the peripheral and the central. The peripheral theory holds that the initiating change acts on some peripheral organ or structure in such a way as to cause this organ to produce stimuli which are then relayed to the central nervous system. Thirst, in this theory, is explained as being due to dryness of the mouth and throat, and hunger as due to contractions of the stomach. It seems the proponents of such theories (Cannon, 1932, and Carlson, 1916) sought to state what we feel when we feel thirst or hunger. They sought to link the introspectible contents of consciousness to events in the afferent pathway conveying signals from peripheral structures. However, the question of whate sensations we feel when we are thirsty is different from the question of how organisms regulate the amount they drink. This last question concerns us now. Psychologists, such as C. L. Hull, have taken the peripheral theory and attempted to make it a part of a behavioristic theory of food and water regulation, treating hunger contractions, for instance, as the origin of the stimuli which lead to eating responses in the animal.

Whether the peripheral theory is treated as a statement about our feelings or about our regulatory mechanisms, considerable evidence disproves it. Observations which seemed to support the theory attempted to show a correlation between subjective reports of hunger and the peripheral events thought to accompany these reports. For instance, Cannon and Washburn (1912) performed an experiment in which the amount of stomach contraction of a man was shown to correlate with subjective reports of hunger. The technique used to demonstrate this was interesting. A subject swallowed a balloon attached to a tube. When the balloon reached the stomach, it was inflated through the tube and variations in the pressure on the balloon were recorded on a kymograph. The subject was asked simultaneously to signal when he felt hungry. The authors found that, in general, reports of hunger were accompanied by stomach contractions. However, Davis et al. (1959) have shown that this result was an artifact of the insertion of a balloon into an empty stomach. The stomach contractions reported during hunger were caused by the inflated balloon. Otherwise, if the stomach was left empty while the subject was hungry, there was less activity in the stomach than when the subject had eaten, and there was no correlation between any activity of the stomach and reports of hunger.

Further, it has been possible to obtain dissociations between the peripheral changes thought to cause hunger or thirst and the phenomena of successful and normal regulation of food or water intake, throwing strong doubt on the peripheral theory. For instance, it has been shown that the removal or absence of structures from which the peripheral impulses arise does not produce an absence of hunger, as might be expected with the peripheral theory. Sometimes it is necessary in human patients to intervene surgically by removing the stomach, or large parts of it, yet such patients continue to display the usual symptoms of hunger.

Wangensteen and Carlson (1931) report a case of this type (complete gastrectomy) in which the patient emphatically maintained that the sensation of hunger was unchanged after the operation. To make sure that the intestine had not begun to behave as the stomach did normally, a recording balloon was inserted into the intestine as in the experiment of Cannon and Washburn (quoted above). Contractions similar to those of the stomach were not apparent. Parallel results were obtained on animal subjects by Tsang (1938) and Bash (1939). Animals with their stomachs excised still showed hunger and appeared to be normally motivated for food.

Secondly, intensification of the peripheral changes thought to be the basis of thirst has not produced the effects expected by the peripheral theory. Austin and Steggerda (1936) and Steggerda (1941) report the case of a young man who apparently had a congenital absence of salivary glands. Consequently, the mucous membranes of his mouth were always dry. (There was, however, some mucinous secretion from other glands from under the tongue and inside the cheeks.) This man's fluid intake was measured over 18 days and compared with that of four normal subjects. His total water intake was no different, although he did take a small amount (about 60 cc.) of water nearly every hour to relieve the discomfort due to the dryness of his mouth. Zaus (1936) reported the case of a ten-year-old child with a similar abnormality where no excessive drinking was present. Therefore the prediction from the dry mouth or peripheral theory of thirst is not borne out.

Experiments on dogs with extirpated salivary glands have also been undertaken (Montgomery, 1931). No increase in average daily water intake was observed in these animals. Though the mucous membranes of the mouth remained moist due to secretions from other glands in the region of the mouth and throat, such secretions were much more viscid, and it seems reasonable to suppose that the mouths of these dogs were drier than those of normal controls.

Many experiments have been performed which attempt to manipulate the peripheral state of the animal by pharmacological means. For instance, pilocarpine has been administered because it greatly promotes salivary flow. It was predicted on the peripheral theory that this should reduce drinking since the mouth should be less dry than normal. However, such experiments present a methodological difficulty since this drug also has various central actions which make its effect difficult to interpret. Montgomery (1931) showed that pilocarpine reduced water intake in dogs irrespective of whether they had their salivary glands removed. Thus the fact that pilocarpine increases salivary flow appears irrelevant.

In light of the above evidence, it seems that peripheral stimuli are better viewed as the concomitants rather than the causes of the initiation of hunger and thirst.

The Central View

Thirst. A second view of the locus of action of physiological changes has been put forward. According to this view, the physiological changes initiating hunger and thirst act directly on circumscribed sites in the central nervous system. Recent experimental evidence lends strong support to such a view. Andersson and McCann (1955) showed that microinjections (0.003 to 0.01 cc.) of 2 to 3 percent sodium chloride into a circumscribed region of the hypothalamus of unanesthetized goats induced drinking of water. Such drinking lasted from 2 to 5 minutes and began 30 to 60 seconds after the injection. Miller (1957) reported that injections of 0.15 cc. of 2 percent sodium chloride into the third ventricle of a cat produced drinking. An injection of isotonic saline in the same place produced no effect whereas a similar injection of distilled water actually reduced drinking. Miller (1961) reported that an injection of similarly small quantities of sodium chloride caused cats to perform a learned response of working for water and an injection of distilled water produced the reverse effect. Herberg (1962) obtained a similar result with rats. When rats were given a minute injection of hypertonic saline into a cannula implanted in the lateral ventricle, they almost immediately rushed toward the spout of the water bottle for a drink.

The very small amounts of hypertonic saline needed to produce drinking when injected either into the hypothalamus or into the ventricles suggest that there are structures in the hypothalamus highly sensitive to changes in osmotic pressure and that the stimulation of these structures is ultimately connected with the onset and maintenance of drinking behavior.

Electrical stimulation in such structures has also produced drinking. In a study by Andersson and McCann (1955), electrical stimulation initiated drinking within 10 to 30 seconds, and drinking stopped within 2 or 3 seconds after the current had been switched off. Overdrinking of up to 40 percent of body weight could be provoked. This mode of eliciting drinking did not lose its efficacy as swiftly as did microinjection. Greer (1955) also evoked drinking by electrical stimulation. It has further been observed that drinking produced by stimulation of hypothalamic structures will extend to the ingestion of liquids which are normally distasteful to the animal, and that under such stimulation the animal will seek out sources of water which it has previously discovered. Further, if drinking is induced by stimulating an area containing structures which transform humoral changes into neural activity, its destruction should lead to a cessation of drinking. Andersson and McCann (1955, 1956) have shown this to be the case. By electrolytically damaging the areas which upon stimulation produced thirst, a partial or complete loss of thirst was produced, with the degree of thirst depending upon the extent of the lesion.

It could be argued that in the foregoing experiments only the coordinated acts of drinking were induced or abolished and that the structures in which drinking, as a reflexion of thirst, originated were not implicated. It should be stressed, however, that physiological stimuli were used which resembled those causing thirst (hypertonicity of extracellular fluids) and that animals sought out sources of water which they had previously discovered. Further evidence can be produced from the extirpation studies quoted above. Though dogs which had been operated on would not drink water, they readily drank such fluids as milk or broth when hungry. This shows that the motor act of drinking was preserved.

Clinical evidence suggests a similar central mechanism in man. For example, Kourilsky (1950) reported the case of a young woman with an arachnoid cyst in the hypothalamic region who suffered from excessive thirst. A sudden lowering of pressure, due to the incision of the cyst at operation, caused a sudden diminution of thirst, which had been intense before and during the operation. Her water intake after the operation became normal.

Quartermain and Miller (1966) have found that after minute injections of carbachol into the preoptic area of the hypothalamus, rats will drink for about 20 minutes. (Carbachol is a cholinomimetic. It is a drug which has a similar action on the postsynaptic ending as acetylcholine; however, carbachol is resistant to breakdown by the enzyme acetylcholinesterase. This gives carbachol a very much longer period of action than acetylcholine.) However, if the rats injected with carbachol are not given access to water immediately after injection, drinking is induced even if access to water is delayed up to at least 60 minutes. Carbachol-induced thirst persists only if drinking is prevented. This suggests that carbachol-induced thirst can be satiated in a similar way to normal thirst.

Khavari and Russell (1966) have shown that rats learn, remember, and manifest extinction in the same way under cholinergic brain stimulation or water deprivation when running a maze for a reward of water.

Fisher and Coury (1962) were also able to elicit drinking in rats by implants of carbachol (a cholinergic drug) in the septal region, anterior nucleus of the thalamus, the cingulate gyrus, and the lateral hypothalamus. Spread of the drug through the vascular or ventricular systems was not determined.

Routtenberg (1965) presents evidence that spread of drug could account for Fisher and Coury's results.

Fisher (1969) himself has voiced doubts about the actual locus of stimulation by the drug. When carbachol is applied to some loci in one hemisphere, it will produce drinking. However, inhibition of this drinking will occur when atropine is applied to the same loci in the opposite hemisphere. As carbachol and atropine are antagonists when applied to the same synapses, the only straightforward interpretation of this effect is that these drugs cancel each other out by acting on the same synapses. The only way this could be done is by diffusion either through the ventricles or along vascular pathways. Against the interpretation that the effects are due to diffusion is the fact that the carbachol must be applied to specific brain loci to have an effect. However, this might mean only that diffusion occurs more readily, for instance, from certain structures by reason of their proximity to the ventricles. Fisher (1969) also expresses concern because of the somewhat long latency between the administration of cholinergic (and adrenergic) stimuli and behavioral response. Such a latency ranges between two and ten minutes, which is difficult to explain if the drug is acting locally as a neurotransmitter but is easy to explain if diffusion is necessary or some secondary process is really responsible.

It may be that the pathways underlying eating and drinking do not have the same transmitters in all species. For instance, Myers (1969) reports that carbachol or acetylcholine, injected into the lateral hypothalamus of rhesus monkeys, did not evoke eating or drinking. On the other hand, norepinephrine, dopamine, and 5-hydroxytryptamine evoked eating and drinking in satiated monkeys.

Novin and Durham (1969) recorded the activity of single cells and the DC potential change in the region of the supraoptic nucleus. When hypertonic solutions were injected through the carotid artery, many of the cells observed showed excitation, but some showed inhibition. Also observed was a negative shift in DC potential. This shift was not abolished after the area was isolated from the rest of the brain by cutting around it. Novin and Durham argue, therefore, that this DC shift is a generator potential such as is found in sense receptors, and that it is this change in potential which is translated into action potentials in neurons, signaling thirst.

Studies on the central locus of drinking have not generally determined whether they were studying volemic or osmotic thirst. Exceptions are the experiments which employ hypertonic saline as the stimulus to drinking. However, more recent experiments have produced evidence that volemic and osmotic thirst can be dissociated by lesions.

Blass (1968) completely destroyed the front portion of the rat brain, consisting of the olfactory bulbs and the rostral portion of the cortex, and removed some of the septal nuclei, anterior comissure, caudate nucleus, globus pallidus, and preoptic area. When such rats are injected with polyethylene glycol, intravascular volume is reduced without a concomitant cellular dehydration. The response of such lesioned rats to such reduction of intracellular volume does not differ statistically from that of normal rats, subjected to the same injection, either in the latency of drinking or in total amount drunk. However, when osmotic thirst was produced by injection of an NaCl solution, there was a large difference between the lesioned rats and normal controls. The lesioned rats took much longer to begin drinking and drank much less in total volume (Blass, 1968).

In a further experiment, Blass and Hanson (1970) showed that the exaggerated thirst after lesions of the septal nuclei (first described by Harvey and Hunt [1965]) is a disorder of the regulatory mechanism for hypovolemic thirst. When osmotic thirst was produced by an injection of NaCl solution, the increase in drinking of the septally lesioned rats was very similar to that of controls. When, however, volemic thirst was produced by an injection of polyethylene glycol (which reduces intravascular volume), the lesioned rats increased their water intake much more than the controls.

Though it is not known at present where the receptors are located which measure intravascular fluid volume, lesions in the lateral hypothalamus abolish thirst in response to decrease in intravascular fluid volume, suggesting that at least some of the neural circuitry associated with such regulation passes through this portion of the hypothalamus (Stricker and Wolf, 1967b).

Hunger. Similar results have been obtained linking hunger to central structures (as described above in the case of thirst). For instance, Anand and his co-workers (1951, 1955, 1961) found that bilateral extirpation of the lateral region of the hypothalamus produced aphagia, that is, a complete cessation of eating without any other apparent abnormality. Unilateral lesions had no effect on eating. Animals with bilateral lesions made no attempt to eat in the presence of food even though they were dying through lack of nourishment. Similar effects were later shown in cats and monkeys by Anand, Dua, and Shoenberg (1955). However, their effects are not as simple as was first thought. Animals with lesions of the lateral hypothalamus could, as Teitelbaum (1961) has shown, be nursed back so as to "escape" their loss of hunger and of thirst. Teitelbaum and Epstein (1962) have made a careful analysis of this recovery process. Adipsia may be the primary deficit in animals with these lesions. However, it seems that the lesions produced no simple loss of an urge to drink but, rather, what seems like an actual aversion to rehydration.

For instance, Williams and Teitelbaum (1959) found that animals with these lesions would not drink to avoid shock until the shock was made very strong. By using a technique showing that a normal rat can be taught to hydrate itself by pumping water directly into its own stomach, Epstein (1960) found that rats with lateral hypothalamic lesions did not learn this procedure, even though their learning ability was unimpaired. Further evidence that the lateral hypothalamus contains a mixture of pathways—some of them concerned with eating and drinking—has been reported by Grossman (1960). He found that by injecting minute amounts of carbachol (a cholinergic drug) into the lateral hypothalamus with an implanted hypodermic needle, drinking was produced, while similar injections of epinephrine or norepinephrine injected through the same needle produced increased eating. Studies by Miller (1965), using other pharmacological agents than those just mentioned, confirm the notion that an adrenergic system is involved in eating and that a cholinergic system produces drinking. It therefore appears that the pathways mediating eating and drinking have different transmitter substances.

Electrical, as well as biochemical, stimulation of the lateral hypothalamus can also produce marked increase in eating (Coons et al., 1965) (Fig. 16–2). To produce an effect, the electrical stimulation, in contrast

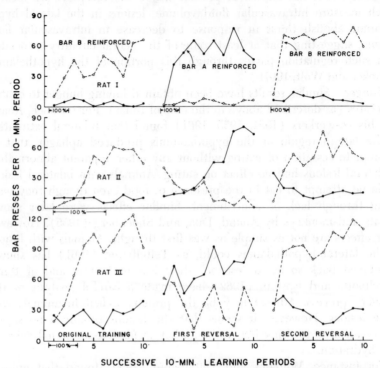

FIG. 16–2. Bar pressing for food, motivated by lateral hypothalamic stimulation. Two bars were available but only one produced a food reward. The rats quickly learned to reverse their choice of a bar, depending on which bar produced a reward. Except where the base line is marked 100% to indicate that every response was rewarded, the reinforcement was on a variable-interval 15-second schedule. Each reversal of reward bar was preceded by extinction for rat I but not for rats II and III. (From Coons, E. E., et al., *Science*, 150, No. 3701, December 3, 1965, 1321, copyright 1965 by the American Association for the Advancement of Science.)

to lesions, need only be unilateral (Delgado and Anand, 1953; Anand and Dua, 1955). Wyrwicka et al. (1959) have shown that food-getting habits could be elicited with hunger induced by electrical stimulation. They trained normally hungry goats to place their left foreleg on a food tray to obtain a reward of oats. Even though the goats were satiated, the same habit could then be evoked when lateral hypothalamic stimulation was turned on. Such an evocation was not that of some automatism because when the reward of oats for the action was discontinued, the habit dropped out as if extinction of the response had taken place, even though electrical stimulation continued. The time course of such extinction of the habit very closely followed the time course and characteristics of extinction under normal conditions of hunger. When reward was again introduced, goats stimulated in this way re-learned after extinction had taken place. On the other hand, when the electrical stimulation was discontinued, disappearance of the learned response was very rapid, though reward was not withdrawn. Only one or two movements appeared after the discontinuation of stimulation.

Stimulation by the biochemical means normally responsible for hunger has not been performed since the precise biochemical change or changes which give rise to hunger have not been established. Until such an effect of stimulation by microinjections in the lateral hypothalamus has been demonstrated, as in the case of thirst, an essential element will be lacking in the argument that the lateral hypothalamus is the structure translating into neural activity the biochemical change or changes that cause hunger. It would be desirable to have all the kinds of evidence for this hypothesis as are available for the case of thirst. Otherwise, it is possible that these structures merely involve the pathway from the structure initiating hunger, rather than the initiating locus itself.

In fact, it seems unlikely that bodily changes are translated into neural activity in the lateral area of the hypothalamus. It is probable that the lateral area contains a pathway leading away from an area which monitors bodily states. Wyrwicka and Doty (1966) elicited feeding from electrical stimulation of loci in the globus pallidus. Fibers from this area pass into the lateral hypothalamus. These fibers then pass into the ventral tegmentum and then to the ventrolateral boundary of the central gray. Electrical stimulation could elicit feeding from the relevant parts of all these structures.

Tenen and Miller (1964) found that increases in the intensity of electrical stimulation of the lateral hypothalamus made rats ready to drink an increasing concentration of quinine in their milk. It has been found that with hunger normally induced by food deprivation, the hungrier rats are, the more readily they will drink a bitter solution.

However, electrical brain stimulation evoking eating does not always produce what would be called normal hunger. For instance, Harwood and Vowles (1966) stimulated the forebrain of the ring dove through an implanted electrode. Such stimulation motivated bouts of pecking and eating directed to food but not to non-nutritious objects such as feces or grit. However, the same stimulation could not elicit the performance of a habit to obtain food previously learned by the ring doves under food deprivation. Further, such forebrain stimulation did not increase the rate of key pecking to obtain a food reward on a schedule which gives only intermittent reward. Ring doves whose hunger is increased by normal means speed up their rate of key pecking when only a certain proportion of responses is rewarded. It seems that fore-brain stimulation in the ring dove elicits not real hunger but only certain components of feeding behavior.

Eating has been evoked by stimulation of other loci besides the lateral hypothalamus. Robinson and Mishkin (1962) experimented with rhesus monkeys and in a small percentage of the animals were able to evoke eating by stimulation of such areas as the anterior cingulate gyrus and the midline thalamus.

A very interesting finding about rats with lateral hypothalamic lesions has recently been reported by Devenport and Balagura (1971). Rats that have recovered from lateral hypothalamic lesions, with body weight staying at 70 percent of normal, displayed greatly enhanced food-motivated behavior. In spite of a relative aphagia, such animals begin eating almost five times as fast as controls after 21-hour food deprivation in both a novel and a familiar environment. The lesioned rats also displayed much faster learning than normals of a Y maze for a food reward when they were deprived of food for 36 hours. The results suggest that lateral hypothalamic lesions dissociate eating behavior from food-motivated behavior.

Specificity of Electrical Stimulation

Valenstein et al. (1968) have questioned the assumption that specific brain loci produce eating or drinking in a fixed manner. They assume that the electrode stimulates a single nonspecific plastic substrate, modifiable by experience to manifest a variety of drive behavior. They have demonstrated two effects. The first is that a rat, in which drinking is evoked by the electrical stimulation of a particular brain locus, may instead begin to eat or gnaw if there is no opportunity for drinking. This could be due to the fact that the electrode stimulates different fiber tracts to varying degrees. The second effect is that once the rat had obtained experience with an activity that was not its first choice because the relevant goal object was unavailable, the introduction of the goal object of its first choice would produce the activity of both its first and second choice. For instance, a rat would eat when electrically stimulated through an implanted electrode when in the presence of food and water. When the food was taken away, it would drink upon being stimulated; when the food was reintroduced, it would continue to drink. Thus it looks as if the specificity of the brain loci evoking drive has changed due to experience.

However, the interpretation of the experiment may not be so simple. Coons and Cruce (1968) have shown that loci evoking drive activity can also, under some circumstances, produce reward. The secondary activity, such as drinking, might, while being evoked, become "superstitiously" linked with reward and so become an instrumental act. Such "superstitions" can be frequently observed in animals receiving rewarding intracranial self-stimulation. Supporting such an interpretation is the observation of Valenstein et al. (1968) that such "superstitious" behavior occurred in some of their animals. For instance, one rat "frequently positioned itself in one part of the cage, and with the onset of stimulation of a specific path was traversed on the way to the drinking bottle."

Another possible explanation of the change observed by Valenstein et al. is that the threshold for the evocation of a behavior decreases as such behavior is repeated. For instance, the threshold for rewarding stimulation decreases as the rewarded act is repeated. It is therefore possible that the threshold for drinking decreases as drinking is elicited and that such a threshold may, as a result of such repetition, become lower than that for, say, eating that was initially lower.

Valenstein's theory of the nonspecificity of hypothalamic drive substrates has been experimentally tested by Roberts (1969), who doubted the lack of postulated specificity because he had found considerable specificity in the oppossum (Roberts et al., 1967). Roberts argued that if eating, gnawing, and drinking evoked by hypothalamic stimulation are produced by the same undifferentiated mechanism merely as the result of differential experience, it follows that any electrode which elicits any of the three responses (eating, drinking, gnawing) should be trainable to elicit either of the other two drive patterns equally well. However, Roberts found that in spite of prolonged training, half of the 12 rats he used showed no increase of the trained responses and the other 6 animals developed only weak responses. It seems that if the initial tendency to perform a particular drive pattern is absent or weak, the substrate cannot be changed. It is therefore more plausible to think of discrete pathways than of plastic substrates for drive.

Theories of Regulation of Amount Eaten or Drunk

An important question is what kind of control system regulates eating or drinking. To answer such a question it is not of primary importance to know where the component parts of such a system reside or to what precise biochemical changes they respond. The important consideration in such a theoretical approach is the nature of the interrelations of the components of which the control system is made.

Simple Homeostat View. It has been a frequent and general assumption that eating or drinking continues as long as the change which induced is in operation. The view that the activity of ingestion is coterminous with the change which evokes it can be called the simple homeostat view because it suggests a system of the same form as that which can be found in simple regulatory devices such as a thermostat. In this device, when the temperature of the environment falls below a certain point, a thermometer switches on a heater. As soon as the temperature rises above this point, the heat is again switched off. An analogous system can be proposed for eating and drinking. The onset of eating and drinking is controlled by a change in some body constituent (which has its parallel in a fall in temperature in the example of the thermostat) which at a certain point switches on the eating or drinking activity via some structure which is sensitive to this change (paralleled by the thermometer). This activity continues as long as the sensitive structure is affected, and ceases as soon as the change which acted on the sensitive structure is reversed.

Such a scheme was suggested by C. L. Hull. He assumed that when a drive (of which hunger and thirst are instances) acts on an organism, a physiological state generates afferent impulses (or stimuli), which in turn evoke relevant responses (e.g., eating in response to the drive stimuli of hunger). In time, such responses reverse the change which evoked the stimuli, with the consequence that the organism stops eating. (Hull also believed that by the operation of other mechanisms the animal's overall behavior could be modified by learning.) Hull thought that the drive stimuli generated by a particular physiological deficit originated from peripheral structures. The drive stimuli of hunger were identified with afferent impulses from the stomach when it was contracting, and the drive stimuli of thirst were posited to be afferent impulses arising from a dry throat. Though this suggested peripheral locus of the origin of drive stimuli would doubtlessly be modified by Hull today, since it is not essential to his theory, the character of his theory as a simple homeostat view would not be affected by this change.

Whether such a simple homeostat model is correct in the case of hunger and thirst can be determined by observations on the behavior of animals when they are eating or drinking. One test of the hypothesis is to see whether the change which initiates eating or drinking must be reversed before ingestion will stop.

Relation between the Initiating Change and Cessation of Ingestion

Thirst

Evidence from Preloads. Do animals stop drinking before the deficit which instigated their drinking is replenished? One method of finding out is to compare the time they normally take to drink with the time it takes for the physiological instigating change to be reversed. The time to reversal of such a change can be most directly assessed by placing water directly in the animal's stomach (or preloading). Then, after various time intervals, water is offered to the animal to drink. If the time it takes to suppress drinking after a preload is longer than the time the animal normally spends in drinking the same amount, we can safely conclude that the normal inhibition of drinking is not due to the absorption of water by the system. Bellows (1939) has shown that a dog can drink just over 10 percent of its body weight in 4 minutes, and that it takes 15 minutes after a preload of about 8 percent of body weight is placed directly into the dog's stomach before drinking is inhibited. This result indicates that drinking ceases long before the initiating change is reversed.

Towbin (1949), however, reported that drinking is considerably reduced after a preload of water even when drinking is allowed to occur just after such a preload. However, such immediate inhibition in Towbin's experiment was not due to water absorption or to a reversal of the initiating change because he obtained similar results on immediate inhibition of drinking by injecting air into the stomach or by inflating a balloon in the stomach.

This conflict of evidence is probably due to the fact that Towbin's technique caused nausea due to stomach distention. Miller and Kessen (1954) have shown that rapid distention of the stomach, though it causes cessation of ingestion, can also be aversive. This is inconsistent with the notion that thirst is removed by the stomach distention procedure. In Miller and Kessen's experiment, rats were given a choice between two goal boxes in a T maze. In one goal box a balloon was inflated in their stomachs. Though such an inflation apparently satiated them, they learned to avoid the goal box in which the balloon was inflated. It seems that the rate of water injection is important; if it is too high, nausea will result.

On the other hand, if water injection is too slow, especially in a small animal such as the rat, whose rate of absorption is high, such an experiment may run into another difficulty because there will be a reversal of the initiating change. Miller, Sampliner, and Woodrow (1957) obtained results which apparently showed the inhibitory nature of injecting water into the stomach of a rat, even though extreme care was taken not to inject water at a rate which might produce nausea. Water was injected through a chronically implanted stomach fistula at the rate of 1 cc. each 50 seconds, which is the rat's normal rate of drinking. All in all, 14 cc. of water were inserted into the stomach prior to the tests, which consisted of bar pressing for a reward of water and of ad libitum drinking from a graduated cylinder. An immediate and considerable inhibition of thirst occurred as a result of this preloading procedure.

However, in the case of such a small animal as the rat, where the surface area of the stomach is high in relation to its volume, the rate of dilution of body fluids is probably so high that it may have taken place almost entirely during the 12 minutes when water was being slowly injected. By monitoring changes in conductance (a measure of the concentration of body fluids) while a rat drinks, Novin (1962) was able to show a considerable diminution of body fluid tonicity within the first 12 minutes after drinking began.

In summary, it appears than when the technique of preload is used in experiments on the shutoff of drinking, the results are not completely conclusive. The most likely evaluation of the evidence favors the view that absorption factors are not normally responsible for the cessation of drinking.

Evidence from Use of Esophageal Fistulae. Whether postingestional reversal of the initiating change stops drinking can also be determined by letting an animal drink while preventing water from reaching its stomach. This is achieved by transecting the esophagus so that, as the animal drinks, the water emerges from an aperture in its neck. This procedure of sham drinking was utilized by Bellows (1939), Adolph (1941), and Towbin (1949) in experiments on dogs. It seems clear from their results that the animal does not continue to drink until exhaustion supervenes but stops when it has drunk an amount proportionate to its deficit, as calculated by the experimenter. This supports the idea that inhibition of drinking occurs through factors other than the reversal of the initiating deficit. However, one difficulty of this conclusion is that both Bellows and Towbin calculate that dogs will drink anywhere from 155 percent to 250 percent of their deficit before stopping for five minutes. Such figures are not necessarily accurate as it is difficult to know how much such dogs would have drunk without the esophageal fistula.

Towbin, for instance, attempted to calculate the dogs' deficit in the following way. He assumed the deficit to be the least amount of water which, when placed directly in the stomach, produced an absence of drinking after it had been left in the stomach for an hour (a sufficient time for absorption). However, it is known that a dog will begin to drink only when it has lost 0.4 percent of its body weight in water (Robinson and Adolph, 1943). So if Towbin inserted an amount of water into the stomach which would bring the deficit of water below the 0.4 percent mark, the dog would not start drinking. However, if instead of inserting water into the stomach he had allowed the dog to drink, it would have drunk until its deficit of water was completely reversed. It seems, therefore, that this method of calculating the amount of water which the animal would have drunk under normal circumstances could produce a very considerable underestimate. Therefore Towbin's figure of 250 percent overdrinking when the esophagus is transected is probably a considerable overestimate. Adolphs' (1941) figures are more likely to be correct. He used deficit of body weight as an estimate of how much the dog with an esophageal fistula should drink, and on this basis he found that the amount drunk was almost equal to such a deficit.

As can be seen, most of the conclusions concerning the causes of drinking cessation are based on somewhat circuitous arguments resulting from experiments employing techniques that are difficult to interpret. The technique of esophageal fistulation by transecting the esophagus may destroy some of the metering devices which are important in regulating drinking. Further, animals cannot eat their normal diet after such an operation, and in the author's experience they are essentially sick animals. The technique of preloading the animal's stomach produces critical delays, and so absorption of the preload, and it also complicates interpretation because stomach distention is abnormal.

Evidence from Counterinjection. In order to overcome such difficulties of interpretation, another type of approach was devised by Deutsch and Blumen (1962). One end of a tube was sewn into a rat's stomach and the other end was threaded under the skin, protruding between the ears. As the animal drinks, each lick actuates a pump electronically. This pump drives two syringes. One of these syringes delivers an amount of fluid to the rat's tongue. This amount of fluid is adjusted to be the same as that which the rat obtains by a single lick of a tube from which it normally obtains its water. The other syringe is connected to the tube going into the animal's stomach. This second syringe can be filled with saline of such a concentration as to produce isotonic saline when mixed in the animal's stomach with the water arriving from the other syringe via the mouth and then the esophagus. Only a small amount of the hypertonic solution need be injected if it is sufficiently concentrated. Therefore we can prevent an animal from deriving the normal physiological consequences received from drinking and tasting water, and the animal will in fact derive no short-term physiological reversal of the change which initiated drinking. On the other hand, outside the experimental situation the animal eats and drinks normally, remain healthy, and frequently gains weight. Using this method, one can study the effects of varying the taste of the fluid drunk while maintaining stomach tonicity, and one can also vary the stomach tonicity while maintaining taste factors. By determining the differences in the time course of drinking under these conditions, the relative importance of sensory and absorption factors in the slaking of normal thirst can be assessed.

Rats with a stomach tube inserted were tested under three conditions: (1) when they were tasting water and water was counterinjected into the stomach, (2) when they were tasting water and the hypertonic saline was counterinjected so that isotonic saline would result from the mixture in the stomach, and (3) when they were tasting hypotonic saline (0.6 percent saline) and the resulting mixture due to the counter-injection of hypertonic saline was again isotonic saline. The volume counterinjected in each of these three conditions was in the same proportion to the volume drunk in all three conditions.

The main results of the experiment are clear (see Fig. 16–3). When

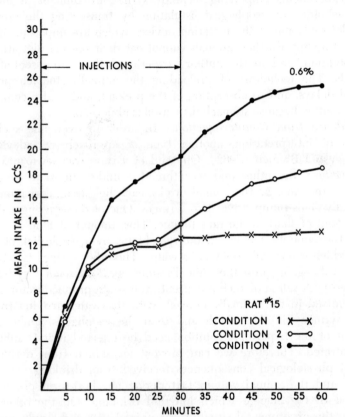

FIG. 16–3. Cumulative records of a rat drinking during counterinjection. The three conditions are explained in the text.

the rat is tasting water, irrespective of what is arriving in its stomach, drinking stops after about 15 minutes (when the rat has been thirsty for 22 hours). Furthermore, as shown by the curves of intake over time, the time course of drinking is the same, irrespective of what is arriving in the rat's stomach when it is tasting water, over the period during which the rat makes up its normal deficit. However, if the normal physiological consequences do not follow, the rat will resume drinking. On the other hand, a rat tasting 0.6 percent saline will exhibit a time course of drinking which is very different from that of a rat tasting water but receiving the same isotonic mixture in its stomach, again showing that taste factors are very important.

The experiments reviewed above bring out two points. First, it seems that placing water in the rat's stomach does not relieve thirst immediately but only after a period of time. This effect appears to work by reversing the change which initiates thirst. Second, there are factors which terminate drinking without the reversal of the initiating change which produces drinking. These factors seem to produce cessation of drinking in the normal case. Therefore the simple homeostat theory of thirst cannot account for the data on drinking, though it does appear to contain a part of the truth when we consider the long-term effect of placing water in the stomach.

Hunger. Experiments similar to those discussed above have been carried out in the study of hunger, but with different results. Food was placed directly in the stomach (Kohn, 1951; Berkun, Miller, and Kessen, 1952) and was found to produce almost immediate satiation, even though explanations in terms of nausea can be excluded. Kohn (1951) measured the frequency of response in a Skinner box. He found that rate of lever pressing in this apparatus declined after stomach injection of food. Berkun et al. (1952) measured the amount actually ingested by the rats after food had been placed in the stomach. There was a decrease in eating which could not be accounted for by a reversal of the physiological change which had initiated eating. It is unlikely that digestion of the inserted food could have taken place to a significant extent in the time allowed. Further, normal ingestion by mouth of the same amount of food as was injected directly into the stomach led to an even greater depression of eating, pointing to an effect of gustatory factors in satiation.

Smith and Duffy (1955) attempted to discover in more detail factors involved in this phenomenon of satiation through direct injection into the stomach. The question posed by Kohn's and Berkun, Miller, and Kessen's results was what aspects, such as sheer bulk or nutritive properties of the injected substance, produced satiation. Accordingly, Smith and Duffy trained rats in a Skinner box on an aperiodic reinforcement schedule to obtain food when they were hungry. After training was completed, they used a stomach tube to fill the rats' stomachs with various substances in order to determine the effect on the rate of subsequent bar pressing.

Smith and Duffy's first experiment was similar to Kohn's. They injected three different substances—10 cc. of isotonic saline, 10 cc. of enriched milk, and 10 cc. of sugar solution (30 gm. of sugar to 70 cc. of water)—in a rat's stomach. They found that saline had little effect on the rate of bar pressing whereas the milk and the sugar had a considerable effect. The number of bar presses in a 46-minute period before injection was 231, and this dropped to 37 bar presses after the sugar injection, and 80 after the milk injection, in the same period. In their second experiment, they attempted to determine if simple indigestible bulk (which could not be assimilated as the saline could) would not account for their results on the basis of simple pressure effects. Accordingly, from a mixture of 40 gm. of kaolin (china clay) to 60 cc. water they injected 10 cc., 7 cc., or 4 cc. into the rat's stomach. Smith and Duffy found that the kaolin injections into the stomach had no effect on response rate. However, in their third experiment they found that when the bulk was of a nutritive substance, it had a depressive effect on the rate of responding. They found that with a 30 percent sucrose solution the depressive effect on the rate of responding was "approximately linear with respect to quantity."

Though this experiment strongly suggests that hunger is decreased before restoration of the level of nutrients is achieved by the rat's digestive system, and though the factors responsible for this decrease are to a certain extent elucidated, the experiment is not completely satisfactory. After the intragastric injection, an average of 7.5 minutes elapsed before a rat was placed in the Skinner box. The test period was 46 minutes. Therefore digestive factors cannot be altogether excluded. It can, however, be said that the experiment seems to establish the point that when non-nutrient bulk is injected slowly so as not to cause nausea, it does not have a satiating effect.

In view of the above experiments, it can be strongly argued that cessation of eating is not due to a reversal of the change which acts on the central nervous system. Even given that digestion may have played some part in lessening subsequent food intake after the direct injection of food into the stomach, it is impossible to dispute the fact that normal ingestion by mouth of the same amounts of food led to an ever greater depression of eating. This shows that there are satiating effects beyond any possible digestive factors.

Hull et al. (1951) have observed eating in a dog with an esophageal fistula. The dog used in this experiment weighed 10 kilos before the operation. At the beginning of this experiment, this dog ate 8 kilos of food before stopping for five minutes. Even then, cessation of eating was probably not due to normal satiation but to sheer exhaustion. It is reported that the dog showed "violent nervous shaking." Here, as contrasted with the study of thirst, the effect of swallowing food when it does not reach the stomach does not seem to be strong enough to make the dog stop eating. Such an observation fits the simple homeostat view of ingestion well, but such a view is contradicted by the finding that the simple placing of food in the stomach inhibits eating before digestion can take place.

Afferent Inhibition View of Satiation

Another view has been elaborated by Deutsch (1953, 1960) and Stellar (1954). This theory resembles the simple homeostat model but adds an important complication. It will be recalled that in the simple homeostat model a physiological deficit excites a center which in turn produces activity. This activity reverses the change which excited the center and consequently switches itself off. In the system we are now considering, all this is assumed to be true, but another factor has been inserted. This factor consists of afferent activity originating in the receptors, and when the activity is conveyed to the excited center, it is rendered progressively less excitable by the initiating physiological change. In the case of drinking, it is hypothesized that such afferent activity is generated by taste receptors on the tongue that signal water, receptors in the throat that signal swallowing, and perhaps some receptors in the stomach. As the animal drinks, these receptors send back messages to the hypothalamic center activated in the thirst state and make the center gradually less excitable, until the animal stops drinking. In this way, drinking will usually cease before the physiological change which evoked the drinking is reversed as a result of advance information on how much has been drunk. On the other hand, insertion of water in the stomach can lead to a nonoccurrence of drinking if enough time is given for the water to reverse the change which would have initiated drinking had water been vailable. An analogous system is believed to operate in the case of eating, except that the main afferent message shutting off ingestion is considered probably to be generated by the upper gastrointestinal tract. Therefore placing food directly in the stomach has an inhibitory effect not found with the introduction of water into the stomach in the study of thirst.

This system can be described as follows. A physiological change acts on a center. This center produces activity, which in turn produces afferent signals that desensitize the center in proportion to the number of signals received. Thus the center is rendered progressively less excitable by the initiating physiological change. In this way the cessation of an activity such as eating or drinking can be brought about in advance of the reversal of the physiological change which initiated these activities. On the other hand, such a reversal of the initiating change can also bring about a cessation, though this is never true in the ordinary situation because the signals generated by the activity, such as drinking, act in advance.

Therefore, in the ordinary case, the amount eaten or drunk will be a function first of the amount of excitation of the initiating central structure, and second, it will be a function of the amount of signal fed back from the receptors to this center. Given a certain level of excitation in the center, the greater the amount of afferent stimulation per unit time, the more quickly the center will be rendered inexcitable. On the other hand, given a certain amount of afferent stimulation per unit time, the greater the excitement of the center generated by the physiological change, the longer the activity will last, because it will take a longer time for such a center to be desensitized.

Diluted Water

It is possible to vary the number of afferent impulses derived from drinking simply by placing sodium chloride (common salt) in drinking water, as long as such a solution remains hypotonic. Zotterman (1956) made electrophysiological recordings from the chorda tympani nerve, which conveys afferent signals from the taste buds. He discovered that the same nerve fiber that is affected when a hypertonic solution of sodium chloride is placed on the tongue also responds to application of water. However, such a fiber responds in an opposite way to these two substances. This fiber has a high and steady spontaneous or baseline rate of firing, presumably due to the normal salt content of the saliva. When a hypertonic sodium chloride solution is placed on the tongue, there is an increase in the steady rate of firing of this nerve fiber. However, when water is placed on the tongue there is a decrease in the steady firing rate of the nerve fiber. Thus the presence of water is signaled by a fall in the amount of discharge in the fibers, which increase their firing when salt is present above the quantity normally found in saliva. When a small amount of salt is added to water—less than the amount in the saliva—the solution continues to have the effect of decreasing the normal rate of firing in the fiber which signals the presence of water or salt. However, such a decrease is not as large as that which is produced by pure water. Therefore the effect of placing salt in water is to diminish the signal usually generated by the water. In some species, such as the rhesus monkey, there is a fiber which signals the presence of water by increases in rate of firing. However, in these animals the addition of salt to the water diminishes such an increase so that salt in the water also diminishes its gustatory effect.

From this neurophysiological evidence it should be expected that when a small amount of salt is added to water, a more prolonged drinking of the slightly salty solution should result. Further, we should expect a progressive increase in the overdrinking of such salty solutions as the salt content of the water increases up to the level of the salt content in the saliva. The more salty the water up to this point of equality with the saliva, the smaller the number of water messages generated by a given volume of fluid. When the salt content of the water applied to the tongue is greater than the salt content of the saliva, there will no longer be a depression of activity, and consequently there will be no activity which can be interpreted as a signal of the presence of water. However, there will be an increase in activity in the water-salt fibers. This is the message for salt. Thus hypotonic saline will act on the taste receptors of the rat as if the solution were diluted water. On this basis, one might hypothesize that the animal will drink more of the hypotonic saline, not because it prefers this solution but because more of the solution has to be drunk to have the same effect as a smaller volume of water.

The fact that rats will drink more hypotonic saline than water has been known for some time; therefore this theoretical prediction seems to be confirmed. Furthermore, overdrinking of saline increases with the concentration of the solution up toward the point where it is isotonic. Overdrinking occurs even when water is freely available at the same time as the saline (Nelson, 1947; Bare, 1949; Young, 1949; Randoin et al., 1950). Of course it could be, as Mook (1963) points out, that more hypotonic saline is drunk because it is less efficient than water in reversing the physiological change which produces thirst; therefore the effect which has been found might not be due to taste factors. However, Stellar and McCleary (1952) and Mook (1963), using animals with esophageal fistulae so that the ingested fluid did not reach the stomach, obtained essentially the same results. Postingestinal factors were not operating.

From Mook's results, it seems that the peak in overdrinking of saline shifts somewhat to more dilute solutions of saline when nothing reaches the stomach. This would indicate that postingestional factors play a part in the situation when water was allowed to reach the stomach. Mook used a situation in which only one fluid was presented to the animal and only the total intake during one hour was measured. Results with such a procedure would reflect mainly the effects of the long-term reversal of the physiological change which produces thirst when the tasted fluid is allowed to reach the stomach. On the basis of taste factors, if the animal drank too little of a solution to produce reversal of the physiological change, this unreversed physiological change would shortly produce drinking again. Thus over a long period total intake of a fluid reflects its efficiency in reversing the physiological deficit which produces thirst. If, on the other hand, drinking occurs without any fluid entering the stomach, total "intake" should be grossly elevated, but the relative amount of intake of various solutions will reflect the influence of mouth factors alone. The afferent inhibition of drinking set up by drinking will occur more rapidly with some solutions than with others and last only a relatively brief time. As a result, more drinking of less orally satiating solutions should occur.

A result which at first appears to be inconsistent with the diluted water hypothesis has been obtained by Mook (1963) by using a variation of the fistulation technique quoted above. He transected the esophagus of rats in such a way that fluid drunk by the animal would drain out before reaching the stomach. However, each lick actuated a pump that would inject a predetermined amount of any fluid directly into the stomach through the lower end of the esophagus. When the animal was given different concentrations of saline to lick while no fluid was injected into the stomach, overdrinking of hypotonic saline occurred (as summarized above). However, if water was injected into the stomach while the rat licked different concentrations of saline, the rat drank the same amount of these as of water. On the basis of these results, Mook concluded that overdrinking of hypotonic saline is due to post-ingestional factors because it occurred only when saline reached the stomach, and did not appear when water reached the stomach only as a result of saline drinking. However, such a conclusion is contradicted by his own finding (quoted above) that overdrinking of saline occurred when nothing was allowed to reach the stomach. Relative overdrinking of saline could not be due to postingestional factors (Fig. 16–4).

As stated above, Mook measured only the total "intake" summed over a whole hour. Let us consider the discrepant case where the rat is "drinking" saline which escapes through the interrupted esophagus but

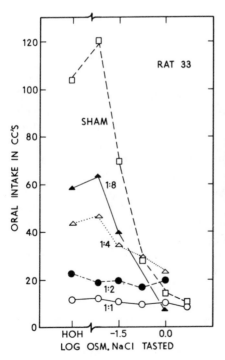

FIG. 16–4. Drinking of saline in Mook's animals as a function of concentration of saline which the rat tastes. The curve marked "sham" is obtained when the rat drinks saline but nothing is allowed to reach the stomach. The curve marked 1:1 indicates the condition in which any volume of saline drunk (but not allowed to reach the stomach) is matched by the same volume of water injected directly into the stomach. The other curves are obtained when different ratios of saline drunk to water injected into the stomach are employed. The numbers on each curve indicate the ratio of water injected into the stomach to amount of saline drunk. (From Mook, D. G., *J. comp. physiol. Psych.*, 56, 1963, p. 656; by permission of American Psychological Association.)

receiving an equal volume of water in its stomach instead. If the rat initially "overdrinks" when it is licking saline, it will simply take more water into its stomach. After a while this will stop the rat from being thirsty by reversing the initiating physiological change. When the rat is no longer thirsty, there will be no further "drinking" during the hour if saline overdrinking is caused only by thirst. If the rat licks water instead of saline, there will be less "drinking" at the beginning (because the shutoff message is more efficient), with the consequence that the rat will take less water into its stomach than when it is licking saline. In this case the rat will stay thirsty longer and continue to lick the water tube. All this adds up to saying again that thirst regulation over a period of an hour is bound to be governed by the cancellation of the initiating factor in thirst, that is, rehydration. If, on the other hand, rehydration is not permitted, the relative amounts drunk will merely reflect the properties of the afferent shutoff message. Mook's results are therefore consistent with the diluted water hypothesis, and are in fact good evidence for it.

However, it might still be said that the evidence concerning the greater volume of saline drunk merely shows that the animal prefers saline to water. Indeed, it has usually been assumed that saline is overdrunk because of some preference for its taste. Rats have a preference for sugar solutions and will drink them in large amounts. To show that this argument is unlikely, Deutsch and Jones (1959, 1960) places rats in a situation so that when they were thirsty they had to choose between equal volumes of water and hypotonic saline. If the rats preferred the taste of hypotonic saline, they should have learned to run to it; if, on the other hand, it appeared to the rats that the hypotonic saline was diluted water and therefore less thirst quenching, they should have learned to seek out the water. The rats learned to run to the water. This did not support the view that rats had a genuine preference for saline. On the other hand, it supported the view that saline is overdrunk because it is less satiating to a thirsty animal (Figs. 16–5a, 16–5b).

To test the view that there is a preference which accounts for the overdrinking even further, Deutsch and Jones experimented with rats that had been satiated with water to see if they would learn to run to a reward of saline (0.2 percent and 0.8 percent), as one might expect if they liked the taste. After six days it was clear that the animals had no appetite for either solution. Although the average running time dropped from 82 seconds on the first day to 30 seconds on the sixth day, the whole reward of half a cc. was drunk on only 4 of the 90 trials. On one-third of the trials the animals sniffed at the reward, and probably took a lick and then left it alone. The rest of the time the rewards were completely ignored. It was therefore concluded that saline

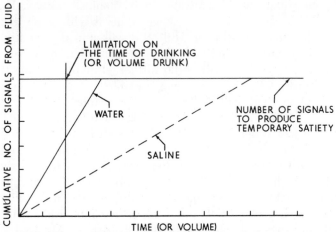

FIG. 16–5a. This figure illustrates the relation of amount drunk of a solution in an ad libitum situation to its reward value when intake is limited. Saline produces fewer safety signals per unit volume. A larger volume is drunk to produce satiety, and the same volume produces fewer satiety signals and so is less rewarding.

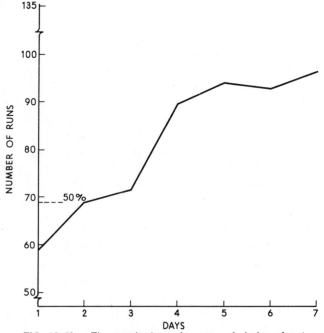

FIG. 16–5b. The graph shows increase of choice of water over 0.5 percent saline in a T maze as the rats learn. (From Deutsch, J. A., and Jones, A. D., *J. comp. physiol. Psych.,* 53, 1960, p. 123; by permission of American Psychological Association.)

does not act as an incentive when the rat is not thirsty. So it appears that excessive drinking of saline is due to a smaller quantity of water signals from this liquid, which means that the rat has to drink more saline than water before the necessary number of signals arrive to switch off the thirst center.

By using a T maze, limited amounts of water and saline as a reward, and some additional controls, Chiang and Wilson (1963) have confirmed the results obtained by Deutsch and Jones. Falk and Titlebaum (1963), on the other hand, found that when the animals used in their experiment were thirsty, there was no preference for either water or saline. However, when they were not thirsty there was a preference for saline; in fact, the animals would run for it.

Exploring this interesting discrepancy, Deutsch and Wiener (unpublished) found that by using the strain of albino rat obtained from the same supplier as Falk and Titlebaum, they could obtain the same results only if the animals were maintained on a salt-deficient diet. That is, when placed in the T maze, salt-deprived rats from the Charles River Laboratories chose saline and water equally when thirsty, and they ran to the saline when not thirsty. (Other peculiarities of the Charles River strain, such as a hyperphagia, have been noted by Sherman, 1963, and Jacobs and Sharma, 1969.)

When placed in the T-maze, however, nonsalt-deprived rats from the same supplier preferred water but would not run for saline when they were not thirsty. In this respect the nonsalt-deprived rats resembled a parallel group of Long Evans hooded rats. However, a group of Long Evans rats maintained on a salt-deficient diet did not prefer water to saline when they were thirsty, although they would not run the maze when they were not thirsty. It appears, therefore, that Falk and Titlebaum's (1963) result was due to their use of a certain strain of rat kept accidentally on a salt-deficient diet. From observation in the laboratory, it seemed that the strain of rat used by Falk and Titlebaum is particularly susceptible to salt deficiency. Therefore in tests of the diluted water theory it is particularly important to make sure that the animals being tested are not salt depleted.

Chiang and Wilson (1963) reported a further discrepancy with the diluted water theory which has not yet been further investigated. Under ad libitum conditions, they measured rats' frequency of drinking bouts from a bottle containing saline and a bottle containing water. It was found that rats would drink more frequently from the saline bottle than from the water bottle. Such a result would not be predicted from the diluted water hypothesis, which would predict a random and equal choice of the two bottles, although longer bouts on the saline bottle would be expected. The two-bottle ad libitum situation may be a very sensitive test for revealing slight salt craving. This may exist even with a diet which is perfectly compatible with growth. A more stringent test of the theory would be to see if overdrinking of saline persists when animals are fed a diet richer in salt, even though choice of the saline bottle is random. With the use of a lesion, overdrinking of saline in the absence of saline deficiency can be dissociated from drinking of saline in response to a salt deficit. Wolf (1964) has shown that lesions in the dorsal part of the lateral area of the hypothalamus will abolish an increase of salt intake in response to treatment producing such an increase in normal animals. Therefore, lesioned animals seem unable to react behaviorally to salt deficiency. However, they show the same pattern of overdrinking the hypotonic saline as normal nondeprived controls. From this dissociation it would appear that normal overdrinking of saline and true salt preference due to salt deficiency are two different phenomena produced by different mechanisms. This supports the diluted water theory of saline overdrinking.

Factors Switching Off Ingestive Activity

As was stated above, if water is placed in a thirsty dog's stomach, the dog will immediately drink approximately the same amount it would have drunk without this preload (Adolph, 1950). However, if the dog is forced to wait from 10 to 15 minutes, he will not drink (Bellows, 1939). This again is to be expected on the hypothesis being reviewed. A reversal of the change which initiates the activity takes place, even though such a reversal would never occur naturally because it would always have to be preceded by tasting and swallowing water.

The evidence concerning hunger can be similarly examined in the light of this theory. In the case of hunger, it seems that the messages which shut off eating arise mainly in the upper end of the gastrointestinal tract (with a minor effect of taste messages on eating, as shown by Kohn, 1951, and Berkun, Miller, and Kessen, 1952). If the stomach acts to generate such inhibitory afferent messages, we can explain why placing food in the stomach, as in Kohn's or Smith and Duffy's experiment, should cause satiation of hunger. It can also be seen why a hungry dog with an esophageal fistula should not stop eating before physical exhaustion sets in. Since no food reaches the stomach, no afferent message is generated to switch off eating.

The Message Causing Satiation

The message sent from the digestive tract to inhibit eating may well be biochemical in nature. Glucagon, a protein secreted by the α cells in the pancreas, has been suggested as a possible factor. It has been found that injections of this substance will diminish hunger contractions and reports of hunger (Stunkard et al., 1955) and will diminish the amount eaten (Schulman et al., 1957). It has been thought that this substance acts by allowing glucose to be taken up by body cells, and that presumably glucagon also affects the central nervous structures (the ventromedial nucleus of the hypothalamus) which may monitor the level of glucose being taken up. This view is based on the discovery (Van Itallie et al., 1953; Stunkard and Wolff, 1954) that in man there is a correlation of satiety with a relatively large difference between arterial and venous blood. This signifies that glucose is being taken up by body cells as it passes from the arterial to the venous system. Hunger, on the other hand, never appears when the difference between the arterial and venous glucose is relatively large. Nevertheless, a small difference can be present without hunger occurring. Therefore some other accompanying factors must be implicated in hunger.

It is tempting to suppose that glucagon, which apparently produces satiety, does this by permitting body cells to take up glucose from the blood and thus increase the arteriovenous difference in blood glucose. Unfortunately, glucagon has various physiological effects. The particular effect necessary for this view has not been completely demonstrated, as is stressed by Behrens and Bromer (1958). It should also be mentioned that Herberg (1962) failed to find evidence for the action of glucagon when it was injected directly into the ventricles of the rat. Herberg found that no significant decrease in food intake resulted from such injection. However, he has reported reduction of food intake under some conditions of glucose injections into the ventricles (Herberg, 1960).

It is of course unlikely that there is a single satiating factor in hunger, just as it is unlikely that there is a single initiating factor. There are many different hungers. For instance, an animal may be hungry for protein while it is satiated for carbohydrate. It appears that the satiating messages originate mainly from the upper gastrointestinal tract. Satiating messages do not seem to be neural because vagotomy (Grossman et al., 1947) does not alter food intake significantly. It seems more probable that the shutoff messages are humoral. The upper gastrointestinal tract secretes a variety of hormones, such as pancreozymin, as a relatively differentiated response to the presence of various components of the diet. These are already known to act as messengers to promote the flow of the appropriate digestive juice ahead of such dietary components. There is a possibility that such hormones also exert a shutoff action on the central nervous system. For instance, the hormone enterogastrone, derived from the small intestine, reduces gastric secretion and gastric motility. Schally et al. (1967) injected hungry mice with this substance to see if it would inhibit eating, and an inhibition of eating was observed. In a similar experiment, Koopmans, Deutsch, and Branson (1972) injected cholecystekinin, another hormone secreted by the digestive tract, and an inhibition of eating was again observed. However, drinking was also inhibited in thirsty mice. As Schally et al. (1967) did not employ controls, it is entirely possible that there was a nonspecific effect of enterogastrone as well. So far, then, it seems that results with intestinal hormones can be accounted for by general factors affecting intake (such as malaise) rather than by a specific effect producing true satiety.

HUMORAL NATURE OF HUNGER

The most direct and convincing evidence that some of the factors concerned with either the evocation or satiation of hunger has been obtained by Davis and his collaborators (1966) when blood is transfused between a pair of rats when one is hungry and the other is satiated. Two cc. of blood are withdrawn through a chronic intravenous cannula from both rats simultaneously, and then the blood from one rat is injected into the other. This procedure is repeated until 26 cc. of blood has been crossed between the two rats. Immediately after the transfusion, each rat is given access to food.

In one study, one member of the pair was kept on an ad libitum diet and the other was kept without food for 23.5 hours each day. The blood of each pair was transfused 30 minutes before the food-deprived animal was fed each day. When the food intake of the 23.5-hour deprived rat was measured after it had received blood from the satiated animal, it was found that its intake dropped to 50 percent of the amount it ingested when no transfusion was given. Thus it looks as if the blood of a satiated rat contains a factor which produces satiety in a hungry rat. However, the reduction in food intake might be due to some nonspecific factor connected with transfusion and not necessarily with satiety as normally produced. To control for this possibility, the donor rat which had been on an unrestricted diet was deprived of food 24 hours before its blood was injected into the recipient. (This recipient was on a 23.5-hour schedule.) In this case the food intake of the recipient was not reduced below the normal level. This showed that the effect of the blood transfusion on the recipient was a function of the satiety or hunger of the donor. Transfusion in itself had not caused a drop in food intake.

However, we still do not know what was being transferred. One possibility, as Davis believes, is that a satiety factor is being transferred from the donor to the recipient rat. The other possibility is that the factor which produces or evokes hunger in the recipient is being diluted by the blood of the donor where it is not present. Either way, there would be the reduction of food intake which was observed.

In an effort to investigate these effects further, Davis kept both members of the pair without food 23.5 hours each day. The donor member of the pair was fed 30 minutes before transfusion, so that it was satiated. However, the recipient of this freshly satiated blood did not show a significant reduction in intake. One interpretation of this is that 30 minutes after feeding the humoral state which initiates eating has not been reversed by the processes of digestion. Therefore, when the blood of a freshly satiated donor is used, it does not dilute the humoral state which initiates eating in the recipient. If this interpretation is correct, it would imply that the signals which normally turn eating off (satiety signals) are not transferred from donor to recipient. This might be because such signals are not humoral or because such signals are humoral but are rapidly destroyed while being continuously secreted by the freshly fed intestine. Their presence would therefore not be detected by a single-shot transfusion (Fig. 16–6).

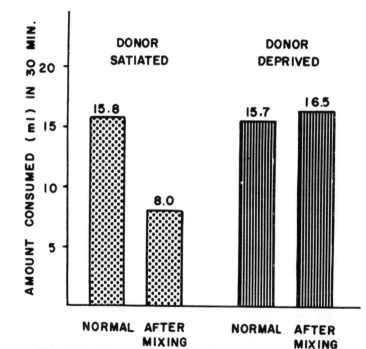

FIG. 16–6. Mean intake of test diet in 30 minutes by animals on the deprivation schedule. On the left (a) the mean intake on the day prior to transfusion (normal) is compared with the mean intake of the same animals immediately following the mixing of their blood with satiated donors (after mixing). On the right (b) the same comparison is made for animals whose blood was mixed with the blood of 24-hour deprived donors. (From Davis, J. D., Gallagher, R. J. and Ladove, R., 1967. Copyright 1967 by the American Association for the Advancement of Science.)

LOCUS OF ACTION OF SATIETY MESSAGE

There is evidence that whatever the message signaling for satiety may turn out to be, its locus of action is in or close to the ventromedial nucleus of the hypothalamus. The destruction of this region in rats produces overeating, which leads to gross obesity (Hetherington and Ranson, 1940, 1952; Brobeck et al., 1943). (However, Reynolds [1963] has not found this to be the case.) Overeating has also been produced by a temporary block of the ventromedial nucleus through procaine injection (Epstein, 1960; Hoebel and Teitelbaum, 1962). Apart from their tendency to overeat, the rats seem physiologically normal (Teitelbaum, 1961). Rats with ventromedial lesions pass through two stages—the dynamic phase and the static phase. In the dynamic phase, immediately after the operation the rats displayed a wolfish appetite, sometimes even choking themselves by their frantic efforts to eat. However, if the animals are artificially fattened before the operation, this phase is correspondingly diminished (Fig. 16–7). The rats enter the static phase as their

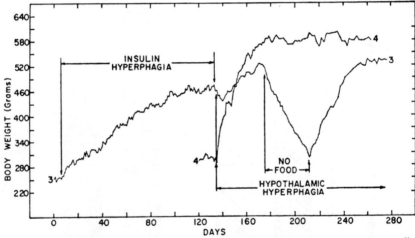

FIG. 16–7. Rate of weight gain in rats with lesions of the ventromedial nucleus of the hypothalamus. Rat 3 is previously induced to become obese by insulin injections. Rat 4 starts from a normal weight. The rate of gain of weight in rat 3 is also illustrated after it has been reduced after operation to its previous weight by being deprived of food. (From Teitelbaum, P., *Excerpta Medica*, No. 47, 1962, p. 700.)

weight increase levels off. The overeating in this phase does not seem to be a result of greater hunger because when animals with ventromedial lesions have attained their final weight, though they overeat and maintain their body weight, they actually seem less hungry than normal animals on indices of hunger other than eating (Miller, Bailey, and Stevenson, 1950; Teitelbaum, 1957).

For instance, if the task of obtaining food is at all strenuous or the food somewhat unpalatable, the ventromedial rat will tend to be more easily discouraged from obtaining or ingesting food than the normal rat. However, under conditions of normal availability of food, the hyperphagic rat will eat a larger meal (Teitelbaum, 1958). These results are to be expected if the path which normally inhibits eating via an advance message has been knocked out. The animal without its ventromedial nuclei would only stop eating when the change which had occasioned eating had been reversed. In fact, the ventromedial animal has been converted into a simple homeostat as far as its food regulation is concerned. As a result, the animal overeats. This was predicted by the simple homeostat view. With larger meals, excess food is stored before it can all be used, resulting in obesity. The reason animals with ventromedial hypothalamic lesions actually seem less hungry though they eat more is, as Teitelbaum's (1957) work strongly suggests, the result of their obesity. These obese animals are not as strongly affected by food deprivation as normal rats. Smaller hunger-initiating changes may occur in an obese animal than in a normal animal when food deprivation conditions are equal.

There is also some likelihood that the reward value of eating is diminished in animals without the ventromedial hypothalamus. It seems (Teitelbaum, 1964) that a normal reward or feedback path is interrupted by lesions of the ventromedial nucleus of the hypothalamus. When normal rats are provided with a lever which they can press to cause delivery of a nutrient solution directly into their stomach, they will learn to press it rapidly and thus regulate their food intake within normal limits. However, rats with lesions of the ventromedial nucleus have great difficulty in learning to do this. Teitelbaum (1964) believes that some rats would even starve to death in this situation if they were not rescued. However, if a sweet taste is coupled with the intragastric injection, a lesioned animal will work hard enough at pressing the lever to become obese again.

It is also possible to produce lesions of the ventromedial nucleus of the hypothalamus by administration of gold thioglucose to mice. This substance tends to be selectively absorbed by the nuclei and destroys them by its toxic action. Such findings have been used to support the notion that the ventromedial nuclei are sensitive to the glucose level and so produce satiation when glucose enters them (Mayer and Marshall, 1956). On the other hand, Perry and Liebelt (1959) have shown that such injections also cause lesions in the fornix, hippocampus, preoptic area, and vagal nuclei, areas where the blood-brain barrier has greater permeability.

An experiment with many interesting possibilities in elucidating the role of the factors causing satiety was conducted by Hervey (1959). He used parabiotic rats (rats which have been made into artificial siamese twins) so that substances present in one rat can diffuse slowly into the other rat. Hervey removed the ventromedial nuclei from one of the rats of such a pair. The lesioned rat became obese, as would be expected. It also could be expected that the nutrients derived from the excessive eating by the lesioned rat would make its partner obese. However, the partner became very thin, which would seem to indicate that only the substance producing satiety had diffused from the lesioned partner (where it would be produced without effect by excessive eating).

However, the nonlesioned partner does not always become very thin. For instance, Fleming (1969) obtains this effect in only a small proportion of his parabiotic rats, and Han et al. (1963) do not obtain the effect. As the factors determining these variations have not been isolated, elucidation of the theoretical importance of this effect must be left to further research. One of these factors may be found in the rate of exchange of blood and body fluids in parabiotic rats in different laboratories. The rate of exchange of body fluids in these rats is slow, and small differences in the rate of exchange may determine just what components are transferred. Some components may be fast decaying, and these would transfer only if the rate of transfer is sufficiently high.

Hoebel and Teitelbaum (1966) have shown that rats will overeat, eat less, or eat the same amount after lesions of the ventromedial nucleus of the hypothalamus depending on their weight at the time of operation. For instance, rats that had been made extremely obese by forced feeding would lose weight after being allowed to regulate their own food intake after a ventromedial lesion and would stabilize their weight at a lower level of obesity. A similar phenomenon has been demonstrated by Powley and Keesey (1969) in the case of lesions of the lateral area of the hypothalamus. Rats whose weight had been reduced by food deprivation prior to the operation would perhaps even become hyperphagic after the operation when allowed access to food, though their weight would stabilize below the point normal for such rats. In less extreme cases, weight loss prior to the operation dramatically shortened the duration of postoperational aphagia and anorexia. These experiments again confirm the notion that these lesions produce alterations in a homeostatic mechanism to produce deviations from the level at which the organism stabilizes.

Stimulation of the ventromedial nucleus produces a decrease in eating (Smith, 1956; Wyrwicka and Dobrzecka, 1960). However, Krasne (1962) showed that this may be due to the aversive effects of the stimulation rather than a specific satiating effect. Further, cessation of stimulation of the nucleus is followed by eating. This is a rebound effect and is very powerful. However, it is interesting that the latency of the eating after stimulation has ceased may be several minutes.

Electrical Recordings from the Hypothalamus

Anand (1961) and his collaborators have measured activity in the ventromedial and lateral regions of the hypothalamus by means of electrical recordings. They reported that during hyperglycemia there is an increase of activity in the ventromedial nucleus and some decrease of activity in the lateral region. Hypoglycemia produced the reverse picture.

Interaction between Hunger and Thirst. Since most food is hypertonic, when an animal eats it also becomes thirsty. It has been shown (Cizek, 1959) that a dog's water intake decreases when available food is decreased and water intake increases when food intake increases. It seems, therefore, that a great deal of drinking occurs because eating has induced thirst. Similarly, it is a common observation that food intake drops sharply when water is not available. It seems as if thirst, or its physiological cause, in some way inhibits eating. (This is a useful arrangement because the consequences of the factors producing thirst damage the organism more rapidly than the consequences resulting from lack of food.) Consequently, the consumption of a hypertonic substance gradually ceases as thirst begins to be induced (Shuford, 1955). In separate tests, rats were given solutions of sucrose and glucose, which were equally preferred. The rats would stop drinking glucose earlier because glucose has a higher osmotic pressure. Experiments by McCleary (1953) and Schwartzbaum and Ward (1958) show that the osmotic pressure of substances placed in the stomach before ingestion of other substances is permitted also influences the amount subsequently ingested. The reduction in subsequent ingestion is a function only of the osmotic pressure of the preload. It is unlikely that these experiments show, as has been suggested, that osmotic pressure produces normal satiation of hunger. Rather, it seems that they illustrate the point made above; namely, that a thirsty animal will not make itself thirstier.

Stimuli Evoking Ingestion and Provoking Aversion

Unlearned Attractiveness of Certain Visual Stimuli Related to Feeding and Drinking. What leads animals to ingest some substances and to reject others? Though many preferences and aversions are learned, there is evidence that others are unlearned. (Some of the unlearned gustatory preferences have already been discussed [pp. 545–50].) Investigations have been carried out concerning the unlearned attractiveness of certain visual properties. For instance, Tinbergen and Perdeck (1950) demonstrated that the newly hatched herring gull chick would peck at objects resembling the beak of an adult herring gull. This chick is fed in the nest by its parent, and the sight of the adult beak is sufficient to evoke responses which are a part of the eating pattern. This responsiveness to stimuli which emanate from the adult beak is probably innate because it was found that these responses can be evoked most effectively by dummies of a normal adult beak. These dummies were far from exact copies of the adult beak, and in a certain sense were beak caricatures. Dummies which were much narrower than an adult beak and which had several adjacent, narrow bands of orange color at the base of the beak were superior to a natural beak. The adult herring gull has an orange patch near the base of its beak. Thus by exaggerating some of the properties of the beak, a much more effective stimulus to pecking was found. If the herring gull chick had learned that the properties of the adult beak were attractive because it had been fed after seeing the beak, we should have expected the natural beak to be the most attractive.

Rheingold and Hess (1957) obtained a similar result when experimenting with the attractiveness of certain visual properties of water to newly hatched domestic chicks. In this experiment, factors of previous reward were more closely investigated. Rheingold and Hess attempted to isolate the cues which evoke a drinking behavior pattern in newly hatched chicks. Such a pattern is distinct from their pecking behavior. When the chick pecks, it begins with its beak pointed down and its head directly above the object it is attempting to ingest, and then it strikes with a quick motion downward, jerking its head up again at the end of the stroke. The drinking response is different in that the downward phase of the movement is slower and the beak is pushed forward when it touches the substance to be drunk, and then it is tilted up. The same stereotyped movement occurs even when a hard substance has evoked the response.

The subjects of Rheingold and Hess were three-day-old chicks which had never eaten or drunk. (Up to this age, a chick can live on the internal yolk sac without undue detriment.) Each chick was placed in an experimental arrangement with six different substances placed around it in a semicircle. These substances were (a) tap water, (b) water colored blue to such an extent that it was no longer translucent, (c) water colored red but still translucent, (d) a circle of polished aluminum, (e) mercury, and (f) a hard, translucent plastic which looked like water to the human eye. In order to eliminate learning, each chick was allowed to respond only once. The results showed that most of the chicks attempted to drink the mercury. Progressively fewer chose plastic, blue water, tap water, aluminum, and red water (in that order). Only a third as many chicks preferred tap water to mercury.

After seven days the majority of these chicks—which had in the meantime been given experience with food and water—were given the same test again. Though they had received four days' experience with water and had been deprived of it for 12 hours, the relative number of chicks approaching the test stimuli was practically unchanged. Mercury again attracted the largest number and tap water the fourth largest. So it seems that mercury, as the artificial beak used by Tinbergen and Perdeck (see above), is more effective in evoking a particular response than the natural stimuli of water. Such stimuli have been termed "supernormal" by the ethologists. They have been demonstrated to exist in other contexts besides eating and drinking. For instance, it has been shown that the oyster catcher will attempt to incubate eggs larger than itself in preference to those in its own nest.

Thus the experiment of Rheingold and Hess convincingly shows that there are certain characteristics of substances which make animals attempt to ingest them without having had any previous process of learning. It further shows that when animals are placed among substances which were not present to the species during its evolution, such innate preferences may actually lead to the ingestion of useless or deleterious substances. Sometimes such substances may possess the characteristics of a supernormal stimulus, and therefore these useless or deleterious substances may be ingested in preference to the substance which is physiologically beneficial because the useless substances in some way, and to a greater degree, possess the attractive characteristics of the beneficial substance.

Fantz (1957) performed a similar experiment on innate, visually controlled food preferences in domestic chicks. He used different test objects of various shapes to see which the chicks peck at. Hess and Gogel (1954) had demonstrated such a preference in the case of colors. In his initial experiments, Fantz used newly hatched, one- to three-day-old domestic chicks which did not have any experience of food or water. They were tested in groups placed in various boxes. These boxes contained stimuli in the form of various small objects which were inedible. These could be pecked but not dislodged. The number of pecks at each object was recorded by means of the closure of an electric contact whenever a peck occurred. The results clearly show that the chicks pecked consistently more at round objects than at angular objects. Though the chicks' order of preference for "edible" shape was maintained even after pecking which was unrewarded and also after feeding, it was possible to alter the preference (though not entirely) by giving the chicks food of an irregular, rather than a round, shape.

It seems clear, therefore, that when the chick hatches, it is already predisposed to ingest objects with certain preferred visual qualities. In the case of drinking, some of the properties of water, such as a shiny and mobile surface, seem attractive; in the case of eating, properties of food such as roundness (seeds and grain) evoke a pecking response. Such an arrangement has a clear biological usefulness because it increases the probability that in its ordinary environment a chick, upon hatching, will begin to drink or to peck at substances which are physiologically beneficial. It will therefore tend to eliminate some of the trial-and-error processes which would be necessary if the chick had to learn, without any initial built-in bias, what objects or substances are edible or drinkable.

Stimuli Provoking Aversion

If it is useful for animals to be so constructed as to be attracted to certain kinds of objects or substances when they are hungry or thirsty, it is even more important that they should not ingest substances that are deleterious or harmful. Though it would be a handicap if a young chick were required to learn every characteristic of food objects in its environment, it would be an even greater danger to its life if it did not avoid certain properties of vision, taste, or smell. There are many substances in an animal's environment which would kill the animal or incapacitate it if they were ingested. Those individuals in a species which do not avoid harmful substances will not survive to reproduce. Therefore there is a high selective pressure for a species where the mechanism for the avoidance of harmful substances is inborn. We should therefore, on evolutionary grounds, expect to find properties or qualities of substances which produce avoidance of a substance. In this way an animal is safeguarded against ingesting harmful substances which are present in the environment during the evolution of the species.

The problem of blocking certain behavior patterns in spite of the presence of the correct stimulating conditions must also be solved during other types of activity besides eating and drinking. For instance, many of the characteristics which evoke mating or copulatory reactions are present in individuals—or even objects—with which mating is unlikely to lead to offspring. Through the process of natural selection, the properties of objects incapable of successful mating become repulsive to the animal, just as eating certain objects becomes aversive. By natural selection, individuals are selected with mechanisms which will block mating when certain characteristics are present, since these individuals are more likely to have progeny.

Amygdalectomy and Aversive Function

Many of the behavioral abnormalities found by Kl (1939) to occur in monkeys following bilateral tempora:

also be produced by ablation of structures in the amygdaloid complex (see Chapter 10). Bilateral removal of this complex results in a whole set of symptoms. The animals become very tractable and tame (though exceptions have been noted), sexually indiscriminate (see also p. 573), and eat objects such as feces. Food selection is altered since the animals will now ingest such foods as meat or fish which they normally reject (Pribram and Bagshaw, 1953). Weiskrantz (personal communication) has established that such indiscriminate eating behavior is not the result of a sensory deficit in taste. Before their bilateral amygdalectomy, he trained rhesus monkeys on a two-bottle preference situation in order to establish what concentration of saccharin these animals preferred. He used four different concentrations of saccharin in successive conditions. He also incorporated trials in which both bottles contained only water. At the same time as he carried out this saccharin solution preference test, he also carried out another experiment on the same animal to determine its absolute threshold for saccharin. He did this by rewarding some of the monkeys with a small piece of apple if they licked up five drops of saccharin and ignored the water from a container, the selection being made by taste. Other monkeys were rewarded with a piece of apple if they chose the water instead of the saccharin.

Weizkrantz repeated all of these tests after bilateral amygdalectomy. He found that the postoperative threshold for saccharin did not change. Trying to obtain a piece of apple, the animals could distinguish a weak solution of saccharin from water, just as they could before the operation. However, preference for solutions of saccharin changed. The postoperative animals would drink the stronger concentrations of saccharin which they had tended to reject before amygdalectomy. (Saccharin tastes bitter in strong concentrations.) Behavior of the control operates (animals which had part of their striate cortex removed) did not appear to be significantly altered. Weiskrantz concluded that preference can be altered without any change in taste sensitivity, as measured by standard discrimination techniques. The results of this experiment also make it plausible to believe that a part of the system which leads the animal to reject certain substances has been removed. As has been argued, from general behavioral considerations it appears plausible that there are two systems which determine what an animal will treat as food. The first system leads an animal to select objects for food on the basis of certain qualities. The second system leads the animal to reject objects as food because of certain other inherent qualities. We may suppose that the second system is damaged in bilateral amygdalectomy.

It is probable that the two systems are usually in balance, and depending on the strength of each system, selection takes its course. The hungrier an animal becomes, the stronger the attractive qualities of food become. As a result, aversive food which the animal would not ordinarily eat will be ingested because the animal is very hungry. Similarly, an animal that is nearly satiated will be more selective about its food than a hungry animal. Since animals with bilateral ablation of the amygdaloid complex are deficient in their aversion to food, they should eat more at each meal than normal control animals, especially if both groups are fed coarse diets. If the diet has fewer aversive properties, the difference in preference of the two groups of animals should be decreased. In fact, animals without the amygdaloid complex become fatter than normal control animals.

Another line of evidence is obtained from ventromedial operates. Here the animal continues to eat, in spite of being in a very low hunger-drive state. We should expect the operation of the aversive factor to be more clearly revealed in such an animal.

Teitelbaum (1955) has observed that the intake of ventromedial operates is very greatly affected by the sensory properties of their diet. Though these animals eat much more than normal animals, they are more fastidious and respond to a coarsening of the diet by decreasing their intake. Such observations on animals with lesions closely agrees with what would be expected of the mechanism as inferred above from behavioral and physiological data.

Some investigators have reported that lesions of the amygdaloid complex produce hypophagia. Green et al. (1957) found that damage to the anterior portion of the amygdala produced a decrease in eating whereas lesions near the junction of the basal and lateral nuclei produced overeating. Koikegami et al. (1955) have also reported hypophagia or aphagia after lesions to the amygdala. It seems that this region is also involved in water intake as well as in food intake. Grossman and Grossman (1963) showed that small lesions in this area produced overdrinking as well as overeating. Further, chronic electrical stimulation reduced both food and water intake. This makes it probable that lesions which produce hypophagia have an irritative effect, since the effects of lesions and stimulation are in the same direction.

Influences on eating and drinking through chemical stimulation of the amygdala have been demonstrated by Grossman (1964). Reliable effects occur only if the animal is already hungry or thirsty. An adrenergic agent (norepinephrine) led to increased food motivation while an adrenergic blocking agent (dibenzyline) led to a decrease of such motivation. A cholinergic agent (carbachol) greatly increased thirst motivation while atropine (an anticholinergic agent) led to its decrease. As mentioned above (p. 597), similar pharmacological sensitivities occur in the hypothalamus. The fact that reliable effects can only be obtained while the animal is in a drive state further supports the view that the amygdala modulates eating or drinking rather than causes it. For instance, increases or decreases of aversion to the quality of food being eaten would mainly become manifest only when the animal was eating.

Lesions of the frontal cortex have also been reported to produce hyperphagia (Richter and Hawkes, 1939; Langworth and Richter, 1939). The relation to ventromedial hypothalamic and amygdaloid hyperphagia is obscure at present.

DIETARY SELECTION

Thus far hunger has been treated as if it were a unitary phenomenon, but hunger is in reality a name for a group of associated appetites. It is possible, for instance, for a rat to be satiated for carbohydrate and yet be hungry for protein. When a rat is kept in a cage by the experimenter and supplied with a prepared compound rat cake, the rat does not have to select the components of its diet in order to maintain itself free of deficiency disease. On the other hand, an animal living in a free environment must select naturally occurring foods in such a way that dietary deficiency is avoided. Such an ability to select an adequate diet in a controlled setting has been demonstrated by Davis (1928), who worked with young children, and by Richter (1942a), who worked with rats. In fact, rats allowed to make such a selection grow more rapidly than those fed on a standard laboratory diet (Richter, 1942b).

Because selection of diet by the animal normally results in maintenance of a healthy condition, it seems plausible to assume that the animal selects its diet on the basis of a physiological need. We would then expect that if the physiological need shifted, diet selection would show a corresponding alteration. Such is the case, for instance, in pregnancy. There is an increase in the intake of fat, protein, and minerals, but sugar intake is lowered. This corresponds to the requirements of the developing fetuses (Richter, 1942a). Dietary selection returns to normal after the young are weaned. Artificially induced deficits similarly lead to corrective selection. For instance, rats in which the pancreas has been removed decrease their intake of sugar to avoid diabetic symptoms but increase their intake of fat to maintain caloric intake (Richter and Schmidt, 1941). Also, after removal of the parathyroid gland, which has the consequence of increasing levels of phosphorus and decreasing levels of calcium, rats avoid phosphorus compounds and increase their calcium intake (Richter, 1939).

A species can adapt itself in relation to dietary requirements in various ways. It is possible to select individuals who have simple requirements concerning food sources. Thus a species may be selected which can live on a single food source, such as eucalyptus leaves in the case of Koala bears or mulberry leaves in the case of silkworms. The silkworm, if it eats mulberry leaves, is supplied with all it needs for healthy development. In this way the animal has adapted so that, provided it eats enough of one particular foodstuff, it will not suffer dietary deficiency. The animal is somewhat like the laboratory rat in a cage. At the other extreme, we may imagine an animal which evolved in an environment in which the combinations of basic food components were very unstable or random. Such an animal cannot adapt by choosing one kind of food-stuff sufficient for all its needs. It must be able to select its diet so that by varying the intake of different foodstuffs the correct proportions of needed nutrients will be ingested. Such an animal might, for instance, learn to detect the various constituents in food which it needs and then regulate its food intake according to the amount of these food components already ingested. A species of animal living in a capricious dietary environment cannot adapt by picking some naturally packaged combination of nutrients because no single package exists in the environment we have imagined. Such a species must separately recognize the various important dietary components.

However, usually the natural food environment of a species is such that the needed combinations or packages of nutrients are present. These nutrients have their own distinctive odors, tastes, and visual properties. Most animals consequently adapt in a manner somewhere between the two extremes outlined above. Many animals are equipped to select their diet from a variety of naturally occurring nutrient combinations in their environment so they can maintain themselves in good health. However, any one environment contains naturally occurring nutrient packages or combinations in which there are large sets of differing food components regularly associated in fixed proportions. On the whole, most animals only have an ability to recognize these packages and not their separate components.

Whether a species of animal has adapted by developing an ability to select naturally occurring combinations of nutrients or to select a variety of foodstuffs, in either case the animal in innately attracted to the sight and taste of the substance as it occurs naturally. In many cases it appears that animals have evolved in such a way that when they have a specific physiological nutrient deficit, it is translated directly into a craving for a certain taste. Epstein and Stellar (1955) (see p. 636) showed that the appetite for salt occurred without learning when the salt deficiency occurred. Thus it is unlikely that tests in the laboratory can reflect the ability of a species to select an adequate diet in the food environment in which it evolved. Food substances offered to the animal in the laboratory may look, feel, taste, and smell unlike those found by the animal in its natural environment.

However, there are cases where animals can select foodstuffs on a basis which does not reflect built-in preferences. In such cases, animals may learn to ingest substances because of their beneficial aftereffects.

For instance, Harris et al. (1933) performed experiments on the ability of vitamin B–deficient rats to discriminate between diets in which this vitamin was either present or absent. If the rats were not given a large choice of diets, after a short period of learning they were able to discriminate and eat the diet containing the vitamin. Having learned that one of the diets was beneficial, the rats would still continue to eat it when the vitamin was left out. Learning in this instance is dependent on the rapid relief of symptoms, since the beneficial aftereffects of ingestion of this vitamin are rapid. When relief of symptoms is slow, as with vitamins A and D, learning does not take place. The same experiments carried out with animals deficient in vitamin A and vitamin D yielded negative results; that is, the animals could not learn to select the right mixture to remedy their deficiency. It was concluded that the amelioration of the animals' condition was not rapid enough in these cases.

While animals cannot learn to select certain vitamins, such as A and D, because the beneficial consequences occur too long after the relevant substances have been tasted, harmful consequences of eating seem to be associated for much longer periods of time. If the ingestion of a substance is followed by some aversive event, such as X-ray irradiation, the rat will show an aversion to the taste which preceded the noxious stimulus (Garcia et al., 1966; Kimmeldorf and Hunt, 1965; Smith and Morris, 1964). Consumption of sucrose, followed seven hours later by X-ray irradiation, produced an aversion to sucrose in rats (Revusky, 1968).

It has been shown by Rozin (1967) and Booth and Simson (1971) that aversive learning is an important component in dietary selection. Rodgers and Rozin (1966) showed that thiamine-deficient rats would show preference for any new diet over the standard thiamine-deficient diet. A similar preference for novel diets in rats deficient in pyridoxine, riboflavin, or minerals has been demonstrated by Rozin and Rodgers (1967) and Rogers (1967). Rozin (1967) has shown that rats kept for a time on a thiamine-deficient diet continue to avoid this deficient diet even after they have been permitted to recover.

It also seems that such long-term associations can be formed by rats only between gustatory or olfactory stimuli and noxious aftereffects, and not between visual or auditory stimuli and such aftereffects. However, Holman's (1968) work suggests that similar long-term associations can be formed by rats between stimuli and their beneficial aftereffects. He found that rats would perform a response to obtain intragastric food only when some interoceptive stimulus was provided when the intragastric injection was made. For instance, rats would press when the food injected into the stomach through a tube running down the esophagus was cold but not if it was at body temperature. Association could apparently be made between beneficial aftereffects and a stimulus when such a stimulus was oropharyngeal. External clicks were not suffi-cient. Holman's work makes it probable that previous work showing reward by direct administration of food into the stomach was mediated by secondary reinforcers arising from various oropharyngeal sensations (e.g., Snowdon, 1969; Borer, 1968).

Scott and Verney (1947) showed that an appetite for the B complex of vitamins was acquired. If the food containing this vitamin was flavored with anise, animals deficient in B complex would learn to ingest the food with the anise taste instead of the plain food. If the vitamin was left out of the diet flavored with anise but added to the plain food instead, the rats would prefer to eat the plain food. In this way the experiment ruled out the possibility that the animals simply preferred food with a particular flavor and that their choice was independent of vitamin content.

Further, in a test which measured food intake over a three-week pe-riod, Scott and Quint (1946) have demonstrated that rats deficient in thiamine (vitamin B_1), riboflavin (vitamin B_2), and pyridoxine (vitamin B_6) will preferentially select foods containing these vitamins. Rats which were not deficient in these substances showed no such preferential selec-tion. On the other hand, when pantothenate deficiency occurred, the rat found it difficult to learn what food to select. Scott and Quint found that an appetite for pantothenate cannot be developed unless the diet containing it is labeled with anise. However, even then some animals made the wrong choice.

It has been shown in the preceding examples that under some circum-stances animals may learn to ingest diets which were at first preferen-tially neural. Provided that the beneficial aftereffects of ingestion are rapid enough and provided that there are not too many alternatives to confuse the animal, it will learn to eat what is good for it. However, such a diet must not, on the other hand, be initially repulsive or aversive. As has been pointed out above (p. 550), an animal will avoid foods of certain tastes, smells, or other sensory properties because its ancestors did not consume such foods and they survived to reproduce and transmit their "dislikes" to their progeny. Animals have many such aversions which often extend to substances which are beneficial or harmless. Human beings also find certain tastes repugnant. The bitterness of qui-nine, for instance, is extremely unpleasant. Rats, monkeys, and other animals also dislike quinine. Jukes (1938) found that even chickens avoided diets containing more than 0.03 percent quinine. They also avoided food containing more than 2 percent salt or 2 percent citric acid. Rats have been observed by Deuel and Movitt (1944) to dislike rancid flavors. Scott and Quint (1946) found that rats previously fed an unflavored diet avoided food with the taste of trimethylamine, which has a fishy flavor. Scott and Verney (1947) further found that rats disliked lactose, and Scott and Quint (1946) found that many more animals refused egg albumen in a mixed diet than other purified proteins, such as casein, lactalbumen, and fibrin.

Since certain properties will produce a strong aversion in animals, it is not altogether surprising that when some animals are given certain choices of purified food components they would die rather than eat the evil-tasting and putrid-smelling beneficial substance offered to them. An experiment performed by Scott (1946) illustrates this point. He used six-week-old albino rats. In their cage were four cups containing the following food components necessary for growth: sucrose, hydrogenated fat, casein, and a mixture of salts. Casein was liked by some rats and not liked by others. If they liked casein, they ate an average of 3 gm. per day and grew well. If they did not like it, they ate less than .01 gm. per day and died within a short time. That there was something unlearned about this dislike of casein is shown by a similarity in appetite between rats that were littermates. This may be interpreted as a failure of rats to select a beneficial diet, as shown in a similar experiment by Pilgrim and Patton (1947). It should, however, be pointed out that purified casein has unattractive properties, at least to the human observer. It seems probable that in its natural environment an animal may avoid a substance with such properties as casein and increase its chances of survival.

Just as beneficial substances which have a taste that usually belongs to poisons and therefore are avoided are found only in the laboratory, nonbeneficial substances are ingested in the laboratory because they share certain sensory properties with beneficial substances. Again, the normal association between the flavor of a substance and its aftereffects which is found in the animal's natural environment may not be present in the laboratory. For example, Hausmann (1933) discovered that rats would drink large quantities of saccharin solution, which to the human tongue tastes sweet but which is of no nutritive value. A sweet taste is usually an indication of the presence of sugars and is characteristic of ripe fruit or young vegetable shoots. Another interesting dissociation which can be demonstrated in the laboratory occurs in the case of diacetyl, a compound found in milk, and which, when used with monobutyrin and butyric acid, produces the flavor of butter. Deuel and Movitt (1944) found that diets to which this substance was added were preferred by rats. They conjectured that this may be manufactured by the lactating female to impart a characteristic taste to her milk. Though the milk itself has great nutritional importance, the dissociated flavoring material, diacetyl, possesses no physiological function as far as is known. It does not, for instance, act like a vitamin—so that, although it is nutritionally useful for a rat in its natural environment to ingest substances such as milk, which tastes of diacetyl, the consumption of the flavoring material itself brings no benefit. It seems likely that an appetite for diacetyl may arise when the rat is short of some of the substances which in the normal environment are always associated with a diacetyl flavor.

A further point should be made concerning laboratory investigation of special appetites. The usual species employed in tests of dietary self-selection have been either domestic or laboratory strains of animals, such as chickens or albino rats. These strains of animals have not, on the whole, been selected for their ability to maintain a balanced diet. They have, rather, been selected for such characteristics as excessive egg laying or tameness. Such traits may be linked to inefficient food selection. That such hereditary considerations are of importance has been demonstrated by Scott (1946), who found that rats that are littermates tend to have similar appetites.

Detailed Investigations of Special Appetites

One of the cases where it has been possible to demonstrate that an animal will make up a specific nutritional deficit is that involving sodium chloride (common salt). Richter (1942) demonstrated that when adrenal-ectomized rats, which lose sodium at a rapid rate (and so usually die in a few days if not provided with excess salt), are given access to salt, they will ingest enough 3 percent solution of salt to survive free of symptoms of salt deficiency. It has been suggested that adrenalectomized rats learn to ingest adequate amounts of salt because of the beneficial aftereffects of the ingestion of salt; that is, the animal learns to eat a substance that alleviates certain deficiency symptoms. Such an argument appears to be supported by the fact that such adrenalecto-mized animals increase their salt intake gradually after operation. However, Epstein and Stellar (1955) point out that this gradual increase in intake might, instead, reflect an increased need for sodium as progressively more if it is lost by the animal after its operation. To decide between the two hypotheses, they tested two groups of rats. The first was allowed access to a salt solution immediately after the operation and the second was given access to it only after a few days. They found that the first group did indeed increase its salt intake gradually. However, when the second group was given the salt solution, it immediately consumed as much as the first group. This study demonstrates that the increased appetite for salt in adrenalectomized rats is unlearned. Further evidence that sodium-deficient rats have a strong innate preference for the taste of sodium salts has been found by Rodgers (1967).

A further experiment points to the same conclusion since it seems that rats cannot learn to ingest salt if they cannot taste it. Richter (1942) found that when he sectioned the nerves which convey messages from the taste receptors (glossopharyngeal, chorda tympani, and lingual), the animals which were salt deficient could no longer select the needed solution. Wolf (1968) has shown that lesions in the gustatory nucleus in the thalamus reduce or abolish the rat's response to sodium deficiency. It is perhaps not surprising that if an animal cannot taste salt, it cannot display a salt appetite.

One may suggest that hunger for sodium chloride is regulated similarly to thirst. A deficit gives rise to excitation in cells which are specifically sensitive to such a deficit. This gives rise to ingestion, which produces afferent impulses. These afferent impulses, originating in the salt receptors, serve to desensitize the cells irritated by the initial deficit. Some evidence relating to the localization of the tissue sensitive to sodium deficit has been found. Wolf (1964) has shown that bilateral lesions in rats in the dorsal part of the lateral area of the hypothalamus produce a loss of reaction to sodium deficiency. Animals with such lesions do not increase their intake of salt after induced salt deficiency.

The appetite for sweet-tasting substances also appears to be a specific hunger, though the precise physiological deficit which occasions the appetite has not been identified. However, it has been noted that during food deprivation, consumption of sweet-tasting non-nutritious solutions increases (Carper and Polliard, 1953). Moreover, it has been demonstrated that the afferent message regulates intake of sweet substances. Hagstrom and Pfaffmann (1959) have produced evidence that the amount of a sweet-tasting substance, such as fructose and sucrose, drunk in an ad libitum consumption situation, correlated inversely with the amount of activity generated by "sweet" taste receptors in the chorda tympani. Hagstrom and Pfaffmann conclude that postingestional factors are responsible for this correlation because they assume that the amount ingested in the ad libitum situation is a direct measure of preference. However, these authors also found that the amount of activity in the chorda tympani was closely correlated with the reward value or preference of the substances when the quantity of various sweet-tasting liquid substances was limited. This is the inverse of the ad libitum situation.

This result is comparable with the result found by Deutsch and Jones (1959, 1960) on the overdrinking and reward value of hypotonic saline, and it fits the diluted water hypothesis. On the basis of this hypothesis, we would expect ingestion to cease when a certain quantity of afferent messages has impinged on the center sensitive to physiological deficit. Two equal volumes of substances such as equiosmolar solutions of sucrose and fructose produce different amounts of a "sweet" signal in the afferent pathway. Then we would expect a greater consumption of the solution which produces a smaller amount of afferent signal because each unit of volume will produce less desensitization of the initiating center. Therefore, on the basis of this hypothesis, the amount drunk in an ad libitum situation is not a measure of preference but a measure of the effectiveness of a substance in producing satiation. This hypothesis also regards the amount of a specific afferent message produced by an ingested substance as being directly proportional to its reward value. Therefore, if the same equiosmotic volumes of sucrose and fructose are ingested, the sucrose should be the more rewarding because it generates a larger number of afferent signals. So we should predict an inverse relation between the satiation value of substances and their reward. Such a finding, hitherto regarded as paradoxical, has also been obtained by Young and Greene (1953). These authors found that the animal preferred more concentrated sucrose solutions when it had to choose between various dilutions of sucrose in a situation where intake was restricted. However, more dilute solutions of sucrose were "preferred" (i.e., larger quantities were consumed) when ad libitum drinking was permitted in another situation.

It seems that this appetite for sweet-tasting substances is inborn. De Snoo (1937) studied 20 pregnant women suffering from polyhydramnios, a painful swelling of the abdomen due to an excess of amniotic fluid in the uterus. He was able to show that this disorder was caused by a failure on the part of the fetus to drink amniotic fluid because (for some reason or other) the amniotic fluid in these patients did not taste sweet. When saccharin (a non-nutritive sweet-tasting substance) was injected, the painful swelling of the abdomen promptly went down. Methylene blue was injected to make sure that this was an effect of drinking on the part of the fetus and not some effect of the saccharin on secretion of amniotic fluid. De Snoo's hypothesis was corroborated when this harmless dye appeared in the mother's urine after, but not before, saccharin was injected. It seems that the fetus begins to drink when the taste of the amniotic fluid becomes sweet.

When given access to saccharin solution, rats will also ingest large quantities of it. Carper and Polliard (1953) found that an animal will consume large quantities of saccharin when it is hungry. As has been mentioned before, saccharin is non-nutritive. The evidence that saccharin is drunk by rats in spite of its non-nutritive value again lends support to the notion that it is an unlearned special hunger, as De Snoo's observation seems to indicate. However, it should be mentioned that Smith and Capretta (1956) dissent from this view. They noted that animals used in experiments on saccharin ingestion could have been digesting food while they were allowed to drink the saccharin. Therefore it is possible that the rats erroneously learned that the saccharin reduced their hunger, causing them to drink it in large quantities. Consequently, an experiment was designed so that some of the rats were given the saccharin solution only after having been deprived of food for a long time. Other rats were allowed to drink soon after they had been fed. Smith and Capretta found that saccharin was treated as less rewarding by the group of rats which received the saccharin when they were hungry than by the control group which had been given the saccharin while the processes of digestion were still occurring. They therefore concluded that saccharin consumption is due to erroneous learning.

However, other interpretations of this experiment are possible. Saccharin has various properties which might have produced such a result. The rate of absorption into the blood stream of hungry animals may have been much higher than in animals which had just eaten. It is known that an injection of saccharin produces a bitter taste in the mouth whereas an injection of sucrose produces a sweet taste. (Saccharin in high concentrations in the mouth also tastes bitter.) In this way a high blood level of saccharin may have produced an unpleasant taste which was aversive to the animals. It would be interesting to repeat this experiment on rats with esophageal fistulae, or to use other sweet-tasting substances without the peculiar properties of saccharin.

Hoarding

An activity which is closely related to eating and food deprivation is hoarding. In their natural state, many animals meet a situation in which food is plentiful at one time and scarce at another. In the temperate zone, a time of plenty occurs in the fall and a time of scarcity in the winter. Many rodents carry food back to their burrows in the fall. One of the signals for such activity is low environmental temperature (McCleary and Morgan, 1946).

Evolutionary pressures have ensured that hoarding takes place in the fall rather than in the summer. Another factor which promotes food hoarding is food deprivation. Hoarding does not normally occur in rats that have always been given unlimited access to food. It is necessary to partially deprive rats for some days before hoarding makes its appearance (Wolfe, 1939; Stellar and Morgan, 1943). On the other hand, hoarding is not due to hunger at the time of hoarding. Once rats have undergone a few days of partial deprivation, they hoard while they are temporarily satiated. In fact, while they are very hungry, rats will eat rather than hoard (Morgan, Stellar, and Johnson, 1943).

Herberg and Blundell (1967) demonstrated that electrical stimulation of the hypothalamic feeding area evokes intense hoarding activity. On the other hand, it is noteworthy that Blundell and Herberg (1970) were unable to evoke hoarding by microinjections of norepinephrine into this area. Further, Herberg and Blundell (1970) showed that hyperphagia produced by lesions in the ventromedial nucleus of the hypothalamus does not in itself produce hoarding. In fact, rats with ventromedial lesions do not hoard if they are allowed to become obese. On the other hand, they hoard if their body weight is reduced below normal. It seems, therefore, that nutritional status influences the propensity to hoard, regardless of the presence of the ventromedial nucleus of the hypothalamus.

Herberg and Blundell (1970) provide an elegant theory to account for their data and those of others on hoarding. They assume that the lateral hypothalamus conveys messages concerning the nutritional status of the organism. Some of these pathways lead to eating activity, and are inhibited by the ventromedial nucleus. Other pathways, also conveying information about the organism's nutritional status, are not connected to the ventromedial nucleus, and they lead to hoarding activity when they are active. In this way both eating and hoarding are evoked by neural activity in the pathways of the lateral hypothalamus signaling depletion. Eating leads to an inhibition of the pathways leading to eating (because of their connection to the ventromedial hypothalamus), while it does not affect the activity of the pathways leading to hoarding. This explains why deprivation is necessary to evoke hoarding and why satiation through eating does not stop hoarding. Removal of the ventromedial nucleus in itself does not affect hoarding, although it produces an increase in eating. It also explains why stimulation of the lateral hypothalamus produces hoarding.

The major unexplained finding is that microinjections of norepinephrine do not produce hoarding but produce eating instead. This is explained by assuming that norepinephrine produces hunger by producing disinhibition of the lateral hypothalamus from the ventromedial nucleus. In this way, when norepinephrine is injected there is a temporary removal of inhibition by the satiety mechanism in the ventromedial nucleus upon the pathway in lateral hypothalamus. That part of the pathway which is inhibited by the ventromedial nucleus leads only to eating and not to hoarding.

Such an interpretation of the effects of the injection of norepinephrine into the lateral hypothalamus is supported by an experiment by Booth and Quartermain (1965). They injected rats with norepinephrine, and these rats showed an enhanced sensitivity to the taste of food to which quinine or saccharin had been added. Such rats also performed poorly on variable interval schedules of one minute or more. Such peculiarities are also characteristic of rats with lesions of the ventromedial hypothalamus.

However, while the theory explains the effects of deprivation on hoarding while the effects of such deprivation are still present, it is unable to explain the effects of deprivation which occurred a long time before a hoarding test. For instance, rats have been kept on a restricted diet for two weeks after weaning. After five months of unrestricted feeding, such animals hoarded more than their littermate controls when given an opportunity to hoard (Hunt, 1941; Hunt et al., 1947). It seems unlikely that there should be an enhanced activity in the lateral hypothalamus after five months of unrestricted feeding.

Bibliography and Author Index

The following is a complete list of books and articles, etc., referred to by authors' names in this book. Volume numbers of journals are in boldface and numbers in parentheses refer to pages in this text.

A

Abeles, M., and Goldstein, M. H. Jr. Functional architecture in cat primary auditory cortex: columnar organization and organization according to depth. *J. Neurophysiol.*, 1970, **33**, 172–97. (111)

Ables, M. F., and Benjamin, R. M. Thalamic relay nucleus for taste in albino rat. *J. Neurophysiol.*, 1960, **23**, 376–82. (263)

Abt, J. P., Essman, W. B., and Jarvik, M. E. Ether-induced retrograde amnesia for one-trial conditioning in mice. *Science*, 1961, **133**, 1477–78. (438)

Ackerly, S. S., and Benton, A. L. Report of case of bilateral frontal defect. In Fulton, J. F. (ed.), *The Frontal Lobes*, Baltimore: Williams and Wilkins, 1948, 479–504. (365)

Adametz, J. H. Rate of recovery of functioning in cats with rostral reticular lesions. *J. Neurosurg.*, 1959, **16**, 85–98. (409)

Adams, H. E., Hobbit, P. R., and Sutker, P. B. Electroconvulsive shock, brain acetylcholinesterase activity and memory. *Physiol. Behav.*, 1969, **4**, 113–16. (443)

Ades, H. W. Central auditory mechanisms. In J. Field, H. W. Magoun and V. E. Hall (Eds.), *Handbook of Physiology*. Vol. 1. (Physiological Society) Baltimore: Williams and Wilkins, 1959. (158)

Ades, H. W., and Felder, R. Acoustic area of monkey (Macaca mulatta), *J. Neurophysiol.*, 1942, **5**, 49–54. (158)

Adey, W. R., Merrillees, N. C. R., and Sunderland, S. The entorrhinal area; behavioral evoked potential and histological studies of its interrelationships with brain-stem regions. *Brain*, 1956, **79**, 414–39. (374)

Adey, W. R., Sunderland, S., and Dunlop, C. W. The entorrhinal area; electrophysiological studies of its interrelations with the rhinencephalic structures and the brainstem. *E.E.G. Clin. Neurophysiol.*, 1957, **9**, 309–24. (400)

Adler, N. T. Effects of the male's copulatory behavior on successful pregnancy of the female rat. *J. Comp. Physiol. Psychol.*, 1969, **69**, 613–22. (556)

Adolph, E. F. The internal environment and behavior: III Water content. *Amer. J. Psychiat.*, 1941, **97**, 1365–73. (606)

Adolph, E. F. Thirst and its inhibition in the stomach. *Am. J. Physiol.*, 1950, **161**, 374–86. (618)

Adrian, E. D. The action of the mammalian olfactory organ. *J. Laryngol. Otol.*, 1956, **70**, 1–14. (269, 280)

Adrian, E. D. Afferent areas in the cerebellum connected with the limbs. *Brain*, 1943, **66**, 289–315. (315)

Adrian, E. D. Effects of injury on mammalian nerve fibers. *Proc. Roy. Soc. B.* 1930, **106**, 596–618. (180)

Adrian, E. D. The electrical activity of the mammalian olfactory bulb. *Électroenceph. Clin. Neurophysiol.,* 1950, **2**, 377–88. (276).

Adrian, E. D. The physical background of perception. Oxford: Clarendon Press, 1947. (420)

Adrian, E. D. Sensory messages and sensation, the response of the olfactory organ to different smells. *Acta Physiol. Scand.,* 1953, **29**, 5–14. (280)

Adrian, E. D., Cattell, McK., and Hoagland, H. Sensory discharge in single cutaneous nerve fibers. *J. Physiol.,* 1931, **72**, 377–91.

Adrian, H. O., Lifschitz, W. M., Tavitas, R. J., and Galli, F. P. Activity of neural units in medial geniculate body of cat and rabbit. *J. Neurophysiol.,* 1966, **29**, 1046–60. (163)

Agranoff, B. W., Davis, R. E., Casola, L., and Lim, R. Actinomycin D blocks formation of memory of shock avoidance in goldfish. *Science,* 1967, **158**, 1600–1601. (484)

Agranoff, B. W., and Klinger, P. D. Puromycin effect on memory fixation in the goldfish. *Science,* 1964, **146**, 952–53. (483)

Aidar, O., Geohegan, W. A., and Ungewitter, L. H. Splanchnic afferent pathways in the central nervous system. *J. Neurophysiol.,* 1952, **15**, 131–38. (243)

Akert, K. Diencephalon. In Sheer, D. E. (ed.) *Electrical Stimulation of the Brain.* Austin: Univ of Texas Press, 1961, 288–310. (356, 357)

Akert, K., Gruesen, R. A., Woolsey, C. N., and Meyer, D. R. Klüver-Bucy syndromes in monkeys with neocortical ablations of temporal lobe. *Brain,* 1961, **84**, 480–98. (355, 373)

Akimoto, H., Yamaguchi, M., Okabe, K., Nakagawa, T., Nakamura, I., Abe, K., Torii, H., and Masahashi, I. On the sleep induced through electrical stimulation of dog thalamus. *Folia psychiat. neurol. Jap.,* 1956, **10**, 117–46. (408, 409, 410)

Albe-Fessard, D., and L. Kruger. Duality of unit discharges from cat centrum medianum in response to natural and electrical stimulation. *J. Neurophysiol.,* 1962, **25**, 3–20. (234, 245)

Albe-Fessard, D., Liebeskind, J., and Lamarre, Y. Projection au niveau du cortex somato-moteur du singe d'afferences provenant des recepteurs musculaires. *C.R. Acad. Sci.,* 1965, **261**, 3891–94. (336)

Albe-Fessard, D., and A. Rougeul. Activités Gilaterales tardives évognes sur le cortex du chat sous chloralose par stimulation d'une voie somésthètique. *J. Physiol.,* (Paris) 1955, **47**, 69–72. (219)

Albino, A. C., and Lucas, J. W. Mutual facilitation of self-rewarding regions within the limbic system. *J. Comp. Physiol. Psychol.,* 1962, **55**, 182–85. (517)

Allen, W. F. Effect of ablating the frontal lobes, hippocampi, and occipito-parieto-temporal (excepting pyriform areas) lobes on positive and negative olfactory conditioned reflexes in dogs. *Am. J. Physiol.,* 1940, **128**, 754–71. (282)

Allen, W. F. Effect of ablating the pyriform-amygdaloid areas and hippocampi on positive and negative conditioned reflexes and on conditioned olfactory differentiation, *Amer. J. Physiol.,* 1941, **132**, 81–92. (282)

Allen, W. F. Results of prefrontal lobectomy on acquired and on acquiring correct conditioned differential responses with auditory, general cutaneous and optic stimuli. *Amer. J. Physiol.,* 1943a, **139**, 525–31. (283)

Allen, W. F. Distribution of cortical potentials resulting from insufflation of vapors into the nostrils and from stimulation of the olfactory bulbs and the pyriform lobe. *Amer. J. Physiol.,* 1943b, **139**, 553–55. (282)

Allen, W. F. Effects on partial and complete destruction of the tactile cerebral cortex on correct conditioned differential foreleg responses from cutaneous stimulation. *Am. J. Physiol.,* 1947, **151**, 325–37. (241)

Allen, W. F. Fiber degeneration in Ammon's horn resulting from extirpations of pyriform and other cortical areas and from transections of horn at various levels. *J. Comp. Neurol.,* 1948, **88**, 425–38. (377)

Allers, R., and Halpern, R. Wechselwirkungen gleichzeitiger Erregung Mehrerer Hautsinne. 1. Die Beeinflussung der Tastschwelle durch die Haut-temperatur. *Pflüg. Arch ges. Physiol.*, 1921, **193**, 595–609. (196, 211)

Allison, A. C. The structure of the olfactory bulb and its relationship to the olfactory pathways in the rabbit and the rat. *J. Comp. Neurol.*, 1953, **98**, 309–53. (279, 282)

Almli, C. R. Hyperosmolality Accompanies Hypovolemoa: A simple explanation of Additivity of stimuli for drinking. *Physiology and Behaviour*, 1970, **5**, 1021–28. (589)

Alpern, H. P., and McGaugh, J. L. Retrograde amnesia as a function of duration of electroshock stimulation. *J. Comp. Physiol.*, 1968, **65**, 265–69. (437)

Alpers, B. J. Relation of the hypothalamus to disorders of personality: Report of a case. A.M.A. *Arch. Neurol. Psychiat.*, 1937, **38**, 291–303. (364)

Alrutz, S. Studien auf dem gebiete der temperatursinne. *Skandinav. Arch. Physiol.*, 1900, **10**, 340–52. (215)

Alston, J. H. The spatial condition of the fusion of warmth and cold in heat. *Amer. J. Psychol.*, 1920, **31**, 303–12. (216)

Altman, J. Some fiber projections to the superior colliculus in the cat. *J. Comp. Neurol.*, 1962, **119**, 77–96. (97)

Altman, Ya. A. Are there neurons détecting direction of sound source motion? *Exp. Neurol.*, 1968, **22**, 13–25. (163)

Amassian, V. E. Fiber groups and spinal pathways of cortically represented visceral afferents. *J. Neurophysiol.*, 1951a, **14**, 445–59. (243)

Amassian, V. E. Cortical Representation of Visceral Afferents. *J. Neurophysiol.*, 1951b, **14**, 433–44. (243)

Amassian, V. E. Interaction in Somatovisceral Projection System. *A. Res. Nerv. & Ment. Dis.*, Proc., 1952, **30**, 371–402. (244, 248)

Amassian, V. E., and DeVito, R. V. Unit activity in reticular formation and nearby structures. *J. Neurophysiol.*, 1954, **17**, 575–603. (401)

Amoore, J. E., Johnston, J. W., and Rubin, M. The stereochemical theory of odor. *Scientific American*, 1964, **210**, 42–49. (278)

Amoore, J. E., and Venstrom, D. Sensory analysis of odor qualities in terms of the stereochemical theory. *J. Food Sci.*, 1966, **31**, 118–28. (278)

Amoore, J. E., and Venstrom, D. Correla-tion between stereochemical assessment and organoleptic analysis of odorous compounds. In T. Hayashi (Ed.). *Olfaction and Taste II*. Oxford: Pergamon Press, 1967, 3–17. (278)

Anand, B. K. Nervous regulation of food intake. *Physiol. Rev.*, 1961, **41**, 677–708. (599, 625)

Anand, B. K., and Brobeck, J. R. Hypothalamic control of food intake in rats and cats, *Yale J. Biol. Med.*, 1951, **24**, 123–40. (371, 599)

Anand, B. K., and Brobeck, J. R. Food intake and spontaneous activity of rats with lesions in the amygdaloid nuclei. *J. Neurophysiol.*, 1952, **15**, 421–30. (373, 376)

Anand, B. K., and Dua, S. Feeding responses induced by electrical stimulation of hypothalamus in cat. *Indian J. Med. Research*, 1955, **43**, 113–22. (600)

Anand, B. K., Dua, S., and Shoenberg, of limbic system of brain in waking animals. *Science*, 1955, **122**, 1139. (363)

Anand, B. K., and Dua, S. Electrical stimulation of the limbic system of brain ('visceral brain') in the waking animals. *Indian J. Med. Res.*, 1956, **44**, 107–19. (359)

Anand, B. K., Dua, S., and Shoenberg, K. Hypothalamic control of food intake in cats and monkeys. *J. Physiol.*, 1955, **127**, 143–52. (599)

Anderson, A. C. *Journal of Comparative Psychology*, 1940, **30**, 399–412. (495)

Andersson, B., and Larsson, B. Influence of local temperature changes in the preoptic area and rostral hypothalamus on the regulation of food and water intake. *Acta Physiol. Scand.*, 1961, **52**, 75–89. (591)

Andersson, B., and McCann, S. M. Drinking, antidiuresis and milk ejection from electrical stimulation from the hypothalamus of goats. *Acta Physiol. Scand.*, 1955a, **35**, 191–201. (595, 596)

Andersson, B., and McCann, S. M. A further study of polydipsia evoked by hypothalamic stimulation in the goat. *Acta Physiol. Scand.*, 1955b, **33**, 333–46. (596)

Andersson, B., and McCann, S. M. The effect of hypothalamic lesions on the water intake of the dog. *Acta Physiol. Scand.*, 1956, **35**, 312–20. (596)

Andersson, S. A. Projection of different spinal pathways to the second somatic sensory area in Cat. *Acta Physiol. Scand.*, 1962, **56**, Suppl. 194, 1–74. (219, 226, 230, 236, 246)

Appelberg, B., Bessou P., and Laporte, Y. Action of static and dynamic fusimotor fibres on secondary endings of cat's spindles. *J. Physiol.*, 1966, **185**, 160–71. (298)

Applezweig, M. H., and Moeller, G. The pituitary-adreno-cortical system and anxiety in avoidance learning. *Acta Psychol.*, 1959, **15**, 602–3. (347)

Apter, Julia T. Projection of the retina on superior colliculus of cats. *J. Neurophysiol.*, 1945, **8**, 123–34. (119)

Araki, T., Eccles, J. C., and Ito, M. Correlation of the inhibitory post-synaptic potential of motoneurons with the latency and time course of inhibition of monosynaptic reflex. *J. Physiol.*, 1960, **154**, 354–77. (18)

Arduini, A. Enduring potential changes evoked in the cerebral cortex by stimulation of brain stem reticular formation and thalamus. In H. H. Jasper, L. D. Proctor, R. S. Knighton, W. C. Noshay and R. T. Costello (Eds.), *Reticular Formation of the Brain*. Boston: Little, Brown and Company, 1958. (465)

Arduini, A., and Arduini, M. G. Effect of drugs and metabolic alterations on brain stem arousal mechanisms. *J. pharmacol. Exper. Therap.*, 1954, **110**, 76–85. (403)

Armstrong, D., Jepson, J. P., Keele, C. A., and Stewart, J. W. Pain-producing substance in human inflammatory exudates and plasma. *J. Physiol.*, 1957, **135**, 350–70. (200)

Aronson, L. R. Hormones and reproductive behavior: Some phylogenetic considerations. In Aubrey Gorbman (Ed.), *Comparative Endocrinology*. New York: John Wiley & Sons, Inc., 1958, 98–120. (553, 554)

Arthur, R. P., and Shelley, W. B. Role of proteolytic enzymes in production of pruritus in man. *J. Invest. Dermat.*, 1955, **25**, 341–46. (210)

Arthur, R. P., and Shelley, W. B. The peripheral mechanism of itch in man. In G. E. W. Wolstenholme and F. O'Connor (Eds.), Ciba Foundation Study Group (Study Group No. 1), *Pain and Itch: Nervous Mechanisms.* Boston: Little, Brown and Company, 1959, 84–97. (209, 210)

Asdourian, D., Stutz, R. M., & Rocklin, K. W. Effects of thalamic and limbic system lesions on self-stimulation. *J. of Comp. Physiol. Psychol.*, 1966, **61**, 468–72. (517)

Auleytner, B., and Brutkowski, S. Effects of bilateral prefrontal lobectomy on the classical (type 1) defensive conditioned reflexes and some other responses related to defensive behavior in dogs. *Acta Biol. Exper.*, 1960, **20**, 243–62. (393)

Austin, V. T., and Steggerda, F. R. Congenital dysfunction of the salivary glands with observations on the physiology of thirst. *Illinois, M. J.*, 1936, **69**, 124–27. (594)

Ax, A. F. The physiological differentiation between fear and anger in humans. *Psychosom. Med.*, 1953, **15**, 433–42. (342)

B

Babich, F. R., Jacobson, A. L., Bubash, S., and Jacobson, A. Transfer of a response to naive rats by injection of ribonucleic acid extracted from trained rats. *Science*, 1965, **149**, 656–57. (475)

Bach, L. M. N., and Magoun, H. W. The vestibular nuclei as an excitatory mechanism for the cord. *J. Neurophysiol.*, 1947, **10**, 331–37. (318).

Bacq, Z. M., and Brown, G. C. *Journal of Physiology (London)*, 1937, **89**, 45–60. (497)

Baker, P. F., Hodgkin, A. L., and Shaw, T. I. Replacement of the protoplasm of a giant nerve fibre with artificial solutions. *Nature*, 1961, **190**, 885–87. (11)

Balagura, S., and Hoebel, B. G. Self-stimulation of the lateral hypothalamus modified by insulin and glucagon. *Physiology and Behavior*, 1967, **2**, 337–40. (528)

Baldwin, M. Electrical stimulation of the mesial temporal region. In E. R. Ramey and D. S. O'Doherty (Eds.), *Electrical Studies on the Unanaesthetised Brain*. New York: Paul B. Hoeber, 1960, 159–76. (364)

Ball, J. Sex behavior of the rat after removal of the uterus and the vagina. *J. Comp. Psychol.*, 1934, **18**, 419–22. (557)

Ball, J. Male and female mating behavior in prepubertally castrated male rats receiving estrogens. *J. Comp. Psychol.*, 1939, **28**, 273–83. (567)

Barber, T. X. Toward a theory of pain: Relief of chronic pain by prefrontal leucotomy opiates, placebos, and hypnosis. *Psychol. Bull.*, 1959, **56**, 430. (250)

Bard, P. A diencephalic mechanism for the expression of rage with special reference to the sympathetic nervous system. *Am. J. Physiol.*, 1928, **84**, 490–515. (367, 371)

Bard, P. On emotional expression after decortication with some remarks on certain theoretical views, Parts I and II. *Psych. Rev.*, 1934, **41**, 309–29, 424–49. (368, 371)

Bard, P. The effects of denervation of the genitalia on the oestrual behavior of cats. *Amer. J. Physiol.*, 1935, **113**, 5. (557)

Bard, P. The hypothalamus and sexual behavior. *Research Publications of the Association for Research in Nervous and Mental Disease*, 1940, **20**, 551–79. (563, 564)

Bard, P., and Macht, M. B. The behavior of chronically decerebrate cats. In G. E. W. Wolstenholme and M. O'Connor (Eds.), *The Neurological Basis of Behavior*. London: J. and A. Churchill, 1958, 55–75. (368)

Bard, P., and Mountcastle, V. B. Some forebrain mechanisms involved in the expression of rage, with special reference to suppression of angry behavior. In J. F. Fulton (Ed.) *The Frontal Lobes*. Baltimore: Williams and Wilkins, 1948, 362–404. (368, 371, 373, 377)

Bard, P., and D. McK. Rioch. A study of four cats deprived of neocortex and additional portions of the forebrain. *Bull. Johns Hopkins Hosp.*, 1937, **60**, 72–147. (369, 371)

Bare, J. K. The specific hunger for sodium chloride in normal and adrenalectomized white rats. *J. Comp. Physiol. Psychol.*, 1949, **42**, 242–53. (613)

Barfield, R. J., and Sachs, B. D. Sexual behavior: stimulation by painful electric shock to skin in male rats. *Science*, 1968, **161**, 392–93. (571)

Barlow, H. B. Purkinje shift and retinal noise. *Nature* (London), 1957, **179**, 255–56. (86)

Barlow, H. B., Blakemore, C., and Pettigrew, J. D. The neural mechanism of binocular depth discrimination. *J. Physiol.*, 1967, **193**, 327–42. (112)

Barlow, H. B., and Hill, R. M. Selective sensitivity to direction of movement in ganglion cells of the rabbit retina. *Science*, 1963, **139**, 412–14. (95, 96)

Barlow, H. B., and Levick, W. R. The mechanism of directionally selective units in rabbit's retina. *J. Physiol.* (London), 1965, **178**, 477–504. (96)

Barlow, H. B., and Sparrock, J. M. B. The role of afterimages in dark adaption. *Science*, 1964, **144**, 1309–14. (115)

Barnes, P. J., Smith, L. M., and Latto, R. M. Orientation to visual stimuli and the superior colliculus in the rat. *Q. Journal Exp. Psychol.*, 1970, **22**, 239–47. (99)

Barondes, S. H., and Cohen, H. D. Puromycin effect on successive phases of memory storage. *Science*, 1966, **151**, 594–95. (481)

Barondes, S. H., and Cohen, H. D. Effect of acetoxycycloheximide on learning and memory of a light-dark discrimination. *Nature*, 1968, **218**, 271–73. (482)

Barondes, S. H., and Jarvik, M. E. The influence of actinomycin D on brain RNA synthesis and on memory. *J. Neurochem.*, 1964, **11**, 187–95. (483)

Barris, R. W., Ingram, W. R., and Ranson, S. W. Optic connections of the diencephalon and midbrain of the cat. *J. Comp. Neurol.*, 1935, **62**, 117–54. (97)

Bartoshuk, L. M., McBurney, D. H., and Pfaffmann, C. Taste of sodium chloride solution after adaptation to sodium chloride: implications for the "water taste." *Science*, 1964, **143**, 967–68. (267)

Bash, K. W. An investigation into a possible organic basis for the hunger drive. *J. Comp. Psychol.*, 1939, **28**, 109–34. (594)

Batini, C., Moruzzi, G., Palestini, M., Rossi, G. F., and Zanchetti, A. Persistent patterns of wakefulness in the pretrigeminal midpontine preparation. *Science*, 1958, **127**, 30–32. (402)

Batsel, H. L. Electroencephalographic synchronization and desynchronization in the chronic 'cerveau isolé' in the dog. *EEG clin. Neurophysiol.*, 1960, **12**, 421–30. (409)

Bauer, H. G. Endocrine and other clinical manifestations of hypothalamic disease. *J. Clin. Endocrinol.*, 1954, **14**, 13–31. (583)

Bauer, J. H., and Cooper, R. M. Effects of posterior cortical lesions on performance of a brightness-discrimination task. *J. Comp. Physiol. Psychol.*, 1964, **58**, 84–92. (118, 119)

Baumgarten, R. J. von. Plasticity in the nervous system at the unitary level. In F. O. Schmitt (Ed.), *The Neurosciences: Second Study Program*. New York: Rockefeller Univ. Press, 1970, 260–71. (458)

Bazett, H. C. Temperature sense in man. In *Temperature: Its Measurement and Control in Science and Industry*. New York: Reinhard, 1941, 489–501. (199)

Bazett, H. C., McGlone, B., Williams, R. G., and Lufkin, H. M. Sensation. I. Depth, distribution and probable identification in the prepuce of sensory end-organs concerned in sensations of temperature and touch; thermometric conductivity. *Arch. Neurol. Psychiat.*, 1932, **27**, 469–517. (229)

Bazett, H. C., and Penfield, W. G. A study of the Sherrington decerebrate animal in the chronic as well as the acute condition. *Brain*, 1922, **45**, 185–264. (367)

Beach, F. A. The neural basis of innate behavior. I. Effects of cortical lesions upon the maternal behavior pattern in the rat. *J. Comp. Psychol.*, 1937, **24**, 393–439. (577)

Beach, F. A. Effects of cortical lesions upon the copulatory behavior of male rats. *J. Comp. Psychol.*, 1940, **29**, 193–245. (564)

Beach, F. A. Central nervous mechanisms involved in the reproductive cycle of vertebrates. *Psychol. Bull.*, 1942, **39**, 4, 200–226. (553, 564, 567)

Beach, F. A. *Hormones and Behaviour: a survey of interrelationships between endocrine secretions and patterns of overt response*. New York: Paul B. Hoeber, 1948. (554, 555)

Beach, F. A. Neural and chemical regulation of behavior. In H. F. Harlow and C. N. Woolsey (Eds.), *Biological and Biochemical Bases of Behavior*.

Madison: Univ. of Wisconsin Press, 1958. (570)

Beach, F. A., Conovitz, M. W., Steinberg, F., and Goldstein, A. C. Experimental inhibition and restoration of mating behavior in male rats. *J. Genet. Psychol.*, 1956, **89**, 165–81. (571)

Beach, F. A., and Fowler, H. Individual differences in the response of male rats to androgen. *J. Comp. Physiol. Psychol.*, 1959, **52**, 50–52. (571)

Beach, F. A., and Holz, M. Mating behavior in male rats castrated at various ages and injected with androgen. *J. Exp. Zool.*, 1946, **101**, 91–142. (553)

Beach, F. A., and Jaynes, J. Studies of maternal retrieving in maternal retrieving in rats. III. Sensory cues involved in the lactating female's response to her young. *Behaviour*, 1956, **10**, 104–25. (576)

Beach, F. A., and Jordan, L. Sexual exhaustion and recovery in the male rat. *Quart. J. Exp. Psychol.*, 1956, **8**, 121–33. (566)

Beach, F. A., and Levinson, G. Effects of androgen on the glans penis and mating behavior of castrated male rats. *J. Exp. Zool.*, 1950, **114**, 159–71. (560, 579)

Beach, F. A., and Whalen, R. E. Effects of intromission without ejaculation upon sexual behavior in male rats. *J. Comp. Physiol. Psychol.*, 1959, **52**, 476–81. (566)

Beach, F. A., and Whalen, R. E. Effects of ejaculation on sexual behavior in the male rat. *J. Comp. Physiol. Psychol.*, 1959, **52**, 249–54. (564, 565, 566)

Beach, F. A., and Wilson, J. R. Mating behavior in male rats after removal of the seminal vesicles. *Proc. National Acad. Sci.*, 1963, **49**, 624–26. (557)

Beach, G., and Kimble, D. P. Activity and responsivity in rats after magnesium pemoline injections. *Science*, 1967, **155**, 698–701. (474)

Beecher, H. K. *Measurement of Subjective Responses*. New York: Oxford, 1959. (250)

Beh, H. C., and Barratt, P. E. H. Discrimination and conditioning during sleep as indicated by the electroencephalogram. *Science*, 1965, **147**, 1470–71. (422)

Behrens, O. V., and Bromer, W. W. Glucagon. *Am. Rev. Vitamins and Hor-*

mones (Academic Press), 1958, 263–301. (619)

Beidler, L. M. Theory of taste stimulation. *J. Gen. Physiol.*, 1954, **38**(2), 133–39. (255, 258, 273)

Beidler, L. M. Facts and theory on the mechanism of taste and odor perceptions. In J. H. Mitchell, Jr. et al. (Eds.), *Chemistry of Natural Food Flavors*. Quartermaster Research and Engineering Command, 1957, 7–43. (264)

Beidler, L. M. Dynamics of taste cells. In Y. Zotterman (Ed.), *Olfaction and Taste*. Oxford: Pergamon Press, 1963, 133–38. (255, 259, 264)

Beidler, L. M. Innervation of rat fungiform papilla. In C. Pfaffmann (Ed.), *Olfaction and Taste*. New York: Rockefeller Univ. Press, 1969, 352–69. (260)

Beidler, L. M., and Smallman, R. L. Renewal of cells within taste buds. *J. Cell Biol.*, 1965, **27**, 263–72. (260)

Békésy, Georg von. *Experiments in hearing*. New York: McGraw-Hill Book Company, 1960. (128, 131, 135)

Békésy, G. von. Olfactory analogue to directional hearing. *J. Appl. Physiol.*, 1964, **19**, 369–73. (281)

Békésy, G. von. Sweetness produced electrically on the tongue and its relation to taste theories. *J. Appl. Physiol.*, 1964, **19**, 1105–13. (253)

Békésy, G. von. Taste theories and the chemical stimulation of single papillae. *J. Appl. Physiol.*, 1966, **21**, 1–9. (253)

Bell, C., Sierra, G., Buendia, N., and Segundo, J. P. Sensory properties of neurons in the mesencephalic reticular formation. *J. Neurophysiol.*, 1964, **27**, 961–87. (426)

Bellows, R. T. Time factors in water drinking dogs. *Amer. J. Physiol.*, 1939, **125**, 87–97. (605, 606, 618)

Benda, C. E. *Developmental Disorders of Mentation and Cerebral Palsies*. New York: Grune & Stratton, Inc., 1952. (313)

Benjamin, R. M. Cortical taste mechanisms studied by 2 different test procedures. *J. Comp. Physiol. Psychol.*, 1955a, **48**, 119–22. (263)

Benjamin, R. M. Effect of fluid deprivation on taste deficits following cortical lesions. *J. Comp. Physiol. Psychol.*, 1955b, **48**, 502–5. (263)

Benjamin, R. M. Some thalamic and cortical mechanisms of taste. In Y. Zotterman (Ed.), *Olfaction and Taste*. Oxford: Pergamon Press, 1963, 309–29. (263)

Benjamin, R. M., and Akert, K. Cortical and thalamic areas involved in taste discrimination in the albino rat. *J. Comp. Neurol.*, 1959, **111**, 231–60. (263)

Benjamin, R. M., and Pfaffmann, C. Cortical localization of taste in albino rat. *J. Neurophysiol.*, 1955, **18**, 56–64. (263)

Bennett, E. L., and Calvin, M. Failure to train planarians reliably. *Neurosciences Res. Prog. Bull.*, 1964, **2**, 3–24. (475)

Beritoff, J., and Chichinadze, N. Localization of visual perception in the pigeon. *Bull. Biol. Med. exp. USSR*, 1936, **2**, 105–7. (446)

Beritoff, J., and Chichinadze, N. On the localization of cortex processes evoked by visual stimulations. *Trans. Beritov Inst. Tiflis*, 1937, **3**, 361–74. (446)

Berkun, M. M., Kessen, M. L., and Miller, N. E. Hunger reducing effects of food by mouth, measured by a consumatory response. *J. Comp. Physiol. Psychol.*, 1952, **45**, 550–54. (609)

Bermant, G. Response latencies of female rats during sexual intercourse. *Science*, 1961b, **133**, 1771–73. (566)

Bermant, G. Rat sexual behavior: Photographic analysis of the intromission response. *Psychon. Sci.*, 1965, **2**, 65–66. (551)

Bermant, G., Anderson, L., and Parkinson, S. R. Copulation in rats: relations among intromission duration, frequency, and pacing. *Psychon. Sci.*, 1969, **17**, 293–94. (565)

Bermant, G., and Taylor, L. Interactive effects of experience and olfactory bulb lesions in male rat copulation. *Physiol. Behav.*, 1969, **4**, 13–17. (565, 568)

Bermant, G., and Westbrook, W. H. Peripheral factors in the regulation of sexual contact by female rats. *J. Comp. Physiol. Psychol.*, 1966, **61**, 244–50. (566)

Best, J. B., and Rubinstein, I. Maze learning and associated behavior in planaria. *J. Comp. Physiol. Psychol.*, 1962, **55**, 560–66. (475)

Bickford, R. G., Mulder, D. W., Dodge, H. W., Svien, H. J., and Rome,

H. P. Changes in memory function produced by electrical stimulation of the temporal lobe in man. *Research Publications of the Association for Research in Nervous and Mental Disease*, 1958, **36**, 227–43. (432)

Biederman, G. B. *Psychonomic Science* (in press). (491)

Biemond, A. The conduction of pain above the level of the thalamus opticus. *A. M. A. Arch. Neurol. Psychiat.*, 1956, **75**, 231–48. (245, 247)

Bignami, G. Pharmacological influences on mating behavior in the male rat. *Psychopharmacology*, 1966, **10**, 44–58. (567)

Bindra, D. Stimulus change reactions to novelty and response decrement. *Psychol. Rev.*, 1959, **66**, 96–103. (445)

Bintz, J. Time-dependent memory deficit of aversively motivated behavior. *Learning and Motivation*, 1971. (347, 348)

Bishop, G. H. The organisation of cortex with respect to its afferent supply. *Annals, N.Y. Acad. Science*, 1961, **98**, 559–69. (171, 246)

Bishop, M. P., Elder, S. T., and Heath, R. G. Intracranial self-stimulation in man. *Science*, 1963, **140**, 394–95. (517)

Bishop, P. O., and McLeod, J. G. Nature of potentials associated with synaptic transmission in the lateral geniculate of cats. *J. Neurophysiol.*, 1954, **17**, 387–414. (22, 23)

Black, A. H. Heart rate changes during avoidance learning in dogs. *Canad. J. Psychol.*, 1959, **13**, 229–42. (345)

Blake, L. The effect of lesions of the superior colliculus on brightness and pattern discrimination in the cat. *J. Comp. Physiol. Psychol.*, 1959, **52**, 272–78. (119)

Blakemore, C. Binocular depth discrimination and the naso-temporal division. *J. Physiol.*, 1969, **205**, 471–97. (112)

Blakemore, C., and Cooper, G. F. Development of the brain depends on the visual environment. *Nature*, 1970, **228**, 477–78. (102)

Blakemore, C., and Pettigrew, J. D. Eye dominance in the visual cortex. *Nature* (London), 1970, **225**, 426–29. (112)

Blass, E. M. Separation of cellular from extracellular controls of drinking in rats by frontal brain damage. *Science*, 1968, **162**, 1501–3. (598)

Blass, E. M., and Hanson, D. G. Primary hyperdipsia in the rat following septal lesions. *J. Comp. Physiol. Psychol.*, 1970, **70**, 87–93. (598)

Block, R. A., and McConnell, J. V. Classically conditioned discrimination in the planaria *Dugesia dorotocephala*. *Nature*, 1967, **215**, 1465–66. (475)

Blum, J. S., Chow, K. L., and Pribram, K. H. A behavioral analysis of the organisation of the parieto-temperopreoccipital cortex in the monkey. *J. Comp. Neurol.*, 1950, **93**, 53–100. (241)

Boekh, J. Electrical activity in olfactory receptor cells. In C. Pfaffmann (Ed.), *Olfaction and Taste*. New York: Rockefeller Univ. Press, 1969, 34–51. (273)

Bogacz, J., St. Laurent, J., and Olds, J. Dissociation of self-stimulation and epileptiform activity. *Electroencephalogram and Clinical Neurophysiology*, 1965, **19**, 75–87. (518)

Bogdanski, D. F., and Galambos, R. In G. L. Rasmussen and W. F. Windle (Eds.), *Neural Mechanisms of the Auditory and Vestibular Systems*, Ch. 10. Springfield: Charles C Thomas, 1960. (141)

Bohdanecky, Z., and Jarvik, M. E. Impairment of one-trial passive avoidance learning in mice by scopolamine, scopolamine methylbromide, and physostigmine. *Int. J. Neuropharmacol.*, 1962, **6**, 217–22. (485)

Bohdanecky, Z., Kopp, R., and Jarvik, M. E. Comparison of ECS and flurothyl-induced retrograde amnesia in mice. *Psychopharmacologia* (Berlin), 1968, **12**, 91–95. (438)

Bohus, B., and Endröczi, E. The influence of pituitary-adreno-cortical function on the avoiding conditioned activity in rats. *Acta Physiol. Acad. Sci. Hung.*, 1965, **26**, 183–89. (347)

Boissonnas, R. A., Guttmann, S., Jaquenoud, P. A., Pless, J., and Sandrin, E. The synthesis of bradykinin and of related peptides. *Ann. N.Y. Acad. Sci.*, 1963, **104**, 5. (200)

Boman, K. On the mediation of cold pain, *Acta Physiol. Scandinav.*, 1959, **45**, 211–15. (193)

Bond, D., Randt, C. T., Bidder, T. G., and Rowland, V. Posterior septal fornical and anterior thalamic lesions in the cat. *A.M.A. Arch. Neurol. Psychiat.*, 1957, **78**, 143–62. (377)

Bonvallet, M., Dell, P., and Hiebel, G. Tonus sympathique et activité électrique corticale. *Electroencephalog. and Clin. Neurophysiol.*, 1954, **6**, 119–44. (578)

Booth, D. A. Localization of the adrenergic feeding system in the rat diencephalon. *Science*, 1967, **158**, 515–17. (622)

Booth, D. A., and Quartermain, D. Taste sensitivity of eating elicited by chemical stimulation of the rat hypothalamus. *Psychonomic Science*, 1965, **3**, 525–26. (620, 640)

Booth, D. A., and Simson, P. C. Food Preferences acquired by association with variations in amino acid nutrition. *Quart. J. Exp. Psych.*, 1971, **23**, 135–45. (633)

Borer, K. T. Disappearance of preference and aversions for rapid solutions in rats ingesting untasted fluids. *J. Comp. Physiol. Psychol.*, 1968, **65**, 213–21. (634)

Boss, W. R. Hormonal determination of adult characters and sex behavior in herring gulls (Larus argentatus). *J. Exper. Zool.*, 1943, **94**, 181–203. (553)

Boudreau, J. C., and Tsuchitani, C. Binaural interaction in the cat superior olive S segment. *J. Neurophysiol.*, 1968, **31**, 442–54. (162)

Bovet, D., McGaugh, J. L., and Oliverio, A. Effects of post trial administration of drugs on avoidance learning of mice. *Life Sciences*, 1966, **5**, 1309–15. (473)

Bower, G. H., and Miller, N. E. Rewarding and punishing effects from stimulating the same place in the rat's brain. *J. Comp. Physiol. Psychol.*, 1958, **51**, 669–74. (356)

Bowman, R. Magnesium pemoline and behavior. *Science*, 1966, **153**, 902. (474)

Bowsher, D. Termination of the central pain pathway in man: the conscious appreciation of pain. *Brain*, 1957, **80**, 606–22. (244, 399)

Bowsher, D. The termination of secondary somatosensory neurons within the thalamus of Macacca Mulatta: An experimental degeneration study. *J. Comp. Neurol.*, 1961, **117**, 213–18. (217, 218, 232, 399)

Bradley, P. B., and Elkes, J. The effect of atropine, hyoscyamine, physostigmine and neostigmine on the electrical activity of the brain of the conscious cat. *J. Physiol.*, 1953, **120**, 14–15. (396)

Bradley, P. B., and Mollica, A. The effect of adrenaline and acetylcholine on single unit activity in the reticular formation of the decerebrate cat. *Arch. itel. Biol.*, 1958, **96**, 168–186. (401)

Brady, J. V. The paleocortex and behavioral motivation. In H. F. Harlow and C. N. Woolsey (Eds.), *Biological and Biochemical Bases of Behavior*. Madison: Univ. of Wisconsin Press, 1958, 193–235. (377, 390)

Brady, J. V. Temporal and emotional effects related to intracranial electrical self-stimulation. In E. R. Ramey and D. S. O'Doherty (Eds.), *Electrical Studies on the Unanesthetized Brain*. New York: Paul B. Hoeber, 1960. (517)

Brady, J. V. Emotional Behavior. In *Handbook of Physiology*, Section I, *Neurophysiology*. Vol. III. (American Physiological Society) Baltimore: Williams and Wilkins, 1960, 1529–52. (346)

Brady, J. V., Boren, J. J., Conrad, D., and Sidman, M. The effect of food and water deprivation upon intracranial self-stimulation. *J. Comp. Physiol. Psychol.*, 1957, **50**, 134–37. (528)

Brady, J. V., and Conrad, D. G. Some effects of limbic system self-stimulation upon conditioned emotional behavior. *J. Comp. Physiol. Psychol.*, 1960, **53**, 128–37. (517)

Brady, J. V., and Nauta, W. J. H. Subcortical mechanisms in emotional behavior: affective changes following septal forebrain lesions in the albino rat. *J. Comp. Physiol. Psychol.*, 1953, **46**, 339–46. (377, 385)

Brady, J. V., and Nauta, W. J. H. Subcortical mechanisms in emotional behavior: the duration of affective changes following septal and habenular lesions in the albino rat. *J. Comp. Physiol. Psychol.*, 1955, **48**, 412–20. (377)

Brady, J. V., Schreiner, L., Geller, I., and Kling, A. Subcortical mechanisms in emotional behavior: the effect of rhinencephalic injury upon the acquisition and retention of a conditioned avoidance response in cats. *J. Comp. Physiol. Psychol.*, 1954, **47**, 179–86. (390, 392)

Brain, R. *Diseases of the Nervous System.* (4th ed.) Oxford: Oxford Univ. Press, 1952. (289)

Brazier, M. A. B. The action of anesthetics on the nervous system with special reference to the brain stem reticular system. In J. F. Delafresnaye (Ed.), *Brain Mechanisms and Consciousness.* Springfield, Ill.: Charles C Thomas, 1954, 163–200. (403)

Breen, R. A., and McGaugh, J. L. Facilitation of maze learning with post trial injections of picrotoxin. *J. Comp. Physiol. Psychol.*, 1961, **54**, 498–501. (470)

Bremer, F. Physiologie nerveuse de la mastication chez le chat et le lapin. Centre cortical du goût, *Arch. Inst. Physiol.*, 1923, **21**, 308–53. (264)

Bremer, F. L'activité cérébrale au cours du sommeil et de la narcose contribution a l'étude du mécanisme du sommeil. *Bull. Acad. Roy. Med. Belg.*, 1937, **2**, 68–86. (397)

Bremer, F. The Neurophysiological problem of sleep. In J. F. Delafresnaye (Ed.), *Brain Mechanisms and Consciousness.* Springfield, Ill.: Charles C Thomas, 1954, 137–63. (410)

Bremer, F., and Terzuolo, C. Contribution à l'étude des mecanismes physiologiques du maintien de l'activité vigile du cerveau. Interaction de la formation réticulée et de l'écorce cérébrale dans le processus des réveil. *Arch. Inter. Physiol.*, 1954, **62**, 157–78. (400, 401)

Bremer, F., and Stoupel, N. Facilitation et inhibition des potentiels évoques corticaux dans l'éveil cérébral. *Arch. Int. Physiol.*, 1959, **67**, 240–75. (424)

Bremer, F., and Terzuolo, C. Rôle de l'écorce cérébrale dans le processus physiologique du réveil. *Arch. Int. Physiol.*, 1952, **60**, 228–31. (401)

Bremer, F., and Terzuolo, C. Nouvelles recherches du le processus physiologique du reveil. *Arch. Int. Physiol.*, 1953, **61**, 86–90. (401)

British Medical Bulletin. The physiology of voluntary muscle. *Brit. Med. Bull.*, 1956, **12**(3). (287)

Broadbent, D. E. The role of auditory localization in attention and memory span. *J. Exp. Psychol.*, 1954, **47**, 191–96. (417)

Broadbent, D. E. *Perception and communication.* London: Pergamon Press, 1958. (417, 418)

Brobeck, J. R. Food intake as a mechanism of temperature regulation in rats. *Fed. Proc. Amer. Physiol. Soc.*, 1948, **7**, 13. (591)

Brobeck, J. R., Tepperman, J., and Long, C. N. H. Experimental hypothalamic hyperphagia in the albino rat. *Yale J. Biol. Med.* 1943, **15**, 831–53. (622)

Brogden, W. J. Sensory preconditioning. *J. Exp. Psychol.*, 1939, **25**, 323–32. (509)

Bromiley, R. B., and Bard, P. A study of the effect of estrin on the responses to genital stimulation shown by decapitate and decerebrate female cats. *Amer. J. Physiol.*, 1940, **129**, 318–19. (563, 564)

Brookhart, J. M. The cerebellum. In *Handbook of Physiology*, Sec. 1. Vol. II. Washington: American Physiological Society, 1960. P. 1245. (315, 317)

Brookhart, J. M., and Dey F. L. Reduction of sexual behavior in male guinea pigs by hypothalamic lesions. *Amer. J. Physiol.*, 1941, **133**, 551–54. (558)

Brookhart, J. M., Dey, F. L., and Ranson, S. W. Failure of ovarian hormones to cause mating reactions in spayed guinea pigs with hypothalamic lesions. *Proc. Soc. Exper. Biol. and Med.*, 1940, **44**, 61–64. (558)

Browder, E. J., and Gallagher, J. P. Dorsal cordotomy for painful phantom limb. *Ann. Surg.*, 1948, **128**, 456–69. (227, 247)

Brown, A. G., and Iggo, A. A quantitative study of cutaneous receptors and afferent fibres in the cat and rabbit. *J. Physiol.*, 1967, **193**, 707–33. (181, 188)

Brown, C. W., and Ghiselli, E. E. Subcortical mechanisms in learning. IV. Olfactory discrimination. *J. Comp. Psychol.*, 1938, **26**, 109–20. (283)

Brown, H. Effect of ribonucleic acid (RNA) on the rate of lever pressing in rats. *Psychol. Rec.*, 1966a, **16**, 173–76. (474)

Brown, H. Effect of ribonucleic acid (RNA) on reversal of a probability matching problem in pigeons. *Psychol., Rec.*, 1966b, **16**, 441–48. (474)

Brown, S., and Schaefer, E. A. An investigation into the functions of the occipital and temporal lobe of the monkey's brain. *Phil. Trans. Roy. Soc. B.* 1888, **179**, 303–27. (372, 433)

Browne, L. B., and Hodgson, E. S. Electrophysiological studies of arthropod chemoreception. IV. Latency, independence, and specificity of labellar chemoreceptors of the blowfly, *Lucilia. J. Cell Comp. Physiol.*, 1962, **59**, 187–202. (256)

Brown-Grant, K., Harris, G. W., and Reichlin, S. The effect of emotional and physical stress on thyroid activity in the rabbit. *J. Physiol.*, 1954, **126**, 29–40. (582)

Bruce, R. H. An experimental investigation of the thirst drive in rats with especial reference to the goal gradient hypothesis. *Journal of General Psychology*, 1937, **17**, 49–62. (521)

Bruce, R. H. The effect of lessening the drive upon performance by white rats in a maze. *J. Comp. Physiol. Psychol.*, 1938, **25**, 225–48. (521)

Brugge, J. F., Anderson, D. J., Hind, J. E., and Rose, J. E. Time structure of discharges in single auditory nerve fibers of the squirrel monkey in response to complex periodic sounds. *J. Neurophysiol.*, 1969, **32**, 386–401. (164)

Brugge, J. F., Dubrovsky, N. A., Aitkin, L. M., and Anderson, D. J. Sensitivity of single neurons in auditory cortex of cat to binaural tonal stimulation: effects of varying intraural time and intensity. *J. Neurophysiol.*, 1969, **32**, 1005–24. (164)

Bruner, J., and Kennedy, D. Habituation: occurrence at a neuromuscular junction. *Science*, 1970, **169**, 92–94. (455)

Bruner, J., and Tauc, L. Long-lasting phenomena in the molluscan nervous system. *Symp. Soc. Exp. Biol.*, 1966, **20**, 457–75. (456)

Brush, F. R. Retention of aversively motivated behavior. In F. R. Brush (Ed.), *Aversive Conditioning and Learning*. New York: Academic Press, 1970, p. 402–65. (346)

Brush, F. R., Davenport, J. W., and Polidora, V. J. TCAP negative results in avoidance and water maze learning and retention. *Psychon. Sci.*, 1966, **4**, 183–84. (474)

Brush, F. R., and S. Levine. Adrenocortical activity and avoidance learning as a function of time after fear conditioning. *Physiol. Behav.*, 1966, **1**, 309–11. (346, 347)

Brust-Carmona, H. C. B., and Hernandez-Peon, R. Sensory transmission in the spinal cord during attention and tactile habituation. *Int. Congr. physiol. Sci.*, 1959, 44 (Abstr. XXI). (422, 423)

Brutkowski, S. Comparison of classical and instrumental alimentary conditioned reflexes following bilateral prefrontal lobectomies in dogs. *Acta. Biol. Exper.*, 1959, **14**, 291–99. (392, 393)

Brutkowski, S., Fonberg, E., and Mempel, E. Angry behavior in dogs following bilateral lesions in the genual portion of the rostral cingulate gyrus. *Acta. Biol. Exper.*, 1961, **21**, 119–205. (380)

Bullock, T. H. Neuron doctrine and electrophysiology. *Science*, 1959, **129**, 997–1002. (21)

Bullock, T. H., and Hagiwara, S. Intracellular recording from the giant synapse of the squid. *J. Gen. Physiol.*, 1956, **40**, 565–77. (17)

Bunch, M. E., and Lang, E. S. *Journal of Comparative Psychology*, 1939, **27**, 449–59. (495)

Bunch, M. E., and Magdsick, W. K. *Journal of Comparative Psychology*, 1933, **16**, 385–409. (495).

Bunge, M. B., Bunge, R. P., and Ris, H. Ultrastructural study of remyelination in an experimental lesion in adult cat spinal cord. *J. Biophys. Biochem. Cytol.*, 1961, **10**, 67–94. (12)

Bureš, J., Bohdanecky, Z., and Weiss, T. Physostigmine induced hippocampal theta activity and learning in rats. *Psychopharmacologia*, 1962, **3**, 254–63. (485)

Bureš, J., and Burešová, O. The use of Leao's spreading depression in the study of interhemipheric transfer of memory traces. *J. Comp. Physiol. Psychol.*, 1960, **53**, 558–65. (448, 449)

Bureš, J., and Burešová, O. Plastic changes of unit activity based on reinforcing properties of extracellular stimulation of single neurons. *J. Neurophysiol.*, 1967, **30**, 98–113. (460).

Bureš, J., and Burešová, O. Plasticity in single neurones and neural populations. In G. Horn and R. A. Hinde (Eds.), *Short-term changes in neural activity and behavior*. Cambridge,

England: Cambridge U. Press, 1970, pp. 363–403. (460)

Bureš, J., Burešová, O., and Fifková, E. Interhemispheric transfer of passive avoidance reaction. *J. Comp. Physiol. Psychol.*, 1964, **57**, 326–30. (449)

Burešová, O., Bureš, J., Bohdanecky, Z., and Weiss, T. Effect of atropine on learning, extinction, retention and retrieval in rats. *Psychopharm.*, 1964, **5**, 255–63. (485)

Burgess, P. R., and Perl, E. R. Myelinated afferent fibers responding specifically to noxious stimulation of the skin. *J. Physiol.* (London), 1967, **190**, 109, 541–62. (176, 194)

Burns, B., Deslisle, Heron, W., and Pritchard, R. Physiological excitation of visual cortex in cat's unanesthetized forebrain. *J. Neurophysiology*, 1962, **164**, 238–181.

Busch, H. F. M. An anatomical analysis of the white matter in the brain stem of the cat. *Thesis, Van Gorcum and Comp. N. V.*, 1961, 116 pp. (218)

Buser, P., and Borenstein, P. Responses somésthetiques, visuelles et auditives, recueillies au niveau du cortex "associatif" suprasylvien chez le chat curarisé non anesthesié. *EEG clin. Neurophysiol.*, 1959, **11**, 285–304. (157, 319)

C

Cadwalder, W. B., and J. E. Sweet. Experimental work on the function of the anterolateral column of the spinal cord. *J.A.M.A.* 1912, **58**, 1490–893. (227)

Caggiula, A. R., and Eibergen, R. Copulation of virgin male rats evoked by painful peripheral stimulation. *J. Comp. Physiol. Psychol.*, 1969, **69**, 414–19. (572)

Cajal, Santiago Ramón Y. *Histologie du système nerveux*. Vol. 2. Paris, 1911. (77, 281)

Cajal, Santiago Ramón Y. *Neuron Theory or Reticular Theory?* M. V. Parkiss and C. A. Fox (Trans.). Madrid: Institutio "Ramon y Cajal," 1954. (3)

Cajal, Santiago Ramón Y. *Histologie du Système Nerveux de l'Homme et des Vertebrés*. Vol. 1. Madrid: Consejo Superior de Investigaciones Cientificas, 1955. Pp. 839–88. (218)

Caldwell, D. F. Effects of adrenal demedullation on retention of a CAR

in the mouse. *J. Comp. Physiol. Psychol.*, 1962, **55**, 1079–81. (344)

Calhoun, W. H. Effect of level of external stimulation on rate of learning and interaction of this effect with strychnine treatment in mice. *Psychol. Rep.*, 1966, **18**, 715–22. (473)

Callaway, E. III, Jones, R. T., and Layne, R. S. Evoked responses and segmental set of schizophrenia. *Arch. Gen. Psychiat.*, 1965, **12**, 83–89. (427)

Cannon, W. B. *Bodily Changes in Pain, Hunger, Fear and Rage*. (2nd Ed.) New York: Appleton-Century-Crofts, 1929. (342, 593)

Cannon, W. B., and Britton, S. W. Studies on the conditions of activity in endocrine glands. XV. Pseudoaffective medulliadrenal secretion. *Am. J. physiol.*, 1925, **72**, 283–94. (367, 368)

Cannon, W. B., and Washburn, A. L. An explanation of hunger, *Amer. J. Physiol.*, 1912, **29**, 441–54. (594)

Capps, M. J., and Harlow, W. A. Auditory frequency discrimination after transection of the olivocochlear bundle in squirrel monkeys. *Exper. Neurology*, 1968, **21**, 147–58 (169)

Carlson, A. J. *The Control of Hunger in Health and Disease*. Chicago: University of Chicago Press, 1916. (591, 593)

Carlton, P. L. In J. T. Tapp (Ed.), *Reinforcement and Behavior*. New York: Academic Press, 1959. (502)

Carlton, P. L., and Vogel, J. R. Studies of the amnesic properties of scopolamine. *Psychonom. Sci.*, 1965, **3**, 261–62. (486)

Carpenter, C. R. Psychobiological studies of social behavior in Aves. I. The effect of complete and incomplete gonadectomy on secondary sexual activity, with histological studies. *J. Comp. Psychol.*, 1933a, **16**, 59–96. (553)

Carpenter, C. R. Psychobiological studies of social behavior in Aves, I. The effect of complete and incomplete gonadectomy on the primary sexual activity of the male pigeon. *J. Comp. Psychol.*, 1933b, **16**, 25–57. (553)

Carper, J. W., and Polliard, F. A comparison of the intake of glucose and saccharine solutions under conditions of caloric need. *Amer. J. Psychol.*, 1953, **66**, 479–82. (637, 638)

Carreras, M., and M. Levitt. Microelectrode analysis of the second somatosensory area in the cat. *Fed. Proc.*, 1959, 18–24. (222, 236)

Castellucci, V., Kupfermann, I., Pinsker, H., and Kandel, E. R. Neuronal mechanisms of habituation and dishabituation of the gill withdrawal reflex in *Aplysia. Science,* 1970, **167,** 1745–48. (456)

Cawthorne, T., Dix, M. R., Hallpike, C. S., and Hood, J. D. Vestibular function. *Brit. med. Bull.,* 1956, **12,** 131–42. (325)

Cerf, J. A., and Otis, L. S. Heat narcosis and its effect on retention of a learned behavior in the goldfish. *Fed. Proc.,* 1957, **16,** 20–21. (436)

Cerletti, A., Stürmer, F., and Konzett, H. Bradykinin, Strukturaufklärung, Synthese, physiologisch-pharmakologisch Grundlagen. *Deutsch. Med. Wschr.,* 1961, **86,** 678. (200)

Chamberlain, T. J., Halich, P., and Gerard, R. W. Fixation of experience in the rat spinal cord. *J. Neurophysiol.,* 1963, **26,** 662–72. (478)

Chambers, R. M. Effects of intravenous glucose injections on learning, general activity, and hunger drive. *J. Comp. Physiol. Psychol.,* 1956a, **49,** 558–64. (549)

Chambers, R. M. Some physiological bases of reinforcing properties of reward injections. *J. Comp. Physiol. Psychol.,* 1956b, **49,** 565–68. (549)

Chambers, W. W., Levitt, M., Carreras, M., and Lin, C. N. Central determination of sensory processes. *Science,* 1960, **132,** 1489. (242)

Chang, H. T., Ruch, T. C., and Ward, A. A. Jr. Topographical representation of muscles in motor cortex of monkeys. *J. Neurophysiol.,* 1947, **10,** 39–56. (336)

Chapman, L. F., Walter, R. D., Markham, C. H., Rand, R. W., and Crandall, P. H. Memory changes induced by stimulation of hippocampus or amygdala in epilepsy patients with implanted electrodes. *Transactions of the American Neurological Association,* 1967, **92,** 50–56. (432)

Chapman, W. P. Studies of the periamygdaloid area in relation to human behavior. *Assn. Res. Nerv. Ment. Dis.,* 1958, **36,** 258–77. (363, 365)

Chapman, W. P. Depth electrode studies in patients with temporal lobe epilepsy. In E. R. Ramey and D. S.

O'Doherty (Eds.), *Electrical Studies on the Unanaesthetised Brain.* New York: Hoeber, 1960, 334–50. (365)

Chapman, W. P., and Jones, C. M. Variations in cutaneous and visceral pain sensitivity in normal subjects. *J. Clin. Invest.,* 1944, **23,** 81. (250)

Chapman, W. P., Rose, A. S., and Solomon, H. C. Measurements of heat stimulus producing motor withdrawal reaction in patients following frontal lobotomy. *A. Res. Nerv. Ment. Dis. Proc.,* 1948, **27,** 754–68. (250)

Chapman, W. P., Schroeder, H. R., Geyer, G., Brazier, M. A. B., Fager, C., Poppen, J. L., Solomon, H. C., and Yakovler, P. I. Physiological evidence concerning importance of the amygdaloid nuclear region in the integration of circulatory function and emotion in man. *Science,* 1954, **120,** 949. (363)

Chapouthier, Georges. Behavioral studies of the molecular basis of memory. In J. A. Deutsch (Ed.), *The Physiological Basis of Memory.* New York: Academic Press, 1973, pp. 1–17. (475)

Chapouthier, G., Legrain, D., and Spitz, S. La planaire en tant qu'animal de laboratoire dans les recherches psychophysiologiques. *Expérimentation Animale,* 1969, **1,** 269–80.

Chapouthier, G., Pallaud, B., and Ungerer, A. Relations entre deux réactions des planaires face à une discrimination droite-gauche. *C.R. Acad. Sci. Ser. D.,* 1968, **266,** 905–7. (475)

Cherry, C. Two ears—but one world. In Rosenblith, W. A. (Ed.), *Sensory Communication.* Cambridge, Mass.: MIT Press, 1961, 99–1117. (137)

Cherry, E. C. Some experiments on the recognition of speech with one and with two ears. *J. Acoust. Soc. Amer.,* 1953, **25,** 975–79. (416)

Chevalier, J. A. Permanence of amnesia after a single post-trial electroconvulsive seizure. *J. Comp. Physiol. Psychol.,* 1965, **59,** 125–27. (440)

Chiang, H. M., and Wilson, W. A. Some tests of the diluted-water hypothesis of saline consumption in rats. *J. Comp. Physiol. Psychol.,* 1963, **56,** 660–65. (617)

Chinn, H. I., and Smith, P. K. Motion sickness. *Pharmacol. Rev.,* 1955, **7,** 33–82. (326)

Chorover, S. L., and Schiller, P. H.

Short-term retrograde amnesia in rats. *J. Comp. Physiol. Psychol.*, 1965, **59**, 73–78. (436)

Chow, K. L. Conditions influencing the recovery of visual discriminative habits in monkeys following temporal neocortical ablations. *J. Comp. Physiol. Psychol.*, 1952, **45**, 430–37. (435)

Chow, K. L. Lack of behavioral effects following destruction of some thalamic association nuclei in the monkey. *A. M. A. Arch. Neurol. Psychiat.*, 1954, **71**, 762–71. (372)

Chow, K. L. Brain waves and visual discrimination learning in the monkey. In J. Wortis (Ed.), *Recent Advances in Biological Psychiatry*. New York: Grune and Stratton, 1960, 149. (466)

Chow, K. L. Effect of local electrographic after discharges on visual learning and retention in the monkey. *J. Neurophysiol.*, 1961, **24**, 391–400. (463)

Chow, K. L., Dement, W. C., and John, E. R. Conditioned electrocorticographic potentials and behavioral avoidance response in the cat. *J. Neurophysiol.*, 1957, **20**, 482. (468)

Chow, K. L., Dement, W. C., and Mitchell, S. A., Jr. Effects of lesions of the rostral thalamus on brain waves and behavior in cats. *EEG Clin. Neurophysiol.*, 1959, **11**, 107–20. (409)

Chow, K. L., and Obrist, W. D. EEG and behavioral changes on application of Al(OH)₃ cream on preoccipital cortex of monkeys. *Arch Neurol. Psychiat.* (Chicago), 1954, **72**, 80–87. (462)

Chow, K. L., and Randell, W. Learning and EEG studies of cats with lesions in the reticular formation. Paper read at the first annual meeting of Psychonomics Society, Chicago, 1960. (409)

Chow, K. L., and Survis, J. Retention of overlearned visual habit after temporal cortical ablation in the monkey. *AMA Arch. Neurol. and Psychiat.*, 1958, **70**, 640–46. (434)

Cizek, L. J. Long-term observations on relationship between food and water ingestion in the dog. *Amer. J. Physiol.*, 1959, **197**, 342–46. (625)

Clark, C. V. H., and Isaacson, R. L. Effect of bilateral hippocampal ablation on DRL performance. *J. Comp. Physiol. Psychol.*, 1965, **59**, 137–40. (387, 392)

Clark, D., Hughes, J., and Gasser, H. S. Afferent function in the group of nerve fibers of slower conduction velocity. *Am. J. Physiol.*, 1935, **23**, 114–69. (198)

Clark, G. Prepubertal castration in the male chimpanzee with some effects of replacement therapy. *Growth*, 1945, **9**, 327–39. (553)

Clark, W. E. Le Gros. The thalamic connections of the temporal lobe of the brain in the monkey. *J. Anat.*, 1936, **70**, 447–64. (319)

Clark, W. E. Le Gros, Beattie, J., Riddoch, A., and Dott, N. M. *The Hypothalamus*. Edinburgh: Oliver and Boyd, 1938. (60, 365)

Cleghorn, T. E., and Darcus, H. D. The sensibility to passive movement of the human elbow joint. *Quart. J. Exp. Psychol.*, 1952, **4**, 66–77. (301)

Cohen, B. D., Brown, G. W., and Brown, M. L. Avoidance learning motivated by hypothalmic stimulation. *J. Exp. Psychol.*, 1957, **53**, 228–83. (355)

Cohen, H. Lettsomanian lectures on the mechanism of visceral pain *T. M. Soc. London.*, 1944, **64**, 65–99. (248)

Cohen, H. D., Ervin, F., and Barondes, S. H. Puromycin and cycloheximide: Different effects on hippocampal electrical activity. *Science*, 1966, **154**, 1557–58. (482)

Cohen, H. D., and Barondes, S. H. Further studies of learning and memory after intracerebral actinomycin D. *J. Neurochem.*, 1966, **13**, 207–11. (483)

Cohen, L. A. Analysis of position sense in human shoulder. *J. Neurophysiol.*, 1958, **21**, 550–62. (301)

Cohen, M. J., Hagiwara, S., and Zotterman, Y. The response spectrum of taste fibres in the cat: a single fibre analysis. *Acta Physiol. Scand.*, 1955, 33, 316–32. (259)

Cohen, M. J., Landgren, S., Strom, L., and Zotterman, Y. Cortical reception of touch and taste in the cat. *Acta Physiol. Scand.*, 1957, **40**, 1–50. (263)

Cohn, Z. A., and Hirsch, J. G. The isolation and properties of the specific cytoplasmic granules of rabbit polymorphonuclear leucoytes. *J. Exp. Med.*, 1960, **112**, 983. (200)

Cole, K. S., and Curtis, H. J. Electric impedance of the squid giant axon during activity. *J. Gen. Physiol.*, 1939, **22**, 649–70. (11)

Collias, N. E. Hormones and behaviors with special reference to birds and the mechanisms of hormone action. In E. S. Gordon (Ed.), *Symposium on Steroid Hormones.* Madison: University of Wisconsin Press, 1950. (553)

Collins, W. E. Effects of mental set upon vestibular nystagmus. *J. Exp. Psychol.,* 1962, **63,** 191–97. (325)

Collins, W. F., Nulsen, F. E., and Randt, C. T. Relations of peripheral nerve fiber size and sensation in man. *Arch. Neurol.,* 1960, **3,** 381–85. (198)

Comis, S. D., and Whitfield, I. C. Influence of centrifugal pathways on unit activity in the cochlear nucleus. *J. Neurophysiol.,* 1968, **31,** 62–68. (167)

Cook, L., and Davidson, A. B. Effects of yeast RNA and other pharmacological agents on acquisition, retention and performance in animals. In D. H. Efron et al. (Eds), *Psychopharmacology: A review of progress 1957–1967.* Washington D.C.: U.S. Government Printing Office. PHS Publ. No. 1836, pp. 931–46. (474)

Coombs, J. S., Curtis, D. R., and Eccles, J. C. The interpretation of spike potentials of motor neurons. *J. Physiol.,* 1957, **139,** 198–231. (276)

Coombs, J. S., Curtis, D. R., and Eccles, The electrical properties of the motoneuron membrane, *J. Physiol.,* 1957, **139,** 198–231. (276)

Coons, E. E., and Cruce, J. A. F. Lateral hypothalamus: Food current intensity in maintaining self-stimulation of hunger. *Science,* 1968, **159,** 117–19. (602)

Coons, E. E., Levak, Milena, and Miller, N. E. Lateral hypothalamus: Learning of food-seeking response motivated by electrical stimulation. *Science,* 1965, **150,** 1320–21. (600)

Coons, E. E., and Miller, N. E. Conflict versus consolidation of memory traces to explain "retrograde amnesia" produced by ECS. *J. Comp. Physiol. Psychol.,* 1960, **53,** 524–31. (438, 439)

Cooper, R. M., and Taylor, L. H. Thalamic reticular system and central grey: self-stimulation. *Science,* 1967, **156,** 102–3. (517)

Coppock, H. W., and Chambers, R. M. Reinforcement of Position preference by automatic intrevenous injections of glucose. *J. Comp. Physiol. Psychol.,* 1954, **47,** 355. (548)

Cordeau, J. P., and Mahut, H. Some long term effects of temporal lobe resections on auditory and visual discriminations in monkeys. *Brain,* 1964, **87,** 177–90. (434)

Corkin, S. Tactually-guided maze learning in man; Effects of unilateral cortical excisions and bilateral hippocampal lesions. *Neuropsychologia,* 1965, **3,** 339–52. (433)

Corning, W. C. Evidence of a right-left discrimination in planarians. *J. Psychol.,* 1964, **58,** 131–39. (475)

Corning, W. C., and John, E. R. Effect of ribonuclease on retention of conditioned response in regenerated planarians. *Science,* 1961, **134,** 1363–64. (474)

Cornsweet, T. N. Determination of the stimuli for involuntary drifts and saccadic eye movements. *J. of the Optical Society of America,* 1956, **46,** 987–93. (115)

Correll, R. E., and Scoville, W. B. Effects of medial temporal lesions on visual discrimination performance. *J. Comp. Physiol. Psychol.,* 1965a, **60,** 175–81. (434)

Correll, R. E., and Scoville, W. B. Performance on delayed match following lesions of medial temporal lobe structures. *J. Comp. Physiol. Psychol.,* 1965b, **60,** 360–67. (434)

Correll, R. E., and Scoville, W. B. Significance of delay in performance of monkeys with medial temporal lobe resections. *Exp. Brain Res.,* 1967, **4,** 85–96. (434)

Cowan, W. M., and Powell, T. P. S. Centrifugal fibres in the avian visual system. *Royal Society of London Proceedings,* Series B, Biol. Sci., 1963, **158,** 232–52. (80)

Cragg, B. G. Centrifugal fibres to the retina and olfactory bulb, and composition of the supraoptic commissures in the rabbit. *Exp. Neurol.,* 1962, **5,** 406–27. (281, 282)

Creed, R. S., Denny-Brown, D., Eccles, J. C., Liddell, E. G. T., and Sherrington, C. S. *Reflex activity of the spinal cord.* Oxford: Oxford Univ. Press, 1932. (26, 27, 28)

Crespi, L. P. Quantitative variation of incentive and performance in the white rat. *American Journal of Psychology,* 1942, **55,** 467–517. (532)

Creutzfeld, O. D., Watanabe, S., and

Lux, H. D. Relations between EEG phenomena and potentials of single cells. I. Evoked responses after thalamic and epicortical stimulation. *Electroencephalography & Clinical Neurophysiology*, 1966, **20**, 1–18. (397)

Crisler, G. Salivation is unnecessary for the establishment of the salivary conditioned reflex induced by morphine. *Amer. J. Physiol.*, 1930, **94**, 553–56. (510)

Critchley, M. *The Parietal Lobes*. Baltimore: Williams and Wilkins and London: E. Arnold, 1953. (238, 337)

Crocker, E. C., and Henderson, L. F. Analysis and classification of odors. *Amer. Perfum.*, 1927, **22**, 325–27. (277)

Crosby, Elizabeth Caroline, and Henderson, John Woodworth. The mammalian midbrain and isthmus regions. Part II. Fiber connections of the superior colliculi. B pathways concerned in automatic eye movements. *J. Comp. Neurology*, 1948, **88**, 53–91.

Cushing, H. *Papers Relating to the Pituitary Body, Hypothalamus and Parasympathetic Nervous System*. Springfield: Charles C Thomas, 1932. (364)

Cutting, W. C. *Handbook of pharmacology . . . The actions and uses of drugs*. New York: Appleton-Century-Crofts, 1964. (494)

D

Dale, H. H. Pharmacology and nerve endings. *Proc. Roy. Soc.*, 1935, **28**, 319–32. (17)

Dallenbach, K. M. Pain: history and present status. *Amer. J. Psychol.*, 1939, **52**, 331–47. (204)

Darling, F. F. *Bird flocks and the breeding cycle*. London: Cambridge, 1938. (581)

Darrow, D. C., and Yannet, H. The changes in the distribution of body water accompanying increase and decrease in extracellular electrolyte. *J. Clin. Investigation*, 1935, **14**, 266–75. (587, 588)

Dastoli, F. R., Lopiekes, D. V., and Price, S. A sweet sensitive protein from bovine taste buds. Purification and partial characterization. *Biochemistry*, 1968, **7**, 1160–64. (255)

David, E., Finkenzeller, P., Kallert, S., and Keidel, W. D. Reizfrequenzkorrelierte "untersetzte" neuronale Entla-

dungsperiodiztät im Colliculus inferior und im Corpus geniculatum mediale, 1969, **309**, 11–20. (151)

Davidson, J. M., and Sawyer, C. H. Effects of localized intracerebral implantation of oestrogen on reproductive function in the female rabbit. *Acta Endocrinol.*, 1961, **37**, 385–93. (557, 561, 584)

Davis, Clarence D. The effects of ablations of neocortex on mating maternal behavior and the production of pseudo-pregnancy in the female rat and on copulatory activity in the male. *Am. J. Physiol.*, 1939, **127**, 374. (577)

Davis, C. M. Self-selection of diet by newly weaned infants. *Amer. J. Dis. Child.*, 1928, **36**, 651–79. (631)

Davis, H. Peripheral coding of auditory information. In W. Rosenblith (Ed.), *Sensory Communication*. Published jointly by M. I. T. Press and John Wiley & Sons (New York), 1961, pp. 119–42. (142)

Davis, J. D. Food intake following blood mixing of hungry and satiated rats. *Psychon. Sci.*, 1965, 3, 177–78. (620)

Davis, J. W., Thomas, R. K., Jr., and Adams, H. E. Interactions of scopolamine and physostigmine with ECS and one trial learning. *Physiology and Behavior*, 1971, 6, 219–22. (485)

Davis, R. C., Garafolo, L., and Kveim, K. Conditions associated with gastrointestinal activity. *J. Comp. Physiol. Psychol.*, 1959, **52**, 466–75. (594)

Davis, R. E. Environmental control of memory function in goldfish. *J. Comp. Physiol. Psychol.*, 1968, **65**, 72–78. (484)

Davis, R. E., Bright, P. J., and Agranoff, B. W. Effect of ECS and puromycin on memory in fish. *Journal of Comparative & Physiological Psychology*, 1965, **60**, 162–66. (484)

Davison, C., and W. Schick. Spontaneous pain and other subjective sensory disturbances: clinico-pathologic study. *A.M.A. Arch. Neurol. Psychiat.*, 1935, **34**, 1204–37. (245)

Dawson, R. G., and McGaugh, J. L. Electroconvulsive shock-produced retrograde amnesia: analysis of the familiarization effect. *Communications in Behavioral Biology*, 1969, 4, 91–95. (437, 440)

Dawson, R. G., and McGaugh, J. L. Drug facilitation of learning and memory. In J. A. Deutsch (Ed.), *The Physiological Basis of Memory*. New York: Academic Press, 1973, pp. 78–104. (473)

Dax, E. C., and Radley-Smith, E. J. The early effects of prefrontal leucotomy on disturbed patients with mental illness of long duration. *J. Ment. Sc.*, 1943, **89**, 182–88. (381)

Déjérine, J., and Roussy, G. Le syndrome Thalamique. *Rev. Neurol.*, 1906, **18**, 521–32. (244)

Delgado, J. M. R. Cerebral structures involved in transmisson and elaboration of noxious stimulation. *J. Neurophysiol.*, 1955, **18**, 261–75. (362)

Delgado, J. M. R., and Anand, B. K. Increase of food intake induced by electrical stimulation of the lateral hypothalamus. *Am. J. Physiol.*, 1953, **172**, 162–68. (600)

Delgado, J. M. R., Robberts, W. W., and Miller, N. E. Learning motivated by electrical stimulation of the brain. *Amer. J. Physiol.*, 1954, **179**, 587–93. (351, 355, 511)

Delgado, J. M. R., Rosvold, H. E., and Looney, E. Evoked conditioned fear by electrical stimulation of subcortical structures in the monkey brain. *J. Comp. Physiol. Psychol.*, 1956, **49**, 373–80. (356).

Dell, P. C. The reticular formation of the brain. *Henry Ford Hospital International Symposium*. Boston: Little Brown and Co., 1958, 513–34. (578)

De Lorenzo, A. J. D. Studies on the ultrastructure and histophysiology of cell membranes, nerve fibers and synaptic junctions in chemoreceptors. In Y. Zotterman (Ed.), *Olfaction and Taste*. Oxford: Pergamon Press, 1963, 5–18. (259)

Dement, W. The occurrence of low voltage fast EEG patterns during behavioral sleep in the cat. *EEG Clin. Neurophysiol.*, 1958, **10**, 291–96. (412)

Dement, W. The effect of dream deprivation. *Science*, 1960, **131**, 1705–7. (412)

Dement, W., Henry, P., Cohen, H., and Ferguson, J. Studies on the effect of REM deprivation in humans and animals. *Research Publications of the Association for Research in Nervous and Mental disease*, 1967, **45**, 456–68. (412)

de Molina, F. A., and Hunsperger, R. W. Central representation of affective reactions in forebrain and brain stem: electrical stimulation of amygdala, stria terminalis and adjacent structures. *J. Physiol.*, 1959, **145**, 251–65. (353, 355, 358, 361, 362, 378)

de Molina, F. A., and Hunsperger, R. W. Organization of subcortical system governing defense and flight reactions in the cat. *J. Physiol.*, 1962, **160**, 200–213. (370, 371, 376)

Dempsey, E. W., and Rioch, D. McK. The localization in the brain stem of the oestrous responses of the female guinea pig. *J. Neurophysiol.*, 1939, **2**, 9–18. (563)

Denny-Brown, R. S., Eccles, J. C., Liddell, E. G. T., and Sherrington, C. S. *Reflex Activity of the Spinal Cord*. Oxford: Oxford University Press, 1938. (310)

Desmedt, J. E. Auditory-evoked potentials from cochlea to cortex as influenced by activation of the efferent olivo-cochlear bundle. *J. Acoust. Soc. Amer.*, 1962, **34**, 1478–96. (167)

Desmedt, J. E., and Mechelse, K. Suppression of acoustic input by thalamic stimulation. *Proc. Soc. Exp. Biol. Med.*, 1958, **99**, 772–75. (167)

Desmedt, J. E., and Mechelse, K. Corticofugal projections from temporal lobe in cat and their possible role in acoustic discrimination. *J. Physiol. Lond.*, 1959, **147**, 17–18. (157, 167)

Desmedt, J. G. Neurophysiological mechanisms controlling acoustic input. In G. L. Rasmussen and W. F. Windle (Eds.), *Neural Mechanisms of the Auditory and Vestibular System*. Chapter 11. Springfield: Charles C Thomas, 1960, pp. 152–64. (167)

De Snoo, K. Das trinkende kind im uterus. *Monatschrift J. Gebursh. u. Gynäk.*, 1937, **105**, 88. (546, 638)

Dethier, V. G., and Arab, Y. M. Effect of temperature on the contact chemoreceptors of the blowfly. *J. Ins. Physiol.*, 1958, **2**, 153–61. (255, 280)

Deuel, H. J., Jr., and Movitt, E. Studies on the comparative nutritive value of fats. III. The effect of flavor on food preference. *J. Nutrition*, 1944, **27**, 339–46. (364, 635)

Deutsch, J. A. A new type of behaviour theory. *British Journal of Psychology*, 1953, **44**, 304–17. (512, 515, 611)

Deutsch, J. A. A machine with insight.

Quart. J. Exper. Psychol., 1954, **6**, 6–11. (512, 515)

Deutsch, J. A. *The Structural Basis of Behavior.* Chicago: The University of Chicago Press, 1960. (515, 611)

Deutsch, J. A. Learning and electrical self-stimulation of the brain. *J. Theoret. Biol.*, 1963, **4**, 193–214. (95, 528)

Deutsch, J. A. Behavioral measurement of the neural refractory period and its application to intracranial self-stimulation. *J. Comp. Physiol. Psychol.*, 1964, **58**, 1–9. (533)

Deutsch, J. A. An electrophysiological stimulator with digital logic. *Journal of the Experimental Analysis of Behavior*, 1966, **9**, 399–400. (516)

Deutsch, J. A. Macromolecular change and synapse. In *Macromolecules and Behavior.* New York: Appleton-Century-Crofts, 1972, pp. 279–303. (476)

Deutsch, J. A., Adams, D. W., and Metzner, R. J. Choice of intracranial stimulation as a function of delay between stimulations and strength of competing drive. *J. Comp. Physiol. Psychol.*, 1964, **57**, 241–43. (521, 522)

Deutsch, J. A., and Blumen, H. L. Counter-injection: A new technique for the analysis of drinking. *Nature*, 1962, **196**, 196–97. (607)

Deutsch, J. A., and Deutsch, D. Attention: Some theoretical considerations. *Psych. Rev.*, 1963, **70**, 80–90. (422)

Deutsch, J. A., and DiCara, L. Hunger and extinction in intra-cranial self-stimulation. *J. Comp. Physiol. Psychol.*, 1967, **63**, 344–47. (527)

Deutsch, J. A., Hamburg, M. D., and Dahl M. Anticholinesterase-induced amnesia and its temporal aspects. *Science*, 1966, **151**, 221–23. (489)

Deutsch, J. A., and Howarth, C. I. Evocation by fear of a habit previously learned for intracranial electrical stimulation. *Science*, 1962, **136**, 1057–58. (358, 529)

Deutsch, J. A., and Howarth, C. I. Some tests of a theory of intracranial self-stimulation. *J. Comp. Physiol. Psychol.*, 1963, **70**, 444–60. (521, 522)

Deutsch, J. A., Howarth, C. I., Ball, G. G., and Deutsch, D. Threshold differentiation of drive and reward in the Olds effect. *Nature*, 1962, **196**, 699–700. (532)

Deutsch, J. A., and Jones, A. D. The water-salt receptor and preference in the rat. *Nature*, 1959, **183**, 1412. (548, 615, 637)

Deutsch, J. A., and Jones, A. D. Diluted water: an explanation of the rat's preference for saline. *J. Comp. Physiol. Psychol.*, 1960, **53**, 122–27. (548, 615, 637)

Deutsch, J. A., and Leibowitz, S. F. Amnesia or reversal of forgetting by anticholinesterase, depending simply on time of injection. *Science*, 1966, **153**, 1017. (489, 496)

Deutsch, J. A., and Rocklin, K. *Nature*, 1967, **216**, 89–90. (492)

Deutsch, J. A., and Wiener, N. I. *J. Comp. Physiol. Psychol.*, 1969, **69**, 179–84. (501)

De Valois, R. L. Behavioral and electrophysiological studies of primate vision. In Neff, W. D. (Ed.), *Contributions to Sensory Physiology.* Vol. I. New York: Academic Press, 1965. (89, 90, 91)

Devenport, L. D., and Balagura, S. Lateral hypothalamus: reevaluation of function in motivated feeding behavior. *Science*, 1971, **172**, 744–46. (602)

De Vito, R. V., Brusa, A., and Arduini, A. Cerebellar and vestibular influences on Deitersian units. *J. Neurophysiol.*, 1956, **19**, 241–53. (318)

De Vries, H., and Stuiver, M. The absolute sensitivity of the human sense of smell. In W. A. Rosenblith (Ed.), *Sensory Communication.* New York: John Wiley & Sons, 1961, 159–67. (277)

De Wardener, H. E., and Herxheimer, A. The effect of a high water intake on the kidney's abilities to concentrate the urine in man. *J. Physiol.*, 1957, **139**, 53–63. (167)

Dey, F. L., Fisher, C., Berry, C. M., and Ranson, S. W. Disturbances in reproductive functions caused by hypothalamic lesions in female guinea pigs. *Amer. J. Physiol.*, 1940, **129**, 39–46. (558)

Diamant, H., Funakoshi, M., Strom, L., and Zotterman, Y. Electrophysiological studies on human taste nerves. In Y. Zotterman (Ed.), *Olfaction and Taste.* Oxford: Pergamon Press, 1963, 193–203. (255)

Diamant, H., and Zotterman, Y. A comparative study on the neural and psychophysical response to taste stimuli.

In C. Pfaffmann (Ed.), *Olfaction and Taste*. III. New York: Rockefeller Univ. Press, 1969, 428–35. (264).

Diamond, I. T., and Neff, W. D. Ablation of temporal cortex and discrimination of auditory patterns, *J. Neurophysiol.*, 1957, **20**, 300–315. (166)

Diamond, I. T., Randall, W., and Springer, L. Tactual localization in cats deprived of cortical areas SI and SII and the dorsal columns. *Psychon. Sci.*, 1964, **1**, 261–62. (242)

Dill, D. B. *Life, Heat and Altitude*. Cambridge: Harvard Univ. Press, 1938. (588)

Dingman, W., and Sporn, M. B. The incorporation of 8-azaguanine into rat brain RNA and its effect on maze learning of the rat: an inquiry into the biochemical basis of memory. *J. Psychiat. Res.*, 1961, **1**, 1–11. (478)

Ditchburn, R. W., and Ginsborg, B. L. Vision with a stabilized retinal image. *Nature*, 1952, **170**, 36–37. (115)

Dodge, R. Habituation to rotation. *J. Exp. Psychol.*, 1923, **6**, 1–34. (324)

Dodt, E. The behavior of thermoreceptors at low and high temperatures with special references to Ebbecke's temperature phenomenon. *Acta Physiol. Scand.*, 1953, **27**, 295. (192)

Dodt, E. Schmerzimpulse bei Temperaturreizen. *Acta Physiol. Scandinav.*, 1954, **31**, 83–96. (193)

Dodt, E. Discussion of paper by A. Iggo: A single unit analysis of cutaneous receptors with C afferent fibers. In G. E. W. Wolstenholme and F. O'Connor (Eds.), Ciba Foundation Study Group (Study Group No. 1), *Pain and Itch: Nervous Mechanisms*. Boston: Little, Brown and Company, 1959, 41–59. (216)

Dodt, E., and Zotterman, Y. Mode of action of warm receptors. *Acta Physiol. Scandinav.*, 1952a, **26**, 345–57. (189)

Dodt, E., and Zotterman, Y. Discharge of specific cold fibers at high temperatures (paradoxical cold). *Acta Physiol. Scandinav.*, 1952b, **26**, 358–65. (192, 215)

Dodwell, P. C., and Bessant, D. E. Learning without swimming in a water maze, *J. Comp. Physiol. Psychol.*, 1960, **53**, 422–25. (508)

Doetsch, G. S., Ganchrow, J. J., Nelson, L. M., and Erikson, R. P. Information processing in the taste system of the brain. In C. Pfaffmann (Ed.), *Olfaction and Taste*. New York: Rockefeller Univ. Press, 1969, 492–511. (262)

Dogliotti, M. First surgical sections in man of lemniscus lateralis (pain-temperature path) at brain stem, for treatment of diffused, rebellious pain. *Anesth. et. Analg.*, 1938, **17**, 143–45. (244)

Dole, V. P. Biochemistry of Addiction. *Ann. Rev. Biochem.*, 1970, **39**, 821–40. (31, 32)

Donovan, B. T., and Van der Werff ten Bosch, J. J. Precocious puberty in rats with hypothalamic lesions. *Nature* (London), 1956, **178**, 745. (584)

Donovan, B. T., and van der Werff ten Bosch, J. J. Oestrus in winter following hypothalamic lesions in the ferret. *J. Physiol.*, 1956a, **132**, 57. (583, 584)

Dorfman, L. J., and Jarvik, M. E. A parametric study of electroshock-induced retrograde amnesia in mice. *Neuropsychologia*, 1969, **6**, 373–80. (437)

Doty, R. W. Functional significance of the topographical aspects of the retino-cortical projection. In R. Jung and H. Kornhuber (Eds.), *The Visual System: Neurophysiology & Psychophysics*. Berlin: Springer-Verlag, 1961. (118)

Doty, R. W., Beck, E. C., and Kooi, R. A. Effect of brain stem lesions on conditioned responses in cats. *Exp. Neurol.*, 1959, **1**, 360–85. (409)

Doty, R. W., Rutledge, L. T., Jr., and Larsen, R. M. Conditioned reflexes established to electrical stimulation of cat cerebral cortex. *J. Neurophysiol.*, 1956, **19**, 401–15. (510)

Douglas, R. J. The hippocampus and behaviour. *Psychol. Bull.*, 1967, **67**, 416–42. (391)

Douglas, W. W., Ritchie, J. M., and Straub, R. W. The role of non-myelinated fibers in signalling cooling of the skin. *J. Physiol.*, 1960, **150**, 266–83. (181)

Dow, R. S. The electrical activity of the cerebellum and its functional significance. *J. Physiol.*, 1938, **94**, 67–86. (316)

Dowling, J. E. Synaptic organization of the frog retina: an electron microscopic analysis comparing the retinas of frogs and primates. *Proc. Roy. Soc.*, B, 1968, **170**, 205–28. (78)

Dowling, J. E., and Boycott, B. B. Organization of the primate retina: electron microscopy. *Proc. Roy. Soc.*, Ser. B, 1966, **166**, 80–111. (76, 77, 78, 79, 80)

Dowling, J. E. & Cowan, W. M. An electron microscope study of normal and degenerating centrifugal fibre terminals in the pigeon retina. *Z. Zellforsch. mikroscop. Anat.* 1966, **71**, 14–28. (80)

Downman, D. B. B., Woolsey, C. N., and Lende, R. A. Auditory areas I, II and EP: Cochlear representation, afferent paths and interconnections. *Bull. Johns Hopkins Hosp.*, 1960, **105**, 127–46. (153, 155)

Drake, L. G., and McKenzie, K. G. Mesencephalic tractotomy for pain; experience with 6 cases. *J. Neurosurg.*, 1953, **10**, 457–62. (244)

Drori, D., and Folman, Y. Effects of cohabitation on the reproductive system kidneys and body composition of male rats. *J. Reprod. Fert.*, 1964, **8**, 351–59. (555)

Dumont, S., and Dell, P. Facilitations, spécifiques et non-spécifiques des réponses visuelles corticales. *J. Physiol.* (Paris), 1958, **50**, 261–64. (424)

Duncan, C. P. The retroactive effects of shock on learning. *J. Comp. and Physiol. Psychol.*, 1949, **42**, 32–34. (435, 436, 440)

Duncan, P. M. Effect of temporary septal dysfunction on conditioning and performance of fear responses in rats. *J. Comp. Physiol. Psychol.*, 1971, **74**, 340–48. (388)

Durup, G., and Fessard, A. L'electroencephalogramme de l'homme. *L'année Psychol.*, 1935, **36**, 1. (509)

Dusser, J. G. de Barenne. Recherches expérimentales sur les fonctions du système nerveux central faites en particulier sur deux chats, dont le néopallium avait été enlevé. *Arch. néerl. Physiol.*, 1920, **4**, 31–123. (367)

E

Ebbecke, U. Uber die temperatur—empfindungen in ihrer abhangigkeit von der hautdurchblutung und von den reflexzentren. *Arch. Ges. Physiol.*, 1917, **169**, 395–462. (199)

Ebner, F. F., and Myers, R. E. Inter- and intra-hemispheric transmission of tactile gnosis in normal and corpus-callosum sectioned monkey. *Federation Proc.*, 1960, **19**, 292. (448).

Eccles, J. C. *The Neurophysiological Basis of Mind: The Principles of Neurophysiology.* Oxford: Clarendon Press, 1953. (8, 16)

Eccles, J. C. *The physiology of nerve cells.* Oxford: Oxford University Press, 1957. (8, 12, 14, 15, 16)

Eccles, J. C. The effects of use and disuse on synaptic function. In P. F. Delafresnaye et al. (Eds.), *Brain Mechanisms and Learning.* Oxford: Blackwell, 1961, 335–52. (487)

Eccles, J. (Ed.). *Brain and Conscious Experience.* New York: Springer, 1966.

Eccles, J. C. *The Physiology of Synapses.* Berlin: Springer, 1964. (487)

Eccles, J. C., Eccles, R. M., and A. Lundberg. Types of neurons in and around the intermediate nucleus of the lumbrosacral cord. *J. Physiol.* (London), 1960, **158**, 89–118. (218)

Eccles, J. C., Eccles, R., and Magni, I. Central inhibitory action attributable to presynaptic depolarization produced by muscle afferent volleys. *J. Physiol.*, 1961, **15a**, 147–66. (19)

Eccles, J. C., Magni, I., and Willis, W. Depolarization of central terminals of group 1 afferent fibres from muscle. *J. Physiol.*, 1962, **160**, 62–93. (19)

Echlin, F., and Propper, N. Sensitization by injury of cutaneous nerve endings in frog. *J. Physiol.*, 1937, **88**, 388–400. (201)

Economo, C. Von. *Die Encephalit is Lethargica.* Vienna: Deuticke, 1918. (364)

Edwards, A. S. The measurement of static ataxia. *Amer. J. Psychol.*, 1942, **55**, 171–88. (334)

Edwards, C., and Ottoson, D. The site of impulse initiation in a nerve cell of a crustacean stretch receptor. *J. Physiol.*, 1958, **143**, 138–48. (276)

Egan, J. P., Carterette, E. C., and Thwing, E. J. Some factors affecting multi-channel listening. *J. Acoust. Soc. Amer.*, 1954, **26**, 774–82. (417)

Egger, M. D., and Flynn, J. P. Effect of electrical stimulation of the amygdala on hypothalamically elicited attack behavior in cats. *J. Neurophysiol.*, 1963, **26**, 705–20. (359)

Eisenman, J., S. Landgren, and D. Novin. Functional organisation in the main sensory trigeminal nucleus and in the rostial subdivision of the nucleus of the spinal trigeminal tract in the cat. *Acta. Physiol. Scand.*, Suppl. 214, 1963, **59**, 1–44. (220, 231)

Eist, H., and Seal, U. S. The permeability of the blood-brain barrier and the blood-CSF barrier to C¹⁴ tagged RNA. *Am. J. Psychiat.* 1965, **122**, 584–91. (476)

Ek, J., Jonkees, L. B. W., and Klijn, J. A. J. On the effect of continuous acceleration. *Acta Oto-laryngol.*, 1960, **51**, 416–19. (322, 325)

Eldred, E. Posture and locomotion. In J. Field, H. W. Magoun, and V. E. Hall (Eds.), *Handbook of Physiology.* Vol. II. Section 1. Washington: American Psychological Society, 1960, 1067. (334)

Eldred, E., Granit, R., and Merton, P. A. Supraspinal control of the muscle spindles and its significance. *J. Physiol.*, 1953, **122**, 498–523. (299)

Ellen, Paul, and Butter, John. External Cue Control of DRL performance in rats with septal lesions. *Physiol & Behavior*, 1969, **4**, 1–6.

Ellen, P., and E. W. Powell. Effects of septal lesions on behavior generated by positive reinforcement. *Expl. Neurol.* 1962, **6**, 1–11. (386)

Ellen, P., Wilson, A. S., and E. W. Powell. Septal inhibition and timing behavior in the rat. *J. Comp. Neurol.*, 1964, **10**, 120–32. (386)

Elliott, D. F., Horton, E. W., and Lewis, G. P. Actions of pure bradykinin. *J. Physiol. (London)*, 1960, **153**, 473. (200)

Elliott, D. F., Horton, E. W., and Lewis, G. P. The isolation of bradykinin, a plasma kinin from ox blood. *Biochem. J.*, 1961, **78**, 60. (200)

Elsberg, C. A., and Levy, I. Sense of smell; new and simple method of quantitative olfactormetry. *Bull. Neurol. Inst. New York*, 1935, **4**, 5–19. (283)

Elul, R. Regional differences in the hippocampus of the cat. II. Projections of the dorsal and ventral hippocampus. *Electroencephalography and Clinical Neurophysiology*, 1964, **16**, 489–502. (391)

Endroczi, E., and Lissak, K. Role of reflexogenic factors in testicular hormone secretion; effect of copulation on the testicular hormone production of the rabbit. *Acta Physiol. Hung.*, 1962, **21**, 203–6. (555)

Enomoto, T. F. Unilateral activation of the non-specific thalamic system and bilateral cortical responses. *EEG Clin. Neurophysiol.*, 1959, **11**, 219–32. (409)

Enroth, C. Spike frequency and flicker fusion frequency in retinal ganglion cells. *Acta Physiol. Scand.*, 1953, **29**, 19–21. (114)

Enroth-Cugell, C., and Robson, J. The contrast sensitivity of retinal ganglion cells of the cat. *J. Physiol.*, 1966, **187**, 517–52. (110)

Epstein, A. N. Water intake without the act of drinking. *Science*, 1960, **131**, 497–98. (599, 622)

Epstein, A. N. Reciprocal changes in feeding behavior produced by intrahypothalamic chemical injections. *Amer. J. Physiol.*, 1960, **199**, 969–74. (599)

Epstein, A. N., Fitzsimons, J. T., and Simons, B. Drinking caused by the intracranial injection of angiotensin into the rat. *J. Physiol. (London)*, 1969, **200**, 98–100. (589)

Epstein, A. N., and Stellar, E. The control of salt preference in the adrenalectomized rat. *J. Comp. Physiol. Psychol.*, 1955, **48**, 167–72. (550, 632, 636)

Epstein, R., and Tauc, L. Heterosynaptic facilitation and postetanic potentiation in *Aplysia* nervous system. *J. Physiol.*, 1970, **209**, 1–23. (458)

Epstein, A. N., and Teitelbaum, P. Regulation of food intake in the absence of taste, smell and other oropharyngeal sensations *J. Comp. Physiol. Psychol.*, 1962, **55**, 753–59. (630)

Eriksen, T. C., Bleckwenn, W. J., and Woolsey, C. N. Observations on the postcential gyrus in relation to pain. *Tr. Am. Neurol. Ass.*, 1952, **77**, 57–59. (245)

Erulkar, S. D., Rose, J. E., and Davies, P. W. Single unit activity in the auditory cortex of the cat. *Bull. Johns Hopkins Hosp.*, 1956, **99**, 55–86. (160)

Ervin, F. R., and Mark, V. H. Physiological observations on the human thalamus. *Trans. Amer. Neurol. Assoc.*, 1959, 92–100. (234, 247)

Evans, E. F. Cortical representation. In A. V. S. de Renck and J. Knight (Eds.), *Hearing mechanisms in verte-*

brates. London: Churchill, 1968, 272–87. (141, 158, 159)

Evans, E. F., and Whitefield, I. C. Classification of unit responses in the auditory cortex of the unanaesthetized and unrestrained cat. *Journal of Physiology,* 1964, **171,** 476–93. (141, 147, 164)

Evarts, E. V. Temporal patterns of discharge of pyramidal tract neurons during sleep and waking in the monkey. *J. Neurophysiol.,* 1964, **27,** 152–72. (312, 413)

Evarts, E. V. Representation of movements and muscles by pyramidal tract neurons of the precentral motor cortex. In M. D. Yahr and D. P. Purpura (Eds.), *Neurophysiological Basis of Normal and Abnormal Motor Activities.* New York: Raven Press, 1967, pp. 215–51. (336)

Evarts, E. V. Relation of pyramidal tract activity to force exerted during voluntary movement. *J. Neurophysiol.,* 1968, **31,** 14–27. (336)

F

Falk, J. L., and Titlebaum, L. F. Saline solution preference in the rat: further demonstrations. *J. Comp. Physiol. Psychol.,* 1963, **56,** 337–42. (617)

Fangel, C., and Kaada, B. R. Behavioral "attention" and fear induced by cortical stimulation in the cat. *EEG Clin. Neurophysiol.,* 1960, **12,** 575–88. (362)

Fantz, R. L. Form preferences in newly hatched chicks. *J. Comp. Physiol. Psychol.,* 1957, **50,** 422–30. (627)

Favreau, O. E., Emerson, V. F., and Corballis, M. C. Motion Perception: a color-contingent aftereffect. *Science,* (1972), **176,** 78–79. (110)

Feldberg, W., and Vartiainen, A. Further observations on the physiology and pharmacology of a sympathetic ganglion. *Journal of Physiology,* 1934, **83,** 103–28. (488)

Feldman, E. M., and Waller, H. J. Dissociation of electrocortical activation and behavioral arousal. *Nature,* 1962, **196,** 320–22. (395)

Ferguson, J., Henriksen, S., Cohen, H., Mitchell, G., Barahas, J., and Dement, W. Hypersexuality and behavioral changes in cats caused by administration of p-ohlorophenylalamine. *Science,* 1970, **168,** 499. (555)

Fetz, E. E. Operant conditioning of cortical unit activity. *Science,* 1969, **163,** 955–58. (459)

Finch, G. Salivary conditioning in atropinized dogs. *Amer. J. Physiol.,* 1938, **124,** 136–41. (510)

Fisher, A. E. Maternal and sexual behavior induced by intracranial chemical stimulation. *Science,* 1956, **124,** 228–29. (557, 560)

Fisher, A. E. The role of limbic structures in the central regulation of feeding and drinking behavior. *Ann. N. Y. Acad. Sci.,* 1969, **157,** 2, 894–901. (597)

Fisher, A. E., and Coury, J. N. Cholinergic tracing of a central neural circuit underlying the thirst drive. *Science,* 1962, **137,** 691–93. (597)

Fishgold, H., and Larry-Bounez, G. C. Réaction l'arrêt et l'éveil dans les lésions du tronc cérébral et des hémispheres. *Rev. Neurol.* (Paris), 1952, **87,** 603–4. (400)

Fishman, I. Y. Single fiber gustatory impulses in rat and hamster. *J. Cell Comp. Physiol.,* 1957, **49,** 319–34. (259, 262)

FitzGerald, O. Discharges from the sensory organs of the cat's vibrissae and the modification of their activity by ions. *J. Physiol.* (London), 1940, **98,** 163. (189)

Fitzsimmons, J. T. Drinking by rats depleted of body fluid without increase in osmotic pressure. *J. Physiol.* (London), **159,** 297–309. (588, 589)

Fitzsimmons, J. T. The role of a renal thirst factor in drinking induced by extracellular stimuli. *J. Physiol.,* (London), 1969, **201,** 349–68. (589)

Fjallbrandt, F., and Iggo, A. The effect of histamine, 5-hydroxytryptamine and acetylcholine on cutaneous afferent fibers. *J. Physiol.,* 1961, **156,** 578–90. (189)

Fleishman, E. A. Perception of body position in the absence of visual cues. *J. Exp. Psychol.,* 1953, **46,** 261–70. (333)

Fleming, D. G. Food intake studies in parabiotic rats. *Annals N. Y. Acad. Sci.,* 1969, **157,** 2, 985–1002. (624)

Flexner, J. B., and Flexner, L. B. Restoration of memory lost after treatment with puromycin. *Proc. Nat. Acad. Sci. USA,* 1967, **57,** 1651–54. (479, 480)

Flexner, L. B., Flexner, J. B., and Roberts, R. B. Memory in mice analyzed with antibiotics. *Science,* 1967, **155**, 1377–83. (480, 481, 483)

Flexner, J. B., Flexner, L. B., and Stellar, E. Memory in mice as affected by intracerebral puromycin, *Science,* 1963, **141**, 57–59. (478)

Flynn, J. P., and Wasman, M. Learning and cortically evoked movement during propagated hippocampal after discharge. *Science,* 1960, **131**, 1607–08. (434)

Foerster, O. *Die Leitungsbahnen des Schmerzgefühls und die Chirurgische behandling der Schnerzzustande.* Berlin: Urban, 1927. (238)

Foerster, O. In O. Bunke and O. Foerster (Eds.), *Handbuch der Neurologie.* Vol. 5. Berlin: Springer, 1936. (202, 229, 238)

Foerster, O., and Gagel, O. Die vorder seitenstrang durchschreidung berin neuthen, eire klinische-pathophysiolafische-anatomische grudie. *Ztschr. ges. Neurol. Psychiat.,* 1932, **138**, 1–92. (209, 227, 229)

Folman, Y., and Drori, D. Normal and aberrant copulatory behaviour in male rats (*r. Norvegicus*) reared in isolation. *Anim. Behav.,* 1965, **13**, 427–29. (571)

Folman, Y., and Drori, D. Effects of social isolation and of female odours on the reproductive system, kidneys and adrenals of unmated male rats. *J. Reprod. Fert.,* 1966, **11**, 43–50. (555)

Fonberg, E., and Delgado, J. M. R. Avoidance and alimentary reactions during amygdaloid stimulation. *J. Neurophysiol.,* 1961, **24**, 651–64. (359)

Fortier, C. Adenohypophysical corticotrophin, plasma free corticosteroids and adrenal weight following surgical trauma in the rat. *Archs. int. Physiol. Biochim.* 1959, **67**, 333–40. (347)

Fortier, C., de Groot, J., and Hartfield, J. E. Plasma free corticosteroid response to faradic stimulation in the rat. *Acta Endocr.,* 1959, **30**, 219–21. (347)

Fox, S. Evoked potential, coding, and behaviour. In F. O. Schmitt (Ed.), *The Neurosciences: Second study program.* New York: Rockefeller University Press, 1970, 243–59. (397)

Franchina, J. J., and Moore, M. H. Strychnine and the inhibition of previous performance. *Science,* 1968, **160**, 903–4. (473).

Frank, E., Stein, D. G., and Rosen, J. Interanimal "memory" transfer: results from brain and liver homogenates. *Science,* 1970, **169**, 399–402. (476)

Frank, K., and Fuortes, M. Presynaptic and postsynaptic inhibition of monosynaptic reflexes. *Fed. Proc.,* 1957, **16**, 390. (18)

Frankenhaeuser, B. Impulses from a cutaneous receptor with slow adaptation and low mechanical threshold. *Acta Physiol. Scand.,* 1949, **18**, 68. (189)

Frazier, W. T., Waziri, R., and Kandel, E. Alterations in the frequency of spontaneous activity in aplysia neurons with contingent and noncontingent nerve stimulation. *Fed. Proc.,* 1965, **24**, 522. (458)

Freeman, Ralph D., Mitchell, Donald E. and Millodot, Michel. A neural effect of partial visual deprivation in humans. *Science,* 1972, **175**, 4028, 1384–86. (103)

Freeman, W., and Watts, J. *Psychosurgery in the Treatment of Mental Disorders and Intractable Pain.* (2nd ed.) Springfield: Charles C Thomas, 1950. (250)

French, J. D. Brain lesions associated with prolonged unconsciousness. *Arch. neurol. psychiat.,* 1952, **68**, 727–40. (397)

French, J. D., Amerongen, F. K., and Magoun, H. W. An activating system in brain stem of monkeys. *Arch. Neurol. Psychiat.,* 1952, **68**, 591–604. (401, 402)

French, G. M., and Harlow, H. F. Locomotor reaction decrement in brain-damaged monkeys. *J. Comp. Physiol. Psychol.,* 1955, **48**, 496–501. (392)

French, J. D., Hernández-Peón, R., and Livingston, R. B. Projections from cortex to cephalic brain stem (reticular formation) in monkey. *J. Neurophysiol.,* 1955, **18**, 74–95. (399, 401)

French, J. D., and Magoun, H. W. Effects of chronic lesions in central cephalic brain stem of monkeys. *AMA Arch. Neurol. Psychiat.,* 1952, **68**, 591–604. (398, 408)

French, J. D., Verzeano, M., and Magoun, H. W. A neural basis for the anaesthetic state. *A.M.A. Arch. Neurol. Psychiat.,* 1953, **69**, 519–29. (403)

Fried, P. A. Limbic system lesions in rats: differential effects in an approach-avoidance task. *J. Comp. Physiol. Psychol.*, 1971, **74**, 349–53. (391)

Friedman, S. B., Ader, R., Grota, L. J., and Larson, T. Plasma corticosterone response to parameters of electric shock stimulation in the rat. *Psychosom. Med.*, 1967, **29**, 323–28. (347)

Fritsch, G. T., and Hitzig, E. Uber die elektrische erregbarkeit des grosshirns. *Arch. Anat. Physiol. wiss. Med. Leipzig*, 1870, **37**, 300–346. (334)

Frommer, G. P. Gustatory afferent responses in the thalamus. In M. R. Kare and B. P. Halpern (Eds.), *The Physiological and Behavioral Aspects of Taste.* Chicago: University of Chicago Press, 1961. (263)

Frommer, G. P., and Pfaffmann, C. J. Electrophysiological analysis of gustatory, tongue temperature, and tactile representation in thalamus of albino rat. *The Physiologist*, 1961, **4**, 38. (263)

Fulford, B. D., and McCann, S. M. Suppression of adrenal compensatory hypothalamic lesions. *Proc. Soc. Exper. Biol. and Med.*, 1955, **90**, 78–80. (585)

Fuller, J. L., Rosvold, H. E., and Pribram, K. H. The effect on affective and cognitive behavior in the dog of lesions of the pyriform-amygdala-hippocampal complex. *J. comp. physiol. Psychol.*, 1957, **50**, 89–96. (374)

Fulton, J. F. *Physiology of the nervous system.* New York: Oxford Univ. Press, 1943. (26)

Fulton, J. F. *Frontal Lobotomy and Affective Behavior.* London: Chapman, 1951. (381)

Fulton, J. F. (Ed.). *A Textbook of Physiology.* (17th ed.) Philadelphia and London: Saunders, 1955. (287)

Fulton, J. F., and Jacobsen, C. F. The functions of the frontal lobes, a comparative study in monkeys, chimpanzees and man. *Abstr. 2nd Int. Neurol. Congr.* (London), 1935, pp. 70–71. *Advances Mod. Biol.* (Moscow), 1935, pp. 113–123. (380)

Funderburk, W. H., and Case, T. J. The effect of atropine on cortical potentials. *EEG Clin. Neurophysiol.*, 1951, **3**, 213–23. (396)

Fuortes, M. G. F. Responses of photoreceptors. *J. Psychiatric Research*, 1971, **8**, 289–300.

G

Gad, J., and Goldschneider, H. Uber die summation von hautreizen. *Ztschr. F. klin. Med. Berl.*, 1892, **20**, 337–73. (204)

Galambos, R. Suppression of auditory nerve activity by stimulation of efferent fibers to cochlea. *J. Neurophysiol.*, 1956, **6**, 424–37. (167)

Galambos, R. Microelectrode studies on medial geniculate body of cat. III. Response to pure tones. *J. Neurophysiol.*, 1952, **15**, 381–400. (147, 152)

Galambos, R., and Davis, H. The response of single auditory nerve fibers to acoustic stimulaiton. *J. Neurophysiol.*, 1943, **6**, 39–57. (160)

Galambos, R., and Davis, H. Inhibition of activity in single auditory nerve fibers by acoustic stimulation. *J. Neurophysiol.*, 1944, **7**, 287–303. (160)

Galambos, R., Myers, R. E., and Sheatz, G. C. Extralemniscal activation of auditory cortex in cats. *Amer. J. Physiol.*, 1961, **200**, 23–28. (140, 166)

Galambos, R., Rose, J. E., and Bromiley, R. B. Microelectrode studies on medial geniculate body of cat. II. Response to clicks. *J. Neurophysiol.*, 1952, **15**, 359–80. (160)

Galambos, R., Schwartzkopff, J., and Rupert, A. Microelectrode study of superior olivary nuclei. *Amer. J. Physiol.*, 1959, **197**, 527–36. (139, 147, 160, 162, 423)

Galambos, R., Sheatz, G., and Vernier, V. G. Electrophysiological correlates of a conditioned response in cats. *Science*, 1956, **123**, 376–77. (423)

Gallistel, C. R. Electrical self-stimulation and its theoretical implications. *Psychological Bulletin*, 1964, **61**, 23–34. (531)

Gallistel, C. R. Motivating effects in self-stimulation. *J. Comp. Physiol. Psychol.*, 1966, **62**, 95–101. (522)

Gallistel, C. R. Intracranial stimulation and natural rewards: differential effects of trial spacing. *Psychonomic Science*, 1967, **9**, 167–68. (522)

Gallistel, C. R. The incentive of brain stimulation reward. *J. Comp. Physiol. Psychol.*, 1969a, **69**, 713–21. (522)

Gallistel, C. R. Failure of pretrial stimulation to affect reward electrode preference. *J. Comp. Physiol. Psychol.*, 1969b, **69**, 722–29. (522)

Gallistel, C. R. Self-stimulation: the neurophysiology of reward and motivation. In J. A. Deutsch (Ed.), *The Physiological Basis of Memory*. New York: Academic Press, 1973, 175–227. (516, 517)

Gallistel, C. R., Rolls, E. T., and Greene, D. Neuron function inferred from behavioral and electrophysiological estimates of refractory period. *Science,* 1969, **166**, 1028–30. (540, 541)

Gangloff, H., and Monnier, M. Electrographic aspects of an "arousal" or attention reaction induced in the unanesthetized rabbit by the presence of a human being. *EEG Clin. Neurophysiol.,* 1956, **8**, 623–30. (400)

Ganong, W. F., and Hume, D. M. Absence of stress-induced and "compensatory" adrenal hypertrophy in dogs with hypothalamic lesions, *Endocrinology*, 1954, **55**, 474–83. (585)

Garcia, J., Ervin, F. R., and Koelling, R. A. Learning with prolonged delay of reinforcement. *Psychonomic Science,* 1965, **5**, 121–22. (633)

Garcia-Bengochea, F., Corrigan, R., Morgane, D. R., Jr., and Heath, R. G. Studies on the function of the temporal lobes: the section of the fornix. *Tr. Am. Neurol. Assoc.,* 1951, **76**, 238–39. (377)

Gardner, E. Physiology of movable joints. *Psychol. Rev.,* 1950, **230**, 127–76. (301)

Gardner, E. D., and Morin, F. Spinal pathways for projection of cutaneous and muscular afferents to the sensory and motor cortex of the monkey (*macacca mulatta*). *Am. J. Physiol.,* 1953, **174**, 149–54. (219)

Garner, W. R. The effect of frequency spectrum on temporal integration of energy in the ear. *J. Acoust. Soc. Amer.,* 1947, **19**, 808. (161)

Garner, W. R., and Miller, G. A. Differential sensitivity to intensity as a function of the duration of the comparison tone. *J. Exp. Psychol.,* 1944, **34**, 450. (161)

Garten, S. Über die grundlagen unserer orientierung im raum. *Abh. Maths-Phs. Sachs. Akad.,* 1920, **36**, 431–510. (333)

Gasser, H. S. Pain-producing impulses in peripheral nerves. *A. Res. Nerv. Ment. Dis. Proc.,* 1942, **23**, 44–62. (180)

Gasser, H. S., and Erlanger, J. Role of

fiber size in establishment of nerve block by pressure or cocaine. *Am. J. Physiol.,* 1929, **88**, 581–91. (197).

Gastaut, H. Correlations entre le systeme nerveux vegetatif et le système de la vie de relation dans le rhinecephale. *J. Physiol.* (Paris), 1952, **44**, 431–70. (509, 573)

Gastaut, H. The brain stem and cerebral electogenesis in relation to consciousness. In J. F. Delafresnaye (Ed.), *Brain Mechanisms and Consciousness*. Springfield, Ill.: Charles C Thomas, 1954, pp. 249–283. (394)

Gastaut, H., Morin, G., and Leseure, N. Etude du comportement des épileptiques psycho-moteurs dans l'intervale de leurs crises. Les troubles de l'activité globale et de la sociabilité. *Ann. méd-psychol.,* 1955, **113**, 1–27. (365)

Gastaut, H., Naquet, R., Vigouroux, R., and Corriol, J. Provocation de comportements émotionnels divers par stimulation rhinencephalique chez le chat avec électrodes à demeure. *Rev. Neurol.,* 1952, **86**, 319–27. (359, 362)

Gastaut, H., Jus, A., Jus, L., Morrell, F., Storm Van Leeuwen, W., Dongier, S., Naquet, R., Regis, H., Roger, A., Bekkering, D., Kamp, A., and Werre, J. Étude topographique des reactions éléctroencephalographiques conditionnées chez l'homme. *Éléctroencephalog. and Clin. Neurophysiol.,* 1957, **9**, 1–34. (509).

Gault, F. P., and Leaton, R. N. Electrical activity of the olfactory system. *EEG Clin. Neurophysiol.,* 1963, **15**, 299–304. (466)

Gauss, C. J. Geburten in kunstlichem dammerschlaf. *Arch. Gynak,* 1906, **78**, 579–631. (485)

Geisler, C. D., Rhode, W. S., and Haselton, D. W. Responses of inferior colliculus neurons in the cat to binaural acoustic stimuli having wide-band spectra. *J. Neurophysiol.,* 1969, **32**, 960–74. (163)

Geldard, F. A. The perception of mechanical vibration. III. The frequency function. *J. Gen. Psychol.,* 1940, **22**, 281–89. (210, 211, 212)

Geldard, F. A. *The Human Senses*. New York, London: Wiley, 1953. (210)

Geller, A., and Jarvik, M. E. The time relations of ECS induced amnesia. *Psychon. Sci.,* 1968, **12**, 169–70. (441, 442)

Gellhorn, E., and Loofbourrow, G. N.

Emotion and Emotional Disorders; a Neurophysiological Study. New York: Harper and Row, 1963. (340)

Gerall, A. A. An attempt to induce precocious sexual behavior in male guinea pigs by injections of testosterone propionate, *Endocrinology,* 1958, **63**, 280–84. (554)

Gerall, H. D., Ward, I. L., and Gerall, A. A. Disruption of the male rat's sexual behaviour induced by social isolation. *Anim. Behav.,* 1967, **15**, 54–58. (571)

Gerbrandt, L. K., Skrebitsky, V. G., Buresova, O., and Bures, J. Plastic changes of unit activity induced by tactile stimuli followed by electrical stimulation of single hippocampal and reticular neurons. *Neuropsychologia,* 1968, **6**, 3–10. (437, 460)

Gernandt, B. Pain conduction in phrenic nerve. *Acta Physiol. Scand.,* 1946, **12**, 255–60. (243)

Gernandt, B. E. Vestibular mechanisms. In *Handbook of Physiology.* Vol. I. Section I. *Neurophysiology.* Washington: American Physiological Society, 1959, pp. 549–64. (321)

Gernandt, B., and Zotterman, Y. Intestinal Pain: An electrophysiological investigation on mesenteric nerves. *Acta Physiol. Scandinav.,* 1946, **12**, 56–71. (198, 243)

Gesteland, R. C., Lettvin, J. Y., Pitts, W. H., and Rojas, A. Odor specifications of the frog's olfactory receptors. In Y. Zotterman (Ed.), *Olfaction and Taste.* Oxford: Pergamon Press, 1963, 19–34. (272)

Gibbs, F. A. Abnormal electrical activity in the temporal regions and its relationship to abnormalities of behavior. *Res. Publ. Am. nerv. ment. Dis.,* 1956, **36**, 278–94. (365)

Gibson, W. E., Reid, L. D., Sakai, M., and Porter, P. B. Intracranial reinforcement compared with sugar water reinforcement. *Science,* 1965, **148**, 1357–59. (526, 527)

Gilman, A. The relation between blood osmotic pressure, fluid distribution and voluntary water intake. *Am. J. Physiol.,* 1937, **120**, 323–28. (588)

Gilman, A., and Goodman, L. The secretory response of the posterior pituitary to the need for water conservation. *J. Physiol.,* 1937, **90**, 113–24. (588)

Glees, P. The termination of optic fibres in the lateral geniculate body of the cat. *J. Anat.,* 1941, **75**, 434–40. (105)

Glees, P., and Clark, W. E. Le Gros. The termination of optic fibres in the lateral geniculate body of the monkey. *J. Anat.,* 1941, **75**, 292–308. (104)

Glees, P., Cole, J., Whitty, C. W. M., and Cairns, H. The effects of lesions in the cingular gyrus and adjacent areas in monkeys. *J. Neurol. Neurosurg. Psychiat.,* 1950, **13**, 179–90. (379)

Gleitman, H. Place learning without prior performance. *J. comp. physiol. Psychol.,* 1955, **48**, 77–79. (508)

Glickstein, M., and Sperry, R. W. Intermanual somesthetic transfer in split brain rhesus monkey. *J. comp. physiol. Psychol.,* 1960, **53**, 322–27. (—)

Gloor, P. Amygdala. In J. Field, H. W. Magoun and V. E. Hall (Eds.), *Handbook of Physiology.* Vol. II. Section I. *Neurophysiology.* (American Physiological Society) Baltimore: Williams and Wilkins, 1960, 1395–1416. (365, 374)

Goff, G. D. Differential discrimination of frequency of cutaneous mechanical vibration. Doctoral dissertation, University of Virginia, 1959. (212)

Goldberg, J. J., Diamond, I. T., and Neff, W. D. Auditory discrimination after ablation of temporal and insular cortex in cat. *Fed. Proc.,* 1957, **16**, 47. (166)

Goldberg, J. J., Diamond, I. T., and Neff, W. D. Frequency discrimination after ablation of cortical projection areas of the auditory system. *Fed. Proc. Balt.,* 1958, **17**, 55. (148, 165)

Goldberg, J. M., and Brown, P. B. Functional organization of the dog superior olivary complex: an anatomical and electrophysiological study. *J. Neurophysiol.,* 1963, **31**, 639–96. (152, 162)

Goldberg, J. M., and Brown, P. B. Response of binaural neurons of dog superior olivary complex to dichotic tonal stimuli. Some physiological mechanisms of sound localization. *J. Neurophysiol.* 1969, **32**, 613–36. (162)

Goldberg, J. M., and Greenwood, D. D. Response of neurons of the dorsal and posteroventral cochlear nuclei of the cat to acoustic stimuli of long duration. *J. Neurophysiol.,* 1966, **29**, 72–93. (160)

Goldberg, M. M., and Neff, W. D. Frequency discrimination after bilateral ablation of cortical auditory areas. *J. Neurophysiol.*, 1961a, **24**, 119–28. (148, 165, 166)

Goldfoot, D. A., Feder, H. H., and Goy, R. W. Development of bisexuality in the male rat treated neonatally with adrostenedione. *J. Comp. Physiol. Psychol.*, 1969, **67**, 41–45. (569)

Goldscheider, A. Untersuchungen uber den muskelsinn. *Arch. Anat. Physiol.*, 1889, Lpz., 369–502. Ministry Supply Trans. No. 20825T. (301)

Goldstein, K. Die lokalisation in der grosshirnrinde. In Bethe et al. (Ed.), *Handb. Norm. Pathol. Physiol.* Berlin: Springer, 1927, **10**, 600–842. (240)

Golstein, K. *Aftereffects of Brain Injuries in War.* New York: Grune & Stratton, Inc., 1942. (240)

Goldstein, M. H., Jr., Hall, J. L., II, and Butterfield, B. O. Single-unit activity in the primary auditory cortex of unanesthetized cats. *J. Acoust. Soc. Am.*, 1968, **43**, 444–55. (147)

Goldring, S., and O'Leary, J. L. Cortical D.C. changes incident to midline thalamic stimulation. *EEG clin. Neurophysiol.*, 1957, **9**, 577–84. (465)

Gollin, E. S. Developmental studies of visual recognition of incomplete objects. *Perceptual and Motor Skills,* 1960, **11**, 289–98. (433)

Goodale, H. D. Feminized male birds. *Genetics*, 1918, **3**, 276–99. (567)

Goodman, L. S., and Gilman, A. *The Pharmacological Basis of Therapeutics.* New York: Macmillan, 1965. (488)

Gordon, G., Landgren, S., and Seed, W. A. Responses of single cells in the caudal part of the spinal nucleus of the trigeminal nerve of the cat. *J. Physiol.*, 1960, **193**, 12–13. (231)

Gordon, G., Landgren, S., and Seed, W. A. The functional characteristics of single cells in the caudal part of the spinal nucleus of the trigeminal nerve of the cat. *J. Physiol.*, 1961, **158**, 544–59. (219)

Gorska, T., and Jankowska, E. The effects of deafferentation of a limb on instrumental reflexes. In Czechoslovak Academy of Science, *Central and Peripheral Mechanisms of Motor Functions* (Proc. Conf. Liblice), Prague, 1963. (299)

Goy, R. W., and Phoenix, C. H. Hypothalamic regulation of female sexual behaviour; establishment of behavioural oestrus in spayed guinea pigs following hypothalamic lesions. *J. Reprod. Fertil.*, 1963, **5**, 23–40. (560)

Graham, C. H., and Hsia, Y. Color defect and color theory. *Science*, 1958, **127**, 675–82. (94)

Granit, R. Centrifugal and antidromic effects on ganglion cells of retina. *J. Neurophysiol.*, 1955, **18**, 388–411. (122)

Granit, R. *Receptors and Sensory Perception.* New Haven: Yale University Press, 1955. (122, 298, 316, 424)

Granit, R. The visual pathway. In Dawson, H. (Ed.), *The Eye.* Vol. 2. New York and London: Academic Press, 1962, 537–763. (76, 80, 89, 122)

Granit, R. *The Basis of Motor Control.* London and New York: Academic Press, 1970. (297, 298, 300)

Granit, R., Leksell, L., and Skoglund, C. R. Fibre interaction in injured or compressed region of nerve. *Brain,* 1944, **67**, 125–40. (203)

Granit, R., and Renkin, Barbara. Net depolarization and discharge rate of motoneurons, as measured by recurrent inhibition. *J. Physiol.*, 1961, **158**, 461–75.

Grant, L. D., and Jarrard, L. E. Functional dissociation within hippocampus. *Brain Research*, 1968, **10**, 392–401. (391)

Gray, A. A. On a modification of the Helmholtz theory of hearing. *J. of Anat. Physiol.*, 1900, **34**, 324–50. (134)

Gray, J. The role of peripheral sense organs during locomotion in the vertebrates. In Symp. Soc. Exp. Biol. No. 4. *Physiological Mechanisms in Animal Behaviour.* Cambridge: Cambridge University Press, 1950. (332)

Gray, J. A. B. A morphological basis for pre-synaptic inhibition. *Nature,* 1962, **193**, 82. (19)

Gray, J. A., and Wedderburn, A. A. I. Grouping strategies with simultaneous stimuli. *Quart. J. exp. Psychol.*, 1960, **12**, 180–84. (418)

Graybiel, A., Clark, B., and Zarriello, J. J. Observations on human subjects, living in a slow rotation room for periods of two days. *Arch. Neurol.*, 1960, **3**, 55–73. (327)

Graybiel, A., and Hupp, D. I. The oculo-gyral illusion; a form of apparent motion which may be observed following stimulation of the semicircular canals. *J. aviat. Med.*, 1946, **17**, 3–27. (324)

Green, J. D. Electrical activity in hypothalamus and hippocampus of conscious rabbits. *Anat. Rec.*, 1954, **118**, 304. (559, 562)

Green, J. D. The hippocampus. In J. Field, H. W. Magoun, and V. E. Hall (Eds.), *Handbook of Physiology*. Vol. II. Section I. *Neurophysiology*. American Physiological Society. Baltimore: Williams and Wilkins, 1960, 1373–90. (379)

Green, J. D., and Adey, W. R. Electrophysiological studies of hippocampal connections and excitability. *EEG clin. Neurophysiol.*, 1956, **8**, 245–62. (400)

Green, J. D., Clemente, C. D., and de Groot, J. Rhinencephalic lesions and behavior in cats. An analysis of the Kluver-Bucy syndrome with particular reference to normal and abnormal sexual behavior. *J. comp. Neurol.*, 1957a, **108**, 505–45. (374)

Green, J. D., Clemente, C. D., and de Groot, J. Experimentally induced epilepsy in the cat with injury of Cornu Ammonis (hippocampus). *A.M.A. Arch. Neurol. Psychiat.*, 1957b, **78**, 259–63. (374)

Green, J. D., Clemente, C. D., and de Groot, J. Rhinencephalic lesions and behavior in cats. *J. comp. Neurol.*, 1957, **108**, 505–36. (552, 567, 573, 630)

Green, J. R., Duisberg, R. E. H., and McGrath, W. B. Focal epilepsy of psychomotor type; preliminary report of observations on effects of surgical therapy. *J. Neurosurg.*, 1951, **8**, 157–72. (379)

Green, R. H., Beatty, W. W., and Schwartzbaum, J. S. Comparative effects of septo-hippocampal and caudate lesions on avoidance behavior in rats. *J. Comp. Physiol. Psychol.*, 1967, **64**, 444–52. (392)

Greenwood, D. D., and Maruyama, N. Excitatory and inhibitory response areas of auditory neurons in the cochlear nucleus. *J. Neurophysiol.*, 1965, **28**, 863–92. (141)

Greer, M. A. The role of the hypothalamus in the control of thyroid function. *J. clin. Endocrinol.*, 1952, **12**, 1259–67. (589)

Greer, M. A. The effect of progesterone on persistent vaginal estrus produced by hypothalamic lesions in the rat. *Endocrinology*, 1953, **53**, 380–90. (584)

Greer, M. A. Suggestive evidence of a primary "drinking center" in hypothalamus of the rat. *Proc. Soc. Exper. Med.*, 1955, **89**, 59–62. (327)

Griffard, C. D., and Pierce, J. T. Conditioned discrimination in the planarian. *Science*, 1964, **144**, 1472–73. (475)

Grillner, S., Hongo, T., and Lund, S. Descending monosynaptic and reflex control of γ-motoneurons. *Acta Physiol. Scand.* 1969, **75**, 592–613. (298)

Grindley, G. C. The variation of sensory thresholds with the rate of application of the stimulus: 1. The differential threshold for pressure. *Brit. J. Psychol.*, 1936, **27**, 86–95. (205)

Groen, J. J. Postnatal changes in vestibular reactions. *Acta Oto-laryng.*, 1963, **56**, 390–96. (326)

Groen, J. J., and Jongkees, L. B. W. The threshold of angular acceleration perception. *J. Physiol.*, 1948, **107**, 1–7. (322)

Gross, C. G., and Carey, F. M. Transfer of learned response by RNA injection: failure of attempts to replicate. *Science*, 1965, **150**, 1749. (476)

Gross, C. G., Bender, D. B., and Rocha-Miranda, C. E. Visual receptive fields of neurons in inferotemporal cortex of the monkey. *Science*, 1969, **163**, 1303–5. (121)

Grossman, M. I., Cummins, G. M., and Ivy, A. C. The effect of insulin on food intake after vagotomy and sympathectomy. *Amer. J. Physiol.*, 1947, **149**, 100–102. (619)

Grossman, S. P. Eating or drinking elicited by direct adrenergic or cholinergic stimulation of the hypothalamus. *Science*, 1960, 301–32. (599)

Grossman, S. P. Behavioral effects of chemical stimulation of the ventral amygdala. *J. comp. physiol. Psychol.*, 1964, **57**, 29–36. (630)

Grossman, S. P., and Grossman, L. Food and water intake following lesions or electrical stimulation of the amygdala. *Amer. J. Physiol.*, 1963, **205**, 761–65. (630)

Groves, P. M., and Thompson, R. F. Habituation: A dual-process theory. *Psychol. Rev.*, 1970, **77**, 419–50. (457)

Grundfest, H. Bioelectric potentials. *Ann. Rev. Physiol.*, 1940, **2**, 213–42. (534)

Grüsser, O. J., and Creutzfeldt, O. Eine neurophysiologische Grundlage des Brücke-Bartley-Effectes; Maxima der Impulsfrequenz retinaler und corticaler Neurone bei Flimmerlicht mittlerer Frequenzen. *Pflüg. Arch. ges. Physiol.*, 1957, **263**, 668–81. (115)

Grüsser, O. J., and Kapp, H. Reaktionen retinaler neurone nach lichtblitzen. II. Doppelblitze mit wechselndem Blitzintervall. *Pflüg. Arch. ges. Physiol.* 1958, **265**, 501–25. (114)

Grüsser, O. J., and Rabelo, C. Reaktionen retinaler neurone nach lichtblitzen. I. Einzelblitze and Blitzruze wechselnder Frequenz. *Pflüg. Arch. ges. Physiol.*, 1958, **265**, 501–25. (114)

Guedry, F. E., Collins, W. E., and Sheffey, P. L. Perceptual and oculomotor reactions to interacting visual and vestibular stimulation. *Percept. Mot. Skills*, 1961, **12**, 307–24. (324)

Guttman, N. Operant conditioning, extinction, and periodic reinforcement in relation to concentration of sucrose used as reinforcing agent. *J. exp. Psychol.*, 1953, **46**, 213–24. (548)

Guttman, N. Equal-reinforcement values for sucrose and glucose solutions compared with equal sweetness values. *J. comp. physiol. Psychol.*, 1954, **47**, 358–61. (548)

Guzman-Flores, C., Buendria, N., and Lindsley, D. B. Cortical and reticular influences upon evoked responses in dorsal column nuclei. *Fed. Proc.*, 1961, **20**, 330–50. (242)

H

Habgood, J. Sensitisation of sensory receptors in the frog's skin. *J. Physiol.*, 1959, **111**, 195–213. (201)

Hagbarth, K. E., and Kerr, D. I. B. Central influences on spinal afferent conduction. *J. Neurophysiol.*, 1954, **17**, 295–307. (281, 424)

Hagen, E., Knoche, H., Sinclair, D. C., and Weddell, G. The role of specialized nerve terminals in cutaneous sensibility. *Proc. Roy. Soc.* (London), 1953, **B141**, 279–87. (177)

Hagstrom, E. C., and Pfaffmann, C. The relative taste effectiveness of different sugars for the rat. *J. Comp. Physiol. Psychol.*, 1959, **52**, 259–62. (637)

Hahn, H. Die psycho-physischen konstanten und variablen des temperatursinnes. *Z. Sinnesphys.*, 1930, **60**, 198–232. (207)

Hahn, H. Bertrage zur Reizphysiologie. Heidelberg: Scherer, 1949. (265)

Haider, M., Spong, P., and Lindsley, D. B. Attention, vigilance and cortical evoked potentials in humans. *Science*, 1964, 145–50. (428)

Hain, A. M. The effect of (a) litter size on growth and (b) of estrone administered during lactation (rat). *Quart. J. Exp. Physiol.*, 1935, **25**, 303–13. (576)

Halas, E. S., James, R. L., and Knutson, C. S. An attempt at classical conditioning in the planarian. *J. Comp. Physiol. Psychol.*, 1962, **55**, 969. (475)

Hall, J. L., II, and Goldstein, M. H., Jr. Representation of binaural stimuli by single units in primary auditory cortex of unanesthetized cats. *J. Acoust. Soc. Am.*, 1968, **43**, 456–561. (164)

Hamburg, M. D. Retrograde amnesia produced by intraperitoneal injection of physostigmine. *Science*, 1967, **156**, 973–74. (490)

Hamby, W. B. Reversible central pain. *Trans. Amer. neurol. Assoc.*, 1961, 91–94. (245)

Han, P. W., Jui-Yun, Mu, and Lepkovsky, S. Food intake of parabiotic rats. *American J. Physiol.*, 1963, **205**, 1139–43. (624)

Hanbery, J., and Jasper, H. H. Independence of diffuse thalamocortical projection system shown by specific nuclear destruction. *J. Neurophysiol.*, 1953, **16**, 252–71. (404)

Hansen, K. The Mechanism of insect sugar reception, a biochemical investigation. In C. Pfaffmann (Ed.), *Olfaction and Taste*. New York: Rockefeller Univ. Press, 1969, 382–91. (255)

Hard, E., and Larsson, K. Effects of mounts without intromission upon sexual behaviour in male rats. *Anim. Behav.*, 1968, **16**, 538–40. (563)

Hardy, J. D., and Oppel, T. W. Studies in temperature sensations; stimulation of cold sensation by radiation. *J. Clin. Invest.*, 1938, **17**, 771–78. (206)

Hardy, J. D., Wolff, H. G., and Goodell, H. *Pain Sensations and Reactions.* Baltimore, Md.: Williams and Wilkins, 1952. (193, 202)

Hardy, R. K. An appetitional theory of

sexual motivation. *Psychological Review*, 1964, **71**, 1–18. (570)

Harlow, H. F. Recovery of pattern discrimination in monkeys following unilateral occipital lobectomy. *J. comp. Psychol.*, 1939, **27**, 467–89. (120)

Harlow, H. F. Learning set and error factor theory. In Koch, S., (Ed.), *Psychology: A Study of a Science*, Vol. 2. New York: McGraw-Hill Book Co., 1959. (435)

Harlow, H. F. and Bromer, J. A. Acquisition of new responses during inactivation of the motor premotor and somesthetic cortex in the monkey. *J. gen. Psychol.*, 1942, **26**, 299–313. (510)

Harper, H. W., Jay, J. R., and Erickson, R. P. Chemically evoked sensations from single human taste papillae. *Physiol. Behav.*, 1966, **1**, 319–25. (254)

Harris, G. W. Electrical stimulation of the hypothalamus and the mechanism of neural control of the adenohypophysis. *J. Physiol.*, 1948, **107**, 418–29. (584)

Harris, G. W. The reticular formation, stress and endocrine activity. In H. H. Jasper, L. D. Proctor, R. S. Knighton, W. C. Noshay, and R. T. Costello (Eds.), *Reticular Formation of the Brain*. Chapter IX. Boston: Little, Brown and Co., 1958. (561)

Harris, G. W. Central control of pituitary secretion. In J. Field, H. W. Magoun and V. E. Hall (Eds.), *Handbook of Physiology*. Vol. II. Section I. *Neurophysiology*. (American Physiological Society) Baltimore: Williams and Wilkins, 1960, 1007–38. (581)

Harris, G. W., and Jacobsohn, D. Functional grafts of the anterior pituitary gland. *Proc. Roy Soc.* (London), Ser. B, 1952, **139**, 263–76. (583)

Harris, L. J., Clay, J., Hargreaves, F., and Ward, A. Appetite and choice of diet. The ability of the vitamin B deficient rat to discriminate between diets and containing and lacking the vitamin. *Proc. Royal Soc.* (London), Ser. B, 1933, **113**, 161–90. (633)

Hart, B. L. Sexual reflexes and mating behavior in the male dog. *J. Comp. Physiol. Psychol.*, 1967, **64**, 388–99. (563)

Hart, B. L., and Kitchell, R. L. Penile erection and contraction of penile muscles in the spinal and intact dog. *Amer. J. Physiol.*, 1966, **210**, 257–62. (563)

Hartline, H. K. The response of single optic nerve fibers of the vertebrate eye to illumination of the retina. *Amer. J. Physiol.*, 1938, **121**, 400–415. (115)

Hartline, H. K. The receptive field of the optic nerve fibers. *Amer. J. Physiol.*, 1940, **130**, 690–99. (95)

Hartline, H. K. Inhibition of visual receptors by illuminating nearby visual areas in the *Limulus* eye. *Fed. Proc.*, 1949, **8**, 69. (95)

Hartline, H. K., and Ratliff, F. Inhibitory interaction of receptor units in the eye of *Limulus*. *J. gen. Physiol.*, 1957, **40**, 357–76. (23)

Hartline, H. K., and Ratliff, F. Spatial summation of inhibitory influences in the eye of *Limulus* and the mutual interaction of receptor units. *J. gen. Physiol.*, 1958, **41**, 1049–66. (23)

Hartry, A. L., Keith-Lee, P. and Morton, W. D. Planaria: memory transfer through cannibalism reexamined. *Science*, 1964, **146**, 274–75. (475)

Harvey, J. A., and Hunt, H. F. Effect of septal lesions on thirst in the rat as indicated by water consumption and operant responding for water reward. *J. comp. physiol. Psychol.*, 1965, **59**, 49–56. (382, 383, 385, 386, 598)

Harvey, J. A., Jacobsen, L. E., and Hunt, H. F. Long-term effects of lesions in the septal forebrain on acquisition and retention of conditioned fear. *Amer. Psychol.*, 1961, **16**, 449. (385)

Harvey, J. A., Lintz, C. E., Jacobsen, L. E., and Hunt, H. F. Effects of lesions in the septal area on conditioned fear and discriminated instrumental punishment in the albino rat. *J. comp. physiol. Psychol.*, 1965, **59**, 37–48. (386)

Harwood, D., and Vowles, D. M. Forebrain stimulation and feeding behavior in the ring dove (Streptopelia Risoria), *J. Comp. Physiol. Psychol.*, 1966, **62**, 388–96. (601)

Hashimoto, K., Kumakrua, S., and Taira, N. Vascular reflex responses induced by an intra-arterial injection of azaazepinophenothiazine, andromedotoxin, veratridine, bradykinin, and kallikrein and blocking action of sodium salcylate. *Jap. J. Physiol.*, 1964, **14**, 299. (251)

Hausmann, M. F. The behavior of albino rats in choosing food. II. Differentiation between sugar and saccharin. *J. comp. Psychol.*, 1933, **15**, 419–28. (635)

Hayward, S. C. Modification of sexual behavior of the male albino rat. *J. Comp. Physiol. Psychol.*, 1957, **50**, 70–73. (571)

Head, H. *Studies in Neurology.* London: Frowde, Hodder & Stoughton, 1920. (171, 202, 229, 231, 235, 240, 246)

Hearst, E., and Whalen, R. E. Facilitating effects of D-amphetamine on discriminated-avoidance performance. *J. Comp. Physiol. Psychol.*, 1963, **56**, 124–28. (384)

Heath, R. G., and Mickle, W. A. Evaluation of seven years experience with depth electrode studies in human patients. In E. R. Ramey and D. S. O'Doherty (Eds.), *Electrical Studies on the Unanaesthetised Brain.* New York: Paul B. Hoeber, Inc., 1960, 214–40. (358, 364)

Heath, R. G., Monroe, R. R., and Mickle, W. A. Stimulation of the amygdaloid nucleus in the schizophrenic patient. *Am. J. Psychiat.*, 1955, **111**, 862–63. (364)

Hebb, D. O. *The Organization of Behavior.* New York: John Wiley & Sons, Inc., 1949. (435)

Hécaen, H., Talairach, J., David, M., and Dell, M. B. Coagulations limitées du thalamus dans les algies du syndrome thalamique. Resultats therapeutiques et psysiologiques. *Rev. Neurol.*, 1949, **81**, 917–81. (234, 245)

Hecht, S. Rods, cones and chemical basis of vision. *Physiol. Rev.*, 1937, **17**, 239–90. (83)

Heimer, Lennart, and Larsson, Knut. Mating behavior of male rats after olfactory bulb lesions. *Physiol. and Behav.*, 1967, **2**, 207–9.

Heinbecker, P.; Bishop, G. H.; and O'Leary, J. L. Pain and touch fibers in peripheral nerves. *Arch. Neurol. Psychiat.*, 1933, **29**, 771–89. (198)

Held, R. Adaptation to rearrangement and visual-spatial after-effects. *Psychol. Beit.*, 1962, **6**, 339–450. (339)

Held, R., and Hein, A. Movement produced stimulation in the development of visually guided behavior. *J. comp. physiol. Psychol.*, 1963, **56**, 872–76. (339)

Held, R., and Shattuck, S. R. Color and edge sensitive channels in the human visual system: tuning for orientation, *Science*, 1971, **174**, 314–16. (110)

Helmholtz, H. L. F. *Die Lehre von den Tonempfindungen als Physiologische Grundlage fur die Theorie der Musik.* (1st ed.) Brunswick, Germany: Vieweg-Verlag, 1863. (131)

Helmholtz, H. von. *Treatise on Physiological Optics.* Southall: J.P.C., 1925. Translated and edited from the 3rd German edition for the Opt. Soc. Am. (105)

Henneman, Elwood, Sonjen, George, and Carpenter, David. O. Functional significance of cell size in spinal motoneurons. *J. Neurophysiol.*, 1968, **28**, 560–580. (293, 294)

Henning, H. *Der Geruch.* (2d ed.) Leipzig: Barth, 1924. (277)

Hensel, H. Temperaturempfindung und intracutane Wärmebewegung. *Arch. Ges. Physiol.*, 1950, **252**, 165–215. (207, 208)

Hensel, H. Physiologie der Thermoreception. *Egebn. Physiol.*, 1952a, **47**, 166. (397)

Hensel, H. Afferente Impulse aus den Kälterceptoren der äusseren Haut. *Pflüger Arch. Ges. Physiol.*, 1952b, **256**, 195. (181)

Hensel, H. Electrophysiology of cutaneous thermoreceptors. In D. R. Kenshlo (ed.), *The Skin Senses.* Springfield, Ill.: Charles C Thomas, 1968, 384–99. (191)

Hensel, Herbert, and Boman, Kurt K. Afferent impulses in cutaneous sensory nerves in human subject. *J. Neurophysiol.*, 1960, **23**, 564–78. (181, 194)

Hensel, H., Iggo, A., and Witt, I. A quantitative study of sensitive cutaneous thermoreceptors with C afferent fibers. *J. Physiol.*, 1960, **153**, 113–26. (181, 192, 193)

Hensel, H., and Zotterman, Y. Quantitative beziehungen zwischen der entladung einzelner kaltenfasern und der temperatur. *Acta. Physiol., Scand.*, 1951a, **23**, 291–319. (181, 189, 235)

Hensel, H., and Zotterman, Y. The response of mechanoreceptors to thermal stimulation. *J. Physiol.*, 1951b, **115**, 16–24. (194, 235)

Hensel, H., and Zotterman, Y. Action potentials of cold fibres and intracutaneous temperature gradient. *J. Neurophysiol.*, 1951c, **14**, 377–85. (199)

Hepler, N. Color-motion-contingent aftereffect. *Science*, 1968, **162**, 376–77. (109)

Herberg, L. J. Hunger reduction produced by injecting glucose into the lateral ventricle of the rat. *Nature*, 1960, **187**, 245–46. (592, 619)

Herberg, L. J. Physiological drives investigated by means of injections into the cerebral ventricles of the rat. *Quart. J. Exp. Psychol.*, 1962, **14**, 8–14. (596, 619)

Herberg, L. J. Determinants of extinction in electrical self-stimulation. *J. Comp. Physiol. Psychol.*, 1963, **56**, 686–90. (529)

Herberg, L. J., and Blundell, J. E. Noninteraction of ventromedial and lateral hypothalamic mechanisms in the regulation of feeding and hoarding behavior in the rat. *Q. J. Exp. Psychol.*, 1970, **22**, 133–41 (639)

Hering, E. *Ueber individuelle verschiedenheiten des Farbensinnes*, Lotos, Prague, 1885. (105)

Hernández-Peón, R. Neurophysiological correlates of habituation and other manifestations of plastic inhibition. In H. H. Jasper and G. D. Smirnov (Eds.). The Moscow Colloquium on Electroencephalography of Higher Nervous Activity. *EEG Clin. Neurophysiol.*, 1960, Suppl. **13**, 101–12. (424, 425)

Hernández-Peón, R., Alcocer-Cuaron, C., Lavin, A., and y Santibáñez, G. Regulación centrífuga de la actividad eléctrica del bulbo olfatorio. Primera Reunión científica de Ciencias fisiológieas. Punta del Este, Uruguay, 1957, 192–93. (423)

Hernández-Peón, R., and Brust-Carmona, H. Functional role of subcortical structures in habituation and conditioning. In J. F. Delafresnaye (Ed.). *Brain Mechanisms and Learning*. Oxford: Blackwell, 1961, 393–408. (425)

Hernández-Peón, R., Chavez-Ibarra, G., Morgane, P. J., and Timo-Iarier, C. Limbic cholinergic pathways involved in sleep and emotional behavior. *Exptl. Neurol.*, 1963, **8**, 93–111. (411)

Hernández-Peón, R., Guzmán-Flores, C., Alcarez, M., and Fernández-Guardiola, A. Sensory transmission in visual pathway during "attention" in unanesthe-

tized cats. *Acta. Neurol. Latinoamer.*, 1957, **3**, 1–8. (422)

Hernández-Peón, R., Guzmán-Flores, C., Alcarez, M., and Fernandez-Guardiola, A. Habituation in the visual pathway. *Acta. Neurol. Latinoamer.*, 1958, **4**, 121–29. (422, 423)

Hernández-Peón, R., and Hagbarth, K. E. Interaction between afferent and cortically induced reticular responses. *J. Neurophysiol.*, 1955, **18**, 44–55. (400, 401, 402)

Hernández-Peón, R., Jouvet, M., and Scherrer, H. Auditory potentials at the cochlear nucleus during acoustic habituation. *Acta. Neurol. Latinoamer.*, 1957, **3**, 114–16. (423)

Hernández-Peón, R., and Scherrer, H. Habituation to acoustic stimuli in cochlear nucleus. *Fed. Proc.*, 1955, **14**, 71. (423)

Hernánez-Peón, R., Scherrer, H., and Jouvet, M. Modification of electric activity in cochlear nucleus during "attention" in unanesthetized cats. *Science*, 1956, **123**, 331–32. (422)

Hernánez-Peón, R., Scherrer, H., and Velasco, M. Central influences on afferent conduction in the somatic and visual pathways. *Acta. Neurol. Latinoamer.*, 1956, **2**, 8–22. (424)

Hervey, G. R. The effects of lesions in the hypothalamus in parabiotic rats. *J. Physiol.*, 1959, **45**, 336–52. (624)

Hess, E. H., and Gogel, W. C. Natural preferences of the chick for objects of different colors. *J. Psychol.*, 1954, **38**, 483–93. (627)

Hess, R., Jr., Koella, W. P., and Akert, K. Cortical and subcortical recordings in natural and artifically induced sleep in cats. *EEG clin. Neurophysiol.*, 1953, **5**, 75–90. (408)

Hess, W. R. Stammganglien-Reizversuche, (Verh. Dtsch. physiol. Ges. Sept. 1927), *Ber. ges. Physiol.*, 1928, **42**, 554. (351)

Hess, W. R. Das schlafsyndrom als folge dienzephaler reizung. *Helv. physiol. Acta.*, 1944, **2**, 305–44. (408, 410)

Hess, W. R. *Diencephalon: Autonomic and Extrapyramidal Functions*. New York: Grune and Stratton, 1954. (351, 408)

Hess, W. R. The diencephalic sleep centre. In J. F. Delafresnaye (Ed.), *Brain Mechanisms and Consciousness*.

Springfield, Ill.: Charles C Thomas, 1954, 117–36. (409, 410)

Hess, W. R. *The Functional Organization of the Diencephalon.* New York: Grune and Stratton, 1957. (331, 353, 357)

Hess, W. R. and Akert, K. Experimental data on the role of hypothalamus in mechanism of emotional behavior. *A.M.A. Arch. Neurol. Psychiat.*, 1955, 73, 127–29. (355)

Hess, W. R. and Brügger, M. Das subkortikale zentrum der afektiven abwehrreaktion *Helv. physiol. Acta.*, 1943, 1, 33–52. (351)

Hess, W. R., Brügger, M., and Bucher, V. Zur physiologie von hypothalamus area praeoptica und septum, sowie agrenzender balken under stirnhirnvereiche. *Moshv. Psychiat. Neurol.*, 1945, 111, 17–59. (351)

Hetherington, A. W., and Ranson, S. W. The spontaneous activity and food intake of rats with hypothalamic lesions. *Amer. J. Physiol.*, 1942, 136, 609–17. (622)

Higashino, S., Takeuchi, H., and Amoore, J. E. Mechanism of olfactory discrimination in the olfactory bulb of the bullfrog. In C. Pfaffmann (Ed.), *Olfaction and Taste.* New York: Rockefeller Univ. Press, 1969, pp. 192–211. (278)

Higgins, D. C., and Glaser, G. H. Stretch responses during chronic cerebellar ablation. A study of reflex instability. *J. Neurophysiol.*, 1964, 27, 49–62. (300)

Hilalai, S., and Whitfield, I. C. Responses of trapezoid body to acoustic stimulation with pure tones. *J. Physiol.*, 1953, 122, 158–71. (174)

Hill, H. E., Kornetsky, C. H., Flanary, H. G., and Wikler, A. Studies on anxiety associated with anticipation of pain. I. Effects of morphine. *Arch. Neurol.* (Chicago), 1952a, 67, 612. (250)

Hill, H. E., Kornetsky, C. H., Flanary, H. G., and Wikler, A. Effects of anxiety and morphine on discrimination of intensities of painful stimuli. *J. Clin. Invest.*, 1952b, 31, 473. (250)

Hillarp, N. A., Fuxe, K., and Dahlstron, A. Demonstration and mapping of central neurons containing dopamine, noradrenaline and 5-hydroxytryptamine and their reactions to psycho-

pharmacia. *Pharmacol. Rev.*, 1960, 18, 727. (18)

Hillarp, N. A., Olivecrona, H., and Selfverskiold, W. Evidence for the participation of the preoptic area in male mating behavior. *Experientia*, 1954, 10, 224–25. (560, 573)

Hilton, S. M., and Zbrozyna, A. W. Amygdaloid region for defense reactions and its afferent pathway in the brain stem. *J. Physiol.*, 1963, 165, 160–73. (377)

Hind, J. E. An electrophysiological determination of tonotopic organization in auditory cortex of cat. *J. Neurophysiol.*, 1953, 16, 475–89. (154)

Hind, J. E. Unit activity in the auditory cortex. In G. L. Rasmussen and W. F. Windle (Eds.), *Neural Mechanisms of the Auditory and Vestibular Systems.* Springfield, Ill.: Charles C Thomas, 1960, pp. 201–10. (111, 147, 154)

Hind, J. E., Goldberg, J. M., Greenwood, D. D., and Rose, J. E. Some discharge characteristic of single neurons in the inferior colliculus of the cat. II. Timing of the discharges and observations on binaural stimulation. *J. Neurophysiol.*, 1963, 26, 321–41. (141)

Hinsey, J. C., and Phillips, R. A. Observations upon diaphragmatic sensation. *J. Neurophysiol.*, 1940, 3, 175. (248)

Hirsch, H. V. D., and Spinelli, D. N. Visual experience modifies distribution of horizontally and vertically oriented receptive fields in cats. *Science*, 1970, 168, 869. (102)

Hirsh, I. J. The relation between localization and intelligibility. *J. acoust. Soc. Amer.*, 1950, 22, 196–200. (417)

Hodges, J. R., and Vernikos, J. Circulating corticotrophin in normal and adrenalectomized rats after stress. *Acta Endocr.*, 1959, 30, 188–96. (347)

Hodgkin, A. L. The local electric changes associated with repetitive action in a non-medulated axon. *J. Physiol.*, 1948, 107, 165–81. (22)

Hodgkin, A. L., and Huxley, A. F. A quantitative description of membrane current and its application to conduction and excitation in nerve. *J. Physiol.*, 1952, 417, 500–514. (11)

Hodos, W. H. Motivational properties of long durations of rewarding brain stimulation. *J. Comp. Physiol. Psychol.*, 1965, 59, 219–24. (517)

Hoebel, B. G., and Tetitelbaum, P. Hypothalamic control of feeding and self-stimulation. *Science,* 1962, **135,** 375–76. (528, 622)

Hoebel, B. G., and Teitelbaum, P. Weight regulation in normal and hypothalamic hyperphagic rats. *J. Comp. Physiol. Psychol.,* 1966, **61,** 189–93. (624)

Hoebel, B. G. Hypothalamic lesions by electrocauterization: disinhibition of feeding and self-stimulation. *Science,* 1965, **149,** 452–53. (528)

Hoebel, B. G. Inhibition and disinhibition of self-stimulation and feeding: Hypothalamic control and post-ingestional factors. *J. Comp. Physiol. Psychol.,* 1968, **66.**

Holmes, G. Disturbances of vision by cerebral lesions. *Brit. J. Opthal.,* 1918, **2,** 353–65. (120)

Holmes, G. Croonian lectures. The clinical symptoms of cerebellar disease and their interpretations. *Lancet,* 1922, **202,** 1177–82, 1231–37; **203,** 59–65, 111–15. (317)

Horn, G. Electrical activity of the cerebral cortex of the unanesthetized cat during attentive behavior. *Brain,* 1960, **83,** 57–76. (426, 427)

Horn, G., and Hill, R. M. Responsiveness to sensory stimulation of units in the superior colliculus and subjacent tectotegmental regions of the rabbit. *Experimental Neurology,* 1966, **14,** 199–224. (416, 426)

Horn, G., and Wright, M. J. Characteristics of transmission failure in the squid stellate ganglion: A study of a simple habituating system. *J. Exptl. Biol.,* 1970, **51,** 217–31. (455)

Horridge, G. Analysis of the rapid response of Nereis and Harmothoe (Annelida). *Proceedings of the Royal Society* (*Series B*), 1959, **150,** 245–62. (456)

Horridge, G. A. Comparative physiology, integrative action of the nervous system. *Ann. Rev. Physiol.,* 1963, **25,** 523–41. (21)

Horridge, G. A. The electrophysiological approach to learning in isolatable ganglia. In W. H. Thorpe and D. Davenport (Eds.), *Learning & associated phenomena in invertebrates. Animal Behavior Supplement,* 1, 1964, pp. 163–182. (456)

Horridge, G. A. The electrophysiological approach to learning in isolatable ganglia. *Animal Behavior Supplement,* 1965, **1,** 163–82. (460)

Horvarth, F. H. Effects of basolateral amygdalectomy on three types of avoidance behavior in cats. *J. Comp. Physiol. Psychol.,* 1963, **56,** 380–89. (390)

Houpt, T. R., and Hance, H. E. Stimulation of food intake in the rabbit and rat by inhibition of glucose metabolism with 2-deoxy-D-glucose. *J. Comp. Physiol. Psych.,* 1971, **76,** 395–400. (592)

Howard, I. P., and Templeton, W. B. *Human Spatial Orientation.* London: John Wiley & Sons, Inc., 1966. (333, 339)

Howard, R. L., and Meyer, D. R. Motivational control of retrograde amnesia in rats. *J. Comp. Physiol. Psychol.,* 1971, **74,** 37–40. (442)

Howarth, C. I., and Deutsch, J. A. Drive decay: the cause of fast "extinction" of habits learned for brain stimulation. *Science,* 1962, **137,** 35–36. (524)

Howarth, C. I., and Ellis, R. The relative intelligibility threshold for one's own name compared with other names. *Quart. J. exp. Psychol.,* 1961, **13,** 236–39. (419)

Hoyle, G. Neurophysiological studies on learning in headless insects. In J. E. Treherne and J. W. L. Beament (Eds.), *The Physiology of the Insect Central Nervous System.* New York: Academic Press, 1965, pp. 203–32. (461)

Hubbard, J. I., and Willis, W. D. Reduction of transmitter output by depolarization. *Nature,* 1962, **193,** 1294–95. (19)

Hubbard, R. The molecular weight of rhodopsin and the nature of the rhodopsin-digitonin complex. *J. Gen. Physiol.,* 1954, **37,** 381–99. (80)

Hubbert, H. B. The effect of age on habit formation in the albino rat. *Behavior Monograph,* 1915, **2**(no. 6). (495)

Hubel, D. H. Electro-corticograms in cats during natural sleep. *Arch. ital. Biol.,* 1960, **98,** 171–81. (412)

Hubel, D. H. Single unit activity in lateral geniculate body and optic tract of unrestrained cats. *J. Physiol.,* 1960, **150,** 91–104. (105)

Hubel, D. H., Henson, C. O., Rupert,

A., and Galambos, R. Attention units in the auditory cortex. *Science,* 1959, **129,** 1279–80. (421)

Hubel, D. H., and Wiesel, T. N. Integrative action in the cat's lateral geniculate body. *J. Physiol.,* 1961, **160,** 106–54. (105)

Hubel, D. H., and Wiesel, T. N. Receptive fields, binocular interaction and functional architecture in the cat's visual cortex. *J. Physiol.,* 1962, **160,** 106–54. (106, 107, 110, 115)

Hubel, D. H., and Wiesel, T. N. Shape and arrangement of columns in cat's striate cortex. *J. Physiol.,* 1963, **165,** 559–68. (111)

Hubel, D. H., and Wiesel, T. N. Receptive fields in striate cortex of very young, visually inexperienced kittens. *J. Neurophysiol.,* 1963, **26,** 994–1002. (102, 106)

Hubel, D. H., and Wiesel, T. N. Receptive fields and functional architecture in two nonstriate visual areas (18 and 19) of the cat. *J. Neurophysiol.,* 1965, **28,** 229–89. (108)

Hubel, D. H., and Wiesel, T. N. Receptive fields and functional architecture of monkey striate cortex. *J. Physiol.,* 1968, **195,** 215–43. (111)

Huber, F. Brain controlled behaviour in Orthopterans. In J. E. Treherne and J. W. L. Beament (Eds.), *The Physiology of the Insect Central Nervous System.* London & New York: Academic Press, 1965. (456)

Hudspeth, W. J. Strychnine: Its facilitating effect on the solution of a simple oddity problem by the rat. *Science,* 1964, **145,** 1331–33. (473)

Hugelin, A., Dumont, S., and Paillas, N. Tympanic muscles and control of auditory input during arousal. *Science,* 1960, **131,** 1371–72. (425)

Hughes, R. A., Barrett, R. J., and Ray, O. S. Training to test interval as a determinent of a temporarily graded ECS-produced response decrement in rats. *J. Comp. Physiol. Psychol.,* 1970, **71** (2, pt. 1), 318–24. (442, 443)

Hughes, R. A., Barrett, R. J., and Ray, O. S. Retrograde Amnesia in rats increases as a function of ECS-test interval and ECS intensity. *Physiol. & Behav.,* 1970, **5**(1), 27–30. (442, 443)

Hull, C. L. *Essentials of Behavior.* New Haven: Yale University Press, 1951. (545)

Hull, C. L., Livingston, J. R., Rouse, R. O., and Barker, A. N. Time, sham, and esophageal feeding as reinforcements. *J. comp. physiol. Psychol.,* 1951, **44,** 236–45. (610)

Humphrey, G. L., and Buchwald, J. S. Response decrements in the cochlear nucleus of decerebrate cats during acoustic stimulation. *Science,* 1972, **175,** 1488–91. (426)

Humphrey, N. K., (in press) *What the frog's eye tells the monkey's brain. Brain Behavior and Evolution.* (101)

Humphries, B. Maze learning in planaria. *Worm Runner's Digest,* 1961, 3(2), 114–16. (475)

Hunsperger, R. W. Ahektreaktionen auf elecktrische reizung in hirnstamm der katze. *Helv. physiol. Acta,* 1956, **14,** 70–92. (351, 370, 371)

Hunsperger, R. W. Les représentations centrales des réactions affectives dans le cerveau antérieur et dans le tronc cérébral. *Neurochirurgie,* 1959, **5,** 207–33. (353, 357, 363, 372, 374)

Hunt, C. C. Muscle stretch receptors; peripheral mechanisms and reflex function. *Cold Spring Harbor Symposia on Quantitative Biology,* 1952, **17,** 113–23. (297)

Hunt, C. C. On the nature of vibration receptors in the hind limb of the cat. *J. Physiol.,* 1961, **155,** 75–86. (180, 211, 228)

Hunt, C. C., and Kuno, M. Background discharge and evoked responses of spinal interneurons. *J. Physiol.,* 1959, **147,** 364–84. (238)

Hunt, C. C., and McIntyre, A. K. Properties of cutaneous touch receptors in cat. *J. Physiol.,* 1960a, **153,** 88–98. (175, 188, 189, 195, 228)

Hunt, C. C., and McIntyre, A. K. An analysis of fibre diameter and receptor characteristics of myelinated cutaneous afferent fibers in cat. *J. Physiol.,* 1960b, **153,** 99–112. (171, 180, 188, 189, 228)

Hunt, E. B., and Bauer, R. H. Facilitation of learning by delayed injections of pentylenetetrazol. *Psychopharmacologia,* 1969, **16,** 139–46. (473)

Hunt, H. F. Electro-convulsive shock and learning. *Transactions of the N.Y. Academy of Sciences,* 1965, **27,** 923–45. (441, 442)

Hunt, H. F., and Brady, J. V. Some effects of electro-convulsive shock on a conditioned emotional response ("anxiety"). *J. Comp. Physiol. Psychol.*, 1951, **44**, 88–98. (441)

Hunt, J. McV. The effects of infant feeding-frustration upon adult hoarding behavior. *Journal Abnormal Social Psychol.*, 1941, **36**, 336–60. (640)

Hunt, J. McV., Schlosberg, H., Solomon, R. L., and Stellar, E. Studies of the effects of infantile experience on adult behavior in rats. I. Effects of infantile feeding frustration on adult hoarding. *J. Comp. Physiol. Psychol.*, 1947, **40**, 291–304. (640)

Huppert, F. A., and Deutsch, J. A. *Quarterly Journal of Experimental Psychology*, 1969, **21**, 267–71. (495)

Hursh, J. B. Conduction velocity and diameter of nerve fibers. *Am. J. Physiol.*, 1939, **127**, 131–39. (13)

Hurvich, L. M., and Jameson, D. An opponent-process theory of color vision. *Psychol. Rev.*, 1957, **64**, 384–404. (93)

Hutt, P. J. Rate of bar pressing as a function of quality and quantity of food reward. *J. Comp. Physiol. Psychol.*, 1954, **47**, 235–39. (548)

Huxley, H. E. Ultra-structure of striated muscle. *Brit. Med. Bull.*, 1956, **12**, 171–73. (287)

Hyde, J., and Gellhorn, E. Influence of deafferentiation on stimulation of motor cortex. *Amer. J. Physiol.*, 1949, **156**, 311–16. (299)

Hyden, H., and Egyhazi, E. Nuclear RNA changes of nerve cells during a learning experiment in rats. *Proc. Nat. Acad. Science*, 1962, **48**, 1366–73. (474, 476)

Hyden, H., and Egyhazi, E. Glial RNA changes during a learning experiment in rats. *Proc. Nat. Acad. Sci.*, 1963, **49**, 618–24. (476)

Hyden, H., and Hartelius, H. Stimulation of nucleoprotein production in nerve cells by malonitrile and its effect on psychic function in mental disorders. *Acta Psychiat. Neurol. Scand.*, 1948, **48**, 1–117. (474)

Hyden, H., and Pigon, A. A cytophysiological study of the functional relationship between oligodendroglial cells and nerve cells of Deiters' nucleus. *J. Neurochem.*, 1960, **6**, 57–72. (476)

I

Iggo, A. A single unit analysis of cutaneous receptors with C afferent

fibres. In G. E. W. Wolstenholme and M. O'Connor (Eds.), *CIBA Foundation Study Group*. No. 1. *Pain and Itch. Nervous Mechanisms*. Boston: Little, Brown and Co., 1959a, pp. 41–59. (181, 193)

Iggo, A. Cutaneous heat and cold receptors with slowly conducting (C) afferent fibres. *Quart. J. Exp. Physiol.*, 1959b, **44**, 362–70. (193, 194, 201)

Iggo, A. Cutaneous mechanoreceptors with afferent C fibres. *J. Physiol.*, 1960, **192**, 337–53. (181, 193, 225)

Iggo, A. An electrophysiological analysis of afferent fibers in primate skin. *Acta Neuroveg. (Wien)*, 1963, **24**, 225. (175, 181)

Iggo, A. A single unit analysis of cutaneous receptors with C afferent fibers. In G. E. W. Wolstenholme and F. O'Connor (Eds.), Ciba Foundation Study Group (Study Group No. 1), *Pain and Itch: Nervous Mechanisms*. Boston: Little, Brown and Company, 1959a, 41–59. (181, 193)

Iggo, A. Electrophysiological and histological studies of cutaneous mechanoreceptors. In Daniel R. Kenshalo (Ed.), *The Skin Senses*. Springfield, Ill.: Charles C Thomas, 1968, 84–111. (175, 180, 188, 189, 196)

Iggo, A., and Muir, A. R. A cutaneous sense organ in the hairy skin of cats. *J. Anatomy*, 1963, **97**, 151. (189)

Igic, R., Stern, P., and Basagic, E. Changes in emotional behavior after application. *Neuropharm.*, 1970, **9**, 73. (352)

Ingram, W. R. Brain stem mechanisms and behavior. *EEG clin. Neurophysiol.*, 1952, **4**, 395–406. (351)

Ingram, W. R., Barris, R. W., and Ranson, S. W. Catalepsy: an experimental study. *Arch. Neurol. Psychiat.* (Chicago), 1936, **35**, 1175–97. (387)

Ingvar, D. H. Extraneuronal influences upon the electrical activity of isolated cortex following stimulation of the reticular activating system. *Acta. physiol. Scand.*, 1955, **33**, 169–93. (412)

Ingvar, D. H., and Hunter, J. Influence of visual cortex on light impulses in the brain stem of the unanesthetized cat. *Acta. Physiol. Scand.*, 1955, **33**, 194–218. (122)

Iriuchijima, J., and Zotterman, Y. The specificity of afferent cutaneous C fibers in mammals. *Acta Physiol.*

Scand., 1960, **49**, 267. (181, 192, 193, 194)

Irvine, S. R., and Ludvigh, E. Is ocular proprioceptive sense concerned in vision? *A.M.A. Arch. Ophthal.*, 1936, **15**, 1037–49. (304)

Isaacson, R. L., Douglas, R. J., and Moore, R. Y. The effect of radical hippocampal ablation on acquisition of avoidance response. *J. Comp. Physiol. Psych.*, 1961, **54**, 625–28. (391)

Isaacson, R. L., and Wickelgren, W. O. Hippocampal ablation and panure avoidance. *Science*, 1962, **138**, 1104–6. (434)

Ishiko, N., and Loewenstein, W. R. Temperature and charge transfer in a receptor membrane. *Science*, 1960, **132**, 184. (197)

Iversen, D. D. Interference and inferotemporal memory deficits. *Brain Res.*, 1970, **19**, 277–89. (434)

Iversen, S. Brain lesions and memory in animals. In J. A. Deutsch (Ed.), *The Physiological Basis of Memory.* New York: Academic Press, 1973, 305–55. (434)

Iversen, S. D., and Weiskrantz, L. An investigation of a possible memory defect produced by inferotemporal lesions in the Baboon. *Neuropsychologia*, 1970, **8**, 21–36. (434)

Iwama, K., and Yamamoto, C. Transmission of thalamic somatosensory relay nuclei as modified by electrical stimulation of the cerebral cortex. *Japan. J. Physiol.*, 1961, **11**, 169–82. (247)

J

Jackson, W. J. A comment on the hippocampus and behavior. *Psychological Bulletin*, 1968, **69**, 20–22. (391)

Jacobs, H. L., and Sharma, K. N. Taste versus calories: sensory and metabolic signals in the control of food intake. *Ann. NY Acad. Sci.*, 1969, **157**(2), 1084–1125. (617)

Jacobson, A. L., Fried, C., and Horowitz, S. D. Planarians and memory. *Nature*, 1966, **209**, 599–601. (475)

Jansen, J., and Brodal, A. (Eds.). *Aspects of Cerebellar Anatomy.* Oslo: Tanum, 1954. (315)

Jarvik, M. E., and Kopp, R. An improved one trial passive avoidance learning situation. *Psychol. Rep.*, 1967, **2**, 221–24. (437)

Jasper, H. H., Khan, R. T., and Elliott, K. A. C. Amino acids released from the cerebral cortex in relation to its state of activation. *Science*, 1965, **147**, 1448–49. (413)

Jasper, H. H., and Rasmussen, T. Studies of clinical and electrical responses to deep temporal stimulation in man with some considerations of functional anatomy. *A Res. Nerv. Ment. Dis.*, 1958, **36**, 316–34. (323, 364)

Jasper, H., Ricci, G., and Doane, B. Microelectrode analysis of cortical cell discharge during avoidance conditioning in the monkey. In H. H. Jasper and G. D. Smirnov (Eds.). The Moscow Collogium on EEG and Higher Nervous Activity. *EEG clin. Neurophysiol.*, Suppl. 13, 1960, 137–57. (396, 464)

Jefferson, M. Altered consciousness associated with brain stem lesions. *Brain*, 1952, **75**, 55–67. (398)

Jensen, D. D. Paramecia, planaria and pseudo-learning. *Animal Behaviour Supplement*, 1965, **1**, 9–20. (475)

Jerome, E. A. Olfactory thresholds measured in terms of stimulus pressure and volume, *Arch. Psychol.*, (New York), 1942, **274**, 44. (283)

John, E. R., and Killam, K. F. Studies of electrical activity of brain during differential conditioning in cats. In J. Wortis (Ed.), *Recent Advances in Biological Psychiatry.* Chapter 10. New York: Grune and Stratton, 1960, p. 417. (466)

John, E. R., Leiman, A. C., and Sachs, E. An exploration of the functional relationship between electroencephalographic potentials and differential inhibition. *Ann. New York Acad. Sci.*, 1961, **92**, (Pavlovian Conference on Higher Nervous Activity, N. S. Kline [Ed.]), 1160–82. (466, 468)

Johnson, R. N. Effects of intracranial reinforcement intensity and distributional variables on brightness reversal learning in rats. *J. Comp. Physiol. Psychol.*, 1968, **66**, 422–26. (521)

Johnson, W. H., and Taylor, M. B. G. Some experiments on the relative affectiveness of various types of accelerations on motion sickness. *Aerosp. Med.*, 1961, **32**, 205–8. (327)

Jones, F. N. A test of the validity of the Elsberg method of olfactometry.

Am. J. Psychol., 1953, **66**, 81–85. (284)

Jones, F. N. An olfactometer permitting stimulus specification in molar terms. *Am. J. Psychol.*, 1954, **67**, 147–51. (284)

Jones, F. N. Olfactory absolute thresholds and their implications for the nature of the receptor process. *J. Psychol.*, 1955, **40**, 223–27. (273)

Jones, F. N. An analysis of individual differences in olfactory thresholds. *Am. J. Psychol.*, 1957, **70**, 227–32. (277)

Jones, F. N., and Jones, M. H. Modern theories of olfaction: a critical review. *J. of Psychol.*, 1953, **36**, 207–41. (277)

Jones, M. Second pain: fact or artefact? *Science*, 1956, **124**, 442. (204)

Jones, M. T., and Stockham, M. A. The effect of previous stimulation of the adrenal cortex by adrenocorticotrophin on the function of the pituitary-adrenocortical axis in response to stress. *J. Physiol.*, 1966, **184**, 741–750. (347)

Jouvet, M. Étude neurophysiologique chez l'homme de quelques mécanismes souscorticaux de l'attention. *Psychol. Franc.*, 1957, **2**, 250–56. (422, 427)

Jouvet, M. Telencephalic and rhombencephalic sleep in the cat. In G. E. W. Wolstenholme and M. O'Connor (Eds.), *The Nature of Sleep*. London: Churchill, 1961, 188–208. (412)

Jouvet, M. Récherches sur les mécanismes neurophysiologiques du sommeil et de l'apprentissage negatif. In J. F. Delafresnaye (Ed.), *Brain Mechanisms and Learning*. Oxford: Blackwell, 1961, 445–81. (415)

Jouvet, M. Récherches sur les structures nerveuses et les mécanismes responsibles des differentes phases du sommeil physiologique. *Arch. Ital. Biol.*, 1962, **100**, 125–206. (412)

Jouvet, M. Mechanism of the states of sleep. A neuropharamcological approach. *Research Publications of the Association for Research in Nervous and Mental Disease*, 1967, **45**, 86–126. (412, 413)

Judd, D. B. Color perception of deuteranopic and protanopic observers. *J. Res. Nat. Bur. Stand.*, 1948, **41**, 247–71. (94)

Jukes, C. L. Selection of diet in chicks as influenced by vitamins and other factors. *J. comp. Psychol.*, 1938, **26**, 135–56. (634)

Jung, R., and Hassler, R. The extra-pyramidal motor system. In J. Field, H. W. Magoun, and V. E. Hall (Eds.), *Handbook of Neurophysiology*. Vol. II. Section 1. *Neurophysiology*. (American Physiological Society) Baltimore: Williams and Wilkins, 1960. (314, 477)

Justesen, D. R., Sharp, J. C., and Porter, P. B. Self-stimulation of the caudate nucleus by instrumentally naive cats. *J. Comp. Physiol. Psychol.*, 1963, **56**, 371–74. (517)

K

Kaada, B. R. Somato-motor, autonomic and electrocardiographic responses to electrical stimulation of rhinencephalic and other structures in primate, cat and dog. *Acta. Physiol. Scand.*, 1951, **226**, 24, Suppl. 83. (382)

Kaada, B. R., Anderson, P., and Jansen, J., Jr. Stimulation of the amygdaloid nuclear complex in unanesthetised cats. *Neurology*, 1954, **4**, 48–64. (358)

Kaada, B. R., Jansen, J., Jr., and Anderson, P. Stimulation of the hippocampus and medial cortical areas in unanesthetised cats. *Neurology*, 1953, **3**, 844–57. (362, 363)

Kaada, B. R., Rasmussen, E. W., and Kveim, O. Effects of hippocampal lesions on maze learning and retention in rats. *Exp. Neurol.*, 1961, **3**, 333–35. (385, 386, 391)

Kaada, B. R., Rasmussen, E. W., and Kveim, O. Impaired acquisition of passive avoidance behavior by sub-callosal septal hypothalamic and insular lesions in rats. *J. Comp. Physiol. Psychol.*, 1962, **55**, 661–70. (391)

Kagan, J. Differential reward value of incomplete and complete sexual behavior. *J. Comp. Physiol. Psychol.*, 1955, **48**, 59–64. (547)

Kagan, J., and Beach, F. A. Effects of early experience on mating behavior in male rats. *J. Comp. Physiol. Psychol.*, 1953, **46**, 204–8. (571)

Kaissling, K. E. Kinetics of olfactory receptor potentials. In C. Pfaffman (Ed.), *Olfaction and Taste*. New York: Rockefeller Univ. Press, 1969, 53–70. (273)

Kalant, H., Israel, Y., and Mahon, M. A. The effect of ethanol on acetylcholine synthesis, release and degradation in the brain. *Canadian J. Physiol. Pharm.*, 1967, **45**, 172–76. (30)

Kamin, L. F. The retention of an incompletely learned avoidance response. *J. Comp. Physiol. Psychol.*, 1957, **50**, 457–60. (346)

Kamin, L. J., Briner, C. J., and Black, A. H. Conditioned suppression as a monitor of fear of the CS in the course of avoidance training. *J. Comp. Physiol. Psychol.*, 1963, **56**, 497–501. (345)

Karczmar, A. G., Longo, V. G., and Scotti de Carolis, A. A pharmacological model of paradoxical sleep: the role of cholinergic and monoamine systems. *Physiology and Behavior*, 1970, **5**, 175–82. (413)

Karplus, J. P., and Kreidl, A. Gehirn und sympathicus. VIII, (1) zur zentralen Reguliering der loisbeiregungen; (2) Bemerkungen zur Schinerzemp Findlichklit der vegetativen Hypothalamus Zentren, Pflug. Arch. ges. *Physiol.*, 1928, **219**, 613–18. (357)

Katsuki, Y. Neural mechanism of auditory sensation in cats. chap. 29. In W. A. Rosenblith (Ed.), *Sensory Communication*. New York: M.I.T. Press and John Wiley & Sons, 1961, 561–84. (144)

Katsuki, Y., Murata, K., Suga, N., and Takenaka, T. *Proc. Imp. Acad.* (Japan), 1960, 36, 435–38. (141, 147)

Katsuki, Y., Suga, N., and Kanno, Y. Neural mechanism of the peripheral and central auditory system in monkeys. *J. Acoust. Soc. Amer.*, 1962, **34**, 1396–1410. (143, 147)

Katsuki, Y., Sumi, T., Uchiyama, H., and Watanabe, T. Electric responses of auditory neurons in cat to sound stimulation. *J. Neurophysiol.*, 1958, **21**, 569–88. (142, 144, 147, 160)

Katsuki, Y., Watanabe, T., and Maruyama, N. Activity of auditory neurons in upper levels of brain of cat. *J. Neurophysiol.*, 1959, **22**, 343–59. (160)

Keele, C. A. *Lectures on the Scientific Basis of Medicine.* London: Athlone Press, 1958, **6**, 143. (200, 209)

Keele, C. A., and Armstrong, D. *Substances Producing Pain and Itch.* London: Arnold, 1964. [Quoted in R. K. S. Lim. Pain. *Annual Review of Physiology*, 1970, **32**, 274, 280.] (200)

Keesey, R. E., and Goldstein, M. D. Use of progressive fixed-ratio procedures in the assessment of intracranial reinforcement. *J. Exp. Anal. Behav.*, 1968, **11**, 293–301. (520)

Keidel, W. D. Mechanical frequency discrimination in the cochlea. *International Audiology*, 1962, **1**, 37–52. (133)

Keller, A. D. Autonomic discharges elicited by physiological stimuli in midbrain preparations. *Am. J. Physiol.*, 1932, **100**, 576–86. (367, 371)

Kellogg, W. N., Scott, V. B., Davis, R. C., and Wolf, I. S. Is movement necessary for learning? *J. Comp. Psychol.*, 1940, **37**, 99–117. (510)

Kelly, A. H., Beaton, L. E., and Magoun, H. W. A midbrain mechanism for facio-vocal activity. *J. Neurophysiol.*, 1946, **9**, 181–89. (370, 371)

Kelsey, J. E., and Grossman, S. P. Nonperseverative disruption of behavioral inhibition following septal lesions in rats. *J. Comp. Physiol. Psychol.*, 1971, **75**, 302–11. (381)

Kendler, H. H. The influence of simultaneous hunger and thirst drives upon the learning of two opposed spatial responses of the white rat. *J. Exp. Psychol.*, 1946, **36**, 212–20. (513)

Kennard, M. A. Effect of bilateral ablation of cingulate area on behavior of cats. *J. Neurophysiol.*, 1955a, **18**, 159–69. (380)

Kennard, M. A. The cingulate gyrus in relation to consciousness. *J. Nerv. Ment. Dis.*, 1955b, **121**, 34–39. (380)

Kennedy, G. C. The role of depot fat in the hypothalamic control of food intake in the rat. *Proc. Roy. Soc.*, Ser. B, 1953, **140**, 578–92. (591, 592)

Kenshalo, D. R. The temperature sensitivity of furred skin of cats. *J. Physiol.* (London), 1964, **172**, 439. (199)

Kenshalo, D. R. Behavioral and electrophysiological responses of cats to thermal stimuli. In *The Skin Senses.* Springfield, Ill.: Charles C Thomas, 1968, 400–422. (198, 199)

Kenshalo, D. R., and Gallegos, E. S. Multiple temperature-sensitive spots innervated by single nerve fibers. *Science* 1967, **158**, 1064–65. (206)

Kent, E. and Grossman, S. P. Evidence for a conflict interpretation of anomalous effects of rewarding brain stimulation. *J. Comp. Physiol. Psychol.*, 1969, **69**, 381–90. (522)

Kent, G. C., and Liberman, M. J. Induction of psychic estrus in the hamster with progesterone administered via the lateral brain ventricle. *Endocrin.*, 1959, **45**, 29–32. (561)

Kenyon, J., and Krieckhaus, E. E. Enhanced avoidance behavior following septal lesions in the rat as a function of lesion size and spontaneous activity. *J. Comp. Physiol. Psychol.*, 1965a, **59**, 466–68. (386)

Kenyon, J., and Krieckhaus, E. E. Decrements in one-way avoidance learning following septal lesions in rats. *Psychonomic Science*, 1965b, **3**, 113–14. (386)

Kerkut, G. A., Oliver, G. W. O., Rick, J. T., and Walker, R. T. The effect of drugs on learning in a simple preparation. *Comp. Gen. Pharmacol.*, 1970, **1**, 437–83. (461)

Kerr, D. I. B. Properties of the olfactory efferent system. *Aust. J. Exp. Bio. Med. Sci.*, 1960, **38**, 29–36. (281)

Kerr, D. I. B., and Hagbarth, K. E. An investigation of olfactory centrifugal fiber system. *J. Neurophysiol.*, 1955, **18**, 362–74. (281, 282)

Kety, S. S. Relationship between energy metabolism of the brain and functional activity. *Research Publications of the Association for Research in Nervous and Mental Disease*, 1967, **45**, 39–45. (413)

Keynes, R. D. The ionic movements during nervous activity. *J. Physiol.*, 1951, **114**, 119–50. (12)

Khavari, K. A., and Russell, R. W. Acquisition, retention and extinction under conditions of water deprivation and of central cholinergic stimulation. *J. Comp. Physiol. Psychol.*, 1966, **61**, 339–45. (597)

Kiang, N. Y-S. An electrophysiological study of cat auditory cortex. Thesis (No. 3028), University of Chicago, 1955. (154)

Kiang, N. Y-S. A survey of recent developments in the study of auditory physiology. *Ann. Otol. Rhinol. and Laryngol.*, 1968, **77**, 656–76. (143)

Kiang, N. Y-S., Watanabe, T., Thomas, E. C., and Clark, L. F. Discharge patterns of single fibers in the cat's auditory nerve. *M.I.T. Research Monograph*, No. 35. Cambridge, Mass.: Technology Press, 1965. (149)

Kiesow, F. Untersuchungen über Temperaturempfindungen. *Philos. St.*, 1895, **11**, 135–45. (174, 194)

Killam, E. K., Killam, K. F., and Shaw, T. The effects of psychotherapeutic compounds on central afferent and limbic pathways. *Ann. N.Y. Acad. Sci.*, 1957, **66**, 784–805. (396)

Kimble, D. P. The hippocampus and internal inhibition. *Psych. Bull.*, 1968, **70**, 285–95. (391, 434)

Kimble, D. P., and Pribram, K. H. Hippocampectomy and behaviour sequences. *Science*, 1963, **139**, 824–25. (391)

Kimmeldorf, D. J., and Hunt, E. L. *Ionizing Radiation: Neural Function and Behavior.* New York: Academic Press, 1965. (633)

Kimura, C. Vascular sensitivity. *Acta Neuroveg.* (Wein), 1955, **14**, 170. (200)

Kimura, D. Effects of selective hippocampal damage on avoidance behavior in the rat. *Canad. J. Psychol.*, 1958, **12**, 213–18. (391)

Kimura, D. Right temporal lobe damage. *Arch. Neurol.*, 1963, **8**, 264–71. (433)

Kimura, K., and Beidler, L. M. Microelectrode study of taste receptors of rat and hamster. *J. Cell. Comp. Physiol.*, 1961, **58**(2), 131–39. (256, 258)

Kinder, E. F. A study of the nest building activity of the albino rat. *J. Exp. Zool.*, 1927, **47**, 117–61. (577)

King, F. A. Effects of septal and amygdaloid lesions on emotional behavior and conditioned avoidance responses in the rat. *J. Nerv. Ment. Dis.*, 1958, **126**, 57–63. (374, 377, 386)

King, F. A., and Meyer, P. M. Effects of amygdaloid lesions upon septal hyperemotionality in the rat. *Science*, 1958, **128**, 655–56. (376)

Klein, M. Uterine distension, ovarian hormones and maternal behavior in rodents. *Ciba Foundation Coloq. Endocrinol.*, 1952, **3**, 84–88. (577)

Klein, M. Aspects biologiques de l'instinct, reproducteur dans le comportement des mammifères. In P. P. Grasse (Ed.), *L'Instinct dans le Comportement des Animaux et de L'Homme.* Paris: Masson and Cie, 1956, 287–344. (577)

Klein, S. B., and Spear, N. E. Influence of age on short-term retention of active-avoidance learning in rats. *J.*

Comp. Physiol. Psychol., 1969, **69**, 583–589. (347)

Klein, S. B., and Spear, N. E. Influence of age on short-term retention of active-avoidance learning in rats. *J. Comp. Physiol. Psychol.*, 1970a, **71**, 165–70. (347, 348)

Klein, S. B., and Spear, N. E. Reactivation of avoidance-learning memory in the rat after intermediate retention intervals. *J. Comp. Physiol. Psychol.*, 1970b, **73**, 498–504. (347)

Kleist, K. *Handbuch der Ärztlichen Erfahrungen in Weltkriege.* Vol. 4. Leipzig: Barth, 1934. (238, 245)

Kling, A., and Hutt, P. J. Effect of hypothalamic lesions on the amygdala syndrome in the cat. *A.M.A. Arch. Neurol. Psychiat.*, 1958, **79**, 511–17. (376, 390)

Kling, A., Orbach, J., Schwartz, N. B., and Towne, J. C. Injury to the limbic system and associated structures in cats (chronic behavioral and physiological effects). *Arch. gen. Psychiat.*, 1960, **3**, 391–420. (378)

Klinke, R., Boerger, G., and Gruber, J. Alteration of afferent, tone-evoked activity of neurons of the cochlear nucleus following acoustic stimulation of the contralateral ear. *J. Acoust. Soc. Am.*, 1969, **45**, 788–89. (146, 167)

Klinke, R., Boerger, G., and Gruber, J. Studies of the functional significance of efferent innervation in the auditory system: Afferent neuronal activity as influenced by contralaterally applied sound. *Pfluegers Arch.* 1969, **306**, 165–75. (146, 167)

Kluver, H. Functional significance of the geniculo-striate system. *Biol. Symp.*, 1942, **7**, 253–99. (118)

Kluver, H., and Bucy, P. C. "Psychic blindness" and other symptoms following bilateral temporal lobectomy in rhesus monkeys. *Am. J. Physiol.*, 1937, **119**, 352–53. (372)

Kluver, H., and Bucy, P. C. An analysis of certain effects of bilateral temporal lobectomy in the rhesus monkey with special reference to "psychic blindness." *J. Psychol.*, 1938, **5**, 33–54. (628)

Kluver, H., and Bucy, P. C. Preliminary analysis of functions of the temporal lobes of monkeys. *Arch. Neurol. Psychiat.*, 1939, **42**, 979–1000. (573)

Knapp, H. D., Taub, E., and Berman, A. J. Conditioned responses following

deafferentation in the monkey. *Trans. Amer. Neurol. Ass.*, 1959, 185–87. (299)

Kogan, A. B. The manifestation of processes of higher nervous activity in the electrical potentials of the cortex during free behaviour of animals. In H. H. Jasper and G. D. Smirnov (Eds.), The Moscow Colloquium on EEG and Higher Nervous Activity. *EEG clin. Neurophysiol.* Suppl. 13, 1960, 51–64. (396, 465)

Kohlenberg, R., and Trabasso, T. Recovery of a conditioned emotional response after one or two electroconvulsive shocks. *J. Comp. Physiol. Psychol.*, 1968, **65**(2), 270–73. (440, 458)

Kohn, M. Satiation of hunger from food injected directly into the stomach versus food ingested by mouth. *J. Comp. Physiol. Psychol.*, 1951, **44**, 412–22. (609, 618)

Koikegami, H., Fuse, S., Yokoyama, T., Watanabe, T., and Watanabe, M. Contributions to the comparative anatomy of the amygdaloid nuclei of mammals with some experiments of their destruction or stimulation. *Folia Psychiat. et Neurol.* (Japan), 1955, **8**, 336. (630)

Kolbe, H. Die zeitliche Veränderung der Unterschneidsschwelle wahrend der Einwirking eines stetigen Dauerdruckoder Dauerlichtreizes. *Z. Sinnesphysiol.*, 1936, **67**, 53–68. (205)

Koller, G. Der Nestbau der weissen Maus und seine hormonale Auslosung. *Verh. Dtsch. Zool. Ges. Freiburg*, 1952, 106–68. (577)

Koller, G. Hormonale und psychische steuerung beim Nestbau weiser Mause. *Zool. Anz.* (Suppl.), 1956, **19**, (Verh. Detsch. Zool. Ges., 1955), 123–32. (577)

Kolmer, W. Geschmacksorgan. In W. V. Mollendorf (Ed.), *Handbuch der Mikroskopischen Anatomie des Menschen III.* Berlin: Springer, 1927. (260)

Kolmodin, G. M., and Skoglund, C. R. Analysis of spinal interneurons activated by tactile and nociceptive stimulation. *Acta. Physiol. Scand.*, 1960, **50**, 337–55. (229)

Konorski, J. On the influence of the frontal lobes of the cerebral hemispheres higher nervous activity. In *Problems of the Modern Physiology of the Nervous and Muscle System.* Georgian S.S.R.: Tbilisi Academy of Sciences, 1956. (415)

Koopmans, Henry S., Deutsch, J. A., and Branson, Patricia J. The effect of cholecystokinin-pancreozymin on hunger and thirst in mice. *Behavioral Biology,* 1972, 7, 441–44. (619)

Kopp, R., Bohdanecky, Z., and Jarvik, M. E. Proactive effect of a single ECS on step-through performance on naive and punished mice. *J. Comp. Physiol. Psychol.,* 1967, 64, 22–25. (436, 439)

Kornmüller, A. E., Lux, H. B., and Wintrel, R. EEG-Untersuchungen an tieren mit gekrenzten Kreislant. *Naturwissenschaften.,* 1961, 48, 381–82. (413)

Kornblith, C., and Olds, J. T-maze learning with one trial per day using brain stimulation reinforcement. *J. Comp. Physiol. Psychol.,* 1968, 66, 488–92. (522)

Kosman, M. E., and Gerard, R. W. The effect of adrenaline on a conditioned avoidance response. *J. Comp. Physiol. Psychol.,* 1955, 48, 506–8. (344)

Kourilsky, R. Diabetes insipidus. *Proc. Roy. Soc. Med.,* 1950, 43, 842–44. (597)

Kraft, M. S., Obrist, W. D., and Pribram, K. H. The effect of irritative lesions on the striate cortex on learning of visual discriminations in monkeys. *J. Comp. Physiol. Psychol.,* 1960, 53, 509–19. (462)

Krakauer, D., and Dallenbach, K. M. Gustatory adaptation to sweet, sour, and bitter. *Amer. J. Psychol.,* 1937, 49, 469–75. (264)

Kramer, F., and Moskiewicz, G. Beiträge zue Lehre von den Lage-und Bewegungsempfindungen. *Z. Psychol.,* 1901, 25, 114–15. (303)

Krasne, F. B. General disruption resulting from electrical stimulus of ventromedial hypothalamus. *Science,* 1962, 138, 822–23. (624)

Krieckhaus, E. E., Simmons, H. J., Thomas, G. J., and Kenyon, J. Septal lesions enhance shock avoidance behavior in the rat. *Exper. Neurology,* 1964, 9, 107–13. (386)

Krivanek, J., and McGaugh, J. L. Effects of pentylenetetrazol on memory storage in mice. *Psychopharmacologia,* 1968, 12, 303–21. (473)

Krivanek, J., and McGaugh, J. L. Facili-

tating effects of pre- and posttrial amphetamine administration on discrimination learning in mice. *Agents and Actions,* 1969, 1, 36–42. (473)

Kroll, F. W. Schwellenuntersuchungen Bei Läionen der Afferenten Leitungsbahnen. *Ztschr. ges. Neurol. Psychiat.,* 1930, 128, 751–76. (238)

Kruger, L. Characteristics of the somatic afferent projection to the precentral cortex in the monkey. *Am. J. Physiol.,* 1956, 186, 475–82. (219)

Kruger, L. Nervous mechanisms. In G. E. W. Wolstenholme and F. O'Connor (Eds.), Ciba Foundation Study Group (Study Group No. 1), *Pain and Itch: Nervous Mechanisms.* Boston: Little, Brown and Company, 1959, 67. (235)

Kruger, L., and Michel, F. Reinterpretation of the representation of pain based on physiological excitation of single neurons in the trigeminal sensory complex. *Exp. Neurol.,* 1962a, 5, 157–78. (220)

Kruger, L., and Michel, F. A single neuron analysis of buccal cavity representation in the sensory trigeminal complex of the cat. *Arch. oral Biol.,* 1962b, 7, 491–503. (231)

Kruger, L., and Porter, P. A behavioral study of the functions of the rolandic cortex in the monkey. *J. Comp. Neurol.,* 1958, 109, 439–69. (241, 391)

Kruger, L., Simminoff, R., and Witkovsky, P. Single neuron analysis of dorsal column nuclei and spinal nucleus of trigeminal in cat. *J. Neurophysiol.,* 1961, 24, 333–49. (219, 220, 221, 231)

Kryter, K. D., and Ades, H. W. Studies on the function of the higher acoustic nervous centers in the cat. *Am. J. Psychol.,* 1943, 56, 501–36. (166)

Kuffler, S. W. Discharge patterns and functional organization of mammalian retina. *J. Neurophysiol.,* 1953, 16, 37–68. (94, 95)

Kuhn, R. Topographical pattern of cutaneous sensibility in the dorsal column nuclei of the cat. *Trans. Amer. Neurol. Ass.,* 1949, 227–30. (219)

Kumar, R., Stolerman, I. P., and Steinberg, H. Psychopharmacology. *Annual Review Psychology,* 1970, 21, 595–628. (445)

Kunkle, E. C., and Chapman, W. A. Insensitivity to pain in man. *Proc. Ass.*

Res. Nerv. Ment. Dis., 1943, **23**, 100–109. (249)

Kuypers, H. G. J. M. *Structure and Function of the Cerebral Cortex.* Amsterdam: Elsevier Publ. Co., 1960a, 138–43. (242)

Kuypers, H. G. J. M. Central cortical projection to motor and somatosensory cell groups. *Brain*, 1960b, **83**, 161–84. (242)

Kuypers, H. G. J. M., Fleming, W. R., and Farinhott, J. W. Descending projections to spinal motor and sensory cells groups in the monkey: cortex vs. subcortex. *Science*, 1960, **132**, 38–40. (242)

Kuypers, H. G. J. M., Szwarcbart, M. K., Mishkin, M., and Rosvold, H. E. Occipitotemporal corticocortical connections in the rhesus monkey. *Exptl. Neurol.*, 1965, **4**, 245–82. (121)

L

Laffort, P. Mise en évidence de relations lineaires entre l'activité odorante de molecules et certaines de leurs characteristiques psychochimiques. *C. R. Acad. Sci.*, 1963, **256**, 5618–21. (275)

Laffort, P. A linear relationship between olfactory effectiveness and identified molecular characteristics extended to fifty pure substances. In C. Pfaffmann (Ed.), Olfaction and Taste. New York: Rockefeller Univ. Press, 1969, 150–57. (275)

Landau, W. M., and Bishop, G. H. Pain from dermal, periosteal, and fascial endings and from inflammation; electrophysiological study employing differential nerve blocks. *A.M.A. Arch. Neurol. Psychiat.*, 1953, **69**, 490–504. (203)

Landau, W. M., Goldstein, R., and Kleffner, F. R. Congenital aphasia: a clinico-pathalogic study. *Neurology*, 1960, **10**, 915–21. (166)

Landgren, S. Cortical reception of cold impulses from the tongue of the cat. *Acta. Physiol. Scand.*, 1957, **40**, 202–9. (235)

Landgren, S. Convergence of tactile, thermal and gustatory impulses on single cortical cells. *Acta. Physiol. Scand.*, 1957, **40**, 210–21. (235, 263)

Landgren, S. The response of thalamic and cortical neurons to electrical and physiological stimulation of the cat's tongue. In W. A. Rosenblith (Ed.),

Sensory Communication. New York: M.I.T. Press and John Wiley & Sons, 1961, 437–54. (232, 235)

Langworthy, O. R., and Richter, C. P. Increases in spontaneous activity produced by frontal lobe lesions in cats. *Amer. J. Physiol.*, 1939, **126**, 158–61. (631)

Lanier, L. H., Carney, H. M., and Wilson, W. D. Cutaneous innervation; experimental study. *Arch. Neurol. Psychiat.*, 1953, **34**, 1–60. (203)

Lansing, Robert W. Electroencephalographic correlates of binocular rivalry in man. *Science*, 1964, **146**, 1325–27. (203)

Larsell, O. *The Cerebellum from Myxinoids to Man.* Minneapolis: University of Minnesota Press, 1960. (315)

Larsson, K. *Conditioning and Sexual Behavior in the Male Albino Rat.* Stockholm: Almquist and Wiksell, 1956. (564, 566)

Lashley, K. S. The accuracy of movement in the absence of excitation from the moving organ. *Amer. J. Physiol.*, 1917, **43**, 169–94. (304)

Lashley, K. S. Studies of cerebral function in learning. V. The retention of motor habits after destruction of the so-called motor area in primates. *A.M.A. Arch. Neurol. Psychiat.*, 1924, **12**, 249–76. (509)

Lashley, K. S. Basic neural mechanisms in behavior. *Psychological Review*, 1930, **37**, 1–24. (509)

Lashley, K. S. The experimental analysis of instinctive behavior. *Psychol. Rev.*, 1938, **45**, 445–71. (556)

Lashley, K. S. The mechanism of vision. XVII. The functioning of small remnants of the visual cortex. *J. Comp. Neurol.*, 1939, **70**, 45–67. (120)

Lashley, K. S., and McCarthy, D. A. The survival of the maze habit after cerebellar injuries. *J. Comp. Psychol.*, 1926, **6**, 423–33. (509)

Lashley, K. S., and Sperry, R. W. Olfactory discrimination after destruction of the anterior thalamic nuclei. *Amer. J. Physiol.*, 1943, **139**, 446–50. (283)

Latané, B., and Schachter, S. Adrenaline and avoidance learning. *J. Comp. Physiol. Psychol.*, 1962, **65**, 369–72. (344)

Laties, A. M., and Liebman, P. A. Cones of Living Amphibian Eye: Selective

Staining, *Science,* 1970, **168**, 1475–77. (81)

Law, T., and Meagher, W. Hypothalamic lesions and sexual behavior in the female rat. *Science,* 1958, **128**, 1626–27. (560)

Leavitt, F. I. Drug-induced modifications in sexual behavior and open field locomotion of male rats. *Physiol. Behav.,* 1969, **4**, 677–83. (567)

Le Beau, J. Anterior cinguiectomy in man. *J. Neurosurg.,* 1954, **2**, 268–76. (380)

Lebermann, F. Beobachtungen bei Chemischer Reizung der Haut. *Zeitschrift für Biologie,* 1922, **75**, 238–62. (210)

Leblond, C. P. Nervous and humoral factors in the maternal behavior of the mouse. *J. genet. Psychol.,* 1940, **57**, 327–44. (576)

LeBoeuf, B. J., and Peeke, H. V. S. The effect of strychnine administration during development on adult maze learning in the rat. *Psychopharmacologia,* 1969, **16**, 49–53. (473)

Lecomte, J. Endogenous histamine liberation in man. *J. Ciba Found. Symp. Histamine.* London: Churchill, 1956, 173–74. (210)

Leiman, A. L., and Christian, C. N. Electrophysiological analyses of learning and memory. In J. A. Deutsch (Ed.), *The Physiological Basis of Memory.* New York: Academic Press, 1973, pp. 125–65. (457)

Lele, P. P., and Wedell, G. The relationship between neurohistology and corneal sensibility. *Brain,* 1956, **79**, 119–52. (177)

Leukel, F. A. A comparison of the effects of ECS and anesthesia on acquisition of the maze habit. *J. Comp. Physiol. Psychol.,* 1957, **50**, 300–306. (435, 437)

Leventeau, J., and MacLeod, P. Reciprocal inhibition at glomerular level during bilateral olfactory stimulation. In C. Pfaffmann (Ed.), *Olfaction and Taste.* New York: Rockefeller Univ. Press, 1969, 212–15. (281)

Levick, W. R. Receptive fields and trigger features of ganglion cells in the visual streak of the rabbit's retina. *J. Physiol.* (London), 1967, **188**, 285–397. (96)

Levine, J. Studies in the interrelations of central nervous structures in binocular vision. I. The lack of bilateral transfer of visual discriminative habits acquired monocularly by the pigeon. *J. Genet. Psychol.,* 1945, **67**, 131–42. (446)

Levine, J. Studies in the interrelations of central nervous structures in binocular vision. II. The conditions under which interocular transfer takes place in the pigeon. *J. Genet. Psychol.,* 1945, **67**, 131–42. (446)

Levine, J. Studies in the interrelations of central nervous structures in vision. III. Localization of the memory trace as evidenced by the lack of inter- and intraocular habit transfer in the pigeon. *J. Genet. Psychol.,* 1952, **82**, 19–27. (446)

Levine, S., and Brush, F. R. Adrenocortical activity and avoidance learning as a function of time after avoidance training. *Physiol. Behav.,* 1967, **2**, 385–88. (346, 347)

Levine, S., and Soliday, S. An effect of hypothalamic lesions on conditioned avoidance learning. *J. Comp. Physiol. Psychol.,* 1960, **53**, 497–501. (346, 381)

Levine, S., and Soliday, S. An effect of adrenal demedullation on the acquisition of a conditioned avoidance response. *J. Comp. Physiol. Psychol.,* 1962, **55**, 214–19. (344)

Lewis, D. J., Miller, R. R., and Misanin, J. R. Control of retrograde amnesia. *J. Comp. Physiol. Psychol.,* 1968, **66**, 48–52. (437)

Lewis, D. J., Miller, R. R., and Misanin, J. R. Selective amnesia in rats produced by electroconvulsive shock. *J. Comp. Physiol. Psychol.,* 1969, **69**, 136–40. (437)

Lewis, T. *Pain.* New York: Macmillan Co., 1942. (193, 201)

Leyton, A. S. F., and Sherrington, C. S. Observations on the excitable cortex of the chimpanzee, orangutang, and gorilla. *Quart. J. Exp. Physiol.,* 1917, **11**, 135–221. (334)

Liberson, W. T., and Akert, K. Hippocampal seizure states in guinea pigs. *EEG Clin. Neurophysiol.,* 1955, **7**, 211–22. (362)

Lichtenstein, P. E. Studies of anxiety. II. The effects of lobotomy on a feeding inhibition in dogs. *J. Comp. Physiol. Psychol.,* 1950, 43, 419–26. (392)

Licklider, J. C. R., and Kryter, R. D. Frequency-localization in the auditory cortex of the monkey. *Fed. Proc.*, 1942, **1**, 51. (158)

Liddell, E. G. T., and Phillips, G. C. Thresholds of cortical representation. *Brain*, 1950, **73**, 125–40. (335)

Light, J. S., and Sautt, W. H. Essential part of reflex arc for establishment of conditioned reflex. Formation of conditioned reflex after exclusion of motor peripheral end. *J. Comp. Psychol.*, 1936, **21**, 19–36. (510)

Likuski, H. J., Debons, A. F., and Cloutier, R. J. Inhibition of gold thioglucose-induced hypothalamic obesity by glucose analogues. *American Journal of Physiology*, 1967, **212**, 669–76. (592)

Lilly, J. C. Learning motivated by subcortical stimulation: The "start" and the "stop" patterns of behavior. *International Symposium on Reticular Formation of the Brain.* Boston: Little, Brown and Co., 1958. (521)

Lilly, J. C. Learning motivated by subcortical stimulation. In E. R. Ramey and D. S. O'Doherty (Eds.), *Electrical Studies on the Unanesthetized Brain.* New York: Hoeber, 1960. (517)

Lilly, J. C. Operant conditioning of the bottlenose Dolphin with electrical stimulation of the brain. *J. Comp. Physiol. Psychol.*, 1962, **55**, 73–79. (517)

Lim, R. K. S. Pain. In *Annual Review of Physiology*, 1970, **32**, 269–88. (251)

Lim, R. K. S., Guzman, F., Rodgers, D. W., Goto, K., Braun, C., Dickerson, G. D., and Engle, R. J. The site of action of narcotic and non-narcotic analgesics determined by blocking bradykinin-evoked visceral pain. *Arch. Int. Pharmacodyn.*, 1964, **152**, 25. (a) (251)

Lim, R. K. S., Guzman, F., Rodgers, D. W., Goto, K., Braun, C., Dickerson, G. D., Engle, R. J. Potter, G. D., Guy, J. L., and Rogers, R. W. Mechanism of analgesia and pain. Motion Picture Film: Program 48th Ann. Meet. *Fed. Amer. Soc. Exp. Biol.*, Chicago, 1964. (b) (251)

Lindblom, U., and Lund, L. The discharge from vibration-sensitive receptors in the monkey foot. *Exper. Neurology*, 1966, **15**, 401–17. (180)

Lindsley, D. B. Emotion. In S. S. Stevens (Ed.), *Handbook of Experimental Psychology.* New York: John Wiley & Sons, 1951, 473–516. (341)

Lindsley, D. B. Psychological phenomena and the electroencephalogram. *EEG Clin. Neurophysiol.*, 1952, **4**, 443–56. (394)

Lindsley, D. B. The reticular system and perceptual discrimination. In Henry Ford Hospital Symposium, *Reticular Formation of the Brain.* Boston: Little, Brown & Co., 1958, 513–34. (397, 424)

Lindsley, D. B. Attention, consciousness, sleep, and wakefulness. In J. Field, H. W. Magoun and V. E. Hall (Eds.), *Handbook of Physiology.* Vol. III. Section 1. *Neurophysiology.* (American Physiological Society) Baltimore: Williams and Wilkins, 1960. (403)

Lindsley, D. B., Schreiner, L. H., Knowles, W. B., and Magoun, H. W. Behavioral and EEG changes following chronic brain stem lesions in the cat. *EEG clin. Neurophysiol.*, 1949, **1**, 455–73. (408)

Lippold, O. C. L., Nicholls, J. G., and Redfearn, J. W. T. A study of the afferent discharge produced by cooling a mammalian muscle spindle. *J. Physiol.*, 1960, **153**, 218–31. (195)

Lisk, R. D. Diencephalic placement of estradiol and sexual receptivity in the female rat. *Amer. J. Physiol.*, 1962, **203**, 493–96. (560, 584)

Lloyd, D. P. C. Neuron patterns controlling transmission and ipsilateral hind limb reflexes in cats. *J. Neurophysiol.*, 1943, **6**, 293–315. (296)

Loeffler, J. D. An investigation of auditory responses in insular cortex of cat and dog. Thesis, University of Wisconsin, Madison, 1958. (157)

Loewenstein, W. R. Excitation and inactivation in a receptor membrane. *Annals N. Y. Acad. Sci.*, 1961, **94**, 510–34. (180, 197, 199)

Loewenstein, W. R., and Rathkamp, R. The sites for mechanoelectric conversion in a Pacinian corpuscle. *J. Gen. Physiol.*, 1958, **41**, 1245–65. (180)

Loftus, J. P. (Ed.) Symposium on motion sickness with special reference to weightlessness.   AMRL-TDR-63-25. Dayton, Ohio: Wright-Patterson Air Force Base, 1963. (326)

Loomis, A. L., Harvey, E. N., and Hobart, G. Electrical potentials of the human brain. *J. Exp. Psychol.*, 1936, 19, 249–79. (509)

Lorente de No, R. Cerebral cortex: architecture, intracortical connexions, motor projections. In J. F. Fulton (Ed.) *Physiology of the Nervous System.* (2nd ed.) Oxford: Oxford Univ. Press, 1943, pp. 274–301. (111)

Loucks, R. B. The experimental delimitation of neural structures essential for learning: the attempt to condition striped muscle responses with faradization of the sigmoid gyri. *J. Psychol.*, 1935, 1, 5–44. (510)

Loucks, R. B. Studies of neural structures essential for learning. II. The conditioning of salivary and striped muscle responses to faradization of cortical sensory elements, and the action of sleep upon such mechanisms. *J. Comp. Psychol.*, 1938, 25, 315–32. (510)

Louttit, R. T. Central nervous system stimulants and maze learning in rats. *Psychol. Rec.*, 1965, 15, 97–101. (473)

Lowenstein, O. Labyrinth and equilibrium. In *Physiological Mechanisms in Animal Behavior.* Soc. Exp. Biol. Symp. IV. Cambridge: Cambridge University Press, 1950. (322)

Lowenstein, O. Peripheral mechanisms of equilibrium. *Brit. med. Bull.*, 1956, 12, 114–18. (321, 322)

Lubar, J. F. Effect of medial cortical lesions on the avoidance behavior of the cat. *J. Comp. Physiol. Psychol.*, 1964, 58, 38–46. (383, 384)

Lubar, J. F., Perachio, A. A., and Kavanagh, A. J. Deficits in active avoidance behavior following lesions of the lateral and posterolateral gyrus of the cat. *J. Comp. Physiol. Psychol.*, 1966, 62, 263–69. (385)

Lubar, J. F., Schostal, C. U., and Perachio, A. A. Non-visual functions of visual cortex in the cat. *Physiology and Behavior*, 1967, 2, 179–84. (385)

Lundberg, A., and Oscarsson, O. Three ascending spinal pathways in the dorsal part of the lateral funiculus. *Acta. Physiol. Scand.*, 1961, 51, 1–16. (218, 230)

Lundberg, A., and Voorhoeve, D. E. Pyramidal activation of interneurones of various spinal reflex arcs in the cat. *Experientia*, 1961, 17, 46–47. (19)

Luttges, M., Johnson, T., Buck, C., Holland, J., and McGaugh, J. An examination of "transfer of learning" by nu-

cleic acid. *Science*, 1966, 151, 834–37. (476)

Luttges, M. W., and McGaugh, J. L. Permanence of retrograde amnesia produced by electroconvulsive shock. *Science*, 1967, 156, 408–10. (440)

M

MacDonnell, M. F., and Flynn, J. P. Attack elicited by stimulation of the thalamus of cats. *Science*, 1964, 144, 1249–50. (354)

MacKensie, J. Some points bearing on the association of sensory disorders and visceral disease. *Brain*, 1893, 16, 321. (248)

Maclean, P. D. Psychosomatic disease and the "visceral brain": recent developments bearing on the Papez theory of emotion. *Psychosom. Med.*, 1949, 11, 338–53. (349)

Maclean, P. D. The limbic system ("visceral brain") in relation to central grey and reticulum of the brain stem. *Psychosom. Med.*, 1955, 17, 355–66. (351, 355)

Maclean, P. D., and Delgado, J. M. R. Electrical and chemical stimulation of fronto-temporal portion of limbic system in the waking animal. *E.E.G. Clin. Neurophysiol.*, 1953, 5, 91–100. (362)

MacLean, P. D., Dua, S., and Denniston, R. H. Cerebral localization for scratching and seminal discharge. *A.M.A. Arch. Neurol.*, 1963, 9, 485–97. (562)

MacLean, P. D., and Ploog, D. W. Cerebral representation of penile erection. *J. Neurophysiol.*, 1962, 25, 29–55. (561)

MacLeod, J. G. Thalamic representation of splanchmic nerve afferents in the cat. *J. Physiol.*, 1956, 133, 16. (244, 248)

MacNichol, E. F., Jr. Three-pigment color vision. *Scientific American*, 1964, 211, 48–56. (80)

MacPhail, E. M., and Miller, N. E. Cholinergic brain stimulation in cats: Failure to obtain sleep. *J. Comp. Physiol. Psychol.*, 1968, 65, 499–503. (411)

Macrae, D. Isolated fear. A temporal lobe aura. *Neurology*, 1954, 4, 497–505. (365)

Magni, F. R., Melzak, G. Moruzzi, and Smith, C. J. Direct pyramidal influences on the dorsal column nuclei. *Arch. ital. biol.*, 1959, 97, 357–77. (242)

Magnotti, T. L'importanza dell'olfatto sullo sviluppo e fuzione degli organi genitali. *Boll. Mall Orecch. Gola Naso,* 1936, **54,** 281–92. (568)

Magnus, O., and Lammers, H. J. The amygdaloid complex. Part I. Electrical stimulation of the amygdala and peri-amygdaloid cortex in the waking cat. *Folia Psychiat. Neerl.,* 1956, **55,** 555–81. (358, 359)

Magnus, R. *Köperstellung.* Berlin: Springer, 1924. (328, 330)

Magnus, R. Some results of studies in the physiology of posture. (The Cameron Prize Lectures.) *Lancet* **2,** 1926, 531–36, 585–88. (328)

Magoun, H. W. The ascending reticular system and wakefulness. In J. F. Delafresnaye (Ed.), *Brain Mechanisms and Consciousness.* Oxford: Blackwell, 1954, pp. 1–20. (402)

Magoun, H. W. *The Waking Brain.* (2nd ed.) Springfield, Illinois: Charles C Thomas, 1963. (397, 399)

Magoun, H. W., Atlas, D., Ingersoll, E. H., and Ranson, S. W. Associated facial, vocal and respiratory components of emotional expression: an experimental study. *J. Neurol. Psychopath.,* 1937, **17,** 241–55.

Magoun, H. W., and Rhines, R. *Spasticity. The Stretch-Reflex and Extrapyramidal System.* Springfield: Charles C Thomas, 1947. (313)

Maher, B. A., Elder, S. T., and Noblin, C. D. A differential investigation of avoidance reduction versus hypermotility following frontal ablation. *J. Comp. Physiol. Psychol.,* 1962, **55,** 449–54. (392)

Maher, B. A., and McIntire, R. W. The extinction of the CER following frontal ablation. *J. Comp. Physiol. Psychol.,* 1960, **53,** 549–52. (385, 392)

Makous, W., Nord, S., Oakley, B., and Pfaffmann, C. The gustatory relay in the medulla. In Y. Zotterman (Ed.), *Olfaction and Taste.* Oxford: Pergamon Press, 1963, 381–93. (262)

Malmo, R. B. Slowing of heart rate following septal self-stimulation in rats. *Science,* 1961, **133,** 1128–30. (518)

Mandler, G. In R. Brown, E. Galanter, E. H. Hess, and G. Mandler, (Eds.), *New Directions in Psychology.* New York: Holt-Rinehart and Winston, 1962, 267–343. (340, 342)

Mann, L. Casuistischer beitrag zur lehre von central entstehenden schmerze. *Berlin Klin. Wochenschr.,* 1892, Bd. **29,** 294. (231)

Marañon, G. Contribution a l'étude de l'action émotive de l'adrénaline. *Rev. Franc. D'endocrinol.,* 1924, **2,** 301–25. (342)

Maréchaux, E. W., and Schäfer, K. E. Uber Temperaturempfindungen bei Einwirkung von Temperatureeizen verschiedener Steilheit auf den ganzen Körper. *Arch. Ges. Physiol.,* 1949, **251,** 765–84. (173)

Marquis, H. A., and Suboski, M. D. Hypophysectomy and ACTH replacement in the incubation of passive and shuttle box avoidance responses. *Proc. 77th Ann. Conv. A. P. A.,* 1969, **4,** 207–8.

Marriott, F. H. C. Colour vision: other phenomena. In H. Davson (Ed.), *The Eye.* New York and London: Academic Press, 1962, pp. 273–97. (93)

Marshall, F. H. A. On the change over in the oestrus cycle in animals after transference across the equator, with further observations on the incidence of the breeding seasons and the factors controlling sexual periodicity. *Proc. Roy. Soc. London,* Ser. B, **122,** 413–28. (580, 581)

Marshall, J. Sensory disturbances in cortical wounds with special reference to pain. *J. Neurol. Neurosurg. Psychiat.,* 1959, **14,** 187–204. (238)

Marshall, J. F., Turner, B. H., and Teitelbaum, P. Sensory neglect produced by lateral hypothalamic damage. *Science,* 1971, **174,** 523–25. (599)

Maruhashi, J., Mizuguchi, K., and Tasaki, I. Action currects in single afferent nerve fibres elicited by stimulation of the skin of the toad and the cat. *J. Physiol.,* 1952, **117,** 129–51. (175, 181)

Maruyama, N., Kawasaki, T., Abe, J., Katoh, I., and Yamazaki, H. Unitary response to tone stimuli recorded from the medial geniculate body of cats. *Int. Audiol.,* 1966, **5,** 184–88. (151)

Masserman, J. H. Destruction of the hypothalamus in cats: effects on activity of the central nervous system and its reaction to sodium amytal. *A. M. A. Arch. Neurol. Psychiat.,* 1938, **39,** 1250–71. (371)

Masserman, J. H. Is the hypothalamus a center of emotion? *Psychosomat. Med.,* 1941, **3,** 3–25. (351, 354)

Masserman, J. H. *Behavior and Neurosis.*

Chicago: Univ. Chicago Press, 1943. (354, 371)

Masserman, J. H., and Pechtel, C. How brain lesions affect normal and neurotic behavior: An experimental approach. *Am. J. Psychiat.*, 1956, **112**, 865–72. (375)

Matthews, P. B. C. Muscle spindles and their motor control. *Physiol. Rev.*, 1964, **44**, 219–88. (298)

Maturana, H. R., and Frank, S. Directional movement and horizontal edge detectors in the pigeon retina. *Science*, 1963, **142**, 977–79. (95)

Maturana, H. R., Uribe, G., and Frenk, S. A biological theory of relativistic colour coding in the primate retina. *Archivos de biologia y medicina experimentalis*, Suplemento No. 1., 1968, **5**, 1–30. (97)

Matzusaki, M., Takagi, H., and Tokisane, T. Paradoxical phase of sleep: its artificial induction in the cat by sodium butyrate. *Science*, 1964, **146**, 1328–29. (413)

Mayer, B. A., and Stone, C. P. The relative efficiency of distributed and massed practice in maze learning by young and adult albino rats. *Journal of Genetic Psychology*, 1931, **39**, 28–38. (522)

Mayer, J. Glucostatic mechanism of regulation of food intake. *New Engl. Med. J.*, 1953, **249**, 13–16. (591)

Mayer, J. Satiety and Weight Control. *Am. J. Clin. Nutrition*, 1957, **5**, 184–85. (591)

Mayer, J., and Marshall, N. B. Specificity of gold thioglucose for ventromedial hypothalamic lesions and hyperphagia. *Nature*, 1956, **178**, 1399–1400. (623)

McBurney, D. H. Magnitude estimation of the taste of sodium chloride after adaptation to sodium chloride. *J. Exper. Psychol.*, 1966. (265)

McBurney, D. H., Kaschau, R. A., and Bogert L. M. The effect of adaptation on taste buds. *Perception and Psychophysics*, 1967, **2**, 175–78. (265)

McCann, S. M. Effect of hypothalamic lesions on the adrenal cortical response in the rat. *Amer. J. Physiol.*, 1953, **172**, 265–75. (346)

McCleary, R. A. Taste and post-ingestion factors in specific-hunger behavior. *J. Comp. Physiol. Psychol.*, 1953, **46**, 411–21. (625)

McCleary, R. A. Type of response as a factor in interocular transfer in the fish. *J. Comp. Physiol. Psychol.*, 1960, **53**, 549–52. (448)

McCleary, R. A. Response specificity in the behavioral effects of limbic system lesions in the cat. *J. Comp. Physiol. Psychol.*, 1961, **54**, 605–13. (382, 385, 386)

McCleary, R. A. Response-modulating functions of the limbic system; Initiation and suppression. In E. Stellar and J. M. Sprague (Eds.), *Progress in Physiological Psychology*. New York: Academic Press, 1966, pp. 210–72. (383)

McCleary, R. A., and Morgan, T. Food hoarding in rats as a function of environmental temperature. *J. Comp. Psychology*, 1946, **39**, 371–78. (639)

McConnell, J. V. Memory transfer through cannibalism in planarians. *J. Neuropsychiat.*, 1962, **3** (Suppl. 1), 42–48. (475)

McCullough, C. Color adaptation of edge detectors in the human visual system. *Science*, 1965, **149**, 1115–16. (108, 109)

McGaugh, J. L. Facilitative and disruptive effects of stychnine sulfate on maze learning. *Psychol Rep.*, 1961, **8**, 99–104. (438)

McGaugh, J. L. Drug facilitation of memory and learning. In D. H. Efron et al. (Eds.), *Psychopharmacology: A review of progress*. Washington, D.C.: Public Health Service Publ. No. 1836, 1961, Pp. 891–904. (469)

McGaugh, J. L. Time-dependent processes in memory storage. *Science*, 1966, **153**, 1351–58. (436, 440)

McGaugh, J. L., and Alpern, H. P. Effects of electroshock on memory: amnesia without convulsions. *Science*, 1966, **152**, 665–66. (435, 437)

McGaugh, J. L. and Landfield, P. W. Delayed development of amnesia following electroconvulsive shock. *Physiology and Behaviour*, 1970, **5**, 1109–13. (441)

McGaugh, J. L., and Madsen, M. C. Amnesic and punishing effects of electroconvulsive shock. *Science*, 1964, **144**, 182–83. (438, 439)

McGaugh, J. L., Westbrook, W., and Burt, G. Strain differences in the facilitative effects of 5-7-Diphenyl-1-3-Diazamantan 6-ol (1757I.S.) on maze learning. *J. Comp. Physiol. Psychol.*, 1961, **54**, 502–5. (469)

McNamara, H. T., Long, T. B., and Wike, E. L. Learning without response under two conditions of external cues. *J. Comp. Physiol. Psychol.*, 1956, **49**, 477–80. (508)

McPhedran, A. M., Wuerker, R. B., and Henneman, E. Properties of motor units in a homogeneous red muscle (soleus) of the cat. *J. Neurophysiol.*, 1965, **28**, 71–84. (294)

Mehler, W. R. In J. D. French and R. W. Porter (Eds.), *Recent Contributions of Basic Research and Paraplegia.* Springfield: Charles C Thomas, 1961. (281)

Mehler, W. R., Feferman, M. E., and Nauta, W. J. Ascending axon degeneration following anterolateral cordotomy. *Brain*, 1960, **83**, 718–50. (218, 399)

Meikle, T. M., Jr., and Sechzer, J. A. Interocular transfer of brightness discrimination in split-brain cats. *Science*, 1960, **132**, 734–35. (446)

Melzack, R., and Casey, K. L. Sensory, motivational, and central control determinants of pain. In Dan R. Kenshalo (Ed.), *The Skin Senses.* Springfield, Ill.: Charles C Thomas, 1968, 423–43. (250)

Melzack, R., and Scott, T. H. The effects of early experience on the response to pain. *J. Comp. Physiol. Psychol.*, 1957, **50**, 155. (250)

Melzack, R., Weisz, A. Z., and Sprague, L. T. Stratagems for controlling pain: Contributions of auditory stimulation and suggestion. *Exp. Neurol.*, 1963, **8**, 239. (250)

Merton, P. A. Problems of muscular fatigue. *Brit. Med. Bull.*, 1956, **12**, 219–21. (292)

Meyers, B., and McCleary, R. A. Interocular transfer of a pattern discrimination in pattern deprived cats. *J. Comp. Physiol. Psychol.*, 1964, **57**, 16–21. (448)

Meyers, W. J., Valenstein, E. S., and Lacey, J. I. Heart rate changes after reinforcing brain stimulation in rats. *Science*, 1963, **40**, 1233–35. (518)

Michael, Charles R. Receptive fields of single optic nerve fibers in a mammal with an all-cone retina. I. Contrast sensitive units. *J. Neurophysiol.*, 1968, **31**, 249–56.

Michael, Charles R. Receptive fields of single optic nerve fibers in a mammal with an all-cone retina. II. Directionally selective units. *J. Neurophysiol.*, 1968, **31**, 257–67.

Michael, Charles R. Receptive fields of single optic nerve fibers in a mammal with an all-cone retina. III. Opponent color units. *J. Neurophysiol.*, 1968, **31**, 268–82.

Michael, R. P. Estrogen-sensitive neurons and sexual behavior in female cats. *Science*, 1962, **136**, 322–23. (561)

Michelson, J. J. Subjective disturbances of the sense of pain from lesions of the cerebral cortex. *A. Res. Nerv. Ment. Dis. Proc.*, 1943, **23**, 86–99 (245, 247)

Mickle, W. A., and Ades, H. W. A composite sensory projection area in the cerebral cortex of the cat, *Am. J. Physiol.*, 1952, **170**, 682–89. (156)

Mikaelian, D. O. Single unit study of the cochlear nucleus in the mouse. *Acta Oto-Laryngol.*, 1966, **62**, 545–56. (144, 160)

Miller, G. A. The perception of short bursts of noise. *J. Acoust. Soc. Amer.*, 1948, **20**, 160. (161)

Miller, N. E. Experiments on motivation. *Science*, 1957, **126**, 1271–78. (595)

Miller, N. E. Learning and performance motivated by direct stimulation of the brain. In D. E. Sheer (Ed.), *Electrical Stimulation of the Brain.* Austin: University of Texas Press, 1961, 387–97. (357, 596)

Miller, N. E. Chemical coding of behavior in the brain. *Science*, 1965, **148**, 328–38. (599)

Miller, N. E., Bailey, C. J., and Stevenson, J. A. F. Decreased "hunger" but increased food intake resulting from hypothalamic lesions. *Science*, 1950, **112**, 256–59. (623)

Miller, N. E., and Kessen, M. L. Is distention of the stomach by a balloon rewarding or punishing? *Am. Psychologist*, 1954, **9**, 430–31. (605)

Miller, N. E., Sampliner, R. I., and Woodrow, P. Thirst-reducing effects of water by stomach fistula vs. water by mouth measured by both a consummatory and an instrumental response. *J. Comp. Physiol. Psychol.*, 1957, **50**, 1–6. (605)

Miller, R. E., and Ogawa. N. The effect of adrenocorticotropic hormone

(ACTH) on avoidance conditioning in the adrenalectomized rat. *J. Comp. Physiol. Psychol.*, 1962, **55**, 211–13. (346)

Milner, B. Visually-guided maze learning in man: effects of bilateral hippocampal, bilateral frontal and unilateral cerebral lesions. *Neuropsychologia*, 1965, **3**, 317–38. (433)

Milner, B., and Penfield, W. The effect of hippocampal lesions on recent memory. *Trans. Amer. Neurol. Assoc.*, 1955, **80**, 42–48. (433)

Milner, B., and Teuber, H. L. Alteration of perception and memory in man: reflections on methods. In L. Weiskrantz (Ed.), *Analysis of Behavioural Change*. New York: Harper and Row, 1968, pp. 268–375. (433)

Minnick, R. S., Warden, C. J., and Arieti, S. The effects of sex hormones on the copulatory behavior of senile while rats. *Science*, 1946, **103**, 749–50. (554)

Mirsky, A. F., Rosvold, H. E., and Pribram, K. H. Effects of cingulectomy on social behavior in monkeys. *J. neurophysiol.*, 1957, **20**, 588–601. (380)

Mirsky, I. A., Miller, R., and Stein, M. Relation of adrenocortical activity and adaptive behavior, *Psychosom. Med.*, 1953, **15**, 574–88. (346)

Mishkin, M. Visual discrimination performance following partial ablations of the temporal lobe. II. Ventral surface v. hippocampus. *J. Comp. Physiol. Psychol.*, 1954, **47**, 187–93. (121, 373)

Mishkin, M., and Pribram, K. H. Visual discrimination performance following partial ablations of the temporal lobe. I. Ventral v. lateral. *J. Comp. Physiol. Psychol.*, 1954, **47**, 14–20. (373)

Moncrieff, R. W. *The Chemical Senses*. London: Leonard Hill, 1951. (253, 278)

Moniz, E. Les possibilités de la chirurgie dans la traitement de certaines psychoses. *Lisboa. Med.*, 1936, **13**, 141–51. (380)

Monnier, M. La stimulation electrique du thalamus chez l'homme. *Rev. Neurol.*, 1955, **93**, 267. (221)

Monnier, M., and Hosli, L. Dialysis of sleep and waking factors in blood of the rabbit. *Science*, 1964, **146**, 796–98. (413)

Monnier, M., Koller, T., and Graber, S. Humoral influences of induced sleep and arousal upon electrical brain activity of animals with crossed circulation. *Exp. Neurol.*, 1963, **8**, 264–77. (413)

Montgomery, M. F. The role of salivary glands in the thirst mechanism. *Amer. J. Physiol.*, 1931, **96**, 221–27. (595)

Montgomery, M. F. The influence of atropin and pilocarpin on thirst (voluntary ingestion of water). *Am. J. Physiol.*, 1931b, **98**, 35–41. (595)

Mook, D. G. Oral and postingestional determinants of the intake of various solutions in rats with esophageal fistulas. *J. Comp. Physiol. Psychol.*, 1963, **56**, 645, 659. (613, 614)

Moore, R. M. Some experimental observations relating to visceral pain. *Surgery*, 1938, **3**, 534. (200)

Moray, N. Attention in dichotic listening: affective cues and influence of instructions. *Quart. J. exp. Psychol.*, 1959, **11**, 56–60. (419)

Morgan, C. T., and Fields, P. E. The effect of variable preliminary feeding upon the rat's speed of locomotion. *Comp. Physiol. Psychol.*, 1938, **26**, 331–48. (521)

Morgan, C. T., Stellar, E., and Johnson, O. Food deprivation and hoarding in rats. *J. Comp. Psychol.*, 1943, **35**, 275–95.

Morgan, J. M., and Mitchell, J. C. Septal lesions enhance delay of responding on a free operant avoidance schedule. *Psychonomic Science*, 1969, **16**, 10–11. (387)

Morin, E. A new spinal pathway for cutaneous impulses. *Am. J. Physiol.*, 1955, **183**, 243–52. (218)

Morison, R. S., and Dempsey, E. W. A study of thalamo-cortical relations. *Am. J. Physiol.*, 1942, **135**, 281–92. (403)

Moritz, A. R., and Henriques, F. C. Studies of thermal injury; relative importance of time and surface temperature in causation of cutaneous burns. *Am. J. Path.*, 1947, **23**, 695–720. (193)

Morrell, F. Interseizure disturbances in focal epilepsy. *Neurology*, 1956, **6**, 327–33. (461, 462)

Morrell, F. In Conditionnement et Reactivitéen Electroencephalographie, Supp. No. 6, *EEG Clin. Neurophysiol.* Paris: Masson et Cie, 1957. (461, 462, 467)

Morrell, F. Effects of experimental epilepsy on conditioned electrical potentials. *Univ. Minnesota Med. Bull.*, 1957, **29**, 82–102. (462)

Morrell, F. An anatomical and physiological analysis of electrocortical conditioning. *Proc. 1st Intern. Congr. Neurol. Sci.*, Brussels, 1957. (462)

Morrell, F. Microelectrode and steady potential shifts suggesting a dendritic locus of closure. In H. H. Jasper and G. D. Simirnov (Eds.), The Moscow Colloquium on Electroencephalography of Higher Nervous Activity. *EEG clin. Neurophysiol.* Suppl. 13, 1960. (463, 466)

Morrell, F. Lasting changes in synaptic organization produced by continuous neuronal bombardment. In J. F. Delafresnaye (Ed.), *Brain Mechanisms and Learning.* Oxford: Blackwell, 1961, 375–92. (463, 465)

Morrell, F. Effect of anodal polarization on the firing pattern of single cortical cells. In N. S. Kline (Ed.), Pavlovian Conference on Higher Nervous Activity. *Ann. N.Y. Acad. Sci.*, 1961, **92**, 860–76. (465)

Morrell, F. Electrophysiological contributions to the neural basis of learning. *Physiological Reviews*, 1961, ₊41, 443–94. (466)

Morrell, F., Barlow, J., and Brazier, M. A. B. Analysis of conditioned repetitive response by means of the average response computer. In J. Wortis (Ed.), *Recent Advances in Biological Psychiatry*, Chap. ix. New York: Grune and Stratton, 1960, 123–37. (467)

Morrell, F., and Jasper, H. H. Electroencephalographic studies of the formation of temporary connections in the brain. *Electroencephalog. and Clin. Neurophysiol.*, 1956, **8**, 201–15. (509)

Moruzzi, G. Synchronizing influences of the brain stem and the inhibitory mechanisms underlying the production of sleep by sensory stimulation. H. H. Jasper and G. D. Simirnov (Eds.), The Moscow Colloquium on Electroencephalography of Higher Nervous Activity. *Electroencephalog. Clin. Neuropsysiol.*, Suppl. 13, 1960, 231–56. (410)

Moruzzi, G., and Magoun, H. W. Brain stem reticular formation and activation of the EEG. *Electroencephalog. Clin. Neurophysiol.*, 1949, **1**, 455–73. (395)

Mott, F. W. Ascending degeneration resulting from lesions of the spinal cord in monkeys. *Brain*, 1892, **15**, 215–29. (227)

Moulton, D. G. Electrical activity in the olfactory system of rabbits with indwelling electrodes. In Y. Zotterman (Ed.), *Olfaction and Taste.* Oxford: Pergamon Press, 1963, pp. 71–84. (281, 282)

Moulton, R., Spector, W. G., and Willoughby, D. A. Histamine release and pain production by xanthosine and related compounds. *Brit. J. Pharmacol.*, 1957, **12**, 365–70. (209)

Mount, G. B., and Hoebel, B. Lateral hypothalamic reward decreased by intragastric feeding: self-determined "threshold" technique. *Psychonomic Science*, 1967, **9**, 265–66. (528)

Mountcastle, V. B. Modality and topographic properties of single neurons of cat's somatic sensory cortex. *J. Neurophysiol.*, 1957, **20**, 208. (111)

Mountcastle, V. B. Some functional properties of the somatic afferent system. In W. A. Rosenblith (Ed.), *Sensory Communication.* New York: John Wiley and Sons (and Cambridge: M. I. T. Press), 1961, pp. 403–36. (214, 221, 226, 235, 246)

Mountcastle, V. B., and Henneman, E. Pattern of tactile representation in thalamus of cat. *J. Neurophysiol.*, 1949, **12**, 85–100. (221)

Mountcastle, V. B., and Henneman, E. The representation of tactile sensibility in the thalamus of the monkey. *J. Comp. Neurol.*, 1952, **97**, 409–40. (221)

Mountcastle, V. B., and Powell, T. P. S. Neural mechanisms subserving cutaneous sensibility with special reference to the role of afferent inhibition in sensory perception and discrimination. *Bull. Johns Hopkins Hospital*, 1959, **105**, 201–32. (221, 225, 235)

Mountcastle, V. B., Talbot, W. H., Darian-Smith, I., and Kornhuber, H. H. Neural basis of the sense of flutter-vibration. *Science*, 1967, **155**, 597–600. (213)

Moushegian, G., Rupert, A., and Galambos, R. Microelectrode study of ventral cochlear nuclei of the cat. *J. Neurophysiol.*, 1962, **25**, 515–29. (144)

Mousehegian, G., Rupert, A., Marsh, J. J., and Galambos, R. Evoked cortical potentials in absence of middle ear muscles. *Science*, 1961, **133**, 582–83. (423, 426)

Moushegian, G., Rupert, A. L., and Langford, T. L. Stimulus coding by medial superior olivary neurons. *J. Neurophysiol.*, 1967, **30**, 1239–61. (151, 162)

Mowrer, O. H. *Learning Theory and Personality Dynamics.* New York: Ronald, 1950. (343)

Moyer, K. E. Effect of andrenalectomy on anxiety motivated behavior. *J. Genet. Psychol.*, 1958, **92**, 11–16. (346, 347)

Moyer, K. E., and Bunnell, B. N. Effect of exogenous adrenaline on an avoidance response in the rat. *J. Genet. Psychol.*, 1958, **92**, 11–16. (344)

Moyer, K. E., and Bunnell, B. N. Effect of adrenal demedullation on an avoidance response in the rat. *J. Comp. Physiol. Psychol.*, 1959, **52**, 215–16. (344)

Mozell, M. M., and Pfaffmann, C. The afferent neural process in odor perception. *Ann. New York Acad. Sci.*, 1954, **58**, 96–108. (280)

Muller, G. E., and Pilzecker, A. Experimentelle Beitrage zur Lehre vom Gedaechtniss. *Z. Psychol. Physiol. Sinnesorg.*, 1900, **1**, 1–300. (435)

Muntz, W. R. A., and Northmore, D. D. M. Background light, temperature and visual noise in the turtle. *Vision Research*, 1968, **8**, 787–800.

Murphy, J. P., and Gellhorn, E. Multiplicity of representation versus punctate localization in the motor cortex. *Arch. Neurol. Psychiat.*, 1945, **54**, 256–73. (335)

Murphy, J. V., and Miller, R. E. The effect of ACTH on avoidance conditioning in the rat. *J. Comp. Physiol. Psychol.*, 1955, **48**, 47–49. (346)

Murphy, M. R., and Schneider, G. E. Olfactory bulb removal eliminates mating behavior in the male golden hamster. *Science*, 1970, **167**, 302–4. (568)

Myers, R. D. Emotional and autonomic responses following hypothalamic chemical stimulation. *Canadian Journal Psychology*, 1964, **18**, 6–14. (411)

Myers, R. D. Chemical mechanisms in the hypothalamus mediating eating and drinking in the monkey. *Ann. NY. Acad. Sci.*, 1969, **157**(2), 918–32. (598)

Myers, R. E. Interocular transfer of pattern discrimination in cats following section of crossed optic fibers. *J. Comp. Physiol. Psychol.*, 1955, **48**, 470–73. (446)

Myers, R. E. Function of corpus callosum in interocular transfer. *Brain*, 1956, **79**, 358–63. (120, 446, 447)

Myers, R. E. Corpus callosum and interhemispheric communication: enduring memory effects. *Fed. Proc.*, 1957, **16**, 92. (447)

Myers, R. E. Localization of function in the corpus callosum. *Ann. A. Arch. Neurol.*, 1959, **1**, 74–77. (447)

Myers, R. E., and Henson, C. O. Role of corpus callosum in transfer of tactuokinesthetic learning in chimpanzee. *Arch. Neurol.*, 1960, **3**, 404–9. (448)

N

Nachmansohn, D. *Chemical and Molecular Basis of Nerve Activity.* New York: Academic Press, 1959. (17)

Nadel, L. Dorsal and ventral hippocampal lesions and behavior. *Physiology and Behavior*, 1968, **3**, 891–900. (391)

Nafe, J. P., and Kenshalo, D. R. Stimulation and neural response. *Am. J. Psychol.*, 1958, **71**, 199. (206)

Nafe, J. P., and Wagoner, K. S. The nature of pressure adaptation. *J. Gen. Psy.*, 1941, **25**, 323–51. (206)

Nakao, H. Emotional behavior produced by hypothalamic stimulation. *Am. J. Physiol.*, 1958, **194**, 411–18. (351, 353, 355)

Naquet, R. Effects of stimulation of rhinencephalon in the waking cat. *EEG Clin. Neurophysiol.*, 1954, **6**, 711–12. (361)

Naquet, R., Regis, H., Fischer-Williams, M., and Fernandez-Guardiola, A. Variation in the responses evoked by light along the specific pathways. *Brain*, 1960, **83**, 52–56. (425, 426)

Nathan, P. W., and Smith, M. C. Normal mentality associated with a maldeveloped "rhinencephalon." *J. Neurol. Neurosurg. Psychiat.*, 1950, **13**, 191–97. (365, 366)

Nauta, W. J. H. Hypothalamic regulation of sleep in rats. An experimental study. *J. Neurophysiol.*, 1946, **9**, 285–316. (410)

Neff, W. D. Neural mechanisms of auditory discrimination. In W. A. Rosenblith (Ed.), *Sensory Communication.* Cambridge: MIT Press. (167)

Neff, W. D., and Diamond, I. T. The neural basis of auditory discrimination. In H. F. Harlow and C. N. Woolsey (Eds.), *Biological and Biochemical Bases of Behavior.* Madison: University Wisconsin Press, 101–26. (167)

Neff, W. D., Fisher, J. F., Diamond, I. T., and Yela, M. Role of auditory cortex in discrimination requiring localization of sound in space. *J. Neurophysiol.*, 1956, 19, 500–512. (164, 167)

Nelson, D. Do rats select more sodium than they need? *Federation Proc.*, 1947, 6, 169. (613)

Nelson, P. G., Erulkar, S. D., and Bryan, J. S. Responses of units of the inferior colliculus to time-varying acoustic stimuli. *J. Neurophysiol.*, 1966, 29, 834–60. (142, 159, 160)

Neuhaus, W. Die Unterschiedung von Duftquantitaten bei Mensch and Hund nach Versuchen mit Buttersäure. *Z. Vergl. Physiol.*, 1955, 37, 234–52. (277)

Newman, B. L. Behavioral effects of electrical self-stimulation of the septal area and related structures in the rat. *J. Comp. Physiol. Psychol.*, 1961, 54, 340–46. (521)

Newman, B. L., and Feldman, S. M. Electrophysiological activity accompanying intracranial self-stimulation. *J. Comp. Physiol. Psychol.*, 1964, 57, 244–47. (518)

Niemer, W. T., and Jimenez-Castellanos, J. Cortico-thalamic connexions in the cat as revealed by "physiological neuronography". *J Comp. Anat.*, 1950, 93, 101–23. (122)

Nikara, T., Bishop, P. O., and Pettigrew, J. D. Analysis of retinal correspondence by studying receptive fields of binocular single units in cat striate cortex. *Expl. Brain Res.*, 1968, 6, 353–72. (112)

Nissen, H. W. Instinct as seen by a psychologist. *Psychol. Rev.*, 1953, 60, 291–94. (570)

Noble, G. K., and Zitrin. Induction of mating behavior in male and female chicks following injections of sex hormones. *Endocrinology*, 1942, 30, 327–34. (553)

Novin, D. The relation between electrical conductivity of brain tissue and thirst in the rat. *J. Comp. Physiol. Psychol.*, 1962, 55, 145–54. (606)

Novin, D., and Durham, R. Unit and DC potential studies of the supraoptic nucleus. *Annals N.Y. Acad. Sci.*, 1969, 157(2), 740–53. (598)

O

Oakley, B., and Pfaffmann, C. Electrophysiologically monitored lesions in the gustatory thalamic relay of the albino rat. *J. Comp. Physiol. Psychol.*, 1962, 55, 155–60. (263)

Oatley, K. Changes of blood volume and osmotic pressure in the production of thirst. *Nature*, 1964, 202, 1341–42. (589)

Olds, J. Physiological mechanisms of reward. In M. R. Jones (Ed.), *Nebraska Symposium on Motivation.* Lincoln: University of Nebraska Press, 1955. (520, 521)

Olds, J. Runway and maze behavior controlled by basomedial forebrain stimulation in the rat. *J. Comp. Physiol. Psychol.*, 1956, 49, 507–12. (520, 521, 525)

Olds, J. Self-stimulation of the brain. *Science*, 1958, 127, 315–24. (519, 525)

Olds, J. Effects of hunger and male sex hormone on self-stimulation of the brain. *J. Comp. Physiol. Psychol.*, 1958, 51, 320–24. (528)

Olds, J. Differentiation of reward systems in the brain by self-stimulation techniques. In E. R. Ramey and D. S. O'Doherty (Eds.), *Electrical Studies on the Unanesthetized Brain.* New York: Hoeber, 1960. (517)

Olds, J. Operant conditioning of single unit responses. *Proceedings of the 23rd International Congress of Physiological Science. Tokyo*, 1965, 4, 372–80. (459)

Olds, J., and Hirano, T. Conditioned responses of hippocampal and other neurons. *Electroencephalography & Clinical Neurophysiology*, 1969, 26, 159–66. (459)

Olds, J., and Milner, P. Positive reinforcement produced by electrical stimulation of septal area and other regions of rat brain. *J. Comp. Physiol. Psychol.*, 1954, 47, 419–27. (511)

Olds, J., and Olds, M. E. Interference and learning in paleocortical systems. In J. F. Delafresnaye (Ed.), *Brain Mechanisms and Learning.* Oxford: Blackwell, 1961, 153–88. (459)

Olds, J., and Olds, M. Drives, rewards, and the brain. In T. M. Newcombe (Ed.), *New Directions in Psychology II.* New York: Holt, Rinehart, Winston, 1965. (517)

Olds, M. E., and Olds, J. Effects of lesions in medial forebrain bundle on self-stimulation behavior. *Am. J. Physiol.*, 1969, **217**, 1253–64. (517)

Oliver, G. W. O., Taberner, P. V., Rick, J. T., and Kerkut, G. A. Changes in GABA level GAD and CAE activity in CNS of an insect during learning. *Comp. Biochem. Physiol.*, 1971, 38(B), 529–35. (461)

Oliverio, A. Effects of nicotine and strychnine on transfer of avoidance learning in the mouse. *Life Sciences,* 1968, **7**, 1163–67. (473)

Olivier, A., Parent, A., Simard, H., and Poirier, L. J. Cholinesterogic striatopallidal and striatonigral efferents in the cat and the monkey. *Brain Res.*, 1970, 18, 273, 282. (488)

Oonishi, S., and Katsuki, Y. Functional organization and integrative mechanism on the auditory cortex of the cat. *Jap. J. Physiol.*, 1965, **15**, 342–65. (111, 147)

Orbach, J., and Fantz, R. L. Differential effects of temporal neocortical resections on overtrained and non-overtrained visual habits in monkeys. *J. Comp Physiol. Psychol.*, 1958, 51, 126–29. (434)

Orbach, J., Milner, B., and Rasmussen, T. Learning and retention in monkeys after amygdala-hippocampus resection. *Arch. Neurol.*, 1960, 3, 230–51. (433)

Osborn, A. G., Bunker, P. J., Cooper, L. M., Frank, G. S., and Hilgard, E. R. Effects of thiopeutal sedation on learning and memory. *Science,* 1967, 157, 574, 576. (445)

Oscarsson, O. The projection of group I afferents to the cat cerebral cortex. In R. Granit (Ed.), *Muscular Afferents and Motor Control.* New York: John Wiley, 307–16. (336)

Oswald, I., Taylor, A., and Treisman, M. Discrimination responses to stimulation during human sleep. *Brain,* 1960, 83, 440–53. (419)

Otis, L. S., and Pryor, G. T. Lack of effect of TCAP on conditioned avoidance learning in rats. *Psychonom. Sci.,* 1968, 11, 95–96. (474)

Ottoson, D. Analysis of the electrical activity of the olfactory epithelium. *Acta Physiol. Scand.*, 1956, **35**(Suppl. 122), 1–83. (276)

Ottoson, D. Generation and Transmission of signals in the olfactory system. In Y. Zetterman (Ed.), *Olfaction and Taste.* Oxford: Pergamon Press, 35–44. (276)

Overton, D. A. State-dependent or "dissassociated" learning produced with pentobarbital. *J. Comp. Physiol. Psychol.,* 1964, 57, 3–12. (445)

P

Pagano, R. R., Bush, D. F., Martin, G., and Hunt, E. B. Duration of retrograde amnesia as a function of electroconvulsive shock intensity. *Physiol. Behavior,* 1969, 4, 19–21. (437, 441)

Palestini, M., Davidovich, A., and Hernandez-Peon, R. Functional significance of centrifugal influences upon the retina. *Acta neurol. Lat.-Amer.,* 1959, **5**, 113–31. (423)

Palestini, M., Rossi, G. F., and Zanchetti, A. An electrophysiological analysis of pontine reticular regions showing different anatomical organization. *Arch. Ital. Biol.*, 1957, **95**, 97–109. (401)

Pampiglione, G., and Falconer, M. A. Electrical stimulation of the hippocampus in man. In J. Field, H. W. Magoun and V. E. Hall (Eds.), *Handbook of Physiology.* Vol. II. Section I. *Neurophysiology.* (American Physiological Society) Baltimore: Williams and Wilkins, 1960, pp. 1391–94. (363)

Panksepp, J., Gandelman, R. and Trowill, J. A. The effect of intertrial interval on running performance for ESB. *Psychonomic Science,* 1968, **13**, 135–36. (521, 522)

Pantle, A., and Sekuler, R. Size detecting mechanisms in human vision. *Science,* 1968, **162**, 1146–48. (110)

Paolino, R. M., and Levy, H. M. Amnesia produced by spreading depression and ECS; evidence for time-dependent memory trace localization. *Science,* 1971, **172**, 746–49. (454)

Papez, J. W. A proposed mechanism of emotion. *A.M.A. Arch. Neurol. Psychiat.,* 1937, 38, 725–43. (349)

Passey, G. E. The perception of the vertical. IV. Adjustment to the vertical with normal and tilted visual frames of reference. *J. Exp. Psychol.*, 1950, **40**, 738–45. (333)

Patton, H. D., and Amassian, V. E. Thalamic relay of splanchnic afferent fibers. *Amer. J. Physiol.*, 1951, **167**, 815–16. (243)

Pauker, R. S. The effects of removing seminal vesicles, prostate and testes on the mating behavior of the golden hamster, *Cricetus auratus. J. Comp. Physiol., Psychol.*, 1948, **41**, 252–57. (557)

Pavlov, I. P. *Lectures on Conditioned Reflexes.* New York: International, 1928. (250)

Pavlov, I. P. *Conditioned Reflexes.* Oxford: Milford, 1927. (250)

Pearlman, C. A., Sharpless, S. K., and Jarvik, M. E. Retrograde amnesia produced by anesthetic and convulsant agents. *J. Comp. Physiol. Psychol.*, 1961, **54**, 109–12. (436, 437, 438)

Pechtel, C., Masserman, J., Schreiner, L., and Levitt, M. Differential effects of lesions of the mediodorsal nuclei of the thalamus on normal and neurotic behavior in the cat. *J. Nerv. ment. Dis.*, 1955, **121**, 26–33. (372)

Pechtel, C., McAvoy, T., Levitt, M., King, A., and Masserman, J. H. The cingulates and behavior. *J. Nerv. Ment. Dis.*, 1958, **126**, 148–52. (380)

Peeke, H. V. S., and Herz, M. J. Permanence of electroconvulsive shock produced retrograde amnesia. *Proc. 75th Ann. Conv. Am. Psychol. Assoc.*, 1967, **2**, 85–86. (439, 440)

Peiper, A. *Cerebral Function in Infancy and Childhood.* London: Pitman, 1963. (328)

Penfield, W. The cerebral cortex in man. 1. The cerebral cortex and consciousness. *Arch. Neurol. Psychiat.* (Chicago), 1935, **40**, 417–42. (398)

Penfield, W. Mechanisms of voluntary movement. *Brain*, 1954, **77**, 1–17. (420)

Penfield, W. Functional localization in temporal and deep sylvian areas. *A. Res. Nerv. Ment. Dis.*, 1958, **36**, 210–26. (400)

Penfield, W. *The Excitable Cortex of Conscious Man.* Liverpool: Liverpool University Press, 1958. (363)

Penfield, W. Speech, perception and the uncommitted cortex. *Pontifaciae Academiae Scientarum, Scripta varia 30*, 1965, 319–47. (432)

Penfield, W., and Jasper, H. H. *Epilepsy and the Functional Anatomy of the Human Brain.* Boston: Little, Brown and Co., 1959. (238, 244, 363, 364)

Penfield, W., and Rasmussen, T. *The Cerebral Cortex of Man.* New York: Macmillan, 1950. (264, 334)

Penny, R. K., and Croshery, J. Instrumental avoidance conditioning of anxious and nonanxious children. *J. Comp. Physiol. Psychol.*, 1962, **55**, 847–49. (381)

Peretz, E. The effects of lesions of the anterior cingulate cortex on the behavior of the rat. *J. Comp. Physiol. Psychol.*, 1960, **53**, 540–48. (384)

Perez-Cruet, J., Black, W. C., and Brady, J. V. Heart rate: differential effects of hypothalamic and septal self-stimulation. *Science*, 1963, **140**, 1235–36. (518)

Perez-Cruet, J., McIntire, R. W., and Pliskoff, S. S. Blood pressure and heart rate changes in dogs during hypothalamic self-stimulation. *J. Comp. Physiol. Psychol.*, 1965, **60**, 373–81. (518)

Perl, E. R. Somatosensory mechanisms, *Ann. Rev. Physiol.*, 1963, pp. 459–89. (357)

Perl, E. R. Myelinated afferent fibres innervating the primate skin and their response to noxious stimuli. *J. Physiol.* (London), 1968, **197**, 593–615. (176, 194)

Perl, E. R., and Whitlock, D. G. Somatic stimuli exciting spinothalamic projections to thalamic neurons in cat and monkey. *Exp. Neurol.*, 1961, **3**, 256–96. (232, 233, 234, 236, 245)

Perl, E. R., Whitlock, D. G., and Gentry, J. R. Cutaneous prejection to second-order neurons of the dorsal column system. *J. Neurophysiol.*, 1962, **25**, 337–58. (176, 217, 226, 228)

Perry, J. H., and Liebelt, R. D. Extra-hypothalamic lesions in goldthioglucose induced obesity in mice. *Anat. Record*, 1959, **133**, 322. (623)

Peters, R. W. Competing messages: the effect of interfering messages upon the reception of primary messages. *USN Sch. Aviat. Med. Res. Rep.*, 1954, Project No. NM 001 064.01.27. (418)

Petrinovich, L. F., Bradford, D., and McGaugh, J. L. Drug facilitation of memory in rats. *Psychonom. Sci.*, 1965, **2**, 191–92. (473)

Pfaffmann, C. Gustatory afferent impulses. *J. Cell. Comp. Physiol.*, 1941, 17(2), 243–58. (262)

Pfaffmann, C. Gustatory nerve impulses in rat, cat and rabbit. *J. Neurophysiol.*, 1955, 18, 429–40. (259)

Pfaffmann, C. Taste stimulation and preference behavior. In Y. Zotterman (Ed.), *Olfaction and Taste*. Oxford: Pergamon Press, 257–73. (266, 267)

Pfaffmann, C. J., Erickson, R. P., Frommer, G. P., and Halpern, B. P. Gustatory discharges in the rat medulla and thalamus. In W. A. Rosenblith (Ed.), *Sensory Communication*. New York: Wiley, 1961, 455–74. (262, 263)

Pfalz, R. K. J. Centrifugal inhibition of afferent secondary neurons in the cochlear nucleus by sound. *J. Acoust. Soc. Amer.*, 1962, 34, 1472–77. (167)

Pfalz, R. Gekreuzte, zentrifugale Hemmungen und Erregungen im Nucleus cochlearis durch lange Klickfolgen (Meerschweinchen). *Arch. Klin. Exp. Ohr. Nas. Kehlkopfheik.*, 1966, 186, 9–19. (167)

Phillips, A. G., and Mogenson, G. J. Self-stimulation of the olfactory bulb. *Physiology and Behavior*, 1969, 4, 195–97. (517)

Phillips, G. C. Motor apparatus of the baboon's hand. *Proc. Roy. for B.*, 1969, 173, 141–74. (297)

Phillips, M. I., and Olds, J. Unit activity: Motivation-dependent responses from midbrain neurons. *Science* (Washington), 1969, 165, 1269–71. (459)

Picket, J. B. E., III, Jennings, L. B., and Wells, P. H. Influence of RNA and victim training on maze learning by cannibal planarians. *Amer. Zool.*, 1964, 4, 411–12. (475)

Pierce, J., and Nuttall, R. Self-paced sexual behavior in the female rat. *J. Comp. Physiol. Psychol.*, 1961, 54, 310–13. (566)

Piéron, H. Vision in intermittent light. In W. D. Neff (Ed.), *Contributions to Sensory Physiology*. New York and London: Academic Press, 1965, pp. 179–264. (113, 114)

Pilgrim, F. J., and Patton, R. A. Patterns of self-selection of purified dietary components by the rat. *J. Comp. Physiol. Psychol.*, 1947, 40, 343–48. (635)

Pinsker, H., Kupferman, I., Castellucci, V., and Kandel, E. Habituation and dishabituation of gill-withdrawal reflex in *aplysia*. *Science*, 1970, 167, 1740–42. (456)

Pirenne, M. H. Visual functions in man. In H. Davson (Ed.), *The Eye*. New York and London. Academic Press, 1962, pp. 3–217. (117)

Pliskoff, S. S., and Hawkins, T. D. Test of Deutsch's drive-decay theory of rewarding self-stimulation of the brain. *Science*, 1963, 141, 823–24. (524, 525)

Plotnikoff, N. Magnesium pemoline: enhancement of memory after electroconvulsive shock in rats. *Life Sciences*, 1966a, 5, 1495–98. (474)

Plotnikoff, N. Magnesium pemoline: enhancement of learning and memory of a conditioned avoidance response. *Science*, 1966b, 151, 703–4. (474)

Plotnikoff, N. Pemoline and magnesium hydroxide: memory consolidation following acquisition trials. *Psychon. Sci.*, 1967, 9, 141–42. (474)

Plumb, C. S., and Meigs, J. W. Human vibration perception. *Arch. Gen Psychiat.*, 1961, 4, 611–14. (212)

Poggio, G. F., and Mountcastle, V. B. A study of the functional contributions of the lemusical and spinalthalamic systems to somatic sensibility central nervous mechanisms in pain. *Bull. Johns Hopkins Hospital*, 1960, 106, 266–316. (218, 221, 232, 233, 236, 245)

Pollack, L. J., and Davis, L. *Visceral and Referred Pain in Sensations; its Mechanism and Disturbances*. Baltimore: William & Wilkins, 1935. (249)

Pollock, L. J. Overlap of so-called protopathic sensibility as seen in peripheral nerve lesions. *A.M.A. Arch Neurol. Psychiat.*, 1919, 2, 667. (203)

Pollock, L. J., and Davis, L. The reflex activities of a decerebrate animal. *J. Comp. Neurol.*, 1930, 50, 377–411. (249)

Polyak, S. *The Main Afferent Fiber Systems of the Cerebral Cortex in Primates*. Berkeley: University of California Press, 1932. (157)

Polyak, S. *The Retina*. Chicago: University of Chicago Press, 1941. (117)

Polyak, S. In H. Kluver (Ed.), *The Vertebrate Visual System*. Chicago: The University of Chicago Press, 1957. (75)

Pool, J. L. Posterior cordotomy for relief of phantom limb pain. *Ann. Surg.*, 1946, 124, 386–91. (247)

Pool, J. C. The visceral brain of man. *J. Neurophysiol.*, 1954, **11**, 45–63. (378)

Porter, R. W. Alterations in electrical activity of hypothalamus induced by stress stimuli. *Am. J. Physiol.*, 1952, **169**, 629. (578)

Porter, R. W., Cavanaugh, E. B., Critchlow, E. B., and Sawyer, C. H. Localized changes in electrical activity of the hypothalamus in estrous cats following vaginal stimulation. *Am. J. Physiol.*, 1957, **189**, 145. (562)

Porter, R. W., Conrad, D. G., and Brady, J. V. Some neural and behavioral correlates of electrical self-stimulation of the limbic system. *Journal of the Experimental Analysis of Behavior*, 1959, **2**, 43–55. (518)

Potts, A., and Bitterman, M. E. Puromycin and retention in the goldfish. *Science*, 1967, **158**, 1594–96. (438, 484)

Poulos, D. A., and Benjamin, R. M. Response of thalamic neurons to thermal stimulation of tongue. *J. Neurophysiol.*, 1968, **31**, 28–43. (233)

Poulton, E. C. Two-channel listening. *J. Exp. Psychol.*, 1953, **46**, 91–96. (417)

Powley, T. L., and Keesey, R. E. Relationship of body weight to the lateral hypothalamic feeding syndrome. *J. Comp. Physiol. Psychol.*, 1969, **70**, 25–36. (624)

Pribram, K. H., and Bagshaw, Muriel. Further analysis of the temporal lobe syndrome utilizing fronto-temporal ablations. *J. Comp. Neurol.*, 1953, **99**, 347–75. (373, 629)

Pribram, K. H., and Fulton, J. F. An experimental critique of the effects of anterior cingulate ablations in monkey. *Brain*, 1954, **77**, 34–43. (380)

Pribram, K. H., and Kruger, L. Functions of the "olfactory brain." *Ann. New York Acad. Sc.*, 1954, **58**, 109–38. (349)

Pribram, K. H., Rosner, B. S., and Rosenblith, W. A. Electrical responses to acoustic clicks in monkey: extent of neocortex activated. *J. Neurophysiol.*, 1954, **17**, 336–44. (158)

Prien, R. F., Wayner, M. J., Jr., and Kahan, S. Lack of facilitation in maze learning by picrotoxin and strychnine sulphate. *Amer. J. Physiol.*, 1963, **204**, 488–92. (473)

Provins, K. A. Sensory factors in the voluntary application of pressure. *Quart. J. Exp. Psychol.*, 1957, **9**, 28–33. (303)

Provins, K. A. The effect of peripheral nerve block on the appreciation and execution of finger movements. *J. Physiol.*, 1958, **143**, 55–67. (304)

Purpura, D. P. A neurohumoral mechanism of reticulo-cortical activation. *Am. J. Physiol.*, 1956, **186**, 250–54. (413)

Q

Quartermain, D., and Webster, D. Extinction following intracranial reward: the effect of delay between acquisition and extinction. *Science*, 1968, **159**, 1259–60. (524, 527)

Quartermain, D., Paolino, R. M., and Miller, N. E. A brief temporal gradient of retrograde amnesia independent of situational change. *Science*, 1965, **149**, 1116–18. (436, 439)

Quartermain, D., and Miller, N. E. Sensory feedback in time response elicited by carbachol in preoptic area of rat. *J. Comp. Physiol. Psychol.*, 1966, **62**, 350–53. (597)

R

Raab, D. H., and Ades, H. F. Cortical and midbrain mediation of a conditioned discrimination of acoustic intensities. *Am. J. Psychol.*, 1946, **59**, 59–83. (166)

Rabedeau, R. Retrograde amnesia due to spreading cortical depression; paradoxical effect of shock-SD interval. *Psychonomic Science*, 1966, **5**, 113–14. (454)

Rebedeau, R. G., and Whalen, R. E. Effects of copulatory experiences on mating behavior in the male rat. *J. Comp. Physiol. Psychol.*, 1959, **52**, 482–84. (572)

Radionova, E. A. Reactions of neurons in cochlear nucleus to acoustic signals of varying duration. *Fed. Proc.* (Transl. Suppl.), 1966, **25**, T389–90. (161)

Raisman, G., Cowan, W. M., and Powell, T. P. S. An experimental analysis of the efferent projection of the hippocampus. *Brain*, 1966, **89**, 83–108. (391)

Randoin, L., Causeret, J., and Gabrel-

Szymanski, M. Comportement du jeune rat normal auquel on donne le choix entre de l'eau pure et une solution peu concentrée de chlorure de sodium. *J. Physiol.* (Paris), 1950, **42**, 447–50. (613)

Randt, C. T., Quartermain, D., Goldstein, M., and Anagnoste, B. Norepinephrine biosynthesis inhibition: effects on memory in mice. *Science,* 1971, **172**, 498–99. (486)

Ranson, S. W. Somnolence caused by hypothalamic lesions in the monkey. *A.M.A. Arch. Neurol. Psychiat.,* 1939, **41**, 1–23. (371)

Ranson, S. W. Functional and clinical significance of hypothalamus. *Quart. Bullet. N. W. Univ. Med. School,* 1940, **14**, 137–45. (552)

Ranson, S. W., and Magoun, H. W. Respiratory and pupillary reactions induced by electrical stimulation of the hypothalamus. *A.M.A. Arch. Neurol. Psychiat.,* 1933, **29**, 1179–94. (351)

Rasch, E., Riesen, A. H., and Chow, K. L. Altered structure and composition of retinal cells in dark reared cats. *J. Histochem. Cytochem.,* 1959, **7**, 321–22. (478)

Rasmussen, E. W. Experimental homosexual behavior in male albino rats. *Acta Psychol.,* 1955, **11**, 303–34. (571)

Rasmussen, G. L. An efferent cochlear bundle. *Anat. Rec.,* 1942, **82**, 441. (167)

Rasmussen, G. L. The olivary peduncle and other fiber projections of the superior olivary complex. *J. Comp. Neurol.,* 1946, **84**, 141–219. (167)

Rasmussen, G. L. Descending or "feedback" connections of auditory system of the cat. *Am. J. Physiol.,* 1955, **183**, 653. (167)

Rasmussen, G. L. Efferent fibers of the cochlear nucleus. In G. L. Rasmussen and W. F. Windle (Eds.), *Neural Mechanisms of the Auditory and Vestibular Systems.* Springfield, Ill.: Charles C Thomas, 1960. (167)

Raths, P., Witt, I., and Hensel, H. Thermoreceptoren bei Winterschläfern. *Pflüger. Arch. Ges. Physiol.,* 1964, **281**, 73. (181, 191)

Ratliff, F. The role of physiological nystagmus in monocular acuity. *J. Exp. Psychol.,* 1952, **43**, 163–72. (115, 118)

Ray, O. S., Hine, B., and Bivens, L. W. Stability of self-stimulation responding during long test sessions. *Physiology and Behavior,* 1968, **3**, 161–65. (519)

Reid, L. D., Gibson, W. E., Gledhill, S. M., and Porter, P. B. Anticonvulsant drugs and self-stimulation behavior. *J. Comp. Physiol. Psychol.,* 1964, **57**, 353–56. (518)

Reidemeister, C. and Grüsser, O. J., Flimmerlichtuntersuchungen an der Katzenretina. I. *Z. Biol.,* **111**, 241–53; II. *Z. Biol.,* **111**, 254–70. (114)

Reinis, S. Indirect effect of puromycin on memory. *Psychonomic Science,* 1969, **14**, 44–45. (481)

Renshaw, B. Influence of discharge of motoneurons upon excitation of neighbouring motoneurons. *J. Neurophysiol.,* 1941, **4**, 167–83. (300)

Revusky, S. H. Aversion to sucrose produced by contingent X-irradiation: temporal and dosage parameters. *J. Comp. Physiol. Psychol.,* 1968, **65**, 17–22. (633)

Reyes, V., Henry, G. C., Baird, H., Wycis, H. T., and Spiegel, E. A. Localisation of centripetal pathways of the human brain by recording of evoked potentials. *Trans. Amer. Neurol. Assoc.,* 1951, **76**, 246–48. (232, 357)

Reynolds, R. W. Ventromedial hypothalamic lesions without hyperphagia. *Amer. J. Physiol.,* 1963, **204**, 60–62. (622)

Reynolds, W. F., and Pavlik, W. B. Running speed as a function of deprivation period and reward magnitude. *J. Comp. Physiol. Psychol.,* 1960, **53**, 615–18. (532)

Rheingold, H. I., and Hess, E. H. The chicks preference for some visual properties of water. *J. Comp. Physiol. Psychol.,* 1957, **50**, 417. (626)

Ricci, G., Doane, B., and Jasper, H. H. Microelectrode studies of conditioning: technique and preliminary results. *Excerpta Med.,* 1957, **4**, 401–15. (465)

Rice, C. E., and Kenshalo, D. R. Nociceptive threshold measurements in the cat. *J. Appl. Physiology,* 1962, **17**, 1009–12. (199)

Richter, C. P. Mineral appetite of parathyroidectomized rats. *Amer. J. Med. Sci.,* 1939, **198**, 9–16. (631)

Richter, C. P. Total self-regulatory functions in animals and human beings. *The Harvey Lecture Series,* 1942a, **38**, 63–103. (577, 631, 636)

Richter, C. P. Physiological Psychology. *Ann. Rev. Physiol.*, 1942b, **4**, 561–74. (577, 631, 636)

Richter, C. P., and Hawkes, C. D. The dependence of the carbohydrate, fat, and protein appetite of rats on the various components of the vitamin B complex. *Amer. J. Physiol.*, 1941, **131**, 639–49. (631)

Richter, C. P., and Schmidt, E. C. H. Increased fat and decreased carbohydrate appetite of pancreatonized rats. *Endocrinology*, 1941, **28**, 179–92. (631)

Richter, D., and Crossland, J. Variation in acetylcholine content of the brain physiological state. *Am. J. Physiol.*, 1969, **159**, 247–55. (443)

Riesen, A. H. Effects of stimulus deprivation on the development and atrophy of the visual sensory system. *Am. J. Orthopsychiat.*, 1960, **30**, 23–36. (478)

Riggs, L. A., Ratliff, F., Cornsweet, J. C., and Cornsweet, T. N. Disappearance of steadily fixated visual test objects. *J. Opt. Soc. Amer.*, 1953, **43**, 495–501. (118)

Riggs, Lorrin A., and Whittle, Paul. Human occipital and retinal potentials evoked by subjectively faded visual stimuli. *Vision Research*, 1967, **7**, 441–51.

Riley, C. M., and Witschi, E. Comparative effects of light stimulation and administration of gonadotropic hormones on female sparrows. *Endocrinology*, 1938, **23**, 618–24. (581)

Robbins, M. J., and Meyer, D. R. Motivational control of retrograde amnesia. *J. Exper. Psychol.*, 1971, **84**, 220–25. (442)

Roberts, E. Models for correlative thinking about brain, behavior and biochemistry. *Brain Research*, 1966, **2**, 109–44. (456)

Roberts, L. Activation and interference of cortical functions. In D. E. Sheer (Ed.), *Electrical Stimulation of the Brain*. Austin: Univ. Texas Press, 1961, 534–36. (363)

Roberts, M. B. V. The giant fibre reflex of the earthworm, *Lumbricus terrestris*. I. The rapid response. *Journal of Experimental Biology*, 1962a, **39**, 219–28. (456)

Roberts, M. B. V. The giant fibre reflex of the earthworm, *Lumbricus terrestris*. II. Fatigue. *Journal of Experi-

mental Biology*, 1962b, **39**, 229–37. (456)

Roberts, W. W. Rapid escape learning without avoidance learning motivated by hypothalamic stimulation in cats. *J. Comp. Physiol. Psychol.*, 1958a, **51**, 391–99. (351, 356, 357)

Roberts, W. W. Both rewarding and punishing effects from stimulation of posterior hypothalamus of cat with same electrode at same intensity. *J. Comp. Physiol. Psychol.*, 1958b, **51**, 400–407. (356, 517)

Roberts, W. W. Fear-like behavior elicited from dorsomedial thalamus of cat. *J. Comp. Physiol., Psychol.*, 1962, **55**, 191–97. (351, 363)

Roberts, W. W. Are hypothalamic motivational mechanisms functionally and anatomically specific? *Brain Behavior and Evolution*, 1969, **2**, 317–42. (603)

Roberts, W. W., and Carey, R. J. Effect of dorsomedial lesions on fear in cats. *J. Comp. Physiol. Psychol.*, 1963, **56**, 950–58. (389)

Roberts, W. W., and Kiess, H. O. Motivational properties of hypothalamic aggression in cats. *J. Comp. Physiol. Psychol.*, 1964, **58**, 187–93. (358)

Roberts, W. W., Steinberg, M. L., and Means, L. W. Hypothalamic mechanisms for sexual, aggressive, and other motivational behaviors in the opossum, *Didelphis Virginiana*. *J. Comp. Physiol. Psychol.*, 1967, **64**, 1ff. (603)

Robinson, E. A., and Adolph, E. F. Pattern of normal water drinking in dogs. *American Journal Physiology*, 1943, **139**, 39–44. (606)

Robinson, S. W., and Mishkin, M. Alimentary responses evoked from forebrain structures in *Macaca mulatta*. *Science*, **136**, 260–61. (602)

Rodgers, W., and Rozin, P. Novel food preferences in thiamine deficient rats. *J. Comp. Physiol. Psychol.*, 1966, **61**, 1–4. (633)

Rodgers, W. L. Specificity of specific hungers. *J. Comp. Physiol. Psychol.*, 1967, **64**, 49–58. (633, 636)

Roll, S. K. Intracranial self-stimulation and wakefulness: effect of manipulating ambient brain catecholamines. *Science*, 1970, **168**, 1370–72. (518, 519)

Root, W. S., and Bard, P. The mediation of feline erection through sympathetic pathways with some remarks on sexual behavior after deafferentation of the genitalia. *Amer. J. Physiol.*, 1947, **151**, 80–90. (557)

Rose, J. E. The cellular structure of the auditory region of the cat. *J. Comp. Neurol.*, 1949, **91**, 409–39. (153)

Rose, J. E., Brugge, J. F., Anderson, D. J., and Hind, J. E. Phase-locked response to low-frequency tones in single auditory nerve fibers of the squirrel monkey. *J. Neurophysiol.*, 1967, **30**, 769–93. (149)

Rose, J. E., Brugge, J. F., Anderson, D. J., and Hind, J. E. Patterns of activity in simple auditory nerve fibres of the squirrel monkey. *Ciba Symposium, 1968*, 144–57. (149, 150)

Rose, J. E., Brugge, J. F., Anderson, D. J., and Hind, J. E. Some possible neural correlates of combination tones. *J. Neurophysiol.*, 1969, **32**, 402–23. (151)

Rose, J. E., and Galambos, R. Microelectrode studies on medial geniculate of the cat. I. Thalamic region activated by click stimuli. *J. Neurophysiol.*, 1952, **15**, 343–57. (140, 157)

Rose, J. E., Galambos, R., and Hughes, J. R. Microelectrode studies of the cochlear nuclei of the cat. *Bull. Johns Hopkins Hosp.*, 1959, **104**, 211–51. (151)

Rose, J. E., Greenwood, D. D., Goldberg, J. M., and Hind, J. E. Some discharge characteristics of single neurons in the inferior colliculus of the cat. I. Tonotopical organization, relation of spike-counts to the intensity, and firing patterns of the single elements. *J. Neurophysiol.*, 1963, **26**, 294–320. (141, 147)

Rose, J. E., Gross, N. B., Geisler, C. D., and Hind, J. E. Some neural mechanisms in the inferior colliculus which may be relevant to localization of a sound source. *J. Neurophysiol.*, 1966, **29**, 288–314. (163, 164)

Rose, J. E., and Mountcastle, V. B. Touch and kinesthesis. In J. Field, H. W. Magoun and V. E. Hall (Eds.), *Handbook of Physiology*, Vol. I. Section 1. *Neurophysiology*. (American Physiological Society) Baltimore: Williams and Wilkins, 1959, pp. 387–429. (301)

Rose, J. E., and Woolsey, C. N. Structure and relations of limbic cortex and anterior thalamic nuclei in rabbit and cat. *J. Comp. Neurol.*, 1948, 279–348. (349)

Rose, J. E., and Woolsey, C. N. The relations of thalamic connections, cellular structure and evocable electrical activity in the auditory region of the cat. *J. Comp. Neurol.*, 1949, **91**, 441–66. (157)

Rose, J. E., and Woolsey, C. N. Cortical connections and functional organization of the thalamic auditory system of the cat. In H. F. Harlow and C. N. Woolsey (Eds.), *Biological and Biochemical Bases of Behavior*. Madison: Univ. of Wisconsin Press, 1958, 127–50. (152)

Rosenblatt, J., and Aronson, L. R. The influence of experience on the behavioral effects of androgen in prepuberally castrated male cats. *J. Animal Behaviour*, 1958a, G:3, **4**, 171–82. (553)

Rosenblatt, J., and Aronson, L. R. The decline of sexual behavior in male cats after castration with special reference to the role of prior sexual experience. *Behaviour*, 1958b, **12**(4), 285–338. (553, 554)

Rosenthal, S. R. Histamine as possible chemical mediator for cutaneous pain. Dual pain response to histamine. *Proc. Soc. Exper. Biol. and Med.*, 1950, **74**, 167–70. (201)

Rosenthal, S. R. Histamine as the chemical mediator for cutaneous pain. *Fed. Proc.* 1964, **23**, 1109. (201)

Rosenthal, S. R. Pharmacologically active and lethal substances from skin. *Arch. Environ. Health*, 1965, **11**, 465. (201)

Rosenthal, S. R. Histamine as the chemical mediator for referred pain. In Dan R. Kenshalo (ed.), *The Skin Senses*. Springfield, Ill.: Charles C Thomas, 1968, 480–98. (200, 249)

Rosenthal, S. R., and Minard, D. Experiments on histamine as the chemical mediator for cutaneous pain. *J. Exp. Med.*, 1939, **70**, 415. (201)

Rosenthal, S. R., and Sonnencheim, R. R. Histamine as the possible chemical mediator for cutaneous pain. *Amer. J. Physiol.*, 1948, **155**, 186. (201)

Rosenzweig, M. R. Discrimination of auditory intensities in the cat. *Am. J. Psychol.*, 1946, **59**, 127–36. (166)

Rosenzweig, M. R. Cortical correlates of auditory localization and of related perceptual phenomena. *J. Comp.*

Physiol. Psychol., 1954, **47**, 269–76. (164)

Rosvold, H. E. The effects of electroconvulsive shocks on gestation and maternal behavior. *J. Comp. Physiol. Psychol.*, 1949, **42**, 118–36. (577)

Rosvold, H. E., Mirsky, A. F., and Pribram, K. H. Influence of amygdalectomy on social behavior in monkeys. *J. Comp. Physiol. Psychol.*, 1954, **47**, 173–78. (373, 375)

Rothfield, L., and Harmon, P. J. On the relation of the hippocampal-fornix system to the control of rage responses in cats. *J. Comp. Neurol.*, 1954, **101**, 265–82. (377)

Rothman, H. Zusammenfessender Bericht über den Rothmannschen grosshirnlosen Hund nach klinischer und anatomischer Untersuchung. *Ztchr. Ges. Neurol. Psychiat.*, 1923, **87**, 247–313. (367)

Routtenberg, A. The effects of chemical stimulation in dorsal midbrain tegmentum on self-stimulation in hypothalamus and septal area. *Psychonomic Science*, 1965, **3**, 41. (597)

Routtenberg, A., and Kay, K. E. Effect of one electroconvulsive seizure on rat behavior. *J. Comp. Physiol. Psychol.*, 1965, **59**, 285–88. (433)

Routtenberg, A., and Lindy, J. Effects of the availability of rewarding septal and hypothalamic stimulation on bar pressing for food under conditions of deprivation. *J. Comp. Physiol. Psychol.*, 1965, **60**, 158–61. (528)

Rowan, W. Light and seasonal reproduction in animals. *Biol. Rev.*, 1938, **13**, 374–402. (580)

Rozin, P. Specific Aversions as a component of specific hungers. *J. Comp. Physiol. Psychol.*, 1967, **64**, 237–42. (633)

Rozin, P., and Rogers, W. Novel-diet preferences in vitamin-deficient rats and rats recovered from vitamin deficiencies. *J. Comp. Physiol. Psychol.*, 1967, **63**, 429–33. (633)

Ruch, T. C., and Fulton, J. F. Cortical localization of somatic sensibility. The effect of precentral, postcentral and posterior parietal lesions upon the performance of monkeys trained to discriminate weights. *Res. Publ. Ass. Nerv. Ment. Dis.*, 1935, **15**, 289–330. (241)

Ruch, T. C., Fulton, J. F., and German, W. J. Sensory discrimination in monkey, chimpanzee and man after lesions of the parietal lobe. *Arch. Neurol. Psychiat.*, 1938, **39**, 919–37. (241)

Ruch, T. C., and Patton, H. D. The relation of the deep opercular cortex to taste. *Fed. Proc.*, 1946, **5**, 89–90. (264)

Rupert, A., Moushegian, G., and Galambos, R. Unit responses to sound from auditory nerve of the cat. *J. Neurophysiol.*, 1963, **26**, 449–65. (143)

Rupert, A., Moushegian, G., and Whitcomb, M. A. Superior-olivary response patterns to monaural and binaural clicks. *J. Acoust. Soc. Am.*, 1966, **39**, 1069–76. (161)

Rushton, W. A. H. A theory of the effects of fibre size in medullated nerve. *J. Physiol.*, 1951, **115**, 101–22. (12)

Rushton, W. A. H. Peripheral coding in the nervous system. In W. A. Rosenblith (Ed.), *Sensory Communication.* Cambridge: MIT Press, 1961. (23)

Rushton, W. A. H. Visual pigments in man. *Sci. Amer.*, 1962, **207**, 120–37. (83, 84, 85, 93)

Rusinov, V. S. An electrophysiological analysis of the connecting function in the cerebral cortex in the presence of a dominant area. *Communs. XIX Intern Physiol. Congr.* (Montreal), 1953. (463)

Russell, I. S., and Ochs, S. One trial interhemispheric transfer of a learning engram, *Science*, 1961, **133**, 1077–78. (449, 454)

Russell, W. R., and Nathan, P. W. Traumatic amnesia. *Brain*, 1946, **69**, 280–300. (430, 487)

S

Sachs, M. B., and Kiang, N. Y-S. Two-tone inhibition in auditory nerve fibers. *J. Acoust. Soc. Am.*, 1968, **43**, 1120–28. (143)

Saginor, M., and Horton, R. Reflex release of gonadotropin and increased plasma testosterone concentration in male rabbits during copulation. *Endocrinology*, 1968, **82**, 627–30. (555)

Sano, T. Motor and other responses elicited by electrical stimulation of the cat's temporal lobe. *Folia. Psychiat. Neurol. Jap.*, 1958, **12**, 152–76. (362)

Sato, M. Response of Pacinian corpuscles to sinusoidal vibration. *J. Physiol.*, 1961, **159**, 391–409. (213)

Sato, M., Yamashita, S., and Ogawa, H. Afferent specificity in taste. In C. Pfaffmann (Ed.), *Olfaction and Taste.* New York: Rockefeller U. Press, 1969, pp. 470–487. (262)

Satterfield, J. H. Evoked cortical response enhancement and attention in man. A study of responses to auditory and shock stimuli. *Electroencephalography and Clinical Neurophysiology,* 1965, **17,** 456–57.

Sawa, M., Maruyama, N., Hanai, T., and Kaji, S. Regulatory influence of amygdaloid nuclei upon the unitary activity in ventromedial nucleus of hypothalamus. *Folia. Psychiat. Neurol. Jap.,* 1959, **13,** 235–56. (376)

Sawa, M., Veki, V., Avita, M., and Harada, T. Preliminary report on the amygdalectomy on the psychotic patients with interpretation of oral-emotional manifestation in schizophrenics. *Folia. Psychiat. Neurol. Jap.,* 1954, **4,** 309–29. (379, 575)

Sawa, M., Yukiharu, W., Massaya, A., and Toshio, H. Preliminary report on the amygdaloidectomy on the psychotic patient, with interpretation of oral-emotional manifestation in schizophrenics. *Folia. Psychial. Neurol. Jap.,* 1954, **7,** 309–29. (379, 575)

Sawyer, C. H. Triggering of the pituitary by the central nervous system. In T. H. Bullock (Ed.), *Physiological Triggers.* Washington: American Physiological Society, 1957. (558, 584)

Sawyer, C. H. Reproductive behavior. In J. Field, H. W. Magoun and V. E. Hall (Eds.), *Handbook of Physiology.* Vol. II. Section I. *Neurophysiology.* (American Physiological Society) Baltimore: Williams and Wilkins, 1960, 1225–40. (562)

Sawyer, C. H., and Robinson, B. A. Separate hypothalamic areas controlling pituitary gonadotropic function and mating behavior in female cats and rabbits. *J. Clin. Endocrinol.,* 1956, **16,** 914. (557, 583)

Schachter, S. Pain, fear and anger in hypertensives and normotensives: a psychophysiologic study. *Psychosom. Med.,* 1957, **19,** 17–29. (342)

Schachter, S., and Singer, J. E. Cognitive, social and physiological determinants of emotional state. *Psychol. Rev.,* 1962, **69,** 379–399. (343)

Schachter, S., and Wheeler, L. Epinephrine, chlorpromazine and amusement. *J. Abnorm. Soc. Psychol.,* 1962, **65,** 121–28. (343)

Schaeffer, B. H. Strychnine and maze behavior: limited effects of varied concentrations and injection times. *J. Comp. Physiol. Psychol.,* 1968, **66,** 188–92. (473)

Schally, A. V., Redding, T. W., Lucein, H. W., and Meyer, J. Enterogastrone inhibits eating in fasted mice. *Science,* 1967, **157,** 211. (619, 620)

Scheibel, M. E., and Scheibel, A. Structural substrates for integrative patterns in the brain stem reticular core. In H. H. Jasper, L. D. Proctor, R. S. Knighton, S. Roberts, W. C. Noshay, C. William, and R. T. Costello (Eds.), *Reticular Formation of the Brain.* Boston: Little, Brown, 1958, pp. 31–55. (401)

Scheibel, M. E., Scheibel, A., Mollica, A., and Moruzzi, G. Convergence and interaction of afferent impulses on single units of reticular formation. *J. Neurophysiol.,* 1955, **18,** 309–31. (401)

Scheibel, M. E., and Scheibel, A. B. The response of reticular units of repetitive stimuli. *Archives Italian Biology,* 1965, **103,** 279–99. (426)

Schlag, J. D., and Chaillet, F. Thalamic mechanisms involved in cortical desynchronization and recruiting responses. *Electroenceph. Clin. Neurophysiol.,* 1963, **15,** 39–62.

Schmaltz, L. W., and Isaacson, R. L. The effects of preliminary training conditions upon DRL performance in the hippocampectomized rat. *Physiology and Behavior,* 1966, **1,** 175–82. (387, 392)

Schmidt, M. J., and Davenport, J. W. TCAP: Facilitation of learning in hypothyroid rats. *Psychon. Sci.,* 1967, **7,** 185–86. (474)

Schneider, A. M. Effects of unilateral and bilateral spreading depression on water intake. *Psychonomic Science,* 1965, **3,** 287–88. (451)

Schneider, A. M. Retention under spreading depression. A generalization decrement phenomenon. *J. Comp. Physiol. Psychol.,* 1966, **62,** 317–19. (454)

Schneider, A. M. Control of memory by spreading cortical depression: A case for stimulus control. *Psychological Review,* 1967, **74,** 201–15. (451)

Schneider, A. M., and Ebbesen, E. Interhemispheric transfer of lever pressing as stimulus generalization of the effects of spreading depression. *Journal of the Experimental Analysis of Behavior*, 1967, **10**, 193–97. (454)

Schneider, A. M., and Hamburg, M. Interhemisphere transfer with spreading depression: A memory transfer or stimulus generalization phenomenon? *J. Comp. Physiol. Psychol.*, 1966, **62**, 133–36. (452)

Schnieder, A. M., and Kay, H. Spreading depression as a discriminative stimulus for lever pressing. *J. Comp. Physiol. Psychol.*, 1968, **65**, 149–51. (451)

Schneider, A. M., and Sherman, W. Amnesia: a function of the temporal relation of footshock to electroconvulsive shock. *Science*, 1968, **59**, 219–21. (439, 440, 442, 484)

Schneider, G. E. Contrasting visuo-motor functions of tectum and cortex in the golden hamster. *Psychologische Forsching*, 1967, **31**, 52–62. (99)

Schnieden, H. Solution drinking in rats after dehydration and after hemorrhage. *Amer. J. Physiol.*, 1962, **203**, 560–62. (589)

Schouten, J. F. The perception of subjective tones. *Proc. Koninkl. Ned. Akad. Wetenschap.*, 1938, **41**, 1086–93. (137)

Schreiner, L., and Kling, A. Behavioral changes following rhinencephalic injury in cat. *J. Neurophysiol.*, 1953, **16**, 643–58. (375)

Schreiner, L., and Kling, A. Effects of castration on hypersexual behavior induced by rhinencephalic injury in cat. *Arch. Neurol. Psychiat.*, 1954, **72**, 180–86. (373, 374)

Schreiner, L., and Kling, A. Rhinencephalon and behavior. *Am. J. Physiol.*, 1956, **184**, 486–90. (373, 573)

Schulman, J. L., Carleton, J. L., Whitney, G., and Whitehorn, J. C. Effect of glucagon on food intake and body weight in man. *J. Appl. Physiol.*, 1957, **11**, 419–21. (613)

Schulte, A. Transfer und Transpositionsversuche mit Monokular Dressierten Fischen, *Zeit. f. Vergl. Physiol.*, 1957, **39**, 432–76. (448)

Schultze-Westrum, T. G. Social communication by chemical signals in flying phalangers (*Petaurus breviceps papuanus*). In C. Pfaffmann (Ed.), *Olfaction and Taste.* New York:

Rockefeller Univ. Press, 1969, pp. 268–77. (269)

Schwartzbaum, J. G. Changes in reinforcing properties of stimuli following ablation of the amygdaloid complex in monkeys. *J. Comp. Physiol. Psychol.*, 1960, **53**, 388–95. (375)

Schwartzbaum, J. G., and Ward, H. P. An osmotic factor in the regulation of food intake in the rat. *J. Comp. Physiol. Psychol.*, 1958, **51**, 555–60. (625)

Scott, E. M. Self-selection of diet. I. Selection of purified components. *J. Nutrition*, 1946, **31**, 397–406. (635, 636)

Scott, E. M., and Quint, E. Self-selection of diet. III. Appetite for B vitamins. *J. Nutrition*, 1946, **32**, 285–91. (634, 635)

Scott, E. M., and Verney, E. L. Self-selection of diet. V. Appetite for carbohydrates. *J. Nutrition*, 1947, **34**, 401–7. (634)

Scott, E. M., and Verney, E. L. Self-selection and diet. VI. The nature of appetites for B vitamins. *J. Nutrition*, 1947, **34**, 471–80. (634)

Scott, J. W. Brain stimulation reinforcement with distributed practice: Effects of electrode locus, previous experience and stimulus intensity. *J. Comp. Physiol. Psychol.*, 1967, **63**, 175–83. (522)

Scoville, W. B., and Milner, B. Loss of recent memory after bilateral hippocampal lesions. *J. Neurol. Neurosurg. Psychiat.*, 1957, **20**, 11–21. (433)

Sechzer, J. A. Successful interocular transfer of pattern discrimination in "split brain" cats with shock avoidance motivation. *J. Comp. Physiol. Psychol.*, 1964, **58**, 76–83. (446)

Segundo, J. P., Arana, R., and French, J. D. Behavioral arousal by stimulation of the brain in monkey. *J. Neurosurg.*, 1955, **12**, 601–13. (359)

Segundo, J. P., Naquet, and Buser, P. Effects of cortical stimulation on electrocortical activity in monkey. *J. Neurophysiol.*, 1955, **18**, 236–45. (399)

Sekuler, R. W. Spatial and temporal determinants of visual backward masking. *J. Exp. Psychology*, 1965, **70**, 401–6. (110)

Selye, H. The physiology and pathology of exposure to stress. *Acta. Inc. Med. Publ.* (Montreal), 1950. (582)

Selye, H. Stress. *Acta. Inc. Med. Publ.* (Montreal), 1950. (345, 582)

Sem-Jacobsen, C. W., and Torkildsen, A. In E. R. Ramey and D. S. O'Doherty (Eds.), *Electrical Studies on the Unanesthetized Brain.* New York: Hoeber, 1960. (517)

Semmes, J. S., Weinstein, S., Ghent, L., and Teuber, H. L. *Somatosensory Changes after Penetrating Brain Wounds in Man.* Cambridge, Mass.: Harvard Univ. Press, 1960. (240)

Settlage, P. H. The effect of occipital lesions on visually-guided behavior in the monkey. I. Influence of the lesions on final capacities in a variety of problem situations. *J. Comp. Psychol.,* 1939, 27, 93–131. (120)

Seward, J. P., Uyeda, A., and Olds, J. Resistance to extinction following cranial self-stimulation. *J. Comp. Physiol. Psychol.,* 1959, 52, 294–99. (519)

Seward, J. P., Uyeda, A. A., and Olds, J. Reinforcing effect of brain stimulation on runway performance as a function of interval between trials. *J. Comp. Physiol. Psychol.,* 1960, 53, 224–28. (511, 519, 520, 529, 531)

Shandro, N. E., and Schaeffer, B. H. Environment and strychnine: effects on maze behavior. Paper presented at Western Psychological Association Meeting, Vancouver, B.C., 1969. (473)

Sharpless, S., and Jasper, H. H. Habituation of the arousal reaction. *Brain,* 1956, 79, 655–78. (414, 415, 465)

Sharpless, S. K. Reorganization of function in the nervous system—use and disuse. *Annual Review of Physiology,* 1964, 26, 357–88. (487)

Shealy, C. N., and Peele, T. L. Studies on amygdaloid nucleus of cat. *J. Neurophysiol.,* 1957, 20, 125–39. (358, 359)

Sheffield, F. D., and Roby, T. B. Reward value of non-nutritive sweet taste. *J. Comp. Physiol. Psychol.,* 1950, 43, 471–81. (545)

Sheffield, F. D., Wulff, J. J., and Backer, R. Reward value of copulation without sex drive reduction. *J. Comp. Physiol. Psychol.,* 1951, 44, 3–8. (547)

Shelley, W. B., and Arthur, R. P. Studies on Cowhage (Mucuna Pruriens) and Its Pruritogenic Proteinase, Mucumain. *Arch. Dermatol.,* 1955, 72, 399–406. (210)

Sherman, H. Comparative profiles of various strains of rats used in long-term feeding studies. *Lab. Anim. Care,* 1963, 13, 793–807. (617)

Sherrington, C. S. In Schafer, *Text-book of Physiology,* 1900, 2, 782–883. (562)

Sherrington, C. S. *The Integrative Action of the Nervous System.* New Haven: Yale Univ. Press, 1906. (26, 341, 457)

Sherrington, C. *The Integrative Action of the Nervous System.* Cambridge: Cambridge University Press, 1947. (310)

Shuford, E. H., Jr. *Relative acceptability of sucrose and glucose solutions in the white rat.* Doctoral thesis in Psychology, University of Illinois, 1955. (625)

Sidman, H., Stoddard, L. T., and Mohr, J. P. Some additional quantitative observations of immediate memory in a patient with bilateral hippocampal lesions. *Neuropsychologia,* 1968, 6, 245–54. (433)

Sidman, M., Bradv, J. V., Boren, J. J., Conrad, D. G., and Schulman, A. Reward schedules and behavior maintained by intracranial self-stimulation. *Science,* 1955, 122, 830–31. (519, 528)

Siegel, A. C. Deprivation of visual form definition in the ring dove. II. Perceptual motor transfer. *J. Comp. Physiol. Psychol.,* 1953, 46, 249–52. (446)

Sinclair, D. C., and Hinshaw, J. R. Sensory changes in procaine nerve block. *Brain,* 1950a, 73, 224–43. (205)

Sinclair, D. C., and Hinshaw, J. R. Comparison of sensory dissociation produced by procaine and by limb compression. *Brain,* 1950b, 73, 480–98. (205)

Sinclair, D. C., and Hinshaw, J. R. Sensory phenomena in experimental nerve block. *Quart. J. Exp. Psych.,* 1951, 3, 49–72. (205)

Sinclair, D. C., Weddell, G., and Zander, E. The relationship of cutaneous sensibility to neurohistology in the human pinna. *J. Anat.,* 1952, 86, 402–10. (177)

Singer, J. E. Sympathetic activation, drugs and fear. *J. Comp. Physiol. Psychol.,* 1963, 56, 612–15. (343)

Singer, J. J. The effects of atropine upon the female and male sexual behavior of female rats. *Physiol. Behav.*, 1968, 3, 377–78. (560)

Singer, J. J. Hypothalamic control of male and female sexual behavior in female rats. *J. Comp. Physiol. Psychol.*, 1968, 66, 738–42. (567)

Singh, S. D. Habit strength and drug effects. *J. Comp. Physiol. Psychol.*, 1964, 58, 468–69. (478)

Sjöqvist, O. Studies of pain conduction in the trigeminal nerve. *Acta. Psychiat. Scand.*, 1938, Suppl. 17, 1–139. (231)

Sjostrand, F. S. Electron microscopy of the retina. In G. K. Smelser (Ed.), *The Structure of the Eye.* New York: Academic Press, 1961, pp. 1–28. (82)

Skoglund, C. R. Properties of pacinian corpuscles of ulnar and tibial location in cat and fowl. *Acta Physiol. Scand.*, 1960, 50, 385–86. (180)

Slocum, J., Bennett, C. L., and Pool, J. L. The role of prefrontal lobe surgery as a means of eradicating intractable anxiety. *Am. J. Psychiat.*, 1959, 116, 222–28. (365, 381)

Smith, D. E., King, M. B., and Hoebel, B. G. Lateral hypothalamic control of killing: evidence for a cholinoceptive mechanism. *Science*, 1970, 167, 900–901. (352)

Smith, D. F., and Stricker, E. M. The influence of need on the rat's preference for dilute NaCl solutions. *Physiol. Behav.*, 1969, 4, 407–10. (589)

Smith, G. P., and Epstein, A. N. Increased feeding in response to decreased glucose utilization in the rat and monkey. *American Journal of Physiology*, 1970, 217, 1083–87. (592)

Smith, J. C., and Morris, D. D. The effects of atropine sulphate and physostigmine on the conditioned aversion to saccharin solution with X-rays as the unconditioned stimulus. In T. J. Haley and R. S. Snider (Eds.), *Response of the nervous system to ionizing radiation: Second international symposium.* Boston, Massachusetts: Little, Brown, 1964, pp. 662–72. (633)

Smith, Moncrieff, and Duffy, Michael. The effects of intragastric injection of various substances on subsequent barpressing. *J. Comp. Physiol. Psychol.*, 1955, 48, 387–91. (609, 618)

Smith, M. P., and Capretta, P. J. Effects of drive level and experience on the reward value of saccharine solution.

J. Comp. Physiol. Psychol., 1956, 49, 553–57. (546, 638)

Smith, O. A. Stimulation of lateral and medial hypothalamus and food intake in the rat. *Anat. Record*, 1956, 124, 263–64. (624)

Smith, W. K. The results of ablation of the cingular region of the cerebral cortex. *Fed. Proc.*, 1944, 3, 42–43. (379, 380)

Snider, R. S. Interrelations of Cerebellum and Brain Stem. *Ass. Res. Nerv. Rent. Dis. Proc.*, 1952, 30, 267–81. (400)

Snowdon, C. T. Motivation, regulation, and the control of meal parameters with oral and intragastric feeding. *J. Comp. Physiol. Psychol.*, 1969, 69, 91–100. (634)

Sodetz, Frank J., and Bunnell, B. N. Septal ablation and the social behavior of the golden hamster. *Physiol. and Behav.*, 1970, 5, 79–88.

Sokolov, E. N. Neuronal models and the orienting influence. In M. A. B. Brazier (Ed.), *Central Nervous System and Behavior.* New York: Josiah Macey, Jr. Foundation, 1960, 187–239. (465)

Sollenberger, R. T., and Hamilton, J. M. The effect of testosterone propionate upon the sexual behavior of castrated male guinea pigs. *J. Comp. Psychol.*, 1939, 28, 81–92. (553)

Solley, C. M. Influence of head tilt, body tilt, and practice on reduction of error in perception of the postural vertical. *J. Gen. Psychol.*, 1960, 62, 69–74. (333)

Solomon, R. L., and Wynne, C. C. Traumatic avoidance learning: the principles of anxiety conservation and partial irreversibility. *Psych. Rev.*, 1954, 61, 353–85. (345)

Soulairac, A., and Soulairac, M. L. Effets de lésion hypothalamiques sur le comportement sexuel et le tractus genital du rat male. *Ann. Endocr. Par*, 1956, 17(6), 731–45. (557, 558)

Spameni, P., and Lunedei, A. Sui reflessi. *Rev. Clin. Med.*, 1927, 28, 758. (249)

Spear, N. E., Klein, S. B., and Riley, E. P. The Kamin effect as "state dependent learning:" Memory retrieval failure in the rat. *J. Comp. Physiol. Psychol*, 1971, 74, 416–25. (348)

Spear, N. E. Comparison of the reinforcing effect of brain stimulation on Skinner box, runway, and maze performance. *J. Comp. Physiol. Psychol.*, 1962, **55**, 379–84. (521)

Spencer, W. A., Thompson, R. F., and Neilsen, D. R., Jr. Response decrement of the flexion reflex in the acute spinal cat and transient restoration by strong stimuli *Journal of Neurophysiology*, 1966a, **29**, 221–39. (416, 425, 457)

Spencer, W. A., Thompson, R. F., and Neilsen, D. R., Jr. Alterations in responsiveness of ascending and reflex pathways activated by iterated cutaneous afferent volleys. *Journal of Neurophysiology*, 1966b, **29**, 240–52. (416, 425, 457)

Spencer, W. A., Thompson, R. F., and Neilson, D. R., Jr. Decrement of ventral root electro-tonus and intracellularly recorded PSP's produced by iterated cutaneous afferent volleys. *Journal of Neurophysiology*, 1966c, **29**, 253–73. (416, 425, 457)

Sperry, R. W. The problem of central nervous reorganization after nerve regeneration and muscle transposition. *Quart. Rev. Biol.*, 1945, **20**, 311–69. (337)

Sperry, R. W. Physiological plasticity and brain circuit theory. In H. F. Harlow and C. N. Woolsey (Eds.), *Biological and Biochemical Bases of Behavior.* Madison: Univ. of Wisconsin Press, 1958. (120)

Sperry, R. W. Corpus callosum and interhemispheric transfer in the monkey (Macaca mulatta). *Anat. Rec.*, 1958, **131**, 297. (447)

Sperry, R. W. Preservation of high order function in isolated somatic cortex in callosum sectioned cats. *J. Neurophysiol.*, 1959, **22**, 78–87. (448)

Sperry, R. W., and Clark, E. Interocular transfer of visual discrimination habits in a teleost fish. *Physiol. Zool.*, 1949, **22**, 37–78. (448)

Sperry, R. W., Myers, R. E., and Schrier, A. M. Perceptual capacity of the isolated visual cortex in the cat. *Quart. J. Exper. Psychol.*, 1960, **12**, 65–71. (448)

Sperry, R. W., Stamm, J. S., and Miner, N. Relearning tests for interocular transfer following division of optic chiasma and corpus callosum in cats. *J. Comp. Physiol. Psychol.*, 1956, **49**, 529–33. (446, 447)

Spiegel, E. A., Kletzkin, M., and Szekely, E. G. Pain reactions upon stimulation

of the tectum mesencephali. *J. Neuropath.*, 1954, **13**, 212–20. (351)

Spiegel, E. A., Miller, H. R., and Oppenheimer, M. J. Forebrain and rage reactions. *J. neurophysiol.*, 1940, 3, 538–48. (373, 377)

Spiegel, E. A., and Wycis, H. T. Physiological and psychological results of thalamotomy. *Proc. Roy. Soc. Med. Suppl.*, 1949, **42**, 84–93. (372)

Spiegel, E. A., and Wycis, H. T. Stimulation of the brain stem and basal ganglia in man. In D. E. Sheer (Ed.), *Electrical Stimulation of the Brain.* Austin: University of Texas, 1961, 487–98. (220, 231, 232, 357)

Spiegel, E. A., Wycis, H. T., Freed, H., and Orchnick, C. The central mechanism of the emotions (Experiences with circumscribed thalamic lesions). *Am. J. Psychiat.*, 1951, **108**, 426–32. (232, 372)

Spies, G. Food versus intracranial self-stimulation reinforcement in food deprived rats. *J. Comp. Physiol. Psychol.*, 1965, **60**, 153–57. (528)

Spieth, W., Curtis, J. F., and Webster, J. C. Responding to one of two simultaneous messages. *J. Acoust. Soc. Amer.*, 1954, **26**, 391–96. (417)

Spong, P., Maider, M., and Lindsley, D. B. Selective attentiveness and cortical evoked responses to visual and auditory stimuli. *Science*, **148**, 395–97.

Sprague, D. M. Stimulation of reticular formation in intact unanesthetized and decerebrated cats. *Fed. Proc.*, 1953, **12**, 137. (400)

Sprague, J. M. Interaction of cortex and superior colliculus in mediation of visually guided·behavior in cat. *Science*, 1966, **153**, 1544–47. (100)

Sprague, J. M., Chambers, W. W., and Stellar, E. Attentive, affective, and adaptive behavior in the cat. *Science*, 1961, **133**, 165–73. (409)

Sprague, J. M., and Meikle, T. H., Jr. The role of the superior colliculus in visually guided behavior. *Experimental Neurology*, 1965, **11**, 115–46. (99)

Squire, L. R., Glick, S. D., and Goldfarb, J. Relearning at different times after training as affected by centrally and peripherally acting cholinergic drugs in the mouse. *J. comp. Physiol. Psychol.*, 1971, **74**, 41–45. (490, 491)

Squire, L. R., and Liss, P. H. Control of memory by spreading cortical depression: a critique of stimulus control. *Psychological Review*, 1968, **75**, 347–52. (454)

Stamm, J. S. The functions of the median cerebral cortex in maternal behavior of rats. *J. Comp. Physiol. Psychol.*, 1955, **48**, 347–56. (577)

Stamm, J. S., and Pribram, K. H. Effects of epileptogenic lesions in frontal cortex on learning and retention in monkeys. *J. Neurophysiol.*, 1960, **23**, 552–63. (462, 463)

Stamm, J. S., and Sperry, R. W. Function of corpus callosum in contralateral transfer of somesthetic discrimination in cats. *J. Comp. Physiol. Psychol.*, 1957, **50**, 138–43. (447)

Stark, P., and Boyd, E. S. Effects of cholinergic drugs on hypothalamic self-stimulation rates in dogs. *American Journal of Physiology*, 1963, **205**, 745–48. (517)

Starr, A., and Wernick, J. S. Olivo-cochlear bundle stimulation: Effects on spontaneous and tone-evoked activities of single units in cat cochlear nucleus. *J. Neurophysiol.*, 1968, **31**, 549–64. (167)

Starzl, T. E., Taylor, C. W., and Magoun, H. W. Collateral afferent excitation of reticular formation of brain stem. *J. Neurophysiol.*, 1951, **14**, 479–96. (399, 401)

Steggerda, F. R. Observations on the water intake in an adult man with dysfunctioning salivary glands. *Am. J. Physiol.*, 1941, **119**, 409. (594)

Stein, D. G., Brink, J. J., and Patterson, A. H. Magnesium pemoline: facilitation of maze learning when administered in pure dimethylsulfoxide. *Life Sciences*, 1968, **7**, 147–53. (474)

Stein, D. G., and Kimble, D. P. Effects of hippocampal lesions and posttrial strychnine administration on maze behavior in the rat. *J. Comp. Physiol. Psychol.*, 1966, **62**, 243–49. (473)

Stein, D. G., and Kirby, R. J. The effects of training on passive avoidance deficits in rats with hippocampal lesions: A reply to Isaacson, Alton, Bauer, and Swart. *Psychonomic Science*, 1967, **7**, 7–8. (392)

Stein, H. H., and Yellin, R. O. Pemoline and magnesium hydroxide: lack of effect on RNA and protein synthesis. *Science*, 1967, **157**, 96–97. (474)

Stein, L. Secondary reinforcement established with subcortical stimulation. *Science*, 1958, **127**, 466–67. (531)

Stein, L. Reciprocal action of reward and punishment. In R. G. Heath (Ed.), *The Role of Pleasure in Behavior*. New York: Hoeber, 1964. (545)

Steinbrecht, R. A. Comparative morphology of olfactory receptors. In C. Pfaffmann (Ed.), *Olfaction and Taste*. New York: Rockefeller Univ. Press, 1969, pp. 3–21. (271)

Steinhausen, W. Uber den Nachweis der Bewegung der Cupola in der intakten Bogengansampulle des Labyrinths bei der natürlichen rotatirischen und calorischen Reizung. *Pflüg. Arch. Ges. Physiol.*, 1931, **228**, 322–28. (320)

Stellar, E. The physiology of motivation. *Psychol. Rev.*, 1954, **61**, 5–22. (620)

Stellar, E., and McCleary, R. A. Food preferences as a function of the method of measurement. *Amer. Psychologist*, 1952, **7**, 256. (613)

Stellar, Eliot, and Morgan, Clifford, T. The roles of experience and deprivation in the onset of hoarding behavior in the rat. *J. Comparative Psych.*, 1943, **36**, 47–55.

Sterling, P., and Wickelgren, B. G. Visual receptive fields in the superior colliculus of the cat. *Journal Neurophysiology*, 1969, **32**, 1–15. (100, 101)

Sterman, M. B., and Clemente, C. D. Forebrain inhibitory mechanisms: synchronization induced by basal forebrain stimulation. *Exp. Neurol.*, 1962a, **6**, 91–102. (405, 406, 408, 410)

Sterman, M. B., and Clemente, C. D. Forebrain inhibitroy mechanisms: sleep patterns induced by basal forebrain stimulation in the behaving cat. *Exp. Neurol.*, 1962b, **6**, 103–17. (405, 406)

Stern, J. J. Neonatal castration, androstenedione, and the mating behavior of the male rat. *J. Comp. Physiol. Psychol.*, 1969, **69**, 608–12. (569)

Stone, C. P. The retention of copulatory ability in male rats following castration. *J. Comp. Psychol.*, 1927, **7**, 369–87. (554)

Stone, C. P. Sex drive. In E. Allen (Ed.), *Sex and Internal Secretions*. Baltimore: Williams and Wilkins, 1939, pp. 1213–62. (554, 577)

Stratton, L. O., and Petrinovich, L. F.

Post-trial injection of an anticholinesterase drug and maze learning in two strains of mice. *Psychopharmacologia*, 1963, **5**, 47–54. (485)

Streb, J. M., and Smith, K. Frontal lobotomy and the elimination of conditioned anxiety in the rat. *J. Comp. Physiol. Psychol.*, 1955, **48**, 126–29. (392)

Stricker, E. M. Extracellular fluid volume and thirst. *Amer. J. Physiology*, 1966, **211**, 232–38. (589)

Stricker, E. M., and Wolf, G. Hypovolemic thirst in comparison with thirst produced by hyperosmolarity. *Physiol. Behav.*, 1967a, **2**, 33–37. (590)

Stricker, E. M., and Wolf, G. The effects of hypovolemia on drinking in rats with lateral hypothalamic damage. *Proc. Soc. Exp. Biol. Med.*, 1967b, **124**, 816–20. (593)

Stricker, E. M., and Wolf, G. Behavioral control of intravascular fluid volume: thirst and sodium appetite. *Ann. N. Y. Acad. Sci.*, 1969, **157**, 553–67. (589, 590)

Strughold, H., and Karbe, M. Vitale Färbung des Auges und experimentelle Untersuchung der gefärbten Nervenelemente. *Ztschr. Biol.*, 1925, **83**, 297–308 (179)

Strumwasser, F., and Rosenthal, S. Prolonged and patterned direct extracellular stimulation of single neurons. *Am. J. Physiol.*, 1960, **198**, 405–13. (464)

Stunkard, A. J., Van Itallie, T. B., and Reis, B. B. The mechanism of satiety: effect on glucagon on gastric hunger contractions in man. *Proc. Soc. Exper. Biol. Med.*, 1955, **89**, 258–61. (592, 619)

Stunkard, A. J., and Wolff, H. G. Correlation of arteriovenous glucose differences, gastric hunger contractions and the experience of hunger in man. *Fed. Proc.*, 1954, **13**, 147. (619)

Suboski, M. D., Marquis, H. A., Black, M., and Platenius, P. Adrenal and amygdala function in the incubation of aversively conditioned responses. *Physiol. and Behav.*, 1970, **5**, 283–89. (347)

Suga, N. Recovery cycles and responses to frequency modulated tone pulses in auditory neurons of echo-locating bats. *J. Physiol.*, 1964, **175**, 50–80. (159)

Svaetichin, G., and MacNichol, E. F.,

Jr. Retinal mechanisms for chromatic and achromatic vision. *Ann. N. Y. Acad. Sci.*, 1958, **74**, 404. (89)

Swann, H. G. Function of brain in olfaction; Results of destruction of olfactory and other nervous structures upon discrimination of odors. *J. Comp. Neurol.*, 1934, **59**, 175–201. (283)

Swann, H. G. The function of the brain in olfaction, the effects of large cortical lesions on olfactory discrimination. *Amer. J. Physiol.*, 1935, **111**, 257–62. (283)

Seeet, W. H. Trigeminal injection with radiographic control, technique and results. *J.A.M.A.*, 1950, **142**, 392–96. (229)

Sweet, W. H. Pain. In J. Field, H. W. Magoun and V. E. Hall (Eds.), *Handbook of Physiology.* Vol. I. Section I. *Neurophysiology.* (American Physiological Society) Baltimore: Williams and Wilkins, 1959, pp. 459–502. (227, 357)

Sydnor, K. L., and Sayers, G. Blood and pituitary ACTH in intact and adrenalectomized rats after stress. *Endocrinology*, 1954, **55**, 621–36. (347)

T

Tagiamonte, A., Tagiamonte, P., Gessa, G. L., and Brodie, B. B. Compulsive sexual activity induced by *p*-chlorophenylalanine in normal and pinealectomized male rats. *Science*, 1969, **166**, 1433–35. (555, 567)

Talbot, W. H., Darian-Smith, I., Kornhuber, H. H., and Mountcastle, V. B. The sense of flutter-vibration: comparison of the human capacity with response patterns of mechanoreceptive afferents from the monkey hand. *J. Neurophysiol.*, 1968, **31**, 301–34. (213)

Talland, G. A. Improvement of sustained attention with Cylert. *Psychonomic Science*, 1966, **6**, 493–94. (430)

Tanzi, E. Sulla presenza di cellule gangliari nelle radici spinali anteriori del gatto. *Riv. sper. di Freniatria*, 1893, **19**, 373–77.

Tapp, J. T. Reversible cortical depression and avoidance behavior in the rat. *J. Comp. Physiol. Psychol.*, 1962, **55**, 306–8. (449)

Tasaki, I. Nerve impulses in individual auditory nerve fibers of guinea pig. *J. Neurophysiol.*, 1954, **17**, 97–122. (144)

Tasaki, I. Hearing. *Annual Rev. Physiol.*, 1957, 19, 417–38. (142)

Tasaki, I. Demonstration of two stable states of the nerve membrane in potassium-rich media. *J. Physiol.*, 1959, 148, 306–31.

Tasaki, I., and Davis, H. Electric responses of individual nerve elements in cochlear nucleus to sound stimulation (guinea pig). *J. Neurophysiol.*, 1955, 18, 151–58. (143)

Taub, E. Deafferentiation. Paper read to conference on Adaptation. Massachusetts Institute of Technology, June, 1965. (332)

Tauc, L. Site of origin and propagation of spike in the giant neuron of *Aplysia*. *J. Gen. Physiol.*, 1962, 45, 1077–97. (276)

Teitelbaum, H., and Milner, P. Activity changes following partial hippocampal lesions in rats. *J. comp. physiol Psychol.*, 1963, 56, 284–89. (390)

Teitelbaum, P. Sensory control of hypothalamic hyperphagia. *J. Comp. Physiol. Psychol.*, 1955, 48, 156–63. (630)

Teitelbaum, P. Random and food-directed activity in hyperphagic and normal rats. *J. Comp. Physiol. Psychol.*, 1957, 50, 486–90. (623)

Teitelbaum, P. Disturbances in feeding and drinking behavior after hypothalaic lesions. In *Nebraska Symposium on Motivation*. Lincoln: University of Nebraska Press, 1961. (599, 622)

Teitelbaum, P. Motivational correlates of hypothalamic activity. *Excerpta Medica*, 1962, 47, 592. (697, 704)

Teitelbaum, P., and Epstein, A. N. The lateral hypothalamic syndrome. *Psychol. Rev.*, 1962, 69, 74–90. (599)

Teitelbaum, P. Appetite, *Proc. Am. phil. Soc.*, 1964, 108, 464–72. (623)

Tenen, S. S., and Miller, N. E. Strength of electrical stimulation of lateral hypothalamus, food deprivation and tolerance for quinine in food. *J. Comp. Physiol. Psychol.*, 1964, 58, 55–62. (601)

Terzian, H., and Dalle Ore, G. Syndrome of Klüver and Bucy reproduced in man by bilateral removal of the temporal lobes. *Neurology*, 1955, 5, 373–80. (379, 575)

Terzuolo, C. A., and Bullock, T. H. Diverse forms of activity in the somata of spontaneous and integrating ganglion cells. *Arch. Ital. Biol.*, 1958, 96, 117–34. (18)

Terzuolo, C., and Terzian, H. Cerebellar increase of postural tonus after deafferentation and labyrinthectomy. *J. Neurophysiol.*, 1953, 16, 551–61. (316)

Teuber, H. L. *Visual Field Defects after Penetrating Missile Wounds of the Brain*. Cambridge: Howard U. Press, 1960.

Thetford, P. E., and Guedry, F. E., Jr. The postural vertical in unilaterally labyrinthectomized individuals. *U.S. Naval Sch. Aviat. Med. Res. Rep.*, 1952, Proj. No. NM 001 063.01.26 (Jt. Rep. No. 26). (333)

Thomas, G. J., and Slotnick, B. Effects of lesions in the cingulum on maze learning and avoidance conditioning in the rat. *J. Comp. Physiol. Psychol.*, 1962, 55, 1085–91. (385)

Thomas, G. J., and Slotnick, B. M. Impairment of avoidance responding by lesions in cingulate cortex in rats depends on food drive. *J. Comp. Physiol. Psychol.*, 1963, 56, 959–64. (384, 385)

Thompson, J. C., and Blount, R. F. The age of beginning reactivity of the pituitary-adrenocortical system to stress in the mouse. *Endocrinology*, 1954, 54, 620–26. (582)

Thompson, J. M., Woolsey, C. N., and Talbot, S. A. Visual areas I and II of cerebral cortex of rabbit. *J. Neurophysiol.*, 1950, 13, 277–88. (106)

Thompson, R. Retention of a brightness discrimination following neocortical damage in the rat. *J. Comp. Physiol. Psychol.*, 1960, 53, 212–15. (119)

Thompson, R. Thalamic structures critical for retention of an avoidance conditioned response in rats. *J. Comp. Physiol. Psychol.*, 1963, 56, 261–67. (389)

Thompson, R., and Dean, W. A. A further study on the retroactive effects of ECS. *J. Comp. Physiol. Psychol.*, 1955, 48, 488–91. (435)

Thompson, R., and Pryer, R. S. The effect of anoxia on the retention of a discrimination habit. *J. Comp. Physiol. Psychol.*, 1956, 49, 297–300. (435)

Thompson, R. W. Transfer of avoidance learning between normal and functionally decorticate states. *J. Comp. Physiol. Psychol.*, 1964, 57, 321–25. (448)

Thomson, C. W., McGaugh, J. L., Smith, C. E., Hudspeth, W. J., and Westbrook, W. H. Strain differences in the retroactive effects of electroconvulsive shock on maze learning. *Can. J. Psychol.*, 1961, **15**, 69–74. (435, 436)

Thomson, C. W., and Porter, P. B. Need reduction and primary reinforcement: maze learning by sodium-deprived rats for a subthreshold saline reward. *J. comp. physiol. Psychol.*, 1953, **46**, 281–87. (548)

Thorek, M. Experimental investigation of the role of the Leydig, seminiferous and Sertoli cells and effects of testicular transplantation. *Endocrinology*, 1924, **8**, 61–90. (554)

Thorndike, E. L. Expectation. *Psychol. Rev.*, 1946, **53**, 277–81. (508)

Thunberg, T. Untersuchungen über die bei Einer Einzelnen Momentanen Haut Reizung Aufretenden Zwei Stechenden Empfindungen. *Skand. Arch. Physiol.*, 1902, **12**, 399–442. (204, 205)

Thurlow, W. R., Gross, N. B., Kemp, E. H., and Lowy, K. Microelectrode studies of neural auditory activity of cat. I. Inferior colliculus. *J. Neurophysiol.*, 1951, **14**, 289–304. (158)

Tinbergen, N., and Perdeck, A. C. On the stimulus situation releasing the begging response in the newly hatched herring gull chick (Larus argentatus Pont.). *Behavior*, 1950, **3**, 1–39. (625)

Tonndorf, J. Time frequency analysis along the partition of cochlear models: a modified place concept. *J. Acoust. Soc. Amer.*, 1962, **34**, 1337–50. (132)

Tow, P. M., and Armstrong, R. W. Anterior cingulectomy in schizophrenia and other psychotic disorders; clinical results. *J. Ment. Sc.*, 1954, **100**, 46–61. (380)

Tow, P. M., and Whitty, C. W. M. Personality changes after operations on the cingulate gyrus in man. *J. Neurol. Neurosurg. Psychiat.*, 1953, **16**, 186–93. (380, 381)

Towbin, E. J. Gastric distension as a factor in the satiation of thirst in esophagustomized dogs. *Am. J. Physiol.*, 1949, **159**, 533–41. (605, 606)

Travis, R. P., and Sparks, D. L. The influence of unilateral and bilateral spreading depression during learning upon subsequent relearning. *J. Comp. Physiol. Psychol.*, 1963, **56**, 56–59. (449)

Treisman, A. M. Contexual cues in selective listening. *Quart. J. Exp. Psychol.*, 1960, **12**, 242–48. (419)

Trevarthen, C. B. Simultaneous learning of two conflicting problems by split brain monkeys. *Am. Psychol.*, 1960, **15**, 485. (447)

Trevarthen, C. B. Two mechanisms of vision in Primates. *Psychologische Forschung*, 1968, **31**, 299–337. (97, 98)

Trincker, D. E. W. The transformation of mechanical stimulus into nervous excitation by the labyrinthine receptors. In *Biological Receptor Mechanisms, Symp. Soc. Exp. Biol.*, No. 16. Cambridge: Cambridge University Press, 1962. (323)

Trotter, W. The insulation of the nervous system. *Brit. Med. J.*, 1926, **2**, 103–7. (203)

Trotter, W., and Davis, H. M. Experimental studies on the innervation of the skin. *J. Physiol.*, 1908–9, **38**, 134–246. (203)

Trowill, Y. A., Panksepp, J., and Gandelman, R. An incentive model of rewarding brain stimulation. *Psychological Review*, 1969, **76**, 264–81. (545)

Troxler, J. Über das Verschwinden gegebener gegenstände innerhalb unsers gesichtskreises. *Ophthalmologische Bibliothek*, Vol. 2, 51–53, Himly, K., and Schmidt, J. A. (Eds.). Jena, 1804. (115)

Tsang, Y. C. Hunger motivation in gastrectomized rats. *J. Comp. Psychol.*, 1938, **26**, 1–17. (594)

Tsuchitani, C., and Boudreau, J. C. Single unit analysis of cat superior olive S segment with tonal stimuli. *J. Neurophysiol.*, 1966, **29**, 684–97. (147, 152)

Tsuchitani, C., and Boudreau, J. C. Encoding of stimulus frequency and intensity by cat superior olive S segment cells. *J. Acoust. Soc. Am.*, 1967, **42**, 794–805. (160)

Tunturi, A. R. Further afferent connections to the acoustic cortex of the dog. *Am. J. Physiol.*, 1945, **144**, 389–94. (156)

U

Ulrich, J. L. The distribution of effort in learning in the white rat. *Behavioral Monographs*, 1915, **10**, (No. 2). (522)

Ungar, G. Molecular neurobiology: reflections on the first ten years of a new science. *J. Biol. Psychol.*, 1969, **11**(2), 6–9. (476)

Ungerer, A. Effects comparés de la puromycine et de *Datura stramonium* sur la rétention d'un apprentissage instrumental chez la souris. *Comptes Rendus Academie Sciences Serie D.*, 1969, **269**, 910–13. (482)

Ungerer, A., Spitz, S., and Chapouthier, G. Sur les polypeptides toxiques impliqués par Flexner dans l'effacement de la memoire par la puromycine. *C.R. Adac. Sci, Ser. D.*, 1969, **268**, 2472–75. (481)

Ursin, H. The effect of amygdaloid lesions on flight and defense behavior in cats. *Exp. Neurol.*, 1965a, **11**, 64–79. (374)

Ursin, H. Effect of amygdaloid lesions on avoidance behavior and visual discrimination in cats. *Exper. Neurol.*, 1965b, **11**, 298–317. (390)

Ursin, H., and Kaada, B. R. Functional localization within the amygdaloid complex in the cat. *EEG Clin. Neurophysiol.*, 1960, **12**, 1–20. (358, 359, 361)

Ursin, R., Ursin, H., and Olds, J. Self-stimulation of hippocampus in rats. *J. Comp. Physiol. Psychol.*, 1966, **61**, 353–59. (517)

V

Vaffe, J. H., and Sharpless, S. K. Pharmacological denervation supersensitivity in the central nervous system: A theory of physical dependence. In A. Wikler (Ed.), *The Addictive States.* (Proceedings of the Association for Research in Nervous and Mental Disease) Vol. 4. Pp. 226–43. Baltimore: Williams and Wilkins Co., 1968.

Valbo, A. B. Slowly adapting muscle receptors in man. *Acta Physiol. Scand.*, 1970, **78**, 315–33. (297)

Valenstein, E. S. The anatomical locus of reinforcement. In E. Stellar and J. M. Sprague (Eds.), *Progress in Physiological Psychology.* New York: Academic Press, 1966. (517, 522)

Valenstein, E. S., Cox, V. C., and Kakolewski, J. W. Polydipsia elicited by the synergistic action of a saccharin and glucose solution. *Science*, 1967, **157**, 552–54. (519)

Valenstein, E. S., Cox, V. C., and Kakolewski, J. H. Modification of motivated behavior elicited by electri-

cal stimulation of the hypothalamus. *Science*, 1968, **159**, 1119–21. (602, 603)

Valenstein, E. S., Riss, W., and Young, W. C. Experiential and genetic factors in the organization of sexual behavior in male guinea pigs. *J. Comp. Physiol. Psychol.*, 1955, **48**, 397–403. (571)

Valenstein, E. S., and Valenstein, T. On the interaction of positive and negative reinforcing neural systems. *Science*, 1964, **145**, 1456–58. (517)

Van Balen, A. Th. M. The influence of suppression on the flicker ERG. *Documenta ophthalmologica*, 1964. (440, 446)

Vanderwolf, C. H. Effect of combined medial thalamic and septal lesions on active-avoidance behavior. *J. Comp. Physiol. Psychol.*, 1964, **58**, 31–37. (389)

Vanderwolf, C. H. Medial thalamic functions in voluntary behavior. *Canad. J. Psychol.*, 1962, **16**, 318–30. (383, 389)

Vanderwolf, C. H. Improved shuttle-box performance following electroconvulsive shock. *J. Comp. Physiol. Psychol.*, 1963, **56**, 983–86. (384, 389)

Van Deventer, J. M., and Ratner, S. C. Variables affecting the frequency of response of planaria to light. *J. Comp. Physiol. Psychol.*, 1964, **57**, 407–11. (475)

Van Itallie, T. B., Beaudoin, R., and Mayer, J. Arteriovenous glucose differences, metabolic hypoglycemia and food intake in man. *J. Clin. Nutr.*, 1953, **1**, 208–16.

Vaughn, E., and Fisher, A. E. Male sexual behavior induced by intracranial electrical stimulation. *Science*, 1962, **137**, 758–60. (561)

Verger, H. Sur une modification du scheme de Lemaire pour la conception physiologique de réflexe viscuso-sensitil de MacKensie. *Gaz. Sci. Med.*, 1927, **43**, 419. (249)

Victor, M. Observations on the amnestic syndrome in man and its anatomical basis. In M. A. B. Brazier (Ed.), *Brain Function II: RNA and Brain Function; Memory and Learning.* Berkeley: University of California Press, 1964. (430)

Villablanca, J. The electrocorticogram in the chronic cerveau isole cat. *Electroencephalography and Clinical Neurophysiology*, 1965, **19**, 576–86. (399)

Vince, M. A. Corrective movements in a control task. *Quart. J. Exp. Psychol.*, 1948, 1, 85–103. (305)

Vinogradova, O. S. Dynamic classification of the reaction of hippocampal neurons to sensory stimulation. *Zhurnal Vysskei Nervnoi Deyatel' Nosti imeni I. P. Pavlova*, 1965, Vol. 15, 500; *Federation Proceedings, Translation Supplement*, 1966, Vol. 25, T397-T403. (426)

Vinogradova, O. S. Investigation of habituations in the single neurons of caudate nucleus. *Journal of Higher Nervous Activity*, 1968, 8, 671–80. (426)

von Baumgarten, R. J. Plasticity in the nervous system at the unitary level. In F. O. Schmitt (Ed.), *The Neurosciences: Second study program.* New York: Rockefeller University Press, 1970. Pp. 260–71. (458)

Von Economo, C. *Encephalitis Lethargica.* Translated by K. O. Newman, Oxford, 1931. (364, 410)

Von Euler, C., and Holmgren, B. The role of hypothalamo-hypophysial connexions in thyroid section. *J. Physiol.*, 1956, 131, 137–46. (585)

Von Frey, M. Beiträge zur Sinnesphysiologie des Haut. *Math-Phys. Cl.*, Ber. Sächs. Gessellsch. Wiss., Leipzig, 1895, 47, 166–84. (174, 215)

Von Frey, M. Zur Physiologie der Druckempfindung. *Arch. Neerl. de Physiol.*, La Haye, 1922, 7, 142–45. (209)

Von Frey, M., and Goldman, A. Der Zeitliche Verlang der Einstellung bei den Druckempfindungen. *Z. Biol.*, 1915, 65, 183–202. (206)

Von Frey, M., and Kiesow, F. Ueber die Function der Tast Körperchen. *Z. Psychol.*, 1899, 20, 126–63. (205)

Von Holst, E., and Mittelstedt, H. Das Reafferenzprinzip. *Naturwibs*, 1950, 37, 464–76. (339)

Von Monakow, C. Ueber die localisation *Zeitschr. & Nervenheik*, 1908 s., 36, 124. (231)

Von Skramlick, E. Psychophysiologie der Tastsinne. *Arch. Ges. Psychol.*, 1937, Ergänzungsbd. 4. (205)

Voots, R. J. Periodicity pitch and masking in pathologic ears. *J. Acoust. Soc. Am.*, 1962, 34, 739 (A). (138)

Voronin, L. G., and Sokolov, E. N. Cortical mechanisms of the orienting reflex and its relation to the conditioned reflex. In H. H. Jasper and G. D. Smirnov (Eds.), *The Moscow Colloquim on EEG and Higher Nervous Activity. EEG clin. Neurophysiol.*, Suppl. 13, 1960, 335–46. (414, 415, 420)

W

Wagner, H. G., MacNichol, E. F., Jr., and Wolbarsht, M. L. The response properties of single ganglion cells in the goldfish retina. *J. Gen. Physiol.*, 1960, 43, 45–62. (90)

Wald, G. On the mechanism of the visual threshold and visual adaptation. *Science*, 1954, 119, 887–92. (80)

Wald, G. The photoreceptor process in vision. In J. Field, H. W. Magoun and V. E. Hall (Eds.), *Handbook of Physiology.* Vol. I. (American Physiological Society) Baltimore: Williams and Wilkins, 1959. (83, 85)

Wald, G., Brown, P. K., and Gibbons, I. R. The problem of visual excitation. *J. of the Optical Society of America*, 1963, 53, 20–35. (82)

Walker, A. E. Projection of medial geniculate body to cerebral cortex in macaque monkey. *J. Anat.*, 1937, 71, 319–31. (158)

Walker, A. E., Thomson, A. F., and McQueen, J. D. Behavior and the temporal rhinencephalon in the monkey. *Bull., Johns Hopkins Hosp.*, 1953, 93, 65–93. (373)

Wall, P. D. Two transmission systems for skin sensations. In W. Rosenblith (Ed.), *Sensory Communication.* New York: M.I.T. Press and John Wiley & Sons, 1961, 475–96. (228, 229)

Wall, P. D., and Taub, A. Four aspects of trigeminal nucleus and a paradox. *J. Neurophysiol.*, 1962, 25, 110–26. (231)

Wall, P. D. Cord cells responding to touch, damage, and temperature of skin. *J. Neurophysiol.*, 1960, 23, 197–210. (171, 180, 196, 197, 229)

Wall, P. D., and Cronly-Dillon, J. Pain, itch and vibration. *A.M.A. Arch. Neurol.*, 1960, 2, 365–75. (230)

Walker, A. E. Central representation pain. *Proc. Res. Nerv. Ment. Dis.*, 1943, 23, 63–85. (232, 244, 245, 246)

Walsh, R. R. Olfactory bulb potentials evoked by electrical stimulation of the contralateral bulb. *Amer. J. Physiol.,* 1959, **196**, 327–29. (281)

Walzl, E. M. Representation of cochlea in cerebral cortex. *Laryngoscope,* 1947. **57**, 778–87. (158)

Wangensteen, O. H., and Carlson, A. J. Hunger sensations of a patient after total gastrectomy. *Proc. Soc. Exp. Biol. Med.,* 1931, **28**, 545–57. (594)

Warburton, D. M., and Groves, P. M. The effects of scopolamine on habituation of acoustic startle in rats. *Commun. Behav. Biol.,* 1969. (486)

Ward, A. A. The cingular gyrus: area 24. *J. Neurophysiol.,* 1948, **11**, 13–23. (379).

Ward, H. P. Basal tegmental self-stimulation after septal ablation in rats. *Archives of Neurology,* 1960, **3**, 158–62. (517)

Ward, H. P. Tegmental self-stimulation after amygdaloid ablation. *Archives of Neurology,* 1961, **4**, 657–69. (517)

Ward, J. W. The influence of posture on responses elicitable from the cortex cerebri of cats. *J. Neurophysiology,* 1938, **1**, 463–75. (335)

Ward, J. W. Motor phenomena elicited in the unanesthetized animal by electrical stimulation of the cerebral cortex. *A Res. Nerv. & Ment. Dis. Proc.,* 1952, **30**, 223–37. (335)

Ward, J. W., and Hester, R. W. Intracranial self-stimulation in cats surgically deprived of autonomic outflows. *J. Comp. Physiol. Psychol.,* 1969, **67**, 336–43. (518)

Warren, D. C., and Scott, H. M. Influence of light on ovulation in the fowl. *J. Exp. Zool.,* 1936, **74**, 137–56. (581)

Warren, R. P., and Aronson, Z. R. Sexual behavior in adult male hamsters castrated-adrenalectomized prior to puberty. *J. Comp. Physiol. Psychol.,* 1957, **50**, 475–80. (553)

Warrington, E. K., and Weiskrantz, L. Organisational aspects of memory in amnesic patients. *Neuropsychologia,* 1971, **9**, 67–73. (433)

Wasden, R. E., Reid, L. D., and Porter, P. B. Overnight performance decrement with intracranial reinforcement. *Psychological Reports,* 1965, **16**, 653–58. (522)

Watanabe, T. Electric responses of auditory neurons in cat to sound stimulation. *J. Neurophysiol.,* 1958, **21**, 569–88. (161)

Watanabe, T., Liao, T-T., and Katsuki, Y. Neuronal response patterns in the superior olivary complex of the cat to sound stimulation. *Jap. J. Physiol.,* 1968, **18**, 267–87. (159, 161)

Waterhouse, I. K. Effects of prefrontal lobotomy on fear and food responses. *J. comp. physiol. Psychol.,* 1957, **50**, 81–88. (393)

Watrous, R. M. Methyl bromide—local and mild systemic toxic effects. *Ind. Med. Surg.,* 1942, **11**, 575–79. (210)

Weale, R. A. Photochemistry of the human central fovea. *Nature,* 1968, **218**, 238–240. (93)

Weale, R. A. Photochemistry and vision. In A. C. Giese (Ed.), *Photophysiology.* Chapter 9. New York: Academic Press, 1968, pp. 1–45. (81, 93)

Weber, E. H. Uber den Tastsinn. *Archiv. Für Anatomie, Physiologie und Wissenschaftliche Medicin.,* 1835, **2**, 152. (171)

Weber, E. H. Der Tastsinn und das Gemeingefühl. In *Wagner's Handwörterbuch der Physiologie, Vol. III/2.* Braunschweig: Vieweg, 1846, pp. 481–588. (171)

Webster, J. C., and Thomson, P. O. Responding to both of two overlapping messages. *J. Acoust. Soc. Amer.,* 1954, **26**, 396–402. (417)

Webster, D. B., and Voneida, T. J. Learning deficits following hippocampal lesions in split-brain cats. *Exp. Neurol.,* 1964, **10**, 170–82. (434)

Weddell, G. The pattern of cutaneous innervation in relation to cutaneous sensibility. *J. Anat.,* 1941, **75**, 346–67. (203)

Weddell, G., and Miller, S. Cutaneous Sensibility. *Ann. Rev. Physiol.,* 1962, **24**, 199–222. (177)

Weddell, G., Sinclair, D. C., and Feindel, W. H. Anatomical basis for alternations in quality of pain sensibility. *J. Neurophysiol.,* 1948, **11**, 99–109. (202)

Weil, A. A. Ictal depression and anxiety in temporal lobe disorders. *Amer. J. Psychiat.,* 1956, **113**, 149–57. (365)

Weinstein, S. Intensive and extensive aspects of tactile sensitivity as a function of body part, sex and laterality. In D. R. Kenshalo (Ed.), *The Skin Senses.* Springfield, Ill.: Charles C Thomas, 1968, 195–222. (171, 225)

Weiskrantz, L. Behavioral changes associated with ablation of the amygdaloid complex in monkeys. *J. Comp. Physiol. Psychol.*, 1956, **49**, 381–91. (373, 375, 390)

Weiskrantz, L. Impairment of learning and retention following experimental temporal lesions. In M. A. B. Brazier (Ed.), *Brain Function II: RNA and Brain Function; Memory and Learning.* Berkeley: University of California Press, 1964. (390)

Weiss, P. Self-differentiation of the basic patterns of co-ordination. *Comp. Psychol. Monogr.*, 1941, **17**, 1–96. (338)

Weiss, P. Experimental analysis of co-ordination by the disarrangement of central peripheral relations. In *Physiological Mechanisms in Animal Behavior. Symp. Soc. Exp. Biol. No. 4.* Cambridge: Cambridge University Press, 1950. (338)

Weiss, S., and Davis, D. Significance of afferent impulses from skin in mechanism of visceral pain; skin infiltration as useful therapeutic measure. *Am. J. M. Sci.*, 1928, **176**, 517–36. (248)

Weisstein, N. Neural symbolic activity: a psychophysical measure. *Science*, 1970, **168**, 1489–91. (110)

Weitz, J. Vibratory sensitivity as a function of skin temperature. *J. Exp. Psychol.*, 1941, **28**, 21–36. (210)

Wenzel, B. M. Techniques in olfactometry: a critical review of the last one hundred years. *Psych. Bull.*, 1948, **45**, 231–47. (284)

Wenzel, B. M. Olfactometric method utilizing natural breathing in an odor-free "environment." *Science*, 1955, **121**, 802–3. (284)

Werblin, F. S., and Dowling, J. E. Organization of the retina of the mudpuppy, *necturus maculosus.* II. Intracellular recording. *J. Neurophysiol.*, 1969, **32**, 339–55. (79)

Wernoe, T. B. Viscerocutaneous reflexes. *Pflüger Arch. Ges. Physiol.*, 1925, **210**, 1. (249)

Westbrook, W. H., and McGaugh, J. L. Drug facilitation of latent learning, *Psychopharmacologia*, 1964, **5**, 440–46. (472)

Wetzel, M. C. Self-stimulation aftereffects and runway performance in the rat. *J. Comp. Physiol. Psychol.*, 1963, **56**, 673–78. (521, 522)

Whalen, R. E. Effects of mounting without intromission and intromission without ejaculation on sexual behavior and maze learning. *J. Comp. Physiol. Psychol.*, 1961, **54**, 409–15. (547)

Whalen, R. E. The initiation of mating in naive female cats. *Anim. Behav.*, 1963, **11**, 461–63. (572)

Whalen, R., and Luttge, W. P-chlorophenylalanine: an aphrodisiac. *Science*, 1970, **169**, 1000. (555)

Wheatley, M. D. The hypothalamus and affective behavior in cats. *Arch. Neurol. Psychiat.* (Chicago), 1944, **52**, 296–316. (371, 377)

White, J. C. Autonomic discharges from stimulation of the hypothalamus in man. *Res. Publ. An. Nerv. Ment. Dis.*, 1940, **20**, 854–63. (358)

White, J. C. Sensory innervation of viscera; studies on visceral afferent neurons in man based on neurosurgical procedures for relief of intractable pain. *Res. Publ. Ass. Nerv. Ment. Dis.*, 1943, **23**, 373–90. (243)

White, J. C., and Sweet, W. H. *Pain: Its Mechanisms and Neurosurgical Control.* Springfield; Charles C Thomas, 1955. (247)

Whitehouse, J. M. The effects of atropine on discrimination learning in the rat. *J. Comp. Physiol. Psychol.*, 1964, **57**, 13–15. (485)

Whitfield, I. C. *The Auditory Pathway.* Monographs of the Physiological Society, No. 17. London: Arnold, 1967. (140)

Whitfield, I. C., and Evans, E. F. Responses of auditory cortical neurons to stimuli of changing frequency. *J. Neurophysiol.*, 1965, **28**, 655–72. (142)

Whitten, W. The effect of removal of the olfactory bulbs on the gonads of mice. *J. Endocrinol.*, 1956, **17**, 160–63. (269, 568)

Whitten, W. K. Mammalian pheromones. In C. Pfaffmann (Ed.), *Olfaction and Taste.* New York: Rockefeller Univ. Press, 1969, pp. 252–57. (269)

Whitty, C. W. M. Effects of anterior cingulectomy in man. *Proc. Roy. Soc. Med.*, 1955, **48**, 436–69. (380)

Whitlock, D. G., and Perl, E. R. Afferent projections through ventrolateral funiculi to thalamus of cat. *J. Neurophysiol.*, 1959, **22**, 133–48. (221)

Whitlock, D. G., and Perl, E. R. Thalamus projections of spinalthalamic pathways in monkey. *Exp. Neurol.*, 1961, **3**, 240–55. (218, 221)

Wickelgren, B. G. Habituation of spinal

motoneurons. *Journal of Neurophysiology*, 1967a, **30**, 1404–23. (457)

Wickelgren, B. G. Habituation of spinal interneurons. *Journal of Neurophysiology*, 1967b, **30**, 1424–38. (457)

Wickelgren, B. G., and Sterling. P. Effect on the superior colliculus of cortical removal in visually deprived cats. *Nature*, 1969, **224**, 1032–33. (101)

Wickelgren, B. G., and Sterling, P. Influence of visual cortex on receptive fields in the superior colliculus of the cat. *J. Neurophysiol.*, 1969, **32**, 16–23. (103)

Wickelgren, W. A. Effect of state of arousal on click evoked responses in cats. *J. Neurophysiol.*, 1968a, **31**, 757–68.

Wickelgren, W. A. Effects of walking and flash stimulation on click-evoked responses in cats. *J. Neurophysiol.*, 1968b, **31**, 769–77. (426)

Wiener, N. I. Electroconvulsive shock induced impairment and enhancement of a learned escape response. *Physiology and Behaviour*, 1970, **5**, 971–74. (443)

Wiener, N., and Deutsch, J. A. Effects of salt deprivation and strain differences on tests of the diluted water hypothesis. *J. Comp. Physiol. Psychol.*, 1967, **64**, 400–403. (617)

Wiener, N. I., and Deutsch, J. A. The temporal aspects of anticholinergic and anticholinesterase induced amnesia for an appetitive habit. *J. Comp. Physiol. Psychol.*, 1968, **66**, 613–17. (490, 491, 492)

Wiesel, T. N., and Hubel, D. H. Effects of visual deprivation on morphology and physiology on cells in the cat's lateral geniculate body. *J. Neurophysiol.*, 1963a, **26**, 978–93. (102)

Wiesel, T. N., and Hubel, D. H. Single cell responses in striate cortex of kittens deprived of vision in one eye. *J. Neurophysiol.*, 1963b, **26**, 1003–17. (102)

Wiesel, T. N., and Hubel, D. H. Comparison of the effects of unilateral and bilateral eye closure on cortical unit responses in kittens. *J. Neurophysiol.*, 1965, **28**, 1029–40. (102)

Wiesner, B. P., and Sheard, N. M. *Maternal Behavior in the Rat*. Edinburgh: Oliver, 1933. (576)

Wikler, A. Pharmacological dissociation of behavior and EEG sleep patterns in dog. *Proc. Soc. Exp. Biol. and Med.*, 1952, **79**, 261–65. (396)

Wilkie, D. R. Physiology of voluntary muscle. *Brit. Med. Bull.*, 1956, **12**, 177–88. (291, 310)

Williams, D. The structure of emotions reflected in epileptic experiences. *Brain*, 1956, **79**, 29–67. (365)

Williams, D. R., and Teitelbaum, P. Some observations on the starvation resulting from lateral hypothalamic lesions. *J. Comp. Physiol. Psychol.*, 1959, **52**, 458–65. (599)

Wilska, A. Eine Methode zu Bestimmung Trommelfells bei verscheidenen Frequenzen. *Skand. Arch. Physiol.*, 1935, 161–65. (123)

Wilson, J. R., Adler, N. T., and Le Boeuf, B. The effects of intromission frequency on successful pregnancy in the female rat. *Proceedings of the National Academy of Sciences*, 1965, **53**, 1392–95. (556)

Wing, M. E. The response of the otolith organs to tilt. *Acta. Oto-Laryngol.*, 1963, **56**, 537–45. (323)

Wise, C. D., and Stein, L. Facilitation of brain self-stimulation by central administration of norepinephrine. *Science*, 1969, **163**, 299–301. (518)

Witschi, E. Seasonal sex characters in birds and their hormonal control. *Wilson Bull.*, 1935, **47**, 177–88. (576, 581)

Witt, I., and Hensel, H. Afferente Impulse aus der Extremitätenhaut der Katze bei thermischer und mechanischer Reizung. *Pflüger Arch. Ges. Physiol.*, 1959, **268**, 582–96. (194)

Wolf, G. Effect of dorosolateral hypothalamic lesions on sodium appetite elicited by desoxycorticosterone and by acute hyponatremia. *J. Comp. Physiol. Psychol.*, 1964, **58**, 396–403. (618, 637)

Wolf, G. Thalamic and tegmental mechanisms for sodium intake: Anatomical and functional relations to lateral hypothalamus. *Physiol. Behav.*, 1968, **3**, 997–1002. (637)

Wolfe, J. An explanatory study in food storing of rats. *J. Comp. Psychol.*, 1939, **28**, 97–108. (639)

Wolff, S., and Hardy, J. D. Studies on pain. Observations on pain due to local cooling and on factors involved in the "cold pressor" effect. *J. Clin. Invest.*, 1941, **20**, 521–33. (193, 249)

Wolff, S., and Wolff, H. G. *Human Gastric Function.* New York: Oxford University Press, 1947. (342)

Woods, J. W. "Taming" of the wild Norway rat by rhinencephalic lesions. *Nature* (London), 1956, **178**, 869. (373)

Wood, C. D. Behavioral changes following discrete lesions of temporal lobe structures. *Neurology*, 1958, **8**, 215–20. (358, 373, 374)

Woodworth, R. S., and Sherrington, C. S. A pseudo-affective reflex and its spinal path. *J. Physiol.*, 1904, **31**, 234–43. (367)

Woody, C. D. Vassilevsky, N. N., and Engel, J. Conditioned eye blink-unit: activity at coronalprecruiciate cortex of cat. *Journal of Neurophysiology*, 1970, **33**, 838. (460)

Wollard, H. H., Roberts, J. E. H., and Carmichael, E. A. Inquiry into referred pain. *Lancet*, 1932, **222**, 337–38. (248)

Woolley, D. E., Rosenzweig, M. R., Krech, D., Bennett, E. L., and Thomas, P. S. Strain and sex differences in threshold and pattern of electroshock convulsions in rats. *Physiologist*, 1960, **3**, 182. (436)

Woolsey, C. N. Organization of cortical auditory system. In W. A. Rosenblith (Ed.), *Sensory Communication.* Cambridge: M.I.T. Press, 1961. (153, 157)

Woolsey, C. N., and Walzl, E. M. Topical projection of nerve fibers from local regions of the cochlea to the cerebral cortex of the cat. *Bull. Johns Hopkins Hosp.*, 1942, **71**, 315–44. (153)

Worden, F. G., and Marsh, J. T. Amplitude changes of auditory potentials evoked at cochlear nucleus during acoustic habituation. *EEG Clin. Neurophysiol.*, 1963, **15**, 866–81. (425)

Wurtz, R. H., and Olds, J. Amygdaloid stimulation and operant reinforcement in the rat. *J. Comp. Physiol. Psychol.*, 1963, **56**, 941–49. (517)

Wynne, C. C., and Solomon, R. L. Traumatic avoidance learning: acquisition and extinction in dogs deprived of normal peripheral autonomic function. *Genet. Psychol. Monogr.*, 1955, **52**, 241–84.

Wyrwicka, W., and Dobrzecka, C. Relationship between feeding and satiation centers of the hypothalamus. *Science,* 1960, **123**, 805–6. (624)

Wyrwicka, W., and Doty, R. W. Feeding induced in cats by electrical stimulation of the brain stem. *Experimental Brain Research*, 1966, **1**, 152–60. (601)

Wyrwicka, W., Dobrzecka, C., and Tarnecki, R. On the instrumental conditioned reaction evoked by electrical stimulation of the hypothalamus. *Science,* 1959, **130**, 336–37. (600)

Y

Yamamoto, C., and Iwama, K. Arousal reaction of the olfactory bulb. *Jap. J. Physiol.*, 1961, **11**, 335–45. (242, 287)

Yamamoto, S., Sugihara, S., and Kuru, M. Microelectrode studies of sensory afferents in the posterior funiculus of the cat. *Jap. J. Physiol.*, 1956, **6**, 68–85. (224)

Yensen, R. Some factors affecting taste sensitivity in man. II. Depletion of body salt. *Quart. J. Exp. Psychol.*, 1959, **11**, 230–38. (267)

Young, P. T. Studies of food preference, appetite and dietary habit. IX. Palatability versus appetite as determinants of the critical concentrations of sucrose and sodium chloride. *Comp. Psych. Monogr.*, 1949, **19**, (No. 5), 45–74. (613)

Young, P. T., and Greene, J. T. The quantity of food ingested as a measure of relative acceptability. *J. Comp. Physiol. Psychol.*, 1953, **46**, 288–94. (638)

Young, W. C., Goy, R. W., and Phoenix, C. H. Hormones and sexual behavior. *Science*, 1964, **143**, 212–18. (568, 569)

Z

Zaus, E. A. Discussion of paper bv Austin and Steggerda. *Illinois Med. J.*, 1936, **69**, 127. (595)

Zeman, W., and King, F. A. Tumors of the septum pellucidum and adjacent structures with abnormal affective behavior: An anterior midline structure syndrome. *J. Nerv. Ment. Dis.*, 1958, **127**, 490–502. (365)

Zigler, M. J., and Holway, A. H. Differential sensitivity as determined by amount of olfactory substance. *J. General Psych.*, 1935, **12**, 372–82. (277)

Zimbardo, P. G. The effects of early avoidance training and rearing conditions upon the sexual behavior of the male rat. *J. Comp. Physiol. Psychol.,* 1958, **51**, 764–69. (571)

Zinkin, S., and Miller, A. J. Recovery of memory after amnesia induced by electroconvulsive shock. *Science,* 1967, **155**, 102–4. (440)

Zitrin, A., Beach, F., Barehas, J., and Dement, W. Sexual behavior of male cats after administration of parachloro-phenylalanine. *Science,* **170**, 868–69. (555)

Zornetzer, S., and McGaugh, J. L. Effects of frontal brain electroschock stimulation on EEG activity and memory in rats: relationship to ECS-produced retrograde amnesia. *J. Neurobiol.,* 1970, **1**, 379–94. (437)

Zotterman, Y. Species differences in the water taste. *Acta. Physiol. Scand.,* 1956, 37, 60–70. (612)

Zotterman, Y. Thermal sensations. In J. Field, H. W. Magoun and V. E. Hall (Eds.), *Handbook of Physiology.* Vol. I. Section I. *Neurophysiology.* (American Physiological Society) Baltimore: Williams and Wilkins, 1959, 431–58. (191, 200, 209)

Zotterman, Y. Specific action potentials in the lingual nerve of the cat. *Skand.*

Arch. Physiol.,* 1936, **75**, 106. (181, 185)

Zotterman, Y. Studies in the peripheral nervous mechanism of pain. *Acta. Med. Scand.,* 1933, **80**, 185–242. (205)

Zotterman, Y. Touch, pain and tickling; an electrophysiological investigation on cutaneous sensory nerves. *J. Physiol.,* 1939, **95**, 1–28. (180, 208)

Zotterman, Y., and Diamant, H. Has water a specific taste? *Nature,* 1959, **183**, 191–92.

Zubek, J. P. Studies on somethesis. I. Role of the somethetic cortex in roughness discrimination in the rat. *J. Comp. Physiol. Psychol.,* 1951, **44**, 339–53. (241)

Zubek, J. P. Studies in somethesis. II. Role of somatic sensory areas I and II in roughness discrimination in cat. *J. Neurophysiol.,* 1952, **15**, 401–8. (241)

Zubek, J. P. Studies in somethesis. IV. Role of somatic areas I and II in tactual "from" discrimination in the rat. *J. Comp. Physiol. Psychol.,* 1952, **45**, 438–42. (241)

Zwaardemaker, H. *L'odorat.* Paris: Doin, 1925. (277, 284)

Subject Index

A

Abnormalities of sexual behavior, 573 ff.
Absolute intensity threshold, 166
Absolute refractory period, 7, 13
Acalculia, 239
Acetoxycycloheximide, 481, 482, 484
Acetylcholine, 6, 17, 30, 48, 50, 288,
    289, 355, 411, 413, 414, 443, 496
Acetylcholinesterase, 289, 413, 414, 443,
    444, 597, 598
Acridine orange, 461
ACTH, 345, 346, 381
Actin, 287, 289
Actinomycin D, 32, 441, 481, 483, 484
Action potentials, 79, 544
Adaptation, 264 ff., 276, 284, 285, 565
Adaptation to prisms, 339
Addiction, 31
Adenohypophysis (anterior pituitary),
    60, 582
Adipsia, 599
Adrenal cortex, 341, 345 ff., 578
Adrenal demedullation, 344
Adrenal medulla, 44, 47, 341, 344, 578
Adrenalectomy, 347
Adrenocorticoptropic hormone, 346
Afterdischarge, 308
Aggression, 379, 380, 574
Aggressiveness, 379
Agraphia, 239, 337
Alcohol, 30, 275
Alcoholic psychosis, 30
Alcoholics, 30
Alpha blocking, 420
α-glucosidase, 255
α motor neurons, 24, 293, 294, 295, 299,
    316
Alpha rhythm, 394, 420
Aluminum hydroxide, 462, 463

Amacrine cells, 76, 77, 78
Amines, 200
Aminopyrine, 251
Amnesia, 429 ff., 442 ff., 479, 480
Amniotic fluid, 546, 638
Amphetamine, 473
Ampulla, 319
Amygdala, 348, 352, 356, 358 ff., 370,
    373, 374, 375 ff., 390, 517, 573, 574,
    628, 630
Amygdaloid body, 38, 63
Amygdaloid complex, 283
Amygdaloid nuclei, 59, 62, 63, 281, 282
Amygdaloid stimulation, 359, 362, 363
Anaesthesia, 238, 304, 395, 425, 437
Analgesia, 229, 231
Anatomical methods, 39
Anatomy of the nervous system, 33
Androgens, 552, 554, 567, 569
Androstenedione, 569, 579
Anger, 343
Angiotensin, 589
Annelids, 456
Anomalous trichromatism, 93
Anorexia, 624
Anosmia, 568
Anoxia, 343
Ansa lenticularis, 59
Anterior cingulate gyrus, 382
Anterior cingulate lesions, 380
Anterior cingulate region, 379
Anterior commissure, 281, 282, 378, 598
Anterior ectosylvian gyrus in the cat,
    219
Anterior hypothalamus, 562
Anterior perforated substance, 64
Anterior pituitary, 60, 557, 579 ff.
Anterior pituitary of females, 269
Anterior pituitary gland, 579
Anterior temporal lobe, 379

*This book has been set in 10 and 9 point
Caledonia, leaded 2 points. Chapter numbers
are set in 12 and 24 point Helvetica, and
chapter titles are set in 18 point Helvetica.
The size of the type page is 27 by 45½ picas.*